THE ITALIAN IN MODERNITY

ROBERT CASILLO and JOHN PAUL RUSSO

The Italian in Modernity

UNIVERSITY OF TORONTO PRESS
Toronto Buffalo London

© University of Toronto Press 2011
Toronto Buffalo London
www.utppublishing.com
Printed in Canada

ISBN 978-1-4426-4150-1

Printed on acid-free paper

Toronto Italian Studies

Library and Archives Canada Cataloguing in Publication

Casillo, Robert
The Italian in modernity / Robert Casillo and John Paul Russo.

(Toronto Italian studies)
Includes bibliographical references and index.
ISBN 978-1-4426-4150-1

1. Italy – Civilization.   2. National characteristics, Italian.
3. Italy in literature.   4. Italian Americans.   5. Italian Americans in motion
pictures.   I. Russo, John Paul   II. Title.   III. Series: Toronto Italian studies

DG441.C38 2011   945   C2011-900146-2

This book has been published with the help of a grant from the College of
Arts and Sciences, University of Miami.

University of Toronto Press acknowledges the financial assistance to its
publishing program of the Canada Council for the Arts and the Ontario Arts
Council.

 Canada Council
for the Arts
Conseil des Arts
du Canada
 ONTARIO ARTS COUNCIL
CONSEIL DES ARTS DE L'ONTARIO

University of Toronto Press acknowledges the financial support for its
publishing activities of the Government of Canada through the Book
Publishing Industry Development Program (BPIDP).

Contents

Preface

The title of this book presents a paradox. Although much recent scholarship has questioned Burckhardt's characterization of Italy as the 'first-born' of the modern world, there can be little doubt that late medieval and Renaissance Italy made major contributions to modernity as evidenced by the commercial revolution, humanism, political theory, the scientific mentality, the language of the visual arts, and social refinement.[1] By the eighteenth century, however, Italy's fortunes had fallen so far that, having ceased to be in the vanguard of the West, it was nearly bringing up the rear, its place taken by England, France, and Germany. This book is less about reasons for the decline of Italy than its consequences for Italians, their image in the eyes of others, and the West at large.

We do not pretend to completeness in advancing arguments but instead offer longitudinal cross-sections of a vast historical and cultural terrain. Our assumption is that well-chosen themes and figures can be deployed and reticulated to illuminate the larger (though by no means seamless) totality. We have taken care to avoid overgeneralization, for instance by recognizing the degree to which northern and southern Italy differ with respect to the impact upon them of the Renaissance and other historical factors. Another special concern has been to keep in mind the sometimes questioned unity of Italian experience, whether in treating the relations between north and south or those between Italy itself and Italian Americans. As to foreign responses to Italy and Italian Americans, the perspective extends beyond the anglophone world to French, German, Swiss, and Spanish writers and artists. Nor have we neglected the views of the Italians and Italian Americans themselves in evaluating their historical condition.

Whig historians, trying to cut Italy down to size to fit their ideological imperatives, saw only torpor and degradation after the High Renaissance. In this Arthur James Whyte is typical: 'throughout the seventeenth century there was no sign of life in Italy.'[2] Even the far better known Arnold Toynbee, who regarded the Italians of the Roman period as well as those of the later Middle Ages and early Renaissance as having 'performed feats which have not been outdone by any other people in any other place or time,' thought Italy to have begun its decadence as early as 1475, followed by its 'comparative cultural sterility' over the next four centuries.[3] Yet to argue that Italy had suffered a decline demands a definition of historical decline itself. In this book the term is understood to refer to a major falling off in morals, political power, economic clout and prosperity, creativity, and general cultural influence. By that standard, and conforming to the current consensus among historians, Italy can be said to have declined gradually from the early sixteenth into the later seventeenth century, with the decadence first manifest in politics and economics and then in the arts and culture. This decline proceeded in varying degrees of intensity within the many regions, including Sicily and Sardinia.[4] Politically, by the mid-sixteenth century Italy no longer consisted of numerous self-governing states but was ruled by foreign powers in roughly half its territory, the remaining half being constrained by those powers. As late as the Congress of Vienna in 1815, Metternich referred famously and disparagingly to 'the word "Italy"' as only a 'geographical expression.'[5] Besides its loss of self-determination, Italy, notwithstanding its role as the creator of humanism, underwent a serious decline in literacy from about 1600 onward, as both the Church and local governments neglected the education of their subjects.[6] In 1861 illiteracy stood at 78 per cent, the lowest in Western Europe excepting Spain. These are among the reasons that Italy lacked a public sphere on a par with the leading European states, and that, during the seventeenth and eighteenth centuries, it failed to generate liberalizing revolutionary movements of the type to be seen in England, France, and the United States. At all events the political decline of Italy ends only with the Risorgimento leading to Unification in 1860.

Although some scholars argue that the Italian economy was already showing signs of fatigue in the later Middle Ages, Italian decline can be tied to the general crisis of the seventeenth-century economy that afflicted most of Western and Central Europe. Yet unlike northern nations, Italy rebounded slowly and with insufficient vigour to keep up with its main rivals.[7] The relative weakening of Mediterranean commerce, in combination with the challenge of northern industries, whose cheaply made and mass-produced goods undersold Italian luxury products, are just two of many indicators.[8] Others include a shift from adventurous commercial enterprise to over-consumption,[9] upper- and middle-class investment in rural estates so as to secure profits and capital,[10] the so-called re-feudalization of economic and social relations in the country-side,[11] and the fragmentation of Italy, which had been tending towards economic integration in the Middle Ages and the Renaissance, into regional and local markets.[12] Sicilian nobles who had invested in new towns and agriculture in the sixteenth century were now pouring their profits into lavish urban residences rather than reinvesting and improving their estates (*latifundia*); some two hundred palaces lined the streets of Palermo in 1700. The economist Ferdinando Galiani placed Sicily, the granary of ancient Rome, among the poorest lands in Europe along with Poland and the Balkan countries. In 1792 Paolo Balsamo, who had made a comparative study of national agrarian economies, journeyed into the Sicilian interior: 'a distinct gradation of property size may be observed in England and in other European countries,' he wrote; 'in Sicily one jumps at a bound from those who possess much to those who possess little or nothing.'[13] Perhaps a third to a fourth of the island was under cultivation, producing only a third of what under proper management it might have produced (an acre yielded only twelve bushels of grain as against thirty in Great Britain). Unable to feed itself, Sicily had to import grain from Egypt and Russia. By 1700 even Genoa and Venice, the two great commercial and maritime cities, had become economic backwaters, like Italy itself.

Until recent decades, the Italian Renaissance was thought to be barren of science, but this one-sided judgment has been reversed with the recognition now accorded to the many scientists, philosophers, engineers, and artisans who contributed to the advance of theoretical, empirical, and practical knowledge. Humanism itself, with its emphasis on philology, the historicity of texts, and the objective analysis of subject matter, exerted broad influence on the sciences as elsewhere.[14] Yet at least by around 1650 Italian science was weakening in large part as a result of Church interference, including the Holy Inquisition, the *Index of Prohibited Books* (1559), and reinforcement of Catholic mythology against the ascendant scientific world view. Because science and technology required large sums of money and steady governmental support that only major transalpine nations had the will and resources to offer, the small Italian states inevitably fell behind.[15] In literature, Torquato Tasso, who died in 1595, was the last great writer to have a European impact until Giacomo Leopardi in the mid-nineteenth century. As for the arts, the strength of Italian painting was ensured by a high level of average talent, yet apart from Caravaggio, Guido Reni, and Guercino, the Italians were being challenged by artists from other countries such as Velasquez, Rembrandt, Rubens, and Van Dyke. The last titanic genius in architecture and sculpture was Bernini. Though great artists continued to appear, the numbers dwindled to the point where, in the nineteenth century, Italy failed to produce a single major painter or architect for the first time in six hundred years.

In assessing the role of Roman Catholicism from the later Renaissance onward, one must bear in mind that the corruption of the Church during the High Renaissance (and even earlier) ranks as one of the first harbingers of the decline of Italy, and that the Counter-Reformation therefore deserves praise for its very thorough house cleaning. Burckhardt quite plausibly believed that, had it not been for the Reformation, the Church as an institution would have collapsed.[16] Any fair estimate of the Counter-Reformation will acknowledge that it raised the tone of ritual and worship, introduced a high level of devotional discipline, improved the educational and moral qualifications of its clergy down to the parish level, fostered literacy (at least initially), and encouraged hundreds of Jesuit colleges from Cracow to Lima.[17] The Counter-Reformation should also be seen as a major source of the stupendous baroque culture that pervaded continental Europe, England, and Central and South America, truly constituting an international style of Italian origin. Yet for all the achievements of the Counter-Reformation and the baroque, they ceased to remain vital and creative after their initial burst of energy. The Church condemned Italy's leading philosopher to be burnt at the stake (Bruno), acquiesced in the imprisonment for twenty-eight years of one of its finest poets and thinkers (Campanella), convicted its greatest scientist to prison and house arrest (Galileo), and hounded one of its major historians to his death (Giannone). Book publishing, especially in Florence and Venice, retreated from time to time across the border into Switzerland. Spectacle and formalist extravagance came to set the tone in religion as in culture. Supported by imperial Spain, the Catholic Church not only monitored thought but promoted a theatricalized worship marked by the externalization of religious feeling whereby affect counted more than reflection.[18] In religion as in politics the advantage too often lay with the conformists, hypocrites, and dissimulators. As Italy never experienced a political revolution in which substantial numbers of its population participated, so it lacked a Protestant Reformation as a catalyst of individualism and independent thinking.

There were other causes for the decline of Italy: the rise of the Turks and their obstruction of trade to the east, which wounded the Venetian and Genoese economies; the descent of better-equipped English and Dutch interlopers upon Mediterranean commerce during the 1600s;[19] and the gradual marginalization of the Mediterranean itself, completed around 1700 if not earlier, and owing to the shift of major trade routes to the North Atlantic.[20] However, one especially potent and persistent cause stands out above all others: the inferior leadership the Italians have had to suffer at the hands of their upper classes. For the failure of leadership there is a virtual embarrassment of instances.

Contemptuous of the diplomatic skills of his northern European rivals, the Milanese ruler Ludovico Sforza invited them onto Italian soil with the expectation of manipulating them so as to serve his interests. Because of this arrogant miscalculation, not to mention his underestimation of the political skills of his rivals, Sforza visited countless atrocities upon his people and spent his final years in the solitary confinement of a French prison.[21] His mistaken policy typifies the Italians' inveterate inclination, going as far back as the Donation of Pepin, to solve their problems not through their own direct efforts but by appeals to foreign intervention. Although Pope Julius II is famous for having roused the Italians' nationalistic sentiments with his call to expel foreign invaders, *fuori i barbari* (Out with the barbarians), he had previously allied opportunistically with these same invaders to recover papal territories from the Venetians.[22] Like many predecessors, the Medici Pope Leo X not only ignored the frequent complaints of ecclesiastical corruption emanating from northern Europe, but antagonized the northerners still further by stepping up the sale of indulgences to pay for the building of St Peter's. His conduct affords perhaps the best example of the extent to which the Renaissance papacy, focused narrowly on its Italian political interests, had fallen out of touch with northern Europe.[23] The sack of Rome in 1527, in which thousands were killed or raped, and whose artistic losses could never be compensated, was largely the responsibility of the wayward, tricky diplomacy of another Medici pope, Clement VII, who needlessly brought down upon himself and his people the wrath of the Habsburg armies.[24]

The failure of leadership extended throughout the peninsula and the islands. From 1500 onwards Italy's social structure underwent a pronounced rigidification and aristocratization as the bourgeoisie, rather than fulfilling its potential as a class, attempted to entrench its position within the aristocracy, which itself increasingly claimed a legally exclusive and fixed hereditary status, in contrast with the relative social mobility that had characterized the later Middle Ages and early Renaissance.[25] The hegemony of Spain over many parts of Italy solidified by the Treaty of Cateau-Cambrésis in 1559 would probably not have been possible without the willing collaboration of the Italian aristocracy, which not only benefited from the support of Spain but provided it with military officers who in different circumstances might have served in an Italian national army.[26] During the period of refeudalization in southern Italy, landed aristocrats claimed a host of judicial rights and other proprietary privileges that enabled them to rule over their peasants as a law unto themselves. Characterized fatalistically by the peasants as having been 'sent by heaven along with clay soil and bad weather,' the barons were proverbial for remoteness and stinginess.[27] 'From the houses of the *signori*,' one peasant told Francesco Nitti, 'not even smoke comes out.'[28] Contrary to the longstanding honorific 'myth of Venice,' which paints the patriciate most laudatorily, as the fount of political harmony and social responsibility, that class, much more in keeping with the highly condemnatory though less popular 'black myth' with which the city came to be associated during the fifteenth century, is now widely regarded as having been venal and self-interested in many cases.[29] At the same time, the patriciate's increasing neglect of maritime trade for the sake of imperialistic expansion on the Italian mainland or *terra firma*, a costly and depleting enterprise that began in the fourteenth century and very much intensified over the next, and its subsequent refocusing of its attention away from the sea to a system of capitalized agriculture centred in its newly acquired mainland possessions, a development extending from the mid-sixteenth into the seventeenth century, have been faulted by some historians as misconceived or timid retreats from the potentially greater long-term advantages not only of the city's traditional commercial interests in the Mediterranean but of the defense of those interests against the expanding threat of the Ottoman Empire. In any event the abuse of the peasantry on the Venetian estates is well attested.[30] Although the Italian statesman Count Melzi d'Eril resented Napoleon's refusal to confer autonomy upon the Italians, his good intentions did not prevent him from envisioning the creation of the Italian nation entirely from the top down, an Italy formed 'without Italians,' as Giulio Bollati put it.[31] Even during the Risorgimento, Cavour did not conceive of peninsular Italy as a complete unity, and indeed it might have remained divided had not Garibaldi's courageous intervention guaranteed unification of its northern and southern regions, including Sicily. The decades following the Risorgimento were a let-down, as time-servers, opportunists, unimaginative bureaucrats, and rhetoricians of nationalism descended upon the new capital, the enduring symbol of this period being the Victor Emmanuel II monument, whose gigantism usurps and desecrates half of Rome's Capitoline Hill. Instead of building up Italy's human and material potential, Prime Minister Francesco Crispi entangled his immature nation in overseas ventures that ended catastrophically in Italy's defeat by Ethiopia at Adua in 1896, one of the greatest losses ever suffered by a European imperial army at the hands of a non-European power. With complete disregard for the legal norms of international politics, Gabriele D'Annunzio in the aftermath of World War I took over the Yugoslav city of Fiume with what amounted to a private army, thus providing a dangerous model for Italian Fascism.[32] Mussolini's reputation as a master of bluff and bombast needs no introduction, yet what is one to say of the king of Italy who in 1922 was in a position to order the Italian army to prevent the Fascists' unconstitutional takeover of Rome yet chose to do nothing? It has remained an axiom of Italian politics in the post-war period that, with rare exceptions such as Giovanni Falcone and Paolo Borsellino, political leaders do not hold themselves accountable for their actions, but specialize in denying blame and shunting it to others.

In his quest for the 'reason of reasons' for the decline of Italy, the nineteenth-century literary historian Francesco De Sanctis composed one of the greatest of Italian essays, 'L'uomo del Guicciardini' (Guicciardinian Man), which exposes the petty connivances that had resulted again and again in failed leadership by the ruling class. The essay thus identifies a powerful element of the Italian national character that has endured even into later modernity: a self-interest (*il particolare*) so narrowly focused that the individual finds it difficult if not impossible to enter fully, sincerely, and disinterestedly in a collective enterprise whether civic or patriotic.[33] De Sanctis named this type of person after Francesco Guicciardini, the Renaissance diplomat and historian, whose letters and *Ricordi* (Maxims) extolled the patriotism of his close friend Machiavelli, yet who in his own life often played the particularistic role he was perhaps the first to diagnose so acutely.[34] Assessing the Italians' inept response to their political crisis during the later fifteenth and early sixteenth century, when their inability to join in a common cause led to their surrender of autonomy to foreign powers, De Sanctis realized that Italy had then needed most urgently not its usual quotient of self-serving collaborators and accommodationists but rather a host of patriots like Machiavelli – individuals who, placing their country above their *partico-lare* and throwing caution to the winds, were capable of sacrificing them-selves for the sake of a larger social and national ideal. 'Italy perished [*perì*],' he said, 'because the shrewd [*savii*] were too many and the fools [*pazzi*] were too few.'[35]

Decline does not mean collapse, however, and one should not over-emphasize the extent of Italian decline since the Renaissance. 'Had the failure been total, Italy would have perished –,' writes Benedetto Croce, 'and Italy did not perish.'[36] According to H. Stuart Hughes, Mario Praz, and Croce himself, Italian decline is properly understood in relative terms; only when measured against the Renaissance, an unusually cre-ative age, does it appear steeper than it actually was.[37] Although most of Italy had fallen under foreign political control or influence, Venice retained its autonomy into the late eighteenth century and enjoyed an at least somewhat deserved reputation as the last bastion of Italian lib-erty, where political refugees from despotism were often welcomed, and where toleration and freedom of the press were honoured as nowhere else on the peninsula.[38] Notwithstanding the emergence of the black myth of Venice as a nest of imperialistic, repressive, and clandestinely terroristic oligarchs, the city continued to be regarded in many parts of Europe, including England and Holland, as a model of republican gov-ernment.[39] The Kingdom of Sardinia maintained its independence and, after building up its political and military strength, would provide the nucleus for what became the Italian nation during the Risorgimento.[40] In the Kingdom of the Two Sicilies, the Bourbon dynasty that came to power in 1734 made a concerted and partly successful effort to strength-en the interventionist state and thus to weaken the hold of the feudal bar-ons over the peasantry and economy. In this major reformist enterprise the monarchy was aided by such gifted ministers as Bernardo Tanucci and Domenico Caracciolo along with a cadre of intellectuals who hoped to infuse southern Italy and Sicily with the political and social ideals of the Enlightenment.[41] Although a fully developed public sphere hardly existed at the national level, important steps were taken in this direc-tion by Cesare Beccaria, Pietro and Alessandro Verri, Gaetano Filangieri, and other thinkers.[42] Strictly speaking, Archduke Leopoldo of Tuscany cannot be regarded as an Italian ruler, as he belonged to the House of Lorraine and had close connections with the Habsburg dynasty (he ascended to the throne of the Austrian Empire in 1790), and yet the ex-tensive reformist agenda he carried out in his Italian domains from 1770 onward was a major liberalizing effort, even if Leopoldo was often stymied by aristocratic and ecclesiastical opposition.[43] Whatever one thinks of the culture of the Counter-Reformation after its zenith, eighteenth-century Rome under enlightened popes such as Benedict XIV had one of the most developed and successful social welfare systems in Europe.[44] Even the period of the Napoleonic conquest of Italy, which was obviously undertaken to advance French interests, is seen by some historians as having helped lay the basis for subsequent national unification along with the formation of the Italian state, army, and bureaucracy.[45]

Nor can it be said that Italy declined absolutely in either the arts or sciences following the Renaissance. During this period Italy produced mathematicians like Cardano, Tartaglia, and Cavalieri; physicists like Galileo, Castelli, Torricelli, and Borelli; chemists on the order of Avogadro; the astronomer Cassini; anatomists, biologists, and physiologists such as Falloppio, Colombo, Eustachio, Malpighi, Redi, Morgagni, Golgi, and Spallanzani. Volta discovered the electrical nature of the nervous system. Galvani invented the electric battery; Meucci, an immigrant to New York, the telephone; Marconi, the radio. Although the University of Padua gradually lost the reputation for pre-eminence in medical study that it had enjoyed in the later Middle Ages and Renaissance, it maintained its respectability as did other Italian universities such as Bologna, whose faculty included Volta, Galvani, and the physicist Laura Bassi, the first woman to occupy a chair in Europe (1732). Giannone, Vico, his student Antonio Genovesi who held the first chair of political economy in Europe (1754), Galiani, Giuseppe Maria Galanti, and other members of the Neapolitan Enlightenment brought special distinction to the University of Naples. In the arts, so overwhelming was the momentum of the Renaissance achievement that serious decline did not set in until the later seventeenth century, well after political and economic decline; at least up to that point, the Italians were regarded as pre-eminent in painting, sculpture, and architecture. As late as the eighteenth century Italy was still capable of producing Tiepolo, Canova, Piranesi, Canaletto, Guardi, Piazzetta, Longhi, Batoni, and Rosalba Carriera. As for architecture, the false notion of Italy as having fallen into immediate cultural decadence following the High Renaissance was encouraged by the pejorative view of Italian baroque architecture (and baroque art generally) widely popularized through the fulminations of Ruskin. However, the re-evaluation of the baroque accomplished by such scholars as Cornelius Gurlitt in Germany and Sacheverell Sitwell in England has led to its complete vindication as an architectural style; it is now understood that

Italian architecture was perhaps never more inventive than in the seventeenth and early eighteenth centuries.[46] One recalls the achievements of Bernini, Borromini, Longhena, Pietro da Cortona, Guarini, and Juvarra, a dominance within this art equalled by no other European country before or after. The Italian theatrical tradition, including the commedia dell'arte, has been described as very much the basis of Western theatre.[47] Given the prominence of France and Russia in the ballet over the last two centuries, it is too often forgotten that the Italians not only invented the ballet but rivalled the French in this art form up to around 1900, when Italian creativity flagged. If the French were the acknowledged masters of ballet choreography, the Italians specialized in the physical technique of ballet, and gained an unequalled reputation for virtuoso dancing that extended from the eighteenth to the end of the nineteenth century.[48] In chamber and orchestral music, Vivaldi, 'the main protagonist and establisher of the three-movement soloistic concerto,' stands in the front rank of Italian baroque composers from Arcangelo Corelli and Alessandro Scarlatti to Luigi Boccherini and Domenico Cimarosa.[49] Opera originated in seventeenth-century Italy with Monteverdi; by '1700–1720' Italian opera had become 'the regular and foremost entertainment of the upper classes in much of western and central Europe (but for France)';[50] Italy would produce major operatic composers well into the early twentieth century with Rossini, Bellini, Donizetti, Verdi, and Puccini.

Any judgment of Italian decline must also be qualified by a recognition of the enormous prestige and influence – the exemplary status – that classical, Renaissance, and baroque culture maintained in Europe into the early nineteenth century. Fernand Braudel revised his estimate of the beginning of decline of Italian influence no fewer than three times, initially placing it in 1620, then 1650, and finally 'even 1680.' According to Braudel, seventeenth- and eighteenth-century Italians spread their culture through all parts of Europe, including the Slavic world, and even beyond it, and thus maintained the tradition of 'Italians out of Italy.'[51] Working for Ivan III of Russia in the fifteenth century, Aristotele Fioravanti built the Cathedral of the Dormition in the Kremlin. Alevisio Novi was contracted by the same ruler to design the Cathedral of St Michael the Archangel, also in the Kremlin, in the early sixteenth century, not long before Domenico da Cortona designed Chambord on the Loire for François I. In the seventeenth century Agostino Barelli built the Theatinerkirche and Nymphenburg in Munich, and Francesco Caratti, the Nostitz, Michna, and Cernin palaces in Prague. In the eighteenth century, Juvarra and Giovanni Battista Sacchetti constructed the Royal Palace scoundrel, the servile *cicisbeo*, the adventurer and libertine (Casanova, Cagliostro), the swaggering military coward, the beggar, the corrupt priest, the courtesan, the vagabond, the idler or *lazzarone*, the sycophantic *cicerone*, and the primitive in varying degrees of squalor and even nobility. No other European country offered such a deep and varied rogues' gallery, a testimony to the continued importance of Italy within the European imaginary. Italy seemed to embody the childhood of the West, now grown old, or in a still more extreme interpretation, the land of the dead, hauntingly beautiful even in death. For many northern European and American observers, present-day Italians were out of date, their cities a museum, while the country that produced Castiglione's *The Courtier*, the most popular conduct book of the sixteenth and seventeenth centuries, was seen as strangely uncivilized.

Because of their prolonged period of provincialism and absence from the world stage, the Italians of the new nation state found it difficult to play the game of European and world politics. Their economy was not up to it, nor was their military, but most importantly, their character had to undergo a reschooling in those international behavioural norms that had developed over the centuries, whether in private, social, or diplomatic circles. Unfortunately, a recurrent problem encountered by the Italians has been their failure to grasp not only the nature and scope of many of the persistent negative stereotypes assigned to them by northern Europeans and Americans, but the consequent necessity of correcting such negatives over the long run by means of improved standards of behaviour. As for why the Italians, who invented the art of diplomacy in the Renaissance,[59] and who have traditionally cultivated their own notions of *bella figura* on their native soil, remain so heedless of the impression they create on the international stage, the ultimate reason remains mysterious, but surely self-absorption and lack of national pride have contributed their share. Their inability to gauge the impression they make helps to explain why, whatever the injustices of the Treaty of Versailles, the Italians left the negotiating table with virtually nothing as compared to France and England, despite roughly commensurable losses. This fiasco is largely traceable to the confused and undignified conduct of the Italian negotiators, Prime Minister Vittorio Orlando, whom Clemenceau dubbed 'The Weeper' for his tedious emotional outbursts, and Foreign Minister Sidney Sonnino, who not only disagreed with Orlando on Italy's diplomatic goals, but even quarrelled with him in the presence of foreign statesmen, thus placing Italy in a position of irremediable weakness. Whereas Orlando knew no English, a grave disadvantage in negotiations, the half-Welsh Sonnino exploited his fluency in the language in conversing with British prime minister Lloyd George, a Welshman. Upon learning from the other members of the Big Four that Italy would not be allowed to annex Fiume and the Dalmatian coast, Orlando wept openly; then, after storming out of the conference, he sheepishly returned from Italy for fear of losing the diplomatic crumbs allotted him. At no point did the Italians realize that president Woodrow Wilson brought to Versailles an abundance of anti-Italian nativist prejudices of the worst sort, including supposed Italian propensities to hypocrisy and shady dealing. Sad to say, as Wilson sat at the table in the Hall of Mirrors he saw the very incarnation of those stereotypes in the spectacle of Vittorio Orlando.[60]

The Italians' weak hold on democracy and republican institutions left them a prey to Fascism after World War I, which was devastating to their national reputation and one of the lowest points in their history. After World War II the rapid turnover of Italian governments caused by reshufflings of alliances and power sharing was less a sign of real instability than a strategy of quick-witted politicians to fashion short-term realignments that over the long term amounted to a basically equilibrated national political system. However, such seemingly anarchic behaviour unfortunately has played in the media-driven world culture as another example of at best disorder and at worst buffoonery. Though in the 1980s and 1990s it seemed as if there might be an end to 'politics as usual' with the Vatican and P2 scandals, the Mafia maxi-trial, *Mani pulite*, and a long series of state corruption trials, the improvements have been marginal. To give the most glaring example, organized crime is as strong as ever, though the epicentre has shifted from Sicily to Calabria and Naples.

Even now, the effects of Italy's decline inhibit improvement, most tellingly in the form of the ossified gerontocracies that control the professions, the academy, the government, the Church, and other institutions. This host of impediments makes it extremely difficult for young people to leave home, begin a career, and even start a family in that crucial phase of their lives when they ought to be most hopeful and energetic. Notwithstanding that, with the growing power of China and India and other countries in a now globalized world, the twenty-first century promises to be one of increasingly intense competition, and also notwithstanding that top-notch scientific and technological education is regarded as an essential means to meet the challenge of that world, especially for relatively small nations such as Italy, it may be argued that at the highest levels of education the Italians are not facing up to the seriousness of this challenge. Such is the impression created by the 2006 report published by Shanghai Jiao Tong University. England claims two of the top ten and four of the top thirty world universities, and Italy none; the University of Rome 'La Sapienza' ranks exactly last in the list of the top one hundred.

As discouraging as such rankings may be, a more troubling statistic reveals the Italian birth rate to be one of the lowest not only in Western Europe but in the world. What does this say about Italy's faith in its future? If one views the Italians from the perspective not of national character but of national identity – the former referring to the attitudes and values of a people and the latter to historical and cultural forces that have gone into their formation – then one must acknowledge that, historically and culturally, the Italian constitutes a unique entity compounded in more or less equal amounts of classicism, paganism, Western Christianity, and modernity. Could this entity be fated to disappear?

The decline of Italy was accompanied almost inevitably by the gradual decline in the prestige and influence of Italian culture as a whole, to the point where not just the Renaissance and baroque but the classics themselves came to require apologists in the ongoing modern cultural sweepstakes. Undoubtedly a key factor in Italy's waning influence was the Scientific Revolution, for though it included Galileo as a main figure, it also intensified the struggle between science and humanism that in the twentieth century would be decided in favour of the former. Italy's cultural prestige could hardly benefit from the steady depreciation of what had been acknowledged as one of its chief endowments to modernity. Another factor was the impetus given to modern culture by the French Revolution and all its associated ideologies and 'isms.' Romanticism remains the most prominent of those 'isms,' so much so that in recent decades attempts have been made to claim the French Revolution and Romanticism as the origin of modernity, thus usurping the position of the Renaissance in Burckhardt's path-breaking and widely influential (though by no means uncontested) interpretation of the period.[61] In any case, the ideals and values of the Grand Tour were of decreasing importance amid such relentless competition. Another tendency in scholarship has been to de-emphasize and in some cases even to deny the very modernity of the Renaissance, on the grounds of its medieval and feudal residues, technological underdevelopment, comparative lack of scientific emphasis, Catholic traditionalism, limited capitalism, familism, and other features, so that its relevance to modern experience seems much diminished.[62] Other factors contributing to the growing sense of the cultural remoteness of the Renaissance include the ever-dwindling knowledge of both classical culture and Christian iconography as well as the diminishing attraction of modern artists to Renaissance modes of perception, including mimesis and single-point perspective, such loss of interest coinciding with the rise of modernist painting in the late nineteenth and early twentieth century.[63] One recalls Virginia Woolf's well-known reference to the cultural consequences of the London Post-Impressionist exhibition: 'on or about December 1910 human character changed.'[64] The date coincides neatly with Toynbee's terminus for the third (and final) 'Italistic Age' in 1914.[65]

Although Italy did not perish, it had lagged behind when other countries were on the march. In a patriotic poem Alessandro Manzoni's personified Italy laments her fate: 'io non c'era' (I was not there).[66] 'There' means the making of modernity or what might be called 'second modernity' (post-1650), in which the Italians had participated in lessening degrees, whereas they had been the chief architect of first modernity in the form of the Renaissance. After Unification, Italy still struggled to catch up with northern Europe and the United States. Illiteracy was almost totally eradicated by 1914, a tribute to Unification. If in the period before World War I Italy was disparaged as 'the least of the great powers,' nonetheless it was being ranked with them.[67] Only after its 'economic miracle' of the 1950s and 1960s did Italy stand industrially on a par with France and England, two countries with nearly the same population. It reaped the advantages of being one of the original partners in the Common Market and has steadfastly been a major proponent of the European Union. This is yet another proof of Italy's enduring and paradoxical combination of tendencies: on the one hand, a traditional internationalism as reflected in its frequent origination of and participation in major universalistic institutions and movements, including the Roman Empire, the Catholic Church, the Renaissance, and the baroque; and on the other hand, its lack of national spirit for much of its post-Renaissance history, as can yet be seen in the intense regional, local, and even village loyalties (*campanilismo*) of many Italians.

Any serious study of the Italian in modernity cannot remain content to examine Italians only in their native land. By necessity it must treat Italy as it has come to be represented by '*altre Italie*,' the other Italies, the largest being in the United States. The Italian Americans include not only the millions of Italians who emigrated from Italy to America but their millions of descendants in the adoptive country. Nearly five million Italians entered the United States between 1884 and 1914 in one of the largest mass migrations in modern times, amounting to almost a sixth of Italy's national population. That such vast numbers of immigrants arrived on American soil around the turn of the last century in itself implies their lack of commitment to the Italian national enterprise after Unification. The majority of immigrants were impoverished, illiterate southern Italian peasants in search of a livelihood as well as other decencies and comforts of life that their native country had denied them. Despite the efforts of concerned participants in the 'Southern Question' (the so-called *meridionalisti*), the Italian government did little to stop immigration; it did not, for example, provide incentives for southern Italians to remain at home so as to help propel an economy that was industrializing in the 1890s, nor, except in rare instances such as the murder of eleven jailed Sicilians in New Orleans in 1891, did it address the immigrants' often troubled existence abroad. Whole towns emptied out in the Veneto and Piedmont as well as the south and Sicily.[68] In 1902 the sympathetic Prime Minister Giuseppe Zanardelli toured the south, paying particular attention to Basilicata – the first time a sitting northern prime minister had ventured to visit what was Italy's poorest region. Though seventy-six and ill at the time, he went part of the way by mule. When he stopped at the town of Moliterno, he was greeted publicly by the mayor: 'I welcome you in the name of the 8000 Moliternesi, of whom 3000 have emigrated to America, and 5000 are preparing to follow!'[69]

The deplorable social, economic, and political conditions in their homeland (*la miseria,* as the southern Italians called it) burdened the immigrants with many disadvantages as they attempted to settle abroad. As a mainly agricultural people ill-adapted to a predominantly urban environment, they were often relegated to low-paying unskilled employment, which in turn confined them to crowded ethnic neighbourhoods.[70] Nor was it, apart from improved employment opportunities, a propitious time for the immigrants. In the thirty years prior to World War I, the cultural prestige of Italy had reached a low ebb, not to rise until after World War II. In the eyes of mainstream Americans the new Italian arrivals only confirmed the dominant stereotypes of Italians that had accumulated over the previous centuries – in travel books, gothic novels, opera, memoirs, and soon enough in ghetto dramas and gangster films. As for their co-religionists, the Italians were looked down upon by the Irish-dominated American Catholic Church, which, with its Jansenist strain and emphasis on transcendence, Church discipline, and education, had no use for popular southern Italian Catholicism and its pagan residues. Until the immigrants acquired their own parishes and parish churches, they often celebrated mass at odd hours or in church base-ments. Cleaving to their popular, immanentist Catholicism, embodied in front yard shrines, religious processions and festivals, and 'strange' devotional practices, Italian immigrants clashed again and again with the Church hierarchy. Some of their anger and frustration would have been wrongly directed at the official Church, which, in responding to the immigrants, was only trying to hasten the modernization process based on rules, rationalized procedures, emotional neutrality, and instruction.[71]

Strong cultural ties to the Italian past made it difficult for the immigrants to escape Italy even when on American soil. As the persistence of southern Italian attitudes hampered the group's effort to discard the impeding elements of its ancestral legacy, so it found American values that much harder to embrace. Devoted chiefly to their nuclear (and in fewer cases extended) families, and ill at ease in a foreign and often inhospitable environment, many immigrants had little if any desire to remain in the United States, as is shown by their work schedules carrying them back and forth between the two countries, sometimes yearly.[72] Statistics fail to indicate where these so-called 'birds of passage' finally settled, but their suffering was expressed by the Italian-American poet Emanuel Carnevali. Of the immigrants he writes: 'I have come back with a great burden, / With the experience of America in my head – / My head which now no longer beats the stars'; he ends by apostrophizing, 'O Italy, O great shoe, do not / Kick me away again!'[73] Among all immigrant ethnic groups, the 'birds of passage' syndrome was most frequent among Italians. For those who remained in the United States, educational disadvantages and familial distrust of schools as agents of both assimilation and external authority led to poor academic performance, low graduation rates, and a general disesteem of higher education, especially up to World War II and the G.I. Bill. It did not help that Italian American immigrant parents, who preferred short-term to long-term goals, often required their school-age children to work as contributors to the family income, thus denying them the opportunity to finish high school, much less college. Such factors explain why, for the immigrants and their children, substantial assimilation was delayed for more than a generation and in many cases longer. Well into the 1950s, a significant percentage of Italian Americans remained confined to blue-collar jobs and traditional ethnic neighbourhoods of the kind described by Herbert J. Gans in his oxymoronically titled *The Urban Villagers*.[74]

Beyond economic survival, the immigrants' most critical struggle was to come to terms with their newly acquired ethnic identity. Arriving in the United States from different regions of an only recently unified country, they identified primarily with a village, sometimes a province, rarely a region, and almost never the national government. In short, they did not think of themselves as 'Italians.' By means of what is termed 'chain migration,' people from the same towns and villages often regrouped in close proximity within a neighbourhood, even on the same street or in one or two tenements, and continued to worship their household and local saints among other ancestral traditions. Prejudices against other Italian provinces or regions persisted in the United States: northerners versus southerners, Sicilians versus Neapolitans, Calabrians versus Sicilians.[75] However, Americans viewed the new arrivals collectively as 'Italians' and called them as such. It was not long before the immigrants found in the designation 'Italian' their common denominator, as they applied it to themselves. Thus, ironically, the first-generation immigrants discovered their national identity on American soil. Yet even as the immigrants were acknowledging their Italianness, that identity was being modified in the second generation, with the result that, through the process of acculturation to America, an Italian American ethnic identity came to be formed, made up in more or less equal parts of Italian and American elements. This process had been proceeding in all sectors, as a necessary prelude to the group's assimilation.[76] Schools were a chief agent of Americanization, having an enormous impact on second-generation Italian Americans. It was largely through the schools that Italians as well as American-born children came to learn not only about American values, such as capitalist individualism, upward mobility, civic responsibility, democratic politics, and sexual independence, but other religious and ethnic groups. Predictably, conflicts often arose between members of the first and second generations over issues of value and life-style, such as respect for parental authority, economic and sexual autonomy, use of the Italian language, and even the consumption of Italian cuisine.[77] Only with the coming of World War II, fought against the Axis Alliance that included Italy, did Italian Americans turn decisively towards the American side, and indeed they comprised the largest ethnic group in the wartime army.[78]

The immigrants, whose primary social unit was the inward-looking family, brought with them a clannishness and deep-rooted suspicion not only of strangers but of government and other institutions, including even in some cases the Catholic Church. Although Edward C. Banfield's concept of amoral familism has now been seriously qualified, sociologists from Leonard Covello to Joseph Lopreato and Richard Alba have shown the extent to which the immigrants failed to involve themselves in civic and political life both in the larger American community and in their own.[79] Suspicion of authority made them an easy target for exploitation by mainstream Americans or other ethnics who understood much better how to manipulate the political system. Too few Italian Americans willingly embraced the open-ended, rough-and-tumble American political process, falling back on clientelism, personalism, and the family. In the U.S. Congress, state legislatures, and judiciary, Italian Americans were not represented in any way proportional to their numbers. Even in districts where they constituted an overwhelming majority, the successful candidate was often of another ethnic identity – the most famous example being John F. Kennedy, whose congressional district in the 1946 election was heavily Italian American. There is good reason to believe that the absence of strong representation cost Italian Americans some of their own Little Italies, for example, in Boston and Chicago, when the axe of urban renewal fell upon American cities after World War II. In these instances, the ground was cut quite literally from under their feet.[80] Notwithstanding that Italian American immigrants formed an abundance of mutual aid societies on the southern Italian model, these usually remained of local and temporary significance rather than coalescing into larger associations, and so demonstrated the group's relative difficulty in cooperating both impersonally and at higher degrees of organization. To be sure, a possible exception to the widespread view of Italian Americans' comparative political detachment is provided by what has been termed the 'lost history of Italian American radicalism,' which includes the syndicalists, anarchists, and labour radicals of the early twentieth century. Its unquestioned high point is represented by the famous 1912 'Bread and Roses' strike in Lawrence, Massachusetts, in which many Italian American workers participated, as they did in other strikes of that period. Its major figures include not only Arturo Giovannitti, Joseph Ettor, and Carlo Tresca, all of whom took a leading role in the Lawrence strike, but Sacco and Vanzetti who, leaving aside the still vexed question of their innocence, have been shown by Paul Avrich to have been dyed-in-the-wool anarchists by no means lacking in violent designs against mainstream society. Yet the fact remains that Italian American labour radicalism largely died out in the early 1920s as a result of the Red Scare and the already ongoing tendency of Italian American workers, after an initial period of hesitation during which they rejected unions and even acted as strike-breakers, to choose unionization as their chief means of advancing their political interests – a choice reinforced by the successes of labour unions during the New Deal and the immediate post-war period, when a substantial percentage of Italian Americans remained at the blue-collar level. Apart from unions, Italian Americans have tended not to participate in grass-roots movements, political clubs, or voluntary associations. On the whole, their record remains one of political under-representation for at least two-thirds of their experience.[81]

And in those relatively rare instances in which Italian Americans rose to public office, they did not always distinguish themselves. Mario Cuomo wobbled so often over whether to become the Democratic standard-bearer in the 1980s and 1990s that his party sickened of him. One recalls his notorious description of the U.S. Supreme Court when at the last minute he withdrew his name from what would have been a likely nomination: 'They slam this mahogany door shut. And you're ... entombed.'[82] Rarely have words and actions by an Italian American better illustrated both the group's traditional suspicion of political power and its failure to comprehend the enormous advantages of that power. Various reasons have been proposed for Cuomo's behaviour, which some see mistakenly as Hamlet-like indecision. Yet does not the real reason lie in southern Italian vanity and fear of loss of respect in the event of failure? This was not Caesar's way when, standing at the Rubicon, he flung himself at destiny – *alea iacta est,* 'let the dice fly high.'[83]

As an outcome of slowed assimilation, the Italian American contribution to American culture was seriously compromised. There were, most obviously, few Italian American political figures and jurists on the national stage, which can perhaps best be explained by the legacy of political mistrust and absenteeism transmitted to the United States from southern Italy. Well into the second half of the twentieth century there are few Italian Americans in science and scholarship relative to their percentage of the national population, shown statistically in surveys of the major scientific and literary academies. Nor did Italian departments, guardians of Italian high culture, seek out Italian Americans or even bother to understand them, thereby losing a source of both moral and financial support for themselves, not to mention students. The main intellectual organization, the American Italian Historical Association, was established in 1966, a remarkably late date in the history of the group. The National Italian American Foundation – which proudly announces that it is 'dedicated to preserving and promoting the heritage and culture of Americans of Italian descent, the nation's fifth largest ethnic group' – was founded only in 1975 when the first generation was mostly dead. One questions why it took Italian Americans so long to make such fundamental assertions of group-awareness? Italian American poets and novelists who write on Italian American experience are minor figures, to the point where it remains difficult to form a canon. They were unable to universalize their ethnic experience in the manner of Saul Bellow. The one major novelist, Don DeLillo, finally broke his silence on Italian America with his eleventh novel, *Underworld*, which appeared in 1997, before returning to non-ethnic subjects.[84] In sum, Italian Americans were very slow to assert themselves politically and culturally within what might be termed their ethnic 'window' of opportunity, that is, the period in which their identity retained some degree of strength. By the time the Italian Americans had begun to do so, however, they were already entering as a result of assimilation what Richard Alba terms the 'twilight' of their ethnicity.[85] This is not to deny that, ever since the 1960s, American ethnic groups have sought to assert and justify their ethnicity in the present age of identity politics, by contrast to the previous era in which ethnicity was regarded as a guilty secret. Yet despite the fanfare that ethnicity now elicits, a prudent realism requires one to accept the characterization of such behaviour as for the most part 'symbolic' or low-cost ethnicity, performed incidentally on special occasions and without serious commitment or risk.[86] The truth is that, once Italian Americans had entered their asymptotic twilight, it was already too late for them to make a specifically Italian American cultural and political contribution at once deeply reflective of the group's values and experience and at the same time commensurate in its impact to the percentage of Italian Americans within the American population. The patient was no longer there.

Yet it would be wrong to think that Italian Americans have not made significant contributions to American life in the era of assimilation, or that Italian and Italian American culture have been left by the wayside. Italian Americans have been especially visible in the performing arts, painting, classical and popular music, gastronomy, and fashion. Their cinematic achievement is of international scope, from Capra and Minnelli to Coppola and Scorsese. The prominence of Italian American celebrities in the media and advertising has given their group cachet, as may also be said for the ongoing appeal of Italian and Italian-encoded items in the mass-consumption economy. One has only to think of pizza (the most popular food in the United States), the pasta craze and the obsession with the so-called Mediterranean diet, cappuccino and espresso and espresso machines, Italian cafes and crooners from Sinatra to Bennett, international pop icons such as Madonna, Lady Gaga, and Sylvester Stallone, the mystique of the Mafia as an entertainment staple, and Italian luxury goods, including high-priced designer clothing, handbags, shoes, jewelry, and cars. The tourist trade to Italy, which is as old as the Caesars, never flags. As an index of the commonplace identification of the Italian with pleasure, energy, and liberation, it may be mentioned that over twenty-five recent automobile models have received Italian or Italian-sounding names, for instance Acura, Allegro, Altima, Avanti, Brava, Capri, Corolla, Diamante, Fiero, Forenza, Integra, Largo, Maxima, Murano, Omni, Optima, Pacifica, Piazza, Previa, Scirocco, Sentra, Sienna (*sic*), Sonata, Sorento (*sic*), Stanza, Supra, Volare, and Xterra. So frequently and variously has the 'Italian' served as a selling point in contemporary economy and culture (which amount virtually to the same thing) that some Italian American observers reject the idea of the 'twilight of ethnicity,' arguing instead that American civilization is itself undergoing Italianization, 'becoming Italian.' Apart from its blatant rooting for the home team, such a judgment fails to distinguish Italianization of a essentially superficial and consumerist type from those several extended periods of profound Italianization experienced by the West earlier in its history. Of these one may instance the Roman Republic and Empire, the Catholic Church and its dissemination of Christianity through the monastic system and other institutions, and the Renaissance and baroque periods with their major artistic, scientific, and social impact. By such a standard the current alleged 'Italianization' of American culture must appear as a minor phenomenon destined for quick replacement by some equally ephemeral fashion.

To return to the paradoxical title of the book, the characteristic experience of the Italian in modernity is one of belatedness, whether socially, politically, culturally, or, above all, historically. Italy helped to initiate modernity, then fell behind, and spent the last three centuries trying to recover its status among European nations. Having at last reached parity with its competitors in the Western industrial-technological world, it now faces a double difficulty: to maintain or improve its international position, and to preserve its own distinctive cultural and national identity at an adverse moment marked by European unification on the one hand and globalization on the other. As the planet becomes increasingly globalized, it is likely that the pressure of adaptation to technological society will intensify, with a corresponding flattening of differences among peoples and cultures; indeed, this is already becoming apparent in the highly technicized younger generations. The question thus arises whether an Italian identity can survive in such an environment. Italy's difficulties are compounded by the fact not only that it faces a new array of international competitors outside the European arena, but that, as a smaller nation, it may think it too late to exert upon the modern world a significant and specifically Italian influence on a grand scale.

To this sense of belatedness in the immediate present is added the Italian's larger awareness of the straitened historical possibilities of the present as against those previous epochs in which the world felt Italy's influence in a multitude of ways. Admittedly consciousness of dwindling prestige and visibility has been part of the experience of other European nations over the last century: England with its loss of empire, France with the waning of its cultural and linguistic authority. However, in view of the greater scope and variety of the Italian achievement over twenty-seven hundred centuries, there can be no doubt that the belatedness felt by Italians exceeds that of their competitor nations. This is not to deny that France enjoyed cultural hegemony in Europe during several historical periods, as did Italy during Imperial Rome, early Christianity, the Renaissance, and the Baroque. However, not even with Charlemagne, Louis XIV, and Napoleon to its credit can France claim to have created political and spiritual empires such as the Roman Empire and Roman Catholicism, nor can it show a period of economic predominance over the advanced parts of Europe such as the Italians achieved in the Middle Ages and early Renaissance. By the same token, while the British have exerted economic hegemony in modern times, they have never held political or spiritual dominion in Europe, nor is there a single period of European history, not even the Victorian, in which they have dominated European culture as a whole. Comparisons aside, the special task of the Italian in modernity is to recognize the cultural paradox of double belatedness so as better to comprehend the limits within which he or she can act, the ultimate goal being to shape a credible future. We hope that, as the Italian past throws the shadow of its magnitude upon the national present, the Italians and Italian Americans themselves will continue to learn from its historical examples, draw inspiration from its artists, thinkers, scholars, clerics, and statesmen, preserve the living elements of humanism, classicism, and Christianity, and in so doing prove themselves worthy of their inheritance.

Robert Casillo
John Paul Russo

The ultimate truth with respect to the character, the conscience and the guilt of a people remains for ever a secret; if only for the reason that its defects have another side, where they reappear as peculiarities or even as virtues. We must leave those who find pleasure in passing sweeping censures on whole nations to do so as they like. The people of Europe can maltreat, but happily not judge, one another. A great nation, interwoven by its civilization, its achievements and its fortunes with the whole life of the modern world, can afford to ignore both its advocates and its accusers. It lives on with or without the approval of theorists.

– Jacob Burckhardt, *The Civilization of the Renaissance in Italy*,
Part VI, 1860

Setting out again in 1614, he [the British traveller William Lithgow, as reported in his *Totall Discourse*, 1632] this time ventured into the mountain-country of Calabria, famous for tarantulas and brigands. Here his peregrinations would have come to a painful end, had he not produced for the ruffians who were threatening his life, the best of all passports – the certificate of a visit to the Holy Places. On seeing this, *on lui fit fête*: the whole company made merry with him. He then passed over into Sicily … Faring across the island he discovered the bodies of two gentlemen who had killed each other in a solitary duel. As no one was about he rifled their purses, took their diamond rings, and then coolly announced his discovery.

– A. Lytton Sells, *The Paradise of Travellers: The Italian Influence on Englishmen in the Seventeenth Century*, 1964

It is a sign of arrogance and of insolence, even of ingratitude, to limit oneself to a knowledge of Italy when she was victorious and triumphant, and to turn away from her, when she is defeated and subjected to foreign nations. Italy remains our mother whether victorious or defeated, and it is the duty of her sons to acknowledge the obligation which they owe her, in good and in evil times.

– Ludovico Antonio Muratori, Preface to *Rerum Italicarum Scriptores*,
1723–1751

… a new standard for thousands of things …

– Jacob Burckhardt on Italy, *Letters*, 1846

chapter 1

Stendhal and Italy

ROBERT CASILLO

... this cooling planet ...
– Stendhal

PART ONE
Is Italy Civilized?

I

If Stendhal were not internationally famous for his fiction, he would probably be best known as an incomparable Italophile, for whom Italy was virtually synonymous with happiness. 'All the characteristics of the Italians,' he wrote in 1813, '... are pleasing to me.' On 4 July 1814 he proclaimed: 'Rome, Rome is my mother country, I'm burning to be on my way.'[1] So intense was Stendhal's identification with Italy that he made it his adoptive homeland and, in his fictionalized autobiography *The Life of Henri Brulard* claimed for himself a partly Italian genealogy. He mentions in the same work his youthful interest in things Italian, especially Tasso and Ariosto, whose heroic narratives and landscapes influenced his fiction.[2] 'I daily perceive that at heart I am Italian,' Stendhal wrote to his sister Pauline on 10 September 1811. Two years later he remarked in a diary entry that 'my trips to Italy caused me to become more original, more *myself*.'[3] Anticipating a brief visit to Italy in 1813, he told Pauline that he was 'destined once again to see my beloved land of Italy ... my true home ... It is simply that the country as a whole *matches my tempera-ment*.'[4] As much as Stendhal delighted in Rome, Naples, Florence, and other Italian cities, none awakened in him so deep a passion as Milan, his city *par excellence* of gaiety and music, whose residents had mastered as nowhere else the art of serenely enjoying life. Of the Milanese he said that 'I have never encountered a race of men that were so closely fashioned after my own heart,' adding that, if he had the choice, he would never leave the city. The best known example of Stendhal's *italianità* is his proposed inscription for his tombstone: *Arrigo Beyle Milanese.*[5]

Having first visited Italy in 1800–01, as a soldier in Napoleon's armies, Stendhal returned in 1811 for a stay of three months, during which he saw Rome for the first time, and again in 1813. He lived mainly in Milan from 1814 to 1821, when the Austrians permanently expelled him from their Italian possessions because of his liberal sympathies. After a nine-year absence from Italy, except for a five-month visit to Florence and Rome in 1823–4, he wrangled a minor consular post at Civitavecchia that, from 1830 up to his death in 1842, gave him intermittent access to Rome. Stendhal's knowledge of southern Italy was (it appears) mainly confined to Naples, but he was well-acquainted with the rest of the peninsula – its history, local traditions, architecture, music, painting, literature, sculpture, politics, and society. Apart from *The Charterhouse of Parma,* his greatest masterpiece, and *Chroniques italiennes,* a collection of stories inspired by Renaissance manuscripts, Stendhal devoted a very large portion of his voluminous non-fictional writings to Italian culture, politics, and society during the Napoleonic and post-Napoleonic age. Taken together, these works form a sustained meditation on the relation of Italy to Europe during the period of modernization and also on the failings and virtues of Italy itself. By his own testimony Stendhal visited the peninsula with the aim of elucidating what he claims previous travellers had missed in their one-sided pursuit of art. This unknown element is the Italian character, or *'l'Italie morale.'*[6]

Not a few critics complain that Stendhal idealizes Italy to the point of mythification. He is alleged to have confabulated a romantic nowhereland populated by beautiful ladies, handsome worldly aristocrats, impassioned musicians and painters, swashbuckling bandits and assassins, canny clerics, and naturally vivacious peasants. When these uncompromising individualists are not engaged in tender love affairs, reckless heroics, or subtle intrigues, they devote themselves to leisurely aesthetic delectation. Critics also remain skeptical of what they see as Stendhal's counter-myth of northern Europe and especially France as the realm of emotional aridity and conformist routine. They claim that he does justice neither to France nor to modern European civilization, as if his love of Italy were founded on a hatred of France. Ironically, Stendhal's

Italophilism would then exemplify the *ressentiment* he had diagnosed in Romanticism.[7]

In 1818, shortly after the publication of *Rome, Naples et Florence en 1817*, Stendhal's friend the Baron de Mareste accused him of having snobbishly focused on the Italian upper classes. A century later Paul Hazard described Stendhal's response to Italy as exemplifying the 'crystallization' – the lover's overestimation of the beloved – that Stendhal had analysed in *Love*. Supposedly purging the country of the commonplace, Stendhal had portrayed an 'Italy *de luxe*.'[8] To be sure, although Stendhal criticized foreigners (especially the English) for not mixing with Italians, as he himself did, he usually treats the middle as well as the lower classes or *popolo* from a distance.[9] Notwithstanding Francesco Novati's defense of the at least partial truth of Stendhal's portrayal of Italy, Luigi Foscolo Benedetto takes the opposing view in *Arrigo Beyle Milanese*, and even Novati admits that Stendhal sometimes turns Italian faults into virtues. René Dollot contends that Stendhal's judgments of Milanese society are unreliable owing to his having been denied access to the Italian social elite – a complaint that perhaps applies as well to his critique of French society, whose best salons he could not enter.[10] Although appreciative of Stendhal, Harry Levin borrows Benedetto Croce's reference to Stendhal's 'dream of Italy in Italian disguise,' suggesting that his Italian cult is mainly a 'criticism of France.' Richard N. Coe calls Stendhal's Italy a 'dream-fantasy' or 'Utopia'; for Robert Alter it is an 'imagined sphere'; for Victor Brombert a 'private myth.' In the view of Charles Dédéyan, Stendhal remained a bourgeois for whom Italy and the Renaissance were a romantic '*rêve de compensation*.'[11] Implicit in many of these judgments is that Stendhal falsely imagines nineteenth-century Italy to have preserved the vitality of the Renaissance, a criticism repeated by Italo Calvino.[12]

Admittedly Stendhal sometimes idealizes Italy, and makes basic errors. His claim in *Rome, Naples and Florence* that the family is stronger as an institution in Scotland than in Rome reveals his unfamiliarity with the common people, and Bernard Wall rightly questions his notion that Italians are less vain than other nations.[13] Yet despite such defects Stendhal's Italian writings contain a wealth of acute cultural, political, and historical observations, some speculative, many others based on close knowledge and personal experience. Even Hazard admits that these works hold a measure of truth and penetration.[14] Their virtues justify Jules Bertaut's evaluation of Stendhal as probably unequalled among French travel writers, and Paul Arbelet's observation that, although Stendhal's Italian writings may seem prosaic by comparison with those of other French travellers, it is because Stendhal portrays an Italy 'vivante et réele.' Victor Brombert describes him as the French writer of his time who 'knew and understood Italy best.' In Charles Eliot Norton's view, Stendhal surpassed all other foreigners in his knowledge of Italy. For Luigi Barzini, there remains among foreign writers on Italy 'only one real authority, Stendhal.'[15]

Nonetheless, William M. Johnston questions Stendhal's penetration as a travel writer. He faults him for errors of fact, limited geographical range, inability to characterize sites and works of art, and a supposedly one-sided devotion to opera, local gossip, shallow eroticism, and other ephemera dear to the *bon vivant.* Contending that Stendhal relied more on chatter than on books, Johnston refuses to rank him among the finest French travel writers, placing him below the brothers Goncourt, Rému-sat, and Maurel. Such an evaluation ignores Stendhal's strong suit, which is neither description nor atmospheric evocation nor impressionism – apparently for Johnston the essence of travel writing – but an analysis of Italian society and politics as well as of the psychology and behaviour of the Italians.[16]

Cesar Graña's criticism of Stendhal goes deeper.[17] For Graña, Stend-hal is a literary Bohemian and hence anti-bourgeois; and, while Graña ignores Stendhal's writings on Italy, his anti-Bohemian argument encom-passes Stendhal's Italophilism. Indeed, Stendhal identifies Italians with Bohemians if not of the artistic then of the gypsy variety: 'Les moeurs nationales du pays de Naples sont exactement les moeurs des bohè-miens.'[18] Graña shows that the French Bohemians hated modernity for the very qualities Karl Marx and Max Weber had welcomed. Notwith-standing his radicalism, Marx admired the bourgeoisie for introducing discipline, regularity, and system into social life and thus for banishing the erratic rhythms of medieval production and behaviour. Weber iden-tified modernity with the emergence of bureaucracy, which rationalizes law, politics, and society and thus eliminates the subjective, the unrea-sonable, and the incalculable. The Bohemians by contrast opposed such bourgeois values as discipline, self-renunciation, emotional neutrality, thrift, steady production, and utilitarian efficiency. They identified civil society, its laws, bureaucracies, and republican institutions, with dull routinization, impersonal communications, levelling conformity, and the banishment of 'superior' though subjective value judgments, all of which, they feared, meant the closure of spontaneity, novelty, and creativ-ity. Typifying the Bohemians' political standpoint in Stendhal's descrip-tion of republicanism as the 'real *cholera-morbus*,' Graña describes them as irresponsible, for they were unconcerned with the general welfare and pursued only private utopias.[19] Profoundly attracted to earlier social hierarchies, and rejecting the work ethic for an aesthetic and histrionic way of life coloured by erotic hedonism, the Bohemians embraced the conspicuous consumption and 'predatory efficiency' that Veblen later condemned as typical of the 'high barbarism' of pre-industrial societies. The Bohemians' preference for such models, as opposed to disciplined production, reflects their assumption that the constant oscillation from sloth to prowess, as in the Middle Ages, is intrinsically human. Their cult of the artistic genius, ruthless bandit, and social outcast – all Italian stereotypes – expresses their values. Hence too their glorification of only partially modernized cultures, such as Stendhal's Italy.

Although Stendhal often mocks the bourgeoisie and their values, there are reasons for viewing him as other than a Bohemian, not least his artistic dedication and productivity. True Bohemians are not so much artists as devotees of the 'artistic' lifestyle.[20] It is equally mistaken to suppose, as does Graña, that Stendhal is always hostile to modernity or excessively indulgent towards Italy. Rather, his love of the Italy of his own day and even of the Renaissance is never absolute but heavily qualified. Far from rejecting modernity for the sake of Bohemian or aristocratic rebelliousness, Stendhal is drawn to liberalism, utilitarianism, and certain socialist values. Despite his intermittent disgust with republicanism, Stendhal shares de Tocqueville's view that, whatever its failings, democracy defines the main tendency of modern politics after the French Revolution, and must be accepted. No reactionary defender of the *ancien régime*, Stendhal like Tocqueville condemns the oppression and injustice of the old order and shows no desire to undo the French Revolution, which he regards as impossible in any case. For both writers, the French Revolution and its democratic repercussions hold potential for good as well as evil.[21] At the same time, Stendhal often acknowledges the superiority of France and England, the two leading modern nations, to nineteenth-century Italy, which he never wholly confuses with the Renaissance. If anything his consciousness of Italy is deeply divided because he both accepts and challenges modernity.[22] Not only does this ideological conflict repeat the typically Stendhalian antithesis between analysis on the one hand and passion and personality on the other,[23] but its very ground is Italy itself.

Graña is further mistaken in implying that Italy's attraction to Stendhal fully resembles the *nostalgie de la boue* often motivating the Bohemians' fascination with primitive, non-European societies. Dennis Porter notes that whereas Byron, Hugo, Delacroix, and Flaubert were drawn to the Orient and the primitive, Stendhal's single-minded love of Italy reveals him as a 'champion of traditional Eurocentric cultural values' and especially as the heir of the eighteenth century, when Italy was the climax of the Grand Tour. 'We are traveling in order to see new things,' writes Stendhal, 'not barbarian tribes, like the fearless adventurer who penetrates the mountain fastnesses of Tibet or who alights upon the shores of the South Sea isles. We seek more subtle shades; we wish to see manners of acting closer to our perfected [French] civilization.'[24] Nor could all the cultural relativism of the present day ever succeed in elevating Chateaubriand's Louisiana, Gauguin's Tahiti, and Lawrence's Mexico to the level of Italy, which, by virtue of its historical significance, and as the chief repository of the West's older, traditional culture, has immeasurably greater interest and value. Stendhal recognizes as much when, with amusing indifference to American geography, he refuses to compare Italy to 'Cochin-China or to the State of Cincinnati.'[25] Unlike the peripheral and backward settings favoured by many Bohemians, Italy's cultural legacy renders it far more substantial as the counterweight by which Stendhal measures modernity's strengths and shortcomings.[26] And if Stendhal sometimes idealizes his adopted homeland, critics often fail to realize that the value of his mythical Italy, like all utopias, ultimately derives less from correspondence to actualities than from the critical and imaginative truth it contains. More than simply protesting the dominant forces in modernity, Stendhal's Italian utopia envisions their transcendence – not, however, in one country, Italy, privileged and reified as the sole possible realm of *bonheur*, but in the larger social world.

II

In the broadest sense Stendhal defines Italy's inferiority to modern France and England as a deficiency of *civilization*. For though he sometimes praises Italy's 'civilization' for its historical influence, precocity, variety, and 'many-sided *completeness*,' he more frequently asserts the superiority of contemporary French civilization and all that it implies of political, social, and cultural progress. Complaining of Italy's 'less advanced' civilization, he finds that it gives him 'little annoyances in detail' and will cause him to 'return to Paris with pleasure,' for there society has become 'perfected.' Not only does Italy lack the 'decorum of civilization,' but the Ischians, among some other Italians, have 'scarcely a trace' of it.[27] When one recalls Italy's distinguished cultural record since ancient times, such an evaluation may seem insulting. However, Stendhal measures Italy by the standard of civilization as defined in the West since the Enlightenment, and by this definition, which overlaps with the ideas of modernization and progress, he justly estimates Italy's shortcomings. He also understands the historical and social conditions that form the basis of civilization, and the reasons for their relative absence in Italy.

According to Raymond Williams, 'civilization' as a word and concept 'has behind it the general spirit of the Enlightenment, with its emphasis on secular and progressive human self-development. Civilization expressed this sense of historical process, but also celebrated the associated sense of modernity: an achieved condition of refinement and order.' Sheldon Rothblatt characterizes civilization as a 'comprehensive and even ethical term, designating all those material and institutional, but particularly those religious, moral, or intellectual, changes that separated the tame European from the wild barbarian.' Not only does the term encompass the substitution of 'instinct or unconscious controls such as custom' by 'conscious obligations and specified freedoms,' but it refers to 'control over oneself through the use of reason, judgment, and understanding.' The civilized person exhibits 'self-restraint' and 'self-repression,' acting 'defensively against provocation, and in deference to the wishes of others,' so as to reduce 'violence and cruelty.' Civilization thus demands a 'higher state' of human social response along with an 'improved and higher state of human conduct.' As a concept civilization had been preceded by the ideas of *politesse*, refinement, and civility (*civilité*), but whereas the word 'civility' applies chiefly to good manners, civilization stresses both mannerly behaviour and the higher value of reason.[28]

Descending from the eighteenth century, the concept of civilization refers to a gradual and decisive movement away from medieval to courtly and bourgeois behavioural norms. As Norbert Elias observes, the people of the Middle Ages failed to achieve a high level of 'drive control.'[29] Not only did they feel intense passions, they were often controlled by them. Like Stendhal's Italians, they yielded to their spontaneous impulses and freely discharged their emotions, often violently. Having a short emotional fuse, they responded impatiently to events and failed to calculate the long-term consequences of their actions. With their extraordinary freedom of affect, they lacked a dispassionate, matter-of-fact, and objective evaluation of the world. And because their drives were unchecked, medieval people often shifted abruptly from one extreme to another, from asceticism to luxury, love to violent hatred, bellicosity to religiosity, sin to penance, retribution to forgiveness. Yet they showed little differentiation in their ordinary behaviour, since they felt little internal or external pressure to modify it significantly from one situation to another.

The 'civilized' observer often finds something appealing in primitive or comparatively uncivilized societies, which seem to promise intensity of experience, and whose inhabitants appear to have retained the simple and immediate joys of childhood. Thus in the Middle Ages both pleasure and pain were felt with great force. Less attractively, perhaps, the directness and undifferentiation of social experience implies lack of nuance, while volatile individuals often behave in an incalculable and disorderly manner. According to Johann Huizinga, who influenced Elias, the 'primitive' and 'ingenuous' character of medieval behaviour testifies to comparative underdevelopment in law and civility. In the absence of legal and social restraints, medieval people found further encouragement to succumb to the most intense and contradictory passions. Fueled by the code of vengeance, violent tempers created a social climate of 'chronic insecurity.'[30]

In the seventeenth and eighteenth centuries, argues Elias, the idea of civility emerged as essential to civilization. Civilized life implies a softening and refinement of manners and a suppression of those powerful impulses that gave the Renaissance and Middle Ages their dramatic and unpredictable character.[31] As people attained greater drive control, they yielded less to first impulses. As their emotional fuses lengthened, they responded more patiently to events while calculating the long-term consequences of their actions over extended social chains. Their behaviour also achieved a much higher level of affective neutrality. Learning to conceal subjective responses beneath a mask of public reserve, people developed a less emotional, more objective, and hence patient and matter-of-fact approach to life. With the moderation of responses, they went to extremes less frequently, while the increasing differentiation of social and economic life lessened behavioural 'diffuseness.' Instead of acting in basically the same way on all occasions, people learned the social codes each occasion required. As experience became less immediate, it acquired nuances and life gained in sophistication. With the division of public from private, existence became pychologized and perhaps more interesting. In its orderliness and uniformity, social life permitted (and demanded) greater calculation of behaviour. On the negative side, these changes diminished emotion, spontaneity, and the intensity and unexpectedness of pleasure.

According to Elias, the ascendancy of civilization in the West resulted from a combination of forces, all of which Stendhal explicitly or implicitly recognizes. Of these, perhaps the most important is the absolutist court of Versailles, where Louis XIV subjected his courtiers to social rituals of gallantry, politeness, and reserve. In France the aristocratic ideal of *civilité* was adopted by the rising bourgeoisie, who found it both prestigious and consistent with their own habits of orderliness, and thence transmitted to France as a whole. In other northern European nations the Protestant middle class helped to create the modern idea of civility by exemplifying for the general population the values of self-control, self-examination, privacy, good manners, a matter-of-fact attitude, business discipline, and the idea of respectability as defined by the elimination of the eccentric and unseemly. French and English society thus rejected anything abrupt or savage, all displays of intensity or of extreme or obsessive behaviour.

The civilizing process reflects profound political and economic differences between the pre-modern and modern worlds. Because the Middle Ages lacked a modern centralized state, force and law were often in the hands of private individuals, who applied them capriciously and without restraint. The failure of the Middle Ages to create complex societies and economies integrated within national boundaries, as well as to achieve political and social interdependence on a large territorial scale, goes far to explain the comparative inability of pre-modern individuals not only to cooperate with each other but to calculate the long-term consequences of their actions. In the absence of a national government and economy along with nationally accepted behavioural norms, people felt little pressure to moderate their impulses or to organize their lives in accordance with a strict schedule.

Elias observes that 'self-restraint in its highly regulated form' requires 'relatively stable monopolies' of force and law. Defined as a monopoly of force, and buttressed by an impartial legal system, the modern state compels individuals to moderate their behaviour and thus increases drive control throughout society. In the absolutist court especially, force yields to nuance and restraint of affect. As behaviour becomes less extreme and more predictable, the modern state can plan and administer its affairs rationally and objectively. A further requirement is that citizens observe the law, lest civic order require constant use of force. On the whole, civilization implies some political and social liberalization, although the range varies considerably.

Integrated under the state, the modern economy grows more complex and productive, with increasing division of labour and interdependence over great distances. In turn, society shows a greater differentiation of functions and a wider range of interdependences. Civility is thus promoted through social differentiation and integration, for with the division of labour the social code becomes more complex, and more self-control is needed to read social signs. Likewise, as the chains of social interdependence are extended in time and space, there is greater need for behavioural discipline, regularity, and predictability, and less room for oscillations of impulse. Teamwork becomes the modern social norm, and the expanding interdependences are sustained by newspapers and general literacy.[32]

Civilization marks a shift from particularity to universality, from intimate local communities to comparatively impersonal and anonymous large societies. In requiring objectivity and rationality, civilization shapes an ever more systematic and matter-of-fact existence. If ascriptive status, favouritism, traditionalism, familism, emotionalism, and other subjective factors had formerly figured in political and legal decisions, now politics and society aim for impersonal calculation and bureaucratic regularity. Such rationalization implies secularization, including the separation of church and state. The objective standards and steady rhythms of law and bureaucracy favour other systematic activities typical of civilization such as industry, commerce, science, and technology, all of which depend on large-scale cooperative and administrative structures based on rational principles. As life becomes more organized, people abandon the undisciplined rhythms of medieval times, when, to quote Marx, 'brutal' outbursts of energy were succeeded by the 'most slothful indolence.' For Marx, it was the bourgeoisie who had first employed human energy in a 'rational,' 'consistent,' and productive fashion.[33]

Many Enlightenment thinkers regarded civilization as a universal standard not only of refinement and politeness but of political and social organization, to which all nations should aspire. From this perspective, human societies were to be conceived on the analogy not of a branching tree, whereby each society would possess its own unique characteristics and path of development, but of a ladder, each nation being judged by its competence in attaining civilization as humanity's universal goal. Thus, though Hume and the Scottish school somewhat appreciated distinct national characters, they placed their faith in the final triumph of universal qualities, with civilization absorbing all national differences. It was thus expected that Italy would correct its deficiencies of civilization so as to imitate the more advanced European nations. And yet, in a major development extending from the later eighteenth into the nineteenth century, and possibly because of disillusionment with the French

Revolution, the universal ideal of civilization came to be challenged during the Romantic period and subsequently lost most of its cultural authority. It is within this critique of civilization that Stendhal's writings on Italy should be situated.[34]

Nonetheless, Elias overemphasizes the post-Renaissance French contribution to civility and civilization. Bram Kempers notes that already in Renaissance Italy new codes of conduct as well as of the pictorial arts determined decorous behaviour. He holds that, in general, the Italian republics imposed much stricter controls on behaviour than did the courts, where aristocratic ostentation and extravagant expense prevailed. Peter Burke similarly observes that the Renaissance conduct books of Castiglione, della Casa, and Guazzo exalted conformity to a code of good manners over the expression of personal styles of behaviour. Citing the ideal of dominance over the passions in Alberti and Guicciardini, Burke insists that if self-control is civilization, as Elias contends, then these Italians were civilized. Well before Louis XIV, the Italian courts perfected manners and conversation under the influence of intelligent, educated women. In dissociating themselves culturally from the lower classes, the Italian aristocracy and bourgeoisie anticipated later trends. Nor was Stendhal unaware of these developments, remarking that Italy had civilized Europe in the century of Pope Leo X.[35]

Other features that Elias identifies with civilization Marvin Becker finds to have originated in northern Italy, especially Florence, between 1300 and 1600. Besides noting the new emphasis on good manners, patience, reserve, inwardness, privacy, and the art of conversation, Becker remarks the fluid, expanding economies of the Italian states, the decline of violence and the cult of honour through the extension of legality, the supercession of factionalism by voting in urban politics, substantial literacy, the rise of individual and familial values over those of the corporate group and clan, the emergence of state bureaucracy and other secular institutions, the substitution of contractualism for traditional mutualities, and the capacity to conceive of society universalistically rather than personalistically. Peter Burke similarly observes that, up to a point, the Italian Renaissance achieved bureaucratic states in the modern, Weberian sense. However, Daniel Waley and J.K. Hyde argue that Italy had achieved the basis for civilization before the Renaissance, specifically the last half of the thirteenth century, the time of the northern Italian republican communes. Waley finds in these cities not only a high degree of *étatisme* and complex administrative arrangements but liberty, citizen participation, trust, and cooperation. Because citizens willingly acted in the common interest, and respected universal rules, the communes attained the *civitas* upon which civic culture depends. Education was fairly widespread, streets were kept clean, and impartial laws punished irresponsible behaviour. Undoubtedly these civic virtues contributed to the commercial prosperity of these city-states. Hyde likewise stresses increasing civic participation and responsibility, the rule of law, impersonal bureaucratic administration, and education – key elements in the creation of *la vita civile*, or civil life.[36] Robert D. Putnam builds upon Waley's and Hyde's studies in arguing for the enormous long-term influence within northern Italy of its communal and democratic legacy of civic virtue. This tradition encompasses a sense of community, public-spiritedness, adherence to universal laws and rules, and the ability to foster social and economic welfare through civic associations linked not hierarchically but horizontally. What makes northern Italian civic culture work, contends Putnam, is a spirit of trust and cooperation diffused throughout society, as in the later medieval Italian communes.[37]

Thanks to della Casa, Castiglione, and other writers of courtesy manuals, Italy enjoyed in sixteenth-century England an unsurpassed reputation for civility that lasted into the late 1600s.[38] The British travellers Thomas Coryate (*Coryate's Crudities*, 1611) and Fynes Moryson (*An Itinerary*, 1617) both noted that forks, spoons, and knives were regularly provided at the dinner table in Italian houses and inns; by contrast, the Italian scientist Lorenzo Magalotti, who visited England in 1669, found no evidence of the use of the fork. John Raymond, in *An Itinerary contayning a Voyage, Made through Italy, in the yeare 1646, and 1647* (1648), writes of Italy: 'To her we owe our civility,' to which A. Lytton Sells adds, 'that is, our Civilization (the word was not invented until the eighteenth century).' Richard Lassells (*An Italian Voyage, or a Compleat Journey through Italy*, 1670) recommends the educational value of Italy, 'that nation which hath civilized the whole world, and taught Mankind what it is to be a Man.'[39] Fernand Braudel defines the Baroque period as the height of Italy's (modern) influence on France, when Italian manners were widely imitated notwithstanding the reluctance of the French to acknowledge their social indebtedness to Italy. Describing the civilizing function of the late seventeenth-century salon of the Marquise de Rambouillet, who was of partly Italian origin, Braudel writes: 'French aristocrats and literati learned good taste, distinction, politeness in female company, and the affectations of refined language – all in the name of Italian elegance and under the aegis of Ariosto and Tasso.'[40] Yet as Giuseppe Baretti noted in the 1760s, the 'lively French [soon] rivalled their ultramontane masters in many things; nay, they ... attained so quickly to ... civility and eloquence ... that French politeness soon became a kind of universal pattern' for the whole of Europe.[41]

In referring to the 'tilt toward civility' in Italy and describing its progress as 'glacially' slow, Becker implies its only partial success. He mentions the primitive customs of rural districts and excludes southern Italy from the 'fragile' growth of *civiltà*.[42] Perhaps most damaging to civility was the failure of the late medieval communes to maintain trust, cooperation, and the spirit of compromise, so that violent factionalism led to despotism as the only means of preserving order. Although the Renaissance despots retained the communes' pre-existing forms of administration, they annihilated communal republicanism. One-man rule undermined *civitas* and democracy not only by violating universal legal principles but by discouraging trust, cooperation, and personal initiative.[43] Since Renaissance bureaucracies were corrupted by personalism, they failed to achieve full rationalization. Just as political offices were often bought and sold, so personalism continued to infect social life through clientelism and patronage. Despite its incipient bourgeois individualism, Italian Renaissance society eradicated neither the blood tie and vendetta nor the outer-directed medieval cult of honour. After the later Renaissance Italy was largely subjected to foreign powers that imposed despotic and hierarchical rule. Much of the country was 're-feudalized,' to use a much debated term, while patron-client networks pervaded a political world dominated by the aristocracy. The Counter-Reformation strengthened Italy's ecclesiastical hierarchy, which, though it promoted literacy, also controlled intellectual life through indoctrination and censorship. Possibly by around 1650, and certainly by 1700, Italy's economic and cultural decline were manifest.[44] Nor had civility reached maturity during the Italian Renaissance, despite its conduct books. For though the Italian aristocracy and bourgeoisie preceded their northern European counterparts in detaching themselves culturally and socially from the lower classes, this separation remained incomplete. Ercole d'Este, lord of Ferrara in the late fifteenth century, liked to ride around the city streets throwing raw eggs at young women who looked down from their windows; in a similarly carnivalistic spirit he participated in the egg fight that lasted an hour in the piazza of Ferrara in February 1478. During a visit to Bologna Pope Julius II thrashed a prelate who tried to intervene in his dispute with Michelangelo. Castiglione mentions food-throwing and practical jokes among the courtiers of his day, and amusements of the latter type were often built into the Italian country houses such as the sixteenth-century Medici villa of Pratolino, where, to quote Burke, the 'host was able to drench his guests as they strolled in his garden,' yet without the slightest imputation of bad taste.[45] Whereas the civilizing process was accelerating in northern Europe after 1650, it was being counteracted in Italy. Many Italian aristocrats continued to share popular culture and manners into the nineteenth century, by which point the northern European upper classes had established a definite division in taste and refinement between themselves and the lower orders.[46]

Surveying the Italian Renaissance from the perspective of 'civilization,' nineteenth-century writers such as Hippolyte Taine found it wanting. He observes that Renaissance Italians failed to exercise self-control and that their erratic lives present a 'strange incongruity.' Thus, 'after a life of debauchery and violence, even at the height of his vices, man suddenly becomes changed.' The Duke of Ferrara, according to a contemporary chronicler, 'having been attacked with a grave malady which stopped his secretions for over forty-eight hours had recourse to God and ordered all back salaries to be paid.' Ercole d'Este, after leaving an orgy, 'went to sing divine service with his company of French musicians; he either put out an eye or cut off the hand of two hundred prisoners before selling them, and on Holy Thursday he is found washing the feet of the poor.' As for Pope Alexander VI, 'on learning the assassination of his son [Giovanni Borgia], [he] beat his breast and confessed his crimes to the assembled cardinals.'[47] Taine concludes that during the Renaissance 'people as yet are not very polished. Crudity frightens nobody ... What we call good taste is a product of the *salon*, and is only born into the world under Louis XIV.' For Taine, the Renaissance hung suspended in a 'transitional state' between medieval 'lack of culture' and modern 'over-culture.' Renaissance Italy, he says, was 'almost a modern country.'[48]

In southern Italy, the centralized, rigidly hierarchical state had been the dominant political institution since the eleventh century. Unlike northern European monarchies after the Renaissance, which allied with the bourgeoisie against the aristocracy, southern Italian states never fostered the trust, cooperation, and entrepreneurship essential to *civitas* and economic prosperity. Nor did the feudal aristocratic South permit the formation of a responsible, active middle class, an educated public, the spirit of voluntary association, an efficient, rationalized political administration, and respect for universal legal principles. Instead, the personalism and favouritism of patron-client relations prevailed in a society riddled with suspicion and mistrust. [49]And because the weak states of the South have failed to win a monopoly of violence, they have been long afflicted by anarchic criminality and exploitative criminal associations such as the Mafia, which have taken advantage of a power vacuum in becoming a law unto themselves.[50]

The consequences of the retardation of the civilizing process are felt in Italy into the present. Although Dean Peabody characterizes northern Italy as a variant on the model of northern Europe, where *Gesellschaft* patterns prevail, he identifies Italy, alone among major Western European nations and the United States, with a *Gemeinschaft* pattern of society. Most Italians favour particularism or personalism over universalism, ascription over achievement, diffuseness over specificity in behaviour, and affectivity over emotional neutrality. Because private interests invade the public sphere, the modern Italian state is a 'pseudo-*Gesellschaft*.' Unlike northern Europeans, with their strong 'impulse-control,' Italians exhibit frequent 'impulse-expression' and emotional spontaneity even in public. Yet unlike the familiar identification of *Gemeinschaft* with warmth, mutual loyalty, and association, Italy is a 'negatively toned' *Gemeinschaft*, where community is limited to the family and its allies, while individuals and institutions are mistrusted. Imbued with private values, many Italians cannot imagine that an official could act disinterestedly. Civic spirit is therefore deficient in Italy, while in some parts of the South society approaches Hobbesian anarchy. So, too, some Italians have extreme difficulty in comprehending such capitalist values as trust, teamwork, fair play, and adherence to universal rules.[51]

III

Stendhal wrote in an age that largely accepted the idea of national character, of whose reality he has no doubt. In *Rossini* he refers to the 'French character,' and in *Love* he comments on the 'frightening change' that has 'overtaken it.' As for Italians, he says of Lorenzo de' Medici that though he 'bridled' Florentine republicanism he did not debase the 'national character.' Admittedly this statement refers to the Florentines rather than the Italians as a whole, and thus raises the question of the advisability of referring to Italians unitarily – an issue to which we shall return. Yet Stendhal also says that the personality of the Florentine artist Benevenuto Cellini affords unparalleled 'insight' into the Italian national character, and he elsewhere claims that Cellini's autobiography holds its secret.'[52] One could multiply similar examples.

In relying on the idea of national character, Stendhal is indebted to both the Enlightenment and Romanticism, the two main influences upon his thought. Already in the seventeenth century an interest in national character and national genius was evident in the works of Shaftsbury and other writers, and by the middle of the eighteenth century these concepts were widely accepted. Colbert and Le Brun prophesied a revival of the *génie française*; Bolingbroke and Montesquieu followed up Shaftesbury's inquiry into the 'spirit' of nations; and in 1775 James Barry noted that national character figured usefully in the vocabulary of the day. Probably the most influential theorist of national character was Montesquieu, whose *The Spirit of the Laws* attributes national characteristics to two chief causes: politics on the one hand and environment, especially climate, on the other. Contrastingly, David Hume in his essay 'On National Characters' (1748) stressed the role of morals and government over physical causes, whose influence he deemed negligible. The writer most responsible for politicizing national character was probably Rousseau, who saw it as an essential element in political life and who linked it to programs of national preservation and restoration. Rousseau had a powerful impact on Romantic thinking, as witness Madame de Staël, Stendhal's precursor in the interpretation of Italy, who in *Corinne* as in *L'Allemagne* attempted to interpret the Italian and German characters respectively. Linked closely to Romantic historicist culture, national character was coming to be seen as a growing entity with deep historical roots. The attractiveness of the concept of national character in the Romantic period is owed to an increasing dissatisfaction with Enlightenment universalism as well as disillusionment with the French Revolution as an enactment of Enlightenment values. Insofar as the concept of national character could be used to justify the preservation of the distinctive national identities and traits, it had the potential of undermining the Enlightenment concept of civilization as a universal standard of politics, society, and behaviour to which all nations should aspire, even at the cost of their distinctiveness. Some nations, such as Germany from the late eighteenth into the twentieth century, challenged the concept of universal civilization by preserving and cultivating their own national characteristics. For many German thinkers, civilization represented the artificial, mechanical, and material as against the deeper, non-material values they associated with their own ideal of *Kultur*. In France, as in the writings of Guizot, the concept of civilization maintained considerable prestige, as it did in England, where John Stuart Mill, despite his appreciation of national characters, still conceived of civilization as ultimately absorbing national differences. On all these issues Stendhal remains divided in his allegiances, and that division mirrors his conflicted judgments of Italy in his own time.[53]

The idea of a national character has inspired various definitions, some overlapping, others contradictory. Whereas Benedetto Croce regards national character as nothing but the history of a people, which would make it an object of conscious awareness, Alessandro Cavalli draws upon Norbert Elias's studies of German identity in defining it in terms of the 'traces' history has deposited in the 'inner depths' of a people. Since these are acquired unintentionally, they are not part of a nation's historical memory or tradition. Such a definition seems to contradict Croce's identification of national character with a nation's history. For Peter Mandler, national character refers to the common psychological or cultural characteristics that make a people distinctive. He stresses the relative permanence and continuity of national character, referring to a 'single personality type' rooted in 'stable, deep-seated structures.' Adapting and modifying an earlier formulation of Sir Ernest Barker's, Mihaly Szegedy-Maszák's definition of national character apparently relies on Montesquieu while including perhaps unmanageable behavioural elements drawn from history and culture. According to Szegedy-Maszák, national character is a 'complex of socially transmitted traditions, consisting mainly of ethnic, geographic, economic, political, religious, linguistic, and multinational components.' Such a definition would not satisfy Alex Inkeles, who subjects the concept of national character to close methodological scrutiny. Like other scholars, Inkeles believes that national character must refer to relatively enduring features within a population, and he has no doubt that it results from sociocultural forces, especially social structure, though he prefers that it be studied apart from them. Inkeles notes that scholars have sought to derive it from political and social institutions, public and collective action, and high and low culture. It has been studied as an institutional pattern, as a reflection of culture in the anthropological sense, and as action or behaviour. Yet Inkeles rejects the view that national character consists of the sum of the values, institutions, cultural traditions, ways of acting, and history of a people – a complex mix incapable of being measured. Nor should it be identified as a behavioural trait. Instead, Inkeles derives his definition from Tocqueville, whose study of what he calls American 'manners' focuses on personal and individual attitudes, values, opinions, beliefs, and personality dispositions. What Tocqueville is talking about, argues Inkeles, is national character in its properly restricted, manageable sense. As Inkeles defines it, national character is a property of persons, and consists of the dispositions built into the personalities of those who make up a society. These dispositions are the 'relatively enduring personality characteristics' within a nation. Thus national character is revealed in yet not identical with behaviour; rather, its source lies in the individual personality, which determines behaviour. This definition is much narrower than that of Clark R. McCauley and his colleagues, whose studies of group stereotypes bear upon questions of national character, which inevitably involves stereotyping. In their view, stereotypes have to do with the traits, behaviours, and values of individuals, the first two elements standing outside Inkeles's definition. Finally, in a biological interpretation, Richard Lynn defines national character in terms of personality or temperament and attempts to test national groups for their degree of 'anxiety' or emotionality. Although Lynn regards parental nurture and class as the chief recent influences on national character, he sees heredity or genetics as the long-term underlying factor. He further contends that national stereotypes are often confirmed by ordinary observation.[54]

Stendhal's unsystematic meditations on the Italian national character cover many phenomena. Under the implicit assumption that national characteristics are enduring or at least relatively permanent, he often traces to the Middle Ages the attitudes and behaviour of modern Italians. Culture, in the sense of literature, music, and the arts, he also takes as evidence of the Italian character. In his view, Italy's social structure, its political arrangements, and not least its religion, shape and express the character of its people. Generally, however, Stendhal's interest in the Italian character centres on what he terms *Italie morale*, meaning the personality traits of the Italians, their psychology, temperament, values, emotions, and orientation towards the world – traits reflected in behaviour but irreducible to it, being its determinants.

Nonetheless any attempt to define or write in terms of an Italian national character raises difficulties, especially for the period in which Stendhal lived, which was decades before Italian national unification in 1861. Notwithstanding Stendhal's references to an Italian national character rooted in the Middle Ages, historians have tended to regard the concept of national character as having been hindered in its development as a result of the masses' long exclusion from political and hence national life. From this point of view, the concept emerges only in the modern period of the nation states, when people first became sufficiently conscious of their national groupings to identify with them personally, out of a sense of shared identity. Yet Anthony Smith, in posing the question of whether nations existed before nationalism (and finding only fleeting expressions of national sentiment before 1789), acknowledges that an ethnic identity, conscious or unconscious, can exist prior to the

formation of a nation. Raymond Grew argues that, though a state typically seeks to foster a national identity (of which national character is
often seen as an important part), such an identity and character may pre-
exist state formation. Indeed, nation-building aims to give national identity stability and institutional expression, as in the Risorgimento. Also
worth noting is Ruggiero Romano's point that, though Italy failed to
unify politically until the nineteenth century, foreign observers and the
Italians themselves had long attributed to Italy a common culture and
ethnic identity. This took the form of conscious and articulate awareness
in the educated class, for instance Dante, Petrarch, and Machiavelli, and
unconscious attitudes and shared traits among the common people.[55]

Another difficulty in speaking of the Italian national character is that,
owing to geography and even more so to Italy's failure to achieve national unity before 1861, it had long been fragmented into highly distinctive regions and city-states. More than a century after unification,
the peninsula remains diverse culturally and to some extent divided by
regional loyalties and particularisms. Because of this lack of homogeneity within Italy the eighteenth-century writer Giuseppe Baretti hesitated
to generalize about the Italian character in *The Manners and Customs of
Italy* (1769), in which he sought to acquaint his English hosts with his
much-maligned countrymen. As Baretti noted, for centuries the regions
of Italy have had their own characteristic dialects, customs, behaviours,
and even temperaments. This persistent heterogeneity has led twentieth-century observers such as Giulio Bollati and especially Pellegrino
d'Acierno to suggest boldly that generalizations concerning an Italian
national character are futile owing to its multitude of local differences.
For D'Acierno, Italy beyond any other country embodies the Foucaul-
dian *heterotopia*, where difference and diversity triumph over totalizing
uniformity. Yet the majority of commentators have approached the
problem in less extreme fashion, neither exaggerating the regional
variations within Italy nor attempting to define its character in terms
of a single homogenizing essence or trait. Instead, they have acknowledged Italy's regional diversity but at the same time stressed the many
similarities within the nation as a whole. Notwithstanding his awareness
of regional peculiarities, Baretti repeatedly generalizes on the Italian
national character, one of his main intentions being to overturn negative stereotypes. The same willingness to think in terms of a national
character typifies many of the most important writers on this theme, including Pietro Calepio, Madame de Staël, Sismondi, Giacomo Leopardi,
Carlo Sforza, Silvio Guarnieri, Gabriel Almond and Sidney Verba, Luigi

Barzini, Dean Peabody, Michael Carroll, Carlo Tullio-Altan, Loredana
Sciolla, Alessandro Cavalli, and Stendhal.[56]

Few foreign observers are as sensitive as Stendhal to the distinctive
regional cultures and characters of Italy, in which he takes unending
delight, and he is likewise aware of the problem of Italy's many dialects,
which he rightly sees as a major obstacle not only to state formation but
to the establishment within Italy of a public sphere and national culture.
In *Rome, Naples and Florence* he assigns to an Italian speaker the observation that 'You do not need telling that these different peoples are very
far from forming a homogenous nation ... each city detests its neighbors,
and is mortally detested in return.' In *Love* he observes that 'language or
manners' in Italy change from region to region, and in another instance
he goes so far as to describe the Milanese as having their own 'national
character.'[57] Yet for all his awareness of Italian diversity, Stendhal sees
no contradiction in referring to the Italian national character. He realizes that, when all is said and done, the resemblance is likely to be much
greater between a Sicilian and a Milanese than between a Sicilian and a
Scot.

A further objection to the idea of national character perhaps originates
with David Hume's essay 'Of National Characters.' For though Hume
generalizes about national traits when they appear with high frequency,
he warns against overgeneralizing. It is a mistake, he argues, to ascribe a
trait to a national group without admitting exceptions. What Hume objects to, although he lacks a word for it, is what in the twentieth century
would come to be criticized as stereotyping. In its narrowest yet most
widely accepted definition, stereotypes are rigid behavioural and temperamental attributes applied to all members of a group. In an extreme
example of stereotyping, Daniel Defoe in 'The True-Born Englishman'
(1700) claims that each nation fits a single characterological type, the
Italians being uniformly lustful. Although Madame de Staël in *On Literature* seeks to disprove national stereotypes, she too assumes that each
national group can be characterized by a single national trait; fortunately, she avoids such simplistic thinking in *Corinne*. In 1824 James Morier
introduced the word 'stereotype' into English, though without pejorative implications, yet by the early twentieth century Walter Lippmann
and others were complaining of the prejudicially harmful stereotypes
of national characters. National and other forms of stereotyping came
to be condemned by social scientists as thoroughly false conceptions
whereby individual traits and behaviours are forced without exception
into a rigidly uniform and distorting pattern. Although Gordon Allport

held that all stereotypes need not be false, he regarded the majority as crude exaggerations, and most recent studies of stereotypes have sought to demonstrate their inaccuracy. In common parlance 'stereotype' implies the exaggeration of group traits to the point of caricature. As for national character, it has been largely ignored by social scientists since the 1950s, apparently for fear of unscientific stereotyping.[58]

Perhaps because of the withdrawal of the concept of national character, and also because of the desire to replace it, the period following World War II has witnessed an increasing reliance on the newer concept of national identity, a less rigid formulation that encompasses the combination of political ideals and institutions, common culture and territory, and shared symbolic values that hold a nation together.[59] Yet is national character bankrupt as a category? Does it inevitably produce stereotypes in the sense of reductive, unreliable, overly generalizing caricatures of group traits? Insofar as anthropology depends on the assumption that real differences exist between human groups, some generalization – and stereotyping – seems built into the enterprise. Moreover, over the last two decades many social scientists have arrived at a less one-sidedly negative view of stereotypes. For though stereotypes continue to be condemned for admitting no exceptions, it has been shown that many people who rely on them neither ignore exceptions nor rush to judgment, but instead rightly comprehend them as probabilistic predictions combining truth and falsehood. As stereotypes have been shown to conform to objective fact in some cases, and to exhibit degrees of accuracy in many others, it is understandable that the 'kernel of truth' theory of stereotypes has come back, and that studies of stereotype accuracy proliferate. It has also been noted that stereotypes are mutable, for as the characteristics of national groups change, so do the stereotypes by which observers interpret them – a phenomenon of which the northern European response to Italy affords many examples.[60]

Similarly, the concept of national character makes sense if one limits it carefully. As Alex Inkeles argues, not only is it to be identified with the personality traits of adult individuals within a national population, but it should be conceptualized in multimodal terms, as the sum of such traits across that population. The major error is to assume the existence of a single personality mode, or one set of characteristics, within a society. Rather, one should study the range and distinctiveness of modal personalities, so as to isolate characteristics that appear with the greatest frequency, and in varying patterns. National character thus refers to the modes of distribution of personality variants within a society. Yet

Inkeles' conception of national character also takes history into account, for though it consists by definition in relatively permanent traits, it may change to the point where it no longer resembles itself.[61]

Although Stendhal does not write systematically on national character, he avoids subjecting the Italians to a rigidly static profile based on a single characterological category. The Italian types depicted in his writings remain various. Despite his identification of Italians with grand passions and absence of vanity, he acknowledges that the former are rare even in Italy, and that some Italians are quite vain. Nor does he confuse the rough and somber ferocity of the Calabrians, or the sensualism and largely corporeal eroticism of the Neapolitans, with the elegance, sociability, and emotional delicacy of Milanese high society, whatever the resemblances among these groups. Far from supposing the Italian national character to have remained historically fixed, Stendhal often gives the impression of believing it to have altered since the Middle Ages and Renaissance, under the domination of foreign rulers in alliance with the Counter-Reformation. As Stendhal finds the French to have been transformed in his own time by British models, so the Italians are changing under French influence, and seem less and less what they were in the days of Cellini. Yet he believes that some Italians of his own day closely resemble their Renaissance and medieval ancestors, and that the traits of the Italians are sufficiently persistent historically to justify a substantial belief in their characterological continuity with their ancient past.

IV

A reader of Montesquieu, Helvétius, Volney, and Cabanis, Stendhal holds that a nation's climate, and more especially its government, largely determine its character and hence its way of life.[62] Italy's hot and dry yet caressing climate has thus supposedly shaped the Italians' bilious and choleric temperament, which is variously passionate, sensuous, aesthetic, nervous, irritable, impulsive, restless, fiery, and easily offended. Under the same climatic influence the Italians exhibit extreme sensitivity to stimuli, intense corporeal engagement with their total physical environment, and an explosive energy that, though it often issues in dangerous discharges of violence, has its paradoxical counterpart in a propensity for deep meditation upon personal feelings. Taken together, the Italians' erratic behaviour stands in a virtually antithetical relationship with the phlegmatic and insensitive yet steadily productive northern European.[63] In *Literature in its Relation to Social Institutions*, as in her novel *Corinne*, Madame de Staël had preceded Stendhal in giving climatic explanations of the Italian character, which she borrows from Montesquieu.[64] Like Staël, Stendhal links Italy's geography and its national character, noting the similarity between the volcanic landscapes of Rome and Naples and the fiery temperament of the inhabitants.[65] He further resembles Staël in portraying Italy as the 'garden of Europe,' where natural abundance and an indulgent climate foster sensuality and indolent reverie as opposed to the melancholy labours required in the inclement North. Actually, much of Italy is marginally fertile, and its inhabitants have survived only through hard effort against the environment.[66]

For Stendhal, not climate but government has chiefly determined Italian national character. Nowhere is this more evident than in the medieval Italian republics, which have 'moulded the primal Italian character as we know it today,' and whose role in forming Italy Stendhal came to realize partly through the Swiss historian Sismondi. Defiant of monarchical and papal control, the citizens of these merchant republics demanded freedom in defense of their property and thus preferred to be honoured for their 'useful occupations' rather than hungering for the vain and chimerical honours bestowed by monarchical courts. Or as Stendhal puts it, the medieval republics gave Italy its 'foundation of good sense.' The virtue they displayed in defense of their freedom was inspired by the turbulent factionalism of urban politics, as the democracy and liberty pursued in these republics had only a '*precarious existence*' and was of the 'stormy [*orageuse*]' kind. A premium thus being placed on will and character, the period issued in those prodigies of love and hate that inspire Stendhal's confession that he is '*in love with medieval Italy*.' He has in mind the medieval republics when, projecting his never-written *History of Milan*, he notes that the 'gigantic passions of the Middle Ages break through ... in the undimmed effulgence of their ferocious energy.'[67] A further advantage Italy gained from the republics was that their '*liberty*' and 'heroic' way of life 'first touched off' the 'divine spark' of what came to be known as the Renaissance.[68]

Like Sismondi, who helped to clarify his thinking on this point, Stendhal distinguishes between medieval Italian republicanism and the constitutional type that, through England, France, and the United States, has shaped modern politics. Not only was citizenship in the medieval Italian republics reserved for a small percentage of the population, but the state guaranteed neither personal security nor freedom of industry, opinion, or conscience. Instead, citizens were expected to sacrifice their own private interests to participation in public affairs, which were virtually all-demanding, and which often involved them in violent political rivalries. Yet though the Italian tyrants never bestowed constitutions upon their domains, they compensated for their private lawlessness with a wealth of public virtues. Contrastingly, modern constitutional republics aim for peace, security, and the undisturbed privacy of the domestic sphere, including the legal protection of property. Being much more concerned with citizens' rights and equality under the law, such governments are expected to guarantee freedom of industry, religion, and the press. And so the 'liberty' of the Italian republics 'is not that which one finds in Philadelphia or that is dreamed of on the banks of the Thames.'[69]

All of Stendhal's writings on Italy implicate two facts: first, its failure to achieve political unity during the Renaissance, and second, its centuries-long submission to foreign despotisms, which Stendhal sees as having begun in 1530 when Spain extinguished the Florentine Republic. The loss of Italian liberty had been anticipated in fifteenth-century Florence, when the Medici had ruled the city behind the scenes while using money to corrupt its citizens' republican virtues. Over the next three centuries Italy suffered enslavement under 'cruel,' 'suspicious,' 'execrable,' 'predatory,' 'vexatious,' 'plundering,' 'probing,' 'meticulous,' 'infamous,' 'implacable,' 'jealous,' 'debasing,' 'enfeebling,' 'petty,' 'weak,' and 'timid' governments.[70] The Italians' moral character and passionate energy were degraded, as were their republican virtue and communal pride. In sixteenth-century Florence Cosimo I de' Medici replaced republican virtue with that 'cruel' honour Stendhal regards as the form of vanity fostered by courtly societies. Whereas republican liberty had helped to inspire Renaissance art, with few exceptions foreign despotisms caused Italian art and literature to deteriorate. Fervent in his hope for Italian unity and freedom in the nineteenth century, Stendhal often contends that the revival of Italian art and literature requires Italy to become a constitutional monarchy with two legislative chambers, on the analogy of England and post-Napoleonic France.[71] Having been centuries ahead of Europe during the Renaissance, nineteenth-century Italians are two centuries behind England, whose success demonstrates the link between liberalism, order, and prosperity. Or as Stendhal puts it: '*Rien sans la liberté, tout avec la liberté.*'[72]

Despite his admiration of individualism, Stendhal is neither personally nor ideologically antisocial but accepts several distinctly social values as indispensable to civilization. Not only does he espouse the modern co-operative ideal of 'association' set forth by Fourier and others,[73] but he believes that proper relations between government and society require their mediation through an independent public sphere within which free and informed citizens can express openly their political and other opinions in an atmosphere of mutual trust and good will. Stendhal also appreciates the rule of law and impartial application of justice as a means of limiting antisocial behaviour and of promoting the trust of the citizenry in both each other and their government. From this perspective, the anarchic individualism that signals the absence of civilization in Italy is rooted in at least two long-standing historical causes.

First is the legacy of the Middle Ages, when a politically disunified Italy was wracked by violent antagonisms between and within its individual states, and a public sphere thus failed to develop at a national level. Second is the more recent presence of a 'multitude of petty tyrants' who besides maintaining the political fragmentation of the peninsula have deliberately promoted fear and mistrust among its people, so as to reduce them to 'utter degradation.' Every Italian city since medieval times, writes Stendhal, 'has pursued its neighbor with unabated loathing; and the ingrained habit of such civic discord cannot but sound an echo of mistrust between one individual and the next.' If Italy is the 'native home' of love, it is also the land of '*hatred*,' where people fear strangers and regard their neighbours' opinions with suspicion and disdain. What Stendhal says of medieval despotisms, that they never established impartial justice or reasonable laws, applies equally to the foreign regimes succeeding them. In the absence of political liberty, and because mutual suspicion poisons the relation between the despot and his people, there is no real public and no public sphere, which only adds to the general mistrust. A further liability is that despotic injustice encourages people to yield to impulse and to take the law into their own hands. Without a responsible government, how could the Italians develop the social cooperativeness so productive in the law-abiding North? For more than four centuries the 'life' of Italy had been 'choked' by the 'strangling crop of anti-social practices.'[74]

However, Stendhal sometimes exaggerates the deficiencies of the public sphere in post-Renaissance Italy, for as Brendan Dooley has shown, and as Stendhal realizes, an educated public of some extent existed in the eighteenth century. This was partly attributable to the state, which in the late eighteenth century came to appreciate the role of education in shaping public opinion, and also to the resurgence of Italian universities in the same period. Nonetheless, this public sphere remained underdeveloped from the eighteenth into the nineteenth century, taking a local rather than national form.[75]

For Stendhal, the concept of civilization is inextricable from forms of social behaviour that qualify as civilized and that thrive within a certain type of society of which France affords the best example. Demanding self-control, deference, and respect for one's neighbour's opinion, French high society raises refined manners or politeness to a universal standard for the entire nation. As Stendhal realizes, the ideal of *civilité* originates at the court of Louis XIV, who imposed upon his courtiers new and non-violent codes of honour, politeness, and good taste. Thanks to the prestige of the capital, these social values spread throughout France and were further developed in aristocratic salons and in the drawing rooms of the bourgeois emulators of courtly and aristocratic society. Hence the 'living law' of Louis XIV 'still governs' nineteenth-century Parisians.[76] Yet the French social ideal rests not simply on good manners or the proprieties. Rather, society fulfils itself in sophisticated conversation, the object being not simply to observe social conventions but to extract a high degree of pleasure through the enjoyment of oneself and others. One might describe conversation as the chief adornment of such a society, that for which it exists.[77]

It would be an exaggeration to claim that Stendhal failed to encounter good manners or engaging conversation within Italian society, which at some points he praises over its Parisian rival. Not only does he admire the high society of Bologna, which he finds 'a little more colorful' than that of Paris, and whose leading luminary, Madame Martinetti, could easily hold her own in that milieu, but he claims to prefer Paduan society to the most brilliant Parisian salons, which seem arid by comparison with the charms of Madame Benzoni. Rome in the 1820s supposedly has the most 'preferable' salons in Europe, those of Paris having become dry and serious as compared to the wit and variety of Roman conversation. Regarding Naples, Stendhal reports having been 'treated with ... impeccable courtesy,' adding that 'there is nothing save the rarest *nuances* to distinguish the tone which reigns in such company from that of polite society in Paris.' In Florence, he finds 'unforced politeness' in addition to 'civilized urbanity' and 'worldly wisdom.' Naples with its 'fifty fascinating salons' is 'livelier' than Paris, and nowhere in Italy is Stendhal more delighted than amid the liveliness of Milanese repartee in the salon-like boxes at La Scala.[78]

Yet on the whole Stendhal finds Italian society to exhibit many shortcomings in both politeness and conversation, a judgment that seems quite credible and for which the most likely historical explanation lies in the fact that, having been politically disunited from Roman times into the mid-nineteenth century, the Italians unlike the French have never followed a single courtly model of behaviour. Even during the Renaissance, notes Richard Goldthwaite, Italy's political fragmentation resulted in a variety of court models. Nor were the local nobility of the larger capitals necessarily absorbed in court, as witness those sixteenth-century Florentine aristocrats who hardly involved themselves in the social life of the city's first grand dukes, despite the antiquity of their Medici pedigree.[79] Although the various states and regions within the peninsula possessed their own distinctive social traditions and conventions, these were not necessarily binding on the individual, while the antisocial climate under the later Italian despotisms led to disrespect for common behavioural ideals and standards. The result was that the typical Italian often acted as he or she pleased, in disregard of society at large.

Although Stendhal acknowledges that 'naturalness' may flourish in the absence of a standardizing 'decorum of civilization,' he also knows that a 'riotous luxuriance of foolishness may grow unchecked,' and where does one draw the line between agreeable spontaneity and merely crude behaviour? His claim that the Italians are 'far from being polished' is supported by the evidence of rudeness in their salons, where overbearing people dominate the meek and timid. Similarly, the lack of refinement in Goldoni's characters reflects Italy's social situation, that of a 'less advanced' civilization.[80] At points Stendhal implies that civilization exists only in small pockets of Italian society, such as Bologna. Typifying the absence of 'good form' and '*savoir-vivre*' in Italy, which falls below the 'enormously perfected' standard of French salons, Signor Casati on his visit to a box at a theater showed bad breeding by talking for ten minutes without knowing the ladies. As in the Renaissance, Italians tell jokes of 'excellent indecency' and feel free to accost pretty women in the street.[81] Rome is filled with migrant peasants wearing sheepskins. In small towns disputes over party walls lead to bloodshed, which, however fascinating aesthetically, bespeaks the rule of force over both manners and law. Whereas in France the *honnête homme* conceals the unseemly,[82] Stendhal tells of a man who, in the eyes of an Italian, appeared '*honest and kindly*' while proposing an assassination. Having never been at court, an Italian *marchese* will mouth 'foul indecencies' and express his anger 'in more or less the same language' as his lackey. In scholarly debate Italians reveal the 'urbanity of the fourteenth century,' referring to one another politely as 'ass' and 'animal.' In their academies, should one scholar contradict another, he makes of him a mortal enemy.[83]

Stendhal traces the relative absence of refined and sophisticated conversation in Italy to a lack of sites necessary to its cultivation and refinement: on the one hand, the monarchical court; on the other, the national capital where the upper-class salon and its wits define verbal and social models for the nation. Unlike Italy, the French and more especially the Parisians continued to benefit from the influence of the Bourbon court of the eighteenth century, where politeness had reached unprecedented levels of refinement, and where nuanced conversation had become the 'art *par excellence*,' the 'key to everything.'[84] Another factor impeding the development of conversation in Italy is its despotic governments, whose spies and other forms of surveillance discourage not only a public sphere but free conversation. Other causes include poverty and the long-standing antisocial, self-isolating habits of the Italians, as witness that in nineteenth-century Rome Stendhal finds almost no society to speak of in the sense of dinner parties, balls, and other social invitations, while in Milan, were it not for the boxes of La Scala, society would barely exist. Turning their backs on epigrams, witty anecdotes, and piquant incidents, the Italians treat conversation as 'nothing but a *vehicle* for emotional expression,' with the result that, unlike in France, it is very rarely valued 'for its own sake.' Italians prefer to talk all at once, being impatient of give-and-take, while the Calabrians are ignorant of the art of conversation altogether. The 'rapier-like displays of wit' delightful to the French only 'embarrass' the Italians, who lack the French talent for ready repartee and among whom such brilliance is 'heartily despised.' Yet should the Italians find themselves 'bereft of a riposte to fling back at their interlocutors,' they 'go pale with fury,' which testifies to their 'intolerance in argument.'[85] In the judgment of a fictional Frenchman in Stendhal's *Roman Journal*, personal relations among Italians are immediate and direct, yet their passion and sincerity cause them to reveal too much of themselves too quickly, so that their experience lacks wit, subtlety, and interest. Stendhal also finds the typical Italian to lack irony and brevity in wit, which is why Voltaire and La Bruyère leave him cold and why 'hints and insinuations mean nothing to him, in a book.'[86] Contrastingly, in the French salons all is irony and implication, as verbal nuances register the ever-shifting gradations of social distance and intimacy, irony and sincerity. In short, the Italians' political fragmentation and social habits had deprived them of a highly refined verbal culture and its accompanying social sophistication.

Writing in the 1780s, William Beckford remarked the Italians' lack of 'politeness, refinement of manners, and the true spirit of society,' although he noted many exceptions. The same judgment figures in the writing of numerous eighteenth- and nineteenth-century travellers.[87]

Stendhal's contention that Italian scholars often substituted personal insult for reasoned argument may seem exaggerated, yet during the 1760s Giuseppe Baretti opposed free speech in Italy on the grounds that it would unleash a host of scribblers specializing in *ad hominem* invective and scurrilous defamations.[88] If what Stendhal reports of Italian scholars is true, they resembled their Renaissance (and medieval) predecessors. Becker refers to the '[high] temperature of polemical and fiery civic prose so prevalent in Quattrocento Italian humanist court circles,' and Kerrigan and Braden note that scholars Poggio Bracciolini and George of Trebizond 'slugged it out publicly' over translations of Xenophon and Diodorus Siculus.[89]

Just as Stendhal found good manners and conversation in some parts of Italy, so eighteenth-century Italy was not altogether without a refined society comparable to that of France. Geneviève Gennari notes that Pietro Verri displayed his wit and intelligence in the late eighteenth-century Milanese salons of Paola Castiglione and Mme Serbelloni, and there were other approximations of the Parisian standard.[90] Yet though Vaussard notes that salons became 'all the rage' in eighteenth-century Italy, where 'civilized behavior had spread to new classes and women of high birth in particular were freed from a mass of restrictions,' these salons were largely devoted to parlour games and gambling, substitutes for the outdoor games of the previous century.[91] The English Italophobe Dr Samuel Sharpe, a visitor in the 1760s, found Italian *conversazioni* less diversified and interesting than those of London, since Italians dared not speak on liberty, politics, or religion. According to the late eighteenth-century traveller Patrick Brydone, the Sicilian nobility had informed conversations, but their counterparts elsewhere in Italy attended *conversazioni* only for the 'frivolity and nothingness' of playing cards and eating ices.[92] During his Italian visit of 1780 Beckford complained of the dearth of interesting conversation in Venetian aristocratic drawing rooms, where it had been driven out by mindless gambling and indolence resulting from feverishly erratic debauchery. The poverty of conversation among other Italians he attributed to their love of secrecy and dissimulation, which prevented them from speaking their thoughts, and to their vanity, which led to chatter, pretension, and 'pompous insipidity.'[93] Although Hester Thrale Piozzi praised literary discussions in Venice and Verona, where ladies participated, she concluded that no Italian 'dreams of cultivating conversation at all – *as an art*.' She attributed Italy's lack of novels and sophisticated comedies to the Italians' immediate self-revelation or sincerity, which obviated the need for the psychological exploration of character. Germaine de Staël would make the same point in *Corinne*. Even Baretti, an indefatigable apologist for Italy, found Italian drawing room society boring, since, unlike in France, discussions of literature, trade, and economics were off-limits in feminine company.[94] According to Sismondi, the platitudinousness and lack of moral awareness in Italian conversation stemmed partly from political repression, which had prevented a public sphere while making mind and conscience torpid.[95] Similar criticism of Italian conversation appears in the writings of nineteenth-century travellers such as Lady Morgan, Charlotte Eaton, A.W. Power, Henry James, and Byron.[96]

Another feature of Italian society that Stendhal criticizes for its failure to meet the civilized standard is its comparative lack of hygiene and high tolerance of domestic and public filth. As he observes on more than one occasion, dirtiness is a predominant characteristic of Italy. In contrast with Parisian buildings, with their customary 'cleanliness on the interior,' Rome's newly built Palazzo Ercolani, however magnificent, 'already looks all dirty.' 'I didn't see a single room where I'd be able to work with pleasure,' writes Stendhal, adding: 'the dirtiness shocked me wherever I turned.' The first floor of the 'finest cafe in Rome,' though housed in the Palazzo Ruspoli, strikes one 'by the magnificence of the rooms and by their lack of cleanliness.' It is hardly surprising that Rome, like Italy generally, abounds in nasty smells. Stendhal complains of the odor of rotten cabbages in the market of the Corso, of the stench emanating from the church of San Lorenzo in Lucina, and of the 'affreuse saleté' of the Roman streets, which so nauseate him that that he needs smelling salts.[97]

Stendhal's objections to Italy's dirt and smells are confirmed by both historians and travellers. During the eighteenth century, notes Andrieux, Romans customarily threw not only garbage but human waste into the streets, where it was collected at long, irregular intervals. Imbued with bourgeois ideals of public hygiene and orderliness, eighteenth-century travellers such as Goethe, Grosley, Joseph Spence, Hester Thrale Piozzi, and Marianna Starke were scandalized that Italians of all classes, in the absence of public lavatories and, for many, domestic sanitation, relieved themselves in the porticoes, colonnades, and courtyards of their cities. Similar complaints persisted in the nineteenth century among British and American visitors,[98] and, like Stendhal's annoyance with Roman odours, they indicate rising standards of civilization. As Alain Corbin remarks, in France from the eighteenth century onward the olfactory environment 'became increasingly muted and deodorized' thanks to hygienists and sanitation experts. Relating this to Elias's theory of the 'civilizing process,' Corbin notes that, if public hygiene implies social order, the presence of smells connotes bad manners and proximity to animals.[99]

V

Contrary to what Graña suggests, Stendhal respects rational and orderly behaviour as well as social responsibility. One side of his personality is drawn to the idea that reason can systematize all human behaviour, even the passions. He is also indebted to Helvétius's and Bentham's utilitarian principle of the greatest happiness for the greatest number, which entails an appeal to the state as the minister of social benefits.[100] Broadly speaking, Stendhal views politics as the reconciliation of private and general interests. For him, civilization requires a modern centralized state and all that it implies – efficient, impartial administration, uniform laws, a reliable police force, and a cooperative, literate, and intelligent public. These values underly his harsh criticism of Italian politics and society in the 1800s. The Italians, he finds, are unjustified in their 'backstairs patriotism' (*patriotisme d'antéchambre*), whereby they refuse to allow anything Italian (or local) to be disparaged.[101] This is mere vanity in a land so deficient in civilization.

In *Pages d'Italie* Stendhal asserts that the more a people esteems force, the less civilized it is, and that the force which antiquity admired means almost 'nothing' in modernity. The most dramatic evidence of Italy's uncivilized condition is thus its lawless violence as seen in the vendetta – a social evil often noted from the late sixteenth century onward. As Stendhal puts it, '*insecurity* ... is a chronic malady to be endured' in Italy.[102] Michel Crouzet describes Stendhal's Italy as 'la terre *classique* de l'assassinat, ou de la vengeance,' where people side with assassins, and where the language of criminality is as nuanced as that of love, to which Italian violence is linked inseparably. Yet though Crouzet emphasizes Stendhal's fascination with Italian criminality, he notes his demand for political justice, and indeed, Stendhal's interest in Italian bandits is largely literary.[103] Not only does he support the abolition of duelling, but in *A Roman Journal* he describes himself as a 'peace-loving and law-abiding' man, thus revealing his bourgeois sympathies, and adds that, 'especially when I find myself exposed to the vexations of the [corrupt] Italian police, I wish that the entire earth should obtain the legal government of New York.'[104]

Maurice Vaussard gives the impression that crime, including murder, occurred frequently in eighteenth-century Italy.[105] According to Andrieux, Rome was largely free of theft and burglary, since the people were supplied gratis by the government, and there were no riots; yet several murders were committed daily in Rome, and on feast days roughly five and six. Eighteen thousand people are claimed to have been murdered in Rome between 1795 and 1800. Normally accomplished with the knife, the duelling weapon of the lower class, these crimes usually resulted from quarrels over women and personal honour among a people for whom vendetta was an obligation. The Romans also took the law into their own hands as the alternative to an unreliable judiciary as well as a corrupt police force (the *sbirri*), which the people refused to help.[106] Martin Clark observes that in nineteenth-century Italy known murders averaged three thousand per year, and were often motivated by love, vengeance, hatred, and anger. Under the modernizing post-Risorgimento Italian state, however, such acts were defined as criminal.[107]

Of all Italian governments Stendhal is most critical of the papal 'pure despotism' that, except for the Napoleonic occupation of 1810–1814, ruled Rome from the Counter-Reformation to the Italian unification and which he, like Machiavelli, Guicciardini, Giannone, Sismondi, Burckhardt, and Symonds, views as a major cause of Italy's internal conflicts and ultimate decline. Indeed, Stendhal blames the papacy for Italy's political fragmentation, the 'greatest crime of modern times.' He would have had less cause to complain of late sixteenth- and early seventeenth-century Rome, which, thanks to Pope Sixtus V, Bernini, and Borromini, was then the most modern, best administered city in Europe.[108] However, by the early nineteenth century, Rome's backwardness had long been a topos of travel writers. When in 1780 Martin Sherlock described Rome as the 'worst lighted city in Europe,' he evoked the absence of enlightenment in a nation where 'they love obscurity in every thing.' In 1814 John Mayne cited an Italian who, commenting on Rome's lack of street-lighting, described it as nearly a century behind the major European capitals.[109] Andrieux claims that the Romans preferred dark streets, which provided nocturnal immunity from surveillance by the public and police.[110]

In Stendhal's judgment the political, social, and economic decline of the Papal States began as early as 1595. His criticism of the papal government reflects his preference for a rationalistic, tolerant, sensuous paganism over a putatively sadistic Christianity, but it is more deeply grounded in his disapproval of a system in which the Church is the state.

He contends that freedom of thought lasted in Italy until the reign of Pope Paul IV, who reacted to the Reformation by indoctrinating Italian children with superstition; indeed, the 'art of thinking has always been discouraged' in Rome, and, 'when necessary, persecuted.' As priestly education discourages mind and body, so papal hierarchism promotes obsequiousness while crushing character.[111] The papal theocracy is for Stendhal what Imbert calls a 'gigantic machine of political exploitation' which imposes heavy taxes, ruinous monopolies on the grain trade, and needlessly intricate regulations yet fails to reward or encourage 'patient industry.' Not only does the Roman government have 'a hand in every-thing,' so that private economic initiatives require permission, but its meddling in the grain trade had led to famine on some occasions. Un-der these conditions work is thrown in disrepute, the Romans are con-demned to laziness and impoverishment, and banditry flourishes as the best alternative to an honest livelihood. Like many travellers, Stendhal remarks that, at the frontier between Tuscany and the Papal States, 'wild and suspicious barbarity suddenly replaces the most exquisite polite-ness.'[112] He calls to mind other travellers in deploring the uncultivated Campagna outside Rome, where absentee aristocratic landlords main-tain large holdings, and where, from 1550 to 1826, the feuds of noble families and the depredations of bandits helped in the steady process of depopulation. The Campagna, writes Stendhal, is the 'sublimest trag-edy that ever was conceived.' Within Rome itself murders by the knife remain a chronic problem, for the government provides no security and every man is his own master, living in heroic solitude. Yet because the people hate the government and its corrupt police, they sympathize with murderers rather than their victims. As late as the 1820s the papacy granted ecclesiastical asylum to assassins and other criminals – a long-standing custom that shocked northern European observers, including Stendhal.[113] Given so much violence in Rome, he concludes that Italian civilization stops at Florence, and that the Romans are more savage than American Indians.[114]

If Stendhal finds the papal government 'doux et timide' rather than vexatious and cruel, this partly reflects its gerontocratic incompetence, as when Pope Leo XII taxed heavily the *vetturini* who transported travel-lers to Rome, thus endangering its economy. Save for a brief period of re-formism under Napoleon, the Papal States continue to sacrifice rational and objective administrative standards to preferment and clientelism, earning a reputation for capriciousness and unreliability. Papal elections amount to a series of political manoeuvres following which the aged victor hastens to enrich his relatives. The laity are excluded from important posts, and what few careers this backward society affords are closed to talented lay people. Instead, most prelates derive from noble families, and the least qualified among them receive coveted offices. In politics, as in economics, the middle class encounters a multitude of obstacles. Although the Pope needs a banker rather than a monsignor as minister of finance, he makes due with cardinals of 'superlative ignorance.' At the same time, bureaucratic redundancy and special interests confuse and impede the workings of the government. Not only are 'very few people removed from office in this part of the world,' but positions are granted as favours without regard for ability, and the decisions of 'dignified priests' are determined by their mistresses. Rather than fulfilling one's potential through hard effort, one is better off having a priestly patron or bribing the mistress of a prelate. If for three hundred years the Papal States have been riddled with 'suspicion and mistrust,' it is partly because the majority of the acts of the papal government are a 'departure from a rule.' Nor does there exist within its boundaries anything even remotely resembling public opinion as understood in northern Europe.[115]

As for the judicial system: there is an excess of courts, cases are fraught with all kinds of abuses and legal delays, and people so despise the law and police that they regard property rights as based upon violence. For a Sabine peasant, the 'ideas of *order* and of *justice*, which have been rooted in the heart of the Champagne or the Burgundy peasant since the parceling out of national property [after the French Revolution], would seem the height of absurdity.'[116] Like the residents of other Italian regions, those of the Papal States cannot identify with a government that neither helps nor protects them, and they thus serve it all too reluctantly as soldiers. Here is one explanation for the familiar charge of Italian military cowardice that, as Stendhal notes, Murat and General Carlo Filangieri found confirmed in the Neapolitans and Calabrians but that failed to account for the customary courage of Italians in asserting their private interests.[117] Supposedly originating in Charles V's destruction of Roman liberty in 1530, the bandits were in Stendhal's view the 'only *opposition*' to the Roman ecclesiastical state, but after 1600 their essentially apolitical revolt proved futile as Rome descended into 'chronic *stagnation*.' Although the bandits remained heroes to the Roman common people into the nineteenth century, Stendhal praises the efforts of Cola di Rienzi, Sixtus VI, Napoleon, and, in his own time, Cardinal Ettore Consalvi to put down these desperadoes, who typify a low state of civilization. Napoleon having extirpated the banditti in the Papal States, they flourished again in 1817, because industry once more went unrewarded; yet thanks to Cardinal Benvenuti, organized banditry had disappeared in the region of Rome since 1826.[118]

Attempting to assess Rome's future during the Restoration, Stendhal was initially encouraged by the reformism of Pope Pius VII's prime minister, Cardinal Consalvi, a man of honesty and intellect. Not only did Consalvi introduce laymen into the administration of the Papal States, so as to develop a civic sense among the people, but, immediately following the Pope's return to power in 1815, he had strenuously opposed those many *zelanti* within the Church who had sought to abolish Napoleon's reforms in a return to the *status quo ante*. Instead, Consalvi had preferred to maintain French methods of civil justice as well as to adhere to such Napoleonic reforms as the abolition of feudal rights and the establishment of a centralized and uniform administration. If Stendhal's esteem for Consalvi diminished somewhat, it was because of his opposition not only to Italian national unity but to the introduction of a constitutional government into Rome; for as Stendhal knew, a constitution could never be reconciled with the monarchical and ecclesiastical character of the Roman state, which feared to combine priests with lay people. As Imbert puts it, a priestly government is inherently outside the rhythm of modern life. Having thus settled for a paternalistic despotism, Consalvi was drawn increasingly to political repression, partly because the carbonarist movement threatened the papal government, but also because he was increasingly pressured by the *zelanti* and feared to lose his position. When Consalvi finally had to leave office in 1823, upon the election of Pope Leo XII, Rome became a scene of intensifying political repression, or what Stendhal calls a 'regime of fear.' Political crimes no longer received clemency, but instead the death penalty was announced for *carbonari*. The Papal States swarmed with civilian spies, while their prisons were crowded increasingly with political dissidents.[119]

According to Maurice Andrieux, in late eighteenth-century Rome patronage and clientelism were a fact of life for the upper and lower classes; one needed a patron – best of all a cardinal – to get ahead or merely to protect oneself. Nepotism was also prevalent, especially among the popes, who, because they were normally elected at a ripe age, wanted to advance their relatives as fast as possible. The election of every pope was followed by a great redistribution of offices, benefices, and employments. Yet one should not exaggerate such clientelism, for then as now the Catholic Church was a meritocracy, and, as Stendhal acknowledges, an intelligent young man of whatever class was often encouraged to take holy orders. Andrieux finds the problem of the Roman legal system to have been not so much corruption as the inadequate codification of laws as well as an excess of courts, a defect Stendhal also mentions. This resulted in conflicting decisions, and many cases were decided only after long delays. Being priests, the judges lacked legal training and often made arbitrary decisions while thinking themselves guided by divine wisdom.[120]

Banditry, which has long afflicted the Mediterranean world, plagued Italy in the Middle Ages and Renaissance and persisted in parts of the peninsula into the early twentieth century.[121] Stendhal's view of the Roman banditti is confirmed by Andrieux, who observes that the impoverished peasantry, although often exploited and victimized by banditti, admired them as Robin Hoods. The papal soldiery whose task was to pursue them were detested as representatives of an oppressive government.[122] Charles MacFarlane, a Britisher who lived in Italy in the 1820s, found bandits rampant in many parts of the peninsula, especially the Papal States and the south. Besides citing Stendhal, MacFarlane refers to such bandits as Marco Sciarra, who, as Stendhal notes, operated in the Abruzzi and the Papal States in the late sixteenth century; Benedetto Mangone of Eboli, of the same period; and such nineteenth-century southern Italian bandits as Don Ciro Anicchiarico and the Vardarelli brothers, the 'very Coryphaei of modern banditti,' as MacFarlane calls them, whose exploits Stendhal discusses in *Rome, Naples and Florence*. Not only does MacFarlane, like Stendhal, associate Italian eroticism and banditry, he identifies the latter with Italy's lack of 'civilization.'[123] Although Fernand Braudel laments that historians generally leave the topic of banditry to essayists and novelists, he praises Stendhal's observations on the subject, especially his view of Italian bandits as rebels against political and social oppression. In some ways Stendhal's portrayal of the banditti anticipates E.J. Hobsbawm's now challenged theory of 'social banditry.'[124]

The anti-curialism underlying Stendhal's hatred of what he sees as the morally lax Jesuits also motivates his sympathy towards Gallicanism and Jansenism, two French Catholic Reform movements that had entered Italy in the eighteenth century. 'Based ... on a certain idea of ancient ecclesiastical organization as opposed to the Roman Curia,' as Luigi Salvatorelli remarks, 'Gallicanism was a political-ecclesiastical movement that leaned toward the national autonomy of the Church while favoring close association with the state.' Despite its pre-modern dogmatic and ascetic morality, Jansenism emphasized reason and the inwardness of the moral conscience while combating the absolutist intolerance and temporal power of the Roman Church. For the Jansenists, who sought a more

intimate and sincere religious experience than they found in Catholicism, the primitive Christian Church afforded the only authentic form of
worship, the current church being but a simulacrum. Highly influential
in Lombardy under Maria Teresa and Joseph II, and in Tuscany under
Pietro Leopoldo and Scipione Ricci, bishop of Pistoia and Prato, these
movements supported the jurisdictional claims of governments over the
Church while providing them with what Salvatorelli terms a 'widened
theoretical base and moral impulse.' Indeed, the 'limitation of the power
of the Curia became identified with the independence of governments
from the Curia and with the abolition of ecclesiastical privileges,' such
as exemptions of persons and properties from state control. Gallicanism
and Jansenism were thus agents of secular and civil society in attempting
simultaneously to extend the power of the state and to limit ecclesiastical
authority.[125]

Desiring a return to what he regards as the virtue and simplicity of the
primitive church, Stendhal claims that between 400 and 1200 the popes
were elected by bishops in a popular assembly in which they represented
the mass of Christians. In his view, Catholicism in Rome should abandon
its authoritarian practices and adopt the more egalitarian ways of the
French national church. This is not to suggest that Stendhal is close to
being a Jansenist, as religious controversy bores him, while some elements of Jansenism ill consort with his philosophical orientation, often
referred to as 'Beylism' or 'idéologie.' These elements include asceticism, an emphasis on original sin and holy terror, and a basic otherworld-
liness. Yet Stendhal is drawn to Jansenism because of its anti-Jesuitism,
its goal of replacing Catholicism with a new ecclesiastical organization
based on the primitive church, its insistence on spiritual examination of
the self as opposed to the externals of religion, the relative mildness of
its teaching methods (despite stress on original sin and holy terror), its
interest in history as a source of truth, its fusion of morality and religion,
its demand for justice and utility, its goal of promoting civic responsibility through the Church, its clarity and simplicity in verbal expression,
and its general rebellion against the political repression and injustice of
the *ancien régime*. By the same token, Jansenism's quest for the authentic
parallels Stendhal's pursuit of the *naturel* and *vivant*, while the Jansenist
discipline of soul and spirit resembles his ideal of self-mastery in accordance with scientific method.[126]

The papacy holds no monopoly over misrule in Italy. Despite Stendhal's admiration for the Medici as cultural patrons, he denounces what
he sees as their unofficial tyranny over Florence in the fifteenth century,

and he is even less fond of the Medici who, with the support of Spain, ruled the city after 1530. Marking the extinction of Florentine liberty, that year also initiates what Stendhal sees as a disastrous period of Spanish dominance over much of the peninsula. In 1559, the year of the Treaty of Cateau-Cambrésis, Lombardy, Naples, and Sicily fell to Spain. In 1714, at the conclusion of the War of the Spanish Succession, Lombardy along with the Kingdom of Naples passed from Spain to the Habsburgs of Austria; by 1720 Sicily was in their hands. In 1734, however, Charles of Bourbon defeated the Austrians and established in the Mezzogiorno an autonomous kingdom closely linked to Spain dynastically and culturally; indeed, the Bourbon monarch's 'independence from Madrid was more formal than real.'[127]

Stendhal believes Spain to bear the chief responsibility for the miseries of Italy following the end of the Florentine Republic. The Spanish presence, he remarks, 'has been harmful to Italy in every way, and Charles V ... has been most fatal to the human race,' for 'his despotism subdued the bold genius engendered by the Middle Ages.' Thanks to Spain, the energetic and meritocratic spirit of the medieval Italian republics – and with it the national character – has been 'debased,' 'degraded,' and 'enfeebled.'[128] Like Sismondi and many other observers, Stendhal has some justification for accusing Italy's Spanish and Bourbon regimes of having deprived the people of political, social, and economic freedom through heavy taxes, tariffs, political censorship, clerical education, and centralized control. In an atmosphere of suspicion and mistrust, fed by Spanish fears of revolt, the gaiety of the Milanese fled, and they became as taciturn as their masters.[129] Stendhal complains that Spanish rule had been supported by the Church, and that, in serving tyranny and religion, Saint Carlo Borromeo had 'annihilated whatever *strength* had hitherto resided in the character of the Milanese' by imbuing them with ascetic rather than military values. If Bologna maintains 'far closer ties with medieval Italy than does Milan,' it is because it has not had a Borromeo to 'tame its native character and harness it to a *monarchy*.'[130] The Spanish brought into Italy an 'infamous' administration, the demoralizing custom of the *cavalier sirvente* or *cicisbeo*, and chimerical ideas of aristocratic honour, which fostered vanity and jealousy. Jacob Burckhardt holds similarly that Spanish predominance in Italy had resulted in 'obedience to Spanish ideas,' such as 'contempt for work' and a 'passion for titles'; indeed, everyone in Naples and Florence wanted to be or seem an aristocrat.[131] Although Stendhal realizes that a comparatively enlightened Bourbon despotism ruled over the Kingdoms of Naples and Sicily during the eighteenth century, when reformist Neapolitan intellectuals contributed to the European Enlightenment, and although he also realizes that the period of the French occupation witnessed a number of lasting social and economic reforms, including the abolition of feudalism, he regards post-Napoleonic Naples as a repressive monarchy in which aristocrats stand upon their privileges and continue to lord it over the middle and lower classes. Hence his strong sympathy for the Neapolitans' several failed attempts from 1799 onward to establish their own constitutional republic.[132]

Stendhal's judgments of the Spanish presence in Italy remain questionable nonetheless. Braudel faults him for referring to Italy's 'invasion' by Spanish despotism, when in reality Italian society was 'holding the levers of power' beneath 'the veneer of Spanish rule.' Without the Italians' complicity, Spanish authority would have 'collapsed like a house of cards.' Despite the familiar view that Spain had a largely negative impact upon Italy in this period, scholars now stress its benefits for many parts of Italy and Sicily, and even for Naples into the early 1600s. Besides being needed for military reasons, including protection against Islam, Spain not only kept its Italian possessions out of European wars but poured much money into the country, thus helping the Italians to enjoy a favourable balance of payments and even to maintain cultural and other expenditures at a relatively high level.[133]

Stendhal's condemnation of the Spanish cult of honour was perhaps influenced by Sismondi's view that, having received it from the Arabs, the Spanish introduced it to sixteenth-century Italy. The result was exaggerated 'delicacy' over female chastity, along with punctiliousness regarding masculine bravery, so that bravos, poignards, and poisons multiplied. Like Stendhal, Sismondi distinguishes between the Italian Middle Ages, when republicanism led to factional hatred and violence, and when the sense of both personal and public utility prevented such vain notions of honour as came to prevail in the monarchical courts of Europe, and the later, Spanish-dominated Italy, when private vengeance promoted social decay. However, masculine honour and feminine chastity have long typified Mediterranean societies, and it seems doubtful that Spain brought them to Italy. The Renaissance duel, a main feature of the aristocratic code of honour, does not seem to have come to Italy from Spain, although the code was apparently individualistic, as Sismondi holds, and although it conforms to Stendhal's conception of vanity as an obsession with one's public image. Not only did the Renaissance duel originate among Italian soldiers, but the Spanish yielded to Italians in punctilio, duelling technique, and the dissemination of the duelling ethos through manuals such as Girolamo Muzio's *Il Duello* (1550). Spain outlawed duels in 1480 and may have allied with the Counter-Reformation in a failed attempt to suppress them in Italy.[134]

Long defunct, the Italian custom of the *cicisbeo* has been claimed to originate in the Spanish practice of requiring a married woman to appear in public with her husband or a male chaperone, the *cavalier sirvente* (or *cicisbeo*). Vaussard contends that *cicisbeismo* was invented to protect married women from unseemly attentions, and 'was always kept within the bounds of decency,' so that the *cicisbeo* was never a lover. He adds that, though deriving from Spain, the custom was more common in northern Italy than in Naples.[135] Commenting on eighteenth-century Rome, Andrieux asserts that *cicisbeismo* had first arrived there with Cesare Borgia's Spanish retainers, and that it was practised not only by the aristocracy, as is often assumed, but by all classes. According to Andrieux, the custom of the *cicisbeo* arose because upper-class marriages were often arranged and hence loveless, and because divorce was impossible. A neglected wife thus needed a servant and escort on social occasions. Yet despite the profligacy of eighteenth-century Roman society, in which the Church tolerated adultery, and in which even loving marriages faded into infidelity, Andrieux accepts the Italians' claims for the innocence of *cicisbeismo*. It was bad form for a husband to show jealousy toward a *cicisbeo*, and in any case his affection usually went elsewhere. Nonetheless, many travellers assumed possibly justifiably that the *cavalier sirvente* played the role of lover, the *cicisbeo* being in their censorious eyes the illicit version of the *cavalier sirvente*.[136]

For Stendhal, the appeal of *cicisbeismo* is partly mythical, as the relationship between the lady and her devoted servant conforms to his idealized view of Italy as a 'feminine' country where women display queenly superiority over their male idolators. As he puts it: 'To an Italian woman the limited authority which a French woman can wield in her drawing room would seem quite absurd.'[137] Notwithstanding Andrieux's characterization of *cicisbeismo* as innocent, Stendhal believes passionate eroticism to typify the practice, with the participants often rejecting brief liaisons for relatively long term commitments. And whereas most foreign commentators deplored *cicisbeismo*, Stendhal calls to mind Byron's *Beppo* in regarding it as an attractive manifestation of Italian individualism and hedonism. Insofar as, according to Stendhal, the husband and *cavalier sirvente* are on the most friendly terms, the latter even being specified in the marriage contract, *cicisbeismo* lends support to his contention that

Italians normally lack vanity or amour-propre, of which jealousy is one type. Stendhal further realizes, as do some other northern European travellers, that in a country such as Italy, where marriages are often arranged, the custom enables people to find the love marriage denies them. *Cicisbeismo* thus exemplifies the preferability of voluntary fidelity over mere constraint.[138]

On the negative side, Stendhal regards *cicisbeismo* as one of the vices brought to Italy from Spain, and as such, he blames it for marital and domestic corruption as well as for the waste of many youthful lives; moreover, the custom had degenerated in many cases into promiscuity and passionless flirtation.[139] In *The Charterhouse of Parma cicisbeismo* figures among the 'effeminate ways' of the Milanese during their political servitude under Austria, and contrasts with the civic seriousness and activism introduced by Napoleon's armies. Accordingly Stendhal apparently welcomes the suppression of *cicisbeismo* during Napoleon's occupation of Italy. Although *The Charterhouse*, which largely takes place after Waterloo, implies that this reform was temporary, as witness Gina Sanseverina's passing notion of taking young Fabrizio as her *cicisbeo*, Stendhal finds that by the 1820s Italian love affairs had become 'infinitely less scandalous' than before 1805, the bad examples being provided mainly by older women. Likewise, most liasons lasted longer than previously, and *cicisbeismo* was found only in remote regions untouched by Napoleon.[140]

Stendhal's comments on the social and political condition of southern Italy lack the ring of first-hand knowledge. The evidence suggests that, contrary to his claim to have visited Sicily and Calabria, he never entered southern Italy below Naples.[141] Nor had he any excuse for avoiding the remoter south, as it had been visited by French and other northern European travellers during the Romantic period and even earlier. Leonardo Sciascia holds that Stendhal never saw Sicily, which, had he visited it, he would have fantasized as a land after his own heart, where life consists of violent and amorous exploits, and where the 'man plant,' to use Alfieri's phrase, grows more strongly than anywhere else in Italy. Indeed, Sciascia claims that, exulting in all that would cause a right-minded Sicilian anguish and distress, Stendhal would have glorified the Mafia, soon to arise in the area of Palermo following Italian unification.[142]

In general, Stendhal resembles many other visitors in identifying the south, including Naples, with social and political oppression, poverty, and the constant potential for anarchic violence. Resorting to time-worn clichés, he holds that civilization stops at the Tiber or, at most, Naples; that Rome and Naples are barbarous cities masquerading in European dress; that Neapolitans and southern Italians are African or Oriental; and that the indulgent southern Italian climate fosters idleness and cowardice. The social and material environment of the region having deprived its inhabitants of the capacity for thought, these savages live sensuously in the moment, which they sieze with a violent, half-crazed impetuosity. So too, their easily kindled imaginations drive them nearly to madness. The 'barbaric' Calabrians embody '*impassioned childishness*' and far exceed northern Italians in their emotional intensity. Perhaps the most degraded of the southern Italians are the Neapolitan urban poor, the *lazzaroni*, who so lack refinement that they walk the streets nearly unclothed, and who like other Italians excel in cheating and dissimulation. Although southern Italians and especially the Neapolitans may have a special talent for sensuality and music, such traits are counterweighed by their violence, to which their family honour compels them. These superstitious idolators also practice the *jettatura* or evil eye, the belief in which pervades Neapolitan society. Like many visitors to Naples, Stendhal imagines that the Neapolitans' behaviour is largely determined by their climate and environment and that they thus possess a volcanic temperament reminiscent of Mount Vesuvius, the very symbol of southern Italy.[143]

Although Austria was the dominant power in northern Italy during the Restoration, the region contained a number of other authoritarian states upon which Stendhal cast his critical eye. When Piedmont, which had felt the impact of liberalizing reforms during the Napoleonic occupation, was returned to the House of Savoy in 1815, King Victor Emmanuel I gave the impression that the Restoration would be accompanied by an ambitious modernizing program, including the abolition of taxes, support of agriculture and commerce, and elimination of torture. Actually the king wanted to bring back the *ancien régime* as much as possible, and to this end he implemented a paternal despotism marked by the employment of the Jesuits for educational purposes and a restoration of the feudal system from which the aristocracy had most to gain; what remained of the French system was its imposts, the most burdensome of Napoleon's policies.[144]

If the situation in Tuscany was less discouraging than in Piedmont, this was owed partly to the fact that the former state had been returned to the House of Lorraine, which was closely affiliated with Austria's Habsburg monarchy, and which had a reputation for enlightened despotism in the eighteenth century. With the death of Gastone de' Medici and the extinction of his line in 1737, the Florentine state was received by Francesco

Stefano, husband of Queen Maria Teresa of Austria. Now Archduke of Tuscany, Francesco encountered many problems necessitating an extensive reform agenda initially suspected and resisted by the Tuscans. During the decadence of the Medici regime Tuscany had suffered legal and financial confusion, escalating public debt, enfeebled manufactures, agrarian depression, monopolization of land by a few individuals, unwillingness of the big landowners to improve their properties, widespread reliance on unproductive sharecropping (*mezzadria*), interference in commerce by guilds and other corporations, high imposts damaging to local trade and industry, paucity of exports and over-reliance on imports, and failure to reclaim marshlands for agrarian development. Instead of permitting free trade in grain and other goods, the state controlled the market. The continuing practice of primogeniture and *fedecommesso*, which restricted aristocratic inheritance, impeded the circulation of goods while concentrating large properties in a few hands. The aristocracy with its power and privileges still resisted the jurisdictional authority of the centralizing state. The law of entail or mortmain, guaranteeing perpetual ownership of real estate, and by which the Church extended and protected its properties, not only paralysed commerce but discouraged land improvement. There was also the problem of the relation of church and state, as the church often claimed the right to interfere in state affairs. Yet though Francesco Stefano and his administrators made some progress in solving these problems, they were tackled systematically and aggressively only under his successor, Pietro Leopoldo, who assumed the title of Archduke of Tuscany in 1765 and who ultimately succeeded his eldest brother, Joseph II, to the Austrian throne in 1790, two years before his own death.[145]

Like Friedrich Johann Lorenz Meyer, whose *Darstellungen aus Italien* appeared in 1792, many foreign visitors praised Pietro Leopoldo's devotion to the public welfare.[146] Two of the Grand Duke's most important goals were interrelated: to limit the authority and wealth of the Church, and to promote the economy through land distribution and increased circulation of goods. Thus the Church was denied the right of mortmain and, partly through dissolution of monasteries and confiscation of ecclesiastical property, private land ownership and more especially agrarian holdings were encouraged. Besides restricting transfer of property to the Church, Pietro Leopoldo reduced classical exemptions while requiring monastic institutions to become more public-minded and charitable. The introduction of the Jansenist model to Tuscany challenged Catholic ideas of piety and authority. The state control of the grain market, to which Pietro Leopoldo and his advisers attributed the failure of the Papal States, was replaced by a free trade policy that applied to other goods as well. Sharecropping gave way to tenancy of longer duration under conditions close to ownership, and in a further attempt to stimulate local industry, the number of feast days was reduced. Shorn of feudal privileges, including tax exemptions, the aristocracy yielded to state bureaucrats and a new directive class. Likewise the state broke the power of the guilds to interfere in the economy. Common lands were divided, and grand ducal estates were sold off. The national debt greatly diminished, partly through unpopular legal measures. Unlike the Medici, Pietro Leopoldo introduced a penal system consistent with the humane standards of the Enlightenment. Yet though he hoped to confer a new constitution upon Tuscany, his reforms were imposed from above and often unsuccessfully. Never was the constitution implemented, and it proved virtually impossible either to master the clergy or to place ecclesiastical property in secular hands.[147] Nor does Stendhal, though he acknowledges Pietro Leopoldo's reforms, share the commonly favourable judgment of his regime. Perhaps what he most deplores is the espionage the Grand Duke permitted within his dominions, as this 'piece of philosophical virtue' employed a 'spy in every family.' So too the anticlerical measures of Scipione Ricci, the Grand Duke's Gallican and Jansenist associate, bishop of Pistoia and Prato from 1780 to 1791, had foundered on the shoals of *pretismo*. Ultimately, Pietro Leopoldo's 'celebrated government' and 'mildly benevolent authorities' had transformed the Florentines into a 'race of holy-minded castrati,' among whom passion had become 'extinct.' This judgment consorts with Stendhal's view of the Florentines as a bourgeoisified and depassionated people different from typical Italians. Nor did it help Leopoldo's reputation in Stendhal's eyes that his reforms had 'robbed Italy for ever of its magnificent indigenous popular traditions,' the commedia dell'arte.[148]

As for the Restoration in Tuscany, the people, being tired of Napoleonic imposts and conscription, welcomed the return of Duke Ferdinand III, whose state Stendhal initially regarded as the most liberal in Italy. Rather than restoring the *ancien régime*, Ferdinand had conserved the Napoleonic commercial code while continuing to outlaw feudalism, in keeping with the progressivism of Duke Leopold. It was equally to his credit that Ferdinand had chosen as his prime minister Count Vittorio Fossombroni, a likely model for Count Mosca in *The Charterhouse of Parma*, and whom Stendhal praises for 'sage moderation.' Ultimately, however, Stendhal's enthusiasm for the Tuscan regime dwindled, for though possibly the best of absolute monarchies, its economy remained sluggish, poverty reigned among an indolent peasantry, and police spies were everywhere. Fossombroni had also equivocated on religion, on the one hand refusing to bring in the Jesuits, but on the other allowing the return of the religious orders – not *pretismo* but close to it.[149]

Despite the failings of the Tuscan regime, Stendhal found it benign as compared with the small state of Modena, an absolutist despotism run for the pleasure of its Duke Francesco IV, the very symbol of the Restoration and the Holy Alliance. Regarding himself as the owner of his duchy, Francesco trampled on the political rights of his citizens, against whom he instituted a reign of terror to weed out dissidents. In his hands Modena became a bastion of Jesuitism, where religion served the state, and the Jesuits dominated their students morally and intellectually. So much did Stendhal detest this regime that he refused to sleep overnight in the city.[150]

Since Austria expelled Stendhal from his adopted homeland of Lombardy in 1821, one might expect him to deplore the Austrian imperial presence in northern Italy. Having received Lombardy from Spain in 1714, the Austrians laid claim briefly to Venice before Napoleon drove them from Italy, but thanks to the Congress of Vienna in 1815 they regained their Lombard and Venetian territories. Yet rather than allow personal grievance to colour his judgment of Austrian rule, Stendhal acknowledges the superiority of the enlightened despotism of the eighteenth-century Habsburg monarchs Maria Theresa and Joseph II over the earlier Spanish absolutism, ally of the Counter-Reformation.

Not only was this government anti-curial, consistent with the intransigent rationalism of the Emperor Joseph, who sent the Jesuits packing, but it was dedicated to bureaucratic centralization and therefore anti-feudal as well. Since 1782 the opinions of the clergy and aristocracy counted for nothing. Typified by the minister Carlo Firmian (1759–1782), Austria's rational and competent administration achieved legal, educational, and economic reforms that helped to liberate trade and expand the middle classes. Of Firmian's twenty-year tenure Stendhal remarks that he had rooted out the *méchanceté* (wickedness) Machiavelli had seen as natural in Italy, with the result that great men were again possible among the Milanese. As the clergy lost its fiscal privileges, the aristocracy was required to pay taxes in proportion to its wealth. The great Milanese liberals Beccaria and Pietro Verri, both committed to utilitarianism, flourished under this regime and served it as ministers; the poet Parini, a keen critic of Milanese decadence, was patronized by the

Austrian government, which established a printing press in Lombardy around 1760. Thus, unlike many xenophobic Italian writers, Stendhal believes that Austria's enlightened absolutism helped to form modern Italy by supporting what Salvatorelli calls 'civil society.' As Stendhal writes of Milan, even before 1796, the year of Napoleon's descent upon northern Italy, 'there was *already* a dawning awareness of such concepts as *strict impartiality* and *justice.*' By contrast, the regime of Duke Pietro Leopoldo in Tuscany was hampered by *pretismo* despite its successful war against feudalism. This is not to imply, however, that Stendhal finds the Austrian regime ideal. *Il Caffè*, the Milanese journal founded by Beccaria and Verri in 1762, was shut down two years later because of excessive liberalism. Although Joseph II largely succeeded in 'de-Romanizing' Catholicism in northern Italy while making it more reasonable than anywhere else in the peninsula, he put nothing in its place. Since he and Firmian lacked humanity, they proceeded too slowly in their reformism, and missed the chance to give Lombardy a constitutional government. Amounting to an Austrian colony ruled from Vienna, Lombardy enjoyed at best a tolerant, 'bienheureuse inertie.'[151]

If Stendhal shows qualified admiration for the Austrian regime that the Restoration returned to power in Lombardy, it is partly because he realizes that it had preserved and built upon the comparatively wise and moderate Habsburg traditions. Giving the impression of what Walter Maturi describes as a continuation of the enlightened despotism of the previous century, the Restoration in Lombardy as elsewhere in Italy is for Stendhal the best guarantee of Italy's freedom in the long run, especially by contrast with what he sees as the hapless activities of the *carbonari*. The division between church and state, which Napoleon had enforced, persisted in Austrian policy; the influence of priests was limited while the Jesuits continued to be banished, at least initially; and Napoleon's system of conscription remained. As the Austrians had no intention to revive the *ancien régime*, they did not favour the aristocracy. The Austrian administrators, including Saurau and Bubna, were reasonably popular with the Lombards owing to their politeness and administrative talents, which they applied cautiously and carefully. As Austria supported Lombard agriculture, the region was better off than neighbouring Tuscany, and Milan enjoyed considerable prosperity. For Stendhal, who refers with a certain irony to 'le sage et très sage administration de la maison autriche,' the Austrians had grasped their temporary position in Italy, and expected that by around 1850 it would have returned to its '*position naturelle.*'[152]

Yet the Austrian regime had many failings that only became more offensive to Italians with the passing decades. Lombardy remained as before a colony of Austria, which held it by means of an army, and to which it sent enormous sums in taxes. The Lombard constitution was a pretence, as the Italians were subalterns. The laws in Lombardy were Germanized, a measure shocking to the locals, and its commerce was reoriented towards Vienna and Trieste, the latter an Austrian port city that eclipsed Venice. Because of the cumbersomeness of the Austrian bureaucracy, it often responded slowly to the Lombard's needs. Although Stendhal believes Lombardy to have enjoyed an 'easy' period between 1815 and 1820, during which, with lighthearted gaiety, he himself sampled the cultural, intellectual, and erotic attractions of Milan without fear of government interference, he is painfully aware that, after 1820, the Austrian prime minister Metternich out of a reasonable fear of political revolt not only brought back the Jesuits but instituted a reign of terror. His aim, Stendhal contends, was to return to the status quo of 1760. His victims included not only participants in the revolt of 1821, but Stendhal himself, who was forced to flee from Milan in that year, never to return under penalty of death.[153]

VI

Italy's politically subject and fragmented condition during the Restoration might lead one to expect Stendhal to have been highly pessimistic regarding the possibility of national liberation and unification, which the Risorgimento took several decades to accomplish. Yet what most alleviates Stendhal's worries over the future of Italy is that the Italians had experienced if only briefly the liberating influence of the French Revolution and Napoleonic occupation – the ideals of reason, progress, civil administration, rule of law, republicanism, constitutional government, and the centralized state. This is not to forget his appreciation for the traditions of Enlightenment liberalism in northern Italy. The concept of impartial justice had been recognized in Milan before the French occupation of 1796, and, unlike Alfieri, Beccaria and Verri had understood that Italy's regeneration required institutional, judicial, and administrative reform, economic development, and social order. Becarria had also shared Stendhal's utilitarian faith in the greatest good for the greatest number. However, it was Napoleon who had provided the chief impetus for change when, in 1796 and again in 1800, the year he defeated the Austrians at Marengo, his armies had 'awaken[ed] Italy from her age-old slumbers.'[154]

The Cisalpine Republic, which Napoleon established in northern Italy in 1797, was overturned by Austria in 1799 but restored by Napoleon a year later; after 1802 it was called the Italian Republic. Despite their constitutions and approximations to parliamentarianism, the Cisalpine and Italian Republics were a facade for a French virtual dictatorship. In 1804 Napoleon became emperor of France, and a year later he made himself monarch of the newly created Kingdom of Italy, which by 1808 included Milan, Venice, Bologna, and Ancona. In 1810 the Papal States became a part of the French Empire.[155] Admittedly Stendhal disapproves of Napoleon's despotism in France,[156] and, though rejecting the questionable view (later espoused by Luigi Salvatorelli) of the Napoleonic period as retrogressive, he acknowledges that the French exploited Italy. Napoleon, says Stendhal, acted 'in the interests of his own despotic authority.' Yet he also believes that fourteen years of such authority had given the Italians a 'glimpse of moral conscience.' In Italy, unlike France, Napoleon was the 'scourge of corruption' and 'protector of true merit.' Thanks to him, public opinion at last emerged in Milan in 1796. Because of Italy's many failings, only a temporary 'rational despotism' could foster liberty.[157]

In Rome, remarks Stendhal, Napoleon's Civil Code 'began to civilize' the people and thus demonstrate that 'justice is the first necessity.' The period of French administration, between May 1809 and April 1814, gave Rome a 'glimpse of modern civilization,' so that for five years one could 'obtain something from a prefect without paying his mistress or his confessor.' Having proved a skilful administrator during Napoleon's Russian campaign, Stendhal admires the bureaucracies that Napoleon established for Italy. Chosen strictly by merit, Napoleon's civil servants were 'hand-picked ... enlightened intellectuals' whose 'systematic approach and ... tireless activity' contrasted with the undisciplined rhythms of Italian behaviour. Introducing methods and accountability into politics, so as to reduce Italy's 'strangling crop of anti-social practices,' these rational administrators brought the 'luminous consequences of eighteenth-century civilization.' Thus the Italian civil service became reliable rather than vexatious, as formerly. Thanks to Napoleon, Italy escaped the 'void' and 'at one bound cleared three whole centuries of progress.'[158]

A major achievement of the Napoleonic administration was to improve personal security in Italy through an effective police force and harsh legal punishments, including the death penalty, which Stendhal endorses. He contends that civil assassination declined in Naples after the 'civilizing wars of the French Revolution,' and that in Piedmont, through the death penalty, 'five thousand persons lived who would otherwise have perished by the knife.' In Rome, where the murder rate had been staggeringly high during the reign of Pope Pius VI, the French all but eliminated assassinations, which increased immediately after their departure. Relentless opponents of feudalism, the French divided and distributed property so as to develop the economy; work was no longer disdained; and the gap narrowed between the classes. Money began to circulate more freely as the French not only introduced public works projects but supported agriculture and free enterprise. In Lombardy, aristocrats had to serve the government or else fade away. As *cicisbeismo* dwindled under Napoleon's influence, family life acquired a more elevated tone. Still more important, the Napoleonic Code divided property equally among male and female heirs, thus advancing women's rights while countering the idleness of younger sons. Yet this reform was weakly enforced, and after 1815 some regions reverted to past practice. Stendhal concludes that, had Napoleon's Italian regime lasted another twenty years, the Italians could have had a bicameral constitutional government equal to that of France and England. But the French had proceeded too cautiously in Italy, bestowing not 'ten' but only 'two degrees' of civilization. Southern Italy was hardly touched by liberalism, and much of Napoleon's legacy disappeared during the Restoration.[159]

For Stendhal, Italy's political fragmentation has been a chief cause of its provincialism, sectional vanity, and proliferation of local dialects, all of which prevent a national society and culture. From this perspective, Napoleon's greatest achievement in Italy was to have created a native army that, open to all Italians and hence free of provincial rivalries, embodied the potential for peninsular unity and its patriotic defense. Within less than a decade Napoleon's Italian troops had equaled their French counterparts in courage and effectiveness and had thus helped to overturn the Italians' reputation for military cowardice, to which the charge of *cicisbeismo* had contributed. There had also emerged from this 'confusion of races and temperaments' a 'new language' as the indispensable basis for national consciousness and the spread of civilization.[160] Following Italian unification in 1861, many middle-class Italians similarly admired the national army for uniting men of different regions, providing them with the same language and values, and teaching them to read and write.[161] Napoleon had thus perhaps unwittingly set Italy on the 'right road' to constitutional government, for Stendhal sees in this national army the germ of republican institutions enabling Italians to achieve the rights and responsibilities of representative democracy. He hopes for the recovery of the *virtù* (but not the political divisiveness) of the republican Middle Ages, when freedom led to cultural efflorescence. Indeed, Italian culture and society will revive only when the Italians unite under a liberal constitution.[162]

In the aftermath of the all too brief French occupation, with Napoleon having only partly completed his revolutionizing agenda, Stendhal remains convinced of Italy's insufficient civilization. The Italian economy was still feeling the effects of the crisis of the seventeenth century, when, in contrast with the national economic network developed in the Renaissance, the country was fragmented into regional and local markets. Despite some reforms, especially in the north, the interdependence of the peninsula was impeded by political divisions as well as feudal holdovers and tariffs. In Naples, Napoleon's abolition of feudalism and attempt to distribute aristocratic and ecclesiastical properties failed to benefit the poor but instead opened up a market for land speculation, most of these properties going to the rich. Around Rome, the enforced sale of ecclesiastical lands during the Napoleonic occupation had mainly benefited speculators and wealthy proprietors. Nonetheless, Stendhal hopes that Italian agriculture will follow the pattern of land distribution in France, where, after the Revolution, the sale of national property 'quadrupled' the peasants' well-being while giving them a sense of 'justice.' To revive the Campagna, one half of it must be brought under cultivation, and this requires the purchase of land by the state and its division among the people, so as to make them farmers. Similar reforms are likewise required in the Papal States generally, so as to enable money to circulate more freely.[163] Reformism of this type apparently appealed to French visitors to Italy. Even before Stendhal, a commentator on Joseph-Jérôme de Lalande's *Voyage d'un français en Italie* (1769) had recommended the division of land to remedy the stagnation of the Papal States. Charles-Victor de Bonstetten, in *Voyage sur la scène des six derniers livres de l'Énéide*, complained that agriculture in the Papal States enriched only a few farmers with large holdings. Later in the nineteenth century Alexis de Tocqueville, Francois Lenormant, and Georges Goyau proposed land division and distribution as the key to reviving southern Italian agriculture, long burdened by large holdings (*latifundia*). As Lenormant noted, during the Napoleonic occupation the French civil code had enforced the division of land, but when the Bourbons returned to power, agrarian reform weakened. Yet Goyau recognized that the division of land after Italian unification failed to remedy the ills of the Mezzogiorno, and Atanasio Mozzillo notes the error of regarding this reform as the one thing needful.[164]

If, as Stendhal believes, Italian society remains as retarded as the economy, this is partly attributable to the absence of a large middle class, the presumed basis of economic initiative and rational political discussion. Instead, there remains an immeasurably wide 'gulf,' social and intellectual, between the upper classes and the mass of the people, sunk in 'primeval brutality.' Like Luigi Salvatorelli, Stendhal realizes that this division raises serious impediments to political revolution and genuine national unity.[165] Upper-class marriages are still arranged by agreement between families, so that the husband has a mistress and the wife a *cicisbeo*. To avoid the division of inheritance through the multiplication of dowries, usually only one daughter is given in marriage, the others being farmed out to convents in order to escape suitors; there they idle away their days or conduct clandestine affairs such as Stendhal portrays in *The Abbess of Castro*. Yet if a woman evades the convent and remains unmarried, she cannot live alone or own a home, as social prejudice is against it, and she will suffer ridicule should she try to advance in art or academics. For Stendhal, who harboured some feminist sympathies, these conditions are uncivilized. Upper-class families also want to keep their properties intact, which means that younger sons receive no inheritances; yet being too proud to work, they live in pleasurable idleness without the least civic responsibility.[166] The remedy, Stendhal suggests in *Lucien Leuwen*, is the elimination of primogeniture, a measure which, as Tocqueville notes, helps to distribute national wealth and thus to promote an equitable, responsible, interdependent society.[167]

In view of Italy's comparatively backward governments and society, its sectionalism, its unreliable judiciary and police, and not least its underdeveloped economy and consequent disincentives to work, the Italian character falls short of those standards of drive control civilization demands. According to Stendhal, not only are Italians dominated by 'powerful and *disordered* currents of sensation,' but 'complete surrender to the sensation of the moment is no rarity' in Italy. Indeed, so little are the Italians concerned with the future that 'every waking thought is taken up with the present instant,' from which they seek to derive their full quotient of pleasure. For Stendhal, these traits are most strikingly manifest in the southern Italians, including the Calabrians and especially the Neapolitans, who resemble children in being slaves to their immediate pleasures and desires. Yet even the Milanese performs most actions '*solely because they appeal to him at a given instant*.' Like Montesquieu, Staël, Bonstetten and many other writers, Stendhal attributes such behaviour partly to Italy's warm and indulgent climate. Alternatively he notes social and political factors, including bad governments and the absence of a disciplined economy such as would force the Italians to control and exert themselves in an orderly fashion. Just as, in Rome, the absence of criminal justice encourages people to surrender to their first impulses, so it is easy to yield to present sensation and impulse in a city where industry goes unrewarded.[168] Thus, for all his personal enjoyment of the *dolce far niente*, Stendhal views indolence as a characteristic flaw of modern Italians. 'The laziness of the present-day Roman is so great,' he remarks, that 'it is ... a torture for him to go out of his way,' as witness those waiters who leave unwiped the tables at the cafe in the Palazzo Ruspoli. Not surprisingly, the 'passionate love of gambling,' the desire to get something for nothing, is 'one of the characteristics of the Italian imagination.'[169] The Calabrians similarly shrink from effort, while the Neapolitans, typically Italian in refusing to tolerate boredom, are reluctant to do what they find unpleasant, namely work. Except for the perhaps Frenchified Piedmontese, the Italians lack 'character,' which comes only from performing unpleasant tasks, whereas in the Protestant North such character-building values as duty and asceticism lead to constant application and productivity. Stendhal's observations call to mind those of Andrieux who, noting the indolence of eighteenth-century Romans, attributes it partly to the government's failure to promote industry and commerce but also to the fact that the Papal State, the recipient of funds from all over the Catholic world, provided its people with food, amusements, and tax exemptions. The Romans, he adds, loved to gamble.[170]

This is not to deny that Italians concentrate their attention and energy when gripped by what Stendhal terms 'some overmastering passion.'[171] Yet such behaviour, at once extreme and abrupt, lacks bourgeois steadiness and method. As he observes, both '*systematic approach* and ... *tireless activity* are markedly uncommon among so passionate a nation, ever slave to the sensation of the moment.' With a 'touch of the primitive savage in his make-up,' the Italian tends to 'alternate retreats of silence with outbursts of frenzy,' his character being 'utterly devoid of that steadfast patience and stability of temperament which flourish on the northern slopes of... [the] Alps, and which have enabled the Swiss to preserve at least the semblance of a republic.'[172] Stendhal thus defines the characteristically irregular rhythm of Italian society before modernity, marked by sudden and intense explosions of energy followed by total exhaustion – the medieval rhythm Marx scorned.

It is easy to find parallels to Stendhal's characterizations of the Italians in travel writings of earlier and later periods.[173] According to Martin

Sherlock, who visited in the 1770s, the Roman is 'easily moved; and when he is moved, he is violent to an excess.' Hester Thrale Piozzi identifies the Italians and especially the Neapolitans with abruptly violent activity as well as with sudden shifts of ungovernable emotion, as from torpor to frenzy. The land of extremes, Italy lacks the mediocrity typical of England. Writing of his 1802 visit, Eustace notes the erratic, explosive behaviour of the Italians; John Mayne, a traveller in 1814, observes their excessive gestures and vehement feelings, often over trivial matters, as well as their childlike trait of becoming 'quickly irritated' and 'as quickly calmed.' In Hazlitt's view, Italians exhibit an 'infantilism and lack of control' resembling 'madness or insanity.' For the American George Stillman Hillard, a visitor in the late 1840s, the Italian temperament 'allows only a short transition from gentle courtesy to fiery excitement and the drawing of knives.' Hippolyte Taine says of the southern Italians: 'In all things with this people the first impression is too violent; scarcely is the trigger touched when the explosion takes place ... Two cabmen get into a quarrel and seem ready to burst: a minute after, and all is forgotten.'[174]

What then of the Italian mind under these uncivilized conditions? The 'gross ignorance' Stendhal attributes to the Italians encompasses widespread illiteracy, dislike of reading, superstition, incapacity for or unwillingness to engage in logical, critical, self-reflective thought, and lack of objectivity in the sense of impartial judgment. Of these failings, it is the Italians' comparative indifference to the written word which Stendhal most often mentions. In the Vatican Library, for instance, 'no books are visible,' the emphasis being on its architectural and decorative grandeur. Although Stendhal realizes that most Italians are unable to read, he also knows that, even in a city with relatively high literacy such as Milan, they 'read but little.' As Italian women are little interested in novels, that genre cannot flourish in Italy – a telling example of how the absence of a reading public discourages Italian literature. In *Love* Stendhal says of Italy that 'Nobody reads anything.'[175] Even if one allows for his exaggeration, a public sphere could not prosper under these circumstances.

Stendhal was not the first northern European observer to note the deficiencies of the Italians' literacy and reading habits. As early as 1644–46 the English traveller John Evelyn observed the predominance of frescoes and ornamention in the Piccolomini Library in Siena, commenting: 'When all is done, give me books in a *Library*, not pictures.' He was expressing the attitude of a more literary than visual culture. In the mid-1680s, Gilbert Burnet criticized the poor quality of Italian libraries, the Italians' general illiteracy and ignorance, the vast distance between the educated and the common people, and censorship of the press, all marks of a dying civilization. Like Evelyn, Joseph Addison mentioned the Italians' love of ornamentation and comparative lack of interest in reading. Of the Ambrosian Library in Milan he observed that 'books are, indeed, the least part of the furniture that one ordinarily goes to see in an Italian library, which they generally set off with pictures, statues, and other ornaments, where they can afford them.'[176] In evaluating these comments one must recognize, as Burke notes, that travellers not only find the expected but copy each other, so that three successive generations of British travellers make identical objections to the Ambrosian Library. They also observe a cultural code identifying northern Europe with progress, literacy, enlightenment, and economy and Italy with their negatives. Yet Burke allows for some truth in these reports, adding that one might object similarly to Italian libraries of today.[177]

To some extent Stendhal attributes the Italians' indifference to reading to their desire – supposedly inextricable from the influence of a pleasant climate – to immerse themselves in immediate and pleasant sensations. At the same time, he regards such hedonism as a cause of their unwillingness to subject themselves to the pains of hard, patient, reflective thought, which serious reading demands. As he puts it, '*abstraction* is painful for their minds.'[178] Nonetheless, the Italians are not wholly responsible for their illiteracy, ignorance, and other bad mental habits, as these also result from the system of clerical education that, supported by the state, then prevailed in Italy. Repeatedly Stendhal excoriates clerical teachers who have ruined their pupils' minds whether by giving them inadequate instruction, or by stifling their intellectual curiosity and independence, or by enslaving them to ritualism and superstition. According to Stendhal, Roman society up to 1750 believed in miracles, and superstition still reigns even among the Neapolitan upper classes, as witness the southern Italian belief in the *jettatura*. He satirizes Italian education in *The Charterhouse of Parma*, in which Fabrizio del Dongo discovers that his clerical teachers, enemies of the Enlightenment and Jansenism, had taught him 'nothing, not even Latin, not even how to spell.' Although Fabrizio is an aristocrat, his logical abilities are hardly better than those of illiterate peasants, who live according to superstitious prophecies. In his opinion, astrology is a respectable science like geometry. Yet Fabrizio's logical failings are also moral ones, since his inability to reason prevents that objective '*personal examination*' Stendhal admires in Protestantism. When Fabrizio visits a church to ask God to pardon his sins, it never occurs to him to mention the simony by which he had benefited. Far from treating Fabrizio as evil, Stendhal views him as the innocent, pre-moral victim of Jesuitical casuistry, which had deprived him of the '*courage*' to reflect on '*unfamiliar things.*' In another instance, Fabrizio denounces a man who stole a horse Fabrizio had previously stolen.[179] For Stendhal, such moral irregularity, and the inability to recognize it, is Italian. There are, he notes, no greater devotees of the Virgin than the Italian bandits. In *The Abbess of Castro*, the hero passionately worships the Virgin yet helps to desecrate a convent under her protection.[180]

While Stendhal's portrait of Fabrizio may seem like caricature, it is not necessarily exaggerated. Decades before Stendhal, Pietro Verri had attacked Italian clerical education, based upon what Salvatorelli terms 'blindly and uncritically accepted beliefs, and upon the external observance of rituals and practices without any inner moral life,' as a main reason for the present 'inferiority' of the Italians. Alfieri had similarly denounced an education that had provided him with neither logic, nor information, nor 'measures of self-control,' nor 'maxim[s] of conduct.'[181] Noting that the withdrawal of the upper classes from popular culture was less pronounced in Italy than in England and France, Peter Burke asserts that even in the eighteenth century 'many educated Italians continued to share popular beliefs about magic and witchcraft.'[182] Stendhal's characterization of the religious beliefs of Italian banditti receives confirmation in the writings of his contemporary Charles MacFarlane, who observes that they 'have a strong relish for religion, such as it is, and ... will send a knife into your bosom while a crucifix and reliquary repose upon their own.' MacFarlane quotes fellow traveller Maria Graham on the bandits' Madonna-worship, and her observation that 'this mixture of ferocity and superstition is one of the most terrific features in the character of the banditti of Italy.'[183]

Such traits were apparently of long standing, for in 1614 the British traveller William Lithgow pacified banditti by producing what Sells calls the 'best of all passports – the certificate of a visit to the Holy Places,' after which they 'made merry' with Lithgow. James Jackson Jarves remarks of the early nineteenth-century bandit Gasparone, whom Stendhal mentions in *Pages d'Italie*, that he murdered his confessor for refusing to absolve him of a robbery, and yet refrained from bloodshed on Sundays and church festivals. William Dean Howells notes that the consciences of bandits were assuaged if a priest accompanied them, and that some banditti were priests themselves. The nineteenth-century brigand Don Ciro Annichiarico abandoned his original priestly vocation to become a professional criminal, 'unholy wizard,' and 'devil in reality,' thus earning himself the title 'Priest-Robber.' Yet though he was driven by a libido that caused him repeatedly to break his vows of celibacy, he 'never wholly relinquished his sacerdotal character.' According to Stendhal, the notorious nineteenth-century bandit Fra Diavolo was an ex-monk, and another bandit who abandoned the priesthood for banditry returned to preach in his parish.[184]

Sad to say, even Italian scholars and artists lack objectivity. Stendhal complains that the former typically exaggerate the merit of their discoveries, and that even the most erudite are in need of 'one vital quality,' namely the 'gentle art of not considering as already proven whatever fact is vital to the thesis in question; in this respect, the manner of argument employed defies belief!' In *Pages d'Italie* he notes 'an incredible lack of logic' among academics, who, vicious in attacking their rivals, respond to contradiction with mortal hatred and who, if enjoying a cardinal's favour, consider themselves intellectually invulnerable. Yet perhaps the most damning of Stendhal's allegations against Italian scholars is that they all too often plagiarize from each other's work. Although such a charge may seem ironic given Stendhal's many literary falsifications, including plagiarism from Giuseppe Carpani and other Italian writers, he may have had some justification in criticizing at least some Italian scholars of this period for a cavalier attitude towards facts.[185] In any case, even the great poet Alfieri showed 'more fury than intelligence,' for as Stendhal contends, Alfieri's politics were limited by his aristocratic bias, anarchic individualism, and excessive subjectivity. The 'noblest of intellects,' he 'never managed to realize that, in the field of politics, the *sine qua non* of tolerable writing is a careful act of *dissociation* from all the rubs and trifling personal vexations that the philosopher himself may have suffered.' According to Stendhal, Alfieri's lasting hostility to the French Revolution originates in his outrage over an incident mentioned in his *Autobiography*, namely his banishment from Paris during the revolution and confiscation of his belongings by the authorities.[186]

Stendhal realizes, however, that the deficiencies of literacy and reading in Italy cannot be ascribed exclusively to the bad intellectual habits of the Italians and their education under clerical and other teachers. They also reflect the political condition of the peninsula, where despotic regimes impede active public life through censorship, surveillance, and other curtailments of free expression, whether in speech or print. Further inhibiting factors include not only ecclesiastical interference but the political and linguistic fragmentation of the peninsula, which inevitably produces disincentives to authorship by limiting the size of the audience an author can hope to reach. To be sure, Stendhal acknowledges the existence of a publishing trade in Milan, where many original books are printed, and whose bookshops much surpass those of Florence, despite the fact that the Florentine ruler, Duke Ferdinand III, parades his liberalism. And yet there had been greater liberty of the press in Milan in 1783, when Verri published his *History*, than in 1818, when the writings of Beccaria were banned. The other Italian despotisms of the Restoration likewise censor books, newspapers, and discussion. With its spies and censorship, Rome remains essentially a police regime, while in Piedmont the mistreatment of professors and intellectuals is commonplace. Given the presence of police spies and informers, the most dangerous thing an Italian can do is to talk about forbidden literary subjects, and this is a chief cause of that mysterious, sullen silence into which, notes Stendhal, Italians sink when they consider it unsafe to express their thoughts and passions. Whether as a result of illiteracy or censorship, the discouragement of reading means that Italian writers, even a Vincenzo Monti, cannot earn a living by writing. Adding to these difficulties is the fact that inept legislation and legal irregularities among the Italian states have given rise to a heavy trade in pirated editions, so that even a writer of peninsular reputation is deprived of a large portion of his potential income. Taken together, these despotic inhibitions prevent 'popular democracy' and the literate, civic-minded public essential to civilization. Without a constitutional government, literature and culture are a hopeless sham, as great writers like Alfieri 'work blindly in the dark' and in 'despair of any guidance from a *real* public.' In the absence of public opinion such as exists among northern European nations, aspiring writers find themselves oppressed by the intellectual tyranny of culturally conservative pedants. By impeding the circulation of knowledge from state to state, the despotisms insure that Italy remains fragmented and provincial, with the individual states and regions continuing to view each other with hateful suspicion and misunderstanding.[187]

The cultural retardation of Italy since the Renaissance, combined with the presence of foreign despotisms and local dialects reflecting the peninsula's political fragmentation, had in Stendhal's view left the Italian language in a state of crisis remediable only through national unity and constitutional government. Ever since the Latin revival of the later Middle Ages and Renaissance, written Latin had followed a Ciceronian model that had all too often tempted Italian writers to favour ponderous paragraphs stuffed with inflated, interminable sentences. Their love of hypotaxis and luxuriant high-sounding phraseology made it virtually impossible for them to express themselves with the rapidity and precision the French had perfected in writing and speech. Whereas Dante had brilliantly expressed his poetic individuality, the Italian language was later codified by academic pedants for whom the dialect of Renaissance Florence represented the ideal and permanent norm for Italian writers and speakers. Under the censorious surveillance of the Accademia della Crusca, it was deemed essential to write in not a living but an artificial, frozen language. Instead of communicating simply and directly, writers would reach for the dictionary for fear of using a word rejected by the Della Cruscans. In the long run it became hard for Italians to write clearly on difficult topics, partly because simple things had acquired inflated and multiple names. Nor did the national preference for ornate superlatives and flattering hyperboles encourage linguistic precision. Even Alfieri failed to write in his own language, argues Stendhal, although he knows such a statement is likely to offend. He remains certain nonetheless that post-Renaissance life cannot be expressed satisfactorily in the language of fifteenth-century Florence – this being one reason for the retardation of both the Italian novel and a national comic theater. That Italians speak energetically only in local dialects is no consolation, for as Stendhal realizes, these prevent the development of a national literature and reading public. As Alfieri had complained, Italian authors in lacking an approved stylistic model can only write for restricted audiences.[188]

An immigrant to England in the 1760s, Giuseppe Baretti lamented that, although Italian printers continually published new books, it was virtually impossible for writers to earn a living in Italy, for not only did Italy's dialects deprive them of a national audience, but state and ecclesiastical censors often interfered with publication. Curiously, Baretti said little about Italian illiteracy, which had fallen below the northern European standard, and which much reduced the number of readers.[189] The eighteenth-century reformers Ludovico Antonio Muratori and Gaetano Filangieri understood that civic development and political liberalism required a literate public, yet with the collapse of the Milanese journal *Il Caffè*, which ran from 1764 to 1766, Lombardy lost its chance to create a 'united and organized pressure group' capable of interpreting public opinion.[190] From a more favourable perspective, Vaussard, Hanlon, and others note of eighteenth-century Italy that the book market expanded along with printing and publishing, while many well-visited public libraries sprang up. Censors often lacked vigilance and diligence, and publishers deceived them through various tricks. In addition to books by native and foreign authors (in translation), there were journals, periodicals, gazettes, and magazines on various subjects – all of which confirms Dooley's point that a public sphere of some importance existed in Italy at this time. Stendhal's complaints of the deficiencies of Italy's literary culture in the early nineteenth century may therefore testify to a decline from eighteenth-century standards owing to Restoration censorship. Mrs Jameson, who visited in the 1820s, mentions an Italian playwright who, fearing imprisonment and already under police surveillance, feared to complete his work.[191] In any case, Italy's illiteracy rate was much higher than Scotland's a decade after unification, and it remained high in the late nineteenth century, when the circulation of papers and journals languished. Although the Italian press constituted a 'fourth estate' by 1900, the illiteracy rate was 40 per cent in 1914, an obstacle to fulfilled nationhood.[192]

Like Stendhal, Baretti attributed the persistence of Italy's many regional dialects to the absence of a metropolis that, like London, functioned as a political, commercial, cultural, and linguistic centre for the nation. In turn, Italy's linguistic fragmentation remained a major cause of the lack of mutual comprehension among Italians and of the difficulty of generalizing about them. And though Baretti acknowledged the diffusion of books in Italy, he believed its cultural disunity to be increasing because of the preference for dialect.[193] Hippolyte Taine similarly relates the decline of Italy to the 'want of centralization and a capital essential for the suppression of dialects.' Italy's modern history, he adds, derives 'from one circumstance: she could not unite under a moderate or semi-enlightened monarchy in the sixteenth century at the same time as her neighbors.'[194]

Stendhal's qualified optimism towards Italy's political destiny reflects his belief, somewhat reminiscent of the recent much-disputed theories of Robert D. Putnam, that Italy's republican traditions are dormant rather than extinct, and afford the basis for political, social, and cultural revival. To be sure, Stendhal recognizes that medieval republican city-states like Bologna, having failed to satisfy 'every warring interest,' grew 'weary' of their 'precarious' factionalism and ultimately embraced despotism. Sometimes he suggests that Italian republicanism has been permanently destroyed by foreign despotism and the Counter-Reformation.[195] Yet he more characteristically believes that the medieval republics had established a 'foundation of good sense' for the Italian character, and that Italy has preserved 'some traces of that ancient energy inherited from the Middle Ages.' Despite its degradation under Spain and the Church, 'no other nation has such an abundance of pure republican blood in its veins.' As Italy is 'nothing but an extension of the Middle Ages,' so the 'ethical traditions' of cities like Milan are 'intensely republican.' Yet it is wrong to exaggerate the resemblances between Stendhal's conception of early Italian republicanism and that of Putnam. For whereas Putnam emphasizes perhaps excessively the egalitarian, civic communitarian, cooperative, and pacific values of the medieval republics, in which he finds adumbrations of Italy's modern democratic development, Stendhal celebrates them for the ferocity and violence of their factionalism, which led to prodigious individual exploits, and which testify to a high degree of liberty. Not only does Stendhal distinguish the medieval republics from the constitutionally based democracies of his own day, but, notwithstanding his belief that Italy can draw upon its republican traditions on its way to becoming a constitutional democracy, he fears that its realization must spell the end of the older ethos, now outmoded amid modern egalitarian politics.[196]

The Restoration led Stendhal to moderate, but not abandon, his hopes for a peninsular republic. His qualified tolerance of Italian subjection, at least for the short term, reflects his growing dissatisfaction with what he saw as the immaturity, irresponsibility, and lack of methodical, coordinated effort among the *carbonari*, the spearheads of the Risorgimento, then in progress. These failings, he believes, had been demonstrated by the abortive revolts of 1820, 1821, 1822, and 1831. In his short story 'Vanina Vanini,' the hero Missirilli's commitment to carbonarism is compromised by his passion for Vanina, who finds in revolution momentary excitement but who resents her 'Fatherland' as her rival in love. When Missirilli's subordinates plan to celebrate his return by killing a policeman or two, he protests this senseless act yet later kills two policemen himself. When a prison guard curses the *carbonari*, the impulsive hero deals him a blow and subsequently admits his absence of mind. Nor does Missirilli's superstitiousness help him to think clearly.[197] Though Stendhal acknowledges the rebels' generosity of spirit, he dismisses them as naive and undisciplined and finds nothing worthy in their rhetoric, espionage, and conspiracies. Besides disapproving senseless bloodshed, he rejects revolutionary violence as self-defeating. The Restoration has entrenched itself in Italy for the time being, and the revolutionaries cannot yet hope to impose themselves upon history through heroic action. Reckless courage and enthusiasm are less desirable for the moment than the legal and methodical practices of the more progressive Italian governments, which prepare the orderly institutions and prosperity of a liberal state. Although revolution must come, it will succeed not by erratic violence but by a careful assessment of the mechanism of liberty and the needs of the nation. So too, the public must be educated in patriotism and civic responsibility.[198]

In Stendhal's judgment many Italians of the Restoration remain politically undisciplined and ignorant. Not having been exposed sufficiently to Napoleonic reforms, they lack the maturity required for political unity and parliamentary democracy. Though dreaming of political unity and constitutional government, the average Italian of 1830 has no idea of how to achieve them. Because of the enormous distance between the educated and uneducated, the enlightened class will see its liberal hopes 'founder' repeatedly. The youth of Italy remain idle and hedonistic. Only a Napoleonic type can insure rapid progress towards republicanism, yet 'where is he to spring from?' Accordingly Stendhal describes himself as '*very cool*' towards politics in the 1820s. This statement implies not his abandonment of his liberal hopes but his belief, shared by Count Mosca in *The Charterhouse of Parma*, that a 'very long march,' as H.-F.Imbert describes it, awaits Italy in its quest for unity under a constitution. Yet parliamentary liberalism will prevail in Europe, and Italy's constitutional future is assured.[199]

Franco Venturi rightly faults Stendhal for pessimism towards Italian politics during the Restoration. Besides noting the lukewarm constitutionalism he proposed as a substitute for Italy's medieval republics, Venturi criticizes him for appealing to dictatorial solutions while misjudging contemporary forces, such as the *carbonari*, in whom the Risorgimento was maturing. H.-F. Imbert remarks that, despite Stendhal's assumption that Restoration Italy had sunk into dreamy somnolence, Mazzini was already alertly chastising Italian revolutionaries for lack of method.[200] How accurate were Stendhal's political judgments and predictions? At one point he affirms that Naples will achieve a parliamentary constitution before 1840; at another he envisions an Italian revolution between 1840 and 1845; and at another he asserts that all Europe shall enjoy the two chambers, that is, parliamentary government, by 1830. He also suspects that 'fully a century must certainly elapse before Italy has earned her constitution.'[201] Yet Stendhal's false predictions are less noteworthy than his realization that, because of Italy's weaknesses, the consummation of the Risorgimento was impossible in his own time. Furthermore his Italian writings diagnose many deep-rooted failings of civilization that have continued to afflict Italy up to and in some cases even after 1945.[202]

VII

Thus far post-Renaissance Italy has appeared in many ways deficient when measured by the standard of northern European civilization. Montesquieu, Staël, Bonstetten, and other writers had anticipated or confirmed Stendhal's views in largely attributing to the demanding northern climate what they saw as the distinctive and laudable traits of their fellow northerners: social discipline, calculation, organization, method, concentrated attention, patient and sustained effort, love of freedom, respect for law and legality, and willingness to cooperate in pursuit of common goals. Building on this characterological foundation, northerners had attained a high level of political and social organization in the form of national units such as England and post-Napoleonic France. These nations owed their political and social unity to the presence of a state that, centred on Paris and London, administered national affairs in accordance with rational standards. Not only were these nations unified linguistically, they promoted national identity by legitimating, at least for certain classes, political freedom and participation. The involvement of citizens in the discipline and responsibility of civic life awakened their sense of common interests. Essential to their political participation, the public sphere insured the state's answerability to an informed electorate. In addition to protecting the rights and liberties of individuals, the state guaranteed their safety and comfort by assigning a monopoly of violence to the police and national army. At the same time, these states allied with the rising bourgeosie in order to develop the national economy. As the economy became ever more extensive and organized, an increased value was assigned to bourgeois virtues such as sobriety, discipline, patient application, rational calculation, cooperativeness, and control of affect. The upper-class society centred in the national capital provided a common social standard demanding politeness, refinement, and the banishment of unseemly excess. A person was expected not only to calculate the effect of his or her behaviour in specific social situations, but to observe the proprieties by holding emotions and gestures in check. One's reputation for civility depended increasingly on an ability to participate in drawing-room conversation. The overall tendency within the nation towards increasing socialization intensified as the behavioural norms of the capital spread to the provinces, where they were eagerly though imperfectly imitated.[203]

From the 'civilized' perspective, Italy exhibits many failings and thus seems diametrically opposite to the North. Although neither Montesquieu, Staël, Bonstetten, nor Stendhal regards Italy's sunlit and indulgent environment as the sole cause of the Italians' defects, they attribute to it a major and largely deleterious influence on the national character. In short, the Italians represent 'nature' if not absolutely then far more than 'civilization.' They exemplify neither intelligence nor logic nor rational calculation but unbridled emotionality and sensuality. Endowed by nature with great corporeal receptiveness and extraordinary sensibility, they are naturally enslaved to momentary sensations, which cause them to oscillate between the two poles of Italian existence: physical gratification and the free expression of emotion in art. Formed by nature as erratic, impulsive beings, the Italians often go to extremes, for instance from complete idleness to intense activity, including violence. And because they are so susceptible to the immediacy of sensory and emotional stimuli, they lack the sobriety, calculation, patient application, and method typical of the colder north. The warmth and bounty of their gratifying climate having condemned them to indolence while robbing them of the fibre necessary to a free people, they are fated to servitude under despotism. Nor are they capable of cooperative enterprises with other Italians, as their immersion in present sensation and feeling makes it hard for them to acknowledge the needs of, even the existence of, other people. At heart they are anarchic individualists whose enslavement to the present bars them from historical life and thus from a historical identity.[204]

The Italians' failings cannot, however, be ascribed exclusively to environment but are also owed to political and social causes.[205] First, they have long lacked national unity under a centralized state and capital and have thus been unable to create a common language for the peninsula. Besides being in most cases under foreign control, the existing local states are despotic, exploitative, unprogressive, and minimally concerned with their subjects' welfare. Barred from politics, military affairs, and the public sphere, most Italians have neither civic interests nor the responsibility and discipline required of communal life. The Italians can identify neither with their untrustworthy governments, in which they have no share, nor with their no less untrustworthy Italian neighbours, with whom they rarely cooperate. It is even harder for them to identify with Italy as a whole, as they are cut off from the rest of the peninsula by regional, linguistic, political, and other differences. As the Italians view the state with disdainful suspicion, they embrace anarchic individualism marked by clandestine disregard of the law or outright criminality as exemplified by crimes of honour and the frequency of banditry, with overtones of social protest. Italian society thus resembles a state of war, each Italian going his own way in disdain of his neighbours' interests or opinions. What with the underdeveloped local and peninsular economies, the impulsive and self-indulgent Italians lack industry, discipline, application, calculation, patience, self-control, and sobriety – deficiencies already aggravated by a too agreeable environment. Literacy and numeracy, which require educational discipline, fall well below the northern standard. Deprived of a national capital, Italy lacks a predominant class capable of creating for the rest of the nation a model of social refinement and politeness that would restrain the Italians' habit of behaving as they please, careless of drive control.

All the evidence suggests that the north is decidedly preferable to Italy, and Stendhal often seems to think so. Yet the deepest fascination of his Italian writings lies in the divided consciousness whereby he comes to question northern traits and values from an Italian perspective, Italy serving as the countermeasure by which he exposes the often unacknowledged limitations of the complacent North.

Thus considered, the virtues northerners have supposedly developed through exposure to an inhibiting environment prove limited and even deficient by comparison with the characterological traits bred naturally into the inhabitants of the sun-drenched south. Notwithstanding that the monarchical court and the salon, in having shaped new standards of refinement and politeness, exemplify the high degree of socialization required by modernity, such a society carries with it such drawbacks as personal vanity, hypocrisy, emotional refrigeration, loss of authentic personality, and sacrifice of the individual to social convention – negatives that the Italians, in lacking such a society, have been spared. Nor is Stendhal unequivocally admiring of modern national governments, despite his appreciation of their integrated economies, political, military, social, industrial, and commercial organization, and evident public welfare and prosperity. As he shows, these advantages are accompanied by liabilities arising from the increasingly organized forms of modern life. Unlike Italy, where the absence of a complex society enables the individual not only to express his emotions freely but to pursue his personal desires with maximum intensity, the northern arrangement suppresses human will, energy, and individuality. At the same time, bureaucratic and economic routinization combined with social conformism reduce life to a predictable round from which powerful and disruptive emotions are banished along with other forms of the unbidden and incalculable. The individual is absorbed into a general system of society, with its multiplicity of mediations, in contrast with Italy, where experience retains the force and savour of the present moment.

Although Stendhal may appear to have favoured unqualifiedly northern political systems over those of Italy, closer examination reveals the paradoxical relationship between the 'two liberties,' one northern, the other southern.[206] Admittedly the North can justly claim to provide the individual the benefits of an organized society, including freedom under the law, personal security through the police, guaranteed rights, democratic participation, and other benefits promising happiness. Yet the democratic state and society go hand in hand with a dull regimen of overly mediated existence. Not only do they produce conformism, but they impose a host of restraints and obligations that prevent the individual's free pursuit and expression of his or her most personal feelings and pleasures. The absorption of the citizen in politics, coupled with the supremacy of utilitarian values, further reduce the time available for what Stendhal views as the worthiest human activities, above all love and the arts. In this re-evaluation of the northern model, Italy emerges most favourably, the paradox being that, precisely because of their social disorganization and apparent enslavement under despotism, the Italians are more free, and closer to true happiness, than their northern counterparts. Just as the Italians' social anarchy and lack of legal freedoms enable them to remain true individualists, disdainful of the law, so their exemption from political and social obligations enables them to devote themselves unreservedly to love and art, those true sources of happiness in which emotion and sensuous pleasure achieve apotheosis.

Despite the characterological virtues the northerners have acquired in their cold and exacting environment, their surroundings have kept them from developing other traits that appear pre-eminently in Italians and that in some ways give them an advantage over the North. Whereas the Italian is closely allied with Nature, to which he responds sensuously and without the mediation of abstract reflection, the northerner stands outside Nature as a detached observer. This is not only because, first, he has a limited sensibility owing to his unreceptive thick skin, but also because he lives inwardly to such an extent that his mental preoccupations catch him up inextricably in intellectual tangles. Stendhal even suggests that the northerner is so abstracted that he feels a kind of vendetta against the senses – this being a motivating force in Protestantism, or so Stendhal implies. Nor is the northerner, because of his inwardness, anywhere near as expressive by nature as is the Italian. A further limitation of the northerner is that, driven by his environment to plan and organize so as to insure his survival, he lives not in the present but in the future, which only decreases his susceptibility to sensation. And finally, as the struggle against the environment has caused the northerner to develop habits of social organization and cooperation, he willingly submits to regularity and routine, including the boredom of social conventions. This contrasts with the Italian, impatient with all mediation and eager to assert his autonomy as against the social.[207]

Roughly comparable to the natural environment in its influence on the French character, French political life has long been centered on Paris – an arrangement that, whatever its advantages in forging national unity, also promotes cultural and social conformity. For Stendhal, a provincial from Grenoble, the chief drawback of centralization is the effacement of local and regional features through the flight of talented provincials to the capital along with the irresistible imposition of Parisian culture upon outlying regions. As early as *Lives of Haydn, Mozart, and Metastasio* Stendhal laments that the provinces 'are possessed of a disastrous spirit of *imitation*, which makes them worthless in the Arts, as indeed in many other things.' In music, they are 'utterly barren of originality,' and 'Paris alone, in all this great kingdom, counts for anything in music.' So it is that, 'in France, even in the greatest cities, there is not a note to be heard, save for the thin, shrill squeak of the current *opéra comique* fetched down from Paris.' A student of Bordeaux who aspires to fame in the comic theater pores over the rules of Laharpe rather than attempting a Gascon comedy in local style and spirit. Bordeaux, Lyons, and Marseilles are virtually indistinguishable from parts of Paris, which has reduced France to 'a lot of villages.' In *Lives of Haydn, Mozart, and Metastasio* Stendhal remarks that Paris 'counts for everything,' and as late as *Memoirs of a Tourist* he regrets the loss of provincial traits in Arles through improved access to the capital.[208]

While Stendhal is troubled by the spread of Parisian models throughout France, what most disturbs him is the imposition of Parisian social standards upon his compatriots – a process begun by the monarchical court during the late seventeenth and eighteenth centuries. The special social and cultural status Italy enjoys in Stendhal's writings derives largely from the fact that it has never had a court like Versailles or a monarch like Louis XIV. He is less repelled by the Italians' deficiencies of *civilité*, resulting from their lack of a monarchical model, than by Louis XIV's successful attempt to become the universal model and arbiter of behaviour for the crowd of servile courtiers he gathered round him at Versailles. Not only did he regard artists as slaves to his pompous egotism – a marked decline in the French monarchical spirit since the time when Francis I treated Leonardo da Vinci virtually as an equal – but he inflicted upon his courtiers the chilling tyranny of social propriety, which prevented them as a matter of pride from revealing the slightest personal emotion. As the court with its multitude of public rituals left little time for solitude or leisure, love became a rare flower, and was all too often degraded to a performance intended for public admiration. Thanks to Louis XIV and Louis XV, passion, individuality, and originality faded through the imposition of courtly models, to which aristocrats conformed under threat of ridicule. Courtiers and ladies thrilled to experience the vanity of having faithfully copied the latest monarchically approved fashion, or sought desperately to avoid feeling hateful envy in the presence of social rivals more adept than they in the social code. To be sure, the French aristocracy retained some appreciation of true personal honour, which demands physical courage inspired by heroic models such as the Chevalier Bayard. Yet real merit scarcely counted at the court of Louis XIV. To quote *Racine and Shakespeare*, France now observed the 'principle' enshrined in Molière's comedies, that '*one must be like everybody else.*'[209]

Stendhal's dissatisfaction with such social transformations emerges from his deepest beliefs: that passion, as Helvétius taught, is primary in human life, and the source of human activity; that passion is unpredictable; that the noble man imitates no one, but pursues his own passions and pleasures; that the higher pleasures, which are emotional and the chief of which is love, must strike hard; and that, whereas pride connects with genuine self-esteem, the essence of vanity lies in the unrecognized imitation of others' desires, the abdication of passionate individuality in favour of social models and the satisfaction of others' expectations. The vain person lives in the estimation of others and thus surrenders his autonomy so as to please them rather than himself. At the heart of vanity is illusion, the false overestimation of one's own importance and that of other people. The vain person is obsessed with trivial things that his imagination magnifies beyond all proportion. Oblivious to reality, such a person miscomprehends his or her own true interests, and thus runs from one empty desire to another, without ever attaining 'true happiness' or 'genuine pleasure.'[210]

The behavioural ideals of the monarchical court overwhelmingly influenced French society during the eighteenth century and continued to do so after the French Revolution. Taking the court of Versailles as its model, Paris became a scene of vain emulation, each person seeking to outdo all others in the cold neutrality and self-possession that testified to good taste (*bon ton*) conceived as the effortless mastery of the most complicated and trivial formalities dictated by fashion. Thus the 'flight from vulgarity' led to 'most abominable affectation.' As 'natural simplicity' was extinguished among the Parisians, so the formerly easy-going provincials were soon obsessed with social rules in clumsily self-conscious imitation of the capital. Ultimately the 'failure to act naturally' became the distinctive 'fault' of French provincial women, while the spread of convention and affectation among the Parisian upper classes banished spontaneity to the point where existence became thoroughly predictable. Formerly the French had *brio*, but now they wanted to be sophisticated and blasé, like the Parisians, and so they succumbed to that 'extreme politeness' and 'complete dryness of heart' that, conjoined with hypocrisy and affectation, inhibit the feelings and 'refrigerate' passion. 'What strikes one particularly,' remarks Stendhal of Paris, '... is the extreme politeness and lusterless eyes of all the people one meets.' Tutored by the monarchical court, the French now preferred society to solitude, love and other passions having thus become increasingly 'rare' among them, 'stifled' by that social 'vanity' that had reached 'gigantic proportions' in France and England. Contrastingly, 'a passionate man is only like himself, and not like other people.'[211]

This is not to imply that French society remained unchanged following the monarchy, for though the court had left a lasting legacy, republicanism not only allowed greater originality in behaviour but weakened vanity by encouraging various social models rather than that of the king alone. Whereas at Versailles the courtier had escaped ridicule by satisfying monarchical ideals of propriety and gallantry, the nineteenth-century Parisian was afflicted by 'foolish honor,' which consists of emulating the 'best people' and worrying about what the neighbours think – anxieties and obsessions not of the court but of the salons and boulevards. While the power of public opinion intensified through political liberalization and the growing power of the press, ridicule remained nearly as potent a means of social discipline as in the past, having shifted its focus from the court to the larger society, where the fashionable man had replaced the courtier as the 'object of our cult.' Stendhal recognizes, moreover, that public opinion can be as coercive as the monarchical court, for as he notes in *Lives of Haydn, Mozart, and Metastasio*, 'in all matters pertaining to politics and literature, the wealthier classes are duly told each morning in their newspapers exactly what they are expected to think during the rest of the day.'[212]

Because the French were too busy flattering acquaintances in hope of social advancement, or else seeking social approval through vain demonstrations of superior politeness or knowledge of fashion, they had become almost incapable of appreciating the personal happiness to be derived not only from love but from all other passionate experiences that exist for their own sake and apart from social estimations. At most, what they experienced was 'Mannered Love,' which, unlike passion, does not remove a person from his or her egoistic interests, and which of all forms of love is the most boring, as it consists entirely of calculation. More typically, a young Parisian treated his mistress 'as a kind of slave intended to satisfy his vanity.' What most satisfied the typical Frenchmen was not deep affection but the vain display of vivacious wit before an audience. Society itself having developed into an enormous coercive engine of conformism, each person closely watched his behaviour and that of others, so as to avoid and detect damnable violations of propriety – thus confirming Stendhal's point that politeness serves egotism. 'In France,' he writes, 'you and I will both try to imitate the same pattern, and I shall be an expert judge on the way you do it.' Or as he remarks in *Racine and Shakespeare*, 'it is the *opinion of the majority* that erects in the public square the model to which everyone scrupulously conforms.' French society had thus become a theatre of vanity, snobbery, and envy, the latter being the 'chief obstacle' to happiness in France. As 'French wit cannot exist without the habit of attention to the impression of others,' notes Stendhal, so collective ridicule in the form of slashing wit remained the chief means by which French society held passionate nonconformists in line.[213] This punishment had fallen especially hard upon Parisians, 'frozen by the fear of ridicule even more than by the cold mists of the Seine.' Thanks to the habit of ridicule inherited from the monarchy, the French had learned to avoid extremes, yet their 'excessive politeness' was accompanied by such a loss of energy and force of character that they were now an etiolated people. 'The only trace of originality to be found in France,' writes Stendhal, 'is to be discovered among the common people, too ignorant to have a model to imitate.' The dwindling of love may likewise be attributed to ridicule, which, as 'public opinion's executioner,' 'frightens love away.' Love had further declined through the general taste for reading, which inspired narcissistic imitation of literary models, so that the French again preferred vanity to sincere feeling and genuine pleasure. And since passions are the 'very stuff of art,' being at once their inspiration and message, the arts cannot flourish in the 'sad, cold climate of the North, where *Society* is the universal judge and arbiter of everything,' where people are 'above all things *dispassionate*, ironical, and vain,' and where ridicule chills and shrivels feelings. The musical mediocrity of the French was chiefly owed to these causes. Similarly French audiences were corrupted, as they failed to respond sincerely or deeply to a work of art, but aped majority opinion. Regarding France from his Italian vantage, Stendhal holds that 'civilization blanches souls' and that the French suffer from a 'too advanced civilization.'[214]

VIII

Despite the tendency of northern commentators to stress the negative effect of Italy's environment on its national character, Stendhal remains convinced of the superiority of the Man of the Midi to the Man of the North, and thus emphasizes that nature has imbued the typical Italian with highly desirable traits far less common in the northerner.[215] As seen by apologists of the North, the northerner's natural environment has developed in him abstract intellect as against southern sensuousness and sensibility. Though only feebly appreciative of corporeal pleasures, and too reserved to express emotions uninhibitedly whether in art, language, or gesture, the northerner in his ongoing struggle against nature far surpasses the self-indulgent southerner in ability to plan for the future; he does so, moreover, by entering with fellow northerners in cooperative enterprises for which the individual Italian, self-encapsulated in a world of fleeting sensations and feelings, is incapable. And so, unlike the Italian, the northerner uses his mind to create between himself and nature an alternative world of mediations.

Such is the typically invidious northern judgment that Stendhal turns on its head. In celebrating Italy as the home of the *naturel*, he means among other things that it is the land of the body and senses, where sensation remains unconquered by intellect, where sensibility predominates over logic, and where the inhabitants, unlike the reserved and withdrawn northerners, are so absorbed in the immediacy of sensory pleasure that they have achieved oneness with both their bodies and nature itself. Nowhere is this unity of self and body more striking than in the Italians' vivacity, their unique ability, through language, gesture, and the various forms of art, to transform their own physicality into the vehicle of emotional expression. This is not to ignore Stendhal's awareness that the Italians' uninhibited corporeality sometimes leads to almost animalistic brutishness and savagery, yet he justifies such behaviour on the grounds that, being impatient with all mediation and thus driven to gratify their appetites immediately, Italians surpass northern peoples in receptivity to experience – in short, sensibility – which enables them to feel pleasurable sensations and joyful emotions to the maximum. This trait depends upon not only their lack of reflection but their unwillingness to live for the future, beyond present gratifications – that very absence of calculation Stendhal identifies with the *naturel*. Unlike the reflective calculating Englishman, whose weighty ideas and projects remove him from the present by making him what Crouzet terms the 'victim of thought,' the Italian is never depressed, for as Stendhal contends, depression is impossible in Italy.[216]

For Stendhal, northerners ever pursue a future goal they are bound to replace with yet another. Contrastingly, the Italian does not become but *is*, in the manner of a natural entity; he possesses his own energetic being in a perpetual present, seeking his goals as ends in themselves, for the pleasure they provide. His unique capacity to express his deepest feelings immediately and naturally is evident in his frequent eschewal of language in favour of readily comprehensible signs and gesticulations, notwithstanding that northerners often deride such nonverbal forms of communication as uncivilized. With their instinct for expression, the Italians are for Stendhal a naturally artistic people, the Neapolitans being especially blessed with musical aptitude. Regarding the Italians' reputed inability to form a society or join in common projects, these traits testify to the Stendhalian assumption that to be *naturel* is to be free of others, that is, society and its mediations. In the North, people are burdened by moral and social duties, which must lead to the amputation of self. But in Italy, the individual blossoms in the absence of society, for where society is nothing, the individual is superb. Italy is thus for Stendhal the land not only of the *naturel* but of what Michel Crouzet calls the '*moi*,' the individual conceived as an autonomous monad, indifferent to neighbours and society in general. Driven by passion, such a being is identifiable by that animation of speech and gesture that Italians call *brio*, and which shows that the entire body is engaged unreflectively and at all times in the ardent gratification of the individual's pleasures and desires.[217]

Just as Italy's natural environment has produced in its people characterological virtues far less common in the colder, punishing north, so its lack of national unity under a capital figures in Stendhal's writings as a chief reason for advantages that Italy possesses to a degree unequalled elsewhere in Europe. This is not to minimize his realization that political fragmentation has jeopardized Italian liberty, for as he remarks in

Rome, Naples and Florence, 'The history of the thirteenth, fourteenth, and fifteenth centuries is the tale of those countless vain attempts to *evolve a system of sound government* which harassed the peninsula.' Yet Stendhal rightly regards such sectionalism as a reflection of the extraordinary diversity of Italy's many regions and local centres, each of which prides itself on its own distinctive character. Unlike Paris, which monopolizes French creativity to the point where the rest of the country consists of interchangeable villages, Italy boasts of 'seven or eight centers of civilization ... Everything changes ... every ten leagues. To begin with, the races of men are different.' The various regions of Italy speak languages virtually unintelligible to each other, while the 'simplest act' is performed differently in every region. The customs of Ferrara are 'not at all those of Bologna or of Padua, as everything in Italy changes every twenty leagues.' A drive from Milan to Como, for the purpose of hearing the Mombelli sisters sing, is enough to persuade Stendhal that the 'traditions of the two countries [*sic*] are utterly dissimilar; it would require no effort to believe myself a thousand leagues away.' In France the press trumpets national music, but the Florentines speak of '*our* Benvenuti,' and the Bolognese of '*our* Arrici.' Yet though 'language' and 'manners' change in Italy from region to region, and though 'what is good form in Venice' is regarded as 'odd at Naples,' the final result of such diversity is that nothing is unusual, as Italy lacks universal social conventions such as Paris transmits to all France. What it has is 'originality,' for in the absence of a capital and in the presence of weak local governments, the Italians are able to be their passionate selves, with a margin available for displays of genius. Unlike France, the Italian provinces have not lost their special vitality through submission to a common social and cultural standard. This is not to ignore the fact that Stendhal fears that French influence in Italy will obliterate 'local physiognomy,' yet he is pleased to report a return to local ways following the Napoleonic occupation.[218]

Stendhal's keen appreciation of Italy's regional diversity is matched by his awareness of the mutual enhancement of individual works of Italian art and the distinctive local atmospheres of the towns, cities, and regions in which they originated and in which many continue to be preserved. This is shown in his criticism of the Napoleonic armies that, during the French occupation of Italy, transferred a multitude of paintings from local churches and palaces to Paris in shameless acts of pillage. Despite their pretention to being 'civilized,' these 'barbarians' had failed to realize that in carrying off such treasures they 'of necessity ... left behind the atmosphere ... essential to their enjoyment,' and had thus 'diminished the quantity of enjoyment that exists in the world.' Stendhal adds that 'not a few fine canvasses that now hang solitary and as it were forgotten in some remote corner of your gallery [in France], were once the pride and glory of a whole city, and daily furnished matter for a whole conversation.'[219] Such statements suggest that Stendhal would probably have questioned not only André Malraux's concept of the 'museum without walls' but Walter Benjamin's argument that in an age of mechanical reproduction art objects formerly endowed with an elitist 'aura' based on their non-duplicability must lose that aura through mechanical reproduction, thus supposedly preparing for egalitarian art.[220] To be sure, Stendhal was not the last writer to suggest that the transfer of a locally produced and housed work of art to a metropolitan museum must inevitably deprive it of something essential to its character, namely its connection with a local origin, ambience, or school, call it 'aura' or whatever; Ruskin and Pound, among others, thought similarly. In any case, Stendhal assumes that local works possess aura, which depends not simply on what they are in themselves but on their embodiment and reflection of a local atmosphere and tradition. This in turn means that the experience of a photograph of such a work can never be quite the same as one's encounter with it within the environment from which it emerged and for which it was originally intended.

Although Stendhal takes pleasure in all the major Italian cities of his acquaintance, he does not admire them equally. His nearly consistent disparagement of Florence as the capital of a blandly passionless and inexpressive bourgeoisie eloigns him from a climate of opinion that emerged in the eighteenth century and that persists in those many visitors for whom the sober beauty and rationality of Florence and its landscape distil the meaning of the Renaissance and thus justify the characterization of Florentine-dominated Tuscany as 'l'Italia dell'Italia' – the 'Italy of Italy.' These encomiasts would never apply such an epithet to Rome or Naples, with their mingling of magnificence and squalor, or to Venice, with its suggestions of abnormality and corruption, or to Milan, with its comparatively weak cultural legacy, or to such smaller provincial jewels as Assisi and Verona, too distinctly regional to stand for the whole. For Stendhal, however, the middle-class atmosphere of Florence opposes the true spirit of Italy, which he finds better represented in varying degrees by other peninsular capitals. If Naples ultimately dissatisfies him, it is because, fed by a fervid climate, the all-consuming sensualism and pansexualism of Neapolitan lovemaking seems too immediately physical, allowing the imagination no temporal margin within which to nurture deeper feelings for the other person. Naples is a land of demons where natural impulses run to frenzied excess, and where women are treated as mere flesh, almost as if animals. And because the people lack interiority, their passions can only be fleeting, without fullness or resonance. As for Venice, one would expect the capital of hedonism to have attracted Stendhal, and indeed he praises the libertine city as a place where, thanks to its easy customs, desires of all kinds may be satisfied. Yet despite its voluptuousness, Venice displeases him, as the people are lascivious beyond all morality, while Venetian love, in being all too easy, lacks emotional depth. He characterizes the Venetians as the French of Italy, gay, witty, yet without energy. Unlike France or at least Paris, Venice's one-sidedly sensual form of epicureanism fails to provide the intellectual satisfactions Stendhal requires as the complement to physical pleasure. Fortunately, he finds in Rome and Milan two Italian cities that, however disparate in appearance and atmosphere, are closest to his own heart. For though Rome exemplifies a somber and sometimes appalling roughness rarely if ever encountered in the polite society of elegant and lighthearted Milan, the residents of both cities comprehend that love is the profoundest, most serious of emotions, and thus to be nurtured not only in contemplative solitude but amid the most intellectually and imaginatively exalting stimuli – the art and classical antiquities of Rome, and the passionate operatic strains heard from the boxes at La Scala.[221]

Yet another advantage enjoyed by the Italians is that, unlike the French, they have never been subject to the social ideals and standards of an absolute monarchy and its court. This is not to forget that Italy gave rise to numerous local and regional courts during the Middle Ages and Renaissance, but in contrast with those developed under monarchical absolutism, in which individuality was discouraged in favour of slavish subordination to the monarch, Italian rulers fostered and rewarded talent of all kinds. Nor did they remain disdainfully aloof from their protégés, but welcomed and even mixed with them. The result, argues Stendhal, was socially and culturally inestimable.

The medieval and Renaissance despots whom Stendhal mentions include the Sforza, the Bentivoglio, the family of Pico della Mirandola, the Scaligers of Verona, the Polenta of Ravenna, the Manfredi of Faenza, Girolamo Riario of Imola, and Cesare Borgia. In a statement anticipating Burckhardt's *The Civilization of the Renaissance in Italy*, Stendhal says of the despots that 'princes of such a stamp as these, assuming that they fail to reduce all things to one common level of degradation and brutishness, may conjure up among their subjects some singularly forceful characters.'[222] This was all the more likely when the ruler had 'esprit,' as did Machiavelli's hero Castruccio Castracani, who found it in his interest to be just. King Robert of Naples invited Giotto to work in his capital, where he was showered with honours and encouragement and where he enjoyed the conversation and indulgence of the king. Shunning intellectual mediocrity, such later rulers as Lorenzo de' Medici, Alessandro Borgia (Pope Alexander VI), Cesare Borgia, and Pope Leo X not only appreciated the talents of the great artists whom they patronized but treated them nearly as equals. Indeed, Stendhal finds it almost hard to believe that, in the three-hundred-year interval from the fall of the Italian republics to the coming of Spanish despotism, 'Italian princes ... who had usurped the sovereign power lived with the country's men of wit.' In Crouzet's view, Stendhal regards the Renaissance despots not so much as the destroyers as the continuators of medieval republican individualism – a viewpoint opposed to that of Sismondi, the encomiast of the medieval Italian republics.[223] Lorenzo de' Medici, writes Stendhal, 'spent his life with the superior men of his time, in his fine country houses in the vicinity of Florence,' where Michelangelo was only one of the 'many men of spirit assembled by the Medici.' Although Stendhal believes that Lorenzo had undermined the city's republican institutions, a judgment antithetical to that of William Roscoe, he acknowledges that Lorenzo 'so brilliantly sustained the part of kingship,' his greatness lying chiefly in his having 'established a Court at which, for the first time since the reign of Augustus, military prowess was reduced to a secondary role' in favour of cultural achievement. Thus Lorenzo created a court for his courtiers, rather than courtiers for his court. Imitating the Medici, Ludovico Sforza sought glory as an art patron and thus summoned to his court not only Bernardino Luini but Leonardo da Vinci, who later served Cesare Borgia as a military engineer.[224] Of Pope Julius II Stendhal remarks that he 'felt a need to live with the great artists of his time,' whom he 'raised ... to the ranks of his dearest confidants' and whose works he 'enjoyed ... with passion.' The Renaissance model of the court subsequently influenced the French monarchy, for as Stendhal notes, Francis I proudly patronized Leonardo da Vinci, whom he regarded as a great man, and for whom he wept openly upon his death. The conduct of these Italian rulers contrasts with that of Louis XIV, who treated his artists as lackeys and who, with typical vanity, regarded them only as glorifying himself.[225]

Stendhal likewise distinguishes the society of the late medieval and Renaissance courts from that of the later European monarchies, especially the court of Louis XIV, where forceful displays of passionate individualism were stifled under a multitude of regally enforced social proprieties, where cutting ridicule kept nonconformists in line, and where politeness and good taste, the bywords of a socially regimented regime, masked vanity and hypocrisy. Just as, for Stendhal, the Italians have never respected kings but treated them with the 'remorseless hatred' reserved for a 'public enemy,' so no Italian despot has 'ever succeeded in dictating the laws of taste' for Italy; and this, he concludes, explains its 'thousand advantages.' What Renaissance Italy had was not kings but '*princes naturels*,' men of 'ardent passion' who in the ferocity of their genuinely personal joys and desires valued neither emotional reserve nor vanity nor codes of politeness nor a self-conscious 'theory of life'; men, moreover, who sought not to suppress but to promote similar intensities in the passionate souls they gathered round them. As Stendhal notes, the great paintings of the fifteenth and sixteenth centuries stem directly from such habits and feelings, as in those times an artist's greatness was never allowed to be eclipsed by a prince's vanity.[226]

Far from enshrining the gravely decorous proprieties later apotheosized by monarchical absolutism and Protestantism, these smaller, more intimate courts encouraged natural freedoms that seem indecorous by the standards of later, more straight-laced periods. Commenting on what he sees as Sismondi's and Roscoe's sanitized portrayals of Renaissance Rome, Stendhal notes that the writings of Bandello, with their tales of mischievous bawdiness and practical jokes of dubious taste, reflect an age in which puritanism and its southern counterpart, the Counter-Reformation, had not yet condemned clowning, buffoonery, and indifference to proprieties. A clever and inveterate practical jokester, Pope Leo X liked to be surrounded by 'jovial faces,' which made life 'gay and good-humored' at his court, and 'nothing so attractive has ever existed.' This is not to say that Stendhal regards Italian Renaissance society as savage or barbaric, his point being that good manners were never carried so far as to banish passion, pleasure, spontaneity, and originality. As he puts it, 'a politeness that was reputed perfect was not allowed to impair the originality of minds.' Nor did the example of these local courts fade from the Italians' memory in later periods, when they succumbed neither to the 'despotism of *ridicule*' nor to the 'falsehoods of courtiers feigning happiness,' but easily resisted the chilly vanity and hypocrisy of the monarchical courts their invaders had imposed upon them.[227]

Jacob Burckhardt, who somewhat admired Stendhal's *Charterhouse of Parma*, shared his appreciation not only of the individualistic personalities of the Italian Renaissance but of the joy and gladness Leo X diffused at his papal court. Buckhardt describes him as characteristically Florentine in combining the highest cultural refinement with a love of jesters and buffoons, whom he habitually mocked at public feasts, and upon whom he played good-natured practical jokes (*burle* and *beffe*). Yet though neither jesting nor trickery (whether pleasant or nasty) was deemed offensive in early sixteenth-century Italy, they soon fell from favour through the influence of Castiglione's and della Casa's conduct books, which rejected wounding wit as unseemly while seeking to restrain dramatic gestures in the telling of jokes and stories. Much more the fastidious bourgeois than Stendhal, Burckhardt seems to favour the new values of reserve and propriety over the former coarseness of Italian manners.[228] Taine likewise seems uncomfortable in repeating the social and cultural examples Stendhal delights in, such as Bandello's stories and the carnivalism of the court of Leo X, rather preferring Castiglione and the circle of Lorenzo de' Medici, that is, what he regards as the closest Renaissance approximations of French monarchical and subsequently bourgeois ideals of politeness, civility, conventionality, and conversation.[229] Yet despite the influence in Italy of more 'civilized' standards, a large measure of the old spontaneity and light-heartedness persisted during the eighteenth century even at the papal court. Andrieux observes that all but one of the popes of that century were great practical jokers, who doused ladies and prelates with jetting torrents of water released unexpectedly from underground pipes. One pope enjoyed tripping his cardinals so as to make them fall into fountains, and Clement XIV would 'sit happily with a looking glass in his window in the Quirinal [Palace] and dazzle passersby with the reflected rays of sunshine.'[230]

IX

Stendhal realizes that Italy's lack of political unity, and its consequent inability to establish a monarchical court society within a centralized capital, had prevented the development of a single social standard for the peninsula. Instead, the inhabitants of each region follow their own loose standard, which affords them a wide margin for free-wheeling individuality. Stendhal likewise recognizes the many social failings of the Italians, which trace largely to their never having felt the influence of a national court. Nonetheless Stendhal regards Italy's political situation – the very absence of a centralized capital and monarchical court – as a major reason for the many benefits the Italians enjoy as compensation for their shortcomings. Thanks ironically to its seemingly undesirable political situation, early nineteenth-century Italy not only remains free of the social diseases afflicting post-monarchical France, such as frigidity, vanity, ridicule, and hypocrisy, but preserves those values that Stendhal most esteems. On the one hand is the *naturel*, a mixture of sincerity, spontaneity, and passion in the pursuit of experience; on the other is the cult of the *moi*, the unbridled individual who feels, thinks, and acts according to his own lights, and who, as a social monad, follows his desires and passions in absolute freedom, heedless of his neighbours and the social law.[231]

'I'm in an unalloyed Italian mood,' writes Stendhal in his *Private Diaries*, adding that no requirements of 'good taste' can alter its genuineness.[232] As much as this statement favours Italy, it implicitly criticizes France, where the monarchical court and tyranny of Parisian society had in Stendhal's view poisoned manners and feelings, and against which Italy figures as his perennial counterexample. Influenced by monarchical and Parisian models, the French had acquired a host of conventions setting the standard for politeness and good taste. Through the widespread imitation of such models, polite behaviour came to consist in servile conformity to society regarded as the total weight of others' opinions. Conversation was the means by which the subtleties of social behaviour were registered and evaluated, favourably or unfavourably. As Stendhal puts it, 'everyone well knows that one achieves fortune and fame only through drawing-room relations.' In the long run, the French suffered the nearly complete withering of natural simplicity, passion, depth of feeling, sincerity, and spontaneity, till love seemed to have vanished from the human heart. Passion had been chilled by the proprieties, slavish attention to others' opinions, and obsessive copying of approved models both social and literary. To violate convention through passionate or excessive display was to risk general disapproval of one's taste. Behaviour thus became thoroughly calculable, hence predictable and boring. Love was replaced by malicious envy of social superiors or by amour-propre fed by one's mastery of proprieties as a means of successfully negotiating the treacherous social terrain. Passion and sincerity having fled the field, vanity triumphed over society in various forms. Conversation became a means of showing off, so as to meet others' approval. Thoroughly degraded, love amounted to vain flirtation or coquettishness pursued out of narcissism, the eyes of society being but the reflection of one's own self-admiring gaze. The contamination of love by insincerity was further owed to the narcissistic copying of literary models. Not only was there a vast increase in 'the respect for others that vain people call *honour*,' which consists in an exaggerated investment in one's reputation, but vanity revealed itself in affectation and pretension as well as in an obsessive interest in personal dignity and elegant social presentation conventionally prescribed. One could also demonstrate one's effortless mastery of social propriety by adopting an ostentatiously blasé attitude, the pose of superiority conveyed through feigned indifference to other people and refusal to admire anything beyond oneself – though all the while soliciting others' approving gaze so as to admire oneself indirectly. Snobbery could only proliferate in this unhealthy atmosphere, where bitter ridicule punished violators of the social code.[233]

Among the chief causes enabling Italy to figure in Stendhal's work as the counter to France is that it had escaped the influence not only of a single monarchical court but of generally accepted social standards whether at the national or the regional level. Nor had it developed national or local standards of behaviour through organs of public opinion. The Italian, observes Stendhal, 'has never known the pleasures nor shared the pastimes of that multitude of petty tyrants who, ever since the collapse of the medieval republics, have sought to reduce him to utter degradation.' By the same token, 'since Leo X no one in Rome has taught the courtly graces with which the court of Louis XV has poisoned our [French] literature and our manners.' Rather, one sees 'at every turn' that 'this is a country which, for five hundred years, has escaped the contemptuous despotism of a Court like that of Louis XIV or Louis XV.' Unlike in France, social conventions and proprieties are virtually nonexistent in Italy, and other people's opinions exert only a feeble influence upon an individual's conduct. Being thus free of social mediations, the Italian has no fear of the unseemly, or of disgrace by society conceived as a vast censorious mass. To the contrary, 'the number of things which are accounted "coarse" or "in bad taste" is infinitely small.' As for ridicule, which in more socialized nations checks nonconformity, there is little basis for it in a country free of both social conventions and small talk. 'Ridicule is out of the question in Italy,' observes Stendhal, for how can there be ridicule in the absence of a common social standard? By the same token, 'no creature in pursuit of its own happiness, whatever form this happiness may take, strikes' the typical Italian 'as ridiculous merely on account of the unusual object of the quest.' According to Stendhal, public opinion had no existence in Milan as late as 1796, the year of the French invasion.[234]

Thus in Italy the *naturel* is unleashed in inextricable conjunction with the *moi*. 'There is no society,' says Stendhal of Italy, and 'for a full and interesting life a man does not rely upon the happiness' Parisians derive 'daily' from a dully predictable round of social visitations. For the Italians, the complex social rituals of France are a 'waste of time and energy,' a 'veritable *seccatura*.' Rather than gathering in society, so as to solicit others' approval, Italians go their own way in complete disregard of fellow Italians, whom they disdain often to the point of hatred. In Italy, writes Stendhal in *Rossini*, 'every man has the profoundest contempt for his neighbor, and savagely delights in the pride of his own opinions. This, of course, is the reason no really "fashionable" person could even endure to live [there].'[235] The price of such liberty is frequent yet tolerable 'rudeness' (*grossièreté*) along with a ferocity Stendhal also approves, for as he says, where men are free they are fierce. Of the typical Roman, Stendhal observes that 'he despises his neighbor, and thinks about him only to hate him. The respect for others that vain people call *honour* is unknown to him.' What else can one expect in a city where 'public opinion and contempt mean nothing,' and in which the typical individual whether male or female lives self-encapsulated within a private world of erotic and aesthetic reverie? Most Italians neither follow approved social models nor adjust their feelings or behaviour to suit others' conformist expectations, but, consistent with the *naturel*, pursue their own genuine pleasures with total sincerity and emotional intensity. This is Italian 'force' in the sense of passion as against the extreme politeness of the etiolated French. Whether they give themselves to pleasurable sensation or emotional transport, of which the highest forms are art and love, or whether they suffer physical or emotional pain, Italians respond to experience without falsity or self-deception, and without desire to make an impression or satisfy conventions – that is, to charm or gratify the other. The ideal is to act forcefully from the heart, as the Italian 'lives by his passions' and is 'for ever torn between hatred and love.' And since in Italy by comparison with France a 'man's actions depend more directly ... upon the quality of his profounder emotions,' the Italian 'way of life is almost invariably rooted in the inner experiences of soul.'[236]

Of Italy Stendhal notes that 'the judgments of the public are the humble servants of passion. Genuine passion wields over them the power which is elsewhere in the hand of society; it is quite simply that society, offering almost no pleasures at all ... has very little authority.' If the Italian salon exhibits a greater proportion of geniuses and fools than appear in any other, thus confirming the long-standing northern European view of Italy as the land of extremes, it is because the Italians regard as enfeebling the 'politeness that leads one to prefer other people to oneself,' choosing instead to seek their own enjoyments. Stendhal thus emphasizes the Italians' gaiety, light-heartedness, and happy-go-lucky spirit. 'In happy Lombardy, in Milan, and Venice,' he observes, 'the important, in fact the only, business of life is pleasure. No one there takes notice of what the neighbors do, nor cares very much for what happens to anyone else.' Again, the 'tone of [Milanese] society is utterly *natural*, gay without being boisterous,' and so the Milanese are spared the malicious envy proliferant in France. In Rome, where 'everyone is looking for a good time' and where people are concerned with achieving happiness by satisfying their passions, 'everyone follows the impulses of his soul ... there is no embarrassment, no constraint, none of those conventional ways, the knowledge of which is elsewhere called social usage, or even decency and virtue.' Just as the Roman 'fights only when he is angry,' so he 'want[s] pleasures that are real,' since for him '*appearance* is nothing.'[237] Of Roman women Stendhal notes that, unlike the French, they move about as they wish on social occasions, even if this means disarranging their dresses. Such behaviour typifies Italian women, each of whom has her own manners, ideas, and way of speaking, and who prefer a tenderly intimate tête-à-tête to trivial pleasantries or malicious raillery within a group. A person who had enjoyed himself in an Italian woman's salon would never 'ruin' her reputation through ridicule, as he would rob himself of a precious pleasure. Regarding theatrical performances, Stendhal contends that the 'first condition' of musical enjoyment is well known to the Italians, and consists in a 'state of indifference concerning the figure one cuts and the part one plays in the eyes of others.' Whereas among French audiences musical judgments conform to approved opinion, regardless of whether one has enjoyed a work, the Italian judges music by 'sensibility,' the key to 'real inner happiness.' Similarly, 'laughter among the [Italian] audience is never anything but genuine; it is never a weapon of self-deception, not a means of proving to one's neighbor that one is familiar with the foibles and mannerisms of polite society.' In Italian comedies the characters have their own burning ambitions, rather than being apes of the aristocracy. Because the Italians 'make no pretense at gentle manners, at hilarity, still less at nonchalance,' any 'young man' who 'prides himself on being blasé and cynical stands condemned.' To appear flashily clever, conventional, pedantic – this the Italians hate.[238]

Customarily in the grip of passion, Italians exhibit that vivacity and impetuosity Stendhal calls *brio* and that is the very signature of the *moi*. In

Rome, he remarks, not only is conversation especially lively, but 'clever people have *brio*, which I have observed only once in a man born in Paris ... the superior men [of Italy] despise affectation. They could well say, "*I am like myself; so much the better for you.*"' As the Italians are driven from moment to moment by immediate feelings and sensations, life in Italy can never be boring, as it partakes inherently of the incalculable, the *imprévu*. The same spontaneity and sincerity typifies Italian conversation as against the vanity of the French, for whereas the French converse chiefly to display their coldly ironic invidious wit, Italians never converse for the pleasure of it, but only to express strong and deep passions. To quote Stendhal, conversation for Italians is a '*vehicle* of emotional expression.'[239] The Italians' dislike of reading, about which Stendhal complains, has its favourable side, for unlike France where love is falsified by vain imitation of literary models, the Italians are impelled by their own desires, rather than by those acquired from novelistic characters. Yet this is not to imply that, for Stendhal, the Italians necessarily exhibit roughness and crudity, despite their forceful feelings. Rather, many Italians seem endowed innately with a 'natural' politeness preferable to the 'heavy' type prevalent in France. Having been presented one evening at seven or eight boxes at La Scala, Stendhal describes local manners as being full of naturalness (*pleines de naturel*). Of a Florentine assembly he remarks that its members have an 'unforced politeness' in addition to worldly wisdom and civilized urbanity. One sees why Stendhal, while visiting Milan, wished never to see Paris again, that metropolis 'tainted by the Bourbons.'[240]

From Stendhal's perspective, the social advantages of Italy boil down to the fact that, of all European countries, it provides the least scope for those many forms of vanity that wield 'the despotic scepter' in France. He never denies that vanity exists in Italy, for 'grand passions and noble souls are uncommon everywhere,' yet it does not predominate among Italian passions, since Italians are vain only intermittently. 'As a general rule,' writes Stendhal, 'none but the most phlegmatic among the inhabitants of Italy has the least conception of vanity,' which normally takes the form of *puntiglio*, the cult of honour. Yet 'various other passions ... would have prevented *vanity* from attaining to those gigantic proportions which it has reached today in France and England.'[241]

What explains the absence of vanity in Italy is that 'no one ... has ever dreamed of aping the modes and manners of a glittering Court.'[242] Without social conventions, proprieties, and other approved refinements, people are indifferent to others' opinions and hence without desire to please them. Nor is there an incentive for them to display pride or gravity through mastery of the rituals of politeness. The same can be said for all other forms of affectation or pretention, for who would be impressed by another person's putting on airs, or take him or her seriously? Where people disguise neither their joys nor pleasures, and passion and sensibility receive proper estimation, self-important poses of cynicism or indifference or *nil admirari* cannot win approval. To quote the Preface to *Rome, Naples and Florence*, 'the individual who deliberately cultivates affectation is as rare a bird in Roman or Milanese society as the man who behaves with natural simplicity in Paris.' Where a conversation aims to express feelings, no one talks merely to show off. Such is the 'sincerity' of the Italian language that an Italian is 'withered by the lightest breath of *affectation*, which produces a great strain and weariness of spirit.' Affectation can only be 'deadly' in Italian society, where the 'most harmless formula of conventional politeness, which to us [the French] is as indispensable in conversation as it is meaningless in effect, will fall on Italian ears as mere French affectation and irritate the listener to frenzy.'[243] Intolerant of the grave self-important dignity of carriage which they term *sostenuto*, and which seems to them the '*nec plus ultra* of intolerable weariness,' Italians are typically informal, relaxed, hence 'natural,' rarely standing on ceremony but preferring to let themselves go. It was this 'plainspoken informality of Italy' that 'so promptly won' Stendhal 'heart and soul.' In Milan, the people have been' ruthlessly stripped of *gravity*,' and the casual informality of La Scala would scandalize the French. If, according to Stendhal, there is 'nothing more charming, sympathetic, more truly and unreservedly admirable than the manners and customs of society in Milan,' it is because, amid such lightheartedness and laughter, 'solemnity and self-importance have been banished from the earth.' Maurice Andrieux in his study of eighteenth-century Rome confirms Stendhal's observations, noting that whereas the French took *sostenuto* to mean distinction, Romans found it affected. Andrieux further notes French visitors' complaints that upper-class Roman women lacked a 'grand air,' for being without affectation, they said what they liked and laughed when they liked.[244] So little concerned were Italians with their own and others' dignity that they enjoyed mischievous frolicsome games including such devilish practical jokes as Stendhal experienced at the gardens of Leinate in Milan: 'The park is mined with concealed spouts and fountains, expressly fashioned to produce a fine soaking for the unwary visitor. As soon as I placed my foot upon the lowest steps of a certain staircase, no fewer than six jets of water were set off in a great spurt between my legs.'

One thinks of the childish games – *les enfantillages délicieux* – played by Gina and Fabrizio in *The Charterhouse of Parma*.[245]

Yet another advantage that Stendhal discovers in Italy's freedom from a strict and all-embracing code of social conduct is that it largely avoids snobbism, that form of vanity that chiefly pollutes social relations in France. Unlike French high society, which proudly dissociates itself from the rest of the nation through its mastery of the *bon ton* for which it defines the national model, the Italian upper classes are far less distinguishable in manners and customs from their social inferiors, whose tastes and attitudes they share and with whom they mingle freely, without envy, shame, or embarrassment. As Stendhal remarks, the 'wild displays of primitive and unsophisticated behavior in the midst of the wealthiest and most aristocratic *élite* of Milanese society left so indelible an impression on my mind, that I conceived the notion of coming to settle in Italy for good.' Of the Italians he observes that 'in this land of shameless sensuality, no one is highly born or bred to escape the common touch.' In *Rome, Naples and Florence*, he writes that 'there is far less of a dividing barrier here [in Italy] than in France between the daughters of a prosperous innkeeper and the scions of an ancient family; for no one in the whole of Italy has ever dreamed of aping the modes and manners of a ... court.'[246] Likewise, since 'friendship, in Italy, disdains to recognize the barriers of rank ... a *marchesa*, by birth and breeding second to none, may seek and hold the friendship of a simple drawing-mistress.' Contrariwise, the 'crude arrogance of the banker who has grown rich, and the smile of superiority of the man of high birth, are equally unknown in Rome,' as 'people would openly laugh in their faces.' In *The Charterhouse of Parma* the aristocratic hero Fabrizio converses with a lower-class person 'absolutely as between equals.' A further consequence of the absence of snobbery in Italy is that neither poverty nor a curious personal appearance elicits contempt or ridicule, as people no matter how poor are valued for their genuine qualities. Thus in Rome great painters 'will assuredly keep their reputation intact even if they choose to live in a fourth-floor garret,' where the whole city will pay them homage. In *The Charterhouse*, the high-born Gina Sanseverina treats with the utmost graciousness the impoverished and bizarre-looking revolutionary Ferrante Palla.[247]

Stendhal's observations on the lack of snobbery in Italy confirm Peter Burke's argument that, as compared with northern European societies after the Renaissance, the widening division between the upper and lower classes with respect to culture and social customs was less fully realized in Italy, notwithstanding that Italians had previously laid the basis for this European transformation in the works of Castiglione, della Casa, and other writers of courtesy books. Pompeo Molmenti observes that during the Renaissance the Venetian 'rich and poor' were 'united as it were in the bond of communal existence.' He notes as well the familiarity and kindliness typical of relations between the Venetian patricians and lower classes of the eighteenth century, when even practical joking was permitted though the classes were 'so profoundly divided.' According to Andrieux in his study of eighteenth-century Rome, servants and common people would have laughed at a Roman aristocrat with the affected air of his northern European counterparts. Instead, the aristocrat's manners, tastes, and interests typically resembled those of the common people, and he spoke to his servants easily and as an equal. Andrieux remarks more or less the same state of affairs in eighteenth-century Venice. Luigi Barzini, who cites Stendhal on this point, observes similarly that to this day most Italians pay little attention to social rank. Being mainly 'country folk,' aristocrats out of a sense of 'duty' to their 'caste' have long exhibited a 'rough and uncultivated' manner consistent with 'ancient tradition.' Not only has the Italian aristocrat generally been happiest on his country estate, but he has always conversed easily with local peasants, whom he understands and who understand him. Even today he rubs shoulders with common people, while aristocratic children are 'almost unaware of the names they carry,' and throughout their lives maintain friendships with people of all classes. Barzini acknowledges, however, that during the later nineteenth century and under English influence many Italian aristocratic families dropped their practice of allowing servants to enter into dinner conversations with family members, and with this came other forms of snobbism rarely seen before among Italian aristocrats. Regarding the post–World War II period, Barzini finds it no longer possible 'to preserve completely that living-together of the different classes which went to make up the pleasure of so much of our existence.'[248]

In several ways Stendhal's interpretation of the Italian national character inverts two of its oldest stereotypes. Conventionally in the judgment of many northern European cultural theorists and travel writers the northern European stands for brooding introspection as well as intellectual and emotional profundity. His outer senses having been chilled and inhibited by a grim climate, he looks within and thus becomes a grave and serious introvert. But the Italian has been shaped by his warm and agreeable climate into a superficial extrovert; he lives not in his mind but outwardly through his senses, running from sensation to sensation, emotion to emotion, without staying power or depth.

This dichotomy Stendhal rejects. For him it is the French who are extroverts, living for others in society, shifting from one insincere feeling to another, embracing vanity and frivolity. Contrastingly, the Italians are introverts, for as Stendhal describes them, not only is their customary state one of self-encapsulated reverie, in which they commune with their profoundest fantasies, but they are driven by powerful emotions that, when disappointed, plunge them into melancholy that only musical delights can assuage. In defining melancholy as an Italian trait, Stendhal rejects the view of Germaine de Staël, who regards it as characteristically northern European and more specifically German. On the other hand, he is apparently indebted to Staël's view of the French as an in many ways vain, outer directed, and superficial people, notwithstanding their at least partial claim to being northern Europeans. This is not to deny Stendhal's equivocation at some points over whether to define melancholy as a common Italian trait, for as he claims in *A Roman Journal*, that emotion is rare in Italy, and in *Rossini* he describes the Italian form of love, for all its violence and frenzied intensity, as knowing 'nothing of melancholy,' whose presence would apparently testify to an uncharacteristic 'failing' of that 'energy' so marked in Italians. For the most part, however, Stendhal sees the Italian as a melancholy type, whether from a natural tendency to emotional self-absorption or as a consequence of amatory misfortunes of the sort he describes in *Love*, stemming all too often from inordinate passion. As Stendhal puts it, 'every Frenchman who arrives in Italy falls into the same error' of failing to see that the Italian character is 'of a sovereign melancholy,' without which 'impassioned music' is impossible. And this is 'why the French, lively, vain, feather-light, their emotions already ready-formulated on their tip of their tongue, occasionally bored but never melancholic, will never possess any music.'[249]

Stendhal's conception of the Italian as a passionate creature underwrites his inversion of another centuries-old stereotype, that of the Italian as Machiavellian dissembler and hypocrite, with its associations of artifice, lying, cheating, swindling, scheming, conspiring, and the like. The stereotype has a long history going back to Elizabethan times and counts among those most identified with Italy.[250] This is not to deny that Stendhal sometimes depicts Italians as dishonest and warns against being cheated by them, as do many northern travellers. However, he usually extenuates Italian trickeries, and in any case he far more frequently characterizes the Italian as sincere and honest in his desires and passions. 'In spite of all that common gossip may allege against Italy,' he writes in *Rome, Naples and Florence*, the Italian is no 'hypocrite through and through, forever lying and dissembling,' but 'is the least artificial creature in all the Continent of Europe, and the least concerned with his neighbor's opinion.' Far from being 'the wiliest of schemers, a model of consummate prudence, a very Machiavelli incarnate,' he exemplifies 'childlike naiveté' and 'simple trust in virtue.' Unlike the French, who are all too often dishonest with themselves because they have warped their true desires and feelings in accordance with the false social code they perversely idolize, the Italians are almost entirely free of hypocrisy. And even when they must resort to it, they do so honestly, as does Julien Sorel in *The Red and the Black*, admitting fully to himself his act of deception. This is what Stendhal means in characterizing Italian vengeance as 'honest.'[251] In his view, such a lack of self-deception, or self-awareness in deceit, marks Italian superiority to the overly socialized and self-deceiving French. In similar fashion Luigi Barzini identifies self-honesty in hypocrisy as an Italian national trait as far back as the Renaissance, while A. Lytton Sells notes several examples of seventeenth-century Italians engaging self-consciously in what may be called 'sincere' deception. According to Burckhardt, Renaissance Italians exemplify calculated hypocrisy devoid of self-deception: 'The Italian of that time shrank ... from no dissimulation in order to obtain his ends, but he was wholly free from hypocrisy in matters of principle. In these he attempted to deceive neither himself nor others.'[252]

Yet another advantage of Italy, as what Stendhal terms the 'native haunt of passion,' is that here love flourishes with an intensity, sincerity, and durability found nowhere else in Europe, least of all in France. Yet again the Italians benefit from the fact that, being free of a monarchical court, high society centred in a national capital, and the tyranny of public opinion, they have avoided the conventions and proprieties worshipped in France, and that chill, inhibit, and falsify passion by placing it under the microscopic eye of the other. In France, argues Stendhal, love is chiefly the 'mannered' type, calculated and predictable to the smallest detail, so that it hardly differs from 'all the prosaic affairs of ordinary life.' Since the French prefer society to solitude, their passions are generally vain rather than sincere, and sexual conquests normally serve the selfish aim of social exhibitionism.[253] All too often the confession of passion is withheld, as the lover fears ridicule or regards manifestations of love as evidence of weakness or inferiority. Rarely is love given in a spirit of total devotion uncontaminated by egotism. If the typical French woman lacks sincerity in love, it is because she views it as an indirect means of self-admiration, and thus specializes in fickleness and coquettish narcissism. Rather than being direct or transparent, amatory relations are complicated by hidden motives, rivalries, and obstacles. Hence love among the French tends to be superficial and fleeting.

Since there is 'very little society' in Italy, and hence a corresponding infrequency of vanity, the Italians remain capable of real and intense feeling, and amatory passion of the real or sincere type is bound to flourish among them. Thus, in contrast with the overly socialized French, who continue to suffer from vanity and amour propre, the typical Italian person in love 'avoids' society, preferring not the salon but the tête-à-tête, where passions can be expressed openly. Should passion be awakened in them, Italians conceal neither their emotion nor the pleasure it stimulates. They love without reserve and with total devotion uncontaminated by self-worship. The kind of love they most disdain is that which sells itself for money. The comparative absence of novels in Italy, and the lack of interest in reading, inoculates Italians against the vain copying of romantic models. Because Italian passion naturally exhibits a tumultuous unpredictability, it not only differs from the calculable mannered type prevalent in France but confirms Stendhal's identification of Italy with the unexpected or '*imprévu*.' Pursued sincerely and wholeheartedly, Italian love affairs avoid the rivalries, obstacles, and coquetry by which vanity taints love among the French. Admittedly the custom of the *cicisbeo* had encouraged flirtatiousness during the eighteenth century, yet most Italian women are neither fickle nor coquettish nor tolerant of such behaviour in men. Italy is thus for Stendhal the land of lasting passion, where contempt customarily falls upon the unfaithful, and where in more recent times high-born ladies have typically remained with their *cicisbei* for nearly a decade and sometimes a lifetime. That a woman should sorrow for three years over a lost beloved is no rarity in Italy, 'where *vanity* counts for nothing in the constancy of a resolution.'[254]

Stendhal's treatment of the Italian national character cannot claim absolute originality but extends and deepens earlier travellers' perceptions. As Andrew M. Canepa shows, many eighteenth-century British visitors came to see the Italians in Rousseauvian and Romantic terms, not as degenerate Machiavellian scoundrels but as attractive examples of emotional freedom, casualness, spontaneity, sincerity, and authenticity. They now embodied the ideal of life in accordance with Nature rather than as exemplars of an artificial and hypocritical society. Dr John Moore portrays lower-class Italians as living in virtually Adamic innocence, and Hester Thrale Piozzi dissociates Italian naturalness from the snobbish affectation and over-refinement of the English and French.[255] Notwithstanding her discovery of preoccupations regarding birth and lineage among the Milanese, Piozzi claims that, in general, Italians 'measure no man's merit by the weight of his purse; they know how to reverence even poverty.' She often heard Italians call their own servants and those of their friends by 'tender names,' and speak to social inferiors with a 'graciousness not often used by English men or women even to their equals.' This is not to ignore the fact that Piozzi attributes such behaviour to Italy's class system, which, unlike England's, afforded aristocrats the luxury of being warmhearted and tender without fear of losing rank and dignity – a point similar to that of Tocqueville in contrasting Europe and America.[256] According to Piozzi, whereas in France people are 'folded or driven all together in flocks ... with one fashion to serve for the whole society,' so that 'a man may easily contract a similarity of manners by rubbing down each asperity of character against his nearest neighbor, no less plastic than himself,' there is in Italy 'little spirit of imitation, [and] monotonous tediousness is almost sure to be escaped.' In Paris, 'the people can scarcely be termed *polished*, or even *varnished*; they are *glazed*, and everything slides off the *extérieur* of course, leaving the heart untouched.'[257] A visitor to Italy in 1770, Patrick Brydone characterizes Sicilians as a 'frank and sincere' people, and thus devoid of the ostentatious and joyless affectation he had seen on the 'polite' Continent.[258]

During this period a similar view of the Italian was emerging in France and other European countries, as witness Montesquieu, Goethe, DuPaty, Duclos, Roland, Delécleuze, Creuzé de Lesser, Simond, and Staël, all of whom anticipate or concur with Stendhal's identification of Italy with the '*naturel*.' Delécleuze finds a republican equality of manner in Italy; Roland sees Italians as not yet torn to pieces by society; and Duclos characterizes the Venetians as natural beings enjoying a perfect identity between self and world. For DuPaty, the Neapolitans are 'végétation humaine,' obedient to the 'law of nature.' Less favourably, Creuzé de Lesser complains that Italian women, like Italians generally, ignore propriety. The travellers' praise of Italian naturalness often coincides with their criticism of northern societies as a breeding ground for vanity as well as slavish submission to false emotions engendered by public opinion. Roland, Delécleuze, DuPaty, Creuzé de Lesser, Staël, and Bonstetten had preceded or paralleled Stendhal in noting the absence of society and thus of the 'tyranny' of opinion in Italy, where people lived in desert-like isolation. Like Dr John Moore, Germaine de Staël finds Italians to lack vanity, whose absence Delécleuze traces to a native preference for pleasure.[259] Even Stendhal's identification of Italy with love had been anticipated by Addison, De Brosses, Montesquieu, Duclos, DuPaty, Grosley, Delécleuze, Saint-Réal, Cabanis, and Grimm. In Duclos's judgment Italians take love seriously, while Delecleuze sees love as the Italians' only pleasure, engaging them at every instant. According to Saint-Réal, Italian women cannot be seduced, being neither affected puppets nor coquettes. Reminiscent of Stendhal on Italian naturalness, Giuseppe Baretti acknowledges that Italy perhaps falls short of English and especially French refinements, yet he insists that the 'politeness of the Italians to strangers has been allowed by almost all travel-writers.' Numerous travellers' reports suggest that this assertion is largely true, despite the Italians' tendency to outbursts of violent emotion.[260]

One wonders whether Stendhal, in extolling the Italians' passionate, expressive, and uninhibited behaviour, has embraced a dubious myth of the 'natural.' Tears may flow 'naturally,' observes Peter Burke, yet they are governed by cultural conventions none the less. Although Burke identifies the Italians with 'spontaneity,' he shares Stendhal's awareness that such an evaluation depends on social rules and definitions of the natural.[261] 'For after all,' writes Stendhal, '*indecency* is, by and large, a matter of convention.' Besides referring to the 'supreme art of happiness,' which implies that happiness depends on a degree of skill and artifice rather than occurring purely spontaneously or 'naturally,' he holds that the 'art of being natural, or simple, or candidly impassioned ... is a nuance which attaches to every action that a man might perform.' Thus, however direct it may seem, Italian naturalness remains a matter of forms, calculations, artful controls. Yet Stendhal also grasps what Peabody remarks, that there tends to be less internalized and rigorous 'impulse-control' in Italy than in northern European countries, so that, from a northern European perspective, Italians seem spontaneous or 'natural.'[262] That Peabody finds a similar lack of inhibition typical of France does not necessarily mean, however, that Stendhal refuses unfairly to acknowledge in the French traits he lauds in the Italians. Although Peabody fails to distinguish between northern and southern France, the impulse restriction to which Stendhal objects in his compatriots seems to be a mainly Parisian and northern French phenomenon, as he observes it far less frequently in the southern French (and Spaniards), whom, as people of the Midi, he likens to Italians in attitudes and behaviour.[263]

As much as Stendhal acknowledges the comparative lack of emotional inhibition among the Italians, he differs from those many travellers who, seeing only this trait, mythify the unconstrained Italian.[264] With a more complex view of Italian behaviour, he recognizes that Italians often exhibit 'impulse control' and other kinds of self-suppression. In his view, the chief curb on Italian impulse has been the fact that since 1530 Italy's tyrants have fostered a climate of mistrust and suspicion, so that the 'average Italian is scared to death of the least untoward happening,' which will cause him to 'sulk indefinitely in forbidding and melancholy silence.' The fate of Giannone, Silvio Pellico, and other political victims compels an Italian to be mistrustful and cautious. Because the Italian knows himself to be capable of opening the 'floodgates' of 'violent passion,' he is 'full of attention' and even appears unfeeling in moments when his French counterpart yields completely to emotions that, though seemingly stronger than those of an Italian, are weaker. Contrastingly, a 'genuinely angry' Italian is 'silent and self-controlled.' Yet though an Italian's mistrust prevents him from showing joy and familiarity among strangers, he 'lays his suspicions aside' in 'intimate surroundings,' in which he is all 'simplicity and good nature.'[265]

Although it jars with stereotypes, Stendhal's interpretation of the Italians' impulse-control conforms with that of Richard Gambino, who notes the restraint and gravity of southern Italians. It also agrees with that of Luigi Barzini, who traces the wariness and self-inhibition characteristic of Italian social life to centuries of political oppression, anarchic violence, legal corruption, and other evils. Because 'fear lurks in every fold of Italian life,' says Barzini, Italians 'mind their own business,' behaving with 'circumspection, caution and even cynicism ... They cannot afford to be carried away by emotions. They keep them under control.' Yet 'when it is safe to do so,' Italians enjoy genuine and unrestrained emotions as well as anybody. They know, however, that the 'free expression of genuine emotions is a luxury for the privileged, often a dangerous and expensive luxury.' Although Peabody finds less restriction of impulse-expression among the Italians and French than among other Europeans, the former nations exhibit what he terms a pragmatic 'deliberate rational choice of the circumstance of impulse-expression.' Whereas the English and Americans, with their internalized morality, tend to yield to the inhibiting conscience even where external restraints are absent, the egoistic Italians and French express their impulses when circumstances permit it.[266]

Stendhal stresses both the Italians' uninhibited expression and their candour as 'sincere, honest folk' who 'say what is in their minds.'[267] Well aware that Italians often appear thus in travel writings, Barzini observes that in the ferment of Italian streets and piazze the people's words, expressions, and gestures seem to reveal them transparently. Then, reversing himself, Barzini insists that foreign observers have succumbed to an illusion whose deceptiveness lies only partly in the fact that Italians are, in instances unknown to visitors, careful and inhibited. Its chief cause is that, however transparent, the Italians' behaviour exemplifies both their love of theatrical spectacle and the performative, illusion-ridden character of their social life. For these 'sincere' Italians are actually showing off, with an eye on the public's response to their carefully crafted self-image. As an example of Italian theatrical artifice, Barzini cites Castiglione's *Courtier*, which urges its readers to attract public notice and esteem and to construct artificially the illusion of spontaneity – the artful concealment of artifice that Barzini finds typically Italian, and that Castiglione calls *sprezzatura*.[268] Peter Burke similarly describes Baroque Italy as a 'theater society,' in which one was expected to make a *bella figura* (good figure) according to theatrical stereotypes. Even today Italy remains in many ways a shame-culture, where social controls are largely imposed externally through the power of public opinion. On this basis Burke contrasts Italy with northern Europe, the latter being a 'sincerity' culture in which conduct depends much more upon inward or 'internalized' states of moral self-awareness.[269]

The question arises how Stendhal could have made the mistake, if it is a mistake, of identifying Italy with sincerity and the North with hypocrisy – the North of Rousseau and Goethe and of those Protestant traditions of self-examination Stendhal admired. The question also arises how, given the theatricality of Italian society, its concern for *bella figura*, and its vendettas typically driven by the desire to maintain a public reputation, Stendhal can describe the Italians as less vain than northern Europeans. His difficulty seems all the greater when one considers that vanity for him implies showing off before other people to whom one thus unwittingly surrenders one's personal autonomy.

Despite his praise for the Italians' sincerity, Stendhal recognizes their artifice and skill in dissimulation. In describing them as having mastered the art of being natural, he implies that Italian sincerity is compatible with, indeed inextricable from, role-playing. Yet one need not assume that Stendhal fails to call hypocrisy by its proper name. According to Burke, because northern European guilt-cultures demand sincerity or self-honesty, the burden of responsibility often issues in self-deception as people convince themselves of their sincerity when they are actually role-playing in a dishonest concession to social expectations. Contrastingly, Italians adopt a social role wholeheartedly, without self-deception, in full awareness of its mask-like character, and hence they are sincere in performing it, despite their relatively low esteem for sincerity.[270] Unlike northern European observers who often regard Italian Catholics as hypocritical in seeming to run from repentance and asceticism to uninhibited hedonism in the flash of an eye, Stendhal finds no hypocrisy, as they are as sincere in their fear of God as they are in their pleasures.[271] He typifies Italian sincerity in referring to the very honesty of Italian dissimulation, for though Italians may fool others they rarely deceive themselves. Like Burckhardt and Barzini, Peter Burke recognizes this Italian trait, citing Torquato Accetto's *Della dissimulazione onesta* (1641), a Baroque treatise in which Accetto emphasizes not only the playing and perfecting of roles but what he calls honest (*onesta*) dissimulation, free of self-deception.[272] Nor are the Italians themselves unaware that they are the intended victims of such stratagems, for as Stendhal finds Italy to be filled with suspicious souls, so Barzini finds the people 'incredulous: they do not want to be fooled by seductive appearances and honeyed words.'[273] Yet at least externally, Italians usually enter into the spirit of such artifice and, rather than showing mistrust, indulge in deliberate, transparent flattery.

X

Among the points of reference by which Stendhal measures the advantages of early nineteenth-century Italy is the limited republican and democratic politics emergent in France and England after the French Revolution and Napoleonic Wars. It was widely assumed by the exponents of this new political arrangement that, through its superior reasonableness, it would inevitably increase security, freedom, prosperity, and felicity. As Stendhal recognizes, the liberalization of politics and society had coincided with the growing political power and economic influence of the bourgeoisie, which, building on behavioural norms established by the monarchy and aristocracy, shaped society increasingly after its own values. Not only did society become more organized under the rational control of the administrative state, which improved individual security while enlarging the scope of the law, but the parliamentary system promoted party politics and thus the politicization of hitherto uninvolved segments of the population; inevitably ideological obsessions and partisan hatreds came to the fore. Improvements in education were needed to train people for a responsible civic life and to enable them to participate usefully in politics and the economy. The expansion of the press was crucial to the formation of public opinion on political, economic, and social issues. In addition to a growing esteem for legality, social behaviour was characterized increasingly by bourgeois regularity, discipline, objectivity, and impassivity. In high society, to which the bourgeoisie now had greater access, the emphasis was on good manners in the sense of reserve and the restriction of passionate or extreme behaviour. And yet, in assessing these developments from his Italian vantage, Stendhal finds that they have failed to live up to their vaunted promise of a major increase in happiness, pleasure, and liberty. Paradoxically, he believes that in Italy, a land ruled by oppressive despots, the people not only possess greater happiness than in the North but enjoy a higher degree of actual freedom. Probably more than anything else, this explains why he fled the progressive North to Italy.

This is not to suggest that Stendhal fails, at least from one side of his personality, to appreciate the advantages of liberalization in northern Europe, which he hopes will extend to a united Italy. As a liberal, he favours the rule of law and an increase in guaranteed individual rights as provided by progressive modern governments. In his view, a modern liberal state must monopolize violence through the military and the police and so guarantee the security of its citizens. Stendhal further recognizes the role of constitutional government, civic participation, and the death penalty in maintaining the rule of law. Besides performing necessary administrative functions, the national capital helps organize and discipline the population through the press, the main organ of public opinion, and high society, which defines a national behavioural model. By these standards, the Italians are sorely wanting. At the same time, however, Stendhal responds to the modern liberal state with intense skepticism. From his perspective modern republics seem limited when measured against those of the Italian Middle Ages, which represent a different political ideal. As Stendhal writes in *Rome, Naples and Florence*, 'We in our own generation, happier in this at least than our forefathers in theirs, have learned that any government composed of *two Houses* and a *President*, or *King*, is tolerable.' Yet he adds that 'we should take care lest we delude ourselves; for this most *eminently reasonable* government is ... just as eminently unfavorable to genius and originality in any form; and no period in history can ever hope to rival the fascination of the Middle Ages.'[274]

In contrast with Sismondi, who attempted to trace modern liberalism to the medieval Italian republics, Stendhal stresses the differences between medieval and modern republicanism. While both types of republic limited citizenship and the franchise to a relatively small portion of society, the percentage was much smaller during the Middle Ages. Not only did the medieval republic show little to compare with modern security or protection under the law, but it failed to guarantee the freedom of its citizens under the banner of individual rights. Medieval republics differed as well from their modern counterparts in their comparatively underdeveloped capacity to maintain civic order as the basis of collective happiness. What existed in those times was what Stendhal, after Sismondi, terms '*liberté orageuse*,' or passionate liberty. This was a period of 'gigantic passions' and 'ferocious energy' among a citizenry that, owing to imperfect socialization, altogether lacked affectation. Since the government failed to offer security, and since in the absence of a constitution guaranteed rights did not exist, danger appeared everywhere, in the form of personal vendettas and violent factions. Instead of social cooperation, there was daily competition and conflict with a host of neighbours who did not scruple to ignore or circumvent the law. Under these circumstances not the collective but the individual came to the fore, as he was thrown back upon himself as a kind of social monad. The result was that special non-collective virtues developed in the citizen of the medieval Italian republic: egotism, force of personality, energy, passion, resourcefulness, self-reliance, originality, even genius. According to Stendhal, these virtues carried over into the period now known as the Renaissance, and were manifest in the tyrants of that age; he even finds traces of them in the Italy of his own day.[275]

Unlike the medieval Italian republics, those of the early nineteenth century guarantee a host of freedoms under the law, and yet Stendhal complains that this amounts to freedom *de jure* rather than *de facto*, as the individual is actually restricted in his possibilities. Although the legal system protects the individual, it limits his personal freedom to the extent that he agrees to follow the legal order. The widening of liberty and equality to include more and more people as citizens represents not an individual but a collective triumph and must therefore lead to levelling. In this revolt against individuality are to be found a multitude of egos but no egoists in Stendhal's sense of the energetic individual capable of thinking and feeling according to his own joys, passions, and desires. There is moreover a limit to what even the most liberal governments can do in promoting happiness, for as Stendhal observes in *Love*, happiness by its very nature demands personal choice, while its essential objects have remained much the same since ancient times. Anticipating the views of Sebastian de Grazia, Stendhal suggests that the demand for equality will lead to the total removal of all aristocratic and other social exemptions, with everyone without exception being obliged to work.

The older individualism having been replaced by cooperative values, a person now relies less upon himself than upon a host of social ties and dependencies. Concurrently there has emerged a new kind of society, which imposes upon the socialized individual the conformist tyranny of politeness and good taste, so that desires and interests increasingly resemble each other, and life takes on a uniform character. As Stendhal remarks, the peaceable Parisians exhibit an 'excessive politeness' that keeps them from developing 'the kind of strong souls that abound in half-savage places' like Corsica and Piedmont; indeed, 'one finds everything in Paris except force.' Now liberated from the censorship of the old regime, the free press supposedly exemplifies liberty of speech and communication, yet it actually promotes the tyrannical conformity of public opinion and thus adds to the growing sameness. Here is yet another cause of what Stendhal refers to as the '*ton mouton*' (sheepish tone) of modern society, whose hallmark is the absence of force of character. Despite the pretensions of the Parisian system of education, which boasts of being progressive, its end result is the loss of will, energy, and individuality, as the student is swallowed up in a vast standardizing mechanism. 'One of the great features of the nineteenth century, in the eyes of posterity,' writes Stendhal in *A Roman Journal*, 'will be the total absence of boldness needed in order not to be like everyone else,' this being the 'great machine of modern civilization.' He adds that 'It brings all the men of a century to approximately the same level, and eliminates the exceptional men, among whom some obtain the name of genius.'[276]

Stendhal finds the new political order to have coincided with as well as promoted a major change in social experience. In his view, as the discipline of political and social life exerts increasing influence upon the public, fewer opportunities arise for the pursuit of pleasure and passion, of all those things that, being essential to happiness, make life worth living. In attempting to explain the 'frightening' and 'obvious change which has overtaken the French character,' Stendhal refuses to blame it on his hero Napoleon, but attributes it largely to imitation of the English parliamentary model. It was the French government that had committed the 'frightful atrocity' of '*anglicizing*' the French people and of increasing their 'resemblance to the gloomiest people on earth.' The 'sober governments' of France and England exhibit 'wary vigilance,' with 'their eyes on public opinion, and their tame journalists to prove that whatever they do is right.' Herein lies a chief reason for the 'spirit of partisanship which has sprung up' in recent times, and which 'separates the different classes of citizens by hate.' Party politics, complains Stendhal, has 'done ... [its] worst to make the French serious' and nowhere more regrettably than in the salon or drawing room, where they had come to prefer the cold rationality typical of English conversation. Formerly upper-class French society had gaiety and linguistic play to recommend it, for all its conformism and vanity, but in the age of republican politics and freedom of discussion the salon had become indistinguishable from a political debating society, and wit and passion had become even more attenuated than under the old regime. In following the English political model the French had succumbed to 'gloomy conventions' and the 'spirit of dignity,' so that their 'faculty of amusing [themselves]' had been 'destroyed.'[277]

Stendhal further complains that constitutional governments attenuate the private passions not only by replacing leisure with political responsibilities but by focusing citizens' attention on political issues in which matters of industry, productivity, and progress are decided on utilitarian grounds. An example of this, as Crouzet notes, is the British character Oswald in Staël's *Corinne*, a staunch utilitarian whose devotion to the duties and obligations of political liberty forces him to renounce sexual passion.[278] Although representative government 'happens to be the sole passion of the nineteenth century,' and although the conscientious citizen's time is bound to be occupied with 'all the interminable arguments over possible improvements in the constitution,' Stendhal has no wish to share 'the state of mind of those patriotic souls who are forever worrying about the *Law of the Land* or the *Balance of Power*,' yet who have no time for love, art, and other enjoyments. Nor should one forget as a cause of the eclipse of passion the increasing materialism of modern social life amid a commercial and industrial expansion encouraged by the state and bourgeoisie, so that people had become what Crouzet terms the 'prisoners of their objects,' of the very means rather than the ends of life, with nothing left over for the things that really count, being of the heart.[279]

Ironically 'bound up with liberty and with all the wealth of happiness it promises to mankind,' the 'joyless system' of the North results not simply in conformism and gloomy sobriety but, thanks to its rational order and discipline, in that numbing form of unhappiness that Stendhal identifies with 'monotony' and 'boredom.' It is not France, however, but the Protestant nations – England, the United States, and Switzerland – that had made the greatest strides in this direction. As Stendhal remarks in *Rome, Naples and Florence*, the 'most rational variety of Protestantism' cannot favour 'art and human happiness.' Regarding the 'Federated Republics of America,' he wonders whether they will ever 'cast off' the 'drabness of Puritanism' along with their 'Old Testament heritage' of repression. Of Geneva, that supposed land of liberty, he writes that the women bore him yet afford a chance to study prudery. As the virtues of the Genevans amount to proprieties, their lives consist of repeating the same approved phrases. Naturalness is driven out, no new ideas are allowed, and one cannot step out of the circle. And of course marriage is upheld in its most conventional, dispassionate form. This is a horribly pinched society, filled with hypocrisy. The faces are cold and lacking in interest, and Stendhal prefers Naples or even Paris.[280]

Yet another failing Stendhal attributes to the North is the inevitable decline of the arts and artistic creativity through the general tendency of modern politics and society, with their egalitarian, civic, utilitarian, and industrial proccupations. To quote *Rome, Naples and Florence*, 'We are moving towards an era of universal suffrage; and universal suffrage, being wholly concerned with *government*, will have no leisure to dwell with impassioned fervor upon the subtleties of art.' Remarking in *A Roman Journal* that iron rails or a warehouse are a 'hundred times more worthwhile than St. Paul's,' Stendhal adds that 'these so useful objects do not give the sensation of the beautiful,' from which he concludes that 'freedom is inimical to the fine arts.' This is not to imply that Stendhal always adopts a pro-aesthetic stance on this issue, as he sometimes argues for the priority of the political and social over the aesthetic.[281] He assigns to Francesco, probably a fictional Italian, the statement that the '*essential* element of life is liberty and the security of the individual: art, in this nineteenth century of ours, is nothing but an inferior substitute.' In a similar vein, 'liberty is the necessity of necessities, while art is merely a *luxury*, whose lack can be endured without distress.' In *Rome, Naples et Florence en 1817*, Stendhal acknowledges that the 'things that are needed in order for the arts to prosper are often the opposite of those which nations need in order to be happy.' He also sees literature and politics as inextricably related, and seriously doubts whether modern literature could exist save under democratic liberty. Nor does Stendhal always assume the inherent incompatibility of art and republican politics, for as he suggests in *Histoire de la peinture en Italie*, a constitutional monarchy on the English model need not be inimical to art, English deficiencies in that department having chiefly to do with lack of sun and leisure.[282] Yet these statements are counterweighed by the greater frequency with which Stendhal laments the dwindling of art through its alleged incompatibility with the mass mobilization of a democratic society.

As Richard N. Coe remarks of Stendhal's 'persistent and paradoxical' theory, in a democratic republic 'it is necessary for the stability of the state for all the citizens to devote themselves, with single-minded rationality and purpose, to the business of politics.' Thus 'they can have no real leisure,' which art requires, and 'art is impossible in a democracy.'[283] In one of his earliest works, *Lives of Haydn, Mozart and Metastasio*, Stendhal mentions his inability 'to see what pleasure one may hope to derive from constantly fretting oneself to a shadow over constitutional and political problems,' as the English model must lead to the 'Decadence of the Arts' among the French, formerly a people of sensibility. 'Ever since that day when humanity turned its footsteps towards the goal of *democratic government*,' remarks Stendhal, 'I have learned to despair of art; for in no circumstances imaginable could it be deemed anything but a rank absurdity to build so vain an edifice as Saint Peter's'; instead, people now want to spend public money in a '*useful*' fashion. The coming of democracy will thus mark 'the end and death of art in Italy,' and 'we shall be greeted by the cold blast of earnest political discussion, as though Venice were no longer Venice, but rather London, or Washington.' In addition to 'republican dreariness,' the threat to art comes not only from 'budget economies,' marking the triumph of monetary evaluations over all else, but from the 'most rational' and 'chill spirit' of Protestantism, which is always 'fatal to art.' It comes as well from modern commerce and industry, as a result of which humanity has been deprived of the 'idleness' conducive to contemplation and reverie, which Stendhal regards as indispensable to artistic creation. To quote Imbert, when political passions are 'freely unleashed' in Italy, 'in battles over elections and assemblies,' the 'beautiful reveries of lovers' and artists must die out. Regarding the nineteenth century generally, 'everything foreshadows the downfall of the arts.'[284]

In comparing the 'two liberties,' the northern European and the Italian, Stendhal attempts paradoxically to show that, contrary to expectations, the greater freedom in Italy reflects and follows from its social and political defects. He identifies the North with the centralized state that, with its legal and administrative apparatus, rationalizes society, attends to public welfare, guarantees personal rights, freedoms, and security, and exerts an intrusive, often inhibiting force on individual behaviour. The modern state furthermore expects a great deal of its citizens in the form of political awareness and civic participation, not to mention military service and other requirements. Contrastingly, the fragmented states of Italy are dominated by oppressive governments that, far from promoting equality and the public welfare, burden people with irrational, punitive laws. Yet because these governments tend to be poorly administered, they intrude infrequently upon peoples' lives while asking very little of them, Italy being thus characterized by what Stendhal describes as 'suspicious' yet 'weak' tyranny. For instance, Rome's 'unexacting little government' is a 'puffed-up Leviathan,' 'fundamentally *futile*' and 'insignificant.'Admittedly there are exceptions to the rule, such as Venice, yet there the state uses its considerable power to create a climate of gaiety rather than oppression and fear. Because the legal system is both unjust and unreliable in most if not all the Italian states, the people have little or no respect for legalities; and because the law is weak, an atmosphere of physical insecurity prevails, in which people out of aggression or self-defense can only take the law into their own hands. One may say of most Italian governments what Stendhal says of the Roman, that 'from time immemorial' it has been 'abhorred and despised,' that it 'sways no opinion and wields no influence whatsoever; it straddles the society beneath it; but it is not *of* that society.' Or as Stendhal puts it in *A Roman Journal*, one encounters in Rome the 'purest freedom' and the 'most complete despotism.'[285]

Although it may seem that Italy's political condition could only inhibit and thwart the individual in his quest for freedom, Stendhal finds it to afford a most favourable environment for the formation of the *moi*. Typically Italian, such a being represents not simply ego but the idea of egoism in the sense of an autonomous, unrestricted, self-reliant individuality whose hallmarks are force and energy manifest in action as well as feeling. Apart from political factors, the Italians contribute powerfully to the emergence of the *moi* through their lack of a social code, undeveloped public sphere, refusal to accept social mediations or obligations, and indifference to their neighbours' opinions. For Stendhal, the passionate sincerity and spontaneity of Italian behaviour stems largely from this complex of anti-social circumstances and attitudes whereby the Italians, in being 'natural,' enjoy liberty without society.[286]

Even more than society, Italy's political circumstances have called the *moi* into being. Its most favourable setting is that of a despotic yet weak legal state whose subjects not only distrust it but disrespect its arbitary laws and failure to guarantee individual rights and security. Amid these virtually anarchic conditions, danger and the use of private force are facts of life, and the Italian becomes a law unto himself. In *Histoire de la peinture en Italie* Stendhal contrasts the 'flat and insipid' world of the North with the travellers' impression of force and terror upon arriving in Italy.[287] Because the Italian *moi* rejects all dependence and subordination, especially that demanded by the state and its institutions, he can only be a remarkably resourceful individual. He alone is responsible for his personal security amid the threats and dangers posed by an untrustworthy corrupted state and his no more trustworthy neighbours; and as Stendhal contends, distrust creates forceful personalities. The daily life of the Italian *moi* is a constant struggle for survival by means of wits, arms, and muscles. Not only does he insist upon defending his private rights rather than relying on empty guarantees of state and police, but he typically shows his character by operating as a law unto himself. Whatever virtues he possesses are of a private rather than public nature.[288] Or as Stendhal puts it in *Rossini*, the papal government 'makes no effort to introduce any element of *security* into the society for which it is responsible. Every citizen is his own master, to do and speak the first thing that comes into his head, and to satisfy his own particular interests in whatever way he thinks best.' The *moi* in such instances represents Italian 'energy' as displayed in acts of will rather than feeling. Of the Roman upper and lower classes Stendhal observes that their capricious and unreliable governments have required them 'to invent and to will.' His cult of Italian energy, in the sense not of emotion but of will, is manifest in his fascination with Italian bandits, the ferocious plebeians of Rome's Monti and Trastevere districts, and in the sanguinary episodes of Italian history down to his own day.[289] Insofar as, for Stendhal, willpower is 'in the last resort ... nothing but the courage to expose one's person to the threat of danger,' the Trastevereans have will, which is increasingly stifled in the well-administered North. The Trastevereans seem to him 'superb,' for 'there is *energy*, that is to say the quality that the nineteenth century most lacks. In our day the secret has been found of being very brave without energy or character. No one knows *how to will*; our education causes us to unlearn this great science.' In Stendhal's view, only the northern European lower classes possess will and energy – the very idea that inspired his novelistic creation of Julien Sorel. While the industrious northerners enjoy the securities and routinized comforts of civil society, the Italians' anarchic conditions foster those independent assertive personalities that arise only when life is put to the test.[290]

For Stendhal, who sees Italy as having restored something like the natural state of humanity, outside of politics and society, there is no denying Alfieri's famous statement that the 'man plant' grows most robustly in Italy, the Romans surpassing all others. Although Stendhal accepts Alfieri's judgment that the man plant needs a good rather than a 'wicked cultivator,' and although he admits that under better governments the Italians would do better things, he fears that they would 'need less energy in order to live, and would consequently be less fine.' Indeed, a just administration and cooperative society must cause Roman personalities to disappear, while the 'absence of danger' in modern life makes 'us all so insignificant.' The great irony of the nineteenth century is that the Turinese, Modenese, and other Italians want liberal freedoms like those of New York, and yet in New York a man is less free than in Venice or Rome. [291] This paradox receives its fullest expression in Stendhal's *The Charterhouse of Parma*, where the lives of the aristocratic protagonists are most interesting not in spite of but *because* of an oppressive yet incompetent government that challenges them to ever more inventive assertions of selfhood.

One can hardly overestimate Stendhal's emphasis upon the role of force and violence in creating the Italian *moi*. If peril is the school of Italian freedom, whereby Italians acquire the courage to be self-reliant and resourceful, 'the great inconvenience of modern civilization is the absence of danger,' which fosters the blandly compliant inhabitants of the northern metropolis. What makes the average Englishman 'greatly inferior to the Roman,' writes Stendhal in *A Roman Journal*, is that, being 'led by a more or less just government, ... [he] is not obliged, ten times a month, to make up his mind in small hazardous cases that may very well later lead him to his ruin, or even to prison and to death.' One is reminded of Stendhal's observation in *Love* that 'a perfect civilization would unite the delicate pleasures of the nineteenth century with a more frequent presence of danger.' He is thinking not simply of warfare but 'of perpetual danger of every kind, threatening every interest in life, which is the essence of the life of the Middle Ages.' [292]

In disparaging modern as against medieval society, Stendhal holds that the absence of insecurity in nineteenth-century civilization has deprived people of the force and character once nurtured in their medieval predecessors under hazardous conditions. Of the Middle Ages he remarks that 'men's hearts were infused with an ever-present sense of danger,' and this goes far to explain the 'astonishing superiority of the men of the sixteenth century,' an age in which 'originality, nowadays so rare, ridiculous, dangerous, and often affected, was ... general and unvarnished.' Stendhal's observation that 'danger still shows its iron hand often' in Corsica, Spain, and Italy reflects his belief that the political and social conditions as well as the prepotent personalities to be found in the

Italy of his own day retain something of the spirit of the medieval Italian republics, with their 'liberté orageuse.'[293] As Crouzet notes, the absence of the nineteenth-century Italian from political life is for Stendhal a survival from medieval republicanism.[294] In *Rome, Naples and Florence* the nineteenth-century tyrannies of Modena and Milan are 'said to preserve ... [Italian] superiority in the field of *strength of character*. What prodigy of nature bestowed on us those great men of the fourteenth century, if not the dangers of the century preceding?' Bologna likewise preserves 'traces of that ancient energy inherited from the Middle Ages.' This is not to suggest, however, that Stendhal devalues the influence of Renaissance individualism upon contemporary Italy, for in referring to the later Middle Ages he often has in mind what we would term the Renaissance, the chronological scope and identity of that period not having yet been established by historians. Despite the surrender of the medieval republics to Renaissance despots, he sees the latter as having been influenced by republicanism not only in their individualism but in their patronage of talented persons like themselves. Hence Stendhal's statement that, for insight into the Italian character, the *Life of Benvenuto Cellini* is the 'book *par excellence.*' In his admiration of Renaissance egotism Stendhal anticipates (and influences) Nietzsche's defense of amoral self-assertion, as Nietzsche, another great enthusiast of the period, himself recognized.[295]

Whatever one thinks of Stendhal's hope of increasing the danger of modern life, which can seem attractive only to hearty souls, he rightly attributes the Italians' lack of vanity not simply to the absence of society but to the presence of danger in Italy, a state of affairs opposite to that of the pacified North, where vanity and 'foolish honor' luxuriate in their pastureland. In Stendhal's view, vanity thrives amid comparative security and tranquillity, as in nineteenth-century Paris or London, where little that is serious is at stake, and where the desiring imagination freely indulges its delusions regarding oneself and others. But in Italy, a land of violence, political surveillance, mistrust, and fear, where life remains insecure owing to the unreliability of the government, one has neither time nor opportunity to indulge in vain illusions, as the social and political environment constantly demands realism and practicality of the Italians, who need to know where their interests and those of other people really lie. 'What is one to expect,' asks Stendhal, 'of an energetic and sovereignly passionate people, deeply suspicious of fate and of men, and consequently not frivolous in its tastes?' The Roman 'resorts to no subterfuges to disguise the *harshness of the reality of life,*' for society is 'sown with too many mortal dangers for him to run the risk of indulging in faulty reasoning, or that of giving false counsel.' To which Stendhal adds that this '*respect for truth* and the *permanence of desires* are ... the two great features that most separate the Roman from the Parisian.' Commenting on the Italians in *Love*, he writes that 'the fear of princes and their spies results in a respect for what is *useful* and there is no such thing as foolish honor' such as flourishes on the boulevards. Because Italians cannot allow vanity to cloud their realism, they possess 'profound psychological insight' that amounts to a 'kind of premature old age.' They relinquish their awareness of sordid reality on few occasions, chiefly the experience of art and music, which 'sets them free to wander in a world of tender fantasy.'[296] Barzini concurs that the Italians' oft-noted love of artistic display and fantasy originates not in realism but in the attempt to palliate or escape the burdens of reality.[297]

Called into existence as the result of incompetent governments and the absence of society or public, the *moi* reveals itself in two forms of energy of which one is centred in the active will. Its other energizing force is passion as manifest in the individual's quest for enjoyment, pleasure, and above all feeling, the highest form of the latter being love and its attendant state of erotic reverie. Largely untroubled by political and social restraints and interferences, Italy qualifies as that privileged site where the private individual is able to pursue his own joys and pleasures more freely than anywhere else. In Crouzet's summary of Stendhal's views, Italy's pure despotisms ironically allow 'perfect social independence,' as each individual has the opportunity to be himself, or 'natural.' Italian passions are oppressed by neither their 'fugitive' society nor their despotic governments, which, being largely incompetent and undemanding and thus leaving the majority of people alone, 'freeze' society in joy and voluptuousness. Stendhal, however, was not the first to note such ironies, which, as Crouzet shows, appear in numerous eighteenth-century travel writings, many of which Stendhal had read. Remarking the weakness and inactivity of the papal state and its inquisition, as witness the considerable freedom of thought in Rome, the President de Brosses concluded ironically that Europe's worst government was the sweetest. For the Chevalier DuPaty, papal Rome represented apparent political slavery combined with very real liberty. Authority was 'sweet and light,' leaving a happy people to enjoy itself amid a detestable power. For Roland, the Romans as compared to the English lived for themselves.[298]

According to Stendhal in *Rome, Naples and Florence*, 'the Roman [social] system ... makes no provision for families; but in compensation, each individual is free to pursue his own private ideal of happiness.' Commenting on papal Rome in *Rossini*, he writes that the 'unexacting little government, of which I have sketched so libelous a portrait, is infinitely more propitious towards the passions and their untrammeled development than are the more sober governments of France or England, with their wary vigilance, their eye on public opinion.' Stendhal acknowledges that Italian passion may issue in bloody criminal violence, yet he finds something noble and beautiful in such crimes precisely because they are motivated by passion, unlike the vulgarity of northern criminality, in which the typical motive is greed.[299] This is not to argue, as Maurice Bardèche claims, that Stendhal enjoys depicting bloodshed, as he rarely treats it in detail; rather, he admires crime and violence not in themselves but for the passion and energy which inspire them, as these bespeak intensity of life.[300] Moreover, the passions that most interest Stendhal centre not on criminality but on love, which, as it requires by its very nature the opportunity for leisure, meditation, and reverie, is bound to flourish in Italy as nowhere else, for here governments and society make small claim upon a person's interests and time. To quote *Rossini*: 'The very defects of those curious forms of government, which are the bane and blight of Italy, favor the art of love, and so further the cause of art.'[301] Yet Stendhal fears that, upon the day political passions are freely unleashed in Italy, in the battle for elections and assemblies, erotic reverie will have become an anachronism.

Since Stendhal believes art to be based on passion, of which it is the finest flower, it follows logically that Italy, as the land of passion, is also for him the native ground of art. Yet what needs special emphasis is that Stendhal attributes the vitality of art and artistic sensibility in Italy not simply to climate or lack of society or to the passionate nature of the people but to the presence of its despotic regimes, which deny political participation to the Italians. Admittedly Stendhal shows ambivalence on this issue, as he sometimes hopes that a modern Italian republic will encourage the arts, and he acknowledges that some forms of despotism may hinder or vulgarize art by debasing the feelings. Despite his dislike of Sismondi's writings, he apparently shares his identification of the medieval republics with cultural vitality.[302] Yet when in *The Abbess of Castro* Stendhal remarks that, 'unfortunately for the general welfare, for justice, for good government, but fortunately for the arts, the medieval republics were overthrown,' he implicitly extols the artistic taste and originality nurtured by such despots as Lorenzo de' Medici and Pope Leo X. Regarding his own time, Stendhal holds that political oppression and insecurity in Italy have contributed to what Crouzet terms a 'pathé-tique sensibilité' in contrast with the numbed sensations accompanying the monotonous regularity of more civilized life. Each Italian despotism allows its subjects few if any spheres of public or intellectual activity out-side the arts. In Naples, 'there is precisely *one* distraction, *only* one, which the law does not forbid to those passions which the climate breeds in Neapolitan hearts, and that is *music.*' A further advantage of political repression is that, where people feel no political obligations, they have plenty of unoccupied time, this being essential to the formation of sen-sibility. As Stendhal says of Italy, 'for *a creative imagination working in the emptiness of unwanted leisure*' an abundance of time is the 'first and neces-sary condition which produces music.' This same 'idleness,' moreover, favours eroticism, which, as we have seen, he regards as a chief source of artistic inspiration.[303] In *Rossini* Stendhal notes that the repressive re-gimes of Cosimo de' Medici of Florence and the Farnese of Parma drove the people into solitude by banishing conversation, and yet this was all the better, for they not only took refuge in love but developed their musical talents. Thus for Stendhal a major question of his own time is whether, in Italy as in Europe, 'budget economics and republican dreari-ness' will 'paralyze everything in the arts.' Writing optimistically in *Rome, Naples et Florence en 1817,* he claims that 'what renders precious the moral desert of Italy is that, even amid discussions of the two [parliamentary] chambers, this country will always place its happiness in the Beaux Arts.' Yet consistent with his belief that art and modern republicanism cannot mix, he also claims that an Italian republic, in focusing attention on politics, and leaving no time for 'sweet leisure' and 'revery,' will deprive Canova and Cimarosa of 'true judges.' He even predicts – incorrectly – that parliamentary politics spells 'the downfall of the arts in the nine-teenth century.'[304]

Italy's political and social situation has yet another consequence of which Stendhal can only approve. For here as nowhere else in Europe humanity triumphs over boredom, the insidious and pervasive disease of modern life. In Stendhal's characterization the North represents a 'joyless system' in which the dictates of order and discipline crush spon-taneity and thus leave virtually nothing to the unexpected. Contrastingly, and notwithstanding Stendhal's competing love of system, Italy appeals to that no less powerful side of his personality which, delighting in im-provisation, rejects rational calculation as the bane of free and varied existence.[305] If Italy escapes the joylessness of the North, it is partly be-cause it lacks a competently rational administration or bureaucracy that would intrude upon and regulate the lives of the people. Italy's weak governments and laws and consequent climate of illegality lead to anarchic and therefore unpredictable behaviour, often of the violent type. And because society and public opinion exert little inhibiting influence, the Italians are free to unleash passions and impulses of what Stendhal describes as 'inconvenient intensity.' Thanks to the combination of these and other factors, Italy escapes the deadly monotony and emotional numbness of a routinized civil society. It is thus for Stendhal the land of the 'divin imprévu,' the divine unexpected, from which tedium is always banished.[306] Being too impulsive to accept a planned existence, the Italian is a perpetual improviser for whom the least suggestion of predictability spells intolerable boredom. Indeed, Stendhal suggests that boredom cannot exist in Italy, where people refuse to be bored. His concept of the improvisatory Italian, and of Italy as the land of the imprévu, culminates in the character of Gina Sanseverina, the heroine of The Charterhouse of Parma, of whom Count Mosca observes that she shuns calculation and trusts to her 'first impulse,' so that, 'when it is time for action,' she 'upsets everything' by rapturously following 'a new idea as it comes into her head.' From this perspective, the worst threat to Italian life comes from 'progress' in the sense of modernizing political and social reform: 'This country could be civilized in eighteen months by a French or English general,' observes Stendhal of Italy, 'and would thereupon be as estimable as it was interesting; something like New York.' Despite his conscientious support of the removal of bandits from the area of Rome, he adds that in such a 'highly moral country boredom would put an end to my existence in a very few months.'[307]

Yet Stendhal's reading of Italian behaviour is subtler, and in at least one instance more dubious, than has yet been shown. In endorsing Alfieri's assertion that the 'man plant' grows more robustly in Italy than anywhere else, Stendhal seems to imply that, under Italy's political and social circumstances, its inhabitants' self-assertive individuality is usually manifest in not public but private virtues. So much is implicit in the following observation from Rome, Naples and Florence, that 'the Italian, for whom the pleasures of society on a grand scale are prohibited, while the attractions of a salon are likewise forbidden fruit, brings to his individual relationships a proportionately greater measure of ardor and susceptibility.' Barzini confirms this point, remarking that, without a public sphere, Italians have developed highly individualistic values of their own, which they reveal in private.[308] Nonetheless, Stendhal much overestimates Italian individualism, as witness his plainly mistaken assertion that the family, as an institution, is stronger in Scotland than in Rome – a misperception perhaps attributable to Stendhal's relative ignorance of the Italian lower classes as opposed to the free-wheeling, often adulterous upper-middle class and aristocracy. 'The family,' writes Barzini, is the 'only fundamental institution' in Italy, where 'anarchy is a way of life ... Italy of the families is definitely the real Italy.' Barzini cites Gramsci's observation that the Italians are not as individualistic as is often assumed; Francis A.J. Ianni characterizes Italy as a 'nation of families, not of individuals' in which the 'family is the chief architect of the social structure.' On this point Hester Thrale Piozzi surpasses Stendhal, recognizing the greater importance of the family in Italy than in England. According to Peabody, although the Italians are somewhat individualistic, they usually display their virtues for families and friends. It is, however, possible for perceptive observers such as Stendhal to misinterpret the Italians' private or anti-social acts as individually motivated. Jacob Burckhardt described Renaissance Italians' behaviour as highly individualistic, when in reality even the period's overreachers were typically familial or corporate in their motivations.[309] Andrew Molho concurs with many other historians of the Renaissance that the Florentine circulated in society not as a 'free individual' but as a family member, and moreover, that the family 'remained an extremely cohesive social force' in fifteenth-century Florence. Giuseppe Baretti cites the view of clergyman Gilbert Burnet, a prominent late seventeenth-century Scottish visitor, that Italians exhibit a 'passion' for their families unknown to other countries, an observation Baretti regards as 'certainly just' and thus as a worthy rejoinder to the defamations of Dr Samuel Sharp, who had charged that arranged marriages had robbed Italian parents of feeling for their children. Over a century later Thomas Adolphus Trollope observed that family feeling 'will be found to be at the root of the Italian national character,' adding astutely that this loyalty had impeded nation formation.[310] What is even more ironic is that, despite Stendhal's disparagement of French conformism, his appreciation of Italian 'individualism' and authenticity reflects French values, for as Peabody notes, the French and Germans more than other European nations favour the ideal of personal individuality.[311]

XI

Pre-eminent in beauty and sensation as in love and all other forms of human feeling, Italy never ceases to be for Stendhal the privileged home not only of the *moi* but of art itself, for here more than anywhere the vast range of music, literature, and the visual arts reflects and distills the life of a passionate, highly expressive people. Like Burckhardt, Ruskin, Pound, and Adrian Stokes, Stendhal knows that Italian life and art exist in constant interplay, mirroring and enhancing each other. Bolognese faces remind Stendhal of the Caracci, those of Parma recall Correggio, those of Rome, Raphael. In the vicinity of Bologna, one constantly encounters 'heads' by Domenichino and Albano. Likewise the 'vivacité sauvage' of gondoliers' gestures animates the canvasses of Tintoretto.[312] The special aesthetic status of Italy in Stendhal's writings reflects his conviction that here more than anywhere else the artist has had at his disposal the full range of emotional expression that, for Stendhal, is the stuff of art. In his view, art is rooted not in reason but in passion, whether that of the artist or of the audience, while the appreciation of art depends on its being felt rather than reasoned over. Accordingly, Stendhal endorses the Abbé Du Bos's view that painting properly focuses on human passions and that the highest art achieves maximum intensity of expression. He was probably influenced as well by Du Bos's belief that the Italians, with their '*sentiment intérieur*,' surpass the French in sensibility. As Stendhal contends, French artists are no more than overdressed workers who know little of humanity, but the great Italian artists are carried away by the passions they depict. Likewise, the fact that the Roman reasons over art most pitifully in no way prevents him from feeling it with 'surprising strength, depth, and accuracy.'[313] In *Écoles italiennes de peinture* Stendhal insists that in the pictorial arts all is properly subordinated to expression, the movement of the soul. Yet lest energy become mere vulgarity, truth of expression must be combined with the idealization typical of the best Italian artists.[314]

Since art, to quote *Histoire de la peinture*, 'connects with a sentiment, not with a system,' artistic passion and original genius resist academic models, rules, and techniques. The greatness of Renaissance painters is that they refused to imitate other artists or to follow formulas, but developed their own personalities: in short, they were themselves.[315] This aesthetic advantage results from the painters' passionate temperaments but also from social and historical circumstance. As excessive rationalism and politeness had not yet triumphed, feelings were then keener, and there were no Old Masters to copy. A great admirer of Roman and Venetian Renaissance painting, Stendhal disparages their Florentine counterpart for a 'pedestrian rationality' manifest in drily linear design (Vasari's *disegno*), 'squeamish decorousness,' 'desiccation,' passionlessness, and

lack of expression. He traces these alleged defects to the fact that bourgeois Florence, whose present-day inhabitants he despises, stood 'much
closer in spirit to the true meaning of civilization.'[316] Although Stendhal
questions the quality of Italian visual art in his own time, he finds the
older Italian genius to have revived in Rossini, Paganini, and Canova,
whom he praises as virtual forces of nature, all instinct and no theory.
Endowed with vegetable force and tenacity, Canova confirms Stendhal's
view of the Italian as the hardiest 'man plant.'[317]

If, as Stendhal argues, French painting falls below the level of the
Italian, it is largely because Louis XIV employed not the forceful Guercino but the affected Charles Le Brun, whose heavy neoclassicism and
absurd solemnity condemned French painting to the formalized representation of the passions.[318] Since court and salon condemned drama,
enthusiasm, and surprise as violations of *civilité*, French artists favoured
pomposity or elegance over force and energy, and even Voltaire rejected Michelangelo's works as inferior or ugly.[319] Stendhal complains that
nineteenth-century French artists and audiences, fearing ridicule, and
still influenced by courtly interdicts against strong expression, strive for
neoclassical coldness by means of soft, harmonious colours and flat and
uniform shades of grey. David and his academicizing followers manifest
frigidity, Ingres is dry, and other French painters lack the 'tenderness'
of chiaroscuro. When visiting the Cathedral of Milan, with its forcefully
'seductive' representations of Eve, Judith, and Deborah, French travellers object irrelevantly that Italian art lacks the decorum of the salon.[320]

In contrast with the Renaissance, whose art mirrors the lawless passions and physical force typical of that age, civilization requires peaceable and decorous behaviour, and this as Stendhal notes can only mean
that, in the arts, 'another fifteenth century is impossible.' The new 'beau
idéal moderne' is the 'amiable man,' one who, though passionate, has
more spiritual than physical energy, and whose chief qualities include
nobility, charm, wit, an alert and sensitive expression, and strength combined with slimness and agility. One thinks of Julien Sorel and Fabrizio
del Dongo. As for the Italians, their aesthetic sensibility will enable them
to appreciate the *beau idéal*, but they will never achieve it if their society
remains riddled with violent illegalities, amid which the new elegance
must seem feeble. Yet Italian painting has a major role in the revival of
art, for as Stendhal notes in *Histoire*, the Napoleonic wars have reawakened in France an appreciation of energy and emotion, and so 'the taste
for Michelangelo will come back.'[321] The prediction was correct, as witness Delacroix and Géricault.

What Stendhal views as the superiority of Italian to French architecture lies in a bold forcefulness and individuality that he attributes to Italy's freedom from monarchical and bourgeois restraints. Many French buildings suggest the 'dry and sterile execution of a miniature,' writes Stendhal, but Italian buildings often have imposing gravity and are said to have style if they inspire '*respect.*' The Danish art historian Christian Elling finds Stendhal's observation 'shrewd' and of 'far-reaching importance,' as he grasps the stress on mass typical of Italian building since the Romans.[322] 'Never would the combination of the prettiest houses of London and Paris, were they to be whitewashed with a hundred times more of elegance, give the slightest idea of this,' observes Stendhal, adding that, in Rome, a 'simple *shed* is often monumental.' Whereas viewers are likely to find the portico of the Farnese Palace 'horribly gloomy,' he praises it for its 'fierce and truly Roman majesty.' In contrast with Milan's Casin di San Paolo, which elicits '*awe,*' its French counterparts have the 'rococo effect of a boudoir or of a fashionable shop.' Unlike French buildings, which often display '*prettiness*' resulting from a '*super-abundance of detail,*' Italian buildings typically seem massive and fortress-like and thus suggest danger.[323] Although Italian palaces are often unclean and frequently sacrifice comfort and convenience to visual splendor, the smell of rotting cabbages does not prevent Stendhal from finding the Roman Corso, with its churches and palaces, perhaps the 'most beautiful ... in the universe.'[324] Sensitive to the customary irregularities of Italian urban planning, which provide welcome relief from the symmetry favoured in France, Stendhal praises Rome's Piazza Monte Cavallo as one of the most beautiful in the world not in spite of but because of its asymmetry; and he likes it all the more because of the napkins hanging out to dry from the Pope's Quirinal Palace – a lapse of decorum unimaginable in Paris.[325]

The originality of Stendhal's response to Italian townscapes is evident by contrast with his eighteenth-century northern European predecessors. Despite her fondness for Italians, Hester Thrale Piozzi was dumbfounded that Italian noblemen, whose income she no doubt mistakenly deemed equal to that of their English counterparts, would 'hang wet rags from their palace windows to dry, as at the mean habitation of a pauper; while looking in at those very windows, nothing is to be seen but proofs of opulence, and scenes of splendour.'[326] Completely lacking Stendhal's appreciation for asymmetrical urban design, Président Charles de Brosses demonstrated his rationalism when he extolled Turin (the most 'French' city in Italy) for the regularity of its squares, battlements, and streets. The Comte de Caylus similarly criticized Italian cities for their irregular streets, and in 1773 and 1774 the French traveller Bergeret de Grancourt complained of the characteristic asymmetry of Roman *piazze*, even criticising Michelangelo's trapezoidal plan on the Campidoglio. French travel writing of this period abounds in similar judgments justifying Stendhal's disgust with those 'hidebound idiots,' his countrymen. He was probably also referring to the French when, noting the 'reproach levelled against' the irregularity of the Piazza Montecitorio, he dismissed those 'simpletons whose taste is wholly learned.'[327]

Stendhal's contrast between Italian and French or northern European musical taste follows his Romantic assumption in *Lives of Haydn, Mozart, and Metastasio* that music by its very nature not only excites and expresses the passions but provides more physical and emotional than intellectual pleasure. Italian composers are therefore correct to concentrate neither on the orchestral complexities favoured in the North, which Stendhal dismisses as the product of coldly pedantic analysis, nor on the flawless virtuosity sought after by northern instrumental soloists, which likewise kill sensibility and enjoyment, but on vocal music and more especially on the expression of dramatic situations through melody, which, as the triumph of untaught genius over mere mathematical rule, he regards as the most expressive and pleasurable part of music.[328] Although he holds that Italian musicians often lack the patience and interest to learn difficult techniques, and that they are too individualistic to handle complex orchestral works, he finds them unsurpassed in the spontaneous expression of feeling, above all vocally. In short, the Italian musician is a *dilettante* in the sense of one who delights personally in the arts. Despite Paganini's technical virtuosity, Stendhal sees him as a man possessed by a *daimon*.[329]

The characteristic differences between French and Italian music are reflected in the divergent behaviour of native audiences. Stendhal contends that the French, lacking *brio* and being overly mannerly and theoretical, violate the very principle of musical pleasure by thinking about music rather than feeling it. This he sees as the characteristic habit of a people lacking the very quality that distinguishes Italian audiences, namely an 'instinctive feeling for music.' Typical of France, not only is the Théâtre Louvois cramped and uncomfortable, but its solemn audiences conceive of music as a grave 'duty' that requires listening to every note. And yet out of the vain desire to conform to conventional opinion the French are often insincere in their appreciation of music, praising works that displease them. In Italy, by contrast, people are so much at home in local theatres that they talk freely during performances save for those moments when the choicer passages of music inspire maddened shouts and gesticulations.[330] Andrieux observes similarly of the Romans of this era that they thought of theatres as enormous drawing rooms, which they attended so as to enjoy pleasant company in their boxes, to gamble, and to amuse themselves. Here the Italians showed 'bad manners,' for they talked during performances, and noise and disorder reigned. Audiences remained silent only during their favorite arias, over whose merits they often quarrelled violently, sometimes hurling missiles at unworthy performers, who threw back missiles of their own. Unlike northern visitors, who objected to the noisiness of Italian theaters – Hazlitt likened them to Milton's Pandemonium – Stendhal views conversation as a necessary means of relieving the tension beautiful music induces in sensitive souls. Aroused in their deepest feelings and uninhibited in expressing them, Italian audiences confirm his view of Italy as the land of passion.[331]

Nonetheless, Stendhal sometimes has less flattering explanations for the Italians' virtues. If they lack vanity, it is perhaps because their political degradation gives them no cause for self-importance or affectation. Despite his identification of Italy with the unexpected, *The Charterhouse of Parma* and other works emphasize the boredom of a politically and economically stagnant country where, owing to police surveillance and the relative absence of books and newspapers, conversation affords no pleasure. Italian art and love are perhaps only an escape from the 'lack of all interesting novelty.' The Italians' extreme fondness for art and music may result from their rulers' prohibition of conversation. As much as Stendhal celebrates Italian energy, he admits in *Rome, Naples and Florence* that Rome sometimes fills him with a 'sort of languid torpor' absent in the North and more particularly Paris, with its stimulating intellectual life. Having become thoroughly Parisian between 1821 and 1830, he was often bored by Rome while serving as French consul in Civitavecchia from 1830 to 1842, complaining that *dolce far niente* kills wit.[332]

Nor does Stendhal in his more realistic moments suppose that modern Italy much resembles its Renaissance predecessor. As he writes in *A Roman Journal*, 'the Italians, unfortunately for them and for the world, are beginning to lose their national character.' Italian energy having dwindled if not disappeared under mean-spirited despotisms, the common people are much less somber, vindictive, and passionate. The level of education and quality of customs have deteriorated, while the invasion of French social practices threatens to eliminate 'all those habits that give a local physiognomy' to the Italian upper classes, who now exhibit a 'somewhat heavy politeness' inspired belatedly by eighteenth-century French models. At the same time, upper-class Italian women are becoming fickle and depassionated coquettes like those of France. Though exemplifying Italian passion untrammeled by courtly models, Stendhal's collection of stories, *Chroniques italiennes* (1838), suggests that by the late sixteenth century social relations in Italy had grown corrupted by a vain concern for aristocratic honour, family reputation, and money. Don Francesco Cenci, the villain of 'The Cenci,' claims to challenge hypocrisy, yet his egoistic criminality is motivated by a vain desire to shock. In 'Vittoria Accoramboni,' Cardinal Montalto's apparent insensibility at his nephew's murder testifies to a self-control worthy of a courtier at Versailles or an English bourgeois. These spiritual deformations culminate in 'Vanina Vanini,' set in the early Risorgimento, whose heroine, as her name suggests, incarnates vanity itself. In *The Charterhouse of Parma*, whose subject is Italy in the post-Napoleonic era, Stendhal debunks his own cherished mythology in depicting numerous Italians – and even his hero at some points – as marked by vanity. This is the emotion underlying nineteenth-century Italians' *patriotisme de l'antéchambre*, their refusal to accept criticism. So too, the visual arts have faded since about 1600 and remain stagnant except for the solitary figure of Canova. Of all the arts in which the Italians had formerly excelled, music alone 'still retains a hold on life.'[333] Yet Stendhal's wishful hope that a few 'Renaissance' characters still exist in Italy inspires his creation of Fabrizio, the hero of *The Charterhouse*, a throwback to the days of the Borgias and Medici.

PART TWO
Leisure, Tourism, and Their Discontents

I

Stendhal's Italian writings do not totally contradict Cesar Graña's estimation of his critique of modernity. Although Stendhal sees the advantages of 'civilization,' he shares the Bohemians' aesthetic hedonism and nostalgia for pre-technological culture. Never completely checking his aristocratic impulse to self-assertion, he remains fascinated by anarchic and irrational individualism and the predatory norms of pre-modern societies. Yet the Byronic ideal of the dangerous life, which inspired genuine rebelliousness in the nineteenth century, is now an impossibility and a cliché. Perhaps Graña is right: Stendhal's response to modernity is misguided, and modernity stands invulnerable to the objections of its discontents. Admitting only at the end of his study that some value inheres in the Bohemian critique, Graña quotes Bertrand Russell on the dangers of excessive rationalization, and, with an approving nod to Stendhal, criticizes Veblen, whose technocratic values Graña had marshalled against the Bohemians, for having overvalued industrial production and efficiency.[334]

Notwithstanding that Stendhal precedes Marxism and often opposes its assumptions, the Marxist critics of the Frankfurt School suggest a more fruitful, if not entirely reliable, approach to Stendhal's meditations on modernity, especially his Italian writings. Unlike Graña, the Frankfurt critics refuse to endorse or defend modern society as a whole, but focus on the oppressions and deformations caused by its prevalent forces, which they regard as the interlocking spheres of capitalism, bureaucracy, and technology. Protesting that organized production under capitalism has imposed universal 'asceticism,' these critics argue that, in falling under the rule of instrumental reason, not only things but human beings have become instrumentalities – calculable functions of commercial profit, or tools of society's administrative or technical apparatus. The cold organizational rationality and affectlessness that the Frankfurt critics find typical of modern life connect inseparably with the triumph of commercial calculation and technological and bureaucratic efficiency. These critics further contend that, as the propagandized public has been led by advertising to identify happiness with conformist consumerism, so cultural consumption is organized in order to extend and strengthen the sphere of production. Entertainment and advertising, themselves the product of industrial methods, merchandize and thus nullify opposition to the existing culture, while high or 'affirmative' culture, in pretending to occupy an 'ideal' realm beyond material existence, falsely espouses ascetic values that only reinforce (while rendering endurable) social oppression.[335]

To be sure, major differences exist between the nineteenth-century society against which Stendhal protests and the early and mid-twentieth-century society that provides the chief target of the Frankfurt School critique. Stendhal lived amid emergent bourgeois liberalism and democracy, a society characterized by residual aristocratic cultural values and a commitment to individual self-development. Since neither bureaucracy nor technology nor the media dominated society as much as they do today, it was less difficult than in later periods for Stendhal to assert some measure of independent choice and critical resistance to the social order. However, the Frankfurt critics identify the first two-thirds of the twentieth century with monopoly and corporate capitalism, 'total mobilization' of mass society and culture, and a gigantic technological and administrative order, whose combined effect in their view is to reduce most people to uncritical acceptance and integration within the system of social organization and production. As much as he admires Stendhal, Marcuse acknowledges that the great nineteenth-century novelists often celebrate a pre-technological world now gone forever. Not only are the heroic rebels of the last two centuries figures of the affirmative culture, but cultural nostalgia and the dangerous life are invalid, the true goal being to correct social injustice.[336]

Yet Marcuse finds that the imaginary world represented by Stendhal and others retains its value as social criticism. This is *because* its celebration of feudal values bespeaks a 'conscious, methodical alienation from the entire sphere of business and industry,' speculation and profit, in short the tyranny of production and the 'performance principle.' Although that earlier world knew inequality and toil, 'man and nature were not yet organized as things and instrumentalities,' and at least some people had the 'time and the pleasure to think, contemplate, feel, and narrate.' And, while this is an 'outdated and surpassed culture, and only dreams and childlike regressions can recapture it' – Marcuse might be describing Stendhal's Italy – the 'most advanced images and positions' of such writers as Stendhal not only 'survive their absorption' into the administered world but project a culture in which technology serves humane ends.[337]

Commenting on Stendhal's Italophilism, Richard N. Coe finds it partly apt that Maxime Le Roy classed him among 'Utopian socialists.' Stendhal's importance to critics of the Frankfurt School is evident in their frequent allusion to his definition of beauty as *la promesse de bonheur*, the promise of happiness. For them, the phrase evokes the 'other,' non-repressive society, which Marcuse defines in terms of 'images of a gratification that would dissolve the society which suppresses it.' As Patrick Brantlinger notes, the Frankfurt School reinterprets Stendhal's phrase as the utopian promise of social liberation into happiness.[338] Yet for Stendhal, *la promesse de bonheur* has a specifically Italian context, as the phrase appears in *Rome, Naples and Florence*: 'I am just home from the *Casin' di San-Paolo*,' he writes. 'Never in all my life have I beheld so much radiance gathered together under one roof, nor such beauty: beauty so intense that I was fearful to gaze upon it.' He adds that 'to a French observer it was a species of beauty that seemed haughty and somber, promising distant felicity beyond the storms of passion, rather than the transient pleasures of wit, gallantry, and gay flirtation. For beauty – this I believe – is nothing but a *promise of happiness.*'[339]

Happiness figures in this passage as an intensely pleasurable prolongation of consciousness into an alternative realm of aesthetic and erotic beauty. The experience unfolds outside everyday routine, and thus presents itself as a daunting, even fearful challenge demanding the maximum of emotional and sensory powers. For though physical desire and somatic pleasure contribute their share to happiness as Stendhal conceives it, the more important element is passion in the sense of intensity and profundity of feeling, whose 'storms' carry a potential for conflict and even tragedy not to be found in the superficial flirtations and velleities of the passing moment, but which in fulfilling itself affords a 'felicity' unattainable through less powerful emotions and certainly not through sensory gratification alone. And when, five years later, in *Love*, Stendhal again refers to beauty as the promise of happiness, the context is also Italianate and Italophilic, as this work defines Italy as that country where erotic passion and pleasure escape social convention and hypocritical imitation.[340] Nor does it much matter whether Stendhal depicts Italy in its actuality or as invention, although his portrayal combines elements of both. Italy more than any other place awakened in him that predominantly though not exclusively libidinal impulse of fantasy in which Marcuse locates the power of art not simply to protest against domination, production, and the 'performance principle,' but to construct liberating images of a future society in which the contradictions of the present are overcome in the reconciliation of reality and desire. In short, Italy is the primary focus and embodiment of the utopian impulse that the Frankfurt School discovers in Stendhal.[341]

Stendhal's evocation of *la promesse de bonheur* calls to mind the utopian content that Marcuse regards as a chief justification of the 'affirmative' culture of the bourgeois epoch. Yet like Stendhal, the Frankfurt critics diagnose in this culture a perhaps less overtly dystopian implication. Just as the values of the affirmative culture – the good, the true, the beautiful – have been presented as universal and thus obligatory, so that culture has been conceived in ideal, formal, and above all 'spiritual' terms, as a realm at once removed from and 'transfiguring' corporeal pleasure and worldly desire. The result is that, besides disguising and palliating social oppression with its pleasant illusions, affirmative culture exhibits an ascetic, renunciatory, and dutiful character similar to that of the commercial-industrial world, the world of 'mere' materiality from which it claims independence. Contrariwise, the Frankfurt School follows Stendhal in validating that utopian impulse which, in imagining a realm of gratification beyond repressive work, identifies culture with corporeal pleasure and happiness. Not only do these critics, like Stendhal, appeal to Epicurus's argument that the higher pleasures require discrimination, thus challenging certain utilitarian claims that no determinable differences exist among the forms of enjoyment, but they are indebted to Nietzsche's interpretation of *la promesse de bonheur* as a counterclaim to the ascetic and sublimatory assumptions of Kant's aesthetic. For them, as for Nietzsche, Stendhal affirms legitimately and necessarily a sensuously hedonistic and 'interested' response to art, a desire for worldly gratification and happiness as against the Kantian ideal of beauty as the object of disinterested rational understanding and purely formalistic appreciation.[342] To quote Marcuse, 'the autonomy of art reflects the unfreedom of individuals in the unfree society. If people were free, then art would be the form and expression of their freedom.' This statement points to the double revolutionary goal of the twentieth-century avant-garde and its advocates among the Frankfurt School, namely the desublimation of art and thus the end of its autonomy. Whereas the bourgeois had sought to maintain the separation between life and art, though to the detriment of pleasure and happiness, and whereas artists such as Goethe and George had insisted upon the formal and organic autonomy of the artwork, the avant-garde aimed to fulfil the *promesse* of art within everyday life and empirical reality, to infuse expressive rather than merely formal aesthetic values into society itself. This then was the modernist vision of the artistic redemption of modern life.[343] And while it is true that Stendhal was sufficiently a part of bourgeois culture to retain a belief in artistic autonomy, the avant-garde could nonetheless have quoted in support of their agenda his statement that our response to art is a 'special matter, something very close to our mistress's thighs,' or his description of art in *Rossini* as 'only love in another language,' or his proposal in *Lives of Haydn, Mozart, and Metastasio* that composers follow the Italian example of aiming above all to give 'physical pleasure,' or 'sensual delight,' this being, by contrast with the other arts, the very 'root' and aim of music.[344] The Frankfurt critics' attack on ascetic culture consorts well with Stendhal's opposition between France, where a conception of culture as duty requires theatres to be uncomfortable, and Italy, where music ravishes performers and listeners, each alike *dilettanti*.[345]

Nonetheless, the cultural environment of the early and mid-twentieth century led Marcuse and Adorno to argue that contemporary art cannot legitimately honour, as did the art of the bourgeois epoch, Stendhal's demand for ideal beauty and pleasure. Rather, they hold that in the present state of culture and society, characterized by 'total mobilization,' the abolition of the individual subject, and fabrication of exploitative images of happiness for mass consumption by the 'culture' industry, art must deliberately spurn the traditional values of beauty, harmony, and pleasure in favour of dissonance and atonality, lest it proffer spuriously agreeable images of reconciliation disguising the inhuman contradictions of the social order. 'Art survives only where it cancels itself,' contends Marcuse, 'where it saves its substance by denying its traditional form and thereby denying reconciliation: where it becomes surrealistic and atonal.' In its actual as opposed to ideal circumstances art can achieve impact only to the extent that it concentrates on negative moments. Nor can art under these conditions hope to fulfil the avant-garde goal of the desublimation of art, but must continue to maintain its autonomy or 'closure' apart from society so as to preserve its objectivity while resisting absorption into the world of mass consumption.[346] Writing at mid-century of the experience of twentieth-century music, and of the asceticism that 'has today become the sign of advanced art,' Theodor Adorno observes that 'all "light" and pleasant art has become illusory and mendacious ... the promise of happiness, once the definition of art, can no longer be found except where the mask has been torn from the countenance of false happiness.'[347] Elsewhere Adorno observes that, while Stendhal's concept of art's *promesse de bonheur* 'implies that art owes something to empirical life, namely the Utopian content which is foreshadowed by art,' this debt 'keeps on diminishing as life resembles only itself and not art. If art wishes to be faithful to that *promesse*, it has to break it, for any happiness that we may gain in, or in relation to, the existing world is vicarious and false.'[348]

Cesar Graña musters against the Bohemians Veblen's argument for useful and efficient production over conspicuous consumption and aesthetic-erotic hedonism. Stendhal survives this criticism because his divided consciousness of Italy – and modernity – enables him both to understand and to question it. No mere aesthete, he regards the 'vanity' of St Peter's as all the more wasteful in a democratic and utilitarian age of 'state-budgets,' just as he criticizes the popes for building churches when they ought to have aided the sick, suppressed bandits, and distributed land. At the same time, however, Stendhal fears that the industrial and business organization so often entailed by modern schemes of 'tranquil and enduring felicity' must inevitably carry an unacknowledged germ of 'unhappiness.'[349] Not only does the joyless regularity of industrialized existence reduce the individual's capacity to respond to the world variously and spontaneously, but the imperative of production limits opportunities for art and love, those Italian virtues which Stendhal defines as the supreme happiness, and which, being forms of play, demand leisure and hence freedom from the merely necessary or useful.

Well aware that social organization and industrial efficiency had been most fully developed in the England of his time, Stendhal finds in the English an economical and disciplined '*pattern of conduct*' or 'methodism' that the French and Americans are adopting and that he exemplifies in prison-like, Protestant Geneva – a boring 'dismality' of existence any Italian woman could 'smell ... a mile off.' 'Not one Englishman in a hundred has the courage to be himself,' writes Stendhal, 'whereas not one Italian in ten can so much as conceive the possibility of being otherwise.' He adds that 'in England, a man is lucky if he encounters a genuine emotional experience once in a month; but in Italy, the same phenomenon occurs three times a day.' Identifying life with work and duty, and hence absorbed in business and politics, the English sacrifice personal happiness by amputating their capacity for aesthetic and erotic pleasure. The average Englishman is so obsessed with utility that he has only one question concerning any object: 'How can I *use* that *here and now?*' Stendhal had observed the stolid moroseness of the English in Italy, their superhuman gravity, their lack of *esprit* and incapacity for leisure, their preference for dependable, trivial comforts over intense sensations. In his view, the unresponsive British seemed to carry within themselves a 'secret principle of unhappiness.' Lacking that 'passionate sensibility without which one is unworthy of seeing Italy,' they could not grasp that one must transcend the 'merely *useful* or *convenient*' to acquire 'that true degree of culture which seeks out only the *beautiful*.'[350]

Often in his Italian writings Stendhal distinguishes between native Italians, with their expressive gestures and emotional range, and the undemonstrative British, who, numbed by work, seemed never to laugh.[351] He was, as Coe observes, one of the earliest writers to 'react against what he dimly discerned to be the threat of the Great Victorian Seriousness,' which pervaded northern European culture from 1830 to about 1930. Yet Stendhal is no less troubled by the matter-of-factness and affective neutrality demanded by the increasingly disciplined forms of modern life. He fears that the prohibition of expression must attenuate the emotions themselves and thus destroy art, which in his view not only originates in emotion but has emotional expression as its chief aim. These fears underly the passage in *A Roman Journal* in which, referring to a trial, Stendhal remarks: 'Nowadays good form forbids gestures,' so that the accused 'is a man of good breeding ... precisely because the man beside him, if he is completely deaf, cannot tell by looking at him whether he has just been acquitted or sentenced to death.' Stendhal goes on to speculate that, as the world becomes civilized, the 'absence of gestures to which all nations will come sooner or later' will 'do away with sculpture.'[352] Perhaps his most anxious vision of modernity is that of a world from which art and emotion are banished.

Looking ahead, Stendhal fears that architectural distinctiveness, something he found more frequently in Italy than anywhere else, must disappear from modern cities under the imperatives of administrative efficiency and a utilitarian functionalism whose foreshadowings he discerned in his own day. Unlike Italian cities, with their irregularities in layout, the newly constructed city of Lorient has been built by the 'hand of reason,' so that its straight streets lack all picturesqueness. In Marseilles, a city of that French Midi which Stendhal likens to Italy, the newer streets are well paved, bordered by sidewalks, 'straight as a string,' and wide enough to eliminate crowds while permitting public surveillance of all passers-by. Furtive assignations are impossible, and husbands are no longer deceived in Marseilles. Noting that these new streets lack 'character,' as they resemble those being built throughout Europe, Stendhal comments: 'It is fate,' for 'everything modern ... precipitates us into a *boring* manner without trying to.'[353] What Stendhal encountered in Lorient and Marseilles anticipates the 'geometric rationalism' and 'panoptic schema' that would spread inexorably through the developing urban and industrial world in the twentieth century, and that were more notably embodied in Chicago's Columbian Exposition of 1893, where urban vistas were consciously defined so as to establish a 'cohesive and orderly urban environment' promotive of 'public spirit and morality.' As the arch in New York's Washington Square was introduced for the purpose of ordering, regulating, and hierarchizing its urban surroundings, and thus to structure the public's response to it, so the principle of the 'panopticon,' ironically the creation of the utilitarian Jeremy Bentham, one of Stendhal's intellectual heroes, became the 'midwife' to the 'concept of a standardizable, regulated order' in American and European planning from the turn of the century onward.[354] Stendhal would no doubt have preferred Naples' Via Toledo, with its swarming, unpredictable, unmanageable crowds, each person intent on his own pleasure.[355]

As Stendhal surveyed the industrial capitalist complex emergent in his own time, he ventured in an admittedly tentative and at points contradictory fashion interrogations of the accompanying modern ideologies of work and production, sometimes addressing them from his customary utilitarian position, in other instances criticizing utilitarian assumptions from within. Del Litto notes that as a young man Stendhal projected an essay entitled 'Influence de la richesse sur la population et le bonheur,' in which, with what del Litto describes as a degree of 'originality,' he took to task contemporary economists for stressing production to the nearly total exclusion of consumption, as was typical during the heyday of 'orthodox' or laissez faire economics. Among the chief targets of Stendhal's polemic was Jean-Baptiste Say's argument that increased production is properly the chief economic goal since goods will supposedly always find buyers and consumption thus takes care of itself. Although Stendhal does not anticipate later 'underconsumptionist' arguments against Say's Law, he shares Ruskin's view that the final aim of an economy is neither to increase production nor to amass material riches but to promote 'happiness' (*bonheur*) by improving the quantity and *quality* of consumption. To quote Strickland's summary: 'The only justification for productivity ... lies in the enjoyment of what is produced and it is because of the variation in men's capacity for various kinds of enjoyment that markets are so often saturated or exploited. How then can the general good be either measured or foreseen?'[356] Not only must production be fulfilled in gratifying consumption, so as to realize its utility to the utmost, but there is also the problem that, notwithstanding the utilitarian ideal of the greatest good for the greatest number, that is, of maximizing enjoyment throughout society, enjoyments differ in kind and in quality. As Stendhal had learned from Epicurus, it is necessary to discriminate between higher and lower pleasures. One thus discerns in Stendhal's thinking on consumption a tension between Bentham, who took for granted ordinary standards of enjoyment, and Epicurus with his emphasis on a hierarchy of pleasure whose most exalted delights are accessible only to the few.[357]

Stendhal's more mature though ambiguous inquiry into industrialism appears in his polemical pamphlet *D'un nouveau complot contre les industriels* (1825), a little-known work that Geneviève Mouillaud describes as his last attempt to construct a coherent ideology. The pamphlet's inspiration was Stendhal's troubled awareness of the increasing influence of the recently deceased Henri Count de Saint-Simon and his devoted band of disciples, who had in the year of his death launched the short-lived Saint-Simonian journal *Le Producteur* (1825–6), in which they set out the blueprint for a new society organized on industrial technocratic lines. In many ways the prophet of modern industrialism and prototype of technocrats like Thorstein Veblen, who placed work and production at the centre of his utilitarian social agenda, Saint-Simon like his disciples regarded himself as a kind of engineer of happiness and thus a benefactor of humanity. In more conventional terms he is a utopian socialist who repudiated, though not entirely, his connection with liberalism.[358]

For the Saint-Simonians, the predominance of the now challenged aristocratic class had resulted not only in inequality and the exploitation of the lower orders but in the valorization of idleness and corrupted leisure as against productive work, the result being stagnation in the struggle for mastery over external nature. Even after the Revolution the aristocracy had persisted in its selfish, antisocial, slothful behaviour, while intellectual culture was all too often represented by 'parasites' specializing uselessly in the *bon mot*. Contrariwise the Saint-Simonians advanced a productive agenda based on universal work combined with the utilitarian principle of the greatest good for the greatest number. Work was to be vindicated against *oisiveté* as the source and essence of human happiness. Dominated technically by the forces of production, nature would be made to serve human material needs in accordance with a universal tendency towards progress and human perfectability. Class conflict and exploitation were to vanish, for everyone would have become a worker, and all workers of whatever class or type would be united by their common interest in social utility. Work thus defined society, while workers, or the *industriels* in the most comprehensive sense, were society itself. However, not all workers were equally valued or rewarded, for Saint-Simon and his followers envisioned a social echelon that, by virtue of its superior intelligence and technical expertise, received the highest emoluments. This class also determined disinterestedly the allocation of work and its direction, so that for reasons of wealth, power, and influence it dominated the new industrial society. These persons included big manufacturers, major commercial interests, bankers, engineers, inventors, and scientists, the last of whom Saint-Simon at first conceived as a transcendent, even priest-like social intelligence acting independently of property owners and the state and decisively influencing them. The scientists received this special status because positive knowledge, being useful, was the key to moral progress. However, in his later writings Saint-Simon placed scientists within the larger category of intellectuals, which included artists and most other non-artisanal types of mental workers. It was possible for literary intellectuals to become productive workers within the new order only if they transformed themselves from parasites into servants and exponents of industrial values. Although Saint-Simon vacillated initially over whether scientists should dominate society or share authority with the major *industriels*, that is, the manufacturers, entrepreneurs, and financiers, he ultimately favoured the latter, whose supreme wealth, capacity, power, and influence assured them the paramount political and social position. So convinced were Saint-Simon and his followers of the importance of the leading *industriels* that they viewed them not as subalterns of the state but as the premier capacity within the nation, and thus as a technocracy, with all major decisions being submitted to the predominant class and determined on the basis of productivity, utility, and profitability. Respecting artists, whom Saint-Simon in his early works placed in a position close to the scientists, he required them to enlist their talents in awakening enthusiasm for his industrial schemes by projecting visions of the utopian future. The kind of art proper to the new industrial society was to be functional, utilitarian, morally didactic, and easily accessible to the masses, having as its goal the replacement of egoism with brotherhood and social welfare. Should artists lend themselves to the new productive society, they like the intellectuals were assured of inclusion among the important producers. Indeed, whereas in his early writings Saint-Simon had ignored artists, he later saw them as a kind of priesthood on the leading edge of social reconstruction. He placed them alongside the savants and major *industriels*, the latter being *primus inter pares*. It was the artist's job to create the new society by promoting reform, love of liberty, and utilitarian values. For their part, the Saint-Simonians shared their master's view of the artist as the 'priest' of a New Christianity grounded in production and utility. According to Fernand Rude, the Saint-Simonian Leon Halévy even proposed that the arts, lest they die out, serve industrial progress. Drawing from military vocabulary, Saint-Simon defined the entire leadership class of his new society as its avant-garde, a description later applied to social radicals as well as to modern artists in their revolt against tradition.[359]

By no means uniformly hostile to the Saint-Simonians, *D'un nouveau complot contre les industriels* is notoriously difficult to pin down, being marked by contradictions, diffuse argumentation, logical lacunae, and uncontrolled irony. As polemic the work is a failure, for just as one cannot say where Stendhal stands ideologically within it, so he never defines his pamphlet's ideological target – a problem that Mouillaud traces to his at least partial solidarity with the Saint-Simonians despite his criticism of them. To the extent that Stendhal remains within liberal ideology, he shares with the Saint-Simonians the values of productivity (or work), utility (the greatest good for the greatest number), and exchange value or profit as a measure of utility. It does not matter in this comparison that Saint-Simon finally deserted liberalism in the hope that the Restoration monarchy would help him implement his ideas – a disaffection that Rude regards as the motive behind Stendhal's attack on the Saint-Simonians in *D'un nouveau complot*. Nor can one forget Stendhal's technocratic interests and inclinations. Just as he aspired to be a *polytechnicien* during his first youthful sojourn in Paris, so his writings acknowledge technical advance as necessary to the liberal and national-building efforts he favours. Not only did he wish that Napoleon had bestowed an *école polytechnique* upon Italy, but he makes Octave, the hero of *Armance*, a *polytechnicien*. Similarly, in the post-Napoleonic period Stendhal proposed that Cardinal Consalvi tackle the 'Augean stables' of Italy through a national polytechnic school. Stendhal also welcomed the founding of *Le Producteur*, and when its editor complained that *D'un nouveau complot* contained passages offensive to the Saint-Simonians, Stendhal volunteered to remove them.[360]

Nonetheless, Stendhal intensely disdained the manufacturing classes, especially those of England and America, whom he paints repeatedly as money-grubbing, workaholic Philistines. Contrary to the Saint-Simonians, who attributed America's prosperity to industrialists, Stendhal emphasizes its good laws and absence of frontiers. His willingness to accept the Saint-Simonian position in its entirety would have been diminished by his anxious awareness that, as an intellectual and rentier living largely on unearned income, he was vulnerable to charges of idleness and parasitism, at least from the Saint-Simonian point of view. From that perspective Stendhal had less in common with the *industriels* than with aristocrats and Bohemians, each alike 'unproductive' and selfishly antisocial in their leisure. In *D'un nouveau complot* he places himself among the 'thinking class,' whose ideological unity he much exaggerates, and which he defines arbitrarily as consisting of intellectuals with unearned income of six thousand francs per year. That figure is the amount Stendhal thought he should have received under ideal circumstances, as in reality his father's legacy left him with three thousand per year, the rest being compensated for through journalistic and other writings. As if to deflect imputations of parasitism and thus to legitimate his own 'class,' Stendhal insists not only that he and other intellectuals add to the social good through their productions, but that they do so freely, with small concern for material reward. The irony is that, even as he defends the interests of his own 'class,' he claims it to be disinterested and public spirited. The intellectuals are thus contrasted with the upper ranks of the *industriels*, whom Stendhal suspects of concealed vanity, ambition, and special interest.[361]

Broadly speaking, Stendhal's pamphlet warns against taking the Saint-Simonians' claims at face value. Far from being the only useful social group, or even the most useful, the major *industriels* are one of many professions whose products – like those of Stendhal's 'thinking class' – are useful and thus valuable. As esteem is properly bestowed on all who work with probity, one need not honour the major *industriels* above all other groups. Nor do their avowals of disinterested concern for the social welfare stand up to scrutiny, as they aim for private wealth and power. One should therefore think twice about empowering them. Stendhal further complains that, being self-interested, the *industriels* lack the heroism of great patriots and soldiers who have sacrificed themselves for humanity. This, however, marks a contradiction in his argument, as the values of sacrifice to which he appeals ill consort with the utilitarian and liberal ideology of exchange value – an ideology of self-interest – which he accepts unquestioningly. Mouillaud also notes that Stendhal nowhere acknowledges the contradiction between his embrace of both technocratic rationality and the liberal doctrine of exchange value. Her elliptical criticism may rest on a point that Veblen would reiterate, that technocratic canons of efficency and economy jar with competing capitalist canons of pecuniary expenditure and waste. At the same time, Stendhal's attack on the *industriels* finally centres on not the manufacturing or commercial classes but the banking sector, which Saint-Simon and some of his disciples had proposed to place at the head of society, but which Stendhal denounces for lending to immoral causes, such as the Turks' suppression of the Greeks. According to Stendhal, there is no justification for elevating bankers to the '*première ligne*' of society. Yet so far as industrialism in the broad sense is concerned, *D'un nouveau complot* treats it with respect, admitting both its probity and claims to honour, and even finding some justification in the *industriels'* right to judge and choose productive capacities.[362]

Although Mouillaud stresses the importance of bankers (and money) as the ultimate target of Stendhal's pamphlet, it also questions if only intermittently the value of work and production, an issue Stendhal clarifies in a letter written soon afterwards. However much the editor of the journal *Le Pandore* exaggerates in claiming that the pamphlet would discredit all work, Stendhal asks the reader to consider the nature of life in a fully industrialized society such as arose in the next century and of which Saint-Simon was the prophet – a society in which work is universal, in which society is identified with work, in which industry, to quote Stendhal, takes over '*tout estime*,' and in which industry is regarded as the cause of *tout le bonheur*. This was the consequence of what, in a letter to Stendhal, the editor of *Le Globe* characterized as the '*apothéose industriel*.'[363] As for what Stendhal thought of this coming apotheosis, one infers it from the letter he wrote on 9 December 1825 to Mira, the director of the Théâtre of Variétés. Recurring to a favorite theme, which Richard N. Coe characterizes as the fundamental hostility of the bourgeoisie to the 'higher ends of art,' Stendhal complains that industrialism, in requiring the whole world not only to work, but to work to excess, would eliminate the *dolce far niente* necessary to the creation and enjoyment of the masterpieces of Ariosto and Canova. This was a loss, it should be emphasized, of both the capacity and time in which to enjoy them. Stendhal thus challenges the claim that Saint-Simonianism tends inevitably to utility and felicity, contending rather that it cannot but lead to boredom and sadness, since its concentration on productive work leaves no place for *paresse* or idleness, that freedom from work which forms the necessary condition for varied enjoyments. Such a viewpoint is perfectly consistent with that passage in *Love* in which Stendhal observes that, had the industrial capitalist the time to do so, he would hate the dreamer or contemplative for his possession of leisure.[364]

II

It can hardly be emphasized sufficiently that Stendhal lived at a time when the classical ideal of leisure had begun to decline, and that his importance lies partly in his Italianate defence of this ideal. And herein lies a major difference between Stendhal and the Frankfurt School. However much they appreciate aspects of the classical ideal, Marxists typically criticize it as falsely conceiving a privileged or 'timeless' sphere of personal and cultural freedom outside material necessity. As they see it, leisure has hitherto been the creation and possession of a materially privileged class, and has always depended upon exploitation and oppression. To defend the classical ideal is to cling to pre-technological or feudal values while tolerating injustice. The proper goal is to extend leisure so as to include the mass of humanity, a task requiring political and social justice along with the reorganization of the economy and technology towards broadly beneficial social ends, including economic abundance.[365] Stendhal's view of leisure is closer to that of Sebastian de Grazia, champion of the Aristotelian concept.[366]

Based on classical precedents, de Grazia's definition of leisure is unapologetically universal and absolutist. In some respects leisure may be defined purely negatively, as having nothing to do with mere idleness, ascetic withdrawal, or purposiveness. Nor does it exist in a determinate or antithetical relation to work or time or their demands. Valuable in and of itself and thus for its own sake, leisure is a state of being in which one is free from labour along with other everyday necessities and obligations. Objective or clock time does not enter into the definition or description of leisure because it is an inward state, what Epicurus calls the 'time of the soul,' in keeping with the Epicurean view that time has no connection with the good life. Although leisure by no means excludes activity, those who possess it manifest not the doggedness and busy-ness of persons active to some end but the tranquillity, serenity, and composure of those detached from temporal obligations and whose activities are their own end. Thus they have achieved happiness in its highest, most worthy form. Yet it is an error to define leisure as freedom from something, as it is in itself free. Nor is it to be understood as a specified block or chunk of 'free' or idle time away from work, as such a definition would bind it in a logical antithesis to time while compromising the inherent value and integrity of leisure as a timeless state of being in which time effectively 'stops.' Indeed, free time can be calculated but leisure cannot, and the very concept of 'leisure time' is an oxymoron. Nor is leisure recreation or recuperation from work, as this would make it a purposive instrument and thus rob it of its self-sufficiency. As de Grazia observes, the ancient Greeks regarded leisure as a tranquil, unfragmented state of personal being, one which, because untroubled by time constraints and practical necessities, can be devoted without interruption to freely chosen and self-directed pursuits valued in themselves, rather than as means to some other end. The person of leisure dedicates him or herself to a life of intellectual play whose chief objects are self-enjoyment and knowledge. The primary forms of leisure include disinterested philosophical contemplation of reality, conversation or debate enlivened by wit and curiosity, the arts, music, and love. That de Grazia regards love itself as a form of leisure is evident from his citation of Baudelaire's observation that love is the 'natural occupation' of the leisured; moreover, that without the slowness and patience required in order to achieve the depth, subtlety, and momentum of a genuine love affair, love would be but a plebeian orgy – a judgment consistent with the views of both Stendhal and his admirer Ezra Pound. Yet though leisure is an anti-ascetic ideal, and although it often yields enjoyment, its result, de Grazia holds, need not be pleasure. Its essential feature is that it is sought freely, as a personal choice. Rather than being formed primarily by others, the person of leisure forms himself and thus avoids the fate against which Epicurus had warned, of the loss of personal being through captivation by society. It follows that leisure cannot take an organized or collective form, as the person of leisure does not depend for his satisfaction on other people. One must also emphasize de Grazia's rejection of the Marxist and Veblenesque idea that leisure belongs necessarily to an ostentatious and materially exploitative 'leisure class' dedicated to the invidious display of its special privilege of wasting time and material. Rather the desire for leisure springs from a deeply personal attitude and need. The person of the 'leisure kind,' as de Grazia insists on calling it in opposition to the idea of a leisure class, 'may be poor or rich, noble or commoner, of the strong or the weak, but he is always powerful in that he is the only one who, by his daemon, forms himself.'[367]

In Veblen's analysis leisure is economically and socially determined. It is identified with a materially advantaged social class for whom leisure consists not of self-elected freedom from temporal and material constraints, as in the classical definition, but of the opportunity to enact publicly its privileged possession of time and goods in a wasteful, that is, non-utilitarian manner. Leisure is thus valued not for its own sake but as a means of publicizing invidious comparisons between oneself and less advantaged individuals and groups, whom the leisure class infects with emulative envy to the point where leisure comes to be identified with the conspicuous consumption of time and goods. In short, the real purpose of leisure is supposedly to advertise social status. Being thus indistinguishable from snobbism, whose essence is invidious comparison, leisure apparently exists inescapably in bondage to the estimations of society or the other. It is a performative activity and symbolic value that by its very nature needs to be enacted socially so as to be seen and emulated. Solitude or contemplation would seem to have no part in it. As for higher culture, it is for Veblen only an 'insignia of honor' reserved for the wealthy, and is desired chiefly for invidious comparison – again, snob value. To be sure, the leisure class studies ancient languages and fine arts, but does so not for their own sake but to dramatize its removal from mundane considerations. Daniel Thomas Cook argues approvingly that, for Veblen, leisure is not an autonomous 'time out of time,' or a means of escaping the world, but a form of display and social interaction.

Although Veblen concedes that art objects preserved by the rich possess intrinsic aesthetic value, the fact that their market prices far exceed their real value demonstrates the crucial role of 'canons of expensiveness' in their social estimation.[368]

Contemporary leisure theory has drawn from Veblen and other writers (such as Bourdieu and Baudrillard) in arguing that, despite the current absence of a leisure class such as Veblen described, capitalism still places enormous pressure on individuals to advertise their social position through wasteful and conspicuous expenditure. Characterizing as leisure off-work practices that de Grazia would dismiss as 'free time,' leisure theorists see leisure as bound up indissolubly with social and economic considerations, as it not only depends on consumption but entails a goal-oriented 'performative' agenda as demanding as that of the workplace and in some sense an extension of it. In being performative, leisure is also tied inextricably to society and its estimations, as consumption practices not only serve to confer 'distinction' upon individuals, to use Bourdieu's term, but enable them to display their material or cultural superiority over other people. According to Baudrillard, it is improper to refer even to 'free time,' as its chief purpose is social display. Reminiscent of Veblen, his successors leave the impression that, being a form of consumption, leisure cannot but be contaminated by social judgments and the quest for status. Nor is there any doubt of Stendhal's familiarity with social environments similar to those described by Veblen and later leisure theorists, for Chris Rojek notes that modern capitalist society and culture closely resemble the court of Louis XIV. As we have seen, Stendhal dissected the court of Versailles as a nasty hotbed of vain emulation and invidious distinctions extending to the most trivial details of display and expenditure – the king's desires and consumption habits providing the emulative standard not only for his court but for French society. Stendhal similarly reads the bourgeois society of nineteenth-century Paris as a nest of snobbism where, unlike Italy, the tyranny of the other prevails through public opinion, individual autonomy surrenders to others' judgments, contemplative solitude vanishes amid idolatry of society, and even love and culture are sacrificed to the demand for social approval. The question remains, however, whether leisure must be identified with the tyranny of the other in the form of the pursuit of status and symbolic performance, or whether a margin exists within which the individual may freely choose to go his own way. The further issue is whether, despite the social, economic, and political factors that influence and limit leisure, a person may nonetheless remove him or herself either through leisure or at least free-time experience from work, obligation, and social purposes, so as to enter, however temporarily, a 'time out of time.'[369]

Regarding the possibility of the individual removing him or herself from considerations of status and the snobbery that often accompanies them, even contemporary leisure theorists concede that this has occurred historically and remains an option. Although Gary Cross values Veblen's and Simmel's emphasis upon status and fashion as behavioural motivations, he insists that the social meaning of consumption transcends invidious comparison. He also notes David Riesman's point that some working-class people show no interest in status or any other symbolic value in choosing residences. More recently Rojek acknowledges evidence of the independent choice of leisure (or, in de Grazia's terms, free time) among the nineteenth-century working class, a choice that, contrary to Veblen, did not consist in the passive imitation of 'leisure class' canons. According to Rojek, 'it is relatively easy to show that, historically speaking, many social formations have been hostile to the social standards of the rich and wealthy.' Notwithstanding his emphasis on leisure as a temporally bound and purposive performance determined by material factors, Rojek seems to allow that, within the experience of leisure itself, it remains possible to escape if only fleetingly the demands of work, time, and social obligation. This seems implicit in his description of the leisure experience of what he terms a 'taste culture,' a group of like-minded individuals whose leisure preferences are consciously intended to distinguish them from the rest of society, but who in their experience of leisure totally exclude all thoughts of the other. As Rojek remarks, 'references to work are banished from taste cultures. Instead personal identity is focused on the activity in question. The rest of society is bracketed out of consciousness.' To be sure, such a taste culture is likely to value leisure as a recreative escape from work, without having contemplation as its object, and would thus fail to meet de Grazia's definition. Yet these examples show that, just as it is possible to ignore status interests in the pursuit of leisure, so even the experience of 'free time' enables a person to screen out mundane and temporal considerations, even if failing to qualify as leisure in de Grazia's sense.[370]

Although de Grazia refuses to identify leisure with economic privilege or a particular leisure class, least of all the Veblenesque travesty, he has no doubt that leisure by its nature can fulfil itself only as a culturally elitist form of experience available only to the relatively small number of people capable of pursuing and enjoying it – that is, capable of self-formation based on disinterested contemplation. His position agrees with that of Epicurus, who insists upon the necessity of discriminating between experiences and the kinds of pleasures they afford. What remains for the rest of humanity is not leisure but free time away from work; free time, moreover, in which to pursue not leisure in the true sense but ease, material consumption, and primarily sensual gratification, which the masses regard mistakenly as leisure, and which social theorists such as Veblen, with his technocratically grounded denunciation of a materially wasteful and ostentatious leisure class, imagine to be its essence. De Grazia's name for the paradise of non-leisure humanity is Cockagne (Italian, *cuccagna*), a never-never land of unfailing yet exclusively appetitive and sensual delights in which one may always 'take it easy' free of the demands of time and work. Unlike the person of leisure, the inhabitant of Cockayne lacks personal autonomy, being formed by others, or society. De Grazia further holds that, just as leisure in its highest sense remains unassailable in its definition over the centuries, so Cockayne has endured more or less as the utopia of the mass of humanity throughout history, even into the twentieth century. It is this incapacity for leisure on the part of average humanity that underlies de Grazia's conviction that leisure, as an ideal, can be realized only imperfectly in a democracy, especially a mass democracy. Yet if the masses have remained basically the same in their pleasures, they have also experienced cataclysmic intensifications of their work rhythms and work output, so that the modern industrial worker no longer enjoys the relaxed pace of work and abundant free time available to his preindustrial counterparts. As de Grazia remarks: 'The poorest weaver of palm baskets in Sardinia working from dawn to sunset on the stoop of her house can eat, drink, laugh, and talk, watch the passers-by, stretch and keep an eye on the children.' This is a state if not of leisure then of what de Grazia terms 'leisureliness' marked by considerable independence from time constraints defined by the clock. It confirms E.P. Thompson's and Henri Lefebvre's point that pre-industrial work and leisure lacked that clear differentiation into separate spheres that came to typify work under industrialism. Workers in traditional societies suffered no enslavement to the workplace but could anticipate long stretches if not of leisure then of free time authorized by social custom. In the Middle Ages there were 115 church-sanctioned holidays during a year. The normal work rhythms of agrarian societies are remarkably slack by modern industrial standards, as it is only during planting and harvesting that work becomes especially demanding. Of contemporary Greece de Grazia observes that 'the intense work of cultivating and harvesting takes only a few weeks. Outside of these periods

Greek farmers have an evening with ample spare time,' which they pass sitting in a café where they drink coffee, read newspapers, talk politics, and watch the local women at the fountain. Juliet B. Schor presents a similar picture of work in traditional societies.[371]

Greek and Roman views of leisure differed significantly, observes de Grazia, for whereas the Greeks gave it priority over productive work and participation in public affairs, the latter affording the only justification for a person's relinquishment of leisure, Cicero and Pliny thought of leisure or *otium* as something that came *after* business or public life (*negotium*), as a means of recreation enabling one to return refreshed or 'recreated' to everyday activity. Medieval monks such as St Benedict of Norcia somewhat corrected the classical world's perhaps one-sided emphasis on leisure by preaching the dignity of work, but in de Grazia's view medieval thinking remained fundamentally close to that of the classical world, as contemplation continued to be deemed superior to practical life. In Aquinas, contemplation is the highest good. Although the Italian Renaissance tended to favour activity and mastery of nature over contemplation, the Florentine Cristoforo Landino envisioned an ideal balance between activity and contemplative leisure, *negotium* and *otium*. Many of America's founding fathers had received a classical education and thus keenly appreciated the traditional concept of leisure, their views on the issue being much closer to the Greeks than to the Romans. Yet despite these differences in the interpretation of leisure, what remains constant in its evaluation into the twentieth century is its contrast with and superiority to work, defined as a realm of temporal constraints and material necessities.[372]

De Grazia notes that the classical ideal of leisure had its late efflorescence during the eighteenth century, in the Venice of Guardi and Canaletto. Yet even before the triumph of the industrial revolution the assault on leisure was proceeding apace in northern European countries with the rise of Protestantism and its puritanical work ethic, thanks to which, according to de Grazia with a more than casual nod to Max Weber, traditional holidays went by the board and a new emphasis was placed on industry, worldly practicality, rational calculation and discipline, self-control, and time-saving. From the nineteenth into the midtwentieth century leisure was increasingly suppressed in America and the 'progressive' European nations as industrialism and technology defined productive work as a universal imperative, and as mass democracy allied with the state embraced work as the right of all humanity and the means of general felicity. Under this new regime leisure could only be condemned as unproductive idleness, and so for the first time in history work and leisure were consigned to separate spheres. Inevitably the democratic ideal of education had to be an almost exclusively practical one. Like their Puritan predecessors, factory owners and their regimented armies of workers held beauty and the arts in suspicion, deeming them a useless waste of time. Not only did industrialism contribute to the banishment of the classics – and with them the classical concept of leisure – from modern education, but it created a time-ridden workday world bound to the clock and the machine, in which work was far less leisurely than in the past. Gradually leisure was degraded to what it has meant from the later nineteenth century into the present, a fixed chunk of 'free-time' activity outside work, a definition fulfillable by any off-work occupation no matter how time-bound, indolent, inattentive, or interrupted. Thus defined as the antithesis of work and therefore indissolubly bound to it, leisure in the sense of 'free time' was seen conventionally as a means of relaxing and 'recreating' body and mind in preparation for a return to the workplace.[373]

De Grazia readily admits that, since around 1850 up to his own decade, workers had gained seemingly enormous increases in free time owing to concessions by employers along with improvements in labour-saving machinery. He also acknowledges the increased desire for leisure in his own time, with the gradual erosion of the Protestant ethic. Combined with wage increases for the worker, the expansion of leisure was conceived by twentieth-century economists as indispensable to promoting the high levels of consumption needed for economic prosperity. Nonetheless, de Grazia very much doubts whether workers had gained anywhere near as much free time as had been claimed, as they spent much of it in social and family obligations, travel to work, moonlighting so as to keep up a costly lifestyle, the performance of chores, and do-it-yourself domestic improvements intended to save money. Often interrupted and broken into bits, free time could provide little more than distraction. For all his professed desire for leisure, the typical American happily exchanged free time for work and the money derived from it. Still another problem was the machine, which had produced a scarcity of time owing to its frenetic pace, yet which the work-obsessed public continued to worship out of a belief in its inalienable right to technology, Saint-Simon being its unacknowledged hero. Because the fatigue of tedious, demanding, and excessive work left most people with only enough mental and physical energy to pursue trivial, passive, and standardized pastimes, thus robbing them of the possibility of real leisure, their so-called leisure time was shaped increasingly by advertising and other exernal forces and issued in little more than the consumption of goods and gadgets, whose purchase demanded additional work. Like many adherents of the 'mass society' thesis, de Grazia apparently sees the typical consumer as deprived of choice and utterly at the mercy of compulsions and suggestions incited by advertising. The technique of market segmentation that was then being pioneered failed to conceal the presence of the mass, since products that offered 'something for everybody' still produced an 'impression of uniformity' in an America filled with 'nothing but sameness.' Even those who had grown wealthy through work, and whose hard-won freedom from work afforded them a chance of genuine leisure, usually failed to obtain it since their work-centred habits and routines kept them from understanding its meaning. Many people whose wealth freed them from work remained by choice in the workplace for lack of a preferable occupation, thus confirming the point that one can escape necessity yet not have leisure. In contrast to the Greek idea that only leisure prepares one for politics, and that politics, or responsibility to the state, is the only thing that can inspire one to abandon leisure, John Stuart Mill proposed politics as a way of keeping citizens busy in their spare time, and thus of saving them from idleness.[374]

The persistent valorization of work over leisure under modern democracy is shown in the UNESCO declaration of human rights, which mentions the right to work, and in the motto, *Travail, Famille, Patrie*, which appeared on French coins and official documents after the dissolution of the Third Republic in 1940. The first article of the current Italian constitution, which was put into effect in January 1948, and whose workerist terminology shows the intervention of the Italian socialist leader Palmiro Togliatti, defines Italy as a 'democratic Republic founded on *lavoro*' or work. The constitution's fourth article states that the Italian Republic recognizes the 'right of all citizens to work and shall promote such conditions as will make this right effective.' Commenting on the Italian constitution, de Grazia observes that 'it is hard to recognize from this definition [of leisure] the same Italy where the fervor of laboring monks had least shaken the Greco-Roman ideal of tranquillity ... [and] where Venice had become the queen of serenity.'[375]

Besides having traced the political causes of the decline of leisure, de Grazia raises the question of how to recover it in modern society, and this, with the issue of decline, leads him inevitably to politics. Like James Fenimore Cooper, and also like the contemporary leisure theorist Chris Rojek, de Grazia realizes that the character and status of leisure in any society depends crucially upon its reigning political ideology as well as the distribution of political power. In short, politics and culture are inextricable, notwithstanding that, since the time of Goethe and Schiller, leisure has tended to be seen as a purely private realm apart from politics. Yet whereas Rojek deplores what he sees as persistent inequalities in the distribution of what he calls leisure, but which de Grazia would view as only 'free time,' de Grazia more resembles Cooper in attributing the deterioration of leisure (in the classical sense) to the rise of mass democracy, with its egalitarianism, anti-intellectualism and anti-elitism, practical-minded education, and obsession with the production and consumption of material goods. Leisure, which in its true form can be possessed by only a small percentage of persons, had been levelled to the status of any free-time activity. If leisure in the classical sense were to recover any of its lost ground, the conversion of free time to leisure would require a considerable retreat of democracy along with the adoption of an ideology little concerned with time and work. Neither political ideology nor religion should insist that all persons work, while the identification of work with happiness must be severed. The concept of progress would also have to be discounted, so as to counteract the sense of striving that places a person in a constant state of necessity, and the role of advertising would need to be lessened or modified, in order to temper the desire for goods (and, indirectly, work). There would also have to be an economic surplus, and a culture that respected ideas and thinking. Unfortunately, the modern state continues to promote work, consumption, and free time while remaining powerless to intervene in the choice of free-time activities. Yet government intervention in leisure as in any other cultural sphere would probably lead to bureaucracy, though without necessarily solving the question of what people should do after work. And because work would probably remain unchanged, public taste would likely remain the same during evening hours.[376]

Stendhal's writings on Italy demonstrate his understanding of leisure in close if not exact conformity with de Grazia's conception. However, any discussion of Stendhal on this subject must anticipate the charge that he was able to enjoy what he and de Grazia deem leisure only because he was a rentier, living off a small inheritance; moreover, that without this unearned surplus capital to fund his 'idleness,' he would have had to work for a living along with most people. The rejoinder is that though Stendhal's funds gave him the opportunity for leisure and were thus, under the material conditions of his time, a necessary cause of it, they were insufficient to provide him with leisure in de Grazia's sense.

For though a rentier may have free time at his disposal, that is, mere freedom from work, he does not necessarily possess the leisure, or the capacity for leisure, that Stendhal shows in his Italian writings.

Besides belonging temperamentally to the 'leisure kind,' Stendhal acquired his understanding of leisure partly through his youthful instruction in Latin literature, which is sometimes evident in his writings on Rome,[377] and by his indebtedness to French writers of the eighteenth century, which de Grazia terms the swan-song of the leisure ideal. Of these writers, perhaps the most important is Rousseau, to whom Stendhal's ideas of time, nature, and society owe much of their Romantic colouring.

At the core of Rousseau's critique of European civilization stands the opposition between society and nature, each of which holds varying attractions for the freedom-questing individual. According to Rousseau, humanity in its original unfallen state of nature enjoyed an unalienated state of true being, the original unity and independence of the self. This was marked by a special relationship of the individual to time on the one hand and human beings on the other. As society did not exist, he was as yet free of human mediations and dependencies along with the myriad social labours, projects, duties, and obligations that would force him to live in the consciousness of past and future. Nature had not only spared him the utilitarian effort of productive work but enabled him to live joyfully and self-sufficiently in a perpetual present. Content with his own state of being, and fully capable of satisfying his own passions and desires by means of immediately accessible objects apprehended through the senses, the individual felt no need to look beyond the present moment. Neither social ambition nor approval could possibly attract him, and he had no awareness of the temporal horizons opened up by social life. As he experienced the most intimate unity between himself and the outside world, and as he lacked all interest in the past and future, he preferred neither activity nor knowledge but the feeling or sentiment of his own natural existence (*être*) in its familiar state of continuous repose, each idle moment untroubled by consciousness of time. And so the self was present to itself. Yet with the fall into society the unity of the individual's being was fractured through self-alienation, and time came to dominate consciousness. Deprived by society of its passions and immediate self-satisfactions, the self grew alienated from itself as a consequence of its mediated relations with other persons. And so the self was drained of its original energies. Now dependent upon, indeed enslaved to the demands and opinions of society, the individual acquired socially determined ambitions and desires that entailed a multitude of social duties and obligations – all of which unfold in time. Just as the fall into society brought the necessity of work or the 'performance principle,' thus confirming the inextricable link between society and the consciousness of time, so the ambitious individual was absorbed in planning, organization, and a host of projects coordinating the temporal horizons of past and future. Social organization and future-orientation now dominated the mind. It was no longer sufficient for the individual to feel or to be; he must act and know, both of which imply time-consciousness. Calculation and foresight became essentials of life, which ceased to provide novel and unexpected moments. No longer lived in the present, life lost its immediacy. No longer present to itself in its original unity, freedom, and independence, the self was robbed of true being. The further irony is that, owing to the *maladie du projet*, society could not make good on its promise of happiness, since those ambitious ones who labour strenuously to satisfy their long-deferred desires only spend their lives in the non-being of past and future, wasting their chance for unmediated enjoyment of passion in the present. This opposition between nature and society would be taken up by Stendhal, who like Rousseau stresses the value of repose and *paresse* as against work and ambition, and who envisions as he does an order of being in which time, rather than being 'forced,' passes without seeming to pass, the present instant of passion being so intense and prolonged as to seem 'eternized.'[378]

Although Stendhal frequently disparages Madame de Staël for what he regards as weak thinking and rhetorical excess, and although he attempts to minimize his indebtedness to her, he was profoundly influenced by her novel *Corinne, or Italy*, which helped to shape his ideas of Italy, including its relation to time and leisure. At the centre of the novel is the intense and fatally conflicted love affair between the Italian Corinne and the Scotsman Oswald, who exemplify two radically different conceptions of time rooted in southern and northern cultural attitudes respectively. A typical northerner, Oswald is obsessed with saving and using time productively and is thus afflicted with an anxious sense of the urgency of action. He is virtually incapable of enjoying the present and seeks escape from it in restless activity. As a believer in progress, and also as a soldier, he belongs to the Faustian world of the *projet* or 'project,' of duties, schedules, and planning, whereby the experience of the present is hollowed out and the as yet unrealized future goal dominates consciousness. The past only adds to Oswald's burdens by preying upon him through his guilty consciousness of failed obligation to his dead father. Contrastingly identified with Corinne, Italy is portrayed as that specially favoured place where passion mingles with repose and timeless reverie. It is an atemporal realm where, under the seductive influence of nature, art, and love, and amid surroundings of nearly death-like tranquillity, the self willingly surrenders its awareness of time and all the social duties and obligations that accompany it. 'Love,' remarks the narrator in a voice that might be mistaken for that of Corinne, 'offers such sweet hours, casts such sweet charm over each minute, that, requiring an indefinite future, it still revels in the present – welcoming a day as if it were a century of happiness or sorrow.' The experience of love is thus prolonged to seeming timelessness, as if 'eternized.' 'Unquestionably,' adds the narrator, 'it is through love that we can understand eternity! Love muddles all sense of time; it erases the notion of beginning and end. It is so difficult to imagine living without the loved one, that we believe we have always loved him.' The sense of temporal dislocation that Corinne experiences in erotic reverie is reinforced by Rome's abundant historical remains and those of its surrounding landscape. In Rome the co-presence of ancient ruins and modern buildings, which are often built into each other, cause these structures to appear related not so much in time as in space, and thus to create a tranquillizing impression of timelessness. 'You cannot take one step in Rome,' observes the narrator, 'without bringing together present and past, without juxtaposing different pasts.' The narrator adds that, in 'seeing the eternal mobility of man's history, you learn to take the events of your own day calmly; in the presence of so many centuries which have all undone the work of their predecessors, you feel somewhat ashamed of your own agitation.' It as if the timeless and immobile ruins of Rome, where so many historical efforts had come to naught, had diagnosed the *maladie du projet* by proving its ultimate futility. Outside the city the landscape of ruins contributes similarly to Corinne's identification of Italy with a dream of seemingly infinite duration, in which one moves slowly and calmly amid the low murmur of streams and fountains, which itself seems to express the slow, almost noiseless passage of time.[379]

Stendhal finds in Italy an exceptionally fertile ground upon which to cultivate leisure and the 'leisure kind.' For if, as Stendhal and Rousseau believe, society is also the order of successive time, in which the passionate individual is entrapped by a host of self-alienating mediations, projects, duties, and obligations, Italy has thankfully escaped this condition through the virtual absence of the social idea. As Stendhal argues, society in the sense of an approved pattern of behaviour does not exist in

Italy, where each Italian constitutes an autonomous monad driven by his private passions – the *moi*. Not only is such a being utterly indifferent to social claims and estimations, he rejects ambition and civic responsibility. Because of his antisocial temperament, but also because of his repressive, suspicious governments, the Italian seeks his private enjoyments in solitude. Nor can society capture him through the medium of books, since the Italian never reads and thus ignores literary models, preferring instead the self-communing experience of art or the intimacies of love. With the lightening and virtual disappearance of social requirements, the individual enjoys a more immediate relationship to nature and his own natural self.[380]

These antisocial attitudes are combined among the Italians with a distinctive attitude towards the closely interrelated concepts of time and work. To be sure, Stendhal in criticizing the idleness of the Italians often attributes it to their ill-run and unprogressive governments as well as to their depressed economies, the reform of which will lead to a more dedicated, rationalized, and organized workplace. Yet Stendhal repeatedly praises Italy as that land where, unlike contemporary northern nations, the obligations of organized work weigh least upon the individual and thus provide him with the greatest amount if not of leisure in the full sense then of untroubled free time in which to enjoy himself: 'Even those who work the hardest suffer little encroachment on their liberty, if one compares the lightness of their occupations which never stretch beyond early afternoon' with those of northern industrial labourers, from which Stendhal concludes that the Italians, though politically crushed, are at least masters of their own time. Goethe had formed similar impressions of the indolent Neapolitan *lazzaroni*, whose serenity and composure he contrasted with the exacting routine of northern workers. For Stendhal, Italy is the home of the *dolce far niente*, the 'sweet to do nothing,' where the man who does nothing is a distinctive national type, and where the demands of work count far less than the tranquil quest for happiness and pleasure – the *carpe diem* – amid a caressing, gratifying climate. Because the Italian shuns industry with its schedules and organization, whereby past and future prey upon one's thoughts, and also because he remains unaffected by social or utilitarian preoccupations with material riches and conveniences, he is present-minded far beyond his northern counterparts. As if by instinct he ignores work and the false quest for superfluous riches because he realizes that this must lead to more work. 'Save only in money-matters,' writes Stendhal, 'the blandest unconcern with the future is an outstanding characteristic of Italy; every waking thought is taken up with the present moment.' The Italian's immersion in the present is an attempt to preserve the integrity of the *moi* against the order of successive time, which is that of society (and others) on the one hand and of work, or the *projet*, on the other. Living in the immediacy of his present corporeal sensations, the Italian experiences no temporal interval in his response to the external world and is therefore closer to nature than the northerner – this trait being especially characteristic of the Neapolitans, whom Stendhal describes as virtual slaves to momentary sensation. Or as Crouzet puts it, the primacy of the present in Italy is linked to the physical and sensory plenitude experienced by its people. Yet this present is the occasion for the awakening not of sensation alone but of feeling, emotion, passion, as the Italian exemplifies sensibility. His characteristic motto might well be *Sentio ergo sum*: I feel therefore I am. Contrastingly, the Italian shuns thought, as this would shatter his affective plenitude and rob him of immediate oneness with both nature and his own being. Without need to calculate, organize, or economize, or to consider the consequences of his actions, he lacks obligations and responsibilities, which belong to the order of time.[381]

Thus liberated from time, and knowing that the art of enjoyment has no equivalent in the realms of science or work, the Italian gives himself to eroticized pleasures that he enjoys without effort, merely by existing. If the northerner is defined by doing and acting, and devotes himself obsessively to goals and purposes pursued in successive time, the Italian contrastingly stands for tranquil being, and is thus farthest removed from the Faustian preoccupation with *l'avenir*, the *maladie du projet*. The order of the perpetual present is also that of the *imprévu* or uncalculated, as anything can happen where, in disregard of successive time, people surrender freely to the passions and sensations of the moment. The Italian love of gambling, which Stendhal sometimes deplores but which he also finds fascinating as evidence of the national temperament, well expresses the *dolce far niente*, as it betokens the desire to gain money without foresight and effort, as a pure gift of the present – a present of the present, one might say. And because to be liberated from time is also to be exempted from merely utilitarian considerations, the Italian can offer himself freely and immediately to the pure beauty of art, which stands outside of time. Finally, notwithstanding that Italy has a long history embodied in its monuments, its historical identity for Stendhal as for Staël constitutes a kind of illusion, as in their view Italy has neither declined nor progressed over the long term, but has returned again and again to that historical immobility that is its true timeless identity. This is supposedly because its present-minded inhabitants never really complete anything, but are always beginning anew in the freshness of each moment. Accordingly Stendhal is pleased to claim at points that Italy has barely changed since the Middle Ages.[382]

Italy with its special relation to time and work is also the privileged domain of leisure, which the Italians cultivate in subtly differentiated forms. In some instances *dolce far niente* means for Stendhal no more than the *paresse* or idleness in which one experiences the pure sentiment of corporeal existence through one's pleasurable sensations of the environment. This experience is directed outward, with no emotional or reflective or contemplative element, and it does not fit de Grazia's definition of leisure. In *Rome, Naples and Florence*, however, Stendhal says that the 'famous phrase, *dolce far niente*,' which is identified with the Italian way of life, 'should always be understood to imply the delights of voluptuous contemplation inspired by those sensations which possess the soul.' He adds that 'if one day *leisure* should forsake the shores of Italy, if ever Italy should have to work like England, then farewell half her happiness!' According to Stendhal in *Love*, the '*dolce far niente* of the Italians is the pleasure of indulging in the emotions of the soul as one lies languidly upon a divan, a pleasure inconceivable' to active, time-conscious, extroverted people who take no pleasure in solitude. Stendhal adds that this experience is also unavailable to those who 'have nothing in their souls for them to reflect upon.' Thus, though the *dolce far niente* in all its forms affords rich corporeal sensation, it encompasses more varied and prolonged pleasures combining sensation with the contemplation of one's feelings and emotions, and which Stendhal explicitly identifies with the soul. Such moments as these, in which the present seems suspended and 'eternized,' are occasions for both self-formation and self-enjoyment untroubled by time. As Crouzet observes, Stendhal refuses to content himself with mere sensory immediacy or bodily pleasure, as he does not equate these in themselves with happiness. He is more deeply interested in *volupté*, passion, and the *promesse de bonheur*, each of which requires leisure for its fulfilment. Unlike mere sensation, these experiences promise a more serene unity of the *moi*, whereby sensation combines with 'soul' in the sense of emotion and reflection. What Stendhal calls *volupté* means joy or delight, yet it is not as powerful a feeling as passion, which may be directed at a variety of objects, and which in the case of love may lead to tragedy.[383] In Stendhal's characterization passion is a private experience oblivious to time and thus free of social mediations: 'The truly passionate character ... forgets all elegance save that which has become second nature to him.' Likewise, the Italian 'blindly surrenders' to his passion, which 'needs all the energy' of a person's mind. The reverie that Stendhal identifies with Italians and with the experience of Italy consists of the 'tender, solitary,' time-unconscious state within which one loses oneself to passion during one's waking hours. Sometimes he refers to it in its conventional meaning of daydreaming, as when he remarks the Italians' 'habit of daydreaming for hours at a time,' a description consistent with his view of the Italian as a daydreamer. In other instances, reverie promises a more intensely reflective and contemplative experience of the 'soul,' which lifts one out of time, as happened during Stendhal's visits to the Colosseum and St Peter's. To quote *A Roman Journal*, the Colosseum awakens 'Roman revery, which seems so sweet to us and makes us forget all the interests of active life ... depending on how our souls are disposed.' So intensely enjoyable is his immersion in this contemplative state that he would not trade it for the office of 'king of the earth.' In a later passage Stendhal advises the visitor to St Peter's to 'rest and contemplate at leisure the immense void suspended above his head,' adding that in no sense did '*duty*' compel his own admiration of the building. If, for Stendhal, the Midi is the land of both meditation and repose, and Rome the 'abode of quiet contemplation' par excellence, this is partly because, as Crouzet remarks, these are for him timeless settings, where history is stagnant and unmoving, and where one can therefore escape the temporal and social world, as love, art, and spirit flourish there.[384]

Of all the passions nurtured on Italian soil, and whose flowering depends on leisure, Stendhal regards love as the 'strongest.' However, he distinguishes between merely physical love, whose chief aim is immediate sensation and corporeal gratification enjoyed in a transitory discharge of pleasure, and passionate love, which 'has always been rather the infrequent and curious exception than the rule.' Holding out the possibility of the greatest happiness or the greatest misery, passionate love consists of a physical, emotional, and mental state within whose ongoing development time is suspended and prolonged beyond the mere present, and which therefore requires leisure for its unfolding. Hence for Stendhal sexual intimacy is only the final step on the road to happiness, at which point the 'raptures of passionate love have practically effaced the memory of bodily delights.' Like Ezra Pound, Stendhal attributes to the Provençal troubadours the invention of love as an experience transcending immediate physical pleasure, whereby patience and deferral of gratification enable the male lover to advance by degrees through the various stages of love. Just as, with the expansion of the temporal interval between the onset of passion and its fulfilment, the troubadours' beloved was transformed into a spiritual and contemplative as well as sexual object, so the 'language of love' acquired a 'subtlety delicate enough to define the most fleeting shades of feeling.' Occupying a realm outside the normal comprehension of time, passionate love does not 'conform to any rules,' or to anything that 'is in essence calculated and rational.' In short, it rejects successive time, which is inseparable from regulation, calculation, and rationality. The same idea is implicit in Stendhal's observation that love differs from all other desires, which 'have to adapt themselves to cold reality.' For him, true love 'pervades the whole consciousness and fills it with pictures, some wildly happy, some hopeless, but all sublime'; it 'blinds one to everything else in the world,' including time, and leaves the lover without 'interest in anything.' Insofar as, according to Stendhal, passionate love acts 'quite independently of the will,' it apparently circumvents consciousness of time. Again, 'nothing is so interesting as passion; everything about it is so unexpected,' while 'nothing could be duller than mannered love, where everything is calculated.' Passion thus rejects the expectations of society and the other, which belong to the predictable order of successive time rather than to the unexpected or *imprévu*, which belongs to passion. Or as Stendhal puts it, the 'capacity' for love requires leisure 'above all,' and makes a man 'quite incapable of any rational and consecutive undertakings.' Contrariwise, that person suffers a grave misfortune who lacks the 'leisure [necessary] for indulging in a passionate love affair.' At once intense and leisurely, true love inspires in the lover that mood of reverie conducive to soulful contemplation, enabling him to form within his consciousness a multitude of 'pictures' and to meditate upon them.[385]

For Stendhal, art is second only to love in strength among the characteristic Italian passions, and closely resembles it in its causes and effects. As he writes in *Rossini*, 'it is easy to see why Italy, the land of love and of *dolce far niente*, should be at the same time the homeland of art.' To quote *A Roman Journal*, the 'feeling [for art] is [regarded by many as] immoral, for it inclines a man to the seductions of love, it plunges him into laziness.' Like love, art is nourished emotionally on 'sweet leisure' as well as imaginative 'reverie,' the second of which is especially inspired by music. The arts also benefit in Italy from the antisocial attitudes of its people, who instead of embracing the mediated world of society and the other, with its myriad temporal distractions and obligations, take refuge in a timeless realm of leisurely solitude, wherein they cultivate their private feelings and imagination. To quote *Rossini,* people learn to love music 'where *solitude* and *imagination* go hand in hand.'[386] Having few means to occupy his leisure other than the creation of music, as the local economy is stagnant and the government bars him from public life, the Neapolitan composer escapes into solitude and there 'contemplate[s] at length images and impressions formed within his soul ... analyzing every aspect of his emotions.' Yet though the composer has become '*sensually conscious,*' the experience of composition cannot be entirely pleasurable, as it is painful and sorrowful to take the 'plunge into the depths of one's own soul.' Whereas Parisian audiences criticize music as if from a distance, their Italian counterparts abandon themselves entirely to the experience to the point where they lose all sense of time. Unlike the typical Parisian who responds to music with one eye on the rest of the audience, so as to calculate the 'proper' response to a work, the Italian even when part of an audience listens to music as if in solitude, allowing nothing to intrude upon his self-encapsulated and self-elected state of leisurely enjoyment. And since, for Stendhal, all good music appeals immediately to the senses, a work that fails to do so is bound to receive only 'half-hearted appreciation' among the Neapolitans, in whom music provokes an 'immediate and physical nervous reaction.'[387] Yet the impact of music extends beyond the senses, for 'great music is nothing but *our emotion,*' and 'you need a soul in order to feel.' Nor can one forget the contemplative element Stendhal ascribes to music, which induces a 'sensation of pleasure by compelling the imagination to sustain itself temporarily upon a peculiar kind of fantasy.' In stating that 'private self-communion is essential to savor the sublimest charms of music,' he identifies musical experience not only with sensation and emotion but with meditation and thoughts about oneself, and thus assigns it to contemplation.[388]

However much Stendhal extols Italy as the land of leisure, he does not suppose that the majority of Italians enjoy this experience, or are even capable of it, but evaluates their pleasures and enjoyments in terms of a strict hierarchy grounded in the Epicurean concept of true pleasure or enjoyment. When in *Love* he cites Epicurus's view that 'discrimination is necessary to the achievement of true pleasure,' he implicitly challenges the utilitarian and democratic assumption that no real or determinable difference exists among satisfactions, and that pleasure and happiness may be defined simply according to common estimation. What is no less interesting is that Stendhal's hierarchy of pleasure closely resembles that of Sebastian de Grazia. For de Grazia, leisure though in no sense ascetic centres on mental satisfactions actively pursued in contemplative solitude and for themselves. Leisure is thus to be distinguished from what de Grazia calls Cockayne, which he describes as a kind of utopia of the masses, where exclusively somatic or sensory pleasures are enjoyed in a perpetual fleeting immediacy, and whose attractions consist only of taking it easy amid unlimited consumption of material abundance – a kind of fantasy before the fact of the consumer paradise. Stendhal anticipates de Grazia's distinction in his portrait of what Crouzet calls the two Italies, in which the superior is identified more or less with leisure, and in which the inferior, or *l'Italie brute*, remains confined to sensation, and thus holds comparatively little interest for Stendhal. This distinction operates on geographical lines, as it corresponds to the familiar antithesis between northern Italy, identified with civilized refinement, and southern Italy, long denounced for 'African' sensuality and savagery. Succumbing to meridionalist prejudice, Stendhal exemplifies this inferior, brutish Italy in the Neapolitans, for all their attractive qualities.[389]

On the positive side, the Neapolitan stands for *carpe diem* and the rejection of the superfluities of civilization as purchased through needless or painful labour. He experiences intensely the immediacy of gratifying sensations and thus lives pleasurably in the present, in intimate relation with his physical environment. Yet the price of his immersion in the present instant is banishment from culture into animal sensation and appetite. Because the Neapolitan cannot overcome the tyranny of bodily sensation, he remains trapped in a perpetual succession of equally fleeting present moments, void of memory and prevision. The limitation of his experience to the epidermis results in total lack of interiority and capacity for self-reflection, so that he meditates and ruminates on nothing. Being driven by sensation alone, and confined perpetually within the present moment, the Neapolitan lacks real passion, which requires both reflection and gradual development in leisurely contemplation. Although in one instance Stendhal suggests that Neapolitan composers 'contemplate ... the images and impressions' formed within their souls, most Neapolitans appreciate music merely for its 'immediate sensual appeal,' and show little interest in the other arts. Nor, as we have seen, is the Neapolitan capable of more than merely corporeal love, for unlike the Milanese and Romans, he does not reflect upon his feelings, but responds to them appetitively, as an opportunity for fugitive and entirely physical pleasure. Thus Stendhal's Neapolitans call to mind de Grazia's Cockayne, and perhaps not coincidentally the Neapolitans were notorious during the early modern period for their 'Cuccagna,' which was sponsored periodically by the city's rulers as a gift to the Neapolitan people, and which consisted of an enormous scaffolding stocked with all kinds of consumption goods, including bread, cooked meats, cakes and candies, and live animals. It was this paradise of plebeian pleasure that the Neapolitan masses were bidden by their rulers to ransack in what sometimes turned into a bloody and even lethal free-for-all.[390]

Despite Stendhal's appreciation of leisure and the *dolce far niente*, he does not want them to absorb the entire world of work and public affairs, which he recognizes as both impossible and undesirable. 'There are in France fifty thousand women who are wealthy enough to be exempt from all work,' remarks Stendhal in *Love*, adding: 'but where there is no work there is no happiness.' Not only does he appreciate work as a builder of character, as it often involves unpleasant tasks, but he finds in his own labours as a writer, which were motivated partly by economic necessity, a source of enjoyment and self-fulfilment. Stendhal also acknowledges in his Italian writings the undesirability of what he calls *loisir forcé*, the excessive or otiose leisure that contemporary Italians possess and that too often leaves them idle through their inability to use their time worthily. Even those Italians who possess creative imagination often produce their works in the emptiness of '*unwanted leisure,*' as Stendhal describes it. 'Truth to tell,' he writes, 'the *ideal* existence would consist of an active daily life, alternating with intervals of leisure to enjoy that unique and wondrous richness of sensibility which is conjured into being beneath the peerless skies of Rome.' Such a life is devoted not entirely to leisure but, like that favoured by Roman and Italian Renaissance writers, balances *otium* or leisure and *negotium* in the sense of practical and public life, though perhaps as with the Greeks emphasizing the former.[391]

Not only does Stendhal predict the decline of leisure, he attempts to diagnose its causes, and in at least one instance he anticipates the well-known theory of Max Weber's upon which de Grazia also relies in seeking to explain that decline. For Stendhal, perhaps the greatest nemesis of leisure in modernity has been what is often termed the Protestant (or Puritan) ethic, which Weber identified with the English commercial and industrial bourgeoisie, along with those of other Protestant countries, and by which he sought to account theologically for the devotion of that class to such ascetic values as work, discipline, time-saving, impersonality, commercial rationality, and bureaucracy. [392]Although Stendhal does not use Weber's terminology, he is aware of the Protestant ethic from his observations of the English upper-middle class in Italy. As he discovered, they allowed themselves leisure only on Sundays, which, however, they devoted to the Bible. As people of affairs, they preferred money over leisure, and ultimately were left with what little spirit their Bible reading and lack of leisure (*manque de loisir*) permitted. Reminiscent of de Grazia, Stendhal realizes the insufficiency of having an innate gift for leisure, for the right kind of education is also needed in order to develop a taste for it, and if this taste is not developed early it is not likely to develop at all.[393] Stendhal's distrust of the rising class of industrialists and technocrats stems as well from his perception that in winning mass allegiance their ideology must destroy leisure universally by transforming the world into a workhouse. Commenting on Stendhal's visit to a Midlands factory around 1820, Graña remarks that he objected not to capitalist exploitation *per se* but to the worker's loss of happiness, the ineradicable tension between regimented industrial organization and the individual's ability to choose an enjoyably varied life. Stendhal really believed that Neapolitan paupers, having abundant leisure in a caressing climate, were happier than Birmingham labourers.[394] Yet it is a mistake to think that Stendhal sees the expansion of work as the only threat to leisure, for in the case of the salon, the decline proceeds from within. As Marc Fumaroli notes, Stendhal realized that until the French Revolution the Parisian salon was primarily an aristocratic institution dedicated to the art of lighthearted conversation for its own sake. He also knew that, as soon as it had been appropriated by the ascendant post-revolutionary bourgeoisie, the salon had ceased to resemble its former self, having acquired the aspect of a labourious discussion group centred on the gravest public issues. This hijacking of the salon was chiefly engineered by Stendhal's *bête noire* Madame de Staël, which further explains his dislike of her.[395]

If one considers Stendhal's many observations on Britain and the United States, which he rightly regards as spearheads of modern industrialism and commerce, one notes how frequently he links the limitations of the English and Americans not simply to their dutiful work habits but to their attitudes towards time stemming directly from that work-obsession. More than anything else, England is for Stendhal the place where people 'have to work,' and where, to quote the phrase that Stendhal takes the liberty of attributing to none other than Lord Byron, the 'hideous necessity of work appears on every hand.' The English industrial system, he writes in *Rossini*, is perhaps most objectionable because of its claims on workers' time, as witness fourteen-year-old children working sixteen to eighteen hours per day. The young men of England endure the extirpation of their emotions through the demands of the workplace, with the 'appalling necessity of devoting an average of fifteen hours out of every twenty-four to some ungrateful labour.' It is this obligation, remarks

Stendhal in *Love*, that has deprived the English of the *dolce far niente*, whose pleasures are 'inconceivable to those who rush about all day on horseback.' Whereas the Neapolitan makes music and loses himself in the timeless depths of his soul, his English counterpart reads the *Morning Chronicle* and thus remains enslaved to successive time through his all-absorbing interest in business and politics.[396] A direct result of the Englishman's constant need to amass money is the paralysis of his imagination, which can only be cultivated in leisure. While in Rome Stendhal made the acquaintance of the absurdly named (and probably fictitious) American Mr Clinker who, incapable of leisure, found nothing of interest in Roman art and monuments, but discoursed at length upon the speed and cost of canal-building in his native country. As a further indication of the bondage of his consciousness to time and the *projet*, Clinker's conversation focused entirely on money, wills, investments, and other entailments of past and future. Such a person has become what Crouzet terms a 'prisoner of his objects.' The citizen of New York '*does not have the time to feel the beautiful*,' writes Stendhal, 'though he often has the pretention.' Nor have the English and Americans a capacity for love as Stendhal conceives it, that is, as a leisure occupation, for as he says, 'people who pay two thousand workmen at the end of every week do not *waste their time* like this.' Rather 'their minds are always bent on useful and positive things,' the result being that their extreme consciousness of time kills love along with all other possible opportunities for contemplation. In Stendhal's view those who work to become rich are bound to lose 'tender sensations. Little by little the hearts of these gentlemen ossify; things positive and useful possess them utterly, and they lose the capacity for that sentiment [love] which, above all, requires leisure and makes a man quite incapable of any rational and consecutive undertakings.'As Crouzet observes, the northerner works and thinks and plans for the future yet never lives in the present, as he has confined himself unwittingly through deferred gratification to a state of non-being between present and future, while in the exhausting effort to win the objects of his desire he has robbed himself of the ability to enjoy them.[397]

Stendhal again calls to mind de Grazia in attributing the ills of leisure to democracy, towards which Stendhal was ambivalent. Admittedly he overstates his case in arguing that leisure must decline in a democracy because citizens are increasingly robbed of time through absorption in political duties. Although John Stuart Mill envisioned citizenship as a filling up of spare time, it has probably contributed only somewhat to the decline of leisure, as political apathy and absenteeism are common in modern society, especially the United States. Stendhal more perceptively recognizes that democracy, in embracing work, production, and utilitarianism as essential to progress and prosperity, has little use for leisure, and therefore suppresses it in a mood of not very well disguised envy and resentment. Hence Stendhal's mordant observation in *Love* that the man of affairs would surely hate the man of leisure, if only he had the time.[398] Sharing Mill's and Tocqueville's awareness of the often unrecognized opposition between freedom and equality, Stendhal understands that democracy's egalitarian values (whether of the liberal or subsequent mass variety) tend to conformism, and hence hatred of leisure, which from the resentful democratic perspective seems reprehensibly individualistic and elitist. Thus witnessing the assault upon his most cherished values, Stendhal chose to live in Italy, where leisure was still largely unaffected by industrialism, democracy, and a slowly emerging mass society.

III

Despite divergences, some overlap is discernible between de Grazia's critique of contemporary industrial society and leisure and that of the Frankfurt School theorists into the 1960s. Like de Grazia, they recognize the inadequacy of Veblen's concept of leisure, which mistakes the real thing for the conspicuous expenditure of money and material wealth by industrial parvenus and their bourgeois emulators. Offering a totalizing theory of mass society and culture as supposedly uniform or homogeneous, the Frankfurt theorists concur with de Grazia that an absolute division exists between the world of work and what they see as regimented consumption and leisure. For them, the public is gulled and manipulated by producers and advertisers to the point where it has been deprived of its powers of choice and forced to settle for standardized forms of leisure consumption marked out in advance. Indeed, the consumer's attitudes have largely been shaped even before he receives the product and its content. So too, product diversification only disguises mass production. At every turn the possibilities of true leisure, as choice and genuine pleasure, are compromised by capitalist imperatives of work, production, and mass marketing, which integrate the conformist masses within the system. The ascetic values of work and production predominate, while leisure cheats and disappoints. However, for the Frankfurt theorists, the blame lies less with mass democratic politics than with capitalism, from which technology needs to be extricated so as to fulfil its utopian potential – a possibility rejected by de Grazia.[399]

Confirmation of de Grazia's analysis of the fortunes of leisure under industrialism appears in writings by American and European leisure theorists from the late 1940s into the 1970s. The vast majority of commentators on leisure during these decades regard it as having emerged in modernity with the industrial system, which led for the first time to a rigid differentiation between work and leisure. Yet they define leisure not in de Grazia's terms, as a state of being apart from clock time, but in an antithetical and determinate relation to work measured by the clock. For them, leisure consists of discrete and calculable blocks of discretionary 'free time' left over from work and apart from job obligations. It is valued not for its own sake but extrinsically, as an industrial instrument. Its purpose is fundamentally recreative, relaxing and recuperating individuals so that they can perform effectively at work. Additionally it functions as social control. For Joffre Dumazedier, work and leisure form an indissoluble unity in technical civilization. Free-time activities and amusements are assumed by most leisure theorists to consist of diverse types, rather than being judged by high cultural standards of contemplative leisure. As H. Douglas Sessions puts it, de Grazia's concept of leisure defines it essentially as an attitude, which is hard to 'operationalize.' Despite earlier predictions that more free or so-called 'leisure' time would result from increasingly sophisticated machines, leisure theorists of these decades admit that such expectations have been disappointed. In analyses similar to de Grazia's, they show that the twentieth-century industrial system has led to a scarcity of time, partly because of an increasingly hectic and interrupted life-tempo but also because of consumption needs driven by demands for ever higher living standards. Thus people work more to buy more, and shopping takes time as well. Even where free time has increased, it is reinvested in job-related activities or other paid work. The leisure theorists also focus on the organization of leisure, noting that, whereas in totalitaritan nations this task is undertaken by the state, capitalist nations normally consign it to the free market, including advertising; however, the United States government had sought actively to organize leisure during the Depression, and unions sometimes adopt a similar policy. Although Dumazedier, a writer of socialistic background and tendencies, regards the USSR as excessively authoritarian, he not only praises its government-organized leisure programs but envisions the increasing bureaucraticization of leisure in the liberal West, seeing it as a matter of public policy and planning. Psychologists would also have to intervene.[400]

The persistent inability of most commentators to comprehend free

time as it has existed in traditional societies is exemplified in Martin
Clark's study of modern Italy, in which he claims that, after the Risorgimento, the relatively impoverished Italians could enjoy few leisure pursuits for lack of time and money. It must be kept in mind that, for Clark,
leisure and free time are interchangeable. Unlike industrial England,
where the proletariat was winning periodic wage increases, and where
periodicals promoted leisure of various kinds, Italians had only traditional feast days, wine-shops (which cost money), ball games like *bocce*
and *pallone*, and brothels. Clark thus falls into the category de Grazia
mentions, of writers who, because they identify free time with the spending of money, cannot imagine that the poor people of the past ever possessed free time. And yet Clark undermines his whole argument: 'Above
all,' he writes, 'there was [in Italy of this period] much free, or almost
free entertainment to be had on the streets, as anyone who has walked
round, say, Naples, will appreciate.' What Clark fails to mention is that
the spectacle of crowded, active, diverting Italian street scenes – which,
as he observes, exists in parts of Italy to this day – is possible only because
many Italians possessed if not the higher form of leisure then the abundant free time he imagines the absence of industrialism to have denied
them. As an example of what was 'not available' to nineteenth-century
Italians, Clark mentions Blackpool and Llandudno, seaside holiday resorts whose names sound concocted respectively in a spirit of Dicken-
sian and Swiftian ugliness, and to which English factory hands were then
'already flocking' – as if these places, with their commercialized mass
entertainment, mechanized amusements, and industrialized multitudes,
could substitute for the anarchic, spontaneous, mischievous, and voluptuous hedonism of Naples' *dolce far niente.*[401]
    Nor can one agree with Clark's claim that, 'with greater prosperity' in
the twentieth century, Italians 'had more leisure,' and 'some had it in
abundance.' Actually, the Italians' cherished leisure was being degraded
to mere 'free time.' A historian with revisionist Marxist leanings, Clark believes that modern Italians most desperately needed leisure in the sense
of after-work occupations requiring expenditure of money, frequent reliance on gadgets, and use of modern communications and organized
consciousness: magazines, newspapers, radio, and advertising. Clark also
supposes that the Italians, whose hatred of routine has long been noted,
required organized mass leisure, or what Dr Johnson terms 'schemes of
merriment.' Clark therefore has kind words for Mussolini's Dopolavoro
(After-Work) program, a successful attempt to determine and direct the
'leisure time' of the Italian masses. Insisting that these activities were

'recreative fun' (read preparation for more work), Clark observes enthusiastically that Dopolavoro marked the 'first time in Italian history that mass leisure activities existed, let alone been encouraged and subsidized by politicians.' If anything, such an event is a cause for lament that the Italians, under a totalitarian dictator, had betrayed their native traditions of leisure – selling their birthright for a mess of 'fun' and 'free time.'[402]

Another reason for Stendhal's continuing importance as a philosopher of leisure is that he exemplifies and illuminates what in the transition from the nineteenth into the twentieth century was probably the single most important development within modern leisure, namely tourism. Not only did Stendhal coin the word 'tourist,'[403] but he was himself a tourist intermittently over many years, primarily in Italy but also in England, Germany, and France. (This is not the place to discuss whether he ought to be described as a tourist or traveller, the latter being for many the more honorific term). Stendhal's works also contain an unsystematic theory of tourism that was largely worked out through his experience of Italy. This theory is continuous with his ideas of leisure, whose presuppositions it shares, and it also affords a basis by which to evaluate modern tourism, which Stendhal saw only in its embryonic form but whose main trends he anticipated and judged as it were before the fact.

As with leisure, Stendhal sees tourism as something valuable for its own sake rather than as recreation or as the fulfilment of a preconceived cultural duty. The former would reduce it to an instrumentality, while the latter would rob it of freedom by making it obligatory. Since Stendhal regards tourism as a self-forming activity, it must also be self-elected and active rather than passive. As for travel preparations, he read many books on Italian subjects both before and during his visits to Italy, yet he did so out of interest rather than obligation, and his reading enjoined no specific program or programmed response. Shunning calculation and system, which necessarily entail temporal preoccupations, his favoured form of tourism was tranquil and unhurried, characterized typically by long sojourns at preferred sites as well as by complete immersion within them so as to banish any interrupting awareness of time or necessity. Consistent with his abhorrence of calculation Stendhal greatly values the experience of the novel or *imprévu*, the unexpected, which he finds typical of touristic experience in Italy. In general, he is much more interested in intensities of pleasure than in comfort, which may be characterized as the least common denominator of pleasure, and which lends itself far more readily to utilitarian and collectivistic schemes of regulated felicity. Yet for Stendhal, pleasure does not exclude the choice of strenuous and even painful effort, should a tourist elect it, and in any case the highest object of tourism is not physical pleasure alone but the accompanying emotional and spiritual satisfactions of love and aesthetic contemplation.

Many writers on tourism stress its novelty as a distinctly modern phenomenon marked by increasing industrial and technical organization as well by the inclusion of ever larger segments of the population. It is also a commonplace of the history of tourism that, unlike the traditional 'traveller,' the mass tourist first appeared in the later nineteenth century, soon acquired his current reputation for unprecedented conformism, Philistinism, and vulgarity, and gradually came to represent the 'tourist' generally. Despite these standard views, Maxine Feifer and Lynne Withey seem to think that tourism has remained essentially the same since the Middle Ages and even Roman times. Not only did mass tourism exist in earlier periods but, like his or her successor, the ancient tourist was vilified for herd-like passivity and lack of culture.[404] Unfortunately, such arguments ignore the extent to which modern tourism depends on mass society and technology. Like modern totalitarianism, which, by virtue of modern technical inventions, far surpasses earlier forms of authoritarianism in its capacity to invade, pervade, and control society, modern mass tourism could only exist through modern communications and the superior organization made possible by a sophisticated technical civilization. And it is this technical apparatus that insures that tourism in the modern context greatly differs from anything preceding.[405]

If one acknowledges that travel has changed significantly in the last two centuries, one does not want to idealize the eighteenth-century Grand Tour. Since these travellers were primarily aristocrats without need of employment, their activity cannot be characterized as recreative preparation for work, and yet it is wrong to think that they therefore embodied leisure in de Grazia's sense. Turner and Ash fault the travellers' frequent lack of culture, curiosity, and insight. Ideally conceived as a cultural and educational enterprise, the Grand Tour sometimes reached its climax in the fleshpots of Italian cities rather than in their monuments and works of art, to which many visitors gave but a passing nod. Yet on the whole, English visitors rarely mingled with foreigners, including Italians, but preferred the familiarity of their compatriots' company. Although Graham Smith characterizes the typical Grand Tourist as self-directed, this seems not to have been so. Rather, the Grand Tour was already exhibiting the conformism and routinization typical of later periods of travel, as many travellers followed almost unthinkingly a prescribed route or 'beaten track' linking the standard urban sites.[406]

Following the defeat of Napoleon in 1815 Continental Europe was opened up for the first time to ever-increasing tides of English (and American) upper-middle and middle-class travellers who, having grown wealthy through commerce and industry, sought a vacation (often with their families) from the workplace. Social display and the prestige value of travel motivated them as well. According to Erik Cohen, never had so many people travelled to foreign countries for pleasure. The beaten track of the eighteenth-century Grand Tour was largely maintained, and like their aristocratic predecessors British middle-class tourists tended to move in herd-like groups. These were the people whom Stendhal saw in Italy and whom he excoriated for their grim joylessness and incapacity for leisure – a portrait John Pemble finds accurate. In similar fashion Byron initiated the English version of 'antitourism,' bitterly lamenting that the Grand Tour had been invaded by the bourgeoisie. As these travellers were mainly Protestants raised on an ascetic work ethic, and as they had therefore valued industry, orderliness, and organization throughout their lives, they were troubled by the prospect of varied pleasure and an abundance of free time in Italy. This explains why prospective travellers were often exhorted to prepare diligently for their trip abroad, and why so many subjected themselves to highly demanding courses of reading before departure, as if to lend to their free time the moral legitimacy of work. Indeed, Stendhal's *Promenades dans Rome* (*A Roman Journal*) was disparaged for lacking the degree of historic study that Rome, more than any other city, required. Apparently believing that leisure lacks its own justification, and cannot exist for its own sake, many middle-class travellers justified their vacation from work by turning it into an occasion for further work in the form of travel writing. The completed travel book, as the product of their labour, assuaged the guilt of otherwise troubling inactivity. The rise of middle-class tourism coincided as well with the increasing routinization and conformism of modern touristic experience, as it was during the mid-nineteenth century that such compendious guidebooks as Baedeker's and Murray's became standard accompaniments of informed travel. The appeal of these characteristic products of the burgeoning tourist industry lay partly in their meticulously careful day-to-day planning, which left little to chance and thus economized the traveller's precious time. The traveller now had a predictable and, if he wished, punishingly detailed itinerary of conventional sights along with cues as to how to respond to them. Increasingly there were complaints of

travellers filing slavishly through museums in what Graham Smith calls
'an inflexible regimen of forced marches.' For many, travel consisted not
of exploration and discovery of the novel but of the recognition of the
already familiar. It also tended to become dutiful or necessary labour, as
the traveller, his initiative provided less by himself than by his guidebook,
rushed from site to site in a frenetic effort to check off every item in an
approved list. Such an experience, time-ridden, minimally self-directed,
and virtually indistinguishable from work, could only be mechanical and
superficial. Contemplation was driven out by restless activity, while the
means of travel, mere locomotion, frequently swallowed up its ends.[407]

This is not to imply that that nineteenth-century aristocrats were necessarily in a better position than the bourgeoisie to appreciate leisure
in Italy. Writing in 1837, Lady Blessington in the title of her best-known
book characterizes herself as *The Idler in Italy*, of which Maxine Feifer observes uncritically that it 'expressed a mood of perfect leisure, the mark
of the aristocrat, since "leisure" was only for those who could command
their own time.' Evidently Lady Blessington lacks the middle-class obsession with justifying leisure by turning it into work, yet she does not grasp
leisure in the classical sense, since for her leisure consists not of self-
formation or contemplation but of doing nothing, the idleness of the
dolce far niente, which for her has meaning only with work as its antithesis.
She thus dissociates the 'delicious habits of the *dolce far niente*,' which 'engenders' a 'dreamy sort of reverie,' during which the 'book or the pen is
often thrown down,' from the activities of those young Englishmen who
come to Italy and 'read attentively, compare places with the descriptions
given of them in history, and make themselves well-acquainted with the
policy of the country, its laws and constitution,' all of which classically
minded observers might regard as worthy leisure pursuits in themselves,
but which, Lady Blessington observes approvingly, the Englishmen regard as a source of 'much useful information to fit them for a future
career of utility in the senate at home.' One has a choice, then, only
between the 'effeminate pleasure' of mere indolence, the book and pen
abandoned, and a strenuous useful life of public affairs; leisure in the
classical sense of a state of being *and* activity is not entertained as a possibility. That Lady Blessington implicitly distinguishes between *dolce far
niente* and contemplative leisure is also evident in her observation that
the former 'excludes the brave and sober reflection so essential to the
formation of an elevated mind, or to the support of a well-directed one.'
Rather it results in mere daydreaming, which she calls 'a dreamy sort of
reverie.' If anything, Lady Blessington anticipates the current popular

idea of Italian travel as a mere vacation or taking it easy, that is, not real leisure but a grateful refuge from work, as witness her description of Italy as the 'country to which a person borne down by care, or overwhelmed by business, should resort.' Not only is this 'voluptuous region ... ill suited' to things of the mind, but 'to live' is 'so positive an enjoyment' in Italy that the 'usual motives and incentives' to activity are forgotten amid the 'enervating and dreamy enjoyment.'[408]

Although some contend that mass tourism began with the middle-class influx after 1815, pushed by advances in railroad and steamboat transportation, and although the bourgeoisie sometimes prompted anti-touristic sentiments, the beginnings of mass tourism more plausibly trace to mid-century, when the success of Cook's Tours signalled a major expansion of the tourist industry. These were cheap, meticulously organized, and dependable package tours pitched to a middle- or lower-middle-class clientele claiming for the first time its right to enjoy travel – not as individuals or family members, but as members of contracted groups. Soon the mass tourist became the vilified type of the modern tourist, whom other tourists feared most to resemble. Ignorance, passivity, and conformity were commonly associated with mass tourists, who struck their better-heeled counterparts as a commonplace herd pursuing sameness and predictability. The superficiality of their experiences was often assumed, as was their unthinking susceptibility to advertising and inability to appreciate any aspect of travel save locomotion and accommodations. The first Cook's Tour to Italy took place in 1864. By the end of the nineteenth century, notes John Urry, mass tourism was highly systematized. English seaside resorts such as Blackpool were setting the pace for mass tourism, serving as playgrounds for the working class of the mill towns, and thus exemplifying the modern dissociation of leisure-space from the workplace. To quote Adrian Franklin, the seaside resorts afforded tourists a 'world of leisure and consumerism in which new technologies would liberate the human condition.' The democratization of tourism has continued in the twentieth century, gaining powerful impetus after World War II, to the point of becoming a standard feature of global life. It is generally assumed that industrialized tourism on a large scale provides relief from the stress and strain of modern life and more especially work.[409]

IV

The value of de Grazia's critique and those of other mid-century analysts of modern leisure may seem to have much diminished with the advent of postmodern or postindustrial society, which some believe to have witnessed major changes in work, leisure, and tourism, including public attitudes towards them. It has been claimed that work has lost both popularity and importance by comparison with leisure, which in this context is to be understood as free time. As Gary Cross shows, from the mid-nineteenth century onward the central demand of organized labour in the United States as in Britain and France has been the reduction of work hours to allow for increased free time on weekends and paid vacations; this goal was realized through labour legislation in the early twentieth century, when the eight-hour day became standard. From the nineteenth century onward the Protestant work ethic, once the core of life's value and meaning, has been giving way to a 'culture of consumption' called into existence by the need of the capitalist system to find leisure-time consumers for the ever more abundant products of its matured industrial plant. There has also been an ever-increasing need for members of the workforce to escape from industrial routine and monotony by means of consumable free-time thrills and amusements, which industry, business, and advertising have hastened eagerly to satisfy. Despite his portrait of a work-driven society, de Grazia had noted some signs of hostility to work, and in 1979 Alex Inkeles observed a decline in the American work ethic. According to Jacques Ellul, interest in work declined in the United States from 1960 to 1980, when workers showed slackened speed and commitment. Their lack of motivation, which employers tried to correct, adversely affected growth and productivity while causing ethical and disciplinary problems. It has been estimated that free time increased by 10 per cent between 1965 and 1975. By this point leisure theorists such as David Riesman and Daniel Bell had predicted a postindustrial society marked by increased leisure; others envisioned advanced capitalist society as the 'leisure society.' These predictions were often accompanied by the claim that faster machines would save time and enable people to live more leisurely, relaxed lives. Industrial growth, bureaucratic rationalization, and social progress were seen as key factors in the coming reduction of work. Writing in 1979, Dean MacCannell argued that, having been pushed by modern social movements to the 'negative margins of existence,' work and its organization had become merely an 'attribute' of society rather than its 'central' feature. As the industrial epoch concluded, and as workers received more freedom, the Marxian emphasis on work and production lost relevance. Life was expected to be 'fun,' and work failed to mount a 'counteroffensive,' noted MacCannell. Now people increasingly affirmed social values not in work but in leisure, which offered all that work no longer seemed capable of providing: creativity, regeneration, personal satisfaction, self-fulfilment. Leisure was coming to be seen as the site of the authentic, the place, to quote Rojek, where we are ourselves. Alienated from work, people concentrated on lifestyle, a leisure activity often involving increased levels of consumption. Thus production and work further diminished as social values. Not only was creativity identified with leisure rather than with industry, but some envisioned a fusion of work with leisure, so that work would provide more than just economic rewards, and leisure would become productive. Confirming MacCannell's observations, Ellul notes that industrialism is no longer the essence of society, and Urry sees work as dwindling in importance by comparison. More recently Richard Florida finds that many Americans are dissatisfied with routinized and alienating work, especially mass production, and that they willingly give up higher pay in exchange for forms of work which seem to them expressive or 'creative.' These often involve production of cultural rather than utilitarian goods, and exemplify the postmodern intermingling of work with arts, design, and stylization.[410]

Postmodernism and postindustrialism are characterized by major changes not only in the relation of work to leisure but within society, economy, and culture. In its earlier and now superseded form, often termed 'Fordism,' industry followed comparatively rigid and inflexible methods and schedules whose standardized products were valued less for their symbolic or aesthetic or cultural value than for their material utility. Whether conceived by marketing agents or social critics, the individual consumer was assumed questionably to belong to a conformist mass that, incapable of real choice and thus easily manipulable by advertisers, passively received the industrial products assigned to it. With the industrialization and standardization of entertainment or popular culture, it too acquired a mass character, as audiences were manipulated by advertisers into passive acceptance of the products of the so-called culture industry. Yet since work predominated as a social value, only limited amounts of leisure or rather 'free time' were available for these programmed forms of material and cultural consumption. This homogenization and massification of economy and culture inspired Marcuse's description of the modern individual as a denuded 'one-dimensional man.' Contrastingly, the post-Fordist era emergent after World War II has been characterized by much more rapid, fluid, and flexible methods and schedules of industrial production (and advertising) by which it is now possible to offer more individuated patterns of consumption through product differentiation and market segmentation techniques. It is now assumed that consumers buy products for personal or individual reasons that producers, service industries, and advertisers can ignore only at their own cost. The development of more flexible industrial techniques has made it possible to invest products previously valued chiefly for material utility with imagistic, symbolic, and cultural values – in short, commodity aesthetics conjoined with increasing amounts of free time. Besides betokening the convergence of consumption and leisure, these new aestheticized products are valued for their cultural significance as manifest in the amount of 'experience' they deliver. As such, they afford postmodern individuals with perhaps their chief free-time opportunity to express symbolically their personal identity and values, since the individual's lifestyle typically revolves around consumption preferences. Indeed, by the later twentieth century, Juliet B. Schor notes, shopping had become the chief cultural activity in the United States – a classic instance of the postmodern blurring between leisure and other pursuits. Because postmodernism and postindustrialism have assigned special value to individuality, heterogeneity, plurality, and freedom of choice, especially as they relate to the consumer, it is increasingly hard to think of society and culture as a monolithic and homogenized structure imposed by capitalism, as with earlier theories of mass society. Some critics, moreover, stress the importance as sites of resistance to social and cultural conformism of heterogeneous subcultures already existing in the industrial age. Whereas industrial society had observed a distinction between high and popular culture, as well as that between high art and the economic and social spheres, both high and low art are now absorbed into the society and economy through the power not only of commodity aesthetics but of the media, including news, television, film, magazines, and advertising. Having become components of both production and consumption, art and culture can no longer claim autonomy where life itself has become aestheticized. The distinction between high and low art has also broken down, and is largely ignored by consumers and the media. An irony of the contemporary culture of consumption is that Stendhal has been enlisted to advance it: for every person who has read his novels, there are countless more who, ignorant of them, have bought the perfume and toiletry articles bearing his name.[411]

As a highly important form of leisure, making up forty per cent of available free time, and possibly the largest industry in the world, tourism is said to have changed significantly in the transition from a modern to a postmodern or postindustrial society, to the point where, in its contemporary form, it is regarded by many as characteristic of postmodernity itself. During the rise of mass tourism in the later nineteenth century, the typical tourist was dismissed as a de-individualized entity who could only submit to the programmed choices offered by travel agents. The seemingly passive, herd-like behaviour of the mass tourist awakened derision among cultured observers. At the same time, mass tourism and the mass marketing that accompanied it exemplified the totalizing claims of industrial modernity, which, with its inflexible production methods and schedules, found it costly and hence difficult to accommodate differentiation. In postmodernity, however, not only have many tourists rejected the idea of being part of a mass, demanding to be treated as individuals with distinctive interests and needs, but post-Fordist innovations in technology and production have individualized tourism as never before. Although mass tourism, that is, the package tour, has by no means disappeared, the characteristic forms of the so-called new tourism are neither packaged nor standardized. Whereas formerly tourist agencies offered the tourist only a few categories and 'images' to choose from, the range of choices is now highly diversified. Many agencies and advertisers pitch not to mass markets but to segmented ones or 'niches' consisting of targeted individuals whose similar yet special demands they seek to satisfy. There is also considerable customization as the tourist industry attempts to accommodate alternative tourisms and their discourses.[412]

Notwithstanding claims advanced for the arrival of a postmodern age in which the traditional work ethic yields significant ground to claims of leisure, such optimism seems questionable. In an essay anthologized in 1974, a leisure theorist found it unlikely that postindustrial society would be based on anything but clock time. Somewhat over two decades after de Grazia's analysis, Turner and Ash held that 'although people want more leisure, they work harder than they would ideally choose, to save the money necessary to allow them to spend their leisure time in sufficient style.' One recalls de Grazia's point that contemporary leisure is compromised by work and consumption, as the need to earn the money required for free-time spending leads to loss of leisure through compulsive overwork. In *The Technological System*, published in 1980, Jacques Ellul rejected the term 'post-industrial' to describe modern society on the grounds that people still work, and that the phrase 'technological society' more accurately refers to the dominant factor of the present era. Far from having lost its laboriousness through technology, as many had predicted, work had become harder and more exhausting thanks to the increased speeds and services demanded not by the capitalist but by the machine itself, including the computer. A decade later Ellul repeated these arguments, noting that though people worked less, their work was more pressured than ever. In *The Overworked American* (1991) Judith B. Shor scrutinized the consensus view that capitalism had increased leisure and discovered a vast expansion of human effort. True, work hours have declined since about 1850, but in the post-war period they began to climb again – developments also noted by de Grazia. Despite predictions in the 1950s that work would disappear, time on the job expanded from the late 1960s into the 1990s. There were fewer vacations, pay was reduced, and, as people had to do more work for less pay, the stress of work intensified. The increase in work hours reflected the desire of employers for more output and their unwillingness to trade leisure for work. Workers were on the consumerist treadmill de Grazia describes, working increased hours so as to purchase more goods for the sake of style and status. As Gary Cross shows, before World War II the typical American worker rejected free time in favour of money that he or she could earn only through extra work and whose purpose was to maintain or increase the worker's level of consumption. This so-called work-and-spend cycle, triggered psychologically partly by the trauma of the Depression, was promoted by advertising driven in turn by the need to clear the market of the products of a mass consumption economy. Not surprisingly, during the last several decades social critics have often complained of the inauthenticity of leisure, as it has become continuous and even interchangeable with consumption. Despite labour-saving devices, even housework expanded to fill available time, and also to satisfy higher standards of cleanliness pushed by advertisers.[413]

The rise of postmodernism and postindustrialism required leftist critics, including the Frankfurt School and its offshoots, to reposition themselves within a changing culture. Not only had the Frankfurt School identified modernity with mass culture and conformist homogeneity, as if consumers were universally brainwashed, but it had dismissed the leisure satisfactions and cultural distractions afforded by capitalist consumerism as factitious means of maintaining an essentially repressive and ascetic system kept alive through class inequalities and workplace injustices. In order to avoid the absorption of art into so compromising a regime, and despite a theoretical commitment to the avant-garde goal of liberating modern society through the 'desublimation' of art, which was seen as coinciding ideally with the end of art's autonomy upon its immediate sensory transformation of the social world, the Frankfurt School (like the avant-garde itself) chose for strategic reasons to valorize high art, the autonomy of the art object, and formally difficult and challenging art-works as against the satisfying or immediately pleasurable, for in this way art would continue to play a critically adversarial role against injustice and oppression.[414] The postmodern thus posed major difficulties for the Frankfurt School in that, in a kind of general desublimation, the repressive and ascetic features of mass culture were yielding to a consumeristic, hedonistic society of increasing free time. The standardizing and utilitarian features of the older mass production had been replaced by a more differentiated and personalized consumerism, whereby the product was invested with symbolic, cultural, and artistic qualities, and whereby consumption became an expression of personal identity. Even the more unusual kinds of alterity were domesticated thanks to diversified product marketing. As commodities became aestheticized, art was commodified by advertising and the media. The distinction between high and low art having collapsed, art was expected to provide its audiences with immediate pleasure, through expression rather than form. Deprived of its autonomy and absorbed within the system of production and consumption, art had surrendered its critical-adversarial edge. Not only had the avant-garde declined through age, but the eclipse of the bourgeoisie had robbed adversarial art of its traditional foil. And so, to quote Russell Berman, the *promesse de bonheur* had 'lost its credibility.' Although it might appear superficially that the avant-garde dream of the desublimation of art and aestheticization of everyday life had eventuated, thus ending the autonomy of the 'organic' work of art, the Frankfurt critics held that the dream had been co-opted, as in their view the new enjoyments promoted not true freedom but subjection to capitalism. Life-style, again to quote Berman, had become a 'dumping ground' for overproduction, with which leisure and consumption were thoroughly integrated.[415] Not only did Marcuse call for a return to the concept of the autonomy of art, but he used the term 'repressive desublimation' to describe what he saw as the capitalist strategy of superficially alleviating the mechanisms of social oppression through added allowances of leisure and pleasure only so as to impose those mechanisms more effectively and insidiously. Amid these developments Marcuse remained somewhat more hopeful than his colleagues towards the liberating possibilities of technology, which he believed to hold utopian potential only if rescued from capitalist misuse: 'Utopian possibilities are inherent in the technical and technological forces of advanced capitalism and socialism: the rational utilization of these forces on a global scale would terminate poverty and scarcity within a very foreseeable future.'[416]

Similar arguments regarding the fate of leisure echo in leftist writings over the last several decades. Frederic Jameson contends that commodification has submerged all aspects of existence, including aesthetic judgment and consumer choice. Turner and Ash claim that leisure now functions to expel and control 'subterranean' forces so as to protect capitalism itself. No more than a safety valve, leisure enables people to discharge potentially subversive energies through holidays, festivals, sports, etc. According to Rojek, Neo-Marxists reject the theory that postmodern society and economy afford greater choice, flexibility, spontaneity, and self-determination. For them, leisure perpetuates capitalist society, creates the illusion of freedom, and provides surrogate satisfactions for mass audiences – all because leisure products are commodified with the aim of expanding capital. Rojek further objects that under capitalism leisure really prolongs work, as it amounts to a coping and recuperating mechanism. Another of his complaints is that capitalism reduces leisure to a 'performative' activity in that it serves not only to signify symbolically a person's social status but also to fulfil the performance requirements of the capitalist system, which uses leisure to revive the exhausted worker. More recently Lauren Langman and Katie Cangemi dismiss the shift from mass society to more individualistic forms of leisure and consumption, seeing in the latter only commodified forms of pseudo-individualism comfortably integrated within the rationalistic framework of capitalistic culture and society.[417]

If Jacques Ellul's assessment of modern leisure is far more bleak (and convincing) than that of the Frankfurt School and other leftists, it is chiefly because he does not regard technology as a neutral and subordinate instrumentality whose apparent failings will be converted to utopian ends once it has been detached from capitalism and placed under a 'humane' socialism. In Ellul's view, Marcuse's and Baudrillard's acceptance of this unrealistically hopeful evaluation of technology substantially weakens their reading of the postmodern situation – a criticism that extends equally to statements by Dumazedier. Being indifferent to ideology and whatever social or political system within which it happens to function, argues Ellul, technology follows and imposes its own norms and imperatives, which include efficiency, standardization, economy, speed, predictability, self-augmentation, and self-integration. As technology expands, its norms gradually become the socially decisive ones, and finally there exists a technological society and system. In Ellul's unapologetically (and unfashionably) totalizing interpretation, all significant choices are situated increasingly in relation to, and are largely dictated by, technological requirements. Likewise, all major activities including education are dominated by the overriding goal of the technicization or technological adaptation of the individual so as to insure his or her efficient, uncritical integration within the encompassing technological environment. The end result of this universalizing process is a single, because technological, model of life. According to Ellul, technology has been the determining factor since 1960.[418]

Given these premises, Ellul offers a dispiriting evaluation of modern work, education, and leisure. To be sure, he concurs with the Marxist Henri Lefebvre and other writers that modern technology produces diversification and individuality, but he does not conclude hopefully that technology is a heterogenous system holding real possibilities of freedom and personal choice. The error is to suppose that to be totalizing the system must impose conformity and identity, in the manner of the earlier, cumbersome industrial standardization. Actually, the current system is sufficiently flexible as a totality to allow for differences and subsystems, but only those that are compatible with the system and its demands. As the system gets bigger, its computer networks achieve greater integration. Not only does Ellul describe contemporary mass production and consumption as reflecting technology's universalizing imperatives, he speaks of technology as shaping what he does not hesitate to call mass culture. This culture, the underlying reality behind the 'pseudo-diversity of means' and choices proffered by technology, and which are themselves of an overwhelmingly technological character, nullifies both reflection and the communication of humanistic knowledge, as it is absorbed in and by technological ways of thinking. Insofar as all choices are technological or determined by technology, there is no real choice, despite seemingly diverse possibilities. At the same time, the aetherealization and invisibility to which technology aspires well conceal humanity's bondage to it.[419]

Within this system leisure can only be a technological problem, like everything else. Leisure does not exist for its own sake but to adapt humanity to technology, to integrate the individual within its system and to provide him or her with the satisfactions and motivations that enable one to live within a technological universe. 'The organization of spare-time activities,' writes Ellul, 'is mainly a technological task, requiring a high degree of technicity to achieve satisfactory results, i.e. results giving a full impression of leisure and seemingly effacing the technological imperative.' And 'if there is leisure, it is a function of the time that man gains by developing technological means. And these spare-time activities must, in turn, be organized along technological processes.' For all the talk of customized consumption, the segmented markets are technically calculated so as to ensure predictability, and Ellul is well aware of life-style research. Advertising, essential to the normalization and mystification of leisure, is itself a form of technology serving mass production and technological growth. The spare time afforded by technology is largely devoted to escape from the world of work and technological automatism, which humanity hopes to palliate and compensate through leisure. Yet though the 'true state' of leisure is revealed as the ' making up for compulsory submission to the automatism of technological progress,' the technicized individual's absorption into those processes guarantees the 'impossibility' of 'profound experience' in leisure, which can only amount to a distraction, the 'institution of an emptiness.' Ellul will not commit the 'normal mistake' of confusing contemporary 'spare time' with the 'games, fun, palaver, the *dolce far niente*, the relaxations of traditional societies' – the very things that delighted Stendhal in Italy. Finding himself 'forced to state' that contemporary leisure lacks the 'same value' as those enjoyments, Ellul adds that 'it is impossible to "garnish" empty time with such activities, as they cannot be reproduced in our new [technicized] environment.' What passes for leisure is no more than the safety valve or respirator of the technological system, giving the illusion of escape from it. And this, it should be added, Ellul finds equally true of modern tourism as a characteristic form of leisure. The respiratory vacations, holidays, weekend trips, etc., these are escapes into false freedom, disguised means of technological adaptation. What it all means is 'reduction to a single pattern of trivialized life.'[420]

V

The post-war critique of modern tourism owes much to the analysis of Daniel Boorstin, notwithstanding that his arguments often clash with those of later prognosticators of tourism of the new, improved, individuated, and postmodern type. In a well-known formulation of 1964 Boorstin posits an essential distinction between the traveller and the tourist. Typical of the nineteenth century, and largely phased out in the twentieth, the traveller calls to mind the origins of the word 'travel' in the French *travail*, meaning work. He or she is a self-directed individual for whom travel involves active serious effort akin to work and to whom it affords the fruit of authentic experience, a penetrating and primarily intellectual encounter with unfamiliar aspects of the visited territory.

The tourist by contrast emerges with the mass tourism of the nineteenth century, most notably Cook's Tours, and dominates tourism in the twentieth, especially after the increased commercialization and massification of travel around 1950. The tourist is essentially a pleasure-seeker and conformist whose experience of travel remains passive and superficial, without intellectual satisfactions. Not only does he allow his trip to be organized and routinized by travel agencies, but he relies slavishly on guidebooks such as Baedeker's, which Boorstin accuses, as he accuses the tourist industry generally, of reducing tourism to the pursuit of the familiar and expected. What most troubles Boorstin in twentieth-century tourism is the creation by the tourist industry of what he terms the 'environmental bubble' and the 'pseudo-event.' Taken together, these consist of the many artificially constructed barriers, including airports, highways, hotels, shopping centres, and American Express offices, by which the industry encapsulates the tourist against the possibility of immediate and novel experience in a foreign country. Boorstin's contempt for the mass tourist culminates in his description of him or her as a willing gull, a person who actually prefers fake experience, and wants his false expectations to be fulfilled. To be sure, Boorstin's complaints are not altogether original, having been anticipated at least as early as 1869. If one considers Boorstin's ideas from de Grazia's viewpoint, one discerns in him a residual puritanism and asceticism typical of those reluctant to appreciate leisure for its own sake. Thus in arguing that travel be defined properly as a form of work rather than the mere pursuit of pleasure, he resembles those nineteenth-century American Protestant travellers who needed to justify their unaccustomed leisure by filling it with the work of writing or other arduous tasks.[421]

Notwithstanding their reliance on a Marxist-Freudian vocabulary, Turner and Ash's *The Golden Hordes* (1975) is indebted to Boorstin and perhaps Ellul in its almost uniformly negative evaluation of the tourist industry and experience as in its rejection of the emerging postmodern attempt to vindicate modern tourism as an assertion and expression of personal identity. Turner and Ash acknowledge that leisure (or 'nonwork,' as they correctly define it) has become increasingly important, especially with the growing popularity of travel, and yet they characterize tourism as another form of industrialization, an unpleasant truth that the travel industry does its best to conceal. Unimpressed by the claim that mass society has ended, Turner and Ash see the individual tourist as a member of a smaller mass targeted by the tourist industry. The typically passive and manipulated tourist finds himself at the centre of a 'strictly circumscribed world,' where travel agents, hotel managers, and other technicians of 'hedonism and expressivity' secure him artificially against real experience. Although Mediterranean, Caribbean, and other resorts promise the tourist a multitude of intense satisfactions, such highly artificial environments offer only faked primitivism, a contained and 'safe' expression of potentially liberating 'subterranean' values. The tourist dreams of escape into the pleasure principle from the rational and instrumental world of work, a recovery of real identity through the release of suppressed impulses, but what he or she gets is 'performance principle tourism.' For Turner and Ash, tourism is itself an industrial instrument in that it amounts to a controlled and temporary release from the world of alienated labour. Not only is tourism characterized by depersonalized organization and standardization, but it extends and supplements the 'official functional values of productivity, conformity, and obedience to routine.' One is allowed to indulge in touristic pleasure only after the deferral of gratification through submission to the functional demands of the workplace. Far from challenging the system of work, tourism only confirms and supports its values, as the chief function of the tourist industry is to keep the industrial machine rolling by temporarily diverting the worker so as to prepare him for further work. Thus 'non-work' is itself 'merely another marketing opportunity,' motivating workers 'to stay within the system.'[422]

In many ways Dean MacCannell's *The Tourist* (1979) represents the very manifesto of postmodern tourism. For MacCannell, not only is postmodernism typified by increasing emphasis on leisure and consumption over work, but tourism is perhaps the most characteristic of postmodern practices, surpassing even technology.[423] This is not to say that MacCannell conceptualizes leisure (and thus tourism) as do de Grazia or Stendhal, as a form of contemplation chosen voluntarily and apart from obligation or necessity. In some cases MacCannell apparently thinks of it as free or leisure time, or as a vacation providing recuperation from work, while in others he interprets modern tourism as does William W. Stowe, in light of Veblen's concept of leisure as the conspicuous expenditure of time and wealth for the sake of social display and status. Yet whereas Veblen and Stowe identify such behaviour with the pre-World War I 'leisure class' of extremely wealthy social snobs and industrial parvenus, along with their middle-class emulators, MacCannell reports on the democratization of tourism among contemporary mass tourists for whom it too is a form of conspicuous expenditure.[424]

For MacCannell, Boorstin resembles Turner and Ash in going much too far in his negative analysis of touristic experience. Not only does MacCannell question Boorstin's absolute dissociation of the traveller, knowledgeable and self-directed, from the tourist, passive and manipulable, but he rejects Boorstin's argument that the tourist, as the willing gull of the tourist industry, really prefers the inauthentic to the authentic, the 'pseudo-event' and 'environmental bubble' to the real thing. Charging Boorstin with intellectual snobbery and a false sense of moral superiority, MacCannell insists that the modern tourist actively desires and pursues authenticity. Rather than regarding his tour as an opportunity for superficial, contrived experiences, the tourist sees it as a kind of modern pilgrimage from which he would extract the deepest measure of meaning from his encounters. Yet the overall picture of tourist experience painted by MacCannell – one of dullness and disappointment – resembles Boorstin's. As MacCannell describes it, tourism is a comprehensive and 'coercive' system. Too often the tourist has no choice but the pseudo-event and other forms of staged authenticity that, acknowledges MacCannell, Boorstin astutely analyzes. There is also the irony that tourism, supposedly an escape from work, often constitutes a 'perversion' of leisure insofar as it leads back to the workplace, since many postmodern tourist sites are themselves workplaces or at least treat the theme of work. Tourism in this form amounts to 'alienated leisure.' As the tourist runs through lists of the approved or 'true sights,' dutifully checking off each item, sightseeing resembles a moral obligation or job. Fully aware of the frequent superficiality and shallowness of such experiences, their lack of penetration and understanding of the touristic environment, MacCannell laments the untapped potential of tourism, which withholds the authenticity it promises. Although MacCannell admits his inability to explain the cause for such superficiality, Ellul's analysis of the modern technicized consciousness, incapable of self-reflection and humanistic awareness, provides the answer. Yet whereas Boorstin glorifies the nineteenth-century traveller, MacCannell is more skeptical, noting that certain traits of postmodern tourists appear in their nineteenth-century predecessors. And whereas Boorstin implies that intellectuals and other cultured types can remove themselves from the touristic world, and thus occupy an uncontaminated realm of authentic experience, MacCannell regards anti-tourism as self-deluded. Attemping falsely to deny the touristic character of his own experience, the snobbish anti-tourist would vainly hide from himself the truth that tourism is now a universal condition of postmodernity, from which no intellectual or person of culture can escape.[425]

MacCannell's bleak conclusion found an echo in Paul Fussell's *Abroad* (1980), which surveyed resignedly the deterioration of touristic experience from the nineteenth century into the present. Reminiscent of Boorstin, Fussell distinguishes fundamentally between travel and tourism. The former belongs chiefly to the bourgeois age, whose heyday coincided roughly with the mid-nineteenth century; the latter reaches apotheosis after 1900. Travel is bourgeois; tourism is mass-democratic. Travel belongs to a time preceding mass transportation, mass communications, and the tourist industry, with their emphasis on speed, convenience, and comfort. As in Boorstin, the traveller is a self-directed individual who 'knows what he wants and what he's doing.' Deriving from the French *travail* and related to the Latin *tripalium*, meaning torture, travel is a laborious, demanding activity akin to patient study on the one hand and exploration on the other. One recalls that Boorstin, like many nineteenth-century Protestant travellers, had sought to justify travel by turning leisure into hard work. The tourist by contrast lacks the self-direction, inner purpose, and capacity for strenuous effort typical of the traveller. He goes abroad to give the impression of belonging to a higher class, and to feel the power of choosing what to buy; indeed, for him tourism is consumerism and commodification. His conversation is full of references to accommodations and locomotion, as the means of travel swallow up the ends. Yet though Fussell acknowledges the type of the anti-touristic would-be traveller, who fears to be identified as a tourist, who fetishizes travelling beyond the 'beaten track,' and who eschews the camera for the sake of immediacy of experience, Fussell like Mac-Cannell regards tourism as a basic reality of postmodernism: 'We are all tourists now.'[426]

The question naturally arises whether Boorstin and Fussell are justified in favouring the nineteenth-century bourgeois traveller over his or her much-maligned touristic counterpart, or whether their judgments reflect misplaced nostalgia. Also to be considered is whether any of the nineteenth-century travellers (apart from Stendhal) experienced leisure in de Grazia's sense, or whether they knew only the 'free time' of the vacation. As much as the tourist has suffered opprobrium, the traveller has also received harsh, even disdainful criticism. The critics focus on the traveller's inability to enjoy his leisure, which is attributed to Protestantism and its obsessive work ethic. The traveller turned travel into work by writing about it or by slavishly following the most detailed itinerary, as if by obligation. Not only Boorstin but Fussell shares something of this attitude, as he too characterizes travel honorifically as a form of work that among other things includes study. Yet many contrary-minded critics assume that travel cannot be leisure because it is strenuous rather than relaxed. Their objections are often conjoined with condemnations of writers of nineteenth-century guidebooks such as John Murray and especially Karl Baedeker, whom they fault for 'comprehensiveness' of detail, high seriousness, and wide range of learned references and allusions allegedly introduced chiefly for snob appeal, or as a mark of what Bourdieu, in updating many of Veblen's concepts, calls 'distinction.' MacCannell notes that the elevated tone and 'distinctive upper-crustiness' of the Baedeker series has often been ridiculed as a residue of the anachronistic Grand Tour. Contrary to one's expectations, even Boorstin shares this attitude, dismissing the Baedeker guides chiefly as a source of touristic regimentation. Their high cultural bias, emphasizing monuments, works of art, and natural scenery, has also been found objectionable. Although Stowe acknowledges that Murray's guides generally avoid rigid itineraries, and thus allow for alternative choices and improvisation, critics customarily attribute the travellers' routinized and dutiful mentality to their use of guidebooks, with their long lists of required sites. Some critics object to the demanding courses of reading by which many nineteenth-century travellers prepared for their tours, as if these were necessarily recipes for boredom, while Stowe even claims that such superior knowledge had as its motive domination of the host country.[427]

Undoubtedly nineteenth-century bourgeois travellers included many Philistines as well as snobs for whom a visit to Italy, far from being a joyful and sincerely desired experience of leisure in the higher sense, was only a mark of status gained through extravagant eye-catching consumption and based ultimately in invidious comparisons between themselves and less wealthy consumers. Nor can one doubt that some tourists have turned their visits to Italy into a kind of penal servitude, sacrificing themselves dutifully and dolefully to a punishing cultural program. Yet just as the true meaning of leisure has nothing to do with Veblen's leisure class, so it is wrong to think that culture must always be a mere pretext for 'distinction,' as if it could not also arise from self-elected leisure. In short, one must not concede the whole touristic terrain to the tyranny of the other.[428] As much as John Pemble acknowledges the vulgarity of many nineteenth-century travellers, he not only denies that they were all Philistines but finds that some travelled for its own sake, without any other motive or pretext.[429] It is furthermore mistaken to suppose that, if a traveller pursues a high cultural itinerary with unstinting effort, he does so only out of duty and at the cost of real leisure. Such an agenda may be undertaken voluntarily and thus apart from obligation and necessity, as something valued for itself, and where this is so, then de Grazia's requirements for leisure have largely been satisfied. The remaining question, whose answer varies from person to person, is whether the tourist so overtaxes himself that he loses the contemplative poise essential to leisure. Yet a choice of strenuous travel does not in itself deprive one of leisure, the key issue being whether the agenda is freely chosen while affording experience of contemplative value. To think otherwise is to accept the false assumption that leisure means idleness, relaxation, or 'taking it easy.'

Nor is there much justification for the usual criticism of the Baedeker and other guides, as alleged sources of drudgery and pedantry, nor of the arduous preparatory study undertaken by nineteenth-century travellers. Although Fussell compares travel to work and more especially study, this would qualify as leisure were it pursued freely and for itself, no matter how demanding. Unlike many critics, however, Fussell realizes that the Baedeker and similar guides, as typical products of nineteenth-century bourgeois civilization, exemplify a much higher average state of touristic culture than what emerged in the next century under modern technicizing education – a higher average, moreover, from which to foster and develop specimens of de Grazia's 'leisure kind.' Instead of rehashing the predictable yet largely irrelevant charges of pedantry, high cultural bias, and class snobbery, Fussell highlights the quality of the older Baedeker guides, whose 'very tone,' at once 'secure' and 'precise,' suggests the power, knowledge, confidence, and inner-directedness of the true traveller – the person who knows what he wants and what he is doing. Should proof be required of the decline of the Baedeker guides from their nineteenth- and early twentieth-century predecessors, one need only glance at some of the more recent Baedekers, especially the guides to Italy. In light of such a comparison, complaints of 'comprehensiveness' levelled against the earlier Baedekers seem ironic indeed. To judge from the Roman entry in the series, the content of the new Baedekers consists to a large extent of coloured photographs, while the text, besides being noticeably sparse in its details, is typified by crude simplification and superficiality. Vast realms of history, culture, and religion are barely suggested, with no attempt to convey their depth or fascination. Such a guide is intended for those to whom leisure means nothing but rapid locomotion mingled with relaxed or rather enervated attention. Fussell makes a similar point in contrasting the older Baedekers, with their emphasis on seeing or learning, and the now out-of-print

Medieval Towns series, with their modern counterparts, the Fielding's and Fodor's guides, in which consumerism predominates.[430] Although the nineteenth-century traveller has been faulted for his overly conscientious preparations for travel, which allegedly turn leisure into drudgework, there is no doubt of the cultural superiority of the older to the later guidebooks, which participate in and embody that dismantling of Western historical memory and cultural tradition to which Allan Bloom alludes in *The Closing of the American Mind*. Although Bloom's text deals infrequently with Italian authors, it is telling that, in attempting to define the enormous cultural and historical attritions suffered by American education in recent decades, Bloom illustrates the deficiencies of that education by pointing out its inadequacy to prepare a student for the experience of Italy.[431]

Another inescapable question is whether Fussell and MacCannell rightly claim – the latter less regretfully than the former – that we are all tourists now. Is it possible to escape universal tourism so as to achieve an individual touristic experience? Has mass consciousness obliterated the least chance of self-determination? Does the omnipresence of the pseudo-event and environmental bubble preclude the possibility of novelty, the *imprévu*, the authentic? In a series of disturbing speculations with which she concludes her essay on 'postindustrial tourism,' Giuli Liebman Parrinello considers the possibility that an 'excess of cognitive factors,' that is, advertising signs, will have 'debilitating effects on the tourist image,' to the point where the tourist, overwhelmed by previously experienced manufactured images of the tourist site, will no longer be able to dream about it. She adds that 'it is as if the tourist of the future will want in some way to safeguard an element of surprise in his or her personal itinerary, even if the destination no longer holds any secrets.' Yet many writers on postmodern tourism reject the dismal possibilities envisioned by Parrinello and more especially Fussell. According to Maxine Feifer, since 1985 tourists have been more confident and independent than ever before, and fewer package tours are being offered. Writing in 1985, John Urry refers to a new tourism in which, in a seeming portent of the end of mass marketing in the tourist business, packaging and standardization yield to segmented, flexible, and customized tourist practices. As tourist companies cater increasingly to the customer's individual needs, tourism is being transformed into travel. During the 1980s many cities have sought to attract tourists and other kinds of business by developing spectacles of diversity through market segmentation, such as the upper-class shopping mall. In a more recent book Steven Meethan opposes the common view of consumers (and tourists) as passive recipients of advertising and media cues. Although tourism remains a form of commodity production and consumption under capitalism, consumer demand is driven not by material utility alone but by diverse cultural, symbolic, and personal values. Mass tourism still exists, but the older modernist spaces of mass tourism are being replaced by more diversified markets, while holidays have become mobile and various. There is moreover widespread resistance to global standardization.[432]

Yet the new tourism described by Urry and Meethan exhibits some disconcerting features. Besides remarking that tourism is largely media constructed, Urry notes that many tourists treat tourism as a strategy for accumulating photographs, a tendency especially marked among those with a strong work ethic, such as Americans, Germans, and Japanese, who feel that they simply 'have' to take pictures. In such instances not only has leisure been contaminated by a sense of duty bred by the routine of work, but it has itself acquired a technological and conformist character.[433] Meethan defines tourism not in de Grazia's sense but as consumption of non-working time, thus situating it in relation to work. Besides noting the continuing predominance of the package tour, in which, as he claims, many tourists are controlled and programmed, Meethan recognizes that tourism qualifies as a rational technique, as Ellul argues. Although Meethan attributes the driving forces of modern tourism more to capitalism than to technology per se, he acknowledges that customized tourism may actually result from instrumental rationality, that is, technology.[434] Unfortunately, neither Urry nor Meethan addresses Ellul's point that the diversification of the tourist industry and other forms of leisure results from an increase in the speed, efficiency, and flexibility of the technological system, so that tourism and leisure, for all their seeming variety, testify to an underlying uniformity that they only conceal.

Meethan may seem overly confident of a non-standardized and serious cultural tourism, and yet it would be excessive to claim that it has ceased to exist. Among the most insightful inquiries into the possibilities of touristic experience is provided by Erik Cohen in a series of articles published between 1972 and 1979 – articles still relevant despite the vicissitudes of the tourist industry. Although Cohen basically accepts the functional theory of leisure as a non-serious temporary recreative escape from work, and although he predicts the increasing standardization of tourism in postmodernity, he shows that some features of the older forms of tourism – or travel – remain available. To be sure, he finds much truth in Boorstin's analysis of the pseudo-event and environmental bubble, conceding the superficiality, standardization, and predictability of much touristic experience, in which the mass tourist is cheated of profundity by a false front. However, Cohen doubts MacCannell's claim that all tourists seek authenticity, even if they fail to find it, and that modern tourism resembles the pilgrimages of old. What Cohen most objects to is the attempt, which he identifies with Boorstin, MacCannell, and Fussell, to reduce the tourist to a single kind. In an early article he dissociates the mass tourist from the 'explorer' type, who avoids mass tourist routes and traditional attractions yet looks for comfortable accommodations and reliable transport, at once associating with locals yet refusing immersion in the host environment. Subsequently Cohen proposes that the tourist experience falls into five categories, of which the most superficial and least demanding are the Recreational and Diversionary. Alienated from work, the Recreational tourist uses touristic leisure as his means of adjusting to it. Far from being a gull, as Boorstin claims, he has no interest in authenticity, and pseudo-events satisfy his desires. With the Diversionary tourist, one finds neither alienation nor a desire to be recreated, the goal being only distraction. Cohen's remaining three categories are the Experiential, the Experimental, and the Existential, each of which represents a quest for authenticity, the final two being the 'hardest.' The Experiential tourist, who resembles MacCannell's 'universal' tourist, seeks authenticity through vicarious aesthetic participation in the life of others. The Experimenter is an eclectic who tries out experiential possibilities unsystematically. The Existential is the most demanding and by far the least frequently represented category, as it requires the most sophistication, application, and knowledge, and holds out the greatest possibility of self-determination and profundity of experience. It is also the riskiest of modes, being highly susceptible to falsification. The Existential traveller elects a spiritual centre outside his own country and culture of origin, so that life outside that centre is felt as a kind of exile. Yet the elected centre may also be part of the Existential traveller's own culture, for instance a nation other than one's own that has contributed greatly to one's cultural heritage. To judge from Cohen's typology, it remains possible to approximate the tourist experience of a Stendhal, whose elected spiritual centre, Italy, lay outside his country of origin, but which he valued for its contributions to European civilization as a whole.[435]

While leisure and tourism thus appear to hold out greater possibilities for freedom and initiative than Ellul, with his technological pessimism, would allow, even Cohen's Existential traveller can only operate within the narrowing interstices of a contemporary touristic system affording highly standardized and commodified experience to the vast majority of consumers. Nowhere is this more evident than in current touristic responses to Italy and the Italians.

The contemporary conception of Italy as seen in leisure and touristic advertisements has been long in the making and draws from a tradition of northern European representations to which Stendhal himself contributed and which say much about northern European and American attitudes towards Italy and Italians. In a pioneering article Andrew M. Canepa notes that from the later Renaissance into the mid-seventeenth century Italians had acquired the reputation of degenerate scoundrels, culturally sophisticated yet morally corrupted and dissimulating – a negative stereotype partly stemming from Italy's historical decline. However, Canepa believes that the predominantly unfavourable view of Italians among the English began to change somewhat in the later eighteenth century as a result of industrialism and the emergence of the English working classes, whose increasing congregation in cities along with their uncouth and vulgar habits much offended members of the English upper middle class, those most likely to make extended visits to Italy. The upper echelons of English society were fearful that the commercial and industrial growth of their nation, which was then proceeding, would lead to a coarsening of manners as well as a one-sided emphasis on work over civilizing leisure pursuits. Another reason for the changing English view of Italy and Italians during the later eighteenth century was the 'revolt against civilization' soon to issue in Romanticism. This may be summarized as a suspicion of civilized restraint, artifice, convention, and hypocrisy as against the spontaneity, sincerity, and 'naturalness' of less civilized and even primitive societies. In light of these new values and attitudes, the Italians, especially the common people, came to be regarded much more favourably by some English visitors, who assimilated them to the 'primitive,' and who found in them a praiseworthy leisureliness and relaxation, robust and healthy physicality, free expression of feelings, disregard of convention, honesty and lack of affectation, and a childlike and pre-moral 'Adamic' innocence – all that an overly abstract, intellectual, and formulaic civilization had stifled.[436] A similarly favourable re-evaluation of the Italians occurred in this period among not a few French and German travellers. Yet although this new positive image persisted into the nineteenth century, as witness Stendhal, Staël, Byron, and the English travellers cited by Pemble in *The Mediterranean Passion,* and although some travellers identified Italy as a place of relaxation if not of leisure in the true sense,[437] many nineteenth-century northern Europeans and Americans continued to disdain Italians, condemning their alleged dirtiness, lack of impulse control, indolence, and other vices. These negatives reflect the northern European and more especially English and American commitment to capitalism and industrialism, as a result of which Italians could only appear as offensive exemplars of sensuality, appetite, and uninhibited enjoyment. Such traits were out of favour in a nineteenth-century capitalist economy in which work and production were the main imperatives, and consumption was expected to take care of itself.

So far as Italy's representation in twentieth-century England and America is concerned, the watershed appears to be World War I, whose impact on the English upper and middle classes has been treated brilliantly by Martin Green and Paul Fussell. This conflict triggered a profound disaffection with the values of industrial civilization among those classes and with it a further 'rehabilitation' of the Italian. It must be kept in mind, first, that up to 1914 most educated Englishmen had had little firsthand acquaintance with the regimented and depersonalized industrial world; and second, that modern mechanized armies such as those deployed in World War I are what Lewis Mumford rightly describes as prime examples of modern mass industrial organization. The battlefields of First World War thus exposed the sons of the English upper and middle classes to an experience of industrialism such as they would have otherwise found hard to imagine – and they did not like it.[438] Not only did the unprecedented battlefield carnage made possible through modern technology awaken in these war veterans a deep dissatisfaction with industrial civilization, whose tendencies to life-denial and 'repression' seemed manifest in the wastefulness of the trench warfare for which they held their patriarchal Victorian fathers responsible, but they transformed themselves in the war's aftermath into what Green describes as 'children of the sun,' turning to the Mediterranean and especially to Italy as the scene of alternative values beyond the orbit of industrial civilization – warm weather, physical health, bodily grace, leisurely repose, hedonism, sensory immediacy as against over-abstraction and intellectualism, sexual and emotional freedom, self-expression, retreat from the work ethic, and a generally less inhibited and disciplined life. In not a few instances these young men were 'decadent' homosexuals and dandies drawn to regions of Italy and periods of Italian culture that had hitherto suffered a seemingly unredeemable reputation for corruption and cultural decline, and which they undertook to publicize and vindicate: Naples and southern Italy generally, and the Baroque especially. The result of this seismic shift in values was the further rehabilitatation of Italy and the Italian, whose stereotypical qualities of indolence, natural healthfulness, impulse, appetite, and expressive exuberance were evaluated far more favourably than in the past. Some of these 'sun children' not only identified with Italians but sought to be like them, even to become them – so complete was the revolution in their reputation.[439] Although negative stereotypes of Italy and Italians have by no means vanished, often drawing on those of the past, the trend towards positive stereotyping has continued into the twentieth century and beyond, with mass tourism, the fading of the Protestant ethic, the substitution of consumption for Victorian asceticism, and the supercession of modernity by postmodernity and postindustrialism.

Inevitably and predictably Italy and Italians have become instruments of organized consumption through advertising and the other media. Italians now typically figure in films and commercials as travesties of those Italianate qualities that, with licensed exaggeration, Stendhal did as much as anyone else to define but that are now marketable clichés. Although during the Victorian period Italians stood for a hedonism threatening to productive routine, advertising now identifies them with the unforbidden commodified pleasures of travel, sex, gastronomy, and even art. A true 'original,' the Italian of advertising has absurdly excessive *brio* conveyed through self-parodic gesticulations and snatches of familiar Italian music. Often appearing as an amorist versed in the products that insure seduction, he also figures as a lower-class type exemplifying a reckless romantic existence outside the norm. Sometimes he is an urban desperado of somber intensity, who combines the dangerous life and approved tastes. In general, advertising celebrates Italy as the favoured land of leisurely pleasures, yet where one escapes only temporarily the dominant world of production while consuming products and services that extend its dominion.[440] The deeper irony is that such standardization betrays the passionate individuality Stendhal identifies with Italian happiness.

In historical terms the decline of leisure as a cultural value, which de Grazia documents, must be traced largely to the decline of Italy itself, as the chief repository and source of transmission of the leisure ideal to the rest of Europe from classical times, through medieval monasticism and scholasticism, and finally the Renaissance and Baroque periods. In *Stones of Rimini* Adrian Stokes refers to a massive cultural shift from the Mediterranean, centred in Italy, to the northern European and American world, a transfer adumbrated by Columbus's discovery.[441] The rise to cultural preponderance of the so-called North Atlantic civilization has coincided with the historical success of northern European peoples who, lacking classical traditions of their own, and receiving them mainly as southern imports, have over the last several centuries devoted themselves to massive industrial and collective enterprises in an unremitting and colossal expenditure of labour facilitated by ever-developing machine technology. And so the question arises whether it will ever be possible to restore Mediterranean or rather classical ideals of leisure in a contemporary context. As much as one admires the cogency and firmness with which de Grazia defends these ideals of leisure, one senses that he argues in a vacuum, that his position, however stubbornly argued and unassailable in its own strict logic, lacks contemporary relevance and resonance, even for Italy. Though contemporary leisure theorists respect de Grazia's arguments, they rarely find it necessary to engage them. Regarding capitalism, Margaret Thatcher has said quite credibly that it is the only 'alternative.'[442] According to Terry Nichols Clark, following the collapse of communism no one has found a substitute for the mass consumption economy, which remains supreme as an international model.[443] Assessing Italy's situation during the decades post-1945, Fabio Luca Cavazza complains that an archaically aristocratic classical and humanistic education receives disproportionate emphasis in the schools, and that Italians ought to pay more attention to science and technology as the 'fruit of a better humanism,' consistent with democratic world trends.[444] Notwithstanding that Mill, Tocqueville, and Burckhardt sought to maintain the classical and humanistic character of nineteenth-century education, they were sufficiently historicist to acknowledge what has been called the '[in]commensurability of the present and the classical past ... the vast gap that separated the modern world from the past.'[445] Still more stringently, Jacques Ellul insists that 'we have to avoid posing the present-day problems in classical moral terms,' since for various reasons these terms 'are incapable of taking man's actual situation into account.'[446] From this vantage one can perhaps indulge momentarily in the nostalgia that is so widely interdicted nowadays and think of Stendhal's Italian writings as containing the fading echoes of a lost world of leisure, one which, having been lost, is not likely to be found again.

chapter 2

The Unbroken Charm: New Englanders in Italy

JOHN PAUL RUSSO

I

The earliest American tradition of travel writing on Italy was actually a New England tradition, and it grew out of the fact that so many New Englanders followed one another to Italy in the nineteenth century, leaving a wealth of journals, letters, travelogues, newspaper articles, poetry, fiction, and translations. In 1833, on a spring day in Rome, Emerson counted fifteen Bostonians in the Piazza di Spagna. Fourteen Lowells were visiting Italy in 1852; James Russell Lowell said he was 'going abroad to become acquainted with his family.'[1] Many travellers aimed to recover the lessons of an old country for the purpose of educating a young one. They came not as blank slates, but charged with conflict; and they departed not as complete converts, but enjoined by the wisdom of *incipit vita nova*, here begins the new life. With their eclectic intellectual roots in the quasi-aristocratic, neoclassical eighteenth century as well as in the neo-Romantic, broadly bourgeois tradition of self-culture, they set instruction above entertainment, though they knew that their message had the better chance of success if it were leavened with pleasure.

In their long careers Henry Wadsworth Longfellow (1807–82), James Russell Lowell (1819–91), and Charles Eliot Norton (1827–1908) promoted a cultural image of Italy before an academic and popular audience. Each began by publishing an Italian travelogue, as if to show that their counsel was proven on the pulse: Longfellow's *Outre-Mer: A Pilgrimage beyond the Sea* (1833) went through nine editions in thirteen years; Lowell's *Fireside Travels* (1854–64) depicts the Italian national character; Norton's *Notes of Travel and Study in Italy* (1859) was a scholar's guide for several generations.[2] In Cambridge they were neighbours; at Harvard, like dynasts, they succeeded one another at twenty-year intervals from 1836 to 1898, lecturing on Italian culture; in Boston they gathered together in the 1860s to read Dante, which was the origin of the Dante Society of America (1881).[3] Longfellow and Norton translated the *Divine Comedy*, the first into poetry (1867), the second into prose (1892); Norton translated the *Vita Nuova* (1867); Lowell's 'very influential' *Dante* (1872) was the most widely read American study of the poet in its era.[4] In his final years Longfellow laboured over an epic drama on Michelangelo, in which he was 'more distinctly declaring his artistic creed than in any other of his works.'[5] Norton, an 'estranged American Protestant, set adrift in the world of art,' taught classical and medieval art and architecture, and was 'of all the art teachers in nineteenth-century America, undoubtedly the most important, the best known, and the most influential.'[6] His students included Irving Babbitt, George Santayana, Barrett Wendell, Bernard Berenson, George Woodberry, C.H. Grandgent, Jefferson Butler Fletcher, and William Roscoe Thayer; Henry James acknowledged Norton's impact on his understanding of Italy.[7] The humanism of Norton reached his second cousin's grandson, T.S. Eliot, a Harvard undergraduate in Norton's old age, who would pay him tribute in his Charles Eliot Norton Lectures.[8] Italophilic themes inform the work of James Russell Lowell's collateral descendants, Amy Lowell and Robert Lowell.

While Longfellow, Lowell, and Norton are the major figures in the recovery of Italy for mid-nineteenth-century America, many thinkers in the generation or two before them had already expanded intellectual boundaries beyond Lockeian empiricism, Scottish intuitionism, and French encyclopedism. Washington Allston followed up his studies at Harvard with a long period in Italy (1804–8), gathering impressions and deepening his knowledge of the classical world. He would write the first novel by an American with an Italian setting (*Monaldi*, 1822; pub. 1841); 'profoundly influenced by his experience there, Allston more than any other American may be said to have introduced that country [to Americans].'[9] Though in 1814 George Ticknor complained of being unable to locate a single Italian grammar in Boston, the Boston Anthology Club was stimulating interest in Italian studies through its *Monthly Anthology* (1803–11). The founding of the Boston Athenaeum in 1807 furthered these goals; its holdings of Italian travel books would become so extensive that shelf sections would be labelled by individual cities and towns, a proud reminder of Italophilic Boston in the past two centuries. The first issue of the *North American Review* in 1815 contained a spirited defense of the Italian language against the Abbé Prévost's attack.[10] Jared Sparks, the future president of Harvard, lamented the exclusion of Italian 'from the catalogue of acquirements necessary for an accomplished scholar': the Italian language is 'vastly better adapted to every species of composition, than the French ... it has more dignity and strength, a greater felicity of expression, and infinitely more sweetness and harmony.'[11] The *North American Review* from 1815 to 1850 and the *American Quarterly Review* in its brief career (1827–37) published more essays and reviews on Italy than on any other European country except England. George Bancroft and William H. Prescott were in Italy between 1817 and 1821, not only as Grand Tourists but as enthusiastic students of its culture. Bancroft, future Secretary of the Navy and founder of Annapolis, was so eager to reach the Italian shore that he leaped from his ship off Livorno and swam the final two miles.[12]

Epitomizing the New England tradition on Italy, Longfellow, Lowell, and Norton are the Big Three against whom their contemporary and later writers may be compared and contrasted. Essentially, the Big Three subscribe to a series of dialectical oppositions between Italy and America that is indebted to eighteenth- and nineteenth-century travel literature: aristocratic, hierarchical, traditionalist culture versus modern, democratic, industrial society; Catholicism versus Protestantism; individuality versus Tocquevillian levelling; the free, spontaneous, expressively theatrical, and anarchic versus the artificial, the socially imposed, and the increasingly rationalized and administered (under the guise of capitalist freedom); female versus male; leisure (or indolence) versus work (and time-keeping); past versus future; and so forth. 'An entire network of opposing terms can be perceived in the pattern of the discussion as a whole,' remarks William Vance, who warns against reducing a 'complex reality to the simple question of American or Roman superiority in one particular respect.'[13] Writing towards the end of his career, Norton reflects upon the interaction of terms: 'there are always two aspects of Italy, – the one which makes its appeal to the poetic imagination': this is the land of smiling nature, magnificent art, of 'splendour' and 'poetic and historic associations which add a deeper charm to the beauty of the scene.' The other Italy captures 'one's immediate sympathies, with a sense of the pathos of the lives of the vast mass of men, women, and children,' and of 'their squalor.' The two Italies 'conflict with each other' but, he adds, 'each intensifying the other,' not diminishing it (NL 2:207–8).

The New Englanders write as exiles from themselves, from a buried life to which, as they think, Italy will help gain access. They connect the discovery of Italy with self-discovery. A psychic topography of extremes, an 'other' that strangely mirrored aspects of themselves, Italy brought to the surface deep-seated fears and desires as they attempted to come to terms with themselves and achieve unity in their intellectual and emotional life. Because the country is so ancient and, just as importantly, continuous in its historical deposits down to the present, it mixes life, death, and rebirth in ways that are suggestive and homologous to an individual life. The travellers returned home feeling restored to themselves; their Italian sojourns provided the balance they found lacking in America; and they had been given the central clue to their educational mission. 'Nowhere are such study and knowledge more needed than in America,' comments Norton, 'for nowhere in the civilized world are the practical concerns of life more engrossing; nowhere are the conditions of life more prosaic; nowhere is the poetic spirit less evident, and the love of beauty less diffused' (NL 2:8). In 'Cambridge Thirty Years Ago,' a memoir of the quaint, provincial background of the 1820s, Lowell affirms that 'an orbed and balanced life would revolve between the Old and the New [Worlds] as opposite, but not antagonistic poles' (FT 3). While the spheral image expresses the ideal of a rounded education and varied life, there is a utopian colouring in the *not* antagonistic poles. He wants the best of both worlds, though surely the author of the *Biglow Papers* knew that self-knowledge, equilibrium, and wholeness are won only by closer understanding of the extremes and the dialectic interplay between them ('each intensifying the other').

For all three writers Italy is so old that it makes them feel like children; but on the other hand, Italy is the childhood of the West and its present inhabitants are themselves children, and the adults are the Americans and foreign travellers like them. In this sense, Italy is in a separate world from England, France, or Germany, each of which played a leading role in shaping modernity after the Renaissance. Although the writers admired the medieval communes for their independence and economic aggressiveness and extolled Renaissance achievement in art and literature, not to mention the classical world, they found present-day Italy sadly wanting in the virtues of commerce, efficiency, political nerve, republicanism, and domesticity. Nor did they recognize the signs of vitality in literature (Leopardi, Manzoni), music (Bellini, Donizetti, Verdi), or politics (the Risorgimento). The very idea of the modern Italian struck them as oxymoronic. Yet if Italy was not 'modern,' it furnished a standard by which they could examine, condemn, and resist what they regarded as the evils in modernity: the loss of individuality and ironing out of difference, vulgar materialism, bigness, the rush of time, the artificiality and crudity of manners. When Italy finally unified itself, attempted to modernize, and unveiled its Washington in the heroic, anticlerical, republican Garibaldi, these Americans who previously protested Italian tyranny, poverty, indolence, superstition, and vice turned about and longed for pre-Risorgimento Italy. They hated aspects of it, they attacked it, yet they preferred it.

II

Van Wyck Brooks and Paul R. Baker saw little evidence that nineteenth-century Americans in Italy moved outside Anglo-American circles. The same held for other foreigners: each colony (Russian, British, French, German, Scandinavian) kept mostly to itself.[14] There were exceptions, but for the most part American travellers met customs officers, carriage organizers, porters, clerks, and guides. In 1828 the twenty-one-year-old Longfellow found 'excellent society' in Florence 'chiefly composed of French and English' (HWL 1:253). 'I have been nearly a year in Italy,' wrote Henry James in 1874, 'and have hardly spoken a word to an Italian creature save washerwomen and waiters.'[15] The Americans were often on the move and did not return for years, if at all, with little opportunity to form more than fleeting acquaintances or to break through stereotypes. Even when they stayed for extended periods, they might not choose to write about the Italians. Longfellow said he had trouble speaking Italian and 'would make my way through Italy with the little I had acquired.' Then he boarded with the Persiani family in Rome and befriended the three daughters, all of whom could speak English, and he changed his plans: 'I shall make my residence in Italy something longer' (HWL 1:257). Yet, though he wrote home of the daughters' accomplishments and credited the family with saving his life when he caught rheumatic fever (HWL 1:277), he gives them only half a sentence in *Outre-Mer* and conveys nothing of their domus-centred life, instead devoting pages to beggars, dwarfs, charlatans, carnivals, funerals, fireworks, and bravos.[16] Either he was not interested in writing about the modern bourgeois family in Italy or his audience did not want to read about it. His visit left him in a divided frame of mind: 'everything in Italy is really picturesque – yet strip the country of its historic recollections – think merely of what it is – and not of what it has been – and you will find the dream to be fading away' (HWL 1:279).

Although everything had not been 'really picturesque,' the dream of Italy proved more substantial than the reality. Longfellow told his students that 'the mind resolutely refuses to associate anything disagreeable with Italy'; there were disagreeables that time melts away, or the mind suppresses, though not without force. To the poet, Italy is the 'land of his predilection'; to the artist, the 'land of his necessity'; to all, the 'land of dreams and visions of delight' (HLB 2:187). 'Amalfi,' a late poem (1875), expresses the ambiguous nature of the dream. In the poem's framing device, the geographical distance separating Longfellow in wintry Cambridge from a 'land beyond the sea' functions as a metaphor for the psychological distance that the poem aims to collapse through the power of memory. In an attractive personification Amalfi 'Sits ... in the heat' amid mulberry trees, its 'white feet' bathed in the 'tideless summer sea.' A river 'rushes down' the narrow gorge to fill the city's fountains and to turn its mills. Suddenly, as if his increasing closeness to the town were diminishing its charm, the idyllic scene is interrupted by less appealing images: peasant girls carry heavy burdens up streets as steep as stairs, while a monk looking down from the heights asks what 'inexorable fate / Dooms them to this life of toil.' Longfellow then evokes, in a Romantic topos, the former glory of the maritime city whose wharves and quays are now sunk beneath the waters. Just when the dream is on the point of dying, an apostrophe reignites it: 'This is the enchanted land!' Following the 'sickle of white sand' that lines the 'blue Salernian bay,' Longfellow suddenly defies the geographical reality of the scene in imagining, at the farthest distance, the temples of Paestum and its legendary roses, praised by Virgil, which 'Seem to tinge the fatal skies / Of that lonely land of doom.' In the rose-coloured twilight the negative again intrudes as the monk desires a repose as deep as the 'sunken city' of the dead. In the final stanza Longfellow returns to the frame; instead of Amalfi's warmth and panoramic view, Cambridge is 'Walled about with drifts of snow'; instead of rushing torrents, its river is 'cased in ice,' He calls out to 'a long-lost Paradise / In the land beyond the sea' – the dream prevails, or does the poem begin again and with the same results? In 1877, reading the Italian letters of Charles Sumner prompted Longfellow to write George Washington Greene, with whom he shared rooms in Rome fifty years earlier, that from Italy he had 'brought away ... a kind of golden atmosphere, which has always illuminated my life' (HWL 6:268).[17] In a similar mood Norton recalled standing on a promontory in the Italian Riviera, 'the sea so blue and smooth as to be like a darker sky,' and viewing an old castle in a olive grove: 'a scene out of that Italy which is the home of the imagination, and which becomes the Italy of memory' (NTS 1–2). As for his 'two aspects' of Italy, 'in the long run, in memory, the appeal to the imagination proves the stronger and the most abiding' (NL 2:208).

Yet when they were in Italy itself, the Arcadian dream was broken again and again by hard fact. Anyone who visits Rome can understand Lowell's 'rude shock': 'for a few days one undergoes a tremendous recoil'; one feels 'disappointment,' elation, and confusion that may last 'a great while' (FT 222, 224; JLB 1:342). Similar reactions were felt by Goethe and J.M.W. Turner.[18] Rome can be a 'parody upon itself' (FT 224), lost within the thickness of its representations, as one adjusts to the difference between images known from childhood and the reality of their contexts. One confronts the sharp discontinuity between past and present, between the 'imperial ghost among the Roman ruins' on one hand, and the 'modern houses,' 'muddy streets,' 'dingy *caffès*,' and 'cigar-smokers' on the other (FT 223-25). Lowell might have acknowledged that any comparison between the golden age of Rome and mid-nineteenth-century Italy would be self-defeating. Moreover, one should speak of *pasts*, since the past does not manifest itself in an orderly fashion; this is the unsettling experience of Rome as compared with a history book. The city resembles 'what one finds in his pockets after a walk'; the Yankee metaphor is pedestrian, spare, monetary, reductive, but gradually the travellers arrange their pocket 'cubes,' pagan and Christian, into a satisfying 'Roman mosaic' (FT 226; JLB 1:342).

On first approaching Rome Longfellow imagined 'a city of the dead' from which there was no return; 'we had entered the desolate Campagna; we passed the Tomb of Nero ... no sound of active life, no thronging crowds, no hum of busy men, announced that we were near the gates of Rome. All was silence, solitude' (OM 318). But while the ruins were 'grand and beautiful beyond conception' as to make him 'almost delirious,' and the view of the Campagna 'with its ruined acqueducts diverging in long broken arcades' unsurpassed anywhere, he was appalled by the 'buffooneries of Carnival,' the 'dissoluteness of manners,' the 'misery of the people,' and the religious 'mummery' and 'superstition': 'how different from Ancient Rome is Modern' (HWL 1:271–2, 279), as if he had lived in ancient Rome. On return visits, Norton reiterates his antithetical response to Rome: 'far more than I believed it, and yet far less too'; 'the same dirty old place – damp, mouldy, sunny and delightful – that it ever was'; 'more splendour and pomp and more poverty than usual'; 'conservative not only in good old ways, but in bad ones also.' One paragraph begins by deploring the 'oppressed,' 'restless,' 'divided,' and 'impotent' Romans and ends by applauding them, with reservations: 'no people so delightful as this, and no city where nature holds her rights so firmly and asserts them so clearly, spite of Berninis and Borrominis, of priests and forestieri [foreigners]' (NL 1:143, 158, 160–1, 384).

The New Englanders often dwell on the more disturbing facts of contemporary Italy, for example, noise, filth, impulsiveness, idleness, improvidence, begging, ecclesiastical corruption, social distrust, and stagnation. Before his first visit Lowell's opinions had been shaped by gothic fiction and Puritan prejudice: the modern Italian was either a monk or a bravo. The monk did 'nothing but enter at secret doors and drink your health in poison'; the bravo 'lived behind corners, supporting himself by the productive industry of digging your person all over with a stiletto' (FT 210). If living in Italy raised his opinion of the inhabitants in some respects, it confirmed their low status in others. Italians 'quarrel as unaccountably as dogs' and display the 'utmost pitch and agony of exasperation.' They do not 'grow warm, but leap at once from zero to some degree of white-heat, to indicate which no Anglo-Saxon thermometer of wrath is highly enough graduated'; yet, he notes, the 'subsidence is as sudden' (FT 196). If he were asked to name a 'universal characteristic' of an Italian town, it would be 'two men clamoring and shaking themselves to pieces at each other' and a woman 'leaning lazily out of a window, and perhaps looking at something else' (FT 197), knowing they are unlikely to come to blows. Lowell saw physical contact only three times in eight months. In 1857 Norton said 'nightly robberies are common' in Rome, though he himself was not troubled (NL 1:161). As for alcoholism, though Lowell never saw anyone drink water in Florence, 'I also never saw a single drunken man'; in Rome drunkenness is 'exceedingly rare' (JLB 1:316). Longfellow comments on the 'loud laughter,' the 'noisy crowd,' the 'discordant voices' that 'rise louder than the roar of the loud ocean,' the 'noisy burst' of military music (OM 323–4). He sketches an old women who 'pierced my ear' trying to sell him his fortune; the violent gestures, expressive attitudes, and wasted energies of a person merely lighting a pipe; a vendor hawking saint's lives in a 'sharp, cracked voice, that knows no pause nor division in the sentences it utters'; a muleteer beating his donkey mercilessly (OM 322, 333).

Idleness was another complaint about which the New Englanders remarked with varying degrees of displeasure. To Longfellow, the Romans are an 'idle populace,' 'poor – and lazy, and happy' (OM 330; HWL 1:279). As Juvenal decried their 'degraded propensities' with the phrase *panem et circenses*, 'modern Romans are likewise strongly given to amusements of every description' (OM 322, 330). He remarks upon a 'profligate clergy' and 'fat priests [who] waddle about the streets with fans in their hands,' citing Thomson's *Castle of Indolence* against them; the 'idle facchino' playing mora, and loungers almost everywhere (OM 332). Idleness leads to begging: 'Beggars all, – beggars all! The Papal city is full of them; and they hold you by the button through the whole calendar of saints.' The generous Longfellow became so used to giving alms that he mistook a threadbare gentleman for a beggar, and for his pains the insulted gentleman 'showered upon me the most sonorous maledictions' (OM 332). Some forty or fifty 'dirty, laughing, ragged, happily-wretched' children surrounded Lowell on the beach at Terracina begging for *caccose* or *cecco* (*qualche cosa* = something), while their 'nasty and contented' mothers encouraged them from their doorways (JLB 1:343). Norton found a word of praise for the papal administration and public charities 'of the most efficient character,' unrivalled in Europe; yet the adverse result was an increase of begging and poverty, 'for which no excellence of intention can serve as excuse' (NTS 86).

Though the least censorious of the Big Three, Lowell connects idleness and begging, which he blames on the unproductive classes and innumerable feast (i.e., non-working) days (FT 242), as many as three per week. However, he distinguishes idleness or laziness from 'indolence' or 'leisure'; a Neapolitan is a 'loafer,' but 'when a Roman does nothing, he does it in the high Roman fashion.' Leisure is a productive activity in its own right, and not the mere absence of work. According to Lowell, it is found less often among Americans, who are time-constrained by external forces such as banks and newspapers. Lowell satirizes the hubristic pretension of a bank-holiday announcement: 'the world will close to-day at twelve o'clock, an hour earlier than usual.' By contrast, the Roman is 'still the Ancient, with a vast future before him to tame and occupy'; he 'spends from a purse of Fortunatus' and his '*piccolo quarto d'ora* is like his *grosso*, a huge piece of copper, big enough for a shield, which stands only for a half dime of our money' (FT 156–7, 243). The metaphor is northern: time, money, schedules, the clock as a symbol of rational organization as opposed to individual licence and spontaneity. For the spendthrift Roman, the piccolo is like the grosso, a fifteen-minute period can expand usuriously, indefinitely; yet if one translates the cash value of Roman time into American terms, the grosso may be large in appearance but it is worth *piccolo*, small change (the way Americans used to make fun of the large number of lire that made up a dollar). The 'huge piece of copper' is the big show that is reduced satirically for its lack of value. How does one measure modern time in the Eternal City? Stymied in expressing his 'natural temperament,' Lowell confesses 'I have grown wary and don't dare to let myself go'; America is 'too busy, too troubled'; 'there is no *leisure*, and that is the only climate in which society is indigenous, the only one in which good-humour and wit and all the growths of art are more than half-hardy exotics ... Democracies lie, perhaps, too far north' (JLL 2:112–13).[19]

While the *difference* of Italy is the most frequently adopted point of departure, either the positive differences eventually weighed more heavily than the negative ones or these travellers saw the positive in the negative. In contrast to America where 'everything seems shifting like a quicksand, where men shed their homes as snakes their skins,' Lowell admires the sense of 'permanence' and 'repose' (FT 149). A four-hundred-year-old guidebook is serviceable; Montaigne's Roman hostelry in the Via del Orso still stands; and he enjoys the *lucerna* and the *vettura* despite the availability of gaslight and railroads. Trying to explain the mechanism of the St Peter's fireworks, he accuses himself, an artist, of being 'bitten with the Anglo-Saxon gadfly that drives us all to disenchant artifice' (FT 236); this use of 'disenchant' resembles the concept that Schiller used before him, and Max Weber after him, to describe the 'demagification' (*Die Entzauberung*) of modernity by which 'one can, in principle, master all things by calculation.'[20] With yet another reference to time, Lowell applauds Pius IX's decision not to build a railroad linking Rome to its port at Civitavecchia: 'one would not approach the solitary emotion of a lifetime, such as is the first sight of Rome, at the rate of forty miles an hour'; then he mocks Pius's motive: 'because it would be profitable' – the papacy is hopelessly non-capitalistic (Pius later reversed his decision and rode the line in celebration of its opening in 1863) (FT 179). This mixture of rapture and satire, common in Lowell, suits the Italian complexities.[21] Despite his criticism of the Church, Norton was so appreciative of the survival of the Middle Ages, he felt he could be a contemporary of Boccaccio; the daily life of Italians 'has much the same aspect as it had centuries ago'; the ceremony of the Immaculate Conception in the Pietrasanta cathedral (1223) was a 'scene from the Middle Ages,' indeed an 'inheritance from Heathenism rather than the natural growth of Christianity'; 'Italy has undergone many vicissitudes, but few changes' (NTS 3, 6).

To the practical Yankee, Italy means 'antiquity with good roads,' 'cheap living,' and 'freedom from responsibility.' As if from a prison of conformity and duty, writes Lowell, one 'escapes' to Italy; 'fetters' drop upon reaching its shore, where one 'rejoices in the recovery' of 'individuality.' There a person is 'no longer met at every turn with "Under which king, bezonian? Speak, or die!'" (*II Henry IV* 5:3): Whose side are you on, rascal? One is not obliged to take sides on 'table-tipping, or the merits of General Blank, or the constitutionality of anarchy' (FT 148–9). Curiously enough, an American, from the home of individualism, can recover selfhood in Italy, expressed in images of wholeness, health, and regeneration: 'sense and spirit are fed together,' 'body and soul ... sit down together at the same board' (FT 206). The land is an 'Eden' where a person 'need not hide his natural self in the livery of any opinion' (FT 149); our first parents went naked in the Garden; today we hide our true selves under borrowed notions. Lowell means by 'natural' that thoughts and feelings arise spontaneously from the occasion as opposed to responses that are calculated or overly mannered. The Italians combine naturalness with an artistic instinct, even in simple things: 'They contrived to make the commonplace graceful – or rather they could not help it' (JLL 2:119), for the idea of form was so deep-engrained from the sight of beautiful things that they seemed possessed of an inborn standard of taste. Lowell compliments the beauty of an innkeeper's daughter, to which the wife replies: 'Ah, she is nothing to her eldest sister just married ... If you could see *her!* She is bella, bella, BELLA!' The wife later tapped on his door and brought the sister, all dressed up, and 'showed her off to us as simply and naturally as if she had been a picture'; 'the girl, who was both beautiful and modest, bore it with the dignified *aplomb* of a statue. She knew we admired her, and liked it, but with the indifference of a rose.' Lowell marvels at the 'wholly unsophisticated consciousness, with no alloy of vanity or coquetry' (FT 222) – without exhibitionism or solicitation.[22]

While the Enlightenment had treated the child as an imperfect adult, the Romantic idealization of the child as father of the man reached its zenith in America in the 1820s and 1830s, to the great benefit of the Italian stereotype. Italians as unself-conscious children is a common theme in the New England travellers, a contrast with Anglo-American seriousness and work. Closer to nature, the child is in contact with spontaneous, emotional life, like a 'naive' artist: the child and the artist are quintessential symbols of the unified sensibility. Lowell's guide Leopoldo, full of 'perennial boyhood' (FT 159) and effusiveness, is a constant source of merriment, and his most fully realized Italian. The Catholic religion 'wisely provides for the childish' in man and for the 'weaknesses of human nature' (FT 231). Early Italian painters, the so-called Primitives, 'say so much in their half-unconscious prattle, and talk nature to me instead of high art,' writes Lowell, 'children talk so.' He prefers the 'simple honesty' of the early self-portraits to the 'conscious attitudinizing' of the later ones (JLL 2:113–14).

Italian emotionalism gives point and differentiation to personality, which Lowell reads (or perhaps overreads) as strong individualism and a rebuke to American blandness: 'in proportion as man grows commercial, does he also become dispassionate and incapable of electric emotions' (FT 200).[23] Anticipating later writers and critics, these descendents of the Puritans believe that one's emotional nature ('impatience and fire') had been denied its full share. 'Brain is always to be bought, but passion never comes to market' (FT 201). Or: 'Puritanism – I am perfectly aware how great a debt we owe it – tried over again the old experiment of driving out nature with a pitchfork, and had the usual success' (FT 43); Lowell warns his countrymen against feeling through their minds, or at one remove, rather than confronting experience in its immediacy. By going out of oneself and breaking 'habitual associations' one finds 'the common rallying-point' of one's life (FT 10). Lowell extends his observation to the old Italian towns, which have 'originality,' 'an individuality of character as marked as that of trees'; by contrast, 'the sameness of modern cities' is 'tiresome' (FT 249). Norton, too, comments on the organic nature of Italian town-planning: builders give to 'the poorest house in the dullest town or village a delightful individuality'; 'there are no streets built by contract with houses cut to measure on one pattern; but the streets look as streets ought to look, as if they had grown into shape and form out of the various will and taste of the men and women who first built [them]' (NL 1:369). Drawn into the orbit of Berlin, Dresden loses its 'original, native flavour' in the way cities surrounding New York are losing theirs; there is 'no Bologna such as Stendhal describes, no Venice such as Beckford saw'; 'individuality of this sort is fast disappearing in Europe' (NL 1:411).

Lowell ponders over the *difference* of Italy in terms of kinds of knowledge. 'If there be anything which a person of even moderate accomplishments may be presumed to know,' he says, 'it is Italy' (FT 152). The remark, made almost casually, indicates the cultural orientation of individuals in Western civilization (even with a modest education) before 1914. But Lowell takes greater risks: 'there is, perhaps, no country with which we are so intimate as with Italy' (FT 150), where 'intimate' (from the Latin for 'innermost,' 'secret') suggests the closest relations bordering on awe (as in Wordsworth's 'Intimations of Immortality'). The passage affirms the definition of intimacy by Karan J. Prager and Linda J. Roberts: an 'interaction that is distinguished [by] ... self-revealing behavior, positive involvement with the other, and shared understand-ings.'[24] Through these delicate interactions Lowell grows more aware of his true self: 'Surely the American (and I feel myself more intensely American every day) is last of all at home among ruins – but he is at home in Rome' (JLB 1:342); differences fall away as the traveller intuits an underlying kinship. The American side is actually strengthened the longer he stays in Rome, paradoxically his 'mother country' (FT 149). Quoting Byron on Italy as 'my country!' (*Childe Harold's Pilgrimage* 4.78), Lowell writes that the feeling of Rome as the familial mother 'comes to one slowly, and is absorbed into one's system during a long residence. Perhaps one does not feel it till one has gone away' (FT 222), gone home to America where one's new-found awareness can be fully absorbed, inte-grated, and rationally understood.[25]

Norton, too, expressed himself in the language of intimacy, returning to Rome as to a 'dear old friend'; 'we have not got to get acquainted; no tedious preliminaries, no uncertainties; we know each other's hearts' (NL 1:147). A similar feeling attends his departure: 'It was with a home-sick sinking of the heart that I left Italy,' he writes; imagining himself back (home) in New England, he is 'homesick' for Italy (NL 1:404, 406). Since Americans are inevitably divided between geographical or psy-chological spaces (nations, ethnicities, traditions), they are always exiles *somewhere*: for Norton, 'Italy is the country where the American, exile in his own land from the past record of his race, finds the most delightful part of that record' (NL 1:349). During his studies in Dresden Norton turned forty-four and, feeling both 'wonderfully young' and 'wonder-fully old,' he contrasts the effect that Italy and Germany exerted over him, with the paradoxical sense of being both younger and older in these countries for different reasons. 'In Italy one feels as if one had had experience, had known what it was to live, had learnt to know *something* if but very little, and could at least enjoy *much*. Here [in Germany], on the contrary, one is convicted of inexperience and ignorance at every turn, everybody is hard at work learning and knows already a vast deal, and you are forced to begin to go to school again with the sense of hav-ing much lost time to make up for, and of the impropriety of enjoy-ment unless the pleasure is united with instruction' (NL 1:410).[26] At an early date (1871) Norton assesses the heavy price of progress, with its all-pervasive spirit of competition ('at every turn'), constant threat of inadequacy ('convicted'), necessity of playing catch-up ('school again'), demand ('forced') to be forever looking over one's shoulder ('lost much time'), and even its enjoyments contaminated by the gospel of utility. By contrast, mid-nineteenth-century Italy still offered a poignant view of a world elsewhere. But the price inevitably had to be paid, concludes Norton, 'So *we* are all hard at work here.' Longfellow, Lowell, and Norton each studied in Germany to prepare for their teaching careers.

All three writers undergo experiences that partake of a kind of death and restoration to a new life. They might be taken by surprise, like Longfellow, at the most touristic of sites, the Colosseum by moonlight – all the more powerful, he thought, because 'you are disarmed when most upon your guard, and betrayed into an enthusiasm which perhaps you had silently resolved you would not feel.' As he crosses the Forum on a 'midnight visit,' the enormous ruins begin to dematerialize: the column of Phocas becomes a 'thin vapor,' the 'dim, shadowy, indistinct' arches of the Temple of Peace 'seemed to melt away.' The Colosseum stands before him beneath a 'full moon,' 'half in shadow, half in light'; the signs of liminality are the midnight hour, full moon, and the shifting balance between darkness and light, a prelude to revelation. Entering, he hears the ancient crowds only to dispel them, so that a silence pervades the scene. As he walks higher in the amphitheater its arches 'crumbled away'; the dissolution of the real is almost complete, leaving the imagined in its place: the arena below 'seemed less an earthly reality than a reflection in the bosom of a lake.' Some figures 'mingled grotesquely with their fore-shortened shadows,' their voices reduced to 'whispers.' In an intense moment of imaginative transcendence, 'I did not conjure up the past, for the past had already become identified with the present'; 'the arbitrary distinctions of time, years, ages, centuries were annihilated. I was a citizen of Rome!' (OM 337–41). Even the cross in the centre of the arena looked like a dagger in the sand.

For Lowell, the lost natural self can be found again in Italy where one can be 'as happy as Adam' (FT 149), a recurrent theme (FT 139, 149, 153, 168, 229, 242, 243). To be, or return to being, Adam is one of the male American writer's obsessions and, as against Lowell, usually thought to be attainable only by abjuring, not by embracing, Old Europe. But one must die before being reborn; for Lowell, the Tiber was the Styx, the ravaged face of a 'dirty, blue' customs officer to whom he paid an obolus was 'Charon,' and Rome was the 'city of the dead' (FT 223). He loses track of time, he delays returning to Germany, his health improves: 'Since I have been in Italy ... I am quite another man – the color has come back to my cheeks,' adding in one of his characteristic similes, 'I seem to have had all my standing-rigging braced and tautened, like a ship after getting to sea,' that is, in its natural habitat. The climate in Naples is like 'a Medea's bath, fit to make an old man young again' (JLL 1:258–9). In order to kill King Pelias, Medea tricked his daughters into thinking that if they cut him up and boiled him, he would rejuvenate.

A few months in Italy transformed Norton. 'Every day that I am here I love Rome more and more, and it becomes more and more a part of myself' (NL 1:161): four times he repeats 'more.' On 1 March 1857 he revisited the Villa Celimontana, built on the ruins of Roman villas in the late sixteenth century by a 'person of uncommon feeling and taste.' The time, between late winter and early spring in Italy (and the first of the month), is a liminal moment of intensified awareness, which in Horace (*Odes* I.4, IV.7) marks the passing and renewal of life. Revisitation underscores the theme of time and memory, not only regarding Norton's life but, in this landscape strewn with bits of ancient pottery, of other lives. Beneath a statue of Juno that imparts an aura of the sacred, Norton gathers violets, the flower of memory, and picks up a piece of 'red-veined marble,' which seems to convey to him a sense of life's transience. 'More carefully' than on previous visits, as if he were to discover something of greater value by perseverance, he searches for inscriptions, one of which was hidden behind the 'damp unfolding leaves' of the acanthus like the pages of a sibylline book. Another he found incised on an arch: *Redde Diana diem*, Bring back, O Diana, the day (NL 1:162–3) – a prayer to the goddess of the moon (and night) to hurry along so that the new day will come. Diana being the protectress of youth, the inscription could also mean, Bring back my youth. Afterward, the violet's 'perfume fills the air' of his room, prolonging the memory. Such experiences would lead Norton to write some years later, 'If I ever come back, may I be born Italian' (NL 1:404). Having recovered the deepest currents of his life and his cultural past, he felt reborn, expressed in terms of coming back or returning home.

Modelled after Irving's *Sketch Book*, Longfellow's *Outre-Mer* records his three-year journey to Europe (1826–8), the last of which was in Italy. Almost always the spectator, he paints 'scenes' – direct, present tense, al fresco – to entertain a distant audience; the theatrical metaphor, repeated some nine times in fifty pages, enables him to play upon the shift between appearance (or dream) and reality, ever likely to change poles. In Florence he rents a room overlooking the Piazza S. Maria Novella, the 'opening scene' of Boccaccio's *Decameron;* in Rome, he lives in the Piazza Navona where, leaning out of his window, he remarks on the 'busy scene,' the 'animated and curious scene,' 'better than a play,' a 'scene of mirth' (OM 320–3). It was a good seat because this was then Rome's main marketplace, and once a week in August its fountain drains were blocked to make an artificial lake. Carriages drive axle-deep through the waters; someone gropes after a hat that is floating away; a man chases a splashing spaniel who has stolen his shoe (OM 321, 330). In Florence he was much taken by an *improvvisatore* reciting the *Invasion of Italy* and the *Battle of Navarino* with a piano accompaniment, with nine rhymes and nine subjects required (HWL 1:254). Lowell, too, sees the Italians as a histrionic people performing a continuous 'exhibition': they have only *recitare* (recite) to denote acting, 'for their stage is no more theatric than their street' (FT 207). By unifying gesture, rhythm, and animating will, Italians transformed themselves into pictures or, more exactly, the picturesque.

In contrast to his scenes of life, Longfellow's morbid theme becomes obsessive: readings of tomb inscriptions, Tasso's death-chamber, malaria, a bandit's execution, a pilgrim's march, an Irish monk's death from tuberculosis, the 'mournful scene' of another monk's funeral (OM 334). Of all works of art to write about in Florence, Longfellow focuses upon just two, both dealing with the plague: the *Decameron*, when the ten young men and women abandon the 'infected city' for the purity of nature; and a waxwork of the plague by the little known Sicilian artist Gaetano Zumbo (1656–1701), bespeaking 'death, corruption, and the charnel-house,' and haunting him like 'a dream of the sepulchre' (OM 313). 'Humpback dwarfs' that 'tumbled into the dirt by the masked horns of young bullocks' near the tomb of Augustus (OM 330–1) bewilder him – is it a parody of a pagan ritual? Longfellow frowns upon Sunday card-playing, dancing, and theatre-going; 'at the same time no one thinks what they are doing is immoral.' The custom of the *cavalier servente* shocks him during the *passeggiata* in the Corso: 'I see a lady of the highest ton [quality] – who has a rich young banker for her "cicisbeo" – riding in her carriage with her daughter – her husband and her lover!' (HWL 1:272). The seventeenth-century poet Vincenzo da Filicaia's 'To Italy' summarizes his view of the modern scene; Longfellow has chosen a poem that was composed at the outset of the Italian decline:

> Italy! Italy! thou who'rt doomed to wear
> The fatal gift of beauty, and possess
> The dower funest of infinite wretchedness
> Written upon thy forehead by despair;
> Ah! Would that thou wert stronger, or less fair.

Filicaia makes a causal, even fatalistic, connection between an extraordinary gift and an equally extraordinary punishment. Trading upon the traditional topos of a feminine Italy, to be found in Dante, Petrarch, and Leopardi, to name a few, he accuses his country of being a beautiful but morally weak woman. The masculine topos of Cain evokes the country's fratricidal violence, for which she must wear her shame and despair as publicly as her beauty, indeed, as a mark on her forehead. Filicaia therefore urges his country to rectify its failings by being 'stronger' morally or 'less fair' and tempting physically. Elsewhere in the New Englanders' writings Italy is a Venus, a Siren, and a Madonna.

Longfellow typically starts out as the spectator, but often he can be so absorbed by a scene that 'outside' becomes 'inside.' At night in Genoa, which has one of the largest, best-preserved medieval districts in Europe, he gazes from his hotel terrace over the sea – the prospect is like a 'dream' (OM 308), until the midnight church bells wake him to what becomes a nightmare:

> I descended from the terrace, and, groping my way through one of the dark and narrow lanes which intersect the city in all directions, soon found myself in the Strada Nuova. The long line of palaces lay held in shadow, half in light, stretching before me in magical perspective, like the long, vapory opening of a cloud in the summer sky. (OM 308)

His promenade has aspects of an inward, transgressive journey in which he 'descended' through 'dark and narrow' lanes, a labyrinth, an esoteric symbol for the realm of the dead that at the same time encrypts the hidden, interlocking pathways of the mind. We see by a shadowy half-light, not the full light of consciousness, at the liminal hour of midnight. 'Magical' signifies the non-rational powers of imagination, and the 'vapory opening' is the mist that hides and reveals *myst*eriously. The church presents a scene of gaudy, satanic orientalism:

> Midnight mass was to be chanted. A dazzling blaze of light from the high altar shone upon the red marble columns which support the roof, and fell with a solemn effect upon the kneeling crowd that filled the body of the church. All beyond was in darkness. ... And yet, among that prostrate crowd, how many had been drawn thither by unworthy motives, – motives even more unworthy than mere idle curiosity!

Who has seen an Italian crowd 'prostrate' at mass? Ever since Herodotus (1.87) prostration has been linked to oriental despotism in contrast to Western bowing or handshaking. Longfellow's response betrays a moral anxiousness over what he sees as submissive, idolatrous Catholicism; the crowd's confusion, born of an exaggerated emotionalism, perhaps suggested non-rational and even monstrous forces.[27] His fascination has a covering motive, curiosity; the crowd's motives are 'more unworthy' and 'sinful' for mingling religion and eroticism, though his own response has a similar mix: 'How many a heart beat wild with earthly passion, while the unconscious lip repeated the accustomed prayer! ... Is not the long day long enough, is not the wide world wide enough, has not society frivolity enough for thee, that thou shouldst seek out this midnight hour, this holy place, this solemn sacrifice, to add irreverence to thy folly?'

The darker motive emerges in a gothic encounter between a young man and woman who meet by a pillar described in language weighted toward the negative ('shadow,' 'low,' 'veiled,' 'hide,' dimly'):

> In the shadow of a column stood a young man wrapped in a cloak, earnestly conversing in a low whisper with a female figure, so veiled as to hide her face from the eyes of all but her companion. The young man continued leaning against the column, and the girl, gliding silently among the dimly lighted aisle, mingled with the crowd, and threw herself upon her knees. Beware, poor girl, thought I, lest thy gentle nature prove thy undoing!

Then he wonders, 'Perhaps, alas, thou art already undone!' The idler, Longfellow's surrogate, is 'leaning' in a relaxed manner against a pillar, the male symbol; the woman is filled with the panic of temptation, divided between her love for man and God. Longfellow's fantasy is that he is the young man, and would be as nonchalant in the same circumstances. He hears the 'evil spirit' Mephistopheles tempting Margaret, for it is midnight, the in-between moment, when devils slip from eternal into human time and roam the earth. The scene contains an inner journey, satanism, a black mass, temptation, sexuality, and guilt.

Because Italians share a long, close history with their landscape, the one shaping the other, nature may be read allegorically for insight into their character. One episode in Lowell expresses more nearly than any other the depth and complexity of his response. On a fall afternoon he rode on horseback from Hadrian's villa in Tivoli to the Ponte S. Antonio, the ruin of a Roman aqueduct beneath Monte Cavo. 'All the other accessories of our ride were delicious,' he writes, recalling a plenum of sensation: 'It was a clear, cool day, and we soon left the high-road for a bridle-path along the side of a mountain, among gigantic olive-trees, said to be five hundred years old, and which had certainly employed all their time in getting into the weirdest and wonderfullest shapes' (FT 165–6). Leaving the 'high-road' or beaten track for a byway invites something unusual. Olive trees, big as oaks and extremely old from their size, are a synecdoche for the ancient land; the olive is totemic for fecundity, health, and longevity. 'Gigantic' implies monumental, like classical ruins; the trees, too, are in ruins, knobbed, gnarled, and full of the 'weirdest' and 'wonderfullest' forms. 'Weird' conveys its Anglo-Saxon sense of 'fated.'

These olive trees, similar to those that Rodolfo Lanciani photographed fifty years later (thought by some to be seventeen hundred years old),[28] seem possessed by the controlling *daimon* of their individuality:

> Clearly in this green commonwealth there was no heavy roller of public opinion to flatten all character to a lawn-like uniformity. Everything was individual and eccentric. And there was something fearfully human, too, in the wildest contortions. It was some such wood that gave Dante the hint of his human forest in the seventh circle, and I should have dreaded to break a twig, lest I should hear that voice complaining, –
> 'perchè mi scerpi?
> Non hai tu spirto di pietate alcuno?'

Public opinion in America suppresses what it considers the unseemly and excessively idiosyncratic to make for bland conformism. As with the blades of grass, the individuals in a commonwealth are cut down to the same size. Lowell had previously contrasted natural metaphor, which he found appropriate to Italy, with technological metaphor, which he applied to America, where 'railways and omnibuses' have 'rolled flat all little social prominences and peculiarities' (FT 20). Pursuing the contrast more deeply and bearing in mind other, not always flattering, references to Italians as laws unto themselves, Lowell suggests that the un-modernized Italians are rather like these olive trees: 'individual,' 'eccentric,' larger than life, ancient, and characterized at once by an otherness and a shared resemblance, summed up in the phrase 'fearfully human.' The insight is accompanied by a feeling of horror ('I should have dreaded'), while the scene is placed beyond the ordinary by the three superlatives ('weirdest, 'wonderfullest,' 'wildest'); the trees seem so imbued with the human that one of them might almost 'speak.'

In the forest of the suicides Dante breaks a dead twig from a bush, unlocking the voice of Pier delle Vigne (*Inf.* 13): 'Why do you tear me? Have you no spirit of pity at all?' Lowell connects a natural scene of great age, an olive grove planted by human hands, to a topos with a long textual history: the voice in the Dantesque wood, which Tasso employs for Clorinda's tree in *Gerusalemme liberata* 13, and which traces to Polydorus' burial mound in a phantasmagoric passage from Virgil (*Aen.* 3.22–44). 'Why do you tear me?' Would you know my secret? In all these writers, breaking the twig signifies the transgression; then the contexts take over and deliver up different secrets; Lowell's is the terrible otherness of Italy, 'fearfully human ... in the wildest contortions,' which in such scenes as this he had the courage to recognize. What Lowell learned about Italy was much less than what he was learning in Italy about himself.

On another occasion Lowell draws on the Romantic distinction between self-enhancing solitude and self-threatening loneliness: the 'solitudes of Rome ... are without a parallel; for it is not the mere absence of man, but the sense of his departure, that makes a profound loneliness' (FT 225–6). In the common acceptation, writes John C. Woodward, *loneliness* is feeling 'disconnected or alienated from positive persons, places or things,' whereas *solitude* is 'something we may choose for ourselves,' a period of refreshment; William Desmond comments that 'loneliness is a solitude that has become mindful of itself, and in this, mindful of a longing for something it lacks.'[29] In Lowell's Rome, solitude is 'without a parallel' because nowhere else looms the presence of death in so all-pervasive a manner; because the collective presence of humanity – and therefore its 'absence' – over two and a half millennia has left a record of itself in monuments, tombs, and ruins from every age; and more so because this record gives an acute sense not only of death but of dying, the 'sense of his departure.' The uneasiness provoked by the images of mortality focuses individuals on their own death, thereby preventing them from achieving some replenishing communion with the past or the dead. Robbed of the power of choice in the matter, one cannot connect with 'persons, places or things,' and therefore instead of enjoying a self-nourishing solitude, one faces the inescapable truths that one's relation to time is brief and that one dies alone: the 'profound loneliness' contains the intuition of death. Rome is often taken as an example of the classical or Longinian sublime of noble, ego-enhancing emotions; yet it is equally an expression of the Burkean or modern sublime of ego-destroying negation.[30] For Lowell, those individuals who seek improving solitude may find themselves exposed to crippling loneliness. This exposure resembles the very thing that destroys the sublime: a threat of death so physically or psychologically real and alienating that the aesthetic pleasure of the sublime disappears.

Norton's view of Italy was the most informed of his fellow New Englanders because he returned for longer periods and made Italian art and architecture his special field of study. His brief tour in 1850 (at twenty-three) left mixed responses. In Florence he seems to have remembered only the negative aspects of his conversation with the Brownings: Italian literature in 'as low a state as her art,' widespread religious 'infidelity,' the 'low character' of priests, a thieving servant, a corrupt judiciary (NL 1:76–7). A comment by Goethe's grandson, 'that he felt that he was not an artist, for he was conscious of moral preferences,' troubled Norton; it was not the 'right view of an artist,' though an 'advance' over Goethe's (NL 1:76). For Norton, art began with moral precepts; expression came after. Narrow scruple within a provincial sensibility brought him to scorn the supposed amorality of Goethe's private life and of Faust, thereby preventing him from comprehending the larger moral scope of Goethe's genius. By the time Norton was writing his *Notes*, the product of a second sojourn in 1856–7, he had befriended John Ruskin whose influence, together with that of Thomas Carlyle, on the relation between art, morals, and society would loom large in his career. Norton was predisposed to interpret art as an expression of the moral character of a nation; Ruskin provided him with an all-encompassing historical framework and a sense of mission.

Acquiring a theory of history and interpreting it for his own purpose was only half of Norton's achievement; his pedagogical effort would be to promote not only a concept of the Middle Ages but of Western civilization that went against the American grain.[31] The Reformation considered the Middle Ages as 'a long period of institutional and doctrinal deformity,' writes Angelina La Piana; Protestantism 'linked itself directly with ancient Christianity and dropped the intermediary period from the chain of history.'[32] This occlusion was more the case in America, which lacked physical reminders of the period. Some idea of the resistance that Norton faced can be glimpsed from a remark by Hawthorne, who was in Italy at nearly the same time as Norton. Though it is impossible to conceive of Rome without the Middle Ages, the Church, or the Renaissance, Hawthorne nonetheless wrote in *The Marble Faun* that 'Rome, as it now exists, has grown up under the Popes, and seems like nothing but a heap of broken rubbish, thrown into the great chasm between our own days and the Empire, merely to fill it up.'[33] Moreover, many Americans rejected 'classic history' as well as the classical education, even during the so-called golden age of the classics in the antebellum period. Edward Tyrell Channing, a professor of rhetoric and oratory, decried an 'excessive fondness' for 'models in literature' for which we have 'hardly any thing of real congeniality'; the barbarians might better have demolished the 'fair fabricks of Greece and Rome' instead of leaving us to 'grow tender among ruins and fragments.' He championed the 'nativeness' of American literature which 'has, or should have, nothing to do with strangers.'[34]

In Norton's cultural politics, the Italians' 'conscious spiritual relation' with one another reached its 'highest level' in the late Middle Ages (1150–1300). This is the age of the commune, the 'lay democracy,' 'when men painted from their hearts ... the days when Florence was capable of the noblest things, – the days just before Dante's time, just before Giotto began to build his Campanile' (1334) (NTS 18–19, 109, 303).[35] The first signs of a turn appear in the late thirteenth and early fourteenth century, with 'a decline in simplicity and purity and depth of feeling, and an increase of worldliness.' He instances the difference between Dante's *Vita Nuova* (1293/4), with its 'purity of youth' and 'touch of archaism,' and the *Divine Comedy* (?1307–20) marking the 'power of maturity' and a 'more material epoch'; the ideal reconciliation of purity and power has never been accomplished (NL 2:48). Because architecture is, among the arts, the 'most quickly responsive to the instincts and the desires of a people,' cathedrals were Norton's principal symbols for medieval solidarity, illustrating the retreat of feudalism in Italy and the rise of a 'democratic element': 'no sooner did a city achieve its freedom than its people began to take thought for a cathedral.' In the wave of religious enthusiasm that followed, 'instead of being carried away by the wasteful current of feeling, they were able to guide and control to great and noble purposes the impulsive activity and bursting energies of the time' (NTS 105–6, 125).

Orvieto cathedral, whose cornerstone was laid in 1290, is Norton's favourite example, the subject of perhaps his best pages on Italy. According to tradition, its founding took inspiration from the Miracle of Lake Bolsena, which the citizens wanted to memorialize. The town levied taxes, proprietors deeded lands, neighbouring cities and towns paid generous tribute, and pilgrims contributed offerings. Lorenzo Maitani, the architect of the Siena cathedral, was commissioned to lead the project, and agents were dispatched across Italy to purchase various kinds of stone and precious materials: black marble from the Sienese quarries, alabaster from Sant'Antimo, white marble from Carrara, the finest used stone from Roman ruins and villas. Some of the very marble that embodied pagan images would be transformed by artists into a display of Christian symbolism. Though mixed motives might have played a role for some persons (civic rivalry, private ambition), for the vast majority of people a work of such scope and grandeur demanded a higher faith, one that required a commitment of generations, and one that was sustained by the sight of the glorious edifice slowly rising above their own humble dwellings. When the wagons of stone arrived at the bottom of the hill, the townspeople, male and female, from all ranks, harnessed themselves alongside the horses and buffaloes to pull the loads up the 'steep ascent to the uplifted city.' Norton draws a memorable portrait of immanental Catholicism: 'As cart after cart was dragged in by its band of devotees, it was set in its place in a circle of wagons around the church. Candles were lighted upon them all, as upon so many altars. At night the people watched, singing hymns and songs of praise, or inflicting discipline upon themselves, with prayers for the forgiveness of their sins' (NTS 124–5). For once Norton forgot to deplore the papal indulgences that were an added inducement.[36]

The fourteenth century, which began with faith in God, virtue, the principle of 'retribution,' and even the 'future regeneration of Italy,' witnessed the first signs of decline; 'faith disappears' and the cause of Italy is lost. By the fifteenth century a general malaise had set in as people sought relief in 'self-forgetfulness among the delights of sensual enjoyment' (NTS 299–300). For Ruskin, in Venice the Ducal Palace's Porta della Carta (1441) built in the 'new' Renaissance style marked the spot where 'vice reached its climax.'[37] Similarly for Norton, the construction of Brunelleschi's dome in Florence beginning in the 1440s was the turning point; it completed the cycle of great cathedrals begun in the Middle Ages and adumbrated the grandiloquence of Renaissance architecture: 'in the fifteenth century, canons of taste were established ... which, symptomatic as they were of a general change in the spiritual condition of society, debased the standard of an art whose capacities of execution were daily [!] growing more limited' (NTS 103). The Christian purity of Giotto, Fra Angelico, and Perugino was swallowed up in the vanity, excess, and insincerity of later artists, whose saints did not look saintly but rather like 'heathen images' or the 'lowest earthly characters.' Though Michelangelo had given 'just expression to the character of the Papacy in its period of greatest splendor,' he was, with Raphael, a 'forerunner of decay.' In the Renaissance – the notion would be outlandish to Burckhardt – 'original thought was discouraged' by slavish imitation of classical forms: 'art was degraded to the service of ambition and caprice, of luxury and pomp, until it became utterly corrupt and false' (NTS 62–3, 305). Bernini and Borromini stood for 'Roman taste and Roman feeling since Michel Angelo died. It is worse now than ever' (NL 1:144). Norton was a born prognosticator: 'I wonder ... whether we are not to have another period of decline, fall, and ruin and revival, like that of the first thirteen hundred years of our era,' he confided to Ruskin. The fall from 1300 to the mid-nineteenth century had been catastrophic: 'no man who knows what society at the present day really is, but must agree that it is not worth preserving on its present basis' (NL 1:372). One could only wait for the cycle to complete itself.

In April 1856 Norton joined Lowell and two others for a five-week, two-hundred-mile mule-back tour of Sicily culminating in their ascent of Mt Etna. 'Tremendous work, but worth doing at any cost and discomfort,' said Norton, 'such inns as it never entered the heart of man to conceive ... But one lives and likes it' (NL 1:145). Though the island is 'very interesting in scenery and associations,' Lowell lambasted it as being the 'worst governed country in Europe'; its trade was tightly controlled; 'with every advantage of climate and soil, it is miserably poor, – there are no roads, and vexatious restrictions repress trade in every direction. The people struck me as looking more depressed than any I have seen' (JLB 1:384). Regrettably, this was a lost opportunity to write more extensively on the island in the midst of a major historical transition.[38]

In the lull between political storms, 1848 and 1859, Norton looked in vain for signs that the Risorgimento might reach a positive conclusion. An agnostic and the most secularized of the Big Three, he laid the evils of the present at the door of the Church – so fiercely condemning its 'corrupt doctrines' and 'method' in the *Notes* that he apologized in its preface to Italian Catholic friends (NTS vi).[39] Pius IX is a 'known gettatore' (evil eye); Cardinal Antonelli, secretary of state, is a 'dictator' who, like Iago, 'can smile, and smile ... he is a villain'; 'priests, the princes and the churches – they are all alike, untouched by the sacred genius of the place' (NL 1:143–4, 158, 165–6). In one poem (1857) 'priests' rhymes with 'beasts': 'the worst government is that of priests, / And poverty and discontent grow fast, / Where superstition chains men down like beasts.' If he were less indiscriminate, he would have distributed the blame among the Italian ruling class as a whole. Recalling the failure of 1848, he writes Lowell that Italy needs 'another revolution' so that Rome may be 'battered down and depopulated if in that way we can get rid of these churches and these priests. I think I could roast a Franciscan with pleasure, and it would need only a tolerable opportunity to make me stab a Cardinal in the dark' (NL 1:144). This is the Norton whom Ruskin in *Praeterita* singled out for his 'all-pervading sympathy.'[40]

Despite his call for revolution Norton did not want a repetition of 1848. In *Considerations on Some Recent Social Theories* (1853), he inveighed against Mazzini's concept of the people, political liberty, and democratic republicanism; though he applauds the 'republican spirit' (with 'less caste and rank division') in the Middle Ages, leadership must still be left to an enlightened elite.[41] In the 1850s, even while he campaigned for proper housing and schools for the immigrant poor, he supported the Know-Nothing Party, which urged stricter naturalization laws and the exclusion of both immigrants and Catholics from public office. Still, he saluted Garibaldi's popular invasion of Sicily and the march up the Italian peninsula, raising money for The Thousand at garden parties in Newport, Rhode Island, in 1860. The war in Italy, he writes Arthur Hugh Clough, absorbs him more than Lincoln's electoral campaign: Italy's 'new birth' is the 'grandest event of the modern period' (NL 1:210) – which shows both the depth of his Italophilia and his loss of proportion. Though the months leading up to Unification of Italy were 'full of hope' (a 'new life seems to have begun') (NTS vi), he coolly tallied the factors against its future: an 'ignorant people' whose temperament was 'passionate rather than rational,' 'an unintelligent and dissolute king,' 'an upper class unaccustomed to administration,' 'public men unused to debate,' 'civic virtues and political discipline' in abeyance 'for centuries,' and the 'idea of Italy' itself in need of creation. Norton predicts dire consequences: 'constitutional monarchy may lead to a constitutional republic, that to an unconstitutional Despotism' (NL 1:370).

Longfellow and Lowell also fretted through the years of Unification. In his last lecture on Italian literature Longfellow wrote of his 'strong predilection for the Italians ... Particularly at this moment, in the hour of their tribulation and anguish, I would be careful not to say anything which might chill your enthusiasm on their behalf' (HLB 2:186–7). In 1869, on the eve of the annexation of Rome, employing yet another theatrical allusion, Longfellow compares 'depressing' Rome to 'King Lear staggering in the storm and crowned with weeds,' a 'death-in-life.' In a state of anticipation, 'bombarded by public opinion' and 'new ideas,' the Eternal City was 'still holding out, ringing its alarm bells and living on old shoes. It is quite unchanged since you and I were here forty years ago. I said so to Cardinal Antonelli the other day; and he answered, taking a pinch of snuff, "Yes, thank God!"' (HLB 2:450). Less pessimist than either Longfellow or Norton, Lowell in 'Villa Franca, 1859' assails the surprise treaty between France and Austria that halted the drive towards unification and confirmed Austria's dominance of the Veneto. Louis Napoleon 'is not Fate'; Emperor Franz Joseph 'is not Time'; their ship of state sails towards the 'sharp-tusked reefs / Old instincts hardening to new beliefs.' Fate is on Italy's side:

Patience a little; learn to wait;
Hours are long on the clock of Fate.
Spin, spin, Clotho spin!
Lachesis, twist! and, Atropos, sever!
Darkness is strong, and so is Sin,
But surely God endures forever!

Fate is in the hands of a Calvinist God who will deliver the Italians from their depraved oppressors. Yet does 'Darkness' and 'Sin' belong only to the oppressors or to the Italians as well? Beyond liberation, the future is uncertain; Italians would be responsible for themselves: 'the Idea of Rome will incarnate itself again as soon as an Italian brain is found large enough to hold it' (FT 226).

After Rome fell in 1870, completing the work of the Risorgimento, the New Englanders began to complain of the decline of Italy – into modernity. In 1874 Lowell said, not without irony, that Naples has 'changed for the worse'; 'Fancy, there are no more lazzaroni [mendicants], there is no more *corricolo* [an inexpensive public vehicle]' (JLL 2:120). The huge copper coins are gone, he reflects, 'at present it is paper money, and the practical instead of the picturesque':

Is the day of the railways worse than that of Judgment? Why could not one country be taken and the other left? Let them try all their new acids of universal suffrage and what not on the tough body of the New World. The skin will heal again. But this lovely, disburied figure of Ausonia, they corrode her marble surface beyond all cure. *Panem et circenses* wasn't so bad after all ... America gives the *panem*, but do you find it particularly amusing just now? (JLL 2:120)

The 'day of the railways' is the judgment day of modernity: if so much is to be damned, cannot a country like Italy be saved? In 1881 the fashion for 'brazen-faced models' and 'hateful boots with a high heel in the midst of the sole' ('a cloven hoof') annoys him; when he first came to Rome, peasant women wore sandals. '[I] am growing into a furious socialist at the sight of these upstart palaces [in Piazza Barberini] that shut out the sun from Diogenes' (JLL 2:263–4).

The rapidity and extent of change appalled Norton on his return after a twelve-year absence in 1869; uniformity trumped diversity in all directions. Modern Italy, 'in losing tyrants, in becoming constitutional, in taking to trade, is doing what she can to spoil her charm'; it 'has developed the commercial and trading taste, – the taste of New York and Paris' (NL 1:369–70). Florence, then the capital, 'has greatly changed' on account of 'Americanism out of America' (NL 1:372). Other places have withstood; four months before annexation, Rome maintains a 'prerogative of immobility, – and resists with steady persistency the flood of "American" barbarism and of universal materialism which is desolating Europe' (NL 1:384).[42] He often singles out America rather than another industrial nation. Siena, too, is 'Italian of the true stamp ... before the tyrants were driven out and America was discovered'; it is 'not yet revolutionized, – free from the taint of the ten per cent stock-broking age'; 'I could be content to live here' (NL 1:395). Exemplifying technological ahistoricism, the 'railroad whistle just behind the church of Santa Maria Novella, or just beyond the Campo Santo at Pisa, sounds precisely as it sounds on the Back Bay or at the Fitchburg Station; the common school are Americanizing the land to a surprising degree' (NL 1:369–70). '"Costume" has died out except in the remotest districts; dress has become uniform all over Europe' (NL 1:411). On Lake Como in 1883 he complains in his set antitheses (imagination and reality, leisure and speed, individuality and levelling, etc.): 'imagination has to exclude much of the intrusive life of the prosaic days in which we live. The little smoky steamers are puffing about with bustling speed too constantly, there are too many second-class travellers with their second-class style, the vulgar democracy invades the sacred retreats of the Muses.' Now tourism has ramped up the numbers. 'Most romantic' Bellagio has become a 'cheap modern watering place,' a 'place of trivialities and trinkets,' 'dust and fashion'; hotels are 'vast, conspicuous, enormous democratic palaces,' where 'democratic' has negative associations (unlike in his descriptions of the Middle Ages) and 'conspicuous' implies the mimetic desire that robs one's selfhood (NL 2:154–5).[43] Progress had brought on 'the destruction of old shrines, the disregard of beauty, the decline in personal distinction, the falling off in manners.' In America material well-being had a balancing effect: 'the superb and unexampled spectacle of fifty millions of human beings living at peace and in plenty ... compensates in a certain measure for the absence of high culture, of generous ideals and of imaginative life' (NL 2:156–7). It would compensate, too, in Italy, but Norton was not seeing it.

Norton's antagonism drove him to revise upward his opinion of the Church. 'In spite of its obscurantism, and its elevation of itself about the State,' he came to prefer it to 'our modern sects'; 'Protestantism has failed.' The Church, with its 'dignity, and splendid ceremonial, and noble traditions, and secular sympathies,' stood as one of the last bastions against the modern. It seemed to support his social agenda: 'one of its greatest services,' he said in 1901, has been its 'control ... over the Irish immigrant' with regard to 'pecuniary honesty' and 'chastity' (NL 2:308–9). He might have appreciated the irony that Irish American Catholicism, which from the 1850s imposed its doctrinal and cultural orientation on the official Church in America, shared certain features with northern European and American Protestantism (emphasis on transcendence over immanence, juridical formalism, Jansenist neo-puritanism, instruction) and played a large role in the Americanization of the Irish and other immigrants.[44] Norton understood the Church culturally, though not without condescension: 'I cannot enter an old church, worn by the feet and knees of generation after generation of those who have brought their cares, and sorrows, and desires there for relief, for comfort, for new hope, but my heart shares with them in their emotions, and the tawdry adornments and trifling *ex votos* only adds to the impression' (NL 2:208–9).

One of the enduring achievements of Longfellow, Lowell, and Norton was their concerted promotion of Dante as a vital force in American literature. Unfortunately, it came at the expense of Milton, his nearest rival. As James Turner comments, Dante provided a needed 'alternative' to the radical Puritanism that the New Englanders shared with Milton, and also a 'cosmopolitan bridge' to the 'ancient culture of the richly imagined Continent.' For K.P. Van Anglen, Dante was favoured on political grounds: in the struggle between the antinomian demand for 'liberty, equality and personal autonomy' and the Arminian one for 'hierarchy and order,' the Boston Unitarian elite found Milton with his revolutionary Satan less amenable than Dante to their leaning towards order. According to Kermit Vanderbilt, Norton felt that the *Divine Comedy* was 'more congenial to the modern poetic spirit,' representing an ideal of wholeness in contrast to the 'shattered unity of the modern consciousness.'[45]

The Big Three adumbrated the elevation of Dante over Milton in the High Modernism of Pound and Eliot and their successors.[46] While Milton is a '*doctrinaire*, ready to sacrifice everything to what at the moment seemed the abstract truth' 'with no regard to historical antecedents,' Lowell writes, Dante is not a 'mere partisan,' a 'Luther before his time,' because with a doctrinal core that is 'simple, human and wholesome' he could 'generalize his special experience into something mediatorial for all of us' (AB 51, 63, 129, 271). Milton's politics are those of the controversialist whose issues are 'ephemeral' (AB 270); though Dante was similarly enmeshed in the politics of his times, his audience has 'widened in proportion as men have receded from the theories of Church and State which are supposed to be its foundation' (AB 57). Both poets inform their work with an autobiographical presence; whereas Milton is a 'self-opinionated, unforgiving, and unforgetting man' who 'never lets himself go,' Dante is 'individual rather than self-conscious' and 'pliable as a field of grain at the breath of Beatrice' (AB 278, 311). Against Longfellow's preference for linguistic analysis or Norton's for moral allegory, Lowell stresses Dante's personal drama of sin and redemption; his epic is an 'autobiography of a human soul, of yours and mine, it may be, as well as Dante's' (AB 124). As the bridge between the ancient and modern worlds, 'the theme of his poem is purely subjective, modern ... romantic; but its treatment is objective (almost to realism ...), and it is limited by a form of classic severity' (AB 52, 129, 131). Unlike Eschenbach's *Parzival*, which shows 'good feeling' rather than 'settled conviction,' and which is 'wandering' in its design, Dante's epic is a 'Gothic cathedral,' continually unfolding before the pilgrim reader: the effect 'of its leading thought is that of aspiration' (AB 134, 140). As against Milton's 'Calvinistic Zeus,' 'nothing in all poetry approaches the imaginative grandeur of Dante's vision of God'; 'since Dante, no one had stood on these visiting terms with heaven' (AB 54, 311).[47]

Only fleetingly could Longfellow, Lowell, and Norton recognize the links between the modern Italians and their historical past. Perhaps, by hindsight, their inability to come to terms with emergent Italy was a missed opportunity, because their misapprehension carried forward and inadvertently contributed to a climate of opinion that did little to prepare for the great wave of immigrants to the United States beginning in the 1880s. Yet from time to time, amidst all their moralizing, the New Englanders glimpsed the persistence of the historical character, seeing the modern Italian as the heir, and the only possible heir that fits the empty space in the historical puzzle. 'How this people kept any spark of sweetness and charity and humanity alive through the burnings and massacres of the middle ages and through the wanton wickedness of the Renaissance, must always be a matter of wonder,' remarks Norton, taking the long view, though in his puritanical vein. 'And now, if one knows how to live with them, they are the sweetest people on earth' (NL 1:404); the conditional clause contains a wealth of experience.[48] Mentioned are sweetness, humanity, and charity, but other enduring traits can be found in his and the other New Englanders' pages: individuality, anarchic tendencies, sensuousness, virtuosity, love of novelty, a convincing combination of sincerity and rhetoric or theatricality, and fascination with violence. If the Italophiles could not connect the past with the present and preferred the past, increasingly as the years wore on, their writings are witnesses to the continuity, a vivid record of Italian life in a moment of swift transition.

III

Longfellow, Lowell, and Norton have been grouped together because they and their followers were arraigned together under a satiric label, the 'Genteel Tradition,' which has endured to this day. In books and essays beginning with 'The Genteel Tradition in American Philosophy' in 1911 and culminating in *The Last Puritan* and an autobiography, Santayana criticized these writers and thinkers for failing to bring their art close to the life of their times: 'about the middle of the nineteenth century, in the quiet sunshine of provincial prosperity, New England had an Indian summer of the mind; and an agreeable reflective literature showed how brilliant that russet and yellow season could be'; yet it yielded a 'harvest of leaves.' The Genteel Tradition drew on its Puritan heritage for its scrupulous conscience and sense of duty, softened by the Boston Unitarians and culminating in Transcendentalism with its mild optimism and personalist mysticism. For Santayana, the Genteel writers were too timid, elevated, moralizing, and lacking in tragic spirit; they maintained a fastidious distance between *belles letters* and the raw, energetic world of business, democracy, and popular culture.[49] In their belief that America needed 'culture' they showed 'a special deference and attraction to Europe, where "culture" was thought to have its native home.'[50] Santayana had known some of the Genteel writers in their old age; as he recalled, Norton 'would tell his classes, shaking his head with a slight sigh, that the Greeks did not play football.' Norton did not deplore football's roughness (the Greeks had even rougher sports), but its collectivism, routinization, and boosterism, which seemed like an epitome of his country's utilitarian future.[51] Genteel writers were powerless before those forces.

After Santayana, the Genteel Tradition was eviscerated by Van Wyck Brooks ('highbrow,' 'unsocial,' 'desiccated,' 'remote,' 'vaporous'), Vernon Parrington (a 'nation-wide nuisance'), Randolph Bourne ('a little thing of Brunelleschi's'), Sinclair Lewis, Malcolm Cowley, Edmund Wilson, Ludwig Lewisohn ('professorial exercises'), Mumford (not 'organic,' i.e., sufficiently 'American'), and Mary McCarthy, by social realists, High Modernists, and liberal reformists, until by the 1950s the critique became a tradition in itself, hollowed out to the point where even the virtues of the originals were condemned, ignored, or forgotten.[52]

After nearly a century, the Genteel writers deserve revisionist attention. But first one must allow that some of Santayana's and the others' critique can be sustained. However personally committed were the Genteel writers, their major works did not engage the great issues of their times – the Mexican War, slavery and the Missouri Compromise, the Civil War. Their sympathies were meliorist; and when those sympathies were abused, they did not rouse themselves to significant action, but instead tended to temporize, 'always busy applying first principles to trifles.'[53] Nor, in the shadow of the European masters, did these writers exhibit great originality or experimentation. Teachers more than writers in their criticism, they should have written books, not textbooks. Against the Genteel Tradition Santayana brought forward Shelley, Whitman, and Browning as poets who, connecting their idealism to the political or practical world, unified their morality with their aesthetics and took the battle into the camp of the enemy; and both Shelley and Browning had spent years in Italy and drew upon it for inspiration.

At the same time Santayana does not credit Genteel achievements. Though he respected the enlightened Boston of the 1850s, he condescends: 'There were gentle lights burning in some of those houses, with no exaggeration of their brilliance: Ticknors, Parkmans, Longfellows and Lowells with their various modest and mature minds.'[54] Parkman's for one was no 'modest' mind. When American culture was still narrow, rigid, insecure, and dominated by British models, the Genteel writers served and improved their times; they succeeded in introducing Americans to foreign cultures (German, Italian, French, Spanish, Hindu) and expanding their knowledge of foreign languages, thereby paving the way for cosmopolitanism later in the century. As for the charge that they were too European, it begs the question whether 'creativity could or should respect national boundaries.'[55] They also founded or inspired numerous cultural institutions that have prospered down to the present time. In their Dante studies and translation, they surpassed Britain itself. Their legacy of Dante to the generation of Eliot and Pound secured his place among the foremost influences on High Modernism and twentieth-century literature in English.

In the past thirty years, critics and historians have levelled a new attack on the Genteel Tradition, seeking its origins in the political, economic, and professional elite of coastal Massachusetts.[56] On this view, the New England elite felt threatened by the violent forces of modernity, unleashed by the American and French Revolutions and 1848. Genteel culture supposedly acted as a barrier against the rising tide of disorder and anarchy. Authors (Dante) or periods (the medieval) are enshrined on the basis of how well they can be enlisted in support of class hierarchy and order. One difficulty with this interpretation is that, in making economic materialism or 'consumer culture' to be the motor of history, it turns genuine culture into a kind of front, superstructure, or mere snobbery, where the chief function of artists and thinkers is to lend authority and tone to the elite. This view based on economic reductionism denies any possibility of self-transcendence, or the kind of influence a Dante or Shakespeare might have on the formation of character. Moreover, it imposes one interpretation on an author or period; in the later nineteenth century, Dante or the Middle Ages served the cause of socialist communitarianism as much or more than capitalist hegemony. To give some idea of the complexity of the issue, Norton believed that the teaching of art history would foster spiritual values; he urged that Americans take up art collecting and museum building. He got his wish: in the Gilded Age the big American industrialists started buying up European treasures to compete for status, to the point where one could say that art collecting had become 'a product of materialism, not an alternative to it.'[57] Yet today, their museums are among the foremost public institutions adorning scores of American cities.

The Boston elite felt threatened both from populist politics and from the moneyed interests centred in New York and Philadelphia, where money would dominate populist politics. Yet it could be as plausibly argued that the progressivist Boston elite protected an ideal of high culture against what they perceived to be blind self-interest and crude materialism. They placed an enormous value on education, on philanthropy, and on social and legal reform. They succeeded in making their city 'the most important literary center in the United States' and 'eastern Massachusetts ... the most intellectually exciting part of the country' between the War of 1812 and the Civil War, and vital and productive in architecture, philosophy, the arts, and literature in the decades after.[58]

IV

George Stillman Hillard (1808–74), at one remove from the Genteel writers though still to be classed with them, approached Italy in an empirical spirit, well suited to his writing a comprehensive guide. After graduating from Harvard, he embarked on a career in law and politics, but a high-pitched voice prevented his making his mark in the age of American oratory. A Jacksonian Democrat, he served in the Massachusetts House and Senate, and held down the Boston office of his radical classmate and law partner, the abolitionist U.S. senator Charles Sumner. When Hawthorne, of whom he was the close friend and personal attorney, was in financial straits, he came to his rescue by raising a fund among Boston literati. Hawthorne praised the 'classic refinement of Hillard's culture.'[59] In its time *Six Months in Italy* (1853; 887 pp.), the product of a tour made in 1847–48, was 'probably the most popular book about Italy written by an American,' running through twenty-one editions before 1900.[60] John Lothrop Motley said that 'nothing can be more scholarly and elegant than the whole expression of his book'; 'his pages have the effect of finely coloured photographs of the scenes he has visited.'[61] Today it ranks among the finest travelogues in English in the past two centuries.

  Six Months in Italy covers more ground than the work of Hillard's fellow New Englanders. While the Grand Tour provides the book with a sturdy trunk (Milan, Venice, Florence, Rome, Naples), it branches out more extensively to the smaller cities and towns (Verona, Parma, Arezzo, Lucca, Pisa, Todi, and many others); 'Life, indeed, is short, and art is long, and all things cannot be seen; but thrift and resolution can do much, and let them not fail to see Perugia and Assissi (*sic*)' (2:335). His interests included religion, economics, agronomy, universities, and hospitals, as well as art, architecture, and popular culture, all of which inform his book. He wants travellers to be prepared for Italy, say, by reading on winter nights, but he is not unreasonable, making an epigram out of an epigram: 'the more learning the better; but a little is not dangerous' (SM 2:454).[62] He urges surveying the land with an unprejudiced gaze: 'the traveller must leave all his notions of progress and reform at the gates, or else he will be kept in a constant state of protest and rebellion ... he must try to forget such things as a representative government, town-meetings, public schools, railways, and steam-engines.' In sum, travellers in modern Italy need imagination, the 'power of going out of one's self, and forgetting the actual in the ideal' (SM 1:204). Roman ruins do not stand as a 'shrine for memory' apart from a city. Hillard captures that mixture of past and present one finds in Piranesi's engravings; 'we can nowhere escape from the debasing associations of actual life' (SM 1:204, 291). In what seems an almost contemporary approach, ruins are not merely aesthetic phenomena or moral symbols: 'they are texts,' to be read depending on particular, expressed interests. 'The scholar, who finds in a bath or a temple a nucleus for his vague and divergent reading to gather around, feels for it something like gratitude as well as attachment' (SM 1:292). A monograph-length study of travel writing on Italy, which concludes the book, is the first of its kind in English, as if he wanted to place himself in the line of northern European visitors to the south.

Hillard's tour, extensive even for six months, makes large demands on travellers, and so he warns against mental exhaustion in one of his homespun similes: 'as an overcrowded trunk cannot be shut, so an overcrowded mind falls short of its natural capacity of retention ... . Choose what seems most interesting, and let the rest go' (SM 1:100). Happily for posterity, Hillard would not let things go. His energy is prodigious, but he knows that strength must be husbanded. On Rome and the Campagna, almost half the entire work, he advises not to hurry with epigrammatic force: 'The Rome of the mind is not built in a day' (SM 1:203). With its sententiousness, alternation of Latinate and Anglo-Saxon diction ('natural capacity of retention,' 'let the rest go'), energetic rhythm, alliteration, parallelism, antithesis, and precision, his style shows the influence of Samuel Johnson (perhaps the strongest on any American style), revealing its roots in the more factual eighteenth-century travel writing. He conducts his readers like Rasselas touring Cairo:[63] 'many things must be forgotten, in order that a few may be remembered'; the Trevi Fountain 'sounds worse in description than it looks to the eye ... we begin with criticism, but we end with admiration'; 'let no one, therefore, who is meditating such a journey be discouraged by the amount of what he cannot do; but rather take encouragement from the thought of how much can be done' (SM 1:249; 1:413; 2:454).

Hillard reaffirms the central themes of the New Englanders: the sense of plenitude, spontaneity and love of play, sobriety, realism, individuality, lack of hypocrisy, natural vivacity, and 'uniform courtesy and civility,' even among humble contadini (SM 2:334; cf. 7). He also echoes the Italophilic contempt for customs officials, thieving coach drivers, 'dirty inns, bad dinners, comfortless sleeping-rooms, bells that will not ring, servants that will not come, and horses that will not go'; an Englishman in Italy 'exchanges quiet efficiency for noisy inefficiency' (SM 2:272). The numerous beggars, 'dark shadows which haunt all the bright points' (SM 1:190–1), appall his humanitarian conscience. At the same time Hillard often strikes out on his own: he is 'almost unique in American travel books of the period' for his study of the agricultural conditions of the Roman Campagna.[64] Supported by research in French, German, and Swiss sources, in tight lawyer-like paragraphs, the politically liberal Hillard examines the historical origins of the latifundia, land management, absentee ownership, middle men, depopulation, and malaria. Two decades before the famous government report of Sidney Sonnino and Leopoldo Franchetti, he condemns 'the prevalence of a system by which enormous estates were gathered into a few hands, while the mass of the community was doomed to a depth of poverty which was fatal to virtue, because fatal to hope' (SM 2:76). In contrast to Boston with its growing suburbs, Rome had poor economic relations with its surrounding environment; with the benefit of hindsight Hillard predicts political trouble from a 'fierce and rebellious spirit' (SM 2:99). He even blasts what would come to be known as the 'tourist gaze,' the imaginary of information, opinion, prejudice, and expectation by which the tourist confronts the Other:[65] 'We have no right to look upon a landscape only as a picture, or to view it merely as a harvest-field for dreamy emotions' (SM 2:72). This is no Genteel lawyer.

Limited contact with Italians not connected to the business of travelling prevented Hillard from tackling the problem of cultural stereotypes instead of repeating them. The Italian nature is 'rich in the various modifications of sympathy, but poor in the products of principle'; 'amiable, vivacious, good-natured' yet 'passionate and vindictive' (SM 2:237). He tends to support the notion, advanced by Leopardi, that Italians abound in private virtues and lack public ones. Like most American travellers, he did not move outside Anglo-American circles, mixing with 'agreeable English society' (SM 1:175) in Florence but not with Florentines, and remarking on English children in the Boboli Gardens, not Italian ones. Like many Anglo-Americans, he would choose Florence (for its supposed bourgeois coziness) above all Italian cities as a place of residence (SM 1:182). In Naples the image of the adult Italian as the natural child takes on a negative colouring. The lower classes resemble the 'inmates of a nursery,' 'grown-up children,' 'civilized savages'; their only verb tense is 'the present' (SM 2:181–3) – they yield to immediate impulse. In sum, Hillard can be trapped by the very tourist gaze that he had elsewhere resisted. Still, the longer he remained, the more he revised: 'when I compared my last impression of the Italians with my first, I felt that I had taken one lesson more on the rashness of hasty judgments'; the pleasures of Italy are not 'to be purchased by any thing more than trifling discomforts and inconveniences' (SM 2:334).

Insufficiently knowledgeable of the medieval period, the classically trained[66] Hillard sees only a deep gulf separating ancient and modern Italy in language, literature, and culture ('strength to softness,' 'power to emotion,' 'masculine' to 'feminine' [SM 2: 267]), and not continuity and preservation. Oddly, he does not mention John James Blunt's

Vestiges of Ancient Manners and Customs, Discoverable in Modern Italy and Sicily (1823), and it was almost too soon for him to have taken advantage of the rising interest in the Middle Ages. 'In Italy, strangers seem to be at home, and the natives to be exiles' (SM 1:184). Had he understood the natives better, he would have realized that they are not 'exiles' in their own land, uncomprehending of their heritage and (what he likely means) unworthy of it. Yet, like the Big Three, he is right that many 'strangers' found themselves 'at home.' In the heyday of the Empire, writes the Anglophilic Hillard, the English are the 'legitimate descendants of the old Romans' and 'stalk over the land as if it were their own' (SM 2:267–8). William Ware, a fellow Bostonian, said that 'the old Roman, in truth, survives not in any of the Italian family; and if any where on the face of the earth now, in the modern Englishman.'[67] This is the theme of *translatio imperii*, one civilization holding imperium at a time, and beginning in the Near East, the direction was west: 'Westward the course of empire takes its way,' in Bishop Berkeley's words.[68] A few years later, Lowell claimed the inheritance for America: 'we represent more truly the old Roman Power and sentiment than any other people. Our art, our literature, are, as theirs, in some sort exotics; but our genius for politics, for law, and above all, for colonization, our instinct for aggrandizement and for trade, are all Roman' (JLB 1:342).[69]

'Vulgar Protestant cant' (SM 2:144) over Roman Catholic clergy and festivals offends Hillard's tolerance. Travellers are urged 'to look upon pope, cardinal, and monk, not with a puritan scowl, but as parts of an imposing pageant, which we may contemplate without self-reproach, though without approving' (SM 1:204). The English are scolded for their 'countenance of irreverent curiosity,' 'careless deportment,' and 'inveterate staring' in churches (SM 2:270); Hillard's Anglophilia was obviously not uncritical. He denounces the 'sneering protest' against the 'mummeries of superstition' (SM 1:332) and ridicules those economy-minded Protestants who wander through a noble church worrying that something might have to be paid for to be visited. He argues on behalf of the ritualism and public quality of Italian religious life: 'the Romish Church, especially, is wiser in providing so much more liberally for that instinct of worship which is a deep thirst of the human soul.' The boxed pews of spare New England churches are synecdochic of social hierarchy, personal coldness, and privacy compared to the inviting, spacious interiors of the Italian ones that permit easy mixing (SM 1:330–2; cf. 2:190, 230). Also, the Italian churches are much more frequently open.

Hillard's taste was formed before the massive cultural shift pioneered by Ruskin and the Pre-Raphaelites (the Brotherhood was founded in

1848, the year after Hillard was in Italy). Though Hillard respected *Modern Painters*, it failed to open his eyes.[70] Generally he adhered to the standard and taste of his times, without, however, succumbing to dryness and rigidity or losing his distinctive voice. On his view, Greco-Roman classicism is succeeded by a long blank; then Giotto; then another blank, with a few exceptions; then the peaks of Italian art, Raphael and Michelangelo, and their successors; then gradual decline in the seventeenth century. After insightful pages on classical sculpture in Florence and the Vatican, he skims over medieval art and architecture. St Mark's in Venice is a 'strange jumble' whose interior is 'too crowded and too dark' (SM 1:41), and San Zeno in Verona 'left no impressions' (SM 189); these are two of the most important churches in Ruskin. Ghiberti's Baptistery Doors, declared worthy of being the 'Gates of Paradise' by Michelangelo, are the 'inadequate result of forty years of labor' (SM 1:132), and Luca della Robbia's glazed ceramics suggest 'soup tureens and tea drinking' (SM 1:165). For Hillard's taste, there is too much Quattrocento love of concrete particulars. His observation that the 'exclusive admirers of Christian art ... the Pre-Raphaelite school ... value an angular virgin, with limbs that look as if they had been cut out of tin, beyond the best forms of Guido [Reni] or Domenichino' (SM 1:364) reveals an entire aesthetic or rather two competing aesthetics. In Heinrich Wölfflin's terms, Hillard prefers the 'chastened flow of line,' broad volumetric masses, vitalized spaciousness, economy of detail, inevitability, and compositional integrity of High Renaissance artists over the 'abrupt intricacy' of line, angularity, flat planes, realism, wealth of incident and 'anarchic' detail, and 'multiplicity' of earlier Italian artists: in terms of Adrian Stokes, for modelling over carving.[71] Raphael's *Entombment of Christ* (1507) is the painting at which the Pre-Raphaelites drew the chronological line.[72] For them, it was the end; for Hillard, a beginning. Yet he leaned this time to the Pre-Raphaelites and called it the 'gem' of the Borghese, while they 'esteem it one of Raphael's highest efforts, and one of the last expressions of his uncorrupted pencil.' Perhaps his high estimation of Raphael's early painting owed something to Ruskin and the Pre-Raphaelites after all, because he distinguishes himself from more traditional critics who judged the painting to be 'stiff and feeble, at least in comparison with the artist's later works' (SM 1:364).

Set-pieces on Michelangelo's Medici Chapel and the Sistine Ceiling, Raphael's Stanze and *Transfiguration* ('at the head of all the oil-paintings in the world' [SM 1: 251]), and Titian's *Assumption*; his chapters on Roman fountains, palazzi, and the Colosseum; the Vatican sculptures, which 'not only [surpass] any other collection, but all other collections put together' (SM 1:234); the museum of antiquities in Naples: these passages show Hillard at his analytical and appreciative best as a travel writer. He is discerning on classical sculpture such as the Niobe; having studied Winckelmann and Lessing, he offers an original explanation of why the Laocoon group arouses such controversy – not because it epitomizes spatial over temporal art, but because it 'stands upon the very line by which the art of sculpture is divided from poetry and painting' (SM 1:238). Hillard does not like sculpture that is overly mimetic or tells a story: 'when a statue becomes too expressive, it ceases to be statuesque and begins to be picturesque' (SM 1:353). The *Apollo Belvedere* reveals limitations: 'a little of the fine gentleman,' 'not enough of the serene unconsciousness of the immortal Gods,' less of the 'simple grandeur' of other Greek masterpieces (an allusion to Winckelmann's ideal of the Greek, 'noble simplicity and tranquil grandeur') (SM 1:237). He explicates the *Dying Gaul* at length without so much as mentioning another piece in the same room, the *Marble Faun*, which was to attract Hawthorne ten years later. If Hillard does not enlarge the taste of his audience, he enriches the taste they already have.

Baroque art receives conventional disparagement, as Hillard disapproves of three main preoccupation: *violence:* the grasping of the mother's hair is 'too violent,' her lips 'too revolting' in Guido Reni's *Massacre of the Innocents* (SM 1: 98); *theatricality:* Bernini's baldacchino resembles 'a colossal four-post bedstead without the curtains' (SM 1: 218);[73] and strained emotion: Carlo Dolce is 'a painter against whom one gets in time to feel a sort of personal spite' (SM 1:154–5). Reservations creep into mostly laudatory readings of Andrea del Sarto, Correggio, and the Bolognese school; the Carracci 'want vitality' (SM 1:99). Against Ruskin, he pleads the case for Domenichino's *Last Communion of St. Jerome,* appreciated well into the nineteenth century, in terms of the neoclassical antithesis of genius and art: 'the fire of genius never burns along his lines; but skill, taste, correctness, judgment, and decorum always wait upon his pencil' (SM 1:255). The *Apollo and Daphne* and *David* of the young Bernini show the 'natural vigor of his genius' ('*at least* equal to that of Chatterton in poetry'! [my italics]); later works such as the *Ecstasy of Saint Theresa* and the *Chair of Saint Peter* show 'bad taste and corrupting patronage' (SM 1:393). His *Pluto and Proserpina* is both 'violent' and 'theatrical' (SM 1:387); the Fountain of the Four Rivers is 'one of the heaviest sins against good taste that ever was laid upon the much-enduring earth' (SM 2:45). With his *Venus* Canova aimed for something 'more beautiful than beauty' and ended with 'prettiness': a 'veteran belle' hides a blush with a fan, while peeking through the sticks to 'observe the effects' (SM 1:155). He similarly objects to the sculptor's statue of Pauline Bonaparte where her awareness of her own nudity 'obtrudes the fact offensively upon the attention' (SM 1394). The American sculptors Hiram Powers and Horatio Greenough receive much more positive commentaries. Hillard is weakest on architecture, especially the baroque: 'in the middle of the seventeenth century, architecture had reached its lowest state of degeneracy, under the corrupting influence of Borromini' (SM 1:359). Yet these are among the most important decades in the history of Italian architecture: Bernini, Longhena, Guarini, Da Cortona – and Borromini.

It would be unfair to hold Hillard's critique of baroque art and architecture against him. Anti-baroque sentiment became practically universal in European taste after Winckelmann, and especially in the post-Romantic period. Lowell went through San Luigi dei Francesi without so much as mentioning Caravaggio's St Matthew paintings, while his general comment on Roman architecture is absurd: 'Going to see [the churches] is like standing to watch a procession of monks, – the same thing over and over again, and when you have seen one you have seen all. There is a kind of clumsy magnificence about them ... no spring or roar in their architecture as in that of the Lombard churches I have seen' (JRL-B 1: 321–2). As late as 1907 Camillo von Klenze deplored the 'meaningless grace' of Bernini; he dated the shift away from the taste for the baroque to the final decades of the eighteenth century.[74] Only Jacob Burckhardt towards the end of his career argued for a reassessment, which commenced with his pupil Heinrich Wölfflin and Cornelius Gurlitt in the 1880s.[75]

However much they embraced the Risorgimento, the New Englanders remained ambiguous on the subject of technological modernization in Italy. In the first volume of *The Stones of Venice*, which appeared in 1851, two years before Hillard's book, Ruskin decried the two-hundred-and-twenty-arch railway bridge connecting Venice and the mainland for ruining the panorama. However, Hillard defends the bridge in practical, political, and aesthetic terms. It is 'an artery by which the living blood of to-day is poured into the exhausted frame of Venice'; it proves how 'wealth and genius are spent in lightening the burdens of common life'; it bespeaks 'the growth of an age of schools, hospitals and almshouses, in which the privileges of the few are giving ground before the rights of the many'; and it extends 'the pleasures of travel' to a 'continually increasing class.' Aesthetically, the bridge is also 'noble,' is 'grander from its very incongruity.' The 'great results and achievements of modern civilization'

have 'a certain feeling of their own' – he is groping towards the technological sublime, but that bridge will never get him there. In sum, the
railway bridge that links Venice to the coast connects 'the past with the
future' (SM 1:86–7). The train to Pompeii likewise juxtaposes two different worlds.

Taken together, the travellers' remarks illustrate the changing attitude
towards time, of which the train had become a modern symbol. Hillard
reports how the train saved him a potentially wasted day. At 10:30 a.m.
he went from Livorno to Pisa, spent an hour in and around the cathedral, took the train to Lucca for the afternoon, then retraced his steps
and was back in Livorno at 6:30 p.m. That the train was manufactured in
Philadelphia was 'a small dividend contributed in the shape of the useful arts, by the new world, towards paying off that great debt of gratitude
which all mankind owes to Italy for what it has done in the fine arts' (SM
2:339). Yet the day's images produced blurred pages. The emphasis falls
on the schedule out of which he makes a kind of game. He ignored della
Quercia's tomb monument of Ilaria del Carretto (1408) in the cathedral
of Lucca; had he noticed it he certainly would have mentioned it – he
speaks of other works there and had read Ruskin's unforgettable description of it in *Modern Painters* II (1846). The whole focus on speed, schedules, and locomotion adumbrates a broad theme in twentieth-century
travel writing, which concerns itself more with the technical means as
opposed to the ends of travel.

Hillard's sense of time contrasts with what he and his fellow Americans
find so characteristic of Italians: their love of leisure, appealing to the extent that it does not become outright laziness. 'Time is of no value, and
the whole movement of life is adagio' (SM 2:101); the people of Terni
'strolled about in a leisurely way, as if they had a great deal more of the
capital of time than they knew how to invest' (SM 2:314); oral culture
requires 'abundant leisure' (SM 2:230); and so forth. When he compares
the villagers of the Alban Hills with those of rural New England, organization and gadgetry are key factors: 'in handiness and management, in
labor-saving contrivances, in the adaptation of means to ends, in economy of time and labor, [Italians] are lamentably, ludicrously deficient'
(SM 2:238). Still, Hillard approaches the question from both sides, as
when he lounges at a cafe in St Mark's Piazza, he spurns the moralist's
injunction against wasting time: 'a week of such evenings leaves very
pleasant recollections behind.' At such a table, in what Napoleon called
the drawing-room of Europe, he may have recollected the noisy streets
of downtown Boston: 'it was agreeable to one coming from our restless

country, to breathe for a while the soothing atmosphere of repose –
to see men sitting quietly in their chairs, and evidently not struggling
against an impulse to whittle at the arms by way of safety-valve to their
nervous unrest.' Yet he is not James's Lambert Strether, such pleasure
being virtuous only if it rewards 'discipline and struggle' (SM 1:47). If,
however, the unresting Hillard cannot fully yield himself to leisure, he
knows what it is and can appreciate it in others: it was 'a refreshment
to see so many happy faces' (SM 1:47) The Italians are at home in the
world, enjoying the pleasures they find in it, mostly the ones they make
for themselves: 'that unconscious enjoyment of the mere sense of existence, which ... was to the benevolent mind of Paley the most convincing
proof of the goodness of God, is stamped in expressive and unmistakable
lines upon the general Italian face' (SM 1:48).[76]

One consequence of modernization that Hillard noticed in the Italy
of the 1840s was the weakening of individuality and particularism. The
'peculiarities of Naples are growing less and less marked, and those racy
traits of life and character which so much impressed the travelers of a
earlier period, are fast disappearing' (SM 2:174). The *lazzaroni* are gone,
owing to the 'greatly extended net-work of communication between
Naples and the rest of Europe' (SM 2:174). 'Are gas lamps, cheap cali-
coes, and railways inconsistent with Titians and Sansovinos?' (SM 1:57).
Perhaps so: Hillard disliked foreigners' bourgeois bonnets with their
'bold staring front and incongruous ornaments' in contrast to the beautiful headdresses and veils of the local Italian women: 'before a bonnet
the poet drops his pen, the sculptor his chisel, and the painter his brush'
(SM 1:90). Yet while the Old World was on the wane, Italy was not reap-
ing the benefits of the New, and he doubted whether in its present state
of 'half slumber and half despair' it could throw off foreign controls and
the weight of its past to join the ranks of modernity. 'As we have no past,
so Italy seems to have no future'; 'he who is without opportunity exists
but does not live'; 'who would wish to share in a decline?' (SM 2:452).
Building towards his conclusion, Hillard recommends a modest sojourn
(six months?), which enlarges the mind, raises the spirits, and relaxes the
nerves, with the additional benefit of giving an American 'fresh cause of
gratitude for having been born where he was' (SM 2:452). Permanent
residence, however, he rules out. While England and Germany are each
remembered as a 'valued and esteemed friend,' he declares on the point
of departure that 'the image of Italy dwells in our hearts like that of a
women whom we have loved' (SM 2:450). The scrupulous attorney had
tried avoiding stereotypes and largely succeeded, but when it came time
to reject Italy, he fell into the trap of bourgeois sentimentality.

V

Like Hillard, Margaret Fuller was steeped in Italy's 'great past'; unlike him, she believed in its 'great future.'[77] Hillard was an 'old acquaintance' of Fuller's long before they met up in Rome in April 1848, when she entrusted him with a small mosaic to bring home to her mother (L 5:61, 68, 103). She had earned the sobriquet of the American Corinne by New Englanders for her superior culture, her feminism, and her linguistic ability, even before she went to Italy and became even more deeply identified with the Staëlian heroine. She did not live to write an Italian travel book, nor do we know how seriously she may have contemplated one. In October 1847, after six months of touring, she said, 'I begin to know as well as to feel' about the country to the point where 'a book would be too short' (L 4:305–6). Another time, praising Rome, she admits it is 'useless to try and write of these things, volumes would hardly begin to tell my thoughts.' Then she reverses herself, 'the Italian sun has wakened a luxuriant growth that covers my mind'; 'Oh how much I might write, if I had only force!' (L 5:100–1). Passing remarks on her desire to 'gather the fruit of my travels' (L 4:301) and write the 'narrative of my European experience' (L 5:73) may refer to her history of the Roman revolution, or an autobiography, not travel writing per se, though some comments are tantalizing. While she cannot present 'all the details' of her stay in Ravenna to *Tribune* readers, 'I shall write them out some time ... Padua, too.'[78] Each day in Italy, she wrote in 1849, has been 'so rich in joys and pains, actions and sufferings, to say nothing of themes of observation, I have never yet had time to know the sum total – to reflect' (L 5:283). Her travel sketches in the letters and newspaper dispatches would make a book longer than many travelogues.

If the idea of an Italian travel book crossed her mind, what form might it have taken? The genre was congenial: it mixes description, historical fact, fiction, commentary, argument, and autobiography; it can absorb almost anything into its plastic form and include a wide range of authorial tones. She had already published one such book, *Summer on the Lakes in 1843*, and as Jeffrey Steele notes, 'many of her succeeding texts – *Women in the Nineteenth Century*, her New York essays, and her Italian dispatches – were also shaped by the model of travel writing.'[79] Fuller, always in need of money, might have been wise to publish a travel book because 'no other genre of American literature enjoyed a greater popularity or a more enduring prominence in the nineteenth century.'[80]

Writing in 1845, the year before travelling to Europe, Fuller theorized

on the genre: a traveller should (1) be 'in good health' lest 'partial' or
'exaggerated' comments arise from a 'morbid state'; (2) have an alert,
cultivated mind not 'too much burthened with theories and opinions';
(3) have knowledge of both science and the fine arts to receive the 'peculiar influences and the most expressive features of life in each land'; (4)
have 'poetic sensibility' and 'sympathy' for what is 'special and individual
in nations and men'; (5) balance intellectual power to generalize with
well-reported particulars, lest 'we have only an inference, when we want
the facts also'; and (6) have 'no special object in traveling, beyond the
delight of new and various impressions, or, if he has one, it should only
absorb enough of his time and attention to give earnestness and spirit to
the rest' – in other words, it is the journey, not the arrival, that matters.[81]
A seventh quality, unlisted but exemplified by Fuller herself, is humility: in Rome 'you rise in the morning knowing there are a great number
of objects worth knowing, which you may never have the chance to see
again. You go every day, in all moods, under all circumstances; feeling,
probably, in seeing them, the inadequacy of your preparation for understanding or duly receiving them' (AHA 258). Fuller singled out Goethe's
Italian Journey, the supreme masterpiece of European travel writing, and
Joseph Forsyth's *Remarks on Antiquities, Arts and Letters during an Excursion in Italy, in the years 1802 and 1803* as 'two that could not fail to be of
great use to the student who wishes really to see the Italy of Italy, and to
take, not Italo-American, but Italian views of the garden of the world.'[82]
Elsewhere she recommends De Staël, William Beckford's *Italy*, John Bell's
Observations on Italy (1825), and Luigi Antonio Lanzi's *History of Painting
in Italy* (1828).[83]

'To speak with any truth of Italy ... requires *genius*,' writes Fuller; '*talent*, which is made to serve most purposes now, entirely fails here' (L
4:272). She does not mean that only geniuses can get to the truth about
Italy, but that mere quick study and verbal facility will not suffice. Fuller
had the '*genius*' to write the truth, first, because of her preparation in
Italy's language, history, and culture. That she spoke Italian moderately
well enabled her to become close to the people; she would never have
been entrusted with a hospital directorship during the revolution if she
could not communicate quickly and accurately. Her method for learning the language is direct and uncompromising: 'six months total absti-
nence from English' (L 5:172); 'I have been quite off the beaten track
of travel, have seen, thought, spoken, dreamed only what is Italian' (L
5:251). Her Roman letters tell how she pored over books on the city and
Italian history. Watching travellers waste large sums of money, she is dis-

consolate that she 'cannot afford reference books, little journals, many things that would be of great use' (L 5:213), such as prints for teaching and lecturing. Ovid's birthplace, Sulmona, had to be passed up 'for the want of a few dollars' (L 5:103). When Fuller wanted to buy her sister a gift, she said that an engraving of Titian's *Assumption* is 'one of those I should like most, if I had money' (it cost $4.50) (L 5:47).

Fuller's intellectual preparation was greatly enhanced by a knowledge of the local scene, so much so that, in an essay published many years ago, A. William Salomone focused upon Fuller as the 'shining exception' among American travellers before 1860 in her comprehension of the fundamental ideological issues of the Risorgimento.[84] How did this come about? She lived in the cities and the countryside; she travelled alone as often as in company (or with fellow Americans); she had a balanced interest in the past and the present, and in pagan mythology and Catholic Rome; and while she could savour the 'last hours of [Italy's] old solemn greatness' (L 5:158), she threw in her lot with the future. Her understanding of the present – what would be her special contribution – meant a more than passing acquaintance with Italians, 'of all ranks, from the very highest to the lowest' (L 4:299), from Princess Cristina Belgioioso and Marchioness Arconati Visconti in Milan, to the central Apennines where 'I see no one but Italian Contadines' (L 5:75).[85] Her lack of funds, if it had a blessing, brought her nearer to common life: 'foreigners cannot live [on a few cents a day], but I could' (L 5:149), implying she is no longer a traveller, but a resident.[86] That she was familiar with the extremes is illustrated by an offhand comment, made shortly before she embarked for America, and playing on the contrast between splendour and squalor: her ship is 'laden with mar[ble] and rags, a very appropriate companionship for wares of Italy' (L 6:83).[87] One can only speculate whether the heavy cargo of marble contributed to the shipwreck of the *Elizabeth*, which hit a sandbar in a gale off Fire Island in July 1850; Fuller, her husband, and son were drowned.

Though she knew the larger cities, she was, like Hillard, fascinated by the smaller ones, 'those true Italian towns, where the old charm is unbroken' (L 4:301). The charm is 'unbroken' because of the strength of the social, cultural, and historical bonds between past and present. That deep organic connection endured longer in Italy than it did in northern Europe and America, and still remains in some measure. For Fuller, Italy will be one of the last places in Europe to break completely with its past. Siena is 'a real untouched Italian place' (L 5:43); Vicenza, 'a truly Italian town, with much to see and study' (L 4:298); Bologna, 'full of expression, of physiognomy' (AHA 232), 'really an *Italian* city, one in which I should like to live, full of hidden things' (L 4:291); Perugia, 'so much to see which excites generous and consoling feelings' (L 5:265); 'Brescia[,] in fact almost all Italian towns' (L 5:274). Writing from Rieti where her son was born, Fuller expresses an ideal of happiness: 'living peaceably in one beautiful provincial town after another' (L 5:254–5). These words, coming near the end of her sojourn, could only have been written by someone who knew Italy well.

The use of 'charm' (or 'magic,' 'grace', 'dream') was common in nineteenth- and twentieth-century travel books on Italy. It refers to the pleasing as opposed to the disturbing, and was frequently connected to the feminine. It is the kind of word that Santayana would put down as 'genteel.' Mary McCarthy fulminates against this breed ('old maids of both sexes, retired librarians, governesses, ladies with reduced incomes') in *The Stones of Florence*.[88] Yet Fuller did not fall victim to the 'tourist gaze.' If charm was all that some tourists felt, it formed only part of her complex response to what is strange, heathen, Catholic, dangerous – the 'fearfully human.' Stendhal said, 'I feel a charm [*charme*] in this country which I can hardly define; it is like love'; and no one would accuse Stendhal of being a bourgeois gazer; far from it, he loved Italy because it was so anti-bourgeois.[89]

Like Goethe and Ruskin, Fuller stresses the need to see things slowly, 'quietly *looking* one's fill' (her italics) (L 4:273): this kind of seeing completes a physical process and is the beginning of spiritual growth, 'fill' being an image of plenitude.[90] A long list might easily be compiled of Fuller's references to the two kinds of seeing, outward and inward, often contrasted in the same passage: 'I cannot look merely with a pictorial eye on the lounge of the Roman dandy, the bold, Juno gait of the Roman Contadina'; 'the natural expression of these fine forms will animate them yet' (AHA 260). Staring (eyes wide open, fixed gaze, potential rudeness) gives way to 'natural' or essentialist seeing. 'I am ... no longer a staring, sight-seeing stranger, riding about finely dressed in a coach to see the Muses and the Sibyls. I see these forms now in the natural manner' (L 4:310). While 'staring' is a kind of unnatural seeing that does not penetrate the surface, and can even be threatening and removing, 'seeing' lessens the distance between subject and object: 'it must be torture merely to *travel* to Italy and give a passing stare at the beautiful body without ever having time or peace to come in contact with its soul' (L 4:306). Titian's *Sacred and Profane Love*, then in the Palazzo Borghese, 'has developed my powers of gazing to an extent unknown before' (AHA 223). The English stand out as the 'most unseeing' of travellers (AHA

220): 'Ah! How joyful to see once more *this* Rome, instead of the pitiful, peddling, Anglicized Rome, first viewed in unutterable dismay from
the *coupé* of a vettura' (AHA 259). Fuller did not embrace New England
Anglophilia, though there is no reason to suppose that the English were
any more or less 'unseeing' than the Americans or, for that matter, any
other nationality.[91] 'Now I saw the true Rome ... I came to live in tranquil companionship, not in the restless impertinence of sight-seeing' (L
4:298): deliberateness over speed, seeing over sightseeing, friendly relations over rudeness. Spurning a 'coffee-house intelligence' (L 4:295),
she writes that 'I am really seeing Italy, differently from what mere travellers do' (L 4:304). To take in the whole of Italy is impossible, so Fuller
resorts to synecdochic condensation by which 'the great features of the
part pursue and fill the eye' (AHA 220), another image of plenitude.

Fuller's Italian journey resembles a pilgrimage in which the religious
feelings of her youth are secularized and subsumed. Her ideal traveller
undergoes a loss of self through 'intimacy of feeling' with, and an 'abandonment' to, the 'spirit of the place' (AHA 220). The moment captures
the Coleridgean 'coalescence of subject and object'; this is the transcendent intuition or 'revelation,' 'the real knowledge, the recreative power
induced by love,' which is succeeded by the imaginative 'assimilation'
of 'soul and substance' within an enlarged self (AHA 258). In December 1847 she wrote that the driving rhythms of the saltarello danced by
humble folk (perhaps Trasteverini) beside the Colosseum 'carried me
quite beyond myself.' Bored and 'catching cold from the damp night-
air,' and probably fearful of Roman fever, her American companions
wanted to leave and 'remember it against me' for keeping them waiting
(once again, the outsider). But Fuller would not be denied the 'delight';
though she might have been just as cold, she was 'heated by enthusiasm,'
and the dance was like 'Italian wine,' 'Italian sun.' Afterward, she kept
returning to the scene to absorb its meaning: 'I love to see and study it
much' (AHA 267).[92] The episode is structured along the contrast between life and death: sun, light, heat, wine, health, artistry, ecstasy versus
night, cold, dampness, illness, boredom. Fuller experiences heightened
moments with the intensity of satisfying a natural instinct: 'I thought and
drank in the spirit of Rome' (my italics) (L 5:40); the 'spirit' of Rome
'must be *inhaled wholly*, with the yielding of the *whole* heart. It is really
something transcendent, both spirit and body' (my italics) (L 4:290). In
the 'painful process of sight-seeing,' 'there is no quiet to let that beauty
breathe its life into the soul' (my italics) (AHA 258).[93] Again, as external to
internal, sightseeing opposes the kind of seeing that informs both 'heart'
and 'soul.'

The Chapels of the Cemeteries on the slopes of the Janiculum provide the setting for one of Fuller's most memorable encounters.[94] She happened upon the scene on one of her solitary, undirected walks in early November 1847, following All Souls' Day, so that thoughts of death must have been in mind.[95] A Franciscan friar, a pregnant woman, beggars, and a few boys among others are kneeling in prayer before the Stations of the Cross; the boys chant a hymn. Longfellow in *Outre-Mer* had recoiled at the emotionalism of prostrate church-goers in Genoa; tolerant and fastidious, Hillard warns against disrespect. Only Fuller overcame the cultural and religious distance ('as from pole to pole') to join the people in prayer:

> It was a beautiful moment, and despite the wax saint, the ill-favored friar, the professional mendicants, and my own removal, wide as pole from pole, from the position of mind indicated by these forms, their spirit touched me, and I prayed too; prayed for the distant, every way distant, – from those who seem to have forgotten me, and with me all we had in common; prayed for the dead in spirit, if not in body; prayed for myself, that I might never walk the earth 'The tomb of my dead self'; and prayed in general for all unspoiled and loving hearts, – no less for all who suffer and find yet no helper. (AHA 261)

Repeated four times, 'prayed' emphasizes her desire to collapse the distance between herself and others, and to dispel the loneliness of a single woman in a foreign country. Lest she walk the earth as the 'tomb of my dead self,'[96] she prays in earnest for that spiritual rebirth that so many of her fellow New Englanders associated with Italy. In love, and to be a mother herself within a year, she may identify with the pregnant woman praying for the yet unborn child. Fuller then 'took my road by the Cross, which marks the brow of the hill' and in an *imitatio Christi* climbed the Janiculum and is rewarded for her prayers: 'Before me lay Rome – how exquisitely tranquil in the sunset! Never was an aspect that for serene grandeur could vie with that of Rome at sunset' (AHA 262). As in the episode of the saltarello, the antithesis of death and rebirth, further supported by the liminal hour, helps structure the concrete details and the symbolism: cemetery at sunset and resurrection; loneliness and community; low ground, depressed spirits, cordoned view versus hill-top panorama, the Longinian sublime, and serenity; turmoil and peace.

These examples of her travel writing – and they could easily be multiplied – reveal that Fuller is neither abstract, nor laboured, nor excessively concerned with the self. Like the finest travel writers, she shares the palm with the object.

The intensification of her spiritual life through travel represents a stage in the secularization of Protestant inwardness, within just a few decades to take various directions in American life, from the therapeutic, to the aesthetic, and the revivalist. With Fuller, however, the goal is post-Romantic self-realization through an active interchange with the universe: 'a full communion with the spirit of Rome' (L 5:192), the 'much more full and true way' (L 5:283) of living that she found in Italy. Perhaps here as elsewhere, she puns on her name, a mark of plenitude. In one of her strongest statements on travelling, she draws on religious metaphor: 'All these things [the country, the people, the spectacles] are only to me an illuminated margin on the text of my inward life' (L 4:271). Bearing the mystery of the inward life, the spiritual self as text is read like a sacred word, which the travels and commentaries in the 'margin' help to interpret and 'illuminate.' As in her Puritan-Protestant background, the word is central, the image is *outside*. Fuller's hospital work during the siege of Rome brought her life in Italy – public and private, political and cultural – to its highest point in self-understanding and fullness of being. Her 'rebirth' on a small scale participates in Italy's spiritual and political renewal on the grand scale.

With a knowledge of Italy and Italians deeper than that of most of her American contemporaries, Fuller could give the major topoi a more personal interpretation. Like the Romantics, she believed the child to be the 'father of the man' and accepted the common notion of the Italian as having a childlike simplicity and naturalness. But she goes further and identifies with the child, for its imaginative wholeness and happiness. Within a few months of her arrival, Fuller writes, 'Italy receives me as a long lost child' (L 4:293). Soon after she confides in her mother, 'I have not been so well since I was a child, nor so happy ever' (L 4:312), implying Italy and Rome are mothers too: 'Rome! oh my mother! How sadly tender I return into thy arms' (L 5:156). She speaks of her 'passive child-like well being' (L 5:43) in Italy. Not least of the reasons for this metaphor, as Margaret Allen writes, Italy enabled her to 'recapture some of [her] lost childhood.'[97] Though Fuller recognizes the intellectual differences between her and her husband, she also enjoys what she finds wanting in herself: his 'unspoiled instincts' (L 5:270), a 'simple child-like piety' (L 5:301), a 'perfectly unconscious character' (L 6:46); he is 'simple and uniform though not monotonous more than are the flowers of spring' (L 5:302; 5:271). No one has loved her more 'except little children or mother' (L 5:300). Perhaps his innocence and sincerity, misunderstood by others as ignorance or doltishness, was part of what captivated her.

Connected to the theme of the child is that of 'coming home' to one's true self. The metaphor recurs in letters from early in her sojourn. At first, she 'could not yet find myself at home in Italy' but quickly became 'absorbed in [Rome's] peculiar life' (L 4:290); within weeks, 'I feel myself at home' (L 4:293), 'really *in* Rome,' but the 'English and Americans are not at home here' (L 4:310). More readily than her fellow New Englanders, the Italians appear to have accepted her individuality and circumstances: they 'sympathize with my character and understand my organization, as no other people ever did,' and 'highly prize my intelligent sympathy'; 'they say "I am so '*simpatica*'"' (L 4:299; 5:86). In other words, there is mutual sympathy. She understands her Americanness through her separation from America: 'since I have experienced the different atmosphere of the European mind, and been allied with it, nay, mingled in the bonds of love, I suffer more than ever from that which is peculiarly American or English' (L 4:310). The more one sees and experiences, the more the lines of one's character become sharper: 'The American in Europe, if a thinking mind, can only become more American' (AHA 250–1) – with which Lowell would agree. No phrase rings more commonly in the letters than a passage from Byron's *Childe Harold's Pilgrimage* (4.77), 'Oh Rome! my country! city of the soul! / The orphans of the heart must turn to thee, / Lone mother' (L 5:68, 147, 156, 157, 240, 241, 274, 275). The images combine the themes of the child, exile, 'home,' and the 'Lone mother' who is lonely from the child's absence. Fuller thought of herself as an 'orphan,' as when she wonders if she could ever return to Boston, '*I* have no "home," no peaceful roof to which I can return' (her italics) (L 5:76-77). But later she writes, again citing Bryon, Rome is '*my* country' (L 5:147), 'my *home*' (L 5:274), 'oh Rome, *my* Country!' (all her italics) (L 5:275). During the revolution she regarded herself, in Robert N. Hudspeth's words, as 'a Roman defending her home' (L 5:12). Exiled to Florence, she is 'home-sick for Rome' (L 5:274). As with other members of the tradition, the recourse to the home metaphor also signals a desire to recover and make familiar the relation to the cultural past.

One speculates further on the travel book Fuller might have written. It is possible she would have devoted more attention to politics, class, and the common people. She appreciates the 'winning sweetness' of the poor, their 'ready and discriminating love' of beauty, and their 'delicacy in the sympathies,' lack of which made her 'sick' in America (AHA 425); when they are lazy, it is with a difference – they are 'indolently joyous' (L 4:273).[98] As in Hillard, the 'unaffected' (AHA 262) behaviour of Italian women ('you can see what Heaven meant them to be' [AHA 262]) contrasts with the artificiality of foreigners. Much more than Hillard, she can be caustic and judgmental, as if separating the quick from the dead: 'No; Rome is not a nine-days wonder; and those who try to make it such lose the ideal Rome (if they ever had it), without gaining any notion of the real. To those who travel, as they do everything else, only because others do, I do not speak; they are nothing. Nobody counts in the estimate of the human race who has not a character' (AHA 258) – a statement that could have come from a Unitarian pulpit. Her comments on the fine arts would likely have been developed; as they stand, they are within the boundaries of taste that Hillard inhabited. Michelangelo is a 'demigod'; his *Moses* is 'the only thing in Europe, so far, which has entirely outgone my hopes' (AHA 224). A great admirer of Titian, she finds Domenichino 'very unequal' or uneven in his paintings, 'but when he is grand and free, the energy of his genius perfectly satisfies' (AHA 223) – which is the modern judgment. Unlike Hillard, she recommends the Carracci, though her interest in Guercino wanes. The Certosa outside Pavia, which Ruskin detested, impresses her; but she does not mention his much-praised Romanesque San Michele. She comments less on architecture than on painting and sculpture.

Some of the memorable set pieces in the letters and dispatches could pass directly into a travel book: the Campagna when the Tiber had overflowed its banks and her coach seems to glide on moonlit water. Or, the Roman Carnival, during which the heavy downpours fail to dampen the spirits of the crowd. Or, the mountain chapels beyond Rieti (Hillard, by contrast, thought the Apennines dull compared with the Alps and almost dismisses them [SM 1:103]). William Vance comments on 'the People' as the true hero of Fuller's dispatches, and Brigitte Bailey shows that her view of Rome is 'defined by citizens in motion, by political processions, funerals, troop movements, and religious festivals whose meaning is increasingly political': the crowd 'shapes itself into a political community.'[99] At the same time Fuller does not let the individuals dissolve into the crowd like drops in the ocean. When she could not walk from the Corso to St Peter's owing to the 'most vivacious, various, and good-humoured crowd,' she paused, 'so I saw only themselves; but that was a great pleasure. There is so much individuality of character here' (AHA 267). Fuller's attitude towards crowds diverged from the nineteenth-century theories of Lombroso, Le Bon, and Sighele, for whom crowds are undifferentiated, atavistic organisms thinking with one mind and ruling by hard instinct, that of the lowest common denominator. She invests the Italian crowd, from revolutionary crowds to religious *feste*, with rational choice and constructive values. A funeral cortege down the Corso 'had that grand effect so easily given by this artist people, who seize instantly the natural poetry of an occasion, and with unanimous tact hasten to represent it' (AHA 268).

Fuller's attitude towards Catholicism changed on living in Italy, or rather, opposing sides of her response matured. As a reporter in New York she 'spoke positively of Catholics in order to goad her readers,' for example, praising the Catholic family ideal; but in Italy she 'associated political and social progress with Protestant rather than Catholic versions of Christianity.'[100] Yet she felt the tension between her skeptical views and the aesthetic attractions of Italian Catholicism, not unlike British women who travelled to Italy. For Dorothy Wordsworth, Mary Shelley, Hester Thrale Piozzi, and Charlotte Eaton, 'Italian Catholicism provided two conflicting versions of the sublime,' comments Jane Stabler, 'one based on absolute political papal authority and one on the transcendent aesthetic possibilities of music, art and communal festive joy.'[101] Though Fuller rejects doctrinal Catholicism and expresses extreme displeasure at the ceremony of the nun taking the veil, she can appreciate papal Rome as a 'united and poetic' whole (AHA 259). Referring paradoxically to the rituals as a 'gorgeous mummery,' she admits to being 'charmed' by their 'poetry' and 'picture' (AHA 243). Her relationship to Catholicism exemplifies her ability to balance various viewpoints, in this case, moral suspicion, emotional attachment, and aesthetic feeling. This capability, which expands her scope of vision and colours her observations not only on religion but on other issues as well, accounts for 'her constant effort to transcend the otherness of Italian culture.'[102]

Almost defiantly, Fuller preferred Rome to Florence. Why, on the contrary, did Hillard (L 1:182) and so many Anglo-Americans prefer Florence to Rome? Smaller, more manageable, tidily bourgeois? Unbaroque, i.e., less overtly Catholic, less Counter-Reformation? In Oliver Wendell Holmes's 'Boston to Florence' (1881), Boston sends a 'sister's kindliest greeting.'[103] Giuliana Artom Treves entitled a chapter of her book on the Anglo-Florentines 'The Boston of Italy.' The Catholic Mary McCarthy, who comments upon the supposed likeness to Boston, admires the 'protestant,' 'iconoclastic' nature of 'four-square' Florence, a 'city of progress,' 'sobriety,' 'decorum,' and Savonarola, a 'puritan' town, in contrast to Rome with its 'snaky' baroque Catholicism: the baroque is 'a style utterly un-Florentine.'[104] In one of the *Tribune* dispatches Fuller says, 'I do not like Florence as I do cities more purely Italian' because the 'natural character is ironed out here, and done up in a French pattern' (AHA 231), that is, more organized, administered, 'civilized' as Stendhal (who disliked Florence[105]) would say. Florence is 'more in its spirit like Boston than like any Italian city,' 'a kind of Boston to me, – the same good and the same ill; I have had enough of both'; Florentines are 'busy and intellectual' (L 4:291; 5:161). She likes Mrs Greenough, 'but not the Boston part of her' (L 6:77): provincial, inbred, emotionally inhibited, highly cerebrated: perhaps Mrs Greenough reminded her of weaknesses that she had overcome in herself. Florence 'will never charm me as have ...' – and she lists a string of Italian cities and towns (L 5:274). 'Rome is not as cheap as Florence, but I would not give a pin to live in Florence' (L 4:310; cf. 4:278); 'it is a place to work and study in; simple life does not seem so great' (L 5:274), 'great' (or sublime) as opposed to business- and work-oriented. In 1850, having passed six months in Florence, she writes that Rome 'is worth ten million Florences' (L 6:69). Despite her association with bourgeois republicans (who stood in the forefront of the Risorgimento), her choice of sublime Rome over bourgeois Florence is another indication of the profound temperamental and intellectual divide separating her from so many American travellers. She was not one of them and they resented it – most of them silently; some, like Lowell, Hawthorne, and Joseph Mozier, openly.

They disliked her anti-bourgeois nature, her radicalism, politics, and sexual freedom, the more shocking in a woman. Unlike the New Englanders, for whom Boston was the 'hub of the universe' or at least the 'Athens of America,' Fuller was, in Hudspeth's phrase, 'the de facto citizen of a cosmopolitan world' (L 6:15), the international European culture of George Sand, Belgioioso, Mickiewicz, and Mazzini, among others, who recognized her as one of their own and who are, in her words, 'exquisitely witty, original, and no less generous and kind' (L 6:78). Her disapproving brother Richard, however, is 'amazed at [her] *worldliness*' (L 6:66); her wealthy uncle Abraham, who had teased her in withholding cash, 'far from aiding, wished to see me fall' (L 5:71); her 'Aunt Mary' Rotch, aware of her plight, bequeathed a large fortune to her lawyer and another friend, when a small fraction of it would have made an enormous difference to Fuller. It is true that at times Fuller might have exaggerated her isolation. In the fall of 1848 Eliza Farrar raised money from among Fuller's friends to provide her with an annuity of three hundred dollars for life. Yet so used to being slighted had Fuller become that she might have overlooked those rare instances when she was met with generosity. There was always some slight for her to point to. For Hawthorne she was a 'great humbug.'[106] When Lowell pilloried her in *A Fable for Critics*, William Wetmore Story came to her defense, more pleading and sentimental than principled and firm: 'because fate has really been unkind to her, & because she depends on her pen for her bread & water (& that is nearly all she has to eat) & because she is her own worst enemy, and because through her disappointment & disease, which embitter every one, she has struggled most womanfully & stoutly, I could have wished you had let her pass scot free.' Lowell spoke for a multitude in his cruel reply: the 'general verdict was "served her right"' (L 6:80n). After her death she was poorly edited by her friends and treated in a caddish way by Henry James, who referred to her 'poverty of knowledge' and 'magnificent ... egotism,' calling her 'a somewhat formidable bore'; she 'left nothing behind her,' except for the 'unquestionably haunting Margaret-ghost.'[107]

She was 'odd and unpleasing' (L 6: 59), to quote her on herself; 'people rarely think one like me worth serving and saving' (L 5:104). Yet if she was spurned by many of her fellow countrymen, she found herself at home in Italy: 'Who can ever be alone for a moment in Italy? Every stone has a voice' (AHA 229). Drawing on the trope of death and rebirth, she described a walk in Rome, passing the house 'where Keats died where he lived' on the Piazza di Spagna, then by the houses of Raphael, Goethe, Poussin, and Claude Lorrain: 'Ah, what human companionship here, how everything speaks' (L 5:181). She recalls, too, that Hans Christian Andersen had set his *L'improvvisatore* in the apartment where she was living; she knows her link in people's minds to De Staël's Corinne, an *improvvisatrice*. In sum, the artists and writers are dead, yet live again and 'speak' to her, while those back home are living but no company at all. Perhaps she knew that Keats had written a sonnet on this theme, 'Great Spirits now on Earth are sojourning.' Emma Keats, the poet's niece, had been a pupil of Fuller's in New England.

In a review of Alfieri's autobiography Fuller digressed to consider how various countries like Greece, France, and Germany can instruct America: 'But there is not on earth, and, we dare to say it, will not be again genius *like* that of Italy, or that can compare with it in its own way.'[108] She left the 'tomb of my dead self' in the city of tombs, was reborn in the country that symbolized rebirth, and repaid the debt by contributing, like Alfieri, to its own renewal.[109] Had she survived the shipwreck on her return to the United States in 1850, she would have published her history of the Roman revolution of 1848 which was lost with her. But she would doubtless have written many other books, among which might have been an Italian travel book worthy to be placed beside Goethe, Stendhal, and De Staël.

VI

By half a century New England writers had quietly anticipated Santayana's critique of the Genteel Tradition. Though (so far as I know) he mentions Fuller only once in his writings, and never Hillard, he might have conceded that they overcame its limitations.[110] Even while assaulting the Genteel thinkers and artists in essay after essay, however, he was intermittently at work on *The Last Puritan: A Memoir in the Form of a Novel* (1935), a project stretching back to 1889 and as revealing as his three volumes of autobiography. In the novel, he explained to his friend, the Yale critic William Lyon Phelps, he wanted to portray 'the fate of a whole string of Harvard poets in the 1880's and 1890's – [Thomas P.] Sanborn, Philip Savage, Hugh McCullough, Trumbull Stickney, and Cabot Lodge: also [William Vaughn] Moody,' 'friends of mine ... visibly killed by the lack of air to breathe.' Santayana may have wondered whether, as a poet, he suffered a similar Genteel fate in the 1890s, his last book of poems appearing in 1901. 'People individually were kind and appreciative to them, as they were to me; but the system was deadly, and they hadn't an alternative tradition (as I had) to fall back upon'; 'they hadn't the strength of a great intellectual hero who can stand alone.'[111] The system is progressive liberal Protestant, increasingly secularized, industrial-utilitarian America, which the novel's protagonist, Oliver Alden, embodies, questions, and attempts to transcend. The alternative is southern European Catholic and cosmopolitan culture represented by Alden's 'half Italian and half American' cousin, Mario Van de Weyer, and by 'Professor Santayana,' author, narrator, and minor character; Santayana referred to the novel as *Oliver & Mario*, its oppositional paradigm.[112] The 'intellectual hero' could be Goethe, Whitman, Nietzsche, William James, Henry James – or Santayana himself, 'who can stand alone.'

By birth and background Santayana was well suited to explore the oppositions, being the product of Spanish and American culture. His father and his mother's father belonged to the Spanish diplomatic corps; his mother, Josefina Borrás, married a Boston merchant, George Sturgis, whom she met in the Philippines. A few years after Sturgis's death in

1857 she took her three children from Boston to Madrid where she became reacquainted with Augustín Ruiz de Santayana. They were married and their only child was born in 1863 and named Jorge after her first husband. Later she decided to fulfil a vow and raise her Sturgis children in Boston, where the family could assist her financially, and where at the age of eight Jorge was reunited with his mother and half-siblings. At some point during the next years, 'Jorge' became anglicized to 'George'; 'George Santayana' was the mark of his dual perspective.

In 1884–5, Santayana studied Dante under Norton. The influence is apparent in Santayana's *Interpretations of Poetry and Religion* (1900), particularly in its proposition that a scientific age reads a religious work by treating religion poetically and the imagination morally. Though Norton always topped the list of persons to whom Santayana sent copies of his books, in his autobiography he treats Norton harshly, finding his cultural 'nostalgia' to be 'fastidious' and 'secondary' because his 'fidelity to the conscience of his ancestors' was 'fundamental,' and using the past not to open the mind but to confirm belief. Santayana found him 'so saturated with morality that when anything seemed to him morally right, he couldn't notice whether it was vulgar.'[113]

Similar, though deeper, was the relationship with another of his instructors, William James, who taught him the importance of the instinctive and immediate, 'the unadulterated, unexplained, instant fact of experience.'[114] Santayana had studied James's *Principles of Psychology* under James the year before its publication, then reviewed it in laudatory terms; and *Interpretations* seems almost to expound James's will to believe as a test of truth, as when Santayana comments that the Crucifixion can 'transform' a modern soul, whereas the doctrine of eternal punishment has ceased to do so; we 'acknowledge poetic propriety or moral truth to be the sole criterion of religious credibility.' For James's part, reading *Interpretations* was a 'great event' in his life; he praised the 'imperturbable perfection' of its argumentation. But he balked at its seemingly Platonist 'anti-realistic' stance, its reproof of science's imperializing tendency, and its defence of 'harmonious and integral ideal systems,' both philosophical and ecclesiastical, from the Mediterranean world. And he must have bristled at Santayana's mocking characterization of a contemporary philosophy resembling James's own as the 'higher optimism,' a 'glorification of impulse,' a belief that evils will be subsumed in the march of progress but meanwhile faced down with a 'radiant countenance,' and the substitution of 'the dignity of success for the dignity of justice.'[115] In a letter to their colleague George Herbert Palmer, James vented disapproval: 'what a perfection of rottenness in a philosophy! I don't think I ever knew the anti-realistic view to be propounded with so impudently superior an air. It is refreshing to see a representative of moribund Latinity rise up and administer such a reproof to us barbarians in the hour of our triumph.' In the spirit of honest exasperation James told Palmer to show Santayana the letter. More offended by the reference to his moribund Latinity than to the rottenness of his philosophy, Santayana shot back: 'You tax me several times with impertinence and superior airs. I wonder if you realize the years of suppressed irritation which I have past in the midst of an un-intelligible sanctimonious and often disingenuous Protestantism, which is thoroughly alien and repulsive to me, and the need I have of joining hands with something far away from it and far above it.'[116] The battle lines of world systems in *The Last Puritan* were being drawn. Although the two patched up their differences, Santayana threw off his debt to James in his autobiography: 'I trusted his heart but I didn't respect his judgment'; America was delighted 'at the way he started, without caring where he went. In fact, he got nowhere.'[117]

Santayana taught at Harvard from 1889 to 1912 when, nearing fifty, he repudiated what he felt to be the intellectual sterility and materialism of American life and retired to Europe, living on a small legacy and royalties. He spent the war years in Oxford, moved to Paris, and considered living in Avila, Monaco, and Florence before settling in the mid-1920s in Rome, where he died in 1952. 'It might seem that I turned to Italy and especially to Rome as a last resort, but that was not the case. Italy and Rome were my first choice, my ideal point of vantage in thought, the one anthropological centre where nature and art were most beautiful, and mankind least distorted from their complete character.'[118] He couches his defence in the language of classical humanism: the normative in nature, choice, completeness, beauty, ideal vision, and universality.

The Last Puritan has been largely ignored and remains outside the canon. Written in a period of crisis and innovation in fiction, yet breaking no new ground formally, the novel combines elements of the *Bildungsroman*, family chronicle, philosophical letters, apologia, novel of manners, university novel, and the international novel in which an innocent, upright American confronts cosmopolitan, decadent Europe and suffers a loss of innocence. Its conflict of world views descends thematically from the Genteel Tradition and antecedents in travel literature. 'Although he was the most penetrating of the many critics of the Genteel Tradition,' remarks David Perkins, 'Santayana was also, in some respects, its greatest exponent.'[119] The *critic* explains why Genteel thought had failed and

what might replace it; the *exponent*, why artists need not confine themselves to an expression of their age, but through imagination may rise
above it and range freely across time and space.

In a prologue, set in Paris shortly after World War I, 'Professor Santayana' is visited by his former student, Mario Van de Weyer. As so often
happened when they reminisced, their thoughts turn to Mario's cousin,
Oliver Alden, scion of an old Boston family, and 'of all the victims of
the war the nearest to us both.' Mario suggests that the professor write
Oliver's life: he was 'The Last Puritan,' 'last' in the sense of ultimate or
representative; in him 'puritanism worked itself out to its logical end'; he
'convinced himself, on puritan grounds, that it was wrong to be a puritan,' yet remained one out of duty, which was the 'tragedy' (LP 6). The
professor accepts the task because, as a classmate of Mario's father, he
knew the complex family history;[120] because the diaries and letters are
preserved; and because Oliver, 'the most gifted of my pupils in my last
days at Harvard (LP 6), illustrates one of the great problems of his generation: the spiritual and emotional decline of a hegemonic class and its
implications for modernity.

Oliver's father is a wealthy Bostonian doctor who never practised and a
dilettante epicurean who roams the world in his private yacht; he is separated from Oliver's mother who, hating Boston, raises her son (born ca.
1890) in rural Connecticut. The boy grows up in an emotionally pinched
environment, though the situation is relieved by a *sentimentalische* German governess who inspires him with a love of nature and Goethe. He
attends the local high school – a boarding school would have removed
him from his mother's watchful eyes – where he excels in his studies and
sports. At sixteen Oliver joins his father for a cruise, becomes friends
with the yacht's young English captain Jim Darnley, and is introduced to
his elderly cousin Caleb Wetherbee, a Catholic convert who has founded
a monastery in the Puritan stronghold of Salem. From a standpoint of
extreme humanist Catholicism, Wetherbee represents one way of attacking the system. In a lengthy monologue, one of the novel's high points,
he urges Oliver to break out of himself and go to 'old honest sharp-
witted Boston' to complete his education: 'if under your smooth blank
egg-shell of polite humanity you have a soul in you, go and hatch it in
Boston.' Moreover, the city needs fresh blood because it is 'becoming
too much like the rest of the country, choked with big business, forced
fads, and merely useful knowledge' (LP 187). Touring England, Oliver
meets Mario, a year and a half his junior and a pupil at Eton, a 'penni-
less orphan' (LP 292) who impresses him with his inner strength, poise,

and culture. Inheriting a fortune on his father's death, Oliver follows his mother's wishes and applies to Williams College in western Massachusetts (far from Boston, at least within her geography), though he eventually transfers to Harvard, at which Mario is an undergraduate. Afterwards the cousins take a year-long journey around the world. When war breaks out, Mario enlists in the UK's Royal Flying Corps, Darnley in the navy; Oliver waits in Oxford for America to enter, reading philosophy with the now retired Professor Santayana. Finally, Oliver goes to war, but never sees action. He dies in a motor accident soon after the Armistice.

The epilogue takes place circa 1935 in Rome, where Professor Santayana has chosen to live and where Mario, married with a family, works for the Vatican. Returning the hefty manuscript of 'The Last Puritan,' Mario recommends publication because, while the professor may have exaggerated the facts, he expresses a deeper truth, described elsewhere in his writings: 'After life is over and the world has gone up in smoke, what realities might the spirit in us still call its own without illusion, save the form of those very illusions which have made up our story?' (LP 602).

In presenting the Puritan configuration of values and its Genteel residues, Santayana endows Oliver with the virtues of his race: integrity, courage, self-scrutiny and self-discipline, personal austerity, love of hard facts, hatred of sham. Neither is he fanatical, nor calculating, nor ungenerous; he has the will to question his upbringing and grow beyond it. How far? is the real question. With the advantages of superior intelligence, wealth, and character, Oliver's life seems not his own, and not so much predestined as pre-dedicated to duty. 'All sensation in Oliver was, as it were, retarded; it hardly became conscious until it became moral' (LP 159).[121] Santayana's irony flits across the free-indirect style: 'he knew it was his duty to marry some day, as it was his duty to go to college and to play football and to choose a profession. Fortunately the duty of marrying didn't come round at a fixed date like the other duties' (LP 236). Football immerses him in concreteness, a welcome deadening of conscience and his 'mystic alienation' (LP 228) from his family and others. Yet even sports become imprisoning, like his daily two-hour gymnastic regimen. He plays football 'with a cold heart' (LP 382) and questions the loss of the self in the delirium of the game: 'Was it right to be transported out of oneself at all? Wasn't it just shirking, a mere escape and delusion?' (LP 413). He is happy when he breaks his leg in a game for the excuse not to play any more, whereupon he is persuaded out of a sense of duty into rowing, yet another routine, another team as opposed to individual sport, one of the traditionally preferred sports of the elite. Oliver decries both the killing programs and the remedies: 'I hate pleasure. I hate what is called having a good time. I hate stimulants. I hate "dope." It's all a cheat' (LP 371).[122] 'Dope' probably killed his father, a suicide. Mario's buoyant *modus vivendi*, behaving 'irresponsibly, even licentiously' though 'within the limits of kindness and honour,' is rejected as 'enviable if you wish to be happy but impossible if you wish to do right, to make yourself and the world better' (LP 508).

Oliver's conflicted nature is reflected in his name: Alden, his genealogical descent from the gentle John Alden, about whom Longfellow wrote in *The Courtship of Miles Standish;* Oliver, from the implacable Cromwell. 'Either the truth or nothing' (LP 582) is Oliver's ramrod standard, what the fleshly Jim Darnley calls his 'moral tantrums' and 'blooming principles' (LP 169), though he is not priggish. Illustrating what Santayana describes as the late-Protestant 'combination of earnestness with waywardness,' Oliver sinks into a desperate minimalism of spirit and action: 'Enough if on occasion I practice charity and keep myself ... from wrong' (LP 583).[123] This is not the faith of his forefathers who crossed oceans, moved mountains, and tamed a wilderness.

Eliseo Vivas faults Santayana for not making a better case for late Puritan Protestantism, and for not presenting Oliver with defined goals, a career, a mission in life to put his integrity to the test. Oliver strives for perfection, with nothing specific to be perfect about; as for pleasure, 'he sought to persuade himself that what he missed was not worth having.'[124] Better for Oliver had he one touch of nature that makes the whole world kin, but that would be a different character. Vivas wants a bourgeois melodrama, whereas Santayana aimed at a '*tragedy*' (his italics): Oliver 'wouldn't be commonplace, there are plenty of people to be commonplace.'[125] Many college students from the 1890s up to the war underwent a crisis of faith and emerged to choose careers in law, medicine, business, diplomacy, or the academy. As with characters in Henry James and Proust, however, Oliver's money frees him from dependence on a career so that he can pursue his existential crisis to its 'logical end'; his is not a case of the rich playboy whose money, not scruple, takes the will away. Though Oliver fancies becoming an unsalaried professor, he cannot be said to have a Weberian 'calling.'[126] Oliver prefers philosophy because of its abstraction, its strength of reason, and substitute spirituality, in tune with his Puritanism. Santayana could have given Oliver more to do, for instance, by making him an ambulance driver in the war (Oliver almost does so), by having him survive to become a professor or philanthropist, or even by having him die in battle. Mario is his chief foil, but there are lesser ones, characters from his generation who seek answers to the loss of religious faith and lack of self-fulfilment. His cousin Edith volunteers in hospital work (according to T.J. Jackson Lears, many young upper-class Americans of the period responded to feelings of spiritual weightlessness by devoting themselves to something intensely 'real,' say, by working among the lower classes, or in settlement houses).[127] Senator Lunt has Homer's poetry to guide him, at home in Montana or in the thickets of Washington politics. Darnley has his swagger and sensualism – he dies in the war.

For Santayana, such solutions and compromises can obscure the underlying problem: the shallow life of secularized modernity, dedicated to power and materialist culture, lacking measure, flattening individuality, and jettisoning its historical and religious traditions. Oliver faces the loss of faith knowingly and unflinchingly and endures the consequences, but not without some minimal returns, like his scattered epiphanies. H.T. Kirby-Smith allows him 'philosophical enlightenment, if not emancipation.'[128] Thus, Oliver intuits an 'eternal self' (LP 296) that seems at times to stir beneath a mundane self. Or, at Concord, he sees into the life of things (again, in a brilliant deployment of the free-indirect style): 'The meagre woods, the sluggish river, the frail monuments were eloquent in their pathetic inadequacy, as if the spirit that had blown here had disdained to stop and to become material, and had spread and transformed itself to infinity into unexpected things' (LP 404).[129] Among Oliver's 'few moments of physical pleasure,' writes Jonathan Levin, are his friendship with Jim Darnley and his love of nature – as when, after Jim's death, he comes upon a black swan floating on the Thames in flood at Oxford, another of the novel's highpoints; in these moments, his 'spiritual nature is not so much abandoned as brought into fleeting contact with overwhelming, sensually stimulating psychical realities.'[130] However, either from his epiphanies or moments of pleasure, Oliver does not attain to the visionary power of, say, Hans Castorp's in the 'Snow' episode of Mann's *Magic Mountain* (though, as with Oliver's aperçus, this does not lead to action) or the curé of Ambricourt in Bernanos's *Diary of a Country Priest*. Professor Santayana tells Mario that Oliver's was 'the tragedy of the spirit when it's not content to understand but wishes to govern' (LP 10). Yet Oliver is discontented even when he understands; contemplative leisure does not compensate for his loss of faith and feelings of worthlessness. The traffic accident that kills him is as much a moral comment on his inability to commit himself as an aesthetic decision to bring the novel to a close. Otherwise he would have lived a life of quiet desperation to the end of his days. He is a younger, later version of Dürer's Knight, the ideal type of the Protestant's lonely spiritual quester in secular modernity, 'and often in his wintry day the sun sets without shining.'[131]

As Oliver's chief foil, Mario has been judged both a success and a failure, with Ross Posnock's reference to him as the novel's 'moral center' as strongly positive and Vivas's negatively dismissive 'Mario is not real at all.'[132] A literary descendent of Pater's *Marius the Epicurean*, he is the first character introduced, gives the author his subject and even his title, and while he does not appear until halfway through the story, he is never thereafter far from the main action and has the last speech in the epilogue. When Oliver meets him at Eton, he seems so 'merry' and 'innocently sparkling' that he was like a 'Chinese figurine, all ivory and silk' and 'hardly seemed human at all' (LP 289). He has two names (Mario and Vanny), two languages (English and Italian), and two nationalities (in his theatrical self-description, he should be 'half a Neapolitan beggar-boy on a door-step picking fleas' and 'half a cowboy spitting tobacco') (LP 289). The animal, aesthetic, and flight metaphors that characterize him express a harmony of natural, artistic, and spiritual qualities. Against Oliver's 'academic Saint Sebastian' (LP 292), Mario is like a prince out of the *Arabian Nights,* Titian's Bacchus leaping (high in the air) from his chariot, a fashionably dressed Gabriel descending (in flight) in an Old Master's painting (LP 291–2), a 'faun' like Hawthorne's Donatello in *The Marble Faun* (LP 384). He speaks in a 'beautiful bird-language,' the Etonian accent, and might appear 'flighty' (LP 281, 346, 412); he is an aviator in the war. His American grandmother, a throwback to an earlier pre-'system' generation, praises his 'terrible pagan Italian stamina' in contrast to 'our northern flabbiness'; he is a 'ray of light' (LP 456) in her stodgy household.[133] When he leaves college to be near his dying mother and remains in Europe, she alone applauds his decision to seek his own way in life. Santayana may have been patting himself on the back.

To portray Mario, Santayana drew upon the Genteel and travel-writing model: instinct and feeling, force of personality, imagination and play, the child, sincerity, the feminine, virtuosity. Mario's Italian mother to whom he owes his 'deeper side' (LP 346) sacrificed her opera career to raise him and tries returning to it afterward; Oliver's mother has no career and lives through her son. Mario's mother breastfed him – 'it makes all the difference' (LP 408);[134] Oliver's gave him the bottle and does not kiss him in public. Mario's mother is not possessive, he remains close to her, yet is no mamma's boy; Oliver's is so domineering that he rebels, psychologically, geographically, and at length legally. Mario is likened to Mozart's Cherubino, in love with love (LP 291), and has a shipboard romance with an opera star twice his age, 'Madame Gorgoroni,' an incident (as the name suggests) treated with light satire. Mario can sing and accompany himself at the piano; he arranges an amateur theatrical. 'Quite Italian in a sort of speculative glorification of the facts, a dash of cockiness and personal challenge' (LP 523), he is attractive to women (another gift from his mother), whereas Oliver, who is more handsome, more intelligent, more athletic, and wealthy into the bargain, has no luck at all. Mario has limitations: he can be glib and superficial, and on their visit to Emerson's house at Concord, while with poignant intimacy of feeling Oliver dreamily scans the village memorials, Mario is thinking ahead to lunch (LP 404). Lowell saw a balance of intellect and feeling in the Italian and a suppression of feeling in the American; Santayana endows Mario with both rationality and emotion, with the 'courage of his full human nature' (LP 6), whereas anhedonic Oliver suffers from a division between mind and feeling, and between self and world. Mario is an aesthetic pagan, 'corrected and civilized by his Catholic and Italian connections.'[135] Professor Santayana calls Mario 'more American, more modern, than Oliver himself; or rather he is what men of the world had always been, brilliant slaves of their circumstances' (LP 509), not exactly a compliment, but a good example of an essence in Santayana's philosophy.[136]

On first inspection, Oliver finds his cousin 'alarming and strangely formidable' (LP 291); he cannot fit this elusive, paradoxical personality into conventional categories. Mario is both sincere and theatrical (the name 'Mario' has something of the stage Italian); a 'child in his delight' yet 'ageless and inscrutable' (like Pater's Mona Lisa); 'hyacinthine' and 'delicate in his strength' but 'strangely agile and supple,' 'sporting,' though not in the 'homely, hard-working, sailor fashion of the Anglo-Saxon' (LP 347, 384, 507). He is amazed at how well Mario converses with all kinds of people, in contrast to his American friends who seem only to talk when they want something or complain. Oliver does not relish conversation. Mario's sport is solo flying, linked more closely to an instinctual sense of play than an embrace of technology. He lives intensely in the moment, 'all sparks of fire, all shifts of quick feeling and brilliant light' (LP 296). When he visits his cousin after a two-year interval, there was 'not the least hesitation on his part in recognizing, embracing, clinging to Oliver in the old way' (LP 384), though Oliver probably did not much occupy his consciousness in the intervening years: Italian present-mindedness trumps nostalgic sentimentalism. Oliver defends his cousin against his mother, to whom he is dandified and 'effeminate' like 'all young Italians' and only wants her son's money. 'Of course I paid for everything,' Oliver replies, '– except the kindness' (LP 346–7).

On their world tour Mario plays the *cicerone* with his guidebooks, always at home with himself, never repelled by what he sees as the other, but also 'never shaken in his own judgments' (LP 507) because he is secure in them, perhaps too secure. The theme of the Italian 'at home in the world' is Genteel; it does not mean that Italians are all by nature cosmopolitan; rather, that they carry within them a strong, satisfying (to them) cultural construction wherever they go (even if at times it is inappropriate). Often bored with sight-seeing, Oliver reads the Western newspapers and financial reports; there is, he muses, 'no private space any longer in the world, and no freedom; every chink and cranny was choked with the same vulgarity' (LP 507). Yet with greater perspicacity and depth than his cousin, he questions if what he sees might be better than his own culture.

In Santayana's political writings Mario illustrates the 'liberalism of liberty' or 'classic liberty' (the individual, independent entrepreneurs, risk and acceptance of instability, spontaneity, 'inequality,' 'moral diversity') in contrast to the 'liberalism of control' or modern liberalism (cooperativeness, the administered society, egalitarianism, progress, 'moral uniformity'). The liberalism of control is 'wholly out of sympathy with the wilder instincts of man, with the love of foraging, of hunting, of fighting, of plotting, of carousing, or of doing penance.' These instincts express the tragic Mediterranean spirit that was tamed by religious submission; the liberalism of control tames the instincts by rules and procedures. 'Classic liberty, though only a name for stubborn independence, and obedience to one's own nature, was too free, in one way for the modern liberal.'[137] The liberalism of liberty is 'absolute' and 'fierce'; incalculable in the strict sense, not able to be measured; associated with radical system-building and the arts, with penitence and martyrdom, criminality and capriciousness; 'impracticable,' 'tragic and ridiculous,' a 'deep tragedy, because the narrower passions and swifter harmonies are more beautiful and perfect than the chaos or the dull broad equilibrium that may take their place.' On the other hand, the liberalism of control, which is 'English' or 'American,' is guided by the spirit of work, responsibility, social pressure, reformism, compromise, and optimism, all necessary for a modern society to prosper. Santayana ranks himself with the absolutists, like 'the luckless American who is born a conservative, or who is drawn to poetic subtlety'; 'in remote places you sometimes find such a solitary gaunt idealist – or else he flies to Oxford or Florence or Montmartre to save his soul – or perhaps not to save it.' At the same time, while classic liberty would be 'more beautiful if we were birds [Mario?] or poets,' we all are obviously not so, and in a carefully reasoned volte-face Santayana concludes that 'co-operation and a loving sacrifice of a part of ourselves – or even of the whole, save the love in us – are beautiful too, if we are men living together.' The two liberties are 'incompatible'; '[we] must make a painful and a brave choice between them.'[138]

In Europe, where Mario thrives, Oliver cannot decide whether to transcend the world like Plato, Plotinus, and Christianity, or to capitulate and be harmonious with it (LP 509, 520); his choice lies between the liberalism of control and ascetic withdrawal. When the war forces him to reconsider his beliefs under the sign of ultimacy, he hammers out the issues with his cousin, in whom the war brings out the inborn classical realism. For Mario, the war is 'horrible,' like death, yet it is, like Virgilian tears, 'in the nature of things.' No one would consciously design either nature or human nature as they are, with all their imperfections: 'but we have to make the best of them as they are' (LP 524). Mario does not mean that one should acquiesce, but rather accept the fact that life is a battle: 'the world is always full up with people, hungry people, pushing people, barbarous people: you've got to crush them or be crushed.' Oliver might well have drawn these conclusions from what he already knew of Mario. Then, Mario surprises him – Professor Santayana could have uttered the same words: 'I'm no conservative, I don't want to preserve myself, or things as they are, nor to move backwards and restore the past.' The present is 'horribly mixed,' the past was 'rather nasty,' what of this war that will determine the future? 'Chivalrous' Mario believes that he fights against the only thing worth fighting against: 'The Devil, the Tempter, the Father of Lies. That's what we're up against, what everybody has been up against who has ever done anything beautiful' (LP 524–6). Mario will fight for the preservation of the higher culture, beauty united with goodness and truth. He, too, has an element of Dürer's Knight.

Oliver takes refuge in his private moral outrage against the 'stupid' war and the civilization that cannot contain its savagery. Adrift, he allows external events to decide things for him: 'he wasn't very happy or useful in modern society,' but he 'couldn't conceive of any other' (LP 524, 526). He joins up after America enters: 'the mere momentum and mechanism of war continued to move the body, leaving the soul in profound apathy' (LP 564). Though Mario's martial spirit and 'slapdash' motives are distressing, Oliver intuits in him 'something great, something ancient and fundamental'; by contrast, he felt 'helpless and disinherited' and caught in a 'nasty spider's web of convention' (LP 525). Mario obtains a commission outside of his American citizenship; he goes to the front, is wounded, returns, is wounded again. Oliver remains behind the lines and suffers from unspecified illnesses. The war does nothing to change him. 'A critical faculty fearless but helplessly subjective,' he remains 'miserably caged' in himself, 'psychologically,' 'socially,' 'morally,' on his 'last pilgrimage' (LP 507–8, 602).

On reading *The Last Puritan*, William Lyon Phelps wrote Santayana that he had not created one good (i.e., moral, exemplary) character; that he did not 'love life'; and that he did not recognize that 'faith is necessary.' From an old friend it was a stinging rebuke and, given Santayana's identification with the project, a harsh judgment on his life. Santayana replied that Oliver was 'very good': there is his moral courage to overcome the religious and spiritual emptiness of his generation; that he failed does not negate the value of the endeavour. Second, it was 'Oliver, not I, who didn't love life'; he sought for something worthy of his belief – a 'tragic vocation,' like a poet's or a philosopher's – and found nothing worth his sacrifice. If temperamentally, he did not possess an 'animal Epicurean faculty,' love of life is in the novel, in Mario, among others.[139]

As for the third charge, 'faith is necessary,' Santayana declared an oblique indebtedness to James's pragmatic theory of belief: 'faith is an assurance inwardly prompted, springing from the irrepressible impulse to do, to fight, to triumph. Here is where the third sloppy wash in the family tea-pot is insufficient. And without robustness an imposed intellectual faith wouldn't do.' For him, doctrinal religion in the early twentieth century had lost its spiritual force; intellectual faith, say, a political credo or commitment to science, might suffice if it had 'robustness'; but such a 'faith' must be constructed by individual effort. Were such a 'faith' to be imposed, it would lack the power to make one act upon it. Having lost the faith of his fathers, and failing to construct an intellectual faith of his own, and lacking temperamentally the Epicurean option, Oliver is left with an anguished awareness of vacuity. The one other option lay in mystical transcendence of the world, and here Santayana admits to Phelps his artistic failure: he had not shown that Oliver was 'a mystic ... and *couldn't* give way to the world, the flesh, or the devil. He ought to have been a saint.' Yet Santayana was right not to make him a mystic, saint, or 'intellectual hero,' which would have violated the canons of realist fiction (even at that, in the epilogue Santayana slyly has Mario say that he [Professor Santayana] made Oliver 'much more intelligent' than he actually was [LP 601]). Oliver's 'deepest tragedy,' wrote Santayana, lies in the fact that he came of age in a 'spiritual vacuum': if one is 'born a poet or a mystic in America he simply starves, because what social life offers and presses upon him is offensive to him, and there is nothing else. He evaporates, he peters out.'[140] *Pace* Phelps and Vivas, Oliver is a good, even 'very good' person, above average, though not too much so (as Aristotle said of the ideal tragic hero), involved in an action that is serious, complete, and of magnitude, flawed by an inability to act or to compromise, and ultimately defeated by the hostile system. The frequent use of 'tragedy' to depict Oliver's fate is justified.

VII

Santayana or his surrogate narrator, Professor Santayana, can claim the moral high ground from Professor Phelps for several reasons, first because he has entertained so many points along its circumference. Formally, this 'memoir in the form of a novel' results from the dialectic interplay of fact (memoir) and fiction (novel), the thinnest of partitions dividing the genres. Then, most eclectically, he exploits the resources of numerous subgenres (*Bildungsroman*, apologia, international novel, etc.) and the satiric mode. Its central characters and many minor ones are representative types of wide variety, 'masks for my own spirit,' the more finely etched for his having lived with them for so many years, 'spirit' in his materialist philosophy being defined as the most intense consciousness (an 'immaterial invisible inward intensity of being').[141] In their capacity as frames, the prologue and epilogue give further vantage points. Santayana's external commentaries blend in with those of Professor Santayana in the frame; and Mario's voice in the frame and the novel is in the same. Characters seen from so many angles enhance narrative possibilities – fact, fiction, outside the novel, in the frame, in the novel itself. 'Mario is the man I think I ought to be,' said Santayana to Corliss Lamont, 'but I can't help liking Oliver; and that's the trouble.'[142] In the frame Mario confides without a trace of jealousy or bitterness, 'I always knew that you thought more of Oliver than of me' (LP 7). Also in the frame Santayana describes Mario in terms of harmonious equilibrium – the 'outward sign of an inward grace' (LP 600) – yet this is the phrase by which he described the 'very essence of poetry' thirty-five years earlier in *Interpretations*, so it is highest praise.[143] In one of the best examples of ironic self-reference on Santayana's part, Mario in the frame slyly recommends that the professor publish the manuscript because it has 'a better philosophy in it than in your other books' (LP 602).

Beyond formal devices, Santayana has constructed his own 'intellectual faith,' the 'better philosophy,' which is the axis around which the other viewpoints in the novel revolve. Unlike Oliver, who in the end had neither a religious faith nor its intellectual replacement, Santayana had the transformed myths of a religious faith and his own intellectual constructions to guide him. From Homer and Lucretius, as he said, he had a 'humourous animal faith in nature and history, and no religious faith: and this common sense world suffices for *intellectual satisfaction,* partly in observing and understanding it, partly in dismissing it as, from the point of view of spirit, a transitory and local accident.'[144] Homer's poetry, Platonic forms and Aristotelian naturalism, history, Lucretian materialism, Spanish Catholicism, and scepticism, these make for a broad-based 'alternative tradition.' Santayana 'savored all that European culture had to offer,' writes Irving Singer, 'and he did so by treating his Catholic origins as a resource rather than a burden.' Unlike Caleb Wetherbee, Santayana believed that religion is justified not by its dogma and institutions but by its myths and rituals, which 'could embellish everyday experience by making it orderly, ornate, and meaningful.' Not a conservative justification in the narrow sense, it is a historical one: 'he cherished Catholicism,' continues Singer, 'as the living residue of Greek and Latin civilization that had survived in the modern world despite the inroads of Nordic and Romantic barbarism.'[145]

Yet he was not backward-looking. In 1927, in an exchange of letters with Van Wyck Brooks, he questioned why so many American writers 'peter out' (the same idiom used for Oliver) 'unless they go and hibernate in Europe?' Having lived long on both sides, Santayana gave freely of advice that echoes his critique of the Genteel Tradition. 'Instead of being interested in what they [American writers and artists] are and what they do and see, they are interested in what they think they would like to be and see and do: it is a misguided ambition, and moreover, if realized, fatal, because it wears out all their energies in trying to bear fruits which are not of their species.' Amassed, these interests become an *'applied culture,'* resembling the 'imposed intellectual faith' or the European zeal of the Genteel writers unable to produce works of importance and originality. Cautioning against such a culture, he suggests a range of new topics by way of answering one of his staunchest critics. 'What Lewis Mumford calls 'the pillage of the past' (of which he thinks I am guilty too) is worse than useless'; 'art, etc. has a better soil in the ferocious 100% American than in the Intelligentsia of New York. It is veneer, rouge, aestheticism, art museums, new theatres, etc. that make America impotent. The good things are football, kindness, and jazz bands';[146] also the wilderness, the California 'forests,' the 'Sierras.'[147]

The football reference as one of the 'good things' brings him full circle. In the 1890s Santayana, who enjoyed watching the game, wrote that football was a 'symbol of all the prehistoric struggles'; it had 'vitality with disinterestedness'; 'heroic virtues shine in miniature' and the 'passion' is not 'excessive'; fans with 'keen and intelligent interest' remark upon the players 'like the crowd in Homer upon the prowess of their chief.' Admittedly, the game lacks the aesthetic quality of Greek athletics; yet it 'borrows from the bleak and autumnal landscape something of a pathetic earnestness and natural horror.' A side-benefit of liberal education, football is among the 'fruits of leisure.' At one point the 'frenzy' of the game must have scrambled his reason: 'our athletic life is the most conspicuous and promising rebellion against this industrial tyranny.'[148] Even in the 1890s, though much more so today, sports like football are a synecdoche of the system, not a rebellion against it. When he noted, admiringly, the tight planning of the games, he was closer to the truth.[149]

By the time of *The Last Puritan* Santayana steeps his descriptions of the game in satire: a 'great passion about nothing' (LP 228); 'every move ... forced and planned and fussed over and pushed into you against the grain,' a 'horrid tyranny' (LP 397). Classical allusion is now turned against it; fans are 'two compact masses of humanity on opposite sides of the field, whose aspect could change instantly from that of Rome after Cannae to that of twenty thousand demons frantic with joy' (LP 231). Christian Messenger thinks that the later Santayana had rejected the playing field that had once been a symbol for 'hearty American energy and optimism'; by the 1930s 'the America of concerted group action is not for him.'[150] Yet the letter to Van Wyck Brooks suggesting 'football, kindness and jazz bands' does not sound like a rejection. Rather, it is in keeping with Santayana's measured acquiescence to the liberalism of control, with football embodying teamwork, planning, competition, heft, and the future. American authors should study the 'good things' for their critical insights into their cultural reality, which is the use to which he put the game, albeit negatively, in *The Last Puritan*. Maybe Norton was right after all for shaking his head about the Greeks and football.

As this example may show, Santayana had carved out for himself a unique position that took from both liberalisms. The central issue had always been individual freedom, and his objection to the Puritan and Genteel traditions, revivals like the New Humanism of the 1920s and 1930s, and to the deadly system itself is that they narrowed one's freedom by interposing one or another notion of 'reason' or 'goodness' between the individual and immediate experience. Though there is certainly no experience without some mediation, the premise of Santayana's 'animal faith' is that the initial response to life should be immediate and spontaneous. By the same token, his concept of 'prerational morality' (or 'morality proper') does not lack a kernel of reason but is embedded in habits, acts on instinct or intuition, and is akin to aesthetic taste.[151] If rationalism and ethics impose their particular grids before the person has had the chance to be affected – a kind of moral prior restraint – the person will not be free to try wide ranges of human experience, will not be as open to possibility and change, will not have the 'courage of [one's] full human nature' (LP 6). The ethical philosopher, however, was content to let reason and goodness have the last word.

If Oliver's death is Santayana's conflicted rejection of the America of his youth, Mario's settling in Italy answers to another side of his experience. Echoing the New England Italophiles, Mario makes his claim for Italy: 'in one sense it's everybody's country who is conscious of the past' (LP 587). The remark (as one might expect) resembles Santayana's autobiographical comments: 'In Rome ... I feel nearer to my own past, and to the whole past and future of the world'; 'inhabited by a people that more than any other resembles the civilised ancients,' possessed of an 'eternal dignity,' Rome is 'my fated centre of gravity and equilibrium.'[152] So he left America, making a conscious choice between the two liberties, of freedom and control, and if he acceded to the latter in some respects, it was done critically and with reservations, and he kept alive the former by making his reservations public in book after book. Professor Santayana's last remark to Mario is wistful, as if to say, the two of us merely need to carry on in our differing ways: 'You are at home in the grand tradition ... you will hand on the torch of true civilisation; or rather, in this classic Italy, you have little need of tradition or torches' (LP 600). But in America? Santayana as the self-described 'American writer' knew that if his 'alternative tradition' had little chance against the tide of modernity, he would exercise his 'irrepressible impulse to do, to fight, to triumph.' Meanwhile, the tradition still cast its twilight glow and offered refuge. That is why, like Mario, he chose to live in Italy.

chapter 3

Isle of the Dead

JOHN PAUL RUSSO

As a new Italy emerged in the nineteenth century from its fragmented territories, foreign visitors sought for the older land into which they read their desires and fantasies. They were reacting against industrial society, attacking it, resigning themselves to it, or searching for a way out. Many visitors chose a funerary theme or a classical underworld to express themselves and their yearning for death or a lost world in which they might be reborn. 'If orthodox religion was crumbling, and if nature was emptied of spiritual meaning,' wrote Douglas Bush, 'classical myth might seem to be the last symbolic medium for transcendental longings.'[1] Italy offered a rich soil for these melancholy wishes to germinate, with its monuments, tombs, and ruins, and with a history so long that life, death, and rebirth can lie in the midst of one another. Hesperia, from the Greek *Hesperios* for Twilight Land or the western Mediterranean, was used by Virgil for Italy; it also refers to the 'land of the dead'; Strabo identified Cumae and Avernus with Homeric Hades.[2] 'Renaissance' itself contains the metaphor of life and death (as does 'Risorgimento'), signifying either a 'continuing "survival" of antiquity' or a 'discontinuity' but with cycles of death and rebirth.[3] From Venice to Sicily, the land was dotted with chthonic sites and place names; it was pierced by caverns and grottoes, raised by hellish volcanoes, plagued by malarial marshes, ringed by mysterious islands. At Pompeii one could see the living world frozen in time; at Rome one could visit the catacombs. In its mellow and seemingly endless decline, visitors found a land that, unlike their own, had not yet broken irrevocably with its pre-modern past. Hence the mood of nostalgic yearning only deepened when they realized that Italy was on the march as a unified state, and had begun to modernize and narrow the distance between itself and the northern nations.

Insights into this fascination and yearning may be extrapolated from studies by Geoffrey Gorer, Alberto Tenenti, Michel Vovelle, Philippe Ariès, and others who have investigated Western attitudes to death and the afterlife.[4] The sociological model of Ariès, the 'most prominent pioneer' in the field, is adopted here in a heuristic spirit.[5] In this model, nature is an unceasing dynamism in which death as such may not exist; rather, it may be 'a notion cultivated by man that disappears in the overall plan of nature.' Yet if death hardly exists for nature, from a human standpoint death is nature's most brutal fact. Seeking its own survival, culture erects defensive barriers to control or mitigate nature's savagery by religion, morality, law, and other institutions. Culture opposes nature and nature's death, attempts to rob nature of its victory or at least to subtract from it, by running a gamut of options, which Ariès historicizes from classical antiquity to the present time.[6]

The 'first' Middle Ages (ca. 550–1100) held a 'naive and spontaneous acceptance of destiny and nature,' neither denying death nor exaggerating its importance, but treating it as natural and familiar, 'half-way between passive resignation and mystical trust': this is 'tame death.' Medieval eschatology, liturgy, and religious literature stress community survival over individual death. Death was a public affair, from the protocols of the dying person's room with relatives and neighbours around the deathbed, to a funeral banquet reaffirming communal life. Physical death was an intermediary sleep between this life and the Second Coming. Where the Romans buried their dead in tombs with personal inscriptions, these disappear in the medieval 'forgetting of the self.' The deceased was handed over to the church, to be placed in a charnel house and a common grave; death is anonymous. Cemeteries, which had been set outside city walls in the classical period, were moved back. In life people wanted to be near the dead, and in death to be buried *ad sanctos*, in churches and churchyards in town centres, symbolizing the eternal 'coexistence,' the 'unbroken family' of the living and the dead.[7] Though the 'first' Middle Ages is one of its exemplary moments, tame death is universal, 'the oldest death there is.'[8] Found among Homer's warriors, American cowboys, and Tolstoy's peasants, it endures in pockets of society to this day and, for Ariès, it is the most acceptable attitude.

From here Ariès maps out his 'devolutionary' model in which 'death reverts through several successive stages from the tame to the savage state.'[9] In the 'second' Middle Ages (1100–1350) and early Renaissance (1350–1500), eschatological ideology shifted its focus from community survival to the loss of personal identity; this stage is 'one's own death.'

Hitherto, physical death had not meant death itself, which occurred only at the end of time; 'as long as this interval existed, the person was not altogether dead, the balance sheet of his life was not closed.'[10] Now brought forward, the Last Judgment took place at the moment of physical death when the elements of an individual life were tallied and judged. No longer a brief sojourn, writes Tenenti, earthly life was an 'end in itself,' 'a period that was always sufficient to construct one's own salvation'; 'henceforth one treats not of saving the soul, but the man.'[11] The humanists decried wasting time, of which there was so little for earning fame, and revived the classical theme of a hero's memory-survival. Tombs of public figures and rich testators were individualized; funeral inscriptions appeared after an eight-hundred-year interval; even the middle class had funeral plaques.[12] Death was losing its anonymity.

In what may be termed 'first' modernity, from the High Renaissance to about 1750, Western culture exhibited the earliest signs of the 'great modern fear of death.'[13] Summoned by Julius II, the Fifth Lateran Council (1512–17) 'affirmed in dogmatic decrees the doctrine of individual immortality, which proclaimed personal rather than collective integrity in eternity as well as in history; this doctrine provided a context for the colossal egos of both the patron and the artist.'[14] Heroic individualism coupled with the scientific ambition to master nature provoked a counterattack on nature's part. Instead of 'tame' resignation and belief in the harmony of living and dead, death becomes terrifying, obsessive, and highly personal: a total '*break*' with life. Ariès's paradoxical name for his third stage, 'remote and imminent death,' implies that attempts to distance death or hide from it only bring it insistently nearer. In the conflict between denial and fascination, culture enlists the erotic to reduce the terror of death by making it desirable; baroque sensibility abounds in images of suffering and death informed, not by shrinking horror, but by erotic arousal: the iconography of Donne and Crashaw where 'Death raped the living'; Caravaggio's *Martyrdom of St. Matthew* depicting torture and death at the hands of athletic nude executioners; Poussin's *Dying Adonis;* the tomb scene in *Romeo and Juliet;* Bernini's *Ecstasy of Saint Theresa.* 'Like the sexual act, death was henceforth increasingly thought of as a transgression which tears man from his daily life, from rational society, from his monotonous work, in order to make him undergo a paroxysm, plunging him into an irrational, violent, and beautiful world.'[15] Ariès finds no evidence that matters were much different for the Reformation or Counter-Reformation, in German pietism or early evangelical Protestantism, in southern Europe or Puritan America.

Fear of death was thus assuaged by desire, by aesthetic beauty, and at length by the beautiful in nature itself. From Thomas Gray and the Graveyard School to Wordsworth, landscape poets accept death as a longed-for return to primordial nature.[16] In his *Essay on the Sublime and the Beautiful* (1757), a signpost in cultural transition, Edmund Burke went so far as to make death both beautiful and sublime. As Giuseppe Sertoli comments, the Burkean sublime implicates terror, a thrill in the nerves, sadomasochistic pain, and loss of self by 'eroticized death'; the beautiful involves a relaxation of the nerves, languid melancholy, a kind of post-orgasmic stupor, a 'pleasure-like dissolution hardly distinguishable from death.' The choice lies between the sublime's 'frenzied' death and the beautiful's 'melancholy' death, gothicism and sentimentalism, 'the coordinates of sensibility and culture in the second half of the eighteenth century.'[17]

Around 1750, at the outset of 'second' modernity, the sublimations of the imaginary forced their way into practice. In this fourth stage, 'thy death' or 'death of the other,' cemeteries that for a millennium had been located in town centres were removed, often under the pretext of sanitation and seemliness.[18] Set in a landscaped meadow, the tomb site is a family property in which the dead are 'at home,' to be visited 'as one would go to a relative's home, or into one's own home, full of memories.'[19] The cult of the tomb reaches its limit in the great national cemeteries, the nation being one family. There is renewed interest in embalming techniques, funeral regulations, fetishization (vivisection, the lock of hair), and ruins. [20] From his study of Provençal wills Vovelle argues for a 'dechristianization' or 'desacralization' of death that reverses baroque religiosity, a 'major mutation of collective sensibility' on the eve of the French Revolution.[21] It synchronizes with what Lawrence Stone calls 'affective individualism,' in which the focus is upon neither the (medieval) community nor the (Renaissance) individual but on an intermediate zone, the survivors, which may include the nuclear family and an inner circle of friends.[22] The survivor displaces the fear of death from the self onto the loved one, who must appear not to have died or even to be sleeping, but to await us in a nearby world. For believers, the afterlife may be traditional or occult; for non-believers, it may take the form of personal memory or private cult. Few took the Last Judgment seriously. Who could put one's friends through such an ordeal? Even hell as the great image of despair fades from sight. Fauré removed the *Dies Irae* from his *Requiem.*

'Thy death' triumphs in the Romantic cult of the dead, a 'substitute re-

ligion of Nature and family affection.'[23] Starting with Gothic novelists and
Romantic poets, the beautiful death became a set-piece in nineteenth-
century European and American art and literature. 'This apotheosis
should not blind us to the contradiction it contains, for this death is no
longer death, it is an illusion of art,' warns Ariès: 'Death has started to
hide'; 'the compromise of beauty was the last obstacle invented to chan-
nel an immoderate emotion that had swept away the old barriers.'[24] In
the English Romantic elegy 'the mourner displaces the mourned as the
principal subject.'[25] Writers stress the union of the living and the dead
within the family or between lovers and friends: the Brontes, the Rosset-
tis, Cambridge Apostles, spiritualists.[26] Victorians went into mourning
as if they invented it – 'the very idea of death moved them' – and their
obsessive observance of traditional conduct subverted the ritual control
of grief (its original purpose) by indulging in quasi-hysteria.[27] Beyond
these manifestations, Terry Castle sees in the Romantic cult 'not just a
new response to death, but a new mode of thought altogether – a kind of
thinking dominated by nostalgic mental images.'[28]

Today 75 per cent of Americans die alone in a hospital or nursing
home, surrounded not by family and friends but by machines: death is
a 'technical phenomenon.'[29] Labelling this fifth and final stage 'forbidden' or 'inverted' death (1914–), Ariès laments its lack of moral dignity.
'Death untamed' is shameful, a non-subject, at the furthest remove from
natural acceptance of the biological fact.

One may extend Castle's observation by considering how the geographical and historical region 'which the Apennines divide and the sea
and the Alps surround' became the object of intensified reverie. Italy was
proof that what might have appeared dead in Western modernity was
still 'alive' in the world of its survivors. Their record in the arts not only
enshrined a way of life vanishing before their eyes, but articulated an
eschatology that was personal in the extreme. The beauty and historical
depth of the Italian landscape, cities, and towns were necessary components, Ariès's 'compromise,' which shielded visitors from contemporary
realities. As Ruskin said of Italy, 'her name and her strength are dwelling
with the pale nations underneath the earth; the chief and chosen boast
of her utmost pride is the *hic jacet;* she is but one wide sepulchre.'[30] He
crystallized his feelings with a line from Milton's *Il Penseroso,* two adjectives in the superlative degree, 'Most musical, most melancholy' (1.542).
Of deepest melancholy for Ruskin is the belief that the real Italy lies in its
illustrious past, which is dead and can never be sufficiently mourned for.
Yet its past stands forth eternally alive through the musical or aesthetic

element that breathes life into its natural scenery, its towns and cities, its art and culture, and its ruins. In his earliest definition of the beautiful, 'what is most musical will always be found most melancholy'; 'there is no real beauty without a touch of sadness.'[31]

The power by which Italy stirred feelings of the past and the dead is exemplified by the work of James Fenimore Cooper, Sheridan Le Fanu, Ouida, Arnold Böcklin, and Maurice Barrès. The common link between an American New Worlder, an Anglo-Irish writer of Huguenot antecedents, an English popular novelist, a Swiss artist of German culture, and a French nationalist is their intimation of death in Italy, which inspires them to pursue their longings to untold depths and transmute their secret revelations into an art of spectral ultimacy.

1. Frontoni's Confession in J. Fenimore Cooper's
The Bravo: A Venetian Story

When James Fenimore Cooper crossed the Alps and heard the coachman shout *Italie!* he doffed his hat. The author of the *Leatherstocking Tales,* a myth-maker of the American West, Cooper grew attached to Italy 'as one loves a dear friend'; it 'haunts my dreams and clings to my ribs like another wife'; 'the very name excites a glow in me, for it is the only region of the earth that I truly love.' Certainly he loved America more, yet that love was mixed with anger and bitterness, not the unalloyed love of Italy: 'I could wish to die in Italy.'[32]

From October 1828 to May 1830 Cooper travelled with his family through the peninsula, residing nine months in Florence, four in Naples and Sorrento, and five in Rome, with ten final days in Venice. To be nearer everyday life he rented houses instead of hotel rooms, and he broke through stereotypes (falling victim to others, as so often happens in the process): 'in grace of mind, in a love, and even in a knowledge of the arts, a large portion of the common Italians are as much superior to the Anglo-Saxon race as civilization is superior to barbarism.' He extends his observations through the social scale: 'I do not know any peasantry in which there is more ingenuousness, with less of rusticity and vulgarity, than that of Tuscany.'[33] Not entirely avoiding court life, however, he writes that the Italian gentleman is 'more gracious than an Englishman,' 'less artificial than a Frenchman,' and 'the nearest a true standard, of any gentleman of Europe'; 'there is a sincerity in this class, also, that took me by surprise; a simplicity of mind rather than of manner, that is not common on the other side of the Alps.'[34] The natural American had seemed to have found his counterpart. Cooper sailed the coast from Genoa to Naples and visited as far south as Paestum. In *The Water Witch* (1830), written in Sorrento, the Bay of Naples is contrasted with the low-lying New York coast, which he thought scenically less interesting. *The Bravo* (1831) is set in Venice, *The Wing-and-Wing* (1842) in Elba and the Sorrentine peninsula. His letters, notebooks, and travelogue *Gleanings in Europe: Italy* testify to his belief that 'there is no place where mere living is such a luxury.'[35] His wife said Italy was the only country he ever left 'looking over a shoulder.'[36]

Yet Cooper's attitude towards Italy was deeply divided. *The Bravo*, finest of his Italian writings and his contribution to the subgenre of the Venetian novel, denounces the various governments of Italy in decline, and one of its most memorable scenes is an assassin's nocturnal confession in an island graveyard. In his preface to the novel he outlines a case against despotism and the tyranny of the minority, and takes artists to task for neglecting the 'history of the progress of political liberty,' something that his own novel will presumably help correct.[37] He then clarifies the definition of 'republic' since Venice prided itself on the title: in a republic, rights ideally belong to the individual, not the state, and are only yielded up for self-protection: the state cannot dispense or withhold rights as it pleases. 'A government not properly based on the people possesses an unavoidable and oppressive evil of the first magnitude, in the necessity of supporting itself by physical force and onerous impositions, against the natural action of the majority' (iv). Cooper was putting the Ninth and Tenth Amendments to the U.S. Constitution into his own words and defining his novel's didactic purpose: to expose the vices of the 'system ... of Venice' (241), 'a narrow, a vulgar, and an exceedingly heartless oligarchy' (144). And not only Venice: in the eighteenth century there were 'several of these self-styled commonwealths, in not one of which, however, was there ever a fair and just confiding of power to the body of the people, though perhaps there is not one that has not been cited sooner or later in proof of the inability of man to govern himself!' (145).[38] Cooper could not resist taking a swipe at the American system.

'The many layered confection known as the myth of Venice,' writes James S. Grubb, 'is no single myth but an accumulation of historical explanation and contingent propaganda.'[39] For novelistic purposes, Cooper reduced his own eclectic research to just two myths: liberty and decadence. Venice had been for centuries an 'asylum for refugees of many kinds,' comments William Bouwsma, and had 'long realized one major Renaissance ideal in abundance: her subjects enjoyed a high degree of personal liberty.'[40] Though its economic decline dates from the second quarter of the seventeenth century, its myth of political liberty and moral rectitude was celebrated as late as 1797 in Wordsworth's sonnet on the dissolution of the Venetian Republic. By this time, however, La Serenissima was far better known as the most liberal, licentious city in Europe, with an inherently aesthetic value for a writer pursuing a theme of corruption. The black myth of Venice had its roots in the fifteenth century but was greatly popularized by Casanova and Byron, among many others. Cooper betrays his own leanings by depicting Venice as a beautiful, unreal, death-haunted city. But since he wanted to show the interrelation of social, economic, religious, and political factors in decline, he set his scene in the early eighteenth century, the beginning of the end, when Venice clung to the last shreds of power, and when its 'lethargy' was only 'incipient' (2); and not in present-day Venice (1820s), the end of the end, in which the decadence had completed its course. Though the 'wings of our lion are a little clipped,' remarks senator Gradenigo, 'his leap is still far, and his teeth dangerous' (75).[41] What would be the point of a tale of a lion without teeth?

The Bravo tells the story of Don Camillo Monforte, a Calabrian lord and heir to a fortune from the Venetian branch of his family. To secure absolute loyalty and enrich the state, the 'jealous,' 'arbitrary' law of Venice stipulates that its nobles 'dispose of any foreign possessions they might acquire' (224) and invest in the republic. Since Monforte will not relinquish his Calabrian fiefs, his legacy prompts interminable legal action; the Senate has kept him waiting five years. As the novel opens, he has just saved the life of Violetta Tiepolo whose gondola has been mysteriously run down in a canal. In this 'accident' arranged by the state, her rich and titled Roman uncle has drowned; she is the legatee. Like Monforte, then, she inherits landed wealth outside Venice, though in her case the Senate has made her its own ward, with the intention of marrying her to a Venetian and so keeping her fortune within the state. When Violetta and Monforte fall in love, the state conspires to prevent a marriage from which it cannot benefit. Gradenigo, a member of the all-powerful Council of Three and Violetta's appointed guardian, schemes to marry her to his spendthrift son. Thus, while the sophistic Gradenigo justifies his private interest on behalf of Venice, the same state thwarts the natural desires and flouts the economic freedom of Monforte and Violetta. 'I wish there were less of luxury and more of liberty within its walls' (47), says Violetta on hearing of Monforte's legal woes: the two myths in opposition.

Enter Jacopo Frontoni, a bravo, go-between, secret agent, and state assassin employed by the Council of Three, one of the most brilliantly realized figures in Cooper's fiction. In a highly coloured, gothicized portrait,
indebted to the Burkean sublime and the figure of the Romantic villain,
Frontoni is tall, athletic, slim, with a 'firm, assured, and even' walk, and
an 'erect' bearing 'strongly characterized by a self-possession.' His face is
'bold,' 'noble,' showing 'that strong and manly outline which is so characteristic of the finer class of the Italian countenance' (9). 'Frontoni,'
from *fronte*, means 'large or strong face.' But he typically conceals this
'face' or identity; as he says, 'Call me Mask' (108). When Monforte asks
his gondolier if he knows 'the countenance of one named Frontoni,'
he exclaims, 'His countenance, Signore!' as if to say, Who has seen it?
or Who dares look into his dangerous face if one could? 'By what else
wouldst thou distinguish a man?' says Monforte (18), implying that as
the face signifies the identity, an *open* face signifies the inner identity.
Actually, Frontoni rarely wears a mask; his face is mask-like. The name
Jacopo is a version of Iago, another Venetian master of disguise. Frontoni's 'bloodless' cheeks 'betrayed rather the pallid hue of mental than
of bodily disease,' pallor being the sign of death in gothic fiction. His expression is 'melancholy rather than sombre' (9) – not sombre by nature,
but melancholy by experience and self-reflection – and his voice is 'low'
(342), close to nerve-wracking silence. His most striking feature is his
eye, described so often and variously that it is ultimately indescribable:
'glittering' (9), 'full of brilliancy, meaning, and passion' (9), 'searching' and 'riveted' (39), 'dark' (41), 'glowing' (67), 'kindled' (72), 'glaring' (205), 'speaking' (231), 'contracting' (236). 'The eye is all that is
revealed of the masked and suspicious Venetians; suspicion generates
surveillance and surveillance generates suspicion.'[42] Yet the bravo's eye
is so various and inscrutable, it reveals nothing.

The state has imprisoned Frontoni's father on false charges, and
though having subsequently determined his innocence, it refuses to
admit its error. Instead, as a condition of his father's release, Frontoni
must serve as a public bravo, 'front,' and scapegoat for the state's crimes,
including clandestine murders carried out by its agents. His reports
have sent people to their deaths, though, he protests, he himself has
not committed murder and has even saved lives (389–90). His presence
strikes terror into the heart of patrician and commoner alike: 'he knows
more family secrets' than the prior of San Marco who spends 'half his
time in the confessional' (10) – a proleptic comparison. Frontoni is also
the friend of Antonio, an impoverished old fisherman and Gradenigo's

'foster-brother,' who appeals unsuccessfully to the Senate to exempt his grandson from the galleys.[43] In a gondola race at the regatta celebrating Venice's Marriage of the Sea, Frontoni shows a selfless side by letting Antonio win the prize and beg the doge for his grandson's release.[44] When Antonio's plea is rejected, the prize is passed to Frontoni, who boldly makes the same request. Such contumacy marks the onset of the Senate's disfavour.

The Council of Three orders Antonio's secret execution for fomenting a populist uprising.[45] From a distance Frontoni helplessly observes the drowning of his friend and seeks consolation in the distant heretics' graveyard on the Lido. To thwart the state's intentions, Violetta marries Monforte in a secret ceremony conducted by Father Anselmo, who had earlier been tricked into confessing Antonio and had watched in horror as the police threw him into the lagoon. As the ceremony draws to a close Violetta and Monforte are betrayed by their servants. She is abducted from the palace and Monforte sets out to rescue her with his men, eventually reaching the graveyard where he encounters Frontoni. This chance meeting draws together the principal strands of the plot. In his confession to Monforte, Frontoni breaks with his past and offers to help Monforte find Violetta and flee Venice. In the end Monforte and Violetta make a daring escape to Calabria in the very felucca that the Senate employs for smuggling.[46] Frontoni is arrested on the false charge of murdering Antonio and sentenced to death. When the appeals of Father Anselmo and Frontoni's beloved Gelsomina are rejected, he is beheaded before the doge's palace.

A tense, hallucinatory atmosphere hangs over these events. Though the novel opens and closes amid scenes of revelry and, as Alberta Fabris Grube notes, though contrasts of noise and quiet and of light and darkness figure prominently, noise and light only reinforce the prevailing tone of darkness, secrecy, and silence.[47] Venice is 'sombre' (43), 'despotic' (147), 'specious' (240), 'pretending' (288), and 'vicious' (413). If some squares are lively, 'the rest of the town was as silent as the grave' (43). Moonlight spills over domes, roofs, and lagoons – Cooper exploits these ghostly, spectacular effects for symbolic purposes. Gradenigo's praise is undercut by his own imagery: 'I often compare the quiet march of the state, contrasted with that troubled movement of some other of our Italian sisters, to the difference between the clatter of a clamorous town, and the stillness of our noiseless canals' (70).

Daylight is oppressive in its own way, as people remain hidden by the omnipresent mask. Male and female masquers glide up and down

flights of marble stairs, across piazzas, through shady arcades. On the
rule permitting masks unless expressly forbidden by the Senate, Monforte remarks cynically, 'without this narrow privilege, the town would
not be habitable a day' (211). 'Sacred' in Venice, the mask is 'the glory
of our excellent and wise laws,' says the 'Mask' Frontoni himself, mocking Venetian propaganda: 'he who seeketh to dwell within the privacy
of his own thoughts, and to keep aloof from curiosity by shadowing his
features, rangeth our streets and canals as if he dwelt in the security of
his own abode' (108). The mask is synecdochic of Venice, its Girardian
double: beautiful facades and hidden crimes. Where suspicion, mistaken
identity, and corruption are common, one's closest servants cannot be
trusted. Violetta's are paid informants, as is evident in her abduction:
'One flew along the narrow streets of the islands, to the residence of
the Signor Gradenigo; another sought his son; and one, ignorant of the
person of him he served, actually searched an agent of Don Camillo, to
impart a circumstance in which that noble was himself so conspicuous
an actor' (221). Monforte moves among the senators as in a pantomime,
not unlike Rigoletto after his daughter's disappearance: 'none might
have discovered that an heiress of so much importance had been so near
being lost to the state, or, on the other hand, that a bridegroom had
been robbed of his bride' (245). In a novel with prison scenes, drowning,
and assassinations, the principal means of conveyance, the gondola, is
likened to a coffin ('hearse-like' [53, 204]).[48]

The Venetian patriciate controls events with a power that seems demonic or god-like, depending on viewpoint: 'The sparrow does not fall
in Venice, without the loss touching the paternal feelings of the Senate' (71). Never one to keep his readers unenlightened, Cooper inter-
polates critical tracts on the Senate, the Inquisition, the Council of Ten,
and the Council of Three; the latter meets in masks and issues decrees
'without communication with any other body, and had them enforced
with a fearfulness of mystery, and a suddenness of execution, that resembled the blows of fate' (147). As with the love between Monforte
and Violetta, so too with Antonio's relation to Gradenigo, and with the
kindly Gelsomina's to her spying cousin Annina, state policy cuts across
familial bonds. Nor is religion beyond corruption: when Father Anselmo
leaves Violetta's palace, an agent warns him of the slippery marble steps,
'treacherous to an uncertain foot,' leading to the water. 'Mine,' replies
Father Anselmo, is 'too practised in the descent to be unsteady. I hope I
do not now descend these stairs for the last time?' (190). When he does
return, after confessing Antonio, a maid asks why he looks so ill 'with

the hue of death': 'deceive us not,' she says, 'haply thou hast more evil
tidings – Venice –,' and Father Anselmo interrupts her to complete her
sentence: 'Is a fearful state' (207). Despite signs of unrest the entire system is locked in place: authoritarian power masquerading as a republic,
rigid class division, religious intolerance, smuggling, propaganda, to the
point where change seems futile. Seeing himself – and his city – as without hope, Frontoni speaks with epigrammatic force: 'we are certain only
of the past' (342). *The Bravo* anticipates the political novel of state terror
in such writers as Conrad, Kafka, and Solzhenitsyn.[49]

Where secrecy and crime are prominent, Cooper found his counter-
theme in confession: personal, political, secular and religious. The word
'confession' appears twenty-eight times in the novel and is associated
with every major character. Besides incidental references to both true
and false confessions (and confessors), there are four confession scenes.
In a forced confession, Frontoni is interrogated by the Council of Three
(367–8). In two religious confessions, Father Anselmo shrives Antonio
(200–3) and Frontoni (386–92) before they are executed. The longest
confession (229–42), the turning point of the novel, does not take place
before a priest and is not forced; it involves two main characters, Frontoni
and Monforte, representatives of the poorest and richest classes, united
by mutual sympathy and outrage against Venice. 'Frontoni's Confession,'
to give it a name, is so imaginative in scope that one scarcely overpraises
it to say it looks ahead to Stavrogin's confession in Dostoevsky's *The Possessed*.

Appropriately for a confession made outside the Church, the encounter between Monforte and Frontoni takes place on a moonlit night in
the Jewish, Protestant, and heretics' graveyard near the northern end of
the Lido, the 'outer edge' (230) of Venice. 'In the nineteenth century,'
says Giorgio Bassano's Ermanno Finzi-Contini, it 'was considered one
of the most romantic spots in Italy.'[50] The twenty-year-old William Beckford, anticipating the new sensibility in *Dreams, Waking Thoughts, and Incidents* (1783), had visited this 'forlorn' corner: crossing the graveyard, he
plunged into the sea in a quasi-religious reverie: 'the tide rolled over me
as I lay floating about, buoyed up by the water, and carried me whereso-
ever it listed.' Unlike the biblical wind of the Spirit that 'bloweth where
it listeth' (John 3:8), Beckford's tide appears malign, enticing. 'It might
have borne me far out into the main, and exposed me to a thousand per-
ils, before I had been aware ... My ears were filled with murmuring, unde-
cided sounds; my limbs, stretched languidly on the surge, rose, or sunk,
just as it swelled, or subsided. In this passive, senseless state I remained,

till the sun cast a less intolerable light.'[51] On visiting the graveyard in September 1833 Chateaubriand likened its scanty grasses to the hair on the head of a corpse. The visit inspired *Rêverie au Lido*, which, like his *La Lettre à M. Fontanes* on Rome and the Campagna, expresses his sense of transience and loss. He recalls tracing a name in the sand and counting to sixteen the number of waves before it was entirely washed away. 'Venice, when I saw you a quarter of a century having flown away, you were under the empire of the great man, your oppressor and mine; an island awaited his tomb; an island is yours' (Venice is its own grave). 'But you perish unknown to yourself; I know my ruins.'[52]

Failing to locate Violetta and at a loss to know what to do, Monforte allows himself to drift towards the outskirts of the moonlit lagoon 'in pure indecision' (229), the more to be taken by the surprise in store for him. He disembarks near the 'retired graves of the proscribed,' sends his men away, and walks across the dunes into the graveyard. Cooper had ample precedent from the Graveyard School and gothic fiction for choosing such a site for contemplation. Though lack of trees is typical of Venice, their absence on this end of the island is felt painfully because evergreens serve in Christian graveyards as consoling emblems of eternity. 'Solitary, exposed equally to the hot airs of the south and the bleak blasts of the Alps, frequently covered with the spray of the Adriatic, and based on barren sands, the utmost that human art, aided by a soil which has been fattened by human remains, can do, has been to create around the modest graves a meagre vegetation, that is in slight contrast to the sterility of most of the bank' (230). The desolation ('solitary,' 'barren,' 'fattened') mirrors Monforte's psychological disgust (Beckford was nauseated by toads and locusts). The division of Protestant and Jewish graves rouses Cooper's anger: such distinctions should not be preserved in death when all are, democratically, before God.

Monforte had not 'threaded more than half the graves' – he is at the allegorical centre – 'when a human form arose from the grass' (231). Fearing robbery or murder, he raises his rapier and 'the stranger faced the moon, in a manner that threw all of its mild light upon his features' (231), the first of the references to *light upon the face* as indicative of a revealing truth. 'Why art thou here?' asks Monforte. '"Why are these here?" demanded Jacopo, pointing to the graves at his feet.' Essentially he is saying, I am a dead man; there is no place of safety. His irony typifies the scene; questions followed by questions, one undeceiving the other, confessor and confessed exchanging roles. 'My spirit hath need of room,' pleads Frontoni, 'I want the air of the sea – the canals choke me –

I can only breathe in freedom on this bank of sand!' A distant corner of an 'outer' island lies farthest possible from the core of claustrophobic Venice ('choke,' 'need for room') as well as a liminal point ('breathe,' 'freedom'). 'The deep tones of his voice appeared to heave up from the depths of his chest': his last reason is uttered *de profondis*, 'I loathe yon city of crimes!' (232). Suicide by his own stiletto is more honourable than the sword of 'pretended' Venetian justice. While Monforte knows that the state has condemned Frontoni, he also suspects, wrongly as it happens, that the bravo assisted in Violetta's disappearance. With the rapier at his throat, Frontoni has the temerity to invoke the dead beneath him to re-mark on the topsy-turvy world of Venetian violence: 'Arise, ye Israelites and bear witness ... A common bravo of the canals is waylaid, among your despised graves, by the proudest Signore of Calabria!' (233).

Frontoni's sardonic jest amounts to saying that the main characters have much in common, beyond social and moral differences: they are the same age, they are betrayed by the state and want justice, they feel the redeeming power of love. Their names, 'Monforte' and 'Frontoni,' have similarities in length, letter, and sound that reinforce the sense of doubling. 'All of Venice's stigmatized "subversive" outcasts form a com-munity of potentially countersubversive "Jews." Appropriately, it is at the burial grounds that these two "Jews" discover their fellowship.[53] They feel a mutual need to confess and purge themselves. When Monforte says, 'I have cursed the whole race for its treachery,' Frontoni replies that 'this is rather for the priore of St. Mark, than for the ear of one who car-ries a public stiletto' (234). Monforte learns to his surprise how closely he has been spied upon. 'A year hence,' the bravo says with candor bor-dering on indiscretion, as he refers to Violetta, 'you may know what it is to have your own wife turning your secret thoughts into gold.' With Antonio's murder, Frontoni has reached the limit of his endurance. His 'delusion' having been removed, 'I serve them no longer' (236). Mon-forte sheathes his rapier 'unconsciously,' willed by instinctive sympathy.

Just as Frontoni recommended a confessor to Monforte (though ironi-cally), Monforte counsels Frontoni to 'ease thy soul by confession and prayer.' Remaining silent, Frontoni 'turned his eye wistfully into the countenance of the other.' He is countenance to countenance, 'face to face' (*a fronte a fronte*), playing on the significance of the name. Often the symbol of appearance or the superficial, the face now conveys open-ness and sincerity. In the topsy-turvy world of Venetian morals, where the mask is the symbol for hiding, the face stands for the plain truth. In an exchange of name attributes that reinforces their bond, Cooper plays on Frontoni's name by referring to the opposing 'countenance' of Monforte; and in the next sentence, he plays on Monforte's name ('high mountain') by referring to the 'mountain' of guilt in Frontoni. 'Speak, Jacopo,' pleads Monforte, 'even I will hear thee, if thou wouldst remove the mountain from thy breast' (237). Frontoni thanks him for his sympathy and explains that he has taken to visiting the graveyard to 'commune with the hated dead.' Hated like himself, and so he can sympathize with the outcasts; and dead, because they alone can be trusted. Since Venetian corruption has penetrated the administration of the sacraments, he has not 'dared to trust my secrets even to the confessional' (237). Only the obstacle of class remains to be overcome before a 'confession' can take place between them.

Frontoni puts the matter most directly, though his remarks might seem forward for an illiterate bravo. Such articulated awareness of class division is what Hegel called the necessary anachronism in good historical writing: 'You are noble, I am of humble blood,' declares Frontoni, 'your ancestors were senators and Doges of Venice, while mine have been, since the fisherman first built their huts in the Lagunes, laborers on the canals, and rowers of gondolas. You are powerful, and rich, and courted; while I am denounced, and in secret, I fear, condemned. In short you are Don Camillo Monforte, and I am Jacopo Frontoni!' (237). Monforte is moved – Jacopo has spoken 'without bitterness' and in 'deep sorrow' – yet still refuses to hear out the bravo, urging him to seek a priest. Then Frontoni implores him, 'I must speak or die!' (238). When for a third time Monforte urges him to confess to a priest, the estranged bravo relates how he used to confide in Antonio to ease his guilt. With his friend murdered, and no one to take his place, he has come to the graveyard to commit suicide.

Mention of Antonio raises Monforte's suspicion anew because the fisherman had been implicated in the populist riot. Though Monforte's ideal of *noblesse oblige* often echoes Cooper's federalist democratism, he remains a southern Italian baron in a world imbued with feudal residues, and he has Cooper's fear of the mob. Monforte therefore accuses Frontoni of repenting from fear of political reprisals after a bungled insurrection, instead of true contrition for misdeeds, political and otherwise. When with his characteristic 'bitter,' 'smothered' smile (238; cf. 233), Frontoni says that Venetian 'justice' executed Antonio, Monforte replies angrily that Venice was putting down a rabble rouser. 'Jacopo seemed choked.' This is a kind of death: in examining Frontoni's despair, Cooper reintroduces the theme of equality. If the dead are without religious or class distinction before God's mercy, the living *in extremis* and over the very bones of the dead should be able to depend on universal compassion: '[Frontoni] had evidently counted on the awakened sympathy of his companion, not withstanding the difference in situations' (238). Again, there is a silence in which Monforte gathers in the moment and feels a wave of sympathy, though he remains afraid or unwilling to hear the crimes or to stare into the bravo's soul. Sensing hesitation, interpreted as a failure of sympathy, Frontoni entreats him – 'with a pathos in his voice that went to the heart of his auditor' (238) – to leave and let him die.

At this point Monforte transcends himself: 'Speak, I will hear thee,' he says, at last willing to hear the confession. 'Unburden thyself; I will listen though thou recount the assassination of my dearest friend' (238). Once again, the face-to-face imagery conveys a wordless message of mutual understanding and compassion: 'the oppressed Bravo gazed at him, as if he still distrusted his sincerity. His face worked, and his look became still more wistful; but as Don Camillo faced the moon, and betrayed the extent of his sympathy, the other burst into tears' (238–9). Hitherto, the bravo 'faced the moon' (231), now it is Monforte; Frontoni's face *worked* – a peculiarly American way of expressing the efforts of his soul becoming visible. At the same time, light shows the consoling sympathy in the face of Monforte.

'You have saved a soul from perdition' (239). Like the Ancient Mariner, with whom he shares a 'glittering' eye, Frontoni expresses gratitude for an opportunity to relieve his misery. While the confession of the bravo is not recorded – the deeds done, the guilt endured – Cooper has provided enough evidence from elsewhere in the novel to substantiate his crimes and his guilt. (Besides, Monforte tells him to hurry because he has his own problems!) Were Frontoni's particular crimes to be told, one wonders whether the reader's, if not Monforte's, sympathy could have been long sustained. For Monforte, 'every shade of disgust had given place to an ungovernable expression of pity' (239). As Cooper sketches in the act of confession, one imagines an expressive show of theatrical skill: '[Frontoni] seemed to play with the sympathies of the listener, as the improvisatore of that region is known to lead captive the passions of the admiring crowd' (239–40). Cooper's point is that the improvisitory show or appearance does not imply insincerity in a naturally expressive people, that rhetoric and sincerity are not necessarily at odds, but serve each other (many foreigners in Italy fail to understand this paradox). The confession comes to an end just as they step beyond the graveyard and reach the liminal shore: 'when the low tones of the Bravo were no longer audible, they were succeeded by the sullen wash of the Adriatic' (240). That his voice should fade ominously into the lugubrious surf suggests his fate.

By contrast, Monforte does not confess much beyond his curse of vengeance. Yet when he tells Frontoni not to reproach himself 'beyond reason,' he concedes his own wrongdoing on both personal and class grounds: 'even my name and rank have not, altogether, protected me from their arts' (240). Since Frontoni excuses him ('I know them capable, Signore, of deluding angels'), Monforte has meant that he has been unable to protect himself from the state's machinations, and also that he has participated in them. There was, Monforte says, a 'vicious deception of seemliness,' an exercise of power 'without any other responsibility than that which is exacted by the selfishness of caste!' (240). In meditating upon Venetian falsehood and his own complicity, Monforte stops short of confessing the 'sins' of his class, an act that would strain credibility. Hence he 'soliloquized, rather than addressed' Frontoni: one should not admit too much to a poor bravo. Monforte launches upon an interior monologue, a Cooperian diatribe on the despotic city which 'leaves none of us masters of our own acts.' Echoing the preface, Monforte's thoughts on the abuse of power and the corrupting relation of money to politics apply as much to America's post-Hamiltonian plutocracy as to Venetian aristocrats:[54]

> The wiles of such a combination are stronger than the will. It cloaks its offences against right in a thousand specious forms, and it enlists the support of every man under the pretence of a sacrifice for the common good. We often fancy ourselves simple dealers in some justifiable state intrigue, when in truth we are deep in sin. Falsehood is the parent of all crimes, and in no case has it a progeny so numerous as that in which its own birth is derived from the state. I fear I have made sacrifices to this treacherous influence, I could wish forgotten. (241)

The bravo seems to catch the drift but knows his place, and does not presume on any advantage: he 'uttered a few words of a general nature, but such as had a tendency to quiet [Monforte's] uneasiness' (241). Monforte's is a different sort of confession, but a confession nonetheless.

Then words become deeds. Frontoni offers to assist Monforte in finding Violetta and escaping with her, while Monforte will make the bravo his vassal, rescue him to Calabria, and use his connections with Rome to have him absolved, exemplifying the very dependence on religious politics that Frontoni decried in Venice. In this secularized version of the Catholic sacrament, one confesses the other in a Protestant priesthood of individuals. The far more stricken soul, Frontoni will confess again to Father Anselmo. However, mutual understanding and sympathy have already acted like the free gift of grace, saving one from suicide, winning the other new hope of recovering his bride. The scene stands above and outside the endless plotting and duplicity that characterizes Venice: 'the schemes of the selfish may be foretold,' says Frontoni, 'it is only the generous and the honest that baffle calculation' (235). True to his word, he arranges the lovers' rendezvous and successful escape – from the very graveyard on the Lido that again functions as a locus of freedom. Only Venice thwarts the bravo's end of the deal.

Jacopo Frontoni exemplifies a major tenet of Cooper's republican faith, that the individual moral life can redeem commercial and political evil and reinvigorate society.[55] 'The most distinctive element in Italian civilization to Cooper, which made him deprecate American civilization in contrast,' comments Nathalia Wright, 'was the recognition by Italians that the greatest values were other than pecuniary ones.'[56] Wrought by immense labour from the sea, built upon commerce and austerity, Venice had been the rule that proves the exception; falling into luxury and decadence, abusing power, Venice had become the exception that proves the rule: its fate is held out as a warning to a new nation across the Atlantic. When Frontoni rises from the cemetery ground, he presages his moral resurrection; he is reborn, purged of his crimes and prepared to die, not by suicide, but rather like Dickens's Sidney Carton, by sacrificing himself to save the lovers and achieve some final moral purpose. This is the life-giving burden of Frontoni's confession on the isle of the dead.

2. Sheridan Le Fanu's Grand Tour of Hell

In its beautiful and grotesque versions, the Romantic cult of the dead informs the work of the Irish novelist Joseph Sheridan Le Fanu. Grandnephew of the playwright Richard Brinsley Sheridan, Le Fanu (1814–73) belonged to the Anglo-Irish Protestant Ascendency that ruled Ireland well into the nineteenth century, when it was eclipsed by the rising movement of Catholic, commercial Ireland. His father was a rector, and Le Fanu grew up in a religious atmosphere in Dublin and County Limerick. After studying classics and law at Trinity College, Dublin, he was called to the bar but never practiced, turning instead to journalism and fiction. His wife's early death in 1858 was a devastating experience from which he never recovered. Thereafter he led a reclusive life, waking after two o'clock at night and working for the next hours, 'when human vitality is at its lowest ebb and the Powers of Darkness rampant and terrifying.'[57] His greatest success came with his suspense novels, *The House by the Churchyard* (1863) and *Uncle Silas* (1864), and supernatural tales such as 'Borrhomeo the Astrologer' and 'Carmilla.' Though admired by Henry James and W.B. Yeats, and 'gifted with a sombre power which has seldom been equalled in painting the ghastly and the macabre' (Dorothy Sayers),[58] this master of the occult and the 'obscenity of violence'[59] remains too little known.

The setting of Le Fanu's mystery novel *Wylder's Hand* (1864) is the country estate of Brandon in the English midlands. Mark Wylder and Captain Stanley Lake are rivals for the hand of Wylder's cousin, Dorcas Brandon, a wealthy heiress.[60] Wylder is engaged to Dorcas, though Dorcas is in love with Lake. Shortly before his marriage Wylder vanishes. Soon letters that appear to be in his hand begin arriving to excuse his absence, each one postmarked at a farther distance from the novel's epicentre, Brandon: London (97), Boulougne (130), Marseilles (196–7), Frankfurt (201), Geneva (223), and finally Italy with Genoa (235) and Venice (239–40), where the letters stop. Thereupon, Dorcas breaks the engagement and marries the unscrupulous Lake, who is only interested in her inheritance.

Yet Wylder is not in Italy. He was stabbed to death by Lake in an altercation and buried on the estate grounds. Lake has arranged that the letters, which he has written as a set in 'Wylder's hand,' be posted at discrete intervals in time and space by a hired agent. Lake has confided in his sister Rachel, who unwittingly served as an accessory to the crime and who lives in seclusion on the estate. It was predictable that Lake should have chosen Italy, and particularly Venice, as the locale for Wylder's disappearance, presumably to die or enter a madhouse, because Italy is 'the abyss' (231).

The point is driven home in a singular conversation between Lake and the aged, half-mad, prophetic Uncle Lorne who haunts the estate and, one learns later, has witnessed the murder. Breaking in on an evening party, Uncle Lorne speaks in a kind of Jacobean prose, an expressive medium with its overtones of ghosts, secrecy, revenge, and violence. He relishes his role as Lake's guilty conscience, hinting as much by an elaborate periphrasis of 'Italy.' Mark Wylder, says Uncle Lorne, is 'in an evil plight' (the narrator Charles de Cresseron, a family acquaintance, is the 'me'):

'Is he?' said Lake, with a sly scoff, though he seemed to me a good deal scared. 'We hear no complaints, however, and fancy he must be tolerably comfortable notwithstanding.'

'You know where he is,' said Uncle Lorne.

'Aye, in Italy; everyone knows that,' answered Lake.

'In Italy,' said the old man, reflectively, as if trying to gather up his ideas, 'Italy. Oh! yes, Vallombrosa – aye, Italy, I know it well.'

'So do we, Sir; thank you for the information,' said Lake, who nevertheless appeared strangely uneasy.

'He has had a great tour to make. It is nearly accomplished now; when it is done, he will be like me, *humano major*. He has seen the places which you are yet to see.'

'Nothing I should like better; particularly Italy,' said Lake.

'Yes,' said Uncle Lorne, lifting up slowly a different finger at each name in his catalogue. 'First, Lucus Mortis; then Terra Tenebrosa; next, Tartarus; after that, Terra Oblivionis; then Herebus; then Barathrum; then Gehenna, and then Stagium [*sic*] Ignis.'

'Of course,' acquiesced Lake, with an ugly sneer, and a mock bow. (230–1)

This partial list of the ten kingdoms of hell traces to various 'catalogues' from the Faustus legend to Emanuel Swedenborg's extensive commentaries on the Book of Apocalypse.[61] Since Lake does not suspect Uncle Lorne's awareness of the circumstances, he pretends to agree: 'everyone knows' Wylder is in Italy. What Lake himself does not know is the truth of Uncle Lorne's metaphor, that Wylder truly is 'in an evil plight' and in 'Italy,' land of death and eternal damnation. '"I know where he is," resumed the old man with his finger on his long chin, and looking down upon the carpet' (231).

For two centuries the Grand Tour of Italy had been the crowning experience of an English gentleman's education, while the association of Italy as next door to hell goes back much earlier.[62] Uncle Lorne's Italy offers a 'great tour' of the varied hells in Western tradition. Vallombrosa ('Shadowy Valley') is the glen near Florence with a Dantescan background, the inspiration of Milton's description of the fallen angels 'who lay intrans't / Thick as Autumnal Leaves that strow the Brooks / In *Vallombrosa*, where th' *Etrurian* shades / High overarch't imbowr' (PL 1.301–4). Lucus Mortis is the grove of death; Terra Tenebrosa, the dark-shadowed land. The classical underworld consisted of three levels: topmost Erebus is a passageway from the upper or living world to Hades, the underworld proper. Below Hades lies a third level, the pit of Tartarus, the place of punishment for the Titans and others who offended the gods. Italy thus contains all three levels. Further, it is Terra Oblivionis (land of oblivion), signifying the loss of memory on crossing Lethe (or sitting, like Theseus and Pirithous, in Pluto's Chairs of Forgetfulness). 'Stagium Ignis' (Rev. 9:14) is Lorne's 'error' for Stagnum Ignis, 'pool of fire.' Since elsewhere the narrator notes Wylder's bad Latin, Lorne's 'error' may indicate that the ancient language is undergoing corruption. Barathrum (Barathron) was a cleft or pit at Athens where the bodies of executed criminals were thrown (Xen. *Hellen.* 1.7.20; Herod. 1.133). Gehenna, from the Hebrew *Ge-Hinnon*, is a valley south of Jerusalem where Kings Ahaz and Manasseh sacrificed sons to Moloch (2 Chron 28:3, 33:62). Gehenna became a garbage dump; smoke rising suggests the burning of refuse, and in the New Testament it symbolizes hell and punishment.

In Lorne's sly humanist pun, after his Grand Tour of Italy Wylder will be *humano major* (Ovid, *Fasti* 2:491), 'more than human,' 'greater than human,' applied to the Olympian gods since they are anthropomorphic but nonetheless greater (i.e., taller, stronger, etc.) than merely human in form and all other attributes. Wylder will have grasped the essential Italy because he is 'more than human' in a demonic sense. Lorne himself is a very old man, and his fascination with Italy underlines the theme of ancientness. 'Lorne' points to deprivation – deprived of life. The 'Uncle' is the oppositional tag that familiarizes. If Lake knew his Swedenborg as well as Uncle Lorne, he would have realized that the wise uncle knew him for the murderer and would have killed him too. As Lorne prophesizes, Wylder 'has seen the places which you are yet to see': you, too, are headed for damnation. Lorne's 'Italy' is only explicable by reference to Le Fanu's absorption in Swedenborg's demonology and angelology.

In Swedenborg's theology, the human world lies between two spirit worlds, both *humano major*, antechambers to final heaven and final hell, and is linked to them by a system of correspondences: 'The world of spirits is not heaven, nor is it hell, but it is the intermediary place or state between the two. For to that place man comes at first after death, and then, after a certain time, he is either raised up into heaven or cast down into hell, in accord with his life in the world.'[63] The 'angels' or 'demons' that populate the respective spirit worlds began as human beings, and their actions on earth determined their place in one or the other antechamber after their mortal life. 'Instead of working off in punishment or purification the consequences of sin prior to final salvation,' remarks

W.J. McCormack, 'souls in the world of spirits are gradually attuned either to heaven or hell by a process of self-revelation.'[64] Only in death does the full meaning of one's earthly life manifest itself. Wylder's 'evil plight,' his 'Italian' tour, is his coming to terms with the evil he created on earth; and Italy in the Anglo-Irish imaginary functions as a realm of spiritual degradation, the antechamber of his soul's final resting place in hell. Still alive, Lake has 'yet to see' this hell of Italy and does not grasp the implications of Uncle Lorne's catalogue. So his 'Nothing I should like better [to see]; particularly Italy' (with internal rhyme at the end for emphasis) comes off as a passing touristic wish, to be fulfilled in inexorable Swedenborgian terms. In the present, Lake cannot read his fate. Like the Ascendancy's doomed sense of itself, Le Fanu's individuals are 'bound by the same tyranny of a static present and a knowing, active, and retributive past.'[65]

The son of a Protestant minister in Catholic Ireland, Le Fanu would have little difficulty in trading on public associations of Italy with damnation and retributive justice. As the 'oracle' Uncle Lorne concludes his conversation, he almost seems to be playing with Lake:

'Don't be frightened – but [Wylder]'s alive; I think they'll make him mad. It is a frightful plight. Two angels buried him alive in Vallombrosa by night; I saw it, standing among the lotus and hemlock. A negro came to me, a black clergyman with white eyes, and remained beside me; and the angels imprisoned Mark; they put him on duty forty days and forty nights, with his ear to the river listening for voices; and when it was over we blessed them; and the clergyman walked with me a long while, to-and-fro, to-and-fro upon the earth, telling me the wonders of the abyss.' (231)

The town clerk, who does not know his Swedenborg either, jokingly breaks in to humour Uncle Lorne and to ask if Wylder has been writing his letters 'from the abyss.' Lorne takes him with sardonic seriousness:

'Yes, yes, very diligent; it behoves him; and his hair is always standing straight on his head for fear. But he'll be sent up again, at last, a thousand, a hundred, ten and one, black marble steps, and then it will be the other one's turn. So it was prophesied by the black magician.' (231)

Wylder, like his double Lake, is a wicked soul whose 'Italian' sufferings bespeak his damnation; his hair standing straight is a physiological image of the terrified animal ready to flee. The passage treats of a living death, witchcraft, the desert, the river of the underworld, and racism. In Swedenborgian terms, Wylder is 'alive' and working out his self-awareness in his infernal antechamber in Vallombrosa, with its 1,111 black marble steps, the number symbolizing the repetition of infinity. When *he* is finished, 'it will be the other one's turn' and Lake will take his place. The phrase 'to-and-fro upon the earth' refers to Satan's self-description of terrestial mischief-making (Job 1:6). Lorne envisions Satan as a black Catholic priest, 'chief of the lying prophets with thick lips' (231), the swarthy Italian who tempts Wylder for forty days and forty nights, a parody of Christ's sojourn in the desert. Surely Lake must have realized the wisdom of the town clerk's statement when Uncle Lorne first broke in upon the party: 'Let him alone ... don't cross him, and he'll not stay long' (230). But Lake crossed him.

In the novel's climactic scene Captain Lake, a candidate for Parliament, is riding with his political supporters through the woods when his horse rears at the smell of decaying flesh: Wylder's hand is sticking out of the ground:

> It was, indeed, a human hand and arm, disclosed from about the elbow, enveloped in a discoloured coat-sleeve, which fell back from the limb, and the fingers, like it black, were extended in the air ... In this livid hand, rising from the earth, there was a character both of menace and appeal; and on the finger, as I afterwards saw at the inquest, glimmered the talismanic legend 'Resurgam – I will rise again!' (369)

The horse throws Lake, who dies from his injuries, and the facts of the case are finally made known. Wylder's hand is both his false hand (writing) and his real hand, which causes the horse to throw Lake and which stands for retributive justice beyond the grave. The Latin motto of his signet ring points to his 'resurrection' in hell.

Just as Italy as hellish antechamber is the symbolic punishment for wicked men, so Italy as heavenly antechamber is offered as the tangible reward to the two worthy women, tragic victims of male iniquity. Dorcas's love fails to redeem Lake and she can find no peace, while Rachel, having been forced to assist him on a mysterious errand connected with Wylder's disappearance, lives a guilt-ridden life at 'Brandon,' the mark or brand of sin. Both times, when Lake whispers the crime in her ear, and when Rachel admits her complicity, Dorcas faints. Is she an innocent victim, or might she have conspired in her own way by breaking the original engagement? 'All three characters move paradoxically in a situation of love and distrust,' writes Michael Begnal; 'only the fatal accident can resolve the tension.'[66] Rachel turns down a good marriage proposal, the sign of her guilt and her rejection of the social world. Thrown together in their misery, Rachel and Dorcas share a deep mutual sympathy and long for a kind of beautiful death and release: 'we shall be old maids,' says Dorcas, 'and live together like the ladies of Llangollen.' Lady Eleanor Butler (?1739–1829) and Sarah Ponsonby (?1735–1831) left their families and retired to this Welsh valley ('some of the loveliest brook and glen scenery in the world'[67]), where they redecorated Plas Newydd in the Gothic style, a shrine of pilgrimage for late neoclassical and romantic writers. As Dorcas says to Rachel, 'with the winter's snow we'll vanish from Brandon, and appear with the early flowers at our cottage among the beautiful woods and hills of Wales.' In Swedenborgian terms, this is one of the antechambers of heaven. There is another: during those winter months they will 'vanish' to Italy. Dorcas's fantasy underlines her plight: 'the only sort of personal relationship that is possible in *Wylder's Hand* is the homoerotic relationship between the principal female figures.'[68]

In the novel's final paragraph de Cresseron, visiting Venice, sees Dorcas and Rachel in a gondola. Venice had hitherto served as the final stop of Wylder's Grand Tour: where Rome is typically the culmination of the Grand Tour, the substitution of Venice cannot have been accidental. Yet 'equivocal'[69] Venice takes on its opposite, equally powerful representation: a visionary paradise, with the attraction of poetic beauty and sexual freedom. As Lake had said 'everyone knows' about infernal Italy, de Cresseron now says 'everyone knows' about edenic Italy too:

> Some summers ago, I was, for a few days, in the wondrous city of Venice. Everyone knows something of the enchantment of the Italian moon, the expanse of dark and flashing blue, and the phantasmal city, rising like a beautiful spirit from the waters. Gliding near the Lido – where so many rings of Doges lie lost beneath the waves – I heard the pleasant sound of female voices upon the water – and then, with a sudden glory, rose a sad, wild hymn, like the musical wail of the forsaken sea: –
> 'The spouseless Adriatic mourns her lord.'
> The song ceased. The gondola which bore the musicians floated by – a slender hand over the gunwale trailed its fingers in the water. Unseen I saw. Rachel and Dorcas, beautiful in the sad moonlight, passed so near we could have spoken – passed me like spirits – never more, it may be, to cross my sight in life. (387)

De Cresseron adopts the same wistful, Ruskinian tone with which Dorcas describes her Welsh fantasy, and is absorbed by the dream-like song.[70] The line from Byron's *Childe Harold's Pilgrimage* 4.11, 'The spouseless Adriatic mourns her lord,' refers to the annual Marriage of the Sea. With the extinction of the Venetian republic, Napoleon had the Bucentaur destroyed and the ceremony discontinued: so the feminine sea is 'spouseless,' lacking the male Venice. Under the spell of the chaste moon-goddess and like the watery lagoons, Dorcas (whose husband is dead) and Rachel (who has turned down a proposal) are 'spouseless' mourners, which in their case, Le Fanu implies, is no bad thing given the viciousness of the males. What was melancholy for Byron is transformed into a consolatory pleasure.

'Unseen I saw' develops out of a later passage in the same canto when Byron, before the Colosseum in Rome, states that 'we become a part of what has been, / And grow unto the spot, all-seeing but unseen' (4.138). The individual spirit survives in the locale of its deepest experiences. 'Unseen I saw' suggests the ghostliness of both the narrator-viewer and the viewed; as in Swedenborg, only as a ghost himself may he see the disembodied souls in Ariès's Romantic cult of the dead, with the endurance of friendships in the life after death. The intermediate spirits are 'not bodies of flesh and blood; they do not obey the law of gravity; but neither are they pure spirits, unheard and unseen. Someday they will even leave impressions on photographic plates. They are imagined, even before then have been seen, as shapes clad in a luminous glow, gliding through the air.'[71]

McCormack argues that Le Fanu changed Venice from its historically masculine gender to the feminine and 'substituted as a consequence a doubled feminine in Venice/Adriatic': the novel moves from lake (Lake) to lagoon (Venice); from wicked men, Captain Lake and the historical General Lake who was a savage repressor of the Irish Rebellion in 1798, to the happiness of the formerly victimized women in ethereal Venice. If so, then one must think of the enclosed body of water or 'lake' as a symbol of male egoism as opposed to the open merging of the city's canals with the larger lagoons and the boundlessness of the feminine sea.[72]

The doge's ring recalls Wylder's signet ring with its motto *resurgam*. If the women refuse the male wedding rings, the slender hand that trails its fingers in the water recapitulates the doge's ancient rite and signifies a symbolic marriage with the feminine, complete with the gondolier's Byronic song. In this rite of purification, the 'ring' finger trailing in water is proof of love and prepares for resurrection into heaven. In perfect symmetry, Italy functions as the antechamber of the Swedenborgian heaven for Dorcas and Rachel as it serves as the antechamber of the Swedenborgian hell for Wylder and Lake.[73] The narrator says the women's 'spirits' will not 'cross' his sight again: they are on the brink of the spirit world. Yet 'cross' is a strong word, used earlier of Uncle Lorne: does it mean to hex or trouble de Cresseron, and the surrogate reader, by their memory? In Le Fanu's imagined Italy, one learns to fathom one's eternal destiny.

3. Arnold Böcklin between Classical Hero-Cult and the Romantic Cult of the Dead

In 1880 Marie Berna, a young widow, went to Florence to commission a painting from the Swiss artist Arnold Böcklin. He proposed a spring festival with children dancing or something similar, but she wanted 'a landscape, preferably "a landscape over which one could dream."'[74] Within months Böcklin completed a large painting of a hauntingly beautiful island rising out of a sea, with marble burial vaults embedded in its cliffs and tall cypresses clustered around its centre, the dark atmosphere heavily charged with a brooding solemnity. Böcklin made altogether five versions of this painting, varying somewhat from one another in size and detail: two in 1880, one each in 1883, 1884, and 1886. He referred to it vaguely as 'silent island,' 'island of the tombs,' even 'a picture to dream over.' In 1883 a gallery owner gave it a permanent title: *Die Toteninsel,* Isle of the Dead.[75]

By 1900 it was the most famous contemporary painting in the German-speaking world, the 'very symbol of man's inevitable passing,'[76] 'a kind of icon for universal grief.'[77] Conrad Ferdinand Meyer said he would want to die beneath it. Strindberg employed it as the backdrop for the final scene of *The Ghost Sonata* (1907).[78] Max Klinger made an engraving after the third version, which in turn inspired Rachmaninoff's *Isle of the Dead* (1909), his 'orchestral masterpiece.'[79] Böcklin influenced Jules Laforgue, Stefan George, Emil Nolde, De Chirico's metaphysical style (*The Enigma of the Oracle* [1910]), Max Ernst, and Dalì (*The True Painting of Arnold Böcklin's 'Isle of the Dead' at the Hour of the Angelus* [1932], *Interior Court of the 'Isle of the Dead'* [1934]).[80] A postcard of *Isle of the Dead* was popular with German soldiers writing home in World War I. The third version was found in Hitler's Linz Collection.[81] It appears in two of Val Lewton's horror films, *I Walked with a Zombie* (1943) and *Isle of the Dead*

(1945). When in 1926 the Metropolitan Museum of New York acquired Berna's original, to which Böcklin had given more flowers to lend it a 'softer expression,' Bryson Burroughs wrote that it was 'perhaps more widely known than any other German work of art since the sixteenth century.'[82]

In the history of European painting Böcklin (1827–1901) is situated between German Romanticism and symbolism; his mythic themes, his experiments in the irrational, his unsettling iconography and bold palette anticipate surrealism and expressionism. He secularizes the religious symbolism of Caspar David Friedrich and Philipp Otto Runge, though his mode of secularization, while retaining Christian elements, more often looks backward to mythological antiquity.[83] Yet Böcklin's ancient world lacks noble simplicity and tranquil grandeur; it is perhaps closer in spirit to Nietzschean Dionysus or Stravinsky's *Le Sacre du Printemps*. Wagner was so admiring of Böcklin that he commissioned him to design the dragon for *Siegfried* in 1876 (the dragon was built in England and shipped in pieces to Germany; the neck went to Beirut instead of Bayreuth, so that on opening night the dragon's head was attached directly to its body).[84] Mystery, melancholy, the grotesque, sacral Dionysian joy – together with an uncanny dread that results from mixing these themes – are the dominant emotional keys in his finest works. In their psychological effect, writes Simmel, his landscapes are 'timeless, not as eternal but as primordial – timeless in the sense that reflection and nature had not yet started developing in the direction of opposite poles.'[85] De Chirico said Böcklin's art evokes '*déjà vu*.'[86]

Böcklin's knowledge of Italy was indebted to Jacob Burckhardt, his elder contemporary and fellow resident of Basel who may have prompted his first Italian journey in 1850. He settled in Rome and married Angela Pascucci, an orphan, with whom he had fourteen children. For years the family lived in straightened circumstances. Angela used to carry his sketches and canvases around the Roman cafes to sell to tourists. Sometimes Böcklin returned north to earn money. In the early 1860s he was teaching in Weimar, from which he wrote Burckhardt: 'I am now able to say I know Germany very well, its spirit, culture, art, poetry, etc. which being able to, I would take my leave of it on the first train towards the not-yet-civilized South.' He wants to flee south, but chooses the train, the new symbol of 'northern' progress, as means of transport to return to an older civilization 'not-yet-civilized' in the modern sense. 'I am waiting for the first opportunity to take the way out and flee this airless atmosphere ... and then farewell grand duke, farewell university career and attached stipend, farewell fields of potatoes and turnips.'[87] He spent thirty-one of his last fifty years in Italy and died at his villa in San Domenico, near Florence.

Classically educated, Böcklin was prepared to absorb Burckhardt's conception of Italy as the land of high culture and humanism, 'first-born among the sons of modern Europe,' and of its ideal of the self-aware, self-realizing individual.[88] In the 1850s he painted Italian landscapes with technical proficiency, if little originality. Then in 1858 he fell ill with typhoid and appears to have had a near-death experience that affected his outlook.[89] Shortly afterward he painted *Pan Frightening a Shepherd,* and subsequent works recall not merely a pagan but a pre-civilized, ahistorical world, where Venus rises from the waters on the back of a monstrous red fish, or where nereids and lusty tritons sport among the shoals. Pan 'is no more than a stone or a clump of reeds until the talismanic moment in which he turns his head to throw a baleful gaze upon the unsuspecting wayfarer, and from that moment the god and his dissolute satellites invest the scene with a rudimental energy in which man and beast participate without distinction or hindrance,' comments Robin Ironside; it is an occasionally ludicrous, at any rate incongruous, world in which 'its impossible inhabitants, its satyrs, centaurs and tritons subsist, not as poetic accessories or even as suggestive symbols, but as hitherto unnoted, somewhat unpleasant natural phenomena.'[90] The figures are not classical as the ancients or Renaissance Italian artists envisaged them; nor do they bear any resemblance to the harmonious Greek myths in Winckelmann, Goethe, and Schiller. Böcklin's flight from history in the age of historicism constitutes a critique of his times, with its self-satisfied middle-class culture, materialism, and notion of progress. Whereas an exuberant vitality frequently informs his mythological figures, his painting of contemporary settings is pervaded by a deep melancholy.

Villa by the Sea II (1864–5) was considered by Heinrich Wölfflin, also a Baseler, indispensable to understanding the 'psychic emotion of our century.'[91] In this large painting of a desolate Italian villa, a woman dressed in black stands on the shore, leans her head on her left hand, and stares in perplexity over the sea. After initially referring to her as Iphigeneia (presumably exiled in Tauris), Böcklin left open the reference, and Rudolf Schick hewed to this line in commenting that the work suggests a mood of grief on the part of 'the last descendent of an ancient family.'[92] Since the personification of Italy as the grieving, victimized woman has a tradition extending from Guittone d'Arezzo and Dante to Foscolo and Leopardi, one could regard her and her ancient race *in extremis* as Italian.[93] The skies are blue gray and whitish; Böcklin said he wanted to convey an oppressive scirocco. Though the woman's shawl is blown back and the cypresses lean away from the sea, the waters near shore remain calm. Waters are often smooth near protecting cliffs and buildings; also, Böcklin is reported to have said that trees by the sea, owing to persistent off-shore wind, are bent back even in good weather. Some trees have lost part of their foliage or are slightly brownish. In all, nature is not a comforting presence; in Böcklin's painting, 'in the conflict [with civilization] nature always emerges the victor.'[94] Since neither the fountain with sea horses nor the shrine to the Virgin Mary offer consolation, ancient myths and traditional faith have lost their power. The water falls from the basin of the fountain, across some rocks, and over the edge of a low cliff into the sea pool, making a thin veil-like shower before the mouth of the cave or grotto. A transitional zone between the upper world of light and the chthonic world of the occult, the cave is the focal point of the painting whose deep shadows pick up the black of the women's clothes.[95]

Another accent is the blood-red panel by an Ionic pillar; the villa's pale colour would seem to take its departure from this panel, life and energy having faded in a beautiful death. Everywhere nature and architecture are intertwined as in a death-grip. Yet all seems still and inevitable, as if decline had been in progress for centuries. For Böcklin, 'historical associations are only fleeting'; trees and ruins 'do not suggest other dimensions but only their eternal unchanging being'; whereas summer in a northern landscape would suggest its opposite by implication, the 'lack of change between temperatures and vegetation' in his Mediterranean landscapes supports a sense of timelessness.[96]

Simmel argues that ruins represent a balance and tension of opposing forces, the upward striving of the spirit and the downward-dragging force of nature. 'The moment decay destroys the unity of the form, nature and spirit separate again and reveal their world-pervading original enmity – as if the artistic formation had only been an act of violence committed by the spirit to which the stone unwillingly submitted.' Though victorious nature takes its revenge on spirit, the ruin nonetheless conveys peacefulness to the extent that the opposing forces 'are working serenely together.' Nor is a ruin merely half a classical arch or a broken wall; it could be a dilapidated or inhabited building, 'often found in Italy off the main road.' The impression of peace and aesthetic harmony is disturbed, not because 'human beings destroy the work of man – this indeed is achieved by nature – but that men *let it decay*.'[97] Either by choice or circumstance, they have not withstood the decline. Though Böcklin would have thought that nature's revenge in the ruin was a lesson against human pride, he has balanced this moral theme in *Villa by the Sea* by a mood of tragedy and nostalgia for a vanished glory.

Böcklin's art succeeds by crossing themes and conflating oppositions. Natural and non-natural elements appear together, or natural features lie in odd juxtapositions such as 'geology and flora in purely imaginary congruences.' Without a horror of mixing, he experiments with 'contamination' and freely allows present and past, dream and reality, light and dark, northern gothicism and southern humanism, to interact with each other in 'metaphysical time.'[98] Even where his subject matter is ancient myth and his visual reality is Italian, the treatment and mood is German and gothicizing, with painterly indistinctness, free rhythmicality, glaring tonalities, and spontaneous irregularity.[99] Thematically, Cristina Nuzzi writes that 'love tied to death or as a presage of death dominates the most mature work,' as in *Villa by the Sea, Triton and Nereid* (1873/74), *Isle of the Dead* ('beauty and dissolution'), and *Calm at Sea* (1887).[100] In all, it is the composite nature of a Böcklin painting and its unification of opposites that universalizes: with this result, that many of his paintings 'strike one as the only convincing statement of a given theme.'[101]

Given this generalizing tendency, one cannot pretend to identify the island that served as the model for the *Isle of the Dead*. In her memoirs Böcklin's wife said it was the Castello on Ischia built by Alfonso V of Aragon; Böcklin began vacationing in Naples in the late 1870s. 'The huge solitary cliff rises majestically from the deep blue water,' writes Herbert M. Vaughan:

> Whether viewed in brilliant sunshine under a cloudless sky, or in foul weather, when the sea is hurling its waves over the stone causeway that connects the isolated crag with the little city of Ischia, the first sight of this historic castle is singularly impressive. Nor is its grandeur lessened on a near approach, for the ascent to its topmost tower takes us through a labyrinth of staircases and mysterious subterranean passages, through vaulted chambers and curious hanging gardens to an airy platform, which commands a glorious view in every direction over land and sea.[102]

Others have proposed Gorgona, site of a prison in the Tuscan archipelago; Ventotene, a crater's rim, one of the Pontines; the English cemetery in Florence; the island of San Michele in Venice; San Vigilio on Lake Garda; or an island off the Dalmatian coast (which Böcklin never visited). Alberto Savinio (De Chirico's brother), who interviewed

Böcklin's son, states that the artist was inspired by the volcanic island of Ponza, which has some Roman ruins.[103] Böcklin obviously drew on many memories from travelling along the rocky Italian coasts as well as from his reading in classical literature. The massed cypresses are not native to any Italian island; he lived in Tuscany for many years and transposed them. Cypresses are a symbol for what Italians call *la mestizia toscana*, Tuscan sadness, heard powerfully in the music of two Tuscans, Puccini and Mascagni. Beyond the classical topos of the marshy shore of Hades, the association of death and the crossing of water appears to be primitive and vestigial.

Although its literary program should not be separated from the total response, the painting impresses in purely pictorial terms.[104] An island of high cliffs looms in the middle distance. Böcklin associated horizontals with serenity (smooth waters and horizon) and verticals with solemnity (cliffs, cypresses). But on a diagonal axis, eliciting tension, a boat with two figures and a coffin approaches the shore. The theme of crossing is thus expressed in a way entirely appropriate to the natural scene and aesthetic requirements: 'focusing on the boat, the viewer then glides with it towards the center of the island, also the center of the painting,' observes Sharon Hirsh; 'this dark central passage of the painting is Böcklin's most dramatic compositional feat: an essentially "negative" space that not only dominates the painting's center but also serves as its focal point.'[105] An unfinished version shown to Berna did not have the boat, but even without it (and its disturbing diagonal) one is pulled into the painting's dark centre, a grotto, which is not uncommon among such islands (the Blue Grotto); it is 'as if we are being drawn on, in the cold, humid darkness, towards some inevitable place of destiny'; 'we are caught by a silence which seems to scream; we are hypnotised by the weight of representation.'[106] Silence was a typical symbolist theme for the condition or the actual perception of supra-sensuous reality.[107] Böcklin's more-than-silence may signify metaphysical silence in mythic reality or in dream process or nightmare.

In the two 1880 versions, where the atmosphere is dark and starless, light far too brilliant for moonlight bathes the figures and white marble vaults: such non-natural brightness also suggests the hyperreal. In the last three versions, a storm darkens the horizon but, as one looks higher, the sky brightens with patches of blue amid tempestuous clouds. The light or the blue might imply hope in a Beyond or the fact that death lies in the midst of life. The pink and golden flowers that lend a (slightly) 'softer expression' have a countereffect. The flower of death is in all likelihood the asphodel, the 'plant of death' that the Greeks placed in their cemeteries and that is 'pre-eminently the flower of Southern Italy and Sicily':[108] 'There glowing ghosts of flowers / Draw down, draw nigh' (Swinburne, 'Before the Mirror'). Another contrast lies between the fury of the rising storm and the still waters surrounding the island. Böcklin requires flat waters for the boat, with its cargo of death, to make a calm and stately approach. Silence, solemnity, darkness, and death are features of the Burkean sublime. Instead of Charon, the cruel bureaucrat of hell (Böcklin had painted this figure as old and unkempt in *Charon* [1876]), an elegantly turbaned, richly costumed Egyptian rower guides the boat to the shore. He is expert in these waters from his knowledge of the *Book of the Dead;* leaning to his oar, he blends with the blue-black waters lest he detract from the standing celebrant, perhaps Marie Berna herself, conducting her husband's body to its grave.[109]

Rigid and hieratic, she stands in an intensely focused light that falls on her white robe wrapped tightly as a shroud, on the white cloth draping the coffin, and on the white marble tombs in the cliffs. The colour white, which Böcklin associated with calmness, contrasts with the surrounding darkness By the use of the Rückenfigur, the visual motif of a person seen from the back, the viewer is drawn into the painting by seeing what the person sees. Moreover, 'as in Caspar David Friedrich, a standing figure drawn from behind stands for man in general.'[110] The stiff posture, picked up by the cypresses, shares the solemnity of the vertical. Like the cypresses, her height is exaggerated, a psychic distortion reinforcing uncanniness. Even the jagged cliffs, Hesiod's 'tall rocks' of Styx (*Theog.* 776), seem distorted in their height. Gert Schiff complains that the cypresses are 'implausible on a rocky island,' but contradictoriness is exactly the effect Böcklin intended to produce.[111] In the 1883 version, the cliff on the extreme right and the celebrant are homologous, up to the sloping shoulders and the tilted head; detached from the island, the rock rises out of the water like another celebrant leaning towards the isle. Burroughs wrote that the final two versions (1884, 1886) lack the 'mysterious serenity' of the earlier ones for being 'painted in bright colors with violet-red sky and sea, the island and cypresses towering ever higher.'[112] Yet there is nothing decadent; Böcklin pursues the evolution of the experience, with its tendency to unreality. The expressionistic colouring contrasts with the shadowy, colourless darkness of the first two versions. Land and water, storm and calm, light and darkness, flower and rock, bending male rower and standing female celebrant, all make for a series of tensions, so that the painting more resembles a dream with its contradictions than a physical reality.

Marie Berna had received her 'picture to dream over,' a quintessential expression of Ariès's 'death of the other.' As Böcklin promised her in his letter: 'you will be able to enter into a dream of an obscure world of shadows, feeling the light breath that wrinkles the sea and being afraid of disturbing the solemn silence by a single word.' Another time he said apropos the painting: 'one is startled if there is a knock upon the door.'[113] Startled because a single word or a knock breaks the spell, or possibly completes the spell, the word or knock being the final summons.

Isle of the Dead has Böcklin's major themes (love and death), his preferred locale (Italy), and his artistic strengths as a landscape artist, without his flaws as a portraitist (the figures are small and emblematic, like the woman in *Villa by the Sea* II).[114] It involves a layering or silting of attitudes to death, Ariès's tame and untamed, as if only through a *coincidentia oppositorum*, formal, thematic, and historical, could Böcklin reconcile and transcend the complexities and ambiguities of his own approach to death.[115] *Die Liebeninsel* (*Isle of Life*) (1888), a less successful companion piece, gives further evidence of the artist's thinking in terms of opposites. Oddly enough, *Isle of Life* fits the description of his first proposal to Berna, a spring festival with children dancing.

What are these oppositional attitudes to death? To begin with, *Isle of the Dead* depicts 'Homeric' death, a matter-of-fact acceptance of a universal fate characteristic of the Mycenaean warrior caste: death as *terminus*. In the *Iliad* and *Odyssey* Hades (the 'Invisible') is a remote and gloomy underworld where the dead exist in a kind of negative trance with little or no memory of their previous existence. There the *psyche* or soul is an object of neither love, worship, nor fear and cannot aid or threaten the upper world. Homer writes sparingly of the 'ends of the earth,' a 'barren coast,' and a 'grove' of Persephone with dark poplars and willows, beyond the Cimmerians who 'never see the sun' (*Od.* 10.539–40). Odysseus grows faint with fear when Circe says that he must journey to Hades for Tiresias's prophecy. On his visit there Achilles tells him that he would rather be a migrant day-labourer in the land of the living than king of the dead (*Od.* 11.489–91). Homeric death is always tame: 'there is no death-avoidance, either in the sense of avoiding contact with death and the dead, or in that of excessive concern with avoiding one's death'; 'death is familiar, hateful rather than frightening.'[116]

In support of the Homeric view, all five versions of the *Isle of the Dead* leave the strongest impression of finality. Ironside notes 'occult features' in the landscape such as the cypress avenue that in the 1886 version is like a dark tunnel, a 'passage-way not to Elysium but, more probably, to the abdomen of mother earth.'[117] Savinio observes that the cypresses are smaller and the cliffs larger as the series progresses, as if to indicate a reduction in the overall quotient of life, 'assuming it is legitimate to speak of life in connection with cypresses.'[118] Yet it is legitimate because the cypresses are alive, the natural cycle continues. By the same token, the cliffs of death are limestone, the fossilized deposits of organic life. Ruskin eulogized the cypress, Italy's 'national tree,' in a watery classical underworld: 'whoever has marked the peculiar character which these noble shadowy spires can give to her landscape, lifting their majestic troops of waving darkness from beside the fallen column, or out of the midst of the silence of the shadowed temple and worshipless shrine, seen far and wide over the blue of the faint plain, without loving the dark trees for their sympathy with the sadness of Italy's sweet cemetery shore, is one who profanes her soil with his footsteps.'[119] In the 1883, 1884, and 1886 versions, storm clouds almost encircle the island. Böcklin would have known that the Homeric Harpies ('gusts of wind,' 'stormblasts') are 'wind-deities of a peculiarly sinister kind,' handmaidens of the Furies (Erinyes), the underworld goddesses. Telemachus laments that he will never see his father because the 'Harpies have abducted' him (*Od.* 1.241), and Penelope mourns similarly for Telemachus (*Od.* 4.727). Rohde compares the wind-deities to the German folk myth of the Devil's Bride or Whirlwind's Bride 'who rides in the whirlwind and also carries off men with her.'[120] Lastly, in the 1886 version, instead of holding her head erect, the celebrant bows before the island, as if reverencing its power and acknowledging the victory over life.[121] All these features underline Homeric death, 'the work of resignation, not of hope.'[122]

In contrast to Homeric death, a second attitude informing *Isle of the Dead* is marginally hopeful, death as *transitus:* this is 'Hesiodic' transport (*Works and Days*, 170ff).[123] Transport (in German, *Bergentrückung*) refers to the 'translation of individual heroes to a solitary after-life in secluded abodes of immortality,' where they enjoy the pleasures of feasting and like-minded company.[124] The sole mention of transport in Homer occurs in a speech by the sea-god Proteus, who prophesizes that Menelaus will not die like other men but be spirited away with Helen to the Elysian Fields (*Od.* 4.560ff). This may be a late addition, just outside the traditionalism of both the *Iliad* and *Odyssey* in which 'there is no overt prediction of impending immortality for either Achilles or Hektor.'[125]

Hesiod and later poets elaborated upon transport for the sake of a more positive attitude to the afterlife, at least for exceptional persons. In *Works and Days* Zeus rescues 'fortunate heroes' from death and grants them 'a living and an abode apart from men ... at the ends of earth. And they live untouched by sorrow in the islands of the blessed along the shore of the deep swirling Ocean' (168ff). Although absent in Homer, hero cults flourished after the seventh century and are mentioned by Aeschylus (*Choeph.* 324ff), Sophocles (*El.* 836; *Oed. Col.* 621ff), Euripides (*Helen* 1013–16), and Pindar (*O.* 2.68–74).[126] As Sourvinou-Inwood comments, Hesiod's advance over Homeric traditionalism parallels the growth of the city-states, social complexification, and individualism beginning in the Archaic period (700 BC–480 BC); the development implies an 'affirmation of one's individuality in death which now appears primarily as the end of one's person and one's life, rather than an episode in the history of the community and the life-cycle'; psychological tension; 'concern for survival in memory and hope for a happy after-life'; and 'a certain loss of familiarity.'[127] In Ariès's model, the shift from tame death to one's own death is repeated in the later Middle Ages, also a time of social complexification and incipient individualism.

Consistent with a Hesiodic *Bergentrückung*, Böcklin gives every indication that the barge bears the remains of a person of high status, possibly a hero. In four of the five versions the white coffin is draped with wreaths of flowers. The figure of the Egyptian rower is a positive sign. Like Charon, though more romantically, he would function both 'to guide the shades in the (awesome) transition from life to death, and so provide reassurance for the individual'; and also to police the borders between life and death – which hints at a 'greater anxiety about one's own death seen now as an individual experience, and a greater concern with separating firmly, and securing the margins between life and death, that is, ensuring that death is kept securely away.'[128] Portrayals of Charon may be positive: 'even under the management of Charon the ship or boat retains its – relatively speaking – felicitous connotations,' observes Erwin Panofsky, 'and there were those who derived the name of the grim ferryman from χαίρειν, "to be of good cheer."'[129] The tombs do not preclude immortality; there is no contradiction between the grave cult and belief in the hero's afterlife '*so long as the promise of immortalization aims not at the here-and-now but rather at a fulfillment in the hero's future.*'[130]

Also suggestive of a *Bergentrückung*, the scene is no dismal, marshy shore but a Mediterranean island of sublime beauty, fit for the blessed ones, a race of heroes or hero-artists. In Homer, Oceanus 'sends up the gusts of shrill-blowing Zephyros / at all times, so as to reanimate men' (*Od.* 4.567–8); the heroes died and went to Hades, then were 'reanimated' by the breath of life. Hesiod refers to 'islands of the blessed' and heroes for whom 'the grain-giving earth bears honey-sweet fruit flourishing thrice a year' (*Works and Days* 172–3), that is, without interruption. Pindar mentions 'ocean-breezes that blow around the Islands of the Blest' and 'flowers of gold' (*O.* 2.72–4).[131] Such breezes assist the dead, as the islands are 'accessible only by ship'; and the Harpies are present in a mild form, the *aurai pontiades* or Sea Breezes, 'spirits of the benevolent elements which ... help the souls of the departed to attain the Isles of the Blessed or the upper reaches of the atmosphere.'[132] Examining similarities among earthly paradises, Gregory Nagy notes the fresh sea wind; continuous growing season ('*suspension of a vegetal cycle*') and hence neither winter nor bad weather; golden plant life in which gold suggests 'the artificial continuum of immortality, in opposition to the natural cycle of life and death as symbolized by the flourishing and wilting of leaves'; and divine aura, as in Hesiod's heroic age.[133] In the two 1880 versions of *Isle of the Dead* there is no bad weather, though Böcklin reverses himself in the last three versions with their storm clouds. Golden flowers provide a bright note and, in Hesiodic terms, even the pitch-black darkness in the centre of Böcklin's island may not be *the end* but only a passage, perhaps to the Elysian Fields. As for the cypresses, their phallic shape suggests the male principle, 'the tree of life, associated with the genealogical tree of the whole human race'; the female principle (Gaia, Hestia's circle) is symbolized by the dark cave of earth.[134] In one nineteenth-century dictionary of symbolism, though cypresses signify 'death' and 'desperation,' they may also elicit feelings of 'freedom' and 'relief from affliction.'[135] For Simmel, Böcklin's landscapes express a 'mixture' of freedom and confinement or 'an uplifting sense of release from imprisonment in the necessary.'[136] Release into freedom, even at the cost of death, is one of the noble emotions of the Longinian sublime. Cypresses (and other evergreens) stand for immortality in the traditional Christian graveyard.

Connected with the hero cult and Hesiodic death is memory-survival: 'in the epic tradition the tomb is the locus of the hero's posthumous fame.'[137] Only eight years earlier, Böcklin had painted his *Self-Portrait with Death Playing the Fiddle* (1872), in which instead of Venus or the Muses he is inspired by Death: 'with the awareness of mortality that comes with middle age, the artist conveyed his sense of urgency as he realized that his time was growing short and that his painting had not yet made its mark upon the world.'[138] *Isle of the Dead* is one of the artist's vehicles of secular fame. Norbert Schneider proposes that the white-robed figure represents the 'heroization of the grand solitary,' which Franz Zelger reinterprets as Böcklin's 'melancholy self-heroization.'[139] In the last three versions, Böcklin ceased signing his name on the rocks and painted a carved *A B* above a marble burial vault in the cliff, as if he himself wished to be buried there – indeed, *is* spiritually buried there. Earlier he had carved his initials on Charon's boat (*Charon*), as it were the name of the boat; again, the artist's signature does more than name the artist *ab extra*, it incorporates itself within the monumental iconography.[140] He would have recalled Horace's ode beginning *Exegi monumentum aere perennius* (I have built a monument more lasting than brass [*Odes* I.36]). On the Doric column that marks his tomb near Florence is inscribed, from the same ode, *non omnis moriar* (I shall not wholly die).

The Hesiodic dead keep the memory of their existence while survivors celebrate them in song and ritual. The dream-like island aestheticizes and relieves or conceals the bare fact of death. In his critique of the Romantic cult of the dead, Ariès warns that the 'compromise' of beauty is an illusion; it thrives on hope, but also on pride. Böcklin knew it instinctively and qualified the Hesiodic attitude to death. Although the beauty of a Böcklin landscape evokes sympathy with nature, as Simmel writes, this feeling oscillates with a sense of detachment, objective distance, and the 'capacity to reflect upon that which nature does not share with us,' thereby deepening our sense of loss.[141]

Consistent with these qualifications, the third attitude to death in the *Isle of the Dead* is a natural-metamorphic notion according to which life and death have ways of changing places under the forms of nature itself. Ischia, Ventotene, and Ponza – if not Böcklin's main inspiration, still his painting depicts something similar – are remnants of an 'extensive submarine volcanic complex.'[142] In the painting, steep-sided lava and tufa cliffs rise out of the sea on a volcanic base; the landing dock appears to be a kind of limestone and the in-built marble tombs are a metamorphic recrystallized limestone. With its fossil materials 'the very substance of limestone suggests concreted Time,' writes Adrian Stokes on the 'living' quality of this stone in the art of the Mediterranean basin: 'the sea and the limestone dominate those lands.'[143] The isle of the dead is a living memorial to nature itself.

Böcklin has taken marble and limestone as the two major architectural and ornamental building materials both to give the island its 'architectonic elements' and to suggest an organic quality.[144] Quattrocento limestone architecture, comments Stokes, is 'the spectacular translation of time into space.' So too is classical building, which, more than other types of architecture, recalls 'the horizontal bedding of stones'; 'the jutting cornice, the architrave mouldings, the plinths and blocks, have a definite relation to the joints of stones as seen in quarry or cliff; and particularly to limestone, medium between the organic and the inorganic worlds.'[145] Böcklin's structured cliffs with their 'jutting cornice,' 'plinths and blocks,' and geometric burial vaults express the interfusion between the inorganic, the organic, and the architectural. The overall shape of the island recalls a classical amphitheatre, as if one were to behold a timeless scenario, the mystery of death.[146]

Yet if this natural form has the appearance of an amphitheatre, it is in ruins, with the peace and harmony of a ruin. Simmel grants exceptions to the ruin norm in which man made the building and nature made the ruin. Wholly *natural* ruins such as alpine forms may also express the conflict of the opposing forces, the upward striving and the downward sinking: 'volcanic eruptions or gradual stratification have built the mountain upward; rain and snow, weathering and landslides, chemical dissolution, and the effect of gradually intruding vegetation have sawed apart and hollowed out the upper ledge, have cast downward parts of what had been raised up, thus giving the contour its form.'[147] Böcklin conspires with nature in appropriating a natural ruin for a purpose peculiarly fitted to it, tomb vaults, and in conformity with his belief that the ruin embodies nature's victory over human pride. 'The destruction of the spiritual form by the effect of natural forces,' writes Simmel, '... is felt as a return to the 'good mother,' as Goethe calls nature; 'between the not-yet and the no-longer lies an affirmation of the spirit whose path, it is true, no longer ascends to its peak but, satiated by the peak's riches, descends to its home.' Perhaps to heighten this spiritual affirmation, Böcklin includes a religious cult and a sacred grove, thus sanctifying the heroic spirit in the face of tragic destiny. Simmel compares the deep peace of a ruin to 'a holy charmed circle'; the ruin conveys

the obscure antagonism which determines the form of all existence, now acting among merely natural forces, now occurring within psychic life, and now taking place between nature and matter. This antagonism – although here too it is in dis-equilibrium in that it lets one side preponderate as the other sinks into annihilation – nevertheless offers us a quietly abiding image, secure in its form. The aesthetic value of the ruin combines the disharmony, the eternal becoming of the soul struggling against itself, with the satisfaction of form, the firm limitedness, of the work of art.[148]

Isle of the Dead presents an imaginary pagan cult, within a classical setting, as a private romantic reverie.

Time and eternity intersect in the sacred isle, an emblem of geological eons and the human lifespan, and the work of art that asserts itself over time. Regarding this panorama of time, F.H. Meissner concludes that *Isle of the Dead* is a history (one should say, an ahistorical history) of the planet and the species, 'from the summits of craters on diluvial soil, to cypresses, and from these to man and the traces of his civilizing action'; 'the place inspires the seriousness of death, like a pyramid.'[149] It is a natural and a man-made monument, and not merely the hand that made the tomb-vaults, but the celebrants and the ritual in their extensive social, religious, and cultural contexts. Thus the widest oppositions, between past and present, organic and inorganic, spirit and nature, life and death, all come together in these natural-metamorphic forms. Perhaps they express Böcklin's deepest and most conservative wish: in death to be repatriated, like Castor and Pollux, in the 'life-giving earth' (*Il.* 3.243).[150]

With three attitudes to death and five versions of the painting, it is reasonable to expect one attitude to predominate in one or another version without completely effacing its rivals. In the first and second versions, Homeric death holds priority, the original inspiration. The sky and sea are very dark; the island is remote and 'forbidding';[151] the celebrant stands erect and faces death. Such an expression of tame death is as much northern as it is Homeric: the Twilight of the Gods theme, which runs from the *Völuspà* to Wagner, 'contaminates' this southern island, renders it uncanny, while remaining faithful to the native German spirit. The third version marks a departure in mood and tone, which persists in the last two versions: all three are less disturbing than the first two, the main reason being that there is so much more reassuring light. They may even be considered Hesiodic and hopeful, as if Böcklin were recapitulating the historical development in his own working out of the themes. The natural-metamorphic forms emerge quite distinctly; the atmosphere is luminous, the cypresses soft and feathery; the water like crystal. Yet in the fifth, a storm appears to be intensifying and the celebrant bows to the island; the anxiety is aroused and is quietened. In the fourth the celebrant merely holds out her hands as if in greeting. In the third, the 1883 version, the contrasting attitudes seem in balance: the storm may be rising or dissipating; the colours are neither overly sombre nor exotically brilliant; the trees of life and cliffs of death are evenly distributed; there is only a slight bow of the head. Nothing tips the balance, and this suspension before death adds the final note of mystery.

4. Ouida and the 'Death of the Other':
the Etruscan Tomb in the Maremma

Who reads Ouida today? It was not always so. In 1899 Max Beerbohm declared Ouida was 'one of the miracles of modern literature'; only Meredith among living novelists rivalled her in 'sheer vitality.' In the same year G.K. Chesterton wrote that 'though it is impossible not to smile at Ouida, it is equally impossible not to read her.' Thackeray and Meredith admired her novelistic art, while G.S. Street spoke for the Decadents in praising her 'passionate love of beauty' and 'passionate hatred of injustice.' Ambrose Bierce lamented Ouida's 'expenditure of intellectual force, of which she wasted enough to have made a half-hundred better novelists than herself.' For Stephen Crane, her *Under Two Flags* was 'a song of the brave.' Not one to praise beyond merit, Norman Douglas admired Ouida's novels for 'their tone, their temper, for that pervasive good breeding, that shining honesty, that capacity of scorn,' but also, one suspects, for their pagan quality.[152] Vernon Lee, who traced Ouida's influence in Edith Wharton, Maurice Barrès, the Comtesse de Noailles, and Anatole France, wrote of an Italy 'entirely believed in because entirely interesting, entirely lovely, terrible, picturesque, entirely Italian. The Italy of Ouida and J.A. Symonds (let alone of Childe Harold), made solely for the heart's desire of the imaginative tourist.'[153]

Ouida's forty novels and short story collections are today virtually unread. The Modern Language Association bibliography for 1980–2005 lists eight articles on her. If she is read at all, it is because of the interest in popular culture and feminism. Yet, while her language has occasional weaknesses, her narrative is always direct and precise, and one strategy suited to her strengths is to map the psychological plot running beneath the rapid romance narrative. Ouida fits Elaine Showalter's profile of women 'sensation' novelists who, though 'thwarted in a full exploration of their imaginative worlds by Victorian convention and stereotypes ... did move well beyond the code of renunciation and submission that informed earlier fiction.'[154]

Ouida (1839–1908) was born Maria Louise Ramé, the only child of a French father and an English mother, and grew up in Bury St. Edmunds. She later referred to herself as de la Ramée, which sounds like a pseudonym. Her own pseudonym 'Ouida' derives from the sound she made as a child in trying to say Louisa, in her mind a sign of uniqueness and essentiality, 'my very own as children say.'[155] The choice of this oddly sounding baby name expresses a private fantasy and a demand for self-definition (and redefinition) for which she found abundant outlet in her fiction.

Louis Ramé, her father, was a teacher of French who pretended friendship with Louis Napoleon and was rumoured to be connected with secret political societies. More likely something of an adventurer, he appears to have run through his wife's dowry in a year and was absent for long stretches of Ouida's childhood. Perhaps he was trying to escape his creditors. He instilled in his daughter the love of nature so evident in her novels.[156] She idolized him, preferred the foreign strain in her background, and looked down on her English roots. He disappeared after 1871, and was believed to have died in the Paris Commune, but this may be another family myth. Ouida's mother, who had endured her 'mercurial' husband, waited upon her 'capricious' daughter as chaperone, secretary, confidante, and hand-wringing accountant. Ouida brought her to Italy, 'never appearing anywhere without her mother – an unassuming if sombre ghost draped in black.'[157]

Ouida's fictional formula emerged in *Granville de Vigne: or, Held in Bondage* (1863), *Strathmore* (1865), and *Under Two Flags* (1867): aristocratic life, a chivalric code, exotic locales, charismatic and independent-minded women, dashing faithless men, narrative drive, intrigue, chance, steep rises, steeper falls. 'By rejecting the prudish moral tone that characterized popular fiction of the 1850s and by devouring novels filled with crime, passion, and sensuality,' writes Natalie Schroeder, 'Victorian women readers began in the 1860s to rebel against the establishment.'[158] High life or low life was Ouida's métier, and the clash between, which usually resulted in tragedy for all concerned. '[She] travelled, as some of us travel in trains, first or third class, never second.'[159] In the early 1870s she moved to Tuscany, the principal setting of her eight Italian novels. She fell in love with an impecunious Italian marchese who took advantage of her wealth but refused to marry her. A series of novels 'passionately defending the Italian peasant' treat the upper class as egotistical, predatory, and sadistic. Ruskin praised *A Village Commune* (1881) for its 'photographic' portrayal of rural life in Tuscany and the Romagna.[160] A lover of nature and champion of antivivisection, Ouida told the story of her novel *Puck* from the viewpoint of a Maltese terrier; she was evicted from her Florentine villa for refusing to trim its foliage.

As long as her audience remained loyal, Ouida could afford to live luxuriously, like the very aristocrats she derided. Comparing herself to

Aspasia and De Staël, to Semiramis and Cleopatra, she preferred the company of worldly aristocrats to bohemians, professors, and critics. At her peak, in the 1870s and 80s, she was earning five thousand pounds a year – on one visit to London two hundred pounds a week were spent on flowers alone. But the fate of the popular novelist is tied to public taste: it changed in the 1880s and Ouida did not. After her extravagance caught up with her, she moved from place to place, each less attractive than the one before, ending in a miserable house on the road outside Viareggio. There, with her big dogs and other strays, beloved by the local poor, she died almost destitute in 1908.[161] In the English cemetery at Bagni, an unknown admirer paid for a monument, meant to recall Della Quercia's tomb of Ilaria del Carretto in nearby Lucca, down to the little dog at the statue's feet.

'A little terrible and finally pathetic grotesque' was Henry James's gratuitously cruel remark, which Norman Douglas dismissed as the smear of a 'feline and gelatinous New Englander.'[162] Sir Francis Vane, who visited Ouida shortly before her death, eulogized her: 'she was the first of a series of writers who brought the true Italy and the true Italian home to us, forced us out of our insular prejudice, and made us friends in a more intimate manner than even national *ententes* can ever do, and in that manner gave sight and understanding to the people of both races.' Through her Vane pays tribute to the heyday of English-language writing, particularly travel writing, on Italy.[163]

In Maremma (1882), the last of the peasant novels, is set in the coastal marshland of southwest Tuscany and Latium. From the eighth to the third centuries BC the region was ruled by Vetulonia and Vulci, two of the twelve states of ancient Etruria. The 'Maremma,' a dialect word deriving from the Latin *maritima* (marine), afforded fine harbours from which the Etruscans exported copper, tin, and iron, mined in the nearby mountains. By the second century BC the harbours were silting up, the Romans discontinued the drainage system, and the coasts reverted to sea lagoons and flood lands.[164] The terrain furnished Dante with the wood of the suicides ('No brakes so harsh and dense have those savage beasts that hate the tilled lands between the Cecina and Corneto' [*Inf.* 13.7–9]); and Pia de' Tolomei dies there ('Siena mi fè, disfecemi Maremma,' 'Siena made me, Maremma unmade me' [*Purg.* 5.134]). Pia's story became a Romantic setpiece, as in Felicia Hemans's *The Maremma* (1819) and William Herbert's *Pia della Pietra* (1820), and the tradition persists in Eliot's ironic allusion ('Highbury bore me. Richmond and Kew / Undid me,' *The Waste Land* III).[165]

In *Cities and Cemeteries of Etruria* (1845), which joins the qualities of a travelogue to a scholarly monograph, George Dennis wakened interest among the Victorians in the mysterious Etruscan culture. His title was well chosen, for he balanced his study between its cities and its ancient cemeteries or great cities of the dead, which at the time were yielding seemingly boundless archeological riches. (Ouida expressed her outrage at their despoliation.)[166] Among his finer pages are his landscape descriptions of the Maremma. From May through early autumn, the littoral is a 'desert seashore swamp,' a 'preserve of wild boars and roebucks'; 'stagnant pools along the shore send forth intolerable effluvia, generating deadly fevers, and poisoning the atmosphere for many miles around'; 'no one remains in this deadly atmosphere, who can in any way crawl out of it.' Then, from late October to May, it is a land of 'beauty peculiar and somewhat savage ... like that of an Indian maiden, yet fascinating in its wild unschooled luxuriance'; 'a tall underwood of tamarisk, lentiscus, myrtle, dwarf-cork trees, and numerous shrubs unknown to me, fostered by the heat and moisture ... and matted together by parasitical plants.'[167] Ouida occasionally borrows from Dennis (e.g., the land is 'overgrown with thickets and low timber and matted parasites' [568]). *Nel mondo, o in Maremma,* meaning 'in the world or out of it' (like the Maremma), was proverbial (614). In combining seasonal renewal and the classical underworld, with its confusion of land and water, form and decay, life and death, Ouida stands closer to Dennis than to her near-contemporary Vernon Lee, who focuses on the end of the life cycle ('The dead, in the Maremma, are too dead. And the living are not sufficiently alive').[168]

Maremma's flora and fauna, its daily and yearly round of life, and its Etruscan materials capture a mythic timelessness. Though, like *A Village Commune,* the novel is set in the near present, Ouida avoids direct treatment of political or social issues. The recent Unification of Italy passes in a single reference as if it were the loss of natural autonomy; 'Dependence' is Ouida's cutting word for what was more often called 'independence,' of which the peasants 'heard much but understood little' and, as yet, had received no benefit (479). As the 'first English writer to chronicle the sense of growing disillusion with the actual achievement' of the Risorgimento, Ouida criticizes the government's tax policies that pushed small villages like her fictional Santa Tarsilla into oblivion (479).[169] The railway to Grosseto is mentioned; it is flooded out in the autumn rains. Nature has not entirely yielded to technology. Ouida mentions a prison on the island of Gorgona where the government had established a penal colony in 1869. Without these few references, the story could have happened almost any time from the seventeenth to nineteenth centuries; or, more precisely, the story lies in what may be called Fictional Italian Time, so cherished by foreign travellers and writers in Old Italy down to 1914.

Beyond its geographical and political affinity with decline and death, Ouida's Maremma has a cultural affinity through its Etruscan legacy. In many ways, her Etruscans are her quintessential Italian types, and though Kenneth Churchill claims that Etruscan references proliferate 'whenever Ouida wishes to evoke the graceful and joyous response to life,' this is neither their sole nor even their central function in the novel, where Etruscan lore figures so prominently.[170] Like the Maremma itself, Ouida's concept of the Etruscans manifests antithetical qualities. There is joy and vivacity, to be certain, but with their violence, sacrificial cults, profound belief in an afterlife, and elaborate concentration on funerary art and architecture, the Etruscans inspired Ouida's major themes, the lost father and the survival of the past.[171]

By 1880 the Italian government had begun to drain wide tracts of the Maremma, so Ouida's portrait of its primitive beauty is suffused by nostalgia, the kind seen in Macchiaioli artists like Giovanni Fattori and Telemaco Signorini. Following Dennis, she presents the background of her story in terms of an immemorial pattern of life. From May to October the land is 'one vast smoking morass,' 'sunburnt,' 'storm-harassed,' and 'fever-stricken' (454); 'poisoned air, so hot, so damp, so laden with the seeds of disease' (480); 'windless, vaporous, silent' (627); the population dwindling to a sickly few (568). 'An almost absolute silence reigned here, only broken by the booming of millions of mosquitoes and the tinkling now and then of the one feeble church-bell' (479). Intense, brooding heat and pestilence reach their height in August, when the novel's critical events occur: Mastarna's rescue, Joconda's death, the meeting with the deceitful Count Este, Sanctis's death, Este's abandonment, Musa's trial. The convention of romance permits Ouida to speed up the months to get to the 'canicular heats' (816) for a major scene. The healthy season begins in late October: the Maremma 'awoke to motion and noise of men' (627). This is the transhumance of which she gives as memorable a portrait as D'Annunzio's : 'down from the mountains of the Lucchese and Pistoiese districts laborers troop by the thousands; shepherds come from the hills with long lines of flocks; herds of horses and cattle go daily by the roads; hunters chase the boar and buck, and charcoal-burners and ploughman pour themselves in busy legions over the plains and the woods' (454). The height of this season is mid-winter, at which time

Ouida fixes the novel's turning point, Este's seduction of Musa. By May, the migrants are mostly gone and the land turns malarial. Ouida paints the two faces of the Maremma in broad contrast: the 'erect, healthy, smiling, stalwart,' 'mountain-born' people from the Apennine chestnut forests are ranged against the 'pale, swollen, ague-shaken creatures' of the low-lying villages 'like life beside death' (455). The men are 'bitter foes and hot lovers; faithless ones, too.' The women suffer the consequences: 'when the Maremma girl sings of her lover he is always some Pistoiese or Lucchese *damo* from the Apennines, and the burden of her song is always one of absence, of doubt, and of inconstancy' (455).

As the story opens, the elderly Joconda Romanelli travels on foot to sell her linen in Grosseto. Half a century before, she flouted the wishes of her alpine family and married a trader from the Maremma. Later he died at sea, and her three children and grandson fell victim to malaria and other diseases. The trader is the first of the 'lost' fathers in the novel, while Joconda is a study of long-suffering Mrs Ramé: prudent and responsible, both women committed one devastating 'error' out of passionate love. The trader was from the south like Mr Ramé; by contrast, Joconda is from the Gran Paradiso in the north. Yet, to give her an element of her beloved French father, Ouida makes her a Savoyard. Her name means 'cheerful,' though in the novel she is dour and laconic. Possibly Ouida wants to indicate that Joconda had chosen love over family and society, and however high the price, had found happiness. Also, her name connects her to the much-prized Etruscan joy of life and to the most famous of Joconda myths, da Vinci's Mona Lisa.

Too proud to return home, Joconda has eked out a living by spinning and herb-gathering in Santa Tarsilla, which lies on the coast between Telamone (or Talamone) and Orbetello. Dennis, who travelled these twelve odd miles, depicted a 'swampy shore, with low bare heights inland, once crowned by one of the proudest cities of Etruria,' the 'most maritime nation' of its time, home of the 'sea-kings'; Telamone and the villages 'are almost deserted in summer, and the few people that remain become bloated like wine-skins, or yellow as lizards.'[172] As Montgomery Carmichael wrote in 1901, Telamone is 'scarcely worth a visit. It is crumbling away, and the malaria here is very deadly.'[173] Ouida's fictional Santa Tarsilla lies on a small bay 'that scholars affirmed had once been, like its neighbors Telamone and Populonia, a port of those sea-kings, the Etruscans.' Since the young emigrate, its population consists

of 'the feeble, the old, and the very poor' who are 'nearly all dropsical,'
'listless and shivering,' with the children lying on the sand 'too weak to
care to play' (467, 478–9). Known for her charity, St Tarsilla or Tharsilla
(Dec. 24) was the virgin aunt of Pope Gregory the Great. She had a vision of her great-grandfather Pope St Felix and was given a glimpse of
heaven. The choice of this patron saint affirms Ouida's ideal of the caring, virginal woman and the exalted, remote father.

In Grosseto all attention is fixed upon the captured brigand Saturnino
Mastarna. Of massive build, Saturnino has 'sombre,' 'terrible' 'black'
eyes, 'rich and red' lips, 'straight and handsome' features, and long 'dark
locks'; his earrings have been taken from him, but a gold medallion of
the Madonna is worn at his throat (460). For local folk, distrustful of the
government, he is *nostro Saturnino* (455). For literary critics, he descends
from the Bryonic hero, the handsome rebel-outcast of melancholy or saturnine disposition. Years before he had found Joconda's missing grandchild, and she now repays the deed by daring to give him refreshment.
He begs her to save his baby daughter, abandoned after the ambush
in his mountain hideout. Her mother Serapia, named after the Roman
saint and martyr of Syrian origin, was 'half a captive' and 'half a willing
mistress,' a 'second Proserpine' carried away 'to a night of oblivion, peril
and crime' (474) by Saturnino's Pluto; she died either by fever or (some
think) at the hands of Saturnino in a jealous fit. Joconda goes into the
mountains to rescue the child, who has survived exposure, a sign of mi-
raculous intervention. Within her childhood fantasy, Ouida has reduced
the power of the child's rival for the father by splitting the mother image
between Serapia and Joconda. Serapia is the Mrs Ramé who broke with
convention to marry the stranger. Joconda is the Mrs Ramé who is the
practical-minded duenna; however, Joconda's own youthful choice of a
love-match shows Ouida's reluctance to rob even the foster-mother of an
assertion of freedom and love against convention. The child will grow
up to become a new 'Persephone' (625, 653), Serapia's replacement as
queen and consort. The allusion to the woman who lives half the year as
Demeter's daughter on earth and half as Pluto's queen in Hades underscores the Maremma's seasonal shift from life to death. Saturnino is imprisoned for life on Gorgona, named for the three mythical figures, one
of whom, the Medusa, turns men to stone by her gaze. Later, when the
girl asks about her father, Joconda says he is 'dead in the sea' and looks
north 'where she knew that the isle of Gorgona rose from the waves'
(488), a monstrous parody of the birth of Venus.

Naming and renaming, first and last steps in definition, are an obsession with self-named Ouida, so it is worth noting that Mastarna did not think of telling Joconda his child's name; it is his secret, a detail that comes to signify complicity in a forbidden love. As if the child will atone for the father (or repeat his transgression), Joconda names her Maria Penitente after an obscure Eastern sinner-saint, the 'Syrian Magdalene' (481) (Ouida thus links her to Serapia), and keeps the identity of the child's father a secret from all save the parish priest who soon dies.[174] The child grows up resembling her beautiful mother and the angel in Dolci's *Angel of the Annunciation*. Like Joconda's, her character is proud, self-sufficient, and innocent; and like her father's, it is bold and courageous. No more than Joconda, still 'an alien and a stranger' (461) in the village where she has spent fifty years, do the people accept the young girl, who remains apart from the other children. Ouida compensates for her alienation by making her, unlike the other children, immune to malaria and other diseases: she lies under the protection of Artemis, a plague goddess, with whom she is identified. She is nicknamed Velia, after the fierce seabird (shrike, sea-mew); Musoncella, 'one who pulls the long face' or 'the girl that turns her face away' (484–5), from social or sexual advances (*far il muso*, to be sullen); and, among a 'contagion of ... nicknames' (484), the pagan Musa, or poetic inspiration, which wins out over all the others. An artist-surrogate for Ouida, and with her 'very own' nickname, she learns to play the lute and sing of the 'melancholy' and 'abandonment' of the land; her 'power of improvisation' and 'inborn melody' disturb Joconda, 'a Puritan at heart' (511). When Musa is eight, Joconda expresses her fear of dying before Musa has grown up. Musa responds that she would die too: 'Do you love me so much, then?' asks Joconda. 'I should not like to live if you were not here. I do not know if you call that love,' replies the child, joining love and death. 'It is love,' said Joconda (491). Musa tries to comprehend death through the one experience she has had that might equal it in strength.

At twelve, roaming the Maremma, Musa discovers a tomb complex of an Etruscan *lucumo* or king and experiences a sexual awakening. (Though by 1856 some fifteen thousand tombs had been located in the territory of Vulci alone, a *lucumo*'s tomb of this size would have been a major find.)[175] The frescoed walls are covered by figures 'seated before a banquet,' 'playing on lyres,' 'dancing before an altar,' 'riding on many-colored steeds,' 'leading strange forest beasts,' surrounded by 'lotus-flowers' (502). In death the Etruscans celebrate life. 'But ... what made her tremble in every limb, was the recumbent figure, stretched upon a bier of stone, of a man in armor and casque of gold,' with a golden-

winged sceptre and golden shield, lamp, and cup (502). Her sudden
dread provokes the memory of her father, the brigand king with his
flashing gold. One chamber after another is filled with funerary objects,
utensils, and jewellery. When she returns to the *lucumo*, however, she
watches in horror as the dead warrior crumbles away, 'all in an instant,'
leaving nothing but ashes (504). He has disappeared as mysteriously as
her father. Ouida crosses romance and science: 'The air and the light entering with her, after exclusion for two thousand years or more, reached
the oxidized armor, the recumbent corpse, and melted them back to
dust' (504).[176] The contents of the other chambers do not suffer oxidation because they had been exposed to air, a circumstance that only magnifies the *lucumo*'s disappearance. In a 'trance' Musa feels 'sublimity of
awe,' but also 'infinite pity' for the dead king; her Christian upbringing
confuses her. 'Was it death? was it life?' a 'god' or 'devil'? 'Why had he
not taken her too? She would have been glad to go.' Most likely, mixing
love and death, she yearns for the lost father: '"This is death!"'... Death
had been here so long alone and in peace, and she had broken in upon
his rest, and he in wrath had claimed her' (504–5). On this thought she
loses consciousness.

   Waking at nightfall, Musa feels as if she were resurrected from the
dead and struggles to the cave entrance where the sounds of nature revive her. As she gazes at the night sky she imagines that 'the dead had ris-
en and fled'; he is in the 'lustre' of the moonlight; the *lucumo*'s shield is
the moon, the shooting star his spear (506). In her reverie she has transformed the dead *lucumo* into an all-powerful god. 'I have seen Death,
and it is beautiful' (506), she later tells Joconda, as if beauty no less than
love were to ease the path between life and death. 'Child,' admonishes
Joconda, 'you have not yet seen what you love die!' Musa is told to keep
the discovery of the tomb a secret – the 'father' remains the secret –
though Joconda, who knows nothing of oxidation, puts down the
lucumo's disappearance to Musa's dreaming. 'But the earth, – is it all
a grave?' Musa asks, 'Did God make men and women?' She was abandoned by her real father; the vanished *lucumo* as a substitute father has
prompted her curiosity: 'Those people are my kindred.' Joconda replies:
'no one knows whence you come' (507).

   From time to time Musa visits the tomb, half fancying the *lucumo*
would return to tell her the 'secrets of the grave' (510), which are fused
in her mind with sexuality and symbolized by the sensuous, orgiastic
frescoes. The tomb becomes a shrine, more familiar to her than those
of the saints, though her curiosity about the Etruscans remains unsatis-
fied because of local ignorance. She removes nothing from the tomb

in stark contrast to the landowners, like the Italian duchess who dances
the night away wearing an Etruscan gold necklace. A few years pass and
Joconda makes Musa, now fifteen, vow not to give herself in love without
the 'blessing of Church' (517), just the kind of conventionalism Ouida's
heroines are born to transgress. In a letter to her alpine family Joconda
relates Musa's story.

One August night Musa pulls a drowning man to shore and revives
him – an iteration of the theme of crossing between life and death. She
assumes he is a galley-slave, but it is Masterna escaped from Gorgona.
'I have no name,' he murmurs, 'I am dead and buried'; then, 'I was
Saturnino.' She recognizes the name of the brigand and he threatens to
kill her if she informs on him. A false name might have been more prudent under the circumstances; within the novel's economy of naming,
however, his real name asserts his power of identity. 'But if I had a knife!'
(533): if he had a knife he could return among the living and to be the
real Saturnino again. His 'bronze-like shoulders glistened with the salt
of the sea; he sat erect on the beach, regaining strength and consciousness with each breath; the heat of the night was around them like steam:
it seemed to her startled fancy as if his eyes and his mouth gave out
fire' (533). Musa witnesses a demonic return of the dead *lucumo* with the
breath of life. 'She was rooted to the ground as by some spell' (533). He
even has the 'bronze-like' sheen of the *lucumo*'s 'lustre,' bronze imagery
being associated with the *lucumo* and Mastarna (483, 489, 533, 743, 755,
800). The one childhood memory that Musa retains of her father is his
embracing her so tightly that 'something cold and bright,' his dagger,
'hurt' (488), while the smoke and gunfire of the ambush mix confusedly
in her memory with the oxidation of the *lucumo*. Now he returns asking
for a knife, which she will shortly steal for him, thus giving him back his
'life.' She does not report him to the police because of her 'immense
pity' and her distrust of authority.

Saturnino's last name Mastarna, meaning leader or master, traces
to the Etruscan warrior and strongman Macstrna, one of the heroes of
Vulci. According to legend he appears to have been in the service of the
revolutionary aristocratic brothers Caelius and Aulus Vibenna who attempted to grab power within the Etruscan kingdoms in the late sixth
century BC. After one battle Caelius was taken prisoner, but later freed
by Aulus and Macstrna. In a frescoed tomb discovered by the Florentine
archaeologist Alessandro François in 1857, Macstrna uses a dagger to cut
the cords that bind Caelius.[177] The action coincides with the expulsion of
the Etruscan royal family of the Tarquins by the Vibenna party, with which
Macstrna was allied. In Roman tradition Macstrna is commemorated by

being identified with the sixth king, Servius Tullius, *magister populi*, 'the original name of the Roman dictator': 'Macstr-na = mag(i)st(e)r-na.'[178] Following a now largely discredited interpretation, Ouida links Masterna to Servius Tullius (460). As for Mastarna's first name, Sarturnino, Saturnia is an Etruscan city named after Saturn, 'the sower,' an Italian agricultural god and legendary king of Rome in the age of gold. Saturnino Mastarna's name encodes the polarities of life and death.

By the time Musa returns to the tomb with a knife, Mastarna has fled with the jewellery, another link between him and the *lucumo*. Returning home she finds that Joconda has died in her sleep. In mythic reciprocity, the tomb having been robbed, Death exacts vengeance by claiming a life. When the villagers demand Joconda's pitiful legacy to pay her alleged debts, Musa throws the jar of coins at their feet and leaves Santa Tarsilla to make her home in the tomb. There, freed from the constraints of society, she lives out her incestuous fantasy: 'Here was her refuge, her palace, her place of sanctity and dreams; here the native unconscious poetry and passion in her found a likeness to themselves' (564). Utensils and pottery intended for use in the afterlife serve Musa's daily needs, while at night she sleeps on the 'stone couch' of the *lucumo*'s bier, watched over by Chimaera, Typhon, the Dii Involuti, and other 'terrible shapes' of the monstrous Sacred. Gradually these presences of death infect her: 'their cold repose, their ineffable indifference, their passionless defiance of mankind' (565). One night, in a Herculean effort, she disinters Joconda's coffin and transports it across the Maremma to one of the inner chambers of the tomb. This act of piety provides her with a votive shrine. In thematic symmetry, like her father, she has robbed a grave and, like him (though unfairly), will be punished. Meanwhile, Mastarna is recaptured trying to sell the gold. While Ouida lets her imagination wander widely in these episodes, her childhood fantasy reconstituted in the *lucumo*'s tomb remains intact.

Musa's grief is assuaged by the changing seasons (565–78). The transference of love from the dead onto nature, seen already in the *lucumo*'s apotheosis, may recall young Ouida, who associated her own disappearing, reappearing father with the natural world that he taught her to love. Musa identifies with birds and animals, destroying hunter's nets and traps wherever she can. She herself is likened to Antinous, the favorite of Hadrian (489), Dante's Pia (511), and Francesca da Rimini (741), Artemis (571, 596), Tanaquil (572), Cleopatra (603), Psyche (608, 609), Maia (611), Atagartis (611), Persephone (625, 653), Luna, Cupa (646), Circe (676), Penthesilea (688, 695, 704), Britomart (695, 704) and Una

(695, 705), Eve (745), Electra (748), Glauca (755), Laena (792, 803), and a priestess of Fauna or Pales (598). Though Ouida is not a careful mythographer, the figure in the carpet is the young virgin pledged to her father or traumatized by sex. While the list includes a sorceress, a licentious queen, a murdered bride, and an adulteress, references to Homer's Nausicaa (614, 625, 655, 656, 717) outnumber any of them. Musa's rescue of Masterna recalls Nausicaa's 'saving' Odysseus (*Od.* 6).[179] As often in classical mythology, the multiple names (like the nicknames) invest the subject with the varied powers that the names connote. Her beauty, of which she is either unaware or unconcerned, is also a source of power (564). For Joconda, Musa's face recalled Masterna's 'terrible beauty' (489) and when Musa first sees her face – in an Etruscan mirror – a scorpion crosses the glass (615); this awareness of beauty with its potential destructiveness terrifies her.[180] Count Este likens Musa to 'Gorgona,' which serves to strengthen her identification with her bandit father (727).

Three men now enter Musa's life. Villamagna is a Sicilian trader, 'very handsome, with a glowing, sun-warmed beauty, like one of his own Sicilian fruits' (578). He falls in love at first sight, for in Italy 'this sudden birth of love is still a truth' like the 'red in the pomegranate's flower' (579): Hades' fruit, given to Persephone, is a symbol of 'heterosexual union with its seeds and blood-red juice,' but also a reference to Side (Gr. 'pomegranate') (603), the mythical virgin 'who commits suicide in order to avoid the sexual violence of her father.'[181] Enna in central Sicily was among the many sites in the ancient world where it was claimed that Hades abducted Persephone. Musa rejects his proposal flatly: she distrusts such suddenness; also, Ouida implies, while Villamagna would surely love her, she would be stifled within his Sicilian world. The second suitor is Joconda's grand-nephew, Maurice Sanctis, who learned of Musa through Joconda's letter and seeks to bring her back to the Alps. Older than Villamagna, tall, spiritual, with an 'entirely Northern' face (but 'not much beauty': count on Ouida for blunt appraisals) (588), and 'by custom a Parisian' (610), Sanctis (the 'holy' one) is an artist of rising fame and heir to a fortune. His prudent 'Teuton' (593, 594) demeanour and intellectuality contrast with Villamagna's southern passion. He is related to one of Ouida's major types, 'the languid male dandy connoisseur,' which she popularized in late-Victorian fiction.[182] Musa spurns him too: 'there was about him the atmosphere, as it were, of another world than hers, – a sort of look of ease, of culture, of success ... which alienated her' (593). (Ouida was obviously writing as fast as her pen could move.)

He is too sublimated to be a lover, too weak for the wild and passionate Maremma. After a few weeks he succumbs to malaria and leaves without telling her the secret of her origins.

The third person is the imperious Count Luitbrand (*sic*) d'Este, convicted on a trumped-up charge of murdering his mistress, wife of a powerful lord in Mantua, and sent to prison on Gorgona. His name joins the fierce Lombard king Liutprand with the courtly Renaissance Este, though his own family has fallen on bad times. Haughty, possessive, and 'wonderfully handsome, with the beauty of the Greek ideal' (612), Este escaped from Gorgona with Mastarna, from whom he has learned of Musa's tomb as a possible hideout; Mastarna said if the girl gives him trouble, 'a fawn's neck is soon slit' (613). One of Ouida's decadent, faithless aristocrats, Este had led 'the usual tranquil, amorous, unoccupied life of young Italian men in old Italian cities' (653). He would row along a canal, wait among the reeds, then climb up to his lover's room in a tower; one night he found her stabbed to death by her husband – an event from which he has never recovered and which has left him callous and bitter. The marshy environs of Mantua connect him with the destructive forces of the Maremma, while the identification with snakes will be borne out in his treachery. The three men have the qualities Ouida values in her protagonists: eroticism (Villamagna, Este), money (Villamagna, Sanctis), the artistic nature (Sanctis, Este), aristocracy (Este). Besides having three of the four requirements, Este is psychologically the fair side of Mastarna, Apollo to the other's Dionysus, the 'Greek ideal' to 'terrible beauty,' though he has Mastarna's cruel streak. Narratively, the aristocratic Este is right to be associated with the escaped brigand king.

Searching the Maremma for the tomb, Este (like Sanctis) falls seriously ill with malaria and fears he is dying. The narrative pauses while Ouida explores why 'Death appalls at all ages the Latin temperament' (664–5). Este hates death as the extinction of his pleasures, suppressing thoughts of suicide and looking out to nature, the sun, the fields, and love. Ouida supports his presentism in a lengthy description of the Maremma in November, while she admires even more the way Musa combines her love of nature with a mythic appropriation of the past and her love of her family. In Ariès's terms, Este's attitude is natural and tame, whereas Musa embraces the 'death of the other' in the form of a Romantic cult of the dead. Musa finds Este and slowly nurses him back to health, and falls in love. The one suitor to win her love is the one who cares nothing for her. Her innocence and restraint soon irritate the manipulative, predatory count, who accuses her of a provocative passivity. To fetch quinine for him she travels to Orbetello, where she sees Mastarna behind a prison fence. Ouida must find a way to express Musa's ambivalent feelings towards the father consistent with her plot; so she makes Musa angry with Mastarna for robbing the grave (the dead *lucumo*) and grateful to him for sending Este (a living one). As she decides to help him with money, he recalls Serapia in her features and realizes that Musa is his child. But he does not tell her. Perhaps he is ashamed, or he wants to make opportunistic use of his knowledge.

Villamagna notices Masterna talking with Musa and, still hoping to marry her, approaches Mastarna, who shows no compunction in divulging her true origins. With their common love for Musa as his self-serving plea, Mastarna seizes the chance to get help for another escape. In Ouida's reiteration of the stereotype, while Villamagna does not share the 'common Sicilian sympathy' for the '*malandrini*' (ruffians), neither did he deplore their crimes 'as Northern nations or people of the cities might do' (651) (Joconda had a 'cooler, sturdier Northern sense of right and wrong' [480]). The fact that the 'fierce blood' of the Mastarna ran in Musa's veins only enhances her in Villamagna's eyes, 'as Persephone looked to her lover when the darkness of the shades was about her'; by contrast, to Sanctis's 'Northern mind' and 'worldly knowledge' the secret of her birth had been the 'most terrible of all inheritance' (653). Eventually, every main character in the novel knows the secret of Musa's origins except Musa herself.

Although she means as much to Este as a *lucumo*'s 'slave' (655, 660) or 'dog' (721), he instructs her in classical and Etruscans myths from an historical viewpoint. These studies (and it is appropriate that Este, not Sanctis, should be the corrosive analyst) fail to undermine Musa's mythopoeic imagination, which responds enthusiastically to his tales of prehistory. 'The ardor of the Sicilian left her hard and scornful'; 'the gentleness of Sanctis had left her cold and thankless'; yet 'one languid smile from Este's eyes, one listless word from his mouth, made her grateful and full of joy' (656). Musa's fatal choice of the 'bad' suitor arises out of the contemporary women's situation. As Natalie Schroeder comments, though writers like M.E. Braddon and Ouida 'were forced to bow to convention and punish aggression and self-assertiveness, the predominantly female reading audience was regaled with woman's potential for power.' Ouida's heroines are strongly self-assertive and make bold choices, but she then punishes them for doing so, according to the social conventions of the times: 'feminine rebellion is more openly determined through overt sexuality.'[183] Like Ouida, Musa prefers the scandalous aristocrat over the merchant or the artist. Finally, Este must be 'bad' because he awakens love that Musa confuses with the incestuous love of the father and magnifies into criminal dimensions. In the plot this is reinforced by Este's ties to Masterna and the archetypal *lucumo*.

Having failed to win Musa and having discovered Este's intentions, Sanctis offers to clear Este's name if Este will marry Musa and rescue her from the Maremma. Incapable of self-sacrifice himself, Este mistrusts it in others but has nothing to lose by pretending to agree. Likewise, when Musa tells Este of Villamagna, he suspects a thieving southerner will return to steal her away. Ouida's imagery can be rather clichéd: 'Jealousy darted from the dreamful gaze of Este: it is a hooded snake that always lies beneath the amorous smile of all Italian eyes' (715). Besides the phallic snake, 'hooded' suggests the secretive nature of sexual jealousy. Este's determination to possess Musa is founded on mimetic desire: 'all at once he saw, and his dulled desires leaped from their ashes into fire, because other men also saw, other men also desired' (717).

Musa's vow to Joconda holds until Este rescues her in a boating accident. While the thought of losing her makes Este think himself in love, she in her weakened condition allows him to kiss her – again, love is connected to illness – and they become lovers. For Musa, her near-drowning has been a kind of rebirth: 'she had descended into the grave of the deep waters, and been delivered by the hand that she loved' (749). The Syrian Magdalene has broken her vow, just as Joconda had gone against her family's wishes. Musa possesses traits of the Romantic Fatal Woman as analysed by Mario Praz: beautiful, exotic, often innocent and therefore more enticing, associated with the moon and Artemisian coldness, and older than the rocks among which she sits.[184] Sanctis thinks she is 'eternally young' and 'preserved in the secrecy of these forests, without change, whilst all the rest of earth grew old' (683); she preferred Este's tales of prehistory; she is an innocent fawn to Mastarna; she is at home among Etruscan tombs. During this time, in Mantua, Sanctis extracts a confession from the husband who murdered his wife, Este's mistress, and this clears Este. Yet Sanctis's midsummer exertions have ruined his health and he too falls victim to malaria. In Ouida, they die who sacrifice for love.

Musa's relations with the young men fall into the categories of female protagonist outlined by Pamela K. Gilbert, whose principal texts are *Under Two Flags* and *Folle-Farine:* (1) 'ice-princesses' who, though they may be love objects for men, 'manage to stay outside this realm [of capitalist exchange and commodification] whether through aristocratic birth or through their identities as artists'; and (2) 'active (and poor) "good" women' who, 'against their will, ... must enter the realm of exchange, into which they are inexorably drawn, thus losing their identities as subjects, a process figured as the opening of their bodies by sex, violence, and illness.' With Villamagna and Sanctis, Musa is the ice-princess. With Este, she is the 'poor,' 'good' sacrificial woman. Ouida makes the villain of the plot neither the middle-class southern trader nor the frail northern artist, but the dissolute aristocratic playboy; '[Ouida] both exposes the upper classes to criticism for their sexual morals and seals them off from such criticism (they are members of 'The Order'; they are not comparable to or understandable by other mere mortals).'[185] With Mastarna, however, Musa is both ice-princess and sacrificial women.

As Musa half suspected, on learning of his pardon Este departs with vague promises. She compares him to the vanishing *lucumo* (768), a repetition of her abandonment by her father. 'The instinctive fatalism, the strange passivity, that are in the Southern temper, and succeed its gusts of passion, its heat of rage or love, made her accept her abandonment as a thing not to be questioned' (774). Musa acquiesces because she has violated social convention and her vow: she desires punishment both for what she has done and for what she has *not* done, sexuality in this novel being partly identified with incestuous longing.

Este sends a messenger with a little money, which she refuses, indicating her desire to re-establish her selfhood as ice-princess. Nor does she inform anyone that she is pregnant by Este. Her son, child of another absent father, dies shortly after his birth. During the summer Musa is found with the dead baby and Joconda's coffin and is arrested for trespassing and grave-robbing. A court imprisons her with a prostitute, word spreads, and the summer-stricken townspeople accuse her of having the evil eye and want to execute her, a scapegoat for all the ills inflicted by the Maremma. As her once robust health fails her, the loyal Villamagna comes to her aid. Proven innocent, she is released and returns to her home in the tomb. Summer passes to autumn, the malaria relents, news spreads of her goodness, and the townspeople begin to think well of her. In Ouida's myth-making, Musa is a plague goddess who controls the seasons.

In the mountain forests of Sardinia, Villamagna reaches Mastarna surrounded by his bandits. The 'ancient blood' of the 'Etruscan Mastarna' (806) – the *lucumo* himself – demands vengeance against Este. Mastarna visits his daughter and, in what Ouida calls his 'first instinct of any nobility' (811), again withholds the secret of her origins, lest he deepen her grief. Then he leaves for Este's palazzo in Rome. In the melodramatic conclusion, having followed Mastarna, Musa struggles physically with him to prevent Este's murder and faints from exhaustion; meanwhile, Este's henchmen have been given enough time to subdue Mastarna. She has saved the life of her faithless lover. But she is unconscious when Mastarna curses Este, cries out that Musa is his daughter, and dies of apoplexy. Now Este knows the secret. The next day, discovering Este with a courtesan, Musa flees Rome and wanders distractedly back to the tomb, 'wondering where God was' (831). There on the tomb she commits suicide with Este's dagger, descendent of the original dagger of Masterna that she had felt as a child. Ouida borrows the Virgilian metaphor of the wounded deer that depicts Dido in love (831), and however distant the comparison between the two characters (and Este's abandonment is not motivated like Aeneas's by a higher mission), there is something of the same violation of convention (Dido's vow of not remarrying, Musa's of marrying within the Church) and the same tragedy of the heart. After burying her in the tomb, with 'half his life,' Este went home: 'But men forget, – and he forgot' (832).[186]

If there is any consolation, Musa finds Mastarna in death, which in the Etruscan religion ensures a vital, compensatory afterlife. Yet Ouida does not pursue this path, instead crying out against fate, the gods, Darwinian determinism, hunting, the suppression of women, and social injustice. Ouida first gives Musa's thoughts in the free-indirect style, '"God cannot care,"' then her own, closely parallel thoughts: 'No one cared: the terrible, barren, acrid truth, that science trumpets abroad as though it were some new-found joy, touched her ignorance with its desolating despair' (718). Ouida's credo denies a benign divinity in the face of a dynamic nature: 'Life was only sustained by death. The harmless and lovely children of the air and of the moor were given over, year after year, century after century, to the bestial play and the ferocious appetites of men.' These men in the abstract seem not to be merely hunters and trappers, but the men who have preyed on Musa, including her father. Hence, the pathos of the concluding lines: 'The wondrous beauty of the earth renewed itself only to be the scene of endless suffering, of interminable torture ... The slaughter, the misery, the injustice renewed themselves as the greenness of the world did. No one cared. There was no voice upon the blood-stained waters' (718). No voice of the *father*.

Musa's last thought, 'If God care' (832), is questioning, not prayerful. Her family romance, like Ouida's, is a self-enclosed, asexual intimacy with a father, a Pluto figure whose most prominent attributes are greed,

secrecy, sexuality, and violence. 'Love can live upon itself alone, rootless like an orchid' (741); the only time Musa had felt rootedness was
when she met her father and was 'rooted to the ground as by some spell'
(533). Any possibility of incest is eliminated by the fact that the *lucumo*,
the first Mastarna, went up in smoke at the breath of life. That the second Mastarna is a violent brigand and has been incarcerated implicates
the forbidden desire and protects against its fulfillment. The feeling of
abandonment is prolonged by Musa's never learning of her origins, not
even from the father whose withholding the secret prevents the removal
of its stigma and proves destructive of life. Isolate, transient beauty in a
sickly land is the recurrent metaphor. Musa's innocence is 'grand and
noble' like 'one of the large white lilies that rose up from the noxious
mud of the marshes' (655; cf. 517, 568, 570, 579, 646, 801), the poisonous creatures around her. Yet her death leaves strangely unresolved the
conflict between her and them, only where it could have been resolved,
in the utmost depths of the self; in tomb-like memory that celebrates life;
in a land whose name contains the sea and that mingles life and death:
in Maremma.

5. Maurice Barrès and the Death of Venice: Where 'night is more beautiful than day'[187]

'If one were to ask me what is the greatest happiness,' said Maurice
Barrès, 'I would not hesitate to reply: "It is to be 22 and have one's first
trip to Italy"' (*Notes* 13). In the footsteps of his *maîtres*, Chateaubriand,
Stendhal, and Taine, he began visiting the country in the 1880s, and at
each subsequent phase of his life it was the mirroring pool in which he
could gaze intently and read the fluctuations of his soul. Among his diverse legacies – a theory of nationalism, a social platform that influenced
French politics down through De Gaulle, novels of ideas, travel books
– are his quasi-symbolist meditations upon Venice, Pisa, Siena, Ravenna,
and other Italian scenes. 'La mort de Venise' (1903), which ranks among
the finest travel essays on any Italian city, bespeaks the cultural mood of
Europe in the years leading up to 1914.[188]
    It was said that Barrès had a penchant for just two or three figures of
speech: antithesis (or paradox) and apostrophe. As to the first, one finds
almost throughout his career a sensation-seeking aestheticism and political engagement; an obsession with a personal life force and an attraction
to death; anarchic individualism and the most stringent discipline of tradition and nationalism; a feeling for 'the uprooted' and 'rootedness.'[189]

As for apostrophe, Barrès laments the decline of regional differences and the cutting of historical ties to the past in the emergence of modern society, though he is not one-sidedly anti-modern and was no monarchist. Summing up these losses and addressed as if present, Barrèsian Italy is what is gradually lost to modernity, though the beauty of its death makes possible its restoration, however fleeting and subject to the same process of dissolution, within the individual soul. Yet Italy does not carry one symbolic valence for Barrès, any more than it could for any writer with a complex understanding of the country. Besides traditionalist Italy, there is a modernizing Italy and a romantic, exotic Italy that contrasts to the almost ascetic geography of his native region. 'The "magic" gardens' of radiant spring in Italy are something that Barrès 'would close to his son until he has learnt to prefer "a garden in Lorraine in September."'[190]

People living on frontiers can be hypersensitive to questions of national identity; borders and mingling capture ideas of purity and dangerous pollution. Born in Charmes-sur-Moselle, Barrès (1862–1923) as a young boy witnessed France's defeat in the Franco-Prussian War, and he later said that his main goal in life was the return of Alsace-Lorraine. At twenty he went to study law in Paris, though he turned to journalism and affected the air of a dandy. Subscribing to a leftist, anti-bourgeois agenda, he won notoriety for his critique of Decadence 'from within' in *Sur l'oeil des Barbares* (Under the Eye of the Barbarians) (1888), the first novel of a trilogy titled *Le Culte du moi* (The Cult of the Self). The second novel, *Un homme libre* (A Free Man) (1889), charts a way out of Decadence through rigorous mental exercise and monk-like discipline. He had found his voice and his audience, which hailed him 'Prince of Youth.' In 1889, at twenty-seven, he upset all expectations by winning a parliamentary seat on a Boulangist platform. After Boulangism collapsed he crossed over to the Socialists, but his Socialism was lukewarm and he lost his seat in 1893.

For thirteen years he languished in the political wilderness, losing five elections. During this time he founded *La Cocarde* (1894–5), which promulgated protectionism, anti-liberalism, anti-positivism, and a smattering of socialist projects.[191] His journalism confronts the decline of French power by contrasting his country politically, economically, and militarily with Germany and England. During these years his theory of 'integral nationalism' took shape; it promoted religious, historical, and cultural unity, while opposing both an abstract nationalism based on a diversity of groups and special interests, and also internationalism. His organicist concept of the nation became the subject of his second trilogy, *Le Roman de l'énergie nationale* (The Novel of National Energy), in which he poured out his love for Lorraine and 'my internal Lorraine' (7:55), to complete his life's journey from the cult of the self to *la terre et les morts* (the earth and the dead).

Barrès saw the young people of France streaming towards the cities, breaking ties to their region, and losing their religious beliefs. He had been one of them himself. In *Les déracinés* (The Uprooted) (1897), the first of the novels of National Energy, he blamed the lycées and the universities for their complicity with this situation, among other reasons, for having adopted Kantianism as the 'state religion' (1:141) of the Third Republic. This foreign import 'has the effect of molding the youth of present-day Lorraine, Provence, Brittany or Paris after a constant, abstract, ideal type. Yet what we need are men who are strictly rooted in our soil, in our history and in the national consciousness' (*Scènes* 177–8). The novel follows seven young men who studied philosophy together in Nancy and then left for Paris. Their teacher Bouteillier instils in them Enlightenment rationalism, skepticism, cosmopolitanism, and Kant's categorical imperative interpreted as duty to the centralized state. Descending from a revolutionary type, possessed of unquestioned belief in his own rectitude, Bouteillier falls upon 'indigenous populations like a despotic bureaucrat doubled by the fanatical apostle' (1:141). His millenarian ideal of transcendence opposes the concrete particulars of individual memory; it 'fails to do justice to the rich diversity of real human conditions. Worse, it smacks of intolerance, of intellectual pride, and of a will to homogenize and dominate,' writes Fritz Ringer, who thinks that Kantianism was less at issue than the rigid sameness of French Republican educational practice.[192]

To Bouteillier's moral universalism, Barrès responds: act in the interests of France. He protests on behalf of difference, though chiefly so far as nations or local milieu, and not individuals, are concerned. The self is subordinated to a particular community or group over whom it may have little or no control, a problem that absorbs Barrès's fiction. Like many late-nineteenth-century thinkers wishing to express the depths of non-rational being, he dipped into heterogeneous vocabularies of psychology, biology, and social theory for solutions: 'our thoughts are not the products of our own individual intelligence; they are the physiological translations of primeval physiological dispositions' (*Scènes* 162). There is nothing original in this aspect of his thought; he merely pushes naturalistic ideas to their limit and applies them to novelistic and propagandistic ends. We are determined not by universal reason but, on the contrary, by the forces of an ancestral homeland, ethnicity, cultural descent, group, family, and moment. To embrace this geo-biological reality is the beginning of wisdom, both as an individual and as a people: 'nationalism is the acceptance of a particular kind of determinism' (*Scènes* 159).[193] In a lurid example from *Les déracinés*, two men murder and decapitate an Armenian woman, the sacrificial immigrant, female victim. Though the protagonist Sturel learns who the murderers are, he will not report them because the government press manipulates facts for political ends; the men are fellow Lorrainers and his region would lose prestige.

When liberals and Dreyfusards like André Gide and Anatole France repudiated Barrèsian nationalism on behalf of European humanism, skepticism, and personal freedom, he brushed their objections aside.[194] Be it Paris, Lorraine, or Italy, the merit of a place or an idea (or even another person) lay in its capacity to promote self-actualization and guide service to the nation. 'What I have pursued everywhere, in doubling myself by Lorraine and France, in traveling, in seeking power, is an immense increase of my personality' (15:47). If the centre held, its expressions would be consistent with one another. If literature and politics 'have on the surface been at variance and divided me,' he said later in life, 'I have made a unity.'[195]

Although Barrès accepted the parliamentary system, he did join an ill-fated government putsch in 1899; he was let off with a small fine. At this time he published what is said to be the first French essay in which the word 'intellectual' was used as a term of abuse.[196] In 1906 he was elected to the Académie Française and was re-elected to the Chamber of Deputies, holding his seat until his death. Among his projects, in an anticlerical parliament, he proposed that French churches built before 1800, many in serious disrepair, should be designated national monuments so that the state would provide for their upkeep. During the war he threw himself into journalism and propaganda. When the bells in the church towers, 'whose foundations arise from amidst the dead' (8:294), sounded the call to arms in 1914, he delivered patriotic speeches in provincial graveyards as if the dead spoke through him. In *Les Traits éternel de la France* (1916), conceiving the 'holy' war as a 'resurrection,' he extolled its regenerative virtues and whipped up audiences with images of trenches 'saturated with blood ... saturated with spirituality' (8:301). One student protested that Barrès 'spent too much time recounting his mental struggles that preceded his return to integral nationalism. "We love our country *spontaneously* and *without mental effort.*"'[197] In sum, Barrès may have spoken too well. Works of this period, notably *La Colline inspirée* (The Sacred Hill) (1913), commend ancient traditions and disclose his reversion to Roman Catholicism. In 1921 the Surrealists put him on mock trial and pronounced him guilty for 'subverting the human spirit.'[198] Youth had a new prince.

If Barrès's geographical and psychological poles were Lorraine and Paris, this ardent regionalist and nationalist was also one of the great travel writers in an age of travel writing, with books on Spain, Greece, and the Near East as well as Italy. By his own admission the theorist of the self and integral nationalist had 'found himself' on foreign soil. 'It was in Venice that I decided upon my life' (he was twenty-three), and Venice remains 'my most beloved place in the world' (1:40). This declaration on his larger mission is tied to another insight into the origins of his literary vocation: 'if I have succeeded in any measure, it is necessary to pass the honor to Italy, where I learned the nature of form' (1:40).

As applied to his novels, 'form' must be taken in a special sense because, by the standards of French realism and naturalism, his trilogies are relatively plotless; they combine elements of the *Bildungsroman*, the novel of ideas, travel writing, autobiography, and sermon. Yet unifying their diverse materials is a 'form' of self-discovery, though the comparison is less to the youthful heroes of Balzac, Dickens, or Zola than to Huckleberry Finn and Holden Caulfield. In *Sur l'oeil des Barbares* Philippe arrives in Paris from Lorraine and finds himself adrift. However, to adopt contemporary modes of thought and behaviour would only be to replace one despotism by another and live 'under the eye of the barbarians,' a collective term for 'all that can injure or resist the self' (1:31). Barrès alludes to the distinction of the ancient Greeks between themselves and all others (*barbaroi*), though Zeev Sternhell makes a claim for Darwin ('existence is only an eternal battle between the self and the non-self ... one must either conquer or disappear'), and Robert Soucy detects *épater le bourgeois*.[199] Philippe wants the self enlarged on his own terms, and rather than follow the dandy's treacherous path and dissipate his energies, he undertakes a series of intellectual experiments that point to the ego as the one, fixed, inviolable reality. Barrès distinguishes Philippe from bourgeois careerists who pretend to personal autonomy but are driven by social and political conformism, from the Decadents who sacrifice the stability of the self to nihilism, and from left-wing intellectuals with their universalist notions. Philippe also struggles against solipsism and his mediocre situation; just seeing his ugly shoes in a corner can throw him into fits of despair.[200]

In *Un homme libre* Philippe retreats to the country; 'the first need for one who wants to live is to surround himself by high walls' (1:200). Fortified by his study of Loyola, he examines his conscience. This sojourn in Lorraine convinces him that, despite its bleakness and boredom, his links to his past define him absolutely and remain amazingly strong. Yet the novel's (and the trilogy's) turning point occurs not on French soil, but in Venice, the chapters on which, remarked Barrès, are 'perhaps the most precious in the book' (1:32.) After three weeks of exhaustive touring with his Baedeker, the morbid ambience and a superfluity of intense impressions overwhelm him. With a touch of humour he observes, 'one is disposed to forget that Venice, on account of its languid atmosphere and from perpetual cups of coffee, is slightly unhealthy anyway' (1:237).

Again, Philippe withdraws, now more deeply, to his darkened room in the Fondamenta Bragadin, named after the doge who was flayed alive in 1570 and with whom he feels a spiritual kinship (in 'La mort de Venise,' self-analysis is a 'fate analogous' to Bragadin's [7:47]). That the Turks captured and tortured Bragadin has special meaning for Barrès since it expresses the assault by external enemies, the foreign, non-Christian Turks, who were also Venice's enemies. In his meditations Philippe concedes that 'external beauty never truly moved me' and that 'my most beautiful spectacles are only my psychological tableaux' (1:236). These 'always unexpected' impressions are so imbued with meaning that they detach themselves from their biographical contexts. For instance, standing in the twilight on the Zattere, he was suddenly transfixed by the sun, which appeared 'like an enormous beast blazing on a slope of delicate sky, above a sea indifferent to its brutality, thoroughly elegant and of a vaporous tenderness' (1:236); it made him late for dinner. Such impressions swim before him and produce the 'anguish' of transience. In an epiphany he cries, 'Finally, I knew Venice. I held all the documents by which to extract the law of this city and to make it conform to myself' (1:237; cf. 234): a pattern in the impressions had (to use one of his metaphors) 'wakened' to awareness what was naturally 'instinct' within himself. 'I was the artisan.' This is the opposite of Bouteillier's forced imposition of abstract notions. 'My memories, rapidly deformed by my instinct, presented me with a Venice that existed in no particular place' but in its 'forms' or 'law' within himself (1:237–8).

The transitoriness of Venice, accentuated by its dissolving splendour prolonged over the centuries, gives birth to the idea of secular immortality. Whereas he had thought of himself in finite terms, with perhaps thirty years to live, he was now aware of himself *sub specie aeternitatis;* he is 'an instant of a long development of my Being, just as Venice at that moment is an instant in the Venetian Soul' (1: 238–9). The self is liberated by embracing its past and future, though not abstractly because not too distantly: 'I hold to my historical conception like a shipwrecked person to his boat. I do not dwell upon the enigma of the beginning of things, nor to the dolorous enigma of the end. I clamp on to my brief solidity. I place myself in a collectivity a little longer than my individual self; I invent a destination a little more reasonable than my puny career ... my thought arrives at constituting its dependence on this land and these dead' (1:141–2). Philippe imagines this Being in the future 'aggrandized and nearer and nearer to God' (1:239). In its transcendent desire, the self has surmounted its final barrier of death, though the cost to the self is yet unknown. In *L'Ennemi des lois* (Enemy of the Laws) (1893), a novel written between the trilogies, allegiance to *la terre et les morts* is not so easily purchased. Our dead are killers that deal out a fate: 'our malaise arises from precisely the fact that though we are unlike [our forebears], we live in a social world imposed by the dead, not chosen by us. *The dead poison us!*' (4:3). When the past importunes too strongly, Barrès tilts towards the self, and vice versa.[201] Besides, the past is not simply the Other and death, and the self does not exclusively possess vital energy: dialectically, death haunts the self in its isolated, bourgeois autonomy, and life informs the dead. His is an extreme version of Ariès's Romantic cult, with the local and national cemeteries (not excluding tame soldierly acceptance, especially in the war), and with an anchoring community that extends into the historical past. 'What is it therefore that I love in the past? Its sadness, its silence, and above all its fixity' (14:186).

For Philippe, Tiepolo epitomizes the fate of Venice. While not surpassing Bellini, Titian, Tintoretto, and Veronese, each of whom contributed a particular mode of feeling to the Venetian soul, Tiepolo is its 'analyst,' the last survivor who inherits the qualities and completes the picture (1:242). The tradition is still alive in Tiepolo, then expires; with a genius that is 'reflective,' he looks back to a glorious past and ahead into a doubtful future and is saddened. Replete with 'fragmentary reminiscences' of the earlier artists, his vast, shimmering frescoes are 'dazzling' (energizing) and 'melancholy' (debilitating), 'fantasy almost too unexpected'; unity overcomes the antitheses through his 'skeptical' (detached) and 'voluptuous' (embracing) recognition of his moment on the slope of decline. 'Tiepolo contemplates in himself his whole race' and is its 'central conscience'; 'all the souls of Venice are reunited' in his *Caprices* (1:243–4). His art is possessed of the 'floating' quality of Barrèsian Venice. His figures seem to have drifted to their place in the fresco, like images on water, weightless even while seeming volumetric, and stopped – if only for an instant – because the artist has chosen the ideal moment to arrest them. Tiepolo has unlocked something kindred in himself. 'Tiepolo has expressed his melancholy – our own'; 'I recognized his soul – mine'; both are 'concerned with classifying all the emotions which they have felt over the centuries' (*Notes* 8, 10; 1:244). In the Venetian artist Barrès has found the qualities he wanted to cultivate in his art: rhetorical grandeur, cool analysis, the sense of lateness, pleasure, and certainty. 'There is, at the very bottom of our souls, a fixed point, a delicate nerve; if it is probed the result is a total reaction which I cannot mistrust, a movement of my whole being. It is not the awakening of the sensibilities of a mere individual; what frightens me is the awakening of my whole race' (*Scènes* 159) – and the responsibility for interpreting and representing it.

Philippe's hard-won knowledge of the past empowers him in time-present, and his personal contribution to the Lorraine-French Being will modify its future. Pleasure informs the mystical apparition of the soul's future, even while melancholy attends the sense of feeling at the historical end of the line: Venetian art, the French cultural past in modernity, or the contemporary fear of French decline vis-à-vis Germany and England. *Un homme libre* points to a way beyond the self, without denying it; this is why Barrès considered it 'my central expression,' 'a tree planted in my youth and of which I have taken fruit in season after season' (18:106).

Barrès's artistic process resembles the creation of the symbolist *paradis artificiel.* Acolytes gain access to this mystical world of Beauty by interpreting the precisely rendered, highly metaphorical language. It lies above and beyond prosaic reality and ordinary language, which would seem, on first view, to make it off-limits to a travel writer. But as there must be an external setting to the vision, it is 'seen through the poet,' it 'exists in his sensations,' and 'the crisis takes place in him personally.'[202] In Venice he exchanges his Baedeker with its implication of empirical study for spiritual discipline and materials derived from his own impressions. Symbolist art is an attempt at making 'the soul of things visible.'[203] Artists possess hieratic powers: only what 'wakes my dead' (7:14) is meaningful;[204] Goethe and Chateaubriand are 'caryatids' (7:34) of the temple of Venice. 'La mort de Venise' is a 'hymn' (7:9), a 'psalm' (7:23, 54), a 'pilgrimage' (7:22); recurrent metaphors are of embarkation, clearing an obstacle, running past dangers, crossing a threshold, releasing the self (*franchir* [7:18, 23, 59], cognate with 'freedom'), and attaining the 'silence' of mystical perception. 'In quest of the absolute,' the artist finds 'analogues' for this higher reality: Bragadin, Tiepolo, Venice,

Ravenna, Italy, Lorraine, France.[205] With its heightened aura, its working by 'suggestion, connotation, and deliberately indefinite reference,' its avoidance of 'whatever might seem denoted or external,' Barrès's hypotactic prose poetry shares symbolist *fluidité* and 'musicality'; this means not only greater attention to the words' sonic, non-mimetic qualities but to their being 'knit together, flowing, the "words" interacting to the point where they are comparable to a melody in which the alteration of a single note would destroy the effectiveness of the whole.'[206] Venice is the symbolist city above all others for its musicality, which at the outset of his description he acknowledges by a music metaphor: 'The orchestra attacks the prelude' (7:55). Commenting on Wagner's influence, Enzo Caramaschi writes that Barrès works like a musician with just a few key leitmotifs (fever, poison, waking, floating, freedom, slow time, death): 'poetry aspires to attain the musical like a river that loses itself in the ocean.'[207] Musical time, 'not told on dials,' is another device to distance the self from the workaday world.

Just as the Venice of time-present is only a moment in the Venetian soul, and just as Tiepolo is a link in a tradition of Venetian painters, so Philippe, threatened by vertiginous memories and solipsism, anchors himself by deep ties to his personal past and his race. These concepts adumbrate Barrès's historical nationalism: 'When each of us looks over his shoulder, he sees a succession of indefinable mysteries, which in more recent times have come to be called France. We are the sum of a collective life that speaks in us' (*Scènes* 192). In the final volume of the Cult of the Self trilogy, *Le jardin de Bérenice* (The Garden of Berenice) (1891), Philippe finds a practical solution to the question of the self in relation to the Other by entering parliamentary politics: he will lead others, represent others, exhibiting a new-found respect for the soul of the masses. Barrès applauded Saint Simon's remark, 'patriotism is nothing but national egoism' (1:29), and showed a special affinity with artists who engaged in political action: Byron, Wagner, D'Annunzio.[208]

Soucy contends that foreign influences over Barrès diminish in the 1890s as Otherness shrinks to Barrès's specific race and tradition in a narrowly conceived environmental and psychological determinism. This is not yet the case in 'An Education from Italy' (1892) in which Barrès expounds upon Italy as the land of the *moi*: 'If German idealism has given the most profound analysis of the individual ego, it is in Italy that I saw this individualism realized'; the very particularism of Italian history 'protests the excessive centralization which has killed the greater part of a people's originality, or at least their variety' (*Notes* 18). Whereas England and France had only one major city, the large number of Italian cities that stand relatively on the same footing made it easier for individuals to master their environment and advance their self-interest. The republican tradition of the northern Italian communes took its rule 'from the citizens of each generation' (*Notes* 19). Perhaps as a convinced regionalist, Barrès does not fully appreciate how the lack of centralization played a determining role in Italy's decline, leaving it subject to foreign powers and creating the very conditions explored in his travel writings. However, for Soucy, by the time of *Du sang, de la volupté et de la mort* (Of Blood, Pleasure, and Death) (1894) Barrès was heading into his turn towards integral nationalism and becoming more circumspect with regard to foreign influences: 'Italy was to the *moi* what water was to litmus paper, it brought out the essential qualities – French qualities – without adding anything new.'[209]

This statement does not do justice to the interactive quality of Barrès's encounters, nor does it connect the blossoming of his travel writing in these very years to his efforts to extend the boundaries of his sensibility. When Barrès identifies his 'soul' with Venice or Tiepolo ('I recognized his soul – mine'), he means that Venice or Tiepolo have enabled him to discover something of vital importance, of a psychological and spiritual nature, which would have otherwise remained hidden in himself. Even before the decisive turn to integral nationalism, Barrès had been unwilling to let anyone or any place dictate to the self. Wherever he goes in his travels, comments Jules Bertaut, 'he searches for himself.'[210] The Italian cultural heritage provided him with the sensuous and intellectual experience to further that pursuit. Italy was not his *parens* – that was Lorraine and France – but, as he said, the older '*magna parens*,' the 'eternal educator, who continues to soften [subdue, *adoucir*] young barbarians' (5:494). Yet he was no mere vessel into which the sacred wine was poured. He faults the Goncourts for making such an exhaustive description of 'things' (too much objective reportage) and Taine for wanting to extract an 'intellectual system' (too much abstraction) ('The Benefits of a Voyage' [1894]). The point is to render the 'meticulous psychology,' the refinements of awareness:

When we are living in the environment in which we were born, and for which a long succession of our ancestors have prepared us, few things badly wound us or make us feel acutely happy. Our life is a series of repeated efforts against the same difficulties. Our sensations are profound but not unforeseen or precipitated. How much better we feel living in an exotic environment where each day brings us something new to savor or dislike. This multiplicity of small sensations – which after a time becomes singularly destructive and unhealthy – helps us to distinguish the nuances of our personality and at the same time its limits. In the enormous sum of possible sensations a civilization represents, we distinguish very quickly what we can appropriate and what we must reject. In doing so we reveal our true qualities. (*Notes* 30–1, trans. Soucy)

While too much travel, like too much reading, can undermine the self, a certain amount can be healthily absorbed and assimilated. Barrès may err in optimistically assuming one can 'very quickly' determine what one can appropriate or reject.

The strongest argument against Soucy's diminishment of the foreign element as the career wore on is that Barrès wrote his finest travel books *after* his nationalist turn. He is more objective as he gets older and recreates both the essence and the atmosphere of his cities with greater expressive power. His Italian sojourns, which in his early career had played so clarifying a role, figured as significantly in his later one. Earlier, Italy helped teach him the nature of Being; later, a harsher lesson, the nature of non-Being. If he loved the 'fixity' of the past, Italy would teach him that the past itself does not stop living and dying in us, that the past itself can die.

The new lessons commence in his frenzied *Du sang, de la volupté et de la mort* at a midpoint between *Un homme libre* and 'La mort de Venise.' The premise of its 'voyageur lyrique' is that to shake off habit and expand the self one must seek out the opposing, exotic emotions.[211] In an imaginary portrait a Vatican official conducts daily business with efficiency and probity, while privately indulging in the most sordid conduct: his 'marvelous secret' prevents his going sterile, so that Barrès admires the amoral capability of leading multiple lives (Henry James said Barrès had 'an intelligence that was frightening').[212] Where Spain presents an atmosphere of penitential *sang* and ascetic denial that excites ecstatic, animalistic responses to intensify the self, by contrast Italy is 'designed for rather weak, elegant dilettantes' (2:124), decadents suffering from over-refinement, subjectivism, and melancholy, in love with *la mort*. 'Designed' captures the idea of self-conscious artificiality. Italian life 'compels them to sterility in the very way it leaves them to their sensual amusements': their pleasures have no further end than the self and thus become repetitive and deadening. Artists lacking genius can only 'taste pleasure and dally' in 'this atmosphere of paradise' (2:124). As a design for living, Italy either strengthens or destroys the will altogether as by a fatal disease (*fièvres*). Decadence is being used as an experiment against itself.

The dialectic of *sang* and *mort* frames Barrès's commentary on Tuscan art. Following Taine's formula (race, milieu, moment), he argues that 'a people evolves according to the same laws as individuals' (2:153).[213] Painting is the art in which the Tuscan soul fully expresses itself. After sketching the Quattrocento background, he comes to a fork in the road: Leonardo or Michelangelo. This is in Arièsian terms a choice between tame and untamed death. In the Medici and Sistine Chapels Michelangelo defies nature and 'with a brusque *élan* bears us beyond.' Unfinished statues think to themselves, 'What do I wish to become? and their duty, which they impose upon themselves, is to conform, in spite of everything, to their own destiny,' a phrase with a special value to Barrès's Cult of the Self. Michelangelo epitomizes the artist who 'creates a universe' (2:160). By contrast, in *The Last Supper* Leonardo turns away from heroic individualism and towards renunciation and 'acceptance': 'the gesture of the hands and the face, which are, for our constant unworthiness, the most grief-stricken of reproaches, signifies that to understand all and to distinguish the irremediable baseness that lies at the bottom of each of our feelings, the wise one ... pardons all' (2:159–60). Barrès might have pointed to the erosion of geologic form in the background of da Vinci's paintings, signifying the immersion of the human in the nonhuman.

Between *sang* and *mort* is the equivocal *volupté*, stimulating to excitement and teasing to weariness.[214] Autumn has stricken Italy with a perishing beauty: 'here is the country of silence, of the universal effacement of things.' Her greater poetry is not of museums, decorous cities, gardens, and literature; rather, it is 'poetry in a floating state, essential and disengaged from all human change' (2:123); Italy personified has accomplished what Philippe had striven for, the *paradis artificiel*. This partly man-made, diffused beauty haunts Lake Como; the promenades of Pallanza along the shore of Lake Maggiore; and the carefully tended gardens of Isola Bella, from which Watteau's figures might have embarked for Cythera with 'his melancholy, hope in life, and sensuality excited by the unknown' (2:129), and from which 'Tasso's nymphs have disappeared, though their chant still floats over the landscape' (2:131). 'Melancholy' Parma is clad in the 'grey-blue vestments' of October; there Correggio manifests 'the feminine soul in its graduated degrees of nervous contraction to fainting pleasure,' and the dead surrounding Paganini's tomb contrast with the living memory of the fiery violinist and the larger-than-life characters in *The Charterhouse of Parma* (2:137-8). In Pisa near which Byron cremated the body of Shelley, Barrès is pleased not to find a single memorial: 'silence and bareness' are 'eloquence and beauty' (2:147). In Siena, 'solemn and sensuous in its most modest quarters as in its famous promenades' (2:149), Sodoma learned from da Vinci how to portray corporeal pleasure but went further; what in da Vinci is a smile, in Sodoma suffuses the whole body (2:151). In many of the references *volupté* rises to a high degree only to be drained away (*épuisement*, 'exhaustion,' is a repeated word) seemingly without replenishment.

In Barrès's time Ravenna stood in the midst of mud flats and malarial swamps. He came in 1887, two years before Berenson for whom it 'seemed to lie at the bottom of the sea of time ... a footfall made an echo.'[215] An old gardener tends roses at Theodoric's tomb, mingling life and death. Plaques that commemorate where someone was assassinated arouse 'neither curiosity, nor shame, nor pity'; so ancient, they have no connections; history itself can die. Love struggles against death, death wins: 'Was it not here that Byron forced himself to love Guiccioli, to whose bed he finally preferred the tomb?' (2:141). After a fire only a small grove remains of the pine forest that once inspired Dante's vision of the Earthly Paradise: the trees, the 'stagnant water' in and around them, and the 'moaning' of the Adriatic, 'instill in the stroller an idea of eternity'; 'from here, life is nothing more than a distant sound of yapping dogs' (2:142). The crypt of Sant'Apollinare in Classe is filled nearly to the main floor with greenish waste and pungent water: 'things are tired of holding themselves up and want to go where the people already are: under ground' (2:144). Yet men still make bricks from the same red-ochre mud that provided the bricks of the ancient churches.[216] 'Among all these towns, rich with a weighty past,' writes Bertaut, 'will not the palm belong to the most decrepit, the oldest, to that which offers us the most lamentable spectacle of its decomposition under the most joyous, luminous, marvelous sky?'[217] He was thinking of Venice, but Ravenna is even older. Barrès's chapter title, 'Dans le sépulcre de Ravenne,' makes the town its own tomb; its Byzantine mosaic figures are the 'deadest of the dead' (2:141).

In 1898 Barrès's father died, followed in 1901 by his mother. In the period of mourning he conceived of 'La mort de Venise,' a fifty-page travelogue or 'poème symphonique'[218] in which the central themes of his career received consummate expression. It appeared as the first part of *Amori et Dolori sacrum* (Consecrated to Love and Suffering) (1903); the title, taken from an inscription in Santa Maria della Passione, Milan, invokes a dialectic of passion and death found in other essays in the collection, 'Une Impératrice de la Solitude' and 'Le 2 Novembre en Lorraine.'[219] Though he had been to Venice on three occasions, at different times of the year, he has chosen autumn for this most private of visits, and since his subject is dying, he travels alone. Venice is seen at different hours of the day, symbolizing the cycle of a life, a city, and a civilization: a morning ride; a late afternoon and evening tour of the outer islands; and a nocturnal reverie. Since 'Venise' is also the record of the imaginative experience it inspired, Barrès gives half his essay to reflecting upon nine previous visitors, 'shadows that float over the sunsets of the Adriatic' (7:30, 33), including Goethe, Chateaubriand, Byron, Sand, Gautier, Taine, and Wagner. 'Float' conveys the liquid atmosphere and insubstantiality of the 'shadows,' his 'Council of Ten.' He would be the 'candidate' for the tenth seat (7:54); the passage is meant to recall Dante's meeting the five great poets of antiquity in Limbo, 'so that I was the sixth among those high intelligences' (*Inf.* 4.102). These artists 'speak' through Barrès as well as in their own voices and even in music. Beneath Wagner's window in the Palazzo Giustiniani he 'hears' the *Liebstod:* 'When deepest darkness weighs down upon the canals, neither colour nor form appearing, and when the mighty and radiant Church of the Salute itself seems like a ghost, when it is only with difficulty that a silent boat forces the water to form a reflection ..., then the bewitching city finds its own way of piercing the density of night, and from this solemn secret she breathes like a sacred hymn, overwhelming in its desolation and its nostalgia' (7:51).[220]

The narrative perspective of 'La mort de Venise' is most often from a gondola. The undulating prose simulates gliding noiselessly through the canals, the more preferred as they are the more remote, away from the touristic sites that would distract from the intended purpose. Barrès depicts not death *in* Venice, but the death *of* the city itself and, more nearly, the Venice in himself, which stands for the most exquisite, most delicate, yet strongest ties to life, love, and beauty. Aspects of the city are a mimesis of his soul where he achieves his stated goal of making 'his external life conform to his internal life' (7:35).[221] The incandescent imagery and fluctuant rhythms of this symbolist elegy convey the experience not so much of death – Ravenna was dead – as of dying, and dying so slowly and among such beauty that it allays fears and wears down resistance, comes at one from all sides, becomes a matter of analysis, reconciliation, and even ennui (a boy, aged ten and stricken with a terrible illness, said to his father: 'it bores me to die' [7:56]).

The Venice of the casual traveller and collector of curious beauties, the market atmosphere in the Piazzetta next to the doge's palace, the ceremonies, the museums, these hold no interest for him on this visit. Nor does he come imploring death, like the neurotic crying, 'When will your sword emerge from its scabbard? Strike then, O beauty!' (7:14). He is not exhausted – he is more intensely alive. Also, the republican tradition, the commercial empire, and Venetian history mean little compared to his own 'natural overlords,' the 'adventurous cavaliers of Burgundy and Champagne' (7:15), such as Godfrey of Boulogne, Duke of Lower Lorraine, one of the leaders of the First Crusade and the hero of Tasso's *Gerusalemme liberate* (8:312). Further, like Ruskin, Barrès denounces the architectural restorations and admits the contradiction between his lamenting the end of Venice and yet not wanting it brought back to life. Restored luxury leaves him cold; the mystery has disappeared. The fourteenth-century Cà d'Oro once awoke 'pleasure' of a 'dolorous quality,' opposing his 'fevers' to its 'graces'; the antithesis contains one of his motifs, 'dying beauty which excites us to enjoy life' (7:22).[222] Then financial help rescued the 'home of Ariel' until the 'airy abode no longer begs for pity, it claims our admiring homage' (7:16). When the campanile of St Mark's crumbled to the ground in 1902, Barrès opposed its reconstruction. The collapse proved his theory.[223]

All of this has been by way of prelude and regards what he does not seek in Venice; now he arrives. Venice, which 'always made me feverish' in the past (7:14), greets him viscerally as he descends the steps of the train station to the gondolas, and a breeze from the lagoon hits him with its taste of morbidity: 'in vain am I immunized by quinine, I feel millions of bacteria reawakening in me. Every poison that was lying dormant in me recaptures its virulence' (7:55). What had been the conclusion of his earlier travelogues becomes his starting point; the essence of Italy is Venice, and the essence of Venice is 'sensual sadness' or 'sensual melancholy' (*tristesse volupteuse, tristesse melancholique*) (7:14, 15):

This city's power over its dreamers is that, along its livid canals, walls of Byzantine, Saracen, Lombard, Gothic, Renaissance, and even Rococo making, overgrown with moss, reach, under the action of sun, rain, and storm, the equivocal turning-point where, more encumbered from their very artistic grace, they begin their decomposition. So it is with some roses and magnolias which never possess more intoxicating fragrance or show more intense coloration than at the moment when death projects onto them its secret sparks and sets our minds swirling. (7:15)

The prose is a simultaneous journey through the canals and through the mind of the lyrical voyager, to the point where the gradual dissolution of the one reflects the other. 'Sparks' (*fusées*) are the small reflections of light on the canal waters, hardly able to illuminate anything more than themselves, but also the mental illuminations that accumulate in the gondola's journey; and *fusées*, the title of Baudelaire's uncollected writings, underlines the artistic contributions to the Venetian experience. Such passages represent an advance in expressive power over *Un homme libre* where he had put down the 'external beauty' of the city in favour of his psychological recreations. Now his willingness to share the palm with his object has both increased his acuteness of perception and strengthened his *moi*. One 'sees' less in the novel than the prose poem 'because its ideology leaves one less to see.'[224] Towards the end, the 'fever' in Venice is like a stick of dynamite: 'All is broken, it flies into the air; then nothingness' (7:59). The spark has become dynamite to the psyche.

In the forgotten quarters and the 'secondary ways, narrow, obscure, mysterious, serpentine,' like an active agent Venice 'conducts its hidden business' (7:21) with the help of sun, rain, wind, and time. Did Barrès choose the Gothic church of Sant'Alvise (1388) for his morning goal because it was, Lorenzetti writes, 'one of the most distant and solitary spots in Venice' where 'grass sprouts and everything has an almost countrified air,' or because it was dedicated to the French saint, Louis, Bishop of Toulouse?[225] So accessible by gondola are even the farthest districts that it pleases him to say he can reach Sant'Alvise in twenty minutes from anywhere in the city: the most secret truths are near at hand. He raises his eyes to the palaces of the Grand Canal, Venice at its apogee, then chooses to pursue 'the little pathways of stone or water – *rio, fondamenta, salizzada, calle* – that slowly pursue their regression' (7:16). The Venetian words, with their strangeness and technical precision, evoke an aura better than lengthy descriptions, a symbolist technique. Street cries, clopping wooden sandals, lapping water, sounds remain distinct within the 'great silence' (7:17), for the silence of Venice is the absence of the muffled roar of the European metropolis, not the absence of sound in itself. For Barrès, the sounds of Venice are like the trills of forest birds that do not interrupt but deepen the sense of repose. Moreover, nothing to the eye is 'uncertain or confused' in the images of solid things, though sea and sky present palpitating, ever-shifting, ever-mingling, non-tactile surfaces. Anticipating Pound, Barrès extols the 'inestimable vividness of these sensations which come with abundance to steep our organism in a delicious hyperaesthesia'; where a dry climate might make such a nervous tension unbearable, Venice 'bathes the nerves, keeping them alive': a 'slow death' (7:17, 18).

At length he reaches Sant'Alvise, 'exquisite and defenseless' as a 'modest woman,' a hint of Decadent sadism; she cannot withstand the elements of sun and damp, 'but for me in this prolonged agony lies the most powerfully seductive charm of Venice' (7:21). So often in his travelling, one goal substitutes for another; the church's three Tiepolo masterpieces engage Barrès's attention less than what he believed, on Ruskin's attribution, to be works of Carpaccio's childhood. ('Ruskin attributed them, absurdly, to Vittore Carpaccio, then a child of eight or ten'; they are now thought to have been painted by an unknown pupil of Carpaccio's teacher Lazzaro Bastiani.)[226] A new theme, or rather counter-theme, rises from the Barrèsian orchestration, that of the innocent child: 'tourists inclined by their temperament, feminine gender, Anglican religion, and especially their virginity to put up with Ruskinian chatter will have the fullest pleasure if they remember that when he was working on these daubings, sweet child of the people in a picturesque costume, he certainly resembled the street urchins on the campo Sant'Alvise who lie in wait for a gondola and run to find the sacristan to have him open the door of the church' (7:20–1). Barrès would expect his readers to recall Carpaccio's most famous paintings, the *Legend of St. Ursula* series depicting the child and young martyr, now in the Accademia in Venice. Ruskin loved Carpaccio as the last exemplar of the fresh, pure Venice as opposed to the mature, luxuriant corruption of Veronese. For Barrès, the public buildings and palazzi do not move him so much as the slight but persistent micro-'shocks' that these ordinary impressions have on him, 'when disintegration liberates beauties and unexpected harmonies that contain its earliest perfections' (7:21).

Meandering among the last canals and then exiting onto the broad lagoons is 'like opening a breach' where wind and silence 'prophesy the end of Venetian civilization.' The wind off the lagoons is another of those sounds that conspire so well with silence, the natural force above and beyond the visitor, who may hear in it a reminder of mortality, as it functions in Fellini's films. San Michele, Murano, Mazzorbo, Burano, Torcello, the Island of Women, and St Francis-in-the-Desert are the islands on which 'men formerly tried out several Venices; the present city may read its own destiny in them as with maquettes (7:22). The afternoon journey begins with the cemetery on San Michele, the 'island of the dead,' which reminds him of Böcklin's painting. Yet while the artist evoked tragic feeling by means of lombard poplars, cypresses, slabs of stone, black waters, and 'silence,' he missed the joy of the idle gondoliers who stood about joking on the wharves. 'To despair of our final dwelling place, it is not necessary to surround it by general horror,' Barrès responds mordantly, 'that is to flatter ourselves, and it is a lie; instead make me see the indifference: only two or three helpless people weep and they themselves are soon swept away, so that for our little clan it is exactly as if we never existed' (7:23).

In search of 'stranger,' 'more funereal' impressions, as if to approach a vanishing point, he passes on to Murano whose canals are lined by dilapidated palaces taken over by industrial companies. These once elegant buildings should have met a dignified death instead of being attacked by fetid 'pusses' depriving them of repose and anonymity. Open sewers run where rooms had once been filled with 'music, poetry, and love' (7:24). Repulsed (for once!), he seeks the more distant islands, crossing 'vast liquid spaces ... sad as the Roman Campagna,' with a 'desolation almost palpable and heavy, like true beauty' (7:25). Mazzorbo and Burano lie ahead on the lagoon like 'water-lilies.' Barrès could not possibly have seen all these islands by gondola in the time allotted – this is a composite visit.

Sixteenth-century doge Andrea Contarini prided himself for having spurned the blandishments of the Benedictine nuns on Mazzorbo.[227] 'These pleasing beautiful souls, without a doubt as fat as their quails, have long since augmented the island's soil with their sinful flesh.' They survive in the 'pomegranate trees,' 'figs,' and 'vigorous' ivy (7:25), emblems of death and fertility. Since the Catholic Barrès did not believe (at least, at this time) in the resurrection of the body, his metaphors of decomposition are always sinister and more violent even than Thomas Hardy's in poems like 'Drummer Hodge' or 'Transformations.' In the branches Barrès sees 'the lovely arms of the impenitent nuns reaching up over the banks in the overhanging acacias' (7:25), as if still enticing, and still refusing to change their ways. His espousal of *la terre et les morts* enables him to project these tactile feelings into the soil itself, so close to death that he is kin: 'I said to the sepulcher that it is my father; to the worm, you are my mother and my sister' (7:55). On Burano different impressions await: 'misery begets filthiness': outside impoverished houses lining the banks, while their husbands fish in the lagoons, the lace-makers sit and ruin their eyes to make precious embroideries. They too sacrifice for the sake of beauty. 'These poor people rot their earth which in turn rots the lagoons. In this nest of mud, I wished the desolation would increase to a point where humanity would disappear from the site where it can no longer nourish itself.' This alone would break the cycle. The essay reaches its first peak: 'Death took nothing away from a spectacle of which it made its own magnificence' (7:25).

Soon after, 'having navigated ... though this eternal silence,' his gondola arrives at Torcello 'fixed in a death as strong as Ravenna's,' and he wends through a canal to the Cathedral of Santa Maria Assunta, Santa Fosca, and the Baptistery. A woman wearing 'long veils,' who seemed in a hurry to return home 'to sit up late by a cadaver' (to 'wake,' *veiller*), opens the door of Santa Maria, whose mustiness is at first almost suffocating. The sun strikes the pavement, a sign of *Rest in peace*, then the door slams shut from a sudden breeze, and the claustrophobic moment is like being shut in a tomb. In a series of antitheses, he comments on witnessing the 'purity' and 'youthfulness' of the early monuments of Venetian culture in 'eternal November'; 'Torcello's unhealthy mud' and 'three sepulchers' (7:26) contrast with 'the Pisan plain where the Duomo, the Baptistery, the Leaning Tour, and Campo Santo keep a spring as sweet as a Sicilian April' (7:26). While Pisa is a marvel of new invention, Torcello adhers to ancient tradition, both teaching that 'man receives his motives of action from tombs and cradles' (7:27). Torcello rose from the ruins of Altina, which was built by those fleeing the Huns. As it declined, Venice rose. Intruding on these distant thoughts are noisy children playing and crowding the sides of the canal as his gondola departs. He cannot imagine anything 'more pitiable or abandoned' as they chase along the canal, beseeching him to buy some four-leaf clovers. 'Enchanted by my credulity, they scream and wreak havoc all around; but my gondola is already too far away, and these unfortunate merchants of happiness stretch out in vain their fists full of talismans' (7:27). Here as elsewhere Barrès proves his originality, hard to do in writing on Venice.

Once the site of beautiful churches, the Island of Women is a nest of serpents and thieves, on which bodies were once buried indiscriminately. Here the remains of Doge Marino Faliero, assassinated in 1355 for attempting to overthrow the aristocratic oligarchy, were translated, his final 'humiliation,' a pun on the Latin *humilis* (lowly) and *humus* (earth). Heaps of organic matter on the island were later used industrially to refine sugar, and about this time Byron's *Marino Faliero* furnished material for Donizetti: 'To end up in molasses and an opera libretto is too much of a platitude': Barrès would rather lie in Jezebel's charnel house, where he could at least satisfy the hunger of her dogs (7:27–8). Still farther on, he peers down to locate the sunken town of Anania – divers have visited the houses. A symbolist topos, it recalls the Breton legend of Ys,

the magnificent city drowned by the tide for its sins. Suddenly music
crosses the lagoon, and made aware of the hour, he visits the last island,
St Francis-in-the-Desert, where by legend the saint tarried on his way
back from Egypt. Then the birds sang so loudly that he asked them to be
quiet till he could finish his prayers. Where in Umbria his request would
have been taken as 'a sign of gentility,' in this setting it was 'completely
devastating.' The birds never sang again.

At sunset, the time of 'busiest unrest,''monstrous spiders' struggle
to bind themselves by their filaments to puny shrubs and crabs hoist
themselves from the water: precise correspondences for the unpleasant,
non-human, and obscure forces of nature. No other subject is suitable
in this zone but the 'preparation for death' (7:28). The swamp pools surrounding St Francis-in-the-Desert are 'deader than anything ...'; and at
this zero point he realizes that he must hasten back, 'warned that the day
was coming to an end by the torrents of blood mingling together on the
lagoon.' Now unfolds the tragedy's final act, Barrès abandons the pose
of indifference (never entirely convincing) and expresses with all his
artistry the grandeur of his return to an utterly transformed Venice: 'did
not the sun, in abandoning her [Venice], wish to leave behind only an
assassinated beauty?' (7:29). In an optical illusion that becomes visionary, he 'floats' on the sky's reflection on the water. 'Fantastic colorations
succeeded one another with a power to move the most unworthy soul,'
urging final repentance. The *moi* is now submerged in the 'we'; the self
is at such a distance as to be in another world, the mystic impersonality
of the symbolist:

> There were so many somber degrees of the color scale and deep greens
> which are only in the mysterious canals; so many yellows, oranges, and
> blues with which the Japanese decorators play. While in the west the sky was
> liquefying in a burning sea, above our heads some clouds intoxicated by
> magnificence were perpetually renewing their shapes, and the crepuscular
> light penetrated them, saturated them with its innumerable flames. Their
> colors, so tender and excruciating by this lyric fire, reflected upon the la-
> goon, as if to make us glide upon the sky. They covered us, they bore us away,
> they enveloped us by a splendor as complete as, I can say, it was palpable.
> Vanquished by these grand magicians, we lost any notion of the real, when at
> last some dark stains appeared, grew larger on the waters, then gathered us
> within their shadows. They were the monuments of the doges. (7:29)

If the essay's first peak was the death of Venice, the second, greater one is its apocalypse. The sky liquefies, the water takes fire, the world turns upside down, the many-coloured reflections seem the vehicle of the final journey. Relating the city to the East, the Japanese decorators and the other references to artifice, sorcery, and theatricality underline the imaginary nature of the voyage. Yet, not merely the end of a day, it is the end of Venetian art with its striking chromaticism, often linked to the city's atmospheric effects, now reducing to colourless shadow. 'Vanquished,' with no 'notion of the real,' Barrès comes upon what appear first as 'dark stains,' then 'within their shadows,' the extended reflections of the city of the dead. The realization occurs in the concluding sentence, which, following so much hypotaxis, comes as a paratactic exclamation point. 'Monuments' of the doges, not buildings, suggests commemoration, from the Latin 'monere' meaning both to remind and to warn. Immersed, from above and below, in the spectrum of colour, Barrès witnesses the final loss, when God takes back His first gift, *light*, sending the sun 'to declare with its last ray: "And now, forget; it is not necessary that certain things be revealed"' (7:30).

Having risen from the sepulchral islands *to* or *in* Venice, Barrès feels the 'stupor,' 'regret,' and 'stiff achiness such as Lazarus felt' on his return to the living world. Normally epic writers, not travel writers, undertake the journey to the dead. On their return the heroes feel reborn or twice-born and ready to take on new challenges like Odysseus's defeating the suitors or Aeneas's establishing a city. Instead, Barrès is disempowered, his self is catapulted by the negative sublime onto the steps before the monuments of the doges.

But now the palazzi have closed their blinds and windows, as if to hide their crimes and shame, 'dishonored' for having permitted such decline. Venice 'chants an eternal opera to the Adriatic,' a reminder that for a century the city had been the center of innovation in opera. Barrès imagines catching a last glimpse of Jezebel behind a loggia. Is she the 'old corruptress' or a 'sacrificial virgin' that he hears singing? 'In the morning, sometimes, I hear Iphigeneia but evening's blushes cast my thoughts back to Jezebel' (7:55). The Greco-Roman and Judeo-Christian traditions contribute their imagery to the end of a long chapter in the history of the West. His sensibility having been stretched to its extremes, Barrès stands on the brink, ready to 'plunge into an abyss of ineffable lassitude' (7:59). Then, in a phrase his feelings crystallize: 'Désespoir d'une beauté qui s'en va vers la mort' (Despair for beauty that departs towards death) (7:59). Unusual for his writing, the sentence fragment lacks a verb, as if he wanted to extract the last trace of energy and achieve a static moment outside of time, the perfectly expressed symbol. Surrounding it, the chant echoes in his memory, informs the attenuated prose rhythm, and is answered by his final apostrophe delivered pianissimo to the city now engulfed by its waters. 'Sleep, Venice, under your lagoon. The plaint sings still, but the beautiful mouth is dead. The ocean rolls in the night, and its waves break into foam, orchestrating the eternal motif of dying from too great a love of life' (7.59).

chapter 4

From Italophilia to Italophobia:
Italian Americans in the Gilded Age

JOHN PAUL RUSSO

There were Italians and Italian Americans in American literature before the Civil War, and they figure significantly in twentieth-century American literature.[1] Nonetheless, one may second a remark by Richard Brodhead: 'Never before or since has American writing been so absorbed with the Italian as it is during the Gilded Age.'[2] By far the larger part of this fascination expressed the desire for high culture and gentility, an 'aesthetic-touristic' attitude towards Italy exemplifying 'High Cosmopolitan Civilization.' It resulted in a flood of travelogues, memoirs, historical novels, poems, etc., peaking at the turn of the century and declining after World War I. The golden age of travel writing lasted from 1880 to 1914, and for many Americans in these years one of the richest treasures was Italy. This chapter, however, focuses upon Brodhead's other category, the Italian immigrant as 'alien-intruder' exemplifying 'Low Domestic Barbarism.' Travel writing's golden age corresponded exactly with the period of greatest Italian emigration to the United States. The causes of this negative attitude went back several generations before the arrival of the mass of Italian immigrants: 'economic transformations that had been underway at least since the 1830s had produced, by the mid-1880s, a sense of widespread crisis in America ... the new, more 'foreign' immigrant of the 1880s could easily be read as the cause of the painful changes of the present.'[3] Shortly after the Civil War, Italian immigrants appear on the margins of American fiction. Their representation would change dramatically with each passing decade, a warning paradigm of how quickly the stereotypes of one culture can be reshuffled by another.[4]

Among American writers William Dean Howells was well suited to portray the fortunes of the Italian immigrant. He possessed broad social sympathies, a Midwesterner's curiosity in the burgeoning cities on the

Eastern seaboard, and a realist orientation in fiction. For having written
a campaign biography on Lincoln, he was rewarded with a consulship in
Venice (1861–4).[5] Subsequently he published *Venetian Life* (1866) and
Italian Journeys (1867), which won the praise of James Russell Lowell and
Charles Eliot Norton; the Venetian sketches, over 450 closely printed
pages, are 'the most careful and picturesque *study* I have ever seen on any
part of Italy,' wrote Lowell; 'they are the thing itself.'[6] Howells's originality consisted in examining the middle and artisanal classes, everyday work
habits, entertainments, housekeeping, marriage and funerals, foods,
and local customs; 'his way of seeing Venice was transformed from one
of exclusively visual externality to one of dramatic involvement, vision
enlarged by language.'[7] A strong admirer of the Risorgimento, Howells
offered a written panegyric when he could not attend an event in honour of Italian Unification in New York: 'the liberation of Italy is a fact
that all real Americans will celebrate with you ... since the citizen of every
free country loves Italy next to his own land, and feels her prosperous
fortune to be to the advantage of civilization.'[8] In 1870 he delivered the
Lowell Lectures in Boston on 'Modern Italian Poets';[9] he taught at Harvard on the same subject, and periodically reviewed Italian literature. His
Italian was so good, better than that of most Cambridge Italophiles, that
he allows one of his fictional immigrants, a Trieste journalist, 'as if too
zealous for the honor of his beautiful language to endure a hurt to it,' to
correct the narrator's verbal blunder in warning of the dog: 'Morde, non
morsica, signore!' ('Bites, not nibbles, signore!').[10] Howells's knowledge
of Italy and Italians provided him with an ideal vantage point from which
to survey the immigrants and their confrontation with Americans and
other ethnic groups.

In Venice Howells had become engrossed in Carlo Goldoni's realist
drama with its wide variety of professional, middle- and lower-class characters. It was a passion that lasted through his life. Situated within a bourgeois perspective, Goldoni printed 'transcripts from life' and maintained
'simple truthfulness' in his portrayals of 'average' persons, which can
'deepen into powerful situations.' Howells did not seek 'great ethical or
aesthetical proportions,' admiring instead how Goldoni worked within
his limitations, never betraying common sense, nor trying to prove that
'suffering of one kind can atone for wrong of another.' A neoclassic in
his ideal of instruction and delight, he is 'almost English, almost American, indeed, in his observance of the proprieties'; and though propriety
is not morality, it ranks among the 'good things.'[11] James L. Woodress
only slightly exaggerates when he claims that Goldoni, 'more than any

other writer, turned him from Romantic poet into prose Realist.'[12] Four
of Howells's ten travel books concern Italy and five of his three dozen
novels have an Italian setting. Many characters in his other novels have
visited it and discuss it. Moreover, Italian immigrants appear in five of
his novels with an American setting. [13] His first work of fiction, *Suburban
Sketches* (1871), is sprinkled with ethnics of various race and nationality.

The episodes in this little book take place mostly a few miles from Boston, across the Charles River in the fictional suburb of 'Charlesbridge'
– Cambridge, where Howells lived from 1866 to 1877. Its ten chapters
treat the urban growth and social dislocation following the Civil War.
Charlesbridge is a place of mixing, between city and country, upper and
lower classes, Yankee and immigrant, one ethnic group and another. The
onomatopoetic title of one chapter, 'Flitting,' about setting up or breaking up house, captures something new in the air: that the 'fundamental
reality of modern American life was its impermanency.'[14] 'Doorstep Acquaintance,' another sketch, conveys transience, borders, superficiality,
and informality. The expansion of the suburbs, their ethnic quarters,
public spaces, street life, festivals, and transportation, these provide the
background and in some cases the main matter for the book. The narrator's study of horse-car passengers anticipates Basil March's meditations
on the elevated train to the Lower East Side in *A Hazard of New Fortunes*.

Collected from brief essays in the *Nation* and the *Atlantic* in the previous years, Howells gives the Italians space out of proportion to their
numbers in the late 1860s. This may reflect his fond familiarity with Italians and his willingness to defend and excuse them. Besides, it was only
a step from writing about Italians in their own country to writing about
them in the United States. Kenneth Lynn, like Woodress, thinks that it
was 'comparatively easy' for Howells to make the transition.[15] In fact,
the sketches show him grappling with the presentation of ethnics in the
midst of American customs and prejudices; his narrator is in some sense
his foil. This is not the case in his travelogues, where he writes in his
own voice. Yet the Italophiles were convinced that Howells had brought
the suburbs to life, as he had with Italy; indeed, in some sketches he was
mixing Italy and the suburbs together. In 1869 James Russell Lowell expressed his own pleasure upon reading 'Doorstep Acquaintance,' citing
Sara Eliot Norton's praise of it: 'I am not quite sure whether Cambridge
is in Italy – though, now I think of it, I know Italy is sometimes in Cambridge!'[16]

The narrator of *Suburban Sketches* has 'had the fortune to serve his
country' in Venice (91) and has just returned to America. He is set-

ting up house in a new section of a suburb and shares the novelty with his fellow suburbanites, which is a convenient levelling device. His Italian enables him to speak to immigrants with relative ease; dialects never seem to present a problem, perhaps somewhat implausibly in view of their diversity. Yet Howells had spent four years in Italy and knew his way around the language. In short, the narrator is closely modelled on Howells himself. At the same time, as with Washington Irving and his fictional 'Geoffrey Crayon,' Howells distances himself from his narrator and his materials, ethnic or otherwise, and this distance permits a gently satiric treatment of traits, foibles, and stereotypes.

The sketch of Ferry Street in 'Doorstep Acquaintance' is among the earliest portraits of an Italian neighbourhood in American fiction.[17] 'Ferry' means a passage over water, with the implication of regularity: Italians have crossed over, more are coming, yet one of Howells's themes is the Italian desire to return to Italy. Because they had left the home country for economic reasons, not on account of religious or political persecution, repatriation was common, distinguishing them from all other immigrant groups. As many as half of the so-called birds-of-passage Italians at the height of immigration repatriated, though some of them returned to America either permanently or on a seasonal basis.[18] Ferry Street is situated in Boston's North End, by the wharves, 'since the 1840s the first place of settlement for the poorest immigrants.'[19] The original of Ferry Street might be Ferry Way, off Prince Street, and now absorbed into Commercial Street; during the seventeenth and eighteenth centuries, a nearby ferry took people across to Charlestown.[20] In the late 1860s a single street, with perhaps a few side streets, suffices to contain a future Little Italy.

The winter setting emphasizes the displacement of the Italians 'born to a happier clime' (37) and balances any tendency to romance by a framing image with a realist bite. 'It was winter even there ...' (36) begins the sketch. 'Even': as if to say the collective and colourful Italian presence in Ferry Street cannot dispel the snows and chill of New England:

> It was winter even there in Ferry Street, in which so many Italians live that one might think to find it under a softer sky and in a gentler air, and which I had always figured in a wide unlikeness to all other streets in Boston,– with houses stuccoed outside, and with gratings at their ground-floor windows; with mouldering archways between the buildings, and at the corners feeble lamps glimmering before pictures of the Madonna; with weather-beaten shutters flapping overhead, and many balconies from which hung the linen

swathings of young infants, and love-making maidens furtively lured the velvet-jacketed, leisurely youth below: a place haunted by windy voices of blessing and cursing, with the perpetual clack of wooden-heeled shoes upon the stones, and what perfume from the blossom of vines and almond-trees, mingling with less delicate smells, the travelled reader pleases to imagine. I do not say that I found Ferry Street actually different from this vision in most respects; but as for the vines and almond-trees, they were not in bloom at the moment of my encounter with the little tambourine-boy. As we stood and talked, the snow fell as heavily and thickly around us as elsewhere in Boston. (37)

While the Italians make Ferry Street look like an ordinary street in an Italian town, in Boston it is an extraordinary 'vision,' an imaginative re-presentation of the concrete, in this case overturning Yankee Boston in the very site of its origins by the wharves. Ferry Street differs from 'all other streets' in the city because it is 'haunted' by Italy. The people have their own sacred imagery in this quintessential Puritan town (with its distaste for religious icons): the Madonna (queen of heaven as opposed to the Calvinistic Father-God). There are noise-making (instead of bour-geois quiet) and cursing (potential violence); clutter (and by implication dirtiness); perfume (sensuousness) and 'less delicate' odours (smells of urine, strong cooking, as of primitive encampments); 'leisurely' conduct (laziness instead of the work ethic); and Romeo and Juliet figures (al-most figurines) as symbols of art and breakaway sexuality. Though the negatives lurk on and just beneath the surface and give a disturbing ten-sion to the narrator's 'vision,' the general impression is that Italians suc-ceed in making themselves at home in an otherwise hostile environment.

As it opened with a winter image, the passage ends abruptly with a second winter image, as if to enclose the picture of enchantment within a sturdy realist frame. The implied contrast is between communal life and pleasure on the one hand, and coldness and fatality on the other. One long sentence (143 words) continually unfolds and extends itself, sending out imaginative tendrils in all directions, hardly able to contain the richness and plenitude of the street scene of which the syntax is a mimesis. Two shorter sentences (39 and 18 words) convey the narrator's mental return to the winter's day.

No immigrant emerges from *Surburban Sketches* as a fully formed, com-plex character, and many are no more than picturesque stereotypes in the Anglo-American cultural tradition.[21] Nonetheless, some are conceived with sufficient imaginative force to establish a point of human contact;

many are given dialogue, which is facilitated by the Italian-speaking narrator, upholding a canon of realist fiction.[22] The Italian immigrants are associated with peddling, vagabondage, street entertainments, child-like joy, and uncomplicated pleasures. Though Americans in Italy complained unceasingly of the *lazzaroni* and nasty beggars, Howells in Charlesbridge does not object to panhandling. As for idleness, the 'children of the summer' (35) (thus Howells refers to adult Italians) protest that the lack of English prevents their 'practicing some mechanical trade': "What work could be harder," they ask, "than carrying this organ about all day?"' (35). Yet the narrator thinks that they protest too much and love their open-air life. Open, but not countrified; Italians are a town-oriented people, even if their town had been a small southern village. With typical American bonhomie (and gentle irony) the narrator calls them 'friends'; yet they are barely 'acquaintances' and he does not expect to see them again. They are a displaced instance of the picturesque, a 'vision' constantly undercut by their being out of place, and this opposition between romance and realism is intensified by the Italians' and the narrator's capacity to find themselves at home and take pleasure wherever they are.

One 'friend' is a coal-heaver in winter and an organ-grinding 'troubadour' in summer: the opposition of industrial drudge and carefree singer corresponds to the seasons with their alternation of death and life that had characterized the Ferry Street 'vision.' The friend's 'lazy,' 'soft-eyed' boy, who collects coins with his tambourine, announces that the family has enough money to return to Italy. His mother is an 'invalid' and 'must be taken home' (37), as if to die. Many of the immigrants are 'sick' for home; one recalls that nostalgia was originally diagnosed as a disease (of sailors, to be precise). With one exception, the immigrants say nothing of economic necessities that have driven them across the sea, and do not complain about them, nor does Howells question them on the matter. The exception is the journalist from Trieste, then under Austrian rule; having left his 'ungrateful land' (44) for political reasons, he had worked under Maximilian in Mexico, then fled following the emperor's execution and made his way across the United States. He is the immigrant without a country. Though in 'a tone of bitter and worldly cynicism' (44) the journalist voices unspecified criticism, he sings a Venetian barcarole at the thought of repatriating himself.

Another 'friend' is a chestnut-roaster from Tuscany who sells twice as many chestnuts for the same money as could be bought from an English-speaking merchant. In other words, he is not trying to undersell his competitors but simply lacks business sense, at least in America, where language is a problem. Many Italians failed to learn English because they lived in the hope of speedy repatriation. Yet they paid dearly for their failure, as they could not find more remunerative jobs that would hasten their return. The disincentive for learning English had another untoward consequence: 'the tendency of Southern Italian immigrants to return to Italy and their cultural and physical isolation from Boston's Yankee culture made them particularly unsuitable American citizens.'[23] Howells depicts the immigrants from all over Italy, not just southern Italians, as clinging tenaciously to their native language. The chestnut-roaster addresses the narrator in Tuscan, as if unaware that 'Tuscan is not the dialect of Charlesbridge' (38). The tacit assumption is that there is 'no other tongue in the world but Italian' and that this 'makes all the earth and air Italian for the time' (39) – another instance of the at-home-in-the-world theme recurrent in Howells's treatment. The narrator enjoys speaking in Italian because it 'flatters [him] with an illusion' of being in Italy; if he stood and stared in astonishment, even a moment, at the chestnut-roaster's speaking to him in Italian, the pleasing illusion would vanish and their exchange would shrink to 'vulgar reality' (39). The ingenuous 'swarthy fruiterer' in *The Rise of Silas Lapham* is 'not surprised when he is addressed in his native tongue' by a Boston Brahmin Italophile.[24]

With his wares before him on the ground, an 'image-dealer' from Lucca reclines before a meeting house and answers questions, at his own speed, as he drops morsels of food into his mouth. He barely notices the busy life that goes on around him. Although the narrator is amused, his Yankee neighbours would probably have disdained the lack of ambition and industry. In quiet sympathy with him, however, the narrator becomes an image-dealer, too, as he imagines the peddler 'doing his best' to transform the meeting house into the 'cathedral' of Lucca, the piazza of which 'probably has a fountain and statuary' and is 'not like our square, with a pump and horse-trough in the midst' (40). Again, romance balances realism. And to compensate for the lack of romance, the Cambridge square has a 'towering' elm tree: if Italy has art, America has nature. The Italian peddles plaster statuettes of Apollo, classical deities, and 'Canovan dancers': paganism and Dionysian life. As the narrator thinks, the Puritans beneath their 'moss-grown headstones' in the cemetery would start if they saw such eroticism in their midst. The occasionally iconoclast Puritans prized the biblical Word above colourful imagery, the mark of Roman Catholic culture.

Among the other immigrants is an old Lombard scissors-grinder, an anarchist 'very red in his sympathies' (42), who had worked in Naples and Athens before coming to America. He also wants to repatriate 'per goder un po' di clima prima di morire' (to enjoy a bit of good weather before dying) (41). He marvels at the new Boston Public Library, designed by McKim, Mead, and White after a Renaissance palazzo, and recently opened, from which he, a poor man, may borrow books. The narrator shows his embarrassment that the immigrant knows more than himself about American history, from having studied Carlo Giuseppe Botta's *History of the War of the Independence of the United States of America* (1809), the most celebrated account until George Bancroft's *History of the United States* began appearing in the 1830s.[25] An elderly Genoese lady, who has delicate manners and the face of a child expressing 'kindliness' and 'sympathy,' sells pins and needles, thread, tape, 'and the like *roba*' (45), and she trusts people so much that she does not even count the money paid her; again, the narrator drops in the occasional Italian word. Wondering how she manages to eke out a living from her basket, he recalls Italian simplicity and economy from his days abroad. The lady will not end the conversation before she graciously offers two or three tiny gifts from her now seemingly boundless basket, which takes on a magical quality: 'the truth is, we Northern and New World folk cannot help but cast a little romance about whoever comes to us from Italy, whether we have actually known the beauty and charm of that land or not' (45).

Despite having been cheated of his wages and left destitute in South America, the 'swarthiest' of Neapolitan organ-grinders possesses 'that lightness of temper which seems proper to most northern Italians, whereas those from the south are usually dark-mooded, sad-faced men' (though they have 'fine eyes,' they are 'not so handsome as the Italians of the north') (50). 'South' connotes trouble in Howells's text: South America, the U.S. South, southern Italy. 'Brahmins distinguished between Northern and Southern Italians from the very beginning of the Southern Italian invasion of Boston in the 1880's,' John F. Stack observes. For the Brahmins, only northern Italians were 'part of Western civilization'; their 'Germanic blood and artistic achievements sharply distinguished them from the ignorant peasants of Southern Italy.'[26] *Suburban Sketches* shows this distinction already in place a decade earlier. The narrator's stereotyping of the Neapolitans as sad and sullen deliberately contradicts their reputation for cheerfulness and amiability. 'Nothing surpasses for unstudied misanthropy of expression the visages of different Neapolitan harpers who have visited us; but they have some right to their dejected countenances as being of a yet half-civilized stock, and as real artists and men of genius' (50). Again, the narrator indulges in Romantic primitivism, which he mocks gently in calling them 'artists' and 'men of genius,' who are conventionally saturnine. Yet Howells is not deceived by appearances: however rough in look, the Neapolitans are 'not so surly at heart as they look' (50). In the late 1860s and early 1870s, when perhaps a thousand Italians lived in Boston, there was not yet the preponderance of southern Italians, so they do not dominate Howells's panoramic sweep. The immigrants of *Suburban Sketches* are drawn rather evenly from the entire length of the peninsula.

As if to subvert the defensive pose implied by 'doorstep acquaintance,' the narrator remarks that he invited one Italian acquaintance into his home. Glad 'but not ... surprised' (38) to be greeted in Italian, she is the widow of a 'Vesuvian lunatic,' Giovanni Cascamatto ('crazy helmut'), who kept setting fire to their homes until he perished in a blaze, another pejorative allusion to the fiery southern temperament. Yet the widow epitomizes 'tranquil courtesy.' Since her 'object in coming to America was to get money to go back to Italy,' she is raising a subscription to which the narrator makes a pledge. When he invites her to dinner, she answers with an 'insurpassably flattering' compliment that 'she had just dined – in another palace.' Quite likely she had not – she is being courteous – and just as likely the word *palazzo* was spoken. Saying it, she touches his house 'with the exquisite politeness of her race.' Her graceful action has a talismanic quality because the real house, a 'little box of pine and paper,' suddenly becomes in the narrator's mind 'a lordly mansion, standing on the Chiaja, or the Via Nuovissima, or the Canalazzo' (38). By word and gesture she expresses the longing for a home, humbler than his imagining, but in the same city, Naples, her husband having burned down her own. Such an act is more terrifying because of the sense of the sacral with which Italians invest the domus.[27] In his fiction Howells attaches enormous significance to the house as a symbol both of the individual and of social status: Silas Lapham's new Back Bay house, which also burns down, is the most prominent example. The narrator concludes: 'we had made a little Italy together' (38), meaning not a 'Little Italy' in the sense of an urban neighbourhood – it is too early for that – but the make-believe, the enchantment of being in Italy. With its diminutive, affectionate wording and with the inner rhyme of 'little' and 'Italy,' the phrase suggests the pleasing, the informal, the gracious, at once concrete and yet seen by the light of imagination. As Norman Douglas said, 'Italy is a delightful place to remember, to think and talk about.'[28]

But is this a false communion? a cozy sentimentalism? It could be that the woman's plight has given the bourgeois narrator a sense of aristocratic exclusivity with a palace on the Bay of Naples. Perhaps, too, the woman is faking it a bit; Italians are masters of playing up to foreign travellers in their land and of participating in the fantasy in an ingratiating way. On Howells's 'self-satisfied exercises in multiculturalism,' Brodhead remarks that 'speaking their language verbally may only conceal how little Howells "speaks their language" in any other sense.'[29] This is too harsh: the passage strikes the note of sincerity; and the narrator assists the lady financially, not merely emotionally, and without theatrics or condescension. Moreover, he demonstrates his ability to communicate with different types of Italians and other ethnics throughout the sketches.

Charlesbridge, then, is a place of mixing. Yet where distinctions are threatened or lost amid rapid social change, scapegoating is likely to follow. In Boston of the 1860s and 1870s this role had been filled by the Irish, far more numerous than the Italians.[30] Though Howells's narrator, who has seen Dublin as well as Italy, notes the equal pleasure taken by the Irish and Italians in noisy street life, gossip, and lounging, he brushes aside as superficial these observations because 'there is beneath all this resemblance the difference that must exist between a race immemorially civilized and one which has lately emerged from barbarism "after six centuries of oppression"' (66). Southern Italians, who had earlier been described as only 'half-civilized' (50), are included among the 'immemorially civilized.' Perhaps Howells means that southern Italians are civilized of long standing historically in comparison to the Irish, an instance of his favouring the Italians.[31] In her study of race and class in Howells, Elsa Nettels comments that 'the Italians are not stigmatized by the solecisms and the eye dialect that disfigure the speech of Irish and black figures.'[32] Venting his prejudices, the narrator employs the Italian as a stick to beat the Irish by the carefully built-up theme of *cortesia*. 'You are likely to find a polite pagan under the mask of the modern Italian; you feel pretty sure that any of his race would with a little washing and skilful manipulation, *restore*, like a neglected painting, into something genuinely graceful and pleasing; but if one of these Yankee-fied Celts were scraped, it is but too possible that you might find a kern, a Whiteboy, or a Pikeman' (66–7). The painting simile presents the 'neglected' Italian as unclean; yet uncleanness is superficial and the underlying image is aesthetically pleasing.

The narrator's prejudice towards the Irish was hardly unusual after the Civil War among both Brahmins and the Yankee middle class of bureaucrats, shopkeepers, and tradesmen. Oscar Handlin and Stack note the increasingly bitter edge given to anti-Irish prejudice. Though identified by common ancestry and religion with the Brahmins, the Yankees differed from them by never tolerating the Irish immigrants who were competitors in the labour market and whose Roman Catholicism was anathema. More idealistic and far more insulated economically and socially from the immigrants, the Brahmins had initially accepted Irish immigration and 'deplored the excesses of anti-Catholic and anti-Irish hysteria during the 1840s and 1850s'; 'the Irish assault on Boston did not provoke xenophobia and nativism until after 1860,' writes Stack; 'the egalitarianism of the Adamses and of Hancock and Emerson persisted in spite of the unpleasant burdens that Irish immigration presented to the Brahmins.'[33] When the Irish population of Boston jumped from 3,936 in 1840 to over 50,000 in 1855, and when the Irish formed a political bloc opposed to the Brahmin program of reform, the Brahmins closed ranks with their Yankee brethren. 'At that moment,' writes Handlin, 'the tradition of tolerance was breached and long repressed hostilities found highly inflammable expression.'[34] The rising tide of Italian immigration takes place against this backdrop.

In another sketch some Neapolitan boys are performing with violin and harp, while Yankee boys stand around with 'impassive' faces, 'warily guarding against the faintest expression of enjoyment' (51).[35] Suddenly the 'minstrels played a brisk measure, and the music began to work in the blood of the boys'; one boy shuffles his initially 'reluctant' feet, then breaks into 'a sudden and resistless dance,' as if caught up by a life force. However, the boy dances 'only from the hips down': the music has only taken over half his body. The split between mind and body results in his dancing 'in an uncoordinated way' and with 'no expression'; dancing neither comes naturally nor gives pleasure. The Yankee is ungainly, his gestures stiff and awkward. Is this in contrast to the musical Italian with fluid gestures and graceful comportment?[36] None of the other boys is 'infected' and the narrator turns away: 'The spectacle became too sad for contemplation' (51).

The musical Italian appears in 'Jubilee Days,' referring to the National Peace Jubilee in liberal Boston in June 1869. As would Caruso fifty years later, the Italian diva 'Parepa-Rosa' sings 'The Star-Spangled Banner' and various arias in a make-shift coliseum erected for the occasion in Back Bay (203). In a rendition of Verdi's Anvil Chorus one hundred 'fairies in red shirts' marched like 'garibaldini' and played on invisible anvils, while one hundred fireman beat on anvils with sledgehammers, a thousand musicians played, and ten thousand people sang at the top of their lungs.[37] 'Never in my life, neither at Torino, nor at Milano, nor even at Genoa,' says an Italian immigrant, 'never did I see such a crowd or hear such a noise, as at that Colosseo yesterday' (212). New World gigantism and populism combine to make a public spectacle, and if the immigrant seems excited by American demographic muscle, the narrator says *he* prefers the 'chorus' of birds in the tree outside his surburban window.

Just as Italians were beginning to emigrate to Boston, African Americans arrived from the upper South; between 1865 and 1880 they doubled their number.[38] Howells's comparison of African Americans and Italians is more complex than the one with the Irish. Like Ferry Street, the African American quarter of Charlesbridge has a 'ragged gayety'; like the Italians, who are 'children of the summer' (35), the African Americans have 'summer in the blood' (20); both stand in contrast to the thrifty Yankees who take their pleasures in either the 'pocket' or the 'conscience' (20), that is, anhedonically. Like the Italian quarter, too, the African American one is contrasted with the 'aggressive and impudent squalor' of the Irish one and, as well, with the 'surly wickedness' of a 'low American street' (20). Strolling through the black neighbourhood, the narrator has the pleasing illusion that an 'orange-peel' in the street might have come from an orange tree 'in the soft atmosphere of those back courts' (20); the orange is also a totemic fruit of the Italians. The African Americans have 'supple cunning' and 'abundant amiability' (28); the Italians are 'wily and amiable' (39). The African Americans possess an 'inward music' (20); music is often linked to the Italians (though Richard Gambino points out differences between black and Italian music, the one emphasizing rhythm, the other melody).[39] Lynn observes that Mrs Johnson, the narrator's part African American, part Native American servant, is a 'turbaned, pipe-smoking, black equivalent of an Italian servant.'[40] Howells refers to skin colour, Mrs Johnson's being 'coffee soothed with the richest cream' (20, 26); Italians are often 'swarthy' (114), one of Howells's ethnic code words.[41] Mrs Johnson is so 'full of guile' and 'goodness,' the same odd pairing of qualities found among the Italians, and she reminds him 'pleasantly of lowly folk in elder lands' (30). What other 'elder' land did Howells know better than Italy? Like the Italians, she has a 'lawless' (21) side, a 'child-like simplicity' (22), and manners marked by 'tranquillity and grace' (20). Not having been bourgeoisified, again like the Italians, Mrs Johnson only works when she wishes, though she gets the job done. Having the culinary disposition of the Italians, she is particularly noted for having learned how to prepare Italian dishes: 'visions of the great white cathedral, the Coliseum, and the "dome of Brunelleschi" floated before us in the exhalations of the Milanese *risotto,* Roman *stufadino,* and Florentine *stracotto* that smoked upon our board' (22). Finally, in unspoken sympathy, the ex-slave learns a Garibaldi liberation song, 'Camicia Rossa' (28).

The type of the mysterious, uncanny Italian is explored in the sketch 'By Horse-Car to Boston.' Tall and dressed in black, a women on the trolley has arms that 'showed through the black gauze of her dress with an exquisite roundness and *morbidezza*' (93); this aesthetic term refers to the softness, realistic flesh tones, and chiaroscuro-like qualities of a painting. She wears 'heavy bracelets of dead gold, fashioned after some Etruscan device,' gold Etruscan earrings that touch her 'white columnar neck' (the column as symbol of Italy), a 'massive' Etruscan necklace, and 'a multitude of rings.' The Etruscan link enhances the association with her dress of mourning, death, and the primitive history of Italy. Her 'very expressive' hand 'took a principal part in the talk which the lady held with her companion, and was as alert and quick as if trained in the gesticulation of Southern or Latin life somewhere.' Her face is 'strange,' 'death-white'; her eyes are 'liquid.' She was 'altogether so startling an apparition, that all of us jaded, commonplace spectres turned and fastened our weary, lack-lustre eyes upon her looks, with an utter inability to remove them.' This Medusa-like 'mystery' (94) is in the vein of the Fatal Woman: entrancingly beautiful, pallid (the colour of death), with an uncanny, dreamlike gaze, and possessing a vampire wisdom.[42] When she departs, everyone 'woke from a dream,' or 'as if freed from a potent fascination,' and she never 'reappeared' again (94).

While Howells's leisure-loving Italians receive the benefit of every doubt, he reserves harsh criticism for a Yankee vagrant. A veteran of the Civil War, 'American, pure blood' (56), he has fallen so low on the social scale as to have been employed by an Irishman, a descent in social status that the narrator considers especially disconcerting. The vagrant refuses to work hard and prefers panhandling and an occasional day job to steady employment. Without friends or family he expresses the essential plea of the immigrant: 'What I want is a home' (59). But the narrator, whose patience has been exhausted, responds, 'Why don't you get married?' and dismisses him callously: 'Do you know now, I shouldn't care if I *never* saw you again' (59). What for an Italian immigrant is acceptable or at least tolerable behaviour in the new country is considered outrageous and humiliating in an American.

By the mid-1880s it was evident that many Italian immigrants were not returning home. On the contrary, they arrived each year in greater num-

bers, and their presence was beginning to assume weight and density in
Boston. The geographical triangle of *The Rise of Silas Lapham* (1885) consists of the lower-class North End (with a slowly growing Italian population), the South End (Yankees and Irish middle and lower-middle class;
Lapham's old house), and patrician Beacon Hill with its recent adjunct
Back Bay ('New Land') reclaimed from the Charles River (Lapham's
new house). 'Its first streets thrown open in 1872, the present Back Bay
filled up in the next thirty years, and became equal to Beacon Hill in the
status it conferred on inhabitants. Its air of Victorian prosperity and gentility made the North End appear even more squalid and the South End
even more dreary.'[43] Lapham builds his house on Beacon Street, Back
Bay, with the rear of the house facing the river, 'the clean, fresh smell
of the mortar in the walls mingling with the pungent fragrance of the
pine shavings neutralized the Venetian odor that drew in over the water'
(906). Though knowledgeable of the cleansing action of the Venetian
tides, Howells cannot resist appropriating the negative topos of foul-
ness and morbidity, which opposes Puritan cleanliness and New England
forest 'fragrance.' On his view, like Venice in being reclaimed from a
tidal lagoon, Back Bay exudes a miasma that, far from being neutralized,
portends catastrophe: his unfinished house goes up in flames, bringing
ruin. Three of Howells's five Italian novels have a Venetian setting, and
in each an aura of decadence stands for the 'demoralizing influences' of
Italy on American character.[44]

The Italian immigrant as an 'explosive' element is a topic of conversation at an elegant Beacon Hill dinner party at the home of Bromfield
Corey in *The Rise of Silas Lapham*. This Italophilic Brahmin dabbled in art
studies as a young man in Rome and, though he may not have fought in
the American Civil War, he boasts 'a little amateur red-shirting' (1047)
with Garibaldi in 1848. His tastes are described as 'simple as an Italian's'
(948), and his amiable nature, if shallow and ineffectual, is put down
to 'Italianized sympatheticism' (1186) – the phrase shows Howells in
command of this subject. Lapham's house is linked to morbid, Corey's
to touristic Venice: the 'carved Venetian *scrigni*' (1034) (jewel-boxes,
strongboxes) that decorate Corey's walls evoke the former mercantile
power, and might remind him of his family's slipping domestic economy (e.g., letting the butler go). Still, Lapham on the way up and Corey
on the way down are sufficiently distant socially not to see the other in
himself. At the dinner party Corey slyly proposes a scheme to help the
Italian immigrants with their severe housing problem: 'The occupation,
by deserving poor of neat habits, of all the beautiful, airy, wholesome

houses that stand empty the whole summer long, while their owners are away in their lowly cots beside the sea' (1040). When the ladies exclaim their disapproval, Corey, stung to the quick, teases his guests: 'nothing but the surveillance of the local policeman prevents me from applying dynamite to those long rows of close-shuttered, handsome, brutally insensible houses. If I were a poor man, with a sick child pining in some garret or cellar at the North End, I should break into one of them, and camp out on the grand piano' (1041). The squatter image combines Italophilic and Italophobic elements, the grand piano denoting high culture and music pre-eminent among the Italians (Lapham's daughters take dancing lessons 'at Papanti's' [883][45]), 'camping out' referring to the desperate plight of the immigrants, 'dynamite' conveying their anarchic, potentially violent character typically directed in Howells against a house. When one of the matrons asks about the fate of the furniture, Corey slyly withdraws his proposal. A minister adds, 'It's wonderful how patient they [the Italians] are' (1041) – southern Italian fatalism – and the subject is dropped. Howells's British editor Richard Watson Gilder insisted that he remove the word 'dynamite' lest he give the immigrants or their sympathizers any ideas: 'Not but a crank would misinterpret your allusion, but it is the crank who does the deed.' His British publisher Roswell Smith wrote that the reference to dynamite 'suggests nihilism, destructiveness – revenge.'[46] Fearing a legal ban, Howells removed the passage, which has been restored by later editors.

In the North End Corey buys an apple from a 'swarthy fruiterer' (993) with whom he enjoys exercising his Italian. These visits remind him of the carefree days of his youth in Italy. Later Howells satirizes Corey's 'sympatheticism' to the point where the proper Bostonian loses some of his dignity – significantly, over fruit. Corey eats a breakfast orange 'in the Neapolitan fashion' (1184), a habit probably picked up as an art student in Rome. It means to cut the orange in quarters and to tear and suck out the pulp of each piece with one's teeth: voracious, full of gusto, but in upper Boston a trifle *volgare*. Giuseppe Gaddi Conti claims an 'intimate sympathy' between Howells and Bromfield Corey and notes that on occasion Howells chooses him as his mouthpiece. Corey is a Howells surrogate, like the narrator in *Suburban Sketches.*[47]

Howells's *The Vacation of the Kelwyns* was written around 1906–7 and published posthumously in 1920, but its setting in New England of 1876 places it in the pre-immigration period, and its view of the Italians is accordingly mild and suffused with nostalgia. Parthenope Brook, the main character, was born in Naples of American artists who named her after the siren protectress of the city. They themselves died of fever in Rome, leaving her to be raised in rural New England. In Parthenope's wistful remembrance of her Italian childhood, Nathalia Wright reads Howells's poignant memories of his own youth, as Howells writes, 'in those simple days when living in Italy was almost a brevet of genius.'[48] At one point an itinerant Italian family of organ-grinders pass by the New Hampshire vacation house:

> There were two men – an older man who sat silently apart in the shade and a young man who came forward and offered to play. He had the sardonic eyes of a goat, but the baby in the arms of a young mother had a Napoleonic face, classic and mature. She herself was beautiful, and she said they were all from the mountains near Genoa and were presently on their way to the next town. They were peasants, but they had a grace which made Parthe-nope sigh aloud in her thought of the contrast they offered to the manner-less uncouthness of the Yankee country-folks. (151)

From the 'goat' (and scapegoat) to 'Napoleon,' 'classic and mature,' Italians in Howells have come full circle. To their credit, they appear courteous, sincere, individualistic, quick-witted, and artistic. On the debit side, they are anarchic, though non-violent, slow to adapt to American commercial society, and weakened by their lack of English. Wright contends that Howells's Italian immigrants are 'representative less of their own country than of the American melting pot.'[49] But they have not yet 'melted.' They bear a nuanced resemblance to the ideal of the Italian in European and American Romantic literature.[50]

The representation of Italian Americans alters for the worse when, like the Irish, the Italians were perceived to be in America to stay. An occasional nuisance, more often colourful and kindly characters, Howells's Italians of the 1860s and 1870s in *Surburban Sketches* plan to repatriate; yet their steadily growing number poses a nagging social problem in the 1880s in *The Rise of Silas Lapham*. By the 1890s Howells wonders by what 'malign chance' the Italians have metamorphosed from the 'friendly folk' they are 'at home' in Italy to the 'surly race they mostly show themselves here: shrewd for their advancement in material things, which seem the only good things to the Americanized aliens of all races, and fierce for their full share of the political pottage' (*Impressions and Experiences* [1896]).[51] From 'friendly' to 'surly,' from carefree to 'shrewd' and materialistic, Italians are being 'Americanized' into Italian Americans and, as such, have begun to claim their social and political rights.

Let us remain in the 1880s, the transitional decade, in examining the American representation of Italians. In 1884 Arlo Bates published *The Pagans*, the first of a series of novels once known for their brisk satire on Bostonian art circles. The Italophilic theme emerges in the situation of two of the central characters who had studied art in Rome, and in the fateful circumstance of one of them becoming betrothed to an Italian. The novel also contains Italophobic scenes in the North End, and what only a decade earlier seemed picturesque was now disturbing. Although Bates's Little Italy has none of the simple charm of Ferry Street, his immigrants are no huddled mass. Hitherto Italian immigrants appeared on the margins of American fiction. As their presence grew in Boston, the point was to find some way of bringing them forward into the central plot, of mixing the Americans and the Italian immigrants in a convincing manner. This too was the task of *The Pagans* and its sequel *The Philistines*,[52] which Bates accomplished by means of a protean character who moves between both worlds: a southern Italian peasant female art model. In this way ideological and social conflict between Italophilia and Italophobia comes narratively to life.

In the circle of George Whitefield Chadwick, who may figure in *The Pagans* as the 'musician,' Bates (1850–1918) was the son of a surgeon from East Machias, Maine, and was graduated from Bowdoin College in 1876. Like Howells, he pursued a literary career as a journalist and novelist in Boston, becoming editor-in-chief of the Boston *Sunday Courier* in 1880 and professor of English at the Massachusetts Institute of Technology in 1893. But the rise of Arlo Bates was neither as fast nor as high as the rise of William Dean Howells. Howells came from genteel, well-connected Ohio stock, married into a prominent New England family, and on arriving in Boston was invited to attend Dante Club meetings with Longfellow, Norton, and Lowell. He subsequently became editor of the *Atlantic*, taught at Harvard, and was asked to succeed Lowell in the Smith Professorship of Modern Languages there. He was the friend of presidents Hayes and Garfield, two fellow Ohioans. Bates was a Sunday magazine editor and taught in the English department of what was then a new technical school. Nonetheless he was a respected member of the Boston community and, like Howells, gave a set of Lowell Lectures, *Talks on the Study of Literature*, published in 1895.

An informal club of seven artists, the 'Pagans' stand for 'the protest of the artistic soul against shams,' by which they mean custom and authority; profess an 'unformulated although by no means unexpressed antagonism against Philistinism'; and believe truth is 'that which one sincerely believes.' For them, Puritanism is the 'preliminary rottenness of New England' while Philistinism is the 'substitution of convention for conviction.'[53] They obviously like thinking in big abstractions. In surroundings that are not inimical to artists – rather, too hospitable, for Bostonians champion their artists into dull submission[54] – the Pagans endeavour to open a space between the Puritanism of their ancestors and the Philistinism of their contemporaries, as they hover between gentility and bohemia. Theirs is an altogether precarious situation, a Bostonian outpost of the Decadence: drifting beyond this space spells disaster for all but the hardiest souls, and the space ultimately proves too small for any of them to produce genuine art. To hear them talk, it is hard to say whether the Philistine or the Puritan is the bigger threat. Arthur Fenton, a Pagan with a penchant for making epigrams, sells out to become a society portrait-painter.[55] Another Pagan complains that Emerson did not go far enough – he 'lacked the loftiness of vice; he was eternally narrow' and knew 'only half of life' (80). In *The Philistines* Bates extends his critique: even where individuals have liberated themselves intellectually from Puritan dogma, it leaves its mark upon conduct. The 'essence' of Puritanism is 'its strenuous earnestness, its exaltation of self-denial, and its distrust of the guidance of the senses.'[56] Santayana and Van Wyck Brooks have been anticipated.

In *The Pagans* Bates connects the two Italies, of high culture and the impoverished immigrants, by means of the 'peasant girl' Ninitta whom Grant Herman, a Boston sculptor, met on an excursion to Capri, 'loved or believed he loved,' and 'induced' to come to Rome and be his model (37, 38). 'Loved or believed he loved' and 'induced' (or seduced?) are among the many vague words or phrases employed to excuse Herman whenever his behaviour is scrutinized. 'Black-haired' (159), Ninitta has a 'dark, homely face, only redeemed from positive ugliness by her deep, expressive eyes' (34). Perhaps her face is not at issue because Herman is a sculptor and initially is attracted by her body: 'rather slender, lithe and sinewy,' long limbed 'like Diana,' 'superb,' 'splendidly shaped' (34, 159). In terms of the novel's thematic conflict, the division between beauty and ugliness, between body (sexuality) and head (conscience), expresses the split response to the Italian.

The diminutive 'Ninitta' conveys slightness, a ninny, a nonentity; we never learn her family name, as if she had none, having cut her ties in running off to Rome. With an 'Italian's passionate nature' (110), 'passionate southern heart' and 'crude, simple emotions,' Ninitta is the archetypal 'undisciplined Italian' (171).[57] Lacking a bourgeois manner and drive

control, she is 'tender, loving, pathetically submissive' one day, jealous as
a 'fury' (116) on another. She is 'superstitious' (114); jealous (109, 110,
114, 215); suspicious (120); impulsive (270) and theatrical (12, 139);
but also 'a good girl' (40, 119), 'true and pure' (118) in her loyalty; and
finally, unpredictable and dangerous: she holds her hair up with what
appears to be a 'stiletto' (119) (which is silly and melodramatic – Bates
is descending). The stiletto, the Mafia, and the crime of passion constituted the stereotype that conditioned every major anti-Italian outburst
in the 1890s, less than a decade after Bates's novel.[58] One pagan, who
employed her as a model, tried kissing her against her will; she 'offered
to stab him with some sort of a devilish dagger arrangement she carries
about like an opera heroine' (12); 'offered' as opposed to 'threatened'
implies the theatrical. When he hollers for help and other artists rush in
like a 'chorus,' she leaves 'without a fuss' (13) – she can fight her own
battles. Ninitta's mind is a 'strange' amalgam of 'simplicity' and 'worldly
wisdom' (75). She thus combines purity, sincerity, strength, 'character,'
and violence (when justifiably provoked): the noble savage. Capri is the
geographical equivalent of stage Italian for natural beauty and promiscuous sexuality. It is located in the 'aesthetic-touristic' south, the origin of
an increasingly larger percent of the 'alien-intruders.' Eventually almost
80 per cent of Italian immigrants came from southern Italy.

In Rome, Herman had faint-heartedly proposed to Ninitta and was 'too
honorable to betray her' (38). Then, believing mistakenly that Ninitta
is having an affair with his friend, he flees Rome. Perhaps he wants to
believe anything that will soothe his conscience and paper over difficulties in leaving her. Though he learns after his friend's death that Ninitta
had been faithful to him, he is not so honourable as to renew his pledge
of marriage because he has meanwhile fallen in love with a sculptress,
Helen Greyson, who is estranged from her husband. As the novel opens,
as it were *in medias res*, Ninitta has just arrived in Boston after seeking Herman for seven years. Her presence on the scene throws the Pagans, the
Puritans, and even some of the Philistines into consternation. Ninitta is
the one and only pagan.

When Ninitta confronts Herman with his obligations, he is cool towards her, gives her a handshake, says he has a headache, and asks her to
come back tomorrow (40). It is hard to think of a character who has ever
recovered in the eyes of the reader from such an initial poor showing.
Bates faults Ninitta for not understanding why, even on having learned
the truth of her chastity, Herman would still renege on his offer of marriage. But Ninitta cannot be held accountable; Bates, who appears never

to have read *I Promessi Sposi*, shows no comprehension of Italian *rispetto* involving 'obligations and reciprocal arrangements.' Since Herman has given a ring and Ninitta has remained faithful, his personal feelings do not override the principle: 'affection did not constitute an essential component of *rispetto*, even if its presence was desirable.'[59] Bates would have us believe that, coming from her background, she should accept Herman's change of heart and end the engagement. To understand her betrothed, writes Bates, 'would have required not only a knowledge of facts of which she could have no cognizance, but far keener powers of reason than were centered in Ninitta's shapely head' (77). (Though this is badly written, 'shapely' implies a sculptural quality – the face itself, symbolic of identity, has a 'positive ugliness.') The 'facts' are seven years of separation, cultural and class differences, a new country, and another woman. While the first three mean nothing to Ninitta, 'instinct' (77) leads her to suspect another woman. Herman's unfounded suspicion of Ninitta in Rome is passed over lightly; Ninitta's well-grounded suspicion of Herman manifests a glaring defect in her character.

Embarrassed and seeking reconciliation, Herman visits Ninitta's threadbare attic room, which her aesthetic flair has rescued 'from the common-place'; 'a bit of flimsy drapery, begged from some studio, hung over one of the windows; a rude print of the Madonna was pinned to the wall, and under it, on the wooden table, was a bunch of withered flowers' (114). The Madonna is her religious ideal and a proof of her sincerity. In these surroundings, and apparently for the first time, Herman sees her as a person: 'she was no longer simply the model, she was an Italian woman in her own home' (115). Against much of what one already knows about her, Bates allows Ninitta an extraordinary act of self-transcendence, as if he would make her do what is 'right' from the point of view of the other characters' interests. Ninitta rejects Herman's renewed proposal because she refuses to force him into a loveless marriage. The psychological motivation is surprising, and just barely plausible, but the scene has unquestionable impact, and if Bates could have multiplied such scenes, he might have deepened understanding of the immigrants. Soon afterward, looking to make a living, having agreed to pose for a statue by Helen, Ninitta discovers that Helen is sculpting a large work, *The Flight of the Seasons*, and that Herman is the model for the head of December (at thirty-five, Herman is prematurely gray and already complaining of his age). It is noteworthy that Helen is sculpting a face and head, with Herman as the model; with Ninitta, only the physical body (and head insofar as it is 'shapely,' but not the face) is seen as beautiful. In a sudden outburst of fury, Ninitta goes to Helen's studio and smashes the head of December to bits. 'She didn't make any attempt to conceal it,' reports Helen, 'she came stalking melodramatically into his studio with the mallet and laid it down. "There," said she, "now kill me. I have broken her work." It was like a fashion magazine story' (139). Helen does not get angry; that would be bad behaviour, the histrionic emotion she mocks in Ninitta. If her sculpture meant more to her, she might not compare its destruction to cheap sensationalism.

Ninitta's action has the immediate effect of freeing Herman from the obligation of being 'Her Man'; will he now be Helen's man? In the novel's chief moral crisis Herman's conscience does not let him off so easily with regard to his pledge to Ninitta, and he has second thoughts. Meanwhile, ill and bereft, Ninitta grows despondent and drifts aimlessly towards the North End, her surrogate home country. Ferry Street has grown into a large Italian neighbourhood, which social workers at the time called 'Boston's classic land of poverty':[60]

The poorer classes of foreigners in any city [writes Bates] are led by similarity of language and occupations to gather into neighborhoods according to their nationality, and the Italians are especially clannish. The fruit-venders and organ-grinders form separate colonies, each distinguished by the peculiarities incident to the calling of its inhabitants, the crooked courts in the fruit-sellers' neighborhood being chiefly marked to outward observance by the number of two-wheeled hand-carts which, out of business hours, are crowded together there. (164)

An immigrant family, recognizing her speech, takes pity on Ninitta and brings her home to their tenement. She is eventually found by Mrs Edith Fenton, wife of the 'Pagan' Arthur and an upper-class volunteer in social work.[61] Already involved in social service, many Brahmins and Yankees would shortly embrace the settlement house movement, as T.J. Jackson Lears writes, '[searching] in the slums for the intense experience they felt they had been denied at home.'[62] A noted settlement house was the North End Union, founded in 1892 by the Benevolent Fraternity of Unitarian Churches.[63]

The interior of the tenement is presented through Mrs Fenton's eyes: 'The children have just been put into our schools, but they have not advanced very far as yet ... they are wretchedly poor. I wish you could see the place, Mrs. Greyson. Eight people in a room not so large as this, and such poverty as you could hardly imagine. Yet these people had taken in another' (160). It was not uncommon for whole families to live in a single room, and the population density led frequently to health and sanitation problems.[64] Hoping to make conversions, Protestant churches set up 'missions' in the slums, but with limited success. 'They are Catholics, naturally,' Mrs Fenton says, 'but they do not seem to have much religion of any kind, and keep clear of the priest for some reason' (161).[65] That they lack 'much religion' is plainly wrong, but their keeping clear of priests seems to have been the case with many arriving immigrants. According to Anna Maria Martellone, 'even if [the immigrant] was a practicing, convinced Catholic, the conditions in which he found himself within the ambience of English-language parishes, governed by the Irish clerics, distanced him after a short time from the influence of the Church.'[66] But it was not long before the Italians had their own priests. Italians in the North End and West End made a point of having their children baptized by Italian priests in Sacred Heart Church in the North End.

Mrs Fenton returns to the North End with Helen, whose knowledge of Italian will be helpful in persuading Ninitta to come back with them – yet another 'crossing' for Ninitta. In addition to charity, virtues mitigating the situation are (Yankee) thriftiness and cleanliness, seen as exceptional: 'Ninitta was found in a room tolerably clean for that portion of the city, the old fruit woman who was its mistress having retained more of the tidiness of thrifty peasant ancestors than most of her class. One room was made to accommodate the mother and seven children, and during the absence of the former from home the premises were left in charge of a girl just entering her teens [who] was engaged in preparing the family dinner of maccaroni' (164–5).Why is there no mention of the father? Here only women are helping other women, from Helen and Mrs Fenton to the young Italian girl doing the cooking. If a woman is scapegoated as the cause of trouble, women are the only ones who appear actively sympathetic. Yet Bates draws upon another stereotype and feminizes the Italians, rendering them (in his eyes) weak, abandoned, and vulnerable to exploitation, a mimesis of their historical condition.

After Ninitta goes back to proper Boston, Helen persuades Herman to honour his pledge and marry Ninitta. Since Helen's husband has just committed suicide and she is free to marry, her self-sacrificing act is attributed to a Puritan conscience. Similarly, Herman's temptation to marry Helen is great, and so his sacrifice in marrying Ninitta is made to seem the greater. Bates leaves the impression that the sacrifice is wrong, that the Puritan conscience is at fault; at the same time Ninitta represents dangerous sexual desire that must somehow be controlled or repressed. The novel ends with Helen's gloomy departure for Rome, Herman's reluctant marriage, and the disbanding of the Pagans. Yet this is not the real ending, only a suspension that awaits a sequel, because everything points to a marriage that is doomed and a love between Helen and Herman that will not die.

More disposed towards Herman's indecisiveness and opportunism than sympathetic with Ninitta's seven-year odyssey and social ostracism, Bates scarcely conceals his prejudices where a Brahmin, at least in public, would have been more detached and oblique. If with an air of social superiority Helen says that Ninitta's behaviour is like a magazine story, Bates's own writing rarely rises above the level of the Sunday papers. Whether he was shaping the moral perceptions of his audience or merely expressing them, crudity of presentation is altogether stronger in *The Philistines*, published in 1889, five years after *The Pagans*. At the end of the first decade of large-scale Italian immigration to Boston, the expansion of their community has intensified nativist social prejudice.[67]

In *The Pagans*, virtually against the intentions of the novelist, Ninitta is a forceful, if impractical, individual with a capacity for love and endurance; in *The Philistines* she is blamed unjustly for a failed marriage, commits a single indiscretion, and pays with her life. Six years have passed and Herman and Ninitta have grown emotionally apart. As he looks across the breakfast table, he 'continually tried to discover what process of reasoning led Ninitta to given results' (60). Not fluent in English, she still speaks to him in Italian, which Bates implies is a failure to adapt. They have a 'swarthy' (62) boy, named Nino after Ninitta, who is also 'swarthy' (388). To the inheritance of physical traits are added psychological ones. Herman accuses his wife of spoiling Nino and is angry that the *bambino*, as she insists on calling him, is not at the table: 'He has all the Italian laziness in him,' says Herman, who goes to rouse the boy and finds him lying 'luxuriously' in his little bed (he is only five). One recalls the 'lazy' boy with the tambourine in *Surburban Sketches*. Child-like themselves, Italians infantilize their children, which is no way to prepare them for real life. 'He will be a *bambino* to you when he is as big as I am' (62): Nino is a mama's boy.

Isolated in Boston, Ninitta has made sacrifices to conform to her husband's society. 'She used to have a few Italians come to see her; people she met that time she ran away, you remember, and we brought her home,' Mrs Fenton says, 'but they don't come now.' She raises her eyebrows, 'A question of caste.' Rejecting her compatriots for the sake of social climbing for her child, Ninitta told her Italian friends that 'the *bambino* was born a gentleman' and 'couldn't associate with them' (108). Yet when Ninitta is desperate, she goes to see 'Italian friends of former days' (436), the only people to whom she can turn. With unbecoming prejudice, Helen jokes that Ninitta is as out of place at an afternoon tea as 'the pope at a dancing-party' (107).

Herman's attempt to fathom his marital troubles and Ninitta's conduct involves him in rationalization and self-deception: 'as the larger nature, it should be his place to make concessions, to master the situation, and to secure Ninitta's happiness.' For her, he had made the 'great sacrifice of his life,' and Bates never lets the reader forget it:

> But his patience, his delicacy, his steadfastness counted for little with Ninitta. She had been separated from him for long years of betrothal, during which he had developed and changed utterly ... Even Ninitta, little given to analysis, could not fail to recognize that her husband was a very different being from the lover she had known ten years before. One fervid blaze of the old lover would have appealed more strongly to her peasant soul than all the patience and tender forbearance of years. (222)

He has all the patience; she, all the passion; and Bates would have us think that, were it not for her 'peasant soul,' she would know better. If Herman had been more cruel towards her, had he made a 'slave' of her, she would have 'accepted her lot as uncomplainingly as the women of her race had acquiesced in such a fate for stolid generations.' Given her unfulfilled desire Ninitta is tempted to model again, her work supposedly being an outlet for her sexuality; an opportunity is provided by the Pagan-turned-Philistine Arthur Fenton. Vice attracts itself and then feeds on itself: 'the time came when her ardent Italian nature was so kindled that she became involuntarily the tempter in her turn' (223–4). While Herman had posed for the married Helen Greyson in *The Pagans* without a trace of shame, Ninitta's modelling for Fenton is seen as scandalous. Bates traces Ninitta's fault to her background: 'There was, too, who knows what trace of heredity in the readiness with which Ninitta tacitly adopted the idea that infidelity to a husband was rather a matter of discretion and secrecy; whereas faithfulness to her lover had been a point of the most rigorous honor' (223). Again, not comprehending Italian mores, Bates misreads his central character.

Fenton's *Fatima* (Shining One) portrays Ninitta as an oriental beauty 'lying with long sleek limbs amid bright-hued cushions' (379), linking

the Italian woman to oriental luxury and wantonness (a familiar stereotype: the Venetian courtesan, the *dama* of the *cicisbeo*). Fenton has tried
to conceal Ninitta's identity by only taking her body for the model and
by transposing a beautiful head from another model, but the ruse will
not work: her 'true' identity is the body and will be recognized as such.
The dichotomy between Italophilia and Italophobia, already present in
Ninitta's person (beautiful body, ugly face), is now expressed by decapi-
tation. The theme appears in both *The Pagans* and *The Philistines*. The
destroyed head of December modelled on Herman might also be read
as a castration image, December being the month of death. Helen's
last name 'Greyson' also contains a deathly colour, her first name being
the mythical beauty; in her own way she, too, evokes a split response, of
love and death. Helen and Herman are entering middle age, typified by
Helen's *The Flight of the Seasons*. The various doublings express fears of
dwindling potency and a consequent arousal of sexuality. Bates himself
was in his later thirties at the time of writing the novel and his wife had
recently died, leaving him with a young son about Nino's age.

At the gallery exhibition Herman recognizes his wife's body (with its
'sensuous enticement') and it 'choked' him (382–3). Scandal has broken out over Ninitta, and it fills Herman with shame and anger. He confronts Ninitta, whose 'swarthy passionate face was an image of terror'
(388). The rhetoric is racist and sexist: 'She was not far enough away
from her peasant ancestors not to be moved by the size and strength of
her husband's large and vigorous frame. Many generations and much
subtlety of refinement must lie between herself and savagery before a
woman can learn instinctively to fear the soul of a man rather than his
muscles in a crisis like this' (388–9). This is a roundabout way of saying
that Italians are wife-beaters, an Anglo-American stereotype.[68] Herman
asks how she could have betrayed him, though whether she has ever
sexually betrayed him is only insinuated and highly doubtful. Besides, an
artist like Herman might have understood, at least vaguely, her desire to
pursue her line of work in the studio instead of staying home. So he punishes her where it hurts most: what will Nino think of her when he grows
up? The question, a veiled threat, plunges her into deeper grief. 'Could
he have known what was passing in her heart; it would have moved him
to a deeper respect and a keener pity than he had ever felt for her. No
more than a dumb animal had she any language in which she could have
made him understand her feelings had she tried' (391). Not Ninitta,
but Bates himself lacks the language of her feelings, for it is the gift of
language that a novelist should bestow upon such a character, either di-

rectly through speech and action, or indirectly through description and symbol.

Ninitta decides to flee Boston, and return to Italy, leaving Nino with his father. This is also unlikely, given her maternal instincts, her southern Italian background, and her special devotion to the Madonna. But the further away the novel goes from 'nature' or Italian mores, the more its ideology becomes clearer. A second exile is not a sufficiently severe penalty for her; she might return, as she did in the past; and she is blocking the marriage of Herman and Helen. There is no other solution to the scandal but for the scapegoat to die. And the partner of the deed, Arthur Fenton, must die for 'seducing' Ninitta and (it is another part of the plot) for trafficking in bad business ventures, thereby compounding his sexual with his financial transgressions. Moreover, he is a Pagan turncoat. On a steamer bound for New York she meets Fenton on his way to placate his creditors. In dense fog the steamer crashes into another ship and Ninitta and Fenton are drowned. As Bates explains, Fenton would have survived the disaster, were it nor for his heroic attempt at trying to save her. If this is to grant Fenton a measure of redemption, Ninitta must again appear responsible for wreaking havoc on the entire tribe. Further, since both Ninitta and Fenton believe that Boston will think they had run off together and never learn the truth, their deaths are psychologically as well as physically tormenting. In a swift dénouement Herman and Helen marry and plan to raise Nino in Boston. Bates does not speculate on his upbringing or the influence that his Italian background might have on his life.

Thanks to the research of Martino Marazzi, Francesco Durante, and Joseph Cosco, among others, the picture of the Italian American in the period around 1900 is being filled in.[69] In two works of art just before World War I, Italian immigrants are of central interest, and it seems appropriate that those works should be in opera, a genre to which the Italians were closely tied: *The Padrone* (1912) by Bates's friend George Whitfield Chadwick, and *The Immigrants* (1914) by Frederick Shepherd Converse. Regrettably, neither opera has been performed in its entirely or even published. Victor Fell Yellin's recent biography raises hopes for an improvement in Chadwick's fortunes, particularly regarding his stage works.[70] A portion of *The Padrone* was performed in concert version in the 1960s.

Dean of American composers, Chadwick (1854–1931) wrote one of the first large-scale musical works portraying Italian immigrants in the United States. Set in Boston's North End in the 'Summer of the Present Day,' the opera capitalizes on the verismo style of Puccini and Mascagni to paint a dark picture of social conditions, exploitation, immigration politics, and violence. Chadwick submitted *The Padrone* to the Metropolitan Opera, under the management of its director Giulio Gatti-Casazza, who had left La Scala in 1908 to accept the American post, where he would hold sway for twenty-five years. In an open spirit he had instituted a policy of staging one new opera by an American composer each season. Yet Gatti-Casazza turned Chadwick down without explanation, the more unusual given the composer's eminence. Chadwick made his own inquiries and later told a friend that Gatti-Casazza 'disliked the book because it was a drama of life among the humble Italians,– and probably too true to life.'[71]

What was Gatti-Casazza's motivation? It was not on account of the music because the prize went (in part, according to Yellin, for political reasons) to Victor Herbert's *Madeleine*, 'theatrical fluff' set in the eighteenth-century salon of a French actress. Was Gatti-Casazza, a bourgeois 'northerner' from Udine, embarrassed by the revelations of sordid life among fellow Italians, mainly from the south? Or was he trying to protect them and prevent their image from being further maligned on the main stage of an already famous American institution? In the event, Chadwick locked away his stage masterpiece. Yellin speculates that, at fifty-nine and in failing health, Chadwick may have wanted to devote his remaining years to teaching and administration and to the promotion of his orchestral works. He never wrote again for the stage.

The son of a New Hampshire carpenter turned insurance salesman, Chadwick grew up in the mill town of Lowell, Massachusetts, amid crowded immigrant conditions. His stepmother may have been a mill worker. He entered the New England Conservatory of Music in 1872, travelled abroad to study in Leipzig and Munich, and returned to Boston where he established a career in teaching and composition. He became director of the New England Conservatory in 1897. Known as one of the Boston Six, he developed a distinctively American tone in his symphonic music, as anyone who listens to his impressive *Symphonic Sketches* will feel immediately. (One should place it alongside the *New World Symphony* by Dvořák, who also taught at the New England Conservatory in the 1890s, to hear the difference.) Yellin writes that *The Padrone* is a 'sympathetic outsider's understanding, far in advance of its time, of the way cultural forces act on the everyday lives of ordinary people of a specific ethnicity.' When Chadwick wrote *The Padrone*, however, in some sense he was returning to the scenes of his youth and may have had an 'insider's' understanding too. The 'completed orchestral score bears all the hallmarks of a noble, viable work,' notes Yellin, who praises its 'sensitivity to the intimate relationship between the prosody of the words and his musical invention.'[72]

The plot of *The Padrone* with its verismo style would do justice to *The Godfather*; even its title seems prophetic. Divided into two acts with an orchestral interlude, it tells the story of Marietta, a tambourine girl in the pay of a local *padrone* named Catani (from the city Catania?). She lives in hope of saving enough money to pay the passage of Marco, with whom she is in love. The opening scene is laid in a North End restaurant where Marietta rejects Catani's advances. Vowing revenge, Catani convinces Francesca, Marietta's elder sister who has been spurned by Marco, to denounce Marco to the immigration authorities on a trumped-up charge of abandonment. Marietta's savings would then go for naught and she would be forced to stay in Boston and marry Catani, while Francesca would be free to return to Italy with Marco. After the interlude, the scene switches to the docks where Marco is about to land. Three choruses interact: wealthy Americans returning from a tour of Italy, the Italian immigrants disembarking, and the dockside Italian Americans to welcome them and to celebrate the wedding festivities (Broadhead's categories hold good). Marietta and Marco meet, but Francesca's denunciation succeeds, and he is led back to the ship. In a rage Marietta stabs Catani to death.

'As a dramatic composer,' concludes Yellin, 'Chadwick advances into the big leagues of continuous lyric drama, the most flexible and theatrical medium before the invention of cinema.'[73] Oddly enough, the work that could have been the bridge between the classical American composers and the new generation of young immigrant composers or first-generation Americans was denied a hearing: 'The very process of immigration, which *The Padrone* sympathetically examined, was to be the cause of a gap in the continuity of American musical history between older composers of Yankee stock and young modernists, many of whom were first- or second-generation immigrants. As the Yankee "fathers" tended not to recognize the ethnic (i.e., American) legitimacy of the upstart "sons," the sons, in turn, denied their musical "parents" the usual filial affection and respect and even, at times, their existence.' Unpublished, *The Padrone* could not influence the next generations of American or Italian opera composers: George Gershwin, Virgil Thomson, Marc Blitzstein, and Gian-Carlo Menotti.[74] Wilfrid Mellers writes that 'on the strength of [*The Padrone*] – dealing with low, modern American life – it would seem that Chadwick had the aptitude and technique to have anticipated Menotti': it is 'a major opera of genius like Gershwin's *Porgy and Bess*.'[75]

Frederick Shepherd Converse (1871–1940) was another American composer engrossed by the saga of the immigrants. According to Robert Joseph Garafolo, Converse visited Naples in 1909 and was 'moved by the plight of the Italians emigrating to America.'[76] Three years later he began composing *The Immigrants*, with a libretto by Percy MacKaye. Its original title appears to have been 'The Emigrants'; the change indicates that Converse had decided to establish the viewpoint in the United States rather than the land of departure. He finished the work in 1914 and submitted it unsuccessfully to the Los Angeles Prize Contest. Meanwhile, Henry Russell wrote Converse that he would arrange to have the work reviewed by Gatti-Casazza and Cleofonte Campanini at the Metropolitan. In 1910 Gatti-Casazza had produced Converse's *The Pipe of Desire*, the first opera by an American at the Metropolitan, but 'it appears as though the Metropolitan Opera Company was unwilling or unable to produce these works [*Beauty and the Beast* and *The Immigrants*].' The Boston Opera Company, with which Converse was associated, went into bankruptcy in 1914 after five seasons, dashing any hopes that the opera would find an audience. Like *The Padrone*, it was the inspiration of Italophilia and the victim of Italophobia.

Epilogue

To jump forward several generations, Italophilia and Italophobia inform two books that examine urban redevelopment in the 1950s, Fred Langone's *The North End: Where It All Began* (1994) and Walter Muir Whitehill's *Boston: A Topographical History* (1959, 1968).

Langone, a lawyer and Boston city councillor, came from an Italian American family long settled in the North End. In 1927 his grandfather Joseph A. Langone, Sr, state representative and owner of a funeral home, organized and led the massive funeral procession of Sacco and Vanzetti. Langone's father was election commissioner and state senator; his mother was a powerful figure in state and national immigration politics. William Foote Whyte was often a guest at Langone's home when he was conducting research for his classic study of American ethnics, *Street Corner Society*; Langone's father appears in the book as the political figure 'George Ravello.'[77] *The North End* is both a personal memoir and a historical portrait of a neighbourhood over two centuries of changing ethnic groups and economic fortunes, with the Italians lodged in it as the majority ethnic group for roughly the past century (90 per cent at their height in 1910; 42 per cent in 2000).

Langone's strongest theme is protecting one's community from opportunistic politicians, Panglossian city planners, 'greedy developers,' special interest groups, and Washington. He had fought a losing battle against the expansion of Logan International Airport, which meant increased noise pollution and the destruction of neighbourhoods and marshlands in the predominantly Italian East Boston. He also lost out when in the 1950s the Southern Artery, an elevated superhighway, tore through one side of the North End and left it hemorrhaging for years and choking with congestion. (In the 1990s, planners decided that the Southern Artery was a big mistake and decided to put everything underground, the now-completed Big Dig.) Yet Langone had his successes: when politicians wanted to shut down the open market in the old Haymarket Square, which predated the American Revolution, he not only helped save it, but was able to give it an extra day. He won the fight to preserve the famous North End waterfront, site of the Boston Tea Party.

His book's most painful chapter does not concern the precariously preserved North End, but the West End, contiguous and fluid with it, and as Langone says, vibrant, safe, even more cosmopolitan in its ethnic mix of Italian American, Irish American, Jewish American, Polish American, African American, Ukrainian American, and many others. In the late 1950s and early 1960s the West End was 'redeveloped' in what some sociologists consider among the worst examples of its kind in American urban history. The West End is the North End's dark shadow.

Showing little understanding of the heritage they were enjoined to protect, lacking in any real culture to guide them in their momentous decisions, planners and politicians seized and condemned the West End's forty-eight acres and thirty-two hundred households and cut the heart out of the city. Along with the demolition of Haymarket, Bowdoin, and Scollay squares to make room for the architectural catastrophe of Government Center and a no less hideous 'new' city hall, the razing of the West End sundered the North End from Beacon Hill and Back Bay, forever destroying the architectural integrity of Old Boston. If the reclamation of the marshlands to make Back Bay was the finest urbanistic achievement for the nineteenth-century city, the West End demolition ranks as its most significant twentieth-century event. Back Bay enhanced Boston, the West End Urban Renewal Project was an unmitigated disaster.

One may wonder where were the city elders and the venerable sages when the West End and the colourful, old squares were on the chopping block. One can find no better example of political decadence after World War II than the way Boston's leaders turned a blind eye to what was happening to their city. In *Boston: A Topographical History*, published in 1958, a year after the unveiling of the West End redevelopment plan, Walter Muir Whitehill, director of the Boston Athenaeum, blandly reviewed the decision: 'This [plan of redevelopment] is the less to be regretted in that the area, having been open country in the eighteenth century, had fewer points of historic interest than the other parts of the town.'[78] How easily the sentence slips from the mandarin's pen: Elevation of a 'historic' eighteenth century of Brahmin-Yankee pride; 'open country,' the pastoral myth; suppression of the immigrant-laden nineteenth century that had its own storied myths; 'fewer points' revealing that he is merely counting, not seeing the West End (as would Camillo Sitte, Lewis Mumford, or Robert Venturi) in its aesthetic and urbanistic relations to other quarters; no hint of the human cost, 'less to be regretted.'

Ten years later, in a second edition, Whitehill sang a different tune, harsh and grating. Now that the character of the central city had been transmogrified, he woke to a nightmare. Conducted by the Boston Redevelopment Authority, the West End project 'brutally displaced people, disrupted neighborhoods and destroyed pleasing buildings, only to create a vast approximation of a battlefield in the center of the city ... [the new apartment towers of Charles River Park are] as complete a break with the traditional architecture and habits of Boston as the adjacent shopping center-motel-movie house in Cambridge Street, which has the air of having wandered in from the suburbs of another city.'[79] Yet there is no admission of his earlier error in judgment, and the new chapter in which he reviews the West End fiasco is called, in the language of advertising, 'A Decade of Renewal.' As if he had just come upon the scene, he writes: 'total demolition of large areas, without regard for the feelings of people, and their eventual reconstruction – after long periods as a desolate dump – in unfamiliar form for new uses was neither good sense nor good politics.' In an endnote, however, the critic expresses some of the feelings that may have guided him: 'there were streets and courts that were quite as suitable for economical living in the center of the city as the streets of the north slope of Beacon Hill or of Bay Village'; the West End had 'many of the virtues that Jane Jacobs found' in Greenwich Village. So the West End was not a slum after all; this had been one of the reasons given for its redevelopment. 'In Poplar Court, for example, a number of young physicians and their families lived pleasantly in nineteenth-century red brick houses converted into apartments.'[80] These future members of the elite are the only specific group that Whitehill mentions as displaced among the thirty-two hundred households. 'They were near the Massachusetts General Hospital, and their wives made full use of the nearby foreign groceries and bakeries.' In fact they were American groceries and bakeries of various ethnicities, not 'foreign' ones.

Langone made certain that the lessons of the West End would not be lost on the North End or, for that matter, elsewhere in the city. Developers did not tear down a single house in the North End, which, having retained its distinctive character, is one of the major tourist attractions on the East Coast. Yet Langone's *pietas* includes not only his own heritage; he embraces all the ethnic populations who have nourished the spirit of the place, from the early British immigrants to the most recent arrivals. Then, he welcomes future inhabitants of whatever origin, as if to say that the 'twilight' of one ethnicity (in Richard Alba's phrase) only just precedes the dawn of another. The book's subtitle *Where It All Began* calls attention to the birth of the American Republic and to its rebirth in the consciousness of each successive ethnic group. Balancing many expressions of passing, nostalgia, and death in Langone's memoir are metaphors of birth and living process. 'The North End will never die out as a good, viable community because it is here that our great country was born. No matter what ethnic strain of immigrants came here, it never changed its character.'[81] Its people have always pulled together as a community, a fact powerfully expressed in their participation in numerous civic and religious events. One of the most culturally engaging – and one that Langone himself had no small hand in saving after World War II – is the annual Veterans Parade.

In the spirit of renewal, this parade starts from Paul Revere's grave in King's Chapel Burial Ground and proceeds to the original Paul Revere House in North Square, North End. Here the mayor of Boston hands a scroll to 'Paul Revere,' who, crying 'The British are coming!,' rides on horseback down Prince Street, near the Old North Church where the warning lanterns were hung, across Charlestown Bridge, and onward to Lexington sounding the alarm. The city preserves its heritage.

chapter 5

Puccini's American Theme

JOHN PAUL RUSSO

Giacomo Puccini's operatic career, from *Le Villi* in 1884 to *Turandot* in 1924, corresponds exactly to the period of mass emigration from Italy. During these forty years, fifteen million Italians left their homeland, mainly for the Americas, one-third of them for the United States. Today the movement is viewed, with Fascism and industrialization, as 'perhaps the most significant social phenomenon in Italian post-unification history.'[1] Even in the 1890s, Francis Marion Crawford deplored Italy's being 'depopulated' and in a sweeping historical parallel said that 'in parts' emigration 'is so extensive that it can only be compared with the westward migration of the Aryan tribes.'[2] Of Verdi's twenty-seven operas only the minor *Alzira* (1845) has a New World character, theme, or setting; its libretto derives from Voltaire's drama *Alzire* on the Spaniards and Incas in sixteenth-century Peru. Yet Verdi composed before the mass emigration, and his social and political themes reflect the Risorgimento. By comparison, three of Puccini's twelve operas involve North America in some way: the final act of *Manon Lescaut* (1893) takes place in a dreary waste in the French territory of Louisiana; U.S. Navy lieutenant Benjamin Franklin Pinkerton abandons Cio-Cio-San in *Madama Butterfly* (1904); a mining town nestled in the Sierra Nevada in California is the scene of *La fanciulla del West* (1910). Two of them contain English words in their titles, a rarity for Italian opera. In these works Puccini takes up his characteristic themes of erotic sensualism, violence and sadism, betrayal and desertion, self-pity, degradation, and tragic guilt. But he also insinuates an oblique commentary on the main social movement of his day, as North America is associated with a full cycle of the immigrant experience: escape, hope, exploitation, material success, destruction of the family and traditional culture, and nostalgia for the Old World.

Puccini was born in 1858 into a family that claimed four successive generations of ecclesiastical composers, each of whom held the post of organist and choirmaster in the Duomo (San Martino), Lucca. In a singular expression of classical *pietas* their names appear, in chronological order, in Puccini's: Giacomo Antonio Domenico Michele Secondo Maria. Because great-grandfather Antonio also bore the name of Maria, Puccini became Secondo Maria. His early *Messa di Gloria* pays them homage, and some of his operas display a power to secularize and eroticize religious themes and pageantry: *Suor Angelica*, *Tosca* (the act 1 procession in church, during which police chief Scarpia sings of his desire for the title heroine), *Butterfly* (the choral song at Cio-Cio-San's marriage ceremony), and *Fanciulla* (Minnie's Bible-reading scene).

In Puccini's youth Lucca was a small city of thirty thousand inhabitants. The duchy had only recently been absorbed into Tuscany, according to the plan laid down by Metternich in 1815; but the pieces of the Italian puzzle had long become unstuck, and were about to be pieced together again in the form of Unification. Socially if not economically, the Puccinis had risen to the upper middle class. Then, in 1864, Puccini's father died suddenly, leaving a pregnant wife and six children and plunging the family into financial ruin. Puccini was five and the only son; a younger brother was born a few months later. In time he took upon himself the burden of rescuing the family musical tradition. Everyone expected it of him, from his stern, practical-minded mother to the town fathers. For years, these men left vacant the post of organist and choirmaster of San Martino's, secure in their belief that young Giacomo would someday occupy it. There could hardly be a more noteworthy expression of *Gemeinschaft* culture.

Biographers have consistently drawn Puccini as an apolitical creature, at best 'forever a *laudator temporis acti*' of the bourgeois epoch, at worst an early if silent supporter of Fascism (he died in 1924, when Italy was two years into the regime).[3] Harvey Sachs concludes that Puccini's occasional responses to Fascist rule were 'uninformed' and, regarding his music, 'insignificant.'[4] Yet earlier in his career Puccini insulted democratic instincts and applauded government ministers who ruled with a strong hand. He tended to associate his country's artistic genius with its pastoral and agrarian traditions. He shunned cities even as small as Lucca. Though rehearsals and premieres forced him to Milan, Rome, Paris, London, Berlin, Vienna, Madrid, Buenos Aires, and New York, he inevitably longed for his 'lairs' at Torre del Lago on Lake Massaciuccoli, St Lucia d'Uzzano (Pescia), Monsagrati, Chiatri high in the wilderness above Lucca, Boscolungo (Abetone) in the Apennines, and Torre della Tagliata down the coast in the remote Tuscan Maremma. Surely the ecclesiastical and aristocratic patronage that served his forebears was preferable to modern bondage to the opera producer and publishing house. (In 1880 Puccini's mother had appealed successfully to Queen Margherita for a scholarship to help her son through the Milan Conservatory.) One should not forget that such patronage survived much longer in Italy than in France or Great Britain. Oliver Goldsmith had lamented the decline of the aristocratic patron before the bookseller in his *Enquiry into the Present State of Polite Learning in Europe*, published in 1759, during the career of the first Giacomo Puccini (1712–81).

Like many members of his social class and generation, Puccini snubbed the rampant industrialization in northern countries and parts of Italy. Yet he contradicted himself too and was passionately fond of the latest consumer goods. 'Lucky you,' he wrote Sybil Seligman in London, 'who live in a country of great resources,' and he praised German 'orderliness' and 'conservatism.'[5] He favoured the Central Powers over France and England before Italy's entry in World War I; either refused or was not asked to sign protests against German atrocities; and was suspected of philogermanism during the war. His patriotism was supposedly proven by his mediocre *Inno a Roma* (1919), which during Fascism became 'a sort of third national anthem' after *Giovinezza* and the Royal March; Puccini referred to his *Hymn* as 'una bella porcheria' (a nice piece of trash).[6] 'What do you think of Mussolini?' he wrote his librettist Giuseppe Adami shortly after the Fascist March on Rome, 'I hope he will prove to be the man we need. Good luck to him if he will cleanse and give a little peace to our country!' (30 Oct. 1922).[7] When Mussolini dangled the post of honorary Senator of the Realm in 1924, Puccini accepted, barely three months after the assassination of the Socialist opposition leader Giacomo Matteotti. Then, in bad faith, he made light of the fact and signed himself 'Sonatore' (Player, Musician) instead of 'Senatore.'

Altogether Puccini's is not an attractive political portrait, especially in contrast to Verdi's or Toscanini's. Verdi put his opera to the task of rousing an unformed nation against their Austrian and Bourbon oppressors; Toscanini went into exile and attacked the Fascist dictatorship from abroad. If Puccini had lived longer into the Fascist period, he would not have actively supported the regime (he never actively supported any regime), but he probably would have acquiesced. 'As a highly intelligent musician who had quickly recognized the virtues of Debussy and even of Schoenberg, and as a cosmopolite whose friendships cut through all national and religious barriers,' Sachs observes, 'he certainly would have found absurd the provincial anti-Europeanism and racism of the later, imperial brand of fascism. Given his love of law and order, however – concepts so often extolled by Mussolini – and of strong, even repressive, government, he would most likely have allowed himself to become one of the regime's sacred cows.'[8] While an appraisal of Puccini's American theme might not alter the judgment of his political character, it should qualify its harshness. The plight of suffering, grief-stricken, emarginated individuals always worked on his imagination to bring out the best in his music. His choice of librettos everywhere confirms the strength of his emotions in this direction. The mass emigration of Italians might have acted upon him in this way, but Puccini also had deep, personal reasons for his sympathies.

In 1890, at age thirty-two, Puccini had reached the lowest ebb of his career. Although his first two operas, *Le Villi* and *Edgar*, had met with some critical success, both had failed commercially. He was heavily in debt and had to struggle to support a growing family. At this juncture, like so many Italians of his generation, he turned his eyes to the Americas. There, writes Mosco Carner, 'the fabulous fees which artists were said to earn among the large colonies of Italian immigrants seemed a potent enough inducement to forsake his native country.'[9] In *One Hundred Years of Solitude* Gabriel García Márquez paints their portrait in the figure of Pietro Crespi, the itinerant Italian dancing master. Puccini's younger brother Michele, a music teacher, had already emigrated to Argentina, and some of their correspondence survives. In one letter to him Puccini expresses his anxiety over *Edgar*: 'I fear terribly for the opera, because all are making a bitter war against me. If you find work for me, after *Edgar*, I will come. Not in Buenos Aires, but in the interior, among the redskins!' (6 Feb. 1890).[10] Desperate for work, he still resists the metropolis, preferring wild, primitive nature.

Biographers tend to minimize these letters, claiming that Puccini had no intention of leaving Italy. The fact that he would not or could not take that final step does not mean, however, that he could not imagine such alternatives to his present condition, and as Samuel Johnson said, no man thinks much of that which he despises. 'If you are coming along well where you are, I'll come too, if there were something to do,' Puccini wrote Michele a few months later, 'Write me about this. I am fed up with the struggle with poverty, always!' (24 Apr. 1890). The next week he resumes in a letter filled with details of his wretched finances: 'If I could find a way of making money, I would come where you are. Is there anything to do? I would quit everything here and leave ... I am ready, extremely ready, if you write me to come, I will come, and one will get along. However, money is needed for the trip, I warn you!'[11]

If Puccini harboured any illusions about the Americas, one of Michele's replies would have dispelled them: 'I warn you – do not come here! You cannot imagine what I have been through. What a life! I left Buenos Aires, where I worked like a slave, with nothing to show for it on account of the high cost of living. Then they told me that in the province of Yoyoy [Jujuy, a mountainous region in northern-most Argentina] I would obtain a position teaching voice, piano and Italian for 300 *scudi* a month. I crossed the Andes, and after innumerable sufferings came at last to Yoyoy.'[12] Through the offices of the Argentine vice-president, the son of an Italian, Michele was put in touch with Don Domingo T. Perez, a parliamentary deputy who arranged the teaching post in Jujuy. Even before departing Buenos Aires, Michele caught influenza, which he exacerbated by attempting to teach before he was well. The journey was every bit as astonishing as Michele said, including a storm that swamped his train and a stage hold-up by Indians that led to a furious gunfight (Michele packed a revolver and a stiletto). In Jujuy Michele at first seemed to prosper, but he fell in love one of his pupils – the wife of Perez, according to a friend who later wrote Puccini.[13] After eight months the lovers were discovered. Perez challenged Michele to a duel in which the deputy was wounded in the shoulder. Michele fled the region, first to Buenos Aires, then out of the country. He ended up in Rio de Janiero, then in the throes of a yellow fever epidemic. Michele caught the disease and died on 12 March 1891, at the time when Puccini was at work on *Manon Lescaut.*

Puccini, who had assumed responsibility for his younger brother ever since their mother's death in 1884, was crushed by the news. Michele had dropped out of the Milan Conservatory, the scene of his elder brother's triumph, after three years. Then he had 'drifted from job to job, between Lucca and Milan, always in the shadow of his older brother and often acting as little more than an errand boy for him.'[14] The promise of South America had turned to nothing. 'Oh my God, what torture, I am almost a dead man!' Puccini wrote his sister Ramelde on learning of his death; 'I could say that such pain I did not feel even for our poor mother, and it was tremendous. What a tragedy! I cannot wait to die; what am I now doing in this world? Poor Michele. Whatever might happen to me, glory, honors, satisfactions – all will leave me indifferent.'[15]

Manon, too, dies in the New World. She has been deported by the

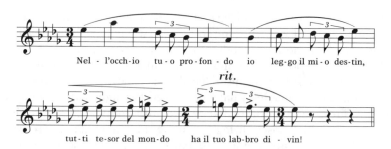

Figure 1

French police, ostensibly for prostitution and theft, actually for double-crossing a powerful lover. In the Abbé Prévost's novel, on which the opera is based, Manon is a flirtatious sixteen-year-old country girl who, instead of entering the convent, runs away with an aristocratic seventeen-year-old philosophy student, the Chevalier des Grieux. She is ensnared by Parisian high life and turns to rich men to satisfy her love for clothes and jewels. In Puccini's opera, towards the end of act 2, des Grieux confronts Manon with one such betrayal and she begs forgiveness. A creature of pure impulse, she actually does have a soft spot for des Grieux. 'I dreamed of a bright future,' she implores him; and at this point, with des Grieux caught between his belief in Manon's sincerity and his own blind romantic passion, Puccini introduces a musical theme that will have five prominent appearances in the opera (fig. 1).[16] Des Grieux's lines declare the attainment of a future that vastly transcends the present: 'Nel l'occhio tuo profondo / io leggo il mio destin, / tutti tesor del mondo / ha il tuo labbro divin!' (In the depths of your eyes / I read my fate; / your divine lips / have all the treasures in the world!). Charles Osborne thinks that this final section of the love duet (where the theme first appears) is less successful than the opening section; the 'music takes on a quasi-martial aspect which leads one to suspect that Puccini may here be making use of music conceived to fit words of a different temper.' The overall impression is that 'one is listening to two Verdi characters exulting at the moment of victory rather than two Puccinian lovers in passionate embrace.'[17] While Osborne correctly notes a shift in mood, his misreading of the emotional motive for the shift leads him to fault Puccini's intention. Knowing what lies ahead for the young lovers, Puccini needed a powerful heroic theme in their duet as a foreshadowing device. All his early operas show this ability to exploit a kernel theme to point forward and backward in psychological and narrative texture. In the present context, the theme that expresses the courage needed to attain the 'bright future' may be more appropriately described as heroic rather than martial, though the former may include the latter. One may compare the briefer 'Trionfal! di nova speme ...'of Tosca and Cavaradossi in act 3 of *Tosca*.

What lies in that future? Puccini must have thought of his brother and the wife of Senator Perez. The heroic theme next appears in the final moment of the Intermezzo (between acts 2 and 3), which Puccini entitled 'The Imprisonment; The Journey to Le Havre.'[18] It is meant to signify the lovers' reunion and their embarkation for America. Then, true to its anticipation, the heroic theme appears at the climax of act 3 when the ship is about to embark for New Orleans. This act, the finest Puccini had composed to date, had given him the most trouble, so much that he was only to complete it after he had finished act 4. Manon has been arrested and taken to Le Havre where she awaits deportation. Trailing her, des Grieux bribes the police to secure her escape, but plans go awry. As Manon is led on board, des Grieux in a brief impassioned e minor aria beseeches the captain to take him along: he will be a cabin boy, he will do the most menial task, he cannot live without Manon: 'Guardate, pazzo son' (Look at me, I'm going mad). In the middle of the aria a much-contorted version of the heroic theme forces its yearning quality to the breaking point: a dotted eighth note followed by a sixteenth note and a sustained dotted half-note. Writing on the first movement of Beethoven's *Moonlight Sonata*, Wilfrid Mellers describes this particular rhythmic motive as 'traditionally a representation of fortitude.'[19] At the end of the aria – or is it interrupted? – a cannon shot signals that departure is imminent. The vocal line halts on middle C while the sympathetic captain ponders taking des Grieux aboard. Of particular interest are the captain's words, which do not appear in Prévost's novel:[20] 'Ah! popolar le Americhe, giovinotto, desiate? ben ... ebben ... sia pur! Via, mozzo, v'affrettate!' (Ah! young man, so you want to populate the Americas? Well, well, so be it. Get going, cabin-boy, hurry up!). Then the orchestra breaks forth in the most optimistic rendering of the heroic theme, now in sunniest E major, rising from *ff* to *ffff*, 'like a fanfare to mark the reunion of the two lovers and their departure for the freedom of the New World.'[21]

Puccini handled his heroic theme with great invention. The theme is shaped like a *V*. Emphasis can be placed on its plunge downward in despair as in des Grieux's e minor aria. But its upward rise can be marked in bold E major chords towards triumph, as in the embarkation scene, and here it is possible to feel a 'quasi-martial' air (Osborne). Its chord progression can even sound 'hymn-like' (Carner), and the descendent of church composers would not have forgotten the Baroque convention whereby E major, 'the sharpest major key in common use [that] was associated with heaven' (Mellers), signifies Manon's 'bright future.' In its rolling, wave-like rhythm, the theme may well suggest the ocean voyage. Most important, as act 3 rushes to its climax, the heroic theme conveys the 'noble passion' of the Longinian sublime. Freedom imagery (release from prison, embarkation) and ocean imagery are, claims Longinus, particularly suitable for expressing emotional release into transcendent existence. The general tone is romantic yearning for future bliss, a cosmic emotion that Romain Rolland labelled the 'oceanic sensation.'[22]

Everyone agrees that young Puccini committed an act of musical hubris in writing *Manon Lescaut* because Jules Massenet had chosen the same novel as the vehicle for his own masterpiece *Manon* (1884) only nine years before. Hoping to stave off the most blatant comparisons, Puccini directed his librettists to concentrate where possible on scenes from Prévost that Massenet did not use. Thus, in Massenet, Manon dies on the road to Le Havre. There is no cannon shot, no ship captain, no embarkation, no final act in America. Carner approves of Puccini's act-three embarkation scene, but wishes the opera ended there, with Manon dying 'on board ship': Puccini was 'compelled to put his lovers to the inconvenience of undertaking a voyage as far as the New World.' The opera has a 'lame ending' with the 'inevitable risk of monotony,' the 'biggest dramatic blunder of all.'[23] If, however, the mass emigration of Italians and Puccini's personal circumstances are kept in view, the decision to capitalize on these scenes in the novel makes both psychological and dramatic sense. Puccini depicts the arrival at Le Havre, embarkation, and dénouement in the New World.

Nothing heroic attaches to the last appearance of the heroic theme in the final act, titled 'In America.' Des Grieux has fought a duel over Manon with the governor's nephew, and Manon and des Grieux are fleeing the territory. The story was bearing an uncanny resemblance to Michele's fate. The theme now assumes a true Puccinian form: 'limping,' 'sagging,' 'dragging,' broken, meandering, melancholy. We heard the triumphant upward motion of the theme in the embarkation. Now in the deepening gloom of Louisiana (described as a 'desert,' it was probably damp, deadly marshland or a thick forest; Puccini had read James Fenimore Cooper in translation), the theme conveys a sad listlessness and sense of the void. Michele Girardi describes it well as a 'mirage just before those isolated chords introduce desperate, lonely awareness' in Manon's act 4 aria, 'Sola, perduta, abbandonata.'[24]

The second of Puccini's operas involving America or Americans, *Madama Butterfly*, is based on John Luther Long's magazine story 'Madame Butterfly' (1898), which in turn inspired a one-act play of the same title (1900) by the American playwright and producer David Belasco (1839–1917). The story tells how Cio-Cio-San, reduced to poverty and forced to become a geisha, is married on contract to Pinkerton, an American naval lieutenant, on his stop in Nagasaki. He leaves, three years pass, and, having broken the contract, the lieutenant returns with an American wife to claim his son by Butterfly. Deeply in love, she awaits his return and makes inquiries in person at the American consulate. There she learns of Pinkerton's remarriage and even meets the American wife, who is patronizing to her. In the story she goes home and attempts suicide; but she survives and vanishes, perhaps back into her previous occupation. In the play she succeeds in killing herself. The story is in two parts. In part one, Pinkerton and Butterfly are together in the early days of their marriage. The second part covers Butterfly's waiting, the consulate scene, and the suicide attempt. Belasco's play includes just that second part.

Puccini was entranced by the play's London production in 1900. Perhaps his total lack of English stimulated his imagination to wander over the storyline because he at once recognized its operatic possibilities. Originally he thought of writing a one-act opera closely following the play. Then he considered a separate 'North American act,' set within the American consulate at Nagasaki, ostensibly to situate the action on 'Western' ground and enforce the East-West contrast. In either case there would be next to nothing for Lt Pinkerton. In both story and play Pinkerton's is a bit part: he first appears on page sixteen of a nineteen-page play and has just six lines (his American wife has eight). Therefore Puccini shrewdly directed his librettists Giuseppe Giacosa and Luigi Illica to quarry the story's first part and create a 'first act.' In the opera Pinkerton remains on stage throughout act 1 so that the audience can observe and assess his character in a variety of scenes. Thereafter Puccini bowed to circumstance and could only slip in a short *arioso* for Pinkerton, and not sung to Butterfly, but to her little house, in act 3. With his superb sense of theatre, Puccini cut the consulate scene and transferred the entire action of act 2 to Butterfly's house, to which the consul must now pay a visit. 'The Consulate was a great mistake,' he wrote his publisher Giulio Ricordi, 'the action must move forward to the close without interruption, rapid, effective, terrible.'[25]

Pinkerton's expanded role gave Puccini wide room to manoeuvre and elaborate upon his American theme. Dramatic conflict between the principals is minimal – Pinkerton and Butterfly never speak to each other after their act 1 love duet – so Puccini pursued the conflict of East and West. But as he knew about Japan even less than he knew about the United States, he universalized the conflict by setting Old World against New World on a variety of issues, from religion, law, and the family to such abstract concepts as time and space. To learn about speech patterns and customs, he consulted a Japanese actress and the wife of the Japanese ambassador to Italy. The latter even sent home for music. While the Japanese musical themes and ideas that he eventually borrowed are no mere window dressing, social and historical reconstruction was not his specialty. All his evidence for Old World culture lay close at hand, in the very ritualism, hierarchism, and patriarchy of Italy. As for the New World, Puccini could draw upon his own understanding of the 'northern' character and the personal experience of Giuseppe Giacosa.

Giacosa visited the United States in 1893 and published his findings in *Impressioni d'America* (1898), described as 'the most important record of the Italian perception of America towards the end of the last century.'[26] He toured widely, from New York to the Deep South, Chicago, Detroit, and Boston. In a generally balanced account he admired Americans for their 'vigorous feeling of social equality and personal dignity' and their 'proud awareness of physical energy,' while deploring the ostentatious display of wealth, the miserable conditions of their slums, and such personal habits as strong, antisocial drinking ('they enjoy being drunk more than drinking'). However, some of his observations are prejudicial stereotypes: Chicago's 'chief characteristic' is 'violence': 'I wouldn't want to live there for anything on earth; but I believe that those who ignore it do not completely understand our century, of which it is the ultimate expression.'[27]

Giacosa found Italian Americans slow to catch on to the American way of life, partly for cultural reasons and lack of English. They signed citizen papers forswearing allegiance to Italy but did not vote or participate in their new country's affairs, with disastrous results. Nor did they band together like the French or Germans. The Americans held them third lowest in public esteem, with only the Chinese and the African Americans beneath them. Prejudice was especially true on the eastern seaboard, whereas in Texas and California the Italian was more of an equal in the battle for financial and social success. Italians were victimized not only by Americans but by one another. The Italian consul in Chicago told Giacosa that when he asked the immigrants how they protected their money (and just about anything else), they always answered, 'il compare' (the friend, crony, godfather). The immigrants laboured as hard as the Americans, often in the most menial and dangerous occupations, and saved carefully. Yet while American workers considered 'prosperity to be an indispensable condition of life' and lived in 'nice, comfortable, solid homes, similar to those in which ... almost only lawyers, doctors, and judges live in Italian towns,' the Italian went on living in impoverished conditions. The blood-spattered butchers in Chicago changed to 'clean new clothes' on leaving the slaughterhouse and went home like the petty bourgeois to whom they aspired. But the ill-clad Italian immigrants were often sending their salaries back to Italy, a mark of familism that ran against self-interest: 'Where the dollars go, there go the mind and heart, and a little later (if he can afford to), the person.' Americans were baffled by the immigrant's self-sacrifice. 'But we, who know our domestic conditions, must judge our compatriots in an entirely different light'; 'the greatest part of their misery is the fruit of ignorance. But it is certain too that the greatest part of their suffering is an exercise of deep and lasting courage.'[28] Finally, he notes that the professional or upper-class Italian Americans were either too few or unwilling to be of much help, another illustration of the great failure of Italian culture to generalize itself, to spread more deeply through its population. At a feast honouring an Italian consul, various immigrants got up to defend Italy against its detractors; as Giacosa's eye travelled across the immigrants' strained faces, he noticed their rancour, suspicion, and bitterness and imagined what they could accomplish if they were united.

The Americans in *Madama Butterfly* are Sharpless, who is U.S. consul at Nagasaki; Pinkerton; and Pinkerton's second wife Kate. Then, there is the offspring of Butterfly and Pinkerton, the love child 'Trouble,' with 'blue eyes' and 'blond hair.' Kate has one of the most awkward roles in all opera. She asks Sharpless for the child in Butterfly's presence and then begs her forgiveness. Butterfly merely waves her off, telling her faithful servant Suzuki that she will talk only with Pinkerton, then commits suicide. In a tradition that probes the devious machinations behind the coronation of Poppea, eulogizes moral triumph in the immurement of Aida, and magnifies even a verismo character like Mascagni's Santuzza into heroic proportions, an ordinary American housewife on an Asian tour almost breaks operatic illusion. Kate is a minor variant of the American theme that Puccini does not develop. She was only left in, as on the margin of a painting.

The essence of Sharpless is sympathy – for Butterfly, for Suzuki, for Pinkerton. In many ways he is the kind of person the lieutenant might well become, a man who has learned human compassion through age and experience. (Sharpless is completely out of breath after climbing up to Butterfly's house and must be well past his youth.) Used to travelling about the world, he perhaps once lived according to young Pinkerton's 'easy-going creed' ('facile vangelo') of no ties and brief affairs. It 'makes life enchanting,' he sighs, and 'saddens the heart.' Yet the worldly diplomat has not been embittered by experience. Maybe his name, Sharp-less, is meant to connote his gentleness; or is it because he must offer 'sharp,' painful counsel in a most understanding fashion? He issues the warning signals to Pinkerton; he consoles Butterfly when suspicions are raised about her husband's return. Not especially defined by any national traits, he is the familiar avuncular type in Italian opera: Sir Giorgio Walton in Bellini's *I puritani* and Raimondo Bidebent in Donizetti's *Lucia di Lammermoor* are cut from the same cloth.

The more appealing the tenor, the finer the voice, the less mean will appear Lieutenant Benjamin Franklin Pinkerton. Yet in some ways he exemplifies the Ugly American, a symbol of his country's imperialist expansion, a lieutenant in the very navy that 'opened up' Japan in the 1850s. He was Uglier in the opera's original version. Puccini cut Pinkerton's nasty comments on the exotic foods ('candied fruits and flies') and 'nauseating gluttony' of the Japanese and his reference to Butterfly's servants as 'Mug One – Mug Two – Mug Three.'[29] Like the composer himself, he bears a heavy freight of names. 'Benjamin Franklin' is the quintessential hero of the pragmatic individual and American entrepreneur. 'Pinkerton' refers to Allan Pinkerton (1819–84), the Scottish-born American who founded the famous detective agency in 1855. Pinkerton had been a Chartist and was even detained for radical behaviour in England. In the United States he altered his opinions to suit his fortunes, becoming deputy sheriff of Cook County, Illinois, then chief spy for the Army of the Potomac and a head of counter-espionage. After the Civil War his agency protected railroad lines and was involved in strike-breaking. Pinkerton agents were widely criticized for their actions in the Pullman Strike of 1894, and so at the time of Long's story the name would have been recently in the public eye. Finally, Lt Pinkerton's warship is the

U.S.S. *Abraham Lincoln*. Self-interest and imperialism masquerade under the most cherished symbol of liberty.

With all these clues, Pinkerton has rarely been understood as a political and sociological phenomenon. Richard Specht calls him a 'Tristan disguised as a modern naval lieutenant ... too cowardly to meet the woman whom he has abandoned ... brutal enough to bring his "legal" wife with him and demand the child through her agency.' For Vincent Seligman, he is a 'cold-blooded and thoughtless seducer, in many respects a more repulsive character than even the wicked Scarpia.'[30] If the young lieutenant is heartless and morally wrong to desert Butterfly, he is not a sadist or ruthless killer like Scarpia, a chief of police and master of a secret service that Allan Pinkerton might well have envied.

We first meet Butterfly's self-styled 'Yankee vagabond' bargaining for a rented house in the opening scene. Goro, the Japanese agent, says the house is 'strong as a tower,' but Pinkerton, never to be taken in, sees it as light as a 'featherweight' and easily blown away in the wind. With a combination of fulsome affability and low cunning, traits of the Yankee trader, he twice flatters Goro as a 'great pearl,' thus demeaning one of the most famous of biblical images of the soul (Matthew 13:46). Two deceivers recognize each other. Goro has arranged the wedding ceremony, and Pinkerton asks if there are many relatives. In a rare moment of humour, Goro responds: 'The mother-in-law, the grandmother, the uncle Bonze (who will not grant us the honor of his presence) and male and female cousins ... we have about two dozen of these counting the older relatives and collateral descendents.' Gently satirizing an Italian institution, Puccini opposes the modern American Pinkerton as naval adventurer and loner to a chorus of a landed traditional family.[31]

Sharpless enters and Pinkerton brags of a nine-hundred-ninety-nine-year bargain that can be cancelled at the end of each month. Sharpless chimes in with 'And the clever man profits by that,' Pinkerton underlines his remark ('Certainly'), and with this reference to the profit motive, the opening bars of 'The Star-Spangled Banner' ring out, band fashion, in brass and woodwinds. The national anthem is the pivotal theme in the first scene where Pinkerton expatiates on his mode of life, the 'easy-going creed' of love and irresponsibility (fig. 2). Puccini, who wanted Pinkerton to 'sing like an American,' gave him a jaunty, relaxed aria, to be sung 'frankly.'[32] His opening words put a pleasant face on the anthem's first bars, a rising fourth (the anthem's 'you see' in 'O say can you see'), then a gentle fall corresponding to the anthem's 'by the

Allegro sostenuto con spirito

Figure 2

dawn's early light': 'Wherever the Yankee vagabond [lo Yankee vagabon-
do] goes all over the world, he enjoys himself and makes his fortune
taking risks. He drops anchor trusting to his luck ... until a sudden storm
upsets the ship, moorings, riggings ... He is not satisfied with life until he
makes his treasure the flowers on every shore ... a beautiful girl, his love.'
Naval and travel metaphors apply equally to both sexual and imperialist
desires. Sharpless breaks in gently, counselling that this way of life 'saddens the heart.' Perhaps he says this to himself, because the words sail
over Pinkerton, who keeps singing: 'Defeated, he'll take a plunge and
struggle back. His cleverness serves him everywhere. So I am marrying
for nine hundred ninety-nine years Japanese style.' Over 'milk-punch or
whiskey' both men stand up and toast, in English, 'America forever!' to
the melody of 'The Star-Spangled Banner.' Now it sounds harsh and grating, in keeping with the crudity of language and emotion.

The two men talk of the wedding, to begin shortly. It is another bargain that can be cancelled each month, 'for nothing, only a hundred
yen' ('per nulla, sol cento yen'). The music rises in tension as Sharpless
foresees danger and compares Pinkerton's infatuation ('smania') with
an impoverished, fifteen-year-old geisha's 'sincere' love ('sincer l'amor'),
but is *smania* to be compared to *sincer l'amor*? Taking up the metaphor of
the butterfly from Pinkerton, he warns that it would be a terrible wrong
to tear its wings. Pinkerton ends the conversation by calling for another
toast, 'to the day when I will marry in a real wedding to a real American
bride.' The ideal of the ceremonious has been totally perverted. Toasting
personal betrayal followed fast upon a toast to American imperialism.
This crass behaviour is interrupted by a procession of women leading the
way before Cio-Cio-San as the music turns enthrallingly beautiful. She

calls them her 'amiche' (friends) and they are almost certainly geishas. Their ethereal ode to love overwhelms Pinkerton's cavalier treatment of the subject.

The wedding scene sets in motion the doomed conflict between two ways of life: the ancient, ritualistic, hierarchical society represented by Butterfly and her uncle Bonze, a Buddhist priest, and Pinkerton's new 'easy creed' of independence and self-interest. But first Butterfly makes a telling error in introducing herself. The commissioner gives Pinkerton's first names as Benjamin Franklin; then Butterfly refers to herself as Mrs 'F.B.' Pinkerton. Her 'error' can be traced to Long's original story where in another scene Butterfly is identifying herself, mixes up three long, foreign names, and delicately corrects herself: 'Missus Ben-ja-no! Missus Frang-a-leen Ben-ja-meen – no, no, *no!* Missus Ben-ja-meen Frang-a-leen Pikkerton.'[33] The name given wrong may show a nervous insecurity as well as unfamiliarity. She both is and is not the wife and 'familiar': reversal cancels. Butterfly then tells her family's story, showing that the Japanese traditional family has its rigidities that hardly make it the ideal opposition to Pinkerton. Her father was involved in some impropriety serious enough to be asked to commit hara-kiri by the emperor, symbolized by the ritual presentation of a sword. The family fell into poverty and Butterfly became a geisha to take herself off their hands. In love with Pinkerton, she realizes a way to rescue herself, only to find that her uncle, the Bonze, a Buddhist priest, refuses to solemnize her marriage to a non-Buddhist. The actual ceremony is, therefore, a civil one, with the Japanese commissioner and registrar, the American consul, and a minimum of formality. The American anthem sounds, for the third time in the opera, at the moment Pinkerton's name is called. The process of identification continues.

After Sharpless and the Japanese officials make their exit, the private family festivities proceed. Isolated amid a dozen or so relations, Pinkerton comments playfully, but a trifle cynically, 'Here I am a family man,' and then adds the cutting 'Let's hurry and be rid of these people as soon as we decently may.' The typical American is always in a hurry, and Pinkerton's politeness merely facilitates efficiency; it does not spring from the heart. The Japanese toast is more like a libation, as the chorus of women sing to the Japanese god 'O Kami! O Kami!' In the midst of the mystical Kami theme, the Bonze is heard shouting angrily for Butterfly. He arrives preceded by two lantern bearers and followed by two priests. The contrast to the rather cool, dull ceremony will be a fiery, hieratic, familial excommunication. Both uncle and priest, significantly combining the familial and religious functions in a culture where the family is a religion (not unlike Italy), the Bonze already knows the answer to his question, whether by marrying a foreigner Butterfly has 'denied the ancient cult.' Butterfly's mother tries to intervene but the Bonze pushes her aside. Pinkerton steps forward and cries, 'Hey, you, I say enough is enough!' ('Ehi, dico: basta, basta!') As the Bonze summons the clan and orders them to leave, Pinkerton seizes the moment: 'Get out of here this instant, In my house there'll be no uproar and no "bonzery."' A man's home is his castle. Initial sympathies are with the lovers and against the priest, whom the devious Goro, Pinkerton's ugly double in business and ceremonies, shunts aside with a typically Italian curse, 'Un corno al guastafeste' (Horns to the spoil-sport). But Pinkerton has not been a source of understanding and diplomacy in this scene. Likewise, in the love duet, he brusquely insists that Suzuki quiet down – she is saying her evening prayers, invoking the gods, more in need now than ever. Incidentally, in this scene he calls Butterfly his 'little toy.' Butterfly turns the 'compliment' into a pretext for analogies: 'We are a people accustomed / To little things, / Humble and quiet.' She later conceives of the United States as 'un gran paese,' a *big* country.

During the three years that pass between acts 1 and 2, Butterfly holds out hope of Pinkerton's return. She identifies him with his country and believes in America as the land of justice and freedom, unlike her own land, which has rejected her. Again, Suzuki prays to the Buddhist gods, now to stop Butterfly's weeping; in unconscious imitation of Pinkerton, Butterfly interjects blasphemously: 'Fat and lazy / Are the Japanese gods. / The American God, I am sure, / is more prompt to answer / Those who implore him.' The lines may contain an ironic comment on the Yankee values of speed and efficiency. Butterfly welcomes Sharpless to her 'American' house, which we know is a house of cards, and asks if his 'grandparents and ancestors are well.' To her innocent way of thinking, America stands for all that is good in her own culture, along with justice and fairness. When Goro explains the Japanese law on divorce, completely favouring the male, Butterfly interrupts him – 'Not my country's law,' she sings of the triumph of her love as the orchestra strikes up the 'Star-Spangled Banner' theme. 'Which country?' Goro asks. 'The United States,' she answers. Butterfly turns to Sharpless: 'We know that to open the door / And chase the wife out the shortest possible way, / Means divorce here. / But in America / you cannot do that. Am I right?' Sharpless hesitates to answer, 'You are ... But ... ' The point is that Butterfly suffers beneath the law of both her native and adoptive lands.

Ernest Newman said that Puccini's sympathy for victimized women proved him a 'strong feminist.' Sympathy alone does not make a feminist, and Puccini never translated his sympathies into a public agenda. More likely, he was re-enacting his own need to victimize, projecting his own guilt-ridden desire and longing for its extinction.[34]

In the second part of act 2, Butterfly's patience seems to have proven her right. Pinkerton has returned. She sees the American flag flying from the warship *Abramo Lincoln*, singing the name of Lincoln as if he were her own personal liberator. Handing the spyglass to Suzuki, she extols the triumph of love in a moment of ecstasy over an orchestral line containing an implacable repetition of the 'Star-Spangled Banner' theme, in its fifth and final appearance in the opera. For Puccini, Butterfly's attitude towards the United States expresses the hope of immigrants generally. He himself did not believe in the dream, so he loaded each reference to America, either on Pinkerton's or Butterfly's part, with an almost savage irony. In the final moments of the opera, Butterfly puts a tiny American flag in her child's hand before she hides behind a screen and stabs herself to death with her father's ritual sword. The child is waving it, as in victory, when his father rushes in, calling Butterfly's name.

Madama Butterfly ranks as one of the most popular works in the history of opera. Its theme was eminently of the nineteenth and twentieth century: the individual caught between traditionalist and 'modern' (commercial, industrial, technological) culture. This conflict is deeper than – because it subsumes – the incompatibility between East and West. Puccini took a sensational magazine story and turned it into a powerful tragedy, winning an audience far broader and more lasting than the turn-of-the-century audience of the *Century Magazine* and Belasco's plays. The opera stands up to what Samuel Johnson called the test of great art, the portrayal of 'general nature,' the 'length of duration' in the public mind and its 'continuance of esteem' (*Preface to Shakespeare*). Puccini's was perhaps the last generation before the split between popular and sophisticated art drove itself through modern culture, and his work as a whole may serve as a reminder of how great art, in the novel, symphonic music, and grand opera, was also popular art in the nineteenth century. The union of high and popular culture that he achieved with Belasco in *Madama Butterfly* would fall apart in his next effort with the American director.

The running thread in Puccini's musical biography is the search for a libretto and its 'creative reconstruction.'[35] After his Japanese opera Puccini had the double burden of finding both a libretto and a librettist. The partnership of Giacosa and Illica, from *La Bohème* (1896) to *Tosca* (1900) and *Madama Butterfly* (1904), ended with Giacosa's death in 1906. Puccini was in his late forties, at the height of his musical powers, an international celebrity, wealthy far beyond his expectations. Whatever he composed would receive the greatest attention. Houses would vie for its premiere, Toscanini would probably conduct it, Caruso would probably sing in it. What would he do next? The world was waiting.

Seven troubled years were to pass between *Madama Butterfly* and his next premiere. While he explored a dozen possibilities for a libretto, including one by D'Annunzio, he received an invitation to make a visit, his first, to the United States. The Metropolitan Opera offered him eight thousand dollars to superintend the American premiere of *Madama Butterfly*, and he agreed. During the 1906–7 season, the Met was mounting four of his operas (producing four operas by a living composer who had so far only written six is utterly astounding). He was taking note of an English *Butterfly*'s enormous success in the United States and Canada, a fourteen-thousand-mile, sixty-city tour, with about two hundred performances over six months. 'Never before was a single opera taken on such an extensive journey, traveling with double understudies required for the nightly, and some additional matinee, performances.'[36]

Yet Puccini immediately regretted his decision. In December 1906 he was supervising a production of *Madama Butterfly* in Paris, and it was going poorly. Though his recently discovered diabetes was under control, he was suffering nervous exhaustion and longed for Torre del Lago: 'The thought ... of going to America is getting on my nerves.'[37] Impulsively he had mistaken an invitation for an escape and he always despaired of public life: 'An invitation to dinner makes me sick for a week,' he wrote in similar circumstances on a previous sojourn in Paris, 'I wasn't born for the life of drawing rooms and receptions.'[38] Still, he went and caused a sensation at dockside in New York when he announced that he was 'thinking of writing an opera with western America as a background.' The morning headlines read: 'Would write THE American Opera / M. Puccini Fired to Compose "The West" / Will consult Mr. Belasco.'[39] Actually, he had reached no conclusions on the subject of his next opera.

Rehearsals absorbed much of his attention during his stay in New York (Jan.–Feb. 1907), for Puccini was a scrupulous observer of these events. He published an open letter in the *New York Herald* on gramophone royalties. He dined at Del Pezzo on Mulberry Street in Little Italy and 'sat for a special photograph, copies of which were given free to all those who contributed to a building fund for a school planned for poor children of Italian parentage.'[40] Then, after three weeks, boredom set in: 'I have had all I wanted of America.' He was on a boat back to Italy two weeks later.[41] Note his language: 'all I wanted of America.' He had not travelled from New York City: what drew his interest were the latest gadgets and consumer goods like automobiles, radiators, gramophones, telephones, refrigerators, and cameras. At a dinner at the Vanderbilt's, Clarence Mackay, a banker and Metropolitan Opera board member, said he 'would give anything' for a manuscript copy of Musetta's Waltz. Puccini, who had seen a three-thousand-dollar motorboat in a shop window, wrote out the opening bars and signed it.[42] There is a touch of vulgarity in such an action; Verdi would never have done it.

Unexpectedly, the New York visit proved the turning point in Puccini's search for a libretto because he saw three plays by Belasco, including *The Girl of the Golden West*, which had been brought to his attention the previous year. 'I like the ambience of the West,' he informed Tito Ricordi near the end of his trip, 'though in all the pieces I have seen, I have found only a scene or two here and there. Never a simple line, all farrago and, at times, in bad taste and old hat.' 'We've had enough now of *Bohème*, *Butterfly*, and Co. Even I am sick of them.'[43] Enough of fainting heroines and tragic outcomes, it was time for New World optimism and rough-and-ready characters that the Wild West could provide in abundance; Belasco called the Girl a 'bully' role. Again, Puccini could not understand most of the English of Belasco's play, though this had not impaired his judgment of *Butterfly*. The story was direct in emotional appeal and as easy to follow as a silent film. Like a silent film, too, Belasco's play was dotted with 'folk' and popular music. Girardi notes the possible influence of the cinema western, like Edward S. Porter's *The Great Train Robbery* (1903), and 'the classic devices of spectacle, Manichaean contrasts, and simple morals.'[44] Apparently it was when the camp minstrel sang 'The Old Dog Tray' that Puccini turned to Belasco and said 'Ah! there is my theme at last.'[45]

Puccini grasped Belasco's intention, to trade on the aura of the Wild West. Belasco said his play was a 'drama of love ... against a dark and vast background of primitive characters and untrammelled nature.' The Far West was one of the genuine myths of American modernity. Custer's Last Stand, its quintessential episode, occurred in 1876. The frontier had vanished by 1890 and at the outset of the new century the West completed a process of mythicization that had begun with the Leatherstocking Tales. In the (nostalgic) Hegelian twilight, Frederick Jackson Turner announced his thesis on 'The Significance of the Frontier in American History' (1893), where he claimed that the ever-receding frontier was the strongest explanatory force behind American history. It stripped its inhabitants of Old World habits and values and forged them anew by dint of circumstance. Frontier life accomplished in one generation what took two or three in cities on the Eastern seaboard: immigrants are 'Americanized,' 'liberated,' and 'fused into a mixed race, English in neither nationality nor characteristics.'[46] In Puccini's opera the Mexican 'Ramerrez' is also 'Dick Johnson' as ethnic (cultural, physical) differences collapse as if by magic. On the other hand, O.E. Rölvaag's *Peder Victorious* portrays the extreme difficulty of acculturation. Nevertheless, for Turner and his school, the American identity was the grandest product of the frontier. A new national character had been thrust upon the world stage – with its laconic, colourfully expressive idiom.

As Belasco's ambivalent title implies, the Golden West is not just the age of gold, a vision of innocence and true love in a primitive setting. Belasco did not paint the West of fur trappers, daring scouts, and Indians, nor even the 'second' West of Frederic Remington's cowboys and Bret Harte's town folk. Belasco's West is the white man's greed, false identities, bandits, alcoholism, manhunt, and lynch-mob justice. It is 'yellow fever,' the gold in the hills that drives the denizens of the mining towns to criminal excess. Belasco was hardly prepared to disentangle the competing forces that shaped the myth of the West, even if he wished to do so. Difficulties were papered over with stock characterization, romantic sentimentality, melodramatic twists and turns, and a happy ending. Nor did he realize that the West could not be disconnected from the East. Economic historians have severely qualified or dismissed Turner's thesis, showing that Eastern entrepreneurs and market conditions affected the frontier at every stage of its development. New immigrant populations took low-paying jobs in the East and drove out earlier immigrants, who went West to make their fortunes. The West joined hands with the East, and its myth of rugged individualism and the wide open spaces was at least partly orchestrated in Eastern centres of wealth and power. Its hidden side was manifest destiny, raw capitalism, the exploitation of nature, and genocide. Belasco exploited the myth of exploitation.

Turning Aristotle upside down, Belasco emphasized spectacle over plot and character and captured his audience with special effects, like the long, rolling scenarios or the blizzard on Cloudy Mountain that required the combined efforts of thirty-two stagehands. He structured the play around a character, and not even a character but an actress, Blanche Bates, whom he had helped raise to stardom as Cigarette in a stage adaptation of Ouida's *Under Two Flags*. An early manifestation of the star system, the Girl served as a vehicle for Bates's versatile style. The Girl Minnie is not so much a person as an actress featured from various emotional sides, and if the sides did not add up to a whole, so much the worse for the play. 'Minnie' calls up the diminutive, fragility; she is more often generalized as 'the Girl,' a synecdoche of the Golden West, something pure and virginal, and at the same time in danger, in need of protection, open to trade, plunder, rape. 'I've got my first kiss to give still,' she tells Johnson. Yet if Belasco's and Puccini's Girl possesses the sweet innocence of a Mary Pickford, she has the cool nerve of a Belle Starr. Both proprietress and barmaid of the Polka Saloon, she is a mini-capitalist and social outcast, for as we know from countless westerns, barmaids in the Old West were typically loose, hard women. 'In a world in which money rules, Minnie is also a commodity exploited by the bartender, Nick, who says to her in "low tones": "please walk around / every one of your words, every smile / is a sale."'[47] The Girl is not to be distinguished from the Golden West: she is that youthful West in all its projected fantasy and exemplifies Belasco's commercialization and false mythicization. The Girl, the Gold, the West, these are interlocking, almost interchangeable symbols. Had Belasco been born twenty-five years later, he would have been a Hollywood mogul.

La fanciulla del West opens with a rousing prelude, with its 'American' sound, its theme of 'love as redemptive force,' and its cakewalk rhythm from African American dance associated with Johnson as the bandit Ramerrez.[48] It is nightfall at the Polka Saloon. Jake Wallace, the camp minstrel, sings a song that awakens thoughts of home, and all the miners join in. The saloon in American popular culture was 'for a long time felt as the antitype of the home, a refuge for escaping males, nearly as archetypal as the wilderness and the sea.'[49] The miners drink, gamble, and fight, nearly lynching one of their own until Sheriff Jack Rance steps in. Ashby, a Wells Fargo agent, informs them that the bandit Ramerrez and his gang are in the neighbourhood. A miner taunts Rance about his love for Minnie, a quarrel breaks out, and a shot is fired, at which point Minnie makes her entrance. She has won the miners' hearts with her simple charm, and they are willing to entrust their money to her (which they almost live to regret), though Ashby cautions that the money were better left with Wells Fargo. Minnie transforms the bar into Sunday school by giving them a Bible lesson on Psalm 51 and how the soul can be born again. Puccini's religious theme has fought its way into the most recalcitrant materials. Rance confesses his love, but Minnie knows he is married and is not in love with him. Too many episodes and too much circumstantial detail, more appropriate for a play or a novel than an opera, are crowding this libretto.[50]

Ramerrez enters, disguised as Dick Johnson. His 'bad' side is covered by his Mexican name; his gang is all Mexican, as is his mistress, Nina Micheltorena, 'a proper siren, who paints herself with chimney black and gives a languid eye.' On his own report, Ramerrez has been forced to a life of crime and his true nature is good, so he can assume an American identity, Dick Johnson, a stage name. Moreover, Johnson comes from Sacramento, suggesting *his* pure soul; and the chaste Minnie, yet to give her first kiss, is the perfect foil to Micheltorena. This is a racist, good guy/bad guy characterization of Ramerrez/Johnson (he is Leslie Fiedler's grown-up Good Bad Boy.)[51] Johnson and Minnie, we learn, had once met on the road to Monterey. They go off dancing while the miners force a bandit to give a (false) confession as to the whereabouts of Ramerrez. Despite a rising storm and the pitch blackness, the miners rush out in pursuit and leave Minnie and Johnson to end act 1 in an inconclusive love duet, betraying Puccini's lack of conviction. Johnson is so enamoured of Minnie that he refuses to steal the gold.

Act 2 takes place in Minnie's cabin halfway up the mountain. A blizzard rages as Minnie and Johnson renew their pledge of love in a second duet that also fails to convince. Shots go off, Johnson hides, and the miners enter and tell Minnie that Johnson is Ramerrez. She does not betray him, but after they leave she turns him out into the storm for lying to her. He is immediately wounded at the door, and she drags him back and conceals him in the loft. Rance enters and discovers the outlaw's presence by the blood dripping from above. To save his life Minnie proposes a card game: if she wins, Rance must let Johnson go free; if she loses, she gives him up and goes with Rance. She cheats and wins – and where could she have learned to trick a wily sheriff? In act 3, set in a redwood forest, Johnson has been caught and is about to be hanged; with his neck in the noose he sings the opera's single excerptable aria, 'Ch'ella mi creda libero.' Minnie rides up with a pistol clenched between her teeth and pleads for his life. After she reminds them of Psalm 51 and her many acts of mercy, the angry miners melt with sympathy. When Sonora sings, 'It's not the gold that he stole, but your heart,' to the strains of Jake's nostalgic song, the lovers ride off together to a better life.

Puccini's 'American opera' is burdened with the weakest of his twelve libretti.[52] In his major operas, problems of plot and character resolve themselves in the light and heat of his musical genius. Here, he did not grasp the extent of such problems, much less that his arias and his narrative, incidental, and transitional music were not dispelling those problems simply because the problems were too great and the music not quite great enough. 'I read and reread Belasco's play until I felt I knew my characters thoroughly,' he said at the time; 'once I understand and catch the spirit of my characters, melody comes very easily to me.'[53] Given the paucity of solid musical characterization, the absence of defining arias, and the failure of not one but two love scenes, the maestro's comment now seems an unintended and ironic admission of defeat – and how long had it been since Puccini wrote a love scene that did not sweep all before it? Even his sense of structure deserted him. The act 2 love duet follows too closely on the heels of the act 1 duet; there has been neither sufficient action nor psychological development to warrant the second, which is repetitious. In the second duet, the lovers finally kiss each other, and it is the fact that she has given her first kiss to a liar that brings her to throw him out of the cabin. Though the orchestral score is technically and musically brilliant, so much so that Girardi speaks of its being 'the real protagonist of the opera' and cites Ravel and Webern in its defence, with the exception of Johnson's act 3 aria and a few other passages, the vocal writing is under-inspired.[54] Special effects like the blizzard and the spectacular scenery merely highlight dramatic weaknesses. The humour, broad as a prairie, fails to charm. When the miners cry 'La posta! La posta!' they sound like children at summer camp awaiting mail from home. When they shout 'Whiskey per tutti,' they sound like those same children crying for milk. They cannot recover from these scenes and be credible as a lynch mob.

Girardi and others have demonstrated that Puccini, absorbing new influences like Debussy, Strauss, and Schoenberg, composed his opera in a more dramatic, transitional style, which would bear fruit in *Turandot.* They point to his use of the whole tone scale, the black minstrel songs, and the Latin rhythms. At the same time, Puccini knew his strengths and must have realized his opera's deficiencies. In an interview in 1910 he said, 'I am an Italian and I love melody. Melody must always be queen in music.'[55] The reviewer from *The Nation* wrote that 'In the whole opera there is not one of those stirring, broad, sensuous melodies which have made "La Bohême" [*sic*], "Tosca," and "Madama Butterfly" famous' (15 Dec. 1910).[56]

With *Madama Butterfly* Puccini had the example of his native land for a traditionalist culture. But apart from some Fenimore Cooper and Harte stories, he knew little of the frontier or the American West, though he pretended otherwise. 'For this drama I have composed music that I feel sure reflects the spirit of the American people and particularly the strong, vigorous nature of the West. I have never been West, but I have read so much about it that I know it thoroughly.'[57] His lack of curiosity, which normally made an exception of libretti, now hurt him terribly. Giacosa's death cast its shadow, for he had written insightfully on the American scene and character. Puccini tried to remedy the situation by choosing as librettist the Bolognese writer Carlo Zingarini, whose mother was American and taught English (unhappy with the results, he added a second librettist, Guelfo Civinini, who also disappointed him). For Puccini the West was mostly fantasy, and he surely remembered seeing one of its greatest myth-makers, Buffalo Bill Cody, who had brought his Wild West Show to Milan in 1890. 'I enjoyed Buffalo Bill,' he wrote to his brother in Argentina, 'It is a company of North Americans with a number of red indians and buffaloes, who perform splendid feats of shooting and make genuine recreations of frontier scenes. In eleven days they made 120,000 lire!'[58] Puccini distinguishes the North Americans from the Red Indians (the original North Americans now displaced; white versus red); and he categorizes the Indians in a prepositional phrase with buffaloes (the Indians are feral nature, as opposed to culture).[59] One of the 'realistic scenes' was the stagecoach hold-up. Puccini might also have seen a re-enactment of Cody's single-handed combat with the young Cheyenne chieftain Yellow Hand at War Bonnet Creek in 1876. Cody killed and scalped the Indian, crying 'First scalp for Custer!'[60] Also, to the impoverished Puccini, the Wild West Show looked like a money maker, though in fact Cody rarely made money on his shows, on account of huge expenses due to his scrupulosity for detail and authenticity. In 1907 Puccini may have felt that he could capture the vast American public as he had with *Madama Butterfly*.

If Puccini's understanding of the West was weak, he knew nature and had a deep sympathy for the miners. For him, nature was not pleasant parks and gardens, but some of the wildest terrain that Italy afforded, and this might have attracted him to Belasco's play. His love of rugged wilderness was not at all typical for an Italian, who is urban in general character. Rather, it seems more American in spirit. Each of his rural retreats was one degree more remote than the previous one; he negotiated a house in the Maremma (for hunting) in his late fifties; by his mid-sixties it was abandoned because it had even become too difficult for him to reach.[61] 'I am sick of Paris,' he writes in spring 1898 when rehearsals for *La Bohème* wore on:

> I am panting for the woods with their sweet smells and fragrance. I am panting for the free movement of my belly in wide trousers and no waistcoat; I pant after the wind that blows free and fragrant from the sea; I savour with wide nostrils its iodic salty breath and stretch my lungs to breathe it! I hate pavements! I hate palaces! I hate capitals! I hate columns! I love the beautiful column of the poplar and the fir; I love the vault of the shady glades; and I love, like a modern druid, to make my temple, my house, my studio therein![62]

At length he returned home and went to Monsagrati, which resembles Grendel's den in *Beowulf*. 'I am in a hideous, hateful place, drowned in the middle of the woods and pine-trees, so that one can see nothing, shut in by mountains, and lighted by a broiling sun with no breath of wind.' He had gone there for the purpose of finishing *Tosca:* 'I am very happy to have fled to this tedious place where the human being is the exception'; his family, 'for whom it is a real sacrifice,' had to be dragged there.[63] Years later, when he sought inspiration, he felt that the wilderness might revive him: 'without fever there is no creation; because emotional art is a kind of madness, an exceptional state of mind, over-excitation of every fibre and every atom of one's being, and so on *ad aeternum*. I am going to the Maremma towards the end of the month to become still more brutish.'[64] Giuseppe Adami, his friend and one of the librettists of *Turandot*, wrote of him: 'if anyone suggested how much better the society of men would be for him, he would extol some distant haunts of his down in the Maremma, with the woods and sea for company, and buried antiquities of Etruria, pale dawns, fiery sunsets, and vast silences in which there was no deception. Perhaps there alone did he succeed in dispelling his constant melancholy. But no one knew.'[65] It was tantamount to a desire of death, Puccini's wish to disappear 'in a wood where the foliage is thick'; 'my melancholy is immense, unspeakable, frightening.'[66]

Connected with his love for the wilderness, hunting was his only real pastime: 'Here life is as usual: shooting.'[67] This love of nature and hunting crystallized slowly, but it traces to his earliest awareness. The major figure in Puccini's pre-conservatory musical background had been Carlo Angiolini, who taught at the Pacini Institute in Lucca. Angiolini became a substitute father for the boy, to whom he also imparted his passion for hunting: 'His ideas on hunting were remarkably sound. It stood to reason, therefore, that his ideas on music must be equally sensible.'[68]

Puccini installed a special gunroom at his home in Torre del Lago. A short corridor separated it from the music study, so that a few steps would bring him from his piano to his gun collection, hunting boots, and stuffed heads. He himself was a nocturnal creature, composing from 10 p.m. to 4 a.m., the time of dreaming, when animals are 'smothered in their lairs.' Sometimes a few friends would play cards in a further room, a quiet background noise that he preferred; it lent the air of a hunting lodge.[69] At his piano Puccini would sit wearing a soft felt hat, 'cocked at a slightly jaunty angle,' as if after guiding a heroine to her death (in nine of his twelve operas) he might grab a gun, rush outdoors, and kill an animal, or was it the other way around? 'I wrote *The Girl of the Golden West* in a year and a half, at night and on coffee. During the day I hung about my home, Torre del Lago, at Viareggio, in Tuscany, fishing and hunting.' 'I went out shooting with my guns and had a good deal of sport, but still thinking of Minnie and the Sheriff.'[70]

Vincent Seligman defended Puccini's passion for hunting as 'normal' for a Tuscan of his generation. The testimony of the letters reads otherwise, and one should speak of an obsession with hunting, with victimizing, with killing. 'In the green rustic wilderness of the wonderful Maremma, where nice people go, I think I shall pass the best days of my life! But are you mad? To be out shooting – where there is really something to shoot – and after a success! It is the moment – the supreme moment – when the mind is really at peace! I want to make the most of it and I shall abandon myself to it. What do I want with banquets, receptions, and official visits?' Bad productions of his operas feel like '*executions*' and in the next sentence he adds: 'nothing new here – the usual life; I'm going to have a day's shooting.' His humour can be harrowing, as when he sends dead butterflies to his druggist: 'As corpses let them remind you that when evening comes we must all die. While my brain is silently giving life and colour to my Roman heroine [Tosca] I act as executioner to these poor frail creatures. The Neronian instinct manifests and fulfils itself.' Pinkerton and Sharpless will soon talk of these dead butterflies. Puccini loved to eat his prey. In the last year of his life he wrote a poem that ends: 'Passano i tordi ... Tira la corda / nel buon momento. / Oh, che contento!' (The thrushes pass ... Pull the trigger / at the right moment. Oh, how content I am!). On his deathbed in Brussels, following an operation for cancer, he said he wanted both to get back to the final scene of *Turandot* and to 'wreak destruction on the birds.'[71] But his fate was to die of a cancer that was possibly either begun or exacerbated by a goose bone stuck in his throat.[72]

Puccini required the products of industrial society to insulate himself

Andante tranquillo (*interno, molto lontano*) ♩ = 46

Figure 3

further from that society. He loved driving motor cars into the hills, the faster the better, and he always had the latest models. Seligman called him 'one of the pioneers of motoring' in Italy. In the winter of 1903 he insisted on being driven home in dense fog at night. His chauffeur went off the road and Puccini, knocked unconscious, was pinned beneath the car and nearly asphyxiated. He was eventually pulled free, with a badly broken leg. It took a year to heal and left him with a permanent limp.[73]

Nature and hunting are crucial to understanding Puccini's decision to compose *La fanciulla del West*. 'I have in mind a magnificent scenario, a clearing in the great Californian forest, with some colossal trees ... eight to ten horses on the stage.'[74] No other work by him to this time had exploited the difference between indoors and outdoors, and as Robert K. Wallace notes on romantic music, 'the contrast between indoors and outdoors can be expressed both literally and metaphorically.'[75] From the prelude, perhaps his finest, the orchestration breathes with musical images of wind-swept mountains and distant panoramas, the blizzard, dawn in a mining camp, meadows of wild flowers, horses, and other elements of local colour (eight horses galloped across the stage in the spectacular American premiere in December 1910). On the metaphorical level Puccini aims, if less successfully, to capture the 'spirit of nature ... as a primal force.'[76] As for his passion for guns and hunting, he himself devised the sensational Johnson manhunt on a few hints in the Belasco original.[77] Beyond nature and hunting, it was the minstrel's song that first attracted him to Belasco's play.

'*Nostalgia. / Mal di terra natìa*' (Nostalgia. / Homesickness!), says Nick to explain a miner's depression. The nostalgia theme (to give it a name) weaves through the entire opera (fig. 3). First stated briefly in its most elemental form by an off-stage chorus moments after the prelude in act 1, it is given full treatment by Jake Wallace, then taken up by the chorus of miners, and sung by Minnie in her Bible lesson, conditioning the entire atmosphere of the act. It serves again as one of the high points of the act 2 love duet. In act 3 Minnie recalls how her affection for the miners had knit them into a family to the strains of the nostalgia theme, and it is heard in the finale when the lovers ride off into the mountains.

Are the miners as close to Puccini's heart as the contradictory Girl or the bad guy/good guy Ramerrez/Johnson? The plight of the immigrants was once again exerting pressure on the composer's imagination. In Belasco's play the lyrics for the song were adapted from 'The Old Dog Tray,' also known as 'Echoes from Home,' which was sung in the Californian mining camps in the 1850s. Belasco's father had been a gold miner, and Belasco himself had roamed across California and Nevada in the 1860s. For a long time it was thought that the melody of this song was related to either the mining song 'The Old Dog Tray' or to Stephen Foster's completely different song with the same title. Following the lead of the American composer-ethnologist Arthur George Farwell in what may be the first published article on the opera in 1910, Allan W. Atlas has shown conclusively that Jake Wallace's aria is unrelated to either 'The Old Dog Tray' or Foster's song, but is instead a modified version of the 'Chorus of Virgin Maidens,' which is the second section of the Zuni Indians' 'Festive Sun-Dance.' This was the theme that Puccini heard – 'Ah! there is my theme at last' – that night in 1907, and this was the music that he asked his friend Sybil Seligman to procure for him. Only Puccini took a song that was originally in a *tempo di marcia* and transformed it into a 'sentimental minstrel song that expresses the white man's nostalgia for home, "mamma," and faithful pet dog.'[78] Since the tune in the tempo Puccini gave it is a trifle boring, especially for such a prominent structural motif, one wonders why this genius of melody did not tap his own imagination for a better one. Perhaps his desire to convey an authentic 'American' spirit misled him to rely too heavily on this particular quotation. He needed something on the order of Wally's 'Ebben? ne andrò lontana' from his fellow Lucchese Alfredo Catalani's *La Wally* (1892) or, to look ahead, his other great aria with a nostalgia theme, Liù's lament 'Signore, ascolta' in act 1 of *Turandot*.

The saloon scene in the first act of *Fanciulla* is organized around the nostalgia theme. One of the miners, Jim Larkens, has been writing a letter home and his spirits are low. Nick explains Larkens's trouble: 'He's thinking of his dear old Cornwall / and his mother who's waiting for him there.' Jake Wallace is now heard singing offstage, 'Che faranno i vecchi miei / là lontano, ... ?', as if to emphasize the sad, far-away quality of the theme: 'What will the old folk do / way back home, far away ... ? / Sad and lonely my old folks / will weep and think / I'll not come home any more.' Jake enters the saloon and continues singing to the theme: 'La mamma mia / ... che farà / s'io non torno ...?': 'What will ... my poor mother do / if I return no more?' The miners pick up the melody: 'At the loom she'll spin flax and sorrow / for a shroud to wind her in.' Missing her son, she will die of a broken heart. There is a brief reference to an old dog and a house 'al rivo accanto' (by the shore). Larkens breaks down in tears and the miners take up a collection to send him back to Cornwall. In Belasco's play, it is to Pennsylvania. As in *Manon Lescaut*, however, Puccini required the absolute separation implied by the Atlantic Ocean. Also, the original song refers to a dog – the Anglo-Saxons' best friend, a latent memory of their past as hunters and wanderers through the northern forests. In Italy, where the classical tradition persists, the distinction between the human and animal world is clear-cut, and few Italians would shed tears in public for an old dog. (De Sica's *Umberto D* is the exception that proves the rule.) So Puccini reduces the dog and magnifies the mother, the traditional southern Italian woman. In a cinema western, nostalgia is rarely a theme, let alone a dominant one.[79] Never is anyone heard crying for 'my mother.' As the chorus develops the theme, it begins to sound more like a hymn sung in the cathedral of San Martino, Lucca, than in a mining saloon in the Old West.

The nostalgia theme is also heard as Minnie winds up her lesson. In Psalm 51 the sprig of hyssop grows in the purified heart; even the meanest sinner can be saved: 'let each one of you keep with you / this supreme truth of love.' With 'amore' the theme commences, linking religious love to one's love for family, community, and native land. No sooner is the lesson over but the mail arrives, bringing fresh cause for nostalgic sadness. Joe learns that his 'grandmother has passed away,' Bello that his girl Ketty has married someone else, Harry that disasters have struck his old village. Even the hard-bitten Sheriff Rance thinks of his old home 'dai monti, sopra un altro mare' (by the mountains, above another sea): 'Nobody regretted my going, Minnie, / and I shed no tears at leaving.' Minnie sings both of her poor family 'down in Soledad' ('Oh, how well I recall everything'), and of the miners, 'Poor men! How many of them / have left a family far away.' Joe offers Minnie flowers in act 1; 'Back home,' he says, 'there are lots of them.' In act 3, pleading for Johnson's life, she reminds him of these flowers 'like the ones that used to grow on your heath' ('brughiere'), suggesting Scotland.

In the act 2 love duet, with the posse at the door, Johnson declares his love to the nostalgia theme: 'I cling to you, our hearts as / one, alone with you!' Then Minnie and Johnson sing together: 'How sweet to live and die and never part again!' The theme also reappears later in act 2 when Johnson re-declares his love and tells his sad life's story: 'I dreamed of redeeming myself through work and [the nostalgia theme begins] love ... And my lips murmured an ardent prayer.' In these scenes the nostalgia theme conveys the collapse of distance through romantic love. At the end of act 3, Minnie sings the nostalgia theme as she reminds the miners of the good deeds she has done for them. She was 'little Maud, the sister you adore,' to Harry, when he was delirious. She declares them 'fratelli del mio cuore' (brothers of my heart). Puccini has employed a single musical theme to depict three forms of love – the familial, the religious, and the erotic, ultimately (in his view) deriving from one source.

American and English audiences, writes John DiGaetani 'often find it difficult to identity with Puccini's miners, especially when the miners cry out that they miss their mothers. Anglo-Saxon audiences often find that these are not real westerners but Italian sissies.' Yet Puccini is probably closer to the truth of things in his portrayal of men like Larkens, Rance, Bello, Harry, and Joe, who seemed to have gone directly west for gold without an intervening period of acculturation. Puccini may also have had in mind his countrymen who would think of their native land in terms of the mother and, as Joe does, of flowers. DiGaetani's answer is to deconstruct the whole staging and emphasize its 'mythic qualities'; the miners are 'doomed figures from a faraway land engaged in an alienating quest.'[80] The whole problem with this opera is too much 'myth' as it is, and insufficient historical analysis. If one appreciates the immigrant's story, the miner's plight and Puccini's musical expression of it may become more real and therefore comprehensible; to mythicize here is to fall into the same trap as Puccini and Belasco.

What are the larger reasons for Puccini's wrong turn in *La fanciulla del West*? Part of the answer lies in that period of libretto searching, 1904–8. He had just completed two full-length verismo operas, *Tosca* and *Madama Butterfly*. The principles of verismo, which derive eclectically from theorists like Zola and the realists, stipulate that 'mythological,' 'historical,' and 'dynastic' subjects be avoided in favour of scenes and characters drawn from everyday life, preferably from the lower classes.[81] Artists should concentrate on rendering strong, even brutal passion, in a straightforward plot. Mascagni's *Cavelleria Rusticana* (1890) is often taken as the operatic touchstone for the style. Biographically, *La fanciulla del West* is Puccini's last full-length verismo opera. But is it sufficiently verismo? Myths are not merely of the past, but of modern making too, and one can be as easily captured and controlled by the one as the other. He did not examine the 'Golden West' under verismo standards by which it might be exposed, transformed, and rendered aesthetically convincing, admittedly a rare feat. (Examples would be John Ford's films *The Searchers* and *The Man Who Shot Liberty Valence.*) Only occasionally does Puccini break through the Far West myth in this opera – as in his nostalgia theme and the recollection of the mother – and get to the truth of things: *verismo.*

Did Puccini ever approach genuine verisimilitude in treating the lower classes? Years before, just after *Manon Lescaut,* he considered a libretto based on Giovanni Verga's *La Lupa,* and went to Sicily to see the terrain, take photographs, and discuss the matter with Verga himself. Specht says he gave up because there was 'something within him that protested against certain scenes, especially the last, in which blood is shed while a procession is passing by, singing the litanies.' If Puccini was not above violence in his operas, he was above sacrilege. In act 1 of *Tosca* Scarpia merely courts sacrilege in betraying his overriding lust during the Te Deum procession in Sant'Andrea delle Valle; in act 2 he shuts a window to stop the sound of the religious chorus, while Cavaradossi's torture proceeds offstage (violence shuts out religion). More to the point, Puccini complained that *La Lupa* did not have 'a single *luminous,* pleasing figure standing out from the general gloom.'[82] He had the same problem with the heroine of many another rejected libretto. The overriding objection is always the lack of central characters with whom he could establish sympathetic identification.

Could Puccini have taken another path? Given his earlier leanings towards verismo principles and the fact that he was already dealing with the American character in *Butterfly,* one wonders if the thought of an opera on the Italian immigrants ever crossed his mind. Did he meet any immigrants in New York apart from those working in the Metropolitan Opera House? The great Italian stars of *Fanciulla,* Caruso and Amato, were immigrants; many in the Met chorus and orchestra were immigrants (Italians among them). Had he ever read Giacosa's book? (Having interviewed many Italians, Giocosa filled his book with their stories, like the coal mine disaster in Pennsylvania that gives the lie to the gold mine fantasy in California.) There is no reason to believe that he did or, if he did, that it made a difference. Could Puccini have applied a truly caustic verismo style that the immigrant setting would require? The evidence can be read both ways. *Il Tabarro* (1918), a one-act opera, shows his capabilities for writing about the urban poor. Yet a full-length opera about Italian immigrants would have forced a closer look at his own society and culture. He would have had to re-examine his patriarchal version of a failing agrarian tradition and to come to terms with the modern metropolis. The more one questions, the further away seems the possibility. Puccini achieved a high degree of realism in *Tosca* and *Butterfly* with their studies in tyranny and exploitation. His goals were uncertain in *La fanciulla del West*, and where Puccini's judgment failed him, so too did his imagination.

Nevertheless, some promising imaginative turn on Puccini's part might have led to operatic results in the Brutal East that did not happen in the Golden West. On that visit to New York in 1907 Puccini, at forty-nine, stood at a crossroads. He had mulled over libretto after libretto. The mass emigration was a topic rolling right under his feet, literally below decks when he sailed to North and South America. Leoncavallo and Mascagni wrote splendidly about southern Italians in their native villages. Why not write about the ones who emigrated? It was the major Italian social issue of its day, and immigrant life was not without its deep pathos and its storied, dramatic power. The usual Puccini themes, especially his sympathy for the downtrodden, were closely involved. Instead of dallying in the California mountains, which he had never seen, in a dramatic action that was stilted, sentimental, and unconvincing, he might have approached his American theme directly and lighted the way for other composers. It almost seems as if Puccini were determined to remain unconscious of the matter. Since suppression often brings forth its polar opposite, the proof may be found in his next opera, set in an atmosphere that he so often despaired of. *La Rondine*, least affecting of his mature works, takes place in high-bourgeois Paris.

chapter 6

'To Die Is Not Enough!'
Hemingway and D'Annunzio

JOHN PAUL RUSSO

Morire non basta.

– D'Annunzio

Given the historical legacy of particularism, no one city epitomizes Italy in modernity, though Venice probably comes closer than any other in the popular imagination. It has been 'painted and described many thousands of times,' said Henry James, 'and of all the cities of the world is the easiest to visit without going there.'[1] Or, as one would say, it is the world's most 'virtual' city. With its wealth of historical, literary, artistic, and political associations, unique urbanism and architecture, contrary myths and polarities of East and West, deeply engrained and often contradictory stereotypes, putative autochthonous identity, and not least, mingling of strangeness and familiarity, Venice has thwarted the attempts of all but a few writers to deploy and shape their Venetian materials into an original vision. On the contrary: in a study of thick intertextuality Rosella Mamoli Zorzi writes that most nineteenth-century travellers brought their own readings of a 'totally dead' Venice so that 'the energy of the real city [the politics of 1848, struggles against bad restoration, etc.] is not sufficient to break through the assumed perception of its beauty.'[2] There were notable exceptions. 'To avoid trite and clichéd descriptions' of Venice in *Pictures from Italy*, Dickens fractured the stereotypes by portraying his own visit in the form of a dream, 'a series of *juxtaposed* images, immersed in silence, using the visual process typical of dreams'; 'this technique seems also to underline the lack of reality of the object which is being represented.'[3] His dream was the cultural archetype of nineteenth-century Venice.

Another rare exception is Hemingway, whose Venetian novel came late in his career, after several stalled efforts, in 1950, with *Across the River and Into the Trees*. This contribution to a subgenre of European fiction, the Venetian novel, has long been misinterpreted and undervalued by readers who have failed to understand it within its numerous intertextual contexts. As if confirming belief in Hemingway's presumed decline, Leslie Fiedler's reference to the novel as a 'complete fiasco' was typical of the earliest reviews and commentaries. On the Italian side, Alberto Moravia also called it a 'fiasco.' Most recently, Stephen L. Tanner remarks that it is 'not a very good novel.' Among its few defenders, however, Agostino Lombardo writes that Hemingway never 'reached such consonance with the Italian soul and soil' as in *A Farewell to Arms* and that this 'consonance is the real artistic motivation also of *Across the River and Into the Trees*, a novel to my eyes greatly undervalued.'[4] To follow up on Lombardo's suggestive comment, one should resist the temptation to take this novel merely as a reprise of his familiar themes: the soldier hero, code behaviour, stoicism, vanity, mysterious wounds, love and death. The key to this novel is Venice, whose myths impart organizational strength and subtlety, and help explain odd structural features, integrally linked symbols, and tangled linguistic undergrowth.

Historically, the 'bifrontal myth' of Venice may be labelled 'classical' and 'black' (or 'romantic' – essentially an anti-myth).[5] Though the former is considerably older and, from the eighteenth century, less suited to aesthetic purposes, Hemingway valued them both and they inform his novel almost equally. Renaissance humanist historians and their successors celebrated Venetian republican virtue, mixed government, and political liberty; Gasparo Contarini claimed that Venice even 'surpassed the constitution of ancient Rome.'[6] This classical myth, a 'civic cult of mystic patriotism,' traces to the early medieval period and the translation of Saint Mark's body from Alexandria to Venice (ca. 827), and ultimately to the city's origins in the sixth and seventh centuries.[7] Venice owed its life to the resourcefulness, economic enterprise, and civic and moral discipline of a people who withstood barbarian invasions from the north and marine invasions from the south and east. No state, wrote Burckhardt, 'has ever exercised a greater moral influence over its subjects.'[8] For a thousand years (2,212 according to Thomas Coryate's *Crudities* [1611]), La Serenissima was inviolable save by the tidal waters of the lagoon bathing her 117 islands. Modern readers are more familiar with the 'black' myth that came into prominence in the Renaissance: the city of luxury, decadence, greed, tyranny, carnival, aesthetic refinement, orientalism, illusion, perverse sexuality – and, in Thomas Mann's phrase, the 'voluptuousness of doom.' Georg Simmel referred to Venice as the 'ambiguous' city, and Mann agreed: this was the 'humblest adjective that can be applied,' 'this musical magic of ambiguity still lives.'[9] Hemingway often crosses mythic patterns, which is the case with the opening chapter; this 'story about death'[10] begins with allusions to the watery outskirts of Hades.

The swamp is the real origin of Venice – the novel begins and ends there, and nowhere do we long forget the presence of dark water. Traditionally, the swamp is a Western symbol for the unhealthy mixture of land and water, uncontrollable life and decomposing matter, pollution, disease, and death. In the Book of Job, Behemoth (the hippopotamus) and Leviathan (the crocodile) are swamp monsters; and in Isaiah, Rahab is a marine dragon or chaos-monster. The sublime vision of new heaven and new earth in Revelation begins: 'there was no more sea' (Rev. 21:1).[11] Flaubert and Pound, two writers whom Hemingway revered, place the swamp in the same metaphorical zone with the feminized Orient, luxury, decadence, and non-rational powers. These writers present the 'familiar paradox of Oriental fecundity and sterility, enormous abundance and enormous barrenness'; in Pound specifically the teeming undifferentiated swamp stands for the 'parthenogenetic feminine.'[12] With its organizing mark of the phallus, the sign of plough and stylus, the male principle preserves hierarchy against the chaotic energies of the swamp-feminine. As in Pound, where Venetian history is one of the scenes in which these warring principles engage, so in Hemingway, the swamp is a culturally charged symbol: Venetian lagoons and canals frequently represent the feminine and the lure of death. The title itself, *Across the River and Into the Trees*, taken from Gen. Stonewall Jackson's dying words, announces the theme of the watery passage to death.

Richard Cantwell is an American colonel stationed in Trieste in the years after World War II. *Cant*ankerous, given to exposing *cant*, no politician, he has been demoted from general to colonel for losing too many men in following impossible orders in the battle of the Hurtgen Forest (where Hemingway had been a war correspondent); most likely, he was a scapegoat for his superiors' folly – he certainly thinks so. Having been wounded many times and suffered 'maybe ten' 'real' concussions (10), and with a serious heart condition, he is thinking of retiring to Venice, where he has a few soldier friends from World War I and has become infatuated by Renata, a young Venetian contessa. The novel tells the story of a brief visit to Venice that ends in his death. One learns these details in the second chapter, because the first chapter opens at a duck-shoot in the lagoons near Venice, at low tide, in the pre-dawn hours, on a cold, windless winter night.[13] The light comes up to a 'gray dim sky' by the end of the chapter.[14] People are unidentified except by the generic 'boatman' and 'shooter.' Like Charon, the irascible ferryman of the underworld, the boatman is surly ('What the hell is eating him?' [4]), powerful ('tall, heavily built' [4]), violent ('shoved the boat savagely,' 'smashing with his oar at the ice,' [4]) and inhuman ('big brute' [4]; but Cantwell will describe himself as 'brutal' too [65]). The shooter (Cantwell) has overtaxed himself in rowing out, complains to himself of discomfort, and asks for water. The boatman replies 'No water' (no life) and warns with a cruel sadism that the lagoon waters are 'unhealthy' (4) too. The shooter manages to kill two birds, as it were, sacrifices for the god of death. The boatman continues to be unhelpful. 'To hell with him,' thinks the shooter, who says to himself 'keep your temper, boy,' because 'every time you shoot now can be the last shoot and no stupid son of a bitch should be allowed to ruin it' (7). The shadowy light, the marshy waters, the Charon figure, the curses ('hell'): this is the outer precinct of Hades.

Hemingway laboured over the progression and disjunction of the opening and closing chapters and complex narrative structure, about which commentators have disagreement.[15] Chronologically the novel begins with chapter 2 (fig. 1), Cantwell's medical check-up in Trieste, a Thursday. Chapters 3 to 15 comprise Friday, the motor journey from Trieste to Venice, the late afternoon and night in Venice at the Gritti Palace Hotel, ending with a nocturnal gondola ride. Chapters 17 to 39 narrate events of morning and midday of Saturday; Cantwell leaves Venice in the afternoon (chapter 39) and repairs to a country villa in preparation for the duck-shoot on Sunday: the duck-shoot that began in chapter 1 and was interrupted by 39 chapters resumes in chapter 40 precisely where it left off: the shooter (Cantwell) alone in the sunken hogshead, the boatman's surliness still unexplained, and the shooter's 'anger' (281) intensifying to a point where he must take heart pills. When from his advanced location the 'sullen boatman' starts killing the birds that would have come to the shooter, the shooter 'fired at him twice' (281) – warning shots, but the implication is obvious: he wants to 'kill' the boatman and defeat the power of death. He learns after the duck-shoot that the boatman's 'hatred' (302) is due to the fact that Moroccans had raped his wife and daughter during the Allied invasion; in the boatman's mind, an American colonel shares in the crime. Cantwell dies shortly afterward on the road back to Trieste (chapter 45). The swamp thus encloses the

Fig. 1. Time and Form in *Across the River and Into the Trees*

Chronological Time		Narrative Time	Cantwell's Time
Italy, late fall, 1946 or 1947			
Chapter 1	Day 4	'tomorrow'; duckshoot in swamps near Venice, two hours before dawn	'boatman' and 'shooter' in marshes
Chapter 2	Day 1	'day before yesterday'; a medical examination in Trieste	prognosis
Chapters 3–15	Day 2	'yesterday'; drive from Trieste to Venice; afternoon drinks at Gritti; evening with Renata; nocturnal gondola ride; returns to hotel; portrait	memories of early career in WWI: first visit to Venice
Chapters 16–39	Day 3	'today'; morning and lunch with Renata; leaves Venice for duck-shoot	recounts later military career in WWII to Renata
Chapters 40–45	Day 4	'tomorrow'; dawn; the duckshoot; and death on road back to Trieste	realm of the dead

novel with its central events in Venice, surrounding the city and permeating its atmosphere by the merging waters of the canals. Beside this framing effect, the swamp as the biological mixture of life and death is outside historical time.

The long drive from Trieste ('itself a near homonym of *triste*')[16] to Venice gives Cantwell an opportunity to reminisce about his early experiences in northeastern Italy during World War I, while establishing Venice itself as both the day's goal and the morbid attraction of the feminine love-object. Reflective of his mood, he crosses a 'secret and sad' Veneto landscape, 'quite different from the splendor of Venice,' the descriptions setting up an opposition between the land and the 'sea' city.[17] His 'big' wound (33) was received defending the 'queen of the seas' (35), giving him a taste of death, or rather the 'loss of the immortality' (33); from youth Venice is implicated among the causes of death. Then, he fought to protect Venice without having seen 'her' (45) (a lack), without even having 'command of the language' (45). He means Italian, though the context suggests a helpless child who does not have a 'language' to speak its needs or its love. For a commander like Cantwell, not to have 'command' is a breach in his armor. Hemingway's fondness for turning idiomatic expressions inside out is succinctly illustrated.

If his first wound was suffered in defending, without seeing, an idealized Venice, a second 'small wound' (45) required going to the city itself for treatment. So it could not have been *that* small. What is it? Again, Venice is linked to wounding, and a 'small' wound might indicate not only a physical but a symbolic wound. On this first journey he sees Venice as a 'queen ... rising from the sea' (45), an allusion to the birth of the goddess Aphrodite/Venus from the sea foam, the sperm and severed genitalia of the castrated Uranus (no part of the deity loses power). Later, Renata will describe herself as 'rising from the sea' (97). This conjunction of city, goddess, and sexual desire occurs in the best-known example of the topos in English, by another soldier-writer-celebrity, Byron, in *Childe Harold's Pilgrimage* (4.11): 'She looks a sea Cybele, fresh from ocean, / Rising with her tiara of proud towers.' In Byron's amalgamation of classical and black myth, Venice as both queen and fertility goddess wears her 'towers,' the male sexual symbol, her trophies. Venice is 'a sea Cybele' because the real Cybele, the eastern fertility goddess whom the Greeks assimilated to Rhea, mother of the Olympians, is normally associated with the land. In the older strata of Cretan and Phrygian religion, Cybele is the mother goddess who is accompanied by a 'subordinate figure of the male attendant, half son, half lover,' e.g., Adonis or Attis.[18] The terrified Attis castrates himself after sleeping with her; Cybele's priests castrate themselves in ritual commemoration. Towers also stand for the mural wall or battlements; they form the woman's headdress signifying the city as a protective enclosure; the 'goddess crowned with an image of her city is the Mediterranean's oldest emblem of sovereignty.'[19]

His next thought after the 'small wound' is, '*Merde* ... we did very well that winter up at the juncture' (45), an event or place of military engagement. Death is also undesirable, the enemy; 'Death,' he thinks later, 'is a lot of shit' (219). By swearing '*Merde*' (Italian, 'excrement'), he desecrates the city near which, after a few near-misses in his youth, he is fated to die. His thought – doing very well 'at the juncture,' a joining (English ed.: 'junction,' which is more a place than an act) – contains a buried reference to successful sexual penetration and also to a fateful crossroads. A similar layering of geographical, sexual, and fate metaphor is employed by Sophocles to depict Oedipus' killing his father Laius at the crossroads and marrying his mother. In Hemingway's assimilation of these materials, since the juncture originally concerns a fight with the Austrians, one concludes that in defeating the male enemy, Cantwell re-enacts the Sophoclean scenario and incestuously claims the mother.

Throughout the novel Cantwell is obsessed by loss: his youth, his health, his generalship, his 'three battalions,' 'three women' (a doubling): 'where the hell does it end?' (95). Psychic energies are consumed in fighting thoughts of death, which must be continually suppressed as 'morbid,' a favourite word (34, 47, 78, 168, 291). Efforts fail because he longs for death as the end of loss and suffering. '*Komm süsser Tod*, he thought' (88): Bach's choral melody 'Come, Sweet Death' on death and rebirth. Cantwell turns things into death, projecting his desire onto the birds that he shoots; onto the many types of fish and crustaceans in the market, 'boat-tailed bullets, dignified in death' (192) (the bullets, his projection of warfare; alliteration, Joycean in its beauty); onto a cooked lobster, 'a monument to his dead self' (115); onto General Custer's body, 'unspeakably mutilated'; onto the 'metallic agony' (46) of the *motoscafo* engine, bought in one of the 'grave-yards of automobiles' (43); onto 'cripples' – 'he was a sucker for crips' (71); onto 'mutilated' soldiers (a 'German dog eat a good German soldier's ass' [257]). He displaces his anxiety onto his wife, 'Deader than Phoebus the Phoenician' (213). Unlike Eliot's 'Phlebas' (*The Waste Land*, 4), Phoebus Apollo returns every day from 'death'; the feminine antagonist, compared to a male plague god, will rise to claim her victim. Cantwell, misremembering, identifies himself with Eliot's 'Phlebas the Phoenician, a fortnight dead' by drowning; yet Phoebus ('bright one') means that he wants to rise again. 'Phoenician' may also relate to Cantwell's frequent references to his 'trade.' In the city of trade and death, death is his 'strange trade' (40); 'killing armed men' is 'my trade' (63), his 'sad trade' (94), his '*sale métier*' (114), a 'sad science' (133), the '*triste métier*' (253); and so forth. Planning his own burial, Cantwell imagines the 'mulch' (a swamp image) (34–5) of his buried body, and thinks his brother's corpse may have 'deliquesced' on a Pacific island in the war (another swamp image) (257), thus conceiving both in terms of organic decomposition by water.

Cantwell dwells on numbers, a military trait that has become an obsession. In battle, by his own count, he has a record of 'one hundred and twenty-two sures' (123), a real killer. Now he has recurrent anginal pains and takes two heart pills at six-to-seven-hour intervals (12, 33, 92, 166, 266, 281, 294): it gives him pleasure to 'take them dry' (33) – 'dry' activates the associations against water, the swamp, and death – or with gin (281); the pills are his 'bullets' to protect him from death. Hemingway gives prominence to his heart trouble and its medication, devoting the second chapter to a medical examination.[20] The surgeon flatters Cantwell that his 'cardiograph' is 'wonderful' and 'could have been that of a man of twenty-five' or a 'boy of nineteen' (9). While a 'normal' cardiogram of a healthy teenager might be slightly different from a 'normal' cardiogram of a healthy fifty-one-year-old, there is nothing to warrant the surgeon's remark. Most likely he is trying to cheer up the ailing colonel, who is even more seriously ill that he thinks. The 'boy of nineteen' brings him back to his precise age during the Italian campaign in World War I (a line of demarcation after which he says he was a 'man' [31, 96, 179]) and makes him a few months older than Renata's present age, 'nearly nineteen' (75). Renata calls him Richard 'lion-hearted,' which he corrects by way of an aggressive reference (defecation) to the 'crap-hearted' (229). When, on what will be his final journey to Venice, Cantwell suddenly realizes that he will arrive in half an hour, he takes two heart pills (33), a doubling and overcompensation, to lower his blood pressure and pep up his heart, as if protecting himself from the city, another killer.

It takes four chapters to arrive in Venice, reminiscent of Gustav von Aschenbach's long-delayed arrival in Mann's *Death in Venice*. One does not start from but ends in Venice. The journey across the Veneto, with its many stops and detours ('where I grew up very rapidly' [93]), enables Hemingway to elaborate upon Cantwell's growth from 'boy' to 'man.' Throughout the journey Cantwell tries to keep 'strictly controlled' (20), repressing his thoughts of death and 'unthinking his great need to be there' (20), conscious of the mortal danger in his strenuous pastime (winter duck-shooting) and his passion (Renata).

The butt of Cantwell's frequent outbursts is the 'driver,' a feckless, somewhat insensitive American soldier named Jackson; the name parodies the great general's. Cantwell's regular driver is away, and the substitution is a sign of the new and unknown. Initially uneasy (to add to his uneasiness), Cantwell is comforted at finding Jackson a 'good driver' (he is a garage mechanic – his trade is driving itself). Cantwell's 'big Buick' (20) is fit for this fatal journey, a 'tumbril' (228), 'god-damned,' 'over-sized,' and 'luxurious' (307) – a hearse; he is 'still paying for it' (23), and it will never be paid for, except by his life.

It may be the effect of the pills that the countryside passes dizzily by Cantwell. Or, 'I'm not sure I like speed' (14), his longing for stillness and repose. His thoughts travel back to the scenes and battles of his youth. Only three weeks earlier, he had revisited the ground nearby where he had suffered his severest wound in World War I, to his 'right kneecap' (19) (where Hemingway had been seriously wounded, serving as a volunteer ambulance driver on the Italian front in July 1918). Fixing the spot by triangulation, he had desecrated it by defecating and then burying a knife along with a 'brown' (18) (colour of organic death) ten thousand lira note, a considerable sum at the time.[21] Cantwell surrenders his weapon and offers a worthy tribute of money to the victor Pluto, the god of death whose name in Greek means 'wealth.' From the earth all wealth comes and to it all returns. Cantwell's youthful behaviour typifies his desire to get rid of death, to project it onto the other. The money he gives to the earth is a kind of payment as substitute for himself or as an advance. By making the exchange, he buys time (and time is money): no one escapes the Plutonian economy. The act that attempts to cancel or negate violence here only repeats it. Cantwell will defecate as a sign of protest again in Venice, one of the many doublings in the novel, on the morning after he has had to sleep alone, Renata having refused him (167–8). As he 'sat there' in the bathroom, he first thinks of Renata: her absence, his long wait for her telephone call, her depriving him of company and pleasure. The train of thoughts that follows is: the army (where there is as much privacy as in a 'professional shit-house'), 'shit-house' ambassadors, 'wives.' Linked together are violence, '*Merde*,' the system that has denied him his generalship, and the feminine. There are other links between the expulsion of human waste, anal sadism, and protest against Renata (or the feminine) along with the deep desire for privacy, which represents male independence. On first arriving at the Gritti he asks a porter to get Renata on the telephone while he (Cantwell) goes to urinate (68). In his earlier reverie he had linked '*Merde*' and 'her' (Venice) (45). Another time he jokes with Renata, who cannot grasp the colloquial use of the word 'go' in 'going to the bathroom': 'That,' he says, 'is the one thing we do alone' (228). Dying is the other.

Nearing Venice, Cantwell asks Jackson to stop so that they can admire the 'square tower' (28) of Santa Maria Assunta on the island of Torcello lying in the distance.[22] Built in 639 and modified in 864 with the addition of a bell tower, it is later described as 'old' (39, 61) only to distinguish it from the eleventh-century Santa Fosca next to it. Cantwell likes to think in patterns of division: we/they, boy/man, water/land, Torcello/Venice, Santa Maria Assunta/Santa Fosca. In the language of the American frontier, which the driver can understand, he gives Jackson a thumbnail sketch of the men who 'pioneered' (28) Venice. Visigoths, Lombards, and 'other bandits' (i.e., foreigners) had driven local inhabitants from the mainland to Torcello. However, its lagoons silted up and mosquitoes brought malaria, so the 'Torcello boys' moved on and built Venice, which was more 'defensible.' Cantwell makes the transition earlier and smoother than it was. According to Lorenzetti, Torcello flourished well into the Middle Ages, when it was overtaken by the 'greater wealth and power of Venice' and suffered the 'gradual silting up of its water': Venice is a predator.[23] A 'Torcello boy' smuggled the body of Saint Mark out of Alexandria to Venice to give the Venetians their patron saint (29). Numerous references to 'boys' indicate a priority over the father: the 'boys' were there at the origins and lay claim to autochthonous authenticity. If Venice is 'tough,' 'the boys from Torcello ... were very tough' (28), though they also had 'very good taste in building' (28) and brought the stones in barges to build Venice: the ideal combines strength of will and aesthetic appreciation. He later defines a 'tough' man as one who 'backs his play' (49), surely a Cantwell.

The founding myth, which Cantwell embraces, and which enables him to share possession and claim priority by identification with the 'pioneers,' is reinforced on many occasions, as when he says that Venice is a 'tougher town than Cheyenne' (35) on the scale of toughness (Jackson is from Wyoming); and though Venetians have 'good manners,' Venice is 'tough as Cooke City, Montana' (36) (Cantwell is from Montana, another doubling – the juxtapositions are becoming more bizarre).[24] As with Torcello, strength does not rule out manners and taste; so despite its reputation for aesthetic refinement, carnival, and pleasure, Venice preserves its founders' independence and resourcefulness and 'makes a living on its own' (35), the classical myth. Cantwell – and Hemingway – hated and feared the dependency syndrome, though both fell victim to it. He thinks of Venice as 'my city' (26) and wants to live there; he is 'part owner' because he had defended it in his youth, on account of which the Venetians 'treat me well' (26). They accept him as one of their own, unlike the French who only resent him for having shamed them in World War II.

Cantwell identifies his own youth with Venice's, which is Torcello. One of the attractions of the 'square tower' is that it rises beside the old church and is not attached to it; it has its independence from the feminine. Cantwell prefers the 'good taste' and 'geometrically clear' (28) simplicity of Santa Maria Assunta to Saint Mark's, which is feminized as 'pretty Byzantine' (29), with a pun on 'pretty.' Moreover, he sees the square tower on Torcello against the bell tower on nearby Burano where men 'make bambinis' (29), but these phallic tower images hardly need the extra associations – to wit, a bartender whom Cantwell befriends 'seemed to feel that he had invented, or at least, erected the Colonel as you might be happy about participating in the erection of a *campanile*, or even the old church at Torcello' (39). The head waiter imagines staging an event with Cantwell for the fictitious military 'Order of Brusadelli' (the in-group, the Happy Few) 'in some historic place such as San Marco or the old church at Torcello' (61). Still another waiter refers to local gossip involving Cantwell: 'Some people don't understand the Torcello part' (75).[25] This has no clear referent in the novel, suggesting in-group knowledge. Cantwell wonders when they will tear down the 'Cinema Palace,' a reductive reference to Saint Mark's (Jackson calls it a 'moving picture palace' [29]), and build a 'real cathedral' (161). When they bring back Saint Mark's body a second time, replies Renata. Venice is already a doubling or displacement: Saint Mark's body is moved from its origin to establish another origin. 'That was a Torcello boy,' says Cantwell, about the hero who brought back the body. 'You're a Torcello boy' (161), the Venetian contessa confers honorary status upon him.

To summarize the opposition between Torcello and Venice: Torcello with its square tower is linked to Cantwell as the young soldier, masculine pride, heroic exploits, and autonomy. Venice signifies the feminine, the unattainable, the sense of lack, and the lure of the swamp. Death ties in with lack because it implies otherness and difference; the individual is neither complete nor self-sustaining, and hence not immortal. Torcello was silted up in its later history, its inhabitants driven out by invaders and malaria, its churches abandoned, and it was absorbed by Venice. The fate of Torcello is the fate of all things.

If Cantwell protests on behalf of Torcello, he delights no less in the romantic myth of Venice, one of whose major motifs is play and carnival. In the novel 'fun' is one of those quite ordinary words (like 'boy,' 'trade,' 'engine,' 'pills,' 'lovely,' 'sad,' 'jerk,' 'tough,' 'hell') on which Hemingway's linguistic magic works the changes. Often enough Cantwell must remind himself that he has come to Venice to 'have fun' (27, 71, 101, 152, 281), because he fears that he is not and that time is running out. On the way up the Grand Canal, he passes the palazzo of Gabriele D'Annunzio (1863–1938) and Eleonora Duse (1858–1924): 'Christ they are dead,' he thinks, hoping 'they had fun in that house' (51). Gliding by the contessa Dandolo's palazzo, he notes that, though 'over eighty,' she acts 'as gay as a girl,' does not 'fear dying,' and colours her hair 'red' (47). Dandolo is an ancient Venetian name, proving the blood remains strong; her visitors are 'cheerful' because 'they are going to see the Contessa Dandolo.' Cantwell never walked in Venice 'that it wasn't fun' (45), even though climbing the bridges triggers anginal pains. 'No one is ever old in Venice' (93), a typical example of Cantwell's self-deception. Venice transforms reality and is contrasted, much to its advantage, to Milan. Only gondoliers and waiters seem to work. The 'Order of Brusadelli' is a source of humour (it sounds like stage Italian) and magic 'spell' for Cantwell, who is its 'Supreme Commander,' with his former sergeant, now a headwaiter, as Gran Maestro. Cantwell enjoys the in-jokes and for a time the 'spell works' (62); the Gran Maestro notices that 'this taking of towns had pulled him out of his depth' (62). Yet appearances cannot be kept up for long, the 'spell was broken' (64), his brooding depression resumes. Revealed by Cantwell at the end of the novel, the 'Supreme Secret' of the Order combines 'love,' 'fun,' oriental opulence, and death by water: 'Love is love and fun is fun. But it is always so quiet when the gold fish die' (271). Here possibly the symbolism is precious and top-heavy.

With an element of child-like play, Cantwell and Renata 'have fun' (116, 127) with their food. Shopping together is 'fun' too (141), as is changing places in a gondola (152). Cantwell has had 'as much fun shooting' at the duck-shoot 'as I ever had' (281), more self-deception, considering his condition; and so forth. Though the weather is cold and windy, Cantwell likes his bedroom windows wide open and guesses that a 'hell of a tide' will flood the piazza San Marco: 'That's always fun' (167). The pleasure derived from inundation is another sign of projected aggression. Maybe if he tears down the great cathedral he can restore the origin, Torcello. The flooding of the piazza is a version of the Romantic-Decadent topos of the sunken city (Poe, Longfellow, Lalo, Barrès, Debussy's 'engulfed cathedral,' Ungaretti's 'porto sepolto,' De la Mare), an apocalyptic vision of stillness and sunken beauty. Irked by the fact that Jackson worries too much, will not drink with him (41), and does not know how to 'have some fun' (58), Cantwell orders him to 'have yourself some fun,' a command Jackson rephrases absurdly in military terms (58), unable to understand the meaning. The Gran Maestro assumes that Jackson is 'one of those sad Americans' (58), mechanical, unimaginative, not one of the Happy Few.

Heavy drinking on a delicate heart condition and strong medication can be dangerous 'and he knew that it was bad for him' (70). Cantwell's fun is self-destructive. He drinks his first 'double' upon arriving at the garage (39) in Venice and has seven more drinks of hard liquor *before* dinner (55, 63, 69, 82, 92, 101, 116).[26] At dinner with Renata he shares a bottle of Valpolicella and a bottle of expensive champagne; another bottle of champagne is placed in the gondola; a bottle of Valpolicella is by his reading light in his hotel room (164). He drinks it before going to sleep and, on rising, he finds a second bottle of the same wine (172) and starts drinking. His entire experience of Venice is suffused in a haze of alcohol, a 'drug' that undermines the effect of the heart drugs. The drinking may also explain why he does not notice much in Venice, except in general terms. The occasional, highly revealing 'stupidity' of the dialogue may be the result of intoxication.

With empathic insight Hemingway creates an atmosphere around Cantwell consistent with theme and characterization, and only indirectly alludes to Venetian beauty, mystery, and decay, even ironizing these qualities. He chooses the least touristic season in which to set the novel, flouting convention. In D'Annunzio's *Il fuoco* (1900) (The Flame), the 'true spirit' of 'temptress' Venice is 'in the silence and, most frighteningly – be certain of it – in full summer, at noon'; 'demanding, even cruel,' Venice as midday goddess is a 'deathlike suspension of all things,' but also an epiphanic 'intimation of original energy' in the self.[27] In *Death in Venice* Aschenbach arrives in late, inclement spring but stays into the hot summer and the cholera epidemic that kills him. It seems appropriate, in light of Cantwell's precarious health and soldierly virtue, that the 'true spirit' of his Venice reveals itself in winter, and at night, in the 'same strong, wild, cold, wind from the mountains' (184); in evening walks between the Gritti and Harry's Bar, where climbing each little bridge gives him heart spasms; and in a nocturnal gondola ride with Renata under a heavy army blanket, a literary reminiscence of Jordan and Maria in *For Whom the Bell Tolls*.

Crossing over frequently into interior monologue, Hemingway keeps his own perceptions close to Cantwell's, so that Venice is seen largely through Cantwell's sensitive eyes. The Grand Canal looks 'as grey as though Degas had painted it on one of his greyest days' (71). Nothing seems 'dull' along the canals and it 'doesn't all have to be palaces and churches' (44). Yet the churches draw his curiosity. On his way to Harry's he passes Santa Maria del Giglio, thinking to himself that its 'small, 'compact,' 'air-borne' forms resemble a 'P-47' (77), the biggest, heaviest fighter plane in World War II. Given his somewhat inebriated state, one might question his choice of adjectives, especially if one puts down the baroque as a ponderous, intricately ornamented style. But the flight metaphor affirms Hemingway's perceptual accuracy: if a big plane could defy gravity, why not a 'small' church, one that illustrates a Wölfflinian principle of baroque style, 'an urge for upward movement.' That Cantwell anticipates looking it up in a guide deepens one's awareness of the pleasure to be denied him by death, for he would have learned that the marble relief maps of cities decorating its façade celebrate the military service of its patron, Antonio Barbaro: a soldier's church. Santa Maria del Giglio is one of a thousand reasons why Cantwell loves walking through the 'strange,

tricky town,' (45), which is like 'working cross-word puzzles' (45), full of
intersections, byways, and dead ends – like the puzzles of words themselves. For Venice is 'a game you play' (185), fun to be sure, but also an
unknown terrain where one gets lost playing '*solitaire ambulante*' (185)
in the labyrinthine city. Taking a gondola across the Grand Canal, he
sees the 'black-clad people' climbing out of a 'black-painted vehicle,' as
if disembarking on the isle of the dead; 'nobody would give you a penny
for your thoughts' (185). In his youth he tried to pay off death with
(for him) a large sum of money; now, a penny is all that is required by
Charon for passage. The weather during his morning stroll is not only
'*brutto*' (ugly) but '*Brutissimo*' (very ugly) (183); unlike a good Burberry,
his army coat is only 'wind-proof,' 'not water-proof' (184), making him
vulnerable to the Venetian element. He had once had a 'sore throat all
winter' from being near the water in the Veneto (32). It makes him angry that some 'jerk' can send his 'boy to a fancy prep school because he
made these raincoats my ass' and cut a deal with a 'Benny Meyers of the
ground forces,' an anti-Semitic reference (185).

Cantwell's main reason for going to Venice is to visit Renata, a young
aristocrat, known first as the contessa (68), only later as Renata (88),
and never given a last name. A generalized, ambiguous character, she
is presented in vague terms, mistaken for a failure of characterization,[28]
and seems rather a screen upon which Cantwell projects his fantasies.
'Renata,' which means 're-born' in Italian, is both the vehicle and goal of
Cantwell's longing: to be 're-born,' to achieve the 'great miracle' (288)
of love, to regain something of the spirit of lost youth, and to ease his
death. Renata is a Venetian born in Venice (he is a 'Torcello boy') and
closely identified with the city. When Cantwell, evoking the soldierly
classical myth, asks how many people in her family fought for Venice,
she replies proudly, 'Everybody,' 'Always ... and several of them were
Doges' (219). Cantwell thinks,'they were not Othello and Desdemona'
(230), because she is 'better looking' than Shakespeare's heroine and
he 'fought as many, or more times' than the 'garrulous Moor' (230). Yet
Renata still begs her Othello to tell *his* war stories, twice falling asleep
while he is telling them (she is a trifle drunk; he, a trifle garrulous). She
describes the portrait of herself that she gives him as if it were a person
'rising from the sea without the head wet' (97), possible only for a goddess, in other words, Venus 'rising from the sea' (45) or its near homonym 'Venice,' 'queen of the seas' (35).

Venice is a city of oriental splendour, precious gems, and fabled riches.
Besides her portrait Renata gives him two square emeralds, family heir-

looms, green being one of Venice's colours, and squareness signifying the geometric and non-natural, a pairing with Torcello's 'square' tower. The square emeralds are her symbol, just as the square tower on Torcello is Cantwell's. Renata asks him to feel in his pocket for her two 'stones' (103), a sexual referent, which will remind him of her. When Cantwell discovers that the jewels are valued at a quarter of a million dollars, he is embarrassed and returns them. He prefers frugality, simplicity, Torcello.

Besides her associations with innocent heroines and heroic Venice, Renata also embodies the sinister qualities of the Romantic Fatal Woman typified by Keats's 'La Belle Dame Sans Merci':

> I saw pale kings, and princes too,
> Pale warriors, death pale were they all;
> They cried – 'La belle dame sans merci
> Hath thee in thrall!'

Attributes of the Fatal Woman include a diabolical beauty; a Medusa smile; alluring innocence; algolagnia or sexual pleasure from either suffering or inflicting pain (particularly to an erogenous zone); a close relation between the erotic, the aesthetic, and the exotic ('love of the exotic is usually an imaginative projection of a sexual desire'); frigidity; perversion; slaughter-lust; Sphinx-like or cat-like 'knowledge'; a devotion to the cult of the moon; and the desire to be idolized (Venus, the Eternal Feminine) (207); vampirism and Satanism; and a bloodless complexion: 'the typical Fatal Woman is always pale,' writes Mario Praz, pallor being spectral or death-like.[29] Renata has 'pale,' 'almost olive-colored skin,' a 'profile' that could 'break your, or anyone else's heart' (Cantwell has heart trouble), and hair of an 'alive texture' (80), the feral talisman. The 'unnatural' aspect of their intimacy is not so much the age difference, which troubles her (272), but a mock-violation of the incest taboo. Cantwell often calls her 'Daughter' and she goes along with the fantasy (Hemingway was in the habit of addressing even slightly younger women as 'daughter'; he called Marlene Dietrich 'daughter,' which greatly amused her – she was five years younger than Hemingway). Yet when he objects to any suggestion of 'incest' (98), she makes an excuse: 'I don't think that would be so terrible in a city as old as this and that has seen what this city has seen' (98).[30] Either Venice has seen so much sin that one more makes little difference, or Venice is so old that it is virtually pre-social, that is, natural, and therefore sexually permissive and promiscuous. 'Crime is natural, and therefore innocent.'[31] The incest theme relates to the quest for rebirth and the origin: incest-longing, in Byron, Chateaubriand, and Poe, implies a desire to give birth to oneself, not to acknowledge difference.

Renata gives hints of depressive affect and needs to be whipped up by stories of violence. She repeatedly asks to hear war stories, teasing him not to be 'rough,' never giving up on the slaughter-lust (123, 125, 126, 133, 138, 139, ...) until Cantwell finally objects, 'Let's skip war,' on page 217. 'No. I need it for my education,' Renata replies. Then follow chapters 29 to 35 taken up with Cantwell's World War II memories. Finally, he pleads, 'I bore myself, Daughter"; 'Tell me some more please,' she insists, 'and be just as bitter as you want' (240). Renata can be as 'rough' (212) as Cantwell; she is finally enrolled in the Brusadelli, a real killer (270). Her utterance of a crucial 'disappointment' (110) (refusal of sex – this is the second reference lacking a clear referent)[32] sounds to Cantwell like 'the worst' from a battalion commander. As a figure of demand she shakes his monolithic impenetrability: 'you never give me presents' (102). He protests that on a colonel's pay (further reduced by alimony payments) he can only afford drinks, meals, and 'small things from the PX' (102), which will not long satisfy a Venetian contessa. Stopping at a jewelry shop, he wants to buy her one of two 'small negro' (259) figurines: the diminutive Othello, perhaps a servant, seen occasionally beside Venetian ladies in paintings. Just heads and torsos, a mark of her castrating power, the figurines wear turbans of chip diamonds (105): the decorated phallus as trophy. While she prefers the one with the 'nicer' face, he says 'I think I would rather have him [the other figurine] attend you if it was the old days' (259), that is, she wants the beautiful face, he identifies with the strong protector, the two myths of Venice side by side in the two figurines. She accepts his decision and haggles over the price, which even at its lowest he cannot afford and has to borrow the money from her. Later, in silent protest, he claims that he never 'gave' it to her because she had picked it out (290): he is not a servant after all. He calls her 'gentle cat' (155), the animal known for its stealth, silence, and predatory indifference. Feline narcissism – not weak characterization as Hemingway's critics say – may explain her bland affect.

A cat is also a sphinx, possessor of forbidden knowledge: 'how would you like to be a girl of nineteen years old in love with a man over fifty years old that you know was going to die?' (91). Taken aback, Cantwell says, 'you put it a little bluntly' (92). She repeats the remark with astonishing frankness at dinner: 'Oh, I wish ... that you were not going to die' (160); and the next day, 'that is the good thing about you going to die that you can't leave me' (211). A death goddess, she will forever possess him. Can this be 'fun'? Renata's protestations are veiled acts of sadism. She enjoys holding his 'hurt hand' and dotes on his wound: 'all last week, every night,' she dreamt that his wounded hand was 'the hand of our Lord' (84). She thus reverses the roles of divinity and supplicant, making her the worshipper, him the worshipped. Inflicting pain, Renata enjoys pain herself: she makes him kiss her so that 'the buttons of your uniform hurt me' (110).

The power of the Fatal Woman to punish and wound is connected to vampirism. He carries her square emeralds, which (she says) come from 'dead people,' the war trophies of her family. She draws his blood like a vampire, for they kiss so hard that he feels the 'sweet salt' (111) of his blood on his lips. Cantwell's most serious 'blood' wound is his heart condition, which rapidly deteriorates on this visit. At one point he 'reminds' Renata's portrait to 'keep your God-damn chin up so you can break my heart easier' (173).

As implausible as it may first appear, Renata belongs with Semiramis, Marguerite de Bourgogne, and Théophile Gautier's Cléopatre, who had 'massacred in the morning the lovers who had passed the night with her.'[33] In a nocturnal gondola ride Renata exercises her control from the start, makes arrangements with the gondolier, chooses the route, and sets the ground rules for sexual behaviour. The gondolier with his long pole is a mysterious double of Cantwell, a competitor and, in a sense, equally under Renata's power. Cantwell thinks, 'What hand or eye framed that dark-ed symmetry [of the gondola]' (149) and wonders why he has never fully appreciated the beauty of the gondola: the allusion to the 'fearful symmetry' of Blake's 'Tyger' implicates violent energy under aesthetic control. Renata, with her hair blown back in the wind, looks like the 'figure-head on a ship' (149), plowing through the seas. Sorceress, vehicle, and goal, Renata is identified with the gondola and reminds Cantwell of the 'same magic as always of the light hull.' (Brett Ashley has the curves of a racing yacht.) So, too, the gondolier lays 'her partly on her side' to have 'more control' (151). Under the blanket Cantwell feels Renata's body with what she calls his 'hurt hand' and helps her experience perhaps three orgasms to Cantwell's none. The first orgasm happens and 'the bird' flies out the 'closed window' (154). Then, 'please wait until after we have gone under the second bridge,' she says, but 'please attack gently' (154-5); and, third, 'do you think we could once more if it would not hurt you?' (157). It 'hurts' him because of his heart condition, 'hurt hand,' and the denial of sexual gratification. Yet Renata has satisfied her desire, avoided sexual penetration, and refused her partner. Her conduct the next morning confirms a peculiar sexual terror. Cantwell and Renata meet in St Mark's Square, which, as if in response to his wish, has been flooded (in Venice desire and reality merge). He likes it; she does not, saying, 'It is only really fun toward the last when the children play' (200). She may want children, but not by Cantwell. Renata projects her fear of penetration onto the female Venice who has been violated by the sexual overflow of the male sea god (Neptune, *il mare;* the classical sea, as opposed to the Romantic one, is masculine). At the same time her refusal of sex provokes two of Cantwell's most violent fantasies: he 'jokes' about military secrets such as 'energy crackers' that prevent erections, 'like the atomic bomb, only played backwards' (197). And he wants to destroy Venice, 'give all Venice botulism from 56,000 feet' because 'they give you anthrax' (a disease of sheep).

The feminine body as representative of Venice is a motif that Hemingway may have taken from D'Annunzio's *Il fuoco,* where Venice is the 'magnificent and tempting city in whose canals, as in the veins of a voluptuous woman, a fire was beginning to burn.'[34] In the gondola ride Cantwell's wounded hand 'coasted' (152) along her body as he 'searched for the island,' that is, the clitoris, 'in the great river with the high steep banks'; there is no penetration.[35] She asks that he 'hold the high ground' (153, referring to her breasts). In the symbolic geography of the swamps and lagoons, this is another island, the *riva alto* (Rialto) or high bank on which Venice was founded. Cantwell feels he is 'assisting, or had made an act of presence, at the only mystery that he believed in except the occasional bravery of man' (153). In this sexualization and profanation of religious language, he is like a priest 'assisting' at the revelation of a 'mystery' in which he 'believed,' that is, the body of the woman floating in the gondola in her primeval realm of the swamp. The champagne, which they drink, is the sacramental wine. In *Il fuoco* Stelio Effrena rhapsodizes over the sexual penetration of the male sky-god Autumn into the canals of the goddess Venice, 'the hour of the highest Feast,' not the revelation of the Host as in Wagner's *Parsifal,* but sexual consummation, 'as if the wild bridegroom were waving his purple banner as he drew near in his fiery chariot.'[36]

Searching for, 'finding' and then 'losing,' an 'island' (153) or the 'unknown country' (155) upon which to land and relieve oneself of the burden of a lonely 'nomadic' life (142) is an enduring theme in Hemingway's fiction. The title of *For Whom the Bell Tolls* recalls the celebrated phrase in Donne's sermon, 'no man is an island'; and there is the posthumous *Islands in the Stream*. In Venice the hundred-odd islands, linked by canals and bridges, retain their independent existence even while forming a larger organic whole. In one respect, pioneering Venice and whatever is preserved of that spirit in the modern period may represent Hemingway's ideal of social solidarity and independence. Yet the chief impression is of Cantwell's loneliness and failure to communicate, indicated by the virtually seamless narrative shifts into isolated, interior monologue. In the market, facing the 'attack' of shoppers, Cantwell forms an '*îlot de résistance*' (190) against them. In one of the final scenes Cantwell stands in a sunken oak hogshead waiting for the ducks to fly over, a solitary man-made island in a 'frozen lagoon' and 'far' from the 'sedge-lined shore' (280). As in Keats's 'La Belle Dame Sans Merci,' for this 'pale warrior,' the 'sedge has wither'd from the lake.' Marina Gradoli speaks of the novel in terms of a 'gradual detachment of the Hemingway hero from his own country,'[37] indeed, from any country.

If Venice transforms life into art, and Renata is a true daughter of the city, then her portrait, which she presents to Cantwell, is the icon of that transformation. Everyone and everything associated with the portrait are somehow tainted by her ability to render weak and helpless. It was painted by a '*pédéraste*' who has 'false teeth' (loss of aggressive power) because he was attacked by other pederasts under a 'full moon' (96), almost certainly for being ashamed of his pederasty (he makes a show of dating women).[38] Renata is a devotee of the cold moon, the symbol of the huntress-maiden Artemis in her brightness and the death goddess Hecate in her 'dark spectral side.'[39] When Cantwell says that she can have any 'planet' she wants, she chooses: 'I'll be the moon' (99) (significantly, not a planet). For one course at dinner Renata chooses lobster, a precious luxury food from what Cantwell describes as 'our rich coast' (117), indicating both possession and victimization: 'lobster fills with the moon,' meaning that it feeds better when there is light at night that supplies its lack. When the moon is dark, 'he' is 'not worth eating' (117); the male lobster is being fed and consumed in the presence of the moon, which is female, at the height of her power. Cantwell identifies with the cooked lobster and is fascinated by its obscure world – witness his thoughts in the fish-market, 'the closest thing to a good museum' (192), as he pores over the albacore, bonito, bullets, eels, sole, scampi, clams (he eats six raw), and so on. 'When you want to be the moon and various stars and live with your man and have five sons,' Renata declares, 'looking at yourself in the mirror and doing the artifices of a woman is not very exciting' (118), a disavowal of narcissism that rings false. Like an oriental goddess, she suffers no rival around her and no daughters; but she will have a horde of men ('five sons'). Half-seriously, Cantwell thinks that she wishes to marry him and have children: '"Then let us be married at once." "No," she said' (118).

Maureen O'Shaughnessey comments that Hemingway 'tells us surprisingly little' about Renata's portrait, but that will depend on what one does with information given.[40] Renata says it is 'very romantic': the hair is 'twice as long' as normal, and hence more potent, and she looks as though she were 'rising from the sea.' But the painting falsifies reality, because 'you rise from the sea with the hair very flat and coming to points at the end.' This is 'almost the look of a very nearly dead rat' (97). 'Very ugly,' as she admits, the portrait evokes the face of the Medusa encircled by snakes ('coming to points'). Feelings of horror and repulsion are transferred onto rats, 'very nearly' dead, but still alive, associated with the swamp, predatory vermin, disease, and undifferentiated nature. Renata has 'killed' another potential aggressor ('rat pack,' symbol of male sexual predatoriness). Mesmerized by the real and the portrayed Renata, Cantwell utters, 'I think of you when you come from the sea too' (97); he thinks of her both as in the portrait and as the Medusa-like woman described by Renata. This Medusa does not rise like a queen from the sea but like a rat from the swamp: the other Venice rising from the littoral marshlands.

Since Renata will not spend the night with Cantwell at the Gritti, in her stead – and it is a depressing spectacle – he has her portrait brought to his room and propped on chairs, and arranged with mirrors, near his bed so he can look at and talk to it. His first thought is to blame himself: what 'went wrong tonight ... Me, I guess' (165). Yet the fault must be shared with Renata, who abandons him to this frightening substitute, her iconic double, while she sleeps alone. The picture is silent, unresponsive, 'indefensible' yet menacing, not unlike the real Renata, as life and art fuse together. 'You are two years younger than the girl you portray,' Cantwell addresses the portrait, 'and she is younger and older than hell; which is quite an old place' (176). The remark underlines one of the traits of Fatal Woman: the vampire. Earlier her kiss drew blood; he will soon call 'her' daughter in three languages (266), an eternal presence, a Magna Mater. The locus classicus of the Decadent topos of timeless vampire beauty is Pater's lyric excursus on the Mona Lisa, which Yeats considered the first modern poem:[41] 'She is older than the rocks among which she sits; like the vampire, she has been dead many times, and learned the secrets of the grave; and has been a diver in deep seas, and keeps their fallen day about her; and trafficked for strange webs with Eastern merchants.'[42] Cantwell's 'younger and older than hell' links Renata's portrait to Pater's (and da Vinci's) Mona Lisa; Renata's Venetian ancestors trafficked with Eastern merchants; and 'hell' reinforces the association of her fatal and satanic beauty, which is not reduced but rather accentuated by his attempt to joke about it ('quite an old place'). And Renata will learn the 'Supreme Secret' of the Brusadelli (peace of death). His most frequently used curse, 'hell' is often on his lips (4, 6, 52, 63, 92, 118, 165, 166, 172, 173 ... 245, 253, 279, 281, 282, 289) and therefore on his mind. '"The hell with you," the portrait said, without speaking. "You low class soldier"' (174). He projects this harsh thrust of aristocratic disdain onto the picture, which returns it, punishing him for his social inferiority and psychological insecurity. 'The hell with you': he is in hell, among the swamps.

The Gioconda smile, a variant of the Medusa smile in Romantic tradition, is so hackneyed a motif that one might expect Hemingway, at this late date, not to exploit it or to do so only indirectly. Pater described it as an 'unfathomable smile, always with a touch of something sinister in it, which plays over all Leonardo's work.' While one looks in vain for any smile from the portrait (or from Renata), the smile is subtly displaced from Renata onto her double, the Barone Alvarito, Cantwell's sexual rival. Alvarito is a Venetian aristocrat like Renata; 'about three years older' (130) than Renata; 'almost tall' (but not tall, and certainly not as tall as Caltwell, the 'tower') and 'beautifully built' (129) (not robustly, but beautifully, which is almost feminine), just as Renata has a 'tall striding beauty' (80). He is a hunter (129); she the moon, the huntress. She says that 'we knew each other as children' (130) (regressive merging) and that he was 'born very old' (130) (like the vampire portrait). She is 'pale' and his name Alvarito is 'a diminutive of "the pale one"' (is he too a diminished male in her presence?).[43] Some hidden communication takes place between them (are Renata and Alvarito engaged?) since she 'had been quiet and a little withdrawn, since she had seen Alvarito' (131). She teases Cantwell about the reason why Alvarito did not invite her to the duck-shoot: 'He might not have asked me because he wanted me' (199). Death has been claiming the older men around them: both Renata's and Alvarito's fathers have died recently.

Their mothers, too, share a peculiar trait: still in mourning, Renata's mother 'sees almost no one' (93) and 'can't live' in Venice 'too long at any time because there are no trees' (205); she 'lives' in the country. Alvarito's mother lives near Treviso 'where they have trees'; she is 'tired of there not being trees in Venice'; 'nothing really interests her now except efficiency,' revealing an awareness of the opposition between old Venetian culture and modernity (48). Both De Staël and Barrès had remarked on the lack of life-giving vegetation in Venice.[44] Living in the country, both women are associated with the chthonic powers and rites of the dead – Demeter figures who in a primitive matrilinear era claim priority over the dead fathers. Renata made a point of saying her square emeralds descend through the mother. Alvarito is Cantwell's host at the duck-shoot, surely knows of his heart condition, and is possibly implicated in his death; he purveys a killing form of fun as surely as Renata. Cantwell does not want to die in Venice, but in nature; not in a swamp or swamp-like environment (like his brother), but on dry land: 'across the river and into the trees.'

Alvarito's significance having been established, Hemingway devotes a paragraph to what may be termed his Gioconda smile, as if to give it typographical emphasis:

> It was not the easy grin of the confident, nor the quick slashing smile of the extremely durable and the wicked. It had no relation with the poised, intently used smile of the courtesan or the politician. It was the strange, rare smile which rises from the deep, dark pit, deeper than a well, deep as a deep mine, that is within them. (129)

This smile expresses the remote, the unbidden, the primordial, the 'unfathomable' quality 'with a touch of something sinister' that Pater saw in the Mona Lisa's smile.[45] '[D]ark' and 'deep' came first, then 'deeper,' and finally, with a doubling in place of the superlative, 'deep as a deep mine'; pit, well, and mine lead to the primordial centre of (mother) earth where geologic space merges with time; using both 'deep' and 'strange,' Pater said Mona Lisa was 'older than the rocks among which she sits.' While the 'sinister' interpretation suits Hemingway's context, it does not exhaust the da Vinci portrait, in which the smile could equally signify prenatal bliss or earliest childhood, the first sight of the smiling, nourishing mother. The total meaning points to the eternal cycle of nature: birth and death join hands in celebration of the mystery of life.

Alone at night Cantwell feels the 'stones' which are 'hard and warm against his flat, hard, old, and warm chest.' He notes 'how the wind was blowing' from the north, looks at the portrait, drinks more wine, and reads 'Red' Smith in the *Herald Tribune* (166). The train of associations leads from the emeralds, felt 'against' his chest and parasitically drawing their warmth from his blood, to the death-wind from the north, the drug of wine, and diversion ('fun' – the sports page). When he realizes he should take his medicine, he thinks 'the hell with the pills' (166). At this point the desire for death seems stronger than the desire for life. Then he decides to take the pills. The next morning, he asks the portrait, 'why the hell can't you just get into bed with me?' (172), and concedes defeat. Renata would 'out-maneuver' him every time (173); given his own 'hurt hand,' Renata always gets the upper hand (Latin, *manus*).

The most complex doubling (or tripling) in the novel is Cantwell, Hemingway, and D'Annunzio. As a news reporter in Kansas in 1917 and an ambulance driver on the Italian front in 1918, Hemingway had become aware of the exploits of Italy's most famous living writer, and not only with D'Annunzio the writer, but the soldier, lover, leader, and international celebrity. At twenty, Hemingway looked upon D'Annunzio as 'everything that [he] wanted to be.'[46] Like D'Annunzio, he had been wounded in the war, the token of blood brotherhood that appealed to his primitivism. When in 1919 he returned to Chicago, he made gifts of D'Annunzio's *Il fuoco* in translation to girlfriends, including his future wife Hadley. *The Flame* or *The Flame of Life* concerns artistic creativity, sexual power, crowd hysteria, social coercion, death, and eternal fame; D'Annunzio and his book must have made an odd *galeotto*. Hemingway entitled his first anti-war poem 'D'Annunzio.'[47] In his World War I scrapbook he had a large photograph of D'Annunzio in a troop mess. Two short stories from 1919–20, 'The Woppian Way' and 'The Mercenaries,' examine D'Annunzio's character. Four foreign dispatches to the *Toronto Star* in the early 1920s fill in the portrait. It is not exaggerating to speak of a D'Annunzio obsession.

In nearly all these pieces, as in his correspondence, Hemingway does everything to belittle D'Annunzio, and to reduce his literary and military achievements, not in the spirit of criticism, but out of sheer envy and malice. Idealization and identification underwent the same tortuous process to which he subjected other father figures and potential competitors; yet more so perhaps in D'Annunzio's case because of what the two writers shared in common.

Anthony Rhodes's profile of D'Annunzio's 'strongest instincts' overlaps with Hemingway's: 'heroism,' 'egoism,' 'violence,' 'sensuality,' 'interest in blood and wounds,' the desire 'to excel in everything.'[48] One should add the fascination with weaponry, the military, athleticism, and a massive 'death wish.'[49] Michael A. Ledeen speaks of D'Annunzio's 'totally captivating personality' and 'charisma' that 'extended over men and women,' a remark that perfectly suits Hemingway (four wives, gangs of friends, hangers-on).[50] Praz portrays D'Annunzio's as a 'child of a semi-barbarous race, who, coming into contact with a more than mature civilization, assimilated it rapidly and summarily, with the inevitable discords'; 'beneath the veneer appears from time to time the *spirito crudo*.'[51] No American writer fits this description better than Hemingway, with his suburban love of the virgin wilderness 'up in Michigan' and Idaho, deep-sea fishing off Key West and Cuba, or game-hunting in Africa, and his quick assimilation of the extreme sophistication of Poundian poetics, Stein and Joyce, and the Parisian milieu. Alberto Moravia saw a darker side to Hemingway's linkage of two worlds, making a comparison to D'Annunzio; a 'healthy, youthful, brave and frank view of life was to reveal itself through Hemingway as related to all the most refined, tired and corrupt elucubrations of old Europe,' 'the sort of decadence which, finding literature insufficient, was later to spread to *mores* and politics by way of D'Annunzianism and Nazism.'[52] Yet despite the manifold interrelations between the two writers, Hemingway felt compelled to deny the authority of D'Annunzio. His native cultural tradition required that (as Montale said of Faulkner) 'every American writer' be 'self-made.'[53] For years D'Annunzio vanished from Hemingway's biography and fiction only to reappear in Cantwell's sharply perceived memories in the Venetian novel. Then Hemingway comes to terms with him, in the truest way for an artist, in his art.

When in 1965 Montale spoke of D'Annunzio's 'example' to Hemingway, he warned that the 'two men – and the two writers – were very different.'[54] But Michael S. Reynolds did not heed this counsel in arguing that Hemingway's 'military adventures' in World War II 'were to bear a striking resemblance' to those of D'Annunzio in World War I. His catalogue of resemblances only serves to show how unlike the two men's experiences actually were: 'D'Annunzio led single-boat raids on the Austrians; Hemingway outfitted his fishing boat to attack German submarines single-handedly' (note the two 'singles' – as if they were one-man armies). 'D'Annunzio flew bombing missions; Hemingway flew intercept missions with the R.A.F. as a reporter' (note the dying-fall qualifier, 'as a reporter'). 'D'Annunzio gathered his own army to liberate Fiume after the war; Hemingway gathered his band of irregulars after the Normandy invasion and was the first military group into Paris.' One can hardly find 'striking resemblances' between D'Annunzio's raids, by land, boat and plane, in hostile territory, and Hemingway's fishing boat escapades off Cuba aimed at locating U-boats or journalist adventures in France in World War II. 'Despite what he said and possibly believed in later years, Hemingway did not find a U-boat.'[55] Spruille Braden, the American ambassador to Cuba, was merely humouring his resident celebrity by letting him 'participate' in the war effort.[56] Hemingway never saw a submarine; he threw the grenades into the sea to enliven his (rather dull) drinking parties, and it was fun getting free gas from the government. Nor can Hemingway's arrival in Paris be compared in any way to D'Annunzio's capture and fifteen-month control of Fiume. As a journalist for *Collier's*, Hemingway was (again) a non-combatant; he was not the 'first military group' into the city; he did not 'liberate' the Ritz Hotel – all Hemingway myths, this last a self-parody of his low-cost 'heroism.' By contrast, D'Annunzio was a commissioned army officer, went on some sixty missions, and earned many medals from Italy and foreign governments. Osbert Sitwell compared his Italian Gold Medal for Valor to the Victoria Cross.[57] Hemingway never ran torpedo raids, never took a city, never held up a nation's business for months at a time, nor upset a peace conference. However, in fairness to Hemingway, he received the Silver Medal for Valor from the Italian government in 1918 for rescuing an Italian soldier when he himself was severely wounded.

Nonetheless, the end result of biographical comparisons places Hemingway at a disadvantage. A better approach is to examine Hemingway's long connection to D'Annunzio and his use of the latter's image to construct an ironic antagonist and literary double. To begin with, his antiwar poem 'D'Annunzio' (1920–1) unites the pithiness of American slang and the lapidary tone of an epitaph in the Greek Anthology: 'Half a million dead wops / And he got a kick out of it / The son of a bitch.'[58] D'Annunzio's name as sole title is like a black banner planted on top of the carnage. The pun in the name 'announces' death, not redemptive rebirth, which D'Annunzio promised through war. The one superman is set against the many – indeed, the half million – whom he enthralled: he is a king of the dead. Magnitude ('Half a million'), according to Longinus and Burke, is a component of the sublime; Hemingway deflates the false sublime ('kick') of D'Annunzio's language by coarse, laconic slang and jumpy rhythms.[59] His fictional protagonists (Henry, Jordan, Cantwell) deplore the rhetoric of war, even as they are attracted by war itself. D'Annunzio had no such divided consciousness. The slang of 'wops' and 'son of a bitch' unifies the two categories: he is a 'wop' too.

In 1919 Hemingway wrote his first story with an Italian background, 'The Woppian Way.' At one time, on the advice of an editor, the title was changed to 'The Passing of Pickles McCarty.'[60] The original title is better because it points to the story's thematic distinction between ancient military might (the Appian Way from Rome to Brundisium) and modern degeneracy and vulgarity. More specifically, the Woppian Way refers in the story to the Strada Cadorna, constructed in 1916–17 and running from Bassano to the summit of Monte Grappa; it could also mean '*all'italiana*' in the pejorative sense.[61] Several magazines rejected the story, whereupon Hemingway withdrew it from publication.

A forty-two-year-old American journalist, who functions as narrator, is in Rome 'when the story broke': D'Annunzio's occupation of Fiume, captured and claimed for Italy in September 1919. He rushes to Trieste where he receives a cable from his news office to 'Cover Fiume!' Blockaded by land and sea, Fiume must be entered illegally, so he goes to the Cafe Cesare Battista (*sic*), named after the patriotic deputy Battisti from the Trentino, executed by the Austrians in July 1916, to gather the latest rumours. He is advised to board the Santa Fina, ostensibly bound for Gibraltar, and if anyone asks 'What Flame?' to answer '*Fiamma Nerra*' (*sic*): the black flame, symbol of the Arditi, the Italian shock troops with a 'commando' aura.

Unable to sleep, he comes up on deck at 1 a.m. to get some air and smoke a 'long, black, poisonous "Tuscanis"' cigar. He conjures up the image of D'Annunzio, smoke referring to the demonic, violent nature of the subject matter, to insubstantiality, and to the D'Annunzian symbol of the flame. A touch of the decadent attaches to the world-weary journalist: Wildean characters are always effetely smoking, lounging, musing. He imagines D'Annunzio's military adventurism as a parodic continuation of his sexual exploits. When one Huysmanian extreme has been exhausted, another takes its place:[62]

> As I smoked I thought of the great amourist who had exhausted the love of women and now was wringing the last drops from love of country onto his white hot soul. Of how he had set the decrees of nations aside by his Filibuster. This hero with his occupation gone. A lover who had failed in only one pursuit, that of death in battle. Would he find the death he was looking for at Fiume, or would he be cheated again?[63]

'Amourist' is spelled in the French manner, not 'amorist,' which is American. He ridicules D'Annunzio as 'wringing the last drops,' forcing excitement from an enervated society.[64] In *Forse che sì forse che no* (Perhaps yes, perhaps no) (1910) D'Annunzio's Paolo Tarsis cannot say whether 'it pleased him more to spill sperm or blood' (this is the *spirito crudo*).[65]

Either way, 'drops' fall on a soul that is like an excessively hot plate (not merely hot, or red hot, but 'white hot') and go up in steam, a mock-sacrifice to his own egoism.

At Fiume, so the narrator thinks, D'Annunzio seeks death and secular martyrdom to transcend reality. Mindful of the need for civic holidays and public festivals, D'Annunzio consecrated Fiume as the 'City of the Holocaust' (smoke, fire, destruction, renewal), which initiated the Fascist rhetoric of sacrifice:[66]

> I thought of the last time I had seen him, when he climbed out of the cockpit behind his pilot after the return from the serenissima raid on Vienna. How, looking like a bald headed old vulture he unstrapped the ivory hilted dagger that he wore on a belt around his flying jumper and said to his pilot, 'You achieved what you went after – but not I,' and walked away.

The aging flier D'Annunzio is also an 'old vulture' who preys on the death of young soldiers, and the journalist satirizes D'Annunzio's remark after his leaflet-drop over Vienna on 9 August 1918 ('the zenith and the culmination of his war career'[67]). He had led seven planes from his 'La Serenissima' squadron, named after 'most serene' Venice, on the seven-hundred-mile round trip journey; 'serenissima' combines with 'raid' to make an oxymoron. D'Annunzio distinguishes himself from the others who merely accomplished the mission; *his* mission looks beyond the local one to final victory, and beyond that to possibility of heroic death.

The politician D'Annunzio 'set the decrees of nations aside'; he castigated the Versailles conference and Francesco Nitti's wait-and-see policy. In wresting control of Fiume from the Allied occupation, he acts as a law unto himself. At Fiume, comments Renzo De Felice, D'Annunzio's politics were neither left nor right, but an 'aestheticized' mixture, resembling a Shelleyan, anarchic utopia.[68] He adopted a democratic constitution and promulgated the League of Oppressed Peoples to counter the colonialist hegemony of the League of Nations. However, in the eyes of many in Europe and the Americas, he was at best a troublemaker, at worst an international outlaw.[69] The journalist labels him a 'Filibuster,' a 'freebooter' (from the Dutch, 'free' 'booty'),[70] one who engages in 'private military action in a foreign country,' like William Walker in Nicaragua. D'Annunzio's florid rhetoric is also 'Filibuster,' the emptiest language of all, the mere killing of time, in contrast to the journalist's flat tone and concise speech. With 'Filibuster,' the narrator crosses American and European political and *para*-military fantasies, a key element in D'Annunzio's appeal to him because he, like young Hemingway, had been a recent Red Cross volunteer on the Italian front. D'Annunzio (and the narrator, and Hemingway) is both in the army but not in the army, thus preserving his independence. Or he is a more extreme army.

After the war – like Cantwell in Venice, like Hemingway in Oak Park – D'Annunzio finds his 'occupation gone.' If his occupation is war, what of him as a writer? For all his antipathy to D'Annunzio, the journalist of 'The Woppian Way' is linked to him through both war and writing. Ancient bards sang the deeds of heroes and so kept alive their fame. Today, writes Hemingway in an early poem, 'All armies are the same / Publicity is fame' (ca. 1922). The modern press exerts the power of scandal and publicity to make and break celebrities. Although the journalist wants to deflate D'Annunzio, as the ironic viewpoint indicates, he is irresistibly drawn towards him, not realizing to what extent he is involved in D'Annunzio's celebrity and therefore complicit and morally culpable. Without the fiery D'Annunzio, there is no story. In this regard, Hemingway's personal experience as a reporter is highly relevant: against his parents' wishes he sidestepped a university education to enter literature through journalism in the tradition of Howells, Crane, and Norris, and he was a freelance reporter during both the Spanish Civil War and World War II. Equally relevant, D'Annunzio began his Roman career as a journalist and gossip columnist and learned early how to exploit the organs of mass media.

On deck, enjoying his Tuscanis cigar, the journalist feels a knife poking at his ribs. He gives the password and discovers that his assailant is his friend Neroni, an Italian American from California whom he had met before the battle of Monte Asalone, and who is also heading for Fiume. The name 'Neroni' is stage Italian for someone either with black hair (*nero*, black) or like Nerone (the emperor Nero). In a flashback that comprises the remainder of the story, Neroni explains his 'renaissance' as a follower of 'a certain bald headed adventurer' who 'was able, with a handful of troops, to seize and hold the port of Fiume under the noses of three great allied powers.' Neroni was the once popular boxer who had dropped out of Stanford to enter the ring, fighting under the name of Pickles McCarty (Italian Americans and others frequently adopted Irish names in professional boxing). Unable to get a shot at 'the champ' or too impatient to wait for it, Neroni mysteriously quit boxing – his 'passing' or fading from memory – and joined the Arditi. (In terms of Hemingway's career, 'The Woppian Way' may show him questioning his reasons for joining the war effort, not as a soldier like Neroni, but as a non-combatant.) Neroni's heroism is incontestable: he has fought all across the Italian front, from the stony plateau of the Carso (1915–16) and Monte San Gabriele (August–September 1917) ('one of the fiercest of the lesser battles of the war'[71]), to Monte Asalone (December 1917–January 1918), Monte Corno (May 1918), and the final Piave offensive (June 1918). Hemingway writes 'Gabrielle' with two *l*'s so that at the same time he raises D'Annunzio – a mountain, after all – he deflates him by feminizing the name and emasculating the man. D'Annunzio advocated Italy's entry into World War I; so he is a reason why Neroni and the others fought over his mountain. Then he seized Fiume to gain the territorial rewards he felt that Italy had been denied, so he is the reason why they are fighting now. 'San' Gabrielle brings in the idea of sacrifice, ritual, and heroic sanctification – all the rhetoric and pageantry that took the place of politics during the months of the Fiume affair. Monte Corno was the scene of the capture of Cesare Battisti, a real hero, in 1916, and Hemingway was taking advantage of a ribald pun on Corno.[72]

The journalist had followed Neroni and the Arditi up Monte Asalone to observe the fighting (this is one of Hemingway's earliest battle descriptions). Afterwards Neroni lies exhausted along the ground with other soldiers, 'breathing heavily and drunkenly, like men between the halves of a football game.' The athletic metaphor links up the two strands of the fighter's career. Though the journalist enthusiastically believes Neroni could be the 'Champion of the world,' Neroni will not return to the ring and fight for a cheap trophy after the experience of real fighting in the war. One cannot expect him to 'hit a man with leather gloves more times that he will hit me with leather gloves. And stop every three minutes, while down in the front row a lot of fat, pink faced men will holler "Kill him! Kill him!"' The image of being surrounded by spectators obviously captivates him: 'Hitting men with little leather gloves, while down in the front row pink-faced, pop-eyed bald-headed men yell for blood!' The 'bald-headed' spectators recall the 'bald headed adventurer' for whom Neroni would again sacrifice his life. Yet the war was real; Fiume by comparison is just a sport. Although Neroni wants 'ardently' (Hemingway is punning on 'Arditi') to think that Fiume is an urgent cause, Hemingway treats it as a high-stakes game of an aesthetic filibuster. D'Annunzio is just another spectator of the event that he has created for like-minded adventurers. Pickles McCarty's 'renaissance' is another sign of his 'passing.' Is D'Annunzio's a patriotic act to recover Italian land? Does it inspire the sense of belonging to a new order, the 'city of life' that is drawing radicals from the right and left? Is it the mere love of dangerous, illegal adventure? Whatever the answer, Neroni has succumbed to the spell of the charlatan.

D'Annunzio may figure as the flying ace Il Lupo in 'The Mercenaries,' also entitled 'Wolves and Doughnuts' (1920–1).[73] Reynolds comments that the 'entire fantasy carries overtones of the aging, Italian poet/war hero': D'Annunzio.[74] However, Giovanni Checchin identifies Il Lupo as Fulco Ruffo di Calabria, the Italian flying ace, citing three references in the story. First, Il Lupo is 'second only to the dead Baracca,' and in real life the much-decorated Ruffo did succeed Francesco Baracca, the most famous Italian flying ace in the war, as commander of the 91st Squadriglia da Caccia in July 1918. Then, like Ruffo, Il Lupo is a southern Italian. Lastly, the story exactly reverses one of Ruffo's exploits: Il Lupo brings down Baron Hauser behind Italian lines with Hauser's observer dying in the crash; Ruffo brought down an Austrian plane in which the pilot died and the observer survived.[75] Most likely, Hemingway borrows traits and feats from both D'Annunzio and Ruffo in his creation of Il Lupo.

In Hemingway's portrait, Il Lupo has the charisma of D'Annunzio. Both have a distinguishing facial scar. Il Lupo is a 'flyer up in Istery or Hystery or somewheres,' the triple pun bringing together the territory of Istria (and Fiume), history, and hysteria – the compost heap that D'Annunzio created in Fiume. Moreover, this tale is the first in a line of thinly veiled stories where Hemingway attacks living writers and competitors by mocking some real or imagined sexual problem, e.g., 'Mr. and Mrs. Elliot' about T. S. Eliot and his wife; 'The Snows of Kilimanjaro' with its reference to 'Julian' (F. Scott Fitzgerald); and *To Have and Have Not* where the 'joke' is on John Dos Passos for wanting and failing to have children.

'The Mercenaries' is set in Chicago immediately after the war. Like Neroni, Rinaldo Rinaldi, the narrator, is an Italian American who had fought on the side of Italy to be in the war – an American who, unlike Hemingway, found a way to fight. Rinaldi wanders into a speakeasy filled with soldiers of fortune, mobsters, and tough guys, and gets into a conversation with two soldiers. One is a sophisticated Frenchman, Ricaud, with monogrammed shirts and expensive cigarettes; the other, a 'big' American with a 'leather face' and 'cheap' cigarettes by the name of Perry Graves, whose name rather obviously deals with his trade. Graves explains that both he and Ricaud have joined up as mercenaries with the Peruvian army in a war with Chile over a 'doughnut,' a cheap piece of pastry with a hole in the middle, that is, nothing. He mocks patriotic attitudes, so that Ricaud comments: 'Captain Graves is a propagandist to himself.' With the inadvertent result of the Frenchman's shaky knowledge of English, Hemingway probes the D'Annunzian mystique: not *for* or *of* himself, which would imply the *miles gloriosus;* rather, *to* himself, knowing how to play the propagandist game, with a country, with himself.

Graves narrates an extended flashback: a captain in the war, he was demoted after demobilization because 'I was an officer, but not a gentleman. I could command a battery, but I've got rotten taste in cigarettes.' He drinks heavily, smokes and chews tobacco, and yet is sensitive and articulate, Cantwell's prototype. Cantwell too is a professional soldier who has been demoted, from general to colonel, but then Cantwell is older (most Hemingway surrogates age with him; Cantwell is Hemingway's age at the time of his writing the novel). Cantwell similarly refers to war as his 'trade,' drinks heavily, hates politicians and the military brass, blasts propaganda, and is only at home with other similarly emarginated characters like himself. Thus, both Graves and Cantwell make a big show of being friendly with the waiters. They are lords over the servants; yet both, hating authority, identify with the servants, and secretly dislike them for their servility. And, like Cantwell, Graves is fascinated by D'Annunzio. 'Ever heard of Il Lupo?' asks Graves.

'Who in Italy has not heard of Il Lupo? The Italian ace of aces and second only to the dead Baracca,' Rinaldi informs the reader. D'Annunzio is associated with death and fame: Maj. Francesco Baracca, the flying ace killed in action in June 1918; the epithet 'dead' ironically immortalizes him. The choice of 'Lupo' (wolf) for D'Annunzio refers to certain Italian brigades, the Lupi, addressed as such in D'Annunzio's war speeches where, according to Vito Salierno, 'the word assumes tribunal tones' that would be 'typical of fascism.'[76] Since Rinaldi and Ricaud believe that Il Lupo is a 'brave man,' Graves takes it upon himself to demolish the myth. He tells – it is clearly a lie told increasingly under the spell of liquor – how after the war he took a vacation in Taormina. On the train he meets a beautiful signora, wife or mistress of Il Lupo; they had already noticed each other at the Rome racetrack where Graves had won on a dog named 'Dionysia,' an allusion to D'Annunzio's admiration for Nietzsche and greyhounds. The signora is another Fatal Woman, with her great beauty, her pallor ('a face colored like old ivory'), her 'red lips,' her impenetrable eyes like 'inkwells,' the numerous associations with fecund nature ('as good to look at as the scenery'), the immediate presence of danger and death – she is *bella Italia* herself, with all her fatal attractiveness. They enjoy a sumptuous dinner, meticulously described and including 'Bronte' wine from grapes grown on 'Aetna.' Lord Nelson was made Duke of Bronte, and the volcano is a recurrent symbol in *Il fuoco* that Hemingway elsewhere associates with D'Annunzio.

The next morning Il Lupo rushes into the breakfast room ('an Eyetalian can't come into a room without rushing' – lack of drive control) and catches the lovers dining together. He is wearing a 'beautiful blue theatrical-looking cape,' 'shining black boots,' and a sword; his face is 'white' (as death) except for a scar that stood out like a 'bright red welt,' the result of a previous duel.[77] Portrayed as a cuckolded, stage Italian, from one angle Il Lupo is absurd. Yet he astonishes Graves from another: 'the lupo was magnificent. He was doing the dramatic, and he was going it great.' Challenged to a sword duel, Graves insists on pistols, old versus new world. The now-sweating Il Lupo agrees to pistols at extremely close range, across a table 'with their left hands touching,' a token of their psychic union. The entire physical arrangement is so foolish as to call the whole episode into doubt. Hemingway makes the (sexual) victory a foregone conclusion in this American fast-draw context: Il Lupo's gun is 'one of those little 7.65 mm, pretty ugly short little gats' (short and ugly like D'Annunzio), while Graves's is a 'big forty-five' and made a 'big handful.' On the count of two ('before the signal'), Il Lupo breaks down and reaches in cowardly fashion for his gun. Graves still beats him to the draw and shoots him through the hand holding the gun: 'You see, he hadn't never heard of shooting from the hip.' The signora comforts Il Lupo while Graves, embodying classic *disinvoltura* as well as cowboy cool, finishes his coffee ('It was cold, but I like my coffee in the morning'). Il Lupo is not a 'wolf' but the lesser 'coyote,' a desert dog with more howl than bite. In *Across the River and Into the Trees* the contrast between wolves and coyotes, referring back to 'The Mercenaries,' occurs just pages before Col. Cantwell's reminiscence of D'Annunzio and serves as its thematic introduction. The wolf is 'gaited like no other animal,' 'gray' (colour of death), 'sure of himself,' 'carrying that heavy head and with the hostile eyes' (24), a Cantwell icon. Jackson says the wolves were 'gone before my time; they poisoned them out. Plenty coyotes though' (24); which is no surprise.

In a brief denouement on the nature of courage, Rinaldi wonders whether Il Lupo is brave after all. The last word goes to the neutral, observant Ricaud (part 'northerner,' part Latin), who explains that Il Lupo is no coward, his bravery having been proven in many military encounters. Only 'he is Latin. That you cannot understand, for you have courage without imagination. It is a gift from God, monsieur.' Ricaud envies Graves the lack of 'imagination' because imagination raises the spectre of fear and so kills courage. Hemingway could have stolen the notion from D'Annunzio himself.[78]

In a later version of the story, Hemingway substituted himself in the role of Perry Graves: he was 'saved from a duel, he said, when the woman distracted her husband long enough for Ernest for escape.'[79] There are other parallels between him and Graves. To recuperate from his leg wound, young Hemingway travelled to Taormina for a week with his friend James Gamble just after the war. He too possessed a very 'theatrical,' Italian military cape lined with red satin, which he had made for him in Milan and in which he posed for photographers on his return to the United States. Both men end up in wintry Chicago sharing a disdain for propaganda and a fascination with war, etc. Hemingway was carrying on an inner battle with D'Annunzio.

In bylines for the *Toronto Star* Hemingway referred occasionally to D'Annunzio. On 24 February 1921 he jokingly announces that Sweden, in search of sulphur for its match industry, has taken ninety-nine-year leases on Mt Vesuvius and Mt Etna in exchange for the right to select the Nobel Peace Prize for twenty years. In Hemingway's cynical comment, just three years after the war, Alfred Nobel's wealth, built on dynamite, benefits the quest for peace. Later the same day another bulletin reports that D'Annunzio has occupied Mt Etna and Mt Vesuvius and issued an ultimatum: 'I hope to die on both of these glorious mountains if frozen Swedes ever touch one powdered fragment of their holy sulphurs.'[80] Death, Italian territorial claims, patriotism, secular religion, explosive violence both natural and man-made – it adds up to D'Annunzio in the Fiumian imbroglio. Etna and Vesuvius are the most active volcanoes in Europe, and Hemingway was aware of D'Annunzio's volcano symbolism in *Il fuoco*. The greatest of natural *fuochi*, the volcano is identified with annihilation, renewal, the negative sublime, sexual passion, and the will. D'Annunzio further links the image to artistic power. In one scene Effrena helps carry Richard Wagner, stricken with a heart attack in his gondola (Wagner actually suffered his attack in the Palazzo Vendramin, which he had rented); he likens the 'renewed beating' of the 'sacred heart' of the composer to a 'volcano bursting open,' which concatenates Christ imagery and artistic immortality ('renewed') with natural violence.[81] That pacifist Sweden (or Norway, which awards the Nobel Peace Prize) should even consider awarding such a prize to Italy, under the sway of such volatile characters as Mussolini and D'Annunzio, adds to the bite of Hemingway's sarcasm.

In another dispatch, 'Mussolini, Europe's Prize Bluffer' (27 Jan. 1923), the dictator may last 'fifteen years' or be 'overthrown next spring' by D'Annunzio 'who hates him.' Not everyone at the time would have agreed with Hemingway on the relations between the two men, yet there is a certain canniness to the remark.[82] In a letter to Pound in 1924 Hemingway comments on D'Annunzio's being named 'Principe di Monte Nervosa' by King Victor Emmanuel at Mussolini's request. He puns on the real Monte Nevoso overlooking Fiume to call attention to D'Annunzio's neuroticism, and deliberately feminizes it as he did with Monte San Gabriele.[83]

After a quarter of a century D'Annunzio reappears in Hemingway's Venetian novel. Through Colonel Cantwell, Hemingway revives memories both of his own youth and of his former obsession with D'Annunzio. Now internationally famous himself, the mature Hemingway begins to tally up the balance sheet of the two writers, going back to the novel that once inspired him, *Il fuoco*. In both *Il fuoco* and *Across the River and Into the Trees*, Venice, Torcello, and the littoral swamps provide the highly charged subtext of competing classical and Romantic mythographies. There is a sharp division of the principals into young and middle-aged. In *Il fuoco* the composer (poet, dramatist, critic, artist) Stelio Effrena is the younger partner; the actress La Foscarina is twenty years his senior. In Hemingway's novel, they are reversed: Cantwell is fifty or fifty-one (8, 75), Renata 'nearly nineteen.' Cantwell refers to Renata as 'Daughter'; the name is likely taken from D'Annunzio's daughter Renata;[84] and D'Annunzio referred to his mistresses as 'brother' or 'sister.' Both couples have tormented sexual liasons; Cantwell and Renata's is unconsummated, Effrena and Foscarina's long delayed. La Foscarina inflicts a 'wound' by biting Effrena's lip; Renata wants to be hurt by the buttons of Cantwell's uniform (111).[85] All four principals exhibit various forms of algolagnia. Further, both novels have victims of heart disease: Wagner collapses in the final scene of *Il fuoco*. Over-exerting himself physically and psychologically, Cantwell suffers anginal pain and dies of a heart attack.

Beyond these similarities are the private memories of D'Annunzio that Cantwell shares with the reader. Though Hemingway missed seeing D'Annunzio in World War I, he was assigned to the front and would have gathered reports from the soldiers. He gives Cantwell these memories, lending directness and greater impact to the relationship. D'Annunzio enters the novel in a reference by the elderly 'boatman' (46–7) who conveys Cantwell and his driver Jackson in his motor launch up the

Grand Canal to the Gritti. The boatman lost his fifth and last brother on the Grappa in World War I, and he throws some of the blame on D'Annunzio: 'He was a patriot and inflamed by hearing d'Annunzio talk.'[86] 'Inflamed' D'Annunzio's rhetoric and *Il fuoco*. Cantwell is so moved by the story that he decides to give him a much-needed engine (though he dies and the boatman will remain unappeased and impoverished). Riding up the Grand Canal, Cantwell points out the palazzi to Jackson, though he thinks to himself as he passes the palazzo Bryon rented (as it happened, from the ancestors of Alvarito): Byron was 'well-loved in this town' despite his 'errors'; 'you have to be a tough boy in this town to be loved'; the Brownings 'weren't Venetians no matter how well he wrote of it' (48). Cantwell has said that the Venetians treat him like one of themselves. Byron created the Romantic archetype of the poet-warrior-celebrity that culminates in D'Annunzio and Hemingway.

D'Annunzio's 'little villa' (49) on the Grand Canal is the very next one that Cantwell notices: 'little' is not merely descriptive but pejorative, like Il Lupo's pistol, like D'Annunzio's relatively short stature (5'6"). The villa is also 'ugly' (49), the only ugly thing Cantwell seems to notice in Venice, except himself in a mirror ('ugly' [112]). To the tall (six-foot), handsome, well-maned Hemingway, D'Annunzio must have appeared short, bald – and 'ugly': for which reason Hemingway in self-conflict applies the adjective to both his surrogate and his foil. As Cantwell muses to himself, the villa is 'close up against the water' (the destructive element – but what palazzo is not?) and 'overrun with badly administered trees' (49), not an image of nature in the wild but of bad discipline and bad art, perhaps D'Annunzio's occasionally high-flown prose. The villa may have been run down after the war, but Maurice Barrès, who visited D'Annunzio there in 1916, said it was 'a refined setting' (*endroit raffiné*).[87] The villa is 'not a place that you would live in if you could help it. There *he* lived' (49). The italicized *he* shows the psychic pressure and disdain, even before D'Annunzio is mentioned by name, for everyone knows who *he* is. In a parody of D'Annunzio's style, still thinking to himself, Cantwell launches into 'bad' rhetoric tonally at odds with the novel's concise stylistic norm and immediately recognizable as a false note:

They loved him for his talent, and because he was bad, and he was brave. A Jewish boy with nothing, he stormed the country with his talent, and his rhetoric. He was a more miserable character than any that I know and as mean. But the man I think of to compare him with never put the chips on the line and went to war, the Colonel thought, and Gabriele d'Annunzio

(I always wondered what his real name was, he thought, because nobody is named d'Annunzio in a practical country and perhaps he was not Jewish and what difference did it make if he was or was not) had moved through the different arms of the service as he had moved into and out the arms of different women. (49)

D'Annunzio never wrote such bad rhetoric as the first two sentences and was not Jewish, which Cantwell concedes. Though Hemingway knew he was not Jewish, he liked to think him Jewish (and 'ugly' and 'little,' etc.). Hemingway's favourite nickname as a young man was Hemingstein, sometimes shortened to Stein; he used it throughout his life. His mother, whom he disliked, was 'Mrs. Hemingstein.'[88] The anti-Semitic remark is not an isolated case: 'Benny Meyers' (184, 188) is accused not just of staying home but also of making money by cutting deals with army contractors: Hemingway felt that *he* stayed home too. The insulting remarks set D'Annunzio apart, a double and scapegoat for certain qualities that Hemingway secretly admired and wished to reject in himself. Meanness and misery characterize Cantwell and the mature Hemingway, and the note of self-pity creeps in.[89] Jews are the Chosen People, the emarginated, and the scapegoated. Even the small *d* cannot have been an accident, as Hemingway had an equal choice of calling him D'Annunzio. Yet Cantwell appears to be relenting: 'what difference did it make if he was or was not' Jewish. Hemingway may at last be coming to terms with his obsession.

The most self-reflexive element of Cantwell's interior monologue is: 'the man I think of to compare him with never put his chips on the line and went to war.' What man could Cantwell be thinking of – except the world-famous writer Ernest Hemingway? Brave as he was to serve as a volunteer in 1918, Hemingway did not officially go to war as a combatant (which, as an American, he could have done in 1917), in the Spanish Civil War, or in World War II. 'Put his chips on the line' is another reference to war as play, a crossing of the classical and Romantic myths on war. Not serving as a regular soldier must have preyed on Hemingway's mind and made him question his prowess. When it was convenient, he even lied about joining the Arditi. Further, D'Annunzio was fifty-two when he pulled strings to join the Italian armed forces in 1915. Just as famous, Hemingway was only forty-two when America declared war in 1941, but did not sign up; surely with all his connections, he could have done likewise. The author Hemingway is just the kind of person that the sensitive, well-read, 'tough' Cantwell would be comparing with D'Annunzio

– and to Hemingway's disadvantage. That Hemingway lets Cantwell lash out against the hated D'Annunzio *and* Hemingway almost in the same breath gives an indication of Hemingway's masochism as well as his silent identification with the Italian war hero.[90]

Cantwell's reminiscence of D'Annunzio pursues a negative track: the mission that he flew was 'fast and easily over,' which is not true – D'Annunzio made many flying missions; some over the Alps were long by World War I standards and extremely dangerous. D'Annunzio 'lost an eye' in a crash 'flying as an observer'; this is true for the particular flight on which D'Annunzio's plane crashed, but he flew many other missions in which he was no mere 'observer.' It was Hemingway who flew 'as an observer' in World War II. Hemingway deprecates D'Annunzio's military prowess: he 'flew, but he was not a flier. He was in the Infantry but he was not an Infantryman and it was always the same appearances' (50). Hemingway could be, with far more justice, accused of the 'same appearances' and with much less to credit them. Cantwell accuses D'Annunzio of being a wanton publicity-seeker. Thus Renata wants to know if there are any pictures of the Arditi – the Gran Maestro had been one of them. Cantwell says: 'No. There weren't any pictures except with Mr. d'Annunzio in them. Also most of the people turned out badly' (121). 'Mr. d'Annunzio' bourgeoisifies him, reducing his heroic stature, and again, even name, with a lower-case *d*; and his followers suffer because he is just looking out for himself. Frankly, D'Annunzio did the military part so much better than Hemingway, and he also did it first. Through Cantwell's incessant denigration Hemingway attempts to vent his hostility, project his envy and self-hate, and resolve his own contradictory attitudes towards his ideal of the poet-warrior and death.

Colonel Cantwell refers to D'Annunzio as 'Lieutenant Colonel' (50) and seems pleased to have risen higher in the ranks. But Cantwell's (and Hemingway's) hatred stems not only from professional jealousy but from a rejection of D'Annunzio's war mentality and the rhetoric that has less to do with patriotism than with megalomania and Romantic narcissism. In Cantwell's interior monologue, he recalls standing with the troops 'while it was raining' (a Hemingway symbol for misery) and listening to a 'harangue' (51) by D'Annunzio. With his patched eye and his 'white face, as white as the belly of a sole, new turned over in the market, the brown side not showing, looking thirty hours dead,' D'Annunzio is a decaying dead fish, not the 'gold fish' (271) of the Brusadelli. Looking half dead, he is 'shouting': '*Morire non è basta*' (50) (*sic*) (To die is not enough).[91] In a *Toronto Star* dispatch years before, Hemingway had quoted the sentence correctly, *Morire non basta*, and translated it: 'You must survive to win.'[92] Perhaps now he mocks the great writer by making him use a less elegant (though not incorrect) Italian. With years to reflect upon it, Hemingway enriches his own interpretation. Cantwell thinks reasonably to himself: 'What the muck more do they want of us?' (50). Victory, to be sure, but what *more* is the question. In a soldier's 'classical' way of thinking, death is the end of life and life's pleasures. Diminishing death, treating it with contempt, D'Annunzio wants victory, too, yet the emphasis falls on death as lack: hence, one must do more than just die, one must fill death with meaning, be an example to others in dying, dramatize and aestheticize one's death. According to the Romantic myth, in Keats's line, one should be 'half in love with easeful death.' Even so, death by itself is still 'not enough,' not totality, does *not* fulfil life, is not (again, in Keats's words) 'life's high meed.' Besides, D'Annunzio was a hedonist, which cuts into any desire for death. Hemingway had an unmitigated death wish, and that is why D'Annunzio's spasmodic rhetoric strikes him so falsely.

In Cantwell's musings, the soldiers cannot hear D'Annunzio because there are no loudspeakers – that instrument of mass communication would be ready for the next war. When D'Annunzio asks for a moment of silence for 'our glorious dead' (50), the soldiers misconstrue the situation and take it as a cue to shout '*Evviva d'Annunzio*' (50). While others die and are forgotten, 'Long live D'Annunzio!' He is the Superman triumphing over the slaves who exist merely to serve him, while they are automatons who shout mechanically and on (mis)cue. The great writer shouting into the air without anyone hearing him is meant to be ridiculous. The men know what he says because they have heard it so often, 'after victories, and before defeats, and they knew what they should shout if there was any pause by an orator' (50). So they are complicit in his will to power. But, 'loving his platoon' (51), Cantwell wishes to show solidarity; he too shouts '*Evviva d'Annunzio*' in order to 'share their guilt' (51). Hemingway atones for his hero-worship of D'Annunzio by contrary means of satiric reduction and shared guilt.

The mood, setting, and even some of the language of Cantwell's interior monologue recall one of the most famous passages in Hemingway – and American literature – the interior monologue of another soldier who served on the same front in World War I: Frederic Henry in *A Farewell to Arms*. Following the retreat from Caporetto, he hears a friend say that the war effort is not 'in vain' and then thinks to himself:

I was always embarrassed by the words sacred, glorious, and sacrifice and the expression in vain. We had heard them, sometimes standing in the rain almost out of earshot, so that only the shouted words came through, and had read them, on proclamations that were slapped up by billposters over other proclamations, now for a long time, and I had seen nothing sacred, and the things that were glorious had no glory and the sacrifices were like the stock-yards at Chicago if nothing was done with the meat except to bury it. There were many words that you could not stand to hear and finally only the names of places had dignity. Certain numbers were the same way and certain dates and these with the names of the places were all you could say and have them mean anything. Abstract words such as glory, honor, courage, or hallow were obscene beside the concrete names of villages, the number of roads, the names of rivers, the numbers of regiments and the dates.[93]

Henry recalls 'standing in the rain,' which is similar to Cantwell's 'it was raining' when he heard D'Annunzio's 'harangue.' Similarly, Henry cannot completely hear all the words, only the 'shouted' ones, the patriotic clichés; Cantwell says D'Annunzio was 'shouting.' The words that strike falsely – 'in vain,' 'glory,' 'honor,' etc. – are just the kinds of words that Cantwell questions, phrases like 'our glorious dead,' and 'heroes' (he 'did not believe in heroes') (51). Moreover, in the pages immediately prior to Henry's interior monologue, he and his friends discuss one particular battle: 'where it really had been hell was at San Gabriele.'[94]

Cantwell returns from his journey backward in time to the present moment, riding by D'Annunzio's villa on the Grand Canal 'where the poor beat-up old boy had lived with his great, sad, and never properly loved actress.' D'Annunzio could not even treat his lovers right, and Cantwell conjures up the memory of Eleonora Duse, 'her wonderful hands, and her so transformable face, that was not beautiful, but that gave you all love, glory, and delight and sadness; of the way the curve of her forearm could break your heart, and he thought, Christ they are dead and I do not know where either one is buried even. But I certainly hope they had fun in that house' (51). This memory engenders some compensating affection for the hatred that he has shown, and Hemingway's final estimate of D'Annunzio maintains this balance between disdain and respect. Cantwell suddenly interrupts his musings on D'Annunzio to tell Jackson who lived in the villa 'on the left' (the negative path), 'Gabriele d'Annunzio, who was a great writer,' and also to recommend reading him in 'some fair English translations' (51). After a moment Jackson asks for the name again – it is already forgotten.[95] "'D'Annunzio," the Colonel said. "Writer.'" The tone is lapidary, public, final. But it hardly suffices and Cantwell silently resumes his meditation:

> [W]riter, poet, national hero, phraser of the dialectic of Fascism, macabre egoist, aviator, commander or rider, in the first of the fast torpedo attack boats, Lieutenant Colonel of Infantry without knowing how to command a company, nor a platoon properly, the great, lovely writer of *Notturno* whom we respect, and jerk. (52)

A 'jerk' is elsewhere defined as someone who had 'never worked at his trade (*oficio*) truly, and is presumptuous in some annoying way' (97), the opposite of the 'tough' man who 'backs his play' (49). Hemingway, too, may have finally preferred, over the decadent *Il fuoco*, the chastened prose of D'Annunzio's late masterpiece *Notturno:* these meditations in the form of a war diary were written on notecards or dictated to his daughter Renata when, temporarily blinded, he was recuperating from a plane crash in Venice in 1916.[96] Cantwell's recommendation is wasted on Jackson, who will never read D'Annunzio. Later one learns that he is reading 'Comic Books' and can find anything he wants in the PX 'from superman on up to the improbable' (301–2). The Nietzschean Superman and his Italian avatar are brought down to the exchange level of an American comic-book character for mass entertainment.

After 1950, the only significant reference to D'Annunzio in Hemingway appears in an interview with Eugenio Montale in Venice in 1954. Hemingway was in bed, recuperating from two plane crashes in Africa only days before (now something he shared with D'Annunzio). When Montale inquired about his opinion of D'Annunzio, 'he leaps from his bed and tries to imitate him, shouting: "To live is not enough!" Then he remembers, it seems to me with praise, *Notturno*.'[97] The name of D'Annunzio energizes Hemingway, makes him jump out of his sickbed to parody the Italian hero, though he utters a balancing praise for the author of *Notturno*. Both to live and to die are 'not enough,' do not make up a unity, severally or together, and our conceptions of them do not satisfy our human needs. D'Annunzio did not suffer this uncertainty, which may be explained by the greater hold of the nineteenth century. Hemingway only came to maturity in World War I, and post-Romantic conceptions of death leave an absence of fulfilment and a final despair.[98]

Death resolves the two myths in their diverse ways: the classical, by a glorious death fighting for cause or country; the Romantic, by loss of the self into mystic oneness or nothingness. Although Cantwell is denied a soldier's death – he is too good a soldier and too lucky – he does die near the battlefield on which he was almost killed in his youth, where he lost his 'immortality' (33) and his 'death' properly began. His strenuous exertions on behalf of his Fatal Woman in Venice precipitate his other, 'romantic' death. Cantwell's passing may be said to resolve the two myths.

While the trip to Venice hastens Cantwell's death, he does not die in Venice. Death is pollution, and the goddess must not be profaned by the sight of a corpse. Death is natural, and Venice is aesthetic, inorganic ('no trees'), permitting no natural death, so he dies in the country between Venice and Trieste. Cantwell plans a trip with Renata back to Wyoming; she imagines that 'we could see the trees when we woke up' (265); he expresses his love for them by naming them, 'Pines mostly,' 'cotton-wood along the creeks' and 'aspen' that 'turn yellow in the fall' (265). Cantwell says farewell to Renata near the garage, on the edge of Venice, 'under the trees,' though in this season they are 'black' and with 'no leaves on them' (276). On a 'detour' on the road to Trieste Cantwell suffers a heart attack and quotes Stonewall Jackson's dying words, 'let us cross over the river and rest under the shade of the trees' (307). But Hemingway's title is stronger, primal: not under the trees, but 'Into the Trees,' like Frost's 'Into My Own,' where the poet wants to disappear into 'those dark trees,' 'Into their vastness.' As in Frost, Hemingway's deepest affinity is not for the city but for the land, an expression of the Romantic view of nature.

So Cantwell does not die an artist's death, like Wagner, in Venice; or, more exactly, like D'Annunzio's Wagner, to be borne away in a gondola-hearse. Instead, having shut its door 'carefully and well,' he dies in an automobile, his 'timbrel,' symbol of twentieth-century mechanization, on the road away from Venice (307). His final 'order' to Jackson is to return the portrait of Renata and the shotguns, symbols of love and war, to their respective owners, Renata and Alvarito. The insensitive Jackson who, neither understanding nor particularly liking Cantwell, will not act personally but only officially, has the last word: 'They'll return them all right,' Jackson thinks, 'through channels' (308). This mimetic, parodic reduction of the enticing Venetian 'canals' is Hemingway's final comment on the fall from grace and beauty in modern, administered society. A new pestilential form of 'death by water' spreads through the world, where everything feeds through bureaucratic 'channels.'

chapter 7

The Hidden Godfather: Plenitude and Absence in Coppola's Trilogy

JOHN PAUL RUSSO

I

The image of the Italian as criminal, from the virtuoso of crime in the Renaissance to the Italian American gangster of the present, has so firmly embedded itself in popular culture that despite, or perhaps because of, its negative valence, Italian and Italian American artists have long exploited it for their own purposes. In countless works of fiction, film, and drama, the villain-heroes and their shadowy cohorts have been made to reveal themselves from multiple perspectives (social, familial, religious); to represent certain Italian American attitudes (suspicion of authority, anarchistic tendencies, marginality, clannishness, hedonism); and to elicit varied reactions (identification, anger, recrimination, rejection). The only reaction absent seems to be neutrality. The fact remains that the most impressive artistic works of Italian American culture in the past century involve the gangster: the cinema of Martin Scorsese, Don DeLillo's *Underworld*, and Francis Ford Coppola's *Godfather* trilogy.

Before Mario Puzo published an enormously successful novel, he had written a smaller, finer one, *The Fortunate Pilgrim* (1964), in which an immigrant mother raises five children in Hell's Kitchen. Then Puzo, like his fictional heroine, desperate to help *his* children, wrote *The Godfather* (1969). Contrary to what some have thought, he did not write it quickly; yet by his own admission, he did not write it with sufficient care ('below my gifts').[1] After he had gained fame and fortune, he never rewrote it, as he should have, to raise it to the level of his earlier work; nor, when he wrote more novels, did they resemble *The Fortunate Pilgrim*, but only the weaker sides of *The Godfather*. Nonetheless, his gangster novel had a gripping plotline, memorable characters, an 'outpouring of incidents and details,' the 'folklore behind the headlines,' and 'immediacy';[2] and there was Don Vito Corleone, 'popularly accepted as genuinely mythic.'[3] The novel connected gangster fiction to the ethnic novel of assimilation, widening its scope and relevance. Puzo said that he had conceived his novel in cinematic terms, which facilitated work on the screenplay; yet it required a film director reaching his artistic maturity to transform the novel into a unified masterpiece.

Although Coppola absorbed various trends and influences (American gangster genre, the rise of ethnic movements, Vietnam War protest, the critique of corporate capitalism and the Establishment in the 1960s and 1970s), his *Godfather I* (1972) and *II* (1974) were 'new' in T.S. Eliot's sense of the word: 'the existing monuments form an ideal order among themselves, which is modified by the introduction of the new (the really new) work of art among them.'[4] Like many important works of art, the films are difficult to pin down in moral terms – which opens them to multiple interpretations. Robert B. Ray points out how Coppola mixes leftist values ('outlaw,' 'anticapitalist critique,' 'family,' 'romanticized, self-supporting commune') and rightist ones ('efficient authority,' 'uncompromising independence,' 'competitive ethic').[5] On the one hand, the films seem to be attacking a corrupt Establishment and predatory capitalism from the standpoint of the family; on the other, they celebrate a male-dominated hierarchy and bourgeois acquisitiveness, letting the family go to pieces. Similarly, the ethnic factor wakened a sharply divided response in the Italian American community.[6] Many second-generation Italian Americans felt betrayed and loathed the subject matter; having suffered prejudice from the Mafia stigma, they stigmatized Coppola for perpetuating it. Though not unaffected by similar feelings, the third generation embraced the films for their epic proportions, their dramatic power, and their nostalgic mood. According to Hansen's law of immigration, the first generation acts, the second forgets, and the third remembers.

After almost forty years, critical and popular judgment remains unshaken. In 1977 James Monaco wrote that *Godfather I* and *II* were considered together as the 'most significant American film of the decade' (in the 2009 edition, 'of the modern period'). In 1981 John Hess declared *Godfather II* the 'greatest Hollywood film since *Citizen Kane* and one of the three or four best Hollywood films ever made.' Nick Browne extolled *Godfather I–III* as 'monuments on the landscape of American cinema.'[7] The 2005 American Film Institute poll of 1500 critics placed *Godfather I* at number three in the top one hundred films (dropping from number one in 1998); Nino Rota's score was number five in the top twenty-five on the same list. 'I'm going to make him an offer he can't refuse' came in second in the top one hundred famous lines (after *Gone with the Wind*'s 'Frankly, my dear, I don't give a damn'). In 2000 *Godfather I* was voted the number one all-time favourite film in an Internet poll.[8] As Fran Mason comments, *Godfather I* 'no longer exists simply as a screen text but as part of popular consciousness'; 'by century's end,' writes Thomas J. Ferraro, '"The Godfather" referred less to a book or film than to a modern secular mythology.'[9]

Whether one defines myth as a traditional story, an account of origins, or a 'fundamental attitude toward life,' *Godfather I–III* are the strongest cinematic expression of an Eastern urban myth that in the twentieth century took its place beside the great Western frontier myths (Custer's Last Stand, Buffalo Bill, the Alamo, Jesse James).[10] This modern, secular, urban myth became the special province of an ethnicity that began its American experience as neither modern, urban, nor secular, and that had not found the poet, novelist, dramatist, composer, or director to present the story of its migration, one of the largest in modern history, in an artistic form equal to its significance for them. Could the *Godfather I* and *II* fill this void? Pellegrino D'Acierno proposes that the trilogy is not only the 'greatest gangster film of all time,' one 'raised to the level of art film,' but also the 'most symptomatic, if not the most central, cultural text of the Italian American experience.'[11] No one wants to say *most central* because of the Mafia subject. *The Godfather* (novel and films), writes Chris Messenger, 'stands for a great, heroic dream of immigration and family, the epic modern subject so notably missing from our twentieth-century popular classics and sense of ourselves as Americans'; and Mason refers to the first *Godfather* as the 'gangster film as epic.'[12] Coppola himself signalled epic intentions quite directly by giving *The Godfather Saga* (1977) as title to a chronologically rearranged version of *Godfather I* and *II* and by claiming his films were not only ethnic story-telling but the 'Mafia as a metaphor for America.'[13] Though one obviously rejects the American dream through gangsterdom, these claims – 'most symptomatic,' 'epic,' 'classics,' 'saga' – have much in support of them.

C.M. Bowra writes that epic poets (and, to extrapolate, 'epic' directors) imbue their work with lofty aspirations, breadth of scope, 'realism,' and authorial 'objectivity'; the narrative action is made 'to conform to life as they see it.' Protagonists strive 'to pass beyond the oppressive limits of human frailty to a fuller and more vivid life'; amid fierce competition, they prevail through 'superiority in natural endowments,' sense of honour and duty, calculation, risk, and perseverance; success is neither inherited, bought, nor handed over to them. Also, it is insufficient for protagonists merely to be possessed of superior qualities: 'they must realise them in action.'[14]

Godfather I–III fulfil some of the essential elements of an epic. The story of four generations of the Corleone family is vast and cyclical in scope, from an ocean voyage, to a continental crossing, and a *nostos* or return to origins: Sicily, New York, Nevada, New York, Sicily. Its plot has historical plausibility and a high degree of local realism. Coppola remarked that he had 'almost never seen a movie that gave any real sense of what it was like to be an Italian American.'[15] Despite such directors as Borzage, Capra, LaCava, Lupino, and Minnelli, the portrayal of the genuine Italian America as opposed to a stereotypical version had been sidestepped by Hollywood. Coppola's characters were 'the most Italian Italians I'd ever seen in an American movie,' George De Stefano recalls of *Godfather I*, with its 'unprecedented exposure to Italian American history and experience.'[16] Following Thalberg's Fourth Commandment, *Remember you are dealing with a pictorial medium*,[17] Coppola represents *in nuce* the religious rituals (baptism, First Communion, Saint's Day, wedding, investiture, and funeral), daily tone, family life, linguistic register, gesture, habit, private decor, gastronomy, music, and visual reality of Italian America from its heyday to the 1970s, as seen from a third-generation perspective. Even the films' conflicting moralities tend to enhance authorial distance and objectivity.

The *Godfather* films are only marginally about the great migration; they are much more about the great assimilation – still, a worthy subject for epic treatment, if less obviously so. Coppola makes a central thematic interest of what sociologists from Irvin L. Child and Herbert Gans to John W. Briggs, James Crispino, and Richard Alba have shown to be the staircase of (Italian American) assimilation.[18] His films can be mined for examples that substantiate their findings, in not only general plot but also specific incidents and characterization. In the transition-of-power scene in *Godfather I* where the generations confront each other, Michael consoles his dejected father, who wanted his son to succeed in the mainstream: 'We'll get there, Pop. We'll get there'; and he promises his wife Kay that the Corleone family will be legitimate 'in five years.' In *Godfather II*, when Kay complains that seven years have passed, Michael replies, 'I know – I'm trying.' In *Godfather III* (1990) Anthony rejects the family 'business' to become an opera singer, thereby realizing the old dream of preserving his *italianità* and succeeding in the new world.

Beyond subject matter and objective treatment, the protagonists Don Vito Corleone (Marlon Brando, Robert De Niro) and Michael Corleone (Al Pacino) themselves exhibit epic qualities: courage, family loyalty, endurance, sometimes just being 'better' than one's enemies. This was true of earlier gangster heroes: 'Rico [Little Caesar] was in many respects an admirable person.'[19] But viewed from so many angles, particularly from within the family, Coppola's characters prove far more captivating – one thinks of Edmund Burke's 'vice itself lost half its evil, by losing all its grossness.'[20] If this feature seems morally questionable, it is by such an aesthetic route that the director can attract a larger audience and involve them to greater depths. Robert Warshow observes that the 'real city ... produces only criminals; the imaginary city produces the gangster: he is what we want to be and what we are afraid we may become.'[21] Finally, Bowra writes that the epic hero 'gives dignity to the human race.'[22] In this respect, lest one get carried away, *The Godfather I–III* is non-epic, or rather anti-epic.

Fate, too, plays a role in the *Godfather* narrative, an epic convention. Vito's father and older brother were executed in a Mafia vendetta in Sicily when he was a boy. Hiding in a donkey cart, he escapes Corleone. An immigration officer on Ellis Island mistakenly writes Corleone for his name, not his birthplace, another concealment of identity that could save his life. Gazing at the Statue of Liberty, the protective goddess, Vito survives smallpox in a detention centre where he is quarantined for the fate-driven 'three' months (one of the many three's in the trilogy). The baby Zeus hides in Crete and returns to dethrone the child-eating Kronos; Romulus and Remus survive to avenge their mother and grandfather. Fate has a guiding hand in the birth of the godfather as ' hero,' his dynasty, his empire of crime, compared in *Godfather II* to the 'Roman empire.'

Epics evoke the aesthetic experience of the sublime. *Godfather I–III* excite no fewer than eight qualities produced by the sublime in Burke's formulation: terror, obscurity, privation, power, silence, excessive sound ('artillery,' 'natural cries'), suddenness, and pain approaching death.[23] In the opening scene of *Godfather I* the large screen is black, not dark because the film has not begun, but black because the film *has* begun, black as a Rothko, and only after this image fixes itself firmly does one hear a suppliant voice: the perspective is from the darkness of the silent Don Vito himself. In the closing scene the rapid cross-cutting technique creates a tumult of life and death, Coppola's collision montage, from a killing to baptism and back again. Don Vito's threats all have an extra dimension of terror: the brains on the bank check, the horse's bloody head in the director's bed. Not the classical sublime of high, noble sentiments, this is its modern tradition: threatening, violent, emotionally jagged.

The termini of the Godfather films stand at either end of the twentieth century, 1901 and 1997, and it is difficult not to infer some design on Coppola's part. In fact, in *Godfather I* Vito's date of birth as given on his tombstone is 1887; but in *Godfather II* he is nine in 1901; Coppola shifted the action forward to start the action at an iconic date. Also, though *Godfather III* appeared in 1990, Michael's death takes place in 1997, pushing the date closer to the end of the century. The individual termini of the films are *Godfather I*, 1945–1955; *II*, 1901 (1896?)–1959; *III*, 1978–1997. *Godfather I* and *II* proceeded from a sustained inspiration over four years and form an interlocking, complementary unity. *Godfather III* ranks below them in conception, script, casting, production, and direction. Not under discussion is *The Godfather Saga;* in 2002, perhaps recognizing that the *Saga* upset the artistic integrity of the first two films, Coppola produced a DVD collection of the three films.[24] In 2008, working with his cameraman, Gordon Willis, he supervised a definitive set: *The Godfather: The Coppola Restoration.*

II

The two multivalent themes or metaphorical systems that govern the trilogy are the desire for plenitude and an absence or void at the heart of things. These themes should not be essentialized; their boundaries are fluid and problematic. Nonetheless, traced to their radicals, the first is a theme of growth, power, life-enhancement, and self-fulfilment; the second, a countertheme of fear, secrecy, violence, and death. The conflict between them defines the symbolic context of the trilogy.

The most enduring impression made by all three *Godfathers* is of the wide gulf separating the Corleone's family life and the Mafia business; the gulf narrows by the end of *Godfather II*, then widens in *Godfather III* only to close again. One means of exploring the films lies in mapping these codes that seem to confront each other in inexorable opposition. At the family pole are representations of the home, dining scenes, celebrations of family cohesiveness, and a fundamental desire for at-oneness with the world – a desire for plenitude, which is the world. In Lukács's formulation of an integrated totality, these feelings cement 'inside' and 'outside,' leaving no discontinuity between the self and nature, 'no incongruence between soul and deed'; 'the fire that burns in the soul is of the same essential nature as the stars.'[25] According to the Mafia myth adopted in the film, the world of the godfathers in pre-industrial Sicily extends to the mountain's rim and no farther, then closes back upon itself.[26] In Ferdinand Tönnies' distinction, the 'family' is a synecdoche of *Gemeinschaft*, clan or small community, in which associations are based on personal ties and loyalties, favouritism, and vertical hierarchy, as opposed to *Gesellschaft* or impersonal civil society, in which contractual bonds are formed on the basis of individual self-interest and the attainment of ends rather than as ends in themselves.[27] From the Sicilian *latifundia* (large estates typically owned by an absentee baron) to the New York neighbourhoods, the godfathers govern under the forms of paternalism, clientelism, structured hierarchy, and social custom, all of which exert a sense of totality and express their desire for plenitude. Religious ceremonies serve mainly to cement family organization and withstand change.

Since plenitude aims to eliminate desire, it depends upon a lack or absence, an anguished sense of emptiness or dissatisfaction. In the *Godfather* films absence is linked to 'business' and its procedures: plots, secrecy, murder and the threat of murder. Its first representation is the 'black' screen; its last is Michael's death. Vito works for an olive oil importer for 'three' years before buying the company, using the business to cover small-time extortion and thievery with a Robin Hood aura. It leads to boot-legging and a numbers racket and becomes greatly magnified by Michael in the Nevada drug and casino empire. It can be said to reach at least its numerical climax with the figure of five hundred million dollars that Michael will deposit in the Vatican bank to gain control of International Immobiliare. Vito's situation is halfway between that of the feudal don and the casino owner. The old dons were not mainly businessmen; their plenitude was satisfied by what they received in goods, in respect, in the acknowledgement of power over the local territory. This is not the case with the racketeers and the casino owners in Nevada. In *Gesellschaft* culture one tends to level everything ('bottom line'), to rationalize, and to impersonalize. Contracts, laws, and money are the same for everyone; no special clientelistic intimacies, favouritisms, or loyalties apply. 'Tell Michael it was just business, not personal,' says the treacherous caporegime Sal Tessio (Abe Vigoda) as Michael's men 'arrest' him. The secretive nature of the godfathers' activities bears some superficial similarities to advanced corporatism, which otherwise operates by very different rules, but only illegal corporatism allows for 'front' and 'dummy' companies, laundered money, and bribery of government officials, judges, and police. Other aspects of the clandestine 'business' taken over from Sicily are extortion, retribution, and surveillance.

Secrecy is the signature metaphor of the godfathers. Elias Canetti writes that secrecy lies at the core of power and is therefore necessarily full of duplicity; 'lying in wait for prey is essentially secret,' 'the watcher must be capable of endless patience.'[28] Such watchers are the godfathers, who hide from the law, from other underworld families, from friends and brothers; they withhold their innermost thoughts from their wives. Concealment from social and moral scrutiny, physical defense in fortress-like compounds, lawyers to protect them from prying legal arms, little or no written documentation, these are the order of the day. The godfathers' very existence depends on secrecy. Tracking down and assassinating a godfather amounts to the greatest triumph – or catastrophe – because he is the linchpin of the entire structure. Henchmen take elaborate precautions to safeguard him, no one knows more than what is necessary, women know least of all, but not even the *capo dei capi* (boss of bosses) can know all the secrets and is vulnerable to that extent. The men are bound by *omertà* ('solidarity,' 'complicity,' 'silence,' etymologically from 'manliness'),[29] violation of which means exile or death. The faces of the godfathers are impenetrable masks. Their secrets are buried within them and questions are viewed with suspicion. The godfathers speak little and 'act' through four or five 'buffers' and 'button men.' Don Vito and Michael outwit their enemies by learning their secrets. Hyman Roth (Lee Strasberg) knows only what he needs to know since more could be dangerous: 'I didn't ask who gave the order, because it had nothing to do with business.' The intemperate speech of Santino 'Sonny' Corleone (James Caan), the Don's eldest son, rules him out as a godfather and costs him his life. Everyone knows his secret.

The godfathers are not, in the Weberian sense, 'charismatic' leaders (Moses, Gandhi, Garibaldi) who exert authority by force of presence; instead, they are non-charismatic and command from off-stage, though intermediaries, covert activities, lies, perjury, suborned witnesses, coercion, anyone or anything to avoid direct involvement. Men obey orders as 'soldiers' and fit into a rigid hierarchy; women are 'civilians' confined to household and other tasks. Successful godfathers shun notoriety, avoid gunplay, elude prison, and die in their beds. In Puzo's *The Sicilian* (1984), based on the life of the charismatic Salvatore Giuliano and tenuously linked to *The Godfather,* Turi Guiliano [*sic*] is populist, 'lyrical,' and publicity seeking. Ill-suited to be a godfather by the rules of the game, he is betrayed and gunned down by his cousin (that is, from within the family) with the connivance of Mafia bosses.

Over the course of *Godfather I–III* Coppola exposes plenitude on Mafia terms as corrupt and self-defeating, and many of the films' strategies are meant to unmask its falsity: Sicily, Don Vito's expansive feelings towards the business, Michael's megalomania, the Lake Tahoe estate, the Cuban cake, Hyman Roth's 'bigger than U.S. Steel,' International Immobiliare, etc. Given that the desire for power is the shared motive of the godfathers, the build-up and eventual eruption of these competing forces account for the films' climactic moments in the form of treachery and surprise attack. Actually, the men do not speak of murdering so much as assassinating a godfather; an assault on 'constituted authority' is being perpetrated, not a private vendetta: 'just business.' In Michael, the oppositions receive their fullest play and have their most devastating effect.

The wedding party that opens *Godfather I* establishes swiftly and convincingly the thematic opposition of plenitude and absence. In the home 'office' the camera focuses on a petitioner's pallid face enveloped by total darkness. 'I believe in America,' the man begins his credo in heavily accented English, 'America's made my fortune.' Amerigo Bonasera tells the story of his daughter's attempted rape; she saved her honour whereupon her assailants beat her savagely, but they only received a suspended sentence. He seems to speak directly, as it were, into a void. His first name, Amerigo, plays on the Italian for whom the promised land was named and initiates Coppola's metaphorical relation between the powerful Italian American 'families' and corporate America. His last name Bonasera (good evening), profession (undertaker), plea (vengeance), and appearance (black tie and clothes) make him a figure foreboding death. The camera pulls back with the slowness of a predator to reveal the back of Don Vito's unmoving head. The camera at the beginning of a film normally moves towards the action, bringing the viewer into the story; conventionally, at the end, the camera withdraws. At the beginning of *Godfather I,* however, the camera withdraws and 'seems to make the space mysterious.'[30] Like the camera, the viewer shrinks from an unmoving mover, a faceless figure.

With this reversal of convention, Coppola introduces the presence of hidden power felt as a draining away of vital energies, to a point of emptiness and extinction. The face is among the commonest representations in European art and literature for individual identity. The unseen face of the godfather marks an absence of identity, made into an emblem of fear and negation. One cannot gaze upon this face without danger; its invisibility terrifies the more because of its effect upon the petitioner's tormented face in tight close-up, the double of Don Vito's secret terror turned outward. As the lighting comes up to a tenebrous glow, the

impassive Don Vito is seated at his desk. He addresses his suppliant quietly, while playing with a cat, the silent, cunning, nocturnal predator.
The inner sanctum of his Long Island compound is shot in deep shadow; its colours are subdued, leathery browns and golds, like an animal's
den.

Cutting to his daughter Connie's wedding party in the lush, crowded
garden bathed in sunshine, the camera engages in a twenty-five-minute
parallel narration. Formally, this is the first instance of Coppola's cross-
cutting technique, which intensifies to collision montage by the end of
the film; but in each case, and many others between, the formal cross-
cutting emphasizes the thematic alternation. 'The dark-and-light contrast is so operatic and so openly symbolic that it perfectly expresses the
basic nature of the material,' wrote Pauline Kael; 'the contrast is integral
to the Catholic background of the characters: innocence versus knowledge – knowledge in this sense being the same as guilt.'[31] Where is this
guilt and how would the godfathers feel it? One doubts that Don Vito has
a guilty conscience, Catholic or otherwise; Kael mistakes guilt for regret,
and he will surely have regrets. Besides light and dark, the garden scenes
are gendered along lines of nature, women, marriage, and fecundity; the
business scenes in the lair-like office are exclusively male and associated
with aggression, threat, and punishment. Petitioners, clients, and friends
pay their respects to the Don, asking favours and arranging deals. By ancient Sicilian custom a father cannot refuse a request on his daughter's
wedding day, so the powerful Don with three sons but only one daughter
is busy. In the garden he stops a photographer about to take the family
picture – the impatient Sonny does not want to wait – because his youngest son has not yet arrived. Don Vito's first words in the film are, 'Where's
Michael?'

The wedding occurs in August 1945. Michael arrives in the midst of
the celebrations, which in a way are as much his, the returning, decorated Marine (his courage is already a given). At the centre of the receiving
line is Connie (Talia Shire), the Mafia princess whose white purse bulges
with bank bills. The family looks forward to expanding prosperity. 'The
activity is open, social, and inclusive, embracing not only men, women
and children, but even rival Mafia families,' notes William Simon: 'the
dancing, singing, joking and picture-taking are celebratory, privileging
the family as a unifying totality.'[32] Youthful shrieks erupt when the popular singer Johnny Fontane (Al Martino), the Don's godson from the
old neighbourhood, croons a song. Images of natural beauty and sexual
energy are plentiful. Sonny seduces the maid of honour, meeting little

resistance, even while his wife brags unwittingly of his sexual prowess. Guests dine on a sumptuous wedding dinner; food, like song, is a symbol of plenitude. By his military uniform and demeanour, Michael is the outsider; rejecting the *Gemeinschaft*, he chose to fight in the war, go to college, date a non-Italian, and live away from home. Like second-generation 'rebels' in Irvin L. Child's *Italian or American?*, Michael exhibits self-expressiveness, the desire to stand apart, career orientation, and other individualist values.[33] Oddly, to become his own person he must serve as a soldier in his *Gesellschaft*'s battles. His lack of affect, sangfroid, and incipient bitterness provide the first clues that the youngest of Don Vito's three sons will be the one to succeed him and aggrandize his business into an empire, the stages of which constitute the structure of *Godfather I* and *II*. With cool detachment, almost off-handedly, he explains to his girlfriend Kay (Diane Keaton) how the Don pressured a band leader to accept a deal far more favourable to Fontane: 'my father made him an offer he couldn't refuse ... Luca Brasi held a gun to his head, and my father assured him that either his brains or his signature would be on the contract.' At this point, Michael is even detached from his family: 'That's my family, Kay. It's not me.'

Far from being kept separate, the codes overlap and interpenetrate each other: the fat wedding purse or the 'soldiers,' gangsters, and husbands, passing back and forth between the office and the garden. Looking from the window, Sonny cannot keep his eyes off his next prey in the garden; later Don Vito has to send Hagen to find him. Hagen knocks on the door, on the other side of which Sonny is making love: carnal and 'business' knowledge are crossed. In a grotesque mixing of polarities, huge Luca Brasi (Lenny Montana), the Don's most powerful hit man, sits beneath a delicate arbour and rehearses his little speech to the godfather: 'May your daughter's first child be a masculine child.' Born of innocence, the first child will be a capo, perhaps a godfather: a man comfortable with violence. Johnny Fontane is an inherently mixed figure. While his presence elicits the erotic images of young girls running, song, and band sounds, he attends the party because his career, again in crisis, requires the Don's intervention. Another example of code contamination is the racy version of a romantic Sicilian folk song, 'La luna 'mezzu u mari' (The moon in the sea), sung with gusto by Mama Corleone (Morgana King). In the song a daughter asks her mother about a suitable husband, and the mother answers by considering possible bridegrooms, a shoemaker, a mason, a barber, a carpenter. All are rejected because the mother thinks each man could use the tool of his trade to hurt her daughter. The song reflects the mother's reluctance to accept the daughter's sexual growth; the wound that the potential bridegroom may inflict on his bride-to-be is a risqué euphemism for the loss of virginity. Though meant as comic, the song will prove tragically prophetic for Connie, who will be severely abused by her husband Carlo (Gianni Russo). The family must withstand pressures from without, and even greater pressures from within. Thus the wedding, to look ahead, is the beginning of a violent, doomed marriage.

Coppola integrates the smallest details within his framework of opposition.[34] After Bonasera leaves, Don Vito decides to spare the daughter's assailants because they did not kill her; but they can be beaten within an inch of their lives. Olympian calm settles over the office: 'after all, we're not murderers, despite what this undertaker says.' The local undertaker, of all people, knows how people have died. Satisfied, Don Vito sniffs a rosebud in his lapel, a transitional symbol of sensuous pleasure, the feminine, and the garden to which he now proceeds. Inhaling the fragrance, he seems to suck the very power of life from the rose. At his funeral, mourners will each drop a rose on his casket. Almost all the representations of flowers in these films are associated with death.

Tears are shed infrequently in *Godfather I* and *II*; given the killings and funerals, the stoic restraint is admirable. In the opening scene Johnny Fontane breaks down in tears over his career problems, and Don Vito gets as angry as at any time in the film when he tells him to 'act like a man' instead of a 'Hollywood *finocchio.*' When, following the attempted assassination, Don Vito lies on his hospital bed, attached by tubes to machines, Michael visits him only to find that police protection has vanished. Sensing danger, Michael stands guard. 'I'll take care of you,' he says, 'I'm with you now.' Unable to talk, Don Vito looks at his son with tears in his eyes. Are they tears of joy or grief? They are tears of grief because of his realization that Michael will not enter the legitimate world but will throw in his lot with the 'business.' At the same time, the tears are joyful: through love of the father, the most ideally suited of his sons to succeed him will now do so. Tom Hagen was rescued by Don Vito when he was an orphan, living in entrance halls and doorways. Don Vito treated him like a son, sent him to college and law school, and gave him the post of under-consigliere, a high position in the family for a non-Italian. Hagen is German-Scotch-Irish and speaks fluent Sicilian. Though Sonny refers to him as a 'step-brother,' Don Vito never adopted Hagen because, as he says, it would have been an insult to Hagen's family. In *Godfather II*, when there is an inside attempt on his life, Michael turns to Hagen to take over: 'Tom, you're my brother.' Hagen has tears in his eyes. Later, Hagen gives Michael advice contrary to what Michael wants to hear, and Michael dismisses him: 'take your wife, your family, and your mistress – and move 'em all to Las Vegas.' 'Why do you hurt me, Michael?' replies Hagen, 'I've always been loyal.' The concept of familial trust, so clear in *Godfather I*, has greatly diminished. Hagen's tears have a bitter poignancy because the fulfilment of his belief that he has entered the inner circle comes only when that circle has been emptied out. He too discovers the empty centre when he becomes godfather *pro tem* during Michael's 'absence.'

The unmasking of false representations of plenitude takes place on the level of substance, character, incident, and language. Food, for instance, is among the commonest examples of well-being, power, and the family in Italian America. As Puzo remarks in his novel, the older godfathers and their close associates were almost all heavy men. This is true of Don Vito, Tessio, Don Ciccio, Pentangeli, and Clemenza (Richard Castellano), the sardonic caporegime who crosses between worlds of family and business and is a kind of folk spirit and 'instructor.' He shows the 'civilian' Michael how to shoot a gun (what did he learn in the Marines?) and how to make a good tomato sauce because he may one day have to cook for 'twenty men'; meticulous attention to detail makes Clemenza adept at both. Sonny gets testy with him for spending so much time in the kitchen, a domain foreign to his violent nature. The ability of at least one male to cook is essential (and an ethnic marker) when the men 'hit the mattresses' or hide away during a gang war to protect themselves from their enemies and the police.

In one of his major scenes, Clemenza supervises the execution of Paulie Gatto ('gatto,' cat), the driver whose betrayal nearly cost Don Vito his life. Before he leaves home, Clemenza's wife reminds him to buy the cannoli. While his enforcer and the victim wait in the car, he takes an unusually long time eating alone (a rare occurrence in the films), consuming, as it were, his victim. In the next scene, driving along, he needs to relieve himself, a perfect excuse to turn off into a quiet spot, a hideously amorphous marshland. Dumbly looking around, the victim is shot while Clemenza (mercy) urinates, thus symbolically desecrating the ground. Then, in one of the film's most famous lines he tells his henchman, 'Leave the gun. Take the cannoli.' 'Cannolo' derives from the Latin and Italian *canna*, 'reed,' and is related to *cannone*, 'cannon.' A cannolo is a little cannon, a light gun (*cannoncino*). He will bring back the sweets of victory to his family; he has earned them. The pastry, rich in cream, is a luxury item and like many such items (furs, jewels, expensive meats, leather goods) is associated with victimage. Both gun and cannoli are barrelled and phallic, the one stuffed with gunpowder, the other with ricotta. Images of power, they are doubles, and to say leave one and take the other is to put down one gun and take up another. The atmosphere of violence seeps into the language of plenitude. 'Initially, the scenes of the [gangster] soldiers eating spaghetti were supposed to be intercut with shots of them killing their enemies.'[35] Coppola changed his mind, wisely preventing the subtext from overwhelming the text.

The only physical injury that Michael sustains in the entire trilogy occurs after he has saved his father from certain death from Virgil 'The Turk' Sollozzo (Al Lettieri) and the Tattaglias in the hospital. Captain McCluskey (Sterling Hayden), in the pay of the Tattaglias, is so angry at having botched the assassination that he breaks Michael's jaw. His eating mechanism is damaged; he cannot open his mouth and his appearance is brutalized. Later, he has his face remoulded – to everyone's satisfaction: his power has returned. Michael's first murder takes place at a restaurant. Sollozzo and McCluskey think they are 'consuming' a weakened Corleone family, while the nervous Michael retrieves a gun that has been planted behind the toilet in the men's room. Going to the toilet is a symbolic defilement; eating, desecration, and murder are interrelated. The connection between the gun and phallus is strengthened by Sonny's playful remark in cautioning the men who plant the weapon: 'I don't want my brother coming out of that toilet with just his dick in his hand.' Restaurant murders of Mafia hoods all follow the same basic pattern of symbolism.

Also integrated within the oppositional tension is Nino Rota's soundtrack that contains two major themes expressive of absence and plenitude. The Godfather Waltz Theme opens all three films, resembling much less a waltz than a Neapolitan folk song lament. It is the unforgettable trumpet solo in the dark key of C minor; it is a falling melody, plaintive and haunting, and suggestive of a lonely Sicilian shepherd blowing on a reed pipe; but scoring the music for a reed pipe instead of a trumpet would have been distractingly folkloristic. This theme, linked to family survival, may recall the horn solos and brass band dirges at Sicilian funerals, underlining absence. Yet the theme can modulate into a lilting waltz, whence its name, as it does when Don Vito dances with Connie at her wedding, and therefore move to the pole of plenitude. The Love Theme begins as a song associated with romance and fulfilment; even so, Rota delicately tinged this theme, also in C minor, with a shade of melancholy, so that it too can evoke its opposite. The theme, much transformed, was taken from another film that he scored years before; sometimes a theme or aria works better in a new setting, as Rota's does here.[36]

For the dramatic interpenetration of spheres, nothing compares with the transition-of-power scene between Don Vito and Michael at the end of *Godfather I*. In his home garden, nibbling fruit and sipping wine, emblems of his ethnicity, the aging Don Vito drifts back and forth between asking about Michael's family and warning him of assassination: 'your wife and children – you happy with them? ... I hope you don't mind how I keep going over this Barzini business'; 'I spend my life trying not to be careless. Women and children can be careless, but not men ... How's your boy?' The Waltz Theme plays quietly. 'I never wanted this for you. I work my whole life – I don't apologize – to take care of my family.' Michael reassures him that he has everything under control. Then Don Vito expresses his deepest feelings for his son's future, genuine assimilation, and success: 'I never wanted this for you'; 'I thought that ... that when it was your time, that ... that you would be the one to hold the strings. Senator Corleone. Governor Corleone ... something.' Shifting course, Michael tries to cheer up his father by impugning these models, 'another *pezzanovante*,' 'big shot.' But that was not his father's point and he knows it. 'There wasn't enough time, Michael ... wasn't enough time.' 'We'll get there, Pop,' says Michael, 'We'll get there.' If one does not believe Don Vito and Michael's sincerity in this scene, then they are *only* gangsters.

Though contamination of the opposing spheres exists throughout *Godfather I* and helps account for its structural tension, the opening and complementary scene of *Godfather II* shows that the two worlds have become almost indistinguishable: the tension is to be found elsewhere, deeper within the central characters. The wedding in *Godfather I* is the organizing event that gives purpose to the whole occasion, including the business. The beaming Connie holds attention as a bride should on her wedding day. Filmed in sepia-toned colour, the scenes have the look and cheerful spontaneity of a home movie. In *Godfather II*, Anthony's First Communion party at the family compound at Lake Tahoe is a flimsy pretext for a gaudy, heavily staged event where the only spontaneity comes in outbursts of anger, frustration, and disappointment. The boy wanders about lost in his own party. Michael is solidifying his entrance into the corporate world of casinos, the political establishment, and respectable high life. Supposedly summer, the light is intense but cold; and the faraway mountains have an icy, forbidding aura, in contrast to the sunny

garden scene in *Godfather I* but foreshadowing the end of *Godfather II*.[37]
At the wedding party, everyone knows one another; police and FBI are
excluded; Sonny goes outside to smash a camera. At the First Communion party, strangers outnumber family and friends. The family serves
drinks and food to the police and FBI; borders have broken down; the
family pays everyone off. Pentangeli (Michael V. Gazzo), a comic figure
who represents the older generation of Mafia bosses, is completely out
of his element: 'A kid comes up to me in a white jacket, gives me a Ritz
cracker and chopped liver, he says "Canapes." I say, "Can o' peas my ass;
that's a Ritz cracker and chopped liver!"' He is not embarrassed to grab
the nearest source of water available, a garden hose, when he wants to
drink. He tries to teach the band to play the tarantella, which in their
hands quickly turns into 'Pop Goes the Weasel.' The Corleone family
has lost its ethnic roots; Pentangeli's natural discomfort is easily transferred to the viewer. Senator Geary's (G.D. Spradlin) mispronunciation
of 'Corleone' expresses the family's assimilation.

The most serious change between *Godfather I* and *II* occurs within the
family itself. Though only three years have passed, the adults have a worn
look. Fredo Corleone (John Cazale), the weak middle brother and now
underboss, is a dissolute lounge lizard. His wife gets drunk and hollers
obscenities on the dance floor: 'Never marry a wop – they treat their
wives like shit.' Unable to control her, Fredo consents to having her forc-
ibly removed. Later we see them asleep on a huge bed with black silk
sheets, a garishly ornamented backboard with gray stucco carving and
an enormous mirror: a bed of death in a zone of hell. Twice divorced,
Connie shows up a week late, has a new boyfriend in tow, and asks Mama
Corleone to tell Michael she has no time to wait in line to see him (obviously for more money). A repository of the cultural code, Mama is not
appeased by Connie's perfunctory gift and reprimands her. First, Connie
ought to see her children, then wait her turn: she has lost any claim to
special treatment.

In a shark-skin suit and blood-red tie Michael moves slowly, like a sleek
predator. Abstracted and emotionless, he is plotting one of his biggest
deals and things are not falling into place. Marital tension contributes
to his anxiety; this is when Kay complains, 'you promised you'd be legitimate in five years and it's seven' (one can hardly imagine Mama Corleone speaking in this manner to Don Vito). The business dealings lack
even the superficial courtliness of *Godfather I*. Instead of dispensing favours, as Don Vito had done in the parallel scene, Michael turns people
down right and left. *No*, his sister will not marry her latest playboy. *No*,

Senator Geary will not receive twenty-five thousand dollars and a hefty percentage of the gross at Michael's four casinos in exchange for a gambling license worth only twenty thousand dollars. 'I don't like your kind of people,' Geary sneers, 'I don't like to see you come out to this clean country with your oily hair, and dressed up in those silk suits, and try to pass yourselves off as decent Americans ... I despise your masquerade – the dishonest way you pose yourself and your whole fucking family.' Upholding the separation of codes, Michael responds: 'We're all part of the same hypocrisy, Senator. But never think it applies to my family.' *No,* Michael will not let Pentangeli punish the Rosato brothers, though they probably killed Clemenza. 'They do violence in their grandmother's neighborhood,' pleads Pentangeli, whose language connects the mother, home, and the past, evoking vestigial plenitude. Michael even says *no* to Hagen on a business matter; he cannot trust his closest advisor. Then he plans a deal with Johnny Ola, whom Pentangeli denigrates as 'Hyman Roth's Sicilian errand boy': a Sicilian has betrayed his clan and lost his manhood. Outdoors, Pentangeli recklessly accuses Michael of betraying his 'blood' and spills a bloody Mary, a portent of his own betrayal of the family and forced suicide.

It is axiomatic in bourgeois society to separate private from public life. The almost total breakdown of these spheres in *Godfather II* results from a series of crucial decisions that Coppola made in the brief but intensely creative hiatus between shooting the films. Originally, he rejected the idea of a sequel; Michael who started as a 'bright, idealistic, beautiful talented man' had turned into a 'cold, introverted, loveless, horrible monster' by the end of *Godfather I.*[38] Was not the lesson plain enough? Yet Coppola, having second thoughts, said he was 'disturbed that people thought that I romanticized Michael' and made him too sympathetic – which is true. Moreover, 'there is a difference between the Mafia as it really is and the Mafia as we depict it'[39] – which is even more true. Word of the Mafia's enthusiastic response to *Godfather I* leaked out: the mafiosi 'enjoyed the movie's portrayal of its wit and wisdom so much that it dusted off moribund folkways such as kissing the hands of the dons.'[40]

Coppola admitted his troubles in turning the audience against Michael, probably the biggest talking point in his many interviews, e.g., 'if you were taken inside Adolph Hitler's home, went to his parties and heard his stories,' he said, 'you'd probably have liked him.'[41] (Had Coppola read Albert Speer's diaries, which appeared in 1970, he might have thought otherwise.) More probably, like his audience, Coppola simply identified with Michael. To be certain, he leaves no question that Michael's actions are morally opprobrious. The viewer might not deplore his elimination of evil bosses at the end of *Godfather I*, as they are no worse than he is, but he has killed or harmed innocent people, compromised his family, and lied cruelly to his wife (in one of their strongest scenes, at the very end, with the emphatic closing of the door that, then, divided business from family). He has located a conspirator in his brother-in-law Carlo and has him garroted; and Tessio has double-crossed him and has paid the price. Fredo is falling victim to the Las Vegas high life and will soon betray him. Business and family unity show signs of cracking, and Michael's face begins to wear an expression of impassivity and gloom that characterizes him in *Godfather II*.

Yet when the moving vans prepare to bring his operations from New York to Nevada, there is confidence in the air; it is a little like Wagner's gods triumphantly crossing the rainbow bridge to Valhalla, even while the Fate leitmotif casts its dark shadow. The audience has participated covertly in Michael's success and applauds it. The sequel was written to draw to a 'logical conclusion' the unresolved moral conflicts of *Godfather I*: 'I didn't want Michael to die,' Coppola determined; 'I didn't want Michael to be put into prison. I didn't want him to be assassinated by his rivals. But, in a bigger sense, I also wanted to destroy Michael'; 'at the end, he's prematurely old, almost syphilitic, like Dorian Gray.'[42] What he wanted was to make Michael suffer. Balzac might have thought this way of his Lucien de Rubempré in *Lost Illusions:* an aggressive attachment to a character, a refusal to let anyone else teach him the bitter lessons of life. Thus, though Coppola never intended to kill off his protagonist, one of the drafts of *Godfather II* bore the title 'The Death of Michael Corleone.'

III

Coppola's 'destruction' of Michael and the myth of plenitude took two skilful initiatives. The first was structural. In *Godfather I* the narrative is linear: by various technical, cinematic as well as scripted means, the emotional ups and downs of the key family members are so involving that the viewer is almost complicit. Subconsciously we enjoy Don Vito's protection. 'Strangers' are usually enemies and, like false family members, seen as repulsive; they do not gain the sympathy of the audience. Other Mafia families are presented as vicious and double-dealing; politicians are contemptible and police are on the take. In *Godfather II* Coppola broke up the linear narrative by having five alternations of two parallel plotlines:

one is devoted to the rise of young Don Vito (Robert De Niro) in Sicily and Little Italy from 1901 to circa 1925; the other concerns Michael's 'decline' in 1958–59. Remarkably, though the Don Vito plotline runs about 45 minutes (a quarter of the film) and the Michael sequences run over 150 minutes, the asymmetrical balance elicits an aesthetic response more powerful than would chronological parity, while maintaining Michael's centrality as protagonist. The total effect is one of distancing, non-identification, and a more objective view of Michael's situation. If he experiences some self-recognition, there is no catharsis, neither for him nor the audience; though he may suffer inconsolably, and though we fear him, we do not pity him. In Aristotelian terms, he is either 'below average' or (more likely) the 'evil' hero in ethical terms, and so deserves the misfortune he brings upon himself.

For his second and more audacious initiative in *Godfather II*, Coppola mythicizes the five Don Vito sequences, with some ironic undercutting; and he demythicizes Michael by employing various realist and symbolist procedures. Coppola had already shot mythicizing and demythicizing sequences in *Godfather I* where it was Michael in a romanticized Sicily contrasted with his siblings in wintry New York. Far from being a governing technique, however, it comprised only one segment of the film. Further, in *Godfather II* language enforces the opposition of plotlines: young Don Vito speaks almost only Sicilian; Michael speaks almost only English. The nostalgia of the Don Vito sequences with their ghetto crowds, accomplices, and family members counters Michael's lonely mental meanderings and the emptiness of the Nevada scenes. The humble past opposes the opulent present to a point where the past becomes a fantasy of growth, well-being, and wholeness: a false plenitude. These interlocking structures make up the central form of *Godfather II*.

For the five Don Vito sequences in *Godfather II*, Coppola and Mario Puzo brought back the Don, who died in *Godfather I*, and rewrote his life from boyhood to his mid-thirties. They made clear parallels between him and his son. Vito and Michael have their first kill at about the same age: Vito at twenty-eight or twenty-nine when he kills Fanucci circa 1920, which is about the time Michael is born; he holds Michael in his arms in the next scene. Michael shoots Sollozzo and Captain McCluskey when he is twenty-six or twenty-seven in 1946–47. Both godfathers cement their power at a similar age: Vito is in his mid-thirties when he avenges the death of his father, mother, and elder brother by killing Don Ciccio circa 1925; Michael wipes out the last of his major enemies in a cataclysmic barrage of murder in 1958 when he is thirty-eight. Yet these similarities point up serious differences. Vito remains locally in New York, where he builds his 'business' among the families. Michael operates on an international stage and in a rapidly changing world: Las Vegas, Miami, Havana, Lake Tahoe, New York, Sicily, trains, cars, planes. Vito is surrounded by family and retainers. Divorced and alone, Michael consolidates his empire while trying to hang onto the remnants of his family. Vito's inner life remains a mystery; one cannot trap the negative sublime in an argument. By contrast, if Michael himself is a closed book to those around him, Coppola opens it up far more to the viewer. At the end of *Godfather II*, both godfathers have arrived at maturity, worked with the same values, and stand at the summit of power, yet face entirely different futures.

Coppola's unmasking of false plenitude takes on a more somber colouring in *Godfather II*. With food, for example, the salt has lost its savour. Michael refuses Roth's offer of a tunafish sandwich at his house in Miami Beach. The lunch is meagre and unappetizing after the big Italian dinners that have been the rule. Thin and constantly ill, Roth does not eat well and even complains he would 'give four million just to be able to take a piss without it hurting'; he is no Clemenza with his dinner, urinating, and cannoli. To a group of upper-echelon mobsters in Havana, Roth displays a paltry white cake with a green image of Cuba in the frosting and proceeds to divide the cake and the casinos. Sensing Roth's intention to execute him, Michael refuses his cake and denies Roth his victory. Later in Nevada, plotting Roth's murder, Michael eats a big orange, an image of Roth's tropical empire. Oranges, one of the totemic fruits of the Sicilians, appear in plenty in all three films, always in connection with danger, threat, and impending death, or, by opposition, with life, energy, and survival; they stand for control of life and death. Vito as a young man does not have to pay a cart vendor for an orange: it is a 'favor'; his reputation has spread. Don Vito buys oranges just before his attempted assassination, and lives. Barzini (Richard Conte) plays with an orange he has taken from a fruit bowl in the heads-of-families scene, and dies. Fanucci (Gaston Moschin) takes an orange from a cart shortly before he is murdered. Eating an orange, Hagen claims is impossible to kill Roth, to which Michael responds, 'If history has taught us anything, it is that you can kill anybody'; and so forth.[43] Like number painting, such symbolism loses its power by sheer repetition.

According to Thomas Schatz, 'the mythology of the classic gangster film, like that of the Western, concerns the transformation of nature into culture under auspices of modern civilization ... Nature in the gangster film is conspicuous primarily in its absence.'[44] The trilogy does not conform entirely to this critique because the godfathers emerge from a rural southern Italian background and retain a close relation to nature. In *Godfather I* there is the wedding in the Long Island garden, a sacral image of Sicily, where Don Vito grows tomatoes. Paulie dies in a barren marshland. For bucolic Nature one is transported to Sicily where Michael hides out: the warmly lit hills and valleys, the seeming innocence of rural life, peasant dress, impart a sense of peace, relief, and expansion of feeling after the claustrophobic New York underworld. Michael gains a knowledge of his ethnic roots, he learns Mafia lore from Don Tommasino, and falls in love and marries a Sicilian, Apollonia (the name signals mythification). Yet antiquated courtship rituals and the romanticization of nature are set off by cross-cutting to New York to show Kay's feelings of abandonment, the disintegration of Connie's marriage, and Sonny's brutal execution. Even among the Sicilian hills there is no peace. Michael cannot move without his bodyguards, hunters with their *lupara*. One of them betrays Michael and is himself sent to America to hide. Apollonia is blown up in Michael's wired car (twelve or thirteen years later Michael discovers the whereabouts of this betrayer in upstate New York and has him killed the same way – mimetic violence). The Sicilian interlude has only been a step marking Michael's advance to power, intensifying his family loyalty and desire for vengeance. Thus, nature has participated in the unmasking of false plenitude; in a roundabout way Schatz is correct: 'conspicuous primarily in its absence.'

Godfather II abounds in imagery from pre-cultural nature that underlines qualities of negation and otherness. In the opening scene, Vito's father's funeral in Corleone, the procession winds through a dry (or near dry, and therefore absent of life) riverbed on its way to a cemetery among the Sicilian hills in strong, hard sunlight. The body of Vito's elder brother, shot dead by Don Ciccio's men, lies among the rocks. The nature scenes in Nevada seem like the fulfilment of the family destiny, from rural Sicily to New York and then back to a mountainous country in the Far West. For all their unearthly beauty, the Sierra Nevada appears alien and surreal.The family compound is surrounded by walls and guards like the Sicilian *feudo*, but with the addition of electronic sensing devices, alarm bells, and Alsatians in cages. Still, these do not render the fortress impregnable, as proven by the assassination attempt against Michael. It takes place at night in a thunderstorm that heightens the tension in the hunt for the would-be killers. Alarms go off, dogs are unleashed, electronic gates slam, but the would-be assassins are found dead in a dark stream, probably at the hands of Fredo, who had given information on the layout and needed to kill them to prevent them from talking. Curtly Michael says 'fish them out,' like dead fish, perverting the Christian symbol. Fredo disappears mysteriously, a harbinger of his later disappearance 'among the fishes' (he is shot on the lake). In *Godfather I* Clemenza had explained the folk symbolism, 'Luca Brasi sleeps with the fishes.'

Lake Tahoe in *Godfather II* never appeared less touristic. The mountains are coldly purple, gray, and black in the winter light. After months in Cuba and New York, Michael returns, significantly having just missed Christmas. The compound is blanketed in snow, and neither his wife nor his children come to greet him. As he enters the house, he wanders from one empty room to another, until he sees Kay at a distance quietly sewing on a machine, the traditional distaff image technologized. He cannot bring himself to greet her. Nature and family have lost all their replenishing power. Coppola shoots the boathouse from various angles: it is an elaborate structure where expensive craft are hoisted by large cranes and moved by dollies making ear-splitting noises: nature can only be reached through technology.

The one positive reference to mountains in *Godfather II* is a joke made in the presence of dictator Fulgencio Batista. An unnamed 'Cuban ruler' reassures a gathering of American industrialists and Mafia dons that the rebels are 'in the mountains' and that 'we will tolerate no guerrillas in the casinos or the swimming pools'; revolutionary activity linked to the mountain sublime versus gambling and decadent leisure. Michael, who has witnessed a guerrilla sacrifice his own life to blow up an army captain, shrewdly assesses that Cuba is no longer a good investment.

A scene late in *Godfather II* displays the bewitching appeal of natural plenitude. It occurs in the last of the flashback sequences when Don Vito is still consolidating his power and settling old debts. The Don has arranged for a visit to Don Tommasino's estate in Sicily, ostensibly for a family gathering, but mainly as a cover to avenge the deaths of his father and brother, emphasizing the same interaction of family and business. After dining at a long rustic table laden with food and exchanging gifts, they tour the olive oil factory, descending into a deep cellar, which takes on a journey into the past. The camera shoots the scene from a remote perch and looking down, as if distance were a projection of memory. Surrounded by huge oil casks and forming a small circle in the centre of the screen, the extended family drinks a wine toast. Wine is a natural symbol of the earth's fructifying power and is linked to irrational, superhuman strength, Dionysian loss of individuation, and pleasure. The darkness invests the casks with a surreal appearance, and there is just a murmur of warm family voices. This scene is one of the shortest in the film, an almost subliminal image that might have flashed into Michael's memory, no time to focus on an individual, only on the group.

The cellar scene exemplifies the *photogénie* of French impressionist filmmakers: 'the movies' ineffable moments (an actor's walk across a room, the light from a candle) seem to result from the camera's innate ability to record them'; André Bazin's developed a parallel concept of mise-en-scène, which in this instance does not mean 'setting' but the 'untranslatable' essence of a shot, scene, or 'particular set of strategies' (Kay at the sewing machine).[45] Equally potent as a ritual and as an embedded memory, the cellar scene represents the profoundest wishes of the family, survival and plenitude. It shows their most complete at-one-ness with nature, the past, and themselves, with the god of the life force as presider. Don Vito is invincible: and afterward, to underline the point, he personally butchers Don Ciccio.

However much the agonies of the world swirl around it, nothing must contaminate the Italian American family, centre of well-being and psychological protection, the stronger for having grandparents, children, and the nearby wall of uncles, aunts, cousins, honorary members, and other retainers. 'Though we see Don Corleone issuing edicts on his business affairs,' writes William Pechter, 'our predominant images of him are not in his exercise of power but in his domestic role – officiating as father of the bride ... shopping for groceries, playing with his grandchild; not as a Scarface in flashy suits.'[46] Don Vito reminds Johnny Fontane, 'a man who doesn't spend time with his family can never be a real man'; ironically, the sententious remark follows the return of Sonny from his just having committed adultery. Don Vito's family always remains a source of strength for him. One never sees him arguing with his wife or his children; he retains his position of absolute authority. The family name is superimposed upon the business: the Tattaglia Family, the Barzinis, the Corleones: some of these gangs have several hundred 'family members.' In the next generation, however, outside implications of the business reverberate upon all family relationships. Connie's rebelliousness, marriages, dissolute living, and final capitulation (on her knees before Michael) illustrate the condition of women in her American generation (she was born in the late 1920s), but also in her Italian American (second) generation. Mrs Henry Hill is star witness to the condition in Nicholas Pileggi's *Wiseguys*. Sonny has numerous affairs. Fredo cannot control his wife. Michael's first wife is mistakenly killed in his place, and his second marriage ends in divorce.

To be thrust beyond the confines of a family is to be in extreme danger. Two illustrations must suffice: the first involves Michael's frame-up of Senator Geary by taking advantage of his deviant behaviour. Geary wakes up in a drunken stupor beside a dead prostitute while Tom Hagen 'explains' what has happened. Geary cries it was 'just a game' that he had 'done before.' The dead girl, who had actually been murdered by a gang member, lies with a white towel drenched in blood covering her mutilated body. Even Hagen must look away. He assures the senator that no one will know, the girl cannot be traced, she 'has no family.' Furthest from the mother, the prostitute violates the notion of a family; hence from a common Sicilian point of view she can be punished severely. Being without a family, without meaning or value, is the ultimate expression of being expendable. More than any other act in these films, this murder robs the godfathers of every trace of humanity. They justify the murder by setting it within the framework of their most cherished symbol, the family.

The sibling rivalry between Michael and Fredo is one of the more sharply delineated relationships in the films. A gullible, extroverted playboy, Fredo is a comic figure whose flamboyance, vulnerability, and simple-mindedness render him sympathetic in this world of sharks. 'Fredo has got a good heart but he's weak, he's stupid,' says Michael. At the communion party Fredo apologizes to Michael for his wife's conduct: 'You're my brother,' Michael comforts him, 'You don't have to apologize,' words that come back to haunt him. If all seems well on the surface, Fredo dislikes being the family errand boy; and if he knows it was his father's decision to skip over him, he envies his younger brother's ascendency and is ripe for treachery. When Fredo arrives in Cuba with two million dollars to help close a deal, Michael already suspects him. Looking for a good time as usual, Fredo asks, 'Anyone I know in Havana?' Michael gives the icy response: 'Johnny Ola, Hyman Roth.' Michael tells Fredo ominously, 'It is difficult to be a son, believe me.' The godfather has had to sacrifice normal relations with his family. In the film's most lurid sequence Michael realizes his brother's betrayal: Fredo takes him to a sex show in Havana. On stage a woman is tied half naked to a post as other women, dressed to look like nuns, stand around her: a perversion of Catholic ritual and another representation of female victimage. 'Superman' in a gaudy red robe walks before her and drops his robe as the camera switches to the men standing in the audience: Fredo, Michael, the bodyguards, Senator Geary. Fredo jokes about the size of the man's penis, adding that he and Johnny Ola had toured the bars before. Michael's expression turns sullen. Awareness occurs at the moment of the act presumably taking place on the stage.

Fleeing Havana during the revolution, Michael spots Fredo in the panic of the crowd, mimetic of its subject. 'You're still my brother,' Michael yells out in the hope of rescuing him. Fredo is not that foolish and disappears. Michael has him tracked down in New York and brought back to Lake Tahoe. In a late scene Fredo lies helpless on a deck chair and pours out his heart to Michael, who prowls around the room. Fredo recalls how their mother used to tease him, saying he was not a true son but was left by gypsies on the doorstep (perhaps because he is so unlike the other men in his family). He resents being passed over: 'I'm smart and I want respect.' Michael is vehement and repudiates him: 'You're nothing to me now, you're not a brother, you're not a friend. I don't want to know you, or what you do. I don't want to see you at the hotels, I don't want you near my house. When you see our mother, I want to know a day in advance, so I won't be there.' The sin of Cain already weighs upon him; nothing less could have provoked this verbal onslaught, his most extreme in all three films; this godfather suffers guilt after all. Though Fredo betrayed the family not out of premeditation so much as goofy inattentiveness, and he might have been spared, Michael is inexorable. Beseeched by Connie to forgive Fredo, he sits like potentate in the boathouse gazebo; he will not see his brother in the main house where their mother's wake is being held. Then he seems to accept Connie's plea, goes to the main house, walks over to Fredo, wasted thin by anxiety. Fredo turns in his chair and, like a supplicant, clasps his brother and begins to cry. As the Waltz Theme plays softly, Michael's glance meets that of his bodyguard Al Neri. Viewers realize that they, like Fredo and Connie, have been tricked, by Michael's pretense to brotherly love. He will exact the vengeance that he has vowed to do, but only after their mother's death.

Fredo's execution epitomizes Godfather symbolism. Before he takes Anthony fishing, he tells the boy a 'secret,' a parody of the godfather's darker concept of secrecy. When as a boy he went fishing with his brothers, he was the only one who caught a fish because 'every time I said a Hail Mary, I would catch one.' As they are about to leave in the boat, the son is whisked away by his aunt Connie, and Fredo is shot far out on the lake by Al Neri. Inside his house Michael watches from the distance. The shot reverberates across the lake to the mountains, a magnification that is as much symbolic as physical. Nature is again defiled; the Christological association of fish has been inverted.

Given the other proximate causes – competition, changes in Mafia tactics, modernization – it is perhaps commendable that Michael takes responsibility for his family's disintegration. In *Godfather II* he has a brief scene with his mother as the household fire flickers between them, another exceptional example of *photogénie*. In Sicilian Michael asks, 'What did Papa think – deep in his heart?'; 'by being strong for his family – could he – lose it?' His mother answers, 'You never lose your family.' The camera focuses on Michael as he ponders how his father managed, on what sources he drew to maintain his balance and composure. Michael cannot fathom those depths (though he has gone further than ever before), so he replies, 'Times are changing,' and the scene ends. The 'family' that was his father's source of plenitude no longer serves the same for him. Had the times really changed that much, or he been too aggressively demanding of the family? Or both? Coppola prepares in such a scene as this for what comes later, the full disclosure of the secret 'deep in his heart,' absence at the core of being, the godfather's inheritance. Michael's power derives from the control that secrecy gives him. Like a god, he must be seen to be autonomous and absolute, a law into himself, and yet as a human being he is not autonomous. Hagen will say to him: 'you've won – do you have to wipe everyone out?' 'Just my enemies,' replies Michael, 'that's all.' His desires lack limit, so his enemies are legion; the evil god of the godfathers has exacted a horrible price for riches and power. The fact that the fireside scene is conducted in Sicilian, *linguaggio segreto*, which conceals it beneath a linguistic layering, adds to its impressiveness, making it a totally arresting image of the film's central mystery. The camera will not catch Michael in another such moment until the very end of the film.

Masters of the secret, godfathers must be born liars, and Michael is no exception. He does not tell his family that he joined the Marines. He accuses his brother-in-law Carlo of selling out to another crime family and wants a confession. 'Do you think I'd make my sister a widow?' asks Michael. Terrified, Carlo confesses on the spot and, presumably conciliated, Michael gives him a plane ticket to Las Vegas; within minutes Carlo is garroted. Later, in the final scene of *Godfather I,* Kay wants to know if Michael had anything to do with the murder. Michael, suppressing his rage, says that he never discusses business with the women of the family but that he will make this *one* exception. He looks her in the eyes and says 'No.' In *Godfather II* Michael lies to Roth, Hagen, Connie, Fredo, Pentangeli, and the Senate Rackets Committee. The subterfuge by which he is able to overturn what might otherwise have led to a five count perjury conviction is one of his boldest strokes. He brings Pentangeli's rustic-appearing but dressed-up brother from a little town near Palermo to the Senate hearing; the brother's presence reminds Pentangeli of the law of *omertà* and he retracts his testimony. 'Ora la famiglia sta posto,' says Hagen. 'The family is okay again.' Michael's greatest public victory is a prelude to his greatest private defeat.

Kay refuses to return with him to Nevada. In a bitter argument Michael says that he will do everything in his power to prevent her from taking his children away from him. Kay divulges her own secret just after Michael's victory in the Senate hearings: her miscarriage was an abortion and the three-month-old fetus was male. Like our marriage, she taunts him, the abortion was 'unholy, evil,' but the 'only way' she could do something that he 'could *not* forgive' – 'not with this Sicilian thing that's been going on for two thousand years.' She has taken a role usually reserved for a man, become an assassin, and killed a (potential) godfather. After this scene, that there could be any reigniting of their romance in *Godfather III* only goes to show how far Coppola and Puzo would lose touch with their characters. Michael wins custody of his children, with Kay granted some visiting rights (between *II* and *III* he relents, in this as in so much else, because he allows her to share custody).

IV

In point of historical time – Sicily, 1901 – Don Francesco (Giuseppe Sillato), or 'Ciccio' as he is familiarly called, is the earliest of the film's godfathers. His name is stereotypical of a character that went back for generations in an unchanging world.[47] Fat and grotesque, he lives within a heavily guarded estate. He has already killed Vito's father and brother. The mother comes with Vito to beg for his life: 'But [he's] only nine, and dumb-witted. The child cannot harm you.' The motif of the supposedly dull-witted boy who returns to exact vengeance is found in many cultures (Livy's Lucius Brutus, the Hamlet saga, the Anglo-Norman Havelok). Don Ciccio says that the boy will grow strong and return to kill him. The mother buys a few seconds of time by holding a kitchen knife to Don Ciccio's throat while screaming to her son to escape. Freeing himself, Don Ciccio stands back while his henchman shoots her with a *lupara*. Vito looks back in horror, then runs for his life. The men search for him, crying his name at night and threatening his protectors. 'Andolini' echoes ominously in the empty square. Vito is hidden within a basket full of wood carried by a donkey, a providential and appropriate saviour given the importance of this animal in Sicilian culture, and is led out through a labyrinth of streets under his enemies' very noses. The primal nature of the materials, the conflict of good and evil, the initiation of the hero, death and rebirth all lend these scenes a mythic quality. Vito, a younger son like Michael, was probably not the one expected to become godfather. Fate has its own reasons.

Twenty-four years later Don Vito returns to avenge the family murders. Don Ciccio is dozing in a large chair on a sun-baked balcony; surrounded by lethal-looking geraniums, old, bloated, unkempt, and half-asleep, he is monstrous. Don Vito is introduced formally by his original family name, Andolini. Hard of hearing, Don Ciccio asks for the name again and shows a dawning and terrified awareness, at which Don Vito takes out a large kitchen knife, the double of his mother's, and practically disembowels him. Years before, the concealed Vito had escaped the monster by cutting his way out of him, the birth of a hero (Vito = 'alive'). In Hesiodic vendetta, the removal of the curse and the satisfaction of the blood thirst of the dead are typically accompanied by mutilation.[48] This rendering of the entrails of power symbolically discloses the secret: 'Andolini.'

Fanucci is a transitional figure, a link to the legendary Black Hand, a proto-Mafia that reigned in the first two decades of the twentieth century. It was not so much an organization or 'family' as it was a group of freelance racketeers and thugs, each with his own neighbourhood. The black hand is a death or demon sign tracing to illiterate gangs in southern Italy and Sicily (and elsewhere). Since Fanucci's power depends on personal intimidation, he must display his power, and does so after the southernly fashion of *bella figura*. A tall, imposing character, he wears an elegant white linen suit and hat, with a heavy blue coat worn like a cape – a somewhat feminized figure, a matinee godfather. He is first seen in an atmosphere of illusion, a theatre, from a few rows back; his large black silhouette against the stage fills the screen, an image of gothic terror that turns out hollow, all appearance. He extorts money from the theatre owner by threatening to mutilate the nose of his beautiful daughter, the actress who has just appeared on stage in *Senza Mamma:* his actions mimic the histrionics of the play – threats of suicide, death of a mother back in Naples, etc.

Without henchmen, without sons, and with three daughters to provide for (adding to the feminized aura), Fanucci is vulnerable. He wants to buy dresses for them and demands that Vito and his two accomplices, newly entered on a life of crime, pay him almost half their illicit earnings: 'You should let me wet my beak a little.' The buried sexual pun makes Fanucci the feminine bird. In a scene from the longer televised version, cut from the final version, a band of thugs beat him up in an alley. Bleeding and unkempt, he is robbed of his power. Vito watches from a distance, does not bother to help, realizes the hollowness of Fanucci's threats, and sees an opportunity.

In one of the most carefully composed scenes in the trilogy Vito assassinates Fanucci, his first murder. He has reasons: Fanucci's nephew has cost Vito his job, the threatened actress was a friend's *innamorata*. Vito also knows that, learning from Fanucci's mistakes, he can make the better godfather. When Vito sets up his own extortion racket, Fanucci demands a large share of the profit. Awaiting Vito for the payoff, Fanucci drinks an espresso in one gulp, deliberately making a huge sound: another victim is about to be swallowed. Vito arrives while Fanucci rubs a spot of coffee off the cuff of his white jacket: it is a sign of being marked for murder, subtler than the beating by the thugs and accomplishing the same end on a symbolic level. Vito lays the money on the table, and Fanucci covers it with his hat in a grandiloquent manner: a comic concealment. He peeks under it to see if it is all there. Such antics cannot threaten someone of Vito's mettle. All the money is not there, and Vito promises that he will have it later.

They leave and go in opposite directions as Rota's slicing, dissonant chords throw realist time into expressionist ritual. Alongside the procession of San Gennaro honouring the saint whose blood liquefies, Fanucci moves in the crowded street from right to left. He makes a big show of attaching a dollar to the statue of the Madonna, another link to the feminine. From left to right, counter to the movement of the procession, and over the rooftops above, Vito crosses to Fanucci's house. The countermovement signifies Vito's demonic countering of the religious force. Nimble and stealthy, he is an animal stalking his prey. He turns off the light in the hallway and waits. When Fanucci arrives at his apartment he opens the door and turns back to notice Vito; the camera is behind Vito and it is through him that we see most of the scene (and therefore, according to Hollywood cinematography, identify with him). The corridor behind Fanucci is long and dark. Vito shoots him twice in the heart, then gratuitously sticks the gun in his mouth and fires again. Fanucci's *bella figura* has been thoroughly despoiled. He ingests the explosive power of his enemy and explodes from within. The feminine nature of Fanucci is also violated by the phallic gun, while the shots are masked by 'fireworks' and the Madonna's merciful image flashes on the screen. By cross-cutting Coppola contrasts the image of Christian purity and mercy with a violent 'rape.'

What is the key to Vito's motivation? On the more immediate level, it is clientelism. Vito had lost his grocer's job to Fanucci's nephew. The shop owner wanted to give Vito a sack of groceries for his family as a parting gift. This shop owner, who had raised Vito, suddenly abandons him, like a failed or absent father, a double of the real father who was unable to protect him; it is the 'unthinkable Italian crime.'[49] Though Vito is now a needy parent with a young child at home, he refuses to accept the gift. He will not eat someone else's food or power; and he will protect his own family. The deeper motive traces to his mother, who sacrificed herself to save her son. Her murder, which followed upon his father's and brother's, set in motion the events that make him an exile in an epic pattern.

According to Luigi Barzini, the American Mafiosi found that 'the ancient arts were far more useful in America and went further. The Americans were generally trustful, unprepared to defend themselves from guile, often unwilling to fight for what they considered small stakes.'[50] Yet while this may help explain the success of the American Mafia, it cannot by itself account for Don Vito's ascendency over Fanucci, over his peers Clemenza and Tessio, and over other godfathers. Almost casually, Vito falls into the profession for which fate itself has destined him. One important scene in this development takes place at night when he hears a knock on the door and a hushed voice asks, 'Are you Italian?' He agrees to hide something and a few moments later, across a dim light-shaft between apartments, he gets handed a sack of guns by the young Clemenza (Bruno Kirby), whose apartment is being raided by the police. This mysterious scene in which the guns are handed between apartments is one of several scenes that signify a crossing over to a life of crime. In return for this favour, Clemenza promises Vito a present. They go to a wealthy home where they steal a large rug; it is blood red, as if dyed in the gore of its victims.

Next comes Fanucci's murder, where we see Vito smoothly establishing himself over his accomplices. He is superior to the well-dressed, self-important, pompous Clemenza. In the longer television version of the film, Clemenza is somewhat dandified; he makes a big show of buttoning up the fly to his pants on the front steps after visiting his mistress; everyone must acknowledge his power. A craftier Fanucci, but in the same mould. Tessio on the other hand is strong and silent, much like Vito himself, a shadow. When Don Vito is wounded in the assassination attempt, Tessio senses weakness in the family and goes over to Barzini's. Michael figures that it is Tessio, always the 'smarter of the two,' who betrayed the family. In the scene in which the three young men plot against Fanucci they are at supper, about to 'eat' their victim. Tessio and Clemenza are too in awe of Fanucci to attack him; only Vito has a plan, which he does not disclose; it must come as as much of a surprise to them as it does to the victim. They speak Sicilian, except for one, final sentence: Vito says, 'I'll take care of everything.' Again, the crossing into the other language represents the advance across a new threshold.

One of Don Vito's great strengths is not revealing his secret until it is necessary, and then acting with brutal, quick, and overwhelming force. He himself remains hidden behind his paid-off police and judges, behind his security, behind his family, deep in his 'office' at the centre of his home, while others perform the nefarious acts in his name. He does not even dominate the screen time, which might be too revealing. Other characters constantly fill in Vito's portrait, citing him, invoking him, and trying to fathom him. Michael tells Hagen after the assassination attempt in *Godfather II* that 'Pop told me to try to think like those around you think.' Pentangeli warns Michael to be much more careful in dealing with Roth: 'Your father did business with Hyman Roth. Your father respected Hyman Roth. But your father never *trusted* Hyman Roth.' Later, after returning from Roth's home in Florida, Michael calms Pentangeli: 'My father taught me many things ... Keep your friends close, but your enemies closer.' Many characters at one point or another have recourse to the Don's pithy wisdom.

As king of the American underworld, Don Vito is on good terms with death. He comforts his consigliere Genco Abbandando on his deathbed after Connie's wedding, bringing all three sons to the hospital as a sign of respect (Sonny asks why Michael, not a 'soldier,' needs to come; the Don insists on ritual obligation). His name meaning 'abandoning,' Genco fears eternal damnation, and the Don must reassure him. Has it been 'arranged,' Genco asks, surely the Don can 'pull a few strings.' 'Death,' says Genco, 'is afraid of you.'[51] 'You blaspheme,' replies the courtly Don, who stays the night with Genco until he dies. Later we see Don Vito riddled with bullets against a car and then lying near death in the same hospital. Such is his power that he must survive his enemies and die a natural, if monstrous, death. The association of Don Vito with terrifying monsters goes back to the first scene in *Godfather I;* the back of his head in his darkly lit office den. The four-minute death scene is fitting for the master of violence: playing with his grandson Anthony in his tomato garden. The garden is an image of plenitude, the Italian earth, and the blood-red tomato is a totemic vegetable of the southern Italian. Members of Vito's generation often had a plot of ground, a shed or veranda where they took a siesta, tended a few plants, and felt the sacral presence of the old country. The child is plenitude also, a theme stressed poignantly in *Godfather III*. Don Vito puts orange peels – the portentous fruit – into his mouth and transforms himself into a monster with fangs. The boy recoils in horror and starts crying. To cheer him the godfather plays hide-and-seek among the tall tomato stalks. Both the transformation to a monster and the game are metaphors of absence, concealment, and secrecy. The boy chases him around with a can of bug-killer. The exertion is too much for Don Vito, who falls over clutching the stalks. Unaware of what has happened, the boy keeps spraying him with the machine, a kind of gun, which 'kills' the old man. The boy is a killer too, a true member of the family, perhaps a godfather. But Nature never makes a leap. Michael must have his turn.

As a framing device, *Godfather I* opens with Don Vito seated in a chair, and *Godfather II* closes with Michael seated in a chair. Of the human postures that symbolize rank, relationship, and authority, sitting on a raised object is one of the primordial images of power. The throne is the original chair: it 'presupposes subject animals or human beings' who must carry the leader. 'Sitting always involves a downward pressure on something which is defenseless,' writes Canetti. This pressure is the physical manifestation of the leader, his 'weight' of authority measured in degrees of oppression. The ruler sits at ease while others stand and endure their fatigue. The time element is crucial. A standing figure is always ready to move, 'we expect someone who is sitting to *remain* sitting.'[52] The longer he 'sits' in power, the more he controls his situation. Numerous images display the power of the chair in both *Godfather I* and *II*. The 'unseen' godfather in the opening minute of *Godfather I* is seated on his leather office chair. When Michael plots the murders of Sollozzo and McCluskey he 'sits almost comfortably in a chair in a position that will become his most significant one: half at ease, half cornered, simultaneously secure and insecure.'[53] In Las Vegas he tells Moe Greene to clear the party girls out of the room; in a large chair Michael sits down heavily, and waits for his orders to be carried out. When in their last scene together Don Vito counsels Michael how to be a godfather, Michael slumps into a big chair and confirms his authority; his father stands. Like its predecessor, *Godfather II* opens with Michael seated in semi-darkness. Visible are part of his face, the upper part of his body, and his hand, which is being kissed by a kneeling supplicant.[54] The whole title *The Godfather Part II* is shot against the empty leather chair of the old Don, showing the deep impression of his body in its leather, and a deeper crease diagonally across it. Canetti suggests that an 'upholstered chair is not only soft, but also obscurely gives the sitter the feeling that he is sitting on something *living*,' that is, a victim.[55] The crease looks like a wound in the leather; the empty chair superimposes power upon absence, the crease, like a slash, is the signature of the hidden godfather.

Nine-year-old Vito is quarantined on Ellis Island for three months. The viewer faces Vito as he looks out of his window towards the Statue of Liberty. Filmed so, the statue is reflected on the window, lending an illusory appearance, suggesting liberty as both an ideal and a deception. The mature Vito will bring back a souvenir of the Statue of Liberty to his friends at a banquet in Corleone, Sicily: the sacred symbol has been reduced to a touristic commodity. Little Vito sits on a chair so big that his feet do not reach the ground; we see him from the back, precisely the way he is seen at the opening of *Godfather I*. He swings his feet and sings a traditional Sicilian folk song, 'Lu me sceccu malandrinu' (My donkey what a scoundrel), full of sadness and nostalgia. The song begins with 'I had a little donkey that was truly lovely / they killed him, my poor donkey.' A common symbol for the overworked, exploited Sicilians, the animal crucial to the survival of the peasant family, the donkey signifies at once Vito's attachment to and sense of loss of Sicily.[56] It is the first time that we hear little Vito's voice: feeble, frightened. The next shot, while we still hear Vito singing, is that of little Anthony dressed in white and walking down the church aisle for his First Communion: the rich kid and the quarantined immigrant.

A donkey cart saved Vito Andolini. In any gangster film cars figure prominently and have talismanic power; Coppola exploits the fact that cars are moving chairs. Their drivers, near the seat of power, are well placed to be assassins. Clemenza likes to polish his Cadillac. It is Don Vito's chauffeur Gatto who betrays him. The Don is hit five times and stumbles toward his car, as if its magic could save him: he survives. Michael moves him in his wheeled bed halfway across the hospital – to save him. Later Gatto is shot in a car, while Carlo, the other betrayer, is garroted in a car. Michael's wife Apollonia is blown up in a car; the bomb was intended for Michael, fate has again intervened, to the destruction of those around him. Sonny is machine-gunned in his car at a toll-booth. Michael is driven to Hyman Roth's house in Miami Beach in a black car with a fifties-style, gash-like design in red-orange across its side panel. The car looks like a predatory tropical fish. During the second courtship of Kay, in New Hampshire, Michael arrives in a big black car, which is driven in the background as they walk down main street; it represents the lie that she does not want to face and long manages to avoid. One of the most vulnerable moments Michael experiences in both films occurs when he drives through Havana during the revolution. He looks out while youths beat at its windows. Returning to Lake Tahoe after a long period in hiding, he pauses when he sees his son's bright red toy car in the snow, his Christmas gift to his son, purchased by Hagen; it sums up the sacrifice he has made and the suffering he has caused.

The climactic scene in *Godfather II* would not exert such artistic and emotional force were it not long and sufficiently prepared for, going back to the opening of *Godfather I*. The scene takes place at the family estate on Lake Tahoe in autumn 1959. Coppola describes Michael in this scene as 'very possibly the most powerful man in America' (as if there might be one or two others, say, the president); 'But he is a corpse.' He also called it the 'Hitler scene,' after the Berlin bunker, again underlining his sense of his central character as megalomaniacal. More to the point, he is, writes Ray, a 'grotesque parody of the official values.'[57] An earthly counterpart of his patron, St Michael the Avenging Angel, Michael has annihilated his foes. Alone with his memories, he sits in a large block-like easy chair, which seems to engulf him; he is surrounded by other empty sofas and easy chairs, showing the absence of the powerful men with whom he has conferred. The plush room is shadowed in reds, browns, and golds. Never have these colours had a colder glow. It looks like an ultra-modern version of an oriental throne room. He walks to the window so as not to miss hearing the shot that kills Fredo. As he hears it echoing across the vast lake in the cold afternoon light, he bows his head. The camera dissolves to his father's birthday party in 1941; Coppola employs the familiar cinematic convention whereby a dissolve from a character in thought indicates that character's personal thought and memories. The contrast between scenes could not be more vivid. Instead of being immersed in empty silence, Michael sits among his brothers, sister, Hagen, and future brother-in-law at the modest dining room table awaiting their father. One can almost smell the cooking in the kitchen. The birthday is a ritual of fulfilment but also a reminder of aging and the pressing need for a successor, the thought of which weighs on Don Vito.

The object of attention is his empty chair at the head of the table, the chair with equivalent status to his office chair, as it signifies his authority over the realm of the home. Strategically, the camera shoots the scene from behind the chair (with slats, so one can see through it), which is between the viewer and the table; its high back is silhouetted and pronounced, taking the viewer back to the beginning of *Godfather I*. Again, it is as if the audience saw the event from the perspective of the all-seeing, absent father.

The birthday falls on 7 December, which is the day of Pearl Harbor, symbol of massive violence and surprise (secret) attack, two of Don Vito's specialties. The connection between the Don and the Day of Infamy is further strengthened by the fact that the Don also represents a quasi-feudal past and attacks the state; his loyalty is to his family, not his country. Sonny says jokingly, imagine the Japanese 'having the nerve to bomb Pearl Harbor on Pop's birthday'; their father stands on the level of world events. As usual, not understanding the joke, Fredo says innocently, 'They didn't know it was Pop's birthday,' as if the Japanese might have waited a day, out of respect. As Sonny mocks the thirty thousand 'saps' who enlisted that morning, Michael destroys the cheerful mood by telling them that he has just enlisted in the Marines, and everyone knows Michael is no sap. Sonny's position is that men are saps to enlist because they 'risk their lives for strangers,' which is 'stupid.' Michael replies, 'That's Pop talking,' a repetition of the family tradition that he strives to overcome. Hagen intervenes, 'Your father has plans for you' and had to 'pull a lot of strings' for a deferment. Yet Michael says he will be among those who 'risk their lives for their country.' Sonny gets so angry that he has to be restrained when he lunges across the dining table to strike his brother. Don Vito arrives and all rush out to greet him.[58]

All but Michael, the future godfather, who remains quietly seated. He drinks two glasses of wine, gaining strength to withstand his father's displeasure (though we recall that his father saw a different future for this son), and toasting his own victory: of having struck at the core of authority, of having escaped the family, and (ironically) of having succeeded over two elder brothers to the position of authority. The Don's empty chair seems in silent communion with the young Michael. This signification of absence and wine-drinking plenitude renews the oppositions in Michael's memory at a point where their collapse in Nevada has been accomplished.

This scene fades to an even earlier one, the family visit to Corleone in 1925. Michael is a little boy held up in his father's arms at a train window

for all to see; a revelation of the successor. 'Wave goodbye, Michael,' says
Don Vito in a soft haunting voice, truly out of the depths of Michael's
memory. The train is leaving, the relatives are waving, Don Tommasino
sits in a wheelchair, from having been wounded in the Don Ciccio assassination. This scene must stand in Michael's mind for loss itself. If the
father's birthday party represents his attack on authority, the progressive thrust of his individuality, this much earlier memory has a regressive movement, ultimately more profound. The voice of the father, the
ancient homeland, the gathered clan, the train shrouded in steam and
mystery, all are at the furthest possible distance from his present state.

In the film's finest expression of *photogénie*, the camera cuts to Michael
now seated alone outside his house and at lakeside. He wears a heavy
navy-blue sweater against the cold. Moments earlier the lake and mountains appeared in eerie twilight. Now the light is fading and suddenly the
screen darkens quickly as we move from realistic to symbolic time. We
see half his face in tight close-up. The cold light, the otherworldly, unforgiving mountains, the dark and silvery waters, and the silence seem like
the reflection of Michael's gaze turned inward, the mocking symbols of
his spiritual emptiness. Coppola decided against any non-diegetic sound
(another director might have played the *Godfather* leit-motif); nothing
distracts attention from the images, all of which bring us inward to Michael's consciousness.[59] 'His hand covers his mouth and nose; only his
right eye and the deep wrinkles around it are clearly visible,' writes John
Hess; 'it's the two eyes which give us "perspective," and Michael never
had any.'[60] Yet Michael has this moment of recognition. The all-powerful
godfather knows the secret; his power has destroyed everything that he
wanted. The working title for *Godfather II*, 'The Death of Michael Corleone,' is apropos; 'sitting there alone,' Michael is 'a living corpse.'[61] In
the economy of the two films, plenitude that is meant to eliminate desire
has fed upon itself to the point of absence: death-in-life. Having pursued
the matter to its simplest radicals, false plenitude as absence, would Coppola have anything further to say on the subject? There matters rested
for sixteen years.

V

Coppola thought his best work followed *Godfather I* and *II*. Yet only these
films have maintained a continuance of esteem, not *Rumble Fish* (1983),
not *Peggy Sue Got Married* (1986), not *Dracula* (1992), not even *Apocalypse
Now* (1979), and especially not *Godfather III*. 'Characters in *The Sopranos*'

– and they should know – 'have mentioned *The Godfather* trilogy often throughout the run of the series, referring simply to *One* or *Two*. (Never *Three*.)'[62] It is as if an uninspired pupil of the master did the third panel of the triptych to which it is connected by screws and back-joints and not, like the first two, to each other by recurrent themes, subtle characterization, pictorial grandeur, and symbolic linkages. The results might not have been so disturbing were it a totally different film but, in completing the trilogy, it was inevitably compared to its magisterial predecessors. A filmmaker who admires the operatic gesture should know the truth of Wagner's remark: 'The end is everything!' What, then, of the end of 'The Godfather'?

For years Coppola resisted making another sequel and succumbed only out of financial duress. '[He] asked for six months to develop a story and script. [Paramount head Frank] Mancuso gave him six weeks.'[63] He and Puzo rented a suite in a Reno hotel: 'We'd work for hours, and when we ran out of ideas, we'd go down to the casino.'[64] One hopes they had better luck at the gaming tables. *Apocalypse Now* should have taught him that such an approach is too uncertain for a large-scale, multifaceted work.[65] With a looming deadline, Coppola was attempting both to develop a complex narrative and to relate it, however loosely, to films shot a decade and a half earlier. Also, he wanted to bring the story to a definitive conclusion with Michael's actual death thirty-nine years later in Sicily. Production designer Dean Tavoularis said Coppola kept changing the script on the set ('every day'). Often seen as an Italian trait, improvisation functions best with solo performers or a troupe that performs regularly together, as in commedia dell'arte, not with a major film production. George Hamilton recalled Coppola's presenting him with five pages to learn overnight, only to cancel them in the morning: 'He'd say "Just improvise with those lines I gave you." It got to the point where I just threw my lines away ... we were never allowed to do that when I started, with Minnelli.' Hamilton's hair was dyed so often that it became brittle and broke off at the touch; Coppola could not decide on its colour – a telling emblem of failure in preparation. Line producer Chuck Mulvehill tracked the budget; scenes were cut, including Michael's funeral procession. Cast members came and went, some at the last minute. These matters weighed upon Coppola: 'He knew in his heart of hearts. He'd been there before. Francis said to me, "Where did we go wrong?"'[66]

If there is an overarching theme that unifies *Godfather III* it is religion – spiritual, institutional, popular, ceremonial, commercial. Though it was artistically adventuresome to move the trilogy into new territory, Coppola was not on solid ground, religion never having been one of his central concerns.[67] His films lack spirituality; this is not a criticism, only a statement of fact; one cannot speak of Italian Catholic immanence the way one could, for example, in Scorsese or DeLillo. The main story links the Corleone family to the Vatican banking scandal that broke out in the early years of John Paul II's papacy and led to the collapse of the Banco Ambrosiano in 1982, a period that the film compresses into 1978–79. Ritual in *Godfather I* and *II* marked the stages of life and emphasized the disparity between formal ideals and human depravity. In *Godfather III* religion takes on a more varied role: touristic views of old St Patrick's and the Vatican, a conclave in the Sistine Chapel, crowds waiting for the white smoke of election, a plot based on the implausible rumour that the new pope, reformist-minded John Paul I, was poisoned after little over a month on the papal throne. Archbishop Gilday (Donal Donnelly), head of the Vatican bank, becomes involved in a giant swindle, making for a forced parallel between high Church operatives and the mob underworld. 'It's the Borgias all over again,' Michael says; actually it is the Rome of modern canard. Coppola and Puzo gothicize (and trivialize) the Church, perpetuating the old, 'northern' prejudice at variance with an otherwise southern Italian perspective. But they also 'capitalize' the Church, to accommodate their laboured broadside against corporate business.[68] However, in testing Michael's potential for repentance, the film has perhaps the one genuine moment of spirituality in the entire *Godfather* trilogy: his confession to Cardinal Lamberto (Raf Vallone).

Besides the shaky plot, other features of *Godfather III* tell of haste and artistic decline. Compared to the crisp dialogue of the earlier films, *Godfather III* has few specimens of equal quality: Mary Corleone (Sofia Coppola) announces that her father has established the Vito Corleone Foundation 'dedicated to the resurrection of Sicily.' From her lips the phrase sounds sweetly innocent; yet she unconsciously implicates the Mafia in Sicily's 'death' and redemption by money. She hands a one hundred million dollar cheque to Gilday (gilded, gliding) with 'Don't spend it all in one place': the cliché is ironized because he will lose it all in one colossal swindle, and will pay the price. For the most part, however, the script is stilted and banal. On a walk in the Sicilian countryside Anthony (Franc D'Ambrosio) asks his father, 'Why is such a beautiful country so violent?' Michael replies ponderously: 'History.' When Father Andrew Hagen (John Savage), son of the late wily consigliere, departs New York for Rome, Michael's financial advisor B.J. Harrison (George Hamilton) fusses with his bacon and eggs: 'If you hear any rumors flying around the Vatican you let me know, all right?' Hilarious is Michael's paratactic response to a threat of assassination: 'The pope has powerful enemies. We may not be in time to save him. Now let's go back to the opera.'

The earlier films had sententious one-liners, some of which have passed into common usage. In *Godfather III* the pressure to write them pushed Puzo and Coppola to clutch at truisms: 'Never hate your enemies – it affects your judgment'; 'In today's world the power to absolve debt is greater than the power of forgiveness'; 'Finance is a gun; politics is knowing when to pull the trigger'; 'Even the strongest man needs friends'; 'Your enemies always get strong on what you leave behind'; 'When they come at you, they'll come at those you love'; 'Power wears out those who have it'; 'It's dangerous to be an honest man'; 'Every family has bad memories.' The one-liner is a debased form that tries to dazzle and portend, and when it does not, it calls attention to a larger failure of dialogue; in some ways the one-liner is pretentiously anti-dialogue. Coppola and Puzo had lost their ear for language; perhaps too much time had elapsed between films for them to rekindle the magic.

They also fail to name characters well. In *I* and *II* there are the sinister-sounding, clearly southern Italian names Tattaglia, Sollozzo, and Neri; the slight, treacherous Paulie Gatto; the silvery, genial, 'five-angels' Pentangeli; the pot-bellied, jesting, sardonic Clemenza; the tough, blunt Luca Brasi; the slick Barzini; the raffish Johnny Ola; the smooth, corrupt Senator Pat Geary; the flaccid playboy Merle Johnson; the solid Tom Hagen; a police captain named McCluskey. These names suited their characters and the actors who inhabited them. In *Godfather III* the main rival is Altobello (tall, beautiful) (Eli Wallach), a name for a matinee idol without a suggestion of menace. Similarly, Mancini (*mancino*, treacherous) is stage Italian, as is Abbandando; Lamberto is colourless. The flimsy *Zasa* (Joe Mantegna) for the other rival sounds like Zsa Zsa Gabor or Zazu Pitts; Coppola could not restrain a narcissistic identification with the script so he took an inappropriate name from his mother's side of the family.[69]

As with the dialogue and naming, so the symbolism of *Godfather III* has elements of self-parody. With thirteen references to oranges in *Godfather I* and eight in *Godfather II*, this symbol for life and death had played itself out.[70] Yet *Godfather III* opens with a bowl of glowing oranges, first of ten references: oranges topple from the table during the helicopter attack that wipes out many of the old dons. Al Neri peels an orange when he recounts the attack, and sets a glass of orange juice next to the diabetic Michael when Altobello visits him. Joey Zasa dodges an orange stand in Little Italy just before he is gunned down – why not a tomato stand for a change? In the revenge-plotting Vincent Mancini (Andy Garcia) holds an orange, and there are oranges on the table when Calo informs Michael that Don Tommasino (Vittorio Duse) has been assassinated. Suffering a diabetic attack at the Vatican, Michael is given a tumbler of orange juice, and recovers. Altobello throws an orange to the assassin that he has hired. Nor is nature symbolism handled with more care. The Sicilian countryside with humble shepherds and animals resembles travel posters: in the late 1970s this is not the real Sicily. Coppola may have wanted his shot of the Temple of Segesta to be proleptic of the tragic events on the steps of the neoclassical Teatro Massimo; it is merely touristic. At times, however, Coppola shows a sureness of touch. An 'Ellis Ambulance' brings Michael to the hospital after a diabetic attack, recalling the rebirth that immigrants associate with Ellis Island; and Michael survives. Mischievous children play like putti at family events; they sneak behind a blood-red table drapery for 'The Vito Corleone Foundation,' recalling little Vito hiding under a blanket in a donkey cart.

The casting of *Godfather III* further illustrates an exhausted invention. In response to criticism of the earlier films, Coppola made an effort to increase the importance of women. 'Kay resumes a position of equality with Michael in their relationship with their children,' writes Geoff Fordham, 'while Connie, in an assumption of responsibility that would have been unthinkable to her mother, effectively assumes the role of Don during Michael's illness.'[71] If Coppola were to have been successful, though, he would have had to make Kay arrive at the opening ceremony with an escort instead of a husband (and, too obviously, a judge), for the door to be open for a renewal of romance in those later scenes when she and Michael are together in Sicily. It is not in her character to violate her Puritan New England principles and commit adultery, nor in his to tempt her. Given this dead end, it would have been better to have Michael find a new love interest in Sicily, where he had found his first wife. Dressed in loops of dark brocade, a prematurely aged *comare* or *strega*, Connie wrings her hands and thirsts for vengeance. She gives the go-ahead to kill Zasa, something Michael would not have allowed. When she says that the dons will now fear him (had he lost his authority?), he replies, 'Maybe they should fear *you*.' This is supposed to boost her stature. She is relieved when Vincent takes over as godfather, reassuring Michael: 'Vincent knows what to do. Come on outside. Take a rest and – don't think about it,' a pearl of dialogue. She turns out to be woefully wrong.

While Vincent's newness is an asset to the trilogy and while he conveys the ruthless animal aggression of a rising don, the script deprives him of the mental address and sheer *daimon* to inherit the mantle of the imperial godfathers (Brando, De Niro, Pacino). Sonny's illegitimate son, he arrives with his mother Lucy (Jeannie Linero) at the opening party where he starts a brawl to get in. Connie must remind Michael that Vincent is Sonny's child by his mistress. If Vincent is so unknown, why does Michael then tell us that he has followed Vincent's progress and taken care of him all his life, and that he offered him the choice between working 'in the legitimate world' or the underworld? A flashback might have shown Vincent hanging around the margins of the family as a tough, little kid (like young Henry Hill in Scorsese's *GoodFellas*), hoping to gain a foothold, observing the adult world with fascination, and gradually being included. A contrast could have been made with Anthony as foil; young Vincent could have roughed up young Anthony, and Michael might have been impressed. A nice parallel could have been drawn between Michael's familial attentiveness and Don Vito's with the abandoned boy Tom Hagen. When Vincent bites the ear of Joey Zasa, Michael expostulates, 'Temper like his father,' doubting his suitability as heir from the start. After Vincent kills two of Zasa's men, Michael says he should have gone to the police, 'All right, you are what you are. It's your nature.' Though aware of his 'nature,' that Vincent lacks a godfather's cleverness and icy restraint, Michael nonetheless anoints him, something totally out of character. When Vincent receives the homage as the new godfather, echoing scenes of homage in both *I* and *II*, he extends his hand to be kissed as if he were posing for Armani or getting a manicure. The effect is comic reduction, not solemn ritual. His inadequacies prove disastrous at the opera, where he cannot protect the family, thinking everything is under control when a single assassin is killing one guard after another, finally killing Mary.

Godfather I and *II* overflowed with unforgettable minor characters: Luca Brasi, Clemenza, Pentangeli, Senator Geary, Barzini, Mama Corleone, Sollozzo, Capt. McCluskey, Apollonia, Don Ciccio, played by character actors and actresses who could assert their identity indelibly in a few seconds. Similarly, in *Godfather III*, the business magnate Lucchesi (Enzo Robutti) is a pure Italian type of the understated kind, to be encountered over the centuries in politics, in the church, in high finance, at home in the world. One can view them, entrepreneurial, elegantly dressed, enigmatic with their faintly smiling faces, in the political pages of Italian magazines to this day. 'Italian politics have had these kind of men for centuries,' observes Michael, then justifies his own conduct with a specious logic unworthy of his intelligence, 'they're the true Mafia.'[72] Frederick Keinszig (Helmut Berger), the Vatican's chief accountant, is a decadent aristocrat; Don Tommasino has a Sicilian rustic's natural gravitas. Cardinal Lamberto has physical and moral presence; as the only character in the film that can hold his own against Michael, he delivers with immense force. Anthony conveys a youthful idealism and plays a convincing Turiddu in the opera scene; Mary proves her strength and integrity. Both Michael's children, innocents uncorrupted by their family, represent the hope of the next generation.

Generally, however, Coppola gives his characters too little material with which to establish themselves. Inspired supposedly by the 'dapper don' John Gotti, Joey Zasa is an affected suburbanite, not a potential godfather.[73] The other antagonist, Mafia don Altobello, would not scare a fly.[74] Gilday is so obviously slippery where at least he should have *seemed* innocuous; his nervous smoking habit is supposedly evidence of moral corruption, a puritanical American attitude; Coppola is apparently unaware that Italian priests smoke (or used to) heavily and nobody in Italy sees it as a sin. When Father Andrew shows up for his leave-taking at Michael's breakfast table, he brandishes airline tickets like a greenhorn. The scene has no purpose other than to inform of his going to Rome and should imply he will be doing something useful to the plot, i.e., he could have strengthened the Vatican scenes by being a Mafia plant, found out by his enemies and murdered in the crossfire at the end, another victim. Coppola did not waste such opportunities in the earlier films. B.J. Harrison, the WASP advisor, is so solid it is a pity he does not do more; he manages always to look both comfortably part of the action and outside of it.

Perhaps the weakest link in the script is neither the improbable plotting nor frail characterization, but the pervasive mood of weary nostalgia. Returning actors assume their former characters as in a pantomime. Though some attempt to give matters a fresh spin, there is nothing sufficiently original or arresting in the action to carry forward the whole *Godfather* sequence into new terrain, something desperately needed so as not to appear derivative. The finest moments in *Godfather III* belong to Michael, particularly his scenes of Aristotelian recognition and attempted, if ultimately failed, repentance.[75] A film worthy of its predecessors might have been built around his middle-aged predicaments and wish to escape the underworld, without the Vatican chicanery. Ill, older than his fifty-nine years, in an autumnal mood from the outset, he wants to redeem himself in his own as well as his family's eyes.

VI

Having failed to deliver original material, 'new' in Eliot's sense, Coppola did what artists often do and fell back on familiar patterns. *Godfather III* opens with the polarized structure: plenitude and absence, family and business, a celebration party connected with a religious ceremony and the godfather's office. But first a lonely trumpet solo plays Rota's *Godfather* theme. The camera pans across the desolate estate at Lake Tahoe; autumn leaves blow across the grounds under cold, cloudy skies; a statue of the Madonna stands neglected; as the orchestral music enters quietly, flotsam clogs the docks, the camera moves into the dusty interior of the house with a doll and toy cart ... at which point, in a voiceover, Michael begins to read the letter he is writing: 'My dear children, it is now better than several years since I moved to New York, and I haven't seen you as much as I would like.' The abandoned estate images are simultaneous with Michael's writing; if he had been living there, it would not be run down. Connecting back to the end of *Godfather II*, the images exist in the neutral space of epic objectivity, as with Homer's 'long view' on the destruction of Troy and its reclamation by nature in *Iliad* XII. Michael now invites his children to his investiture into the Order of St Sebastian to demonstrate his long-sought public acceptance and to bring the family together: 'the only wealth in this world is children, more than all the money and power on Earth.' Perhaps the key line in *Godfather III*, this is no pious sentiment from a person with a great deal of money and power, but a deeply felt commitment to the next generation. The camera pans slowly across his desk with a photograph of his two children, until he himself appears in a shot reverse shot completing the letter we have just heard: 'I look forward to a new period of harmony in our lives.'

Cut to the investiture ceremony at old St Patrick's on Mott Street, Little Italy: Michael kneels at the altar, with Mary, Anthony, and Connie seated in the front pew, and with Harrison and other members of the family and friends behind them: 'Perhaps you might prevail upon your mother to come to this celebration,' continues the voiceover. While Gilday officiates in Latin, the language of the sacred, Michael recalls his brother Fredo, whom he ordered executed; the camera cuts to Fredo in the boat, saying his Hail Mary; then, back to the ceremony; then, to Michael's watching from the estate while Fredo is shot dead. Cut back to the church, as Joey Zasa enters with his bodyguard, and just as the ceremony ends, Kay with her husband; the children persuaded her to come. Joey shows disrespect by entering in the middle; Kay, even more, by missing the whole ceremony. The first part of the opening scene is Coppola at his best, the free indirect style applied to film. He excels in these fluid movements, here indicating a central reality together with Michael's reflections and memories, from present to past and back again. In just minutes it appears *Godfather II* and *III* have been sutured.

Then matters go artistically wrong. The opening pattern was set with Connie's wedding reception in *Godfather I;* decline in *Godfather II* was indicated by Anthony's Holy Communion party, an excuse for business conducted inside the house. The repetition of this dual pattern a third time takes away surprise and saps the film of energy at the outset. Held in Michael's New York apartment and comprising almost one fifth of the entire script, the scene oscillates between the party festivities and the godfather's office. There are signs of further moral deterioration. Unlike the earlier films that contrasted interior with exterior scenes, the lighting of the party and the office, two interiors, is almost the same: the worlds are virtually indistinguishable. Similarly, the Corleones have even lost the ability to host a good *festa* in *famiglia;* there is plenitude, but only in the nature of consumption, not in familial or personal fulfilment. On the whole, the party comes off in slapdash fashion; Coppola does not create a coherent sense of space; instead of feeling claustrophobic, one is confused. Even the music is less well integrated; Connie and the children sing the relatively unknown Italian American song 'Friscalettu' (Little Whistle): a donkey song would have tied in better with the film's climax and the trilogy as a whole. Rota had died; the film suffers from his absence.

Kay's arrival provides for a transition from the party to the office. Michael greets her with an offer of some cake, which she refuses; his food is his power. She begins on a snide note, congratulating him for 'an honor' that is 'a little expensive' (one hundred million dollars). Michael compliments her looks – they have not seen each other in eight years – but she has come on business and they move to the office. Kay urges him to let their son quit law school, when Anthony himself steps in, not so much to plead his cause but to announce his decision: he is going to be an opera singer. Michael invites his son to work for him. 'I will always be your son,' replies Anthony, 'but I will never have anything to do with your business,' underlining too heavily the polar conflict. Ironically, Anthony answers Don Vito's hope of succeeding in the mainstream, which had been his hope for Michael. After Anthony leaves, Kay says their son is as stubborn and determined as he was, then pours oil on the fire: 'Tony knows you killed Fredo.' Taken aback, Michael asks why she has come: Simply to recall the past? He says that he always acted to save the family, and not for himself: these were his 'reasons.' 'That's your big thing, Michael, Reason. Backed up by murder.' Michael responds, 'You hate me.' 'No, I don't hate you. I dread you' (another blatant example of the poor script). In the end, he agrees to support Anthony's choice.

Then come the dons: Altobello enters ostensibly to donate one million dollars to the Corleone Foundation, in fact to sniff out whether Michael is really going into retirement. Zasa awards Michael a plaque as the Meucci Foundation's Man of the Year.[76] But Zasa, too, has other reasons for the visit: 'I have a stone in my shoe,' an agricultural saying by this point far from the experience of the godfathers (Altobello also employs it). Zasa complains that Vincent cannot take orders and that he disapproves of selling drugs in the old neighbourhood (like Don Vito). Michael calls for Vincent. Seated in his godfather's chair, Michael reminds Vincent that Zasa owns the old 'Corleone family business' and 'out of the kindness of his heart' Zasa gave him 'a job in his family' (more euphemism). 'Contrary to my advice, you took the job. I'd offered you something, better, in the legitimate world.' This is the first of six times the word 'legitimate' is heard, five by Michael, who also uses 'illegitimate' once. The choice of going legitimate, so close to Michael's own 'dream' for himself, had been rejected by Vincent, though not by Anthony. Connie's presence in the office is unusual, but times have changed. She is in league with her nephew, complaining of drugs in the old neighbourhood with that sudden upwelling of scruple typical of her family (her 'we're not murderers' recalls Don Vito's comment on Buonasera). 'That's the past, Connie,' Michael reminds her, then Vincent blurts out: 'I could just kill this bastard.' 'So kill him,' replies Michael quite matter-of-factly to the startled group, 'What has all this have to do with me?' The film comes to life in such moments. Michael refuses Vincent's request to work for him ('I don't need tough guys – I need more lawyers') and insists that he make peace with Zasa. When Vincent and Zasa have the ritual kiss of peace, Zasa whispers '*bastardo*' and Vincent bites hard and deep into Zasa's ear. Biting the ear just enough to draw a drop of blood indicates a challenge, according to the Sicilian custom. Vincent's bite perverts the ritual and, probably unintentionally on Coppola's part, seriously disturbs the audience's relation to Vincent's character; crude, bestial behaviour is not easily forgotten or forgiven. But as he spits out the blood, Connie looks on approvingly; even Michael is impressed – it may recall his own killing of McCluskey and Sollozzo – and decides to let him work for him. When the family picture is taken, Michael asks him to stand in it, surely for the first time.

Mary introduced the financial theme in presenting Gilday with the Corleone Foundation's gift. Afterward, in a private meeting, Gilday asks for Michael's help, 'and not just to light a little candle.' It appears that Gilday had been a good Church fund-raiser and was promoted to the post of Vatican head banker.[77] Yet, as he admits, he is not a banker and the Vatican is now $700 million in debt. Michael corrects Gilday: $769 million. A deal is in the making to further Michael's legitimacy: he will deposit $500 million in the Vatican bank to cover their debt *if* the Vatican agrees to hand over controlling interest in International Immobiliare, the European real estate holding corporation. The word *immobiliare* means 'immovable,' e.g., real estate; this puns on the unmoved mover, God; the 'international' company is a satanic parody. Gilday guarantees that it is only a formality to have the pope sign off on the deal. Michael does not suspect that Gilday is part of a vast scam to rob investors. More likely, Gilday was scammed himself and has joined ranks with the crooks to get out of a hole. How Michael could be fooled by so patent a swindle (and swindler) indicates failing powers or a weak script. Later Altobello urges Michael to open up Immobiliare to the dons' scamming. In the characteristic mix of religion, business, and family, Altobello claims that while the old dons 'worship' Michael, they think he 'abandoned' them; they want to be a 'family' and 'purify' (i.e., launder) their money. Michael stiffens: 'Immobiliare must be legitimate.' Still, he agrees to sit down with the dons; he intends to retire and pay them off, 'so there are no debts or grudges.'

The first signs of trouble occur at the Immobiliare shareholders meeting under Lucchesi in Rome, where a consortium of investors stage a surprise vote against Michael's takeover. Harrison announces that their approval makes absolutely no difference since the Vatican has cast its vote. Now, however, Keinszig informs that Pope Paul has not yet signed over Vatican control, and Gilday hastens to add that the pope is gravely ill. What if he dies? demands Harrison, aware of the risk he has taken with Michael's fortune. Although, to prevent open confrontation, Michael rises to lead in prayers for the pope's recovery, he vents his fury soon afterwards. Lucchesi offers Michael a choice: 'We'll gladly put you at the helm of our little fleet. But our ships must all sail in the same direction.' He threatens that, with papal approval still pending, the money that Michael has deposited will be siphoned away by the European swindlers unless Michael agrees to work with them. That some money may have already been lost only strengthens the threat. Michael has been challenged on both sides of the Atlantic.

At the gathering of the dons Michael hands out generous sums from his casino profits (one exults, 'Fifty million dollars').[78] Zasa gets nothing and feels cheated for having served the Commission without receiving his share. The script fails again: he comes across as vain and peevish: 'It's true – I make more of a *bella figura*, that is my nature.' No godfather would have survived uttering that line, in real life or in the earlier *Godfathers*. As a rich tray of jewels is passed around and the dons each pick a gift as if it were pastry, some grumble that Immobiliare should not be off-limits: it 'is already laundering money in Peru,' 'in Nassau'; 'we should wet our beaks a little.' Michael is alarmed that his operation is so exposed; his secrets are known.[79] The feast is interrupted by the helicopter attack in which many dons are gunned down. The publicity that such an attack on a mob conclave would receive makes any such action unlikely among these masters of secrecy, though there is a historical model. According to Joe Bonanno in *A Man of Honor*, at the close of the Castellammerese War (1929–31), in a resort near Wappingers Falls, New York, Salvatore Maranzano threatened a meeting of bosses by arranging for a plane armed with machine guns to circle overhead; no shots were fired.

Michael escapes unscathed. Though he knows that Zasa lacks the ambition, the backing, and the guts to carry out the attack on his own, 'I respect what he has done. The new overthrows the old.' More sententiousness: how placidly he accepts and even 'respects' the wiping out of his colleagues on the Commission, just the usual conflict between generations. In another plot lapse, though Altobello's well-timed departure should have made him an obvious ringleader, he avoids suspicion. Taking up the legitimacy theme, Michael insists, 'I'm a businessman, first, foremost. I want no further conflict with anyone.' Here he utters the much-parodied line, 'Just when I thought I was out, they pull me back in,' blaming others, not himself.[80] As he suffers a diabetic stroke he says, 'Our true enemy has not yet shown his face,' falling down with the names 'Altobello' and 'Fredo' on his lips; Altobello, the enemy; Fredo, the guilt from whose killing is being overused to drive the plot.

During Michael's convalescence, Vincent eliminates Zasa, wrongly thinking him to be the source of Michael's problems. The assassination occurs during a religious procession of the Madonna in Little Italy, a sacrilege that links this scene to the film's broader religious thematic. Beneath a deathly whitish gray sky, which minutes before had been clear and sunny, Zasa runs down an empty street and is shot dead by Vincent disguised as a policeman on horseback. This scene suffers by comparison to its model in *Godfather II*. In the earlier film the crowds were thick and jostling, the atmosphere tangible with festivity; in *Godfather III* the crowds are so thin that one wonders if lack of funds meant fewer extras, and the atmosphere seems consequently joyless. In the earlier film, young Vito Corleone crosses the rooftops in a movement counter to the street procession (crossing or violating its spirit) and kills Fanucci; in the second, most improbably, the assassins are participants in the procession, wearing masks and white robes and carrying machine guns, and yet, despite the element of surprise, they miss their prey and are all shot dead. It is an additional irony that the earlier film, though shot on a Hollywood set, looks more real that the later one shot on New York streets.

Upon his recovery Michael chastises Vincent, Connie, and Neri for their decision to kill Zasa, who was never high enough to be the source of trouble. Now there will be recriminations, if not all-out war among the dons, making it more difficult than ever to withdraw from the fray. Michael warns Vincent to stop seeing his daughter because it is 'too dangerous,' anticipating the scene when he makes it the condition of being godfather. When Altobello visits and urges Michael to retire, Michael diverts attention by inquiring about the Italians who cause so much trouble with his investments. They decide to meet in Palermo where his son will make his operatic debut.

The last part of the film takes place in Sicily. Michael learns that Altobello has already been playing peacekeeper between the American and Sicilian Mafia: he is 'a saint of reason,' says the gullible Don Tommasino, an example of how religious language permeates the criminal atmosphere. The 'saint' is at the moment hiring an assassin to kill Michael and Don Tommasino himself (all the dons in this film – Michael, Altobello, Vincent, Tommasino – have mental and verbal lapses). As head of the Commission, Michael would have known that Altobello was the traditional go-between. During this conversation Vincent holds an orange, foreshadowing execution. Michael wants to know who might be strong enough to order the Atlantic City massacre and to pressure the Vatican deal. 'Only Lucchesi can reach between these two worlds,' replies Don Tommasino in delphic tones, though help will come from Cardinal Lamberto, a 'wise and good man, very influential.' For Tommasino, Michael deals with 'crooks' without honour; Michael affirms his sense of honour with a thumping 'my word is final.' In the plot's most implausible move, Michael advises Vincent to win Altobello's confidence by convincing him that he (Vincent) wants to betray Michael. Surely Altobello would not be hoodwinked by such a simple trick. Vincent does as he is told, and as Coppola needs to compress, Vincent even meets Lucchesi at Altobello's.

'If we'd known of his [Vincent's] existence,' Altobello brags in front of Vincent, 'we would never have backed Joey [Zasa].' Foolishly, Vincent thinks he has won their confidence.

A sunny cloister in the Vatican, with rose vines climbing the columns, is the setting for the unexpected confession. Michael informs Cardinal Lamberto that he has been victim of a swindle with the Vatican bank as the mediator and guarantor. In retrospect, it seems strange that a respected cardinal would take counsel from a Mafia don. Yet this secret knowledge will be useful to Lamberto in a matter of weeks when he becomes pope. Lamberto takes a stone from a fountain and cracks it open: it is dry. So, he says, Christianity has surrounded Europeans for centuries and has not penetrated to the core. Michael feels the onset of a diabetic attack that is checked by a glass of orange juice. He looks weak, vulnerable, and even undignified. As he recovers, Lamberto asks him if he wants to make his confession. Michael says he has not confessed in thirty years and is 'beyond redemption.' At Lamberto's gentle counselling Michael proceeds, and when he confesses the murder of Fredo, he breaks down in tears. 'Your sins are terrible, and it is just that you suffer,' responds Lamberto; 'your life could be redeemed, but I know that you don't believe that. You will not change.' Yet Michael's contriteness is acknowledged by distant church bells, tolling for Paul VI. Had Coppola more scenes of this quality, he might have had his third masterpiece.

When Connie rebukes him for telling 'secrets' to a stranger, Michael replies in a confessional mode. 'All my life I kept trying to go up in society,' he says, 'where everything higher up was legal, straight. But the higher I go, the crookeder it becomes. How in the hell does it end?' This is Coppola's belief that 'it's the same everywhere,' his penchant for making indiscriminate connections among capitalism, religion, Mafia, government, Italy, and America. Michael's 'politics and crime – they're the same thing,' that is, everyone is corrupt, is a cynical excuse for his own corruption, a refusal to believe that anything is truly 'legitimate.' If Michael had shown the same kind of shoddy thinking as Francis Ford Coppola in this film, he could never have become a godfather.

Kay joins him in Palermo for their son's debut.[81] Perhaps hoping to reignite their passion, he invites her to tour western Sicily that she might better understand him. He plays the chauffeur to avoid having a bodyguard. But the scenes never take fire; they act like middle-aged tourists trying to find something to do – a drive, a wedding party, a 'violent' puppet show. 'I love this country,' he says, though nothing in his actions or even his voice conveys it. 'Though terrible things have happened to its people through its history, they still expect good rather than bad will happen to them.' 'Sort of like me and you, huh?' she replies. Such is the tenor of the conversation. He even protests that he had no choice but to defend his father and save his family: 'You were all that I loved, valued, most in the world. And, I'm losing you – I lost you – anyway. You're gone, and it was all for nothing – so – you have to understand. I had a whole different destiny planned.' This is his third confession and he asks Kay to 'forgive' him. In her own way, she does, admitting 'I always loved you, Michael. I always – I always will.' But news of Don Tommasino's assassination cuts short the scene – which had no where to go, given Kay's marriage and principles – and proves to Kay that they are back where they started.

Soon after his election, Lamberto is reported investigating Vatican finances and Keinszig is missing. Michael attends the funeral of Don Tommasino. As in his scenes with Lamberto, Connie, and Kay, he gives a rare glimpse into his motivations in his words to this dead father-figure: 'You could have lived a little longer. I could be closer to my dream.' 'Why was I so feared, and you so loved? ... I wanted to do good.' What good? The Vito Corleone Foundation? We have too little evidence of concrete action. 'I swear, on the lives of my children: Give me a chance to redeem myself, and I will sin no more.' His oath would have greater impact if Don Tommasino had a stronger role in the film and we knew why he was so loved: the standard of comparison is missing. Still, Michael's lines are meant to bring matters to a head because in a hastily arranged Mafia ceremony he hands over power to Vincent, whose last name is changed from Mancini to Corleone. Vincent agrees to end his affair with Mary, echoing the Wagnerian theme of the renunciation of love for the sake of power. Of the four confessional scenes, only the Lamberto one is adequately realized, and it too needed more dialogue and less orange hysterics to probe into the deeper levels of Michael's character.

As in *Godfather I* and *II*, plotlines converge by collision montage to a climax;[82] only in *Godfather III*, with more plotlines, the sequencing of segments proceeds more rapidly, like the stretto of a finale. The prelude from Mascagni's *Cavalleria Rusticana* creates a sombre mood, as do shots of Palermo's Porta Felice and Teatro Massimo at nightfall. This latter, the masterpiece (1897) of Sicilian architect Giovanni Basile, is a stage-set in itself with a neoclassical-revival façade lending pathos and dignity to the scenes about to unfold.[83] When the Corleones arrive, Altobello whispers to Vincent, '*Et tu*, Vincenzo,' histrionic to the last, citing Caesar's (Michael's) dying words to Brutus (Vincent). 'You can't save him,' Altobello cautions, 'He's lost.' 'Enjoy the opera,' responds Vincent, playing close to the vest, 'all taken care of.' Inside, Connie greets the old don with a ribboned box of poisoned cannoli for his eightieth birthday. He makes certain that she tests one first. A candied orange drop, fatal citron, floats on the ricotta, 'the corruption of Italian food to imply the ultimate disintegration of *la famiglia Corleone.*'[84] She pretends to eat a bit; no don who survived to be eighty would fall for such an act. Harrison brings Michael the welcome news that the new pope, who is 'cleaning house,' has signed off on the Immobiliare deal, keeping up his end of the bargain. Doubtless what mischief Vincent has planned will assist his house cleaning. Family and friends gather in the lobby to toast Anthony's success, to be echoed in the opera's drinking scene. Then, as Michael and Kay preside in the royal box and everyone settles down to enjoy an evening at the opera, the assassin Mosca (Mario Donatone), disguised as a priest, files in with a clerical party.

Why did Coppola choose opera with which to cross-cut his climax, and why *Cavalleria Rusticana?* The family had shown no interest in opera in the earlier films; Anthony's desire to be an opera singer seems insufficient to propel a major scene; Michael cannot even pronounce its title. The Sicilian connection is more suggestive. Set in a Sicilian village, the opera is based on the story and play by the Sicilian Giovanni Verga. Its principal themes are love, betrayal, and revenge. There is a challenge with a ritual biting of the ear and a duel. Taking place on Easter Sunday, the opera conveys the idea of redemption, which *Godfather III*'s preceding scenes had stressed; in *Godfather II* Don Ciccio had been assassinated on Palm Sunday, which would anticipate Michael's on Easter. Then, just as a heightened realism and pessimism characterize Coppola's trilogy, so *Cavalleria Rusticana* (1890) is a principal opera of verismo or naturalism and its music enhances the immediacy of the action, 'making it feel more direct and unmediated, rather than extending or distancing its events in traditional operatic fashion.'[85] (Many non-realist Italian films of the 1940s and 1950s owe their sound tracks to composers influenced by verismo, e.g., Visconti's *Ossessione,* Rossellini's *Il miracolo.*) These reasons were in its favour. On the other hand, a violent opera might seem to fall back on stereotypes, and this particular opera is in any case too obvious a choice. Its gravely nostalgic Intermezzo recently served in Scorsese's *Raging Bull* (1980) and became the unacknowledged anthem of Italian America. More significant, its action does not adequately mirror the film's. *Godfather III* is not about young persons' love, betrayal, and revenge, but about Michael's search for inner peace.

In the opera Turiddu, a young soldier, had come home to find his sweetheart Lola married to Alfio, a teamster. To make her jealous and win her back, Turiddu has seduced Santuzza. The opera opens on Easter morning; its action takes place in the town square flanked by the church and a wineshop owned by Turiddu's mother Lucia. While the chorus sings of love and spring, Santuzza visits Lucia to ask of Turiddu's whereabouts. Alfio enters on his horsecart and wants some wine; Lucia says her son has gone to fetch it in another town, but Alfio replies that he has seen him in the village. After the people enter the church, Santuzza tells Lucia about her son's conduct. Turiddu confronts Santuzza, and when he refuses to return to her, she betrays him. After the Intermezzo, Alfio challenges Turiddu to a duel. He bids farewell to his mother. Soon a peasant women rushes in screaming that Alfio has killed Turiddu.

Coppola excels in his presentation of the opera, holding his own against Franco Zeffirelli's 1982 filmed version. From the opera's sixty-eight minutes he excerpts fourteen, preserving the plotline, the Easter hymn alone being out of sequence. The prelude has already been heard as background music. When Turiddu sings the romantic 'Siciliana,' the camera catches Mary seeking Vincent's eye, but the new godfather looks away; he will not play Turiddu to her – Coppola should have realized the inappropriateness of the opera for this alone. Mosca enters the opera house with the other priests; Al Neri is riding on the train to Rome to kill Gilday; he taps his fingers on the box of cookies that hides a gun; it is in the rhythm of the suspenseful music of Alfio's arrival, which we now hear, with one of the musicians shaking the bells; then, with cracks of his whip, Alfio drives his mule cart on stage singing of his rugged life. Seen across the opera house, first in a full shot, then through Connie's opera glasses, Altobello mouths Alfio's lines, cannoli in hand; Alfio is *his* hero; he even jabs the air, conducting the staccato musical theme. Calo arrives at Lucchesi's house in Rome with a message.

Now that all the elements have been introduced, Coppola jumps over half the opera, including the Intermezzo, to Turiddu's flirting with Lola, and the cross-cutting picks up the pace. Mosca climbs to the upper boxes where he has hidden his rifle and kills a guard with a knife. Turiddu ends his drinking song to a burst of applause. Calo is searched for weapons at Lucchesi's home. In the challenge scene Alfio refuses the wine that Turiddu offers, and Turiddu throws it to the ground. Michael's guards confer with one another; Alfio chats with his friends. In his train compartment Neri eats a cookie and checks his gun. Turiddu accepts the challenge by a ritual kiss and a biting of the ear; the camera cuts to Vincent, who smiles. Mosca props up his rifle and aims at Michael in his sights, when he hears another guard. In an impassioned aria Turiddu admits his guilt but does not want to abandon Santuzza; unmoved, Alfio places his knife on the table. They will meet behind the orchard. Mosca stabs the second and third guards. These are the men Vincent bragged were 'the best.' The challenge scene brings the 'act' to an end to enthusiastic applause.[86]

For the second 'act' Coppola reaches back to the Easter hymn from the opera's pre-Intermezzo scenes, since this music would better accompany the Vatican action. Keinszig eyes his money on a table; Calo is searched by Lucchesi's guards; Neri's train approaches Rome. The chorus sings the *Regina Coeli* hymn as Gilday nervously sips a drink and a 'priest' brings poisoned tea to the pope, 'to help you sleep.' Keinszig, who has been tracked down, is suffocated with a rosary dropped on his mouth in profanation. As the hymn continues, an Easter procession winds across the stage with a raised statue of the Virgin. Harrison says something to Michael, who leaves the box; Father Hagen takes his place next to Kay. Having dispatched three guards, Mosca returns to his rifle only to see Father Hagen in his sights, and leaves to find his accomplice Lupo (Marino Masé). A nun checks on the pope, finds him dead, and runs out screaming as the camera cuts to the chorus singing a hymn to the dead Savior carried on the cross. As Michael and Harrison return to the box, the chorus lowers the cross to the ground, and places a black cloth over Christ. During these moments Altobello eats his last cannoli; it has taken more than one to kill him. With her opera glasses trained on him, Connie whispers 'Sleep, sleep, godfather,' and he slumps over dead. At the hymn's conclusion the risen Christ walks slowly down the steps of the church.[87]

Calo arrives at Lucchesi's office; Gilday, dressed in his purple robe as if for the sacrifice, climbs the long winding baroque staircase, the image of his own deviousness. Turiddu sings his powerful farewell to his mother, and as he runs off, the drumbeat sounds ominously. While in the opera this lasts only for a few seconds before the peasant women rushes in with the news of Turiddu's death, Coppola keeps the drum pounding throughout the rest of the montage, the several parts of which are taking place simultaneously in various parts of Rome and Palermo. Calo tells Lucchesi (in Italian) 'You have lost the faith of the people,' to which Lucchesi cynically responds, 'He who builds on the people builds on mud. And Michael Corleone's message?' Near the top of the staircase, emerging from the shadows, Neri shoots the mitred Gilday three times. Now, like the nun moments before, the peasant woman on stage screams news of Turiddu's death; Calo stabs Lucchesi with his own eyeglasses and is shot dead himself – he was willing to die to avenge his patron, Don Tommasino. The drumbeat ends and the music reaches its thunderous climax as the bloodied Gilday is seen falling down the staircase well; the camera at ground level records his long descent, a treacherous angel falling to eternal hell. In the final shots Keinszig's body hangs and twists from beneath a bridge in an expressionistic blue light, some of his ill-gotten bills falling into the Tiber, with St Peter's (too obviously) in the distance; and there is a bloody Lucchesi with his eyeglasses stuck in his throat. To the audience ovation, the actors take their bows.

Ronald Bergan praises this extended scenario as a 'superlative example of Coppola's use of montage, music, close-up, and sound to create a dramatic effect.'[88] Yet, though he has intercut five plotlines and subplotlines, the technique does not raise the content to a more meaningful level but rather calls attention to itself. In Eisensteinian montage, content and technique inform and enhance each other, as in the finale of *Godfather I*. In *III*, collision montage turns into a jamming, concatenated confusion. The poisoned tea, the assassin disguised as a priest, the nun screaming, the fallen angel, all belong to the gothic novel. The poisoned cannoli is a version of the same, an unconscious parody of the artistic appropriation of the cannoli in *Godfather I*. Also, the risen Christ who walks on stage and is meant to bring the redemption theme to an effective climax fails to connect cinematically or spiritually with Michael. Lamberto was right after all: he 'will not change.'

As Michael and his retinue descend the long staircase outside the opera house, Lupo brays like a donkey, the signal to Mosca. Donkey symbolism reverses itself, from stupidity to canniness, and evokes the rural past: such a signal could have occurred centuries ago. The braying links back to little Vito Andolini's singing the folk song 'Lu me sceccu malandrinu' in *II*: its refrain, an imitation of a donkey, is heard now. Such intelligent use of symbolism is rare in *Godfather III*, though it is common in the earlier films. Mosca hits Michael in the shoulder, shoots again, misses him but kills Mary, then hides in the crowd, where Vincent guns him down. The godfathers have not protected the family.

The child theme, which in *Godfather III* is how the desire for plenitude or fulfilment principally expresses itself, culminates at the opera, where his son's triumph is utterly swallowed up in Mary's death. The film had opened with Michael's seeking to become closer to his children. He had made Mary the head of the Corleone Foundation. Kay concedes that his children love him. He tells Mary, 'I would burn in hell to keep you safe.' His punishment is that she dies as a result of his failure to remove himself from the Mafia, and Coppola spares him nothing. Michael 'tries several times to scream – but no sound comes out. In fact, Al Pacino was actually screaming, but the sound was removed in the editing' – *all* sound, diegetic and non-diegetic, is removed – 'we are dealing here with an *absence* of sound,' writes Walter Murch; 'yet a fertile tension is created between what we see and what we would expect to hear, given the image. Finally, the scream bursts through, the tension is released.'[89] Michael's mouth is opened wide, painfully stretched, a mimesis of its subject matter, its void on the screen is the filmic equivalent of the absence, aggression (teeth), and death.[90]

Coppola saved Mascagni's Intermezzo for Michael's death in Corleone some eighteen years later in 1997. Completing the circle, Michael has left America to die in the land of his origins.[91] Coppola said Michael is 'a man looking for redemption, asking, "What have I done with my life, what have I done with my family?" I was more interested in the story from that point of view than creating yet another nemesis that Michael outsmarts.'[92] If one judges the film on what its director set out to do, the question remains unanswered or is answered in the negative. Michael sits alone in the courtyard; he looks small within the immense panorama. There is neither friend nor family. He falls on the ground and dies; an orange rolls off the table, and a dog comes to sniff him – a death totally lacking in dignity, the symbolism utterly worn out. The Intermezzo fades away; and while it resolves its own musical structure, with its desire for plenitude, the film's action has no such resolution, only an end of pain. One wonders if Coppola realized that the music and the action were at such odds, yet another example of the opera's inappropriateness.

In an earlier draft, the film script ended with a twenty-minute scene of Michael's funeral in Sicily, intercut with a collision montage of enemies being eliminated and Vincent triumphant, as his name suggests. Coppola dropped the scene to save money, instead cross-cutting the murders with the opera. In the film as we have it, Michael dies near where his grandmother was killed in 1901. Though it may be insufficiently indicated in the film, it makes sense in terms of the longing for return. Still, the end has a tacked-on quality, Michael deserved better, and so did Pacino.[93]

VII

Searching for answers to the downward slide of Coppola's career, one turns to his biographers. In 1988 Michael Goodwin and Naomi Wise, who had worked for Coppola in San Francisco, answered those critics who said that there was no decline because in the first place '*nothing* had happened.' Coppola directed four unsuccessful films before *Godfather I* and *II* and nothing 'great' afterward; 'maybe,' as these critics thought, 'he was never more than a moderately talented filmmaker who got lucky.' Goodwin and Wise correctly dismiss this argument, replying that the two *Godfathers* were not flukes, and neither were *The Conversation* and the first half of *Apocalypse Now*. For them, Coppola had burned out, like other directors with brief careers of superior film-making: Buster Keaton, Preston Sturges, Tony Richardson, John Sturges, Arthur Penn, Claude Chabrol, François Truffaut. Out of an 'obsessive hunger for the status of a great artist,' Coppola gambled on being an auteur and lost. Still, 'three and a half great movies outweigh and justify an infinitude of failures.'[94] This is more of a statement of the facts than an explanation of them.

In his biography, which ends with the casting of *Godfather III*, Peter Cowie stresses a few themes: *italianità*, technology, the Renaissance man. 'Nothing has influenced Coppola's life and work so dramatically as his Italian blood'; '[he] loves big, Italianate parties,' throws celebrity 'bashes' at his Napa Valley estate where Carroll Ballard remembers 'people from all over the world, and Francis holding court.'[95] The lifestyle expresses an expansive egocentricity of an innocent kind, a *padrone*'s ego satisfied only if guests and clients enjoy themselves. 'What brings me the greatest joy,' said Coppola, 'is the company of nice people and to be able to go through all the rituals with them, to eat dinner with them, cook with them, talk with them.'[96] For fullness of being, he tapped deeply into his own nature. However, this quality's dark side is lack of limit, one of Michael's flaws. Just after shooting *Apocalypse Now*, which cost him his fortune and some of his artistic independence, 'Francis was in a buoyant mood'; he boarded a private jet, stopped at Rome, went to Cannes 'for a peek at the film festival,' then Madrid for bullfighting, then on to London and New York.[97] Should we be impressed by these exploits? Is this an artist's life? Hemingway fell into this trap. The desire for plenitude went out of control, pleasure turning into its opposite from excess (as his Mediterranean side should have warned him). True enough, Coppola has been an innovator, a talent-finder, a 'neo-renaissance man.'[98] Yet he did not husband his talents, engulfed by one distraction after another: vineyard, magazine, legitimate theatre, restaurant, properties, technology, bashes. His Zoetrope Studios was the biggest distraction; one might call it a breeder of distraction. By contrast, Michael Corleone's problems seem simple. Inevitably, things turned to ashes: 'Francis was very depressed,' wrote Eleanor Coppola in 1990, 'he spoke with such conviction about all the things wrong in his life, how he hated that he was doing the same material he had done nearly twenty years ago, how he hated the process of making movies, and all the time it took. He said the only thing he liked about film-making was the technology.'[99]

Dazzled by Coppola's personality, Cowie fails to chart the decline. 'The years 1976 and 1977 were probably the most fruitful of Coppola's career.' Yet this was the time when Coppola began losing his way. Cowie believes *Apocalypse Now* 'breathes the furnace heat of a personal vision, worthy to stand alongside Goya's *Disasters of War*.' That bombastic film (with brilliant intermittences – the Las Vegas revue in the jungle) cannot bear comparison with Goya's masterpiece. Cowie defends lesser work: 'It is tempting to join the majority and damn *One from the Heart* with faint praise ... But the film is so unpretentious in its emotional content, and the mind behind it so incurably romantic that it eventually seduces you.' 'Unpretentious' is hardly high praise; 'incurably romantic' is a cliché. *One from the Heart* 'may have been made under less taxing conditions, but it lacks the heroic stature of *Apocalypse*.' If conditions were more taxing, would that have meant a better film? 'Ruined by the folly of *One from the Heart*, he recovered with *The Outsiders* and *Rumble Fish*,' which only goes to show how far the standard of recovery has dropped from the *Godfather II*.[100]

Jon Lewis writes that Coppola, captive to the auteur ideal, 'continues to find himself unable to separate his public image from his work.' When auteurism swept Hollywood in the 1970s, Coppola stood in the vanguard. The moguls permitted the youngsters from the film schools to have their day. If they were successful, the studios would profit; if they failed, they, not the moguls, would take the heat. Sure enough, it was not long before Coppola stumbled. But there was another surprise – for the moguls: 'By 1981, all six of the major film studios were either owned by or were themselves conglomerates.' It had become too costly for a single studio to make and market profitable films. Coppola survived for a time on his own money, then fell to the mercy of the studios, themselves bought up by the international conglomerates (he filed for bankruptcy three times between 1990 and 1995). Still casting himself as an auteur, he was a prisoner of his own style or the expectations of his audience for sparks of that style. His problem is his 'seeming abandonment of narrative in favor of a signature style, an abandonment of the nuanced genre revisionism that distinguished the two *Godfather* films in favor of a reliance on the distinguishing factor of *auteurism*'; this is his 'descent into style.' Studio executives who employ him 'believe that his best days – his most creative days – are behind him. Indeed, they seem to be counting on it'; to the editors of *Premiere*, he has become a 'cooperative former genius.'[101]

In 1999 Michael Schumacher published a five-hundred-page biography upon which Coppola commented in draft. Here is Schumacher on the director's career in the late 1980s: 'As an artist, Coppola was nearly as disappointed with some of his recent work as his critics. He longed to return to the kind of movies that he'd made as a young filmmaker,' *The Rain People*, *The Conversation*, and *Rumble Fish*, 'his favorites of his own productions.' Like an anxious parent, he favours the children that need help; the tougher ones can fend for themselves. 'Movies were as formulaic as ever, and if he intended to continue working – and earning the kind of money he and his family needed – he would have little choice but to make the kind of movies that studios and distributors were willing to finance.'[102] So blame the system or the expensive lifestyle. Schumacher's discussion of *Godfather III* focuses on casting, production, and reception, not on the work itself. In another biography (2004), Gene D. Phillips claims that 'to say that *Godfather III* is not in a class with masterpieces like its two predecessors is to recognize that it suffers only by comparison with the standard Coppola had set for himself by his previous achievements.' On the contrary, it is *because of* that standard that the film is not a near-miss, but an outright failure. The film is a 'richly textured,' 'solid follow-up,' though he does complain of the 'brittle elegance of the settings' and the 'formality' of some language (perhaps the so-called epigrams and stilted dialogue that sound at times like Sicilian translated into English, even in third-generation Italian Americans). His promised assessment of Coppola's career never materializes, though he raps the knuckles of naysayers. 'Critics and audiences alike too often are impatient with an artist's need to ripen and develop his talent gradually. A serious artist needs and deserves some degree of tolerance.'[103] Indeed, but for how long? Phillips is writing thirty years after *Godfather II*. For David Thomson, *Apocalypse Now* was the dividing line; it permanently robbed Coppola of his confidence without any compensating benefit; 'he did not learn.'[104]

The failure of *Godfather III* is one of the disasters in Hollywood film history. Coppola had an artistic responsibility to *Godfather I* and *II*, masterpieces of American cinema and Italian American culture; to approach their level of significance he needed resources, time, and inspiration. His interviews present the spectacle of someone looking for excuses: 'But I always sort of resented that the trilogy took up so much of my life, and that it's about shooting people.'[105] Exaggeration betrays him. The films took up a maximum of four years of his creative life; and he resents his greatest artistic triumphs, the only films by which he may be remembered or that made him any real money. What foolish scruple could have led to the terrible reduction of the epic grandeur of *Godfather I* and *II* to 'shooting people?' Coppola disparages the early *Godfather* films as money-makers, as if their success prevented him from doing something really important, like *The Rain People* and *Rumble Fish*. The money he made allowed him to work independently, until he squandered it on ill-conceived projects; sadly, the same was true for Puzo.

Why was Coppola in such a hurry to kill the golden don? Loving the big gesture, he could have realized the full potential of the *Godfather* in sequels that would have branched out in time and space to take in much more of the Italian American immigrant experience or the broader American experience. The epic nature of the materials could have been expanded in many ways: forwards, backwards, sideways; films filling in the gaps in Michael's life; films working out the fate of other family members; films taking up old characters or new ones, but moving in new directions.[106] As models, Coppola might have given thought to Zola's Rougons-Macquart series, some twenty novels, which captures an epoch, or Balzac's *Comédie humaine*, which captures humanity. In that way, Coppola might have succeeded in making his films a 'metaphor for America' or Italian America.

Around 1997 he said that, even while filming *Godfather I* and *II*, he thought it might ruin him; 'And in some ways it did ruin me. It just made my whole career go this way instead of the way I really wanted it to go, which was into doing original work as a writer-director.'[107] What could have been more original than *Godfather I* and *II*? What artists in their early thirties would not feel blessed from heaven by such results? 'The great frustration of my career is that nobody really wants me to do my own work.' Who is this hobgoblin? Studio executives, fans, critics, family members? Who or what is stopping him? 'Basically, *The Godfather* made me violate a lot of the hopes I had for myself at that age.'[108] At least publicly, he appears unwilling to recognize his best work. Were he to do so, he might take pride in a cinematic achievement that could yet serve as a standard to emulate and even surpass.

chapter 8

The Representation of Italian Americans in American Cinema: From the Silent Film to *The Godfather*

ROBERT CASILLO

I

The representation of Italian Americans in American cinema from silent films into the early 1970s has largely been the history of the formation and recirculation of ethnic stereotypes, which most directors have employed unquestioningly, but to which the more talented, while acknowledging that 'grain of truth' stereotypes often contain, have applied strategies of irony and subversion. Although the encounter of native Americans with Italian immigrants helped to form these stereotypes, their deeper origins lie in the relations between Italy and the northern European world. They owe much to Renaissance narratives, not altogether imaginary, of an amorally sensual Italy abounding in seductresses and prostitutes; Elizabethan drama, with its themes of Italian perfidy, intrigue, and assassination; and the gothic novel, in which Italians figure as licentious women or as sinister violators of Anglo-Saxon maidens. Other important stereotypes were provided by grand opera and the nineteenth-century stage. One must also consider the decline of Italy from about 1650 onward, which gave rise to negative stereotypes, many of which were very much alive around 1900, when Italian immigrants were pouring into the United States.[1]

Italy had weakened culturally and economically by the late seventeenth century. The subjection of most Italian regions to foreign invaders delayed state formation and robbed the country of political strength and prestige. Not only was it fragmented politically, socially, and economically, but the Mediterranean had become a backwater. As Italy's prosperity faded, it ceased to lead in cultural innovation. Having initiated what Norbert Elias calls the 'civilizing process,' Italians were now deficient in civility and drive control, and European travellers regarded them as regressive and decadent. The portrayal of Italy was never wholly negative, as it remained a school of art, history, and social refinement, yet though Italians were seen as vivacious and imaginative, many northerners viewed them with contempt.

For Montesquieu and Bonstetten, the Italians' worst defects resulted from an indulgently hot and enervating climate, which had made them lazy, ignorant, and superficial. Incapable of abstract thinking or disciplined effort, this sensual and emotional people lived unreflectively in the present and was especially susceptible to eroticism. Lawless individuality reigned among them. Because they lacked self-control and social discipline, Italians yielded to their first impulses and tended to emotional extremes, exploding into violence in matters of jealous love and personal honour. Subjection to foreign powers had rendered Italian males so servile and cowardly that Italy came to be seen as culturally effeminate. Foreign domination had produced a climate of political surveillance under which the people had become liars and dissimulators. A religion supposedly of externality rather than conscience, Catholicism had encouraged the Italians' love of superficial display while imbuing them with materialistic and idolatrous superstitions. It was widely assumed that Italian Catholic priests, besides spreading moral hypocrisy, engaged in sexual and other intrigues. Of all Italians, the most reviled were the southern Italians and especially the Neapolitans, known proverbially as 'devils.' They were seen as dissolute, sexually depraved, mendacious, and, after the Masaniello revolt of 1647, rebellious against authority.

Nonetheless, the late eighteenth century witnessed the emergence of a more favourable conception of Italians, one that extended into the Romantic period and that influenced American cinema. The Italians and more especially the nation's lower classes were coming to be seen in Rousseauvian terms as noble savages endowed with spontaneity, naivety, emotional plenitude, and expressiveness. Now as never before many northern observers derived from Italy the favourable impression of a primitive, childlike, and pre-moral (if not amoral) people living in Adamic innocence. Dr John Moore marvelled at the Italians' relaxed and sensual attitude toward life – the *dolce far niente* – and their capacity for happiness and enjoyment. Formerly identified with both high culture and uncivilized natural instincts, the Italian now stood as well for the 'natural' in a positive sense. These presumed and often contradictory traits of the Italian national character came to be featured in many nineteenth- and twentieth-century texts, including films on Italian

American subjects. For instance, Italian naturalness figures favourably in Stendhal's travel writings, which romanticize Italian bandits as embodiments of an emotional intensity absent in the administered northern European world. However exaggerated and overgeneralized, the negative and positive stereotypes contained at least a grain of truth.[2]

Notwithstanding the more flattering stereotypes of Italians, the invidious ones persisted even after the Risorgimento. European and English travellers in northern and central Italy still complained of their economic stagnation and of the inhabitants' lazy sensuality and effeminacy. The Italians' emotional volatility sometimes leading to violence, their going to extremes, their lack of self-control and love of gesticulation – these remained proverbial in travel writings, as did their ignorance, illiteracy, and superstition, which were often blamed on the papacy. Although some visitors dismissed the Italians as clowns and buffoons, bandits remained active in the early nineteenth century, and Italy continued to be identified with plotted vengeance and surreptitious assassination with the knife or stiletto. The questionable reputation of the south further diminished with the decline of the Kingdom of the Two Sicilies and the deterioration of Naples as a tourist centre. European visitors and even northern and central Italians came to think of southern Italy as 'Africa,' a realm perhaps even racially distinct from the rest of the peninsula, and synonymous with primitivism, lawlessness, post-feudal poverty, civic disorder, and vendetta. This view of the southern Italians, which appears in William Dean Howells, does not arise from prejudice alone, as banditry persisted in the Mezzogiorno well after its extirpation from northern and central Italy. The social and economic plight of southern Italy only worsened following the Risorgimento, until, in response to the capitalization of agriculture by big landowners, and the ruination of local agrarian economies through foreign competition and tariff barriers, multitudes of peasants and artisans sought their fortunes abroad from the 1880s into the mid-1920s.

Since these immigrants were mainly illiterate peasants of foreign ways and appearance rather than bearers of Italian high culture, they greatly disappointed their native hosts and were soon saddled with old stereotypes along with equally invidious new ones.[3] With their relatively swarthy complexions and short stature (partly caused by malnutrition widespread in the Italian south), the immigrants diverged somewhat from the northern European physical type established during earlier periods of immigration. Most of them could only swell the ranks of unskilled labour, and they were often mocked and ridiculed for taking any job they could. Those who remained in the United States often settled with their families in crowded and impoverished tenements in predominantly Italian neighbourhoods. Within their closely knit ethnic environments, first-generation immigrants largely maintained the elements of their Old World society. Not only did they often fail to learn the English language properly (many refused to learn it), but they devalued schooling in favour of the enforced employment of adolescent family members so as to supplement the familial income. As Italian Americans lived in highly congested areas deficient in sanitation and other amenities, they were often denounced as an unclean people potentially hazardous to national health. Among the more familiar Italian American stereotypes were those of the shoeshine boy, fruit peddler, organ-grinder, boxer, and bomb-throwing radical anarchist. Partly because of the Italian immigrants' seemingly intractable Old World habits, and their apparent unwillingness to embrace American norms, they struck some native observers as unassimilable. In an intellectual and political climate infused with Social Darwinism and various myths of Teutonic, Anglo-Saxon, and Aryan superiority, it was even claimed that Italian Americans were unfit to participate in a competitive industrial society. Early twentieth-century American social theorists complained of their innate mental inferiority, moral depravity, sexual licence, and propensity to violent crime. Identified with loudness, indolence, and disorderly conduct under the influence of wine, the immigrants were alleged to lack the initiative and discipline necessary for democracy. The crimes they were most often associated with included murder, kidnapping, extortion, blackmail, theft, cheating, counterfeiting, gambling, and prostitution. Undoubtedly the stereotype of the sociopathic Italian American contributed to the execution of Sacco and Vanzetti in 1927. More recent scholars claim, however dubiously, that the first Italian American generations were regarded as an 'in-between people,' neither white nor black, and that they achieved assimilation only by proving their 'whiteness' through the adoption of mainstream attitudes and behaviour.

Often played by Irish Americans, Italians soon became visible as stereotypical characters in silent film, and were not always portrayed unfavourably.[4] The closeness and warmth of Italian families, with the nurturing Italian mother predominating, as well as the communal life of the ghetto, seemed enviable to some native audiences. In *One More American* (1918), the drama centres on whether the wife and young daughter of the immigrant Luigi Riccardo (George Beban) can pass their health inspection at Ellis Island and thus join him in the United States. The situation was common during the period of immigration, when Italians and other immigrants were examined medically (and sometimes quarantined) upon their arrival at Ellis Island, so as to prevent disease among the host population. The greatest fear of many immigrant fathers was that their wives and children would be turned away for health reasons at the 'golden door.'[5] In other silent films such as D.W. Griffith's *At the Altar* (1909) Italians appear as happy souls who know how to appreciate life's pleasures spontaneously, their satisfactions being exemplified in the convivial scene of the family dinner table, laden with food and wine. They figure as well as providers of enjoyment, for instance restaurant waiters or circus performers; the latter type appears in *The Wages of Virtue* (1924) and *Head over Heels* (1922). Italian 'naturalness' is often exemplified by emotional intensity, typically exhibited in vehement gesticulations and strong facial expressions, although, as Lee Lourdeaux notes, Italian passion also took the form of compassion, as in D.W. Griffith's *Pippa Passes* (1909). At the same time, Italians are frequently identified with the arts, especially opera, popular song, and instrumental music. In Griffith's *At the Altar*, a violin decorates a domestic interior; in *Pippa Passes*, the heroine's voice and guitar save three separate individuals from despair.[6] Nor was Italian Catholicism necessarily a disfavoured subject during the silent era. Based on an immanentist theology, and emphasizing such non-Protestant values as sacramentalism, mediation, and intercession, Italian Catholic rituals and icons fascinated mainstream audiences in films such as *The White Sister* (1923), among many other examples.[7]

Yet these positive stereotypes easily switched poles. Catholicism awakened in mainstream Protestant audiences fears of superstition, idolatry, papal tyranny, and political conspiracy reflected in rumours of firearms hidden in Catholic churches. The nurturing and procreant Italian family was also a breeding ground for the Catholic masses and thus a demographic threat to the survival of mainstream society. Such families gave the impression of claustrophobic, insular, oppressive, and even tyrannical institutions in which children were smothered by maternal love and enslaved by brutal patriarchy. It would be necessary to extricate the assimilable Italian girl from this environment. In Griffith's *Little Italy* (1921), Rosa Mascani is banished by her father for refusing to marry the man he has chosen for her. Sometimes an Italian girl's only escape is to marry an Irishman, as when Tina Sartori marries Tom in *The Man in Blue* (1925).

Similarly, the attractiveness of the 'natural' Italian yielded to its opposite. The obverse of sincerity and emotional transparency appeared in the old Machiavellian stereotype of the duplicitous schemer and cheater. The image of the fun-loving unreflective Italian degenerated into that of the lazy, irresponsible, good-for-nothing spendthrift. Father Lorenzo in *The Sea Horses* (1926) is a sot, and Ilaria Serra mentions a film in which an Italian girl grows violent after two glasses of wine. The identification of Italians with music and song has its degraded counter-image in portrayals of the low-class organ-grinder and his monkey, as in *The Organ-grinder* of 1909. The natural Italian in his or her appealing emotionality is often replaced by the older stereotype of a person who, dominated by passion, and thus marked by bad manners and unseemly excess, yields abruptly to conflicting and violent impulses. In *Puppets of Fate* (1926) Italians are playthings of their passions, while in *The Wages of Virtue* (1924) they exemplify emotional extremes. The most disturbing of the 'Italian' emotions was sexual desire, especially as embodied in the attractive yet demonic Rudolph Valentino, who though he rarely played Italians was widely identified with the group. Despite complaints in some quarters of Valentino's 'un-American' looks, many American women found his Latin-encoded presentation irresistibly attractive even when he played gigolos and other parasitic types whose indolence insulted the Protestant work ethic. Giuliana Muscio holds that the physical and sexual threat Valentino posed for American womanhood was checked through its expression in the artistically mediated form of the dance, thus reconciling culture and nature, the two warring poles of the Italian character. As the object of idolatrous feminine adoration, which placed him in a position normally occupied by a beautiful cinematic female, and also because of his characters' emotional vulnerability, Valentino elicited protests from American men against his unmasculine subservience to women – a commonplace anti-Italian accusation reminiscent of diatribes against the *cicisbeo*.[8] Valentino's wearing of jewelry, including sadomasochistically coded slave bracelets, and the luxuriant effeminacy of his screen personae, also inspired (apparently groundless) insinuations of homosexuality.[9]

In the silent era Italian passion is often conjoined with crime, and more especially revenge stemming from sexual jealousy. Griffith's *At the Altar* depicts a lover who attempts revenge against his rival during his marriage ceremony by planting a loaded gun beneath the wedding kneeler. In *Little Italy* (1909), which Griffith also directed, Maria rejects Tony in favour of Victor, who then stabs his rival: stiletto and wine flask go hand in hand. *Italian Blood* (1911), another of Griffith's films, concerns a wife who, sensing her husband's cooling passion, attempts to arouse his jealousy. Unexpectedly he is thrown into a frenzied rage, and only just barely avoids murdering his children.[10] The young Italian American hero of Griffith's *Cord of Life* (1909) plots vengeance against a friend who had refused him a loan, but is foiled in his attempt to kill the friend and his child. In Alan Dwan's *The Sea Horses* (1926), Lorenzo's wife and children are nearly destroyed by his unnatural passions.

American audiences also identified Italian Americans with criminal gangs, to which they were supposedly drawn by innate instinct. Yet even before such gangs appeared in American silent films, Edwin S. Porter had portrayed Italian banditti in his eleven-minute series of travel vignettes ironically entitled *The European Rest Cure* (1904). In one vignette three Italian bandits surround an American businessman during his visit to an ancient ruin. The film thus evokes the contrast between Italy's monumental past and present squalor. Nor did it matter that old-style bandits had vanished from Italy; indeed, some silent films portray Italian American criminals as if they were banditti from the Old Country.[11] According to Brownlow, most Italian Americans were law abiding, yet silent films often linked them with crime.

In the silent film Italian criminality often took the form of kidnapping, blackmail, and counterfeiting. Released in 1908, *Her First Adventure* presents a happy suburban family whose young daughter is lured from home by the music of an organ-grinder, who then kidnaps her; Italian musicality thus masks crime. In *The Padrone's Ward* (1913), a native American banker rescues a girl from her guardian, the leader of an East Side gang of blackmailers and thieves. Griffith's *Avenging Conscience* (1914) portrays a son who, having murdered his father, is blackmailed by an organ-grinder. The immigrant heroine of *Poor Little Pepita* (1916) becomes involved in a counterfeiting ring. In *A Bum and a Bomb* (1912), as in *Giovanni's Gratitude* (1913), the image of the Italian American gang member is linked with that of the bomb-throwing anarchistic radical. The same conjunction of two of the worst nativist nightmares of Italian Americans would later claim national attention in the accusations against Sacco and Vanzetti.

The most publicized Italian criminals of the silent era belonged to the so-called Black Hand, the name adopted by small groups of blackmailers and extortionists who emerged in the early Italian immigrant communities.[12] The chief difficulty in fighting the Black Hand, which was sometimes referred to as the Mafia, was the southern Italian code of *omertà*, or silence before the authorities, which became a fixture of films concerning Italian American crime. Lieutenant Joseph Petrosino of the New York City Police Department, who formed an 'Italian Squad' of police detectives to pursue Italian American criminals, helped to explode the notion of the Black Hand as a large organization. However, that Petrosino was assassinated during his mission to Palermo in 1909, very possibly by the Sicilian Mafia, encouraged the probably false belief that both the Black Hand and American Mafia originated in Sicily as criminal organizations that were thence transplanted wholesale to the United States. The publicity surrounding the assassination furthermore solidified the identification of Italian Americans with violent criminality and lent renewed force to the nativist effort to stop southern Italian immigration.[13]

One of the earliest films about Italian Americans appeared in 1906 under the title *The Black Hand*. A butcher's daughter having been threatened, her father appeals to the police, who hide in a cold store to capture the blackmailers. These amateurs, who use the name of the Black Hand for purposes of intimidation, drink wine and play cards in a dingy hideout with a witch-like woman. Their clothes call to mind Italian banditti, while their mustaches identify them as old country transplants. Contrastingly, the butcher wears modern clothes, which, like his rejection of *omertà* and reliance on modern refrigeration, implies his willing acculturation. His linguistic competence in labelling his merchandise with properly spelled English words contrasts with the illiteracy ('desperut' for 'desperate') of the ransom note sent by the Black Handers. In 1909 *The Detectives of the Italian Bureau* honoured Petrosino's idea that Italian Americans could best track down the Black Hand. Three years later, *The Adventures of Lieutenant Petrosino* celebrated his exploits as well as depicting his murder.

A few other early films provide a more rounded, compassionate view of Italians. Released in 1915, *The Alien* starred the well-known stage actor George Beban who, notwithstanding his claim to find Italians unusually picturesque, wanted to depict the real Italian rather than 'the individual with a long black mustache and a bandana handkerchief, armed with a stiletto.' Beban played Pietro Massena, an Italian ditch-digger whose beloved daughter Rosina dies in a car accident. Thanks to a WASP ne'er-do-well, Pietro is accused of sending a Black Hand ransom note. When proved innocent, he refuses compensation and returns sadly to his now solitary home, having surpassed the mainstream characters in morality.

Beban also starred in William Ince's *The Italian* (1914), which Lourdeaux describes as a 'landmark' for Italian identity, and whose original title, *The Dago*, was changed at Beban's request so as not to offend. A happy, guitar-strumming gondolier very much at home amid the beauty of Venice, Beppo Donati loves the inauthentically named Annette An-cello, whose house contains a prominently displayed crucifix, and whom he is about to lose through her forced marriage to a rich merchant. Beppo must therefore go to the United States in order to earn money for Annette's transatlantic passage – a romantic situation different from that of the typical Italian immigrant, who fled the poverty of southern Italy (not Venice) out of economic necessity. Yet Beppo is much disappointed by America, where he becomes a bootblack and sells his vote to a ward boss. Consistent with what historians describe as 'chain migration,' he summons Annette and marries her in a civil rather than Catholic ceremony – behaviour again atypical of Italian immigrants. His removal of his gondolier's mustache figures as yet another sign of his Americanization. Doting on their young child Tony, the Donatis live in a domestic environment largely barren of those sacred objects and shrines with which the Italian American immigrant domus typically abounded; contrastingly, the street scenes of New York's Italian neighbourhood, which were shot in San Francisco, lend a realistic effect. During a heat wave Bebbo goes out to buy pasteurized milk, a modern commodity unknown to his former experience, for the gravely ill Tony, but is robbed en route. After the ward boss fails to provide help, Beppo assaults him and is sent to prison, where he learns of Tony's death. At the conclusion Beppo secretly enters the ward boss's house in order to kill his child but is saved from vengeance only by his compassion. Despite its reliance on stereotypes, including Beppo's effusions and gesticulations, *The Italian* handles its ethnic themes with some insight.

Are Italian American stereotypes of the silent film consistent with historical actualities? Lourdeaux correctly remarks that the Italian gangster and hurdy-gurdy man largely reflect the fears and desires of mainstream audiences, and the same can be said of the frequent identification of Italians with kidnapping. Whereas silent films such as *Little Italy* and *The Three Sisters* show Italian Americans acting independently of their families, the vast majority of the wives and daughters of the immigrant generations submitted to patriarchal restraints, and out-group marriages were most unusual. Such representations of Italian American women seem to express the desire of mainstream audiences to detach them from a presumably bad environment. Likewise the portrayal of Italian men as drunks ill consorts with the disapproval of drunkenness in Italian culture. And though silent films like those of later decades typically depict lower-class Italian Americans, the group was already showing signs of occupational and social mobility by 1915.[14]

Ilaria Serra goes so far as to question altogether the credibility of the

Italian American stereotypes of the silent film, claiming that 'in every sense the world of the screen is a projection.' Her case is somewhat overstated, for as Lourdeaux observes, 'the closer movies got to Irish and Italian cultures, the more likely they were to capture brief moments of ethnic reality.' Indeed, 'the realistic tendency of American cinema was never entirely absent.'[15] Thus the centrality of the family is correctly represented, as is *omertà*. The conviviality of Italian Americans, often appearing in these films in conjunction with music and display, calls to mind the many street festivals of immigrant neighbourhoods. Again, the Black Hand did exist. And finally, the short fuses and erratic emotionality of the cinematic Italians testify to Italy's tardiness in Elias's 'civilizing process,' leaving many Italian immigrants deficient in drive control.

Some scholars contend that Italian Americans were initially perceived in the United States as either black or less than white, and that this is reflected in American cinema's persistently demeaning, even 'racist' portrayals of the group. According to Giorgio Bertellini, whereas most of the newer European ethnic groups gradually 'became white,' a status they were initially denied upon their arrival in the United States, Italian Americans never fully gained such acceptance, but owing to mainstream racial prejudice and a 'deeper ideological necessity' have been 'confined in urban enclaves.' These same mainstream prejudices also explain why Italian Americans supposedly remain, 'ultimately, unassimilated.' Even when Italian Americans moved from their ghettoes, the 'old neighborhood just moved elsewhere,' without real change. Although Bertellini acknowledges the widespread perception that the representation of Italian Americans, though prejudiced, has not been racist, he believes that, even in the 1950s and 1960s, and perhaps beyond, Italian Americans formed a racially liminal group shunned and feared by the mainstream.[16]

For Francesca Canadé Sautman, European ethnic groups arrived in the United States in the category of not-fully-white and only gradually, after submitting to WASP-Teutonic culture, betrayed their true ethnic identity by 'buying into whiteness.' Not only does film legitimate 'racial exclusion,' but Italian Americans occupy an intermediate position, neither white nor black, their otherness being accentuated by their identification with violence and unassimilable ethnic enclaves. Sautman acknowledges that Italian Americans have made social and political advances, yet she sees them as powerless to undo film and media repesentations that force them to inhabit the racial 'middle ground' as a sexually explosive and inferior group. 'It is ... [the] system of representation, a stolen identity,' claims Sautman, that today defines being Italian American, rather than such particulars of Italian American life as social and economic status.[17]

What undermines Bertellini's and Sautman's arguments is the empirical evidence compiled over three decades by Thomas Kessner, James A. Crispino, and Richard Alba. Kessner shows that even first-generation immigrants were more mobile occupationally and socially than had been suspected. Crispino and Alba note that, consistent with the straight-line theory of assimilation, successive generations of Italian Americans have achieved increasing levels of acculturation and assimilation, the typical Italian American having now entered the middle class.[18] Like Bertellini, Sautman must explain how Italian Americans have successfully assimilated while supposedly suffering constant demonization through racial stereotypes. However unflattering, these stereotypes have contained an at most incidental racial component and have obviously been much less crippling than Sautman imagines. As for why this is so, part of the explanation lies in the research into stereotyping and stereotype accuracy conducted in recent decades, which neither Bertellini nor Sautman cites.

The subject of stereotyping accuracy was largely off limits for research for many decades following World War II, on the assumption that stereotypes, defined as universal, rigid, and typically negative generalizations concerning population groups, cannot but promote prejudice because of their inaccuracy. However, recent research demonstrates the possibility of accurate stereotyping when it is understood that the stereotype represents a trait or behaviour only of relatively high rather than universal incidence within a group. Research into stereotyping accuracy has also demonstrated that those who interpret group traits and behaviour on the basis of stereotypes arrive at reliable conclusions regarding that group in some instances, and that in doing so they are usually aware that the stereotype admits of many exceptions. And this is why, contrary to what Sautman thinks, a WASP can enjoy *The Godfather* series without supposing that his Italian American co-office worker belongs to the Mafia.[19] Yet unwilling to accept that the increasing assimilation of the group explodes her racialized conception of Italian American identity, she takes the extreme position that the mainstream perception of Italian Americans remains uninfluenced by their actual social existence, but is revealed only by the 'system of representations' that generates their invidious and supposedly racial portrayals. Not only would Sautman's ideology trump observable fact, but she attributes implausibly to cinematic and other media representations a significance far greater than that of social behaviour itself and the everyday perceptions and attitudes that emerge from such behaviour.[20]

Far from characterizing Italians as blacks or quasi-blacks, Carlos Cortés notes that from the beginnings of silent cinema they were treated much more favourably than 'colored' ethnics, that is, blacks, Asians, Mexicans, and American Indians. These non-European ethnics were identified with a primitivism, violence, and brutality far worse than the Italian stereotypes, and because of their colour and presumed savagery were deemed unacceptable as candidates for 'Americanization.' Not only did 'their skin color set them apart from other Americans,' but 'silent screen colored ethnics often operated antisocially and resorted to far more violence than did white ethnics.' The key difference between Italians and non-European ethnics in the silent (and later) films is that the former can assimilate, as witness the frequent portrayal of Italians marrying, if not WASPs, then other European ethnics.[21]

II

Although few Italian American actors or directors were associated with the silent film, directors Frank Capra and Gregory La Cava began their careers in the silent era, and by the late 1940s Vincente Minnelli enjoyed a reputation. Yet these artists generally avoided Italian American themes. If one assumes 'Italian American cinema' to require the treatment of Italian American subjects by in-group directors, its emergence came only in the early 1970s, with the arrival of Coppola and Scorsese.[22] As second-generation ethnics working within the studio system, Capra, La Cava, and Minnelli were seeking to assimilate rather than reveal their origins, while commercial necessities and public taste gave little impetus to in-group explorations of Italian American ethnicity.

Given the paucity of Italian American filmmakers, non–Italian American actors and directors were left to interpret the Italian American experience largely through stereotypes. However, the late 1920s and early 1930s saw the emergence of a new stereotype not hitherto associated with Italian American criminality – the Prohibition-style gangster. This is not to suggest that Italian Americans originated organized crime in the United States, as some claim, for it is well known from the work of Herbert Asbury that Irish immigrants to New York City had formed their own large gangs by the mid-nineteenth century. A thriving gangland existed in Chicago in the 1890s, with Irish criminals at first predominating, while in the northeastern United States Jewish gangsters were underworld overlords from about 1910 into the 1930s. Nor is there any doubt that early sound films portray Irish and Jewish along with Italian gangsters. And yet the fact remains that many cinematic gangsters of the early sound film were Italian Americans, and William Everson rightly observes that Italian Americans were coming to be isolated as criminal types in the films of the Prohibition era.[23] This new stereotype coincided with underworld developments of that time, beginning in Chicago where, following the elimination of 'Big Jim' Colosimo in 1920, Johnny Torrio and his successor Al Capone created an organized crime syndicate in which violent inter-ethnic bootlegging rivalries yielded gradually to peaceful cooperation, business organization and expansion, and the corruption of authorities. Subsequently in the northeastern United States Italian American crime families introduced similar innovations, in some cases borrowed from their Jewish predecessors in the underworld, whose dominant position they had usurped.[24] And yet, as David Ruth observes, even during the late 1920s and 1930s, moralists and the public were less concerned with ethnic criminals than with their middle-class counterparts of native stock, a concern reflected in film as well as in fiction and the media. Ruth further notes that the transformation of the Prohibition underworld into consolidated business operations or syndicates enabled it to penetrate far beyond its former habitat in the slums and ghettoes into the very core of mainstream society, with the top-echelon gangster, operating from an office located in the downtown business district, and quite familiar with the commercial advantages of efficiency and specialization, now widely regarded as virtually indistinguishable in dress and manner from the ordinary businessman.[25] Thus the interwar period witnessed the earliest stirrings of national anxiety over the presumed infiltration of the American economic, social, and political system by an invisible and all-pervasive criminal syndicate that masked its nefarious designs under the cover of business respectability. These fears would come to a head during the Kefauver hearings of the early 1950s and the subsequent federal and state assaults against the underworld from the later 1950s onward, by which point Italian Americans had come to be seen as playing the preponderant role in organized crime.

Sometimes described mistakenly as the first gangster film, Joseph Von Sternberg's *Underworld* (1927) nonetheless fused many of the basic elements of the genre for the first time, including nocturnal urban scenes, an underworld café below street level, mid-town crowds of shoppers, a brownstone residential neighbourhood, a dance hall, a criminal hideout, a courtroom, and a prison. Yet though the film refers to 'wop gangs,' its protagonist, Bill 'Bull' Weed, is neither an Italian American nor a Prohibition-style bootlegger, but a bankrobber reminiscent of a Western outlaw. In *Broadway* (1929), Italian American actor Paul Porcasi plays the gangster and nightclub owner Nick Verdis, but the character's ethnic identity remains unspecified, being generically 'Mediterranean.'[26] Contrastingly, *The Racket* (1928) follows the career of Nick Scarsi, a gangster modelled on Al Capone in his dealings with Big Bill Thompson, the corrupt major of Chicago. However, in both the film and its original stage version the character of Scarsi was assigned to two Jews, Louis Wolheim and Edward G. Robinson respectively. Released two years later, *Doorway to Hell* stars Lew Ayres as Louie 'Legs' Ricarno, a Johnny Torrio figure. Not only has Ricarno put his city's bootlegging operations on a 'business basis,' but he controls the operation by arbitrating territorial disputes among the gangs. *Doorway to Hell* claims the distinction of having originated several generic cliches: the identification of the Italian American gangleader with Napoleon; coin flipping as the mark of the gangster's insouciance; the use of a plastic surgeon to make a dead gangster seem alive; the concealment of a machine gun in a violin case; and the theme of the impossibility of leaving the criminal gang. Unfortunately, the bland Ayres resembles a frat boy.

Released in 1931 at the height of the craze for gangster films, William Wellman's *Star Witness* testifies to the angry nativist and mainstream response to the Italian American gangster. A member of an Anglo-American family witnesses a murder carried out by the gangster-extortionist Maxie Campo (Ralph Ince), whereupon Campo escapes through the family home after assaulting an aged grandfather. Having agreed to testify, the witnesses are then terrorized by Campo's gang, which kidnaps a young family member. Implicitly the solidarity of the all-American family – white, Anglo-Saxon, Protestant – is threatened by a false criminal 'family' spawned by the teeming southern Italian influx. Such a scenario may reflect mainstream anxieties, for whereas the Anglo-American family was often feared to be suffering a demographic and moral crisis during the early twentieth century, as witness increased incidence of divorce along with a declining birth rate, Italian American and other immigrant families were widely regarded on account of their high fertility as threatening the demographic dominance of the established American groups. Indeed, Richard Alba and other scholars observe that the southern Italian family in some ways strengthened during the early phases of American settlement, when it shifted from a nuclear to a more extended pattern.[27] In any case, Campo's nefariousness is foiled by the xenophobic and crotchety Grandpa, a Civil War veteran and living symbol of the older America, whose testimony sends Campo to the electric chair. Identifying nativism and patriotism, and even invoking Lincoln, Grandpa lashes out during the trial against 'back-stabbin' yeller-bellied furriners,' meaning stiletto-bearing southern Italians, and at the same time asserts that gangsterism originates on foreign shores, implicitly Italy. Yet though the courtroom audience greets Grandpa's fulminations with resounding applause, his ultimate reward consists only of a return trip to the old folk's home, such being the strength of his family's solidarity.[28]

Directed by Will Hays from 1922 onward, the Motion Picture Producers and Directors Association (MPPDA) aimed to insure the conformity of films to public standards of decency and morality. By 1927 the first code of self-regulation had been issued to Hollywood producers, consisting of eleven prohibitions of the portrayal of nudity, lewdness, drug traffic, miscegenation, and the like. The new production code, officially adopted by Hollwood producers in March 1930, responded to protests against both a perceived increase in sexual themes and the enormous popularity of gangster films, which were feared to promote recklessly immoral and lawless behaviour among youth. A major cause for these complaints was the often xenophobic opposition of rural Protestants to an increasingly influential, hedonic, and permissive urban culture that they identified not only with Jews and Catholic ethnics but with Jewish-controlled Hollywood studios. However, Catholics and more especially Irish Catholics were also beginning to play an ever more prominent public role as guardians of morality in the cinema.[29]

The so-called classic gangster film flowered briefly in the early 1930s in three major works, of which two focus on Italian Americans: Mervyn Leroy's *Little Caesar* (1931), William Wellman's *The Public Enemy* (1931), and Howard Hawks's *Scarface* (1932).[30] Scripted by W.R. Burnett from his identically titled novel, which is preceded by a fictitiously Machiavellian and hence 'Italianate' epigraph endorsing ruthless self-interest,[31] *Little Caesar* follows the criminal career of Rico Bandello, who begins in the provinces, joins an eastern city gang, rises nearly to the top of gangland, and then suffers a sudden calamitous fall followed by a lonely, ignominious death. Unlike Capone, Rico seems not to be a bootlegger, and has no difficulty with the IRS; yet the film often recalls the Chicago underworld during Prohibition. Not only does Rico's removal of gangleaders Sam Vettori and Little Arnie Lorch remind one of the misfortunes of Big Jim Colosimo and Johnny Torrio, but Rico's murder of former associate Tony Passa on the steps of a church is inspired by the execution of Chicago gangster Hymie Weiss by Capone henchmen.[32] Among Rico's underworld associates, Arnie Lorch, proprietor of a gambling operation, and

Devoss, owner of the Bronze Peacock Club, both appear to speak with Italian accents. Not implausibly, Burnett's title mocks Benito Mussolini, who shares Rico's short stature, criminality, and imperial pretentions.

The casting of Edward G. Robinson as Rico typifies Hollywood films about Italian Americans up to the end of World War II, in which the role of the protagonist, including that of the Italian American gangster, was assigned to non–Italian American actors.[33] Yet unlike Lew Ayres in *Doorway to Hell*, Robinson's interpretation captures Rico's ethnicity as well as his pathologically menacing ambition. It would have helped Robinson's performance that he had played not only gangster Nick Scarsi on stage but, in the preceding year, the gangster Tony Garotta in *Night Ride*, in which Garotta incarnates an irrational power of evil. In being both typically and atypically Italian, however, Rico discourages one from identifying him with his group. Marked as an Italian American by his heavy accent, he eats spaghetti and associates mainly with Italian gangsters, including his best friend Joe Massara (Douglas Fairbanks, Jr), thus conforming to images of Italian clannishness. His love of sartorial display, like his craving for honour, respect, and public recognition, conform likewise to conventional notions of the Italian. This cannot be said, though, of his choice of a criminal career, for while some Americans may have equated Italian Americans with organized crime in these decades, the majority are not likely to have thought so, and in any case the percentage of Italian Americans in organized crime has been remarkably small from the 1920s onward. By the same token, Rico's lack of a family diverges from Italian American norms. The 'mother figure' in his life, the gypsy- or witch-like Ma Magdalena, who hides him in a cavernous and womb-like secret room, calls to mind not the conventional Italian mother as Madonna figure, but the prostitute Mary Magdalene. Far from being a nurturer, she keeps all but a hundred and fifty of the thousand dollars Rico has confided to her. Whereas most Italians enjoy wine and other alcoholic drinks, though rarely to the point of drunkenness and still more rarely alcoholism, Rico is a teetotaler who warns his accomplices of the dangers of getting drunk. Consistent with this abstemiousness, he utterly lacks the Italian gift for enjoyment of life. Nor does Rico participate in Italian American Catholicism, notwithstanding his absurd claim that he is as 'religious as the next guy.' His dying statement – 'Mother of Mercy, is this the end of Rico?' – seems drawn from a long occluded religious upbringing, but its content is disappointed vanity. Again contrary to Italian American norms, Rico is either asexual or homosexual, and unlike most Italians, he is painfully uncomfortable in social situations.[34]

For fear that *Little Caesar* might seem to justify or encourage crime, the filmmakers mollified the New York Board of Censors with minor changes including a moralizing opening title: 'He who lives by the sword shall die by it.'[35] In retrospect the film suggests a perverted Horatio Alger story whose protagonist fails because of anachronistically violent methods and characterological deficiencies. In the opening nocturnal scene Rico murders a gas station attendant to eliminate a witness to the holdup. Next he appears with accomplice Joe Massara in a diner where he turns back a wall clock to provide them with an alibi. In addition to revealing, as Stuart Kaminsky remarks, Rico's urge to control time in his own interests, as when he later demands that a holdup be performed exactly at midnight, his turning back the clock may imply symbolically his regression to an earlier stage of crime.[36] Just as Rico's nickname suggests Latin authoritarianism, so he aims for total domination and control, and he therefore has no use for America's cherished brand of laissez faire capitalism, even in its underworld version. Notwithstanding that the very name 'Rico' refers to wealth or riches in Italian, he himself states that rational goals such as monetary wealth interest him far less than recognition, esteem, and power: 'Money's all right but it ain't everything ... Have your own way or nothin'. Be somebody.' Whether Burnett realized it or not, Rico expresses values that by the 1920s were yielding in the underworld to a more business-like approach. As Francis A.J. Ianni notes, the southern Italian is a Mediterranean for whom material acquisition is secondary to power, influence, and respect.[37] Clinging to Old World values, the trigger-happy Rico refuses to accept that Italian American gangs had come to eschew violence in favour of a comparatively cooperative, low-profile, business-like approach to crime based on the corruption of public officials. As Sam Vettori tells Rico: 'The rod don't go around here. That's old stuff.' The business-like WASP Big Boy, corporate mastermind of the underworld, favours non-violence.

Rico exemplifies not so much traditionalism pure and simple as the conflict between Old World values and those of a newly encountered technological and material civilization. Although his attitudes towards crime reflect southern Italian norms, he and his rivals perform their depredations by means of sophisticated modern machinery. Like many of his fellow Italian Americans, whose southern Italian ancestors had long remained confined to their pre-modern culture of *miseria*, with its low rates of production and consumption, and had developed within that environment a sense of limit manifest in their proverbial frugality,[38] Rico experiences the exhilarating discovery that the low expectations typical of southern Italy and the Italian American neighbourhood had been raised incalculably within American mainstream society, which afforded hitherto unimagined possibilities of consumption as visible tokens of social status and personal power. Yet whereas most immigrants resolved to acquire such objects slowly and laboriously, Rico would win them quickly and in excess, and thus provides the first major cinematic instance of the Italian American gangster as a figure of lavish consumption and the mass-consumption economy.[39] The conspicuous expenditure that had formerly been the exclusive prerogative of the leisure class had become proletarianized, and was now to be seen in the ethnic criminal aping the dress and manners of high society.

In rising to the heights of crime, Rico flaunts such visible tokens of underworld success as a fedora, a pinky ring (a stereotypical gangster adornment), and expensively tailored clothes, including spats and a double-breasted overcoat. Nonetheless, Rico's triumphal party at the Club Palermo only exposes his social limitations as well as his associates' baseness. Not only do they present him with a stolen watch as a gift, thus calling in question their proclaimed loyalty, but his clumsy address altogether lacks fluency and polish. Having already demonstrated his social ineptitude, Rico is even more uncomfortable on this public occasion. The next day, as he searches alone in broad daylight for a newspaper account of the party, he is nearly murdered by a rival gang as the price of his vain love of publicity. During a visit to Big Boy's lavish residence, he mistakenly supposes the fifteen-thousand-dollar price tag on a painting to refer to the frame, whose showiness attracts him. Whereas the low-profile Big Boy hangs on to his clandestine power, the deposed Rico is lured from hiding by an insult planted in a newspaper, only to die in a hail of bullets in a foolish attempt to defend his public 'reputation.'

What also brings Rico down is the personalism that, most salient in his friendship with Joe Massara, prevents him from maintaining a business-like approach to crime. Noting Rico's devastation when Joe leaves the gang for a dancing career with his fiancée Olga, most commentators view Rico's emotional investment in Joe as homoerotic, although Bondanella identifies it with Italian American homophilism.[40] One wonders, however, whether this cultural trait was as familiar to Burnet as the long history of the attribution of aberrant sexuality to Italians. In one scene, Rico's gestures and expression become suggestively effeminate as, dressed in his newly tailored tuxedo or 'monkey suit,' he primps before a mirror with his adoring underling Otero looking on. One is invited to view Rico's disdain of 'softness' both in himself and in his male associates as overcompensation for his own 'feminine' side. In any case, Rico's affection for Joe undermines his criminal career, for though Joe informs against him, Rico cannot kill his friend but goes 'soft' in his presence. Unlike Rico, Joe assimilates not only through his career but through love of a non-Italian woman.

Little Caesar contributed substantially to the Italian American version of the gangster genre. Already present in *Doorway to Hell*, the theme of the difficulty of leaving the underworld appears in the conflict between Rico and Joe; it figures later in such films as *Brother Orchid* (1940), *The Brothers Rico* (1957), and *The Godfather* series. Like Rico, many screen gangsters have a 'sartorial moment' marking their arrival – Scorsese's *Goodfellas* (1989) is a recent example.[41] Similarly, Rico's phallic cigar contributes to the conventional cinematic image of the mob boss to be seen in later characterizations, including those by Robert De Niro, Neville Brand, and Robinson himself. Tony Passa's murder on the steps of a church evokes the opposition between crime and Catholicism that figures in *Cry of the City* (1948), *The Godfather* (1972), *Mean Streets* (1973), and *The Funeral* (1996). Rico's 'going soft' has parallels in *Scarface*, *Key Largo* (1948), and *The Big Combo* (1955). And finally, in charting Rico's 'progress' from an obscure western American locale to a teeming Eastern metropolis, *Little Caesar* like many later gangster films implies that in the post-immigration period the latter has become the new American frontier, the ethnic underworld criminal having replaced the cowboy-gunman.[42]

Based loosely on Armitage Trail's novel of the same name, which amounted to a loose biography of Al Capone, *Scarface* (1932) was produced by Howard Hughes and directed by Howard Hawks. The script was provided by journalist Ben Hecht, the scenarist of *Underworld*, who knew Chicago's burgeoning crime scene. *Scarface* tells the story of Italian American Tony Camonte who, like Capone, rises to underworld supremacy. The film's emphasis on incest, violence, and betrayal was inspired by the Borgias as well as Elizabethan stereotypes.[43] *Little Caesar* also influenced *Scarface*, yet whereas Rico seems only a glorified holdup man, Tony becomes a bootlegging lord during Prohibition, as did Capone. However, both Rico and Tony are killed by police, unlike Capone, who went to prison in 1931 for income tax evasion. Though derivative, *Scarface* remains the best of the classic gangster films thanks to its lively script, dramatic intensity, tense spatial composition, expressionistic lighting, and inventive camera work.

Played by Paul Muni, Tony begins his career as gangleader Johnny Lovo's henchman and on his orders executes gangster Louis Costillo, whose refusal to enter bootlegging has blocked Lovo's ambitions. While Lovo reorganizes Costillo's territory using rational business methods, Tony sabotages various rival establishments so as to open up new markets for his boss, yet he grows hostile to Lovo because of his refusal to expand into the North Side. Upon killing Lovo and taking over his operation, Tony claims his WASP girlfriend Poppy and then proceeds to kill Northside gangleaders O'Hara and Gaffney. Concurrently Tony's personal life is filled with turmoil and frustration, partly because his Italian American mother disapproves of his criminality, but also because he unconsciously desires his sister Cesca (Ann Dvorak), whose suitors he will not tolerate. Unaware of Cesca's marriage to his trusted friend and subordinate, Guino Rinaldo (George Raft), Tony kills Guino upon discovering him with his sister. Later surrounded by the police in his fortress-like apartment, Tony is reunited with the forgiving Cesca who is then killed by gunfire. Tony then goes to pieces and, having been gunned down by the police, collapses in a gutter. The Cooks' Tours sign outside his apartment, proclaiming 'The World Is Yours,' which he had taken to refer to himself, comments ironically. Hawks had originally intended for Tony to die in the street in a pile of horse manure, so as to confirm the prophecy of a police detective who had told him that he would 'die right where the horses had been standing.'[44]

The two-year delay in the release of *Scarface* reflects the fact that the Hays Office greatly objected to it. Not only did it contain much more violence than *Little Caesar*, which many audiences had regarded as too brutal, but the censors believed that its apparent glorification of gangsters required editorializing inserts. Dozens of cuts were demanded, both to tone down the violence and to lessen the protagonist's attractiveness; Tony was to die as a betrayed coward; and the title was to be changed to 'Scarface: The Menace.' As a compromise, the film was released as *Scarface: Shame of a Nation*. Further to mollify the censor, a preface described the film as 'an indictment of gang rule in America, and of the callous indifference of the government' to this problem. It concluded with a challenge to the government: 'What are you going to do about it?' In a specially added scene, a police chief rejects the notion of the ethnic gangster as 'colorful,' contrasting the 'crawling louse' Tony with the Western gunmen of old who, though antisocial, at least fought each other face to face. Thus the honest, forthright WASP tough guy proves superior to the back-stabbing Italian.[45] Another modification is the scene that, set in a newspaper publisher's office, appears distractingly at the film's midpoint, and that represents concerned citizens and city fathers as mainly upper-crust Anglo-Americans with vaguely English vocal intonations. The publisher proposes to fight gangsterism by means of rigid anti-gun legislation and, in the last resort, through martial law. When he claims that half of America's gangsters 'aren't even citizens,' and proposes to put 'teeth in the Deportation Act,' an Italian American civic leader supports him: 'Dats-a true. Dey bring-a nothin' butta disgrace-a to my whole people.' The film's ending exists in two versions, one of which has a cowardly Tony dying in a gutter.[46]

Tony amounts to a collection of ethnic stereotypes with curious wrinkles here and there. As he approaches the unsuspecting Costillo to murder him in a phone booth, he whistles the famous sestet, with a revenge motif, from Donizetti's *Lucia di Lammermoor*: 'What restrains me in such a moment?' The Italian markers in this scene include vendetta, gunplay, amorality, lack of restraint, and, not least, opera, which figure often in cinematic representations of the upper-echelon underworld. In expressing his violent passions operatically, Tony calls to mind one of the most enduring Italian stereotypes, that of the artist-criminal or criminal-artist, of which Hollywood's mob bosses are partly derivative.[47] Next Tony appears in a barber's chair, his face covered in towels which, once removed, reveal his coarse, almost ape-like handsomeness. Unlike Capone, who was born in this country, Tony speaks broken English, yet he shares with Capone and Rico Bandello an excessive concern for his public appearance that may suggest effeminacy but that, however stereotypical, was anomalous for mob bosses of those times. Overall Tony suggests the lowbrow type, primitive if not quite simian, yet seemingly less so as the film proceeds. An illiterate, as were many Italian American immigrants, he wants to 'write ... [his] name' across the city – in bullets. He displays his ignorance in mispronouncing '*habeas corpus*' as 'hocus pocus,' in conformity with the long-standing stereotype of the Italian American as a primarily corporeal, linguistically challenged entity. What somewhat qualifies this characterization of Tony are his cultural aspirations, these being a reflection of his presumably innate Italian affinity for theatrical spectacle as well as his desire for legitimacy through the imitation of high society. Thus in the company of his hooligan associates he attends a performance of the stage play *Rain* and even criticizes them for what he sees as their ignorant and insensitive evaluations of its promiscuous heroine. At the same time, Tony exhibits the combined childishness, savagery, and amorality that many northern European travellers had come to identify with southern Italians. This is evident when, having retrieved a tommy gun from his enemies during their failed attempt to assassinate him, Tony returns their fire with a reckless glee reminiscent of a pre-adolescent trying out a new Christmas present, as he has never seen so destructive a weapon. Robin Wood's characterization of Tony as an 'over-grown child' seems justified, for besides sporting a suit of 'all different colors' as his means of seduction, he loves fancy dressing gowns, ornate ties, and jewelry, the last of which Wood identifies with the savage's love of beads.[48] Such behaviour consorts with another eighteenth- and nine-teenth-century stereotype, to be examined later, that identifies Italians with American Indians. This is not to say that *Scarface* portrays Italian Americans as Indians, but that, as Wood observes of *Monkey Business*, one of Hawks's later comedies, the 'juxtaposition of apes, savages [Indians in fact], and children is clearly related to the presentation of the gangsters in *Scarface*.' And finally, Tony's childishness is inextricable from that lack of self-reflection that prevents him from recognizing both his incestuous impulses and the immorality of his violence.[49]

Although Tony differs from Rico in having a family, his domestic life is highly disorganized and anomic as compared to the 'father-dominat-ed, mother-centred' Italian American families typical of those decades, when the nuclear family was often strengthening ties with relatives.[50] In contrast with such a norm, Tony's father has either died or disappeared, thus creating a void in parental authority that helps to explain the son's waywardness as well as Cesca's keeping late hours and running around with men, behaviour quite unusual among Italian American women of the second generation. Nor is there a trace of an extended family of Camontes. Although Camonte's mother stereotypically offers him abundant wine and spaghetti during his infrequent visits home, she at best reproves rather than controls him, and he denies her the mother-respect typical of Italian America. If anything the Camonte household confirms the mainstream view not only that Italians have 'distinctly im-proper families,' but that they are an inbred people, a trait implicit in the film's incest theme.[51] In view of Tony's bizarre family background, one is tempted to agree with Fran Mason's claim that, to the extent that he has a family, it is his gang.[52] Nonetheless one must accept Warshow's standard characterization of Tony as being, finally, a desperate individu-alist who, like Rico, dies alone after shooting it out with the police. Such individualism stands out in Tony's credo, in which the gang has no place: 'Do it first, do it yourself, and keep on doing it.'

If Tony's relations with his ethnic group and family are strained as a result of his extreme individualism, his entry into mainstream society is rendered impossible by his antisocial behaviour combined with the vestiges within him of Old World culture, all of which prevents him from adapting to the challenge of modernity. This is not to deny that, even more than Rico, Camonte applies the latest forms of technology to his criminal purposes: toy-like tommy guns, armoured cars equipped for careening car chases and motorcade bombardments, and steel-plated fortress-like apartments. From the mainstream point of view, however, Tony embodies outrageous excess in violence as in materialism and therefore must be killed off as unassimilable. So too, for all his attraction to America as a wide-open and free-wheeling society, Tony cannot shake off the outmoded sexual norms of his ethnic culture, for just as he insists on restricting his sister's sexuality according to Old World standards, thus preventing her from dating in the relaxed experimental style typical of the United States, so he kills Guino in retaliation for a supposed insult to his and Cesca's sexual honour, this being the immediate cause of Camonte's downfall.

Although Tony, like Rico Bandello, has no discernible ties with the Church, and is if anything the incarnation of the gangster as secular materialist, many filmgoers of the early 1930s probably regarded Tony's Catholic cultural background as an explanation for his criminal violence and hence his inability to transcend his Old World origins. Les and Barbara Keyser characterize *Scarface* and *Little Caesar* as 'Prohibition parable[s]' pitting a 'puritanical Protestant nativist establishment' against 'free-spirited Catholic' immigrant minorities.[53] Paul Giles relates the themes of mother- and sister-incest in *Scarface* to the idea, common to Anglo-American core culture, of the 'Mother' Catholic Church, which, besides refusing to surrender its children, demands that they shun the 'confusion and difference' of American society.[54] Not only does Tony bear an obtrusive cruciform scar on his cheek, notes Wood, but the image of the cross, whether as a Christian symbol or death symbol, pervades the film. Indeed, every killing is accompanied by a cross or, as with the St Valentine's Day Massacre, crosses.[55] It is unclear whether such imagery implies that gangster violence is sacrilegious or identifies it somehow with Catholic mysteries; but in any case, American Catholics felt themselves besmirched by *Scarface*.[56]

Consistent with stereotypes of the effeminate and even homosexual Italian, Tony exhibits an ambiguous masculinity.[57] Having initially shown his vanity by examining himself approvingly in a barber's mirror, he indulges in a massage that makes him seem effete, pampered, and self-indulgent; in another scene he wears jewelry, a habit regarded in those days as unsuitable for males. After rising in the underworld, the ignorant

Tony takes as a compliment what Poppy describes as his 'effeminate' collection of fancy shirts and ties. When, like Rico, he breaks down in his shoot-out with the police, he implicitly goes 'soft' and thus shows a presumed feminine trait.

Scarface contains a gallery of Italian American portrayals, not all of them negative. Whereas in the original script Tony's mother willingly accepts his stolen cash, the final version has her caution Cesca against accepting blood money from her brother, for whom she predicts a bad end.[58] Perhaps to placate ethnic audiences, the policeman Guarino figures as Tony's nemesis in an early instance of the good wop–bad wop theme, yet he pursues Tony not for moral reasons but from hatred. In a still less flattering portrayal, Tony's male 'secretary' answers to the stereotype of the ignorant Italian American speaking in broken English. Prevented by his coarseness and irascibility from acquiring good telephone manners, this buffoon botches his secretarial duties and, unable to grasp modern impersonalism, shoots an 'uncooperative' telephone in a fit of rage. Such behaviour exemplifies Italian American childishness, as does Guino's cutting up of paper dolls. While doomed gang boss Louie Costillo plainly lacks Tony's unrestrained appetites, Lovo exemplifies another type, that of the gangster who favours business-like methods. In contrast with Tony's erotic pathology, the scene in which Guino and Cesca fall in love is one of the film's best. The organ-grinder in this scene exemplifies Italian joyfulness, or the 'natural.'

Typical of the early sound era, the Italian Americans in *Scarface* were played mainly by non-Italians. Yet though it is possible for a non-Italian to portray an Italian convincingly, Muni's performance approaches caricature and thus exemplifies what Martin Scorsese, otherwise an admirer of *Scarface*, describes as the 'Mamma mia!' school of acting: 'Muni's scenes with his mother were embarrassing. No one talks that way,' notes Scorsese, though 'George Raft and Ann Dvorak ... were so good, so natural.'[59] Yet for all Muni's shortcomings, *Scarface* contributed substantially to the screen image of Italian Americans as well as to the gangster genre. The Italian American mother nurturing her criminal son with ethnic specialties appears in countless films, as does the gangland summit meeting and code of *omertà* that Tony honours in refusing to turn police informant. His sensual fondness for creature comforts anticipates the self-indulgence of other cinematic gang bosses, who share his taste for blonde mistresses, while Tony's and Guino's visit to a hospital to perform an execution anticipates a famous scene in *Godfather I*. Guino's habit of flipping a coin, which Hawks borrowed from *Doorway to Hell*, is taken up by other screen gangsters. Many later films call to mind *Scarface* in their depiction of cars smashing into fire hydrants and the shooting up of restaurants.

However influential, the image of the Italian American gangster that emerges in *Little Caesar* and *Scarface* is hardly representative. This inaccuracy has less to do with Hollywood's tendency to romanticize its subjects than with the fact that both films are inspired by Al Capone, the most publicized and perhaps the least typical major Italian American crime boss of the twentieth century. With his flashy clothes, flamboyant demeanour, and loud mouth, which won him the publicity he craved but also brought about his downfall by attracting the IRS, Capone failed to conform to the gangster ideal in the Sicilian tradition to which most Italian American crime leaders belonged.[60] Whereas Capone flaunted the operatic style of the Neapolitan Camorra, running to extremes of emotion and violence, Sicilian bosses had long favoured quiet, sober, even anonymous behaviour. Suspicious of Capone's Neapolitan origins and temperament, they found him lacking in the self-discipline demanded by the Sicilian code of *omertà*. As they saw it, Capone's plot to kill federal agent Eliot Ness was sheer madness.[61] Sicilian-born crime boss Joseph Bonanno observes of Capone's Neapolitan gangster associates that they 'went in for loud clothes, roughhouse and maudlin outbursts of violence. The archetypal Sicilian, by contrast, is stoic, self-possessed and given to violence only to restore order, not out of display.' Bonanno claims that the Mafia, as a Sicilian institution, was gradually undermined by Neapolitan recruits such as Joe Valachi, who lacked understanding of Mafia tradition.[62] Sicilian American gangsters' preoccupation with maintaining a low profile is evident in Lucky Luciano's insistence, upon his formation of the 'new' syndicated Mafia in the 1930s, that his fellow bosses and underlings wear sober, unostentatious, and tasteful clothing similar to that favoured by respectable businessmen; and indeed, at least into the 1960s most Italian American crime bosses eschewed showy dress.[63] The much publicized sartorial splendour of John Gotti, who controlled the Gambino family in the 1980s and early 1990s, and whose kinship family originated in Naples, not only offended gangleaders of the older generation but attracted media attention and thus helped to land Gotti in jail for life.[64] Thus an irony of the gangster film is that Al Capone, its most durable icon, embarrassed his peers. Had Capone not called attention to himself, Hollywood would have had to invent him. As Muscio notes, for much of the sound era the cinematic image of the Italian American gangster has largely followed the 'explosive' Capone-like model established by Rico and Camonte, while only a small number of characterizations, chiefly those of George Raft, Eduardo Ciannelli, and Jack LaRue (all Italian Americans, incidentally), exemplify the 'implosive' gangster, that is, a criminal who intimidates not by displays of violence or emotion but by menacing hints and insinuations, which is closer to the reality of the Mafioso.[65] Subsequently Mario Puzo and Francis Ford Coppola were to realize that the modest, austere, and low-key Don Vito Corleone is more interesting (and fearful) than Capone and his celluloid imitations.

The question arises to what extent Rico's and Tony's violence is attributable to their background and social environment. Neither film implies the existence of a biologically inescapable Italian criminality, or portrays organized crime as solely Italian American. Just as in *Little Caesar* Joe Massara wins mainstream success contrary to Rico's chosen path, so the leading underworld boss proves to be the WASP Big Boy, a low-profile corruptor of non-ethnic public officials. In *Scarface*, Camonte's mother brands him as family scapegrace, while Costillo and Lovo shun violence in favour of business methods. Regarding environmental causality, Stephen Karpf and Paola Casella claim that for the socially disadvantaged Rico the only means of advancement is crime – a proposition belied by Joe Massara's success in entertainment.[66] Actually, Rico and Camonte are driven to crime not by environment but by power-lust.[67]

Another question is whether *Little Caesar* or *Scarface* legitimates or glorifies crime, as the censors feared. Given that, in the face of a most unpopular law, Prohibition gangsters like Al Capone provided a highly demanded service, they came to be seen in some quarters as national heroes, and were treated sympathetically in some films of the 1920s. According to David Ruth, the chief attraction of the gangster of that era was that of a rebellious individual pursuing his personal goals at all costs amid the massive, over-organized, and restrictive bureaucratic society the United States had become during the early twentieth century. Ruth contends further that the apparent or presumed resemblance between the entrepreneurial methods of Prohibition-era gangsters and those of so-called respectable capitalists of the same period raised concerns among the American middle class over the possibly inherently rapacious morality of capitalism itself. The strong anti-capitalist sentiments of the Depression era subsequently inspired leftward-leaning critics to invest the gangster with the aura of a romantic rebel who, stuck unfairly at the bottom of the social ladder, only claimed his rightful share of the American pie. Gradually it became a commonplace that crime films awaken ambivalence and even attraction towards the gangster, whose violence and brutality, however objectionable from a strictly legal point of view, supposedly betoken opposition to capitalist injustice. Thus Jonathan Munby recently argues that Leroy's and Hawks's protagonists represent unprecedented ethnic protest against capitalism. Besides noting that Prohibition originates in WASP America's attempt to suppress the alcohol-imbibing after-hours lifestyle of newly arrived and mainly Catholic ethnic groups, Munby closely links capitalism and organized crime, whether in methods, organization, or morality. In his view, *Little Caesar* and *Scarface* portray the underworld as a justifiable path of social mobility for individuals otherwise immured by the capitalist host society within their impoverished neighbourhoods. Exposing the unfairness of American capitalism in virtually seditious fashion, the gangster represents his ethnic group and, through his protest, provides it with its hitherto absent 'dialogic' voice. Such a voice rejects the idea of ethnic assimilation into WASP ideals of Americanness, but rather proposes non-WASP ethnicity as a legimate American tradition in its own right. The censor-dictated inserts in *Scarface* cannot control a pro-ethnic film challenging WASP hegemony.[68]

Unfortunately, Munby not only misreads the films but misunderstands American ethnic groups. It is astonishing to hear that *Little Caesar* and *Scarface*, often taken as slurs against Italian America, and most especially by Italian Americans themselves, exemplify ethnic protest in the 1930s.[69] Ironically, not only do these films rely mainly on non-Italian actors, but their directors and scenarists are either Jews or WASPs. Who gave them the right to speak for Italian Americans? And why should they want to? Burnett's statement that he intended *Little Caesar* as an 'Italian picture,' as if he wrote it from the 'inside,' and which statement Munby accepts, only demonstrates self-delusion.[70] Even if Munby's identification of capitalism with the underworld were justified, the protagonists of *Little Caesar* and *Scarface* favour inefficiently violent methods by comparison with their more business-like underworld contemporaries. One wonders too how Rico and Camonte, with whom we are invited *not* to identify, can exemplify 'dialogic' ethnic protest. With their minimal verbal skills and brutal physicality, they exemplify the almost animal-like speechlessness that Pellegrino d'Acierno recognizes as a negative Italian American stereotype.[71] It is also difficult to see how these self-serving gangsters, men of *omertà*, could serve as the mouthpieces of anything. Although *Little Caesar* and *Scarface* may seem at points to invite audience identification, they ultimately portray the gangster as an aberrant, self-destructive individual.

Munby further holds that, at the time of these films' release, Italian Americans like other ethnics remained confined in virtual racial segregation owing to their limited social and political opportunities. Actually, Italian Americans' comparative lack of political success at this time stemmed partly from their weak civic consciousness, a carry-over from southern Italy.[72] Munby furthermore overestimates the social confinement of Italian Americans during this period, when some members of the first generation were not just acculturating but assimilating. The period's more typical figure was certainly not the gangster but the hardworking Italian American who had 'bought into' America and for whom the gangster, far from being a mouthpiece, was a stigmatizing obstacle to ethnic progress, including assimilation. Contrary to Munby's contention that the censor-demanded inserts in *Scarface* register only the mainstream's prejudicial opinion of ethnics, the words assigned to the Italian American civic leader exemplify a characteristic view of his ethnic group towards the few though highly visible home-grown gangsters within it: 'Dey bring-a nothin' butta disgrace-a to my whole people.' Not accidentally, *Scarface* was condemned by the Order of the Sons of Italy.

III

The classic gangster film enjoyed a brief heyday, as audiences and concerned groups such as the DAR and American Legion were outraged by its questionable moral content and possible incitements to criminality. An outcry also arose against defamatory representations of ethnic groups, including Italian Americans, as gangsters. In March 1931, Will Hays pronounced the gangster film a dead letter, and by September 1931, more than six months before the release of *Scarface*, he had convinced the MPPDA to halt the production of gangster films. Other factors in the decline of the genre were perhaps its naturally waning popularity as a result of overexposure and lack of new ideas, and also the increasing emphasis on sex in the films of the early 1930s, which led to a moral backlash from such pressure groups as the Catholic Legion of Decency. In order to avoid government intervention and regulation, the Hollywood studios agreed to comply with a more stringent production code that was instituted in July 1934. Henceforward the Hays-Breen Office forbade not only the heroization of the criminal but the incitement of 'bigotry or hatred among people of differing races, religions, or national origins.' In 1935 Will Hayes declared a complete moratorium on gangster films.[73]

By the late 1930s, self-regulating Hollywood had largely tamed the gangster genre, which, in a sure sign of decadence, now poked fun at itself in 'gangster comedies.' In *Brother Orchid* Edward G. Robinson plays gangleader 'Little John' Sarto who, after taking a leave of absence in order to pursue higher culture in Europe, loses control of his gang, wins it back, closes it down, and ends up more or less contented as a monk in a monastery, where he cultivates exotic flowers. It is an indication of the sanitization of the genre that Sarto specializes in fraudulent forms of crime rather than in violent illegalities such as bootlegging. Whereas Rico and Camonte had seemed self-generated in their megalomania, in contrast with Tom Powers in *The Public Enemy*, whose more modest underworld career had resulted partly from circumstance, the gangster film now resumed a trend of the 1910s and 1920s in representing the gangster as the passive product of social forces, as in *Dead End* (1937) and *Angels With Dirty Faces* (1938). The gangster film also lost much of its flavour owing to the removal of most indications of the gangster's ethnicity, while the requirement that historical gangsters not be mentioned by name made cinematic biographies of Capone and Luciano impossible.[74] Sometimes, however, as in Raoul Walsh's *The Roaring Twenties* (1939), the gangster is evidently Italian without being specified as such. Thus the film depicts a top-level gangster named Nick Brown (Paul Kelly), who despite his Anglo-Saxon name must be regarded as an encrypted Italian, as repeated attention is called to his eating spaghetti in an Italian restaurant. The character is almost certainly inspired by Al Capone, who called himself Brown.[75] In Mervyn Leroy's *Johnny Eager* (1942) Robert Taylor plays the secretive mastermind of a powerful underworld operation who, despite his unspecified ethnicity, fulfils the stereotype of the Italian criminal virtuoso through comparisons with Michelangelo, Machiavelli, and the Medici. Not only is Eager's front man the improbably named A. Frazier Marco, but he employs the killer Giulio (Paul Stewart), with whom he reminisces over wars with rival Italian American gangs in the old days. Further conforming to an Italian American gangster stereotype, Eager attracts the interest of a beautiful upper-class blonde (Lana Turner) while exhibiting more than a hint of homoeroticism in his otherwise inexplicable friendship with the WASP Jeff Hartnett (Van Heflin), an alcoholic intellectual.[76]

Based on Maxwell Anderson's stage play, Alfred Santell's *Winterset* (1936) dramatizes the Sacco and Vanzetti case and its aftermath. In the film as in the play the two victimized social radicals are condensed in the figure of Bartolomeo Romagna (John Carradine), who is falsely accused of a holdup committed with the use of Romagna's stolen car by the demonic Italian American gangster Trock Estrella (Eduardo Cianelli) and his gang. After Romagna's execution, his tormented son Mio (Burgess Meredith) wanders the country attempting to clear his father's name. In the shadow of Brooklyn Bridge, and in a series of most improbable coincidences, Mio encounters an immigrant family, one of whose members had been Estrella's accomplice; the judge in the Romagna case, now suffering guilty doubts; and the dying Estrella who, with his dwindling gang, aims to conceal his role in the holdup.

Pellegrino d'Acierno complains that the pro-ethnic liberal thrust of *Winterset* is compromised by the fact that the film largely denies Italian American actors the opportunity to portray their fellow ethnics, thus preventing the group from speaking in its own voice. Romagna and Mio are interpreted by WASP actors, while the Italian American Cianelli plays Estrella in an ethnically demeaning role.[77] Not only does Estrella casually betray his colleagues, but, in a recurrence of the theme of the vain and pampered gangleader, he is introduced without dignity, as he is being shaved. *Winterset* thus exemplifies those films in which the 'good' Italian American is impersonated by a WASP, and in which an authentic Italian American portrays his unassimilable counterpart. Nonetheless, Estrella's gang includes non-Italian members, in keeping with the production code, while as in *Scarface* an Italian organ-grinder represents ethnic vivacity and enjoyment.[78]

Although Nick Donati, the main character of *Kid Galahad* (1937), makes his living as a boxing promoter rather than a gangster, he is interpreted by Edward G. Robinson, who often portrayed Italian American gangsters. Nick furthermore has close underworld connections, including the racketeer Turkey (Humphrey Bogart), as well as a gangster's taste for fedoras, double-breasted suits with broad lapels, handkerchiefs, and flashy ties. Making no secret of his ethnicity, he speaks fluent Italian (as did Robinson) in conversation with his barber and immigrant mother. The scene with the barber – a stage Italian who cries '*magnifico!*' – takes place at a three-night party where Donati conforms to the highly questionable stereotype of the spendthrift Italian with a weakness for alcohol. His worst fault is a rigid authoritarianism not uncommon among first-generation patriarchs yet increasingly difficult to maintain among second-generation Italian Americans, a category that includes Donati. Strict in his demand for absolute obedience from his fighters, Donati also adheres to the Old World sexual code and thus comes to fear for the virtue of his sister Marie, who secretly loves the WASP 'Kid Galahad' (Wayne Morris), the top boxer in Nick's stable. Shortly before his murder by Turkey's thugs, Nick finally surmounts his stubborn nature (and ethnic backwardness) both by forgiving Galahad's professional disobedience and by accepting his sister's romance with a non-Italian. Her subsequent marriage to Galahad exemplifies the theme of the Italian American or ethnic woman who escapes the suffocating influence of her ethnic group by marrying outside it. As Daniel Sembroff Golden rightly notes, *Kid Galahad* is unusual for its era not only in allowing Italian Americans to speak Italian on screen but in exploring the tensions between ethnic generations.[79]

In contrast with the likeable Donati, the gangster Johnny Vanning (Eduardo Ciannelli) in *Marked Woman* (1937) calls to mind the antisocial viciousness of Rico Bandello and Tony Camonte while more closely resembling Trock Estrella in his preference for quiet intimidation. Not only is Vanning Italian in appearance, accent, and gesture, but his obviously fictitious and WASP-sounding name seems an odd scrambling of 'Giovanni.' Although the film's title disavows any resemblance to existing persons, Vanning's inspiration is Lucky Luciano, recently sentenced to a long prison term for his domination of New York's prostitution rackets.[80] At the film's opening Vanning has taken over the Club Intime with the aim of increasing its gambling profits. His team of prostitutes, euphemistically termed hostesses, is led by Mary Dwight (Bette Davis), who ironically bears the name of the Virgin Mother, and who imagines that she can avoid being scarred by her world. Mary's sole source of joy and purity is her sister Betty, whom she is putting through college, but who during her visit to the city learns the truth of Mary's occupation. Betty seems about to sink into prostitution herself when, intimidated by Vanning, she falls down a flight of stairs and dies. After beating Mary nearly to death, Vanning's henchmen mark her cheek with a disfiguring X. The other prostitutes take revenge on Vanning by testifying against him in court, where, like Luciano, he receives from thirty to fifty years in prison.

As Luciano reorganized the New York underworld, so Vanning announces upon his takeover of a formerly 'penny-ante business' that 'I'm organizing it.' Yet he differs from Rico and Camonte in his level-headedness and self-containment. Reliant on henchmen, Vanning projects the image of a businessman who, preferring to keep his hands clean, uses violence only if necessary. For him, as for Rico, profits are of less interest than ego-gratification through power. When in the final scene the district attorney denounces Vanning as the 'czar' of an 'empire of vice and crime,' he draws upon the theme of gangland imperialism popularized in *Little Caesar*. At the same time, Vanning resembles Tony in his dandyish vanity, self-indulgent sensuality, and linguistic inadequacy, as witness his ignorance of the word 'intime.' Like many screen gangsters, he combines vicious brutality with hints of homosexuality, for though he owns the Club Intime, he has no female companions but exhibits the misogyny typical of Italian American crime bosses in the gangster film. Not only does he arrive at the club with his pampered dog in tow, but he conducts business during a rubdown by his masseur. Apart from suggestions of effeminacy, such behaviour violates Protestant assumptions of the separateness of business and pleasure, work and free time.

During the 1930s gangsters of whatever ethnic background entered into criminal organizations that, though often of greater size and scope than previously, were also more cooperative, secretive, and peaceable in both their internal operations and dealings with each other. Thus Hollywood and its public came to entertain the reassuring though false notion that organized crime had lost its bite after Prohibition. The imprisonment of Capone and Luciano, and the subsequent deportation of the latter, had further encouraged such assumptions, which appear to have been shared by John Huston and Richard Brooks, co-scenarists of *Key Largo* (1949). The film was directed by Huston and is based loosely on Maxwell Anderson's play of that title. Its main characters include Frank McCloud (Humphrey Bogart), a retired U.S. Army officer who has come to a Key Largo resort hotel to visit the family of a soldier killed while under his command in World War II, during the Italian campaign; Mr Temple (Lionel Barrymore), the owner of the hotel and father of the dead soldier; Nora Temple, the widow of Mr Temple's son; and deported gangster Johnny Rocco (Edward G. Robinson), who dreams of reclaiming his underworld empire formerly centred in Chicago. It is a measure of Rocco's decline in status that he and his small gang have secretly descended upon Key Largo with the minor purpose of receiving payment from another gang for a shipment of counterfeit bills. One calls to mind the deposed Al Capone as well as Lucky Luciano, who following his deportation initially spent time in Cuba. Present at the hotel upon McCloud's arrival, Rocco's underlings pretend to be tourists while their boss hides upstairs under the name of Mr Brown, the pseudonym favoured by Capone. It suggests not only excrement but moral contamination, for as Mr Temple says, Rocco is 'city filth.' His concealment behind an ill-fitting WASP name may imply the threat posed by Italian Americans who pretend to assimilate yet retain criminal propensities.

As romance buds between McCloud and Nora, the Temples invite him to stay overnight. Then, with a hurricane approaching, Rocco appears downstairs where he announces that, in order to complete his scheme, he intends to hold the Temples and McCloud captive. McCloud's reluctance to challenge Rocco reflects the cynical world-weariness he must surmount. When Rocco asks incredulously why he had fought in World War II, McCloud answers that he had hoped to prevent a repetition of the interwar years by purging 'ancient ills, ancient evils.' He thus identifies fascist lawlessness with the Prohibition underworld. A parallel is also implicit between Mussolini, short, imperialistic, violent, and defeated, and the diminutive Rocco. Having only recently fought to protect the world against evil, McCloud is depressed to encounter the threat of gang-rule in his own backyard and thus rejects Mr Temple's idea that America can 'do without the Roccos.'

Nonetheless McCloud proves that he retains the best qualities of the American hero, ultimately taking arms against the Italian American imposter. Rocco having mocked McCloud's small means, he answers that he was 'educated in impractical things,' a statement already ironized in a previous scene in which he demonstrates his seamanship by securing Temple's boat. Contrariwise Rocco shows his impracticality when he orders his yacht to be anchored in a dangerous place just before the hurricane, which destroys it. When in exchange for a shakily inept performance of a song Rocco offers his alcoholic mistress the drink she craves, only to retract sadistically his offer, McCloud pours her a stiff whiskey. After being commandeered to drive Rocco and his gang back to Cuba by motorboat, and knowing he will be killed on arrival, McCloud guns down the gangsters, his final victim being Rocco, who dies cowering at the bottom of the boat. Thus the WASP hero drives the undesirable alien back into steerage and eliminates him like a plague-bearing rat. Indeed, Mr Temple had said that Rocco should be not 'deported' but 'exterminated.'

Robinson's portrayal of Rocco calls to mind Italian American film gangsters of the 1930s, a stereotype to which Robinson had contributed. Reminiscent of Leroy's *Little Caesar*, in which the Italian American gangster aspires to the gangland equivalent of Roman imperial power, McCloud describes Rocco as having been an 'emperor.' Yet unlike Rico Bandello, Rocco is a hedonist who fondly recalls those days in Chicago when he dined on pompano flown in from Florida and washed down with champagne. When Rocco first appears he is taking a bath, phallic cigar in hand, a glass of liquor on the bathtub ledge. The cigar is reminiscent of Rico Bandello and anticipates other cigar-smoking crime bosses such as Rico Angelo in *Party Girl* (1958), Uncle Giovanni in *Mean Streets* (1973), and Al Capone in *Capone* (1975). One thinks of a Roman potentate at his leisure, or some sodden habitué of the Roman baths – not the American work ethic. As previous gangsters had exuded a homoerotic aura extending from dandyism to a taste for massages to male jealousy to sadistic misogyny, so Rocco, having finished his bath, appears nude before his leading henchman (Thomas Gomez), to whom he then casually exposes his backside as he dries himself with a towel. Not only does Rocco's silk bathrobe and flashily expensive clothing suggest effeminacy, but he answers to the misogynistic gangster stereotype in mistreating his mistress. This is not to deny Rocco's heterosexual credentials, as he prefers 'wildcat' women. In one scene, Rocco is immersed in shadow as he whispers obscenities – or 'city filth' – into the ear of Nora Temple, whose name evokes sanctity.

Rocco exemplifies the gangster stereotype so thoroughly that he seems almost to sum its elements. As the gangster is identified traditionally with excess – physical, sexual, gastronomic, sartorial, etc. – so Rocco announces his desire for 'more.' When McCloud asks what he would do after achieving 'more,' he replies: 'I want more of more.' (Such omnivorousness, however, seems ironically reminiscent of the emerging postwar consumer society.) In nearly assaulting the wheelchair-bound Mr Temple, Rocco flouts the Anglo-American ideal of fair play. Although Rocco resembles Rico Bandello in his admiration for toughness – Rico insists that gangsters must know how to 'take it' – he is no more capable than his predecessor of fulfilling the ideal. Thus at the height of the hurricane the anxious Rocco's hands join as if he were unconsciously to pray, his long-abandoned Catholicism revealed in an unguarded, fearful moment.

In other instances the Rocco character anticipates Francis Ford Coppola's portrayal of the underworld, as when he expresses disbelief that McCloud had risked his neck for his country. Notwithstanding that Italian American participation in World War II exceeded the group's percentage of the national population, Rocco's statement exemplifies the lack of national loyalty evident in some members of the group, especially before World War II.[81] The same opposition between private and public commitment appears in the final scene of *The Godfather II*, when Sonny Corleone interprets his brother's voluntary enlistment after Pearl Harbor as an affront to, even a betrayal of, his criminal family. Yet Rocco somewhat contradictorily insists upon his Americanism in protesting

that, in being deported, he had been treated like a 'Red.' His allegiance
to the United States, such as it is, like his annoyance at having been taken
as a leftist radical, conforms with underworld reality, as crime bosses typically loathe communism and idealize the America on which they have
fattened. In *Godfather I* crime boss Barzini announces at a gangland summit meeting: 'We're not Communists.'[82]

Most crime films of the 1940s are less concerned with mob bosses
than with lower-echelon Italian American criminals working as freelance
hoodlums or within small gangs. Some Italian American actors such as
Ted de Corsia, Anthony Caruso, and Jack LaRue carved out minor careers devoted in varying degrees to these secondary roles, which, however, the studios by no means assigned exclusively to Italian Americans.[83]
The more memorable examples include Lash Canino (Bob Steele), the
most dangerous of Philip Marlowe's antagonists in Howard Hawks's version of Raymond Chandler's *The Big Sleep* (1946); Bill Fico (Paul Fix), the
numbers racket enforcer who after killing small-time numbers operator
Leo Morse (Thomas Gomez), nearly kills his brother (John Garfield)
at the climax of Abraham Polonsky's *Force of Evil* (1949); and the Italian
American thugs who, working for local politician Walter O'Neil (Kirk
Douglas), beat up gambler Sam Masterson (Van Heflin) in Lewis Mile-
stone's *The Strange Love of Martha Ivers* (1947). In Jacques Tourneur's
Out of the Past (1947), the menacing black-clad gunman Stefano (Italian American Paul Valentine) penetrates the woodland hideout of the
unjustly accused Jeff Bailey (Robert Mitchum), only to be pulled from
a cliff edge to his death after having been hooked to the line of a cast-
fishing rod. It is as if the pastoral world and its serene pastimes were
taking vengeance on their alien, ethnic violator, who carries with him
metropolitan pollutions. In William Wyler's *Detective Story* (1951), set in a
New York police station, 'virtually every criminal ... from ordinary thug to
wealthy gangster was depicted in the crudest, most insulting stereotypes
of Italian Americans.'[84]

Two other films of the late 1940s, *Kiss of Death* (1947) and *Cry of the
City* (1948), not only interrogate the causes of ethnic crime but, in the
spirit of *film noir*, introduce moral ambiguities uncharacteristic of previous crime films. Directed by Henry Hathaway from a script by Ben Hecht
and Charles Lederer, *Kiss of Death* was shot entirely in New York City and
neighbouring locales and thus reflects Italian neo-realism. It begins with
a Christmas Eve burglary heist in which the unemployed Nick Bianco
(Italian American actor Victor Mature), hoping to provide Christmas
gifts for his family, is captured by the police. Having refused to inform

on his fellow gang members, and gone to prison with the gangleader's promise to look after his family, he learns that his wife has committed suicide and that his two children are in a Catholic orphanage. He then decides to bargain with the ironically named D'Angelo (Brian Donlevy), an ambitious assistant district attorney. In exchange for parole, he will inform on the gang members while helping D'Angelo to trap and convict Tommy Udo (Richard Widmark), a psychotic gunman. Nick thus chooses to become a 'stoolie' – the underworld's most detested figure. While on parole Nick remarries and becomes a bricklayer. When Udo comes to trial, D'Angelo forces Nick to testify under threat of loss of parole but botches the case, allowing Udo to go free. Now vulnerable to Udo, Nick waits for him at an Italian restaurant and, after provoking him, takes five bullets in the belly; however, he had earlier phoned D'Angelo, who arrives on the scene with a police squad that kills Udo.

Kiss of Death treats familial and social environment as only one cause of lower-class criminality. That crime is not entirely environmental in its causality is implicit in Udo, a born sociopath. Nor does the film imply that Italians exhibit some innate propensity for crime, as Udo, with his unplaceable name, qualifies as a generic ethnic. Nonetheless, one learns that as a child Nick had witnessed his father's murder, whereupon his family sank into poverty from which crime was his only escape. Then, following his imprisonment, Nick's attempts to reform his life are frustrated by employers' unwillingness to hire ex-cons. This is compounded by Nick's wife's adultery and suicide, and his betrayal by his gangland associates. One thus feels sympathy for a character otherwise detestable as a 'stoolie.' Consistent with Italian American values, the film suggests that, as Nick's impoverished and disrupted family had contributed to his criminality, so his redemption lies in his re-established family life. The religious implications of this theme are underscored in the scene in which Nick, visiting his children at the orphanage while on parole, appears before a mural whose subject is Christ calling the little children to come to him.

The dramatic force of Kiss of Death lies in its moral ambiguity. However much the criminal world is riddled with duplicity, the code of silence retains its force in Nick's community, and Nick's betrayal of Udo is all the more disturbing since he deliberately enters into his confidence. Yet there is little to prefer in the legal or 'straight' world, for though the good wop–bad wop distinction typifies the crime film, it loses its credibility in Kiss of Death. Not only is Nick Bianco an in some ways admirable family man who would 'go straight,' but D'Angelo, the assistant district attorney, is a self-important, opportunistic careerist who exploits Bianco while nearly getting him killed. Initially D'Angelo manipulates Nick into informing against his colleagues. When Nick and D'Angelo visit the orphanage, the latter is taken to be the gangster, and indeed he looks and acts like one. Later, violating his promise, he forces Nick to testify against Udo under threat of losing his parole, thus blowing his cover. Ultimately standing alone between the criminal and legal worlds, Nick must settle his problems in his own fashion.

Directed by Robert Siodmak and based on Henry Edward Elspeth's novel *The Chair for Martin Rome*, *Cry of the City* (1948) amounts to a kind of doppelgänger story of the good wop–bad wop type, the former figure being represented as a policeman and the latter as a small-time criminal. Yet unlike conventional treatments of this theme, Siodmak introduces moral ambiguities typical of *noir*. The film begins in a hospital where Martin Rome (Richard Conte), having killed a policeman and been seemingly mortally wounded in a robbery, is attended by relatives, a priest, and his lawyer Kroeger. Another of his visitors is Lt. Candella (Victor Mature), a former friend who grew up in the same ethnic neighbourhood, but whom Rome's younger brother Tony despises for deserting it. Candella interrogates Rome about a ring in his possession, which he suspects he had acquired through the robbery and torture of Mrs De Grazia, but which Rome actually won in a crap game. Much concerned for his young fiancée, Tina Raconti (Debra Paget), Rome advises her to go into hiding lest Candella jail her as his accomplice. When Kroeger offers to defend Rome in exchange for confession to the De Grazia murder, he refuses.

Rome having been transferred from the hospital to prison, Candella visits the Rome household, where the elders welcome him as an old friend. In a familiar motif of the gangster film parodied in Scorsese's *It's Not Just You, Murray!*, Rome's mother supplies Candella with home-made soup to bring to her son. After escaping prison Rome discovers the robbery jewels in Kroeger's safe, kills the lawyer with his switchblade, and transports the jewels to his parents' apartment, his aim being to buy his way out of the country. Although Rome's father disowns him outright, his mother (Mimi Aguglia) does so only after intense anguish; however, the brother remains loyal, notwithstanding that Rome pressures him to steal their parents' savings to finance his getaway. By exploiting the concern of another girlfriend Rome manages to receive treatment from an unlicenced doctor, whom he thus places carelessly in legal jeopardy, and then takes refuge in the cave-like apartment of a grotesquely mannish and menacing masseuse with whom he arranges to trade the jewels. Thus he is wandering ever farther on his desperate night journey from what had been the two main feminine emotional supports of his existence: his nurturing mother, and the beautiful though naïve Tina, whose idealized, almost madonnine innocence contrasts ironically with Rome's ever-deepening descent into criminality. When, in another example of Rome's exploitation of a feminine figure, he attempts to double-cross the masseuse, Candella surprises them, and both men are wounded. Candella finally trails Rome to a church where he has been joined by Tina, who deserts Rome after he threatens to kill Candella. Upon leaving the church, Rome attempts to flee but is killed by Candella with a pistol shot in the back upon failing to heed the cry: 'In the name of the law, Rome, stop!' As in *Little Caesar*, *The Godfather*, and *Mean Streets*, Catholicism is associated with murderous bloodshed, although it can also be argued that the film honours Catholic sanctities in that Rome is killed outside the church. Just before dying on the sidewalk Rome draws his switchblade in a symbolic reversion to the role of hoodlum in which he began. His progress through the nightmarish urban world of the film has carried him back to his origins in the old neighbourhood, as if he (and Candella) were driven by a retrogressive ethnic fatality.[85]

Nonetheless the good wop–bad wop antithesis is too simple to explain the main characters. As a policeman, Candella has abandoned the ethnic neighbourhood's personalistic ties out of a sense of allegiance to state and nation, thus exemplifying second-generation Italian Americans who assimilated by internalizing mainstream values. Yet from the perspective of the neighbourhood code of *omertà*, Candella has betrayed Rome and is not to be helped in pursuing him. If anything, Candella meets with a mixture of contempt and distrust – the attitude of Rome's brother for much of the film. When Candella denounces Rome's conduct in Tony's presence, so as to discredit him, Rome rejoins disdainfully: 'Make an Italian a cop, he's got to make a speech.' The cynical and civically crippling assumption underlying this remark would seem to be that public authorities are driven by motives of self-display and ego-gratification rather than by a genuine impersonal commitment to the general welfare – precisely the attitude Herbert Gans found in the Italian American 'urban villagers' in the late 1950s.[86] And yet ironically, the depressive Candella returns to the old neighbourhood in quest of what the impersonal mainstream lacks. Besides referring to Mrs Rome as 'Mamma,' as if seeking a surrogate family to ease his bachelorhood, he may envy the close familial and social ties available to Rome, a local resident. Unlike Rome, Candella has neither a loyal brother nor a loyal and beautiful girlfriend. With his low policeman's salary, Candella perhaps also envies Rome's criminally acquired wealth. It is as if Candella, in obsessively hunting Rome, sought to destroy a darker, suppressed side of his personality.

Not only is Rome concerned for Tina, shielding her from the overzealous Candella, but he seems more admirable, or at least less despicable, than Kroeger, who tries to manipulate him into a false confession. That Rome receives the affection of his mother, brother, and girlfriend implies attractive qualities, and it also appears that Rome has remained loyal to the neighbourhood by refusing to assimilate. Yet as the film proceeds, he alienates the viewer. Although he loves the virginal Tina, he has another girlfriend, presumably for carnal purposes. Besides jeopardizing the doctor, he robs Kroeger and later envisions Candella's murder. When Rome surprises Candella at gunpoint in Mamma Rome's apartment, Rome seriously entertains the possibility of gunplay in her presence, unlike Candella who, insisting that all violence is to be avoided in such a situation, shows a concern for Rome's mother's welfare greater than that of her son. Having been urged by Rome to steal from their parents, Tony finally realizes that his brother lacks the father- and mother-respect that sustains home and neighbourhood, and that loyalty to him requires the betrayal of family. Rome thus dishonours both the legal written code and the unwritten code of ethnicity. That his is a distinctly Italian American problem is suggested by Candella's words, 'In the name of the law, Rome, stop!' While 'Rome' refers to the character, it also calls to mind the capital of both Italy and Catholicism, two alleged centres of lawlessness needing to be stopped.

Unlike *Kiss of Death* and *Cry of the City*, which attribute Italian American criminality to environmental and cultural factors, Nicholas Ray's *Knock on Any Door* (1949) blames society entirely. Based on Willard Motley's novel of the same title, and directed by Nicholas Ray from a script by John Monks, Jr, *Knock on Any Door* tells the story of Nick 'Pretty Boy' Romano (John Derek). On trial for the murder of a policeman, Nick is defended by attorney Andrew Morton (Humphrey Bogart), who had grown up in the same slum neighbourhood as Nick and who, feeling responsible for his fate, has taken the case despite its potential damage to his career through bad publicity. Nick has lived in the slums since the death of his drug-dealing father, who had been unjustly imprisoned for murder in self-defence. After Nick becomes a juvenile delinquent, his mother sadly recalls his days as a choirboy – a scene perhaps inspired by *Little Caesar*, in which the murdered gangster Tony Passa, a former altar boy, is mourned by his mother. Nick is later sent to a brutal reform school for car theft and upon his release is filled with vengeance against society. Arrested a second time, he is befriended by Morton and subsequently marries a poor girl named Emma. But Nick's hot temper and unattractive past keep him from holding down a job, until at last Emma kills herself, exhausted by his return to crime. Now wearing the fedora hats and double-breasted suits of the aspiring gangster, and cultivating his full head of hair, Nick has become 'Pretty Boy' Romano, whose motto is 'Live fast, die young, and leave a good-looking corpse.' The district attorney (George MacReady) causes Nick to admit his guilt, yet in his final speech Morton characterizes him as the product entirely of his social environment. Nick then goes to the electric chair with head shaved, the last of his socially inflicted indignities.

Knock on Any Door treats its characters chiefly as the self-conscious bearers of a social thesis. Its claim that society has produced Nick's criminality is undermined by his temperament and behaviour, a compound of laziness, corruptibility, vanity, mendacity, violence, and incivility, as Casella notes.[87] He is a stereotype of the antisocial, unassimilable Italian. However, the most obvious contradiction to Morton's arguments is Morton himself, who grew up in the neighbourhood that produced Romano, yet who conquered poverty through hard work. Thus the film itself supplies sufficient evidence to undermine its thesis.

IV

The 1930s and 1940s are widely thought to have witnessed major changes in the underworld that are reflected in representations of Italian Americans in the gangster genre. Following the 'Castellamarese War' that is claimed by many scholars to have raged among Italian American criminal groups in the late 1920s and early 1930s, the underworld is believed to have been reorganized by Lucky Luciano and his Italian American and Jewish associates so as to expand and rationalize operations in response to post-Prohibition. Inter-gang warfare, violence, prejudices against non-Italian gangsters, flashy high-profile behaviour – these were disfavoured. An increased cooperativeness, practicality, efficiency, anonymity, and business-like approach were required of Italian American criminal organizations, which now took the form of syndicates or 'families' operating within assigned territories. Although the Italian American underworld lacked a single dictatorial authority, the leaders of the major New York crime families constituted a 'commission' with regulatory powers and advisory influence. Otherwise, families operated freely in their own spheres. The new comparatively business-like impersonality of organized crime became evident in 1941 with the disclosure of Murder Incorporated, a murder-for-contract service employed by the underworld.[88]

Whereas in the classic gangster film the egoistic protagonist parodies the self-made man, organized crime now appears in films as a large-scale business-like organization known as the syndicate. The organized criminal adopts the guise of a business bureaucrat or corporation member, supposedly sharing the anonymity, impersonality, and amoral efficiency of the organization to which he belongs. The crime boss not only falsely advertises himself as a legitimate businessman but, with his low-key methods and subterfuge, resembles one. Like large-scale business corporations, the criminal syndicate gives the impression of a massive, insidious, all-intrusive organization beyond comprehension. This view of the underworld reflects post-war anxieties concerning the rise of corporate and bureaucratic America and the absorption of the individual within its vast and impersonal systems.[89]

Another major influence upon the representation of the Italian American gangster was the increasing awareness during the post-war period of two Italian American criminal organizations that had largely dropped out of public consciousness. Following the lynching of eleven alleged Sicilian Mafiosi in New Orleans in 1891, the idea of the Mafia lost currency. By the 1920s the Black Hand had become a dead letter not only because of its inability to compete with larger and better-organized Prohibition-style criminal groups, but because, in the view of some scholars, these groups had recruited many Black Handers. During the 1930s Italian American organized criminals were known not as Mafiosi but as gangsters. Nor does the word 'Mafia' appear in *Little Caesar*, *Scarface*, *Marked Woman*, or *Key Largo*, perhaps because of the production code. Yet by the late 1940s the Mafia and the Black Hand were regaining their notoriety.[90]

Directed by Joseph E. Lewis, *Undercover Man* (1949) stars Glenn Ford as Treasury Department operative Frank Warren, who brings down a criminal syndicate run by 'The Big Fellow.' After Warren is nearly intimidated by syndicate threats to his wife, his courage is revived by the wife and daughters of a murdered Italian American front man, who risk their lives by producing evidence sufficient to convict the boss. Notwithstanding that Lewis was handicapped by the production code, 'The Big Fellow' is clearly based on Al Capone. Still more unusual, *Undercover Man* refers openly to the Mafia, a synonym for the syndicate, and implies that it originated in the Old Country. Indeed, the front man's wife and daughters tearfully inform Warren that their grandfather had died fighting the Mafia in Sicily.

The following year saw the release of *The Black Hand*, an MGM production directed by Richard Thorpe from a script by Luther Davis. Starring Gene Kelly as Johnny Columbo, the nemesis of the Black Hand, the film is inspired by the career of New York Police lieutenant Joseph Petrosino, whom J. Carroll Naish interprets as Lt. Lorelli, but whose assassination the film transfers from Palermo to Naples. With its frequent references to Mafia and Mafiosi, *The Black Hand* reflects several misconceptions that influenced public views of organized crime. First, it portrays the Black Hand as a large-scale organization similar to later, large-scale Mafia associations, when it actually consisted for the most part of small and loosely organized groups.[91] Second, the film resuscitates the false notion, which goes back to the silent film era, that the Black Hand and American Mafia originated in southern Italy as criminal organizations with little or no modification following their transfer to the United States; moreover, that the Black Hand represented an initial stage or phase in the continuous development of Italian American criminal organizations.[92] The third error is evident in the opening title, which suggests that the elimination of the Black Hand also terminated other organized forms of Italian American criminality. The film further espouses the conspiratorial notion that the serious forms of American crime derive from foreign sources, as a kind of plague to be 'purged.'

Set in Manhattan's Little Italy during immigration, *The Black Hand* opens with the murder of Columbo's father, who had dared to oppose the Black Hand, and whose death occurs in the presence of a corrupt policeman. Following the mature Columbo's return to the United States from Sicily, he aims both to avenge his father and to rescue the reputation of Italian Americans by destroying the extortionists who prey upon them. Reminiscent of the Black Hand films of the silent era, the Italian American community's observance of *omertà* constitutes a major obstacle to law enforcement, as in the courtroom scene in which a trial witness is intimidated into silence upon observing a throat-slitting gesture.[93] Although Columbo initially has little success, partly because of *omertà* and also because of spies and informants, his luck changes after he meets Lt. Lorelli, who laments that the Black Hand has caused the denigration of his group as an 'inferior race.' Ironically, however, Columbo punishes the Black Hand only when he resorts to its methods, using the knife to extort information from local witnesses. At the climax, having long endured destructive bombings by Black Hand blackmailers and extortionists, Little Italy is rocked by a cathartic explosion as Columbo blows up the Black Hand headquarters and then despatches the ringleader (Jewish American Mark Lawrence) in a knife fight.

The Black Hand was overly optimistic regarding the purification of the Italian Americans' criminal reputation, for within a year America was rocked by a Mafia scare promoted by Tennessee senator Estes Kefauver, whose committee conducted a nationwide investigation of interstate rackets from 1951 to 1952. In attracting enormous television audiences, these hearings raised fears of the strangulation of America by a criminal octopus supposedly generated from Sicily and nearly as threatening to national survival as Russian communism – the Mafia. Kefauver believed the Mafia to exist as a single conspiratorial organization, which he claimed to be 'also known as the Black Hand and Unione Siciliano.' Supposedly forming a nation-wide syndicate in control of gambling, prostitution, and narcotics, the Mafia was seen as a loosely organized but cohesive coalition of crime families that, though it eschewed the precise and public practices of a large corporation, operated as much as possible in a quiet and business-like manner, often with legitimate businesses as fronts. It was comforting for Americans to hear that the worst forms of national crime had resulted from an alien invasion, though Kefauver provided no real evidence. In order for the Mafia to grip the national consciousness, what was required was a highly publicized event such as the arrest of Italian American gang bosses at Apalachin in 1957, and the testimony of gangster-informant Joe Valachi in the next decade.[94]

Unlike Kefauver, who refused to equate the structures and methods of post-war organized crime with bureaucratized business corporations, the syndicate films of the period often represent the criminal organization as a business or corporate arrangement within which the individual criminal amounts to an anonymous functionary, an 'organization man' such as one might find on Wall Street or Madison Avenue. Yet though one might expect American films of the late 1940s and 1950s to have portrayed such syndicates as Italian American organizations, especially given the coincidence of fears of syndicate crime with the Mafia scare, they largely ignore Italian Americans and thus adhere to the production code. There are no top-level Italian American gangsters in *I Walk Alone* (1949), *The Mob* (1951), and even *The Racket* (1951), which the Kefauver hearings inspired. Although the latter film is set in a Midwestern city like Chicago, the criminal organization lacks a distinctly Italian American imprint. *Captive City* (1952), which responded to the Kefauver hearings, and which opens with statements by the senator himself, focuses on non–Italian American criminals, as does *Turning Point* (1952).[95] Nor do Italian American criminals figure significantly in the several films equating syndicate takeover with communism: *Red Menace* (1949), *Woman on Pier 13* (1949), and *I Was a Communist for the FBI* (1951).

To be sure, the word 'Mafia' is heard more frequently in the American cinema of this period, and some of these films portray Italian Americans as syndicate-style gangsters, even at the crime-boss level. One thinks of Triano in Anthony Mann's *T-Men* (1947), Lagana in Fritz Lang's *The Big Heat* (1953), Mr Brown in *The Big Combo* (1955), and Broderick Crawford's Charlie Lupo in the Russel Crouse–directed *New York Confidential* (1955). Lupo heads the board of directors of a vast criminal cartel that, headquartered in Manhattan, aims to cover its tracks by penetrating legitimate business. Lupo himself has entered upper-middle-class society by building a lavish suburban mansion. Yet when the cartel's infiltration of the American oil industry falls through, owing to its betrayal by its Washington representative, the board of directors executes Lupo to prevent his testifying. In *Hoodlum Empire* (1952), which attempts to cash in on the publicity surrounding the Kefauver investigation, syndicate boss Nick Mansani (Luther Adler) testifies before a Senate committee – a scene inspired by Frank Costello's televised difficulties with Kefauver.[96]

In most syndicate films, the gangs and syndicates are non-ethnic or multi-ethnic, while Italian Americans sometimes take orders from WASP bosses or others of non-Italian ethnicity. One sees this in Raoul Walsh's *The Enforcer* (1951), in which Rico (Ted de Corsia), head of the syndicate's murder team, answers to Mendoza (Everett Sloane). The far-flung syndicate in *The Brothers Rico* is directed by Sid Kubik, a non-Italian though born in Little Italy, whose underlings include Italian Americans like the brothers of the title. Although the word 'Mafia' is mentioned in Phil Karlson's *Tight Spot* (1955), the film's crime czar is Benjamin Costain (Lorne Greene). As Mike Hammer discovers in *Kiss Me Deadly*, Italian American crime boss Carl Evello (Paul Stewart) is only the instrument of the sinister Doctor Soberin. Nor are Evello's henchmen Italian American. In Samuel Fuller's *Underworld U.S.A.* (1961), the high-echelon gangster Gela answers to Conners, a kind of boss of bosses, and is himself only the head of the syndicate's narcotic operations, taking his place in a tripartite corporate structure.

In other instances the films depict not 'syndicates' but small gangs of Italian American and other criminals. Portrayed by Edward G. Robinson, Vincent Canelli in *Black Tuesday* (1954) escapes prison on the day of his execution thanks to a guard whose daughter has been kidnapped by

Canelli's gang; the film's climactic shootout is far too violent to appeal to a syndicate boss. Sometimes the small-time Italian American criminal is treated sympathetically, as for instance safecracker Louis Chiavello (Anthony Caruso) in John Huston's *The Asphalt Jungle* (1951). A devoted family man driven into crime by hardship, Chiavello is killed in a robbery; when the police invade his household as the family gathers round his dead body, it seems a desecration. In other instances the Italian American helps the law, as in *The Mob* (1951), in which Johnny D'Amico (Broderick Crawford) exposes the waterfront rackets directed by Blackie Clay. Varying the good wop–bad wop theme, *T-Men* heroizes Treasury Department agents Dennis O'Brien (Dennis O'Keefe) and Tony Genaro's (Alfred Ryder) pursuit of syndicate leader Triano. When Triano kills Genaro in the presence of O'Brien, the latter cannot prevent it for fear of revealing his true identity. In *Johnny Allegro* (1949), George Raft plays a former gangster who helps the government defeat a right-wing conspirator (George Macready).

A standout among syndicate films as well as a classic of *film noir*, Fritz Lang's *The Big Heat* stars Glenn Ford as Police Sergeant Dave Bannion, the self-appointed nemesis of Italian American crime boss Lagana (Greek American Alexander Scourby), who has corrupted the city of Kenport, including the police. While investigating a case, Bannion interrogates a female barfly who is subsequently murdered, as is later revealed, by Vince Stone (Lee Marvin), Lagana's psychopathic henchman, who had applied burning cigarettes to his victim's flesh before killing her. Warned off the case by his superiors, Bannion visits Lagana at his suburban mansion in quest of information and there declares war against the crime boss, whose bodyguard he beats up. Although suspended from the force for his maverick behaviour, Bannion continues his investigation privately. There follows the retaliatory and lethal car-bombing of his wife (Jocelyn Brando), leaving Bannion to look after their only child. Having been a family man, he now feels overwhelming vengeful hatred towards Lagana, whom he arrests at the climax after disarming and mauling Stone.

Marked by a vaguely Italian accent, and portrayed so as to emphasize his Roman nose, Lagana nonetheless resides in a suburban mansion which, protected by policemen "on the take," shows his total extrication from the ethnic neighbourhood. He even has a British butler, the implication being that now the WASPs serve the underworld. As Bannion enters the mansion, the product of what he calls 'twenty years of corruption,' Lagana's daughter is throwing a high-toned dance party across the broad vestibule from the study where Bannion and Lagana meet. The distance between these two domestic settings underscores the latter's desire, typical of mob bosses, to separate his familial life and criminal career, this also being the reason for Lagana's outrage that Bannion has visited him concerning a murder: 'I have an office for that kind of thing!' Rather than dirty his hands with violence, Lagana leaves it to his henchmen. Yet because Stone's brutal methods too much resemble those of pre-syndicate crime – 'It was an old-fashioned killing,' notes Bannion, 'Prohibition-style' – Lagana warns him against attracting publicity. The boss's goal is to avoid the fate of Lucky Luciano who, like Rico Bandello and Tony Camonte, failed to keep out of the public eye.

Nonetheless, Lagana manifests the personal aberrations that had helped to ruin such gangsters as Bandello and Camonte. In an early scene, in which Lagana stretches out in silk pajamas on a lavish bed as George, his bodyguard, hands him a telephone, there is a hint of homosexual perversity, as if George also performed sexual services. So much is implied by Bannion's insulting remark to Lagana after beating up George: 'You wanna pinch hit for your boy, Lagana?' Insofar as, in this context, 'boy' implies a submissive sexual partner, and also given that Lagana is an Italian American male, Bannion has flung at him the most offensive of insults, that of being a homosexual.

Lang's rendering of Lagana carries on from earlier films linking Italian American gangsters with the Madonna or mother-figure, sexual puritanism regarding family members, and, paradoxically, misogyny. In Lagana, however, the stereotypes fuse in a deliberately conflicted portrayal lending support to the view that Italian Americans have strange families. Besides showing his devotion to his daughter Angela, whose name evokes celestial devotion, Lagana calls Bannion's attention to the portrait of his mother displayed prominently in his office. Characterized by her worshipful son as a 'fine old lady,' she is an Old World matron. When Lagana mentions that she 'lived here with me,' he seems a mama's boy. Yet it is hinted that, having somehow disappointed her, Lagana had resented her withholding of complete approval: 'She never got over being surprised at my success.' The obverse of Lagana's mother worship reveals itself in misogynistic violence, as he is responsible for the barfly's death and the car-bombing of Bannion's wife. Moreover, Lagana attempts to neutralize Bannion by murdering his daughter, although he has a daughter of his own. Yet it would be wrong to suggest that Lang contents himself with a one-sided demonization of the Italian American villain, as Bannion's private war against the underworld seems motivated less by idealism than by vengeance. In applying the 'big heat' he comes to resemble his gangster quarry, as if he had unknowingly suffered their moral contamination.

Directed by Joseph E. Lewis, *The Big Combo* (1955) is another film *noir* of the mid-1950s dealing with organized crime. Richard Conte plays Mr Brown, financial mastermind for the Combination, the eastern branch of the national crime syndicate. Born an Italian American, yet seeking to hide his ethnic past, Brown has chosen the same pseudonym favoured by Al Capone and his cinematic counterpart in *Key Largo*. Yet unlike the trigger-happy Rocco, Brown looks and acts like a low-profile business executive. In his view, violence ill consorts with 'impersonal business,' and is only a last resort. Having placed his first wife in a mental institution, for which he feels guilty, Brown claims the blonde and WASPy society beauty Susan Lowell (Jean Wallace) as his sexual trophy. Reminiscent of Lagana, Brown finds his nemesis in Lieutenant Leonard Diamond (Cornel Wilde), a moralist who, like Bannion, detests the gang boss. A further motive for Diamond's hatred is his love for Susan, whom he would rescue from Brown. Thus representing the fascination of evil, which transfixes Susan and Diamond, Brown has no doubt of his magnetism, for as he tells Diamond, he holds Susan not by means of money but by the force of his vice-ridden 'personality.' Again reminiscent of Johnny Rocco, whose nerve fails him during a hurricane, Mr Brown shows his 'soft' side in the final scene at the moment the police arrive to arrest him. However, the Big Combo appears to be a multi-ethnic mob.

If Lang's *The Big Heat* is artistically the best of the syndicate films, Phil Karlson's *The Brothers Rico* (1957) perhaps goes farthest in using the sub-genre to explore Italian American ethnicity, assimilation, and identity. The main character is Eddie Rico (Richard Conte), a former accountant for a nation-wide criminal syndicate directed from New York City by Eddie's uncle, Sid Kubik. Both Eddie and Sid had grown up in New York's Little Italy, where Eddie's mother and grandmother still reside, and where, though crippled, the mother still runs a family store on Mulberry Street. Not only does Eddie regard Sid as a surrogate father, but Sid is indebted to Eddie's mother for saving his life. Eddie, who had left the organization three years previously, lives in Florida with his wife Alice (Dianne Foster), a non-Italian woman with whom he enjoys a loving though childless marriage. The successful laundry business that the self-assured Eddie owns and operates appears to be a 'clean' operation far removed from the syndicate and yet was very possibly funded initially by 'dirty' money. He typifies the many second-generation Italian Americans who sought to assimilate by escaping their ethnic neighbourhoods into suburbia. Well respected by his employees, Eddie has many standard tokens of material success: handsome car, large and expensive house, well-furnished rooms, substantial bank account. His two brothers, Johnny and Gino, who remain in the syndicate's employ, share Eddie's regard for Uncle Sid as their father by adoption.

Eddie's confidence is gradually eroded after the syndicate, which he thought he had escaped, enlists his help in locating his brother, Johnny. Actually, the brother has been marked for execution and the syndicate is using Eddie to find him. His situation resembles that of Michael Corleone in *Godfather III*, who, having achieved his decades-long dream of extricating himself from the Mafia, laments, 'Just when I thought I was out, they pull me back in!' Although the syndicate's request troubles Eddie's wife, he sets out blithely to find his brother without realizing he is being followed. When Eddie meets with Kubik in his Miami hotel room, Kubik calls him 'son' and professes his loyalty to Eddie's family, including his worship to Mama Rico, yet after Eddie leaves on his quest for Johnny, syndicate henchmen are shown beating Gino to death. Upon finding Johnny, Eddie arrogantly discounts his brother's suspicions of Kubik, as he assumes the compatibility of familial and syndicate interests. Then Johnny is executed, and a shaken Eddie is told by syndicate creature La Motta (Harry Bellaver) that his death had been a foregone conclusion. This motivates Eddie's decision to report the syndicate to the district attorney as his only way of protecting his wife and adopted child.

Eddie's relationship to what remains of his Italian American family is detached and compromised. Rather than showing any deep concern for his mother and grandmother, he guiltily makes up for his lack of warmth by plying them with consumer items: a refrigerator for his mother, which ill suits the old-fashioned decor of her apartment, with its religious icons; and a television to amuse his grandmother, who can hardly understand English, and whom he even proposes to send to a rest home (although his mother, faithful to Italian ways, refuses to do so). The overall impression is of a nearly insuperable division between the generations, as the first continues to exemplify what Eddie dismisses as the 'old country,' while the second attempts to assimilate within a new corporate America it cannot comprehend. The film's final shoot-out occurs in Little Italy, where Eddie, helpless in a syndicate-dominated nation, takes refuge in his mother's apartment. When Kubik confronts him there, Eddie kills him with his mother's assistance. The district attorney then prosecutes the syndicate thanks to Eddie's testimony.

Like *The Brothers Rico* Nicholas Ray's *Party Girl* (1958) is a gangster film in the *noir* mode and thus exhibits moral ambiguity. Yet unusually for *film noir*, Ray chose to film in colour, a device that clashes jarringly with the nearly consistent downbeat mood. And whereas *The Brothers Rico* examines organized crime and ethnicity in a contemporary setting, Ray depicts Prohibition era gangsters in a city like Chicago, and whose gang-leader, Rico Angelo, resembles Al Capone.

While attending a party given by Rico Angelo (Lee J. Cobb), Vickie Gayle (Cyd Charisse) is protected by mob lawyer Thomas Farrell (Robert Taylor) from harrassment by Angelo's underling Louis Canetto (John Ireland). An embittered cynic with a crippled hip, Farrell falls in love with Vickie, whom he helps to become the star dancer in Angelo's club. Following Farrell's hip surgery, he and Vickie attempt to start a new life together, but during their European vacation Angelo forces them to return to the United States, as he will not allow his prize lawyer to 'quit.' Subsequently, however, Farrell is arrested and agrees to testify against the mob. Upon learning that Angelo holds Vickie captive, he rescues her from the crime boss who, riddled with bullets by the police, plummets to his death.

Party Girl draws its inspiration from gangland history while building on gangster stereotypes. The scene in which Angelo, at a testimonial for underling Frankie Gasto, initially praises Gasto and then beats him to death with a silver pool cue previously offered him as a gift, is inspired by Capone's use of a baseball bat to kill two perfidious underlings at a banquet. Like Rico Bandello and Tony Camonte, Angelo undermines himself by using violent methods that attract the police. Reminiscent of Rico, Johnny Rocco, and Lagana, he is both a sadist and misogynist. When he confesses his grief over the announced marriage of film-star Jean Harlow, he exemplifies the lacrimose Italian American gangster with the potential for 'going soft.' Next, however, Angelo shoots Harlow's framed photograph to bits with his revolver: 'I took care of her,' he boasts; 'she had it comin'. I got her out of my system.'[97] Later, to coerce Farrell's cooperation, he threatens to disfigure Vickie with acid. At the climax he repeats the threat and tests the acid by pouring it over a red papier-mâché bell – a symbol of partying gone sour. What differentiates Rico Angelo from his generic predecessors is his more active participation in misogynistic brutality.

Party Girl contains an unusual scene dramatizing the opposition in American mainstream attitudes between the socially and culturally déclassé world of Italian America, demonized in the gangster, and the native Italian, whose prestige increased in the 1950s with the rise of American mass tourism, as a result of which travellers became aware of two contrasting Italian types. In the film Farrell and Vickie abandon the American mob for an extended European vacation culminating in romantic Venice. As the lovers enter the lobby of their expensive hotel, the manager and concierge fawn over them with nauseating obsequiousness, chattering voices, and preposterously exaggerated gesticulations. Implicitly the scene dissociates *these* Italians, northern Italians of the preferred 'civilized' type, from the intimidating Italian Americans Farrell and Vickie have left behind. It is as if Ray were articulating the mainstream wish that Italian Americans should incarnate the sycophantic Italian so ingratiating (and unthreatening) on Italian soil. Ironically, Farrell and Vickie's arrival at the hotel coincides with Rico Angelo's phone call summoning Farrell to return immediately to Chicago. In Venice Italians serve Farrell; but back home he serves them.

The late 1950s and early 1960s witnessed a series of events that seemed to many observers – including the long sceptical J. Edgar Hoover – to prove the existence of a Mafia conspiracy. Not only was the Senate Committee for the Investigation of Interstate Racketeering formed in 1957, with Senator John L. McClellan of Arkansas as its chairman, but on November 7 of that year occurred the most disastrous event in the history of Italian American organized crime. In response to turmoil within the underworld, roughly a hundred leading Italian American gangsters met to confer at the country estate of mob boss Joseph Barbara, which was located in the small town of Apalachin in upstate New York. Yet before the participants could get down to business, they were raided by local police, who arrested about sixty of the conference participants, the others having escaped. The subsequent dropping of conspiracy charges against the captured gangsters could hardly undo the damage that had been done, for now Hoover, McClellan, and many others believed the Mafia to exist. As the McClellan Committee intensified its efforts, Hoover made the Mafia the FBI's number-one target. Another blow was struck in 1963 and 1964, when mob underling Joe Valachi reported before a televised Senate investigative committee on what he called the 'Cosa Nostra' – another name for the Mafia, which investigations over the next four decades proved to exist.[98] The repercussions from Apalachin can be read in several films, including *Inside the Mafia* (1959), in which the deported Lucero, a Lucky Luciano figure, plans to announce his takeover of the Mafia at a major conference to be held at a country estate at Apple Lake, which sounds like Apalachin.

Notwithstanding the growing notoriety of the contemporary Mafia, filmmakers from the late 1950s onward remained fascinated by the history of organized crime. The first film since *Dillinger* (1945) to flout the production code's prohibition against gangster biographies, Richard Wilson's *Al Capone* (1959) stars Rod Steiger. Yet though audiences may have preferred to observe the Italian American underworld as projected nostalgically into a glamourized past, Thorpe's film exploits recent fears of a Mafia 'syndicate' in claiming that the current organization of American criminal gangs traces to Chicago of the 1920s. The narrator's asssertion that Capone's story has 'an important meaning for us today' has its correspondent visual in a later scene in which Capone presides over a gangland meeting in a wood-panelled, high-ceilinged boardroom reminiscent of a business corporation. Having grossed over a hundred million that year, Capone announces that his 'working capital' has enabled him to 'organize' and thus to 'move into every legitimate business there is' – the syndicate octopus. To quote the narrator: 'In 1927 the underworld invaded the business world ... Capone set a frightening pattern ... that still exists today.' Actually, the identification of organized crime with a centrally organized national syndicate far exceeds the truth, while whatever organization it does possess is far less attributable to Capone than to Torrio or Luciano.

In the opening scene, set in 1919, Capone enters the Four Deuces nightclub as the new bodyguard for Johnny Torrio, the club's owner and friend of the Capone family. Signposting his parasitism, Capone walks to the free lunch counter, helps himself to cold cuts, and then saunters along the bar with his mouth stuffed with food. Soon Chicago will be his free lunch. The scar running diagonally from his left cheek to his jaw is quite visible. When Capone sees a pile of money on Torrio's table, he kisses it idolatrously, whereupon Torrio reports that Chicago is a 'fat town,' especially with Prohibition coming. When Capone grows physically and metaphorically fat through success, the question is whether he can stay on top.

Torrio introduces Capone to Torrio's boss, the rich and dapper 'Big Jim' Colosimo, who is about to attend the opera with his mistress. Although Torrio orders Capone to remove his hat in the presence of a lady, thus underscoring his bad manners, it is soon evident that Capone shares Colosimo's love of opera, *Rigoletto* being his favourite work, and Tetrazzini and Caruso his favourite performers. Not only is the identification of Italian Americans with gangsters a generic cliché, as witness *Scarface, House of Strangers, Pay or Die, The Untouchables, Some Like*

It Hot, and *Godfather III*, but Capone is known to have been a devotee. However, Colosimo's days are numbered owing to his failure, recalling that of Louis Costillo in *Scarface*, to take advantage of Prohibition. In a meeting with the leaders of the competing Irish gang, including Dion O'Bannion, George 'Bugs' Moran, and Hymie Weiss, Torrio stresses the need to transform bootlegging into a cooperative, centralized, and 'regular business operation.' When Torrio proposes to make Colosimo 'Mr. Big' because of his political influence, O'Bannion mocks Colosimo's Italian accent before the infuriated Torrio and Capone. Just as, to quote Rico Bandello, a gangster 'goes soft' when he 'can't take it any more,' so O'Bannion complains that Colosimo is 'old and soft from easy livin'.'

Soon enough Torrio and Capone form their own plan to replace Colosimo, which Capone helps to carry out in Colosimo's office during a duet in which they accompany a recording of Flotow's 'M'apparit.' Sung in Italian, the lyrics tell of a beloved figure who, in the eyes of the lover, appears and then disappears. Ironically, the song concludes with the arrival of Torrio's two henchmen disguised as workers, who in killing Colosimo cause *him* to disappear. The scene is an overdone take-off on two Italian American stereotypes often fused in the gangster figure (for instance, De Niro's portrayal of Capone in De Palma's *The Untouchables*), namely sentimentality and brutality.

The remainder of the film consists of generic touchstones, recreations of underworld history, and free elaborations of the Capone biography. Colosimo's murder is followed by a basically accurate scene in which Capone orders from Dion O'Bannion's flower shop an extra-large wreath for the funeral. One recalls *Little Caesar*, in which Rico, having eliminated his former driver Tony Passa, orders a large floral wreath for his coffin. Unlike Capone, Torrio drinks heavily in the face of Irish competition and also out of remorse for Colosimo's murder. That Capone also risks decadence is implicit in the scene, now obligatory for the gangster film, in which he is fitted for an expensive suit of clothes in preparation for a high-society opera gathering. According to an underling, Capone is 'getting fat.' However, with the election of an uncorruptible mayor in Chicago, Capone must move his headquarters to Cicero, Illinois, which occurred in 1923.

For the sake of romantic interest, the film invents a historically false love affair between Capone and the young widow of the bartender Capone's henchman had killed – a relationship that begins only after Capone misleads her into thinking him innocent of the killing. Nonetheless the sentimental Capone envisions the widow as his angel in a world of loose women. Although this attitude ill consorts with the reality of a gangster who died of syphilis in 1947 after sampling too often his own bordellos, it conforms to that opposition between ladies and 'broads' typical of the portrayal of Italian Americans. In any case the film concentrates on Capone's criminal career rather than his love life.

Capone's move to Cicero is a time of exile during which Torrio is jailed after a police raid engineered by rivals. Capone retaliates by executing Dion O'Bannion in his flower shop (an actual event), yet despite Capone's reassurances the frightened Torrio leaves Chicago, as he did in 1925. Subsequently Capone is nearly killed in a car-and-machine-gun assault on a Cicero hotel coffee shop, a scene that, inspired by the motorcade that poured a thousand rounds into Capone's Cicero headquarters in 1926, is much inferior to that in *Scarface*, in which Camonte discovers the thrilling possibilities of the tommy gun. Subsequently the re-election of the notoriously corrupt mayor Big Bill Thompson enables Capone to return to Chicago where, with the intention of taking over the American business world, he establishes offices next to the financial district and city hall. He also eliminates his chief gangland competitors in the St Valentine's Day Massacre, with Albert Anselmo and John Scalise doing Capone's dirty work. The later scene in which the assassins themselves are killed by the Northsiders is historically inaccurate, as it is known that in 1929 Capone personally eliminated the duplicitous Anselmi and Scalise. When Capone learns that the journalist Keely, his creature, is betraying him to Moran, Capone has him killed in a subway station. Based on the execution of Jack Lingle, whom Capone henchmen executed in 1930, Keely's rub-out unfolds to the strains of 'M'Apparit.'

Just before his death, Moran describes Capone as 'old, soft, and scared.' The audience thus expects him to fall precipitately through personal weakness, perhaps a breakdown or failure of nerve as with Rico Bandello, Johnny Rocco, and Mr Brown. Instead, Capone's fall comes unexpectedly yet undramatically when he is sentenced for income tax evasion. As if attempting, however ineffectually, to save the film from anticlimax, the final scenes depict Capone in prison where he is set upon by a crowd of resentful inmates and given a brutal beating that, though exaggerated in its violence, calls to mind the harassment and bullying Capone actually suffered while at Alcatraz at the hands of the other prisoners. There follows the narrator's voice-over remarking that Capone ultimately died after having been released from prison because of ill health. What the film fails to mention is that his death resulted from syphilitic paresis, a biographical fact too scandalous for mainstream audiences of that period, and somewhat inconsistent with the film's senti-mentalized portrayal of Capone as capable of romantic love.

Despite its verve, *Al Capone* suffers from Rod Steiger's undisciplined performance, with its externally applied and mechanically produced ethnic markers, such as wild gesticulations, facial tics, loud speech, men-acing swagger, maniacal laughter, and bad manners. Never do his antics convince one of the gangster's ethnicity. Although Capone, as a Neapoli-tan, was more flamboyant than his Sicilian colleagues, this does not jus-tify Steiger's excesses. When Martin Scorsese denounces what he terms the 'Mamma mia' school of the portrayal of Italian Americans, he could be referring to Steiger, who cries 'Mamma mia' while at a gambling table.

By the late 1950s the potential of Prohibition Chicago as television entertainment was apparent to Desi Arnaz, who had bought the rights to Oscar Fraley's *The Untouchables* with the aim of adapting it for his Desilu Playhouse. Fraley's book, which is based on the recollections of Eliot Ness, concentrates on his attempt to destroy Capone's bootlegging op-erations. Produced by Arnaz and directed by Phil Karlson, *The Scarface Mob* aired in 1959 and became the basis for the Desilu-produced televi-sion series entitled *The Untouchables*, which ran from 1959 to 1962. With Robert Stack as Ness and Neville Brand as Capone, *The Scarface Mob*, though reasonably accurate historically, assigned a ludicrous Italian ac-cent to the American-born Capone while attributing to Frank Nitti un-deserved gangland prominence for that period.[99] Yet these inaccuracies pale by comparison with *The Untouchables*, in which Stack and Brand re-prised their earlier roles, and a veneer of historical accuracy was provid-ed through documentary style narration by columnist Walter Winchell. Italian Americans were outraged by the series, which implied that Ital-ian American criminals made up virtually the whole of organized crime, and which they saw with some justification as an obstacle to assimilation through negative stereotyping. Indeed, *The Untouchables* was referred to in some circles as 'The Italian Hour' and 'Cops and Wops.' Ultimately the studio chose to cooperate with the Order of the Sons of Italy by introducing WASP gangsters to counterbalance Italian ones and finally by eliminating Italian American gangsters from the show altogether – a decision that very possibly contributed to the series' demise after a four-year run. Over the next decades Italian Americans protested media identifications of their ethnic group with criminality, even to the point of denying – unjustifiably as it turned out – the existence of the Mafia.[100]

Just as, in the 1930s, the classic gangster film gave rise to gangster comedies, so the later vogue for gangster films inspired its own parodic treatment in *Some Like It Hot* (1959), directed by Billy Wilder from his co-written script with L.A.L. Diamond. Journeymen musicians Joe (Tony Curtis) and Jerry (Jack Lemmon) work in a speakeasy owned by gangster 'Spats' Columbo (George Raft), who conceals his operation within a funeral parlour run by Mr Mozzarella. Raft's rendition of Columbo is effective not only because it recalls his portrayal of Guino in *Scarface* but because it draws upon this Italian American actor's personal knowledge of upper-echelon gangsters. Unemployed following a police raid on the speakeasy, Joe and Jerry witness accidentally the St Valentine's Day Massacre, in which Columbo rubs out 'Toothpick Charlie' and his gang. Now marked for death by Columbo, the two musicians escape to Florida disguised as members of an all-girl band, only to discover that the resort hotel where the band performs is the site of the annual Convention of the Friends of Italian Opera, who include Columbo and his rival Little Bonaparte (Nehemia Persoff). Thus the script contributes to what would become, or perhaps had already become, a standard association between Italian gangsters and Italian opera. In another instance of generic self-consciousness (or self-parody), a desk clerk tosses a coin with studied insouciance, to which Columbo responds: 'Where'd you pick up that cheap trick?' The joke depends on the knowledge that coin-tossing had come to typify many cinematic gangsters after Raft's adoption of it in *Scarface*.[101] Similarly, Columbo's complaint that Bonaparte is going 'soft' calls to mind Rico Bandello's description of decadent mob rivals, while Columbo's machine-gun murder at the climactic banquet plays upon the link to be seen in other films between gangland violence and Italian restaurants.

Although Prohibition remained the preferred era for the historical gangster film, Richard Wilson's *Pay or Die* (1960) focuses on Lieutenant Joseph Petrosino's struggle against the Black Hand. There is, however, a key difference between Wilson's film and *The Black Hand*, the Gene Kelly vehicle of a decade earlier. The historical moment of *The Black Hand* had made it possible for the film to suggest that the Black Hand (and the Mafia) had been banished from the United States by Johnny Columbo, picking up where Petrosino had left off. Contrastingly, *Pay or Die* postdates Apalachin and the early McClellan hearings, and leaves the impression that the Black Hand or Mafia, after rooting itself in America during immigration, had then unleashed its alien blight in succeeding decades. Starring Ernest Borgnine as the immigrant Petrosino, *Pay or Die* is set in New York's Little Italy, where Black Hand extortionists taint the reputation of the ethnic group. When a criminal causes a young girl to be injured seriously during a street festival, Petrosino finds her father too fearful to speak. Although skeptical that the Black Hand constitutes a conspiracy, he changes his mind after observing the victimization of a local baker and his daughter Adelina (Zohra Lampert), with whom Petrosino falls in love. Now convinced of the insidious power of the Black Hand, he forms a squad of Italian American policemen so as to facilitate operations in a neighbourhood faithful to *omertà*. His exploits include the rescue of opera star Enrico Caruso from a car-bombing by extortionists, which the filmmakers adapted from an actual event.[102] Although the film focuses on Petrosino's police career, it also depicts his frustrated attempts to acculturate, as he fails a literacy test six times. When the bomber of a jewelry store is apprehended it becomes known that Zarilli, a respectable citizen of Little Italy, had commissioned the crime, and that he is connected with the Black Hand and the Sicilian Mafia. Subsequently during his visit to Sicily Petrosino learns that New York abounds with criminals wanted in Italy, but before he can use this information he is killed by the henchmen of a Mafia kingpin. Thus the film falsely links the Sicilian Mafia and its American counterpart, implying that, despite Petrosino's efforts, the former organization has given birth to the latter.

Produced and directed by Roger Corman, and scripted by Howard Browne, *The St. Valentine's Day Massacre* (1967) features an improbable yet compelling Jason Robards Jr as Al Capone along with Ralph Meeker as Bugs Moran and Geoge Segal as Moran's torpedo Peter Gusenberg. Despite its low budget, the film recreates convincingly the atmosphere of late-1920s Chicago. Yet though it presents itself as a documentary, factual errors have crept in, and Corman claims imaginative licence. Reminiscent of other films of the 1950s and 1960s, *The St. Valentine's Day Massacre* parallels gangsters and businessmen while tracing contemporary organized crime to Capone's supposed innovations. In his 'anthropological' treatment of the mob, Corman's anticipates Martin Ritt's *The Brotherhood* as well as the films of Coppola and Scorsese.

Capone is introduced as he enters the Hawthorne Hotel, his headquarters in Cicero, Illinois, where he and his underlings await the return of the corrupt Big Bill Thompson to office. In a meeting with his aides, Capone announces that Bugs Moran, leader of the predominantly Irish Northside gang, has targeted him for death. Following a flashback to the motorcade assault on the Hawthorne Hotel coffeeshop, where Capone was nearly killed by Northsiders under Hymie Weiss, Capone assigns the elimination of Moran to protégé 'Machine Gun' Jack McGurn (born Vincenzo de Mora). The outnumbered Moran plans to replace

Patsy Lolordo, Capone's friend and head of the 'Mafia,' with second-rate gangster Joey Aiello, who will use his new authority to remove Capone. Moran's devious deliberations are accompanied by a flashback to the famous flower-shop murder of his former boss, Dion O'Banion, in 1924.

As a first move, McGurn hires unemployed immigrant Nick Sorello to fake the hijacking of a Capone liquor truck and then to inform Moran of his desire to unload the contents. Sorello sells them to Moran's representatives, reporting to McGurn that another pretended hijacking will provide access to Moran. After Aiello betrays Lolordo to Moran's killers, Sorello informs Moran that he will deliver another shipment of hijacked whiskey Thursday morning to his North Clark Street warehouse, with the understanding that Moran will be present. While Capone is personally executing Aiello, his hired killers assemble, including the Sicilian-born John Scalise and Alberto Anselmi. On St Valentine's Day the leading members of Moran's gang are awaiting his arrival at the warehouse when Capone's gunmen, thinking Moran present, enter disguised as police. Having seen their police car, Moran hides in a restaurant as his associates are being tommy-gunned to death. Capone, who is vacationing at his Miami estate, enjoys a foolproof alibi. In the film's subdued coda, public outcry terminates Capone's regime in Chicago, but not before he executes personally the disloyal Scalise and Anselmi at a gangland party. The film concludes with the deaths of Moran in 1957 and Capone ten years previously.

The St. Valentine's Day Massacre announces its documentary intention in a narrator's prologue in voiceover. The film's historical errors include the statement that Capone originated in Castellamare del Golfo, Sicily, when in reality he was born in Brooklyn of Neapolitan parents; ironically, Moran says that Capone, as a non-Sicilian, cannot join the Mafia. Moran's claim that Capone needed permission from the all-Sicilian Mafia and its Chicago representative Pasquale Lolordo before taking any major course of action would have been more accurate had he identified Lolordo as the head not of the Mafia but of the Unione Siciliane. Originally a fraternal organization of Sicilian immigrants in the East and Midwest, the Unione Siciliane appears to have been infiltrated by gangsters in at least some of its branches, including that of Chicago, by the 1920s, thus providing in the opinion of some scholars a basis for what became the American Mafia. Although the film rightly assigns the planning of the massacre to McGurn, it goes too far in claiming Scalise and Anselmi (among others) to have been the killers. The only certain executioner was Fred Burke. Nor is it certain that Scalise and Anselmi killed Hymie

Weiss, as the narrator contends. Rather than having been killed by Capone, Aiello was murdered in a crossfire by Capone gunmen outside his apartment house.[103]

The St. Valentine's Day Massacre honours its generic precursors by quotation or modification of standard motifs. In *Little Caesar*, Rico Bandello consumes spaghetti after murdering a gas station attendant; in *The St. Valentine's Day Massacre*, McGurn twirls spaghetti around his fork as he plots against Moran, the twisting strands suggesting both the serpentining paths of McGurn's devious mind and the victims he will consume. Whereas Rico Bandello answers to the title of 'Little Caesar' and Johnny Rocco thrills to be called 'emperor,' Corman's Capone surrounds himself with classical columns and statuary suggestive of imperial Rome. And finally, Corman alludes to *Scarface* in the large *X* that appears on the door of the abandoned warehouse where the massacre had taken place.

Consistent with gangster films of preceding decades as well as with an emerging current of popular opinion, *The St. Valentine's Day Massacre* reflects anti-capitalist attitudes of the late 1960s in virtually equating organized crime with capitalism. To quote the narrator, 'the nation's underworld rises to power and battles amongst [*sic*] itself just as modern nations and corporations do.' Exemplifying the antiquated approach to crime, Moran conducts his strategy sessions informally and in a run-down setting, whereas Capone gathers his disciplined subordinates in what looks like the corporate boardroom of a successful, well-run business. A later reference to 'syndicate leaders' suggests that organized crime has come to resemble a centralized, hierarchical, rationalized business corporation. As Capone calls to mind a harshly overbearing CEO, so he assigns each associate a specialized sphere of operation, as in a business. Nonetheless, the differences between legal capitalist methods and organization and those of the mob are sufficiently obvious to undermine such comparisons.

What helps to make Corman's treatment of the mob so successful are its smaller details. Whereas Capone goes clean shaven, lacks an Italian accent, and dresses like a businessmen, the Palermitan-born Aiello and Lolordo are 'Mustache Petes,' old-style Italian American gangsters supplanted by the modernizing Capones and Lucianos. Not only does Aiello sport a mustache, but he dresses like a Sicilian don. Lolordo likewise speaks accented English and adopts a courtly Old World manner in contrast to the Americanized Capone's vulgar abrasiveness. In contrast with the ancient 'Roman' furnishings of Capone's suite, which reveal tasteless materialism, Lolordo's apartment though ornate in the Sicilian style contains religious icons, moderate-sized and modestly draped statues, and pictures of ancestors. The crudity of Capone's crowd is conveyed when McGurn twirls spaghetti on a spoon prior to eating it – table manners disfavoured by the Italian upper classes. When Anselmi with ritualistic seriousness smears garlic on the heads of his bullets, an anonymous gangland associate (Italian American Jack Nicholson in an early role) explains this technique in noting that if the victim survives the bullet, the garlic will induce blood poison. Scalise and Anselmi actually used this method, and may have introduced it to the underworld.[104]

A further aspect of the film's 'anthropology' is the gangsters' interethnic hatred, an emotion previously difficult to convey on screen because of the production code. To be sure, Italian and Irish gangsters had traded ethnic slurs in *Al Capone*, but less nastily than in *The St. Valentine's Day Massacre*, in which Moran denounces that 'rotten greaseball!' When the German American Frank Gusenberg asks: 'Since when do we hook up with a bunch of crummy Spics?' Moran responds: 'Don't you pop off to me, you stupid Kraut!' Before O'Bannion's murder Moran tells his boss to 'remember those greaseballs. They'd just as soon put a bullet in your back as eat a pizza' – the stereotype of the back-stabbing Italian. For his part Capone intends to kill Moran, that 'Irish son of a bitch.'

Unlike in Corman's film, the contemporary Mafia forms the subject of director Martin Ritt's *The Brotherhood*, released in 1968 to favourable reviews and public neglect. Scripted by Italian American playwright Lewis John Carlino, this film anticipates *The Godfather* in aiming for an authentic Italian American atmosphere by means of location shots in New York City and Sicily, scenes of weddings, dances, and dinners, sprinklings of Sicilian idiom, and liberal helpings of Mafia lore. *The Brotherhood* also recalls *The Godfather* in exploring the tensions between the older and younger members of the second-generation of the Mafia and thus projects onto the Italian American criminal family a situation that often arose among Italian Americans of that generation, albeit less violently.

The film begins with the wedding of Vince Ginetta, younger brother of middle-aged mob boss Frank Ginetta, and Emma Bertoldo, daughter of mob boss Dominick Bertoldo (Luther Adler), who belongs as does Frank to the five-man board of a major New York syndicate. In contrast to the Sicilian Minettas, however, Dominick is of Neapolitan background, which proves significant. The wedding guests include Frank's business associates, two of whom are non-Sicilians, and a group of Mustache Petes with whom Frank maintains friendly relations. Their leader is the reserved, courtly Don Peppino (Eduardo Ciannelli).

Whereas Frank began his criminal career at a young age under his Mafioso father, Vince has been to college, law school, and the army. Upon being invited to join Frank's operation, Vince assures his wife that he will be involved only in its business affairs. Subsequently, fearing that the syndicate will become 'too big' and thus run afoul of the government, Frank opposes its proposed involvement in an electronics industry crucial to the national space program. His syndicate colleagues, who behave more like businessmen than criminals, reject his traditionalism. When Vince upon Dominick's suggestion attempts to change his brother's mind, Frank is too busy playing bocce with the Mustache Petes to pay attention to Vince, who now fears, as Dominick has suggested, that he and Frank will be thrown out of the syndicate. Contrary to Frank's wishes, the board goes ahead with the electronics venture.

The major turn of the plot comes when Frank is invited into the cryptlike back room of a local grocery store to a meeting of the Mustache Petes. A living relic of the Mafia past, Don Peppino reveals that he and his friends are the last survivors of the crime family ruled by Sicilian-born Salvatore Maranzano who, with forty gang members, was eliminated by Lucky Luciano over a two-day period in the early 1930s. This gang war pitted Mafia traditionalists against business-minded Americanizers led by Luciano, who replaced the older 'Mafia' with a 'syndicate' including alien elements, that is, Irish, Jews, and non-Sicilian Italians. Here then is the origin of the multi-ethnic syndicate to which Frank belongs, and which he hates. Don Peppino then produces letters from the loved ones of the forty-one Mafiosi and calls upon Frank to avenge them. Not only is Frank's father among the murdered, but Luciano had received their names from Dominick. Thus Frank realizes that he must kill Dominick in order to return *onore* to the Mustache Petes.

When Vince informs Frank that he will accept Dominick's invitation to join the syndicate, adding that Frank had been voted down in its recent meeting, Frank punches his brother, who leaves in a suppressed rage. Ever the Sicilian personalist, Frank thinks not of business expansion and profits but of vengeance against Dominick, whom he denounces as a *Cammorista*, that is, a Neapolitan 'bastard.' Subsequently Frank lures Dominick to an abandoned warehouse and kills him with his own hands, but only after reciting the names of the purged Mafiosi. After Frank escapes to Sicily, the syndicate demands that Vince track down and kill his brother, who now realizes that the Mafia is finished, and that Vince's survival requires his own death. Following a country banquet, to which Frank invites the Ginettas' Sicilian relatives, Vince executes his brother with a *lupara* or sawed-off shotgun, a traditional Mafia weapon. Vince then returns to New York, where his future in the syndicate is assured.

Notwithstanding Scorsese's claim that the 'actors [in *The Brotherhood*] did a very good job,' Kirk Douglas exemplifies what Scorsese criticizes as the 'Mamma mia' acting style.[105] Imagining that excessive gesticulations, shouting, clowning, sentimentality, and angrily irrational outbursts suffice to convey *italianità*, Douglas lacks credibility, and his mustache cannot save him. Yet Scorsese justly praises the Jewish American actor Luther Adler as Dominick Bertoldo, one of several Italian Americans played by Adler during his career. Reserved and understated, and with no suggestion of the 'Hollywood Italian,' Adler's Dominick combines wary cunning and obliging good nature, patience and exaggeration, family loyalty and worldly interest. Besides having the requisite Mediterranean appearance, Irene Pappas as Frank's convent-educated wife conveys the seriousness, dignity, and loyalty Sicilian crime bosses expect from their wives. Having portrayed Trock Estrella in *Winterset* and Johnny Vanning in *Marked Woman*, Cianelli is suitably demonic as Don Peppino. The other Italian American in *The Brotherhood* is Alex Cord (born Alex Vespi in 1933), whose understated portrayal of Vince partly counterweighs Douglas's excesses.

Nonetheless Frank Ginetta is an original creation as compared with earlier portrayals of Italian American crime bosses. Not only is the stereotypical boss obsessed with sartorial display, wanting very much to be in style, but, in aspiring to the image of the American businessman, or at least wanting to conform to modern custom, he is typically clean shaven, and is often shown being shaved. Sometimes the crime boss is a psychopathic killer with an inferiority complex, like Rico Bandello, but more typically the unreflectively titanic egos of Camonte and Rocco exemplify a drive for megalomaniac prepotency. In many instances, the misogynistic gang boss inflicts violence on women, and one finds as well suggestions of homoerotic perversity, as with Rico Bandello, Johnny Vanning, and Lagana. Even when a crime boss like Rico or Camonte has family ties, they are warped or perverse.[106]

Counter to these stereotypes, Minetta sports an old-timer's mustache and wears clothes reminiscent of the 1920s. In contrast to the typical cinematic crime boss, who sees no limit to wealth or power, Frank would remain content with his existing operation. Although Frank's business is unavoidably violent, he kills economically, and shows no sadism save in murdering Dominick. Unlike his screen predecessors, Frank has a rich family life, maintaining close ties with relatives at home and abroad. He greatly enjoys his brother's wedding, where he dances with his adolescent daughter. Typically the cinematic crime boss favours loose women, but Frank remains emotionally and sexually devoted to his wife in the manner of an Old World Sicilian don. Unfortunately, Carlino's non-stereotypical conception of Ginetta was weakened by Douglas's overstated performance. What Douglas (and perhaps Carlino) failed to realize is that a Sicilian crime boss cultivates an impression of reserve, discretion, and quiet authority, dominating situations not through overt intimidation but by hints and gestures. Thus the renderings of Italian American gangsters by Cianelli and Scourby are preferable to Douglas's.

Ritt's portrayal of Frank's and Vinnie's relationship handles with some sensitivity the struggle that often arose among second-generation Italian Americans. Largely acculturated but only partly assimilated, the second generation felt the pressure of family and community to remain within its urban neighbourhoods in unflinching loyalty to the ethnic culture. Rather than valuing education for economic and social advancement, many second-generation Italian Americans shared their parents' fear of it as a threat to family and group solidarity. Some members of the second generation, however, especially the younger ones, desired occupational and social mobility as a means of assimilation. Having lost respect for their Italian-speaking fathers and their narrow possibilities, they rejected the Italian language and cuisine. For them, education afforded a path into the mainstream.

For all his success Frank Ginetta remains loyal to the ethnic past, worshipping his father's memory, continuing his business, and avenging him in Sicilian style. Besides speaking Italian to Vince, he uses southern Italian expressions such as *cedrul'* (cucumber), referring to a stupid person. What also marks Frank as an imperfectly assimilated Italian American is his personalism, as when, during a syndicate meeting, he declares that he intends to rely on hand-picked henchmen rather than the syndicate crew. Upon being told that syndicate members must suppress their personalities and 'be like the furniture,' Frank declares with mocking though clumsy humour: 'Okay, I'm a chair.' His impatience with commercial discipline is shown by his casual report of losses at the racetrack – not the behaviour of a respectable businessman. Although Frank appreciates his brother's education and accounting skills, he later informs Vince that learning takes a back seat to tradition. With no place left for him in the United States, Frank flees to Sicily, where he fulfils the role of the Sicilian patriarch before being gunned down by Vince.

Vince stands for the second-generation Italian American eager for assimilation at virtually any cost. Besides being educated, he has entered a profession whose high-level numeracy exemplifies capitalist objectivity and impersonality. His self-contained and nearly affectless demeanour well suits him for the WASP business world. Abstract-minded and matter of fact, and largely detached from family and ethnic loyalties, Vince objects to not only his brother's use of Italian but his friendship with Mustache Petes. In contrast with his brother's father-respect, Vince refers to his father as 'nuthin,' the owner of a 'peanuts and candy store operation.' Indifferent to bocce ball, Vince derives from *The New York Times* a grasp of the international context of the syndicate far beyond that of his insular-minded brother.

Another striking feature of *The Brotherhood* is its genuine flavour of *sicilianità*; no other film went so far in this direction before the *The Godfather.* In the opening scene, as Vince is driven through Palermo to his meeting with Frank, a young man on a motorbike rides along the highway with an old woman clinging to his waist, an apt image of traditionalism impeding modernity. Subsequently Vince encounters local peasants with donkeys, a symbol of Sicily that Coppola employs in *Godfather III.* As Frank and Sicily itself have deviated from modernity, so Vince diverges from the highway and discovers his brother holed up in a ruined medieval castle, possibly a symbol of Sicily as a historical dead end or backwater. It is true that, when Frank tells his brother that his death must occur in traditional style, following a celebration to which 'all the relatives' have been invited, the film falsely implies that the extended family had been the Sicilian norm, when in reality the nuclear family predominated owing to economic scarcity. However, *The Brotherhood* is also about Sicilian ideals and myths, and from that perspective Frank's celebration of the extended family rings true.[107]

The film's American scenes are likewise dense with authentic Sicilian atmosphere. The first murder depicted in the film is followed by the stuffing of a parakeet in the victim's mouth, indicating his violation of *omertà*. After receiving word of the assassination at the wedding party, Frank praises the officiating priest: 'Father, you did a wonderful job' – a compliment equally applicable to his henchmen. This exchange anticipates the baptism scene in *Godfather I* with its ironic cross-cutting between Catholicism and criminality. When Emma learns of Frank's desire to join the Mafia, she exemplifes the Mafia wife's refusal to know of her husband's activities. In murdering Dominic, Frank ties him up Mafia style with a rope attached to his neck and ankles, so that he strangles himself in trying to get free. Frank's denunciation of Dominic as a '*Cammorista* bastard' reflects a historical reality not to be seen in previous films, namely the playing out of southern Italian regional hatreds in the neighbourhoods of remoter decades. Yet *The Brotherhood* errs in Don Francesco's claim that forty-one Mustache Petes under Maranzano were exterminated by Luciano's henchmen in the early 1930s. Although many historians believe the purge to have occurred on 11 and 12 September 1931, Humbert Nelli concludes that the bloodbath never took place.[108]

What also makes *The Brotherhood* remarkable is its treatment of the conflict between the family and syndicate. For though this theme appears in *The Brothers Rico* and *The Godfather* films, *The Brotherhood* in some ways surpasses them in its understanding of the Mafia. According to Dwight C. Smith, *The Brothers Rico* misrepresents the Mafia, as in his view Italian American crime organizations are based not on impersonal business-like or rationally bureaucratic arrangements but on kinship ties both actual and fictional, and thus harmonize or reconcile business and familial loyalties. Smith is indebted to Francis A.J. Ianni who, unlike those criminologists who view Italian American organized criminal groups as centralized, hierarchical, and bureaucratic organizations pervaded by business impersonality, describes them as family businesses in which kinship ties provide the operating principle and bond.[109] Ianni's study has influenced Thomas J. Ferraro, who sees the Corleone family in *The Godfather* as exemplifying the idea of Mafia organization as a family business. Yet while it is unnecessary to refute Donald Cressey's long exploded comparison of the Mafia to a business corporation, Ianni's, Smith's, and Ferraro's views are themselves problematic, since the American Mafia in contrast with its Sicilian counterpart normally places its own organizational interests above all kinship allegiances founded on blood relations. Indeed, the major test of a member's loyalty within the fictionally constituted kinship group making up a Mafia 'family' is to kill a blood relative so as to demonstrate one's stronger ties to the criminal organization.[110] This happens in the case of Vince, whose test of loyalty to the syndicate is to kill his brother. One should not suppose, however, that *The Brotherhood* provides an altogether reliable portrait of Mafia organization and operations, as the criminal group to which Vince Ginetta devotes himself and for which he murders his blood relative amounts to a cartel or business association rather than an artificial kinship group typical of the Mafia.

V

Although the gangster and crime film have been the chief site for the representation of Italian Americans, they have sometimes figured cinematically in a more favourable association with comic laughter, gaiety, conviviality, and pleasure.

Directed by Sam Wood from a script by S.J. Perelman, the Marx Brothers' *A Night at the Opera* (1934) polarizes Italian high and low culture while satirizing the snobbery and cultural pretentions of high society. The elite crowd includes Mrs Claypool (Margaret Dumont), who patronizes opera as a means of social climbing; Herman Gottlieb, the sycophantic impresario; and Rodolfo Lasspari, a highly touted but arrogant Italian-born tenor whose advances are rebuffed by Rosa Castaldi (Kitty Carlisle), his beautiful singing partner. The lower-class crowd includes the bounder Hackensack (Groucho), a would-be opera impresario; Fiorello (Chico Marx), an illiterate stowaway; their friend Tommaso (Harpo), a harp-playing mute; and the Italian immigrant families en route with the others to the United States. Finally there is Rosa's beloved, Ricardo Baroni (Alan Jones), whose singing talents are yet to be discovered.

During the shipboard festival scene, as the first-class passengers look down literally and figuratively upon the immigrant celebrants, one has the impression that the class superiors feel unspoken envy of the immigrants' anarchic energy and enjoyment of life, free of social constraints. Consistent with a long-standing stereotype, the immigrants appear anachronistically in old-style Neapolitan garb, the women wearing bandanas or kerchiefs and affording a vaguely Bohemian impression. The festival unleashes near-frenzied dancing and non-stop consumption of food and wine capped off by musical performances by Ricardo, Fiorello, and Tommaso: singer, pianist, and harpist. The many children in this scene call to mind the positive stereotype of the Italian as a child, direct and open in his responses. The mood of popular anarchism culminates in the final scene, in which Fiorello and Tommaso turn *Il Trovatore* into the equivalent of a three-ring circus, with Italian low culture prevailing over its high cultural rival.

It is sometimes assumed in discussions of the film that both the Marx Brothers and scenarist S.J. Perelman have adopted an anti-elitist and anti–high cultural standpoint without necessarily deriding opera itself. In Italy opera had long been a popular art, and only in the twentieth century did it become a highly exclusive and expensive entertainment of the upper classes. The anarchic invasion of the opera stage in *A Night at the Opera* would figure from this perspective as an attempt to restore to opera its original plebeian energy and sincerity. Thus, after Lasspari is driven from the stage, the real lovers join in a romantic duet. What makes them worthy of revitalizing opera is that, unlike Lasspari, they sing for love and enjoyment rather than money. Could it be then that the film satirizes not opera but only its soulless appropriation by the wrong people? Actually, Ricardo and Rosa have light operatic rather than operatic voices, and *A Night at the Opera* favours not opera but a diluted, vulgarized form of it.

A Night at the Opera draws from longstanding favourable Italian stereotypes of 'fun' and enjoyment. In the American cinema of the 1930s and 1940s Italians and Italian Americans often figure as musicians, from the lowly organ-grinders played by Sicilian American Henry Armetta, to the ambitious violinist in Clifford Odets's *Golden Boy* (1939). They also appear frequently as singers, peddlers, fruit stand and ice-cream vendors, waiters, bar and café owners, and obsequious restaurateurs, with Armetta setting the standard in the latter role.[111] The restaurants have red-chequered tablecloths, with flasks of Chianti in straw containers and Italian landscapes on the walls. Musical performances are sometimes featured, contrasting with the restaurant mayhem in gangster films.

That early-twentieth-century Americans had become somewhat used to Italian food is suggested by *Little Caesar* (1931), in which Rico eats spaghetti in a diner. A year later, however, Chaplin's *City Lights* contained a scene (not unfamiliar to vaudeville audiences) involving an impossibly long strand of spaghetti, which still struck Americans as a bit 'funny.' In *A Night at the Opera*, spaghetti appears on the menu of a pretentious 'Continental' style restaurant (with seemingly Italian waiters), yet its plebian associations are accented in the shipboard scenes where, surrounded by feasting immigrants, Fiorello, Tommaso, and Ricardo gorge themselves. Ricardo then launches into an aria, confirming the stereotypical link between Italian food and song. However, Groucho lauds the man who, as he claims, had the idea of stuffing spaghetti with bicarbonate of soda, thus causing and curing indigestion simultaneously. The increasing familiarity of non–Italian Americans with Italian food, which would ultimately become the most popular of all ethnic cuisines in the United States, is signalled intermittently in various films including *The Best Years of Our Lives* (1946) and *The Blackboard Jungle* (1955), in which the characters, dining contentedly in unpretentious local Italian restaurants, extol what were in those decades were still rather exotic dishes, such as ravioli.

In some films the Italian American restaurant owes its charm to the social and musical gifts of its proprietors along with Italian high cultural associations. Produced by Val Lewton and directed by Mark Robson, *The Seventh Victim* (1943) depicts a Greenwich Village establishment operated by a middle-aged and musically inclined Italian American couple. The restaurant is of the type favoured by pre–World War II Bohemians, who appreciated cheap but wholesome food, cleanliness, fellow-feeling, and tolerance of their artistic lifestyle.[112] Not only does the kitchen resound with the wife's singing, but the dining room contains a prominently displayed mural of Dante's meeting with Beatrice – an artistic touch appealing to Bohemian tastes. In other films, however, the attractive ambience of the Italian American restaurant conceals violence. Thus in *The Strange Love of Martha Ivers* the professional gambler and tough guy Sam Masterson (Van Heflin) visits a restaurant with red-chequered table cloths, where he knowingly compliments the Italian proprietor on the preparation of a dish, yet whose patrons include the ethnic thugs who later beat him up. In George Cukor's *A Double Life* (1947), the feted Shakespearean actor Anthony John (Ronald Colman) is so absorbed in his role of Othello that, without removing his makeup, he distractedly leaves a post-performance celebration and wanders a considerable distance into Manhattan's Little Italy, among ill-lit streets where Italian-speaking locals gather on doorsteps. As he has just concluded his performance as the Moor Othello, the dark 'other' of Renaissance Venice, so he has entered by implicit affinity the realm of white America's dark, fascinating, and violent other, the Italian. No less uncannily, John stands before the Caffè Venezia, which has a gondolier depicted on its front window – an image of transport recalling his own night journey. The otherness of the setting is further accentuated by signs advertising strange and strangely named foods like 'scungilli' and 'calamari,' suggesting both marine depths and, analogously, those of the character's own unconscious. Seated in a shadowy corner of the chiaroscuristically lit restaurant, John meets a blonde-haired waitress (Shelley Winters) whom he later strangles while under the delusion that she is Desdemona. Implicitly his psychosis has something to do with his errant, almost somnambulistic venture into Little Italy, with its mystery, obscurity, and sexual vendettas.

VI

American cinema has also produced a number of what might be characterized as dramas of Italian American assimilation, treating that process in its various phases from the period of immigration onward.

Because most Italian immigrants did not regard themselves as Italian, but identified with their native villages and specific regions of Italy, Italian American ethnicity only emerged after immigration, as a result of the experience of living in America, where the immigrants were regarded collectively as Italians. Initially Italian Americans were very much hybrid creatures torn between the ethnic family or neighbourhood and the mainstream. Following immigration this division was especially evident within the first-generation family, which attempted to preserve the older culture.[113] As in southern Italy, the nuclear and sometimes the extended family were the primary social institutions, the former having been characterized as a 'father-dominated, mother-centred' structure. Yet though the father claimed supreme authority over wife and children, wives often strongly influenced their husbands in addition to enjoying substantial domestic authority. Children were required to be strictly obedient, while familial honour depended on the fidelity and chastity of wives and daughters. Because the Madonna-whore dichotomy prevailed, some sexual licence was permitted to young males. And since familial solidarity took precedence over individual interests, education was disprized, children being expected to work for the family upkeep. Marriages were often arranged, with some allowance provided for the natural affection of the concerned parties.

In the United States these familial patterns were modified through exposure to the New World environment and ideology. Because many wives had to take jobs, their husbands' authority often dwindled. The American school system weakened parental control over children by exposing them to the values of individuality, gainful self-interest, and personal autonomy. Many Italian American children were ashamed of their parents' language, customs, and eating habits. Unknown to southern Italy, and operating outside the home, youthful peer groups sprang up, sometimes becoming breeding grounds for juvenile delinquency.

The period from about 1910 to 1945 witnessed considerable conflict between the first and second generation over acculturation and assimilation. Ultimately the first generation received certain concessions from the second in exchange for the liberalization of practices and attitudes. Children were allowed to keep their earnings, to date more freely, and to choose their spouses, although out-group marriage remained rare. Use of the Italian language was no longer expected of children, who were allowed to socialize with their peer groups. In exchange for these concessions they were expected to live close to home after marriage, which often meant taking blue-collar jobs.[114] Thus education as a means of mobility and assimilation continued to be under-appreciated by many Italian Americans. Another concession was that second-generation family members agreed to be present at the parental residence for Sunday dinners, where the consumption of Italian-style food reaffirmed familial and ethnic solidarity.

Most second-generation Italian Americans showed their loyalty to family and neighbourhood either willingly or grudgingly. A much less common response to generational conflict was that of the so-called rebel. Divesting themselves of all markers of *italianità*, including language, cuisine, and even last names, rebels valued education and used it for occupational mobility. Not surprisingly, they had a higher rate of out-group marriage than most Italian Americans.

Directed by Rouben Mamoulian from the play by Clifford Odets, *Golden Boy* was released in 1939 and stars William Holden. Barbara Stanwyck supplies the love interest, and Adolph Menjou and Joseph Calleia appear as a boxing manager and promoter respectively. The film centres on the young Italian American Joe Bonaparte, torn between boxing and a career as a violinist. Thus the film fuses two contradictory stereotypes of the Italian. Joe Bonaparte's Ruggieri violin exemplifies high culture, art, and music – a stereotype not of Italian Americans but of Italy. The contrasting stereotype is that of the Italian American as a physical, primitive, non-verbal, and virtually animal entity, given to violence and therefore eminently suitable for the boxing ring. In the film, however, the boxing world is identified with mainstream society, whose consumerist seductions nearly corrupt the ethnic protagonist.

Unfortunately, William Holden is miscast as Joe Bonaparte and, despite his long, darkened, and curled locks, lacks credibility. Nor is Lee J. Cobb any better as Mr Bonaparte, Joe's father, a grocer in Little Italy. That the Jewish Cobb plays an Italian American cannot be held against him, as some Jewish actors, such as Edward G. Robinson and Luther Adler, did well in such roles. Cobb's performance, however, affords yet another example of what Martin Scorsese calls the 'Mamma mia' school of acting, as it consists of outlandish gesticulations, tearfully sentimental effusions, and ridiculous pidgin English. With his unkempt hair, handlebar mustache, vest pocket handkerchief, and shirt with puffed-up sleeves, Mr Bonaparte seems to have just stepped off the boat.

His atypicality as a first-generation Italian American father is revealed in the attempt to 'intellectualize' him, by having him play chess in his grocery store. The Italian American immigrant comes vaguely to resemble a long-haired highbrow, an image reinforced not only by his worship of the violin but by the abundant books in his household, indicating an interest in reading atypical of his group. The high cultural afflatus of his residence is owed as well to reproductions of the Sistine Madonna and Madonna della Sedia, the latter a substitute for Joe's deceased mother. Contrary to the authoritarianism of first-generation fathers, embattled with their Americanizing progeny, Mr Bonaparte accepts his son's need for freedom and does not insist on father-respect. Equally improbably, Joe announces his abandonment of the violin on the day Mr Bonaparte gives him a fifteen-hundred-dollar Ruggieri, the result of many years of saving. When Joe confesses to his material aspirations, his father berates him sententiously: 'Money, money, we gotta hearts, we gotta souls – we gotta take care of them.' Whereas Joe's materialism resembles that of the second generation, Mr Bonaparte lacks that hard-headed sense of priorities in money matters typical of southern Italian immigrants. The father's unworldliness is subsequently shown when, distracted by Joe's violin, he fails to hear a customer's request for bread – material necessities have small claim over him. This is not to say that Mr Bonaparte's responses are impossible, yet his portrayal is exaggerated to the point of improbability.

As Joe prepares for his championship campaign, his father gives him the Ruggieri hoping that he will practice. Situated directly between them, the Madonna della Sedia not only calls attention to the absence of the reconciling mother but suggests that Italian high culture divides father and son. When Joe requests his father's blessing upon his career, this being seen in the Italian American culture of those days as essential in all major undertakings, Joe receives an equivocal embrace. Later, Mr Bonaparte refuses the six hundred dollars Joe offers him from his ring earnings, treating it as blood money.

Although in *Golden Boy* boxing belongs to the world of American materialism, it is associated as well with the Italian American gangster-boxing promoter Eddie Fuselli (Joseph Calleia), so that the film maintains the stereotype of Italian American criminality, opposing it to Italian high culture. Impeccably groomed, with an elegant mustache contrasting with Mr Bonaparte's handlebars, and gotten up in expensive, well-tailored style, Fuselli calls to mind Trock Estrella and Johnny Vanning. Like them, he intimidates people less through overt violence than through hints and suggestions. In his most demonic moment, Fuseli deeply inhales a cigarette and, like a dragon, exhales enormous billows of smoke. Yet he is capable of open threats if necessary. Notwithstanding his statement to Joe upon their introduction – 'I'm Eyetalian too, an American citizen' – Fuselli has an Italian accent and exemplifies Old World corruption.

What saves Joe from Fuselli's machinations is his love for Lorna (Barbara Stanwyck), the assistant to Moody, Joe's manager. Having pushed Joe into boxing on Moody's behalf, Lorna comes to realize the true happiness he receives from music and family, and urges him to abandon

Fuselli for the violin. The film's climax comes as Joe prepares for a middleweight title shot in Madison Square Garden. He now dresses in the same style as Fuselli, who plies him with fancy clothes as if he were his double. But Joe regains his integrity upon realizing that Fuselli affords no substitute for Lorna and his family. On the night of the fight, Mr Bonaparte gives Joe his blessing. Yet he pities him, partly because he recognizes Fuselli's role in arranging the bout. Joe's alienation from boxing culminates when he unintentionally kills his opponent, whereupon he rejects Fuselli: 'I'm a cheap edition of you.'

Joe and Lorna can now confess their love and make plans to marry. *Golden Boy* is thus one of those Hollywood films in which the Italian American male protagonist's salvation requires marriage to a non–Italian American woman. Yet whereas the non-ethnic woman usually leads him out of the neighbourhood into the mainstream, in *Golden Boy* the non-ethnic woman returns the hero to the Old World culture – and emotional authenticity – he had nearly betrayed in his zeal to Americanize. In the final scene, after announcing that he has 'come home' to stay, Joe embraces his father before the image of the Madonna della Sedia, which now stands for the Italian artistic tradition uniting father and son.

House of Strangers (1949) ranks among the best Hollywood dramas of assimilation in the post-war period. Directed by Joseph Mankiewicz from Philip Yordan's script, this Twentieth Century Fox production is based on Jerome Weidman's novel *I'll Never Go There Anymore* (1941). Unlike the novel, which treats a small-time Jewish banking family, the film deals with Italian Americans though maintaining the themes of banking malfeasance and family betrayal. Initially Fox producer Darryl F. Zanuck had wanted a story based on the life of Italian American banker A.P. Giannini, who developed the Bank of America, in its time the largest bank in the United States, out of a small lending operation in the San Francisco area. Giannini, however, opposed even a covertly biographical representation. Spyros Skouras, President of Twentieth Century Fox, saw the film's central family as a disguised representation of his own history and limited the film's distribution.[115] Commenting on the film under its projected title, *East Side Story*, Joseph Breen, chief administrator of the Hollywood production code, found its Italian Americans to be 'definitely reprehensible [or] ... at least, unsympathetic.'[116]

Former lawyer Max Monetti (Richard Conte) returns home in 1939 after a seven-year prison term for attempting to bribe a juror during his father Gino's trial for financial crimes. Max owes his imprisonment and career failure to his elder brother Joe, who had betrayed him. Not only does Max seek vengeance against Joe, but he aims to punish his brothers for stealing his father's business. The plaque beside the Monetti Trust and Loan Association in Little Italy announces Joe Monetti (Luther Adler) as its president, and younger brothers Tony (Efrem Zimbalist, Jr), and Pietro (Paul Valentine) as vice-presidents. Initially the fraternal reunion amounts to a cordial exchange of pleasantries. That Joe, despite his hatred of his father, has internalized Gino's tyrannical habits is suggested by the fact that he has duplicated on the interior walls of his office the portrait of Gino that hangs in the family home. Notwithstanding that an American flag decorates Joe's desk, his office contains a prominently displayed bust of Mussolini that, merely by its presence in the office, one associates with Gino, the tyrannical patriarch. This reticulates in turn with a later scene in which Irene Bennet, Max's WASP girlfriend and no friend of his father, mocks the son as 'Il Duce.' The American flag in juxtaposition with Mussolini implies a confusion of social, cultural, and political identity by no means unusual among Italian Americans in the 1920s and 1930s, when the energetic efforts of Italian fascist propagandists, organizers, and interlopers won for Mussolini numerous sympathizers and even some adherents within the ethnic communities, especially among the class of *prominenti* to whom the Monettis belong. Among the reasons for the attraction of Italian Americans to Italian fascism was that, after decades of political and military humiliation, and also after the many indignities suffered by Italian immigrants in America as members of a so-called inferior group, Mussolini had seemed to restore pride and respect to the Italian name. Only with the onset of World War II did Italian Americans reveal their more profound and basic loyalty to the United States.[117]

Max is troubled to learn that their mother, Teresa (Esther Minciotti), has moved from the family house to a humble residence on Little Italy's Mulberry Street, repudiating all her husband's works. Having attempted equivocally to assimilate, Joe mentions that his two half-WASP children are blondes and have learned to 'hate spaghetti.' Finally Max's resentment of his brothers explodes. He refuses Joe's offer of a thousand dollars in compensation and leaves the room. Joe proposes to give him 'blood': 'We'll keep it in the family, where it's always been.' This calls to mind the stereotypical identification of the Italian American with blood: hot-bloodedness, blood vengeance, often familial, and blood in the sense of close family and intra-ethnic ties, as in the phrase 'blood of my blood.' However much the stereotype suggests the closeness of such ties, it also implies their breakage through the blood feud, thus confirming notions of a radically conflicted identity. When Joe insists on family vengeance, he aligns with the Old World.

Max next visits the apartment of Irene Bennett (Susan Hayward), a rich beauty who has remained faithful to him during his prison term. Nonetheless her dream of their new life is jeopardized by Max's plans for revenge: 'Vengeance is a rare wine, a joy divine, says the Arab.' One recalls the films of Valentino, in which the supposed Italian penchant for getting even is transferred to vengeful knife-wielding lovers in Arab garb. Irene wants Max to reject his past and sees his 'vendetta' as yet another undesirable ethnic trait derived from his father, whom she condemns as an 'evil man, a bad man.' But she goes too far in stating that the world is 'better off with your father dead,' whereupon Max, confirming the Italian male's reputation of violence towards women, slaps her and departs for the family house.

In the dark and empty living room Max places a recording on a phonograph. Sung in Italian, Flotow's 'M'Apparit' accompanies a shift of scene to 1932, with Gino Monetti singing the same song in a horrendous voice while bathing. The gigantic bed and multiplication of towels bearing the monogram GM testify to his all-engulfing self-worship. When Joe reminds his father that his creditors await him, Gino rejoins: 'the bank opens when I get there.'

Gino's banking methods seem haphazard and capricious and thus call to mind the practices of not a few small-time Italian American bankers during the early days of immigration.[118] Ignoring a call from an import company, Gino says he must attend to 'friends.' These include a heavily accented Italian American who needs a new horse and to whom Gino lends a hundred and fifty dollars; however, he also deducts thirty dollars as interest in advance – a usurious rate. For good measure Gino orders the lender to speak English rather than Italian, yet when asked a question moments later Gino answers '*si*.' When an Italian American woman requests a loan in order to finance a relative's operation in Denver, which Gino imagines to be in Kansas, thus demonstrating his ghetto insularity, he gladly provides the money, only to regret that he gave her 'too much.' Yet when he receives a call for the renewal of a loan, he barks 'No.' His fusion of business and personalism is summarized in his declaration: 'I am the bank.' The portrayal of Gino Monetti thus conforms to the Italian American stereotype of a lack of business rationality, objectivity, and probity.[119]

Irene Bennet having entered the bank in search of Max, Gino assumes delightedly that her business call really has pleasure as its object. Despite Max's plans to marry Maria, his father would seem to approve of his sexual double-dealing, at least when it involves worldly (and hence unmarriageable) women like Irene. Max's remark to Irene, that 'money is a good cleanser,' rings ironically in view of the earlier scene in which Joe's offer of a thousand dollars leaves Max's hunger for vendetta unappeased. When Joe detects the smell of Irene's perfume in Max's office, his brother attributes it to a 'dame,' which is synonymous with 'broad,' and which suggests that Max sees Irene only as a sexual opportunity, not as a wife.

Joe complains to Max that their father has never honoured his promise of raising his sixty-five-dollar-a-week salary, which fails to satisfy Joe's well-born wife, a Philadelphia WASP used to entertaining friends lavishly. Although he will inherit Gino's business, Joe remains troubled by the fact that, unlike the adored Max, a younger son, his father requires him to work in a teller's 'cage.' Yet despite his independence, Max customarily joins the family at the obligatory dinner cooked by their mother every Wednesday at Gino's house. There is considerable truth to this portrayal, as many first-generation parents accepted their children's Americanizing ways only if they agreed to dine with the family regularly or on at least some occasions. In this instance dinner is delayed on Gino's orders because of Max's tardiness, the dining room being filled in the meantime with the sound of opera, which Gino insists on playing full blast.

The guests include Joe's wife, impatient to return home for a social engagement; the loyal Maria, whom Max takes for granted; and Maria's mother, who fears a bad marriage for her daughter. When Joe's wife, seconded by her husband, complains of the monotony of spaghetti dinners, claiming that they upset her stomach, Gino orders them to continue their Wednesday visits, lest Joe lose his job. Not only do Americans to this day identify Italian food with indigestion, as witness television commercials, but in those decades the family dinner table was the main scene of the conflict between first-generation Italian American fathers and their rebellious second-generation sons. A chief sign of that rebellion was the rejection of Italian cuisine as is typified by Joe's intolerance of spaghetti.

At last Max arrives and gives Maria a passionate kiss, which her mother finds indecorous but Gino welcomes, as marriage spells the end of fun. When Max broaches the issue of Joe's raise, Gino promises that he will inherit the business. The eternal spaghetti arrives, served by the silent, long-suffering Mrs Monetti. Yet scarcely has the meal begun before Max is drawn away by Irene Bennett's phone call, Gino defending him on the grounds that Max's '*professione*' comes first. Before Max and Irene go out on the town, he portrays himself as an unassimilated ethnic who 'still like[s] the smell of garlic and red wine.' He also reports his betrothal to the virginal Maria, who can provide 'kids' and a 'home' and who 'knows only one man.' While defining Max, in contrast with Joe, as the true ethnic, these self-revelations raise problems for Irene, who realizes that Max envisions her as an unmarriageable 'whore.'

Notwithstanding Max's obligations to Maria, he and Irene attend a professional boxing match where Gino, Joe, and Tony have also gathered to watch Pietro, the younger brother, compete. His robe inscribed with the name of Gino's company, Pietro loses the fight and is immediately stripped of the robe by Gino, who derides him as a family disgrace. 'Nice fatherly gesture,' comments Irene, 'the Monettis must never lose.' Upon discovering Irene's jealousy of Maria, Max sees it as a needless complication, whereupon she rebukes his view that 'women live in vacuum-sealed containers.' This is a serious criticism of Max's sexual attitudes, as he has encapsulated the two women in his life within mutually exclusive domestic and sexual realms. Nor can Max decide between them, and this undermines his relationship with Irene. When he subsequently threatens an admirer of hers, she comments that 'This is not Mulberry Street and you're not Il Duce.' In view of his family's origins on Mulberry Street, and of the statue of Mussolini in Joe's office, Irene implies that Max's Italian American heritage divides them. As she puts it, marriage is 'still being done, outside the jungle.' She will not tolerate being treated as a 'dame.' Yet Max forecasts his abandonment of Italian American sexual attitudes, for as he tells Irene, 'You're still my girl, I don't care if you marry ten guys.'

The film's crisis comes when investigators discover irregularities in the Monetti bank. 'Books is no way to run a bank,' cries Gino in defense of his methods on the basis of handshakes and promises to pay. Confronting his outraged patrons, he plays upon their southern Italian animus towards political authority by blaming the shut-down on the state. He also reminds them that had he demanded collateral for loans, as law required, they would not now own their houses and businesses. The implacable patrons' attempt to beat up Gino is prevented only by the arrival of the police.

Joe seems unresponsive to Gino's plight, while the weakling Tony trembles over the potential collapse of the business. Even Max, the most resourceful of the sons, remains baffled as to how Gino had 'gotten in so deep.' His failure to have read the banking acts exemplifies stereotypical

Italian American traits: a lack of interest in reading, and a preference for doing things 'my way,' to quote Sinatra's theme song. Gino thus faces twenty-two counts of misapplication of funds. Nor is it possible, warns Max, to bribe the investigators, as they are dealing with the state government, 'square apples all the way down the line.' Max's statement is 'Machiavellian' in its casualness, as he entertains the possibility of bribing officials. On the other hand, 'square apples' suggests Anglo-Saxon probity and rectitude as against Italian underhandedness.[120]

When Max proposes to split the responsibility for Gino's crimes among the brothers, they totally lack familial loyalty, especially Joe, who mentions his insignificant role at the bank while finding his salary insufficient to 'go to jail for.' Besides accusing Gino of having treated Max as if he were his eldest son, Joe now reveals his envious hatred of Max. The weak Tony joins Joe, as does Pietro, whom Gino had nicknamed 'Dumbhead.' Following the departure of the now conflicted brothers, Gino promises his wife a post-trial vacation in Palermo. She retorts that the family should never have left Sicily, and that it had been happier on Mulberry Street where Gino had owned a barber shop.

Gino's trial goes badly when the prosecutor reveals that he had confiscated family homes and wages following non-payment – practices qualifying as usurious. Gino responds with an Il Duce–style tantrum revealing his misconception of freedom as lawless liberty: 'I do what I want. It's a free country. What I think is right.' After Joe shows no interest in Max's plan to bribe a juror, he attempts to carry out the bribe himself, only to be captured by the police through Joe's connivance. While Max is being sentenced to seven years in prison, the trial concludes with an unexpectedly favourable result, but by now the brothers control the bank. During a visit to Max's prison cell, Gino persuades Max to exact paternal vengeance after informing him of Joe's betrayal and Maria's marriage to Tony. Thereupon Irene, who still loves Max, vilifies Gino for filling his son with 'poison and hate.' Having received a prison pass to attend Gino's funeral, Max bites his thumb as he glares at his brothers, a southern Italian gesture of vengeance. Yet Max's mother refuses to bless his vendetta, however much it 'make[s] Gino happy.' Her refusal is significant, as southern Italian children seek their mother's blessing in important undertakings.

The flashback concluded, Max appears in the darkness of the house. The scratching of the phonograph needle on the turntable evokes the dissonant cycles of family vengeance. As if Gino still lived within him, Max confides to his portrait a scheme to ruin all three brothers, consistent with Gino's teaching 'never to forgive.' Yet realizing the time he has lost in prison, and the possibilities of a new life with Irene, Max repudiates the paternal code: 'I've come back to life, Pa.' He then arranges for Irene to leave with him immediately for San Francisco. Within moments, however, the three brothers show up to kill Max, for despite his disavowal of vengeance, they fear his Monetti 'blood.' When Max attempts to leave, Pietro beats him up and on Joe's orders takes him upstairs so as to throw him from a balcony. 'We were both born on Mulberry Street,' says Joe, 'I can be tough, too.' Joe's speech reveals that, despite his hatred for his father, and despite his attempts at assimilation, he remains in the grip of such supposedly Italian American values as vendetta and disregard of fair play. When Pietro and Tony hesitate to murder Max, Joe orders Pietro to 'Throw him over, Dumbhead,' an insult that, unconsciously imitating Gino, incites Pietro's attempt to strangle Joe. Max then saves Joe by telling Pietro that he will only fulfil his detested father's wishes in killing his brother. Fraternal violence now quelled, Max starts a new life with Irene.

Despite Max's loyalty to Italian ways for most of the film, he surpasses his brothers in acculturation and assimilation. The film implies, though, that his redemption results largely from the intercession of a WASP wife who, in exposing him to superior values, enables him to escape from his ethnic heritage. He lays aside hot-blooded vendettas, learned from the father, in favour of forgiveness and reconciliation. Not accidentally, Max's wife is named Irene, Greek for 'peace.' Her last name, Bennett, derives from Benedict, analogous to *benedetto*, meaning blessed. Whereas Max's mother witholds her blessing, Irene, a mother substitute, confers upon Max the blessing of marriage coincidentally with his repudiation of fraternal vengeance. His marriage demonstrates his ultimate rejection of the dichotomy between virgins and 'dames' (or 'broads'). *House of Strangers* is thus imbued with the mainstream assumption of the retrograde character of Italian American society, and of the need for Italian Americans to transcend their background in order to assimilate.

Among the most significant of the dramas of in-group marriage and assimilation is Tennessee Williams's *The Rose Tattoo*, which premiered on Broadway in 1951 and was released as a Daniel Mann–directed film four years later. Like the play, the film centres on Serafina, a Sicilian American immigrant woman who, following her husband's death, learns of his infidelity yet recovers from the shock of that discovery through her love for a local truck driver. The play was inspired by Williams's recent visit to Italy and Sicily with his companion Frank Merlo, a Sicilian American;

its dedication reads: 'To Frank in gratitude for Sicily.' In preparing the
play Williams had hoped to cast Anna Magnani, whom he often visited in
Rome, as Serafina, but Magnani doubted her English and the role went
to Maureen Stapleton. However, Magnani plays the character in the film
version, with Burt Lancaster as Mangiacavallo, her truck driver suitor.
Shot in Key West, which doubled as a coastal town between New Orleans
and Mobile, *The Rose Tattoo* received three Academy Awards including
Magnani's Oscar for Best Actress. Although the film follows the play's
main outlines, it makes some changes for reasons of economy and also
to exploit its medium. Not only have the play's depictions of anti-Italian
prejudice been toned down to satisfy the censors, but, as Williams complained, the sexual theme has been diluted to suit popular taste.[121]

   The Rose Tattoo testifies to the depth and intensity of Williams's love
of Italy and especially Sicily, a response also present in his other works,
including *Baby Doll* and *The Fugitive Kind*. A frequent visitor to Rome in
the 1940s and 1950s, Williams delighted in what he saw as the Italians'
unabashed sexuality, something which he found very much lacking in his
own country. He also admired the natural grace and emotional warmth
of the Italians, which, in the midst of post-war pessimism, had restored
his confidence in human nature. Nor did Williams patronize the Italian common people for their folk religion, which many travellers have
derided as superstition, but which he portrays without condescension in
the character of Serafina. To quote Williams's preface to the play: 'Our
purpose is to show these gaudy, childlike mysteries with sentiment and
humor in equal measure, without ridicule and with respect for the religious yearning they symbolize.'[122]

   As the film opens Estelle Hohengarten, a blackjack dealer, leaves a
New Orleans tattoo parlor after receiving a rose tattoo over her breast. A
symbol of sexual love, it matches that of Estelle's lover, the Sicilian truck
driver Rosario delle Rose, husband of Serafina and father of Rosa. On
this day Serafina exults to have learned of her conception of a child by
her husband, a moment accompanied, she claims, by the apparition of
a rose tattoo over her own breast. Absolutely loyal to Rosario, she thinks
him equally devoted to her, and describes him to her Sicilian American
neighbours as an incomparable rose. Estelle later appears at the delle
Rose house with the request that Serafina, a self-employed seamstress,
make a pink silk shirt as a gift for her lover, who ironically is sleeping in
the bedroom. Appropriately Estelle works at the Mardi Gras Club, the
Mardi Gras being associated with both carnality and deception. After
Estelle leaves, a boisterous black billy goat escapes from the yard of a

neighbour, an old hag whom Serafina fears to be a *strega* or witch endowed with the evil eye or *malocchio*. When Rosario drives off unexpectedly and noisily in his truck, he is identified implicitly with the billy goat, each standing for unleashed sexual energy. However, Rosario is killed that evening after driving through a police roadblock with a drug shipment concealed under a haul of symbolically phallic bananas. His death devastates Serafina, who loses her child. Yet instead of burying Rosario in accordance with church laws, she has him cremated and his ashes stored in a marble urn placed prominently within her house – a monument to her supposedly ideal marriage.[123]

Three years later Serafina still mourns her husband; her dress, weight, and personal hygiene having deteriorated shockingly. Notwithstanding her refusal to make her daughter a formal party dress, on the grounds that Rosario would have disapproved, the fifteen-year-old Rosa attends a high school dance where she meets Jack Hunter, a young sailor. Upon her return her justifiably suspicious mother demands that she swear before the household statue of the Virgin that she had been studying. In the next scene, the day of Rosa's high school graduation, Serafina keeps her captive at home by withholding her graduation dress. After a female high school teacher shows up to demand that Rosa be allowed to attend graduation, Rosa describes her reluctantly compliant mother as 'disgusting' and races off to the ceremony. Although Serafina at last realizes that she too must attend the ceremony, she is detained unexpectedly by two floozies who insist that she finish for them the racy-looking blouse she had promised. In their open sexuality, and willingness to content themselves with unattractive men, these women contrast with Serafina, who remains fixated on the splendid Rosario. Much annoyed by Serafina's tone of moral superiority and sexual pride, the floozies reveal to her Rosario's affair with Estelle. They mention as well Estelle's rose tattoo – a flesh-and-blood version of Serafina's mystic rose. Serafina now turns in disbelief to the statue of the Virgin, seeking a 'sign' of her husband's fidelity. Her torments only increase when Rosa returns from graduation with Jack, now her beloved. Utterly uninterested in her daughter's diploma, and certain that Jack, consistent with his last name, intends only to steal her virginity, Serafina dismisses his gift of roses and rapturous praise of Rosa, whom she denounces as 'wild.' Yet when the still suspicious Serafina informs Jack that a Sicilian girl may be seen in public only with her fiancé, he confesses his love for Rosa, while Serafina, pleased as well to learn of his Catholicism, persuades him to kneel before the Virgin's statue and avow his sincerity.

Fearing that her husband has given her 'horns,' that is, sexually betrayed her, Serafina visits an Italian American church bazaar in order to
consult with Father De Leo and there is introduced to the truck driver
Alvaro Mangiacavallo (Lancaster), whom she ignores. Her bedraggled
appearance and antisocial behaviour shock the priest, who condemns
her grief as 'excessive' and 'self-indulgent,' and who had foreseen her
decline when she had refused to bury her husband according to church
law. Still incredulous that her husband, to whom she had given 'glory,'
had provided her with 'whores,' Serafina finally scandalizes Father De
Leo when she demands that he reveal the secrets of the confessional.
Amid the commotion Serafina rips Mangiacavallo's shirt, and after calm-
ing her he drives her home.

A kind-hearted bachelor with three dependants, Mangiacavallo sympathizes with Serafina, who reciprocates by mending his shirt. She is
then astonished to discover that he has a torso as magnificent as her
husband's, though conjoined with the head of a clown. For comic purposes Mangiacavallo conforms to the Italian American stereotype of the
lower-class, sentimentally lacrimose muscleman. Neither intelligent nor
articulate, he is a physical, appetitive, and emotional being centred on
love and family. The very name Mangiacavallo, meaning 'Eat a horse,'
implies his corporeality, while his childish reactions and exaggerated
gestures evoke a commedia dell'arte buffoon. Whereas Serafina continues to think of Rosario as a Sicilian aristocrat, Mangiacavallo claims without embarrassment to descend from a village idiot. When he learns of
the rose tattoo borne by Rosario upon his chest, he envisions himself as
Serafina's husband and suggests that the tattoo may return. She informs
Mangiacavallo that, should her husband's betrayal be proved, she will
smash his urn to bits. He then opens a bottle of Sicilian spumanti that, as
it explodes, forecasts Serafina's sexual liberation.

Although Serafina suspects unjustifiably that Mangiacavallo would
marry her as a means of supporting his dependants, his role as Rosario's replacement is signalled when she asks him to wear the pink silk
shirt Estelle had ordered. As an earlier scene had been interrupted by
the escape of a billy goat from a neighbour's yard, representing Rosario's ungovernable energies, Serafina and Mangiacavallo are interrupted
when the same billy goat breaks out again. But now Mangiacavallo uses
a makeshift bullfighter's cape to restrain and in a sense redomesticate
the creature. Implicitly Rosario is the bad husband, incapable of being housebroken, while the more desirable partner is Mangiacavallo,
roughly comparable to Rosario physically but also possessing domestic

virtues. To improve his chances with Serafina, Mangiacavallo has a rose tattoo emblazoned on his chest and then returns to the house where 'The Sheik of Araby' – shades of Valentino – plays on the pianola. When he reveals his tattoo, she is overpowered by the 'coincidence' and, fearful of betraying her husband's memory, drives off with Mangiacavallo to the Mardi Gras Club where Estelle confirms Rosario's adultery. Serafina then breaks the urn and, with a reawakened appetite for life, invites Mangiacavallo to come to the house that evening, but only on the condition of Rosa's absence, lest she observe her mother entertaining a man. After her drunken suitor's arrival Serafina allows him to sleep in an alcove next to the living room – a major modification of the play, in which he and Serafina sleep together. Much disappointed by Jack's scrupulous rejection of her passion the previous evening, Rosa is awakened by the shirtless Mangiacavallo, who initially mistakes her for Serafina. Yet this scandalous moment leads ultimately to Serafina's acceptance of both her daughter's and her own sexuality. At the conclusion she not only blesses Rosa's upcoming marriage but renews her 'conversation' with Mangiacavallo, in some ways a worthier version of Rosario.

Both the play and film of *The Rose Tattoo* suggest that, despite the brevity of his Sicilian visit, Williams had closely observed the locals and acquired a more than superficial grasp of their society and folkways.[124] Reminiscent of an Old World village, the residents of the film's shabby Sicilian American neighbourhood raise goats, drink wine, fear witches, and practise magic spells against the evil eye. The key to understanding Serafina lies in her impoverished peasant origin as well as in her proud self-delusion that, having married a baron, she is herself a baronessa. Like Mangiacavallo, she emerges from the Sicilian culture of *miseria*, including its religious beliefs and customs.

Williams's understanding of Sicily, and Italy more generally, reveals itself in his treatment of the play's sexual theme, which is sometimes misconstrued by critics ignorant of the characters' ethnicity. R. Barton Palmer claims that following her husband's death Serafina adopts such an idealized and aetherealized vision of Rosario that she puritanically rejects her own sexuality. Only the crude and animalistic Alvaro can show her that her refined and elevated notions of sexual attraction merely conceal the essential transitoriness of love and the base reality of animal lust.[125] In such an interpretation Serafina figures as a dualist, incapable of reconciling her erotic idealism with the flesh-and-blood expression of merely physical passion. Actually, the play demonstrates Williams's intuitive grasp of the Italian version of Christianity, which embraces an immanentist view of the divine, and which, far from being puritanical, sees no essential opposition between body and soul. Rather, the flesh is the medium or vehicle through which higher spiritual experience is sacramentally communicated. What troubles Serafina is not physical inhibition or overfastidiousness but her proudly stubborn belief that the sexual sanctity of her marriage had surpassed that of all other women, and can never be duplicated or approached. In her initially exalted conception of her marriage, she had supposedly achieved the perfect fusion of flesh and spirit, in which the animal and higher natures were harmonized and reconciled.[126] However, once she acknowledges her husband's betrayal, she is ready to resume a normal sexual life with somewhat lowered expectations and even entertains the possibility of marriage with the less than ideal Mangiacavallo.

The film's portrayal of Italian and Sicilian religion extends to cultic practices and everyday piety. As ethnologists have noted, Sicilian folk religion mingles orthodox Christian beliefs with animistic and magical notions of pagan derivation. Sacramentalism and immanentism are carried virtually to the point of fetishism and idolatry. Whereas the Trinity typifies conventional Christianity, Sicilian peasants normally pray to statuettes and icons of the Virgin and local saints, in whom, like Serafina, they invest supernatural powers of help and intercession. Should sacred icons prove to be uncooperative or unhelpful, they are disavowed and abandoned in a stream of curses. In the play, Serafina's disappointment with the Madonna results temporarily in her bitter repudiation, although this is omitted from the film, perhaps to avoid the impression of sacrilege. Such behaviour gives unsympathetic foreigners the disturbing though false impression that Sicilians are not quite Christians. Nor do Sicilians or southern Italians regard the church as the primary place of worship, but focus their feelings of devotion and piety upon their private residences and religious festivals. This is why Serafina disregards church law in disposing of Rosario's remains, and also why she preserves his ashes within a household urn. Not only is the typical Sicilian house filled with sacred icons, statues, shrines, holy candles, and pictures of revered progenitors, but family hierarchies are seen as divinely sanctioned and not to be transgressed. A husband wields authority over the household, and children properly observe father- and mother-respect. In general, the individual subordinates self-interest to the larger economic needs of the domus. Sex-segregation is the norm before marriage, while parents have great influence in the choice of spouses, and enormous value is placed upon feminine chastity, lest family honour be impugned.

Another impressive feature of *The Rose Tattoo* is that Williams, without much contact with Italian American life, portrays with sympathetic understanding the conflict that often arose between the first and second generations. This resulted from the opposition between parental attitudes, based on Old World norms, and those of the children, who were becoming Americanized. Seeking to maintain the solidarity of the family and its hierarchical, non-individualistic values, parents often showed indifference or unconcealed hostility to education, which they rightly saw as an agent of Americanization. Through the influence of American society and schools, many second-generation children regarded themselves as culturally inferior and attempted to eradicate their supposedly shameful heritage. These children were embarrassed by their parents' poor English, loud and demonstrative Old World ways, and adherence to ancient superstitions. They resented as well what they saw as their parents' sexual and economic tyranny, and asserted their autonomy as best they could.

Early in the film Rosa is exasperated by Serafina's insistence that the next-door neighbour casts the evil eye. Having been exposed to rationalism through her American school, she informs her mother not only that the 'witch' has cataracts, but that she suffers from rheumatism rather than having shaken hands with the devil. The adolescent Rosa likewise rebels against other Old World attitudes, including parental disapproval of non-chaperoned events such as high school dances. Jack's offhanded remark, that 'it's my money and I can spend it any way I like,' must seem a radical assertion to a second-generation Italian American girl who would have had to yield her earnings to her mother. Rosa's schooling has also made her intolerant of her mother's accented and ungrammatical speech, which, in a display of lack of mother-respect, she mentions in the heat of an argument: 'Why do you talk like you just came over in steerage?' When Rosa's high school teacher demands Serafina's compliance with high school requirements, her objections to Serafina's unseemly 'emotional' outbursts suggest that Rosa's schooling has helped to alienate her from her mother by instilling in her Anglo-Saxon 'drive control.' If, as Rosa says, she is 'ashamed' of her mother and even finds her 'disgusting,' it is partly because she judges her by this standard. Indeed, Rosa tells her teacher not to 'pay any attention' to Serafina, whose authority the school has challenged.

That the delle Rose household contains not a single book testifies to its origin in the Mezzogiorno, where poverty and illiteracy go hand in hand, and where at one time the wealthy had almost exclusive access to learning. Notwithstanding that Rosa's teachers praise her ability, Serafina shows no interest in her mental development but resents the school for encouraging it. What most troubles her is that, unlike the sex-segregated society of southern Italy, where parents monitored children, and where a young man's expression of interest in a young woman often led to marriage, American boys and girls associate freely in the public schools, and even engage in casual dating. Annoyed that Rosa has met Jack at a school-sponsored dance, Serafina bars her from her final examinations and even tries to keep her from her graduation ceremony. When Rosa's high school teacher points out to Serafina that the American government overrides the family in many things, she unapologetically vilifies the school as 'dirt' for allowing her daughter to 'get mixed up with a sailor.' Yet one should not exaggerate Serafina's defiance of her American environment, for besides finally making an effort to attend Rosa's graduation, she gives her a watch as a graduation present. This suggests that, though time had stopped for Serafina upon her husband's death, she concedes at least for Rosa's sake the claims of the time-driven American world.

Directed by Martin Ritt, *The Black Orchid* is perhaps the next Hollywood film of any importance to treat Italian Americans in a romantic vein. It was produced by Carlo Ponti and Marcello Girosi and released by Paramount in 1959. The title role went to Ponti's wife, Sophia Loren, who had recently won an Oscar for *Two Women*, and Anthony Quinn was chosen as male lead. A drama of in-group marriage and assimilation, *The Black Orchid* focuses on the romance between the widow Rosa Bianco, who has one son, and Frank Valente, a widowed businessman. In *The Black Orchid* as in *The Brotherhood*, Ritt sought an authentic portrayal of ethnic life through close attention to the codes and rituals of Italian American neighbourhoods; it certainly helped that he had as his scenarist the Italian American lyricist-composer Joseph Stefano. If *The Black Orchid* lacks deep conviction and full credibility, this is owed partly to the fact that, of the main actors, only Sophia Loren is Italian. That Martin Ritt was Jewish need not have prevented a convincing portrayal, yet he seems to have observed and rendered his Italians from the outside, less as an artist than as a sociologist. While the interiors are well realized, the urban exteriors were shot on a set and thus lack the colour and natural light of a real Italian American neighbourhood.

Like *The Rose Tattoo*, *The Black Orchid* (1958) concerns a black-clad widow who had come to the United States by arranged marriage, and whose husband has been killed because of criminal connections. Rose Bianco resembles Serafina in experiencing sexual deprivations from which an

Italian American male rescues her, and she too has difficulties in raising a second-generation child. In both films the action centres on an Italian American community where Old World attitudes prevail, though in varying degrees. The resemblance extends to the titles, which identify the main characters with flowers. Yet in contrast with Serafina, whose marital delights had compensated her for her lowly social position, Rose wants material comfort and social advancement. Unlike the shabby ghetto of *The Rose Tattoo*, *The Black Orchid* portrays a Northeastern urban ethnic neighbourhood of some prosperity.

The Black Orchid is often identified with the working-class television dramas of Paddy Chayefsky, with which Ritt was well acquainted. In addition to having appeared in one of his teleplays, Ritt was originally slotted to play the lead in Chayefsky's *Marty*, the most famous television drama of the 1950s.[127] Focusing on an Italian American neighbourhood in the Bronx, *Marty* like Chayefsky's other teleplays attempts to find drama in the lives of ordinary working people. It has scenes of the family dinner table, kitchens, living rooms, dancehalls, sidewalks, church-going, butcher shops, and local taverns, the aim being to give the feeling of neighbourhood life. At the same time, *Marty* dramatizes the familial and neighbourhood pressures impinging on the life-choices of its main character. Yet though *The Black Orchid* similarly treats the obstacles to a happy marriage – in the first film, a mother's resistance, in the second, that of a son and daughter – and though it is similarly interested in ordinary ethnic life, these films reveal significant differences. Not only does *The Black Orchid* examine the Italian American upper middle class, in contrast to the lower-middle-class Italian Americans in *Marty*, but whereas in the earlier film the protagonist overcomes a claustrophobic environment through marriage to a non-ethnic woman, the resolution of *The Black Orchid* involves two in-group marriages and thus affirms ethnic solidarity. Another difference is that *Marty* was shot in an Italian American neighbourhood and thus seems more authentic ethnically.

As *The Black Orchid* opens, the widowed Rose Bianco and her young son Ralphie walk behind the hearse containing the remains of Tony Bianco, Rose's gangster husband. During the funeral service she recalls her wedding, when she had asked Tony for a large house with 'lots of closets' and a 'private garage,' and he had advised her to be patient. Having expected him to provide her immediately with a host of material and social benefits, she had contributed to Tony's death by driving him into crime as his only means of satisfying her impatient desire for the American dream. Now, with a son to support and scant funds, Rose is employed in a flower-making factory and even takes work home to supplement her income. Her occupation is ironic insofar as the most typical employment among Italian immigrant women was flower-making, which they performed at home or in factories.[128] Thus, rather than rising socially, Rose has sunk to the condition of her group when it occupied the lowest rung on the social ladder. Even worse, her son Ralphie is a juvenile delinquent whose next attempted escape from a work farm will land him in a 'real prison.'

Rose's opportunity for renewal comes when she attracts the attention of widower Frank Valente, who calls her the 'black orchid' because of her perpetual mourning dress. When he first meets her he remarks the realistic appearance of the flowers she has crafted and thus, besides introducing the film's pastoral theme, anticipates her return to life under his influence. Rose gradually warms to Frank to the point where she allows him to accompany her on her visit to her son. As the landscape unfolds during their bus ride, they each reveal a love of the country. A later scene in which Frank asks Ralphie's permission to marry Rose occurs on prison grounds beneath a spreading tree symbolizing the pastoral retreat to which Frank proposes to take Rose and Ralphie. Located in Somerville, Frank's large suburban lot accommodates even a farm.

One of the more interesting Italian American film characters, Frank Valente in some respects typifies his group and neighbourhood. There are wreaths of garlic cloves in his kitchen, and religious images appear on his walls with the Mona Lisa. As Frank's house contains no books, so he limits his reading to the newspaper – details consistent with the Italian American indifference to reading in those decades. His pastimes include cards and bocce. Yet contrary to stereotype, Frank is neither a criminal nor blue-collar employee but an upwardly mobile businessman. Quinn's sensitive performance contrasts with his sometimes overstated portrayals of Mediterranean males driven by violent physical passions.

While the film's title seems to identify Rose with impenetrable mourning, she is planning to marry Frank by the middle of the film, and if anything the chief obstacle to her marriage comes from Frank's daughter Mary (Ina Balin), who carries the film into a realm of pathology beyond its capacity to handle. Mary is an only child, whose mother had become mentally unbalanced immediately following her birth, and who, her mother having died, now sees herself as her father's caretaker. The mother's unexpected decline not only casts a shadow upon the community's notions of marriage as the path to happiness but helps to explain Mary's hesitation to marry Noble, her fiance. That Mary following

Sunday mass forgetfully wears her devotional cap while in the kitchen suggests that she confuses church and domus. She furthermore exhibits a nunnish reluctance to marry. Her name evokes the Virgin Mother and suits a woman who fears to yield her chastity.

Mary's problem is her love of her father, which may have an unacknowledged sexual component. When Mary learns of Frank's interest in Rose, she denounces her rival as a 'gangster's wife.' When Noble informs Mary of the store he has lined up in Atlantic City, and the marital house he intends to purchase there, she proposes that they live with Frank until they can find a suitable house, her real intention being to look after Frank. Dining out with Noble in a Chinese restaurant, Mary leaves with the excuse that her father – a stickler, it is implied, for ethnic cooking – has no one to prepare his dinner. Ironically, the concluding scenes show that Mary's improving skills in Italian cuisine render her all the more fit for marriage. Initially, however, she is devastated to learn that she and Noble will join Frank and Rose in a double wedding.

Of special significance are the doubling motifs relating Mary and Rose. Whereas Rose begins the film in sorrow and recovers through her love of Frank, Mary descends from relative happiness into mourning, as if *she* had lost her husband. Indeed, her behaviour reminds Frank of his dead wife's condition and raises his fears for Mary's sanity. Her deterioration is suggested in the house-hunting episode, for not only is Mary dressed in black, like Rose in her guise of the 'black orchid,' but she informs Noble that, until recently, Frank 'had never looked at another woman.' She sounds like a possessive wife. Ritt stresses the rivalry between Rose and Mary by posing them similarly, as when Rose and Mary appear in profile together, which shows their strong facial resemblance. Unfortunately, the script needlessly accentuates these visual cues, as when Rose tells Mary: 'We are two of a kind.'

The crisis comes when Rose and Frank are driven apart by their children. Sinking into withdrawal, Mary makes it impossible for Frank to marry for fear of worsening her depression. When Rose tells Ralphie that the marriage has fallen through, he blames her for his father's death and thus indirectly for his juvenile delinquency: 'What did you do to ruin it? Wouldn't he rob a bank for you?' Rose's miseries intensify when she learns that Ralph has escaped the state farm, so that now Frank's child is locked up and hers is on the loose and possibly facing a prison sentence. Helpless in the face of Mary's illness, Frank and Noble resort to prayer in the local church. Rose, however, has no use for religion by this point, telling Frank: 'I need more than church right now.' Though credible, the characters' behaviour is atypical with respect to Italian American religiosity, for in contrast with the traditional piety of southern Italian women, their male counterparts have had a generally poor record of church attendance save on special holidays. If anything, the characters' unusual behaviour only underscores their confusion and difficulty.

What is most dissatisfying about the film is the rapidity and clumsiness of its resolution.[129] Thus Frank unexpectedly meets Ralphie, who like a homing pigeon has found his way back to the local church – the 'miracle' Rose had hoped for. Frank then returns Ralphie to the state farm where a sympathetic warden forgets his infractions. It remains for Rose to visit Frank's house in his absence so as to exorcize Mary's mental illness, though in a trivializing and psychologically incredible fashion. After Rose confesses that she had manipulated Tony as Mary now manipulates Frank, she announces that she will yield Frank in deference to Mary. Then, in a quick descent into utter banality, Mary offers Rose a cup of coffee and in the course of their increasingly amiable conversation learns how to make sausages to Frank's taste. When Frank returns for breakfast he not only reports favourably on Ralphie but praises the sausages. He then sits down to breakfast with Noble and Mary while Rose, now tacitly acknowledged mistress of the house, serves breakfast. As in many films on Italian American ethnicity, the kitchen table is the site of both familial conflict and reconciliation. All that remains is for Frank and Rose to free Ralphie from the state farm before their removal to the suburbs.

All too schematically the ending reverses the opening. In the first scene, Rose wears black; in the last, she wears marital white. Her name, Bianco, meaning white, seems a personal fate. The marriage of Mary and Noble is signalled in the bride's first name, which besides referring to the Holy Virgin, is an imperative: 'marry.' Beginning in urban winter, the film concludes with the transfer of the reconstituted family from the urban neighbourhood, the scene of neurasthenia and juvenile delinquency, to the half-suburban, half-agrarian community of Somerville, which sounds like 'Summerville.' Indeed, they will be living on a farm.

The ending glosses over much too easily the conflicts of both the characters and their ethnic group considered as a historical entity. Although Rose is 'punished' for having contributed to her husband's death through her obsessive acquisitiveness, she fulfils her maternal desires by marrying the prosperous Frank. Time thus grants her what she had formerly demanded so impatiently. It is worth noting that the flight of first-generation Italian immigrants to the United States resulted in the

not infrequently traumatic displacement of a primarily peasant people
to an industrial and commercial society. Those who succeeded in this
environment, and who were thus able to leave their ethnic enclaves, often owned small businesses or factories. However, the suburban flight
of the second and third generations rarely restored old ties to the land,
towards which, incidentally, most immigrant families lacked the sentimental attachments ascribed to them in *The Black Orchid,* so miserable
had been the life of the typical southern Italian peasant.[130] From this
perspective the film's pastoral conclusion seems a wish-fulfilment fantasy contrived to assuage the wound of historical difficulties, losses, and
disappointments. Frank Valente is sufficiently ethnic to savour backyard
mint, to play bocce with neighbourhood oldtimers, and to strengthen
his Catholicism in the course of the film. Rose identifies him with the
joyful, procreant men of her native village, as if compensating for her
loss of southern Italy. This does not prevent him, though, from moving
from the old neighbourhood to the WASPy sounding Somerville, where
his store and factory will be located. Thus Frank, despite his neighbourhood ties, also represents, if only by substitution, a return to the bucolic
atmosphere of a romanticized southern Italian past. For Frank and his
new family are relocating to a farm where Ralphie will be free of gang
pressures and juvenile delinquency. The new locale accommodates three
worlds in equal measure, without any apparent tension between them:
commerce, industry, and agriculture. What is omitted is the city, with
its anomie brought on by historical dislocation. Somerville is thus described as 'Paradise,' magically redeeming historical losses while allowing for the exploitation of historical opportunities hitherto unavailable
to the ethnic group.

Among the more satisfying dramas of Italian American intra-group
marriage is *Love with the Proper Stranger* (1963), directed by Robert Mul-
ligan from a script by Arnold Schulman. Focusing on the character of
Angie Rossini (Natalie Wood), the film examines a third-generation Italian American woman struggling against the repressive attitudes her family has retained from the Old World – a cultural residue reflecting the
fact that these largely unassimilated ethnics remain confined to their
enclave.

Angie, a clerk at Macy's, confronts the sporadically employed jazz musician Rocky Papasano (Steve McQueen) with the news that she is pregnant from their casual encounter; she wants from him only the name
and address of an abortionist. As Rocky is cohabiting with a burlesque
performer (Edie Adams), the question is whether he sees Angie similar-

ly, as a non-marriageable 'broad.' Ironically he performs that very night at a wedding. Although Rocky does not agree initially to help Angie, he is disturbed by their encounter, and comments on the advantages of permanently locking oneself in the bathroom, a motif of entrapment that appears later. Unlike Rocky, who has cut loose from his family, Angie remains under the thumb of her mother and especially her brothers Dominick (Herschel Bernardi) and Giulio (Harvey Lembeck), fruit and grocery store owners who hold Old World concepts of feminine chastity and marriage. Thus, when Angie leaves work, the brothers customarily escort her home in their truck so as to protect her from male attention.

As in many films of this type, the family dinner table embodies conflict and pandemonium, with everyone speaking at the top of his lungs. When Angie's mother and Dominic pressure her to date the clumsy Columbo (Tom Bosley), a successful restaurateur, she insists upon her autonomy: 'This isn't the Dark Ages.' Upon Columbo's arrival, Angie retreats to the bathroom. Returning to the kitchen, she endures his company but is not allowed to socialize with him privately, as her mother holds the peasant belief that a man and woman left alone are bound to engage in sex.[131] Yet a double sexual standard is also suggested in Angie's passing comment that her brother Giulio 'goes out with all kinds.' After Columbo's departure, Angie throws a fit, packs her clothes, attempts to leave the house for good, and returns tearfully that very evening. One suspects that her encounter with Rocky – her sole sexual experience – has been driven by the family's insensitive meddling.

Rocky makes an appointment with an abortionist and even accompanies Angie to the operation. Yet when they arrive at the desolate locale, an extra payment is demanded, and so they hurry uptown in quest of money from Rocky's parents. Happy to find Rocky with a respectable and beautiful woman, his parents offer them not only money but wine, so that the gathering seems like a familial reunion. The run-down locale shown earlier, devoid of society, contrasts with the warmth of the old Italian American neighbourhood, with its social vitality and familial affection. Ironically, Rocky's impromptu visit strengthens his own family ties, which he had abandoned for the rootless musician's life. After the unexpected arrival of Angie's brothers forces the couple into hiding, their love awakens over shared glasses of 'vino,' as Rocky calls it. Although totally unmemorable, the accompanying theme song foregrounds the film's multilayered title, which Paola Casella decodes.[132] Not only does 'stranger' allude to the fact that Angie and Rocky are strangers, at least initially, but Rocky is a stranger to Angie in being outside her family circle, formerly her sole point of reference. It is also implied that Italian Americans, with their peculiar familial traits and marital attitudes, remain strangers within the host society – a view more credible then than now.

Each boarded-up window of the abandoned apartment house where the abortion is to take place displays a large X signifying the negation of both human life and the possibility of marriage between Angie and Rocky. However, Rocky after experiencing a change of heart calls the operation off and installs Angie in a friend's temporarily vacant apartment. The next day Dominic arrives with Rocky, whose eye he has blackened, yet who has agreed to marry Angie. The film's strongest dramatic moment thus comes when Angie resists conformity to family and culture by refusing to marry Rocky merely to satisfy the demand for a 'respectable' marriage. Nor will she marry merely because a man has done her a favour, but only on the basis of mutual love. Notwithstanding her pregnancy and unmarried state, she will leave home and support herself independently. What adds to the force of this scene is Angie's revelation that she is no longer 'scared' but 'terrified' of her future. When Dominick tells her that her decision endangers her mother's life, she repels his emotional blackmail with southern Italian realism: 'She'll live.'

One grasps the momentousness of Angie's decision by the fact that the southern Italy from which most Italian Americans derive exemplifies a shame rather than guilt culture in which violators of social norms risk ridicule and ostracism.[133] Within such a society, and its American counterpart into the third generation, it was rare for an unmarried, pregnant woman to strike out on her own. Instead, some marital arrangement had to be worked out. *Love with the Proper Stranger* thus not insensitively portrays the half-tentative, half-defiant claims of third-generation ethnic women to personal autonomy – a project influenced by the liberalism of mainstream culture. However, the potential difficulties of such a project all too conveniently vanish as Angie's and Rocky's mutual love reveals itself over Sunday dinner at her new apartment, where the defiant working girl emerges as the ravishingly beautiful wife-to-be, serving Italian specialties. Rocky is tired of the musicians' life and wants a steady job. His desire to marry has been signalled all along in his name, Papasano, marked with paternity.

Though charming, *Love with the Proper Stranger* suffers from the leading actors' lack of *italianità*, whose absence amounts to a social comment, witting or unwitting, by the filmmakers. As Casella remarks of Hollywood films, Italian American characters who escape the ethnic enclave are those who, without observable marks of ethnicity, can most easily assimilate.[134] This casting strategy, though, undermines the title, since Wood and McQueen, two box-office sensations each with a generically 'American' appearance, invite strong audience identification and so rob their characters of strangeness.

The best drama of out-group marriage is Fritz Lang's *Clash By Night* (1952), scripted by Alfred Hayes from the identically titled play by Clifford Odets. Yet in contrast with the play, which had treated Polish and other non-Italian proletarians in New Jersey, the film's action has been transferred to Monterey, California, where the main character, the middle-aged Jerry d'Amato, runs a fishing business. For this plot element Hollywood provides analogues going back to the silent film.[135] Still a bachelor, the kind-hearted Jerry lives with and provides for his widowed father (Silvio Minciotti) and Italian American brother-in-law (J. Carroll Naish). At the opening, Jerry renews his acquaintance with the disillusioned Mae Doyle (Barbara Stanwyck), who has returned to town after a vain search for love and fortune. During the ensuing romance Mae answers Jerry's passion with guarded affection and a desire for marital stability. Jerry's friend, the handsome projectionist Earl Pfeiffer (Robert Ryan), is attracted to Mae yet repels her by his cynicism. After Mae marries Jerry and bears him a daughter, she finds her husband dull and ordinary and betrays him with Earl. Finally Jerry welcomes Mae back, on the understanding that their marriage requires mutual trust.

Part of Lang's achievement is to have rendered Italian Americans as Americans who happen to be ethnics, or whose ethnicity is only part of their makeup. Such a portrayal may reflect the Far Western locale, as the relative absence of prejudice in the West enabled Italians to assimilate more easily.[136] This is not to deny that Lang provides his characters with ethnic markers and even invites one to think of them stereotypically, yet in some instances he frustrates such expectations. Not only does Jerry's father play the accordion, an instrument often associated with Italian immigrants, but Jerry addresses a fellow ethnic employee as '*paisan*' (countryman). Yet in continuing in America 'what they did in the Old Country,' the d'Amato family of fishermen counters with its strong work ethic the cliché of the lazy Italian, while the German American Earl prefers the do-nothing job of projectionist. A powerfully built working man of minimal education who expresses himself far more effectively physically than verbally, Jerry calls to mind the Italian American male stereotype of the linguistically challenged brute or primitive. Yet despite his capacity for violence, he exemplifies a contrasting and also more agreeable Italian stereotype in showing a benevolently sweet temper and almost childish naivety. His helpfulness to his father and unappreciative brother-in-law exemplify Italian familism, although this is never presented as a specifically Italian ethnic trait. The same ethnic values are implied when Jerry's father sadly reports the discovery of a dead baby under a bridge, and later in Jerry's troubled mention of a little girl's drowning – the dead children calling to mind the infant daughter whom Mae threatens to 'kill' through abandonment. The film's chief ethnic set-piece is Jerry and Mae's Italian-style wedding, during which Jerry announces: 'God made enough fish, wine, and love for everybody.' Yet Lang avoids what was later to become the stereotype of the uniformly joyous Italian American folk wedding, as the guests include Jerry's parasitic yet fellow ethnic brother-in-law as well as Earl, a glum figure who, amid the celebration, plots to steal Jerry's wife.

In this multi-ethnic community, Italians seem not to be singled out save by the viciously resentful Earl, who responds to Jerry's father's praise of work with mocking imitation of his pidgin English: 'That's right, I no like-a work.' Subsequently, when Jerry's father curses Earl in Italian for having betrayed his son, Earl snaps, 'Cut the Latin, Pop.' The best example of Lang's de-emphasis of ethnicity is the ending, in which he avoids the stereotype of the cuckolded, dishonoured husband retaliating against his betrayers. Far from implying that Italians monopolize domestic violence, the film treats it as part of the lower-middle-class environment, as witness the nasty wrestling match between the young lovers Joe Doyle (Kieth Andes) and Peggy (Marilyn Monroe). So outrageous is Mae's and Earl's betrayal of Jerry that one grasps his nearly murderous anger in purely human terms, regardless of stereotypes. Yet these same stereotypes are overturned when Jerry resists killing Earl and welcomes back Mae as his wife.

Marty remains the best known post-war drama of Italian American out-group marriage. Based on Paddy Chayefsky's identically titled television drama, it was released in 1955 under Delbert Mann's direction and with a screenplay by Chayefsky. The cast included Ernest Borgnine, an Italian American actor, in the title role, with Esther Minciotti as his mother and Betsy Blair as the love interest. Unexpectedly *Marty* won the Academy Award for the best picture of 1955, with Oscars also going to Borgnine and Mann. The film owes its popularity to its sentimental story and perhaps hitherto unequalled realism in portraying working-class Italian American life, which was partly achieved through location shooting around Arthur Avenue in the Bronx.

Marty Piletti is a heavy-set, unprepossessing, and unmarried Italian American butcher who, fast approaching middle age, fears he will never marry. The younger members of his family and peer group have married, and it is assumed by Marty's widowed mother Theresa, with whom he still lives, that he should follow suit. Marty's peer group consists of directionless and loveless Italian American bachelors whose dull existence is typified by the exchanges between Marty and his friend Angie: 'So whaddya wanna do tonight, Marty?' 'I dunno, Angie, whaddya wanna do?' The favoured pastime of Marty's friends consists of sexual encounters with available women, whom they pursue in packs, and whom they regard as unmarriageable. Despite these amusements Marty and Angie attend Sunday mass regularly.

Against all odds, Marty falls in love with a non–Italian American woman named Clara Snyder, a high school teacher. But their path to marriage is difficult. Through conversations with her widowed sister, whose children have abandoned her, Marty's mother comes to fear abandonment by her son, and now prefers not to see him married. She behaves rudely to Clara, and tries to turn Marty against her with remarks concerning her homeliness, advanced age, non-Italian background, and supposed immorality. The only thing in her favour is her Catholicism. At the same time, Marty's friends complain of her age and lack of sex appeal, when actually they envy his marital prospects and fear his departure from the group. Finally Marty's desire for happiness overcomes all opposition, and one understands that he and Clara will marry.

Marty exemplifies a situation common among second-generation Italian American males. Whereas first-generation parents had remained intensely familial and group-conscious, their children had become Italian Americans and often resisted their parents' attempt to impose strict loyalty to ethnic culture, neighbourhood, and society. A minority of second-generation children consisted of 'rebels' who used education as a means of social and geographical mobility. Nonetheless many males, though largely Americanized, remained unreflectively loyal to family and group. Still others, though drawn to the social and economic opportunities afforded by education, submitted to familial and group pressure by taking low-level jobs in their old neighbourhoods.

For much of his adult life Marty has fit the third category. As he mentions to Clara, although he had shown potential for college, and although upon his military discharge he could have entered a university on the G.I. Bill, his family obligations confined him to his neighbourhood as a butcher in someone else's employ. In his loyalty to family and ethnicity Marty contrasts with his assimilating cousin Tommy (Jerry Paris), who not only drives his mother from his house but participates in the white-collar, upwardly mobile world. When Marty proposes to open an Italian food market, Tommy warns that the local people no longer prefer ethnic food. Nonetheless Marty will break from the neighbourhood pattern both in leaving the house (presumably) and in marrying outside the group. As in other films, the northern European wife helps the protagonist to escape a limiting environment.

Marty reveals Chayefsky's grasp of the centrality of the peer group in lower-middle-class Italian American enclaves, especially in the urban Northeast. As Herbert Gans would soon demonstrate in *The Urban Villagers*, these peer groups allowed individual members a small margin within which to show off and thus to provoke only the mild temporary envy of friends. However, peer group members found it hard to initiate activity themselves, preferring to wait for mimetic cues from others. Their individuality existed only in relation to the collective, and any major refusal to conform met with ridicule and the threat of rejection.[137] Similarly in *Marty* the characters have difficulty pursuing their own desires and thus depend on others' suggestions: 'Whaddya wanna do tonight, Marty?' When Marty begins romancing Clara Snyder, he encounters not just the resentment but the ridicule of his peer group, which hopes by this means to control and retain him. His friends mock Clara as a 'dog,' that is, as an unattractive woman below their pornographic standard, and pretend to think her fifty years old. Marty's decision to pursue Clara is an assertion of his autonomy comparable to Angie's rebellion in *Love with the Proper Stranger*.

Considered from a sociological point of view, *Marty* contains an element of truth in portraying the aging main character as family dependent. Writing of Italian Americans more or less of the period of the film, Anne Parsons saw the frequent failure of young adults both to marry early and to achieve occupational status as at least partly the result of the 'centripetal' Italian American family, which by encouraging prolonged dependency limited social opportunity and mobility.[138] Chayefsky also shows sensitivity to Italian American sexual attitudes, which originate in southern Italy. Like its Old World parent culture, Italian American society of earlier generations was typified by sex segregation, great care having been taken to separate young women from males before marriage, so as to insure their chastity. The tendency of men and women to socialize in same-sex groups, even on family occasions, often led to awkwardness and incommunicativeness in sexual relationships. At the same time, Italian American males traditionally identified women either with the young virgin or Madonna figure, suitable for marriage, or with the whore or 'broad' preferred for sex.[139] Marty is thus attracted to Clara partly because she is a respectable woman unlike the local 'broads,' while his aging friends desire young and virginal spouses, however immature this may seem. Their misognyistic objectification of women is shown in their disbelief that Marty had talked with Clara a whole evening without attempting to seduce her. Yet despite their worship of the girlie magazine version of the ideal 'broad,' the sexual behaviour of Marty's friends centres on the pursuit of compliant local women whom they trade among themselves. Although the film remains guarded on this point, even Marty has joined his friends' sexual expeditions, nurses being their usual targets. They reveal their misogyny as well in their fondness for fictional detective Mike Hammer, who follows his murder of a deceitful 'broad' with the throwaway line, 'It was easy.' For them, Hammer's appeal lies in his contempt for the disposable women he sleeps with. However, Chayefsky is less reliable when, in his pretentious afterword to the teleplay *Marty*, he describes Marty's peer group as latently homosexual.[140] Chayefsky fails to see that the sexual segregation typical of southern Italian society has issued not in homosexuality but in homophilism, the strong male bonding manifest in the all-male social clubs of the urban neighbourhoods and tightly knit peer-groups as shown in *Marty*.[141]

The strength of *Marty* lies in its principals, Borgnine, Minciotti, and Blair. Borgnine's impressive performance could easily have gone wrong had he chosen to gesticulate excessively, indulge in buffoonish exaggerations, wallow in self-pity, and milk audience sympathy. Yet under Borgnine's guiding intelligence Marty retains his seriousness and dignity. Cinematically, *Marty* is ordinary, consisting mainly of back-and-forth conversations in apartment interiors. Never more than lackluster, the script favours clumsy foreshadowings and numbingly repetitive ironies. When Theresa Piletti learns of her sister's abandonment, her anguished look telegraphs her sudden determination to prevent Marty's marriage. This change in motivation is all too mechanical, and is needlessly emphasized in the repeated question: 'What are you gonna do when Marty gets married?' In the opening scene in the butcher shop, Marty reports his relatives' recent marriages with the phrase, 'It was a very nice affair,' harped on no less than three times. The heavily ironic implication is that these were tedious events in the routine of an ingrown ethnic community. As if the low-brow taste of Marty's peer group needed emphasis, its most stupid member remarks several times: 'Mickey Spillane, he sure can write.' After repeated suggestions that he search for a bride in nightspots loaded with 'tomatoes,' Marty must content himself with his mother's lasagna, which he extols with unintended irony as 'really rich, loaded with tomatoes.'

The Columbia Pictures film version of John Fante's novel *Full of Life* appeared in 1957. Like *Marty*, this comedy deals with out-group marriage, assimilation, and intergenerational conflict. In contrast with *Marty*, the male protagonist has abandoned his ethnic roots and entered the middle-class mainstream; he does, however, marry a non–Italian American woman. Yet though *Full of Life* shows a grasp of the generational struggle not to be found in Chayefsky's script, it is less satisfying than *Marty*, as it wanders into cloying sentimentality and wish-fulfilment fantasies.

Like the novel, the film reflects the Italian American author's biography. By 1945, having published a number of well-reviewed proletarian novels, John Fante was a well-paid Hollywood scenarist at last capable of buying his family its 'dream house.' The whole structure was later found to be termite infested, a problem he ignored for three years. In 1949, Fante's wife, Joy, berated her now jobless husband after falling through the kitchen floor while heavy with her third child. He returned to work but ignored the termites. When in 1950 Joy again became pregnant, Fante demanded that she have an abortion, which she refused. Although he decided reluctantly to remain with his family, and despite lingering bitterness, he was soon composing rapidly a novel under the working title of *The White Balloon*, an allusion to the main character's pregnant wife. Even as Fante seethed over his wife's pregnancy, the novel transformed his unhappy home life into a celebration of marital love, domesticity, child-bearing, the extended as well as nuclear family, and harmony between ethnic generations. Fante's novel thus casts over his strained relations with his wife and father a glow of generosity, goodwill, and sentimentality. Ironically, when Joy went into labour he did no more than pay her cab fare to the hospital, and showed little affection when he visited his wife and son.[142]

Upon its publication in 1952 *Full of Life* was praised for its life-affirmation as against post-war nihilism. Four years later Fante was working on a screenplay for a film version to be directed by Richard Quine, with whom he closely collaborated. Although he modified the novel, the themes, characters, and situations are basically the same. The film's cast includes Richard Conte as Nick Rocco; Judy Holliday as Emily, Nick's wife; Metropolitan Opera star Salvatore Baccaloni as Nick's father, an Italian-born mason; and Esther Minciotti as Nick's mother. Widely advertised so as to capitalize on the baby boom, the film proved a box-office hit, and like *Marty* was praised for the authenticity of its ethnic characters.[143]

Full of Life begins at night in the Rocco household. Experiencing the cravings of pregnant women, Emily makes herself a sandwich consisting of the processed foods of the suburbs: American white bread, baloney, onion, butter, and mustard. In a later scene, however, Emily consumes the crusty Italian bread offered her by Nick's immigrant father, who also repairs her sunken floor and replaces her fireplace. Just as Nick and Emily's badly constructed American house has soft floors and stucco walls foisted onto unsuspecting buyers, so the food served in such houses is soft, mass produced, and unpalatable. Contrastingly there is Papa's hand-made stone-and-mortar house and the massive stone hearth he provides for Nick and Emily. Not only is the bread substantial and of good quality in Papa's house, but the food consumed there is home-grown and skilfully cooked, Italian American craftsmanship being thus contrasted with American shoddy.

When Nick tells Emily that she will give him babies in exchange for his books, he seems old-fashioned in defining physical and domestic labour as feminine and mental and professional labour as masculine. Yet one should neither suppose Italian American husbands to be tyrants, nor exaggerate Nick's conformity with Old World patriarchy. Despite the official supremacy of the husband in traditional southern Italian and Italian American households, wives enjoyed considerable control within the domestic sphere. This is perhaps reflected in Nick's behaviour, as he allows Emily to act as his intermediary in his dealings with his parents. Indeed, when he avoids discussing floor repairs with his father, she calls him 'coward' – a stern reproach for an Italian American husband, especially in being delivered by his wife. Nor is Emily a pushover, for when Nick playfully smacks her posterior, she orders him never to do it again. At points Nick even seems manipulated by his wife and father, as if they were leagued against him. It is unclear whether his portrayal reflects the Italian American male's wife-dependence, or whether Nick anticipates those emasculated wife-driven husbands soon to populate the 'cutest' of sitcoms.

As an indication of Nick's distance from traditional gender prejudice, it is worth noting that, unlike Old World Italians, who usually prefer male children, Nick has no preference. Contrary to the stereotypes of the gesticulating and explosive Italian American, his gestures are kept in bounds, and he shows only moderate and fleeting fits of anger. When he bristles over his rotting house, proposing to consign the inspector to 'sixty days in Purgatory,' his wife with sweet reasonableness cushions the audience: 'No wonder you lose your patience.' Wearing leisure slacks and cardigan sweater, Nick exemplifies the WASPified Italian American who has mimed mainstream behaviour well enough to produce it in more than rough facsimile. Far from enshrining ethnicity, the Rocco household exemplifies 'progressive' middle-class values of the 1950s. It is rare to see Impressionist paintings and shelves of books in film portrayals of an Italian American domestic interior in this decade. Emily's dabbling in Dianetics shows that, without religious beliefs, she has been captured by therapeutic culture. Her interest in semantics, which she claims to reveal 'true meanings,' implies some vaguely sensed lack of meaning in her and Nick's life.

The crisis comes when Emily falls into a termite-ridden hole in the middle of the kitchen. Unlike Fante, however, Nick addresses the problem immediately. The caved-in floor represents symbolically the weakened foundations of Nick and Emily's life. It is necessary for them to travel to Sacramento to solicit Papa's help. Notwithstanding that Nick and his father have not spoken for years, the master stone mason will have to be told that the house is made of stucco, a substance abhorrent to his feeling for the challenge and durability of stone. The father's preference for hard resistant materials over soft malleable ones like stucco implies his rejection of modelling techniques in favour of that 'carving' approach to craftsmanship that the English art critic Adrian Stokes regards as characteristic of the Italian plastic arts, both high cultural and vernacular, in periods of their greatest flowering.[144]

With cigar in mouth and wine bottle close at hand, Papa sits in his yard in rustic clothes beneath a vast spreading tree symbolically evoking the 'organic' rootedness of Old World peasant life. As he dictates a letter to his wife, giving the impression of patriarchal authority, his illiteracy stands out by contrast with his writer son. The letter is addressed to his sons, whom he orders not to forget their mother, as they have him. Very nearly parodic of an aged *padrone*, Papa's bossy style is belied by his mischievous fondness for a cat to which he feeds wine. When Nick and Emily arrive he greets them ecstatically and commands his wife to prepare chicken cacciatore; in the novel the dinner is liver and bacon, less familiar (and less palatable) to a mainstream film audience. Typical of first-generation immigrants, the interior of Papa's house is filled with sacred icons and images of revered ancestors. Not only does Papa prefer for Emily to give birth to a boy, he even suggests that a male child will result if Nick keeps garlic in his pocket – a folk belief his son derides. Papa subsequently shows Emily the land where he hopes she and Nick will choose to live in the stone house he plans to build for them. Although southern Italians were often forced by necessity to reside within nuclear families, their social ideal while in Italy remained that of the extended family under one roof. What Papa thus hopes for, against the tide of social independence and assimilation, is a partial recovery of the dream of the extended family carried over from Italy.

Nick's underlying submissiveness further reveals itself when, after being slapped by Papa for buying a stucco house, he does nothing. Answering to stereotypes of the violent Italian American, Papa's flare-up precedes the revelation by Nick to Emily that his long-standing conflict with his father arose when Papa attempted to force Nick to remain at home and to follow the profession of stonemason, rather than to pursue an education and writing career, neither of which his father comprehends or respects. This intergenerational struggle continues on the train back to Los Angeles, for whereas Papa brings with him bread, salami, cheese, wine, and other Italian foods for consumption en route, Nick prefers a 'thick steak' and hard liquor in the dining car. His anger over his father's eating habits, which he reveals to other passengers, is consistent with the rejection of Italian foodways by second-generation rebels. Yet though Emily had favoured American white bread and processed foods, she now enjoys Papa's Italian specialties – a first step in her 'Italianization.'

The first thing Papa does upon arriving at the house is to examine not the kitchen floor but the fireplace, which for Italian peasants symbolizes the life of the family. His discovery that the hearth rings hollow indicates that something is missing in the Rocco's family life. There is also a marked inclination in the living room floor – a sign of other familial failings Papa must repair. This is not to minimize the hole in the kitchen, however, as it remains the inner sanctum of the Italian American domus, where the mother prepares its sacred repasts. If the Roccos are planning a family, then the kitchen must be fixed.

Unexpectedly, however, Papa asks Nick to write up the story long current in the Rocco family of their Uncle Mingo (an Abruzzese diminutive for Domenico) and his adventures among southern Italian bandits. It appears that, in a concession to the literate world he deeply suspects, Papa wants his son to accommodate the Old World oral record to print-oriented society. That the subject of banditry, which five decades previously would have touched off both nativist nightmares of Italian American criminality and xenophobic charges of the group's unfitness for assimilation, should appear so casually in a mid-1950s film that not only treats a second-generation suburbanized Italian American but aims to win a middle-class American audience, suggests how far Nick and his fellow ethnics had come in their assimilation. Although never detailed within the film, the story of the bandits relates not to an allegedly noxious presence infiltrating Ellis Island but to a remote and unthreatening romantic past. Situated at an ever widening (and sanitizing) historical distance, the bandits have been transformed from figures of real menace into conventionally picturesque desperadoes made palatable to a mainstream audience. Such an impression is only strengthened by the fact that Nick ultimately sells his write-up of the story to the *Saturday Evening Post*,[145] which was read in millions of middle-class living rooms of that decade. And yet, one may also view the reference to banditry as Fante's effort to deflect or disarm another subject that, for assimilating Italian Americans during those years, was all too close to home, namely the Mafia, which had recently been painted in conspiratorial terms by Senator Kefauver, and a leader of which Conte had already played in *The Big Combo*. In any case, Nick, being occupied with his own freelance work, refuses to supply the story, whereupon Papa runs away only to be retrieved by Emily. After listening to his drunken father repeat the story incoherently, Nick works all night typing it, yet upon its completion Papa tells him to 'save it for my grandson.' He need not read the story, as he has heard it already, but its text will be available when he can no longer tell it. Thus orality and literacy are reconciled, though the hole remains unrepaired.

By now Papa is Italianizing Emily in the peasant mode. At first, she attempts to educate her father-in-law in the 'non-Aristotelian' idea that seemingly solid substances consist largely of void atoms. Espousing perspectivism and relativism as against essentialism, she mentions all the contexts that define her as a person. Yet the old man, repository of peasant wisdom, rejects her ideas, as in his view solid reality is an experiential fact. Nor does he doubt that, whatever her contexts, Emily remains in essence a mother and creator. He adds that, though her house is filled with books and 'pretty' modern pictures, it lacks those images of the Saviour that her children cannot do without.

The decisive change in Nick and Emily's lives comes when, through Papa's intervention, they embrace Catholicism. Indeed, so far as Papa is concerned his son and daughter-in-law are not really married, as they had been joined in a civil rather than Catholic ceremony. For the Protestant Emily, conversion is required, while Nick's return to the fold needs to be seen in relation to changing attitudes towards Catholicism among Italian American families. Because southern Italian immigrants to the United States practised a pagan-infuenced form of folk Catholicism that emphasized not formal church observances but the sanctity of the family and communal festivals, they resisted the legalistic and formalistic religiosity of the Irish-dominated Catholic Church. As in the old country, immigrants often worshipped in their own fashion. Not only did many Italian American males deem church-going to be an activity properly suited to women and children, but many first-generation Italian Americans refused to send their children to Irish-run parochial schools. They did, however, largely follow Church teachings on birth control. With the embourgeoisement of Italian Americans in the post-war period, their church-going increased substantially, partly as a sign of social status, and they were more willing to send their children to parochial schools. Yet now they often opposed the Church on birth control, and their church attendance still fell below that of the Irish and Poles.[146]

From this perspective Nick's father's intense piety may be seen as somewhat atypical. In any case Nick's conversion begins when the local priest, Father Gandolfo, questions his failure to attend mass. When Nick complains that the Church has not changed with the times, the priest appeals as Papa does to eternal human constants. Discussing birth control with his son, Papa regards economic justifications of planned parenting as unacceptable and, as the conclusion suggests, wins Nick over on this point – a result atypical of those decades. Father Gandolfo quickly awakens Emily's interest in Catholicism, although she knows that she cannot become a Catholic immediately or simply because her father-in-law desires it. When Nick acknowledges that he 'used to love the Church,' Emily dismisses his apostasy as having been based on an immature impulse merely to challenge his father. Nick then announces his first visit to confession after seven years.

Having begun to restore his son to first-generation Italian American traditions, Papa can now fix the kitchen floor. He also replaces the existing fireplace with a much enlarged new one built of stone and mortar reminiscent of his own unshakably solid residence. Implicitly Nick's family needed a stable footing through Papa's intervention. Not only are Nick and Emily married in a Catholic ceremony, but on the night Emily is about to give birth, Nick honours ancient superstition by putting garlic in his pocket in the hope of a male child. Before the delivery Nick and Papa pray in the hospital chapel, and subsequently Nick learns that the *Saturday Evening Post* has bought 'Uncle Mingo and the Bandits,' which his father, now reconciled with his profession, had submitted. Predictably, the child is a boy, and the film concludes with a return to the now fortified family house.

In comparison with many dramas of Italian American assimilation and out-group marriage, *Full of Life* benefits from Fante's knowledge and experience of generational conflict. Unfortunately the film and novel fail owing to a schematically predictable plot burdened with heavy-handed symbolism. The meaning of the hole in the kitchen floor, and the reconstructed hearth, is painfully obvious. Emily's conversion, and Nick's reconversion, occur rapidly, sketchily, and unconvincingly. The film's cloying and unrealistically optimistic treatment of its marital and generational theme conveys no real conviction but only contrivance and sentimentality.

Part of the problem lies in the disparity between Fante's unfeeling behaviour toward his wife during her pregnancy, and his novel's 'heart-warming' handling of this situation. For sentimentality arises when an evident disparity exists between what one thinks one ought to feel about something and one's real feelings towards it. Fante did not really feel many of the emotions he depicts in *Full of Life*, and his attempt to compensate for that deficit issues in a basic insincerity – or sentimentality – manifest in both novel and film. One sees this in the handling of the intergenerational struggle, which softens and conceals the rebellious Fante's very real conflicts with his father as well as his deep ambivalences towards his own ethnicity. Nick Rocco caves in before paternal and spousal pressure with less resistance than his termite-ridden kitchen floor. But this is a wish-fulfilment fantasy to which Fante could commit himself only on paper. In the novel and film, the Fante-figure returns to the Catholic Church; but according to Fante's biographer, the novelist remained detached from Catholicism. Whereas the assimilating and exogamous Italian American often suffered eloignment and alienation from family and ethnic group, *Full of Life* presents a never-never land where the antinomies of intergenerational conflict are magically reconciled. On the one hand, Nick marries a non-Catholic wife, moves outside family and neighbourhood, cultivates his reading, and becomes a writer; on the other, he yields to his father's authority, recovers his ancestral religion, converts his wife to that religion, embraces first-generation views on birth control and gender preference, and experiences re-Italianization. All this is manipulated so as to smooth over what in reality would have been fractured and divided.

VII

The portrayal of Italian Americans in the two decades following World War II includes other ethnic types and situations that are difficult to categorize. Broadly speaking, these films portray the Italian American as a misfit, isolated from the host community. This category includes soldiers, boxers, idiots, and juvenile delinquents as well as businessmen. It also includes women as well as men. Some of these films are dramas of marriage, and they always encompass questions of assimilation.

Among the best known portrayals of an Italian American in the 1950s is Frank Sinatra's interpretation of Angelo Maggio in the Fred Zinneman–directed version of James Jones's novel *From Here to Eternity*, which received the Oscar for Best Picture of 1953. Having fallen into a slump, Sinatra believed that this role would recharge his career. As he saw it, to portray Maggio he had only to be himself. When Columbia Pictures president Harry Cohn withheld the part, Ava Gardner, then Sinatra's wife, helped to win Cohn over. Or it may be that Sinatra's Mafia friends pressured Cohn. In any case, Sinatra's performance won him an Oscar for Best Supporting Actor.

Like the novel, the film portrays American soldiers at Schofield Barracks at the time of the attack on Pearl Harbor. Private Maggio, a happy-go-lucky, good-natured Italian American, befriends the Southern career soldier, Private Robert E. Lee Pruitt (Montgomery Clift), whose commanding officer punishes him for refusing to join the company boxing team. Despite his boxing skills, Pruitt shuns ring violence and prefers the trumpet. Victimized for their unwillingness to accept the injustices of the military, Maggio and Pruitt become friends and assuage their sorrows with drink and women. But Maggio runs afoul of Sergeant 'Fatso' Judson (Ernest Borgnine), director of the military stockade. Although their confrontation is initially prevented by Sergeant Milton Warden (Burt Lancaster), Maggio goes AWOL and is sent to the stockade, where Judson tortures him at will. After enduring solitary confinement and numerous beatings, Maggio escapes but only to die in Pruitt's and Warden's presence. Pruitt then avenges his friend by killing Judson in a knife fight in a dark alley.

Maggio is perhaps the best-realized cinematic treatment of an Italian American up to its time in that he has a characterological and sociological roundedness absent from the often cartoonish renderings of the group. Maggio is a misfit only in encountering ethnic prejudice in the military. Otherwise he is a typical lower-class or lower-middle-class Italian American combining in roughly equal amounts Italian and American traits. Like many other males of his ethnic group, Maggio enjoys the normal pleasures (or vices), such as smoking, drinking, gambling, and women. His love of family, and defense of its honour, are characteristically Italian, while his musicality is probably meant to seem an ethnic trait. Thus Maggio appreciates Pruitt's soulful trumpeting, expressing an alienation with which Maggio identifies.

On the other hand, Maggio's occasional drunkenness derives from his American milieu rather than from Italy, where such behaviour is frowned upon. Again unlike his southern Italian forbears, who despised the state, Maggio is a dedicated soldier whose patriotism typifies second-generation Italian Americans. His friendship with Pruitt, whom he calls '*paisan*' and who calls him '*paisan*' in return, likewise diverges from southern Italian and immigrant norms, for as sociologists have noted, first-generation Italian Americans often found their friends chiefly if not exclusively within their own ethnic group, partly because many group members chose to congregate if possible within the same neighbourhoods. However, second-generation sons and daughters developed friendships not only with local ethnics but with non-Italians whom they met in school and especially in institutions such as the military. Indeed, Maggio is not likely to have met Pruitt except in this context.[147]

Whereas Maggio appreciates Pruitt's trumpet-playing, he angers Judson by objecting to his obnoxious banging on a piano. Judson retaliates by calling Maggio 'Wop' and 'Mussolini,' whereupon Maggio protests that only his friends may call him by the former epithet. His later confrontation with Judson draws upon yet also juggles ethnic stereotypes to the point where they lose applicability. As Maggio showcases photographs of his family, including his father and sister, Judson plants a kiss upon the sister's picture and whispers an obscene remark in Pruitt's ear. Maggio's anger over Judson's public insult fits two Italian American stereotypes, that of the son obsessed with familial sexual honour, and that of the impulsive male who favours action over words. Maggio thus grabs a chair and attemps to 'debrain' Judson from behind. Yet though this may evoke the 'sneaky' Italian, he has substituted a chair for the stereotypical knife or stiletto; ironically it is Judson the WASP who pulls a knife when he turns to confront Maggio. In damning him as a 'dirty Wop,' and vowing to cut his heart out, Judson awakens sympathy for his opponent. The stereotype of the bloodthirsty Italian is further undermined when Warden, breaking up the fight, derides Maggio: 'Out for blood, eh? You'd puke your guts out at the sight of a dead man.' Unlike Judson, who plots vengeance against him, Maggio stands back from his violence and appreciates Warden's interference: 'I'm glad he stopped it.' In the end it is the WASP Pruitt who avenges Maggio in a knife-fight.

What destroys Maggio is the corrupt authoritarian system – the U.S. Army – which also ruins Pruitt. Each is a free-thinking, individualistic southerner, one from the American South, the other from southern Italy. Though both men willingly serve the national government, and though neither is wilfully insubordinate, their refusal to submit to the arbitrariness of military authority may reflect their similar regional backgrounds. For both the American and Italian south are agrarian-based and quasi-feudal societies that have been conquered and exploited in varying degrees by an alien state or states. Upon learning of Pruitt's refusal to box, Sergeant Warden tells him that one could go one's own 'way' in the old days, but now one must 'play ball.' Yet Maggio sympathizes with Pruitt: 'Listen, the guy don't have to fight if he don't want to without getting kicked around.' Maggio thus resembles those many cinematic Italian Americans who insist on doing things 'my way': not for nothing did Sinatra adopt the phrase in his personal anthem. Yet when Maggio tells another soldier, 'I just hate to see a good guy get it in the gut,' he is warned: 'You'd better get used to it.' After a sergeant deliberately trips Pruitt in a drill, Maggio cries foul and finds himself running laps in battle gear with Pruitt. His going AWOL, a reckless move motivated by boyish irrepressibility, shows even more glaringly the dangers of doing it 'my way.'

Apart from his difficulties in dealing with an unjust system, Maggio could easily have returned to civilian life, and there is nothing in his portrayal to suggest that he had been involved in the juvenile delinquency that attracted many second-generation Italian Americans in the post-war period. As scholars have noted, transplantation to American soil often disrupted the Old World family structure characterized by paternal and maternal hierarchy. The life of the southern Italian child had been centred on the solidly based nuclear family, which sternly controlled behaviour. However, the second-generation child encountered new contacts, experiences, and possibilities in both school and the urban neighbourhood, and so there developed on American soil the phenomenon of the peer group. Not only did young males spend more time with their peer group than with their families, but parental values sometimes yielded to those of peers. Cut off from parental authority and acting under peer pressure, some young people became juvenile delinquents. Many did so from feelings of low self-esteem resulting from poor education, especially bad job prospects, lack of familial and institutional support, and ethnic self-hate.[148] Now emerged the cinematic stereotype of the Italian American male youth as a member of an antisocial pack, as witness 'Pretty Boy' Romano in Ray's *Knock on Any Door*.

Among the earliest films to focus on juvenile delinquency was *The Blackboard Jungle* (1955), based on a novel by Italian American writer

Evan Hunter, who had adopted a highly WASP-sounding name for its career advantages. Played by Glenn Ford, the protagonist is Richard Dadier, who teaches in an inner-city vocational school attended by Irish, Italian, Puerto Rican, and black students. Despite its reformist ambitions, *Blackboard Jungle* was seen as a scandalous exposé of public education. Its trailer tells of a story 'torn from big city modern savagery,' and the 'startling revelation of those teen-age savages' who terrorize high schools.

Although *Blackboard Jungle* focuses on Dadier's attempt to reform two students, one African American and the other Irish American, played by Sidney Poitier and Vic Morrow respectively, it contains Italian American touches and characters. In the opening scene, as Dadier arrives at the school, nearly naked children are splashing in water released from a fire hydrant. Gesticulating in unmistakeably Italian style, a mother summons a young boy with the angry query: 'You wanna be a bum?' Subsequently Dadier encounters among his students the ever-smiling Italian American Santini (Jamie Farr), whom another student describes as 'an idiot boy,' and who finds his mental ceiling in cartoons. Santini exemplifies the stereotype of the Italian American as a mentally ill-equipped, happy-go-lucky, pre-verbal being. The other Italian American among Dadier's students is the not very bright juvenile delinquent Belazi (Dan Terranova), who joins his fellow gang members in the hijacking of a truck while the leader watches from a safe distance. Dadier's comment that the gang members wear the same kind of jackets calls to mind de-individualized pack animals. At the conclusion Belazi brazenly cheats on an examination and then fails in his attempt to jump Dadier from behind – the stereotype of the sneaky, back-stabbing Italian. When Belazi flashes a knife in the hope of escaping the building, Santini uses the metal staff of an American flag to disempower him. Santini and Belazi thus conform to the good wop–bad wop antithesis, the former, however, being in this case an idiot. As for whether these adolescents are innately delinquent, the image of the empty blackboard accompanying the credits implies that a student's mind originates as a *tabula rasa,* and is largely shaped by environmental stimuli. If the students behave like 'savages,' it is because they live in a 'jungle.' This is not to say, though, that all students can benefit from environmental correction. The insufficiency of environment to explain Belazi's juvenile delinquency is revealed in the remark that, since his 'old man owns a store,' he need not seek a job after graduation. Drawn to crime despite a supportive family, Belazi carries a bad seed.

Directed by Robert Wise, scripted by Ernest Lehman, and with Paul Newman as middleweight champion Rocky Graziano, *Somebody Up There Likes Me* (1956) is based fairly closely on the boxer's identically titled autobiography. Born Rocco Barbella on 1 January 1922, Graziano struggled from the Lower East Side slums to the middleweight championship and lasting minor fame. Although *Somebody Up There Likes Me* is both a boxing film and drama of out-group marriage, it is above all the story of a juvenile delinquent who discovers boxing as his only means to enter the mainstream. Graziano gains not only success through self-help but, in religious terms, his personal redemption. Conscious of its generic precursors, Wise's film looks forward to Scorsese's *Raging Bull.*

Accompanied by Elmer Bernstein's jaggedly nervous score, the opening scene introduces the preadolescent Rocky in the company of his wine-swilling father Nick and his drunken friends in the family's slum tenement. Rocky escapes to the nocturnal streets after being beaten by his father, a failed boxer. 'There goes another little greaseball,' a local policeman observes, predicting that in ten years Rocky will be in the death house at Sing Sing. Although boxer Joe Bonaparte in *Golden Boy* emerges from a fairly prosperous lower middle-class background, most boxers originated within a lower-class milieu like that of Graziano. The film further implies that Graziano's juvenile delinquency stems partly from his environment, which influences his decision to join an antisocial peer group.

In a later scene, which reflects the low self-esteem Graziano exhibits for much of the film, he asks his mother why she alone has not given up on him. Despite its acknowledgement of environmental causality, the film like the autobiography places greater emphasis on character, for as Graziano implies, the cause of his failure lies within himself. Yet it hardly helps his self-esteem that his father sees him as the 'devil.' Cast adrift from family, Graziano leads his gang of juvenile delinquents in robberies as well as the theft of hubcaps, tires, radios, and clothing. These boys disdain school and have never been taught to value education. Having leaped to safety across a precipitous alleyway during an encounter with the police, Rocky is arrested after having leaped back across it in order to come to the aid of his friend Romolo (Sal Mineo). A demonstration of Rocky's capacity for helpfulness, loyalty, and self-sacrifice, this scene anticipates the conclusion when, just before becoming champion, Rocky returns once more to the Italian American neighbourhood to encourage Romolo in his struggle against the defeatism fostered by his brutal surroundings.

While in reform school Graziano nearly kills a guard and is transferred to a penitentiary, where he confesses to his mother his inability to correct himself: 'I tried to turn the leaf but I can't make it ... [There's] something inside of me.' Graziano is subsequently drafted into the wartime army yet shows no patriotism whatsoever. Although such an attitude had once typified southern Italians, Italian American males served in World War II in numbers exceeding the group's percentage within the American population, Graziano being thus atypical of his group. Indeed, he quarrels with his captain, whom he knocks out with a single punch. Later, having escaped to the slums, he plans to pay off the captain by boxing professionally. So complete is his insularity that he cannot imagine the mainstream as following any standard besides that of his neighbourhood.

Operating out of Stillman's gym with Irving Cohen as his manager, Rocky abandons his parental name so as to throw off the military police. Nonetheless he is captured, dishonourably discharged, and sent for one year to Leavenworth prison where, when asked the reason for his imprisonment, he admits: 'For bein' a jerk.' Typically, he blames himself rather than his milieu. The prison boxing coach subsequently persuades Graziano to box seriously, so that he can put his 'hate' to 'good' use: 'Who knows, it may work so many miracles you'll lose that hate someday.' After his release Graziano advances as a boxer and, like many second-generation Italian American males, gives his mother part of his earnings. He also meets a Jewish girl, Norma (Pier Angeli), whose sweetness breaks down his tough-guy impenetrability. *Somebody up There Like Me* thus belongs among those films in which the Italian American protagonist's renewal depends on an understanding non–Italian American woman, sometimes Jewish but more usually WASP. When Graziano revisits his old neighbourhood he finds that his former detractors celebrate his boxing exploits. Boys' clubs around the country have made him their hero. But his championship quest is temporarily thwarted when Tony Zale knocks him out in the sixth round. Graziano encounters a further obstacle when Frankie Pepo (Robert Loggia), a former fellow prison inmate and now a gangster's representative, demands that he throw a fight under threat of the revelation of his dishonourable discharge and military record. Having become what Cohen describes as the 'world's most popular Italian,' after Michelangelo and Sinatra, Graziano fakes an injury to avoid the fix. When asked to identify Pepo and his associates, he maintains his silence out of fear of retaliation and loyalty to the ethnic code. Still haunted by his past on the eve of a championship bout, Graziano attempts to resolve his feelings by revisiting his old neighbourhood.

Most of his friends have been murdered or imprisoned. A soda store owner's counsel, 'never ask for a soda unless you're prepared to pay the check,' emphasizes personal responsibility. When Romolo proposes to buy a flower stand with stolen money. Rocky urges him to 'turn a leaf,' to which Romolo responds with the fatalism Graziano rejects: 'We ain't got a chance, guys like us, do we, Rocky?' After watching the police round up some juvenile delinquents who resemble his former self, Graziano returns to the family apartment where, after exchanging harsh words with his father, he offers him consolation contrary to the theme of self-help: 'You've had nothing but bad breaks. I've been lucky.' Reminiscent of *Golden Boy*, in which Joe's father blesses his final fight, Nick Barbella blesses Rocky and tells him to 'be a champ like I never was.' The benediction balances the beating Graziano suffers in the opening scene. He returns to Chicago and defeats Zale for the championship, which he celebrates with a motorcade procession through the old neighbourhood. He has not returned permanently to the ghetto, however, but has entered the mainstream.

According to Bondanella, while making the film Newman socialized with Graziano in order to learn his slurred, halting, and mixed-up speech patterns.[149] As portrayed in the film, Graziano conforms to the stereotype of the Italian American as a physical being more capable of expressing himself with his fists than through language – a body nearly without a mind. His corporeality is conjoined with volatile and unpredictable emotions that achieve their socially acceptable apotheosis in a flurry of blows unleashed in the ring. Yet behind this menacing physicality remains the endearing adolescent, mischievous, fun loving, unreflective, impulsive, almost pre-moral. Graziano's suburban house contains a pinball machine enabling him, amid his success, to enjoy the crude amusements of the juvenile delinquent.

Inevitably the question arises why Wise's interpretation of Graziano pales before Scorsese's portrayal of Jake La Motta in *Raging Bull*. Both films are based on a boxer's autobiography that traces a spiritual redemption. Like his friend Graziano, La Motta was from the Lower East Side, spent time in reform school, and chose boxing as an alternative to crime. Both married non–Italian American wives. Each won the middleweight championship, yet in doing so met underworld interference, in La Motta's case to the point of having been forced to throw a fight. Although, unlike Graziano, La Motta's fortunes declined after his retirement, he ultimately became a minor celebrity.

The inferiority of Wise's film results partly from Newman's performance, which, with manufactured intensity, consists of externally applied 'Italian American' behaviours. Unlike Newman, who despite his self-conscious swagger lacks the menace of the ghetto bruiser who was Rocky Graziano, De Niro's gestures and mannerisms convincingly express not only La Motta's ethnic culture but his natural truculence and brutality. De Niro also trained with La Motta until he became a skilled middleweight himself, and this only makes him all the more believable. Another clue to the inferiority of Wise's film is its title, announcing God's fondness for Graziano. Despite his savagery, Graziano seems earmarked for success and redemption not through character alone but through an ingratiating likeability or 'personality' consistent with what David Riesman had noted as the increasing outer-directedness of American society during the post-war period. The idea that God embraces such values reflects the American tendency to confuse spiritual election with social popularity and the material success that sometimes accompanies it. Wise's film further implies that, once God has crowned Graziano champion, his success is assured thenceforward. Contrastingly, the withdrawn, suspicious, and sadomasochistic La Motta remains unlikeable. Because his degradation is deeper than Graziano's, his struggle to rise out of it is more painful as well as more powerful dramatically. Contrary to generic convention, La Motta's life goes downhill following his championship, professional success affording no solution to his torments. Nor, in contrast with so many other films of this type, does La Motta's marriage to a blonde non–Italian American woman provide him with his ticket to happiness as the assimilated ethnic, as he needlessly mistrusts his wife and, after inhumanly abusing her, loses his family. And finally, as La Motta's 'redemption' remains tentative and partial, it brings no closure to La Motta's life but requires constant effort and purpose, which makes for a psychologically convincing open-ended conclusion. For these and other reasons De Niro's portrayal surpasses Newman's in characterological depth and dramatic intensity.

The Young Savages (1961) stands out not for artistic merit but for its sociological and criminological themes. Directed by John Frankenheimer, and starring Burt Lancaster as Hank Bell, the film is based on Evan Hunter's story 'A Matter of Conviction.' Insofar as Hunter had adopted a WASP name, he resembles the film's protagonist, Hank Bell, who anglicizes his original name (Bellini) in order to assimilate. The Young Savages in some ways inverts the plot of Knock on Any Door, for whereas in that film a WASP lawyer and former slum denizen attempts to save an Italian American youth from capital punishment, Bell aims to send two young Italian Americans to the electric chair. And whereas Knock on Any Door totally inculpates society, The Young Savages avoids wholly 'environmentalist' explanations of crime, notwithstanding its basic liberalism.

After three members of a primarily Italian American gang enter a Puerto Rican neighbourhood and stab to death a Puerto Rican youth, they are arrested and interrogated by assistant district attorney Bell. The three youths are Rearden, the oldest and most vicious; the mentally retarded Aposto; and the fatherless fifteen-year-old Danny DiPace, for whom Bell seeks the death penalty. Although his zeal seems to reflect unconscious motives, it also stems from the fact that his boss, D.A. Cole (Edward Andrews), finds a vigorous prosecution politically advantageous. What further complicates Bell's relation to the DiPace boy is that he is the son of his old flame, Mary DiPace (Shelley Winters), who has remained in Italian Harlem.

Notwithstanding that Bell enjoys an upper-middle-class lifestyle in an attractive apartment where he lives with his beautiful WASP wife Karin (Dina Merrill) and daughter, his wife's coldness suggests that social mobility and assimilation are disappointing by comparison with the rich familial possibilities formerly available in the abandoned ethnic neighbourhood. Bell's wife also harbours what the conservative Bell terms 'Vassar theories of social oppression,' and thus rejects capital punishment while espousing environmental explanations of crime. Yet when Bell renews his friendship with Mary DiPace, she defends her son with similar explanations: 'You know this neighbourhood,' she says, 'the prejudice against it.' Bell learns not only that Danny had prevented a Puerto Rican boy's murder, but that Mary's marriage to a petty local racketeer had resulted in her immurement within the neighbourhood; moreover, that she had attempted to compensate her son for his no-good father with stories of the former boyfriend she obviously wishes she had married.

Bell demonstrates his fidelity to the impersonal objectivity of the core culture in insisting that Danny face a murder trial. Yet when Danny reminds Bell of his origin – 'your name's Bellini – a Wop just like me' – it appears that Bell would extirpate those who disgrace his ethnic group (and indirectly himself). His conduct is thus more personal than he thinks. Nonetheless, his willingness to help local Hispanics shows that he has largely transcended particularistic loyalty to the old neighbourhood. At the same time, upon learning that Danny DiPace had saved a Puerto Rican boy's life, Bell feels less hostile towards him, as if realizing his undeveloped potential. One has the same impression of the Puerto Rican gangleader who mentions to Bell his admiration of Picasso, whom he compares to Michelangelo. It is implied that the gangleader belongs to the same Hispanic culture that produced Picasso and that, in another environment, his latent talents might dignify his group. Similarly, whereas many films totally dissociate Italian high culture and immigrant low culture, *The Young Savages* suggests that Italian American youth gangs are every bit as Italian as Michelangelo, and that the different levels of cultural performance may reflect not lack of ability or moral endowment but circumstance. Indeed, the group's potentialities are signalled in Bell's original surname, identical to that of the family of Renaissance painters. In anglicizing his father's name he has denied a rich cultural heritage in a one-sided quest for assimilation.

At a rally supporting Cole's gubernatorial bid, Bell and Karin clash over politics. Angered by her self-righteous liberalism, he throws her roughly into their car in seeming reversion to the stereotype of the violent, female-abusing 'wop.' Ironically, upon their return home two Italian American thugs threaten her at knifepoint in order to frighten Hank off the case. Karin's first sobering confrontation with street violence places her liberalism in doubt. In an effort to protect his wife, Bell visits neighbourhood gang leader 'Pretty Boy' Savarese, whose piled-up wavy black hair qualifies as an Italian American youth trademark. Reminiscent of Nick Romano in *Knock on Any Door*, Savarese embodies the two sides of Italian America: good and evil, attractive and terrifying. For though the right side of his face is handsomely profiled, the left is marred unspeakably by the scars of gang warfare. The presentable right side stands for what the mainstream finds acceptable in Italian America – that which, like Bell, it can assimilate.

Although the difficulties of the investigation are compounded by Danny's adherence to the neighbourhood code of silence, the code's declining power is implied when a greengrocer turns in his daughter to the police as a material witness, thus embracing American norms over those of the neighbourhood. Meanwhile, Bell's sympathy for Danny is awakened during a second visit to his mother: 'Thank God, Hank, you didn't have to raise your kid on these streets.' When Bell is later attacked by Italian American hoods, nearly strangling a sixteen-year-old in the fray, he realizes that under the pressure of gang warfare he too could have become a murderer, and thus better comprehends the power of environment over behaviour. Yet though this moment of the narrative links Bell with the ghetto violence he had wanted to disown – the world symbolized by the ugly side of Savarese – he remarks of the attack while recovering from it in a hospital, 'I protected my face so I wouldn't put in a bad appearance' in court. His unmarred face betokens his acceptability outside the old neighbourhood, from which he in his pride still seeks to dissociate himself. However, when Bell assumes with self-satisfaction that his wife has been cured of her liberalism after having been threatened at knifepoint, she remains unpersuaded by 'old Hank Bellini.' There follows Bell's self-recognition, which he confesses to her: 'My old man was ignorant,' says Hank; '... I was secretly glad my name was Bell and not Bellini ... It was part of getting out of Harlem; it was why I married you.' The hard-hearted ethnic has surmounted the self-hate that had fuelled his hatred of Danny and the other defendants, and has modified if not abandoned his conservative view of crime.

The trial scenes contain one of the most disturbing cinematic portrayals of an Italian American. As is revealed under interrogation, Aposto is a moron who, completely illiterate and answering to the name of Batman, favours comic books because of their pictures. He conforms to the stereotype of the Italian American as a sub-literate being who prefers violence to speech. Reminiscent of Santini in *The Blackboard Jungle*, his preference for comic books marks the low point of Italian visual culture in a film that mentions Michelangelo. Morally Aposto belongs with the Neanderthals, having once 'walloped' his father in a stereotypical moment of Italian familial violence. When asked what he would do the next day, were he to return home, he remarks: 'I don't know.' The stereotype of the southern Italian as bound to the immediate present, taking no thought of the next day, and hence without historical destiny, has long been a staple of travellers' reports. If Aposto is spared the electric chair, it is only because of his total lack of moral agency. As if to counterbalance this demeaning image, the film introduces the psychiatrist Androtti, whose Italian identity is as improbable as his British accent.

During the trial it is revealed that only Aposto and Rearden had killed the Puerto Rican youth, the former being sentenced to an insane asylum, the latter receiving twenty years in prison. Out of loyalty to his friends, Danny DiPace initially denies evidence of his innocence in the murder, which causes Bell to wonder about a boy 'whose values are so twisted by the strange social order that he's afraid to admit he didn't kill.' When Danny breaks down on the witness stand, Bell reassures him that crying is for men. Yet Danny has little to cry about, as he receives a year in a boy's prison for third-degree assault. Thus *The Young Savages* refuses to blame society categorically for the crimes of socially disadvantaged individuals but implies that crime has various causes. The psychopathic Reardens must be sequestered from society; the Apostos, lacking moral agency, deserve no blame but require constant surveillance; and the DiPaces are corrigible if caught in time. Yet the film equivocates on these issues, as Bell's illogical final statement to the mother of the slain Puerto Rican seems environmentalist: 'A lot of people killed your son.' What makes the statement illogical is that, like Andrew Morton in *Knock on Any Door,* Bell has himself triumphed by will, intelligence, and character over the social environment to which he attributes such an overwhelming influence upon the individual.[150]

The attribution of savagery to Italian Americans need not require their depiction as gangsters, boxers, juvenile delinquents, and the like, but is sometimes implicit in the kinds of non-Italian social misfits that Hollywood often calls upon them to portray, as if some deep affinity existed between the Italian Americans and dangerous, alien beings. For instance, dark-skinned Italian Americans have often been cast in films and on television as Arabs, one of the traditionally demonic 'enemies' of the West. This identification, which may originate in the tendency of some eighteenth-century British and Continental writers to 'orientalize' Italy, has its likely cinematic origin in Rudolf Valentino and has flourished in many B-movies.[151] Yet Italian Americans have figured much more noticeably in the role of American Indians, another of the West's demonic enemies (but also one of its adored exemplars of healthy primitivism). Given that self-declared Italian Americans make up a small percentage (roughly 6 per cent) of the American population, it is worth noting that Italians and Italian Americans apparently comprise a high proportion of the actors who have played Indians on film. They include Don Ameche, Marco Antonio, Cal Bellini, Delil Berti, Robert Blake, Joe Bonomo, Joseph Calleia, Anthony Caruso, Dolores Cassinelli, Lester Cuneo, Michael Dante, Ted de Corsia, Frank de Kova, Vince Edwards, Paul Fierro, Nick Mancuso, Elsa Martinelli, Robert Miano, Sal Mineo, Tom Nardini, Ric Natoli, Ray Nazzaro, Rigoberto Rico, Claudio Scarchilli, Henry Silva, Armando Silvestre, Charles Soldani, Victor Varconi, Joseph Vitale, and, most surprisingly, Iron Eyes Cody.[152] Sylvester Stallone's Rambo of a more recent era is part Indian and actually looks like an Indian. The identification of Italians with Indians goes back at least as far as James Fenimore Cooper, whose Machiavellian character Magua, in *The Last of the Mohicans,* exhibits an 'Italianate' passion for sex and violence, but whose characters Uncas (in the same novel) and Hard Heart in *The Prairie* possess the nobility of the ancient Romans. During his extended visit to Italy in the late 1820s, Cooper noted a resemblance between American Indians and the tanned, robust, and uninhibited Neapolitan *lazzaroni,* remarking their common proximity to the state of nature.[153] The half honorific, half-derogatory identification of the Indian with the Italian also figures in the lore of the American West, as witness the famed southern Cheyenne warrior Roman Nose, killed at the Battle of Beecher Island in Colorado in 1868. During the preparations for a historical pageant in Philadelphia in 1908 it was suggested that, because of their dark complexions, Italians should play the part of Indians.[154] That this myth lives on, and that some Italian Americans have internalized it, is evident in the widely circulated remark of mob boss John Gotti's daughter, Victoria, as she addressed reporters on the day of her father's sentencing to life imprisonment: 'My father is the last of the Mohicans.'[155]

One of the most memorable of Italian American cinematic misfits from the 1940s to the 1950s is Silva Vacarro (Eli Wallach) in Tennessee Williams's *Baby Doll* (1956). The film was directed by Elia Kazan and freely combines two of Williams's shorter plays, *Twenty-Seven Wagons Full of Cotton* and *The Interrupted Supper*. With its suggestive sexual content, including a voluptuous, thumb-sucking adolescent nymph, *Baby Doll* set off a scandal upon its release in 1956. Initially Williams complained that Kazan had taken a 'grotesque folk comedy' and made it a 'melodrama,' but after a later viewing, he rightly characterized *Baby Doll* as one of the very best cinematic renditions of his work.[156]

Like *The Rose Tattoo*, *Baby Doll* places a Sicilian at the centre of the action, as does Williams's *Orpheus Descending*, which appeared on Broadway in 1957, and which came to the screen as *The Fugitive Kind* two years later. One cannot miss the sympathy and understanding that Williams extends to these Sicilian characters, who figure as objects of local prejudice or hatred, and who often embody values that the playwright admires. One explanation for his sympathy lies in the significant if admittedly partial resemblance between the American South and Sicily.[157] This is not to claim that Sicily has experienced slavery, or has had the problem of a racial minority, or that, strictly speaking, it has suffered civil war, notwithstanding that Italian unification witnessed bloody struggles between Sicilian bandits and the northern state. Nonetheless one gains a sense of the resemblance between these regions if, in reading Richard F. Leavitt's observations, one substitutes Sicily for the South: 'In the mythology of ... [Williams's] work, the South is an antebellum mansion of faded elegance ... always the Gothic focus of his work echoes an awareness of loneliness and loss, a sense of corruption and the physical violence which is an aspect of southern romanticism ... [he shows] passionate concern for dispossessed people living on the border line of despair.' In Leavitt's judgment, Williams is an 'old fashioned Southern romantic who never made any kind of adjustment to the real world,' and whose work is permeated by an 'atmosphere of decay.'[158]

Reminiscent of the American South, Sicily has long been a feudal (or quasi-feudal) and hierarchical society in which power, prestige, and influence have depended chiefly on land ownership rather than industry and commerce. Both aristocracies have pursued cultivated leisure while earning reputations for style and lavishness. Cash on hand is no more important than making a favourable social impression. Imbued with chivalric traditions of masculine and feminine honour, the aristocratic code in both societies requires a man to punish privately any offense to his reputation, and to avenge the sexual honour of the women with whom he associates. Likewise an unmarried woman must preserve her virginity until marriage, and subsequently remain faithful to her husband. The cults of honour and vengeance are not confined to the aristocracy, however, but appear in both regions among the common people, who attempt to emulate the behavioural codes of their superiors. Thus Serafina in *The Rose Tattoo* thinks of her peasant truck-driving husband as a *barone* simply because his family had goats, land, and a farmhouse. In Sicily, and to a lesser degree the American South, the masculine cult of honour has contributed to an atmosphere of lawless violence, whose other causes include social, political, and judicial corruption.

Further reminiscent of the South, the lifestyle of the Sicilian aristocracy has depended upon an exploited peasant population confined to meagre plots of land, whether as serfs or sharecroppers. Both Sicily and the American South have fallen to invaders, who have imposed their own governments while exploiting and dispossessing the locals. Again like its American counterpart, Sicily's agrarian economy has succumbed to more successful industrial and agrarian economies in other parts of the world. As a result, Sicilian aristocrats have found it hard to maintain their lifestyle and have often yielded their domains to bourgeois interlopers and their hired gunmen, precursors of the Mafia. The defeat of the Sicilian economy was also a major cause for the mass migration of the peasantry overseas. Having endured historical catastrophes, Sicily and the American South present a similar impression of traditional cultures once possessed of wealth and grandeur yet now sunken into long decline. The decayed mansions where cotton once was king recall the forlorn country villas of the Sicilian lords, isolated amid wastelands stripped of vegetation through centuries of overgrazing and deforestation.[159]

Archie Lee Meighan (Karl Malden), the proprietor of Tiger Tail, a decayed mansion in the Mississippi Delta, faces bankruptcy because of his deteriorated cotton gin, which he had formerly rented out to local farmers. His voluptuous teenage wife Baby Doll (Carroll Baker) who, with thumb in mouth, still sleeps in a child's crib, and whose bedroom is filled with dolls and other childish knick-knacks, has agreed to consummate their three-year-old marriage on her twentieth birthday, which will occur in two days. However, she vows to cancel their agreement should the rental company reclaim their furniture. When Archie Lee learns that the reclamation will take place that day, he forces Aunt Rose Comfort, Baby Doll's paternal aunt and live-in helper, to say nothing of it, under threat of being sent to a county home. He also tells Baby Doll that he intends to have Aunt Rose cremated rather than pay for her funeral. His malice towards the kindly Rose will help to turn the audience against him while pointing up the more humane treatment she receives from Silva Vacarro who, unlike his American rival, respects the decencies of a traditionalist society.

In the next scene, Vacarro, a Sicilian American recently arrived in the area, throws a party to celebrate his first anniversary as manager of the Syndicate Plantation and Gin. Vacarro is a neatly dressed and handsome man whose thin mustache distinguishes him from the other male characters. His announcement of a Saturday night fish-fry attempts to win over a hostile audience that views him as a 'wop' or 'Eyetalian.' A state senator, the main invited guest, praises Vacarro for having 'brought in the biggest cotton crop in he country,' notwithstanding that people were 'a bit standoffish,' since they 'didn't know you all at first.' The senator adds that, though 'some people suffered' in the competition, the community had benefited. However, a farmer resents Vacarro's success in competing for the cotton crop: 'Hey, Senator, next time run on the Republican ticket and we'll get out the nigger vote for you.'

The insult identifies Vacarro with 'niggers' and thus questions his whiteness. Indeed, Italian immigrants were sometimes regarded as darker whites or else as an 'in-between people,' somewhere between white and black – a prejudice far more pronounced in the South than anywhere else.[160] The disgruntled farmer in the film has thus resuscitated an old slur. In the original screenplay, Baby Doll tells Vacarro that, whereas she suffers from sunburn, 'you're nacherally dark.'[161] Although this exchange is omitted in the film, Vacarro always wears dark clothes. His subsequent all-against-one victimization by the local community calls to mind Southern racial hatred. Thus, following the arson that destroys his cotton gin, Vacarro's first stubborn resistance to mistreatment is accompanied by the lament of a black female singer: 'I shall not be moved.' An African American spiritual that originated in the slave era, this song was adopted by black activists in the 1930s and became popular during the

Civil Rights movement; its presence in *Baby Doll* suggests a commonality between Southern blacks and the Sicilian Vacarro as victims of prejudice. This connection is even more forcefully emphasized at the conclusion when, as Archie Lee is about to be carted off from Tiger Tail by the police, he fears for Baby Doll with Vacarro still on the premises: 'Ain't I a white man? As one white man to another, don't leave him on the place' – the implication being that Vacarro is other than white.

As the senator extols Vacarro, Archie Lee gratifies the locals by burning down his cotton gin. Having just discovered the removal of his furniture, Archie Lee is apparently trying to restore his finances by guaranteeing the profitability of his own cotton gin against Vacarro's otherwise superior competition. Later that night Vacarro confronts the town marshal at a restaurant where, curiously enough, the marshal and a crony share a pizza. If one takes the pizza – a southern Italian dish – as a sign for Vacarro, then the marshal consumes symbolically the community's 'dago' victim, each slice representing each community member's share in the sacrificial feast. Yet when Vacarro encounters a local who, more soberly than threateningly, advises him not to make 'reckless charges,' since he is a 'foreigner' with 'two strikes' against him, Vacarro bristles: 'I don't want no advice, no law, no court in this country. I come from a very old country where it's tradition for each man to make his own justice. Like bootleg liquor, private, in secret. Because there was corruption there too.' He goes on: 'And if justice was executed, it was executed by each man himself, alone. I mean biblical justice, eye for eye, tooth for tooth.' Vacarro conforms to the stereotype of the vengeful Sicilian or Prohibition gangster who takes the law into his own hands. He further implies that the Italian and American South resemble each other in their traditionalism, corruption, lawlessness, and notions of private vengeance.

Vacarro in his plot against Archie Lee calls to mind the stereotype of the Italian as a vengeful conspirator winning his enemies' confidence so as to betray them by assassination. The stereotype, however, is largely inapplicable, for besides seeking redress through the law Vacarro would limit himself to what he sees as fair compensation. He intends not to kill but to prove arson, so as to bring his persecutor to book. Thus on the day after the fire Vacarro arrives at Tiger Tail with twenty-seven truckloads of cotton to be processed by Archie Lee's gin. Having ordered Baby Doll to vouch for his presence on the previous night, her husband is overjoyed to have the job, as he can now reclaim his furniture and Baby Doll's virginity. After Archie Lee calls him a 'wop' and 'dago' to his face, Baby Doll asks Vacarro whether he is a 'wop,' to which he proudly answers:

'No, I'm a Sicilian ... a very ancient people.' Finally Archie Lee drives off to the gin, leaving Baby Doll to entertain Vacarro.

The black-clad Vacarro with his hat and riding whip exemplifies health, vitality, and authority as he strolls amid the physical and moral decay of Tiger Tail. Contrary to the stereotype of the 'dirty Italian,' Vacarro recoils from its garbage-strewn grounds and fulminates against 'ignorance, indulgence, and stink.' Ironically, these terms of abuse have been hurled at Italian immigrants. When he requests a drink of water, Baby Doll directs him to a cold water spring whose pump Archie Lee had never repaired. Her comments on the superiority of cold water over tap implicitly associate the Sicilian with the release of subterranean forces symbolized by water, in contrast with Archie Lee's identification with whiskey, sexual frustration, and destructive fire. When Vacarro gathers pecans from a tree and, after cracking them with his teeth, offers the kernels to Baby Doll, she says she 'would never think of eatin' a nut a man had cracked in his mouth.' Her admission that she still sleeps in her crib interests him far less than her unthinking admission that Archie Lee had left the house the previous evening.

Terrified by Vacarro's claim that Tiger Tail is 'haunted' – a gothic theme that a later scene develops – Baby Doll runs to the mill in search of Archie Lee's protection. She is followed by Vacarro, who learns that the gin needs a new part. Instead of protecting Baby Doll, Archie Lee slaps her publicly for having entered the gin alone in the presence of 'nigger' labourers. This moment signals the end of their marriage. Vacarro's mocking question to the abusive husband, 'How's progress?', derides his violence towards a woman, something of which Vacarro, with his Sicilian 'rustic chivalry,' is presumably incapable. The situation refreshingly deviates from the stereotype of the Italian American male as abuser of women; if anything, Southern chivalry seems dead. At the same time, Vacarro mocks Archie Lee's malfunctioning gin, a far cry from the smooth operation run by Vacarro, who comprehends industrial efficiency though deriving from a 'backward' country. In a malicious improvisation – the improvisatory being yet another Italian stereotype[162] – Vacarro demands that Archie Lee replace the part immediately, which leads him on a wild goose chase across the Mississippi River while Vacarro cultivates Baby Doll.

Returning with her to Tiger Tail, Vacarro learns of her strange marriage. As is evident when Baby Doll unthinkingly eats the kernel of a pecan nut he had cracked in his mouth, she is turning towards the Sicilian. There follows a parody of gothic romance, with its standard situation of the blonde maiden trapped in a haunted castle or mansion by the Latin seducer-rapist. In the film, however, violence and seduction yield to comedy, because the motivations of the potential seducer are more legal than sexual. Initially Baby Doll enters the mansion alone, leaving Vacarro locked out on the rickety porch while she makes lemonade. However, he enters surreptitiously and produces weird noises, thus confirming her fears that Tiger Tail is 'haunted.' Upon finding the kitchen empty, he makes lemonade with liberal doses of gin, thereupon pronouncing 'Mamma mia.' When he encounters the crib in Baby Doll's bedroom, he mutters '*cosa pazza*' – crazy thing – in disapproval of its unnaturalness. Half-erotic, half-childish, Vacarro's and Baby Doll's raucous game of hide-and-seek through the second floor of the rickety mansion culminates in Vacarro's placement of a stuffed stag's head upon his own. The antlers connote the possible sexual threat he poses to Baby Doll, who wears only a slip, as well as the cuckold's horns that, in the Sicilian mode of sexual vengeance, he may intend for Archie Lee. Fearing her own eroticism, Baby Doll escapes to the attic, locks the door, and announces that their game is over. Vacarro threatens to break down the door unless she signs an affidavit testifying to Archie Lee's whereabouts on the night of the arson. Yet Vacarro wants not sex but only the affidavit, which he extracts from Baby Doll as the price of saving her from falling through the floor, the melodramatic possibilities of the scene having turned to grotesque farcicality. The tired Vacarro's afternoon nap in Baby Doll's crib only underscores the childish innocence he shares with Baby Doll, and which is yet another Italian stereotype.

Upon his return Archie Lee invites Vacarro to dinner, wanting desperately to determine his relation to Baby Doll, who now refuses to consummate her marriage, even if the furniture is returned. In her view, her husband's commission of arson reflects his inability to withstand 'fair competition,' a statement with sexual implications. She further suggests that he is headed for jail should his alibi fail. Vacarro's insulting observation to Archie Lee that the mansion contains a nursery and no children counterposes the denatured American to Italian health and fecundity. Needing an object on which to discharge his anger, Archie Lee insults and bullies Aunt Rose, whereupon the chivalric Vacarro again steps in to cool his temper. In making arrangements for local thugs to kill or injure Vacarro, Archie Lee employs methods often identified with Italian American gangsters and cuckolds. The irony confirms Vacarro's comparison of Sicily and the American South: 'there was corruption there too.' *Baby Doll* thus implicitly rejects a pet criminological notion of the 1950s, that crime in the United States originates on foreign shores.

Vacarro is less concerned with violence than with Baby Doll, whom he finds to have 'suddenly grown up.' Wearing a lady-like dress, she now seems comfortable with her sexuality, and Vacarro has caused the transformation. In objecting to her 'Mona Lisa smile,' Archie Lee implies that Baby Doll has not only become 'Italianized' but metamorphosed from thumb-sucking ingénue into an archetype of feminine slyness and mystery. With increasing frustration he derides Aunt Rose's 'unsatisfactory supper' and threatens to throw her out of the house. Vacarro comments that 'when someone feels uncomfortable over something, it often happens he takes out his annoyance on some completely innocent person' – a statement which, though heavy-handed, applies to Vacarro's victimization as much as to Aunt Rose's. However, Vacarro offers to take Aunt Rose as his cook and then, to restore her culinary reputation, joins Baby Doll in gorging on the uncooked greens.

When Vacarro informs Archie Lee that he had sought not to seduce his wife vengefully but to obtain the affidavit, he reveals in his quest for justice a restraint absent in his rival. In addition to his act of arson, Archie Lee intends to injure or kill Vacarro for only a presumed sexual offence. Again the Sicilian code of honour looks better than that of the American Southerner, especially when the latter's jealousy issues in prejudice-laden threats: 'I'm gonna wipe that grin off that greasy wop face for good.' Archie Lee having armed himself, Vacarro and Baby Doll hide in a pecan tree, where they munch on nuts as their adversary vainly scours the yard. When the police inform Vacarro that they cannot hold Archie Lee, he produces the affidavit and announces his upcoming visit to the sheriff. After Vacarro's departure the police tell Archie Lee that, in view of the affidavit, he must go to jail for appearance's sake, thus suggesting that he may never be brought to trial. Nor is the ending any less equivocal for Baby Doll, as her Sicilian Lothario may only have toyed with her.

The final example of post-war Italian American cinematic misfits is Lady Torrance, the female protagonist in Tennessee Williams's *The Fugitive Kind* (1957), who resembles Serafina of *The Rose Tattoo* and Vacarro of *Baby Doll.* Under the hand of director Sidney Lumet the film translates to the screen Williams's play *Orpheus Descending*, which appeared on Broadway in 1957 with Cliff Robertson and Maureen Stapleton in the lead roles and closed after sixty-eight performances. In *Orpheus Descending* the originally non-ethnic Myra of Williams's *Battle of Angels* (1940) is transformed into the second-generation Italian American Lady Tor-

rance, a role that Williams had conceived for Anna Magnani but that
went to Maureen Stapleton since Magnani doubted her command of
English at that time.[163] Unlike the film, in which Lady is a 'dago bootlegger's daughter,' the play specifies that her father had come from Palermo and her mother from Monte Cassino.[164] In the film, which modifies
the play for the sake of greater realism and less clumsy exposition, Magnani has the role of Lady, Marlon Brando plays Val Xavier, and Joanne
Woodward appears as Carol Cutrere. A critical and box-office failure, the
film has a cult following.

Permanently abandoning decadent New Orleans, where he had played
the guitar in local clubs and perhaps worked as a prostitute, Val takes
with him his run-down car, his snakeskin jacket, and his guitar, or 'life's
companion.' When the car breaks down in the small Mississippi town of
Marigold, Vee, the wife of the local sheriff, shelters Val in the local jail. In
an adumbration of the theme of victimization, a prison escapee's death
is signalled by a distant gunshot. However, Val may be able to find work
in the Torrance Mercantile Store, whose owner, Jabe Torrance, will return the next day after a cancer operation, and whose management has
fallen to his wife, Lady Torrance. Val is not only Orpheus within the hell
ruled over by Jabe, a Hades figure, but the Christ whose murder occurs
just before Easter. Lady Torrance is the Euridice whom Val would rescue
from the underworld.

The next day Val meets fellow misfit Carol Cutrere who, disappointed
as a critic-reformer of local racism, has turned to sexual promiscuity and,
with her family's consent, is disallowed from staying overnight within the
county. Her friend, the part-black, part-Choctaw 'conjure man' Uncle
Pleasant, carries a bone that, says Carol, will make a good charm once
'every sign of corruption is burned and washed away' by the sun and
rain. While Carol flirts with Val, two prying women descend from upstairs to report that Jabe and Lady Torrance, who have not yet arrived,
live in separate bedrooms, a sign of the distance between them.

The dark-clad Lady Torrance is a haggard, sleepless, and depressed
woman whom her dying yet still money-obsessed husband rebukes upon
their arrival for placing the shoe display away from the light. Unlike Val,
an Apollo as well as Orpheus figure, and Lady, who was raised among
grapevines and lush orchards, Jabe values the sun only as a source of
profit. Not yet having asked Lady for a job, Val drives Carol to a night
spot where they encounter her brother David, Lady's former lover. Val
and Carol then visit a local cemetery, or 'bone orchard,' which evokes
Hades. It contrasts as well with the real orchards where Lady had grown

up and that lend a golden glow of nostalgia to her existence. After refusing sex with Carol, Val returns to the Torrance store.

There he finds Lady on the phone, frantically demanding sleeping pills from a pharmacist: 'I wish I was dead!' 'No you don't,' says Val, who offers her his snakeskin jacket warmed by his body. She gradually responds to him as a kindred spirit who, as he says, is 'fed up.' Not only does Val divide humanity into the 'buyers' and the 'bought,' but he refers to a special category of people whom he calls the 'fugitive kind,' comparable to legless birds who never light on earth except to die. Touched by his speech, Lady Torrance shows him the confectionery at the back of the store, which she intends to make into an arboured restaurant. 'It's going to be like an orchard in the spring,' she says, mentioning that her immigrant father had transformed his Moon Lake orchard into a highly popular wine garden. Before she can explain why the locals 'burned it up one summer,' the bedridden Jabe knocks on his bedroom floor as a summons to Lady, who quickly offers Val a job. When Jabe learns of the arrangement, he vows that, before he dies, Lady will be too old to take a lover. Her sole consolation is the framed picture of her father above her solitary bed. With his mustache and formal dress, he is a first-generation immigrant type whose image implies Lady's Italian *pietas*.

Lady reveals to Val a major source of her unhappiness in the next scene. Contrary to her wish never to see David Cutrere again, he enters the store so as to remove his unruly sister. Immediately Lady declares her 'hard feelings' towards him, although she rejects his pity. Remarking her aim of recreating her father's wine garden, she asks David to recall those 'wine-drinking nights' when she loved him 'better than anyone has loved him since.' She then reveals what he had not known, that she had aborted his child following his abandonment of her – all this being said within earshot of Val. Lady's rejection had resulted from anti-Italian prejudice, as Cutrere, though in love with her, had succumbed to social pressure to wash his hands 'clean of ... a dago bootlegger's daughter.' Instead, to quote Lady, he married a 'society girl that restored ... [his] home place and gave ... [him] such well-born society children.' Yet Lady too has been 'bought,' since for the sake of companionship and financial security she has sold herself to Jabe at the price of a living death. Her self-betrayal is implicit in the town's name, Marigold, which, though it suggests flowers and sunlight as nature's true bounty, also puns on 'marry gold.' Like Hades, Jabe stands for material wealth, the inert lifeless substance mistaken for true value.

Suspecting unjustifiably that Val and Lady have cuckolded him, Jabe summons Val to his bedroom in order to examine his handsome rival. In Lady's presence he implies that Val is a male prostitute by whom she is 'satisfied' both commercially and sexually. Her desire for a fulfilled existence thus cruelly mocked, Lady takes Val to the ruined wine garden where, as she recalls, young couples went 'to make love' during Prohibition. Yet whereas she and her mandolin-playing father had used to sing as they 'wander[ed] among the white arbors,' now her voice is 'cracked' and perhaps also her face, so that she thinks of herself as a ruin, like the wine garden itself. For after her father had 'made a mistake' by selling liquor to 'Negroes,' the Vigilantes, a Ku Klux Klan organization, had burned it down. Vainly crying for help, he fought the fire alone until he had perished in its flames. 'I'm full of hate,' exclaims Lady, who lives among her father's unidentified killers. However melodramatic it may seem, the violence she describes and the attitudes underlying it consort with known facts of Southern history during the early twentieth century.[165]

One cannot ignore the thematic resemblances between *Baby Doll* and *The Fugitive Kind*. Each film explores the conflict between the Mediterranean personality and ethos, as typified by Vacarro and Lady, and that of the South in its more puritanical, repressive, and life-denying aspects – notwithstanding that the South is also shown to rely on the suspected outsider culture. On the one hand, the Italian or Mediterranean is identified with natural bounty and energy, the warmth and joyousness of animal spirits fed by wine, and expressive emotionality encompassing love and art. The proper setting for such experience is the wine garden, where leisure banishes work. Such a lifestyle is inextricable with that peculiar Italian mixture of paganism, classicism, and Christianity that drew Williams to Italy and Italians. And yet, however much the host community is tempted by the vitality of the foreign culture, it also fears its liberating potential – for instance the selling of liquor to Negroes – and thus confines the wine garden to a single, special place, as if it were under quarantine. Indeed, not only is the wine garden in a sense foreign to the community, but it is operated by and associated with the simultaneously despised and attractive foreigners, Lady and her father. Once the orchard is destroyed, Marigold returns to its repressive social conventions, money-grubbing and money-worship, intolerance of individuality, and suspicion of outsiders, especially those who, like Lady and Val, stand for emotional honesty and freedom as against imprisoning, deadening routine.

Besides being identified with fresh water and trees, Silvio Vacarro rescues a sexually healthy young woman from a much older and domineering husband who, unlike Vacarro, cannot appreciate her. Whereas the
healthy and agile Vacarro combines Old World style with earthiness and
sexual health, his rival Archie Lee exemplifies voyeurism, gracelessness,
ugliness, avarice, joyless drunkenness, and total indifference to culture.
Despite his contributions to the community as a skilled employee of the
Syndicate Plantation, Vacarro is hated for his foreignness and ultimately
becomes the victim of arson, his sexual rival being thus identified with
the destructive element of fire. Vacarro's nearly fatal immolation awakens his awareness of the depth of the community's anti-Italian feeling,
which he answers with retaliatory hatred.

The Fugitive Kind similarly depicts a sterile, loveless marriage, but now
the browbeaten wife is a sexually healthy Italian American woman whom
Val must save from entombment with a man who neither satisfies her
emotionally or sexually nor appreciates her commercial and artistic gifts.
Yet though Lady, like Vacarro, is identified with life-symbols, namely the
water and trees of Moon Lake whose spirit she hopes to revive, she is a
much richer character than the sometimes grotesque Vacarro, as she
taps into deeper sources of human vitality. This is evident in her identification, through her bootlegging father, with wine. Amid the desiccation
of Prohibition, which the play links to the condition of being 'dry,' the
despised Italian Americans had been called upon to satisfy the community's transgressive yet irrepressible Dionysian urges.[166] Lady's father's
wine garden had combined alcoholic ecstasy with the complementary
delights of love and song amid a beautifully cultivated and luxuriant
landscape. Through wine, romance, and art, three classic gifts of life,
the Italians had refreshed the Southern wasteland. It does not matter,
though, that Lady's father had conferred an acknowledged benefit upon
the community, for his work is destroyed by arsonists, as is Vacarro's. Yet
whereas Lady's father dies in the blaze, Vacarro survives the burning of
his cotton gin. Like him, Lady is filled with hatred of her persecutors.

Another resemblance between the two films lies in their understated
association of Italian Americans with blacks. Williams does not imply
their historical or biological identity, yet he does suggest that, in varying degrees, they have been outsiders in the South, and that their status
relates to skin tone. Just as, in *Twenty-Seven Wagons Full of Cotton*, Flora
remarks Vacarro's naturally dark skin, so in *Baby Doll* it is suggested to the
senator who lauds Vacarro that he should look for his support among the
'niggers.' In *Orpheus Descending*, Val tells Lady that she is 'light-skinned

to be an Italian,' to which she answers that 'most people in this country think Italian people are dark,' when in reality 'Some of them are fair, ... very fair.'[167] Although this is omitted in the film, Lady's father's willingness to sell liquor to blacks places him on the wrong side of the social divide, with his forbidden customers.

The problem of the Italian Americans in *The Fugitive Kind* is that, being something of an 'in-between' people in the South of those days, neither white nor black, they are readily associated with ambiguous substances towards which the community feels unresolved ambivalence, and whose dangerous properties the ambiguous Italian Americans are therefore best qualified to deal with. As a bootlegger, Lady's father had produced and sold items and services forbidden by law yet desperately desired by the community. His specialty had been alcohol, which the community had condemned for its evil effects and thus placed under taboo, but which it had also craved and worshipped for its sedative and ecstatic powers, and thus consumed secretly and transgressively. The ambiguities of alcohol, and the community's ambivalence towards it, thus mirror the social construction of Italians in the anglophone world, which envisions them as both evil and attractive, enticing and repellent. The wine garden had been both a sacred place, with its enchantments of nature and art, and a scene of transgressive danger where, had the sanctified powers of wine flowed too freely, social boundaries would have collapsed. The paradoxes of the situation are evident in the fact that, though whites had felt free to consume the forbidden substance, they had consigned its production and sale to quasi-pariahs while forbidding it to blacks.

Notwithstanding that Jabe has ordered the police to watch Lady and Val closely, she offers him the alcove at the back of the Torrance Store as his residence, free of charge. This gesture, which points to future intimacy, troubles the solitary-minded Val who, accusing Lady of soliciting his sexual favours, declares his intention of leaving town. After Lady answers him with a slap, she confesses that she needs Val in order to 'go on living.' Recognizing their mutual need, the couple embrace before the half-transparent alcove curtains decorated with two birds amid foliage. One thinks of Val's earlier speech concerning those nearly transparent and hence invisible birds that fly singly and use the sky as camouflage; yet now the birds form a pair. As Val moves with Lady into the alcove his snakeskin jacket overlaps the birds' wings, as if he were being transformed into a celestial creature: Orpheus ascending. The artificial foliage of the curtain then fades into an exterior shot of foliage through which shines the light of the sun – a sign of the Apolline Val. The luxuri-

ant vegetation of Lady's father's orchard is about to be resurrected in
the refurbished confectionery. The resurrection theme is underscored
when Lady returns from mass on Palm Sunday with two palm branches
in her arms, one for herself and the other for Val, which corresponds to
the return of springtime. Nor does she find anything blasphemous in
the simultaneous reawakening of spiritual and fleshly love. This fusion
of two kinds of experience, which is normally rejected in Protestant cultures, but which is exemplified in Serafina in *The Rose Tattoo*, typifies the
immanentism and analogism of Italian Catholic worship.

Lady enters the nearly refurbished confectionery where Val stands on
a ladder amid its trellises, wind chimes, and artificial grapes and foliage.
Yet though she offers him his 'blessed' Palm Sunday branch, this scene
casts doubts upon the characters' hopes for renewal. In the play Lady's
dreams of recreating the wine garden are associated with the monkey that
accompanied her hurdy-gurdy-playing father, and that collapsed in the
sun and died after singing 'O Sole Mio' too many times. Despite Lady's
claim that the monkey is 'not yet dead yet,' her attempted resuscitation
of the wine garden may be only an impotent 'aping' of the original.[168]
In the film, Val notes the unreality of Lady's enterprise, commenting
that 'these phony grapes got that bird fooled,' and that a windstorm
would 'wreck this place completely.' These pessimistic speculations are
interrupted by the sound of a calliope from the street, where the horse-
drawn cart hired by Lady advertises the opening of the confectionery
that evening. Hung with streamers, the cart is pursued by jubilant children, black and white. The cart and calliope are perhaps inspired by the
play's characterization of Lady's immigrant father as a hurdy-gurdy man.
The circus-like mood at this point in the film consorts with stereotypes
of the natural joyousness of Italian Americans, long identified with entertainment, carnivals, festivals, circuses, mechanically produced music,
children, and – in some instances – childishness. Williams seems to imply
the recovered innocence of the leading characters.

Yet the kingdom that Lady and Val inhabit remains that of Jabe Torrance, who in great pain descends the stairs in order to take 'inventory.'
This includes keeping watch over his wife, whom he regards as a possession like the objects in his store. When Lady proudly shows him the
confectionery, Jabe's nurse responds, 'Well isn't this artistic,' as if art
were utterly foreign to her. 'Artistic as hell,' concurs Jabe resentfully.
The sound of the calliope causes him to wonder whether a circus is in
town, whereupon Lady informs him of the gala opening. 'Boy, I've got a
real live one,' remarks Jake of his wife, as if life were a liability. When he

demands to know the cost of the cart, Val reports that Lady 'got it for a song,' to which he responds: 'What dago song did you sing? O Sole Mio, is that what you sang for it?' He recalls that her father had been 'as much of a live one before he burned up,' and that 'We had to take action' after he had sold liquor to blacks. Thus in his rage Jabe reveals his role in the burning of the wine garden, and Lady realizes in self-disgust that she has married her father's murderer. When Jabe is seriously injured in a fall, Lady totally ignores him.

Later that day it is made known to Val that if he does not leave the county before sunrise, he will be killed. Somewhat contradictorily it is implied that the town's menfolk resent his success with women, and that they also persecute him because of repressed homosexuality. For her part, Lady concentrates on the gala and regards the news of Val's imminent departure as misinformation. Still hoping to win Val, Carol mentions that her brother has offered her gifts to leave the country, including a 'Mediterranean villa ... over the coast of what they call the Divina Costiera, where it's springtime always.' It is pointless, however, for her to attempt to lure Val to this ideal spot, for he refuses to be 'bought' any longer, and in any case her paradisal Italian refuge resembles only superficially the gardens and orchards Lady and her father had created spontaneously at Moon Lake, as it is the product not of love but of money and desperation. At the same time, Carol's reference to a villa 'perched like the nest of a seabird' calls to mind Val's description of those invisible, transparent birds that fly forever and never light except to die.

Although Lady expects Val to work during the gala, he informs her that his life is in danger, and that he must leave the county. Thus the gala cannot take place. What initially prevents Lady from grasping his words is her vengefulness against Jabe: 'I want that man to see the wine garden come again while he's dying tonight,' says Lady, adding: 'Nothing can stop it. It's something got to be done to square things away, to be not defeated. I won't be defeated, not again.' While Lady's indomidability seems admirable, her desire for the wine garden has been contaminated by a sadistic vengefulness, in contrast with Vacarro who had kept his vendetta within bounds. Indeed, on the occasion of Lady's seeming triumph, Jabe has infected her with his ungenerous spirit. There is moreover something sterotypically Italian in her vengefulness and fatalism.

When Lady finally grasps Val's intention to leave, he confesses his love for her, and she extols him as her deliverer from 'hell,' who had made her feel 'alive once more.' As she struggles to prevent his departure, the nurse descends the stairs and, looking disapprovingly upon the lovers, mentions Lady's pregnancy, which she does not deny. For the life-denying nurse this revelation means scandal, but for Lady, an Italian American Catholic, her pregnancy is a miracle, as she had thought herself beyond child-bearing age. The new life in her body contrasts with the cancer growing within her husband. With Val sharing her joy as they walk into the confectionery, she recalls that her father's orchard had contained a fig tree that, seemingly barren, had yielded a small fig unexpectedly.[169] She had then decked the tree with Christmas ornaments, as she wishes herself to be adorned with them now. The fig, or *fica*, which in Italy is taken to symbolize the pudenda, refers to Lady's recent sexual reawakening through Val. Yet within moments there is the rustling sound of flames, for Jabe has set the confectionery afire. With the flames spreading irresistibly, Lady runs indoors only to be shot dead by Jabe, who thus commits a double murder. After the sheriff and his men break down the front door, they encounter Val fleeing from the fire. They turn their firehoses against him and drive him backwards to be immolated. Thus is repeated the destruction of the wine garden by the vigilantes, the vital element of water having been made the instrument of Val's death. Like her father, the Italian American woman is the victim of an envious, spiteful community.

VIII

Francis Ford Coppola's version of Mario Puzo's *The Godfather* (1972), whose sequels appeared in 1974 and 1990, marks the inception of Italian American cinema in the sense of films by Italian American directors treating their own ethnic group. The typical insecurity that first- and second-generation Italian Americans felt towards their ethnic origin had been evident in director Frank Capra, who largely concealed his ethnicity while in Hollywood, and who never treated it explicitly save in the late film *A Hole in the Head* (1959). Yet as a third-generation, college-educated Italian American, Coppola had largely assimilated and was thus able to confront his background with an interest, confidence, and security unknown to previous generations. All this accords with Marcus Hansen's famous "law," which states that what the immigrant wishes to forget his third-generation descendant seeks consciously to remember.[170] What is more surprising, however, is that despite his initial unwillingness to portray the criminal elements that had shamed his ethnic group, Coppola risked the opprobrium of those fellow ethnics in placing the Mafia at the centre of his signature film. The Sons of Italy and the Italian American

Civil Rights League at first opposed the making of *The Godfather*, and only after co-producer Al Ruddy agreed to omit all mention of the Mafia or Cosa Nostra could the production proceed.[171] One of Coppola's advantages in making *The Godfather* was that he and scenarist Puzo understood the gangster genre, which they greatly modify. Coppola also brought to his series a detailed, 'insider' knowledge of Italian American life that seemed immeasurably to increase its credibility and authenticity by comparison with the works of non–Italian American directors. The first of the *Godfather* films had an enormous influence, showing the potential richness of Italian American subjects when treated by a qualified member of the group, and at the same time inspiring other third-generation Italian American directors, such as Martin Scorsese, Nancy Savoca, and Abel Ferrara, to create their own versions of Italian American cinema.

The *Godfather* films build frequently upon conventions of the Hollywood gangster genre. For instance, in *Little Caesar* and *Scarface* the criminal antagonists are shown devouring spaghetti while speaking with heavy Italian accents; Rico has just committed his first murder, and Camonte is already immersed in a life of mayhem. In *Godfather II*, as the young Vito Corleone (Robert De Niro) joins with Tessio and Clemenza over a spaghetti dinner, he hints in heavily accented English at the soon-to-be-achieved assassination of the extortionist Fanucci. Like these generic predecessors, Coppola's film links eating and killing, as if the victim himself were being consumed (an idea later taken up by Scorsese in *GoodFellas*). As John Paul Russo shows, the paradigm for this connection between eating and assassination is Clemenza's remark after the murder of Paulie in *Godfather I*: 'Leave the gun, take the cannoli' – the festive cannoli serving to celebrate Paulie's removal.[172] Gangster films have also traditionally depicted the underworld not unjustifiably in a corrupt, 'symbiotic' relationship with politicians and the police; Coppola elaborates this theme in his portrayal of the police captain McCluskey (Sterling Hayden) in *Godfather I* and Senator Geary (G.D. Spradlin) in *Godfather II*, to whom Michael (Al Pacino) observes that they are 'both part of the same hypocrisy.' Michael's fashionable tailoring at the end of *Godfather I*, and the sleek sharkskin suits he subsequently favours, not only contrast with his early drabness as a soldier and Ivy Leaguer, but call to mind those many films in which the gangster's flashy new clothes signify his arrival in the underworld. What Colin MacArthur describes as the gangster film's characteristic association of the motor car with violence is exemplified in several scenes from *Godfather I*, including the fatal car-bombing of Apollonia, Michael's first wife, the execution from ambush of Sonny at a toll booth, and the assassination of Paulie after he has been 'taken for a ride' by Clemenza.[173] The Senate hearings in *Godfather II* trace to such films as *Hoodlum Empire*, while the mob summit meetings in *Godfather I* are almost *de rigueur* for the genre. Extending the generic association of Italian music and assassination to be seen in *Scarface, House of Strangers, Al Capone*, and many other films, Fanucci's murder by the young Don Vito in *Godfather II* coincides with a street festival in Little Italy, the execution being muffled by the band's crescendo.

Coppola's exploration of possible connections between Italian American crime and the Old World similarly awakens reminiscences of the Black Hand films of both the silent and sound eras. This is not to say that Don Vito Corleone seeks deliberately to extend a Sicilian criminal tradition, or what Kay Adams denounces as 'this Sicilian thing,' for he and his sons are 'forced' into crime by circumstance. And yet Robert K. Johnson rightly complains that Coppola implies without sufficient historical evidence a close historical continuity between the Sicilian and Italian American underworlds. Thus Fanucci, the Black Hand extortionist and Don Vito's earliest enemy, seems intended to represent a form of criminality which, carried over from Sicily, gave rise naturally to the Mafia. With his histrionic and even courtly style, Fanucci leaves the impression of an Old World anachronism on American soil, or what the early Italian Americans would have called a 'Mustache Pete,' whose florid methods the Mafia would improve and supersede.[174]

At the finale of *Godfather I*, Coppola juxtaposes the baptism of Michael's nephew with a series of murders in which Michael's executioners despatch his rivals and thus assure his ascension to power. This parallelism of crime and Catholicism calls to mind not only *Scarface*, in which the proliferation of crosses and *X*'s has been claimed to stand simultaneously for both underworld assassinations and the Church, but *Little Caesar, Cry of the City*, and, to use a non–Italian American example, *The Roaring Twenties*, in which murders occur close to neighbourhood churches. In view of the fact that Michael, during the baptismal ceremony, professes to reject Satan and all his works, Les and Barbara Keyser contend that Coppola aims to show the blindness and even hypocrisy of the Church towards the criminality of some of its most prominent members, so long as they satisfy ritualistic and other external requirements.[175] Yet though the theme of a corrupt Catholicism resurfaces in *Godfather III*, it may equally be argued that the counterpointing of underworld mayhem and Catholic ritual implies the insuperable distance between Michael's behaviour and Catholic ethics. This seems all the more plausible in view not only of *Godfather*

II, whose final scene implies in Catholic terms that Michael is morally damned, but of *Godfather III*, in which, despite the presence of corrupt clerics and interlopers within the Church, Michael nonetheless seeks to obtain absolution for his sins through the intercession of the morally unimpeachable Cardinal (and later Pope) Lamberto (Raf Vallone), whom Michael himself characterizes as a good man. Michael's desire for absolution would make little sense dramatically, indeed could only work satirically or parodically, were the *Godfather* series to have discredited the Church from top to bottom, yet such an interpretation would be extreme. During the absolution scene Cardinal Lamberto traces human depravity not to Catholicism itself but to the impenetrability – like that of stone to water – of humanity to the spirit of Christianity, which Lamberto represents.[176] In any case, the climax of *Godfather I* achieves something like epic grandeur in providing a compendium of the various forms of gangland slaying traditional in the genre.[177] One gangster is killed while trapped in a revolving door, another while shaving, another while receiving a massage, and yet another while in bed with a prostitute; finally, the impeccably dressed underworld boss Barzini (Richard Conte) is killed on the monumental steps of a courthouse symbolic of the law itself.

Another significant theme in gangster films concerning Italian Americans has been the opposition encountered by rebellious second-generation ethnics in their attempt to transfer their primary allegiance from group and family to society and thus the state. In *Cry of the City* Lt Candella prefers legality over ethnic loyalty, yet Martin Rome's mother attempts at first to shield her criminal son from the police. *The Godfather* embodies this tension in Michael Corleone, who enlists in the U.S. Army against his father's wishes and later attends his sister's wedding wearing a U.S. Army uniform. As Paola Casella observes, Michael exemplifes the second-generation Italian American divided between family and mainstream, a division further evident in the fact that Don Vito speaks imperfect English, while Michael struggles with Italian.[178] Nonetheless Michael has internalized Don Vito's desires for the family to attain upper-class or bourgeois respectability. One recalls Lang's *The Big Heat*, in which gang boss Lagana insulates his children from his life of crime. The irony of *Godfather I* is that circumstances and family loyalty prevent Michael from escaping the underworld. As in *House of Strangers*, the protagonist's aim of rejecting his unacceptable origins hinges on the prospect of marriage to an upper-class Anglo-Saxon woman. Yet as a husband Michael must endure Kay's constant complaint that the family remains in the crime business.

Despite many continuities, major differences exist between the leaders of the Corleone family and the representative film gangsters that precede them. Rico, Camonte, and Johnny Rocco are loud and impulsive big spenders, who wear flashy clothes and smoke big cigars as signs of power, and who decline because of vanity and lack of self-control. In contrast to Big Boy, the bland WASP crime overlord in *Little Caesar*, who shuns publicity and continues to prosper by staying out of view, Rico's and Camonte's attention-grabbing behaviour keeps them dangerously in the public eye. Contrastingly, Vito and Michael Corleone reflect Mafia (and Sicilian) folkways in their calculated reserve and detachment, control of events at a distance, and freedom from histrionics. Don Vito would prefer to leave his empire to Michael rather than to Sonny, as Sonny dresses ostentatiously, speaks candidly and out of turn, and has an exceedingly hot head (which gets him killed). Another departure from generic tradition (compare the luxurious residence of Lagana) is that the Corleone family, at least initially, avoids costly expense and lavish display. As Gambino notes, many viewers of *Godfather I* could not believe that Don Vito lived in such unimpressive surroundings.[179]

The Corleone's restraint is inseparable from their allegiance to Italian American familism with its behavioural codes based on respect, loyalty, and duty. Such values set the Corleones apart from such antisocial individualists as Rico Bandello and Tony Camonte who, in their either non-existent or else warped family relations, as in their identification with homosexuality and incest, represent atypical examples of Italian American conduct. To be sure, Don Vito appears to cast an indulgent eye upon Sonny's adulteries, yet he himself is a faithful and basically puritanical husband, and sexual perversion or corruption remains atypical of the Corleone family at least before its decline. Having acquired his father's puritanism along with his role of family leader, Michael is ill at ease when his dissolute brother Fredo takes him to a sleazy sex show in Havana, and even as his marriage collapses there is no suggestion of his infidelity. *Godfather I* and *Godfather II* locate sexual perversion chiefly in the defamilized world outside the Mafia and the Italian American community, in the unmarried Jewish film magnate Woltz who keeps a child star as mistress, and in the married Senator Geary, who apparently practices sado-masochism with prostitutes.

Yet the fact remains not only that Geary gets his thrills in brothels owned and operated by the Corleone family, but that Michael's henchmen delude Geary into thinking that he had murdered a prostitute they themselves had killed, after which, in exchange for Geary's support for Corleone family interests, the family agrees to protect him by obliterating every trace of the prostitute's existence. Michael's apparent assumption that prostitution is merely a source of income typifies the attitude of Italian American criminals that family and business morality should remain separate. Secure in her husband's reliability as a provider, the ideal Mafia wife (such as Mama Corleone) runs her house unconcerned with events in the workplace.[180] From this perspective Michael's mistake was to have married an Anglo-American woman who, incapable of separating public and private morality, questions Michael's business ethics. Although Stephen Farber holds that, in Coppola's view, both Italian American gangsters and Americans typically dissociate their often unscrupulous business practices from the warmth and humaneness of their family lives, he fails to explain why Kay, who represents the WASP point of view, is disturbed by Michael's segregation of the two spheres.[181]

The immeasurable advantage in authenticity that *The Godfather* enjoys over its predecessors must be attributed not to Coppola alone but, at least in the case of *Godfather I*, to Robert Evans, the film's Jewish American producer at Paramount Studios. Although Paramount had recently failed with Martin Ritt's *The Brotherhood*, a solid film on a Mafia theme, Evans blamed the limitations of that and numerous other films concerning Italian American gangsters on the fact that the main participants in these projects were usually Jews without a deep understanding of Italian America. What Evans wanted was a film that, made by Italian Americans, would enable the audience to 'smell the spaghetti' and in which the characters, rather than being mere sterotypes of 'Hollywood Italian[s],' conveyed genuine ethnicity.[182] The appeal of choosing Coppola as director lay in his willingness to work for a low fee, in the fact that an Italian American director would help to placate fellow ethnics sensitive to the subject of the Mafia, and above all in his ethnic background. 'I had faith in him,' said Evans: 'He knew the way these men ate their food, kissed each other, talked. He knew the grit.'[183] Or as Coppola puts it: 'I really saw it as an Italian family, and I knew that if I had one asset it was to do things – textures, what have you – that would be like my own family and not like so-called movie Italians.'[184] Evans also made it clear that he wanted Italian American actors to be cast wherever possible.[185] The gain in authenticity is apparent throughout the film, as when Don Vito dies in a tomato patch, or Clemenza prepares spaghetti for his fellow gangsters at a mob hideout, or characters speak to each other in Sicilian dialect, with subtitles. Unlike the Mafia wedding in *The Brotherhood*, which Casella terms 'anthropologi-cal,' its counterpart in *The Godfather* plunges the viewer into the midst of what seems a living and genuine ethnic gathering.[186]

One does not want to exaggerate, however, the authenticity of *The Godfather* as a document of Italian America, much less to suggest that this is the final test of its merit.[187] As Vera Dika points out, the film's producers were Jewish and, despite their and Coppola's attempt to cast only Italian American actors, two of the principal characters, Don Vito and Sonny, are played by non-Italians. By the same token, Puzo lacked Sicilian an-cestry, as does Coppola. Thus, if the probably unfulfillable ideal of an absolutely 'Italian American cinema' implies a work created entirely by Italian Americans, then *The Godfather* remains a hybrid entity. However, Dika also doubts the film's authenticity on more questionable grounds, claiming that the portrayal of Don Vito Corleone as a man of dignified, sober, patient, and reserved habits presents a misleadingly mystified and unrealistically nostalgic portrait of his family's past, one that contrasts with more familiar stereotypes of the impulsive, hot-blooded Italian American gangster to be seen in Rico Bandello and Tony Camonte.[188] This is not to deny that Coppola ascribes to Don Vito's career and per-sonality romantic and nostalgic elements that require examination, yet the features of Don Vito's behaviour of which Dika complains may be justified on the grounds not of illusion but of authenticity, which she mistakenly regards as nothing more than an 'effect' or construction achieved by the director. Rejecting conventional notions of Italian lav-ishness, Coppola's portrayal of Don Vito as a man of understated dignity agrees with typical Mafia (and Italian) habits of the period depicted in *Godfather I* (mainly the 1940s) and testifies to the sense of limit that the Don, like many other mob bosses, hoped to bequeath to his American-izing sons. As the sociologist Francis A.J. Ianni observes in *A Family Business*, his study of the Italian American crime family to which he gives the fictitious name of Lupollo: 'Despite its rising wealth throughout the 1920's and 1930's, the Lupollo family continued to live conservatively. Their houses in Brooklyn appeared no more luxurious than others in the neighborhood ... [Joseph Lupollo, the head of the family] did not permit himself or either of his sons to take on the lavish life style they could have acquired.' Yet later they did so.[189]

However, Coppola's portrayal of the Mafia is questionable for other, more important reasons, above all Coppola's (and Marlon Brando's) claim that the Mafia amounts to a mirror of American society, and that the Mafia and capitalism share the same methods and corporate organization. Such notions as these, which also appear in varying degrees of explicitness in the syndicate films of late 1940s and 1950s,[190] show how little Coppola – and many of his approving critics – comprehend of the Mafia. 'I always wanted,' says Coppola, 'to use the Mafia as a metaphor for America. Both ... have roots in Europe. Basically, both ... feel they are benevolent organizations. Both ... have their hands stained with blood from what it's necessary to do to protect their power and interests. Both are totally capitalistic phenomena and basically have a profit motive.'[191] When in another interview Coppola was asked whether he regarded 'some corporations' as 'no better and no worse than organized crime,' he replied that everything the Mafia believed in was already 'here,' in the United States: 'In fact, the corporate philosophy that built some of our biggest industries and great personal fortunes was a Mafia philosophy. So when those Italians arrived here, they found themselves in the perfect place.' In the same interview Coppola seems apparently to regard murder as a common business as well as Mafia practice.[192] Marlon Brando similarly claims that *The Godfather* is 'about the corporate mind,' that the Mafia in all its historical forms is the 'best example of capitalists that we have,' and that Don Vito is 'just any ordinary American business magnate' trying to do his best for his group and family.[193] These themes are present in *Godfather II*, in which Michael reminds the corrupt Senator Geary that 'we're both part of the same hypocrisy,' and in which he later attends a board meeting in Havana to which the leaders of major U.S. corporations are invited. Indeed, Coppola's equation between the hated Mafia and the capitalist corporation motivates his animus towards the character of Michael Corleone, to the point where, having failed to convince the audience of his corruption in *Godfather I*, he set about to punish and destroy this 'ultimate corporate monster' in the sequel, until at the conclusion Michael finds himself, to quote Coppola, 'broken,' 'condemned,' and 'alone, a living corpse.'[194]

It is perhaps predictable that mob bosses, with their hunger for social legitimation, have preferred to think of themselves as ordinary capitalists as well as defenders of capitalism. Al Capone considered himself not a racketeer but a businessman, and hated the political left.[195] Steve Carver's *Al Capone* (1975), starring Ben Gazzara, depicts Capone in his last years as riddled with syphilis and inveighing against communism. Joseph Bonanno, in that extraordinary piece of false self-apologetic that is his ghost-authored autobiography, *A Man of Honor*, claims that his family does business in virtually the same way as oil companies, the only difference being supposedly that the former operates in the 'neighborhood' and the latter in the 'international arena.'[196] Yet what is more surprising is that not only Coppola and Brando but many critics of *Godfather I* (and its sequels) accept the idea of the identity between the Mafia and legal capitalism. As Paul Giles apparently lends some credence to Michael Corleone's self-serving belief that his father resembles a typical American businessman, so Stephen Farber finds that Coppola's gangsters conduct business impersonally, as do major American corporation executives.[197] According to Eugene Rosow, the earlier gangster film had frequently identified gangsters with capitalist robber barons (along with Horatio Alger), the gangster being rendered as only a somewhat more brutal version of the capitalist; in later gangster films, including *The Godfather*, the criminal organization is a 'syndicate,' by which Rosow seems to mean a corporation.[198] Although, unlike Coppola, Andrew Dickos does not see the Mafia as initially corporate, he finds that the Corleones adopted a 'sophisticated capitalistic approach' and became increasingly 'like a corporation in a corporate society.'[199] Glenn Man contends that gangsters have typically aped 'the corporate ways of American capitalism,' and that, 'on the whole,' the *Godfather* trilogy 'indicts American capitalism for the rampant materialism within society.'[200] Similar arguments are advanced by Marxist critics, for instance John Hess's contention that Coppola shows 'American gangsterdom' to be the 'perfect microcosm of American capitalism,' and Frederic Jameson's view that *The Godfather* substitutes the myth of the Mafia for American late capitalism.[201]

What is one to make of Coppola's equation between the Mafia and corporate capitalism? Its context is the early 1970s, when a fashionable cynicism towards society and politics was setting in after the ebullient optimism of the preceding decade.[202] It is often claimed that, with the reorganization of the major Italian American criminal groups into 'syndicates' by such criminal masterminds as Johnny Torrio and Lucky Luciano in the 1920s and 1930s, the Mafia to some degree copied rational business methods such as division of territories, cooperation among groups, and reduction of violence.[203] Yet if the Italian American underworld was required to introduce such relatively sophisticated innovations in those decades, it could hardly have followed a corporate arrangement in its Sicilian manifestation, as Coppola contends. In 1969 Donald Cressey offered the influential argument that the Italian American underworld had organized itself along corporate lines, and thus on the basis of a rigidly formal, impersonal, centralized, hierarchical, and bureaucratic structure.[204] However, Cressey's model was subsequently shown to be inaccurate, and the Mafia is now widely seen as being organized for various reasons, including that of security, on a much looser, ad hoc basis. It is also better compared not to a business but to a government or at least a quasi-government that guarantees its members the right to operate as independent entrepreneurs who in return owe tribute to their governors.[205] As for the supposed resemblance between Mafia operations and ordinary or legitimate capitalism, it is true that the Mafia exists symbiotically with its surrounding society, providing it with the illegal services it demands while corrupting judges and policemen so as to win power and influence. Nonetheless the Mafia combines these activities with its everyday practice of forcing 'protection' upon the public along with other forms of racketeering and extortion, all of which in being violent, predatory, and parasitic are beyond the bounds of ordinary legal business.[206] Indeed, Kay's complaints of Michael's failure to divest himself of the criminal side of his operation so as to enter completely into the realm of legitimate business would have no dramatic point or resonance were there no essential difference between the two spheres, a difference that definitely exists and that undermines Coppola's identification of the Mafia with legal capitalism. The same can be said of *Godfather III*, in which the aging Michael Corleone, having tried to 'go legit,' belatedly discovers: 'Just when I thought I was out, they try to pull me back in!'

Notwithstanding that Coppola and his critics often identify the Mafia, both in reality and in the film, with corporate organization, *The Godfather* series and most especially its first installment has given many critics the impression of a different form of criminal organization incompatible with the corporate model that Coppola belabours. This other model is that of the criminal operation organized as a family, and is conceptualized by critics in two basic ways. Most frequently they think of it as a family united by the most intimately personalist ties of kinship and blood loyalty, in which the chief positions of responsibility are customarily filled by leading family members, and in which the control of the organization remains hereditarily within the family itself. As Paola Casella remarks, in the United States the Mafia is widely perceived as a hereditary or dynastic organization.[207] On the other hand, the Mafia organization is also regarded in many quarters as an artificial fictitious kinship group of sworn members who think of themselves as a family and who unite in loyalty and service around the directive core of the organization, which consists of an actual kinship group, that is, a real family like the Corleones.

Apparently for Nick Browne the Mafia best fits the former description, for as he says, in the 'world' of *The Godfather* the 'gang is the family,' while the chief problem for the family leader is the problem of generational succession from father to son. Thus in *Godfather III* it is a family catastrophe when Michael's son rejects hereditary leadership of the Corleone family in favour of an operatic career.[208] In John Cawelti's view, the family is the 'ruling principle of the film,' as it is for Glenn Man, who refers to the Mafia as an exploitative family rather than a corporation.[209] Alessandro Camon observes that those critics who treat the Corleones in terms of a 'capitalist business' or corporate analogy overlook the fact that the 'concept of family is most important to the mafioso, because it is the one that must come first, the one that provides justification and comfort.' Camon further notes that the Mafioso and his associates typically form not a real kinship group but an artificially created 'family.'[210] He does not, however, specify the relationship or interrogate possible incompatibilities or contradictions between real and fictitiously constituted kinship organizations. According to Peter Cowie, the family with its ties of kinship provides the foundation and 'source of ... strength' of the Mafia, which rises and falls according to the family fortunes. Yet though most Mafia members or 'soldiers' are unrelated by blood and thus belong to a fictitiously constituted family, they may, claims Cowie, become members of the predominating kinship group after years of loyal service.[211] Herein lies the importance of the wedding scene in *Godfather I*, as it shows the indissoluble link between business and family.

The question naturally arises how commentators deal with the obvious contradiction between the two competing interpretations of the Mafia as corporate on the one hand and familist on the other. Unlike Camon, some observers seem totally unaware of the contradiction, describing the organization as both corporatist and familist in the same breath, as does Marlon Brando: 'Don Corleone is just an ordinary business magnate who is trying to do the best he can for the group he represents and for his family.'[212] Eugene Rosow describes Mafia organizations as 'crime syndicate[s]' yet also refers to the 'Corleone Clan,' which implies family-based organization. He also refers without explanation to the simultanously 'tribal' and 'corporate' warfare of the Mafia families.[213] No less ambiguous is Martin Scorsese's commentary on *The Godfather* in his documentary on American film, in which he links Coppola's *Godfather* series with the syndicate films of the 1940s and 1950s: 'The syndicate ... even wanted to sacrifice your family ... When you were a Corleone, there was no leaving the outfit. It was an evil family bound by fear and torn by treachery, but you served it without ever questioning it, as if it were your family.' He adds: 'The organization was a state within the state, the gangster a chairman of the board.'[214] Scorsese thus seems to refer to the

Mafia not only as a corporation made up of non-blood relatives, but also as an organization founded on blood relationships, which operates not simply as a business but as a government.

In contrast with these observers, Peter Bondanella notes a definite opposition within *The Godfather* films between family and corporate organization, claiming that the Corleones, though seeking to modernize their organization along impersonal, corporatist lines, fall short in the attempt because they cannot put aside their Sicilian legacy of 'amoral familism,' which continues to enslave them to family-based values such as personalism and the vendetta.[215] This reading reflects the sociological assumption that the ethnic family, with its complex system of private and personal loyalties, and its resistance to rational, bureaucratic, and utilitarian standards of efficiency, impedes the economic and social advancement of ethnic groups and individuals in the modern world. The same assumption figures as well in some of the most insightful and influential interpretations of *The Godfather*, whether in its literary or cinematic version. Whereas conservative critics interpret the film as a celebration of the family as a haven from the harsh encroaching world of capitalism, E.J. Hobsbawm and Frederic Jameson regard Puzo's novel as a falsely reassuring fantasy of the compatibility of family loyalty with capitalist ambition. Yet unlike Bondanella, who reads *Godfather II* as demonstrating the imperfect corporatization of the Corleone organization, owing to its ambiguous adherence to a personalist and vengeance-ridden past, other critics interpret that film as showing how the successfully accomplished impersonal goals of profits, business expansion, utilitarianism, and corporate efficiency destroy familial trust and solidarity. Michael Corleone grows estranged from his wife, neglects his son in favour of business, and murders his disloyal, jealous brother. In *Godfather II* kinship ties and modern capitalism define two irreconcilable structures of social activity and experience.[216]

Contrary to these critics, Thomas J. Ferraro argues that under some circumstances the ethnic family has been and will remain compatible with advanced capitalism, at once providing a structure for the organization of production and services and helping its members to rise economically and socially. Ferraro's primary example is the fictionally titled 'Lupollo' crime family, which forms the subject of Francis A.J. Ianni's *A Family Business*, and whose structure Ferraro compares with that of the Corleone clan. Ianni defines the Lupollo business not as a formal bureaucratic organization dedicated to utilitarian efficiency and the maximization of profit, but as a traditional kinship structure deriving from the southern Italian patriarchal clan. At the apex of the hierarchy is the head of the family. Not only is each family member assured a job within the business but, in contrast with bureaucracies and other types of business, which recruit qualified outsiders, positions are filled exclusively by family members. The binding elements in the Lupollo organization are primarily familial or personal rather than rational: loyalty, respect, trust, honour. Its efficacy is evident in the fact that many of its members enjoy wealth and social prestige.[217] However, Ferraro's main point is that the Corleone family as depicted in Puzo's novel closely resembles the Lupollos. For the Corleones, neither family nor business has priority, since these are inseparably intertwined, each affecting the other simultaneously. As the crisis of the Corleone family is also a business crisis, marked by kinship betrayals and a son's disaffection, so the family's recovery coincides with the defeat of its business rivals.[218]

Judging Puzo's and Coppola's works in the light of the family Lupollo, Ferraro contends that the novel and to a lesser extent *Godfather I* are for the most part historically and sociologically realistic, free from the romantic sentimentalism that Marxist and other critics claim to find in them. As for *Godfather II*, so often praised for debunking its predecessor, he finds it a highly romanticized attempt to show what Ianni supposedly disproves, namely that the inevitable breakup of the nuclear and extended family is the inevitable price of syndicate expansion, Americanization, and modernization. Ferraro describes Michael Corleone's despair at the conclusion of *Godfather II*, his isolation from his family and society, as yet another hackneyed variation on the theme that business success is really failure, that life is lonely at the top. For Ferraro the aesthetic quality of these works largely depends on what he sees as their sociological truth and honesty. He adds that the relative unpopularity of *Godfather II* among non-intellectuals may reflect the public's instinctive unwillingness to accept a 'regressive' sociology that holds capitalism and family to be incompatible.[219]

Unfortunately, Ferraro mentions only those elements of Ianni's analysis that suit his own purposes. While Ianni concludes that in 1972 the Lupollo business was still tied to its kinship structure, he never claims as Ferraro implies that the Lupollo form of organization necessarily corresponds to that of other Italian American criminal organizations. Although Ianni speculates that the same coalescence of family and business may exist elsewhere, he also says that the Lupollos may be more kin-oriented than other comparable organizations and that he cannot 'warrant' the 'centrality' of kinship among them.[220] Given such limited evidence, Ferraro too hastily assumes the typicality of the Lupollos and the Corleones as depicted by Puzo and Coppola. There is moreover good reason to view the Lupollos as an atypical Mafia family. To begin with, the evidence suggests that the vast majority of such so-called families are based not on blood ties but on fictitious or artificially created kinship. Nor is the leadership of such groups determined hereditarily, that is, through succession from father to son or blood relative to blood relative. Instead, family leadership falls upon the most qualified individual regardless of his actual family origin, and sometimes only after a harshly competitive struggle. Indeed, one of the few Mafia families in which hereditary succession is known to have taken place without opposition is that of Florida crime boss Santo Trafficante, whose son, Santo, Jr, inherited his authority. However, when Joseph Bonanno sought to pass on the leadership of his crime family to his son Bill during the mid-1960s, many family members refused to accept the authority of a person they perceived as weak and incompetent. The result was a major war within the family itself.[221] Far from honouring the blood ties of individual members, a Mafia family of the artificially constituted type will often require them to kill a blood relative so as to prove their greater loyalty to their fictional family – a situation similar to the climax of Ritt's *The Brotherhood*, as we have seen. One of the few critics to grasp how this situation applies to *The Godfather* is Gene D. Phillips, who writes: '*The Godfather* offers a chilling depiction of the way in which Michael's loyalty to his flesh-and-blood family gradually turns into an allegiance to the larger Mafia family to which they in turn belong, a devotion that in the end renders him a cruel and ruthless mass killer.'[222]

Yet even if the Lupollos and Corleones are typical examples of Mafia organization, the final part of Ianni's discussion severely weakens Ferraro's contention that the Italian American example proves the continued compatibility of the family with high-level capitalism. Ianni observes that by 1972 (the year *The Godfather* was released) there were definite signs that the kinship structure of the Lupollo family was crumbling, and hence too the structure of its business. Acculturation in the fourth generation had led to an erosion of the father- and mother-respect that form the kinship bond and are essential to the family business. Some prominent family members, in becoming linked to society's rationalized institutions and 'legitimate power establishments,' had also become attuned to such modern capitalist values as utilitarian efficiency and bureaucracy. The family was developing new bases of power that had the clan's increasing respect and that must ultimately challenge the clan chieftain.

Noting instances of small power clashes, Ianni speculated that within a generation the old authority structure would disappear and with it the clan itself. This would likewise mean the collapse of the Mafia, at least as it is embodied in the family Lupollo.[223]

Ianni envisions what Ferraro denies or rather ignores: the eclipse of the family-based business through the dwindling of familial and ethnic ties, each being casualties of modernization and non-familial capitalism. A key factor in this decline is the entry of younger family members into legitimate businesses and the professions; another is geographical mobility, which separates family members and ethnic communities. Although some observers claim that the Mafia remains strong, and that it still attracts younger, reliable members, Richard D. Alba provides support for Ianni's conclusions in noting that the increasing economic mobility of Italian Americans, no longer ethnic centred nor stigmatized as ethnics, has made it difficult for crime families to find recruits. In Alba's view, the unprecedented rash of informants in the early 1980s suggests that the new Mafiosi, often drawn by necessity from outside the web of kinship, lack traditional loyalty and trustworthiness. He explains the persistence of the Mafia partly by the fact that it must take decades for its members to die off.[224]

What is the relevance of Ianni's research to *The Godfather* films? Although a work of art need not be accurate down to the smallest sociological details, these films portray in broad strokes something like the historical process Ianni describes. Contrary to Coppola's claim that the Corleone family resembles a corporation from the start, the films dramatize the difference between Don Vito's version of the Mafia, in which kinship and other traditional ties predominate, and its later 'corporate' manifestation under Michael Corleone, who at the cost of his family ties adopts the most impersonal and ruthlessly efficient business practices. It is not a matter of the family being a corporation or acquiring a corporate form like that of a business, but rather of corporatization destroying the family. In *Godfather I*, the last minute patching-up of a crisis caused by a breakdown in kinship loyalty rescues the Corleones and their business, whose vulnerability has nonetheless been revealed. In the sequel, familial and business interests have become separated, for now Michael Corleone is obsessed with profits, commercial expansion, and the extra-familial contacts that ensure legitimation. Not only is Michael betrayed by his brother, whom he vengefully kills, but Michael betrays his own kinsman, Frank Pentangeli, who had previously betrayed him. The family is further injured by Kay's aborting of her child, behaviour unthinkable in a preceding era, as well as by Michael's brother's and sister's marriages outside the ethnic group, which in a sense only follow Michael's example. Nor can one forget that not the family alone but ethnicity itself is a casualty of these momentous changes, as witness the difference between the Italian American wedding that opens *The Godfather I* and the first communion celebration at the beginning of *Godfather II*. The first is drenched in ethnic custom, music, song, and dance, but the musicians at the second event can only come up with 'Pop Goes the Weasel' when asked to perform the tarantella. An absentee father suffering from nearly catatonic withdrawal, Michael embodies the impersonal, technocratic functionalism of some corporation executives. In an illustration of what Ianni calls 'horizontal' as opposed to the 'vertical' or hierarchical mobility characteristic of familial organization, Michael's power increasingly depends on connections with the power establishment, for instance Senator Geary and the American corporations in Havana. In short, *The Godfather* films present an aesthetically heightened, sometimes melodramatized, but reasonably accurate portrayal of the process of familial devolution predicted by Ianni.[225]

Like Ferraro, Carlos Clarens, Jeffrey Chown, and William Pechter object to what they see as romanticization in *The Godfather* series. Clarens complains with some justification that Coppola is soft on Don Vito in *Godfather I*, and that had he shown the sources of his wealth, the illusion of Don Vito's moral superiority would vanish.[226] For Chown, Don Vito is so thoroughly sanitized and sanctified that we come to empathize with Michael Corleone when in reality we should condemn his ruthless immorality.[227] It also seems unlikely that Don Vito's sense of tradition or limit would have prevented him from entering the drug traffic: Coppola himself recognizes that mob bosses have lacked such scruples, and Puzo's novel is more realistic than the film in portraying Don Vito as a drug dealer.[228] For Pechter, as for Ferraro, *Godfather II* is by far the more romantic work, thanks mainly to its apparently absolute opposition between modernity and the ethnic past. Pechter claims that Michael Corleone's fall from grace necessitates the retrospective elevation of Don Vito into a 'pre-organization gallant bandit'; for Chown, the young Don Vito emerges as a pre-corporate 'Robin Hood' the sources of whose fortune remain conveniently concealed, and who continues to be sanctified notwithstanding his commission of two gruesome murders; and Ferraro questions the credibility of the portrayal of Don Vito's early family life in Little Italy as an idyll or 'romance' of a former ethnic solidarity.[229] This idyllic impression owes much to Gordon Willis's photography, which casts a warm and golden glow over the characters and settings.[230] Although Robert K. Johnson faults the film for its lack of verisimilitude more than for romanticization *per se*, he too notes the implausibility of the episodes depicting Don Vito, which present him as not so much cunning and coldly intelligent as almost simple-minded. Johnson further complains that during his return to Sicily Don Vito exacts an unlikely easy vengeance against a Mafia chieftain, improbably escapes the chieftain's villa after killing him, suffers no reprisals after returning to his native village, and then, with his family, departs the village for America without any apparent concern for his safety.[231]

However perceptive, these critics miss the crucial point that Coppola ironizes his own romanticism, and that his consciousness of the Mafia, ethnicity, and the family is subtly divided. The Sicilian and Little Italy episodes in *Godfather II* are thoroughly convincing if one regards them as Coppola intended, as Michael's vague and distortedly wishful recollections instead of literal representations of actual events. Robert Philip Kolker recognizes not only that the scenes of Don Vito's early career are self-consciously mythic and melodramatic, but that, as flashbacks, they are in large degree a 'subjective relation of Michael's wish-fulfilment fantasies, the content of the familial myth he carries with him.' This narrative method is anticipated in *Godfather I*, in which Michael's visit to Sicily, an affirmation of his familial and ethnic origins, is 'presented almost as a dream of the Don's.'[232] Suffused photographically as if with the golden glow of nostalgia, and laden with obvious implausibilities, Michael's 'reminiscences' less resemble an 'objective' recreation of an actual past than its imagined plenitude; they are the despairing attempt of the shattered Michael, musing in solitude on the autumnal shores of Lake Tahoe, to recapture an unattainable and perhaps non-existent ideal of paternal conduct and familial custom. Not for nothing do the Sicilian and Little Italy episodes intrude upon the more realistic style of the contemporary narrative with their uncanny folk-tale elements and figures: Fanucci, the ogre-like stage Italian, whose death is deserved and so brilliantly staged amid an already theatrical celebration of a street festival; the dapper thug Clemenza, who figures in *Godfather I* as a sort of male godmother, and who in the course of an evening casually introduces Vito Corleone into a life of crime by giving him a fabulous cache of stolen guns; the patriarchal Don Vito strolling at sunset amid the apparent *Gemeinschaft* of Little Italy, known and respected by all the members of the community, dispensing and receiving gifts and favours as if he were some feudal patriarch; his comical chastening of the Calabrian landlord, who would drive a helpless old lady from her apartment; his self-administered killing of Don Ciccio, the murderer of his mother; and finally, the lyrical family reunion, symbolizing the perfect plenitude of love and nourishment. How could Coppola not have recognized the ideality of these situations and images?

And yet, as John Paul Russo suggests, if Sicily is the imagined land of plenitude, it is also, paradoxically, the place of Vito Corleone's separation from his first family and real name. It was here that originary violence divorced Don Vito from the community, pledged him to vendetta, and directed him as if by fate towards his own violent career, mainly against Sicilian fellow ethnics. Noting that Coppola's characteristic mode of irony compels him to unmask false dichotomies, Paul Giles observes that in *The Godfather* series Sicily 'is not a place of pastoral calm, but equally as bloody as New York.'[233] Rather than portraying Sicily primarily as a *Gemeinschaft*, Coppola represents it in ways reminiscent of Edward Banfield's description of southern Italian society as characterized by 'amoral familism' and the Hobbesian war of all against all – socially atomized conditions diametrically opposed to the concept of *Gemeinschaft* as originally defined by Ferdinand Tönnies.[234] Undercutting the fantasy of plenitude of presence, Coppola emphasizes the final remoteness and even the inhumanity of the Godfather, whether as a person or paternal ideal. In *Godfather I*, moments before his death, Don Vito transforms himself playfully into an ogre and terrifies his young grandson. It is as if some unbidden revenant of the Sicilian past had sprung up from within the family's archetypal tomato garden. Yet the last scene of *Godfather II* is still more significant. Having enlisted in the Marines, and thus expressed an allegiance beyond his family, Michael sits alone (once more) in the family dining room, waiting for a father who never appears. This scene aptly symbolizes a division of generations and personalities that no fantasy of *Gemeinschaft* can ever dispel. Earlier Hollywood directors had sensed the conflict in the Italian American experience between the Old and New Worlds, state and family, family and mainstream, but none had even remotely approached Coppola's power of dramatization and depth of understanding.

Notes

Preface

1 Jacob Burckhardt, *The Civilization of the Renaissance in Italy*, trans. S.G.C. Middlemore (Vienna: Phaidon, 1937), 70.
2 Arthur James Whyte, *The Evolution of Modern Italy* (Oxford: Blackwell, 1950), 2.
3 Arnold J. Toynbee, *A Study of History* (London: Oxford Univ. Press, 1934–1961), 4:17, 275.
4 On the decline, see Robert Casillo, *The Empire of Stereotypes: Germaine de Stael and the Idea of Italy* (New York: Palgrave Macmillan, 2006), 4–11, 241–6nn.
5 Clemens Metternich, Richard Metternich-Winneburg, and Alfons de Klinkowstroem, *Mémoires, documents et écrits divers laissés par le prince de Metternich* (Paris: Plon, 1883), 7:415 (6 Aug. 1847).
6 Peter Burke, *The Historical Anthropology of Early Modern Italy* (Cambridge: Cambridge Univ. Press, 1987), 111, 112, 119; Gregory Hanlon, *Early Modern Italy, 1550–1800: Three Seasons in European History* (New York: St. Martin's Press, 2000), 323–5.
7 Thanks to studies by Armando Sapori, Enrico Fiumi, and Robert Lopez, the late medieval and Renaissance economy came to be viewed by many historians as sluggish and contracted owing to diminished incomes and dwindling investment opportunities. Such arguments, however, have been qualified or resisted by Carlo Cipolla, Fernand Braudel, Domenico Sella, Richard Goldthwaite, and Alison Brown. Most historians nonetheless agree that a long-term slump began in the early seventeenth century. See Carlo Cipolla, 'The Decline of Italy: The Case of a Fully Matured Economy,' *Economic History Review*, 2d new series, 5, no. 2 (1952); 178–87; *Before the Industrial Revolution: European Society and Economy, 1000–1700*, trans. Marcella Kooy

(New York: W.W. Norton, 1980), 236–44; Robert Lopez, 'Hard Times and Investment in Culture,' in *The Renaissance: A Symposium* (New York: Metropolitan Museum of Art, 1953), 19–34; Delio Cantimori, 'Il problema rinascimentale proposto da Armando Sapori,' in Cantimori, *Studi di storia*, vol. 2: *Umanesimo, Rinascimento, Riforma* (Turin: Einaudi, 1971), 372–8; Robert Lopez and Harry Miskimin, 'The Economic Depression of the Renaissance,' *Economic History Review*, 2d new series, 14, no. 3 (1962): 408–26; Domenico Sella, *Italy in the Seventeenth Century* (London: Longman, 1997), ix, 19–24, 24n, 29–49, 47n; Immanuel Wallerstein, *The Modern World System, I: Capitalist Agriculture and the Origins of the European World Economy in the Sixteenth Century* (New York: Academic Press, 1974), 81, 84, 216, 219–20, 219–20n; Ruggiero Romano, 'Italia nella crisi del secolo XVII,' *Studi storici*, 14 (1968): 723–41; Benjamin Z. Kedar, *Merchants in Crisis: Genoese and Venetian Men of Affairs and the Fourteenth-Century Depression* (New Haven: Yale Univ. Press, 1976), 16, 18–19, 88–90, 94; Fernand Braudel, *The Mediterranean and the Mediterranean World in the Age of Philip II*, vol. 1, trans. Siân Reynolds (New York: Harper and Row, 1966), 290–1, 320–1, 543–642; Braudel, *The Mediterranean*, vol. 2, trans. Siân Reynolds, 1240–2; Braudel, *Civilization and Capitalism: 15th–18th Century*, vol. 3: *The Perspective of the World* (New York: Harper and Row, 1982–4), 157, 164, 166–74; Braudel, *Out of Italy, 1450–1650*, trans. Siân Reynolds (Paris: Flammarion, 1989), 193, 201–6, 214–15, 218, 221–4; Judith C. Brown, 'Prosperity or Hard Times in Renaissance Italy?', *Renaissance Quarterly*, 42 (1989): 761–80; Richard A. Goldthwaite, *Wealth and the Demand for Art in Italy, 1300–1600* (Baltimore: Johns Hopkins Univ. Press, 1993), 14–67; Alison Brown, *The Renaissance* (New York: Longman, 1999), 18–19.

8 Frederic C. Lane, *Venice: A Maritime Republic* (Baltimore: Johns Hopkins Univ. Press, 1972), 388, 391; Braudel, *Out of Italy*, 223; Giuliano Procacci, *History of the Italian People*, trans. Anthony Paul (New York: Harper and Row, 1971), 158.

9 Overconsumption of costly art objects by Renaissance capitalists may have resulted from the absence of investment opportunities owing to a general market contraction, the long-term consequences being that, when such opportunities arose subsequently, sufficient capital was no longer available, as vast amounts of wealth had been immobilized or 'frozen' in imperishable cultural treasures. See Robert Lopez, *The Three Ages of the Italian Renaissance* (Charlottesville: Univ. of Virginia Press, 1970), 13–14; Carlo Cipolla, 'Economic Depression of the Renaissance?', *Economic History Review*, 16 (1963–64): 519–24; E.J. Hobsbawm, 'The Crisis of the Seventeenth Century,' in Trevor Aston, ed., *Crisis in Europe, 1560–1660* (New York: Doubleday, 1965), 19.

10 It has been assumed that the relocation to the countryside by Italian aristocrats and their bourgeois emulators reflected little more than their desire for a safe, static, unadventurous, comfortable, and hedonistic existence devoted solely to leisure, luxury, and other forms of social and economic parasitism. At least in the Venetian case, however, such ruralization was also motivated by a desire to capitalize agriculture in response both to a declining grain supply from abroad and large increases in the price of food. Thus the villas of the Veneto were not only palaces of pleasure (*delizie*) but working farms, where the two functions were inextricably combined. See Gino Luzzatto, *An Economic History of Italy from the Fall of the Roman Empire to the Beginning of the Seventeenth Century*, trans. Philip Jones (New York: Barnes and Noble, 1961), 145–6; Braudel, *The Mediterranean*, 1:78–80, 78n, 337–8, 598–9, and 2:726, 728; *Civilization and Capitalism: 15th–18th Century*, vol. 2: *The Wheels of Commerce*, trans. Siân Reynolds (New York: Harper and Row, 1982), 284–7; Lane, *Venice*, 306–7, 331; Harry Miskimin, *The Economy of Early Renaissance Europe, 1300–1460* (Englewood Cliffs: Prentice-Hall, 1969), 23, 72; James Ackerman, *The Villa: Form and Ideology of Country Houses* (Princeton: Princeton Univ. Press, 1985), 89, 92–5, 102–3, 105–6, 108; *Palladio* (Middlesex: Penguin, 1984), 47–54; Denis Cosgrove, *The Palladian Landscape: Geographical Change and Cultural Representations in Sixteenth-Century Italy* (University Park: Pennsylvania State Univ. Press, 1995), passim; Reinhard Bentmann and Michael Muller, *The Villa as Hegemonic Architecture* (Atlantic Highlands, NJ: Humanities Press, 1992), passim.

11 For the disputed concept of 'refeudalization,' see Sella, *Italy in the Seventeenth Century*, 63–9; Peter Burke, *The Italian Renaissance: Culture and Society in Italy* (Princeton: Princeton Univ. Press, 1986), 240–1; *The Renaissance* (Atlantic Highlands, NJ: Humanities Press, 1987), 53; Braudel, *Out of Italy*, 204–6; Dino Carpanetto and Giuseppe Ricuperati, *Italy in the Age of Reason, 1685–1789*, trans. Caroline Higgitt (London: Longman, 1987), 23, 38–44; Gregory Hanlon, *Human Nature in Rural Tuscany: An Early Modern History* (New York: Palgrave Macmillan, 2010), 31.

12 Carpanetto and Ricuperati, *Italy in the Age of Reason*, 34–5.

13 Paolo Balsamo, *Memorie economiche ed agrarie riguardanti il Regno di Sicilia* (1802), ctd in Gaetano Falzone, *La Sicilia tra il sette e l'ottocento* (Palermo: S.F. Flaccovio, 1965), 1:264–5. 'Many of Balsamo's observations,' comments Falzone, 'remained valid until the victory of the automonist regulations in 1947' (264). Cf. Ernesto Pontieri, *Il tramonto del baronaggio siciliano* (Florence: G.C. Sansoni, 1943), 9–10, 41, 55–6, 78; Gino Luzzatto, *An Economic History of Italy*, 165–7; and John Paul Russo, 'The Sicilian Latifundia,' *Italian Americana*, 17, no. 1 (1999): 40–57.

14 Although Burckhardt's pioneering *Civilization of the Renaissance in Italy*
(1860) implied that the Renaissance had significant scientific contributions
to its credit, he said relatively little on the subject, focusing on exploration,
geography, and nature study. However, early twentieth-century scientific
historians such as Lynn Thorndike and George Sarton (who later changed
his mind) argued influentially that the Renaissance, including humanism,
was either hostile to or else barren of science. Despite contrary arguments
by Leonardo Olschki and Ernst Cassirer, this view prevailed until the post-
war period, when it was challenged by Eugenio Garin, Paolo Rossi, Frances
Yates, Brian Copenhaver, and other scholars. As Garin contends, Renaissance humanism contributed to scientific advance through its recovery
of ancient texts, insistence upon textual accuracy and critical objectivity,
receptiveness to technology, hostility to Aristotelianism as against Platonism,
rejection of scholastic authority in favour of independent judgment, and
general concern for human agency and autonomy, including knowledge
and mastery of the environment. Just as Garin points out the close alliance
between Renaissance art and science, for instance in Leonardo and Alberti,
so Rossi notes the intimate cooperation of scientists and artisans in their
common quest for cognition and control over the world. Rossi also sees a
link between Renaissance science and occultism, with the former taking
inspiration from the latter even as it supersedes it methodologically, while
Frances Yates goes so far as to claim that Renaissance hermeticism and
neoplatonism played a major role in the development of science through
their fascination with magical control of an analogical universe ordered in
accordance with mathematical and numerological symbols – an argument
largely welcomed by Copenhaver, though received guardedly by Rossi, and
rejected by Mary Hesse and Brian Vickers. See Burckhardt, *Civilization of
the Renaissance*, 146–52; Ernst Cassirer, *The Individual and the Cosmos in Renaissance Philosophy*, trans. Mario Domandi (Oxford: Blackwell, 1963), vii–viii
(Introduction by Domandi), 56–7, 67, 81, 101–2, 142–5, 147–59, 161, 168,
169–91, and passim; Lynn Thorndike, *Science and Thought in the Fifteenth
Century: Studies in the History of Medicine and Surgery, Natural and Mathematical Science, Philosophy and Politics* (New York: Columbia Univ. Press, 1929),
12–13; George Sarton, 'Science in the Renaissance,' in J.W. Thompson, G.
Rowley, F. Schevill, and George Sarton, eds., *The Civilization of the Renaissance* (Chicago: Univ. of Chicago Press, 1929), 78–9; Wallace K. Ferguson,
The Renaissance in Historical Thought: Five Centuries of Interpretation (Boston:
Houghton Mifflin, 1948), 220–1, 338, 383–5; Frances Yates, *Giordano Bruno
and the Hermetic Tradition* (Chicago: Univ. of Chicago Press, 1964), passim,
esp. 190–431, 447–50; Marie Boas, *The Scientific Renaissance, 1450–1630* (New

York: Harper and Row, 1966), passim, esp. 18–19, 22–8, 43, 49, 51, 66, 68–9, 88, 134–7, 345; Eugenio Garin, *Italian Humanism: Philosophy and Civic Life in the Renaissance*, trans. Peter Munz (New York: Harper and Row, 1965), xii, xv–xvi (Introduction by Munz), 2, 3, 24–5, 186–96, 221–2; Garin, *Science and Civic Life in the Italian Renaissance*, trans. Peter Munz (New York: Doubleday, 1969), vii–xi, xiii–xiv, xvi–xxi (Introduction by Munz), 11, 15–16, 147–9; Paolo Rossi, *Francis Bacon: From Magic to Science*, trans. Sacha Rabinovitch (Chicago: Univ. of Chicago Press, 1968), x, xii, 9–10, 11–35, 54, 56–72; Rossi, *Philosophy, Technology, and the Arts in the Early Modern Era*, trans. Salvator Attanasio (New York: Harper and Row, 1970), x–xi, 1–62, 65, 66, 79–80, 112–16, 145, 146; J.R. Hale, *Renaissance Europe: Individual and Society, 1480–1520* (New York: Harper and Row, 1972), 314; Mary Hesse, 'Hermetics and Historiography: An Apology for the Internal History of Science,' in Robert H. Stuewer, ed., *Historical and Philosophical Perspectives of Science* (Minnesota Studies in the Philosophy of Science, 5) (Minneapolis: Univ. of Minnesota Press, 1970), 134–60; Robert S. Westman and J.E. McGuire, *Hermeticism and the Scientific Revolution* (Los Angeles: William Andrews Clark Library, Univ. of California Press, 1977); M.L. Righini Bonelli and William R. Shea, eds., *Reason, Experiment, and Mysticism in the Scientific Revolution* (New York: Science History Publications, 1975); Cesare Vasoli, 'The Contribution of Humanism to the Birth of Modern Science,' *Renaissance and Reformation*, n.s. 3 (1979): 1–15; Pamela O. Long, 'Humanism and Science,' in Albert Rabil, ed., *Renaissance Humanism: Foundations, Forms, and Legacy* (Philadelphia: Univ. of Pennsylvania Press, 1988), 3:486–91, 494–501, 505, 507n; Brian Vickers, 'Analogy versus Identity: The Rejection of Occult Symbolism, 1580–1680,' in Vickers, ed., *Occult and Scientific Mentalities in the Renaissance* (Cambridge: Cambridge Univ. Press, 1984), 95–163, esp. 149–56; Brian Copenhaver, 'Hermes Trismegistus, Proclus, and the Question of a Philosophy of Magic in the Renaissance,' in Ingrid Merkel and Allen G. Debus, eds., *Hermeticism and the Renaissance: An Intellectual History of the Occult in Early Modern Europe* (Washington, DC: Folger Shakespeare Library 1988), 79, 81, 83, 84, 93; David C. Lindberg, 'Conceptions of the Scientific Revolution from Bacon to Butterfield: A Preliminary Sketch,' in David C. Lindberg and Robert S. Westman, eds., *Reappraisals of the Scientific Revolution* (Cambridge: Cambridge Univ. Press, 1990), 8–11, 13–19.

15 John Addington Symonds, *Renaissance in Italy: The Catholic Reaction*, pt. 1 (New York: Henry Holt, 1887), 198–228; Sella, *Italy in the Seventeenth Century*, 213–38; Eric Cochrane, *Italy: 1530–1630* (London: Longman, 1988), 142–5, 152, 198, 201, 216, 218–19, 262, 268–9, 272, 281–3; Hiram Caton, *The Politics of Progress: The Origins and Development of the Commercial Republic, 1600–1835*

(Gainesville: Univ. of Florida Press, 1988), 53–4, 57–8, 60, 67, 72–6, 104, 116–18; H.G. Koenigsberger, 'Decadence or Shift? Changes in the Civilization of Italy and Europe in the Sixteenth and Seventeenth Centuries,' *Transactions of the Royal Historical Society*, 5th ser., vol. 10 (London: Royal Historical Society, 1960), 13.

16 Burckhardt, *Civilization of the Renaissance*, 242.

17 Benedetto Croce, *Storia dell'età barocca in Italia: Pensiero, poesia e letterature, vita morale* (Bari: Laterza, 1957), 14–16; Cochrane, *Italy*, 106–64; Peter Burke, *Popular Culture in Early Modern Europe* (New York: New York Univ. Press, 1978), 220–1, 271, 215–16; Christopher F. Black, *Early Modern Italy: A Social History* (London: Routledge, 2001), 183–7.

18 J.-C.L. Simonde de Sismondi, *Histoire des républiques italiennes du moyen age* (Paris: Furne, 1840), 10:370–4; Franco Venturi, 'History and Reform in the Middle of the Eighteenth Century,' in J.H. Elliott and H.G. Koenigsberger, eds., *The Diversity of History: Essays in Honor of Herbert Butterfield* (Ithaca: Cornell Univ. Press, 1970), 239; Giacomo Leopardi, *Zibaldone*, qtd in Roberto Melchioi, 'Commento,' in Leopardi, *Discorso sopra lo stato presente dei costumi degl'italiani*, ed. Maria Andrea Rigoni (Milan: Rizzoli, 1988), 97n; Francesco De Sanctis, *History of Italian Literature*, vol. 2, trans. Joan Redfern (New York: Basic Books, 1960), 622, 625, 627–8, 692, 715; Benedetto Croce, 'The Moral Life of Seventeenth Century Italy,' in Croce, *Philosophy, Poetry, History: An Anthology of Essays*, trans. Cecil Sprigge (London: Oxford Univ. Press, 1966), 1036–54; Angelo Ventura, *Nobiltà e popolo nella società veneta del '400 e '500* (Bari: Laterza, 1964), 367–71.

19 Braudel, *The Mediterranean*, 1:621–40; Braudel, *Out of Italy*, 218–9, 223; Lane, *Venice: A Maritime Republic*, 388; Samuele Romanin, *Storia documentata di Venezia*, vol. 7, 2d ed. (Venice: Pietro Naratovich, 1853–61; rpt., Venice: Giusto Fuga, 1912), 528–9.

20 The eclipse of the Mediterranean, and most especially of Venice, Italy's greatest maritime power of the Renaissance, was long thought to have occurred almost immediately following Vasco da Gama's circumnavigation of the Cape of Good Hope in 1498, which opened up a commercial route to India, and the news of which apparently plunged Venetian merchants into despair. However, historians since the mid-twentieth century have known that Venice was able to counteract the Portuguese challenge by around 1530, and that it was only in the early 1600s, partly as a result of competition with the Dutch and English, that the Venetian economy experienced a permanent decline, as did many other Mediterranean ports. See Pierre Daru, *Histoire de la république de Venise*, vol. 2, 4th ed. (Paris: Firmin Didot, 1853), 180; vol. 3, 39–41, 84–7, 95–6, 144; vol. 4, 161; William Carew Haz-

litt, *The Venetian Republic: Its Rise, Its Growth, and Its Fall* (London: A. and C. Black, 1900), 2:134–6, 180–1; Horatio Brown, *The Venetian Republic* (London: J.M. Dent, 1902), 137–9; Luzzatto, *An Economic History of Italy*, 151–5; Frederic C. Lane, 'Venetian Shipping during the Commercial Revolution,' in Lane, *Venice and History: The Collected Papers of Frederic C. Lane* (Baltimore: Johns Hopkins Univ. Press, 1966), 3, 10–15, 20–2; Lane, 'The Mediterranean Spice Trade: Its Revival in the Sixteenth Century,' in Lane, *Venice and History*, 25, 30–4; Lane, *Venice*, 285–94, 401–2; Domenico Sella, 'Crisis and Transformation in Venetian Trade,' in Brian Pullan, ed., *Crisis and Change in the Venetian Economy in the Sixteenth and Seventeenth Centuries* (London: Methuen, 1968), 88–105; Harry A. Miskimin, *The Economy of Later Renaissance Europe, 1460–1600* (Cambridge: Cambridge Univ. Press, 1977), 118–19, 145–6, 172; Braudel, *The Mediterranean*, 1:226, 290–1, 312, 320, 387, 391–3, 433, 437, 543, 554, 567; 2:893; Braudel, *Out of Italy*, 219.

21 Francesco Guicciardini, *The History of Italy*, trans. Sydney Alexander (New York: Macmillan, 1969), 7–72, 93, 118, 121, 135, 137–8, 152–5; Guicciardini, *The History of Florence*, trans. Mario Domandi (New York: Harper and Row, 1970), 174–7, 180–1; William Roscoe, *The Life and Pontificate of Leo X* (Philadelphia: E. Bronson, 1805), 1:204–7, 219–20, 224–5, 281, 316–17, 353, 385, 392, 407–8, 413; Sismondi, *Histoire des républiques italiennes*, 7:159–62, 286–7, 295, 345–55, 360–3, 385–7, 401, 470, 473, 475; 8:15, 43, 92–6, 135–6, 139, 145–6, 156–7, 159–61, 163–6, 168–9, 170–5, 177; Burckhardt, *Civilization of the Renaissance*, 23–4, 26, 49–51; Lacy Collison-Morley, *The Story of the Sforzas* (New York: E.P. Dutton, 1934), 192–258.

22 Notwithstanding that Machiavelli admired Pope Julius II for his impetuousness, and that Burckhardt, besides acknowledging his unsurpassed achievement as an art patron, regarded him as both the saviour and consolidator of the threatened papal states, many historians condemn his foreign policy as confused and contradictory, as witness his having invited the Spanish onto Italian soil after driving out the French, with whom he had previously allied against Venice. Pope Julius is also blamed for promoting the ecclesiastical indulgences soon to provide a major cause for the Protestant revolt. See Guicciardini, *History of Italy*, 197–203, 207–29, 230–277; Niccolò Machiavelli, *The Chief Works and Others*, trans. Allan Gilbert (Durham: Duke Univ. Press, 1965), Vol. 1 (*The Prince*), 46, 51–2, 91–2; (*The Discourses*) 523; Daru, *Histoire de la république de Venise*, 3:271–414; Jules Michelet, *Histoire de France*, vol. 7: *Renaissance* (Paris: Flammarion, 1893), 255–6; Burckhardt, *Civilization of the Renaissance*, 63–5; Ludwig Pastor, *The History of the Popes from the Close of the Middle Ages*, vol. 6, 3d ed., ed. Frederick Ignatius Antrobus (Kegan and Paul, Trench, and Trubner, 1901), 217, 232–3, 247–50, 252, 255–7, 290–301,

303–9, 311–20, 426; Federico Seneca, *Venezia e Papa Giulio II* (Padua: Liviana, 1962), passim; Myron Gilmore, *The World of Humanism, 1453–1517* (New York: Harper, 1952), 77–8; Barbara W. Tuchman, *The March of Folly: From Troy to Vietnam* (New York: Knopf, 1984), 91–103.

23 Roscoe, *Life and Pontificate of Leo X*, 1:77–8; 3:183–4; 4:291; John Addington Symonds, *Renaissance in Italy: The Age of the Despots* (New York: Henry Holt, 1886), 436; Symonds, *Renaissance in Italy: The Catholic Reaction*, pt. 1, 8; Ferdinand Gregorovius, *History of the City of Rome in the Middle Ages*, vol. 8, pt. 1, trans. Annie Hamilton (London: G. Bell, 1894–1902), 241–2; James Dennistoun, *Memoirs of the Dukes of Urbino, Illustrating the Arms, Arts, and Literature of Italy, 1440–1630* (London: J. Lane, 1909), 2:306–9; Tuchman, *The March of Folly*, 104–17.

24 From Guicciardini onward historians have seen Pope Clement VII as the victim of his own vacillating, untrustworthy, cryptic, impractical, and unrealistic personality. See Guicciardini, *History of Italy*, 338, 345–7, 360–3, 379–86; Burckhardt, *Civilization of the Renaissance*, 66–8; Gregorovius, *History of the City of Rome*, vol. 8, pt. 2, 701; E.R. Chamberlin, *The Sack of Rome* (London: B.T. Batsford, 1979), 43–9, 66–132; Tuchman, *The March of Folly*, 120–3, 125–6; Judith Hook, *The Sack of Rome*, 2d ed. (New York: Palgrave Macmillan, 2004), passim.

25 Angelo Ventura, *Nobiltà e popolo nella società veneta*, 3–5, 17, 29, 33–4, 39, 297, 300–30; Cosgrove, *The Palladian Landscape*, 49, 69, 90n; James S. Grubb, 'When Myths Lose Power: Two Decades of Venetian Historiography,' *Journal of Modern History*, 58, no. 1 (March 1986): 65.

26 Braudel, *The Mediterranean*, 1:165n; *Out of Italy*, 54–5; Felix Gilbert, 'Italy,' in Orest Ranum, ed., *National Consciousness, History, and Political Culture in Early Modern Europe* (Baltimore: Johns Hopkins Univ. Press, 1975), 33–4.

27 Giuseppe Brasacchio, ctd by Pino Arlacchi, *Mafia, Peasants and Great Estates: Society in Traditional Calabria*, trans. Jonathan Steinberg (Cambridge: Cambridge Univ. Press, 1983), 171.

28 Arlacchi, *Mafia, Peasants and Great Estates*, 172.

29 Although Gina Fasoli believes the myth of Venice to have existed as early as the ninth century, Franco Gaeta more credibly argues that its elements coalesced only in the later fifteenth and early sixteenth centuries. In the myth's initial honorific version, which the Venetians promulgated and which their Italian neighbours sometimes embraced, Venice was identified with perpetual political independence, a 'virgin' invulnerable to invasion, and freedom from internal strife. Subsequently Venice came to be praised by both the Venetians and other peoples as an ideal of balanced republican government, patrician *noblesse oblige*, sound and benevolent administration,

respect for the working classes however disenfranchised, and Venusian splendour. Indeed, in some quarters Venice was seen as the successor of ancient Rome, though in some ways greater. Concurrently, however, there also emerged a competing 'black' or counter myth whereby Venice was identified with oligarchical oppression of both the Doge and the lower orders, imperialistic megalomania in emulation of ancient Rome, terroristic and secretive government, commercial rapacity, the slave trade, colonial cruelties, prostitution, enervating luxury, clerical and monastic corruption, and other offenses. Generally speaking, Venice enjoyed a favourable reputation among most historians into the twentieth century, although the balance has shifted in the post-war period amid a wave of debunking, particularly of the aristocracy, now widely seen as licentious and irresponsible. See Machiavelli, *The Chief Works and Others*, 1 (*The Prince*), 46–50, 52, 78; (*Discourses*) 204–5, 207–8, 209, 210, 268–72, 297, 298–9, 310, 349–50, 380, 418, 458–60, 473–4; Machiavelli, *Florentine Histories*, trans. Laura F. Banfield and Harvey C. Mansfield, Jr (Princeton: Princeton Univ. Press, 1988), 40, 41–2, 89, 189, 253, 259–60, 297–8, 344, 345, 347–9; Guicciardini, *History of Italy*, 8, 30, 37, 76–86, 93, 118, 119, 120–1, 126, 135, 137, 138, 150, 191–203, 207, 208, 216, 221; Guicciardini, *History of Florence*, 6–9, 16–19, 27, 52–7, 61, 87, 98, 104, 112, 120, 151, 154, 157, 174, 175; Gasparo Contarini, *The Commonwealth and Government of Venice*, trans. Lewes Lewkenor (London: John Windet, 1599; rpt., Amsterdam: Theatrum Orbis Terrarum, 1969); Jean Bodin, *The Six Bookes of Commonweale*, trans. Richard Knolles, ed. Kenneth Douglas McRae (Cambridge: Harvard Univ. Press, 1962), 190–1, 221, 235, 249, 711, 785; Baron de Montesquieu, Charles Louis le Secondat, *The Spirit of the Laws*, trans. Thomas Nugent (New York: Hafner, 1949), bk. 5, chap. 8: 'In What Manner the Laws should relate to the Principle of Government in an Aristocracy,' 49–53; Pierre Daru, *Histoire de la republique de Venise*, vols. 1–7, passim; Sismondi, *Histoire des républiques italiennes*, 2:388–98; 3:229–43; 5:185, 443; 6:22–4, 156, 284, 286, 378, 415, 430–35, 458–61; 7:149–50, 177–8, 187–208, 307–8, 450–3; 8:43, 95, 96, 148, 278, 310–12, 331–3, 351–402, 413–89; Edward Smedley, *Sketches from Venetian History* (London: John Murray, 1831), vols.1–2, passim; Romanin, *Storia documentata di Venezia*, 6:67–83, 86–7, 92, 93, 96, 103, 107; Burckhardt, *Civilization of the Renaissance*, 12, 14, 35–41, 49; Symonds, *Renaissance in Italy: The Age of the Despots*, 55, 78, 79, 80, 91, 162, 195, 196, 197, 197n, 198, 202, 214–21, 232, 234–5, 234–5n, 245; Pasquale Villari, *Life and Times of Niccolò Machiavelli*, vol. 1, trans. Linda Villari (London: T.F. Unwin, 1892), 5, 40–8, 353–4, 358, 362–3; Ludwig Pastor, *History of the Popes*, vol. 2, 2d ed., ed. Frederick Ignatius Antrobus (Kegan and Paul, Trench, and Trubner, 1899), 66, 260–1, 279–81, 284–5, 295, 341, 385–6; Pastor, *History of the Popes*, vol. 3, 1st ed. (Kegan and Paul, Trench, and Trubner, 1894), 75–6, 84–5, 120, 126, 242–3, 315, 315n, 322–3, 343–4, 360–5, 366–7; Pastor, *History of the Popes*, vol. 6, 2d ed., ed. Frederick Ignatius Antrobus (Kegan and Paul, Trench, and Trubner, 1901), 232–3, 235–6, 247–75, 290–9, 300; Hazlitt, *Venetian Republic*, vol. 1, passim; Brown, *Venetian Republic*, 28–9, 65–7, 83, 87, 99, 101–4, 107, 111, 120–1, 137–40, 149–50; George B. McClellan, *The Oligarchy of Venice* (Boston: Houghton, Mifflin, 1904), passim; William Roscoe Thayer, *A Short History of Venice* (Boston: Houghton Mifflin, 1908), viii, ix, x, xi, 11–17, 18–19n, 28–9, 40–2, 48, 55–6, 72–3, 93, 97–9, 103–16, 122, 125–7, 164–72, 174, 178–82, 185–6, 190–9, 207–20, 225–9, 251, 267–83, 312; Gina Fasoli, 'Nascita di un mito,' in *Studi in onore di Gioacchino Volpe* (Florence: Sansoni, 1958), 1:447–74; Franco Gaeta, 'Alcune considerazioni sul mito di Venezia,' *Bibliothèque d'humanisme et Renaissance*, 23 (1961): 60–2, 64, 66–8, 71, 72; Franco Gaeta, 'L'idea di Venezia,' in *Storia della cultura veneta*, ed. Girolamo Arnaldo and Manlio Pastore Stocchi, vol. 3, pt. 3 (Vicenza: Neri Pozza, 1982), 565, 568, 570, 572–5, 578–4, 586–9, 591, 594–7, 599–601, 615, 617–34; Z.S. Fink, *The Classical Republicans: An Essay on the Recovery of a Pattern of Thought in Seventeenth-Century England* (Evanston: Northwestern Univ. Press, 1962), 19, 28–51, 53, 73, 73, 126, 130, 138, 177–83; Felix Gilbert, 'The Venetian Constitution in Florentine Political Thought,' in Gilbert, *History: Choice and Commitment* (Cambridge: Harvard Univ. Press, 1977), 179–214; Frederic C. Lane, 'The Enlargement of the Great Council of Venice,' in J.H. Rowe and W.H. Stockdale, eds., *Florilegium Historiale: Essays Presented to Wallace K. Ferguson* (Toronto: Univ. of Toronto Press, 1971), 237, 238, 241, 243, 245–8, 251–2, 268; Lane, *Venice*, 87–8, 100–1, 103–17, 151–2, 174, 220, 244, 248–9, 252–3, 257–8, 271; Brian S. Pullan, *Rich and Poor in Renaissance Venice: The Social Institutions of a Catholic State, to 1620* (Cambridge: Harvard Univ. Press, 1971), 3–5, 7–10, 19, 21, 24–27, 99–100, 103–8, 626–42; Innocenzo Cervelli, *Machiavelli e la crisi dello stato veneziano* (Naples: Guida, 1974), 74, 75, 77n, 122–4, 160–2, 175–9, 185–6, 305–7, 324–5, 331, 351–3, 362–4; Charles J. Rose, 'Marc Antonio Venier, Renier Zeno and the "Myth of Venice,"') *The Historian*, 36 (May 1974): 479–82; J.A. Pocock, *The Machiavellian Moment: Florentine Political Thought and the Atlantic Republican Tradition* (Princeton: Princeton Univ. Press, 1975), 1975), 100–2, 112–13, 255, 262, 271, 284–5, 317, 319–20, 324–5, 327–8, 333, 393; D.S. Chambers, *The Imperial Age of Venice, 1380–1580* (New York: Harcourt, Brace, Jovanovich, 1971), 29–30, 58–9, 66–7, 73, 75–93; Donald Queller, *The Venetian Patriciate: Reality versus Myth* (Urbana: Univ. of Illinois Press, 1986), ix, 3–28; William McNeill, *Venice: The Hinge of Europe, 1081–1797* (Chicago: Univ. of Chicago Press, 1974), 280–1n, 288–9n; Guido Ruggiero, *Violence in Early Renaissance*

Venice (New Brunswick: Rutgers Univ. Press, 1980), xiv, 4, 5, 55, 65–81; Eco O.G. Haitsma Mulier, *The Myth of Venice and Dutch Republican Thought in the Seventeenth Century,* trans. Gerard T. Moran (Assen, the Netherlands: Van Gorcum, 1980), 26–54; Edward Muir, *Civic Ritual in Renaissance Venice* (Princeton: Princeton Univ. Press, 1981), 5, 13–61; Margaret L. King, *Venetian Humanism in an Age of Patrician Dominance* (Princeton: Princeton Univ. Press, 1986), passim.

30 Although Venice has often been faulted for having increasingly neglected its traditional maritime interests as a result of its expansion onto the Italian mainland, an enterprise often attributed to imperialistic ambition and supposedly issuing in materialistic decadence, some scholars contend that the city had economic and political justification for doing so, while others believe that it ought to have protected its holdings with equal tenacity on land and sea. Not only did Venice need to increase its food supply after the closure of eastern markets by the Turks, but its patriciate was attracted by agricultural profits at a time of rising grain prices. The city was also forced by circumstance to secure its overland trade routes to northern Europe as well as to buffer itself against attack by Italian mainland states, especially Milan. See Daru, *Histoire de la république de Venise,* 2:177, 212–32, 283, 374; 3:24, 213; Michelet, *Histoire de France,* vol. 7: *Renaissance,* 248; Romanin, *Storia documentata di Venezia,* 5:150; 6:478, 480–1; Brown, *Venetian Republic,* 65–7; Francis Marion Crawford, *Salve Venetia* (London: 1905), 1:417–18, 444, 483, 489–90; Hazlitt, *Venetian Republic,* 2:101, 123, 132; Miskimin, *The Economy of Early Renaissance Europe, 1300–1460,* 23, 72, 78–9, 125; Lane, *Venice,* 228–9, 248–9, 305–7; Richard Tilden Rapp, *Industry and Economic Decline in Seventeenth-Century Venice* (Cambridge: Harvard Univ. Press, 1976), 144, 147; Cosgrove, *The Palladian Landscape,* 34–6, 40–8, 59.

31 Giulio Bollati, 'Fare l'Italia senza gli italiani: Il tentativo di Francesco Melzi d'Eril,' in Bollati, *L'italiano: Il carattere originale come storia e come invenzione* (Turin: Einaudi, 1983), 14–33.

32 Michael A. Ledeen, *The First Duce: D'Annunzio at Fiume* (Baltimore: Johns Hopkins Univ. Press, 1977).

33 Francesco De Sanctis, *Nuovi saggi critici* (Naples: Morano, 1911), 212–17. See also Francesco De Sanctis, *Storia della letteratura italiana,* ed. Niccolò Gallo (Milan: Mondadori, 1991), 530; and Francesco Guicciardini, *Maxims and Reflections of a Renaissance Statesman (Ricordi),* trans. Mario Domandi (Gloucester: Peter Smith, 1970), 48 (C 28), 58 (C 66), 59–60 (C 71).

34 Guicciardini, *Maxims and Reflections,* 39 (C 1), 48 (C 28).

35 De Sanctis, *Nuovi saggi critici,* 224. In a late *ricordo,* included during the siege of Florence in 1530, Guicciardini concedes: 'it sometimes happens that

fools [*pazzi*] do greater things than wise men [*savii*]' (*Maxims and Reflections*, 75 [C 136]).

36 Benedetto Croce, 'Italian Decadence,' in Croce, *Philosophy, Poetry, History: An Anthology of Essays*, trans. Cecil Sprigge (London: Oxford Univ. Press, 1966), 1029. Cf. 'E l'Italia sarebbe morta, ed ella non morì,' Benedetto Croce, *Storia dell' età barocca in Italia*, 5th ed. (Bari: Laterza, 1946), 44.

37 H. Stuart Hughes, *The United States and Italy*, 3d ed. (Cambridge: Harvard Univ. Press, 1979), 42; Mario Praz, 'Art and Letters in Italy,' in Guy Metraux and Francois Crouzet, eds., *The Nineteenth-Century World* (New York: New American Library, 1963), 437.

38 Writing in the mid-sixteenth century, Marcellino Alberini observed that 'only Venice, which maintains both the form and the reputation of a republic, preserves the honor of Italy.' Ctd in Hook, *The Sack of Rome*, 291. However, Venice's weakened political situation after 1530 sometimes prevented it from living up to its reputation as the last asylum of Italian liberty. Not only did it refuse to antagonize the Hapsburg Empire by tracking down its paid assassins of Lorenzino de' Medici, who was murdered for political reasons in Venice in 1548, but in 1592 Venice bowed to papal pressure by turning over to the Church the political refugee Giordano Bruno, who had been targeted as a heretic, and who was burned at the stake in Rome in 1600. Nor was the Venetian press entirely free of interference from the Holy Inquisition, despite the policy of the Venetian state of subordinating the Church to its own authority. See Michelet, *Histoire de France*, vol. 7: *Renaissance*, 247–8; Symonds, *Renaissance in Italy: The Catholic Reaction*, pt. 1, 9, 51, 190–3, 388–405; Horatio Brown, *The Venetian Printing Press, 1469–1800: An Historical Study based upon Documents for the Most Part Hitherto Unpublished* (London: John C. Nimmo, 1891; rpt., Amsterdam: Gerard Th. Van Heusden, 1969), vii, 40–1, 50–1, 60, 67, 73, 77, 79–80, 89, 92–5, 99–100, 109–10, 122–3, 126–8, 132, 135–43, 145, 147–151, 153–73; Pierre Gauthiez, *Lorenzaccio (Lorenzino de Medicis): 1514–1548* (Paris: Fontemoing, 1904), 238, 332, 346, 357–66; Paul Grendler, 'The Roman Inquisition and the Venetian Press, 1540–1605,' *Journal of Modern History*, 47, no. 1 (March 1975): 48–65; Cochrane, *Italy*, 64–5, 97, 167, 179, 254.

39 J.R. Hale, *England and the Italian Renaissance: The Growth of Interest in Its History and Art* (London: Faber and Faber, 1954), 29–36, 41; Mulier, *The Myth of Venice in Dutch Republican Thought*, passim; Franco Gaeta, 'Alcune considerazioni sul mito di Venezia,' 70–2; Pocock, *Machiavellian Moment*, 285, 321, 324–5, 391–4, 442, 535; Jeanne Clegg, *Ruskin and Venice* (London: Junction, 1981), 13–15.

40 Hanlon, *Early Modern Italy*, 271–82.

41 Aurelio Lepre, *Storia del Mezzogiorno d'Italia, Vol. 2: Dall'antico regime alla società borghesia (1657–1860)* (Naples: Liquori, 1986), 90–1, 93, 97–104; Procacci, *History of Italian People*, 192–7; Carpanetto and Ricuperati, *Italy in the Age of Reason*, 18–19, 61–6, 73, 108–13, 147–9, 154–6, 179–88, 236–48, 250–8; Tommaso Astarita, *Between Salt Water and Holy Water: A History of Southern Italy* (New York: W.W. Norton, 2005), 205–19; Girolamo Imbruglia, ed., *Naples in the Eighteenth Century: The Life and Death of a Nation State* (New York: W.W. Norton, 2005).

42 Brendan Dooley, 'The Public Sphere and the Organization of Knowledge,' in John Marino, ed., *Early Modern Italy, 1550–1796* (Oxford: Oxford Univ. Press, 2002), 209–28; Procacci, *History of Italian People*, 178–9, 216–17; Krystyna Von Henneberg and Albert Russell Ascoli, 'Introduction: Nationalism and the Uses of Risorgimento Culture,' in Ascoli and von Henneberg, eds., *Making and Remaking Italy: The Cultivation of National Identity around the Risorgimento* (Oxford: Berg, 2001), 10.

43 Adam Wandruszka, *Pietro Leopoldo: Un grande riformatore* (Florence: Vallechi, 1968), passim.

44 Hanns Gross, *Rome in the Age of the Enlightenment: The Post-Tridentine Syndrome* (Cambridge: Cambridge Univ. Press, 1990), 175–213, esp. 195, 213.

45 On the question of Napoleon's impact on Italy, see Desmond Gregory, *Napoleon's Italy* (Madison, NJ: Fairleigh Dickinson Univ. Press, 2001), 45–79, 119–43, 144–91; Procacci, *History of Italian People*, 207–9; Luigi Salvatorelli, *The Risorgimento: Thought and Action*, trans. Mario Domandi (New York: Harper and Row, 1971), xvii, 61–8; Harry Hearder, *Italy in the Age of the Risorgimento, 1790–1870* (London: Longman, 1970), 21–30, 163–4; Michael Broers, *The Napoleonic Empire in Italy, 1796–1814: Cultural Imperialism in a European Context?* (New York: Palgrave Macmillan, 2005), passim.

46 Udo Kultermann, *The History of Art History* (Norwalk: Abaris, 1993), 135–7; Sacheverell Sitwell, *Southern Baroque Art: A Study of Painting, Architecture and Music in Italy and Spain of the 17th and 18th Centuries* (New York: Knopf, 1924); Sitwell, *Baroque and Rococo* (New York: Putnam, 1967), 1–132.

47 Eric Bentley, foreword to *The Genius of the Italian Theater*, ed. Bentley (New York: New American Library, 1964), v; in the same volume, see Gordon Craig, 'Carlo Goldoni,' 538–41.

48 Cornelius Conyn, *Three Centuries of Ballet* (Houston: Elsevier, 1953), 24, 26, 35–6, 41, 44–5; Ferdinando Reyna, *A Concise History of Ballet* (New York: Grosset and Dunlap, 1964), passim; Mary Clarke and Clement Crisp, *Ballet: An Illustrated History* (New York: Universe, 1973), 23–30, 42, 45, 48–51, 64, 96–8, 112; Adrian Stokes, *To-Night the Ballet* (New York: E.P. Dutton, 1935), passim.

49 Richard Taruskin, *Music in the Seventeenth and Eighteenth Centuries* (London: Oxford Univ. Press, 2010), 216. Vivaldi was 'a major spur to the so-called "postwar Baroque boom"': his concerti 'have significance in the history of the twentieth century's musical life as well as the eighteenth's' (217).

50 John Rosselli, 'Italian Opera Singers on a European Market,' in Shearer West, ed., *Italian Culture in Northern Europe in the Eighteenth Century* (Cambridge: Cambridge Univ. Press, 1999), 161.

51 Braudel, *The Mediterranean*, 2:894, 1240; cf. 1:604; Braudel, *Out of Italy*, 7, 10–17. Cf. E.J. Hobsbawm, 'Notes,' *Past and Present*, 39 (1968): 174. 'The moral of the story,' comments Braudel elsewhere, 'is that a loss is never the result of a single throw – nor indeed is a triumph. Success depends on seizing the opportunities of a given period, on doing so time and time again, and piling advantage on advantage ... "Growth breeds growth," a country develops because it is already developing, because it is caught up in a movement already under way which helps it. So the past always counts. The inequality of the world is the result of structural realities at once slow to take shape and slow to fade away' (*Civilization and Capitalism: 15th–18th Century*, 3:50).

52 Braudel, *Out of Italy*, 17. 'His twenty-seven *drammi per musica* and other theatre works were given more than a thousand musical settings in the eighteenth century, some of them being set to music as many as seventy times' (Donald Jay Grout and Hermine Weigel Williams, *A Short History of Opera*, 4th ed. [New York: Columbia Univ. Press, 2003], 207). His libretti were adopted by over 250 composers, including Handel (three), Vivaldi (three), Mozart (three), and Gluck (nineteen).

53 Matteo Ricci, *Lettere* (1580–1609), ed. Piero Corradini e Francesco D'Arelli (Macerata: Quodlibet, 2001); Riccardo Scartezzini, 'L'innesto della cultura rinascimentale europea in un contesto confuciano,' Aldo Caterino, 'La generazione dei giganti. Geografi e astronomi gesuiti in Cina,' and Elisabetta Corsi, 'La missione dei gesuiti in Cina tra evangelizzazione e mediazione culturale nella prima età moderna,' in Antonio Paolucci and Giovanni Morello, eds., *Ai crinali della storia. Padre Matteo Ricci (1552–1610) fra Roma e Pechino* (Turin: Umberto Allemandi, 2009), 36–43, 63–93, 94–105; Toby E. Huff, *Intellectual Curiosity and the Scientific Revolution* (Cambridge Univ. Press, 2011), 72–5, 78, 82–3, 266; Francesco Antonio Gisondi, *Michele Ruggeri S.J.: Missionario in Cina, primo sinologo europeo e poeta 'cinese' (Spinazzola 1543–Salerno 1607)* (Milan: Jaca, 1999).

54 For the Grand Tour, see William Edward Mead, *The Grand Tour in the Eighteenth Century* (Boston: Houghton Mifflin, 1914); Christopher Hibbert, *The Grand Tour* (New York: Putnam, 1969); Cesare de Seta, *L'Italia del Grand*

Tour: Da Montaigne a Goethe (Naples: Electa, 1992); Jeremy Black, *The British Abroad: The Grand Tour in the Eighteenth Century* (New York: St. Martin's Press, 1992); Attilio Brilli, *Il viaggio in Italia: Storia di una grande tradizione culturale* (Bologna: Il Mulino, 2008).

55 James Boswell, *Life of Johnson*, ed. R.W. Chapman (London: Oxford Univ. Press, 1970), 742.

56 Charles C.F. Greville, *A Journal of the Reign of Queen Victoria from 1852 to 1860*, *The Greville Memoirs*, pt. 3 (3 vols.), ed. Henry Reeve (New York: Appleton, 1887), 3:263.

57 Lacy Collison-Morley, *Italy after the Renaissance: Decadence and Display in the Eighteenth-Century* (New York: Henry Holt, 1930), 108, 120–1; Garin, *Science and Civic Life*, 85–6; Rosario Villari, *Elogio della dissimulazione: La lotta politica nel seicento* (Bari: Laterza, 1987); Paul Rahe, *Republics Ancient and Modern: Classical Republicanism and the American Revolution* (Chapel Hill: Univ. of North Carolina Press, 1992), 238–9; Jon R. Snyder, *Dissimulation and the Culture of Secrecy in Early Modern Europe* (Berkeley: Univ. of California Press, 2009).

58 Leopardi, *Discorso*, 58–67.

59 Garrett Mattingly, *Renaissance Diplomacy* (Boston: Houghton Mifflin, 1955), passim; Ludwig Dehio, *The Precarious Balance: Four Centuries of European Power Struggle*, trans. Charles Fullman (New York: Random House, 1962), 24–6. Dehio implies the key role of diplomacy in preserving the system of the balance of power for which the major Italian states provided the model for Europe.

60 Obit., *Time*, 8 Dec. 1952, 33; Thomas A. Bailey, *Woodrow Wilson and the Lost Peace* (Chicago: Quadrangle, 1963), 159; Alan Sharp, *The Versailles Settlement: Peacemaking in Paris, 1919* (New York: St. Martin's Press, 1991), 186; Margaret MacMillan, *Paris 1919: Six Months that Changed the World* (New York: Random House, 2002), 279, 292; Spencer Di Scala, *Vittorio Emanuele Orlando* (London: Haus, 2010), 136–9.

61 Jeffrey M. Perl, *The Tradition of Return: The Implicit History of Modern Literature* (Princeton: Princeton Univ. Press, 1984), 10–11, 60.

62 For a sampling of views on these issues, see Federico Chabod, 'The Concept of the Renaissance,' in Chabod, *Machiavelli and the Renaissance*, trans. David Moore (London: Bowes and Bowes, 1958), 149–200; Ferguson, *The Renaissance in Historical Thought*, passim; Denys Hay, *The Italian Renaissance in Its Historical Background* (Cambridge: Cambridge Univ. Press, 1961), 13, 14, 25; Hay, 'Historians and the Renaissance during the Last Twenty-Five Years,' in Audre Chastel, ed., *The Renaissance: Essays in Interpretation* (London: Methuen, 1982), 1–5; *Europe in the Fourteenth and Fifteenth Centuries* (London:

Longman, 1993), 170–1, 374; David Herlihy, 'Family Solidarity in Medieval Italian History,' in David Herlihy, Robert S. Lopez, and Vsevolod Slessarev, eds., *Economy, Society, and Government in Medieval Italy: Essays in Memory of Robert L. Reynolds* (Kent: Kent State Univ. Press, 1969), 173–84; Richard A. Goldthwaite, *Private Wealth in Renaissance Florence: A Study of Four Families* (Princeton: Princeton Univ. Press, 1968), 3, 28–9, 251–75; Marvin Becker, 'Individualism in the Early Italian Renaissance: Burden and Blessing,' *Studies in the Renaissance*, 19 (1972): 274–5 and passim; Michele Ciliberto, *Il Rinascimento: Storia di un dibattito* (Florence: La Nuova Italia, 1975), 11–17, 19–21, 23–7, 31–2, 43–5, 48–53; and passim; Gene Brucker, 'Bureaucracy and Social Welfare in the Renaissance: A Florentine Case Study,' *Journal of Modern History*, 55, no. 1 (1983): 1–21; Burke, *The Italian Renaissance*, 1–2; John Stephens, *The Italian Renaissance: The Origins of Intellectual and Artistic Change before the Reformation* (London: Longman, 1990), 119–21; Alison Brown, 'Introduction' to Brown, ed., *Language and Images of Renaissance Italy* (Oxford: Clarendon, 1995), 7–23; Jack Goody, *Capitalism and Modernity: The Great Debate* (Malden, MA: Polity, 2004), 16, 36, 51–3, 74, 103, 148, 155.

63 Allan Bloom, *The Closing of the American Mind* (New York: Simon and Schuster, 1967), 63; Burke, *The Italian Renaissance*, 1–2.

64 Virginia Woolf, 'Mr. Bennett and Mrs. Brown' (pamphlet) (London: Hogarth, 1924), 4. Although Woolf does not refer to the exhibition itself within her essay, she had it in mind, as it was held at the Grafton Gallery in London in 1910.

65 Toynbee, *A Study of History*, 4:275; cf. 1:19; 3:350–63. Toynbee outlines three 'Italistic' ages in the West: (1) *Roman:* 'the inhabitants of Italy exhibited a pre-eminent energy and creative power during a period of some four centuries running from about the fourth to the last century B.C.' (4:16); (2) *Late medieval and early Renaissance:* 'a period of some six centuries running from the eleventh to the sixteenth century of the Christian Era' (4:16); 'the Italians insulated themselves from the rest of Western Christendom and then worked out a new and higher form of Western culture which inaugurated a fresh chapter in Western history when it was imparted to the Transalpine "barbarians" in due course' (4:17; cf. 3:345–6; 8:102); (3) *'Modern'* (5:637–8): 'the unrivalled creativity of Italy in the fourteenth and fifteenth centuries was thus the original driving force behind the movement of Western Civilization during a span of four ensuing centuries which, on this account, might aptly be called our "Italistic Age"' (4:275); 'the effect of the radiation is sometimes popularly described as "the Renaissance"; but, in application to Transalpine Europe, the expression is misleading. For it was a mimesis of contemporary Italian culture, and not a recapture of some temporarily lost or submerged element in its own Transalpine

social heritage, that was the real secret of the sudden advance in civilization that was accomplished in Transalpine Europe at this date' (4:275n;
cf. 3:375). In 1939, when volume 4 of *A Study of History* appeared, Toynbee
gave 'our "Italistic Age"' as '*circa* A.D. 1475–1875' (4:275n); in 1961, with
the publication of the final volume, he offered 'alternative' dates for the
'breakdown of Western Civilization': the beginning of World War I in 1914,
and the end of World War II with the dropping of the atom bomb in 1945
(12:522). Toynbee's dates for the initial phase of decline are usually 'early,'
marking the point at which a culture first begins to dissipate its most creative and spiritual energies, though political or cultural hegemony might
continue for centuries afterwards. He stipulates a 'transition' period 'from
the Modern Age to that "post-modern" epoch in which we find ourselves
living today' (5:638). Toynbee's concept of the 'post-modern,' a term which
he is sometimes seen as having originated, and which refers to the current
'post-Italistic' age, closely resembles what Geoffrey Barraclough terms 'contemporary' as opposed to 'modern' history (*An Introduction to Contemporary
History* [Harmondsworth: Penguin, 1967]).

66 Alessandro Manzoni, 'Marzo 1821,' in *Liriche e tragedie*, ed. Vladimiro
   Arangio-Ruiz (Turin: UTET, 1951), 1:101.

67 R.J.B. Bosworth, *Italy, The Least of the Great Powers: Italian Foreign Policy before
   the First World War* (Cambridge: Cambridge Univ. Press, 1979).

68 Thomas Sowell, *Ethnic America: A History* (New York: Basic Books, 1981),
   100, 105; Humbert S. Nelli, *From Immigrants to Ethnics: The Italian Americans*
   (New York: Oxford Univ. Press, 1983), 19, 29–35, 39–43; Rudolf J. Vecoli,
   'The Coming of Age of the Italian Americans, 1945–1974,' *Ethnicity*, 5
   (1978): 119, 122.

69 Emilio Sereni, *Il capitalismo nelle campagne (1860–1900)* (Turin: Einaudi,
   1968), 351.

70 Nelli, *From Immigrants to Ethnics*, 19–29, 56–9; Humbert S. Nelli, 'Italians,'
   in *Harvard Encyclopedia of American Ethnic Groups*, ed. Stephan Thernstrom
   (Cambridge: Harvard Univ. Press, 1980), 548–50; Donna Gabaccia, *From
   Sicily to Elizabeth Street: Housing and Social Change among Italian Immigrants,
   1880–1930* (Albany: State Univ. of New York Press, 1984), 54; Vecoli, 'The
   Coming of Age of Italian Americans,' 123–4.

71 Henry J. Browne, 'The "Italian Problem" in the Catholic Church of the
   United States, 1880–1900,' *Historical Records and Studies* (United States
   Catholic Historical Society), 35 (1946): 46–72; Rudolf J. Vecoli, 'Prelates
   and Peasants: Italian Immigrants and the Catholic Church,' *Journal of Social
   History*, 2 (Spring 1969): 217–68; Leonard Covello, *The Social Background of
   the Italo-American School Child: A Study of the Southern Italian Family Mores and
   Their Effect on the School Situation in Italy and America* (Totowa, NJ: Rowman

and Littlefield, 1972), 103–45, 278; Mary Elizabeth Brown, 'Religion,' in Salvatore LaGumina, Frank J. Cavaioli, Salvatore Primeggia, and Joseph A. Varacalli, eds., *The Italian American Experience: An Encyclopedia* (New York: Garland Press, 2000), 538–542.

72 Joseph Lopreato, *Italian Americans* (New York: Random House, 1970), 14–15, 59–60, 78–9, 87; Covello, *The Social Background of the Italo-American School Child*, 1, 149–238, 279–81; Richard Gambino, *Blood of My Blood: The Dilemma of Italian Americans* (New York: Doubleday, 1975), 1–41; Virginia Yans-McLaughlin, *Family and Community: Italian Immigrants in Buffalo, 1880–1930* (Urbana: Univ. of Illinois Press, 1982), 18–24, 34, 36, 48, 52–4, 61–2; Nelli, *From Immigrants to Ethnics*, 43–6, 131–50.

73 Emanuel Carnevali, 'The Return,' in *The Autobiography of Emanuel Carnevali*, ed. Kay Boyle (New York: Horizon, 1967), 201.

74 Herbert J. Gans, *The Urban Villagers: Group and Class in the Life of Italian-Americans* (Glencoe: Free Press, 1965), 199–226; Nelli, *From Immigrants to Ethnics*, 145–8, 173–4; Covello, *The Social Background of the Italo-American School Child*, 241–329; Gambino, *Blood of My Blood*, 37, 38, 89, 91, 257, 264–5; Robert Orsi, *The Madonna of 115th Street: Faith and Community in Italian Harlem* (New Haven: Yale Univ. Press, 1985), 98–9; William S. Engelman, 'Education: Sociohistorical Background,' in La Gumina et al., *The Italian American Experience*, 193–8. John Briggs believes that the Italian immigrants' dis-esteem of education has been much exaggerated (*An Ethnic Passage: Immigrants to Three American Cities, 1890–1930* [New Haven: Yale Univ. Press, 1978], 22–7, 53–5, and passim).

75 Lopreato, *Italian Americans*, 40–2; Nelli, *Italians in Chicago, 1889–1930: A Study in Ethnic Mobility* (New York: Oxford Univ. Press, 1970), 152–3; Nelli, *From Immigrants to Ethnics*, 59; Alexander DeConde, *Half Bitter, Half Sweet: An Excursion into Italian-American History* (New York: Scribner's, 1974), 113.

76 Alba, *Italian Americans*, 9; Nelli, *From Immigrants to Ethnics*, 59–60, 173–93.

77 Irvin L. Child, *Italian or Italian American?: The Second Generation in Conflict* (New Haven: Yale Univ. Press, 1943), passim; Covello, *The Social Background of the Italo-American School Child*, 333–46; Orsi, *Madonna of 115th Street*, 107–29; Jerre Mangione and Ben Morreale, *La Storia: Five Centuries of the Italian-American Experience* (New York: HarperCollins 1992), 215–19.

78 Gambino, *Blood of My Blood*, 122; Nelli, *From Immigrants to Ethnics*, 171.

79 Phyllis H. Williams, *South Italian Folkways in Europe and America* (New Haven: Yale Univ. Press, 1938), 13; Gans, *Urban Villagers*, 90–7, 91n, 100, 102, 105–9, 120–1, 163, 203; Lopreato, *Italian Americans*, 106, 113–15; Alba, *Italian Americans*, 51; Nelli, *From Immigrants to Ethnics*, 96–113.

80 Gans, *Urban Villagers*, 163, 164, 281–304; Gerald D. Suttles, *The Social Order*

of the Slum: Ethnicity and Territory in the Inner City (Chicago: Univ. of Chicago Press, 1968), 100–2.

81 Rudolf J. Vecoli, 'Italian Immigrant Working Class Movements in the United States: A Personal Reflection on Class and Ethnicity,' *Journal of the Canadian Historical Association*, 4 (1993): 299–303; Lopreato, *Italian Americans*, 95–7, 106–7; Nelli, *From Immigrants to Ethnics*, 90–3, 101, 115–18; Gambino, *Blood of My Blood*, 110–11, 115–18; Edwin Fenton, *Immigrants and Unions, A Case Study: Italians and American Labor, 1870–1920* (New York: Arno, 1975); Paul Avrich, *Sacco and Vanzetti: The Anarchist Background* (Princeton: Princeton Univ. Press, 1996); Michael Miller Topp, *Those Without a Country: The Political Culture of Italian American Syndicalists* (Minneapolis: Univ. of Minnesota Press, 2001); Philip V. Cannistraro and Gerald Meyer, eds., *The Lost World of Italian American Radicalism: Politics, Labor, and Culture* (Westport: Praeger, 2003).

82 Ctd in Kevin Sack, 'The Supreme Court; Clinton and "Justice Cuomo": The Real Thing, or Just Talk?' *New York Times*, 20 March 1993.

83 Caesar's famous phrase was originally uttered in Greek and was quoted by him from Menander (Plutarch, *Pomp.* 60, 4). A long-standing crux in classical scholarship, the phrase was given by Suetonius as *alea iacta est*, the die is cast (*Caes.* 32). However, we adopt the translation from Menander favoured by Matthias Geizer in the English translation of his *Caesar: Politician and Statesman*, trans. Peter Needham (Cambridge: Harvard Univ. Press, 1968), 193–4.

84 John Paul Russo, 'DeLillo: Italian American Catholic Writer,' *Altreitalie*, 25 (2002): 4–29.

85 Alba, *Italian Americans*, 159.

86 Herbert J. Gans, 'Symbolic Ethnicity: the Future of Ethnic Groups and Cultures in America,' *Ethnic and Racial Studies*, 15, no. 2 (1979): 173. Cf. Herbert J. Gans, *Popular Culture and High Culture: An Analysis and Evaluation of Taste* (New York: Basic Books, 1974), 102; and Alba, *Italian Americans*, 172.

1 Stendhal and Italy

1 Stendhal, *Private Diaries of Stendhal*, ed. and trans. Robert Sage (New York: Doubleday, 1954), 513, 535; henceforth given as PD in the notes. All other citations of works by Stendhal are indicated in the notes by the following abbreviations – AC: *The Abbess of Castro and Other Tales* (translation of *Chroniques italiennes*), trans. C.K. Scott Moncrieff (New York: Boni, 1926); CP(ENG): *The Charterhouse of Parma* (translation of *La Chartreuse de Parme*), trans. C.K. Scott Moncrieff (New York: Liveright, 1925); CP(FR): *La Chartreuse de Parme*, ed. Michel Crouzet (Paris: Garnier-Flammarion, 1967); EIP: *Écoles italiennes de peinture* (3 vols.), ed. Henri Martineau (Paris: Divan,

1932); JI: *Journal d'Italie*, ed. Paul Arbelet (Paris: Calmann Levy, 1911); HP: *Histoire de la peinture en Italie* (Paris: Calmann-Lévy, 1904); L: *Love* (translation of *De L'Amour*), trans. Gilbert and Suzanne Sale (Harmondsworth: Penguin, 1975); LHB: *The Life of Henry Brulard* (translation of *La vie de Henri Brulard*), trans. Jean Stewart and B.C.L.G. Knight (Chicago: Univ. of Chicago Press, 1958); LHMM: *Lives of Haydn, Mozart, and Metastasio* (translation of *Vies de Haydn, de Mozart et de Metastase*), trans. Richard N. Coe (London: Calder and Boyars, 1972); LL: *Lucien Leuwen* (bk. 1), *The Green Huntsman* (translation of *Lucien Leuwen*), trans. Louise Varese (New York: New Directions, 1950); ME: *Memoirs of an Egotist* (translation of *Souvenirs d'égotisme*), trans. T.W. Earp (New York: Noonday, 1958); MT: *Memoirs of a Tourist* (translation of *Mémoires d'un touriste*), trans. Alan Seeger (Evanston: Northwestern Univ. Press, 1962); PI: *Pages d'Italie*, ed. Henri Martineau (Paris: Divan, 1932); R: *Life of Rossini*, trans. Richard N. Coe (New York: Orion, 1970); RJ: *A Roman Journal* (translation of *Promenades dans Rome*, 1827 ed.), trans. Haakon Chevalier (New York: Orion, 1957); RNF: *Rome, Naples and Florence* (translation of *Rome, Naples et Florence [1826]*, trans. Richard N. Coe (London: George Braziller, 1959); RNF1817: *Rome, Naples et Florence en 1817*, in Stendhal, *Voyages en Italie*, ed. Vittorio del Litto (Paris: Gallimard, 1996); RS: *Racine and Shakespeare* (translation of *Racine et Shakespeare*), trans. Guy Daniels (New York: Crowell-Collier, 1962); SJ: *Selected Journalism from the English Reviews*, ed. and trans. Geoffrey Strickland (New York: Grove Press, 1959); THF: *To the Happy Few: Selected Letters of Stendhal*, ed. Robert Sage, trans. Norman Cameron (New York: Grove, 1952); TSF: *Travels in the South of France*, trans. Elizabeth Abbot (London: Calder and Boyars, 1971).

2 LHB 22, 58, 70, 129, 146, 158–9, 286, 306, 307, 319. For Stendhal's knowledge of Italian authors, see Vittorio del Litto, *La vie intellectuelle de Stendhal* (Grenoble: Presses Universitaires de France, 1959), 23–5, 52–5, 88–93, 130, 243–8, 305, 319, 426. Stendhal had no knowledge of Italian before his first visit to Italy in 1800, at the age of seventeen.

3 THF 133; PD 513; JI 305.

4 Richard N. Coe, Translator's Foreword, in RNF xvi.

5 RNF 143; ME 143; JI 118. On Stendhal's identification with Italy, see Michel Crouzet, *Stendhal et l'italianité: essai de mythologie romantique* (Paris: Jose Corti, 1982), 9, 11.

6 Del Litto, *La vie intellectuelle de Stendhal*, 422–3, and esp. 548, citing *Rome, Naples et Florence (1826)*. See also RNF1817 139.

7 Rene Girard, *Deceit, Desire, and the Novel*, trans. Yvonne Freccero (Baltimore: Johns Hopkins Univ. Press, 1965), 14; Michel Crouzet, 'Stendhal et le "coup de poignard" italien,' in Massimo Colesanti, Anna Jeromidis, Letizia Norci

Cagiano, and Maria Scaiola, eds., *Stendhal, Roma, l'Italia* (Roma: Edizioni di Storia e Letteratura, 1985), 234.

8 Paul Hazard, *Stendhal*, trans. Eleanor Hard (New York: Coward McCann, 1929), 121, 140–2; Margaret Tillett, *Stendhal: The Background to the Novels* (London: Oxford Univ. Press, 1971), 48–9.

9 RNF 2; RJ 69; THF 180; Francesco Novati, *Stendhal e l'anima italiana* (Milano: L.F. Cogliati, 1915), 91–2; Armand Caroccio, *Variétés stendhaliennes* (Grenoble-Paris: B. Arthaud, 1946), 207; Luigi Barzini, *The Italians* (London: Atheneum, 1964), 29, 38. In RJ 84, Stendhal claims to have had a friendly conversation with a *pifferaro*, a lower-class type. In any case he was probably correct that English visitors to Italy kept to themselves. See RNF 125, 236n; RJ 294; RNF1817 80; H. Neville Maugham, ed., *The Book of Italian Travel (1580–1900)* (London: Grant Richards, 1903), 36; William Edward Mead, *The Grand Tour in the Eighteenth Century* (Boston: Houghton Mifflin, 1914), 128; John Pemble, *The Mediterranean Passion: Victorians and Edwardians in the South* (New York: Oxford Univ. Press, 1987), 261, 268; Louis Turner and John Ash, *The Golden Hordes: International Tourism and the Pleasure Periphery* (New York: St. Martin's, 1976), 38–9; Herbert Barrows, 'Convention and Novelty in the Romantic Generation's Experience of Italy,' in Warner G. Rice, ed., *Literature as a Mode of Travel: Five Essays and a Postscript* (New York: New York Public Library, 1963), 74, 80, 82; Jacob Korg, *Browning and Italy* (Athens, OH: Ohio Univ. Press, 1983), 6, 84, 85, 93; Edmund Swinglehurst, *The Romantic Journey: The Story of Thomas Cook and Victorian Travel* (New York: Harper and Row, 1974), 40; C.P. Brand, *Italy and the English Romantics: The Italian Fashion in Early Nineteenth-Century England* (Cambridge: Cambridge Univ. Press, 1957), 12, 15, 22; Maxine Feifer, *Tourism in History: From Imperial Rome to the Present* (New York: Stein and Day, 1985), 96; Lynne Withey, *Grand Tours and Cook's Tours: A History of Leisure Travel, 1750 to 1915* (New York: William Morrow, 1994), 90, 92–4, 357n; Lord Byron, quoted in Oreste del Buono, 'L'eterno mistero della zuppa inglese,' in Oreste del Buono, Gherardo Frassa, and Luigi Settembrini, *Gli Anglo-Fiorentini: una storia d'amore* (Florence: Edifir, 1987), 15; see also 16, 18, 24. Lord Byron, whom Stendhal claimed to have met, enjoyed associating with Italians. See Francesco Viglione, *L'Italia nel pensiero degli scrittori inglesi* (Milano: Fratelli Bocca, 1946), 382–3. According to John Pemble, English writers and other visitors to Italy became more inclined to mix with Italians by the mid-nineteenth century. See Pemble, *The Mediterranean Passion*, 97, 98,128, 133, 134, 135. Perhaps because of a common Latinity, eighteenth-century French travellers were more open than the English to the Italians. See Brian Moloney, *Florence and England: Essays on Cultural Relations in the Second Half of the*

Eighteenth Century (Florence: Olschki, 1969), 16, 19, 20, 26, 46, 156. British travellers cannot be blamed entirely for failing to mingle with the Italians, as local society was often closed to foreign visitors, who complained of the virtual absence of dinner parties. See Withey, *Grand Tours*, 25; Lacy Collison-Morley, *Italy after the Renaissance: Decadence and Display in the Seventeenth Century* (New York: Henry Holt, 1934), 26; Christopher Hibbert, *The Grand Tour* (New York: Putnam, 1969), 116, 123; Robert Casillo, *The Empire of Stereotypes: Germaine de Staël and the Idea of Italy* (New York: Palgrave Macmillan, 2006), 309–10n. For some instances in which foreign travellers (including Hester Thrale Piozzi and Thomas Adolphus Trollope) mixed with Florentines, see Clara Louise Dentler, *Famous Foreigners in Florence, 1400–1900* (Florence: Bemporad Marzocco, 1964), 32, 38, 45, 48, 225, 247, 250–1, 264. In L 26, Stendhal observes that 'it takes years to penetrate intimately into Italian society.' See also PI 224–5.

10 René Dollot, *Stendhal, journaliste* (Paris: Mercure de France, 1948), 258, 258n; René Girard, 'Tocqueville and Stendhal,' *The Magazine of the American Society of the Legion of Honor*, 31, 2 (1960): 74–5.

11 Luigi Foscolo Benedetto, *Arrigo Beyle milanese: bilancio del stendhalismo italiano a cent'anni dalla morte dello Stendhal* (Florence: Sansoni, 1942), 310–11; Novati, *Stendhal e l'anima italiana*, 2–3, 5, 8, 11, 12, 29, 31, 96–7, 101–3; Harry Levin, *Toward Stendhal* (Murray, UT: Pharos, Winter, no. 3, 1945), 12–13; Benedetto Croce, 'Stendhal,' in Croce, *Philosophy, Poetry, History: An Anthology of Essays*, trans. Cecil Sprigge (London: Oxford Univ. Press, 1966), 935; Richard N. Coe, Introduction to RNF, xxi; Robert Alter, *A Lion for Love: A Critical Biography of Stendhal* (New York: Basic Books, 1979), 142; Victor Brombert, *Stendhal: Fiction and the Themes of Freedom* (New York: Random House, 1968), 133; Charles Dédéyan, *L'Italie dans l'oeuvre romanesque de Stendhal* (Paris: Société d'édition d'enseignement supérieur, 1963), 1:223. See also Carlo Sforza, *The Real Italians: A Study in European Psychology* (New York: Columbia Univ. Press, 1942), 79.

12 Italo Calvino, 'Guide to *The Charterhouse of Parma*,' in Calvino, *The Uses of Literature* (New York: Harcourt, Brace, Jovanovich, 1986), 260. See also Dollot, *Stendhal, journaliste*, 259–60.

13 RNF 466; Bernard Wall, *A City and a World: A Roman Sketch Book* (New York: W.W. Norton, 1962), 60.

14 Hazard, *Stendhal*, 141. According to Crouzet, who focuses on the elements of myth and fantasy in Stendhal's *italianité*, his Italian writings are located '*sur la frontière*' between '*récit et de l'expérience.*' See Crouzet, *Stendhal et l'italianité*, 3; also 2, 30–1, 182–3, 350–1.

15 Jules Bertaut, *L'Italie vue par les Français* (Paris: Librairie des Annales Poli-

tiques, n.d.), 236–7; JI, vi–viii; Brombert, *Stendhal*, 132; Charles Eliot Norton, *Letters of Charles Eliot Norton*, vol. 1, ed. Sara Norton (Boston and New York: Houghton Mifflin, 1913), 372; Barzini, *The Italians*, xv. See also Sforza, *The Real Italians*, 78–9. Despite their originality, Stendhal's Italian writings are indebted to eighteenth- and early nineteenth-century French travel writers. See Jean-Luc Seylaz, 'Une fiction stendhalienne: La France du touriste,' in Colesanti et al., eds., *Stendhal, Roma, l'Italia*, 502; Crouzet, *Stendhal et l'italianité*, 4–10, 50–3n, and passim; Brombert, *Stendhal*, 132.

16 William Johnston, *In Search of Italy: Foreign Writers in Northern Italy since 1800* (University Park, PA: Penn State Univ. Press, 1987), 5, 83, 188.

17 Cesar Graña, *Bohemian versus Bourgeois: French Society and the French Man of Letters in the Nineteenth Century* (New York: Basic Books, 1964), passim.

18 Vito Carofiglio, 'Selvaggi, Turchi e intellettuali: Il sud "napoletano" di Stendhal,' in Colesanti et al., *Stendhal, Roma, L'Italia*, 383, quoting *Rome, Naples et Florence*.

19 Graña, *Bohemian versus Bourgeois*, 112; THF 273.

20 Marigay Graña, Preface to Cesar Graña and Marigay Graña, eds., *On Bohemia: The Code of the Self-Exiled* (New Brunswick, NJ: Transaction, 1990), xvi.

21 Like Stendhal, Tocqueville is troubled by mass democracy in its egalitarian levelling, declining standards of culture and political leadership, and sacrifice of liberty to equality. Just as, for both writers, liberty promotes strong individuality and passionate ambitions, so the extension of equality has led to conformity and mediocrity enforced through the tyrannical power of public opinion. At the same time, the decline of liberty under modern democracy results from the increasing organization of society under a centralizing state dominated by the middle class and its values. See Alan S. Kahan, *Aristocratic Liberalism: The Social and Political Thought of Jacob Burckhardt, John Stuart Mill, and Alexis de Tocqueville* (New York: Oxford Univ. Press, 1992), 4–6, 8, 12, 14–33, 34–92; Geoffrey Strickland, *Stendhal: The Education of a Novelist* (Cambridge: Cambridge Univ. Press), 114, 277n; Girard, *Deceit, Desire, and the Novel*, 64–5, 120, 136–7; Girard, 'Tocqueville and Stendhal,' 73–83; Hayden White, *Metahistory: The Historical Imagination in Nineteenth-Century Europe* (Baltimore: Johns Hopkins Univ. Press, 1973), 191–229.

22 Crouzet, *Stendhal et l'italianité*, passim; Dennis Porter, 'Politics, Happiness, and the Arts: A Commentary on Stendhal's *Rome, Naples et Florence en 1817*,' *French Studies*, 24 (July 1970): 254–7. Citing Peter Gay and Mattei Calinescu, Marshall Berman rejects Graña's view of the Bohemians as thoroughly anti-modern. See Berman, *All That Is Solid Melts in the Air: The Experience of Modernity* (New York: Simon and Schuster, 1982), 134–5. In the period

between 1815 and 1848, artistic avant-gardism tended to go hand in hand with both social and political radicalism and Romantic individualism. See Donald Drew Egbert, *Social Radicalism and the Arts: Western Europe: A Cultural History from the French Revolution to 1968* (New York: Alfred A. Knopf, 1970), 118.

23 Leon Blum, 'A Theoretical Outline of Beylism,' in *Stendhal: Twentieth-Century Views,* ed. Victor Brombert (Englwood Cliffs: Prentice Hall, 1962), 101–13; Crouzet, *Stendhal et l'italianité,* 23–4, 30–1.

24 RJ 6; Dennis Porter, *Haunted Journeys: Desire and Transgression in European Travel Writing* (Princeton: Princeton Univ. Press, 1991), 140, 164; 'Reinventing Travel: Stendhal's Roman Journey,' *Genre,* 16 (Winter 1983): 468–73. However, Porter shows that Stendhal rejects the rationalism, didacticism, pedantry, and imperialist fascination of earlier travel writers in favour of his own rebellious, anti-patriarchal cult of hedonism and emotional spontaneity. In this he resembles Goethe, Staël, Byron, and Shelley. See also Turner and Ash, *Golden Hordes,* 45–6; Camillo Von Klenze, *From Goethe to Hauptmann: Studies in a Changing Culture* (New York: Viking, 1926), 3–64.

25 RNF 244.

26 However, Turner and Ash note that many Romantics viewed Italy in ways foreshadowing Westerners' attitudes towards the Third World. See Turner and Ash, *Golden Hordes,* 45–6.

27 RJ 50; JI 238, 267; R 43; PD 456; RNF 207, 384.

28 Raymond Williams, *Keywords* (New York: Oxford Univ. Press, 1976), 57–60; Sheldon Rothblatt, *Tradition and Change in English Liberal Education: An Essay in History and Culture* (London: Faber and Faber, 1976), 17–21; Lucien Febvre, 'Civilization: Evolution of a Word and a Group of Ideas,' in Febvre, *A New Kind of History and Other Essays,* ed. Peter Burke, trans. K. Folca (New York: Harper, 1973), 220–1, 223–9; Michael Timko, 'The Victorianism of Victorian Literature,' *New Literary History,* 6 (1975): 607–27.

29 Norbert Elias, *The Civilizing Process: A History of Manners,* vol. 1, trans. Edmund Jephcott (New York: Urizen Books, 1978), 1–157; Elias, *Power and Civility: The Civilizing Process,* vol. 2, trans. Edmund Jephcott (New York: Pantheon, 1982), passim. See also John Murray Cuddihy, *The Ordeal of Civility: Freud, Marx, Lévi-Strauss and the Jewish Struggle for Modernity* (New York: Basic Books, 1974), 10–14 and passim; John Stuart Mill, 'Civilization: Signs of the Times,' *Westminster Review,* 25 (April 1836): 1–28, reprinted in Mill, *Essays on Politics and Society,* vol. 20 of *The Collected Works of John Stuart Mill,* ed. J.M. Robson (Toronto: Univ. of Toronto Press, 1977), 119–47. C. Stephen Jaeger argues that Elias underestimates the role of educational ideals and especially medieval German culture in the development of civilization. See Jaeger,

The Origins of Courtliness: Civilizing Trends and the Formation of Courtly Ideals, 939–1210 (Philadelphia: Univ. of Pennsylvania Press, 1985), 5–8, 139–40, 212–13, 257–9, 265, and passim. For criticism of Jaeger's argument, see Aldo Scaglione, *Knights at Court: Chivalry and Courtesy from Ottonian Germany to the Italian Renaissance* (Berkeley: Univ. of California Press, 1991), 7, 12–13, 22, 57, 59–63, 68, 230, 309–10, 346n, and passim.

30 Huizinga, *The Waning of the Middle Ages: A Study of the Forms of Life, Thought, and Art in France and the Netherlands in the Dawn of the Renaissance* (New York: Doubleday, 1954), 9–29, 50–5, esp. 23, 24, 26. For qualifications of Huizinga's argument, see J.R. Hale, 'Violence in the Late Middle Ages: A Background,' 25–6, and Werner L. Gundersheimer, 'Crime and Punishment in Ferrara, 1440–1500,' 104, 105, 106–8; both essays in Lauro Martines, ed., *Violence and Civil Disorder in Italian Cities* (Berkeley: Univ. of California Press, 1972). See also Pompeo Molmenti, *Venice: Its Individual Growth from the Earliest Beginnings to the Fall of the Republic*, Part 1: *The Middle Ages*, vol. 2, trans. Horatio F. Brown (Chicago: A.C. McClurg, 1906), 60.

31 On vengefulness in medieval society, see Marc Bloch, *Feudal Society*, 125–6; qtd in V.G. Kiernan, *The Duel in European History: Honour and the Reign of Aristocracy* (Oxford: Oxford Univ. Press, 1988), 32.

32 On the importance of the press, see Alexis de Tocqueville, *Democracy in America*, vol. 2, ed. Phillips Bradley (New York: Alfred A. Knopf, 1980), 111–14.

33 Graña, *Bohemian versus Bourgeois*, 188.

34 Mihály Szegedy-Maszák, 'The Idea of National Character: A Romantic Heritage,' in Peter Boerner, ed., *Concepts of National Identity: An Interdisciplinary Dialogue* (Baden-Baden: Nomos Verlagsgesellschaft, 1966), 46–8, 50; Peter Mandler, *The English National Character: The History of an Idea from Edmund Burke to Tony Blair* (New Haven: Yale Univ. Press, 2006), 18–25. For criticism and defense of Elias's concept of civilization, see Jack Goody, *The Theft of History* (Cambridge: Cambridge Univ. Press, 2006), 154–79, 185, 241, 279; Chris Rojek, *Decentring Leisure: Rethinking Leisure Theory* (London: Sage, 1995), 52–3; Rojek, *Capitalism and Leisure Theory* (London: Tavistock, 1985), 158–72; Eric Dunning, 'The Figurational Approach to Leisure and Sport,' in Chris Rojek, ed., *Leisure for Leisure: Critical Essays* (New York: Routledge, 1989), 36–44.

35 HP 45–6; Bram Kempers, *Painting, Power, and Patronage: The Rise of the Professional Artist in the Italian Renaissance*, trans. Beverley Jackson (London: Penguin, 1992), 9, 213, 215, 239, 241, 307–8, and passim; Peter Burke, *The Italian Renaissance: Culture and Society in Italy* (Princeton: Princeton Univ. Press, 1986), 196, 200, 200n, 211–12; Peter Burke, *Popular Culture in Early*

Modern Europe (New York: New York Univ. Press, 1978), 23–4, 270–3, 275–6; Peter Burke, *The Art of Conversation* (Ithaca: Cornell Univ. Press, 1992), 89–90, 98–108, 115; Peter Burke, 'The Language of Gesture in Early Modern Italy,' in Burke, *Varieties of Cultural History* (Ithaca: Cornell Univ. Press, 1987), 66, 70, 72–3. However, Goldthwaite cautions against seeing Renaissance courts as a strict pattern for the French monarchical court, as there was great diversity among them. See Goldthwaite, *Wealth and the Demand for Art in Italy, 1300–1600* (Baltimore: Johns Hopkins Univ. Press, 1993), 170–5, 245–6, 254. Arnold Hauser underestimates the originality of the Italian Renaissance courts. See Hauser, *The Social History of Art*, vol. 2: *Renaissance, Mannerism, Baroque*, trans. Stanley Goodman (New York: Alfred A. Knopf, n.d.), 48.

36   Marvin B. Becker, *Civility and Society in Western Europe, 1300–1600* (Bloomington: Indiana Univ. Press, 1990), xi–xxii, 10, 12–13, 22, 29–30, 34–5, 38, 55, 61, 66, 77–8, 80–3, 92, 98, 99; Becker, 'An Essay on the Quest for Identity in the Early Italian Renaissance,' in J.G. Rowe and W.H. Stockdale, eds., *Florilegium historiale: Essays presented to Wallace K. Ferguson* (Toronto : Univ. of Toronto Press, 1971), 295–312; Burke, *Italian Renaissance*, 213–15; Burke, *The Historical Anthropology of Early Modern Italy: Essays in Perception and Communication* (Cambridge: Cambridge Univ. Press, 1987), 39, 110–12, 115, 119; Daniel Philip Waley, *The Italian City-Republics*, 3d ed. (London: Longman, 1988), 32–68; J.K. Hyde, *Society and Politics in Medieval Italy: The Invention of the Civil Life* (London: MacMillan, 1983), 94, 115, 154, 166–7, and passim. Machiavelli's anecdote concerning the extremely coarse behaviour of Castruccio Castracani (1281–1328), lord of Lucca, suggests the low level of social refinement during the later Middle Ages. See Niccolò Machiavelli, *The Life of Castruccio Castracani*, in Machiavelli, *The Chief Works and Others*, trans. Allan Gilbert (Durham: Duke Univ. Press, 1965), 2:556–7.

37   Robert D. Putnam, with Robert Leonardi and Raffaella Y. Nanetti, *Making Democracy Work: Civic Traditions in Modern Italy* (Princeton: Princeton Univ. Press, 1993), 83–162 and passim. Putnam attributes the impressive recent civic performance of northern Italy as against the much poorer showing of southern Italy to the superior civic culture of the north extending from the later Middle Ages, when the Italian republican communes arose and flourished, into modernity. Some historians find Putnam's 'path dependency' model too deterministic, while others argue that he fails to specify the mechanism by which to explain the durability of civic attitudes and institutions over centuries of foreign domination. Putnam has also been faulted not only for exaggerating the resemblances between medieval and Renaissance communes and more egalitarian modern democracies, but for

underestimating civic institutions and initiatives in southern Italy. Another complaint is that, contrary to Putnam's attribution of Italy's civic deficiencies partly to Catholic hierarchism and authoritarianism, the Church actually helped to promote *civitas* during the Middle Ages and Renaissance. For other historians, Putnam neglects the more recent cultural forces that have largely determined regional disparities in civic performance, and that lie not in civic culture but in politics and economics. Still other scholars question the very antithesis between a civic northern Italy and an antisocial south. There is, however, some support for Putnam's 'path dependence' model in writings by Michael Broers, Carlo Tullio-Altan, Carlo Sforza, and Domenico Romagnosi. See Sidney Tarrow, 'Making Social Science Work across Space and Time: A Critical Reflection on Robert Putnam's *Making Democracy Work*,' *American Political Science Review*, 90 (June 1996): 389–97; Paolo Feltrin, 'La tradizione civica nelle regioni italiana' (review of *Making Democracy Work*), *Rivista italiana di scienza politica*, 24 (April 1994): 169–72; Leonardo Morlino, review of *Making Democracy Work*, *Journal of Democracy*, 6, no. 1 (1995): 173–7; Per Mouritsen, *What's The Civil in Civil Society? Robert Putnam's Italian Republicanism* (Florence: Badia Fesolana, 2001), 2–5, 11–12; Arnaldo Bagnasco, 'Regioni, tradizioni civiche, modernizzazione italiana: con commento alla ricerca di Putnam,' *Stato e Mercato*, 40 (April 1994): 93–103, esp. 97, 99, 100; Jonathan Morris, 'Challenging Meridionalism: Constructing a New History of Southern Italy,' in Robert Lumley and Jonathan Morris, eds., *The New History of the Italian South: The Mezzogiorno Revisited* (Exeter: Univ. of Exeter Press, 1997), 9–11; John A. Marino, 'The Rural World in Italy under Spanish Rule,' in Thomas James Dandelet and John A. Marino, eds, *Spain in Italy: Politics, Society, and Religion, 1500–1700* (Leiden: Brill, 2007), 412; the following essays in *Politics and Society*, 24 (March, 1996): Ellis Goldberg, 'Thinking about how Democracy Works,' 7–18; Filippo Sabetti, 'Path Dependency and Civic Culture: Some Lessons from Italy about Interpreting Social Experiments,' 19–44; and Margaret Levi, 'Social and Unsocial Capital: A Review Essay of Robert Putnam's *Making Democracy Work*,' 44–5; the following essays in *Polis*, 8 (August 1994): Gianfranco Pasquino, 'La politica eclissata dalla tradizione civica,' 307–11; Samuel K. Cohn, 'La storia secondo Robert Putnam,' 315–24; and Robert D. Putnam, 'Lo storico e l'attivista,' 325–8; Loredana Sciolla, *Italiani: stereotipi di casa nostra* (Bologna: Mulino, 1997), passim; Michael Broers, *The Napoleonic Empire in Italy, 1796–1814: Cultural Imperialism in a European Context?* (New York: Palgrave MacMillan, 2005), 8, 16–17, 26–7, 36–7, 38, 234, 294; Carlo Tullio-Altan, *Una nazione senza religione civile: le ragioni di una democrazia incompiuta* (Udine: Istituto Editoriale Veneto Fruliano, 1995), 65; Sforza, *The Real*

Italians, 1, 2–3, 16–18, 27; Adrian Lyttelton, 'Creating a National Past: Italy, Myth, and Image in the Risorgimento,' in Albert Russell Ascoli and Krystyna von Henneberg, eds., *Making and Remaking Italy: The Cultivation of National Identity around the Risorgimento* (Oxford: Berg, 2001), 44.

38 Lewis Einstein, *The Italian Renaissance in England* (New York: Columbia Univ. Press, 1903), 60–1, 81–2; Ruth Kelso, *The Doctrine of the English Gentleman in the Sixteenth Century*, vol. 16, nos. 1–2 in University of Illinois Studies in Language and Literature, Feb.–May 1929 (Urbana: Univ. of Illinois Press, 1929), 13, 49–50, 51–2, 81–8, 119.

39 A. Lytton Sells, *The Paradise of Travellers: The Italian Influence on Englishmen in the Seventeenth Century* (Bloomington, Indiana: Indiana Univ. Press, 1963), 148, 148n, 159, 167–8, 219, 227.

40 Braudel, *Out of Italy: 1450–1650*, trans. Sian Reynolds (Paris: Flammarion, 1989), 161; Ludwig Pastor, *The History of the Popes from the Close of the Middle Ages*, vol. 5, 1st ed., ed. Frederick Ignatius Antrobus (London: Kegan and Paul, Trench, and Trübner, 1894), 32; Thomas Frederick Crane, *Italian Social Customs of the Sixteenth Century and Their Influence on Europe* (New Haven: Yale Univ. Press, 1920), vii, 1–2, 436–8, 437–8n. Although Burke concedes that the French salon was adumbrated in the Italian Renaissance courts, he contends not only that the Italians failed to follow up these initiatives, but that the French salons associated with Madame de Rambouillet, Madame de Sablé, Madame de Scudéry, and Madame de Lafayette represent an original social formation, in which men and women met on roughly equal terms. According to Gregory Hanlon, the French salon was introduced into Italy during the War of the Spanish Succession. See Burke, *Art of Conversation*, 89–90, 98–105, 113, 115–17; Gregory Hanlon, *Early Modern Italy, 1550–1800: Three Seasons in American History* (New York: St. Martin's Press, 2000), 319; John Addington Symonds, *Renaissance in Italy: The Revival of Learning* (New York: Henry Holt, 1908), 34.

41 Joseph [Giuseppe] Baretti, *An Account of the Manners and Customs of Italy; with Observations on the Mistakes of Some Travellers, with Regard to that Country*, vol. 2, 1st ed. (London: T. Davies, 1768), 172. In *An Account of the Manners and Customs of Italy; with Observations on the Mistakes of Some Travellers, with Regard to that Country*, vol. 1, 2d ed. (London: T. Davies, 1769), 294, Baretti seems to imply French and English superiority in manners.

42 Becker, *Civility and Society in Western Europe*, xx, 1, 94–6, 102–5, 140–1.

43 Hyde, *Society and Politics in Medieval Italy*, 141–52, 178–9, 186; Waley, *Italian City-Republics*, 158–72.

44 Burke, *Italian Renaissance*, 215–6; Ronald Weissman, 'Taking Patronage Seriously: Mediterranean Values and Renaissance Society,' in F.W. Kent

and Patricia Simons, eds., *Patronage, Art, and Society in Renaissance Italy* (Canberra: Humanities Research Center, 1987), 27–33 and passim; Becker, *Civility and Society in Western Europe*, 94–6; Putnam, *Making Democracy Work*, 134–7; Burke, *Historical Anthropology of Early Modern Italy*, 122–4; Anne Jacobson Schutte, 'Religion, Spirituality, and the Post-Tridentine Church,' in John Marino, ed., *Early Modern Italy, 1550–1796* (New York: Oxford Univ. Press, 2002), 128–9; Rosario Villari, *The Revolt of Naples*, trans. James Newell (Cambridge: Polity Press, 1993), 1–2; Hanlon, *Early Modern Italy*, xii, 252–3. According to recent estimates, economic and cultural decline set in not in the early 1500s, as was long believed, but by around 1650. See Braudel, *Out of Italy*, 204–5, 213, 221–4, 226; Braudel, *The Mediterranean and the Mediterranean World in the Age of Philip II*, vol. 1, trans. Sian Reynolds (New York: Harper and Row, 1972), 872–3, 1240–2; Guido Quazza, *La decadenza italiana nella storia europea: Saggi sul Sei-Settecento* (Turin: Einaudi, 1971), passim; Eric Cochrane, Introduction to Cochrane, ed., *The Late Italian Renaissance, 1525–1630* (New York: Harper and Row, 1970), 7–18; Cochrane, *Italy, 1530–1630* (New York: Longman, 1988), 2–3 (Introduction by Julius Kirchner), 33–54, 106–64, and passim; Domenico Sella, *Italy in the Seventeenth Century* (London: Longman, 1997), 19–69 and passim; Casillo, *Empire of Stereotypes*, 4–11. Although Croce complained of seventeenth-century Italy's ethical failings, he acknowledged as did Burckhardt that the Counter-Reformation saved the Catholic Church. Subsequently M. Petrocchi insisted upon the religious fervour of the Counter-Reformation, and more recently Christopher F. Black has emphasized its role in strengthening Italian parish life, in demanding stricter discipline from the clergy, and in greatly improving religious education. See Croce, *Storia dell'età barocca in Italia: Pensiero, Poesia e Letteratura: Vita Morale* (Bari: Laterza, 1957), 14–5; Burckhardt, *The Civilization of the Renaissance in Italy*, trans. S.C.G. Middlemore (London: Phaidon, 1937), 242; Guido Quazza, 'Dall'età barocca' alla ricerca delle forze,' in Quazza, *La decadenza italiana*, 18–9; M. Petrocchi, *La Controriforma in Italia* (Rome: Anonima Veritas Editrice, 1947), 3–38 and passim; Christopher F. Black, *Early Modern Italy: A Social History* (London: Routledge, 2001), 11–12, 167–187.

45 Burke, *Italian Renaissance*, 212; Burke, *Historical Anthropology of Early Modern Italy*, 9; Werner Gundersheimer, *Ferrara: The Style of a Renaissance Despotism* (Philadelphia: Univ. of Pennsylvania Press, 1968), 197, 199–201, 200n; William Roscoe, *The Life and Pontificate of Leo the Tenth* (Philadelphia: Bronson, 1805), 3:294–5. The behaviour of Caterina Sforza during the siege of Forlì in 1488 exemplifies what later periods came to regard as the comparative indecorousness of the Renaissance. See Francesco Guicciardini, *The History*

of Italy, trans. Sidney Alexander (New York: Macmillan, 1968), 152n; J.-C.-L Simonde de Sismondi, *Histoire des républiques italiennes du moyen age* (Paris: Furne, 1840), 7:251; Charles Yriarte, *Cesare Borgia,* trans. William Sterling (London: Francis Aldor, 1947), 158; Hippolyte Taine, *Italy: Rome and Naples* (translation of *Voyage en Italie,* I), trans. John Durand (orig. titled *Voyage en Italie,* vol. 1) (New York: Leypoldt and Holt, 1871), 173; John Addington Symonds, *Renaissance in Italy: The Age of the Despots* (New York: Henry Holt, 1886), 106n, 190. Commenting on the Renaissance, Symonds observes that 'even practical jokes were not considered in bad taste,' although 'irreverence and grossness were tabooed as boorish,' and 'mere obscenity' was 'especially condemned.' Yet 'many jests approved of at that time would now appear intolerable.' Leonardo da Vinci greatly enjoyed playing practical jokes, as did Pope Leo X and Isabella d'Este, for which see also Dmitri Merejcovski, *The Romance of Leonardo da Vinci,* trans. Bernard Guilbert Guerney (New York: Heritage Press, 1938), 175; Isabella Cartwright, *Isabella d'Este: Marchioness of Mantua, 1474–1539: A Study of the Renaissance* (London: John Murray, 1915), 1:10–11; Ronald Lightbown, *Mantegna* (Berkeley: Univ. of California Press, 1986), 103. On the persistence of the taste for practical jokes (*burle* and *beffe*) from the Middle Ages into the Renaissance, and the attempt by Castiglione and other writers of conduct manuals to curb the Italians' taste for such amusements, see Peter Burke, 'Frontiers of the Comic in Early Modern Italy,' in Burke, *Varieties of Cultural History,* 77–93; Baldassare Castiglione, *The Courtier,* trans. Charles S. Singleton (New York: Doubleday, 1959), 133–4, 147, 149, 179, 180–3, 184–90.

46 Burke, *Popular Culture in Early Modern Europe,* 24–5, 27–9, 104, 270–81.

47 Hippolyte Taine, 'The Philosophy of Art in Italy,' in Taine, *Lectures on Art,* trans. John Durand (New York: Henry Holt, 1875), 113–14; Taine, *Italy: Florence and Venice,* trans. John Durand (orig. title *Voyage en Italie,* vol. 2) (New York: Henry Holt, 1875), 25. Patrick Brydone mentions a libidinous eighteenth-century bandit who decided abruptly to enter a monastery, where he failed to resist carnal pleasures. See Brydone, *A Tour of Sicily and Malta in a Series of Letters to William Beckford,* vol. 2, 2d ed. (London: W. Strahan, 1776), 112–30.

48 Taine, *Italy: Rome and Naples,* translation of *Voyage en Italie,* I), trans. John Durand (orig. titled *Voyage en Italie,* vol. 1) (New York: Leypoldt and Holt, 1871), 177–8, 183–5; Taine, 'Philosophy of Art in Italy,' 31, 79.

49 Putnam, *Making Democracy Work,* 92, 99, 104, 111–12, and passim; Anthony Pagden, 'The Destruction of Trust and Its Economic Consequences in the Case of Eighteenth-Century Naples,' in Diego Gambetta, ed., *Trust: Making and Breaking Cooperative Relations* (London: Basil Blackwell, 1988), 127–41;

Casillo, *Empire of Stereotypes*, 196–201, 328–9n. Edward C. Banfield traces the backwardness of southern Italy to 'amoral familism,' the inability of southern Italians to cooperate outside the family in the pursuit of long-term public or civic goals; instead, private and familial interests overwhelmingly motivate social behaviour. Despite its wide influence, Banfield's theory has met with criticism in the United States and Italy, whether as an account of the village from which Banfield derives his evidence, or as a description of southern Italy as a whole. According to Loredana Sciolla, southern Italy exhibits in some ways a greater degree of civicness than northern Italy, contrary to conventional wisdom. See Banfield, *The Moral Basis of a Backward Society* (Glencoe: Free Press, 1958), 16–17, 18–19, 20, 23, 24–5, 28, 30–1, 53–4, 66, 67, 83–163, and passim; Sciolla, *Italiani*, passim; Casillo, *Empire of Stereotypes*, 201–2, 330–1n, 332n.

50 Anton Blok, *The Mafia of a Sicilian Village, 1860–1960: A Study of Violent Peasant Entrepreneurs* (New York: Harper and Row, 1974), xviii, 6, 9–12, 26, 26n, 90–6.

51 Dean Peabody, *National Characteristics* (Cambridge: Cambridge Univ. Press, 1985), 75–9, 83–5, 136–47, 156, 206. See also G.A. Almond and Sidney Verba, *The Civic Culture: Political Attitudes and Democracy in Five Nations* (Princeton: Princeton Univ. Press, 1963).

52 R 205; L 36–7, 135; RJ 261; RNF 233; PI 3, 6; HP 29, 123; THF 180; JI 60, 61, 64, 125–6.

53 Anthony Smith, *National Identity* (Reno: Univ. of Nevada Press, 1991), 84–91; Mandler, *The English National Character*, 19, 22–4, 27–30, 44, 51; Szegedy-Maszák, 'The Idea of National Character,' 45–8, 50; David Hume, 'Of National Characters,' in Hume, *Essays: Moral, Political, and Literary*, vol. 1, ed. T.H. Green and T.H. Grose (New York: Longmans, Green, 1912), 244–58. On civilization as a universalizing concept, and the resistance it has faced in the last two centuries, see Chris Rojek, 'Leisure, Culture and Civilization,' in Chris Rojek, Susan M. Shaw, and A.J. Veal, eds., *A Handbook of Leisure Studies* (New York: Palgrave Macmillan, 2006), 25–6, 33. For German resistance to the concept of civilization for the sake of the often antithetical values of *Kultur*, see Frank E. Manuel, *The New World of Henri Saint-Simon* (Notre Dame, IN: Univ. of Notre Dame Press, 1963), 162–7.

54 Croce, ctd in Giulio Bollati, *L'Italiano: il carattere originale come storia e come invenzione* (Turin: Einaudi, 1983), 39; Alessandro Cavalli, 'Reflections on Political Culture and the "Italian National Character,"' *Daedalus*, 130 (Summer 2001): 123–5; Mandler, *The English National Character*, 2, 8; Szegedy-Maszák, 'The Idea of National Character,' 45; Alex Inkeles, *National Character: A Psycho-Social Perspective* (New Brunswick, NJ: Transaction, 1997), vii, viii, ix,

8–16, 24, 32–4, 36–7, 40–1, 43–8, 55, 59, 66, 74–8, 86, 88–90, 94, 98, 101–4, 135, 162–6, 176–9, 186, 214–15, 218, 236, 237, 244–6, 359–61; Clark R. Mc-Cauley, Lee J. Jussim, and Yueh-Ting Lee, 'Stereotype Accuracy: Toward Appreciating Group Differences,' in Yueh-Ting Lee, Lee J. Jussim, and Clark R. McCauley, eds., *Stereotype Accuracy: Toward Appreciating Group Differences* (Washington, DC: American Psychological Association, 1995), 293–4; Richard Lynn, *Personality and National Character* (Oxford: Pergamon, 1971), ix, xi–xii (Introduction by Sir Cyril Burt), 1, 14, 16–19, 63–4, 70, 156–81.

55 Raymond Grew, 'The Construction of National Identity,' in Boerner, *Concepts of National Identity*, 35; Smith, *National Identity*, 9, 11–13, 14, 19–21, 24, 26, 29–30, 40, 41, 44; Mandler, *English National Character*, 8, 10–13; Felix Gilbert, 'Italy,' in Orest Ranum, ed., *National Consciousness, History, and Political Culture in Early Modern Europe* (Baltimore: Johns Hopkins Univ. Press, 1975), 21–42; Ruggiero Romano, ctd in Silvana Patriarca, 'Italian Neopatriotism: Debating National Identity in the 1990s,' *Modern Italy*, 6, no. 1 (2001): 23. On this point see also Arnold Van Gennep, *Traité comparative des nationalités, I. Les éléments extérieur de la nationalité* (Paris: Payot, 1922), 33–4. Judith Hook and E.S. Chamberlin argue that the impending threat to the whole of Italy posed by Charles V of Spain during the mid-1520s awakened the Italians to a heightened sense of national consciousness which in turn inspired their regrettably failed attempt to unify in the defense of peninsular liberty against the ultimately triumphant Spanish invader – perhaps the last chance for Italian unification before the Risorgimento. See Hook, *The Sack of Rome: 1527*, 2d. ed. (New York: Palgrave Macmillan, 2004), xii, 61–2, 289–90; E.R. Chamberlin, *The Sack of Rome* (London: B.T. Batsford, 1979), 104.

56 Giuseppe Baretti, *Manners and Customs*, 1:15, 56, 59– 61, 63, 65–6, 74, 92–100, 105, 112–13, 122, 225, 235–6, 283, 288–90, 292, 297–8, and passim; Baretti, *Manners and Customs*, 2:25–7, 39, 61, 63, 66, 72, 78, 91–2, 97, 113, 116–19, 127–8, 130–1, 138–46, 160–2, 166–7, and passim. Baretti makes many broad generalizations concerning Italy, yet claims that Italians differ among themselves more than nations differ among each other. See also Bollati, *L'Italiano*, 36–9; Pellegrino D'Acierno, ed., *The Italian American Heritage: A Companion to Literature and the Arts* (New York: Garland, 1999), xxiv, 615–16. Writers on the Italian national character include Pietro Calepio, *Descrizione de' costumi italiani* (1727); Barzini, *The Italians*; Peabody, *National Characteristics*; Giacomo Leopardi, *Discorso sopra lo stato presente degl'italiani*, ed. Maria Andrea Rigoni (Milan: Rizzoli, 1988); Sforza, *Real Italians*; Silvio Guarnieri, *Carattere degli italiani* (Turin: Einaudi, 1948); Almond and Verba, *Civic Culture*; Jacques Le Goff, 'Il peso del passato nel coscienza degli italiani,' in Fabio Luca Cavazza and Stephen R. Graubard, eds., *Il caso italiano*

(Milan: Garzanti, 1971); Michael Carroll, *Veiled Threats: The Logic of Popular Catholicism in Italy* (Baltimore: Johns Hopkins Univ. Press, 1996); Carlo Tullio-Altan, *La Nostra Italia: arretratezza socioculturale, clientelismo, trasformismo e ribellione dall'Unità ad oggi* (Milan: Feltrinelli, 1986); Sciolla, *Italiani*. Unlike the majority of the above writers, and to an even greater extent than Baretti, Carlo Denina opposes any claims for the existence of an Italian national character, arguing instead that only the diverse regions of Italy have maintained their character since Roman times. See Denina, *Essai sur les traces du caractère des italiens modernes* (Paris: Fantin, 1807), 1-24, and passim. On national character generally, see also Ernest Barker, *National Character and the Factors of Its Formation*, 4th ed. (London: Methuen, 1948); Salvador de Madariaga, *Englishmen, Frenchmen, Spaniards: An Essay in Comparative Psychology* (London: Oxford, 1928).

57 RNF 24, 122; L 160; RNF1817 97; RNF 315.

58 Hume, 'Of National Characters,' 244; Mandler, *English National Character*, 14; Francois Rosset, 'Coppet et les stereotypes nationaux,' in Kurt Kloocke, ed., *Le Groupe de Coppet et l'Europe, 1789–1830: Actes du cinquième colloque de Coppet (8–10 Juillet, 1993)* (Lausanne: Institut Benjamin Constant, 1994), 55, 56, 57. On the emergence of the concept of the stereotype, and its negative reputation, see Lee et al., *Stereotype Accuracy*: useful essays include those by Yueh-Ting Lee, Lee J. Jussim, Clark R. McCauley, Victor Ottati, David C. Finder, and Casey S. Ryan. See also the editors' 'Why Study Stereotype Accuracy and Inaccuracy?', 3–27; and Inkeles, *National Character*, 6, 7–8. On the recent decline of interest in the concept of national character, with the exception of writers such as Barzini, Ralf Dahrendorf, and Orwell, see Irving Louis Horowitz, Introduction to Cesar Graña, *Meaning and Authenticity: Further Essays on the Sociology of Art* (New Brunswick: Transaction, 1989), xix.

59 On national character and national identity, see Grew, 'The Construction of National Identity,' 31–5, 39, 40; Smith, *National Identity*, vii, viii, 8–18,71–98; Mandler, *English National Character*, 1–5; Patriarca, 'National Identity or National Character?: New Vocabularies and Old Paradigms', in Ascoli and von Henneberg, *Making and Remaking Italy*, 299–301, 313; Patriarca, 'Italian Neopatriotism,' 26.

60 On stereotype accuracy and inaccuracy, see the essays by the following authors in Lee et al., *Stereotype Accuracy*: Victor Ottati, Yueh-Ting Lee, Richard D. Ashmore, Laura Longo, Monica Biernat, David C. Funder, Guillermo Duenas, and Clark R. McCauley. See also the qualified defence of stereotype accuracy in Penelope J. Oakes, S. Alexander Haslam, and John C. Turner, *Stereotyping and Social Reality* (Oxford: Blackwell, 1994), 186–213 and passim; W. Helmreich, *The Things They Say Behind Your Back* (New York: Doubleday,

1982), 3, 5–6, 38–58 (a chapter on Italian American stereotypes), 243; and Stephen Goldberg, *When Wish Replaces Thought* (Buffalo: Prometheus, 1991), 151–4. A number of scholars cautiously accept the 'kernel of truth argument.' See Benedetto Croce, 'Il paradiso abitato da diavoli,' in Croce, *Uomini e cose della vecchia Italia*, 1st ser., 2d ed. (Bari: Laterza, 1943), 82, 85; Patriarca, 'National Identity or National Character?', 307; Roberto Romani, *National Character and Public Spirit in Britain and France, 1750–1914* (Cambridge: Cambridge Univ. Press, 2002), 1–2, 341; Le Goff, 'Il peso del passato nella coscienza degli italiani'. For criticism of the 'kernel of truth argument,' see Oakes et al., *Stereotyping and Social Reality*, 19–24; Michael Pickering, *Stereotyping: The Politics of Representation* (New York: Palgrave, 2001). On the effect of historical and social change on both Italian stereotypes and the Italian national character, see Andrew M. Canepa, 'From Degenerate Scoundrel to Noble Savage: The Italian Stereotype in Eighteenth-Century British Travel Literature,' *English Miscellany*, 22 (1971): 107–46.

61 Inkeles, *National Character*, viii–ix, 10–7, 35–6, 43, 59, 74, 86, 88–90, 94, 96–8, 101–2, 105, 135, 148–53, 166–7, 214–20, 224–5, 237, 243–5, 359–61. Mandler misleadingly claims that by its very nature 'the idea of national character seeks to connect' many disparate things in a nation 'to a single personality type.' See Mandler, *English National Character*, 2.

62 PI 119; HP 120, 208, 219, 236, 237, 238; R 8, 37–8, 258; RNF 253, 366, 465; RJ 90; PD 412; L 91. Whereas Stendhal agrees with Montequieu that both government and climate influence the character and behaviour of nations, he places, as does Staël, a greater emphasis on the role of government. On the other hand, he disagrees with Hélvetius's claim that climate, as opposed to government, has no influence on national temperament, a view he regards as absurd. See Fernand Rude, *Stendhal et la pensée sociale de son temps* (Paris: Plon, 1967), 26, 28–30, 96; Francine Marill Albérès, *Le Naturel chez Stendhal* (Paris: Librairie Nizet, 1956), 54; Novati, *Stendhal e l'anima italiana*, 13; del Litto, *La vie intellectuelle de Stendhal*, 46n, 85, 208, 271.

63 HP 214–6, 220, 236, 238, 244, 285; PD 91; R 36; RNF 115; Crouzet, *Stendhal et l'italianité*, 39–48; Dédéyan, *L'Italie dans l'oeuvre romanesque de Stendhal*, 1:57.

64 For Staël's climatic theory, and its relation to similar theories previously advanced by Montesquieu and subsequently by Charles-Victor de Bonstetten, see Casillo, *Empire of Stereotypes*, 23–8. See also Charles de Secondat, Baron de Montesquieu, *The Spirit of the Laws*, in *The Great Books of the Western World* (vol. 38, Montesquieu, Rousseau), ed. Robert Maynard Hutchins (Chicago: Encyclopedia Brittanica, 1952), 1–18, 102–15, 153. Stendhal concurs with English, French, German, and Russian travellers on the vivifying and grati-

fying effects of Italy's sunny environment. See Barzini, *Italians*, 34–6. For
the relation between Stendhal and Staël, see Casillo, *Empire of Stereotypes*,
235–6n. See also L 25, 84n, 318, 319; RNF 65, 487n; RS 102, 199; R 61; PI
114, 150; RJ 187; SJ 168, 175, 243–4, 266–7, 295, 308; THF 68; del Litto, *La
vie intellectuelle de Stendhal*, 52, 67–70, 115–6, 132, 163, 183–4, 233, 238, 243,
271–2, 278–82, 279n, 288, 309, 314, 321, 341–5, 400, 422–3, 443, 469–70,
501, 510, 516, 525, 540–2, 575, 633–4; H.-F. Imbert, *Les métamorphoses de la
liberté, ou Stendhal devant la Restauration et la Risorgimento* (Paris: Jose Corti,
1967), 245, 248; Crouzet, *Stendhal et l'italianité*, 6, 13–14, 26–7, 35, 38, 39,
51–2, 51–2n, 56n, 105n, 149–50, 151, 159, 197n, 198n, 244, 261, 296n,
314, 390n, 392n; Michel Crouzet, *Nature et la société chez Stendhal: La révolte
romantique* (Villeneuve d'Ascq: Presses Universitaires de Lille, 1985), 56–7;
Charles Dejob, *Madame de Staël et l'Italie avec une bibliographie de l'influence
française en Italie, de 1796 a 1814* (Paris: Collin, 1890), 62–7, 62n, 91–3, 96,
105–7, 114–5; Bertaut, *L'Italie vue par les francais*, 147–9; Roland Mortier,
*La poétique des ruines en France: Ses origines, ses variations, de la Renaissance a
Victor Hugo* (Geneva: Droz, 1974), 203, 205; Mortier, 'Les états généraux
de l'opinion européenne,' in Kloocke, *Le Groupe de Coppet et l'Europe*, 18;
Benjamin McRae Amoss, Jr, *Time and Narrative in Stendhal* (Athens: Univ. of
Georgia Press, 1992), 36.

65 Dédéyan, *L'Italie dans l'oeuvre romanesque de Stendhal*, 1:218.

66 RNF 11, 58, 60, 114–5, 149, 159, 189; HP 238, 285; L 265. On the harshness
of the Mediterranean climate, see Braudel, *Mediterranean and Mediterranean
World*, 1:232–42, and vol. 2, trans. Sian Reynolds (New York: Harper and
Row, 1972), 1239; John Davis, *People of the Mediterranean: An Essay in Com-
parative Social Anthropology* (London: Routledge and Kegan Paul, 1977), 41;
André Siegfried, *The Mediterranean*, trans. Doris Hemming (New York: Du-
ell, Sloan, and Pearce, 1947), 107–9, 215–16; Barzini, *Italians*, 50–2; Sforza,
Real Italians, 74–5.

67 RNF 39–40, 79, 283, 284, 318; RJ 42; HP 27–8, 30. On the political life of the
medieval republics, with their 'passions orageux' and 'démocratie turbu-
lente, irrégulière, mais énergique,' see J.-C.-L Simonde de Sismondi, *Histoire
des républiques italiennes*, 3:35, 292; 4:45, 83–4, 137–8; 5:168.

68 RNF 12; HP 10, 34, 47, 110, 291, 308; EIP 1:50; EIP 2:142. Although the
origins of the idea of the Italian Renaissance appear in the Renaissance
itself, scholars long lacked a concept of the period as a total cultural complex but referred to it as Stendhal does frequently, in the limited sense of
a renaissance of painting or the arts of civilization. The periodic concept,
which Stendhal comes close to articulating, emerges in the early and middle
nineteenth century, with Seroux d'Agincourt, Michelet, and Burckhardt.

On the development of the concept of the Renaissance, see Casillo, *Empire of Stereotypes*, 248–50n; Lucien Febvre, 'How Jules Michelet Invented the Renaissance,' in Febvre, *A New Kind of History*, ed. Burke, 258–9.

69 PI 13–14, 16–17, 18–19, 51–2, 54–5; HP 13, 14, 27–30; J.-C.-L.Sismondi, *Histoire des républiques italiennes*, 6:456–7; del Litto, *La vie intellectuelle de Stendhal*, 128. On the highly limited political participation within medieval Italian republics, and hence their basically oligarchical character, see Symonds, *Renaissance in Italy: Age of Despots*, 55, 78, 80, 92, 195, 196; William J. Bouwsma, *Venice and the Defense of Republican Liberty: Renaissance in the Age of the Counter Reformation* (Berkeley: Univ. of California Press, 1968), 15; Lauro Martines, *Power and Imagination: City-States in Renaissance Italy* (New York: Knopf, 1979), 139-40, 148.

70 PI 17, 49, 85, 131; HP 16, 28–9, 32; RNF 36, 200–1, 270; RJ 42, 277; SJ 78; R 10–2, 299; L 160, 262, 262n, 265; AC 118; THF 341.

71 RJ 42; HP 16, 34, 40–1; PI 49; RNF1817 8, 74, 78–9, 151; del Litto, *La vie intellectuelle de Stendhal*, 549–50, 614; Imbert, *Les métamorphoses*, 195.

72 PI 49.

73 Rude, *Stendhal et la pensée sociale*, 25, 41, 53–4, 85–9, 237. See also Maxime Le Roy, *Stendhal politique* (Paris: Divan, 1929), 39, 40. Although Croce wrongly holds that Stendhal valued only his private interests, Fourierism attracted artists because of its emphasis on the arts, and despite its appeal to cooperation it verged on anarchism. See Egbert, *Social Radicalism and the Arts*, 118, 135, 136, 138.

74 RNF 11, 36–7, 93–4, 270–1; RJ 258; HP 285; PI 19–20; L 148; Crouzet, *Stendhal et l'italianité*, 165–7.

75 Although eighteenth-century Italy did not altogether lack a public sphere, it was underdeveloped and fragmented by comparison with centralized nations such as England and France, and remained so for many decades even after Italian unification. See Jurgen Habermas, *The Structural Transformation of the Public Sphere: An Inquiry into a Category of Bourgeois Society*, trans. Thomas Berger (Cambridge: MIT Press, 1991); Brendan Dooley, 'The Public Sphere and the Organization of Knowledge'; Anna Maria Rao, 'Enlightenment and Reform'; both essays in Marino, *Early Modern Italy*, 209–28, 246; Hanlon, *Early Modern Italy*, 317–20; Giuliano Procacci, *History of the Italian People* (New York: Harper and Row, 1971), 223–4, 268–9; John Dickie, *Darkest Italy: The Nation and Stereotypes of the Mezzogiorno, 1960–1900* (New York: St. Martin's Press, 1990), 16–17; Krystyna von Henneberg and Albert Russell Ascoli, 'Introduction: Nationalism and the Uses of Risorgimento Culture,' in Ascoli and von Henneberg, *Making and Remaking Italy*, 9–10.

76 RNF 191; RS 33, 47–8, 49, 52, 62, 68–9.

77 On the Parisian salon, see Marc Fumaroli, *Trois institutions littéraires* (Paris; Gallimard, 1994), 114, 119, 136–40, 144–6, 152–54, and passim; Burke, *Art of Conversation,* 115–16.

78 RNF 8, 22, 68, 171, 175, 235, 321, 358; RNF1817 81, 124; RJ 24, 78; LHMM 211, 253; R 451; L 36.

79 Goldthwaite, *Wealth and the Demand for Art in Italy,* 172, 197–9; Barzini, 'The Aristocrats,' in Luigi Barzini, *From Caesar to the Mafia* (New York: The Library Press), 97–8.

80 RNF 207; PD 460; PI 105; RJ 243; del Litto, *La vie intellectuelle de Stendhal,* 248.

81 L 145; HP 282, 286; RNF 442; PD 460, 521, 522; JI 270; RJ 258. See the similar observations of James Jackson Jarves, *Italian Sights and Papal Principles Seen through American Spectacles* (New York: Harper, 1856), 42–4; Hippolyte Taine, *Italy: Rome and Naples,* 279.

82 RJ 47, 60; Cuddihy, *Ordeal of Civility,* 13.

83 RNF 190, 191; PI 237–8; SJ 68; RJ 46.

84 RNF 270. Stendhal's analysis of the negative social consequences of Italy's lack of national unity calls to mind the similar views of Staël and Leopardi. See Germaine de Staël, *Corinne, or Italy,* trans. Avriel Goldberger (New Brunswick, NJ: Rutgers Univ. Press, 1987), 101, 102, 118; Leopardi, *Discorso,* 51, 56–7, 75–6n; in the same volume: Roberto Melchiori, 'Commento,' 90–1n, 95n, 98–100n, 127–8n.

85 RNF 197–9, 200, 242, 245–6, 249–50, 252, 254, 268, 423; RNF1817 166–7; R 454, 457; RJ 290, 292; JI 267; L 161. On the Italians' tendency to treat conversation itself as a kind of combat, with the aim of humiliating the other person, see Leopardi, *Discorso,* 66–9. See also Burke, *Art of Conversation,* 98, 99.

86 RJ 288; RNF 270, 273.

87 William Beckford, *The Travel Diaries of William Beckford of Fonthill* (Cambridge: Constable, 1928), 1:253; Mary Lutyens, ed., *Young Mrs. Ruskin in Venice: Unpublished Letters of Mrs. John Ruskin written from Venice between 1849–1852* (New York: Vanguard Press, 1965), 100; Casillo, *Empire of Stereotypes,* 52–7, 101–7.

88 Baretti, *Manners and Customs,* 1:235–8.

89 William Kerrigan and Gordon Braden, *The Idea of the Renaissance* (Baltimore: Johns Hopkins Univ. Press, 1989), 26–7. For the calumnies and vituperations of the humanists, see Symonds, *Renaissance in Italy: Revival of Learning,* 160, 210, 238–44, 274–5; Georg Voigt, *Il Risorgimento dell'antichità classica ovvero il primo secolo dell'umanesimo,* vol. 1, trans. Diego Valbusa (Florence: Sansoni, 1968), 335–7, 354–60, and vol. 2, 134, 143–51, 435–42; William Roscoe,

The Life of Lorenzo de' Medici, Called the Magnificent (London: David Bogue, 1846), 25–7; Pasquale Villari, *The Life and Times of Niccolò Machiavelli*, vol. 1, trans. Laura Villari (London: T. Fisher Unwin, 1892), 90–2; Philip Jones, 'Le Signorie di Sigismondo Malatesta,' *Studi Malatestiani, Studi Storici*, Fasc. 110–1 (Rome: Istituto Storico Italiano per il Medio Evo, 1978), 5–6; Anthony Grafton and Lisa Jardine, *From Humanism to the Humanities: Education and the Liberal Arts in Fifteenth- and Sixteenth-Century Europe* (Cambridge: Cambridge Univ. Press, 1986), 63, 64, 66, 75–6. Lawrence S. Rainey shows that Pope Pius II's seemingly libellous denunciations of Sigismondo Malatesta conformed to the Renaissance genre of invective. See Rainey, *Ezra Pound and the Monument of Culture: Text, History, and the Malatesta Cantos* (Chicago: Univ. of Chicago Press, 1991), 299n, 136; Villari, *The Life and Times of Niccolò Machiavelli*, 1:92.

90 Geneviève Gennari, *Le premier voyage de Madame de Staël en Italie et la genèse de Corinne* (Paris: Boivin, 1947), 114. The Italian salons described by Brendan Dooley resemble discussion groups rather than conforming to Fumaroli's description of the salon as an aristocratic setting where conversation is pursued for its own sake. See Dooley, 'The Public Sphere and the Organization of Knowledge,' 224–6.

91 Maurice Vaussard, *Daily Life in Eighteenth-Century Italy* (New York: Macmillan, 1963), 152.

92 Moloney, *Florence and England*, 21; Brydone, *Tour of Italy and Malta*, 2:76–7, 315.

93 Beckford, *Travel Writings*, 1:249–50. However, Beckford notes the Italians' wit, talent, and vivacity.

94 Hester Thrale Piozzi, *Observations and Reflections Made in the Course of a Journey through France, Italy, and Germany*, ed. Herbert Barrows (Ann Arbor: Univ. of Michigan Press, 1967), 47, 91, 92, 105; Staël, *Corinne*, 96; Casillo, *Empire of Stereotypes*, 19, 59; Baretti, *Manners and Customs*, 2:127–8. Unlike Maurice Andrieux, who describes conversations in eighteenth-century Venice as uniformly deadly, Molmenti believes some Venetian salons to have exemplified conversation of a higher type, and Alfonso Lowe even claims that the best ones approached the Parisian standard. During the same period, notes Andrieux, *conversazioni* were regarded as the main attraction of Roman society. See Andrieux, *Daily Life in Venice in the Time of Casanova*, trans. Mary Fitton (New York: Praeger, 1969), 77; Maurice Andrieux, *Daily Life in Papal Rome in the Eighteenth Century*, trans. Mary Fitton (New York: Macmillan, 1969), 152–4; Molmenti, *Venice: Its Individual Growth from the Earliest Beginnings to the Fall of the Republic*, Part 3: *The Decadence*, vol. 2, trans. Horatio F. Brown (Chicago: A.C. McClurg, 1906–8), 141–8; Alfonso Lowe, *La Serenissi-*

ma: The Last Flowering of the Venetian Republic (London: Cassell, 1977), 58. On the deficiencies of Italian conversation in the eighteenth and nineteenth centuries, see Gennari, *Le premier voyage de Madame de Staël en Italie*, 67, 111; Burke, *Art of Conversation*, 98; Broers, *Napoleonic Empire in Italy*, 217–18, 248–9; Casillo, *Empire of Stereotypes*, 309–11n.

95 Adolfo Omodeo, 'Il Gruppo di Coppet di fronte a Napoleone,' in Omodeo, *Il senso della storia* (Turin: Einaudi, 1955), 356–7.

96 Lady Morgan, *Italy*, vol. 2 (New York: J. Seymour, 1821), 210; Vittorio Gabrieli, ed., 'Le "Notes on Italy" di A.W. Power,' *English Miscellany*, 3 (1952): 271, 273–4; Charlotte Eaton, *Rome in the Nineteenth Century* (London: H.G. Bohn, 1852), 1:vii–viii, and 2:238–42; Natalia Wright, *American Novelists in Italy: The Discoverers* (Philadelphia: Univ. of Pennsylvania Press, 1965), 203. In a letter of November 1816 Byron writes that 'no society' exists in Milan save in opera boxes, where people play cards and converse; otherwise there are 'neither balls nor open houses.' See Stendhal, *Voyages en Italie*, 1325.

97 PD 437; JI 182; PI 236; RJ 81–2, 139. However, Stendhal finds Milan to have the 'best designed streets in the world, and always clean,' a reflection in his view of medieval and Renaissance civic traditions. See RNF 23, 120–1, 485n; RNF1817 11; JI 129, 131–2; Vittorio del Litto, Introduction to Stendhal, *Voyages en Italie*, 1331n. See also PD 437; RNF 23; PI 236; Crouzet, *Stendhal et l'italianité*, 193. Prior to the modernizing renovations of Baron Haussmann, foreign visitors to Paris complained of its filth, stench, disorder, and congestion, as did Henry Wadsworth Longfellow and Mrs John Adams. See Foster Rhea Dulles, *Americans Abroad: Two Centuries of Foreign Travel* (Ann Arbor: Univ. of Michigan Press, 1964), 22, 37; Withey, *Grand Tours*, 74.

98 Andrieux, *Daily Life in Papal Rome*, 13–14; Sells, *Paradise of Travellers*, 132; Vaussard, *Daily Life in Eighteenth-Century Italy*, 24, 26; Joseph Spence, *Letters from the Grand Tour*, ed. Slava Klima (Montreal and London: McGill-Queens Univ. Press, 1975), 86; Piozzi, *Observations and Reflections*, 25, 88, 212–3; Canepa, 'From Degenerate Scoundrel to Noble Savage,' 129–30; Marianna Starke, *Letters from Italy between the Years 1792 and 1798, containing a View of the Revolutions in that Country, from the Capture of Nice by the French Republic to the Expulsion of Pius VI from the Eccelesiastical State* (London: R. Philips, 1800), 1:335; Lady Morgan, *Italy*, 2:120, 137, 156, 176, 204; John Ruskin, *Letters from Venice, 1851–1852*, ed. John Lewis Bradley (New Haven: Yale Univ. Press, 1955), 31–2; George Stillman Hillard, *Six Months in Italy* (Boston: Ticknor, Reed, and Fields, 1853), 2:8, 21–2, 269; Jarves, *Italian Sights and Papal Principles*, 38, 174, 255, 355, 356; John Chetwode Eustace, *A Tour through Italy, Exhibiting a View of its Scenery, its Antiquities, and its Monuments* (London: J. Mawman, 1813), 1:271–2. English complaints of filth in Italy seem ironic

given that nineteenth-century England permitted industry to befoul its environment. Already in 1661 John Evelyn complained of coal smoke in London, and many Victorian travellers to Italy were happy to have escaped the
polluted air of that city where, to quote Ruskin, 'one cannot place oneself
or one's belongings out of doors without getting dirty.' See Pemble, *Mediterranean Passion*, 152; Carlo Cipolla, *Before the Industrial Revolution: European
Society and Economy, 1000–1700*, trans. Marcella Kooy and Alide Kooy (New
York: W.W. Norton, 1976), 134.

99 For the relationship between the social banishment of odours and Elias's
concepts of 'drive control' and the 'civilizing process,' see Alain Corbin,
The Foul and the Fragrant: Odor and the French Social Imagination, trans.
Miriam Kochan, Roy Porter, and Christopher Prendergast (Cambridge:
Harvard Univ. Press, 1986), 4, 5, 7, 21, and esp. 236n and 89–135. On the
disgust of nineteenth-century northern European and American travel-
lers with the unpleasant smells they encountered in Italian cities, see John
Pemble, *Venice Rediscovered* (New York: Oxford Univ. Press, 1995), 20–1. On
varying responses to smells from culture to culture, see Edward T. Hall, *The
Hidden Dimension* (New York: Doubleday, 1969), 50. What holds true for the
French seems no less true for Italians.

100 Blum, 'A Theoretical Outline of Beylism,' 101, 102; del Litto, *La vie intellectuelle de Stendhal*, 49; Rude, *Stendhal et la pensée sociale*, 24–30, 43, 54, 61–3;
Strickland, *Stendhal*, 270n.

101 RNF 51, 187–90, 191, 192, 395, 486n; R 32–3, 205, 215; PI 42, 141; L 160;
del Litto, *La vie intellectuelle de Stendhal*, 550. The phrase 'patriotisme de
l'antéchambre' was coined by Turgot.

102 PI 100, 110; RNF 251; HP 288–9. On travellers' reports of violence in Italy
during the sixteenth and seventeenth centuries, see Sells, *Paradise of Travellers*, 133, 160, 171, 173, 190–1, 214. According to the late eighteenth-century traveller Dr John Moore, the Italians' 'quick feelings' led to frequent
assassinations. See Canepa, 'From Degenerate Scoundrel to Noble Savage,'
139. Giuseppe Baretti protested allegations that the Italians were 'abominable villains' who '*will treacherously stab on the least provocation*,' whence the
supposed 'frequency of assassination' in Italy. Yet Baretti conceded the
'touchy temper' of the Italian lower classes, whose 'quick feelings' drove
them to reach for their knives. See Baretti, *Manners and Customs*, 1:47,
51, 55, 63, 65, 74. John Chetwode Eustace, a Britisher who visited Italy in
1802, attributed the Italians' violence not to jealousy, irritation, cruelty,
or vindictiveness but to hasty temper and passionate impulsiveness. See
Eustace, *A Tour through Italy, Exhibiting a View of Its Scenery, Its Antiquities,
and Its Monuments* (London: J. Mawman, 1813), 2:579–82. During his visit

to Italy in 1760–64 the artist Benjamin West found that the entire population was by no means criminal, as many had assumed. See Prezzolini, *Come
gli americani scoprirono l'Italia* (Milano: Fratelli Treves, 1933), 23–4. The
nineteenth-century American art critic James Jackson Jarves alleged that,
though Italians tended to commit warm-blooded crimes, they also found
it honourable in cases of vengeance to assassinate by treachery, regarding
such acts as courageous rather than cowardly. See Jarves, *Italian Sights and
Papal Principles*, 338–9. Like the British poet Samuel Rogers, the American
sculptor-writer William Wetmore Story attributed the Italians' alleged inclination to violence and vengeance to fear of judicial injustice under a corrupt legal system. See Rogers, *Italy: A Poem* (London: T. Cadell, E. Moxon,
1836), 149–50; Story, *Roba di Roma* (New York: Chapman and Hall, 1976),
120.

103 For Stendhal on Italian bandits, see RJ 26, 280–3; RNF 20, 237, 417, 419,
426, 428; RNF1817 157–8; R 138; HP 288–9; PI 283–4. See also Stendhal,
Promenades dans Rome, in Stendhal, *Voyages en Italie,* 1234–49. The assumption of Italian lawlessness and vengeance appears in such eighteenth- and
early nineteenth-century writers as Chamfort, Sharp, Eustace, Duclos, Du-
Paty, Bonstetten, and Delécleuze. Yet they often attribute such violence not
to innate criminality but to passion, sensitivity, imagination, and evil governments. See Crouzet, 'Stendhal et le "coup de poignard" italien,' 164,
167–8, 172–3, 180–4, 186, 188, 190–1, 198, 211–12, and passim.

104 RJ 26.

105 Vaussard, *Daily Life in Eighteenth-Century Italy,* 119-20. On the frequency of
murders in eighteenth-century Italy, see Jeremy Black, *The British and the
Grand Tour* (London: Croome Helm, 1985), 104–5; Hibbert, *The Grand
Tour,* 110.

106 Andrieux, *Daily Life in Papal Rome,* 93–9; RJ 98. Andrieux's figures for the
Roman murder rate greatly exceed those of Stendhal, who more credibly
claims that eighteen thousand murders were committed in the Papal States
between 1775 and 1800. See Stendhal, PI 266.

107 Martin Clark, *Modern Italy, 1871–1982* (London: Longman, 1986), 70.

108 HP 26; PI 218; RJ 8, 181, 188, 279; del Litto, *La vie intellectuelle de Stendhal,*
634–5; Imbert, *Les métamorphoses,* 130, 342; Burckhardt, *Civilization of the Renaissance,* 69; Symonds, *Renaissance in Italy: Revival of Learning,* 2; Sells, *Paradise of Travellers,* 220–1; Siegfried Giedion, *Space, Time, and Architecture: The
Growth of a New Tradition,* 5th ed. (Cambridge: Harvard Univ. Press, 1967),
75–106. Alcide de Gasperi, the twentieth-century Italian statesman, similarly
blamed much of Italy's historical misery on papal interference. See Luigi
Barzini, *The Europeans* (New York: Simon and Schuster, 1983), 191.

682 Notes to pages 34–5

109 Martin Sherlock, *Letters from an English Traveller* (London: Nichols, Cadell, Elmsly, Payne, Conant, 1780), 74; Mayne, *The Journal of John Mayne, during a Tour on the Continent upon its Reopening after the Fall of Napoleon, 1814*, ed. John Mayne Colles (London: John Lane, 1909), 181. For street illumination in eighteenth-century Venice, which apparently surpassed that of many contemporary Italian cities, including Rome, see Molmenti, *Venice: Its Individual Growth*, Part 3: *The Decadence*, 2:125–6.

110 Andrieux, *Daily Life in Papal Rome*, 16–17.

111 RJ 7–8, 43, 279; RNF 123; HP 34; Imbert, *Les métamorphoses*, 332.

112 RJ 121, 279, 316; HP 33; PI 260–1; RNF 237, 463; JI 226, 233, 233n; Imbert, *Les métamorphoses*, 290–1, 332–3. On travellers' realization of the difference in administration and prosperity between Tuscany and the Papal States, see Casillo, *Empire of Stereotypes*, 94, 96, 99; Luigi Mascilli Migliorini, *L'Italia dell'Italia: Coscienza e mito della Toscana da Montesquieu a Berenson* (Florence: Ponte alle Grazie, 1995), 40-1. On the high esteem for the political administration of the Grand Duchy of Tuscany in eighteenth-century America, see Howard Marraro, 'Italy and the Italians of the Eighteenth Century seen by Americans,' *Italian Quarterly*, 16 (1972): 55–7.

113 RNF 344, 463; RJ 98, 259, 281, 314–5; PI 229, 232, 261, 286–9; HP 33; Imbert, *Les métamorphoses*, 339; John Addington Symonds, *Renaissance in Italy: The Catholic Reaction, Part 1* (New York: Henry Holt, 1887), 309; Andrieux, *Daily Life in Papal Rome*, 97–8. In eighteenth-century Italy the Catholic Church originally excluded from immunity serious crimes such as murder, yet it became customary for churches to protect their perpetrators, while heresy and free thought were regarded as unpardonable. See Vaussard, *Daily Life in Eighteenth-Century Italy*, 80, 119, 120; Spence, *Letters from the Grand Tour*, 121–2; Piozzi, *Observations and Reflections*, 213; Johann Wolfgang von Goethe, *Italian Journey*, trans. W.H. Auden and Elizabeth Meyer (Harmondsworth: Penguin, 1982), 145; Pierre-Jean Grosley, discussed in Venturi, 'Italia fuori d'Italia,' in *Storia d'Italia*, vol. 3, *Dal primo Settecento all'Unità*, ed. Ruggiero Romano and Corrado Vivanti (Turin: Einaudi, 1973), 1056; Sells, *Paradise of Travellers*, 131. Tobias Smollett and Dr Samuel Sharp were among the many eighteenth-century travellers to charge that Italian criminals customarily enjoyed the ecclesiastical right of sanctuary. Smollett, *Travels through France and Italy*, ed. Frank Felsenstein (Oxford: Oxford Univ. Press, 1979), 210; Canepa, 'From Degenerate Scoundrel to Noble Savage,' 131; Maugham, *Book of Italian Travel*, 41; Baretti, *Manners and Customs*, 1:47, 53–4. Ann Radcliffe's *The Italian* (1797) opens in a church where an assassin has found asylum, this being, a priest claims, an everyday occurence in Italy. See Radcliffe, *The Italian, or the Confessional of*

the Black Penitents: A Romance (Oxford: Oxford Univ. Press, 1981), 1–4. See also Taine, *Italy: Rome and Naples,* 229. In the middle and later eighteenth century ecclesiastical sanctuary was successfully challenged in Tuscany, Lombardy, and other Italian states. See Dino Carpanetto and Giuseppe Ricuperati, *Italy in the Age of Reason, 1685–1789,* trans. Caroline Higgit (London: Longman, 1987), 107, 165–6, 273, 276.

114 RNF1817 68, 69. Lady Morgan, who was indebted to Stendhal's Italian writings, holds the common view that, south of Tuscany, Italian 'civilization' stops. See Lady Morgan, *Italy,* 2:368.

115 RNF 236; HP 32, 33, 39; RJ 8, 48, 78, 100, 113, 181, 188, 189, 202, 204, 239, 258, 316; SJ 264; PI 260–1; R 194, 286; Imbert, *Les métamorphoses,* 159, 290, 337, 341, 359.

116 RJ 188–9, 200, 201, 282; RNF 238–9; Imbert, *Les métamorphoses,* 339.

117 HP 286–7n; RJ 47, 99; L 232, 233. Stendhal regards Italians as very much capable of courage, but only through private passions such as anger rather than out of a sense of civic or military duty. This follows from the individual Italian's worship of himself (*soi*), his disrespect for all honour and esteem deriving from without, and his inability to acknowledge a social value worth fighting for. A further consequence is that the Italians' ferocity is often close to cowardice, for instance killing with a knife in the dark. See Crouzet, *Stendhal et l'italianité,* 132–5, 148n, 329–31. For the stereotype of Italian military cowardice, see Casillo, *Empire of Stereotypes,* 83–6. From late Roman times onward the Italian male population has often proved reluctant to defend its native territory, as was already noted by Ammianus Marcellinus. Nor was the Italians' military reputation helped by the peninsular wars of the Renaissance, which Machiavelli described with some exaggeration as largely bloodless contests. Guicciardini claimed similarly that Italian soldiers of the Renaissance knew the image rather than the reality of war, while Erasmus used the phrase *italus bellax* to exemplify an oxymoron. According to Goldthwaite, the Italian military ethos was declining in the sixteenth century with the notable exception of the Neapolitans, who served impressively in Spanish armies, as Croce remarked. The imputation of cowardice by foreigners intensified during what Gregory Hanlon terms Italy's demilitarization, which occurred in the later Renaissance and baroque periods, when foreign occupation of the peninsula greatly enfeebled the art of soldiering among all classes. Notwithstanding that, during the Napoleonic period, Italian troops serving under French leadership distinguished themselves for bravery and discipline, the reformers of the Risorgimento deplored what they saw as the cowardly effeminacy of Italian males, which they exemplified in the *cicisbeo,* and which they sought to re-

place with republican *virtù*. See Casillo, *Empire of Stereotypes*, 49, 83–6, 273n, 274n, 275n; Benedetto Croce, *España en la vida del Renacimiento*, trans. Francisco Gonzalez Rios (Buenos Aires: Iman, 1945), 236–7, 239–47; Benedetto Croce, *History of the Kingdom of Naples*, ed. H. Stuart Hughes, trans. Frances Frenaye (Chicago: Univ. of Chicago Press, 1970), 104–10; Goldthwaite, *Wealth and the Demand for Art in Italy*, 167, 170; Gregory Hanlon, *The Twilight of a Military Tradition: Italian Aristocrats and European Conflicts, 1500–1800* (New York: Holmes and Maier, 1998), passim. In Carlo Sforza's view, Italy's reputation for military cowardice is the 'work of picayune historians.' See Sforza, *Real Italians*, 10.

118 RJ 278–83; RNF 174, 237–8; PI 254–90; AC 12–3, 14; Imbert, *Les métamorphoses*, 339.

119 RJ 98, 288; RNF 210, 257, 291, 463; RNF1817 24–5, 60–1, 66; PI 229, 287; R 191, 285, 440n; Imbert, *Les métamorphoses*, 159–61, 262–3, 276, 337, 340, 455; Strickland, *Stendhal*, 111; Casillo, *Empire of Stereotypes*, 278n. In 1829 the prestigious French journal *Le Globe* claimed that political repression and surveillance had reduced the Italians so thoroughly to silence that they had been robbed of a public sphere. See Venturi, 'L'Italia fuori d'Italia,' 1245.

120 Andrieux, *Daily Life in Papal Rome*, 30, 38–40, 90–3; RNF 173, 207. For eighteenth-century Rome, see Hanns Gross, *Rome in the Age of of the Enlightenment: The Post-Tridentine Syndrome and the Ancient Regime* (Cambridge: Cambridge Univ. Press, 1990), 1990), ix, 7–8, 11, 40–46, 88–115, and passim; Luigi dal Pane, *Lo stato ponteficio e il movimento riformatore del Settecento* (Milan: A. Giuffré, 1959), 1–53; Hanlon, *Early Modern Italy*, 98, 101, 144–6, 220, 330.

121 For English, French, and American travellers' reports of bandits from the Renaissance into the nineteenth century, see Gino Luzzatto, *An Economic History of Italy from the Fall of the Roman Empire to the Beginning of the Sixteenth Century*, trans. Philip Jones (New York: Barnes and Noble, 1961), 111; George B. Parks, *The English Traveler to Italy*, vol. 1: *The Middle Ages to 1525* (Roma: Edizioni di Storia e Letteratura, 1954), 545–6; Edward Chaney, Jr, 'The Grand Tour and Beyond: British and American Travellers in Southern Italy, 1545–1960,' in Chaney and Neil Ritchie, eds., *Oxford, China, and Italy: Essays in Honour of Sir Harold Acton on his Eightieth Birthday* (London: Thames and Hudson, 1984), 149; Sells, *Paradise of Travellers*, 167; John Raymond, *Itinerary* (1648) in Sells, *Paradise of Travelers*, 214; 'Banditti,' in Samuel Rogers' *Italy*, 178–82; Prezzolini, *Come gli americani scoprirono l'Italia*, 18–9, 227–30; Erik Amfitheatrof, *The Enchanted Ground: Americans in Italy, 1760–1988* (Boston: Little, Brown, 1990), 16; James Fenimore Cooper, *Gleanings in Europe: Italy* (Albany: State Univ. of New York Press, 1981),

295–6; Jarves, *Italian Sights and Papal Principles*, 340; Black, *Early Modern Italy*, 32–3, 188–91; Patrick Brydone, *A Tour through Sicily and Malta: In a Series of Letters to William Beckford* (London: W. Strahan, 1776), 1:2, 3, 73–80; Brian Hill (*Observations and Remarks on a Journey through Sicily and Calabria*, 1792), in Chaney, 'The Grand Tour and Beyond,' 149n; Mayne, *Journal of John Mayne*, 212–3, 256–7; Mrs [Anna] Jameson, *The Diary of an Ennuyée* (Boston: Ticknor and Fields, 1862), 192–3, 253, 254n; Craufurd Tait Ramage, *Nooks and By-Ways of Italy* (1868), excerpted in Atanasio Mozzillo, ed., *Viaggiatori stranieri nel sud* (Milan: Edizioni di Communità, 1964), 121; Howells, 'Italian Brigandage,' *North American Review*, 101 (July 1865): 164–89; Taine, *Italy: Rome and Naples*, 65–8, 72–3. Banditry increased in central and southern Italy with the decline of the agrarian economy in the late sixteenth century. In the Roman Campagna it climaxed between 1577 and 1595 yet was completely suppressed only in the nineteenth century. Its immediate cause was poverty and famine resulting from the Roman government's taxation and mismanagement of the rural economy combined with unequal land distribution and high rents imposed by large landholders and merchants. However, the 'classic country of the banditti,' to quote E.J. Hobsbawm, was southern Italy. During Napoleon's occupation of the south, Joseph Bonaparte and Joachim Murat attempted to extirpate banditry, yet despite the campaigns of General Manhès, the French ignored its underlying social and economic causes, including unemployment and lack of education. According to the French traveller Duret de Tavel, the Calabrians were a 'legion of demons.' Although banditry peaked in the south between 1861 and 1865, as the peasantry resisted Italian unification, it continued in the post-unification period. Francois Lenormant, who visited southern Italy in the late 1870s and early 1880s, saw banditry as inextricable from the region's failure to foster agriculture over pastoralism, which began with Aragon rule in Naples. The decline of brigandage in southern Italy in the late nineteenth century correlates with immigration; impoverished young men took not to the hills but to transatlantic steamships. See PI 254–90; RJ 280–2; Procacci, *History of Italian People*, 156, 182; E.J. Hobsbawm, *Bandits* (New York: Delacorte, 1969), 19 and passim; Villari, *Revolt of Naples*, 38–55, 141–2; Mozzillo, Introduction to Mozzillo, *Viaggiatori stranieri nel sud*, 52–66; Lenormant and Goyau, excerpted in Mozzillo, *Viaggiatori stranieri nel sud*, 621–3, 668–70; Marino, 'The Rural World in Italy under Spanish Rule,' 417–21; Clark, *Modern Italy*, 69–70. On the romanticization of the bandit in painting and literature, see William Gaunt, *Bandits in a Landscape: A Study of Romantic Painting from Caravaggio to Delacroix* (London: Studio, 1937), 123, 126–8.

122 Andrieux, *Daily Life in Papal Rome,* 36–7, 95–6.

123 MacFarlane anticipates E.J. Hobsbawm, who cites his work, in noting that
banditry flourishes in politically fragmented areas where, as in pre-modern
Italy, numerous frontiers and areas difficult of access make it easy for bandits to evade capture. See Charles MacFarlane, *The Lives and Exploits of Banditti and Robbers in All Parts of the World,* 3rd ed. (London: T. Tegg, 1839), 8,
13–14, 16, 21, 25, 26, 27, 29, 91, 181; Hobsbawm, *Bandits,* 16–17; John Mit-
ford, qtd in Jeremy Black, *The British Abroad: The Grand Tour in the Eighteenth
Century* (New York: St. Martin's Press, 1992), 41–2; RNF 426–8, 502n; JI 43.

124 Braudel, *Mediterranean and Mediterranean World,* 2:743–54; E.J. Hobsbawm,
*Primitive Rebels: Studies in Archaic Forms of Social Movement in the Nineteenth
and Twentieth Centuries* (New York: Praeger, 1963), 1–29; Hobsbawm, *Bandits,* 13–14, 15, 19–20, 21, 58, 87. Banditry sometimes serves conservative
interests. See Blok, *Mafia of a Sicilian Village,* 99–102, 100–1n.

125 For Gallicanism, Jansenism, and jurisdictionalism, see Luigi Salvatorelli,
The Risorgimento: Thought and Action, trans. Mario Domandi (New York:
Harper and Row, 1970), 17, 23, 34–7, 50, 57, 70; Furio Diaz, 'La Reggenza,'
in Furio Diaz, Luigi Mascilli Migliorini, and Carlo Mangio, *Il Granducato di
Toscana (Lorena dalla Reggenza agli anni rivoluzionari)* (Turin: Unione Tipo-
grafico-Editrice-Torinese, 1997), 1:129, 134–6, 138; in the same volume,
Luigi Mascilli Migliorini, 'L'età delle riforme,' 293; Adam Wandruszka,
Pietro Leopoldo: un grande riformatore (Florence: Vallecchi, 1968), 125, 135,
423–8, 429–42, 494–8; Carpanetto and Ricuperati, *Italy in the Age of Reason,*
88, 92, 100, 106, 108, 110, 114, 117, 125, 128–30, 132, 145, 147, 148, 151,
153, 155, 159, 164, 165, 170, 175, 176, 178, 181–4, 187–91, 194, 196, 198,
199, 201, 205, 214, 217–9, 228–30, 229, 231, 240, 243–4, 247, 253, 257, 273–
81, 286, 299, 310, 317; Hanlon, *Early Modern Italy,* 253, 311–13, 341, 352,
359–60; A.C. Jemolo, *Il giansenismo in Italia prima della Rivoluzione* (Bari:
Laterza, 1928); E. Codignola, *Illuminati, giansenisti e giacobini nell'Italia del
Settecento* (Florence: Nuova Italia, 1947). Whereas A.C. Jemolo interprets
Jansenism as a purely theological movement, focusing on the dogma and
discipline of the early Church, and concerning itself chiefly with theological controversies, E. Rota and E. Codignola see it as a religion of revolution
and liberty closely linked with other radical systems of thought in Italy and
whose influence was felt into the Risorgimento. According to Carpanetto
and Ricuperati, jurisdictionalism helped to consolidate Piedmont under
the House of Savoy yet failed in the Kingdom of Naples despite the advoca-
cy of the historian Pietro Giannone and Bernardo Tanucci, the chief minister of state. For eighteenth-century reformism, see also Franco Venturi,
'History and Reform in the Middle of the Eighteenth Century,' in J.H. El-

liott and H.G. Koenigsberger, eds., *The Diversity of History: Essays in Honor of Sir Herbert Butterfield* (Ithaca: Cornell Univ. Press, 1970), 239, 240; Vaussard, *Daily Life in Eighteenth-Century Italy*, 79–80; Imbert, *Les métamorphoses*, 332–3, 335, 348–52.

126 PI 25–8; SJ 67; RJ 112, 264, 342–3; H.-F. Imbert, *Stendhal et la tentation janseniste* (Geneva: Droz, 1970), 18, 28–9, 31, 34, 37–8, 41, 43, 48–51, 52, 59, 60, 64, 72, 74–8, 79, 80–1, 87–91, 93–5, 97, 107–8, 109, 112–13, 114, 118–19, 122, 126, 127, 130. Stendhal's attraction to Jansenism is evident too in *The Red and the Black*, in which Julien Sorel, the protagonist, is aided by two Jansenist priests, Abbé Pirard and Abbé Chelan.

127 RNF 305, 337; SJ 78; Procacci, *History of Italian People*, 144–8, 215–16; Carpanetto and Ricuperati, *Italy in Age of Reason*, 179–80.

128 PI 131; RJ 277, 282; L 262, 262n, 265.

129 RNF 36; CP(ENG) 1:9; CP(FR) 36; J.-C.-L. Sismondi, *Histoire des républiques italiennes*, 10:137–4, 194–5, 199–204, 236–54. A visitor to Sicily in 1770, Patrick Brydone had blamed the Bourbon government for widespread poverty, indolence, economic stagnation, and monastic corruption. See Brydone, *Tour of Sicily and Malta*, 2:56–7, 62–3, 285-6, 289–91.

130 RNF 62, 202; Imbert, *Les métamorphoses*, 316–18.

131 PI 131; SJ 78; RJ 282; L 262, 262n; AC 142n; Burckhardt, *Civilization of the Renaissance in Italy*, 188.

132 RNF1817 46–7; RJ 47, 101, 244–5; RNF 123–4, 354, 386; R 5, 153–4, 171, 275n, 299, 450, 451, 495n; Imbert, *Les métamorphoses*, 152–4, 275–6, 300. For a summary of the history of Naples from the Habsburg monarchy into the post-Napoleonic period, see Casillo, *Empire of Stereotypes*, 197–201, 329–30n. For eighteenth-century Neapolitan critics of their city's misrule and poverty, see Venturi, 'L'Italia fuori d'Italia,' 1065, 1106, 1111, 1116–17. Imbert notes Stendhal's only passing awareness of such eighteenth-century Neapolitan reformers as Filangieri, Antonio Genovesi, and Mario Pagani. See Imbert, *Les métamorphoses*, 168.

133 Braudel, *Mediterranean and Mediterranean World*, 1:165n; Braudel, *Out of Italy*, 54–5. For a critique of Braudel's analysis of Spain's relation to Italy during this period, see Michael Harsgor, 'Braudel's Sea Revisited,' *Mediterranean Historical Review*, 1 (Dec. 1986): 142, 154n. Benedetto Croce refuses to blame the Habsburg and Spanish Bourbons for the greater part of Italy's ills, for in his view Italian 'decadence' stems chiefly from internal, moral causes. Not only did the Neapolitans (and other Italians) support the religious and military policies of their Spanish masters, whom they befriended, but Naples may have been an economic liability for Spain. During its occupation of Naples the Spanish government tried to promote economic

conditions (such as roads and other improvements) conducive to a middle class. Although the Neapolitans suffered crushing taxes during the Thirty Years War, which led to the failed revolt of 1647, the later seventeenth century was a comparatively peaceful and fiscally undemanding period for Naples, whose contributions of manpower to the Spanish infantry were now greatly reduced. Regarding the Bourbon regime in Naples, Croce admires its only partly fulfilled reformist agenda, although he attributes its essential energies to the city's intellectual elite. Furthermore Spain had a favourable influence upon the Italian character, if only by reawakening its martial spirit. On the negative side, Croce excoriates Spain's disastrous economic policies in the Kingdom of Naples, including misguided economic protectionism, artificially supported prices, and taxes far beyond the people's capacity to pay. Rosario Villari was later to stress Spanish fiscal policy as a cause for the revolt of 1647. Croce further deplores the destructive influence upon Italian Renaissance culture of 'Spanish barbarism,' noting the Spaniards' militaristic disdain for humanistic culture, and denouncing them for imbuing the Italians with a taste for mindless gallantry, ceremony, luxury, braggadocio, and flattery. At the same time, Spain imposed upon Italy the ignorant dogmatism of the Counter-Reformation, which Croce regards as retrograde and anti-cultural. See Croce, *History of the Kingdom of Naples*, xviii– xix (Introduction by Hughes), 95–101, 110, 113–15, 119–21, 130–40, 126–7, 156, 168–89; Croce, *Philosophy, Poetry, History: An Anthology of Essays*, 976 ('The Sixteenth Century Crisis in Italy: Links Between Renaissance and Risorgimento'); 996, 1000, 1001, 1003–4 ('Italian Culture against Spanish Barbarism'); 1009–11, 1013–15 ('The Character of Spanish Culture'); Croce, *España en la vida italiana del Renacimiento*, 112, 127, 129– 31, 135–42, 145–7, 150–3, 156–62, 179–87, 190–202, 208–46, and passim; Villari, *Revolt of Naples*, passim, esp. 3, 19–55, 74–97, 102–9, 123–4, 138–40, 147, 151–2. On the historical ills of Naples during this period, see also Venturi, 'History and Reform in the Middle of the Eighteenth Century,' in Elliott and Koenigsberger, eds., *Diversity of History*, 235–6. However, Richard Goldthwaite notes that traditional notions of the 'negative effect' of Spanish dominance in later Renaissance Italy have been revised considerably. Despite Spain's political and economic control over much of Italy, including Sicily, and also despite its politically and fiscally oppressive regime, it refrained from exploiting the sources of Italian wealth for many decades from 1550 onward. If anything, Italy profited from Spanish domination, at least in the short run, for though Spain removed great amounts of loot from Italy, it also brought in large amounts of money. Spain very possibly saw Italy as a favoured region, making up for deficit spending in Italy by money transfers from its less privileged possessions. As Italy's subject position saved it from the cost of funding its own military defenses, which Spain paid for at enormous expense, so the peace and stability insured by Spain benefited the Italian economy. Italy's favourable balance of payments up to 1600 is partly attributable to the Spanish presence, and many Italians pursued commercial and financial opportunities within Spain itself. The Milanese and Lombard economy flourished under Spanish rulers, who invested heavily in the countryside, and the same was true of Naples and southern Italy at least into the early 1600s, when Naples's economic development was undermined by a rigid system of land distribution as well as oppressive taxation brought on by the urgent need of the Spanish to finance their military efforts during the Thirty Years War. And finally, not the least advantage of Spanish rule was that it protected Italy against Islamic invasion. See Goldthwaite, *Wealth and the Demand for Art in Italy*, 22–4, 28, 29–33, 35, 51; Thomas J. Dandelet, 'Politics and the State System after the Habsburg-Valois Wars,' in Marino, *Early Modern Italy*, 12–13, 14, 29; Thomas James Dandelet and John Marino, Introduction to Dandelet and Marino, *Spain in Italy*, 3, 5, 7–15; in the same volume, Aurelio Muti, 'The Kingdom of Naples in the Spanish Imperial System,' 85; Dandelet, 'Paying for the New St. Peter's: Contributions to the Construction of the New Basilica from Spanish Lands, 1506–1620,' 182, 184, 185, 195; Giovanni Muto, 'Noble Presence and Stratification in the Territories of Spanish Italy,' 253, 254, 292, 294, 297; Paolo Malanima, 'A Declining Economy: Central and Northern Italy in the Sixteenth and Seventeenth Centuries,' 384–5; John Marino, 'The Rural World of Italy under Spanish Rule,' 411–12, 414, 429; Black, *Early Modern Italy*, 4, 11. In sixteenth-century Italy the upper classes maintained political, social, and economic primacy by supporting foreign conquerors, with whom they had more common interests than with other Italians. See Gilbert, 'Italy,' 33–5. For a contemporary (though uninformed) view of early seventeenth-century Naples, see George Sandys (*A Relation*, 1615), as discussed in Sells, *Paradise of Travellers*, 174–6.

134 See Sismondi, *Histoire des républiques italiennes*, 10:391–9; Kiernan, *The Duel in European History*, 6–7, 46–9, 70–3, 92–3; Frederick R. Bryson, *The Sixteenth-Century Italian Duel: A Study in Renaissance Social History* (Chicago: Univ. of Chicago Press, 1938), vii; Bryson, *The Point of Honor in Sixteenth-Century Italy: An Aspect of the Life of a Gentleman*, doctoral diss., Univ. of Chicago, 1933, 1, 4–5, 8–9, 12, 14, 27, 36, 46, 85; Jonathan White, 'Italy's Romantic Reputation,' in White, *Italian Cultural Lineages* (Toronto: Univ. of Toronto Press, 2007), 182. Croce remarks the Italians' belief that duelling developed in Italy as a result of the Spanish occupation. See Croce, *España*

en la vida italiana del Renacimiento, 141–2, 241–2. According to Pompeo Molmenti, duelling was popular in Venice from the fifteenth into the early eighteenth century, and as late as 1739 the Venetian government threatened duelists with legal punishment. See Molmenti, *Venice: Its Individual Growth*, Part 3: *The Decadence*, 2:71–2. Kiernan (cited above) contends that Italy's lack of a strong aristocratic tradition caused duelling to decline, with business-like assassination taking its place. However, in eighteenth-century Italy one section of the upper classes reacted against duelling and the cult of honour, which suggests that some Italians took them seriously. See Burke, *Historical Anthropology of Modern Italy*, 102–3.

135 Vaussard, *Daily Life in Eighteenth-Century Italy*, 93–5. For possible meanings and derivations of the word *cicisbeo*, see Angelico Prati, *Vocabulario Etimologico Italiano* (Milan: Garzanti, 1970); Alfred Hoare, *An Italian Dictionary* (Cambridge: Cambridge Univ. Press, 1925); *Dizionario Etimologico Italiano*, vol. 2 (Florence: G. Barbera, 1975). Although Stendhal, Burckhardt, and Pompeo Molmenti believe *cicisbeismo* to be of Spanish origin, the eighteenth-century Spanish priest, Fray Joseph Haro, held that it came to Spain from Italy, while many Italians have viewed it as a French import. Luigi Valmaggi describes *cicisbeismo* as a uniquely Italian development responding to specifically Italian social conditions. The anthropologist Julian Pitt-Rivers gives the impression that *cicisbeismo* exemplifies traditional Mediterranean values towards honour and female sexuality. See Casillo, *Empire of Stereotypes*, 291n; for *cicisbeismo* generally, see 108–23. James S. Amelang calls attention to the often noted resemblance between Italy and Spain, including the 'near complete overlap in the eighteenth-century custom of gallants attending on aristocratic women known in Italy as *cicisbeo* and in Spain as *cortejo.*' See Amelang, 'Exchanges between Italy and Spain: Culture and Religion,' in Dandelet and Marino, *Spain in Italy*, 454. On *cicisbeismo*, see also Valmaggi, *I Cicisbei: Contributo alla storia del costume italiano nel sec. XVIII* (Turin: Giovanni Chiantori, 1927), 4, 7–12, 22–3, 227–30, 239–42, and passim. See also Baretti, *Manners and Customs*, 1:77–107, 112–14; Luciano Guerci, *La discussione sulla donna nell'Italia del Settecento: aspetti e problemi* (Turin: Tirrenia, 1987), passim; Mario Barbagli, *Sotto lo stesso tetto: mutamento della famiglia dal XIV al XX secolo* (Bologna: Mulino, 1984), 331–6; Roberto Bizzochi, 'Cicisbeo: La morale italiana,' *Storica*, 9 (1997): 63–90, esp. 89–90; Julian Pitt-Rivers, 'Honour and Social Status in Andalusia,' in Pitt-Rivers, ed., *The Fate of Shechem, or the Politics of Sex: Essays in the Anthropology of the Mediterranean* (Cambridge: Cambridge Univ. Press, 1977), 41–3; Carla Pallandra Cozzoli, 'Dames et Sigisbées,' *Studies on Voltaire and the Eighteenth Century*, 193 (1988): 2029–34.

136 Andrieux, *Daily Life in Papal Rome,* 111–16. Jacob Burckhardt claims that, with the onset of *cicisbeismo* in the late 1600s, traditional Italian jealousy was replaced by indifference. See Burckhardt, *Civilization of the Renaissance in Italy,* 231. Peter Burke comments that travellers' 'contradictory accounts' of Italian women's freedom or lack thereof 'may well have resulted from the difficulty, for newly arrived visitors, of distinguishing courtesans from respectable ladies.' See Burke, *Historical Anthropology of Early Modern Italy,* 16. For travellers' varying responses to *cicisbeismo,* see Camillo Von Klenze, *The Interpretation of Italy during the Last Two Centuries: A Contribution to the Study of Goethe's 'Italienische Reise'* (Chicago: Univ. of Chicago Press, 1907), 28, 75n; Black, *British Abroad,* 43, 199, 201; Canepa, 'From Degenerate Scoundrel to Noble Savage,' 127–9, 138–9; Viglione, *L'Italia nel pensiero degli scrittori inglesi,* 332, 350n; Moloney, *Florence and England,* 19, 20; Maugham, *Book of Italian Travel,* 41; Smollett, *Travels through France and Italy,* 230–1; Baretti, *Manners and Customs,* 1:102–5; Brydone, *Tour of Sicily and Malta,* 2:89–90; Piozzi, *Observations and Reflections,* 52–3; Evelyn Martinengo Cesaresco, Introduction to Hester Thrale Lynch Piozzi, *Glimpses of Italian Society in the Eighteenth Century,* ed. Martinengo Cesaresco (New York: Scribner's, 1892), 12, 14; Eustace, *Tour through Italy,* 2:569–73; Staël, *Corinne, or Italy,* 94, 96–7, 98–9, 330; Casillo, *Empire of Stereotypes,* 108–23. Scholars have never determined conclusively the innocence or licentiousness of *cicisbeismo* (which is likely to have encompassed both possibilities), and its provenance remains disputed. However, it first appeared in Italy in the late seventeenth century and thereafter was widely diffused among the aristocracy of the northern and central regions. Feminist scholars have interpreted *cicisbeismo* as a minor if not frivolous manifestation of feminine revolt against the masculine double standard long prevalent in Italy. Others read it as a reflection of the crisis of patriliny or patriarchal hierarchy that intensified in Italy in the eighteenth century, the custom having supposedly arisen in reaction to the extreme formalism and lovelessness of eighteenth-century marriages. To avoid the dispersion of legacies, these patriarchs often placed their daughters in convents while barring younger sons from the familial inheritance. Yet over the eighteenth century inheritance laws loosened, with the result that women came to enjoy greater freedom and the marriage rate for aristocratic sons and daughters increased. Bizzochi, 'Cicisbei: morale italiana,' 66–73, 75–81, 87–8; Guerci, *La discussione della donna nell'Italia del Settecento,* 95, 97–130, 136–9; Patriarca, 'Indolence and Regeneration: Tropes and Tensions of Risorgimento Patriotism,' *The American Historical Review,* 111, no. 2 (April 2005): 399, 400; Pitt-Rivers, 'Honour and Social Status in Andalusia,' 40–7; Cozzoli, 'Dames et Sigisbées,' 2030–1, 2034, 2034n, and

passim; Gianna Pomata, 'Family and Gender,' in Marino, *Early Modern Italy*, 81–6; Hanlon, *Early Modern Italy*, 322–3; Dédéyan, *L'Italie dans l'oeuvre romanesque de Stendhal*, 1:173.

137 For Stendhal's Italy as the feminine, maternal land of 'woman enthroned,' see RNF 270, 274, 430–1; L 162, 190, 233, 291; RNF1817 25; PI 127–8, 130; HP 121n; Crouzet, *Stendhal et l'italianité*, 4, 11, 15–18, 159, 239–73, 274–84.

138 RNF 22, 85–6, 87–8, 116, 126; RNF1817 81; L 163; Crouzet, *Stendhal et l'italianité*, 265–70, 274–5n, 282–3n; Valmaggi, *I Cicisbei*, 142.

139 RJ 282; RNF 85–6, 116–17, 126; RNF1817 81; PI 131; L 163. See also Stendhal, 'The Women of Italy,' in SJ 244, 246–7, 259–63, 265, and passim. Although the essay is now attributed to Ugo Foscolo, Dollot and other earlier scholars assigned it to Stendhal owing to its congruity with much of his thinking on the social situation of Italian women. See Strickland, *Stendhal*, 235; A.E. Greaves, *Stendhal's Italy: Themes of Political and Religious Satire* (Exeter: Univ. of Exeter Press, 1995), 53, 172–3n; Imbert, *Les métamorphoses*, 148–50, 149n, 169; Crouzet, *Stendhal et l'italianite*, 264–9, 282–3n; Dollot, *Stendhal, journaliste*, 200–7; Dédéyan, *L'Italie dans l'oeuvre romanesque de Stendhal*, 1:88. Having been vilified as immoral by native as well as foreign writers during the eighteenth and nineteenth centuries, *cicisbeismo* was also denounced during the Risorgimento as a symptom of Italian decadence and more specifically effeminacy. See Guerci, *La discussione della donna*, 97–131, 136–8; Valmaggi, *Cicisbeo*, 7–12, 22–5, 230–1, 240–1; Patriarca, 'Indolence and Regeneration,' 382, 387, 389, 391–2, 393; Black, *Early Modern Italy*, 215; Sismondi, *Histoire des républiques italiennes*, 10:238–40, 393–4; Sismondi, *Historical View of the Literature of the South of Europe*, vol. 1, trans. Thomas Roscoe (London: Henry G, Bohn, 1853), 445, 479, 509–10, 523, 531; Sismondi, *Historical View of the Literature of the South of Europe*, vol. 2, trans. Thomas Roscoe (London: Henry G, Bohn, 1853), 26, 75; White, 'Italy's Romantic Reputation,' 189–92. However, in RNF1817 81, Stendhal attributes *cicisbeismo* to nature rather than to Spanish influence.

140 CP(ENG) 1:39; CP(FR) 39–40; RJ 282–3; RNF 88, 116–17; L 163; Imbert, *Les métamorphoses*, 148, 148–9n; Crouzet, *Stendhal et l'italianité*, 264–5, 369–70. Imbert links Stendhal's condemnation of *cicisbeismo* to the Jansenist critique of the moral laxity of Italian society, which parallels that of the eighteenth-century historian Ludovico Antonio Muratori, who likewise denounces *cicisbeismo*, and who is regarded as having been sympathetic towards Jansenism (though not strictly speaking a Jansenist himself). See Imbert, *Stendhal et la tentation janseniste*, 90, 108–9, 114–15. Although Lady Morgan extols Napoleon's apparently largely successful attempt to stamp

out *cicisbeismo*, John Mayne, who visited Italy in 1814, describes it as an ongoing, non-Platonic custom. See Lady Morgan, *Italy* (New York: C.S. Van Winkle, 1821), 1:162, 162–3n; Mayne, *Journal of John Mayne*, 224–5. To judge from other travellers' reports, the custom somewhat revived in the post-Napoleonic period and persisted until around 1850. See Roderick Marshall, *Italy in English Literature: The Origins of the Romantic Interest in Italy* (New York: Columbia Univ. Press, 1934), 80, 103, 244; Viglione, *L'Italia nel pensiero degli scrittori inglesi*, 442; Amfitheatrof, *The Enchanted Ground*, 51; Wright, *American Novelists in Italy*, 81, 119; Prezzolini, *Come gli americani scoprirono l'Italia*, 23, 61, 129, 189–92. For tolerant views of *cicisbeismo*, see Jarves, *Italian Sights and Papal Principles*, 126–9, 315; Hillard, *Six Months in Italy*, 2:242–3.

141 RNF 413–28; JI 67, 67n. On the question of whether Stendhal visited southern Italy below Naples, see Chaney, 'The Grand Tour and Beyond,' 143n, citing A. Mozzillo, 'Stendhal a Calabria?', *Storia e Cultura del Mezzogiorno: Studi in onore di Umberto Caldora* (Roma-Cosenza: Lerici, 1978); Leonardo Sciascia, 'Stendhal e Sicilia,' in Colesanti et al., *Stendhal, Roma, Italia*, 39–41; Sciascia, *Stendhal e Sicilia* (Palermo: Sellerio, 1991), 10, 12; Novati, *Stendhal e l'anima italiana*, 66, 67, 155n; Vito Carofiglio, 'Selvaggi, Turchi e intellettuali,' 387. Unlike most commentators, Carofiglio thinks that Stendhal may well have ventured into the south of Italy below Naples.

142 On northern travellers to southern Italy from the sixteenth to the nineteenth century, see Bertaut, *L'Italie vue par les Francais*, 159–68; John Walter Stoye, *English Travelers Abroad, 1604–1667: Their Influence on English Society and Politics* (London: Jonathan Cape, 1952), 190–1; Chaney, 'The Grand Tour and Beyond,' 134, 146–60; Venturi, 'Italia fuori d'Italia,' 1101, 1105–6, 1108–10, 1116; Edward Chaney, 'The Grand Tour and Beyond: British and American Travelers in Southern Italy, 1545–1960,' in Chaney, ed., *The Evolution of the Grand Tour: Anglo-Italian Cultural Relations since the Renaissance* (London: Frank Cass, 1998), 102, 104, 113–14; Goethe, *Italian Journey*, 179–341; Mozzillo, Introduction to Mozzillo, *Viaggiatori stranieri nel sud*, 9–89; Nelson Moe, *The View from Vesuvius: Italian Culture and the Southern Question* (Berkeley: Univ. of Southern California Press, 2002), 55–76; Black, *British Abroad*, 48, 54; Sells, *Paradise of Travellers*, 169, 171–83, 185–9; Ludwig Schudt, *Italienreisen im 17. und 18. Jahrhunderts* (Vienna: Schroll, 1959), 28, 29, 49, 52, 56, 57, 58, 59, 61, 62, 65, 66, 67; Carlo Ruta, *Viaggiatori in Sicilia: L'immagine dell'isola nel secolo dei lumi* (Palermo: A.A.A. Pittigrafica, 2004), 5–6, 8–9, 13, 21, 73n, and passim; Von Klenze, *Interpretation of Italy*, 59–64; Tommaso Astarita, *Between Salt Water and Holy Water: A History of Southern Italy* (New York: W.W. Norton, 2005), 220–49.

143 RNF 28, 123–5, 179, 188, 350–86, 388–9, 413–28, 435–7; RNF1817 49, 58,
    69, 116; RJ 43, 46–8, 51, 244, 245, 281; R 453–4; AC 207; JI 241–60, 259n,
    336; Crouzet, *Stendhal et l'italianité*, 78–9, 84n, 85n, 116, 119–20, 145n, 174–
    9, 313–4, 331, 361; Carofiglio, 'Selvaggi, Turchi e intellettuali,' 381–7; del
    Litto, *La vie intellectuelle de Stendhal*, 424–5; Burke, *Historical Anthropology of
    Early Modern Italy*, 41; Carpanetto and Ricuperati, *Italy in the Age of Reason*,
    45; Robert Orsi, 'The Religious Boundaries of an Inbetween People: Street
    Feste and the Problem of the Dark-Skinned Other in Italian Harlem, 1920–
    1990,' *American Quarterly*, 44 (Sept. 1992): 315; Clark, *Modern Italy*, 69–70.
    John Larner asserts that, by around 1200, centralizing fiscalism, high taxes,
    and the suppression of commercial enterprise were causing southern Italy
    to sink into 'that economic lassitude which still characterizes it today.' J.K.
    Hyde implies that southern Italy became permanently dependent on the
    northern Italian economy by the late 1200s. See Larner, *Italy in the Age of
    Dante and Petrarch, 1216–1380* (London: New York, 1980), 25–30; Hyde,
    Society and Politics in Medieval Italy, 128. Carpanetto and Ricurperati, *Italy
    in the Age of Reason*, 45, claim that the gap between northern and southern
    Italy became apparent in the seventeenth century. By around 1650, argues
    Rosario Villari, southern Italian backwardness was 'final' and 'irreversible.'
    See Villari, *Revolt of Naples*, 1–2. For the *lazzaroni*, see Casillo, *Empire of Ste-
    reotypes*, 188–97, 200, 328n, 329n; Benedetto Croce, 'I Lazzari,' in Croce,
    Aneddoti di varia letteratura, vol. 3, 2d ed. (Bari: Laterza, 1954), 198–211.
    For the *jettatura*, otherwise known as the *malocchio* or evil eye, see Giuseppe
    Galasso, 'Dalla "fattura" alla "iettatura": una svolta nella "religione super-
    stiziosa" del Sud,' in Galasso, *L'altra Europa: per un'antropologia storica del
    Mezzogiorno d'Italia* (Milan: Mondadori, 1982), 253–85; Casillo, *Empire of
    Stereotypes*, 196, 328n. On the vulcanism of the Neapolitan and southern
    Italian environment and its supposed influence on local character, see
    Casillo, *Empire of Stereotypes*, 212–20, 222; Moe, *View from Vesuvius*, 43–5, 44n,
    45n. See also LHMM 250: 'Naples is the happy land, the land engendered
    of fire, which is the cradle of the finest [operatic] voices.' Rejecting the
    idea of southern Italy's 'immobilism' and exclusion from Europe, Mozzillo
    emphasizes the links between them. See Mozzillo, Introduction to *Viaggia-
    tori stranieri nel sud*, 15–6.
144 PI 60–2; Imbert, *Les métamorphoses*, 62–3, 77–9, 260–1.
145 Diaz, 'La Reggenza,' 3–16, 22, 29, 31, 34–5, 37, 61–118, 119–238. See also
    Wandruszka, *Pietro Leopoldo*, 122–9, 170.
146 For eighteenth-century travellers' admiration for Leopold's reformism, see
    Casillo, *Empire of Stereotypes*, 281–2; Migliorini, *L'Italia dell'Italia*, 46–7, 47n;
    Venturi, 'L'Italia fuori d'Italia,' 1106.

147 For Leopold's reformism, see Hanlon, *Early Modern Italy,* 362–6; Procacci,
    History of Italian People, 235–9; Diaz; 'La Reggenza,' 208, 224, 235–8; Wan-
    druszka, *Pietro Leopoldo,* 13–14, 121–2, 126, 135, 167–73, 175–200, 238–46,
    266–7, 271, 277–85, 288–97, 343–50, 390–406, 408–10, 421–42, 494–506,
    521–5, 547–53, 555–60; Carpanetto and Ricuperati, *Italy in Age of Reason,*
    15, 51–2, 71, 170–4, 210–21, 234, 328, 329; Migliorini, 'L'età delle riforme,'
    258–394; Geoffrey Symcox, 'The Political World of the Absolutist State in
    the Seventeenth and Eighteenth Centuries,' in Marino, *Early Modern Italy,*
    118, 120, 121; Vaussard, *Daily Life in Eighteenth-Century Italy,* 15. Not only
    did Leopoldo's free-trade policies set off peasant revolts in the 1790s, hav-
    ing reduced Tuscan sharecroppers or *mezzadri* to poverty, but his attempts
    to redistribute ecclesiastical properties floundered when they ended up
    in the hands of the few rich landowners who could afford to pay for them.
    See Black, *Early Modern Italy,* 331–2; Procacci, *History of Italian People,* 237–
    9; Wandruszka, *Pietro Leopoldo,* 558–60; Broers, *Napoleonic Empire in Italy,*
    79–80.
148 RNF 123, 250; R 191; HP 286n; L 257; Wandruszka, *Pietro Leopoldo,* 423,
    426, 429–40, 494–506, 508–19, 529; Imbert, *Les métamorphoses,* 152; Miglio-
    rini, 'L'età della riforma,' 370–85; Imbert, *Stendhal et la tentation janseniste,*
    93–5, 99, 113–14. On Pietro Leopoldo's reliance on espionage and anony-
    mous accusation within his dominions, see Wandruszka, *Pietro Leopoldo,* 14,
    313–16.
149 RNF 145, 323; R 11; Imbert, *Les métamorphoses,* 63–4, 151–2, 284–5; Strick-
    land, *Stendhal,* 244–5.
150 Imbert, *Les métamorphoses,* 301–6, 353.
151 RNF 91–6, 122, 235, 237; RNF1817 140–1; RJ 102, 314; HP 150, 285n, 286,
    288; PI 28, 33, 84–94, 147; CP(ENG) 1:24, 102; CP(FR) 54, 113; Hanlon,
    Early Modern Italy, 320, 354–61; Imbert, *Les métamorphoses,* 163–8, 178–80,
    307–8; Imbert, *Stendhal et la tentation janseniste,* 91, 92; Strickland, *Stend-
    hal,* 110; Carpanetto and Ricuperati, *Italy in Age of Reason,* 158–67, 223–5,
    259–72; Greaves, *Stendhal's Italy,* 27–8, 31. On the limitations of Joseph II's
    reformism, see Carpanetto and Ricuperati, *Italy in Age of Reason,* 224–5, 234.
152 RNF 41, 43, 70, 95; RNF1817 148; R 450; PI 144, 145, 146, 147; JI 348; Im-
    bert, *Les métamorphoses,* 154–6, 253–9, 308, 456; Imbert, *Stendhal et la tenta-
    tion janseniste,* 99. Harry Hearder attributes the comparative prosperity of
    Lombardy during the Restoration not to the Habsburgs but to the Italians'
    industry. See Hearder, *Italy in the Age of the Risorgimento, 1790–1870* (Lon-
    don: Longman, 1983), 36–41.
153 RNF 22, 95–6, 122, 146n, 250; RNF1817 149; PI 144–6; Imbert, *Les métamor-
    phoses,* 156n, 179, 181–2, 255, 256, 307, 308.

154 RNF 93–4, 176; PI 91; RNF1817 140; R 12, 65, 98; Imbert, *Les métamorpho-ses*, 168–74, 177; Salvatorelli, *Risorgimento*, 38–42.

155 Hearder, *Italy in Age of Risorgimento*, 18–29, 101, 165–6.

156 For Stendhal, Napoleon's abuses as the dictator of France included the vio-lation of national sovereignty, enslavement of the population, suppression of education, disregard of public opinion, and frustration of the younger generation. Yet Stendhal defended Napoleon against Madame de Staël's harsh criticisms in her posthumously published *Considerations on the Revolu-tion in France* (1817), claiming that Napoleon had aimed at national glory while promoting the individual's right to fulfil his merits and obligations. See RNF1817 1423; RNF 22, 146, 336; RJ 105; Imbert, *Les métamorphoses*, 28, 105, 107, 246, 247–8, 319; del Litto, *La vie intellectuelle de Stendhal*, 576–9.

157 RNF 22, 56, 85–6, 336; HP 287; PI 53; Salvatorelli, *Risorgimento*, xvii, 61; Im-bert, *Les métamorphoses*, 180–3, 183n, 184, 185, 188, 244–6, 318–9; Manuel Brussaly, *The Political Ideas of Stendhal* (New York: Institute of French Stud-ies, Columbia Univ., 1933), 50–1. Aware of Napoleon's Italian (Corsican) origin, Stendhal thinks of him as an Italian sensitive to Italian politics. See RJ 43; RNF 214, 334. However, Stendhal would probably have agreed with Salvatorelli and Hearder that Napoleon thought himself French and always placed French interests first. See Salvatorelli, *Risorgimento*, 61–3; Hearder, *Italy in the Age of the Risorgimento*, 28, 29, 30, 163–4. For an assessment of the positives and negatives of the Napoleonic occupation of Italy, see Desmond Gregory, *Napoleon's Italy* (Madison, NJ: Fairleigh Dickinson Univ. Press, 2001), 65–6, 69–70, 75–7, 119–35, 137–9, 144–6, 150–4, 156–7, 176–7, 179–80, 184, 185–7; Procacci, *History of Italian People*, 258–9; Broers, *Napoleonic Empire in Italy*, 7, 8, 16–22, 25, 26, 35, 49–51, 84, 118, 125–6, 137, 177, 178, 193–7, 201–3, 207, 231, 235, 237–40, 245, 260, 275, 278, 284, 285, 287–98. Contrary to Stendhal's hyperbolic claim, a public sphere existed in Milan before 1796; however, it needed development, as he was well aware.

158 RJ 44, 48, 101, 126; RNF 93–4, 111, 145–6, 174–5, 335; R 267; THF 324; Hearder, *Italy in the Age of the Risorgimento*, 28. Although Stendhal some-times gives the impression that Italians filled the ranks of administrators and bureaucrats during Napoleon's occupation of Italy, Michael Broers observes that the French employed very few Italians for administrative purposes, much preferring to assign such positions to their compatriots. In the view of the disdainful French, the lawless and violent Italian elite was incapable of grasping the rational spirit and workings of the Napoleonic security state. For their part, most Italians regarded the French concept of government as too abstract and geometrical – that is, non-personalistic – for their taste. See Broers, *Napoleonic Empire in Italy*, 7, 8, 16, 26, 70, 137,

141, 157, 158, 166, 175-6, 178, 183-4, 186-97, 203, 207. For all his Italophilism, Stendhal shares something of the conviction of Napoleon's administrators and officers in the superiority of French civilization and its mission over that of the 'decadent' Italians, although he rarely approaches their contempt and disdain for backward, enfeebled Italy. See Broers, *Napoleonic Empire in Italy*, 7, 20, 25, 26–7, 118, 120–1, 163–4, 173, 201, 213–14, 218–22, 245–50, 254–5, 258, 260, 263. Whereas *Rome, Naples et Florence en 1817* harshly criticizes Napoleon's rule in Italy, Stendhal portrays it much more favourably in *Rossini, Rome, Naples and Florence* and *A Roman Journal*. On the negative side he holds that Napoleon dropped his mask to reveal his true despotic intentions, using Italy to test his authoritarianism. Thus Count Melzi d'Eril, who had hoped for an Italian republic, retired in disgust, and Count Prina became Napoleon's instrument. See Stendhal, RNF1817 142–3; R 267; Imbert, *Les métamorphoses*, 318–19, 322, 328; Hearder, *Italy in Age of Risorgimento*, 22–3, 25–9. Although Hearder notes Napoleon's meritocracy and excellent bureaucratic machinery, he regards him as totally immoral and unconcerned with Italy's welfare.

159 HP 287; RNF 22, 125, 145–6, 292, 334, 336, 459; RNF1817 144–5; RJ 98, 115, 259, 282; PI 61, 131, 221–2; R 97, 285, 441. See also Andrieux, *Daily Life in Papal Rome*, 94; Imbert, *Les métamorphoses*, 180, 181, 182, 185, 264, 319; Hearder, *Italy in Age of Risorgimento*, 22, 102–3.

160 RNF 192, 213; RNF1817 142; R 12n, 87; LHMM 258–9; RJ 44; Imbert, *Les métamorphoses*, 188–9.

161 Clark, *Modern Italy*, 49.

162 RNF 12; HP 34, 42; PI 156; LHMM 259; Imbert, *Les métamorphoses*, 319.

163 RNF1817 114–15; Rude, *Stendhal et la pensée sociale*, 233; Carpanetto and Ricuperati, *Italy in Age of Reason*, 34–5; Marino, 'Rural World in Italy,' 426, 428; Imbert, *Les métamorphoses*, 264, 290–1, 299–300.

164 Venturi, 'L'Italia fuori d'Italia,' 1062–3, 1182; De Tocqueville, Lenormant, and Goyau excerpted in Mozzillo, *Viaggiatori stranieri nel sud*, 446, 448, 618, 630–9, 654–6; see also Mozzillo's Introduction, 80. Mozzillo holds that, in addition to civil and social education, the protection of the peasantry (*contadini*) required rigorous juridical discipline in the transfer of property.

165 RNF 220, 429; SJ 78; Salvatorelli, *Risorgimento*, 37.

166 Stendhal, 'Women of Italy,' in SJ 239–67. Though the essay is by Foscolo, it has been regarded as consistent in some ways with Stendhal's views and attitudes. See also Dédéyan, *L'Italie dans l'oeuvre romanesque de Stendhal*, 1:173. On the licentiousness of young Venetian women confined to convents by greedy parents, see Pompeo Molmenti, *Venice: Its Individual Growth*, Part 3: *The Decadence*, 2:81–2, 84–5n. See also Symonds, *Renaissance in Italy: Catholic*

Reaction, 1:315–16; Hugh Honour, *The Companion Guide to Venice* (New York: Prentice Hall, 1977), 71–2; Lowe, *Serenissima*, 26–7. It is misleading, however, to imply that Italian women of the eighteenth and early nineteenth centuries were altogether barred from professional life, for despite the fact that, as in the Renaissance, they were often denied educational, intellectual, and cultural opportunities, it was nonetheless possible for Laura Bassi, Maria Gaetani Agnesi, Maria Pellegrino Amoretti, and others to excel in science, mathematics, and legal scholarship. From this point of view Italian society was perhaps more progressive than its French, English, and German counterparts. See Casillo, *Empire of Stereotypes*, 302–4n.

167 LL 103–4; Tocqueville, *Democracy in America*, vol. 1, ed. Philips Bradley (New York: Alfred A. Knopf, 1980), 47–51. In *Lucien Leuwen* Du Poirier's defense of primogeniture marks him as a reactionary. See Rude, *Stendhal et la pensée sociale*, 221–2; see also MT 110–11. In Italy, primogeniture had been favoured by the feudal aristocracy since the later sixteenth century in combination with the *fedecommesso*, which allowed the head of a family to place constraints on the enjoyment of an estate by future heirs. Ludovico Antonio Muratori warned of the evils of the *fedecommesso*, which among other things impaired the circulation of capital, and which the Lorraine dynasty in Tuscany sought vainly to banish from its domains in the eighteenth century. See Hanlon, *Early Modern Italy*, 169, 172, 424; Pomata, 'Family and Gender,' 75–82; Diaz, 'Il problema delle finanze e l'economia Toscana,' 86–93. Like many eighteenth-century Italian reformers, Gaetano Filangieri argues for the abolition of primogeniture. See Filangieri, *Scienze della legislazione*, in *La Letteratura Italiana: Storia e Testi*, vol. 46 (*Illuministi Italiani*, Part 5 (*Riformatori Napoletani*), ed. Franco Venturi (Milan: Ricciardi, n.d.), 697. Sismondi attributes numerous evils of post-Renaissance Italy to primogeniture, including fraternal resentment, the impoverishment of younger brothers, and their reduction to idleness and vice owing to their lack of property and industry. See Sismondi, *Histoire des républiques italiennes*, 10:388–9. However, Braudel notes that the abolition of primogeniture in France in 1789 led to an irremediable division of land as a result of which French agriculture declined in profitability as compared with England, where large estates prevailed. See Braudel, *Civilization and Capitalism*, vol. 3: *The Perspective of the World*, trans. Sian Reynolds (New York: Harper and Row, 1982), 562–3.

168 RNF 124, 147, 149, 234, 421, 466; RJ 237, 258.

169 RJ 189, 202, 218, 346; see also 81–2. Stendhal describes the 'average Italian' as a 'born gambler.' See R 444.

170 Andrieux, *Daily Life in Papal Rome*, 30, 83–6, 147, 154–5, 171; RNF 421; RJ 202, 245.

171 RNF 130. While in Stendhal's view the Neapolitans remain slaves to the fluctuating sensations of the moment, the Romans and Milanese are capable of passion, which requires feelings of intensity and prolonged duration. See Crouzet, *Stendhal et l'italianité*, 174–5, 176–9, 313–14.

172 RNF 74, 146–7, 199, 284, 466. On the Italians' lack of patience and attention, the consequence of their desire for instantaneous gratification, see Crouzet, *Stendhal et l'italianité*, 123–4.

173 For Taine, Hillard, Paul R. Baker, Misson, DuPaty, Smollett, Sharp, Dr John Moore, Martin Sherlock, Beckford, Piozzi, Henry Swinburne, Eustace, John Mayne, Richard Keppel Craven, Charlotte Eaton, Hazlitt, Ramage, and Ruskin, see Casillo, *Empire of Stereotypes*, 102–4.

174 Sherlock, *Letters from an English Traveler*, 75; Piozzi, *Observations and Reflections*, 232–3, 319; Eustace, *Tour through Italy*, 2:580; Mayne, *Journal of John Mayne*, 136–7; Viglione, *L'Italia nel pensiero degli scrittori inglesi*, 442; Hillard, *Six Months in Italy*, 2:7; Taine, *Italy: Rome and Naples*, 83.

175 PD 434; RJ 114; L 34, 159; RNF 430–1; Hanlon, *Early Modern Italy*, 174.

176 John Evelyn, qtd in J.R. Hale, *England and the Italian Renaissance: The Growth of Interest in its History and Art* (London: Faber and Faber, 1954), 66; Venturi, 'Italia fuori d'Italia,' 993; Addison, *Remarks on Several Parts of Italy*, in *The Works of Joseph Addison*, vol. 1, ed. Richard Hurd (London: Henry G. Bohn, 1854), 370.

177 Burke, *Historical Anthropology of Early Modern Italy*, 17. In a book whose translation appeared in 1964, Luigi Barzini describes Italian libraries as 'pitifully small and out of date.' See Barzini, *Italians*, 103. However, one should not overstate the deficiencies of Italian libraries in early modernity, for not only did aristocrats maintain libraries in their palazzi (though usually secondarily to material splendour), but the Counter-Reformation required local parishes to maintain libraries for parishioners' use, while monastic and conventual libraries served rural priests. Responding to Dr Samuel Sharp, an eighteenth-century English traveller who had maligned Italian libraries (and Italy generally), Giuseppe Baretti claimed that public libraries in Milan, Venice, Florence, and Rome met English standards, that ample collections of books for public use existed in many other important Italian cities, and that most Italian towns and convents had either public or private libraries; indeed, it was 'absurd' to think that Italians kept their libraries for 'mere show.' Luigi Mascilli Migliorini observes that eighteenth-century French travellers such as Cochin, Richard, and Lalande

found excellent public and private libraries in Florence, which also had a sophisticated literary society. Although Christopher F. Black recognizes that 'our knowledge of actual libraries before the late eighteenth century is limited,' Anna Maria Rao notes of that period that governments then began to sponsor libraries, having grasped the value of educated public opinion to the state. See Black, *Early Modern Italy*, 174; Baretti, *Manners and Customs*, 1:196–7; Migliorini, *L'Italia dell'Italia*, 42; Rao, 'Enlightenment and Reform,' 246; Vaussard, *Daily Life in Eighteenth-Century Italy*, 114–15.

178 RJ 37. Like many northern European writers, including Montesquieu and Bonstetten, Stendhal apparently thinks that Italian culture, being supposedly absorbed in the immediacy of sensation or passion, rejects intellectuality and rationality. See Crouzet, *Stendhal et l'italianité*, 99–100, 181. Actually, over the long run Italy has probably surpassed other European countries in shaping that rationality, in the sense of logical, systematic, ends-oriented activity, which Max Weber saw as uniquely Western. Its most significant contributions include Roman and canon law, the monastic system, the creation of an architecture of interior space, the foundations of capitalism in banking and commerce, scholastic philosophy (partly the work of such Italians as Aquinas, St Bonaventure, and Peter Lombard), time-keeping, cartography, the systematization of music and the pictorial arts (perspective), urban planning, bureaucracy, statistics, and the mathematization of nature (Galileo). The self-gratifying northern myth of the purely appetitive, sensual, non-cognitive Italian figures in the works of Robert Browning, for whom Italians have no place in the 'region of ideas,' not being 'thinking, originating souls,' and in D.H. Lawrence, who claims that Italians 'only feel and want; they don't know.' See Korg, *Browning and Italy*, 6, 13, 49.

179 RJ 42, 44, 112, 264; RNF 435–7; CP(FR) 47, 104, 147, 177–9, 223; CP(ENG) 1:14, 90, 148, 188–9, 248. For denunciations of Jesuit education, see RNF 162, 292–3; SJ 81, 108; Francesco de Sanctis, *History of Italian Literature*, vol. 1, trans. Joan Redfern (New York: Basic Books, 1960), 623, 715, 744, 776–81, 783, 793, 796. For Stendhal's anti-Jesuit sentiments, see RJ 102, 114; Greaves, *Stendhal's Italy*, 32, 72–3, 75, 91. The Jesuits had been founded in 1540 by St Ignatius Loyola as a spearhead of the Counter-Reformation and soon developed into a teaching order devoted to the harmonization of Catholic theology with Renaissance humanism. Disbanded by the Pope in 1773, following complaints of interference in secular affairs, the Jesuits were reconstituted in Italy in 1813–14 and came to be vilified in liberal circles as watchdogs of reaction. Stendhal sees the Jesuits partly through Jansenist and Gallican spectacles, as defenders of papal authoritarian-

ism. They thus promote the meaningless externality of ritualism while substituting for reasoned argument appeals to emotion, imagination, and the senses, as in the meditative method of St Ignatius Loyola. At the same time, Stendhal's criticism of the Jesuits in *The Charterhouse* and elsewhere exemplifies what Aldo Scaglione terms the 'liberal conspiratorial' view and is motivated by a distorting bias. The chief goal of a Jesuit education was to foster both citizenship and Christian belief, which were seen as compatible. Its chief instruments were Greek and Latin, especially the latter, as well as grammar, rhetoric, logic, and science. This was essentially a formalistic book-centred education, in which students learned to write like Cicero and to think like Aristotle. The Jesuits, who taught rich and poor alike, dominated secondary schools and helped mightly in saving the Catholic Church during the Counter-Reformation. Thanks largely to Jesuit instruction, the quality and competence of priests greatly improved. Francis Bacon praised the Jesuits for their discipline and learning; Father John W. Donohue refers to their 'civilizing discipline'; and Scaglione sees their pedagogical system as 'undoubtedly the most successful and influential' to have come out of the Renaissance. Hanlon mentions an increasing range of subjects, beyond humanistic training, taught by the Jesuits, and he assigns them substantial responsibility for the increased self-discipline evident in elite behaviour after 1650, when there was a vast expansion of colleges for adolescents. Although the Jesuits were the advance guard of the Counter-Reformation, they sometimes ignored or circumvented papal censorship. They were, however, noted for their harsh authoritarian discipline (which included corporeal punishment) and the suppression of the individuality of students through absolute obedience. The Jesuit didactic method stressed repetition, memorization, and dogma. By the later eighteenth century, amid charges of empty formalism, lack of vocational utility, and the boredom of incessant Latin composition, Jesuit education was widely believed to have failed to keep up with secularization. Some students with great expertise in Latin lacked the skill to write a simple communication in Italian. The suppression of the Jesuit colleges in the late eighteenth century is regarded by Hanlon as a victory for the expansion of literacy by the state. See Imbert, *Stendhal et la tentation janseniste*, 29, 59, 60, 74–5, 122, 124, 125; Aldo Scaglione, *The Liberal Arts and the Jesuit College System* (Amsterdam: John Benjamins, 1986), 1–6, 51–60, 67–73, 138–41, 147–9, 151–8; John W. Donohue, SJ, *Jesuit Education: An Essay on the Foundations of Its Idea* (New York: Fordham Univ. Press, 1963), 63–4, 66–9; Paul Grendler, *Schooling in Renaissance Italy: Literacy and Learning, 1300–1600* (Baltimore: Johns Hopkins Univ. Press, 1989), 363–81; Hanlon, *Early Modern Italy*, 124,

127–8, 175–6, 315, 323–4; Black, *Early Modern Italy*, 173, 186, 214; and the following three essays in Marino, *Early Modern Italy*, ; John Jeffreys Martin, 'Religion, Renewal, and Reform in the Sixteenth Century,' 40; Rao, 'Enlightenment and Reform,' 242; Schutte, 'Religion, Spirituality, and the Post-Tridentine Church,' 140–1.

180 PI 265–6, 278–9; AC 78, 80, 81, 86, 96.

181 Salvatorelli, *Risorgimento*, 49; Vittorio Alfieri, *The Life of Vittorio Alfieri*, trans. Sir Henry McAnally (Lawrence, KS: Univ. of Kansas, 1953), 26, 28. Citing the Jesuit colleges and other institutions, Vaussard contends that clerical education in eighteenth-century Italy was not as useless as Alfieri believes. See Vaussard, *Daily Life in Eighteenth-Century Italy*, 106–7.

182 Burke, *Popular Culture in Early Modern Europe*, 275–6. See also Molmenti, *Venice: Its Individual Growth*, Part 3: *The Decadence*, 2:49–50, on superstition among the eighteenth-century patriciate.

183 MacFarlane, *Lives and Exploits of Banditti and Robbers*, 121–2, 154, 156.

184 RNF 298–300; PI 271–2, 278–9, 282; Sells, *Paradise of Travellers*, 185; Jarves, *Italian Sights and Papal Principles*, 340; Howells, 'Italian Brigandage,' 169; Hobsbawm, *Bandits*, 43; MacFarlane, *Lives and Exploits of Banditti and Robbers*, 117–47, esp. 121. Jarves may rely on Stendhal, PI 278–9. See also Burke, *Historical Anthropology of Early Modern Italy*, 201.

185 RNF 328; PI 102, 237–8; RJ 330. For Stendhal's plagiarisms, see Alter, *Lion for Love*, 125–6.

186 RNF 390n, 391; L 44. Having proclaimed his support of republicanism upon arriving in Paris in 1789, at the onset of the French Revolution, Alfieri was disliked by the revolutionaries because of his aristocratic origins and in 1793 suffered not only the confiscation of his goods but expulsion from the city. This provoked Alfieri to undying francophobia, which he discharged in his poem *Il Misogallo*. See Sforza, *Real Italians*, 85–6. Besides admiring Alfieri's aesthetic relativism and disregard of French classical models of tragedy, Stendhal was impressed by his denunciations of despotism in his dramatic and polemical works. Ultimately, however, not only did Stendhal fault Alfieri's plays for their lack of dramatic action, a failing they shared with those of Racine, but he came to see Alfieri as an ineffectual rebel who, identifying revolution with his own heroic efforts, failed to grasp that it required ideological, economic, educational, and political preparation. See RNF 390–2; RNF1817 8, 51–2, 58, 89, 90–6; RJ 326; Imbert, *Les métamporphoses*, 78–9, 174–8; del Litto, *La vie intellectuelle de Stendhal*, 52–62, 58, 224–8, 228–9n, 238, 271, 368, 404–5, 462–3, 610. Similar personal failings were reported of the Italian writer Ugo Foscolo who, during his exile in England between 1816 and 1827, taxed the patience and

good will of his hosts. Quarrelsome by nature, Foscolo for no reason other than bad temper brought a suit against his friend Cyrus Redding. As Harry W. Rudman notes, 'what annoyed Redding was Foscolo's habit of arguing even when he was in the wrong and knew it ... [Redding] regretted the exile's loud-lunged, passionate, and overbearing manner in disputes, almost always of trivial origin.' See Rudman, *Italian Nationalism and English Letters: Figures of the Risorgimento and Victorian Men of Letters* (New York: Columbia Univ. Press, 1940), 184–5. See also E.R. Vincent, *Ugo Foscolo: An Italian in Regency England* (Cambridge: Cambridge Univ. Press, 1953), 14–22.

187 RNF 11, 97–8n, 142–3, 200–1, 220; RNF1817 75, 75n, 151, 166–7; RJ 126; PI 33, 36–40, 85–6, 90, 96–7; R 10–1n, 11, 286, 441–2, 457; RS 210; SJ 125–6; Imbert, *Les métamorphoses*, 78, 151–2, 155–6, 158, 186, 195.

188 PI 44–7; SJ 81–5; RNF 24, 194–5, 218, 218n, 263–4, 272, 394; RNF1817 71–5; HP 148; PD 57; SJ 82–4; Alfieri, *Life of Vittorio Alfieri*, 154; del Litto, *La vie intellectuelle de Stendhal*, 540–1, 584–9, 591–2, 596; Dollot, *Stendhal, journaliste*, 231–4, 239; Dédéyan, *L'Italie dans l'oeuvre romanesque de Stendhal*, 1:82. Stendhal's complaints of Italian literary language call to mind similar criticisms made by numerous native and foreign observers, including De Sanctis, Croce, Carlo Sforza, Staël, John Stuart Mill, John Addington Symonds, and Ezra Pound, to give only some examples. See Casillo, *Empire of Stereotypes*, 132–4; Sforza, *Real Italians*, 32–4.

189 Baretti, *Manners and Customs*, 1:228–1; Lacy Collison-Morley, *Giuseppe Baretti, with an Account of his Literary Friendships and Feuds in Italy and England in the Days of Dr. Johnson* (London: John Murray, 1909), 57–8. Thanks to the Counter-Reformation, by around 1600 Italian literacy more or less equalled that of Protestant Europe, but soon fell increasingly behind its transalpine neighbours. See Black, *Early Modern Italy*, 174, 186; Hanlon, *Early Modern Italy*, 128, 323.

190 Carpanetto and Ricuperati, *Italy in the Age of Reason*, 153, 226–7; Hanlon, *Early Modern Italy*, 320.

191 Vaussard, *Daily Life in Italy in the Eighteenth Century*, 113–7; Jameson, *Diary of an Ennuyée*, 236–7; Hanlon, *Early Modern Italy*, 317–319; Eric Cochrane, *Florence in the Forgotten Centuries, 1527–1800* (Chicago: Univ. of Chicago Press, 1973), 331, 333; R. Burr Litchfield, 'The Social World: Cohesion, Conflict, and the City,' in Marino, *Early Modern Italy*, 101–2. Litchfield notes that, whereas Italian culture had been dominated by regional courts up to the early eighteenth century, the reading public subsequently gained in importance as a result of the expanding publishing trade, so that, along with the proliferation of library societies and academies, virtually every capital in northern and central Italy had a gazette or periodical by the 1780s. Ac-

cording to Manlio Torquato Dazzi, the influence of the Enlightenment in eighteenth-century Venice is evident in its flourishing publishing trade as well as in its many libraries, which diffused books to all classes of the population. See Dazzi, 'Uno sguardo alla Venezia culturale del primo settecento,' in Carlo Pellegrini, ed., *Venezia nelle letterature moderne: Atti del primo congresso dell'Associazione Internazionale di Letteratura Comparata* (Venezia, 25–30 September 1955) (Venice, Rome: Istituto per la Collaborazione Culturale, 1961), 21–3.

192 Clark, *Modern Italy,* 34–7, 172–3, 177. Writing in the 1960s, Luigi Barzini notes that fewer newspapers per million of the population were sold in Italy than in any other western European country. See Barzini, *Italians,* 102. On illiteracy in Italy, see Hanlon, *Early Modern Italy,,* 324–5.

193 Baretti, *Manners and Customs,* 2:182–6; Rothblatt, *Tradition and Change in English Liberal Education,* 64–5.

194 Taine, *Italy: Florence and Venice,* 78. Stendhal, Staël, and De Sanctis blame Italy's post-Renaissance woes upon its failure to unify politically, a viewpoint later rejected by Croce. See Casillo, *Empire of Stereotypes,* 242–3; Germaine de Staël, *Oeuvres complètes de Madame de La Baronne Staël-Holstein* (rpt.: Geneva, 1967; Paris, 1861), 1:245–7; Andrea Maria Rigoni, Introduction to Leopardi, *Discorso,* 5–6; de Sanctis, *History of Italian Literature,* 2:621–2, 627–8.

195 RNF 284; L 262.

196 RJ 42; RNF 36, 123, 284. See also Crouzet, *Stendhal et l'italianité,* 228–9, 301–2.

197 AC 245, 250–4. See also Imbert, *Les métamorphoses,* 268, 269, 452–7, 605–7.

198 Imbert, *Les métamorphoses,* 14–15, 64, 68, 84, 154–60, 163–4, 174, 193–4, 196–7, 241, 253–9, 284–5, 287, 296, 301, 323–4, 345–6, 347, 354, 456–7, 606–7; LeRoy, *Stendhal Politique,* 35–6.

199 RNF 11–12, 220, 293, 429; RNF1817 8; PI 177–8; Imbert, *Les métamorphoses,* 15, 68, 161–2, 197, 272–3, 283, 354, 606–7.

200 Venturi, 'L'Italia fuori d'Italia,' 1214; Imbert, *Les métamorphoses,* 607.

201 RNF 11–12, 429; RJ 101; RNF1817 139; Imbert, *Les métamorphoses,* 272–3, 346, 607.

202 On the Italian state post-1945, see Clark, *Modern Italy,* 2–4, 327–426.

203 Casillo, *Empire of Stereotypes,* 26–8. Max Weber speculates that the harsh climate of northern Europe may have helped to promote the creation of technological conveniences and supplements. See Weber, *General Economic History,* trans. Frank Knight (Glencoe: Free Press, 1960), 130–1.

204 Casillo, *Empire of Stereotypes,* 26–8.

205 Like Stendhal, Staël thinks of the Italians as living entirely in and for

the present, and hence as lacking a purposive existence. Admittedly they have experienced a historical life at points in their past, yet the flaws of their character and climate must ultimately negate these achievements, returning them repeatedly to a blank point of origin, without having advanced historically. See Casillo, *Empire of Stereotypes*, 146, 218–21, 230–1.

206 On this theme, see Crouzet, *Stendhal et l'italianité*, 24, 28, 43, 44, 45, 141, 212–14, 215–16, 218–29, 232–3n, 233–4n, 290–2, 293, 296–7.

207 Crouzet, *Stendhal et l'italianité*, 97, 100–2, 105n, 113–14, 170–1.

208 LHMM 254, 255, 256; RNF1817 113; MT 293–4.

209 RNF 66, 190–1, 389; HP 39, 39n, 175, 177; RS 33, 47, 48, 49, 59, 62, 67, 68, 69, 70, 72; RJ 210, 255; L 257–8; AC 11–12; del Litto, *La vie intellectuelle de Stendhal*, 234; Stendhal, *Stendhal and the Arts*, ed. David Wakefield (London: Phaidon, 1973), 98–9.

210 L 44, 107, 140–2, 143, 160, 163–4, 250; RNF 155; PD 409; R 15; JI 106; Albérès, *Le Naturel chez Stendhal*, 36, 38; Girard, *Deceit, Desire, and the Novel*, 14–26; Crouzet, *Nature et societé chez Stendhal*, 55–67; Blum, 'A Theoretical Outline of Beylism,' 107.

211 RNF 2, 252, 274, 360, 438; RJ 185, 233, 242–3, 293; LHMM 254; L 61, 120, 138, 140–1, 142, 148, 228; RS 31, 52, 58, 59, 67, 68, 70, 195–6; R 241, 242–3.

212 RS 15, 69, 80; PI 36; L 140, 143, 146, 153, 160; LHMM 256; RJ 187.

213 RNF 149, 274; L 25, 33, 43, 135, 137, 140–1, 142–3, 160, 219, 226, 234, 291; RS 30–1, 52, 68, 70; RJ 290, 293; LHMM 40–3; HP 39; R 241; del Litto, *La vie intellectuelle de Stendhal*, 234; Manuel Brussaly, *The Political Ideas of Stendhal* (New York: Institute of French Studies, Columbia Univ., 1933), 61. For Stendhal on 'Vanity-Love,' see L 43, 145. He appears to have influenced Carlo Sforza's evaluation of French society in *Real Italians*, 143–4.

214 HP 183; PI 19, 42–3; LHMM 256; L 25, 28, 226, 291; RNF 128–9; RJ 185, 243; R 45, 207–8, 308; MT 93. Unlike Stendhal, Harriet Beecher Stowe regards the French as the very opposite of other-directed: 'French life is different from any other. Elsewhere you do as the world pleases: here you do as you please yourself.' See Withey, *Grand Tours*, 80.

215 Crouzet, *Stendhal et l'italianité*, passim; Rude, *Stendhal et la pensée sociale de son temps*, 242.

216 Crouzet, *Stendhal et l'italianité*, 87–104, 107n, 117–31, 136, 174, 180–1; Stendhal, RNF 243, 249; LHMM 40.

217 RJ 24, 131, 233; R 115, 172; Crouzet, *Stendhal et l'italianité*, 21, 29, 41, 80, 89–90, 92, 95, 107n, 137, 152–3, 172–3, 189–90, 194–5. The Neapolitan love of gesticulation, which the local historian Andrea de Jorio describes in detail, was regarded by the Victorian anthropologist Edward Tylor as a

sign of primitivism, supposedy betokening an inability to accept the self-sufficiency of speech in communication. See Michael Herzfeld, *Anthropology through the Looking Glass: Political Ethnography on the Margins of Europe* (Cambridge: Cambridge Univ. Press, 1987), 136–8. On Neapolitan and southern Italian gesticulation see Giuseppe Galasso, 'Lo stereotipo del napoletano e le sue variazioni regionali,' in Galasso, *L'altra Europa*, 149; Barzini, *Italians*, 62–6; David Efron, *Gesture, Race, and Culture: A Tentative Study of the Spatio-Temporal and 'Linguistic' Aspects of the Gestural Behavior of Eastern Jews and Southern Italians in New York City, Living under Similar as well as Different Conditions* (The Hague: Mouton, 1972), passim; Robert Connolly and Pellegrino d'Acierno, 'Italian American Musical Culture,' in D'Acierno, *The Italian American Experience*, 480. Exemplifying the Victorian prejudice against gesticulation, Ruskin denounces the gesticulating Florentines as 'being essentially unable to talk,' as 'they try to make lips of their fingers.' See Ruskin, *The Library Edition of the Works of John Ruskin*, vol. 23, ed. E.T. Cook and Alexander Wedderburn (London: George Allen, 1909–1912), 388–9.

218 RNF 287; L 160, 161, 226; HP 285; RJ 50, 51, 70, 316; LHMM 255; Imbert, *Les métamorphoses*, 328.

219 LHMM 238–9.

220 Andre Malraux, *The Voices of Silence*, trans. Stuart Gilbert (Garden City: Doubleday, 1953), 13–24; Walter Benjamin, 'The Work of Art in the Age of Mechanical Reproduction,' in Benjamin, *Illuminations: Walter Benjamin*, ed. Hannah Arendt, trans. Harry Zohn (New York: Schocken, 1969), 219–53. See also Daniel Boorstin, *The Image: A Guide to Pseudo-Events in America* (New York: Harper and Row, 1964), 101–2. Contrary to Benjamin, Dean MacCannell argues more credibly not only that mechanical reproduction confers 'authenticity' upon the work of art for the first time, but that mechanically reproduced copies of the original are themselves its 'aura.' If anything, mechanical reproduction renders the work of art more valuable by accentuating its uniqueness, which no copy possesses. See MacCannell, *The Tourist: A New Theory of the Leisure Class* (New York: Schocken, 1989), 47–8.

221 Migliorini, *l'Italia dell'Italia*, passim, esp. 8, 11, 38-9, 41–2, 44–6, 48–51, 49n, 59–60, 93–4, 142; Vittorio del Litto, 'Stendhal et Venise,' in Pellegrini, *Venezia nelle letterature moderne*, 105–6; Andrieux, *Daily Life in Venice in the Time of Casanova*, 14. On Florence, see RNF 300–27; L 241–2, 243, 245, 257; RJ 51; JI 336; for Venice, see RNF 69–70, 175; RS 210; PI 20, 29; L 241–2; JI 336, 341; HP 20; RNF1817 17, 85–6, 106, 112, 113, 114, 119, 120n, 121, 124, 128. See also Crouzet, *Stendhal et l'italianité*, 10, 54n, 178–9, 195, 250–3,

313–14; Imbert, *Les métamorphoses*, 285–6, 287. The young John Ruskin, notwithstanding his admiration for Florentine monuments, stated in a letter of 1845: 'Except when I am in the old churches, I don't like Florence. There is no feeling about it. Think what I will, it never touches one – the people are Leghorn bonnetmakers and one feels always in a shop. It is too busy to admit emotion of any kind – busy about nothings.' What disappointed Ruskin was the coldness of an essentially bourgeois city. See John Ruskin, *Ruskin in Italy: Letters to his Parents, 1845*, ed. Harold I. Shapiro (Oxford: Clarendon, 1972), 114, 116–17. Contrastingly, Taine praises Florentine beauty and creativity over that of Rome: Florence and Tuscany are 'truly the heart of Italy.' See Taine, *Italy: Florence and Venice*, 161.

222 HP 14; RNF 157. Jacob Burckhardt similarly acknowledges that Renaissance achievements required the despots' ability to surmount their egoistic and destructive impulses: 'In them for the first time we detect the modern political spirit of Europe, surrendered freely to its own instincts, often displaying the worst features of an unbridled egotism, outraging every right, and killing every germ of a healthier culture. But, wherever this vicious tendency is overcome, or in any way compensated, a new fact appears in history – the state as the outcome of reflection and calculation, the state as a work of art.' See Burckhardt, *Civilization of the Renaissance in Italy*, 2.

223 RJ 42; PI 18–19; HP 13–14, 29–30, 31, 63–4; Crouzet, *Stendhal et l'italianité*, 235n. On Stendhal's cult of the Renaissance and fascination with its forceful personalities, which anticipates the ideas of Burckhardt and Nietzsche, see Wallace Ferguson, *The Renaissance in Historical Thought: Five Centuries of Interpretation* (Cambridge: Houghton Mifflin, 1948), 129–31, 137, 179–94, 199, 206, 254, 295. Yet contrary to the assumption of many critics, Burckhardt's evaluation of the Renaissance differs from that of Stendhal and Nietzsche, as he does not celebrate its ruthless over-reachers operating on the other side of law and morality. See Maurizio Ghelardi, *La scoperta del Rinascimento: L'Età di Raffaello' di Jacob Burckhardt* (Milan: Einaudi, 1991), xix, 3–4, 20–4; Jacob Burckhardt, *The Letters of Jacob Burckhardt*, trans. Alexander Dru (Westport, CT: Greenwood Press, 1975), 235.

224 RJ 42, 261; HP 14, 29, 40, 83, 133; RNF 300–1. Compare Burckhardt's characterization of Castiglione's ideal Renaissance courtier: 'He was the ideal man of society, and was regarded by the civilization of that age as its choicest flower; and the court existed for him far rather than he for the court.' See Burckhardt, *Civilization of the Renaissance*, 200. For William Roscoe's favourable view of the Medici, see his *Life of Lorenzo de' Medici*, passim.

225 RJ 269; HP 42, 125, 177. Not only did the concept of the autonomous artist emerge in the late Middle Ages and Renaissance, but elite artists enjoyed

increasing social and artistic freedom along with a hitherto unprecedented degree of prestige, to the point where they exerted considerable control over the content and treatment of their commissions while being able to move on roughly equal terms with kings, lords, and aristocrats. However, most artists continued to labour obscurely under guild restrictions. See Kempers, *Painting, Power, and Patronage*, 4, 168, 242, 269–70, 303, and passim; Charles Hope, 'Wall Power,' *New York Review of Books*, 25 March, 1993, 61; Hope, 'Artists, Patrons, and Advisers in the Italian Renaissance,' in G.F. Lytle and Stephen Orgel, eds., *Patronage in the Italian Renaissance* (Princeton: Princeton Univ. Presss, 1981), 294, 295, 304, 306–9, 313, 315, 318–19, 328–9, 334, 339; in the same volume: Werner L. Gundersheimer, 'Patronage in the Renaissance,' 11, 16, 19; H.W. Janson, 'The Birth of "Artistic License": The Dissatisfied Patron in the Early Renaissance,' 344-53; Burke, *Italian Renaissance*, 88–96, 103–110; Lisa Jardine, *Worldly Goods: A New History of the Italian Renaissance* (New York: Doubleday, 1996), 23–4, 244–5.

226 RNF 81, 91, 190–1, 270–1; HP 15–6, 26.

227 RJ 21–2, 108, 270, 271–3; RS 72. For Stendhal and Bandello, see Armand Caroccio, 'Stendhal et les conteurs italiennes,' in Caroccio, *Variétiés stendhaliennes*, 41, 48.

228 Burckhardt, *Civilization of the Renaissance in Italy*, 82–4, 96, 193–4, 200, 334n. Burckhardt endorses Stendhal's interpretation of the deep sources of Italian vengefulness during the Renaissance, which 'seems to me to rest on profound psychological observation.'

229 Taine, *Italy: Rome and Naples*, 146, 177–8, 184–5; Taine, 'Philosophy of Art in Italy,' 31, 36–50, 70–2, 77–80.

230 Andrieux, *Daily Life in Papal Rome*, 34. A love of practical jokes persisted in Venice and its territories into the eighteenth century, including the wearing of ghost costumes, the placement of a brazier under a bed during a heat wave or a dead rat in a bed at night, the shrinking of undergarments, the tying down of a sleeping person to a chair, the substitution of salt for sugar, the release of crayfish into a darkened bedroom with candles on their backs, and a host of other tricks. See Pompeo Molmenti, *Venice: Its Individual Growth from the Earliest Beginnings to the Fall of the Republic*, Part 2: *The Golden Age*, vol. 2, trans. Horatio F. Brown (Chicago: A.C. McClurg, 1906–1908), 70n; and Part 3: *The Decadence*, 1:192; Maurice Rowdon, *The Silver Age of Venice* (New York: Praeger, 1970), 122–3.

231 For the Stendhalian *moi*, and its connection with the *naturel*, see Crouzet, *Stendhal et l'italianité*, 14, 23, 24, 41, 45, 48, 71n, 73–7, 78–9, 84n, 87–8, 89, 90, 92, 95, 97, 98, 107n, 117–22, 126, 158, 172–3, 175, 182, 184, 186–9, 191, 192, and passim.

232 PD 416.
233 RJ 24, 208, 290, 313; L 33, 35, 140, 140n, 141, 146; R 463–4; RNF 274; RNF1817 99; RS 194–6.
234 RNF 65–6, 86, 118, 270; RJ 17, 255; R 113; L 159, 226.
235 L 159, 160; RNF 200; R 289, 310.
236 RJ 313; RNF 251–3; JI 137–8, 171, 172, 175, 305–6; L 146, 154, 159; PI 105, 42–3; LHMM 40; RNF1817 58.
237 L 33, 143–4; PI 124; RNF 8, 199; JI 305–6; RJ 24, 25, 208, 293, 313.
238 RJ 29; RS 73; LHMM 242–3; RNF 85, 114, 152–3; L 159; R 19, 416n, 437; PI 122, 123–4.
239 RJ 23, 24, 131; RNF 199, 249; RNF1817 37; PI 79, 126–7.
240 RNF 128–9, 320–1, 430; L 34, 159; RNF1817 6–7; RJ 70; Brussaly, *Political Ideas of Stendhal*, 61.
241 RNF 117, 118, 252–3; RJ 52; L 143, 159; JI 305; CP(ENG) 1:2; CP(FR) 36.
242 RNF 339.
243 RNF 2, 3–4, 22–3, 199, 200, 224–5, 249; L 144; RJ 313; PI 176.
244 RNF 8, 22–3, 30, 31, 200; JI 87; Andrieux, *Daily Life in Papal Rome*, 154, 156. See William Wetmore Story's similar remarks in *Roba di Roma*, 33, 38, 174. For a contrasting view, see Beckford, *Travel Diaries of William Beckford*, 1:249–50.
245 RNF 20; CP(ENG) 1:32–3, 120; CP(FR) 60, 127. See also RNF 33, 421; Brombert, *Stendhal*, 145.
246 RNF 33–4, 58, 98, 104, 339.
247 RNF 117; RJ 100; LHMM 241; CP(ENG) 1:2, 28; 2:237; CP(FR) 36, 57, 440. For similar views, see Barzini, *Italians*, 11; Story, *Roba di Roma*, 308; Crouzet, *Stendhal et l'italianité*, 162, 200n.
248 Molmenti, *Venice: Its Individual Growth*, Part 2: *The Golden Age*, 2:114; and Part 3: *The Decadence*, 2:40–1; Andrieux, *Daily Life in Papal Rome*, 34, 43; Andrieux, *Daily Life in Venice in the Time of Casanova*, 81; Barzini, *Italians*, 49; Barzini, 'The Aristocrats,' in Barzini, *From Caesar to the Mafia*, 88, 92–4, 106–7, 109, 111–12; Sforza, *Real Italians*, 57; Pemble, *Mediterranean Passion*, 143–5. In a work published in 1892, the Marchesa Evelyn Martinengo Cesaresco notes signs of the disappearance of the aristocratic trait of mingling freely with people of all social ranks. However, the absence of snobbery and class arrogance in Italy should not be overestimated, as the southern Italian upper and middle classes have long disdained the local peasantry (*contadini*), whose lowly social position condemns them to shame, humiliation, and self-loathing. See Cesaresco, *Glimpses of Italian Society in the Eighteenth Century*, 18; Joseph Lopreato, *Peasants No More: Social Class and Social Change in an Underdeveloped Society* (San Franciso: Chandler,

1967), 67, 69, 70–3, 74–7. Ermanno Olmi's film *The Tree of the Wooden Clogs* (1978), which treats peasants and landowners in Lombardy around 1900, gives the impression that the upper classes of that region despised the local peasantry almost as if they were another race.

249 RNF 197–9; RJ 69, 223; LHMM 38, 39, 40; R 37; L 43, 65–6; Dédéyan, *L'Italie dans l'oeuvre romanesque de Stendhal*, 1:32–3; Casillo, *Empire of Stereotypes*, 13–14, 80. In *The Italians* Luigi Barzini notes Ignazio Silone's characterization of the Italians as a sad people, which in Barzini's view explains their resort to escapist fantasy as a means of palliating their despair. These impressionistic observations tally with the results of the statistical surveys collected by Alex Inkeles, showing that, between 1960 and 1986, and notwithstanding stereotypes of a 'sunny' country filled with 'smiling workers and singing peasants,' Italians stood out among other nationalities for their frequent reports of unhappiness. See Barzini, *Italians*, 336; Inkeles, 'National Character Revisited,' in Inkeles, *National Character*, 369–70.

250 Casillo, *Empire of Stereotypes*, 86–92; Barzini, *Italians*, 91–2.

251 RNF 4, 471; RJ 46; RNF1817 58; Crouzet, *Stendhal et l'italianité*, 331–3.

252 Barzini, *Italians*, xv, 77–9, 224; Sells, *Paradise of Travellers*, 54, 56; Burckhardt, *Civilization of the Renaissance in Italy*, 227.

253 RNF 92; PI 128–9; L 43, 51, 58, 219.

254 RNF 83–4, 85, 116, 128–9, 252–3, 272–3, 396, 468–9; L 159, 219; RJ 288, 294; PI 120, 126–7, 128-9; RNF1817 37; Crouzet, *Stendhal et l'italianité*, 244–5, 248–9, 258.

255 Canepa, 'From Degenerate Scoundrel to Noble Savage,' 132–43. On the 'rehabilitation' of Italy among northern European travellers, dating to about 1785, see Crouzet, *Stendhal et l'italianité*, 19–20. On the sincerity of the Italians, see Piozzi, *Observations and Reflections*, 51–2, 91, 296, 330–1. The mystique of the natural and sincere Italian (and southern European) persisted at least into the 1920s and 1930s. See Paul Fussell, *Abroad: British Literary Traveling Between the Wars* (New York: Oxford Univ Press, 1980), 131.

256 Piozzi, *Observations and Reflections*, 37, 43, 50–1, 54–5; De Tocqueville, 'Author's Introduction,' *Democracy in America*, 1:8–9. On the warm and friendly relations between the classes in nineteenth-century Italy, see John James Blunt, *Vestiges of Ancient Manners and Customs, discoverable in Modern Italy and Sicily* (London: John Murray, 1823), 249–51; Bertaut, *L'Italie vue par les francais*, 251; Taine, *Italy: Rome and Naples*, 281; Prezzolini, *Come gli americani scoprirono l'Italia*, 177–8; Jarves, *Italian Sights and Papal Principles*, 337.

257 Piozzi, *Observations and Reflections*, 43–4, 332. See the similar views of Lady Morgan, an admirer of Staël's writings on Italy, in Lady Morgan, *Italy*, 1:72,

109, 111. Stendhal, however, did not admire Lady Morgan's works. See SJ 82.

258 Brydone, *Tour through Sicily and Malta*, 2, 84.

259 Crouzet, *Stendhal et l'italianité*, 77, 197n, 198n, 199n, 205n, 278n. On the Italians' independent personalities, see Symonds, *Renaissance in Italy: Age of Despots*, 482; on their freedom from vanity and affectation, see the Italian writer Giovanni Berchet (d. 1851) in del Litto, *La vie intellectuelle de Stendhal*, 630–1.

260 Crouzet, *Stendhal et l'italianité*, 274n, 275n, 280n, 282n; Baretti, *Manners and Customs*, 2:178, 290; Baretti, *Manners and Customs*, 1:56, 63, 294; Barzini, *Italians*, 69. For some examples, see Sells, *Paradise of Travellers*, 167; Richard Lassels in Maugham, *Book of Italian Travel*, 23; Brydone, *Tour through Sicily and Malta*, 2, 20, 44, 350–1; Sismondi, *Histoire des républiques italiennes*, 10: 400; Jameson, *Diary of an Ennuyée*, 83, 274. According to Prezzolini, the more knowledgeable early nineteenth-century American travellers to Italy praised the courtesy of Italians of all classes. See Prezzolini, *Come gli americani scoprirono l'Italia*, 230–1. See also Jarves, *Italian Sights and Papal Principles*, 52–3; Hillard, *Six Months in Italy*, 2, 7, 334; Nathaniel Hawthorne, *French and Italian Notebooks*, vol. 14 of *The Centenary Edition of the Works of Nathaniel Hawthorne*, ed. Thomas Woodson (Columbus, OH: Ohio State Univ. Press, 1980), 438; Taine, *Italy: Florence and Venice*, 163; Story, *Roba di Roma*, 30. For similar responses among Victorian and Edwardian travellers, see Pemble, *Mediterranean Passion*, 133, 134, 135, 138–9. See also Wyndham Lewis, *The Lion and the Fox: The Role of the Hero in the Plays of Shakespeare* (New York: Barnes and Noble, 1965), 55; Wayland Young, 'The Montesi Affair: A Severe Case of Pseudo-Revolution,' *Encounter*, 9 (Sept. 1957): 29–30.

261 Burke, *Historical Anthropology of Early Modern Italy*, 9, 178.

262 RNF 31, 143, 366; Peabody, *National Characteristics*, 128, 141–2, 211–13. See also Stendhal, L 82; 'Clearly, modesty is largely something that is learned.'

263 For the resemblance between the south of France, or the Midi, and Italy, see RNF 132, 154; MT 98, 107, 113, 302; TSF 194, 196; RS 199; R 449n; Crouzet, *Stendhal et l'italianité*, 54n, 73, 74, 101–2, 128–9, 191, 195, 201, 245; L 36, 168. In Stendhal's view the Italians and southern French resemble each other in their prompt feelings, creation and enjoyment of music, and delight in existence.

264 Peabody, *National Characteristics*, 141.

265 RNF 33, 200–1; L 148; PD 429; RJ 288.

266 Richard Gambino, *Blood of My Blood: The Dilemma of Italian Americans*, noted in Peabody, *National Characteristics*, 141; see also 128, 211–13; Barzini, *Italians*, 106, 165, 222–3.

267 CP(ENG) 1:2; CP(FR) 36.
268 Barzini, *Italians*, 74–5, 82–3. Peabody notes Barzini's implication (on p. 56) that even Stendhal took the Italians' spontaneity and apparent simplicity at face value and thus failed to comprehend the role-playing, calculation, and artifice underlying it. Actually, there is reason to think that Stendhal also understood this subtlety of Italian character and behaviour. Peabody, *National Characteristics*, 138.
269 Burke, *Historical Anthropology of Modern Italy*, 9–10, 13–14; Peabody, *National Characteristics*, 138–9; Barzini, *Italians*, 182. On *bella figura*, see Gloria Nardini, *Che Bella Figura!: The Power of Performance at a Ladies' Club in Chicago* (Albany: State University of New York Press, 1999).
270 Burke, *Historical Anthropology of Modern Italy*, 12–3. Barzini registers a similar judgment; see *Italians*, 174. On the difference between guilt and shame cultures with respect to Italy and northern Europe, see Robert Casillo, *Gangster Priest: The Italian American Cinema of Martin Scorsese* (Toronto: Univ. of Toronto Press, 2007), 74–8, 443–7n; Symonds, *Renaissance in Italy: Age of Despots*, 481–7; Thomas Adolphus Trollope, *A Decade of Italian Women* (London: Chapman and Hall, 1859), 2:237–8.
271 RJ 44; Staël, *Corinne*, 180, 182; Casillo, *Empire of Stereotypes*, 60–1.
272 Burke, *Historical Anthropology of Early Modern Italy*, 12–4. Characterizing the seventeenth century as a 'great age of dissimulation,' Rosario Villari identifies Accetto's book with a general tendency within later Renaissance and baroque Italy to justify deception and concealment as indispensable tools of survival in the face of the political oppression, suspicion, and surveillance that then pervaded the peninsula. Yet though Villari connects the *elogio della dissimulazione* (panegyric on dissimulation) with Machiavelli, Pope Paul III, Paolo Sarpi, Tommaso Campanella, Virgilio Malpezzi, and other Italian notables, he regards it as a general European phenomenon of that century. See Villari, *Elogio della dissimulazione: La lotta politica nel Seicento* (Bari: Laterza, 1987), 3–5, 8–9, 17–48, and passim.
273 Barzini, *Italians*, 165; Peabody, *National Characteristics*, 139, 141.
274 RNF 287; THF 324.
275 On the differences between medieval and modern republics, see PI 16–17, 18–19, 51–2, 54–5; HP 28, 30; RNF 79, 446; Imbert, *Les métamorphoses*, 128–9; Venturi, 'L'Italia fuori d'Italia,' 1206–7, 1212, 1213; Crouzet, *Stendhal et l'italianité*, 220–6, 228, 232n, 233n, 234n, 235n. Although Sismondi admired the medieval Italian republics, he regards them as fatally flawed by internal disorder in contrast with Stendhal's celebration of that very turbulence as a source of individual resourcefulness and creativity. Ultimately Stendhal dismissed Sismondi's history as 'ultra-liberal.' For Stendhal and

Sismondi, see Strickland, *Stendhal*, 108. For Stendhal's criticism of Sismondi, see RNF 216; del Litto, *La vie intellectuelle de Stendhal*, 634–5. Whereas Sismondi traces a genealogy of modern democracy from the Renaissance into the nineteenth century, Tocqueville 'explicitly condemns those who judge American by classical example,' arguing that modern democracy is 'not at all the same as ancient,' and denying the relevance of Florentine democracy to nineteenth-century Europe. See Kahan, *Aristocratic Liberalism*, 82–3. Like Stendhal, Taine closely links the disorder of Renaissance society and its artistic vitality. See Taine, 'Philosophy of Art in Italy,' 104–6. Ezra Pound, who admires both Stendhal's writings and Italian Renaissance civilization, traces the pronounced individuality of modern Italians to the persistence of Renaissance influences: 'Modern civilization comes out of Italy, out of Renaissance Italy, the first nation which broke away from Aquinian dogmatism, and proclaimed the individual; respected the personality. That enlightenment still gleams in the common Italian's 'Cosi son io! [That's the way I am]' when asked for the cause of his acts.' Ezra Pound, *Selected Prose, 1909–1965*, ed. William Cookson (New York: New Directions, 1973), 199.

276 PI 20, 42–3, 77; RJ 98, 146; L 163; Crouzet, *Stendhal et l'italianité*, 42–4, 77.

277 L 36–7; R 44–5, 190, 205; RS 79. Stendhal refers to the same modern media-driven ideological partisanship that Jacob Burckhardt would soon observe during his brief stint as a journalist in Basel and that he deliberately escaped through flight to Italy, as he states in a letter to H. Schauenberg, 28 February 1846. Remarking this 'wretched age,' Burckhardt anticipates 'escaping from it to the beautiful, lazy south, where history is dead, and I, who am so tired of the present, will be refreshed by the thrill of antiquity as by some wonderful and peaceful tomb. Yes, I want to get away from them all, from the radicals, the communists, the industrialists, the intellectuals, the pretentious, the reasoners, the abstract, the absolute, the philosophers, the sophists, the State fanatics, the idealists, the "ists" and "isms" of every kind.' Like Stendhal, Burckhardt fled to Italy in pursuit of what he termed in the same letter the 'old culture of Europe' and 'a real eyeful of aristocratic culture.' Not only did Italy provide Burckhardt with a contemplative vantage from which to evaluate dispassionately the political and historical situation of northern Europe at that time, free of the distorting influence of the ideological and political partisanship raging across the Alps, but it afforded him the attractions of leisure (*otium*) in the classical sense, from which he, like Stendhal in his Italian sojourns, extracted the 'joy of pure existence' as against the restless, dissatisfied movement of the industrialized world. See Burckhardt, *Letters of Jacob Burckhardt*, 96–7; Karl Löwith,

Jacob Burckhardt: L'uomo nel mezzo della storia, trans. Laura Bazzicalupo (Bari: Laterza, 1991), 40, 45, 63, 140–4, 162, 165.

278 Crouzet, *Stendhal et l'italianité*, 28.

279 RJ 253; LHMM 10, 256; Crouzet, *Stendhal et l'italianité*, 43.

280 RNF 464–7; LHMM 467; JI 109–11; R 256; RNF1817 172–5. See also 152–3.

281 RNF 401; RJ 222. Stendhal was perhaps influenced by the debate between aesthetic and utilitarian values that runs through Staël's *Corinne*, in which the pro-aesthetic position is represented by the heroine Corinne and the pro-utilitarian stance is assigned to Oswald, her lover. See Casillo, *Empire of Stereotypes*, 74–5, 270-1n.

282 RNF1817 57; RNF 401, 444; HP 42.

283 Coe, Notes to R 489n. See also Coe's Translator's Notes in LHMM 267n.

284 LHMM 256; RNF 445, 463–4, 464–5; RJ 68, 195, 218, 327; R 44, 194n; L 27; Imbert, *Les métamorphoses*, 277–8.

285 R 44, 299; LHMM 10; HP 32; RJ 42; RNF1817 114.

286 Crouzet, *Stendhal et l'italianité*, 290–4.

287 HP 198–9.

288 Crouzet, *Stendhal et l'italianité*, 210–16.

289 RNF 17; R 44; RJ 34, 46, 97–8, 174, 177, 181, 233, 314–15. Influenced by Stendhal, Taine contrasts modern man, secure, tranquil, and spiritually tepid, with Renaissance exemplars of energy and will. However, he complains that Stendhal so overvalues the latter traits that he forgets the greater importance of the social bond. See Taine, *Italy: Rome and Naples*, 11.

290 RNF 154–5, 446; RJ 98, 294–307. See also Imbert, *Les métamorphoses*, 361–2.

291 RJ 182; RNF 218n, 305; HP 285; RS 194–5; L 136; RNF1817 77; Alfieri, *Del Principe e delle lettere*, ed. Giorgio Bàrberi Squarotti (Milan: Serra e Riva Editori, 1983), 155.

292 Stendhal, quoted in del Litto, *La vie intellectuelle de Stendhal*, 671; RJ 181; L 139.

293 L 138.

294 Crouzet, *Stendhal et l'italianité*, 224–5.

295 RNF 123, 233, 445–6; W.D. Williams, *Nietzsche and the French: A Study of the Influence of Nietzsche's French Reading on His Thought and Writing* (Oxford: Basil Blackwell, 1952), 139–40; Jean Prévost, *La Création chez Stendhal* (Paris: Gallimard, 1962), 169, 405.

296 RJ 69, 181; RNF 236; L 142, 160.

297 Barzini, *Italians*, 74–81, 83, 98–9.

298 RNF 92; Crouzet, *Stendhal et l'italianité*, 141, 212, 296–7.

299 RNF 466–7; R 44–5; Brombert, *Stendhal*, 141. Compare the similar views of British traveller John Chetwode Eustace in *Tour through Italy*, 2:581.

300 RJ 237; Maurice Bardèche, *Stendhal Romancier* (Paris: Éditions de la Table Ronde, 1947), 323–4. See also Luigi Foscolo Benedetto, *La Parma di Stendhal* (Florence: Sansoni, 1950), 25–6; Crouzet, 'Stendhal et la "coup de poignard" italien,' 219. Crouzet observes how, in Stendhal's portrayal of Italian violence, horror is mitigated by beauty, while the thrust of the knife is characteristically 'derealized.'

301 R 44. See also L 144; Imbert, *Les métamorphoses*, 277–8.

302 HP 28–30, 54. Stendhal's identification of republicanism with cultural vitality appears to have been influenced by Sismondi's *Histoire des républiques italiennes*. See del Litto, *La vie intellectuelle de Stendhal*, 363; Strickland, *Stendhal*, 108.

303 AC 15; R 44, 458, 462; Crouzet, *Stendhal et l'italianité*, 321.

304 RJ 26, 195, 242–3, 327; RNF1817 123.

305 RNF 467; Blum, 'A Theoretical Outline of Beylism,' 109, 110.

306 PI 120, 126; RNF1817 37; RNF 119; MT 53.

307 CP(ENG) 1:170; CP(FR) 164; RNF 226, 227; RJ 26.

308 RNF 254; Barzini, *Italians*, 157, 235, 327; Barzini, *Europeans*, 157. See also Staël, *Corinne*, 94, 102, 103; Casillo, *Empire of Stereotypes*, 69, 107–8; Edgar Ansel Mowrer, *Immortal Italy* (New York: D. Appleton, 1922), 47; John P. Diggins, *Mussolini and Fascism: The View from America* (Princeton: Princeton Univ. Press, 1972), 14.

309 RNF 466–7; Piozzi, *Observations and Reflections*, 27; Barzini, *Italians*, 190–4, 217–18, 327; Francis A.J. Ianni, *A Family Business: Kinship and Social Control in Organized Crime* (New York: Russell Sage Foundation, 1972), 16; Peabody, *National Characteristics*, 137, 206; Samuel K. Cohn, 'Burckhardt Revisited from Social History,' in Alison Brown, ed., *Languages and Images of Renaissance Italy* (Oxford: Oxford Univ. Press, 1995), 219, 220, 222, 229, 232, 233; Sforza, *Real Italians*, 53–7.

310 Anthony Molho, editorial commentary in Molho, ed., *Social and Economic Foundations of the Italian Renaissance* (New York: John Wiley, 1969), 152, 153; Baretti, *Manners and Customs*, 1:93–4; Trollope, *A Decade of Italian Women*, 2:318; Lauro Martines, *The Social World of the Florentine Humanists, 1390–1460* (Princeton: Princeton Univ. Press, 1963), 50–4; Denys Hay and John Law, *Italy in the Age of the Renaissance, 1380–1530* (London: Longman, 1989), 35–8, 41–2, 43–4; Black, *Early Modern Italy*, 217; John Stephens, *The Italian Renaissance: The Origins of Intellectual and Cultural Change before the Reformation* (London: Longman, 1990), 119-20; Alison Brown, ed., 'Introduction,' in Brown, *Language and Images of Renaissance Italy*, 17; in the same volume: F.W. Kent, 'Individuals and Families as Patrons of Culture in Quattrocento Florence,' 180–2, 187-8; Gundersheimer, 'Patronage in the

Renaissance,' 19; Paul Barolsky, *Giotto's Father and the Family of Vasari's Lives* (University Park, PA: Pennsylvania State Univ. Press, 1992), 133, 135–6. For a more favourable application of Burckhardt's concept of Renaissance individualism, see Marvin Becker, 'Individualism in the Early Italian Renaissance: Burden and Blessing,' *Studies in the Renaissance*, 19 (1972): 274–5, 293; Richard A. Goldthwaite, *The Building of Renaissance Florence: An Economic and Social History* (Baltimore: Johns Hopkins Univ. Press, 1980), 98–9, 104, 111–12, esp. 111. See also Taine, ctd in Crouzet, *Stendhal et l'italianité*, 226, 236n.

311 Peabody, *National Characteristics*, 81.

312 PI 238; HP 272; RNF1817 88; EIP 2:178; RJ 123; RNF 107, 163.

313 David Wakefield, introduction to Stendhal, *Stendhal and the Arts*, ed. Wakefield, 14, 15; see also 38; Crouzet, *Stendhal et l'italianité*, 65n; PI 14–15; HP 90; L 242; LHB 233.

314 EIP passim; JI 207, 209–10; RS 91; Philippe Berthier, *Stendhal et ses peintres italiennes* (Geneva: Droz, 1977), passim, esp. 21, 22–3, 26, 39, 40, 41, 43, 55; Albérès, *Le naturel chez Stendhal*, 103; del Litto, *La vie intellectuelle de Stendhal*, 28.

315 HP 42n, 92–3, 94, 117–18, 119, 165, 167, 178, 179, 180, 182; RJ 32, 39; RNF 12, 76; EIP 1:67, 76; RS 91–2. Taine expresses similar views in 'The Philosophy of Art,' 154–5, and in *Italy: Florence and Venice*, 244–5.

316 L 257; RNF 300–27; RNF1817 17, 74, 85; HP 119, 122, 123, 125; RJ 51; Crouzet, *Stendhal et l'italianité*, 10, 54n, 313–4; Imbert, *Les métamorphoses*, 285–6, 287.

317 RNF 2, 12, 76, 258, 309, 349, 455, 462; RJ 186, 192; Pier Paolo Trompeo, *Nell'Italia romantica sull'orme di Stendhal* (Roma: Casa Editrice Leonardo da Vinci, 1964), 222; Strickland, *Stendhal*, 110.

318 HP 42; RJ 136. Arnold Hauser identifies Le Brun with that historical moment when 'Baroque culture becomes more and more an authoritarian court culture,' and 'court life also passes from a state of comparative freedom to one of strict regimentation.' Le Brun and Boileau became artistic legislators and at the king's bidding promulgated an 'aesthetic of classicism ... guided by the principles of absolutism – the absolute primacy of the political conception over all the other expressions of cultural life.' Like the state, and like an army, 'art should have a uniform character,' at once formally perfect, clear and precise, and governed by absolute rules. Unlike ancient and Renaissance classicism, this modern version sacrificed the artist's subjectivity to 'the typical, the impersonal, the universally valid.' As the perpetual director of the Royal Academy, and the equivalent of minister of the fine arts, Le Brun transformed artists into 'creatures of the state educa-

tional system.' His codification of artistic values and insistence on the slavish observance of technical formulae make him the 'real creator' of French academicism in painting. See Hauser, *The Social History of Art*, 2:190–8. However, Stendhal is perhaps unfair to Louis XIV, who sought to employ the aged Bernini in the completion of the Louvre, but whose aims were undermined by his minister Colbert. Yet Stendhal also disliked Bernini's work, regarding him as an originator of rococo. See Cecil Gould, *Bernini in France: An Episode in Seventeenth-Century History* (Princeton: Princeton Univ. Press, 1982), 1–5, 12–15, 16–22, 38–9, 53–4, 118–19, and passim; Braudel, *Out of Italy*, 162, 173, 176, 178, 180; RJ 59–60, 117–18, 219. Stendhal's judgment of Louis XIV and Lebrun calls to mind Burckhardt, who 'tremble[s] to think what might have happened if Rubens had had to develop under the domination of Louis XIV, and to become his Lebrun.' See Burckhardt, *Recollections of Rubens*, trans. Mary Hottinger (London: Phaidon, 1950), 15.

319 HP 401–2; RJ 39, 136, 256; MT 93; Berthier, *Stendhal et ses peintres italiens*, 72–6.

320 HP 38–9; LHB, 34.

321 HP 258–60, 261, 263–6, 278, 280, 281n, 282, 290, 401–2; R 53; MT 93; TSF 15; RNF 76–7; Berthier, *Stendhal et ses peintres italiennes*, 73, 74, 75, 77–8; Stendhal, *Stendhal and the Arts*, ed. Wakefield, 68–72, 77, 87, 116–17. Michelangelo was on the whole celebrated in England during the period of his anathema in France. See Marshall, *Italy in English Literature*, 3, 71, 72–8, 100, 109, 193, 194, 283, 284–5, 297, 299, 301, 302. See also Lene Ostermark-Johansen, *Sweetness and Strength: The Reception of Michelangelo in Late Victorian England* (Aldershot: Ashgate, 1998).

322 TSF 13, 15, 48, 57; RNF 39, 62; Christian Elling, *Rome: The Biography of Her Architecture from Bernini to Thorwaldsen* (Boulder, CO: Westview Press, 1975), 26.

323 RJ 17, 53, 83, 90, 216–17; RNF 39, 62, 305; RNF1817 43–4. Stendhal seems to have inspired Hippolyte Taine's judgments of Roman buildings. See Taine, *Italy: Rome and Naples*, 18, 103, 104.

324 RJ 82; see also JI 180, 182, 189; PD 417. Stendhal acknowledges that, unlike Paris, the streets of Milan lack sewers, yet adds that 'good order' and 'perfect cleanliness' are not the *sine qua non* of happiness. The contrast between Italian splendour and northern European or American comfort and convenience is commonplace. See Taine, 'Philosophy of Art in Italy,' 59–60; Jarves, *Italian Sights and Papal Principles*, 35–6; Crouzet, *Stendhal et l'italianité*, 193; Casillo, *Empire of Stereotypes*, 135–6, 297–8n. However, in *Rome, Naples et Florence en 1817*, 11, Stendhal says that Milan has the most beautiful streets and pathways in Europe.

325 RJ 138–9. For a discussion of how, by contrast with modern urbanism, Italian cities and piazze typically achieve aesthetic distinction through formal asymmetry and variety, see Camillo Sitte, *City Planning according to Artistic Principles* (first published in 1889 as *Der Städtebau*), trans. George R. Collins and Christiane Craseman Collins (New York: Random House, 1965), 3–59, 83–104. Many of Sitte's insights were anticipated by Théophile Gautier, who complains of the 'immense empty spaces' typical of the urban squares of such modern capitals as London, Paris, and St Petersburg, where 'cold symmetry' prevails, and where the 'great empty fields ... fruitlessly absorb fountains, statues, arches, obelisks, candelabra, and gardens.' In Italy it is understood that a square, 'to produce a fine effect, should not be too large; beyond a certain limit, the glance fails to take in the whole.' Italian squares further differ from the northern in being 'bordered by different buildings of diverse height.' See Gautier, *Voyage en Italie* (Paris: G. Charpentier, 1908), 339. See also Taine, *Italy: Rome and Naples*, 17. Luigi Barzini much exaggerates in referring to the Italians' national compulsion to regularity and rigid symmetry in buildings as in urban planning. See Barzini, *Italians*, 111–12.

326 Piozzi, *Observations and Reflections*, 213. The fastidious Lady Morgan similarly objects to washerwomen's clotheslines hanging from the windows of Roman palaces. See Lady Morgan, *Italy*, 2:137.

327 RJ 138–9; Von Klenze, *Interpretation of Italy*, 24; Vaussard, *Daily Life in Eighteenth-Century Italy*, 25; Stendhal, qtd in Andrieux, *Daily Life in Papal Rome*, 18, 18n. On the contrast between the irregularity and disorder of Naples, which bespeaks the failure of urban planning, and the symmetrically designed and 'rationally planned streets and piazzas' of Turin, which pleases some observers yet wearies others as a result of its 'tame and tiresome uniformity,' see Jonathan White, 'Capital Contrasts: Naples and Turin a Century before Unification,' in White, *Italian Cultural Lineages*, 125–7. However, Stendhal admires Italian neoclassical architects (such as Giuseppe Valadier) for improving the early nineteenth-century Roman townscape. See Claudon, 'Stendhal et le Neo-Classicisme Romaine,' 85, 88.

328 LHMM 12–17, 22–3, 54–5, 63, 75–7, 127, 209, 210–11, and passim; Coe, Translator's Foreword to Stendhal, LHMM x, xii, xxii, xxvii, xxix, xxx; R 10, 20, 61, 67, 122, 128, 132, 133, 170, 221, 242, 300, 301–2, 306, 325, 337–8, 345, 382n, 411, 449, 449n; RNF 57–8, 176, 460, 486n, 492n; RNF1817 15, 121; RJ 194; LHB, 285. Stendhal's animus against technical complexity and proficiency may reflect his failed attempt to learn the cello. See Coe, Notes to R 486n.

329 R 8–9, 39, 316, 340, 355n; RJ 37.

330 LHMM 15, 21, 242, 253; RJ 186–7, 233; R 14, 16, 115, 118, 132, 269, 437–8, 439; MT 148, 151.

331 Andrieux, *Daily Life in Papal Rome*, 160–3; R 118, 315–16, 347, 348; RNF1817 11. See also Beckford, *Travel Diaries of William Beckford*, 1:201; Mead, *Grand Tour in the Eighteenth Century*, 300; Brand, *Italy and the English Romantics*, 20, 178; Viglione, *L'Italia nel pensiero degli scrittori inglesi*, 442; Vaussard, *Daily Life in Eighteenth Century Italy*, 159–60, 166, 167; Bertaut, *L'Italie vue par les francais*, 56–7, 88–90, 110–12. William Wetmore Story found Italian theatre seats uncomfortable, in keeping with the Italian disregard for comfort. See Story, *Roba di Roma*, 204, 205.

332 RNF 442, 457–8; RNF1817 8, 21; RJ 316; L 144, 145; R 12–13, 289, 441–2, 457–8; SJ 126; THF 307, 318, 331–2; LHB 342n; Crouzet, *Stendhal et l'italianité*, 299–302; Alter, *Lion for Love*, 211. Like Alter, Leonardo Sciascia regards Stendhal as very much French rather than Italian in temperament. See Sciascia, *Stendhal e Sicilia*, 20. Carlo Sforza describes Stendhal's temperament as 'essentially Italian.' See Sforza, *Real Italians*, 78.

333 HP 303; RNF 12–13, 37, 146, 349, 462; RNF1817 8, 29; RJ 70, 208, 287, 288; MT 299-300; AC 207–8; SJ 78; Crouzet, *Stendhal et l'italianité*, 237n.

334 Graña, *Bohemian versus Bourgeois*, 168–171, 186–7, 204.

335 Herbert Marcuse, *Eros and Civilization: A Philosophical Inquiry into Freud* (New York: Vintage, 1962), ix, 42–3, 93, 94, 142, and passim; Marcuse, 'The Affirmative Character of Culture,' in Marcuse, *Negations: Essays on Critical Theory*, trans. Jeremy J. Shapiro (Boston: Beacon, 1968), 93–5; Max Horkheimer, 'The End of Reason,' in Andrew Arato and Eike Gebhardt, eds., *The Essential Frankfurt School Reader* (New York: Urizen, 1978), 33–4, 38–9; Marcuse, 'On Some Social Implications of Technology,' in Arato and Gebhardt, *The Essential Frankfurt School Reader*, 141, 142, 143, 145, 158; Martin Jay, *The Dialectical Imagination: A History of the Frankfurt School and the Institute of Social Research, 1923–1950* (New York: Little Brown, 1973), passim.

336 Jay, *Dialectical Imagination*, 215; Marcuse, *One-Dimensional Man: Studies in the Ideology of Advanced Industrial Society* (Boston: Beacon, 1966), 58–9; Marcuse, 'Affirmative Character of Culture,' 124. On the Frankfurt School theorists' qualified optimism towards technology, see Patrick Brantlinger, *Bread and Circuses: Theories of Mass Culture as Social Decay* (Ithaca: Cornell Univ. Press, 1983), 230, 241, 242. Brantlinger quotes Max Horkheimer: 'The fault is not in machines.'

337 Marcuse, *One-Dimensional Man*, 58, 59; Marcuse, *Eros and Civilization*, 40–6.

338 Coe, Introduction to RNF xxi; Jay, *Dialectical Imagination*, 179–80; Marcuse, *One-Dimensional Man*, 60; Marcuse, *Eros and Civilization*, 45; Marcuse, 'The Affirmative Character of Culture,' 114–15; Theodor Adorno, *Aesthetic The-*

ory, trans. C. Lenhardt (London: Routledge and Kegan Paul, 1986), 430; Brantlinger, *Bread and Circuses*, 230.

339 RNF 41.

340 L 66n.

341 Marcuse, *Eros and Civilization*, 127–31, 135, 145. Stendhal's utopianism is manifest in his attraction to Fourier's social theory, whose central idea according to Marcuse is the 'transformation of labor into pleasure' and 'pleasurable cooperation.' See Marcuse, *Eros and Civilization*, 198–9. Positing a 'law' of 'passionate attraction' among human beings, Fourier sought to replace what he saw as the overly rational and repressive regime of modern civilization with a utopian order in which emotion and more especially the passions were allowed their proper gratification, and in which pleasure, having become a social norm or requirement, even ceased to be incompatible with work. See Frank E. Manuel, *The Prophets of Paris* (Cambridge: Harvard Univ. Press, 1962), 9, 197, 210-15, 217–18, 220, 222, 224, 226–8, 230–1, 235, 240.

342 Marcuse, 'Affirmative Character of Culture,' 98, 100, 103, 108–15, 117, 119, 121, 122–3, 126, 129, 131; Marcuse, 'On Hedonism,' in *Negations*, 159–200, esp. 162, 163, 168–9; Marcuse, *Eros and Civilization*, 130–1, 157, 160–2, 164–5, 167–9, 172–7; Jay, *Dialectical Imagination*, 58–9, 179–80; L 55n; Williams, *Nietzsche*, 91, 133–5, 134n; White, *Metahistory*, 368.

343 Herbert Marcuse, *The Aesthetic Dimension: Toward a Critique of Marxist Aesthetics* (Boston: Beacon, 1978), 72–3; Russell Berman, 'Consumer Society: The Legacy of the Avant-Garde and the False Sublation of Aesthetic Autonomy,' 44, 45, 47, 49; and Berman, 'Modern Art and Desublimation,' 82, 85, 92–3: both essays in Berman, *Modern Culture and Critical Theory: Art, Politics, and the Legacy of the Frankfurt School* (Madison: Univ. of Wisconsin Press, 1989); Andreas Huyssen, 'Mapping the Postmodern,' in Charles Jencks, ed., *The Post-Modern Reader* (London: St. Martin's Press, 1992), 62.

344 PD 396; R 15, 17, 73, 173, 442; LHMM 74–5; RNF1817 7, 39; L 231.

345 R 16; RJ 9, 59. In the latter text Stendhal observes that a visit to St Peter's ought not to become a matter of duty after fatigue sets in.

346 Marcuse, *Eros and Civilization*, 132; Berman, 'Modern Art and Desublimation,' 82, 85; Gary Cross, *Time and Money: The Making of Consumer Culture* (London: Routledge, 1993), 50–1.

347 Adorno, 'On the Fetish-Character in Music and the Regression of Listening,' in Arato and Gebhardt, *Frankfurt School Reader*, 274.

348 Adorno, *Aesthetic Theory*, 430.

349 RNF 463, 466; see also 445; RJ 222, 254; Imbert, *Les métamorphoses*, 288.

350 RNF 88–9, 148, 226, 456; RNF1817 18, 105, 155–6; R 46, 410, 449, 461; MT

20; PD 410; PI 160; RJ 20, 22, 67, 130, 131, 191, 256; THF 180–1; HP 81n; L 36, 86n, 233; RS 36, 163. Pemble acknowledges the truth of Stendhal's view of the British in *Mediterranean Passion*, 73–4.

351 L 242, 243. This difference was noted by the British themselves. See Blunt, *Vestiges of Ancient Manners and Customs, discoverable in Modern Italy and Sicily*, 282–3. For a similar American view, see George Stillman Hillard, *Six Months in Italy*, 2:268–71.

352 Coe, Notes to R 499n; RJ 191; Stendhal, *Stendhal and the Arts*, ed. Wakefield, 132. On the suppression of the facial expressiveness of the suffering human being under the legal and administrative discipline of bourgeois society, see Theodor Adorno as discussed by Russell Berman, 'Is Liberty an "Invention of the Ruling Class"?' in Berman, *Modern Culture and Critical Theory*, 20, 22, 23.

353 MT 166, 273, 275.

354 Stuart Ewen, *All-Consuming Images: The Politics of Style in Contemporary Culture* (New York: Basic Books, 1984), 203, 205, 206.

355 PD 457; RNF 350. For Bentham's panopticon, which apparently was intended for workshops for shipwrights, but which he adapted to prisons, houses of industry, poorhouses, factories, insane asylums, schools, etc., see Egbert, *Social Radicalism and the Arts*, 382.

356 Del Litto, *La vie intellectuelle de Stendhal*, 387–91; Strickland, *Stendhal*, 50–1, 264. See also Rude, *Stendhal et la pensée sociale*, 59–61, 166–7; John Tyree Fain, *Ruskin and the Economists* (Nashville: Vanderbilt Univ. Press, 1956), 54, 75–6, 84–6, 147–8, 149; James Clark Sherburne, *John Ruskin, or the Ambiguities of Abundance: A Study in Social and Economic Criticism* (Cambridge: Harvard Univ. Press, 1972), 41, 73, 129, 142, 145–7, 149–53, 179, 284.

357 Crouzet, *Stendhal et l'italianité*, 73, describes Stendhal as being 'under the double patronage of Epicurus and Bentham' (sous le double patronage d'Épicure et de Bentham). See also Stendhal, RJ 147.

358 Stendhal, *D'un nouveau complot contre les industriels* (Paris: Flammarion, 1972); in the same volume, Geneviève Mouillaud, 'Le Pamphlet Impossible: Construction et Deconstruction d'une idéologie stendhalienne,' 89. See also Rude, *Stendhal et la pensée sociale*, 105–14; Egbert, *Social Radicalism and the Arts*, 41, 118.

359 Stendhal, *D'un nouveau complot contre les industriels*: in this volume, see *Le Producteur*, no. I, Introduction, 20–1; *Le Pandore*, 3 Dec. 1825, 38–9; *Journal de Commerce*, 3 Dec. 1825, 42–3; *Le Producteur*, 3 Dec. 1825, 43–6. See also Rude, *Stendhal et la pensée sociale*, 102–3, 107, 113, 115–19, 122, 124–5, 130–3, 135–6, 138–9, 168–70; Frank E. Manuel, *Prophets of Paris*, 9, 10, 109, 111–38, 162-3, 167; Manuel, *New World of Henri Saint-Simon*, 1, 5, 63–77,

81–2, 87, 88, 103, 111, 117–19, 122, 124–6, 131–2, 137, 139, 148, 149, 151, 156–60, 163–6, 171–2, 182–8, 190–4, 196, 197, 200, 202, 204, 208–16, 219–61, 263, 265–70, 273–94, 300–4, 306–10, 312–20, 326, 327, 339; Egbert, *Social Radicalism and the Arts*, 41, 117–33; Robert B. Carlisle, 'Saint-Simonian Radicalism: A Definition and a Direction,' *French Historical Studies*, 5, no. 4 (Fall 1968): 435; Robert B. Carlisle, 'The Birth of Technocracy: Science, Society, and the Saint-Simonians,' *Journal of the History of Ideas*, 35, no. 3 (July–Sept. 1974): 445, 447–8, 450–60, 462–4. For Saint-Simon, writes Margaret Rose, the 'avant-garde' of scientists, industrialists, engineers, and artists was to both 'appreciate a new idea' and 'defeat the forces of inertia,' as well as to 'contribute greatly to the prosperity of manufacturers by the designs and models with which they furnish artisans ... or by making products of use as well as of artistic value.' See Rose, *The Post-Modern and the Post-Industrial: A Critical Analysis* (Cambridge: Cambridge Univ. Press, 1991), 208n; see also 32, 33. Stendhal's essay addresses Saint-Simonianism only as it existed up to 1825, yet the movement to extend and modify its founder's doctrine continued into the 1830s and beyond, to the point where some historians regard Saint-Simonianism as the ideological basis of France as it exists today. Scholars also continue to debate whether the Saint-Simonians remained faithful to their master's teachings. See Manuel, *New World of Henri Saint-Simon*, 1, 219, 260, 344–7, 349, 351–63, 367; *Prophets of Paris*, 2, 161, 165, 166, 167, 169-74, 183; Egbert, *Social Radicalism and the Arts*, 124–33; Carlisle, 'Saint-Simonian Radicalism,' 430–1, 435–45; Carlisle, 'Birth of Technocracy,' 445–6, 457, 462. For selections of Saint-Simon's works, see Keith Taylor, ed., *Henri Saint-Simon (1760–1825): Selected Writings on Science, Industry, and Social Organization* (New York: Holmes and Meier, 1975); F.M. H. Markham, *Henri Comte de Saint-Simon, 1760–1828* (New York: Macmillan, 1952).

360 Mouillaud, 'Le Pamphlet Impossible,' 69–75, 77–8, 81–3, 88; Stendhal, *D'un nouveau complot contre les industriels*, Stendhal to Armand Cerclet, 30 Nov. 1825, 37; in the same volume: Jean-Marie Gleize, 'Présentation,' 63–6; Rude, *Stendhal et la pensée sociale*, 134, 135, 157; del Litto, *La vie intellectuelle de Stendhal*, 390, 401–2, 408–12; RNF1817 24–5. For Saint-Simon's embrace of utilitarianism and liberalism (economic individualism, property rights, and laissez-faire economics), and his abandonment of the latter in the 1820s (and even earlier), see Manuel, *New World of Henri Saint-Simon*, 184, 194, 210, 227, 240–2, 288–91, 294, 312. For the critique of liberalism among Saint-Simon's disciples, see Carlisle, 'The Birth of Technocracy,' 455, 455n, 456, 459. For Saint-Simon's appeal to the Bourbon monarchy, see Manuel, *New World of Henri Saint-Simon*, 283, 284–5.

361 Stendhal, *D'un nouveau complot contre les industriels*, 10–12, 13, 16–17; Mouillaud, 'Le Pamphlet Impossible,' 76, 77, 84–6, 87. For Saint-Simon's high
esteem for the United States as the nation best suited to fulfil his dreams of
a new society, see Manuel, *New World of Henri Saint-Simon*, 196, 236, 280–1.

362 Stendhal, *D'un nouveau complot contre les industriels*, 1, 9–15, 15n, 16–17,
19; Mouillaud, 'Le Pamphlet Impossible,' 74–83, 87; Rude, *Stendhal et la
pensée sociale*, 66–7. On the major economic and social role assigned by the
Saint-Simonians to the finance capitalist, see Manuel, *Prophets of Paris*, 177.
Although Mouillaud finds a contradiction between Stendhal's liberalism,
which stresses self-fulfilment, profit, and utility, and his celebration of socially conscious self-sacrifice, Saint-Simon and his disciples wanted to overcome this contradiction in theory and practice, as they sought to replace
the liberal emphasis on private interest with the ideals of cooperation, the
general welfare, and a self-sacrificial ethos first articulated by Saint-Simon
and later embodied in the Saint-Simonians' business ventures. See Manuel,
New World of Henri Saint-Simon, 351–2; *Prophets of Paris*, 161; Carlisle, 'The
Birth of Technocracy,' 448, 454, 455, 456, 457, 463. On the contradiction
between heroic and utilitarian values in Stendhal, see Albérès, *Le naturel
chez Stendhal*, 47.

363 Mouillaud, 'Le Pamphlet Impossible,' 74–5, 78–9, 83; Stendhal, *D'un nouveau complot contre les industriels*, 11, 12, 13; in the same volume: *Le Pandore*,
3 Dec. 1825, 38–9; *Le Globe*, 17 Dec. 1825, 55. Summarizing Saint-Simon's
ethos of work, Manuel writes that 'modern man had a zest for work,' which
was no burden but an 'expression of free creativity.' He adds that 'productive labor was now an intense passion beyond the pleasure principle,' so
that happiness no longer lies in pleasure but in the enjoyment of work.
Regarding the slogan *Tout par l'industrie, tout pour elle*, Manuel observes that
the 'doctrines of work and progress were the driving ethical concepts of
the new society ... Production was the one positive end of society,' whose
proper maxim could only be 'Respect for production and for producers.'
Again, 'each man ought to consider himself in his social relations as if he
were engaged in a world company of workers.' For Saint-Simon, national
society was 'one vast workshop,' and the 'whole world ... an arena' for
'constantly increasing production and of man as primarily a "working" animal.' By contrast with classical civilization, work 'was the cardinal virtue of
modern society,' 'production was the heart of modern civil society.' In the
'Parable' of *L'Organisateur* Saint-Simon defines work as the 'cornerstone
of progress and the only justification of man's existence.' Or as he put
it in his *Lettres d'un habitant de Genève*: 'All men shall work.' See Manuel,
New World of Henri Saint-Simon, 239, 240–2, 253, 302, 308. Given Stendhal's

questioning of the liberal economic theories of the French economist Jean-Baptiste Say, who emphasized production over consumption and the demand function, it is worth noting Saint-Simon's admiration of Say, whom he regarded as a friend, and of whose ideas he would have been happy 'to consider himself a simplifier and journalistic popularizer,' to quote Manuel. During his later career Saint-Simon held ideas consistent with those of Say, including the elevation of work and production over consumption and distribution, along with the related pre-underconsumptionist view that, as goods will always find consumers, so there can be never enough goods, and the demand function may therefore take care of itself (a simplified statement of Say's 'law'). See Manuel, *New World of Henri Saint-Simon*, 180, 182, 184–5, 189, 197, 240, 312; *Prophets of Paris*, 111, 120, 161; Thomas Sowell, *Say's Law: An Historical Analysis* (Princeton: Princeton Univ. Press, 1972), passim. Manuel writes that because Saint-Simon 'grasped the essence of the new industrialized society before it became bewildering in its complexity,' he accomplished a 'revelation of western social ideals in modern times.' See Manuel, *New World of Henri Saint-Simon*, 5. Margaret Rose stresses the long-term impact of Saint-Simon's ideas, which prophesied many features of modern industrial society as well as postindustrial society. See Rose, *Post-Modern and Post-Industrial*, 32–4.

364 Coe, Notes to RNF 489n; Stendhal, Letter to Mira, 9 Dec. 1825, in Stendhal, *D'un nouveau complot contre les industriels*, 46–7; L 27; Strickland, *Stendhal*, 48–51, 107, 194, 264; Rude, *Stendhal et la pensée sociale*, 170–1. Rude notes that Stendhal's pamphlet failed to do justice to Saint-Simon's doctrine, not only by reducing it to a one-sided apology for industrialists, bankers, and industrialism, but by ignoring its socialist orientation, its condemnation of economic exploitation, and its basic antithesis between workers and non-producers – in short, its moral and spiritual component. See Rude, *Stendhal et la pensée sociale*, 138–9, 162. Manuel observes that Saint-Simon's ideology provided Catholic countries and more specifically France with something comparable to the Protestant ethic. However, Frederick Hayek deplores the Saint-Simonians' lack of humanistic and cultural values, to which he attributes their disregard of history and social tradition along with their crudely reductive technocratic mentality given to the steamrolling methods of engineering. See Manuel, *Prophets of Paris*, 153; Manuel, *New World of Henri Saint-Simon*, 253; Carlisle, 'Birth of Technocracy,' 449–51.

365 Herbert Marcuse, Foreword to *Negations*, xix; Marcuse, 'On Hedonism,' 184; Marcuse, 'Affirmative Character of Culture,' 90–1, 93–4, 95–8; Marcuse, *Eros and Civilization*, vii–viii, ix, 177, 178; Marcuse, 'Some Social Im-

plications of Modern Technology,' 139, 159–61; Max Horkheimer, 'End of Reason,' 31.

366 Sebastian de Grazia, *Of Time, Work, and Leisure* (New York: Twentieth Century Fund, 1962). See also de Grazia, 'Time and Work,' in Henry Yaker, Humphry Ormond, and Frances Cheek, eds., *The Future of Time: Man's Temporal Environment* (Garden City, NY: Doubleday, 1971), 439–78.

367 De Grazia, *Of Time, Work, and Leisure*, 3–4, 7–8, 12–16, 18–25, 35–9, 186–7, 246–8, 252, 316–17, 327, 347–9, 370–1, 372–9, 413–15, 418–21, 478n, 526–7n, 533n. See also Benjamin D. Hunnicutt, 'The History of Western Leisure,' in Rojek, Shaw, and Veal, *Handbook of Leisure Studies*, 66–7; Rodolfo Mondolfo, 'The Greek Attitude to Manual Labour,' *Past and Present*, 6 (Nov. 1954): 1–5. For the limitations of Thorstein Veblen's technocratically motivated conception of leisure, see Theodor W. Adorno, 'Veblen's Attack on Culture,' in Adorno, *Prisms*, trans. Samuel and Shierry Weber (Cambridge, MA: MIT Press, 1981), 75–94.

368 Thorstein Veblen, *The Theory of the Leisure Class* (New York: Viking, 1934), passim; Cross, *Time and Money*, 19; John P. Diggins, *The Bard of Savagery: Thorstein Veblen and Modern Social Theory* (New York: Seabury, 1978), 14–18, 104–7; Chris Rojek, *Leisure and Culture* (New York: Palgrave, 2000), 51–9; Daniel Thomas Cook, 'Leisure and Consumption,' in Rojek, Shaw, and Veal, *Handbook of Leisure Studies*, 305–9.

369 Rojek, *Leisure and Culture*, 37–8, 49, 51–3, 86–7; Pierre Bourdieu, *Distinction: A Social Critique of the Judgment of Taste* (Cambridge: Harvard Univ. Press, 1984); Jean Baudrillard, *The Consumer Society*, trans. Chris Turner (London: Sage, 1998); Cook, 'Leisure and Consumption,' 309–11.

370 Cross, *Time and Money*, 160, 276n; Rojek, *Leisure and Culture*, 58, 94, 99–100.

371 De Grazia, *Of Time, Work, and Leisure*, 8, 36–7, 83, 88–90, 119–20, 197–8, 199–200, 251, 265, 291, 316, 324–6, 348–9, 368–70, 377–9, 381–4, 391, 412. See also Juliet B. Schor, *The Overworked American: The Unexpected Decline of Leisure* (New York: Basic Books, 1991), 6–7, 43–8, 51, 139; Keith Thomas, 'Work and Leisure in Pre-Industrial Society,' *Past and Present*, 29 (Dec. 1964): 50–62; Cipolla, *Before the Industrial Revolution*, 76; Michael Adas, *Machines as the Measure of Men: Science, Technology, and the Ideologies of Western Dominance* (Ithaca: Cornell Univ. Press, 1989), 208, 209, 242; E.P. Thompson, 'Time, Work-Discipline, and Industrial Capitalism,' *Past and Present*, 38 (1967): 56–97; Rudolph M. Bell, *Fate and Honor, Family and Village: Demographic and Cultural Change in Rural Italy since 1800* (Chicago: Univ. of Chicago Press, 1979), passim; Friedrich Georg Juenger, *The Failure of Technology: Perfection without Purpose*, trans. F.D. Wieck (Hinsdale, IL: Henry Regnery, 1949), 5–6; Rojek, *Capitalism and Leisure Theory*, 25. On

Cockayne, see Hunnicutt, 'History of Western Leisure,' 61, 72n. Implicit in
The Theory of the Leisure Class (1899), Veblen's technocratic conception of
society was subsequently deployed in *The Theory of Business Enterprise* (1904)
and *The Engineers and the Price System* (1921). He argues that modern industry should be rescued from businessmen and entrepreneurs, who sacrifice
productive efficiency to pecuniary considerations of profit, wasteful expenditure, and conspicuous consumption. The industrial system belongs
properly in the hands of engineers, technicians, and inventors, for whom
the machine is the essence of objective matter-of-factness, and whose utilitarian values of know-how and efficiency will enable them to restore the
economy to its proper focus, namely production. It has been said of Veblen
that he valued production for the sake of production, and that, placing
work at the centre of life, he confined himself to humanity as producer. In
view of Stendhal's suspicion of the one-sided emphasis placed on production by the technocrats of his own time, especially the Saint-Simonians
and *industriels*, it is worth noting that Daniel Bell ranks Veblen with such
'elitist' theoreticians as Saint-Simon, whom John P. Diggins describes as
a 'technocrat who would give power only to those concerned with the
production of goods.' See Diggins, *Bard of Savagery*, 20–1, 24, 56–7, 78–80,
128, 212, 213; Cross, *Time and Money*, 23. Yet one does not want to exaggerate Veblen's commitment to empiricism, technological rationalization,
mechanization, utilitarianism, and applied science, for as Diggins shows,
Veblen is drawn in roughly the same degree to the non-purposive values of
what he calls 'idle curiosity,' 'aptitude of play,' and 'more or less irrelevant
attention,' which he sees as the basis of scientific progress. Insofar as such
values imply a definite if unspoken respect for the classical ideal of leisure
as the disinterested contemplation of reality pursued for its own sake, they
lead inevitably to the conflict Diggins discerns in Veblen, between humanism and behaviourism. See Diggins, *Bard of Savagery*, 29–30, 56, 70–1, 82–4.
Commenting on Juliet B. Schor's credible argument that medieval society
had much free time, and that its work schedules were much more relaxed
than those of industrial society, Rojek nonetheless refuses to exaggerate
the 'bucolic charm' of the pre-industrial world, for as he notes, Schor fails
to stress the poverty and uncertainty of life in the Middle Ages, when the
economy was locked in a 'low-growth trap,' and starvation often threatened. See Rojek, *Leisure and Culture*, 33.

372 De Grazia, *Of Time, Work, and Leisure*, 3–4, 11–32, 40–1, 44, 280–1, 414–15.
Advancing a view of leisure opposed to that of Aristotle and de Grazia,
David Steigerwald identifies it in Veblenesque fashion with a largely para-
sitic rather than productive leisure class and thus arrives at the conclusion

that 'leisure is by definition incapable of producing culture.' Instead, it is to be equated with little more than expanding consumption as against productive and 'meaningful' work, on which higher culture apparently depends and from which it arises. See Steigerwald, *Culture's Vanities: The Paradox of Cultural Diversity in a Globalized World* (Lanham, MD: Rowman and Littlefield, 2004), 21–2. Rejecting de Grazia's conception of leisure as elitist and exclusive, Hunnicutt apparently regards Cockayne (and its cognate, carnival) as leisure in its own right. See Hunnicut, 'History of Western Leisure,' 66-8, 73n. According to James Ackerman, *otium* is best defined as 'seclusion, or serenity, or relaxation, but the ancients thought of it rather as an opportunity to engage, often intensely, in worthwhile physical and mental pursuits.' See Ackerman, *The Villa: Form and Ideology of Country Houses* (Princeton: Princeton Univ. Press, 1985), 37. Charles Murray implies the Romans' insufficient appreciation of leisure, remarking their limited scientific knowledge, disdain for learning for learning's sake, and general contempt for and suspicion of non-practical activity. See Charles Murray, *Human Accomplishment: The Pursuit of Excellence in the Arts and Sciences* (New York: HarperCollins, 2003), 30–1. Lewis Mumford contends that, whereas the classical philosophers preferred to assign work to slaves if possible, St Benedict and his Benedictine order improved upon classical civilization not only in recognizing the spirituality and moral value of work but in balancing work and leisure in ways that influenced later centuries. Yet Mumford also finds in the Benedictine rule less desirable tendencies towards routinization and mechanization that contributed to modern capitalism, industrialism, and technology. Incidentally, St Benedict was an Italian from Nursia (Norcia), in central Italy. See Mumford, *The Condition of Man* (New York: Harcourt, Brace, 1944), 92, 95; Mumford, *The Myth of the Machine: Technics and Human Development* (New York: Harcourt, Brace, and World, 1967), 263–7. On the difficulty Renaissance humanists encountered in attempting to balance *otium* and *negotium*, see Hans Baron, 'Cicero and the Roman Civic Spirit in the Middle Ages and Early Renaissance,' *Bulletin of the John Rylands Library*, 22 (1938): 72–97; Patricia Labalme, *Bernardo Giustiniani: A Venetian of the Quattrocento* (Rome: Edizioni Storia e Letteratura, 1969), 23–4. De Grazia's concept of leisure resembles that of several twentieth-century observers, although there is no perfect congruity. See Ernest Barker, *Reflections on Leisure* (London: National Council, n.d.); Juenger, *Failure of Technology*; Joseph Pieper, *Leisure: The Basis of Culture*, trans. Alexander Dru (London: Faber and Faber, 1952); Karl Jaspers, *Man in the Modern Age* (New York: Anchor, 1957); Clement Greenberg, 'Work and Leisure under Industrialism,' *Commentary*,

16 (July 1953): 57–61; Hannah Arendt, *The Human Condition* (New York: Doubleday, 1959), 82n 83-4, 85, 131-2n, 132-3, 320-2; Roger Kimball, 'Joseph Pieper: Leisure and its Discontents,' in Kimball, *Experiments against Reality: The Fate of Culture in the Postmodern Age* (Chicago: J.R. Dee, 2000), 335–9, 342, 344–5; Vernon Lee, 'About Leisure,' in Lee, *Ariadne in Mantua* (London: John Lane, 1930), 135–55. Although Lee defines leisure in terms close to those of de Grazia, as inner impulse free of necessity, she seems to view it as a form of dreamy contemplation to the exclusion of activity. In her essay's disappointing conclusion she not only welcomes the democratization of leisure, a socialist agenda de Grazia regards as impossible, but fears that leisure may only mask idleness. She goes on to defend work as the necessary counterweight to leisure, which thus remains in a determinate relation to work.

    Contrary to de Grazia's Aristotelianism, some critics reject all essentialist definitions of leisure as an autonomous experience beyond the mundane. Not only do they argue for the 'performative' character of leisure, which would link it inextricably to the social other, but they stress its close connection with material and political life, focusing on production, consumption, and class domination. See Daniel Thomas Cook, 'Leisure and Consumption,' 304–9; Rojek, *Leisure and Culture*, 37–8, 49–57, 58, 86–7; Rojek, 'Leisure, Culture and Civilization,' 28, 29; Hunnicutt, 'History of Western Leisure,' 58–60.

373 De Grazia, *Of Time, Work, and Leisure*, 5–7, 29, 31–2, 35–61, 63, 89, 118–19, 148, 151, 201–2, 204, 207, 246–8, 252–5, 261–5, 267, 276, 282–3, 287, 290–4, 302–9, 314–17, 323–7, 331–43, 350–2, 353–4, 384, 404–5, 409, 426–7. See also Arendt, *Human Condition*, 4–5, 81, 85-6, 92; Hunnicutt, 'History of Leisure,' 68–71. On the emergence of rigorous mechanical timekeeping in the West, and its effect upon work, society, and individual consciousness, see David Landes, *Revolution in Time: Clocks in the Making of the Modern World* (Cambridge: Harvard Univ. Press, 1983), 58–66, 89–90; Jacques Le Goff, *Time, Work, and Culture in the Middle Ages*, trans. Arthur Goldhammer (Chicago: Univ. of Chicago Press, 1980), 35–7, 43–52. On the 'cult of antiquity' during America's revolutionary period, and the hostility it aroused among exponents of 'useful knowledge,' see Meyer Reinhold, *Classica Americana: The Greek and Roman Heritage in the United States* (Detroit: Wayne State Univ. Press, 1984), 23–93 and passim.

374 De Grazia, *Of Time, Work, and Leisure*, 7– 9, 49–51, 57, 68–78, 81–90, 91–104, 114, 118–120, 131–2, 134–6, 139–40, 143–4, 149–50, 166–7, 183, 185, 189, 203, 208–12, 217–18, 220–3, 225–7, 229, 231, 233, 237–8, 242–6, 250–1, 268–70, 275, 284–9, 293–4, 301, 324–8, 331–2, 336–43, 346, 404–5,

425–6, 493n, 497n. On the inability of those who have been 'liberated' from labour to make worthy use of their time, see Arendt, *Human Condition*, 4–5; Juenger, *Failure of Technology*, 6.

375 De Grazia, *Of Time, Work, and Leisure*, 46–7, 61, 282–3, 284, 409; Jonathan White, 'Justice and the Individual, Torture and the State,' in White, *Italian Cultural Lineages*, 173.

376 De Grazia, *Of Time, Work, and Leisure*, 8, 21, 262, 264–5, 276, 282–3, 290–1, 351–4, 356–9, 361–4, 367, 386–88, 390, 405–6, 409; Rojek, *Capitalism and Leisure Theory*, 7, 16, 32, 93–4, 120, 177, 181; Rojek, *Leisure and Culture*, 52–3.

377 Del Litto, *La vie intellectuelle de Stendhal*, 11, 15, 16–17, 79, 80. Although Stendhal never learned Greek, he was well schooled in Latin literature, as his writings often demonstrate. In RJ 20, he recalls his Latin instruction in secondary school, where he was required to translate Latin into French. Unquestionably he respected classical culture despite his historically conditioned anticlassicism.

378 On Stendal and Rousseau, see Crouzet, *Stendhal et l'italianité*, 7, 21, 83n, 117–20, 120, 122, 185; Crouzet, *Nature et société chez Stendhal*, 47–53, 188–9n, 190n.

379 Staël, *Corinne, or Italy*, 72, 79, 141, 172; Casillo, *Empire of Stereotypes*, 75, 76, 77, 82.

380 Crouzet, *Stendhal et l'italianité*, 121–30, 133, 138, 182–5, 189.

381 R 46, 461, 461n; RJ 69; RNF 199, 234; Crouzet, *Stendhal et l'italianité*, 26, 87–9, 91, 112–31, 138, 174–5, 180–1, 182–4.

382 Crouzet, *Stendhal et l'italianité*, 116, 118–23, 125–7, 131, 136–7, 138–44, 145n, 146n, 183–4, 303–6, 307–9; Crouzet, *Nature et société chez Stendhal*, 190n.

383 RJ 69; RNF 199; L 250; Crouzet, *Stendhal et l'italianité*, 87–9, 177–9, 203n.

384 R 66, 267; L 27, 151; RJ 20–1, 59; Crouzet, *Stendhal et l'italianité*, 37, 91.

385 L 30, 44, 51, 59–60, 63–4, 65, 96, 98, 102, 116, 144, 150, 166, 167, 219, 223, 236–41; Ezra Pound, 'Cavalcanti,' in *Literary Essays of Ezra Pound* (London: Faber and Faber, 1954), 151.

386 R 46, 141, 205; RJ 20, 21, 56, 69, 231, 242–3, 290, 328; L 64, 65.

387 R 15, 17, 20, 21, 57, 73, 140, 173, 205, 290, 325, 457–8.

388 R 404, 405, 436, 437.

389 L 55n; Crouzet, *Stendhal et l'italianité*, 313–14. For the Epicurean concept of true enjoyment in the works of Jacob Burckhardt, see Löwith, *Jacob Burckhardt: l'uomo nel mezzo della storia*, 300.

390 Crouzet, *Stendhal et l'italianité*, 114–16, 119–20, 174–5, 177–8, 179, 314; R 173, 325, 457; RJ 28, 245. On the Cuccagna, see Moe, *View from Vesuvius*,

63, 63n. The Marquis de Sade's highly repellent description of the Cuccagna must be taken cautiously owing to his prejudice against Naples as a
hive of hot-tempered, knife-wielding, ill-disciplined, cheating, and licentious *canaille*. See the Marquis de Sade, *Juliette*, trans. Austryn Wainright
(New York: Grove Press, 1968), 1999–1001; de Sade, *Oeuvres complètes*
(Paris: Au Cercle du Livre Précieux, 1967), 15:440–1.

391 Stendhal, RNF 458; R 463; L 187. Imbert, *Les métamorphoses*, 279–80.

392 Max Weber, *The Protestant Ethic and the Spirit of Capitalism*, trans. Talcott
Parsons (London: George Allen and Unwin, 1948). Weber regards the
Protestant doctrines of predestination, election, and the inefficacy of
good works (as opposed to the free gift of divine grace) as having been
powerful incentives to ceaseless and disciplined labour. The individual
Protestant, in an attempt to relieve himself of the spiritual anxiety aroused
by his unknown otherworldly destiny, strove through worldly material success to gain some indication of divine approval and thus of his ultimate
salvation. Not only was work elevated to a calling, but it became a spiritual
and social duty. What ultimately emerged was capitalism and the capitalist personality, rational as to means yet irrational with respect to ends, for
the Protestant valued work, production, and money-making in themselves,
and sought in work the satisfaction he denied himself in his rigorously
ascetic daily life. However, some scholars trace the origins of capitalism
not to Protestantism but to the later Middle Ages and Renaissance, while
others find early Christian and Catholic examples of the calling. Still others hold that asceticism as well as Protestantism's neo-medieval theological emphasis on community were more impediments than incentives to
worldly acquisition. For Weber's rival Werner Sombart, capitalism develops
out of the hedonistic desire for self-indulgence through luxurious acquisition and consumption. Other critics trace capitalism to the spirit of competitive acquisition in emerging democratic societies. Regarding America,
it has been argued that capitalism began to flourish only after Puritanism
declined. See Diggins, *Bard of Savagery*, 11, 114–23, 129–33; Robert Green,
ed., *Protestantism and Capitalism: The Weber Thesis and Its Critics* (Boston:
Heath, 1959); S.N. Eisenstadt, ed., *The Protestant Ethic and Modernization: A
Comparative View* (New York: Basic Books, 1968). In the latter volume see
S.N. Eisenstadt, 'The Protestant Ethic Thesis in an Analytical and Comparative Framework,' 3, 5, 7–14; Stanislav Andreski, 'Method and Substan-
tive Theory in Max Weber,' 53–8; Ephraim Fischoff, 'The Protestant Ethic
and the Spirit of Capitalism: The History of a Controversy,' 69–71, 77–81;
Herbert Luthy, 'Once Again: Calvinism and Capitalism,' 91–108; Michael
Walzer, 'Puritanism as a Revolutionary Ideology,' 109–34, esp. 113–14, 129.

393 PI 157, 158.

394 Graña, *Bohemian versus Bourgeois*, 94–5; see also Rude, *Stendhal et la pensée sociale*, 166; R 461n. Coe, Notes to R 506, mentions a trip to England extending from October to November 1821. See also Imbert, *Les métamorphoses*, 278. For views similar to those of Stendhal, see Taine, *Notes on England*, trans. Edward Hyams (Fair Lane, NJ: Essential Books, 1958), 64, 219, 227, 229; De Grazia, *Of Time, Work, and Leisure*, 63–90.

395 Commenting on the 'hard labor' of conversation in Parisian salons, Stendhal adds that, 'among the burdens which hastened the death of Madame de Staël,' there was the 'strain of making conversation during her last winter.' See L 231; see also RS 55; RJ 220. According to Marc Fumaroli, the eighteenth-century salon was predominantly an aristocratic institution that pursued the ideal of sophisticated conversation for its own sake. However, in attempting to revive the institution in the early nineteenth century Madame de Staël transformed it into something resembling a discussion group focused on the weighty and burning issues of the day. See Fumaroli, *Trois institutions littéraires*, 92–202, esp. 152, 153, 158, 168–9, 173–5, 176, 177, 182, 185, 186–7.

396 R 46, 461, 461n; RJ 20; RNF 199; L 250; PI 155.

397 RJ 222, 328; L 27, 30; Crouzet, *Stendhal et l'italianité*, 113, 180–1.

398 L 27.

399 Cross, *Time and Money*, 50; Max Horkheimer and Theodor W. Adorno, *Dialectic of Enlightenment*, trans. John Cumming (New York: Herder and Herder, 1972), 120–67; Marcuse, Preface, *Eros and Civilization*, vii–viii; Rojek, *Capitalism and Leisure Theory*, 20–1, 113–4.

400 Joffre Dumazedier, *Toward a Society of Leisure*, trans. Steward E. McClure (New York: Free Press, 1967), ix (Foreword by David Riesman), 4, 11–17, 18–19, 26, 33–8, 59–62, 81–2, 87, 119, 130–8, 151–2, 201–2, 218, 223, 240–3, 248, 263; Rojek, *Capitalism and Leisure Theory*, 13–14; James Frederick Murphy, Introduction to James F. Murphy, ed., *Concepts of Leisure: Philosophical Implications* (Englewood Cliffs: Prentice-Hall, 1974), 3, 12; in the same volume: H. Douglas Sessions, 'Leisure Society Value Systems,' 14–9; Kenneth Roberts, 'A Society of Leisure,' 29; commentary by Murphy, 75–7; Stanley Parker, 'Kinds of Leisure and Their Meaning Today,' 103, 105; Murphy, Introduction to chap. 5, 111; de Grazia, *Of Time, Work, and Leisure*, 269–70, 272–3, 358–9, 361–4, 367, 410, 528n.

401 Clark, *Modern Italy*, 41–2. It is misleading, however, to suggest that English factory workers failed to enjoy themselves at Blackpool, which was pervaded by a 'libertine' atmosphere in which the 'binge' typically provided release from everyday want. See Gary Cross, ed., *Worktowners at Blackpool:*

Mass Observation and Popular Leisure in the 1930s (New York: Routledge, 1990), 162–7; Cross, *Time and Money*, 69, 73, 74, 123, 155, 177–83. For a nostalgic celebration of Naples and its *dolce far niente*, showing how the Neapolitan consciousness of time, characterized by the 'heightened awareness of the present moment,' differs from that of the industrialized north, see Peter Gunn, 'Some Thoughts on Time in Naples,' in Chaney and Richey, *Oxford, China and Italy*, 124–6.

402 Clark, *Modern Italy*, 41, 167, 244–5. For Mussolini's Dopolavoro program, see Cross, *Time and Money*, 99, 103; for the Nazi example, 107, 121. On attempts by national governments, churches, municipalities, employers, unions, political parties, and private organizations to organize and improve leisure during the 1920s and 1930s, see Cross, *Time and Money*, 79–98, 101–14, 119–20, 122–7. Cross concludes that workers generally preferred privatized and commercial leisure to organized or public leisure.

403 Feifer, *Tourism in History*, 2.

404 Feifer, *Tourism in History*, 2–3; Withey, *Grand Tours*, viii, ix–x, 94.

405 Adrian Franklin acknowledges certain resemblances in tourist practices past and present yet rightly stresses the differing needs and desires satisfied by modern tourism. See Franklin, 'Tourism,' in Rojek, Shaw, and Veal, *Handbook of Leisure Studies*, 389, 396–7. For modern tourism as inextricably tied to capitalism and commodification, see G. Llewellyn Watson and Joseph P. Kopachevsky, 'Interpretations of Tourism as Commodity,' in Yorghos Apostolopoulos, Stella Leivadi, and Andrew Yiannakis, eds., *The Sociology of Tourism: Theoretical and Empirical Investigations* (London: Routledge, 1996), 281.

406 Turner and Ash, *Golden Hordes*, 39; Graham Smith, Introduction to Carol Richardson and Graham Smith, eds. *Brittannia Italia Germania* (Edinburgh: VARIE, 2001), 1; James Buzard, *The Beaten Track: European Tourism, Literature, and the Ways to Culture, 1800–1918* (Oxford: Oxford Univ. Press, 1993), passim; Feifer, *Tourism in History*, 118–9; Withey, *Grand Tours*, 5–8.

407 Turner and Ash, *Golden Hordes*, 41; Feifer, *Tourism in History*, 163–5; Pemble, *Mediterranean Passion*, 39–41, 54, 67–74; Withey, *Grand Tours*, 50–1, 59–60, 70–4, 92, 94–5, 103; Erik Cohen, 'Toward a Sociology of International Tourism,' *Social Research*, 39 (1972): 165; Mihaly Szegedy-Maszák, '"Rambles in Rome": Some 19th Century Travelers and Photographers,' in Richardson and Smith, *Brittania Italia Germania*, 7–8; in the same volume, Smith, Introduction, 2, 3; Tony Tanner, *Venice Desired* (Cambridge: Harvard Univ. Press, 1992), 148; William W. Stowe, *Going Abroad: European Travel in Nineteenth-Century American Culture* (Princeton: Princeton Univ. Press, 1994), xii, 10, 18–19, 30, 31, 33, 36, 43–7, 156; Dulles, *Americans Abroad*, 38–9; Graham

Smith, 'Florence, Phototography, and the Victorians,' in John E. Law and
Lene Ostermark-Johanson, eds., *Victorian and Edwardian Responses to the
Italian Renaissance* (Aldershot: Ashgate, 2005), 7–10, 21–2. On American
travellers' troubled response to the Italians' relaxed and even heedless at-
titude towards time, see Paul R. Baker, *The Fortunate Pilgrims: Americans in
Italy, 1800–1860* (Cambridge: Harvard Univ. Press, 1964), 211–2; Diggins,
Mussolini and Fascism, 7–9.

408 Feifer, *Tourism in History,* 166; Lady Margaret Blessington, *The Idler in Italy*
(Paris: Galignani, 1839), excerpted in Manfred Pfister, ed., *The Fatal Gift of
Beauty: The Italies of British Travellers* (Amsterdam: Rodopi, 1996), 94, 295–6.

409 Pemble, *Mediterranean Passion,* 1, 2–3, 18, 39–40; Cohen, 'Toward a Sociology of International Tourism,' 172n; Franklin, 'Tourism,' 394–6; Kevin
Meethan, *Tourism in Global Society: Place, Culture, Consumption* (New York:
Palgrave, 2001), 9–11; Richard Jenkyns, *The Victorians and Ancient Greece*
(Cambridge: Harvard Univ. Press, 1980), 85; Feifer, *Tourism in History,* 2,
184, 188, 220–1, 224, 257; Swinglehurst, *Romantic Journey,* 13–4, 40, 69–70,
189, 201; John Urry, *The Tourist Gaze: Leisure and Travel in Contemporary Societies* (London: Sage, 1990), 5–7, 39, 47–65; Cross, *Time and Money,* 176–83;
Withey, *Grand Tours,* 103, 135–66, 175, 190–1; Dulles, *Americans Abroad,* 4,
5, 65, 102–15, 154; Stowe, *Going Abroad,* 6–10; Pemble, *Venice Rediscovered,*
175, 177–8; Smith, Introduction to Richardson and Smith, *Britannia Italia
Germania,* 1; Dumazedier, *Toward a Society of Leisure,* 125n.

410 Cross, *Time and Money,* 2, 3, 7, 8, 10, 38, 78–98, 114, 118, 121–3, 162–3,
176–8, 187, 195, 197; Gary Cross, *A Quest for Time: The Reduction of Work in
Britain and France, 1840–1940* (Berkeley: Univ. of California Press, 1989),
esp. 215–32, and passim; MacCannell, *Tourist,* 5–7, 35–7, 57–8; Roberts,
'A Society of Leisure,' 31–2, 34–6; Alex Inkeles, 'Continuity and Change
in the American National Character,' in Inkeles, *National Character,* 183–4;
Dumazedier, *Toward a Society of Leisure,* 5–6, 8, 9, 221, 231, 233–4, 236, 259;
de Grazia, *Of Time, Work, and Leisure,* 144–5, 150; David Riesman, 'Leisure
and Work in Post-Industrial Society,' in E. Larrabee and R. Meyersohn,
eds., *Mass Leisure* (Glencoe: The Free Press, 1958), 363–85; John Kasson,
Amusing the Million: Coney Island at the Turn of the Century (New York: Hill
and Wang, 1978), 100; Turner and Ash, *Golden Hordes,* 13; Jacques Ellul,
The Technological System, trans. Joachim Neugroschel (New York: Continuum, 1980), 2; Ellul, *The Technological Bluff,* trans. Geoffrey W. Bromley
(Grand Rapids: W.B. Eerdmans, 1990), 309–13; Juliet B. Schor, 'Overturn-
ing the Modernist Predictions: Recent Trends in Work and Leisure in the
OECD,' in Rojek, Shaw, and Veal, *Handbook of Leisure Studies,* 203, 204–5;
Daniel Bell, *The Cultural Contradictions of Capitalism* (New York: Basic Books,

1976), 19, 53–4, 80–4; Daniel Bell, *The Coming of Post-Industrial Society* (Harmondsworth: Penguin, 1973), passim; Urry, *Tourist Gaze*, 190; Murphy, Introduction to Murphy, *Concepts of Leisure*, 4, 5, 9, 12; in the same volume: commentary by Murphy, 147, 182; Denis F. Johnston, 'The Future of Work: Three Possible Alternatives,' 248–9; Albert Borgmann, *Crossing the Post-modern Divide* (Chicago: Univ. of Chicago Press, 1992), 44; Rojek, *Leisure and Culture*, 90–1, 99–100; Rojek, *Decentring Leisure*, 57; Rojek, *Capitalism and Leisure Theory*, 2; Rose, *Post-Modern and Post-Industrial*, 25, 37; Richard Florida, *The Rise of the Creative Class: And How It's Transforming Work, Leisure, Community, and Everyday Life* (New York: Basic Books, 2002), passim.

411 MacCannell, *Tourist*, ix, 21–3, 28–9, 31, 34–6, 70; Urry, *Tourist Gaze*, 13–14, 82, 84–5, 87, 90, 149; David Harvey, *The Condition of Post-Modernity: An Enquiry into the Origins of Cultural Change* (London: Blackwell, 1989), 3, 5, 121–72, 338–42; Meethan, *Tourism in Global Society*, 20–33, 34, 66–73, 74–81, 117–21; Bell, *Coming of Post-Industrial Society;* the following essays in Terry Nichols Clark, ed., *The City as an Entertainment Machine* (Amsterdam: Elsevier, 204): Clark, Introduction, 'Taking Entertainment Seriously,' 1, 8, 15; Clark, 'A Political Theory of Consumption,' 20, 23, 84n; Clark, 'Urban Amenities: Lakes, Opera, and Juice Bars: Do They Drive Development?', 103–7, 112–13; Franklin, 'Tourism,' 392–3; Andreas Huyssen, *After the Great Divide: Modernism, Mass Culture, and Post-Modernism* (Bloomington: Indiana Univ. Press, 1986), 163–5, 193–4; Rose, *Post-Modern and Post-Industrial*, 21–39, 93–4, 66–7, 230n; Rojek, *Capitalism and Leisure Theory*, 73, 101, 121, 127; Rojek, *Decentring Leisure*, 17–18, 19–20, 88–9; Rojek, *Leisure and Culture*, 27–8, 46–7, 88–90, 94–5, 98–103, 107; Rojek, 'Leisure and "The Ruins of the Bourgeois World,"' in Rojek, *Leisure for Leisure*, 108–11; Rojek, *Cultural Studies* (Cambridge: Polity, 2007), 33, 43; Cook, 'Leisure and Consumption,' 309–13; Cross, *Time and Money*, 158; Patrick Brantlinger, *Crusoe's Footprints: Cultural Studies in Britain and America* (New York: Routledge: 1990), 108–9; Brantlinger, *Bread and Circuses*, 222–48, 278–9; Marshall Blonsky, *American Mythologies* (New York: Oxford Univ. Press, 1992), 48, 55, 95–9; Malcolm Crick, 'Representations of International Tourism in the Social Sciences: Sun, Sex, Sights, Savings, and Servility,' in Apostopoulos, Leivadi, and Yiannakis, *Sociology of Tourism*, 17, 38; in the same volume: Giuli Liebman Parrinello, 'Motivation and Anticipation in Post-Industrial Tourism,' 80; Zygmunt Baranski and Robert Lumley, Introduction to Baranski and Lumley, eds., *Culture and Conflict in Post-War Italy: Essays on Mass and Popular Culture* (New York: St. Martin's, 1990), 12. On the techniques of 'market segmentation' and 'advertising to minorities,' see Daniel Pope, *The Making of Modern Advertising* (New York: Basic Books, 1983), 252–98.

412 Urry, *Tourist Gaze*, 5, 14, 95–6; Feifer, *Tourism in History*, 224–5, 260, 270; MacCannell, *Tourist*, 1–4; Withey, *Grand Tours*, xi; Turner and Ash, *Golden Hordes*, 12; Clark, 'Urban Amenities,' 106–7; Yiorgos Apostolopoulos, 'Introduction: Reinventing the Sociology of Tourism,' in Apostolopoulos, Leivadi, and Yiannakis, *Sociology of Tourism*, 2.

413 Turner and Ash, *Golden Hordes*, 14; Rojek, *Decentring Leisure*, 76; MacCannell, *Tourist*, 5–6; Ellul, *Technological Bluff*, 58, 154, 225, 309, 313; Ellul, *Technological System*, 1–2, 5–11, 72; Cross, *Time and Money*, vii, viii–ix, 1, 2, 5, 9–13, 38, 128–9, 131–5, 143, 147–8, 153, 154, 156, 159–60, 162–4, 166–77, 184, 192–3, 195; Rojek, *Leisure and Culture*, 25–9, 32, 34, 44–5; Cook, 'Leisure and Consumption,' 304–5; Sessions, 'Leisure Society Value Systems,' 15; A.J. Veal, 'Economics of Leisure,' in Rojek, Shaw, and Veal, *Handbook of Leisure Studies*, 142–6; Schor, *Overworked American*, xvi, 1–11, 7–41, 43–4, 48, 49–54, 59–64, 68–73, 76–82, 94–5, 107–38, 139, 141, 163; Steffan Linder, *The Harried Leisure Class* (New York: Columbia Univ. Press, 1970). Schor subsequently rebutted counterarguments to her thesis and has noted more recently a continuing increase in work time in the United States and Sweden. Many nations in the OECD have been less work driven in the last several decades, but she predicts that they will most probably follow the American pattern as a result of employers' insistent demand for expanded hours as well as of the use of advanced technology, which increases labour. See Schor, 'Overturning Modernist Predictions,' 203–4, 206–14. On the ways in which technical organization adds to rather than reduces the amount of work, see Juenger, *Failure of Technology*, 7–8. According to Margaret Rose, Daniel Bell's idea of the post-industrial must be understood as an extension of industrial society. See Rose, *Post-Modern and Post-Industrial*, 33; see also 24, 30.

414 Berman, 'Modern Art and Desublimation,' 82–3, 88–90; Rojek, *Capitalism and Leisure Theory*, 113–14.

415 Berman, 'Consumer Society: The Legacy of the Avant-Garde,' 43–4, 51; Berman, 'Modern Art and Desublimation,' 72, 74, 80–1, 82, 85, 88–90, 94, 95, 97, 98; Huyssen, 'Mapping the Postmodern,' 42–3, 47, 50, 62; Rose, *Post-Modern and Post-Industrial*, 83–4, 227n.

416 Herbert Marcuse, *An Essay on Liberation* (Boston: Beacon, 1969), 4; see also 25; Marcuse, *Aesthetic Dimension*, 32, 35, 72–3; Marcuse, *One-Dimensional Man*, 56–83; Rojek, *Capitalism and Leisure Theory*, 116.

417 Fredric Jameson, 'Post-Modernism and Consumer Culture,' in Hal Foster, ed., *Postmodern Culture* (London: Pluto, 1983); Jim Collins on Jameson's essay, 'Reification and Utopia in Mass Culture,' in Collins, 'Post-Modernism as Culmination: The Aesthetic Politics of Decentered Cultures,' in Jencks,

Post-Modern Reader, 100–1; see also 114, 117; Turner and Ash, *Golden Hordes,* 91; Rojek, *Capitalism and Leisure Theory,* 78, 107–10, 135; Rojek, *Leisure and Culture,* 37–8, 178; Lauren Langman and Katie Cangemi, 'Globalization and the Liminal: Transgression, Identity and the Urban Primitive,' in Clark, *City as Entertainment Machine,* 141–176.

418 Jacques Ellul, *The Technological Society,* trans. John Wilkinson (New York: Knopf, 1964), passim; Ellul, *Technological System,* 1–12, 15–19, 23–5, 34–50, 51–121, 151–2, 157, 331n; Ellul, *Technological Bluff,* 3, 9, 11, 15–16, 18–19, 39, 109–10, 134–6, 144, 157, 223–8.

419 Ellul, *Technological System,* 2, 98–100, 179, 316, 347n; Ellul, *Technological Bluff,* 2n, 45, 109–13, 117, 134–5, 145, 151, 206–7, 223, 337, 347, 349.

420 Ellul, *Technological System,* 8, 39, 149, 249–50, 313–6, 328n, 359n; Ellul, *Technological Bluff,* 39, 62, 137–8, 141, 145, 151, 347. Ellul's view that leisure has been absorbed into technology resembles the concept of a contemporary 'techno-culture' as analysed by S. Aronowitz and W. Di Fazio, but Ellul does not share their optimism regarding the possibility of a social, economic, or political remedy. See Rojek, *Leisure and Culture,* 37–42, 49. Ellul's analysis of modern leisure is influenced by Georges Friedmann, who describes it as the release of 'permanent nervous tension.' See Friedmann, *Le Travail en miettes: specialization et loisirs* (Paris: Gallimard, 1956); Cross, *Time and Money,* 188, 276n. On the incompatibility of technology with leisure, see Juenger, *Failure of Technology,* 45; William Harper and John Hultsman, 'Leisure, Culture, and Progress,' *Journal of American and Comparative Culture,* 15, no. 3 (Sept. 1992): 27, 30–4.

421 Daniel J. Boorstin, *The Image, or What Happened to the American Dream?,* 7–44, 56, 78–80, 83, 87–8, 90, 94, 101–16.

422 Turner and Ash, *Golden Hordes,* 12, 13, 14, 89, 89n, 90–2, 108, 130, 136, 139–40, 209; Urry, *Tourist Gaze,* 7. Turner and Ash's argument resembles that of Watson and Kopachevsky, 'Interpretations of Tourism as Commodity,' 282–90, 292.

423 MacCannell, *Tourist,* 1, 5–6, 15. MacCannell's claim that technology is less suitable than tourism to stand for the universal qualities of postmodernity is belied by Ellul's demonstration that postmodern leisure is itself an extension and form of technology, which uses tourism as one more means by which to impose its universalizing imperatives. It is thus worth noting the frequency with which writers on tourism and leisure stress their historical dependency upon technological developments, although such facts are typically accompanied by warnings that technology is not the predominating factor – a caution more justifiable with respect to earlier periods than to the present one, in which technology holds far greater sway. Boorstin

traces the beginnings of modern tourism to 1850, when the railroad was
bringing leisure travel within reach of the middle and working classes. According to Edmund Swinglehurst, Thomas Cook of Cook's Tours exploited
the 'recently developed power of of the railways and locomotives.' William
W. Stowe concurs that advances in transportation technology lie behind
the vast increases in travel in the nineteenth century. Dumazedier argues
that modern leisure is 'deeply rooted in the conquests of the machine
age,' which include the 'technical determinants' of leisure around 1900,
especially transportation, and the 'technological conditioning of leisure
time' through newspapers, movies, radio, and television. Dumazedier
warns, though, that technology is not the sole determinant, as technical
uses often encounter traditional resistances as well as being influenced
by social and economic forces. For Turner and Ash, tourism is the 'visible
result of the great waves of technology which have changed the face of
the world.' Erik Cohen observes of tourism that 'it would seem that the
technological achievements of the past two centuries have been prime
determinants.' Chris Rojek recognizes the impact of technology on leisure
and tourism, but he sees capitalism as the primary factor. John Pemble's
study of Mediterranean tourism in the nineteenth and twentieth centuries
emphasizes modern technological conveyances, including the steamboat,
railroad, and motorcar. Although Kevin Meetham regards tourism and leisure as explicable chiefly in terms of capitalist commodification and profit-
seeking, he acknowledges that postindustrial tourist developments 'would
not be possible without a globalization of transport and infrastructure
capable of moving people from one destination to another.' He also concedes that advances in technology, including the application of instrumental rationality to leisure, have made possible the post-Fordist revolution
crucial to newer forms of industrialized tourism. Drawing a distinction between 'fast' and 'slow' leisure in the twentieth century, Rojek remarks that
the 'catalyst in each case is often technological,' for instance the pill, the
extension of mass communications systems, especially television, private
transport systems, and the Internet. Yet 'it would be a mistake to fall into a
deterministic mind-set,' as the 'emergence and success of all technologies
is dependent upon a range of cultural, social, and economic factors.' See
Withey, *Grand Tours*, viii; Swinglehurst, *Romantic Journey*, 13–4; Stowe, *Going
Abroad*, 8; Dumazedier, *Toward a Society of Leisure*, 45–52, 53–69, 234; Turner
and Ash, *Golden Hordes*, 11; Cohen, 'Toward a Sociology of International
Tourism,' 165; Pemble, *Mediterranean Passion*, 20–31; Meethan, *Tourism and
Global Society*, 35, 61–2; Rojek, *Leisure and Culture*, 22–4.

424 MacCannell, *Tourist*, 6, 10–11, 32, 37, 51, 55, 80, 103. MacCannell's appar-

ently unconscious Veblenesque prejudice in favour of work or production over the arts and culture is apparent when he approves the inclusion of work sites as tourist attractions as against those who, like Baedeker, would limit guidebooks to artistic and cultural monuments. According to Mac-Cannell, the display of work 'creates the impression in the sightseer of having firsthand experience with society's serious side.' In characterizing work as 'serious' MacCannell implies that art is frivolous, presumably on the basis of the long-standing assumption by economists and the public that what counts socially are the productive and materially useful. Such notions resemble those of Veblen, whose economic theory centred on production, and who identified the arts with wasteful, unproductive leisure. See Mac-Cannell, *Tourist*, 58–62, esp. 62. Stowe concedes that nineteenth-century bourgeois American visitors to Europe enjoyed their travels, yet he defines their driving motive as invidious comparison, the real purpose of European tourism being supposedly to proclaim and confirm social distinctions through consumption of material and cultural goods. Travel thus serves to certify and advertise the superiority of one's taste, while culture becomes a mere pretext for class legitimation – an agenda Stowe claims to discover in the tourist experience and literary production even of Henry James, whom he sees primarily as a middle-class emulator of 'leisure class' values. See Stowe, *Going Abroad*, 19–20, 27, 161–3, 179, 224n. Citing E. Schwimmer, Malcolm Crick characterizes tourism as 'conspicuous consumption of resources accumulated in secular time; its very possibility, in other words, is securely rooted in the real world of gross political and economic inequalities between nations and classes.' See Crick, 'Representations of International Tourism,' 38.

425 MacCannell, *Tourist*, 9–10, 41–5, 51, 53–4, 55, 57–9, 62–76, 91, 102–7, 110–11, 145–7, 152, 164–5. MacCannell's concept of the tourist and of the tourist site as semiotic marker influenced Jonathan Culler's well-known essay, 'Semiotics of Tourism,' *American Journal of Semiotics* (1981): 127–40.

426 Fussell, *Abroad*, 37–43, 47–9, 62.

427 Boorstin, *Image*, 104–6; MacCannell, *Tourist*, 58, 61–2, 64–5, 71; Stowe, *Going Abroad*, 27–54, esp. 45.

428 Terry Nichols Clark warns against thinking that consumption, which now includes both leisure and tourism, always has social conspicuousness or status as its goal, as is assumed in Veblen's *Theory of the Leisure Class*, Bourdieu's *Distinction*, and various writings by Baudrillard. As Clark points out, human beings are not equally concerned about status, while types of status vary considerably, and some people are hardly interested in status at

all. The current social and cultural scene, in which the lower classes dress up and the upper classes dress down, undermines Bourdieu's standard 'explanation' that income or status encourage a person to dress elegantly. See Clark, 'The Political Theory of Consumption,' 65–6, 78, 80, 83.

429 Pemble, *Mediterranean Passion*, 75–6, 96–7.

430 Fussell, *Abroad*, 62–3.

431 Allan Bloom, *The Closing of the American Mind* (New York: Simon and Schuster, 1967), 63.

432 Giuli Liebman Parrinello, 'Motivation and Anticipation in Post-Industrial Tourism,' 85–6; Feifer, *Tourism in History*, 260; Urry, *Tourist Gaze*, 14, 87; Meethan, *Tourism in Global Society*, 4–5, 18–20, 25–6, 32–3, 56–7, 61, 65, 67–8, 72, 79, 88, 93.

433 Urry, *Tourist Gaze*, 2, 13, 139–40. According to Urry, 'tourism is a leisure activity which presupposes its opposite, namely regulated and organized work. It is one manifestation of how work and leisure are organized as separate and regulated spheres of social practice in "modern" societies.'

434 Meethan, *Tourism in Global Society*, 32–3, 50–3, 61–3, 72–8, 116.

435 Cohen, 'Toward a Sociology of International Tourism,' 166–72, 167n, 172n; Erik Cohen, 'A Phenomenology of Tourist Experiences,' *Sociology*, 13 (1979): 179–201; Erik Cohen, 'Rethinking the Sociology of Tourism,' *Annals of Tourism Research*, 6 (1979): 18–20, 22–3, 27-8; Erik Cohen, 'What is a Tourist?: A Conceptual Clarification,' *The Sociological Review*, n.s., 33 (1974): 527–33, 538, 540–2, 544–5, 551n.

436 Canepa, 'From Degenerate Scoundrel to Noble Savage,' 107–46, esp. 122–4, 140–2.

437 Pemble, *Mediterranean Passion*, 12, 14, 100–2, 123–5, 128, 133–5, 142, 145–6, 149–50, 153, 155–7, 163.

438 On the new industrialized mass trench warfare of World War I, see Paul Fussell, *The Great War and Modern Memory* (New York: Oxford Univ. Press, 1975), 36–51, 60, 139–40, 319–20.

439 Martin Green, *Children of the Sun: A Narrative of Decadence in England after 1918* (New York: Basic Books, 1976), 3–35, 41, 44, 60, 68, 78, 79, 119–20, 127, 129, 139–40, 155, 156, 173, 217, 229, 238, 249, 252, 262, 265, 359–60, 389–90, and passim; Fussell, *Abroad*, 3–5, 8–10, 12–13, 15–17, 20–2, 91, 120, 122, 123, 124–5, 129–36, 137, 139. For Victorian precursors, see Pemble, *Mediterranean Passion*, 12, 149–64. Although Green contends that by 1957 the revolt of the 'children of the sun' had been vanquished by the Cold War generation, some of their upper-class and high cultural attitudes towards Italy came to be adopted by their middle-class emulators as well as by mass tourists.

440 Robert Casillo, 'Dirty Gondola: The Image of Italy in American Advertisements,' *Word and Image*, 1 (Oct.–Dec. 1985): 330–350.
441 Adrian Stokes, *Stones of Rimini*, in Stokes, *The Quattro Cento and Stones of Rimini* (University Park, PA: Pennsylvania State Univ. Press, 2002), 62–3; see also 24.
442 Rojek, *Leisure and Culture*, 44.
443 Clark, *City as Entertainment Machine*, 20–1.
444 Fabio Luca Cavazza, 'The European School System: Problems and Trends,' *Daedalus*, 94 (Winter 1964): 414.
445 Kahan, *Aristocratic Liberalism*, 82–3.
446 Ellul, *Technological System*, 109–10.

2 The Unbroken Charm: New Englanders in Italy

1 Martin B. Duberman, *James Russell Lowell* (Boston: Houghton Mifflin, 1966), 127.
2 The following is a list of abbreviations cited in the text and notes: AB, *Among My Books*, in James Russell Lowell, *Complete Writings*, vol. 5 (Boston: Houghton Mifflin, 1904); FT, *Fireside Travels*, in Lowell, *Complete Writings*, vol. 1; HLB, *Life of Henry Wadsworth Longfellow*, ed. Samuel Longfellow, 2 vols. (Boston: Ticknor, 1886); HWL, *The Letters of Henry Wadsworth Longfellow*, ed. Andrew Hilen, 6 vols. (Cambridge: Harvard Univ. Press, 1966–82); JLB, Horace E. Scudder, *James Russell Lowell: A Biography*, 2 vols. (Boston: Houghton Mifflin, 1901); JLL, *Letters of James Russell Lowell*, ed. Charles Eliot Norton, 2 vols. (New York: Harper, 1894); NL, *Letters of Charles Eliot Norton*, ed. Sara Norton and M.A. DeWolfe Howe, 2 vols. (Boston: Houghton Mifflin, 1913); NTS, Norton, *Notes of Travel and Study in Italy* (Boston: Ticknor and Fields, 1859); OM, Henry Wadsworth Longfellow, *Outre-Mer: A Pilgrimage Beyond the Sea* (1833; Boston: Ticknor and Fields, 1859).
3 Longfellow succeeded Ticknor as Smith Professor of the French and Spanish Languages and Professor of Belles Lettres (under which he led the Italian program) in 1836; Lowell succeeded him (1855–77); Norton was professor of the history of art from 1875 to 1898. In 1886 William Dean Howells, whose credentials as a Cambridge Italophile matched his predecessors', turned down the Smith chair.
4 A. Bartlett Giamatti, ed., *Dante in America: The First Two Centuries* (Binghamton, NY: Medieval & Renaissance Texts & Studies, 1983), x.
5 Horace E. Scudder, *Men and Letters: Essays in Characterization and Criticism* (Boston: 1887), 62.
6 Roger B. Stein, *John Ruskin and Aesthetic Thought in America, 1840–1900* (Cambridge: Harvard Univ. Press, 1967), 240, 247.

7 Thayer wrote Norton on his seventy-fifth birthday in 1902: 'I am only one of the score and hundreds for whom you have done so much ... the benefactor through whom they learned *come l'uom s'etterna.' The Letters of William Roscoe Thayer*, ed. Charles Downer Hazen (Boston: Houghton Mifflin, 1926), 119. Norton was the 'Oracle of the Humanities' (*Harvard Graduate Magazine*, Dec. 1908, ctd in NL 2:9).

8 Norton 'had the moral and spiritual qualities, of a stoic kind, which are possible without the benefits of revealed religion,' writes T.S. Eliot; 'and the mental gifts which are possible without genius.' *The Use of Poetry and the Use of Criticism* (London: Faber and Faber, 1933), 13.

9 Nathalia Wright, *American Novelists in Italy: The Discoverers: Allston to James* (Philadelphia: Univ. of Pennsylvania Press, 1965), 17. Allston was in Italy from 1804 to1808.

10 If Prévost had read deeply in Dante, Tasso, Ariosto, and Metastasio, he would have respected a language that 'can express every thing with a simplicity, a grace, a force, in fine, that cannot be approached by any other living language.' Anon. reviewer, ctd in Angelina La Piana, *Dante's American Pilgrimage: A Historical Survey of Dante Studies in the United States: 1800–1944* (New Haven: Yale Univ. Press, 1948), 30.

11 Jared Sparks, 'The Augustan Age in Italian Literature,' *North American Review*, 4 (1817):315.

12 Clifton Waller Barrett, *Italian Influence on American Literature* (New York: Grolier Club, 1962), 6. Rome 'lingers longest,' wrote Prescott, 'the brightest of all I saw in Europe.' Ctd in George Ticknor, *Life of William Hickling Prescott* (Philadelphia, 1863), 42–3.

13 William L. Vance, *America's Rome*, vol. 2: *Catholic and Contemporary Rome* (New Haven: Yale Univ. Press, 1989), 109.

14 Van Wyck Brooks, *The Dream of Arcadia: American Writers and Artists in Italy: 1760–1915* (New York: E.P. Dutton, 1958), ix; Paul R. Baker, *The Fortunate Pilgrims: Americans in Italy: 1800–1860* (Cambridge: Harvard Univ. Press, 1964), 80–104. Vance questions whether 'Americans had no interest in the Italian people' (*America's Rome*, vol. 2: *Catholic and Contemporary Rome*, 109).

15 *The Letters of Henry James*, ed. Percy Lubbock, 2 vols. (New York: Scribner's, 1920), 1:36.

16 'A family of whose many kindnesses I shall always retain the most lively and grateful remembrance' (OM 321).

17 Sumner toured Italy from May to September 1839. 'You gave me the jewel I have,' he wrote Greene, 'for I never should have learned Italian without you.' *Memoir and Letters of Charles Sumner*, ed. Edward L. Pierce, 4 vols. (Boston, 1877–94), 2:119.

18 'If [Turner] was, in truth, disconcerted by his first experience of Italy,'

writes Cecilia Powell, 'this is in itself a measure of his intelligence; it is only the insensitive, narrow-minded and unintelligent visitor to Rome that is not simultaneously overwhelmed, elated and depressed by his experiences. At the end of each day there, any thoughtful and sensitive visitor must surely feel, "Too much for months, let alone for a single day.... Rome is a world, and it would take years to become a true citizen of it. How lucky those travellers are who take one look and leave."' *Turner in the South: Rome, Naples, Florence* (New Haven: Yale Univ. Press, 1987), 192. Powell cites from Goethe's *Italian Journey*.

19 Cf. Sebastian de Grazia distinguishing Aristotle's leisure class from Marx's caught in the class struggle and from Veblen's, which is aristocratic and consumerist: 'The world is divided into two classes, not three or five or twenty. Just two. One is the great majority; the other is the leisure kind, not those of wealth or position or birth, but those who love ideas and the imagination.' *Of Time, Work, and Leisure* (New York: Twentieth Century Fund, 1962), 377–8.

20 Max Weber, 'Science as a Vocation,' in Hans H. Gerth and C. Wright Mills, eds., *From Max Weber: Essays in Sociology* (New York: Oxford Univ. Press, 1946), 139; cf. Gilbert G. Germain, *A Discourse on Disenchantment* (Albany: State Univ. of New York Press, 1993), 28–34.

21 From the Campagna, as the postillion exclaims *Ecco San Pietro!*, the dome of St Peter's can be seen 'hovering visionary on the horizon's verge ... in a moment you are rattling and rumbling and wallowing down into the valley and it is gone' (FT 179). Lowell reduces the lofty vision by a down-to-earth, bumpy ride into the valley; and alliteration is used to good effect in both cases.

22 Cf. Hester Thrale Piozzi: 'The unstudied hilarity of Italians is very rejoicing to the heart, from one's consciousness that it is the result of cheerfulness really felt, not a mere incentive to happiness hoped for.' *Observations and Reflections Made in the Course of a Journey through France, Italy, and Germany* (Dublin: 1789), 378.

23 Cf. Lady Morgan's observation: 'who ever has lived in their society, and visited their capitals, must have remarked that they are the least servile of all the people of Europe; not excepting the English. All their exterior forms are noble and unbending.' *Italy* (London: 1821), 1:180.

24 'Deep Intimate Connection: Self and Intimacy in Couple Relationships,' in Debra J. Mashek and Arthur Aron, eds., *Handbook of Closeness and Intimacy* (Mahwah, NJ: Lawrence Erlbaum, 2004), 45.

25 One finds similar expressions of 'intimate' knowledge elsewhere: 'no place ever took so strong a hold of my being, as Rome,' writes Hawthorne, 'nor ever seemed so close to me, and so strangely familiar. I seem to know it bet-

ter than my birth place, and to have known it longer ... But (life being too short for such questionable and troublesome enjoyments) I desire never to set eyes on it again.' *Works*, vol. 14: *The French and Italian Notebooks*, ed. Thomas Woodson (Columbus: Ohio State Univ. Press, 1980), 524. The opening paragraph of chap. 36 of *The Marble Faun* gives the topos one of its most memorable expressions: 'When we have once known Rome, and left her where she lies, like a long decaying corpse, retaining a trace of the noble shape it was ... when we have left Rome in such a mood as this, we are astonished by the discovery, by-and-by, that our heart-strings have mysteriously attached themselves to the Eternal City, and are drawing us thitherward again, as if it were more familiar, more intimately our home, than even the spot where we were born!' *Works*, vol. 4: *The Marble Faun: or, The Romance of Monte Beni*, ed. William Charvat (Columbus: Ohio State Univ. Press, 1968), 325–6. Cf. Goethe, *Italian Journey*, ed. Thomas P. Saine and Jeffrey L. Sammons, trans. Robert R. Heitner (New York: Suhrkamp, 1989), 104.

26 Still, 'Germany is dull in comparison with Italy' (NL 1:167).

27 Lowell, by contrast, does not become psychologically involved in the religious service, maintaining a satiric distance, crude as it is: 'there was endless Gregorian chanting, then comparative silence, with sudden epidemics among the crowd, of standing painfully on tiptoe to stare at nothing; then more endless Gregorian chantings, more epidemics, and a faint suspicion of frankincense among the garlic; then something incomprehensible performed in dumb show by what seemed automaton candles' (JLB 1:324–5).

28 Rodolfo Lanciani, *Wanderings in the Roman Campagna* (Boston: Houghton Mifflin, 1909), 146–7: the 'most impressive section of the grove lies in the direction of Gericomio,' near Ponte S. Antonio; it could be the terrain through which Lowell travelled. Lanciani thought exaggerated the proposed age of seventeen hundred years; still, the trees grow to great antiquity, the circumference of one being 120 feet. Cf. Thomas Ashby on Ponte S. Antonio, 'one of the most picturesque bridges,' in J.B. Ward-Perkins, ed., *The Roman Campagna in Classical Times* (New York: Barnes and Noble, 1970), 137; and Gilbert Bagnani, *The Roman Campagna and Its Treasures* (London: Methuen, 1929), 204, 242.

29 John C. Woodward, *The Solitude of Loneliness* (Lexington: D.C. Heath, 1988), 4, 5; William Desmond, 'The Solitudes of Philosophy,' in Leroy S. Rouner, ed., *Loneliness* (Notre Dame: Univ. of Notre Dame Press, 1998), 72.

30 Giuseppe Sertoli, 'Edmund Burke,' in Michael Groden and Martin Kreiswirth, eds., *The Johns Hopkins Guide to Literary Theory & Criticism* (Baltimore: Johns Hopkins Univ. Press, 1994), 123–4.

31 One measure of success was the number of undergraduates enrolled in his

course in art history, from 34 in 1875 to 446 in 1895. Richard Norton referred to his father's course as 'Lectures on Modern Morals as Illustrated by the Art of the Ancients' (NL 2:8).

32 La Piana, *Dante's American Pilgrimage*, 13.

33 'And, for the better part of two thousand years, its annals of obscure policies, and wars, and continually recurring misfortunes, seem also but broken rubbish, as compared with its classic history.' *The Marble Faun*, 110; cf. 'nothing is really venerable of a more recent epoch than the reign of Constantine' (*French and Italian Notebooks*, 57). 'Attractive though it may be, Italian art and culture could only defer or misdirect the New Englander's native talents,' comments Clark Davis (*Hawthorne's Shyness* [Baltimore: Johns Hopkins Univ. Press, 2005], 148).

34 Edward Tyrell Channing, 'On Models in Literature,' *North American Review*, 3 (1816): 206. Cf. William Ellery Channing, 'Remarks on a National Literature' (1830), in *The Works* (Boston: American Unitarian Association, 1903), 130; Carl J. Richard, *The Golden Age of the Classics in America: Greece, Rome, and the Antebellum United States* (Cambridge: Harvard Univ. Press, 2009), 88–94.

35 'Lay democracy,' ctd in Kermit Vanderbilt, *Charles Eliot Norton* (Cambridge: Harvard Univ. Press, 1959), 131.

36 Norton ends with Signorelli's fresco cycle on the Apocalypse (1500–1503) in the San Brizio chapel; nothing later brought the cathedral 'new glory'; Norton could not appreciate Francesco Mochi's baroque sculptures, then in the cathedral, but since removed to the church of Sant'Antonio.

37 John Ruskin, *The Stones of Venice*, 3 vols. (London, 1898), 3:11.

38 Evidently, the four travellers kept a journal of this journey, which has not been published (NL 1:145).

39 While Norton wrote that 'the system of the Church cannot coexist with freedom' (NTS 163), Hawthorne thought otherwise: 'Rome,' says Kenyon in *The Marble Faun* (109), 'is not like one of our New England villages, where we need the permission of each individual neighbor for every act that we do, every word that we utter, and every friend that we make or keep. In these particulars, the Papal despotism allows us freer breath than our native air.'

40 John Ruskin, *Praeterita*, in *Hortus Inclusus* (Boston: Colonial, n.d.), 422.

41 Charles Eliot Norton, *Historical Studies of Church Building in the Middle Ages: Venice, Siena, Florence* (New York: Harper, 1880), ctd by Vanderbilt, *Charles Eliot Norton*, 130.

42 'Rome before 1870 was seductive beyond resistance,' wrote Henry Adams; 'no sand-blast of science had yet skinned off the epidermis of history, thought, and feeling. The pictures were uncleaned, the churches

unrestored.' Nevertheless, 'Rome was the worst spot on earth to teach nineteenth-century youth what to do with a twentieth-century world.' *The Education of Henry Adams* (New York: Random House, 1931), 89–90.

43 Cf. Riccardo Cerri and Laura Osella Crevaroli, *The Queen of the Alps: Girovagando a Sud del Monte Rosa. Escursionisti, alpinisti e turisti inglesi dell' Ottocento in Valsesia e dintorni* (Magenta: Edizioni Zeisciu, 1998), 11, 12, 23, 26, 158.

44 Nicholas John Russo, 'Three Generations of Italians in New York City: Their Religious Acculturation,' in Silvano M. Tomasi and Madeline H. Engel, eds., *The Italian Experience in the United States* (Staten Island: Center for Migration Studies, 1970), 195–213; and Richard A. Varbero, 'Philadelphia's South Italians and the Irish Church: A History of Cultural Conflict,' in Silvano M. Tomasi, ed., *The Religious Experience of Italian Americans* (Staten Island: American Italian Historical Association, 1975), 31–52.

45 James Turner, *The Liberal Education of Charles Eliot Norton* (Baltimore: Johns Hopkins Univ. Press, 1999), 198–9; K.P. Van Anglen, *The New England Milton: Literary Reception and Cultural Authority in the Early Republic* (University Park: Pennsylvania State Univ. Press, 1993), viii–ix, 66–68; Vanderbilt, *Charles Eliot Norton*, 172–3.

46 With Lowell, T.S. Eliot shared distaste for Milton's radical partisanship, high esteem for Dante's *Vita Nuova*, belief in the poetic importance of Beatrice, admiration for the final cantos of the *Purgatorio*, exaltation of the *Paradiso* as the summit of Western poetry, and in general a European cultural horizon. Lowell: 'if Shakespeare be the most comprehensive intellect, so Dante is the highest spiritual nature that has expressed itself in rhythmical form' (AB 169). Eliot: 'Shakespeare gives the greatest width of human passion; Dante the greatest altitude and greatest depth' (*Dante* [1929; London: Faber and Faber, 1965]), 11, 27, 47).

47 The Italophiles had their hobby-horses: Lowell's notion that Dante was 'of mixed race, the Alighieri being of Teutonic origin,' and combined the 'deeper and more abstract sentiment of the Teutonic races with the scientific precision and absolute systematism of the Romanic' (AB 8, 53, 65–6, 145).

48 'Treat them with kindness, and call them often by their christian names,' writes Giuseppe Baretti, 'and you may depend upon their most sincere attachment.' *An Account of the Manners and Customs of Italy; with Observations on the Mistakes of Some Travellers, with Regard to That Country* (London: 1769), 57.

49 George Santayana, *The Genteel Tradition: Nine Essays*, ed. Douglas L. Wilson (Cambridge: Harvard Univ. Press, 1967), 78. 'New England attitudes were dominated by attempts to reconcile Protestantism with the romanticism that issued out of German idealist philosophy' (Irving Singer, *George Santayana, Literary Philosopher* [New Haven: Yale Univ. Press, 2001], 47).

50 David Perkins, *A History of Modern Poetry*, vol. 1: *From the 1890s to the High Modernist Mode* (Cambridge: Harvard Univ. Press, 1976), 102.

51 *Genteel Tradition*, 155. Cf. NL 2:358–9. In 1893 Francis Walker, president of MIT, addressed Harvard's Phi Beta Kappa Society on the importance of sports: 'the favorite athletics of today often demand of the contestants the ability to work with others, power of combination, readiness to subordinate selfish impulses, personal desires, and even individual credit to a common end. These are all qualities useful in any profession.' Ctd in Christian Messenger, 'Tom Buchanan and the Demise of the Ivy League Athletic Hero,' *Journal of Popular Culture*, 8, no. 2 (1974): 403.

52 Van Wyck Brooks, *America's Coming of Age* (New York: Huebsch, 1915), 6; Vernon Parrington, *Main Currents in American Thought*, vol. 3: *The Beginning of Critical Realism in American, 1860–1920* (New York: Harcourt, Brace, 1930), 53; Randolph Bourne, 'A Little Thing of Brunelleschi's,' in Olaf Hansen, ed., *The Radical Will: Selected Writings 1911–1918* (Berkeley: Univ. of California Press, 1976), 528; Ludwig Lewisohn, *Expression in America* (New York: Harper, 1932), 76; Lewis Mumford, *The Golden Day: A Study in American Literature and Culture* (1926: Boston: Beacon, 1957), 44.

53 Santayana, ctd by James Ballowe, ed., *George Santayana's America: Essays on Literature and Culture* (Urbana: Univ. of Illinois Press, 1967), 7.

54 Ctd by Ballowe, *George Santayana's America*, 8.

55 Mark Rennella, *The Boston Cosmopolitans: International Travel and American Arts and Letters* (New York: Palgrave, 2008), 8; cf. 35: 'The story of cosmopolitanism in Boston begins with ... Norton.'

56 For the Italophiles' socio-political matrix, see Martin Green, *The Problem of Boston: Some Readings in Cultural History* (London: Longmans, Green, 1966); Daniel Walker Howe, *The Unitarian Conscience: Harvard Moral Philosophy, 1805–1861* (Cambridge: Harvard Univ. Press, 1970); Ronald Story, *The Forging of an Aristocracy: Harvard and the Boston Upper Class, 1800–1870* (Middletown: Wesleyan Univ. Press, 1980); Lawrence Buell, *New England Literary Culture: From Revolution through Renaissance* (Cambridge: Cambridge Univ. Press, 1986); Robert Dawidoff, *The Genteel Tradition and the Sacred Rage: High Culture vs. Democracy in Adams, James, & Santayana* (Chapel Hill: Univ. of North Carolina Press, 1992); Darren Staloff, *The Making of an American Thinking Class: Intellectuals and Intelligentsia in Puritan Massachusetts* (New York: Oxford Univ. Press, 1998).

57 Rennella, *Boston Cosmopolitans*, 36.

58 Howe, *Unitarian Conscience*, 9. Cf. William L. Vance, 'Redefining "Bostonian,"' in Trevor J. Fairbrother, ed., *The Bostonians: Painters of an Elegant Age, 1870–1930* (Boston: Museum of Fine Arts, 1986), 9–30.

59 Pauline Chase Harrell and Margaret Supplee Smith, eds., *Victorian Boston Today: Ten Walking Tours* (Boston: Victorian Society, 1975), 87.

60 Baker, *Fortunate Pilgrims*, 29. George Stillman Hillard, *Six Months in Italy*, 2 vols. (Boston: Ticknor, Reed, and Fields, 1853), hereafter cited in text and notes as SM.

61 John Lothrop Motley, *Correspondence*, ed. George William Curtis, 2 vols. (New York: 1889), 1:189.

62 'I lose infinite pleasure every day, for want of deeper learning,' wrote Hester Thrale Piozzi, Johnson's friend and biographer, commenting in Rome on being unable to read an inscription from Euripides. *Observations and Reflections*, 399.

63 Hillard alludes to Johnson: a tourist in the Vatican is 'like the shepherd in the Rambler who asked to have the river Euphrates flow through his grounds, and was taken off his feet and borne away by the stream ... long before the great circuit is completed, his knees knock together with fatigue, and his worn brain refuses to receive any new impressions. But time and patience, which conquer all things, conquer the Vatican.' SM 1:235–6.

64 Vance, *America's Rome*, vol. 1: *Classical Rome*, 87.

65 John Urry, *The Tourist Gaze: Leisure and Travel in Contemporary Societies* (London: Sage, 1990).

66 Like Emerson before him, and Sumner, Santayana, and Bernard Berenson after him, Hillard attended Boston Latin School (class of 1824).

67 William Ware, *Sketches of European Capitals* (Boston: 1851), 199.

68 Ctd in K.P. Van Anglen, 'Before Longfellow: Dante and the Polarization of New England,' *Dante Studies* 119 (2001): 160. Cf. Ernest Lee Tuveson, *Redeemer Nation: The Idea of America's Millennial Role* (Chicago: Univ. of Chicago Press, 1968), 64–5.

69 He alludes to Anchises' prophecy: 'Others will soften the bronze ... and chart the heavens ... your arts, Rome, are to rule; tame the proud and spare the weak' (Virgil, *Aen.* 6.850), then continues: 'if, in the far-away future, some Gibbon shall muse among our ruins, the history of our Decline and Fall shall be more mournful and more epic than that of the huge Empire amid the dust of whose once world-shaking heart these feelings so often come upon me' (JLB 1:342–3). Cf. Henry Adams, 'Rome was actual; it was England; it was going to be America.' *Education*, 91.

70 'The author of the "Modern Painters" is a great writer on art, and when he is wrong, it is often only from pushing right principles to an extreme. His book is a golden book, steeped in the poetry and the religion of art, just in theory and exquisite in spirit ... , but the author will undoubtedly live to admit that all its vehement and impetuous judgments are not correct.' SM 1:371–2.

71 Heinrich Wölfflin, *Classic Art: An Introduction to the Italian Renaissance*, trans. Peter and Linda Murray (New York: Phaidon, 1953), 210, 216, 235, 239, 252, 254; Adrian Stokes, *The Stones of Rimini* (New York: Putnam, 1934), chap. 4.

72 'With what a sense of relief,'comments Wölfflin, 'the eye turns to Raphael's compositions, with their multitudes of figures – I am speaking of his Roman works, for the *Entombment* is still lacking in this kind of [compositional] clarity.' *Classic Art*, 267.

73 William Wetmore Story's 'hideous' *baldacchino. Roba di Roma*, 7th ed. (London: 1876), 250.

74 Camillo Von Klenze, *The Interpretation of Italy during the Last Two Centuries* (Chicago: Univ. of Chicago Press, 1907), 10, 43.

75 Udo Kultermann, *The History of Art History* (New York: Abaris Books, 1993), 136–7.

76 William Paley, *Natural Theology; or, Evidences of the Existence and Attributes of the Deity, Collected from the Appearances of Nature* (1802; Albany, 1803), 307, 308, 330.

77 *The Letters of Margaret Fuller*, ed. Robert N. Hudspeth, 6 vols. (Ithaca: Cornell Univ. Press, 1988), 4:295; hereafter letters are cited as *L* by volume and page number in text and notes.

78 Margaret Fuller Ossoli, *At Home and Abroad; or, Things and Thoughts in America and Europe*, ed. Arthur B. Fuller (Pt. Washington, NY: Kennikat, 1971), 233; hereafter cited as *AHA* in text and notes.

79 *The Essential Margaret Fuller*, ed. Jeffrey Steele (New Brunswick: Rutgers Univ. Press, 1992), xxii–xxiii.

80 Jeffrey Alan Melton, *Mark Twain, Travel Books, and Tourism: The Tide of a Great Popular Movement* (Tuscaloosa: Univ. of Alabama Press, 2002), 16.

81 'Books of Travel' (1845), in Judith Mattson Bean and Joel Myerson, eds., *Margaret Fuller, Critic* (New York: Columbia Univ. Press), 299–300.

82 'Books of Travel,' 301–2. On Goethe's *Italian Journey* she writes, 'it is this patience, this depth, this serenity consequent on a great scope of vision, and clear discernment of the infrangible links between cause and effect, that are so opposed to our hasty, overemphatic, superficial mode of action' (302). Joseph Forsyth is praised for his 'tone of high culture, refined taste and harmonious thought'; 'one who wanted aid in forming taste, or to be stimulated to a higher point of view and more accuracy and delicacy in observation than contents the crowd will find a preceptor and a friend in Forsyth' (302). *Remarks on Antiquities, Arts, and Letters during an Excursion in Italy, in the Years 1802 and 1803* has been edited by Keith Crook (Newark: Univ. of Delaware Press/Associated Univ. Presses, 2001).

83 Beckford published *Italy*, a neglected masterpiece of travel writing, in 1783 under the title *Dreams, Waking Thoughts, and Incidents, in a Series of Letters, from Various Parts of Europe*; it was withdrawn by Beckford's family, which feared scandal. Fuller probably read the edition that Beckford published fifty-one years later (*Italy, with Sketches of Spain and Portugal*).

84 A. William Salomone, 'The Nineteenth-Century Discovery of Italy: An Essay in American Cultural History. Prolegomena to a Historiographical Problem,' *American Historical Review*, 73, no. 5 (1968): 1378.

85 A common theme: 'the traveller passing along the beaten track, vetturinoed from inn to inn, ciceroned from gallery to gallery, thrown, through indolence, want of tact, or ignorance of the language, too much into the society of his compatriots, sees the least possible of the country'; it is 'quite out of the question to know Italy ... without long residence, and residence in the districts untouched by the scorch and dust of foreign invasion' (AHA 220).

86 'I have screwed my expenses down to the lowest possible peg; at least it seems so now, but I dont know; – that art seems to be capable of ... indefinite perfection in Italy' (L 5:158).

87 Cf. the topos: one must overcome 'Anglicized Rome' ('taverns, lodging-houses, cheating chambermaids, vilest *valets de place*, and fleas!') to see the ancient city; 'it is possible to wash away all this dirt, and come at the marble yet' (AHA 259).

88 Mary McCarthy, *The Stones of Florence* (New York: Harcourt Brace, 1987), 10.

89 Stendhal, *Voyages en Italie*, ed. Victor Del Litto (Paris: Gallimard, 1973), 98 (24 May 1817); for other references to *charme* see 11, 81, 151, 377, 486, 492.

90 Goethe helps 'to stem the tide that hurries us on so fast.' 'Books of Travel,' 302.

91 'a large portion of my countrymen here take the same slothful and prejudiced view as the English, and, after many year's sojourn, betray entire ignorance of Italian literature and Italian life' (AHA 246).

92 Leonardo Buonomo speaks of her 'intense involvement,' her 'desire to participate'; unlike previous travellers, she was 'willing to compromise, to endanger [her] privileged point of view.' *Backward Glances: Exploring Italy, Reinterpreting America, 1831–1866* (Madison, Teaneck, NJ: Associated Univ. Presses/Fairleigh Dickinson Univ. Press, 1996), 29.

93 'This consciousness [the sightseer's eagerness] would be most valuable if one had time to think and study, being the natural way in which the mind is lured to cure itself of its defects; but you have no time; you are always wearied, body and mind, confused dissipated, sad' (AHA 258).

94 The editors of Fuller's foreign dispatches place the Chapels of the Cemeteries 'along the Via Giulia'; in fact, they were in the Cimitero di S. Spirito

near the Porta S. Spirito, across the river on the Janiculum. The editors also claim that 'at the end of the street [Via Giulia] is a good view of Rome.' Yet the land at either end of the Via Giulia does not rise high enough for such a view. Fuller says, 'I went to Santo Spirito. This Cemetery stands high'; from that height on the slope of the Janiculum she walked higher, to the Cross, 'which marks the brow of the hill,' for her panoramic view of Rome at sunset. (Larry J. Reynolds and Susan Belasco Smith, eds., *'These Sad But Glorious Days': Dispatches from Europe, 1846–1850* [New Haven: Yale Univ. Press, 1991], 169–71.) Mariano Armellini published an engraving of the Cimitero di S. Spirito, announcing it is to be demolished (1887); two chapels are described briefly: S. Maria del Rosario and Cappella del Crocifisso. (*Le Chiese di Roma dal secolo IV al XIX* [1887, 1892; Rome: Edizioni R.O.R.E. di Nicola Russolo, 1942], 806–7.)

95 'Each day I am out from eleven till five, exploring some new object of interest, often at a great distance' (L 4:313). 'I now really live in Rome, and I begin to see and feel the real Rome. She reveals herself day by day; she tells me some of her life. Now I never go out to see a sight, but I walk every day; and here I cannot miss of some object of consummate interest to end a walk' (AHA 259).

96 Cf. Shelley, 'The Sunset' (1816): 'The tomb of thy dead self.'

97 Margaret Allen, *The Achievement of Margaret Fuller* (University Park: Pennsylvania State Univ. Press, 1979), 155.

98 'Yes I shall like to go back and see our "eighteen millions of bores," with their rail-roads, electric telegraphs, mass movements and ridiculous dilettant (*sic*) phobias, but with ever successful rush and bang' (L 6:64). The 'eighteen millions of bores' is Thomas Carlyle's description of America.

99 Vance, *America's Rome*, vol. 2: *Catholic and Contemporary Rome*, 132–3; Brigitte Bailey, 'Fuller, Hawthorne, and Imagining Urban Spaces in Rome,' in Robert K. Martin and Leland S. Person, eds., *Roman Holidays: American Writers and Artists in Nineteenth-Century Italy* (Iowa City: Univ. of Iowa Press, 2002), 180–1.

100 Kimberly Van Esveld Adams, *Our Lady of Victorian Feminism* (Athens: Ohio Univ. Press, 2001), 136–7.

101 Jane Stabler, 'Devotion and Diversion: Early Nineteenth-Century British Women Travellers in Italy and the Catholic Church,' in Alison Chapman and Jane Stabler, eds., *Unfolding the South: Nineteenth-Century British Women Writers and Artists in Italy* (Manchester: Manchester Univ. Press, 2003), 16.

102 Buonomo, *Backward Glances*, 43.

103 Vol. 13 of *Works* (Boston: Houghton Mifflin, 1892), 285. Boston, then reclaiming Back Bay from the Charles lagoon, is also likened to Venice.

104 Giuliana Artom Treves, *The Golden Ring: The Anglo-Florentines, 1847–1862* (London: Longmans, Green, 1956), 160–76; McCarthy, *Stones of Florence*, 4, 14, 28, 33, 36, 40, 55, 60, 61, 63, 87, 88, 93. Buying into the myth of the two Italies, McCarthy goes so far as to make Florence almost a northern European city, complete with Irish Jansenist Catholicism. See Paul Giles, *American Catholic Arts and Fictions: Culture, Ideology, Aesthetics* (Cambridge: Cambridge Univ. Press, 1992), 459.

105 Florentines, writes Stendhal, 'have no more passion than beautiful liveries and pretty processions'; the city is 'absolument *sans passions*,' 'too clear and too French,' 'bourgeois.' *Voyages en Italie*, 363, 459, 486, 489, 494.

106 Hawthorne, *French and Italian Notebooks*, 156; 'of course with much talent, and much moral reality, or else she could not have been so great a humbug.'

107 Henry James, *Hawthorne* (New York: Harper, 1880), 68–9, 76, and *William Wetmore Story and His Friends* (Boston: Houghton Mifflin, 1903), 127–8. See Cristina Giorcelli, 'A Humbug, a Bounder, and a Dabbler: Margaret Fuller, Cristina di Belgioioso, Christina Casamassima,' in Charles Capper and Cristina Giorcelli, eds., *Margaret Fuller: Transatlantic Crossings in a Revolutionary Age* (Madison: Univ. of Wisconsin Press, 2007), 201–12.

108 'Italy [Alfieri]' (1845), in *Margaret Fuller, Critic*, 255.

109 On 23 November 2000 a tablet in Fuller's honour was placed in the Piazza Barberini (she lived at no. 60), by the corner of the Via Sistina.

110 After attending a ballet with Fuller, Emerson is reported to have said "This is art!" To which Margaret Fuller replied with added rapture, "Ah, Mr. Emerson, this is religion!" Santayana, *Persons and Places: Fragments of Autobiography*, ed. William G. Holzberger and Herman J. Saatkamp, Jr, vol. 1 of *Works* (Cambridge: MIT Press, 1986), 45.

111 *The Letters of George Santayana*, ed. Daniel Cory (New York: Scribner's, 1957), 306.

112 George Santayana, *The Last Puritan: A Memoir in the Form of a Novel* (New York: Scribner's, 1935), 289 (hereafter cited as *LP* in text and notes); Cory, *Letters*, 303.

113 Santayana, *Persons and Places*, 401 (the 'vulgar' in this instance was Kipling).

114 Santayana, 'A General Confession,' in P.A. Schilpp, ed., *The Philosophy of George Santayana* (New York: Tudor, 1951), 15.

115 George Santayana, *Interpretations of Poetry and Religion*, ed. William G. Holzberger and Herman J. Saatkamp, Jr, introduction by Joel Porte, vol. 3 of *Works* (Cambridge: MIT Press, 1989), 60–2, 148.

116 *The Letters of William James*, ed. Henry James, 2 vols. (Boston: Atlantic Monthly Press, 1920), 2:122–3; Cory, *Letters*, 62. In this letter (Easter 1900)

Santayana also wrote: 'I am nearer to you than you now believe. What you say, for instance, about the value of the good lying in its *existence*, and about the continuity of the world of values with that of fact, is not different from what I should admit' (61–2). As Joel Porte points out, Santayana's belief that 'the highest ideality is the comprehension of the real' is close to James's argument that Whitman and Browning, 'whom Santayana attacked in the book ... were 'in the line of mental growth' because of their insistence that 'the ideal and the real are dynamically continuous.' *Interpretations*, xiv, 168, 169.

117 Santayana, *Persons and Places*, 401.
118 Santayana, *Persons and Places*, 529.
119 Perkins, *History of Modern Poetry*, 1:103.
120 'Professor Santayana' the narrator belongs to the generation of Oliver and Mario's parents, born in the 1860s. However, Santayana the author's generation is more complex: 'In the years 1891–1893 that club [the Delphic] was absolutely my home ... I became so attached to the place, that I kept going there off and on for some years after that, until 1896–7'; 'that second youth of mine was far pleasanter than my first youth, when I was myself an undergraduate, and the original of *Oliver & Mario* was to have been a story set in that club' (Cory, *Letters*, 303). Though his second youth, ten years after his first, still makes him older than Oliver, it draws him closer to Oliver and the members of Oliver's generation whom he mentored at Harvard.
121 '[Oliver's] problem is not that he has no emotions, but rather that they must be moralized before they become acceptable in his own eyes.' Noel O'Sullivan, *Santayana* (St. Albans: Claridge, 1992), 37.
122 In a satiric passage contrasting food habits, Mario praises his cousin, a 'magnificent Nordic' who must be 'fed magnificently.' Oliver eats abundantly but poorly; for him, food is mere energy, 'shovelling in good beef and good mutton every few hours.' By contrast, Mario knows all the best places to eat, expensive and inexpensive, including 'the *Napoli*' in the North End, Boston's Little Italy (LP 428).
123 George Santayana, 'A Brief History of My Opinions,' in Richard C. Lyon, ed., *Santayana on America* (New York: Harcourt, Brace & World, 1968), 8.
124 Eliseo Vivas, 'From *The Life of Reason* to *The Last Puritan*,' in Schilpp, *Philosophy of George Santayana*, 346.
125 Cory, *Letters*, 303, 306.
126 Weber, 'Science as a Vocation,' 134, 135, 140.
127 T.J. Jackson Lears, *No Place of Grace: Antimodernism and the Transformation of American Culture, 1880–1920* (New York: Pantheon, 1981), 80.

128 H.T. Kirby-Smith, *A Philosophical Novelist: George Santayana and* The Last
Puritan (Carbondale: Southern Illinois Univ. Press, 1997), 167.

129 'He liked Concord in its external humility and inward pride, so much like
his own. This place had at least one spiritual advantage over Groton: it was
sad' (LP 404). Cf. Santayana on Emerson: 'There is evil, of course, he tells
us. Experience is sad.' *Interpretations*, 137.

130 Jonathan Levin, *The Poetics of Transition: Emerson, Pragmatism, & American
Literary Modernism* (Durham: Duke Univ. Press, 1999), 112; LP 564.

131 George Santayana, 'Leaving Church,' in Santayana, *Soliloquies in England
and Later Soliloquies* (1922; Ann Arbor: Univ. of Michigan Press, 1967), 90:
'Protestant faith does not vanish into the sunlight as Catholic faith does,
but leaves a shadowy ghost haunting the night of the soul'; '[the Protestant's] idea of God is a vague symbol that stands not essentially, as with the
Catholic, for a particularly legendary or theological personage, but rather
for that unfathomable influence which, if it does not make for righteous-
ness, at least has so far made for existence and has imposed it upon us.'
'The atmosphere of the [Protestant's] inner man is more charged with
vapours, and it takes longer for the light dubiously to break through; and
often in his wintry day the sun sets without shining' (88, 90).

132 Ross Posnock, 'Genteel Androgyny: Santayana, Henry James, Howard Sturgis,' *Raritan*, 10, no. 3 (1991): 61; Vivas, 'From *The Life of Reason* to *The Last
Puritan*,' 349.

133 There is an element of ethnic stereotyping: Mario has stamina, to be sure,
but her so-called flabby Anglos out-accomplished the Italians in the previous three centuries.

134 'You are not comfortable with women,' says Mario; 'It's all because you
never loved your mother and she never loved you. My mother suckled
me at her own breast. She would have given up the stage, given up music,
given up everything rather than not do it, or let anybody else touch me. I
seem to remember it. But suppose I couldn't remember it; the habit would
be there, the impulse, the confidence' (LP 408–9).

135 Kirby-Smith, *Philosophical Novelist*, 166.

136 For Santayana, an essence is like a Platonic idea that requires a consciousness for its survival, hence the mix of Platonism and Aristotelian naturalism or Lucretian materialism. In a book that he particularly admired,
Studies of the Gods in Greece (New York: 1891), Louis Dyer writes that 'all and
each of the greater Greek gods still live their charmed life, and even to-day
each one in some sense is the centre of a scheme of things' (9).

137 Santayana, 'Liberalism and Culture,' 'The Irony of Liberalism,' in Santayana, *Soliloquies in England*, 174, 180, 181, 183: the liberalism of liberty

'implies that the ultimate environment, divine or natural, is either chaotic in itself or undiscoverable by human science, and that human nature, too, is either radically various or only determinable in a few essentials, round which individual variations play *ad libitum*'; on the other hand, 'the transcendental principle of progress ... requires everything to be ill at ease in its own house; no one can be really free or happy but all must be tossed, like herded emigrants, on the same compulsory voyage, to the same unhomely destination' (174, 181).

138 George Santayana, *Character and Opinion in the United States* (1920; New York: George Braziller, 1955), 96, 127, 128, 130; 'The necessity of rejecting and destroying some things that are beautiful is the deepest curse of existence' (130).

139 *Letters*, ed. Cory, 305–7. 'When Santayana says in the Epilogue that any future worth having will come from men like Mario, "not from weedy intellectuals or self-inhibited puritans,"' writes James C. Ballowe, 'he means that Mario's is a modernism that carries with it the lessons of the past. He has not disowned, as Oliver has done, "the living forces of nature."' '*The Last Puritan* and the Failure in American Culture,' *American Quarterly*, 18:2 (1966): 131.

140 Cory, *Letters*, 302, 305.Cf. William James, 'If this life be not a real fight, in which something is eternally gained for the universe by success, it is no better than a game of private theatricals from which one may withdraw at will. But it *feels* like a real fight ...' (*The Will to Believe and Other Essays in Popular Philosophy* [New York: Longman, Green, 1896], 61).

141 Cory, *Letters*, 304; Santayana, 'The Nature of Spirit,' in Santayana, *The Realm of Spirit: Book Fourth of Realms of Being* (New York: Scribner's, 1940), 10.

142 Corliss Lamont, *ed., Dialogue on George Santayana* (New York: Horizon, 1959), 60. Mario's 'warmth, lack of intellectual pretensions, easy-going relations with the ladies, southern European charm, vivaciousness, spontaneity, and lack of reserve epitomize everything that Santayana loved in the Italian character and everything that (and he was acutely aware of this) other people found lacking in him.' Kirby-Smith, *Philosophical Novelist*, 119.

143 Santayana, *Interpretations*, 169.

144 Cory, *Letters*, 305.

145 Singer, *George Santayana*, 48, 57. For Santayana, the culture of Roman Catholicism embodies a long history of human experience, lending it moral weight and authority. Its historical and communal dimension enables it to counter the absolutist subjectivism of Protestantism and German Romanticism. Then, Catholicism has more mythic power than Protestantism,

especially in its Puritan ascetic form. Also, Catholicism believes in divine immanence and the sacredness of nature, whereas Puritanism separates the realm of grace from the realm of nature.

146 Cory, *Letters*, 225–6. Cf. John McCormick, *George Santayana: A Biography* (New York: Knopf, 1987), 270; and Perkins on 'The American Milieu, 1890–1912' in Perkins, *History of Modern Poetry*, 1:95.

147 *Genteel Tradition*, 62–3. 'When you escape, as you love to do, to your forests and your Sierras, I am sure again that you do not feel you made them, or that they were made for you. They have grown, as you have grown, only more massively and more slowly. In their non-human beauty and peace they stir the sub-human depths and the super-human possibilities of your own spirit. It is no transcendental logic that they teach; and they give no sign of any deliberate morality seated in the world. It is rather the vanity and superficiality of all logic, the needlessness of argument, the finitude of morals, the strength of time, the fertility of matter, the variety, the unspeakable variety, of possible life' (62–3). Cf. Levin, *Poetics of Transition*, 113.

148 'A Glimpse of Yale,' 'Philosophy on the Bleachers,' in Ballowe, *George Santayana's America*, 50, 126, 128–9. In Weberian terms, football expresses old Protestantism: 'sport was accepted if it served a rational purpose, that of recreation necessary for physical efficiency. But as a means for the spontaneous expression of undisciplined impulses, it was under suspicion; and in so far as it became purely a means of enjoyment, or awakened pride, raw instincts or the irrational gambling instinct, it was of course strictly condemned.' Max Weber, *The Protestant Ethic and the Spirit of Capitalism* (New York: Scribner's, 1958), 167–8.

149 His stipulating that he meant amateur and not professional sports would not remove this objection.

150 Messenger, 'Tom Buchanan and the Demise of the Ivy League Athletic Hero,' 407–8.

151 George Santayana, *Reason in Science*, vol. 5 of *The Life of Reason: or, the Phases of Human Progress* (New York: Scribner's, 1906), 212–13.

152 *Santayana, Persons and Places*, 467, 536; 'Apologia pro Mente Sua,' in Schilpp, *Philosophy of George Santayana*, 603.

3 Isle of the Dead

1 Douglas Bush, *Pagan Myth and Christian Tradition in English Poetry* (Philadelphia: American Philosophical Society, 1968), 59–60.

2 Virgil, *Aeneid*, trans. Frederick Ahl (New York: Oxford Univ. Press, 2009), 341, 363.

3 Salvatore Settis, *The Future of the 'Classical,'* trans. Allan Cameron (Cambridge: Polity, 2006), 54.

4 Alberto Tenenti, *Il senso della morte e l'amore della vita nel Rinascimento (Francia e Italia)* (1957; Turin: Einaudi, 1989); Michel Vovelle, *Piété baroque et déchristianisation en Provençe au XVIIIe siècle: Les attitudes devant la mort d'après les clauses des testaments* (Paris: Plon, 1973), *La mort et l'Occident de 1300 à nos jours* (Paris: Gallimard, 1983); Philippe Ariès, *Western Attitudes toward Death: From the Middle Ages to the Present*, trans. Patricia M. Ranum (Baltimore: Johns Hopkins Univ. Press, 1974); *The Hour of Our Death*, trans. Helen Weaver (New York: Knopf, 1981).

5 'The theses of Ariès, the methodologies of Vovelle,' writes Joachim Whaley, 'have yet to be tested in depth.' *Mirrors of Mortality: Studies in the Social History of Death*, ed. Whaley (New York: St. Martin's, 1981), 3, 13. Cf. Alan Mitchell, 'Philippe Ariès and the French Way of Death,' *French Historical Studies*, 10 (1978): 684–95; Lawrence Stone, *The Past and the Present* (London: Routledge and Kegan Paul, 1981), 245–59; Robert Darnton, *The Kiss of Lamourette: Reflections in Cultural History* (New York: Norton, 1990), 272–92; Thomas A. Kselman, *Death and the Afterlife in Modern France* (Princeton: Princeton Univ. Press, 1993), 3–5; Ellen Badone, *The Appointed Hour: Death, Worldview, and Social Change in Brittany* (Berkeley: Univ. of California Press, 1989), 12–15; Patrick H. Hutton, *Philippe Ariès and the Politics of French Cultural History* (Amherst: Univ. of Massachusetts Press, 2004), 113–17.

6 Ariès, *Hour of Our Death*, 392. Culture has 'divested death of its brutality, incongruity, and contagious effects by weakening its personal quality in favor of the permanence of society, by ritualizing it and making it only one more transition in every life, only slightly more dramatic than the others,' 394.

7 Ariès, *Western Attitudes*, 14, 103, 105; *Hour of Our Death*, 29, 161.

8 Ariès, *Hour of Our Death*, 28.

9 Badone, *Appointed Hour*, 12. In Ariès's terms, tame death may name the first stage 550–1100 or the larger epoch from 550 to 1914 (four stages), after which death untamed (fifth stage) assumes dominance. Ideologically speaking, Ariès deplores the loss of tame death and the communal values that supported it, a loss that he lays at the door of increasing awareness of 'individual identity' (13) in modernity.

10 Ariès, *Hour of Our Death*, 107. Lawrence Stone argues that the individualizing period dates from the Renaissance, not from the eleventh or twelfth centuries (*The Past and the Present*, 252, 255).

11 Tenenti, *Il senso della morte*, 31, 336. The obsession with the moment of death produced a startling outbreak of the macabre that spread through so-

ciety. Funerary art displays the *transi* or half-decomposed corpse, the danse macabre, and a variety of plague and corruption imagery. Whereas Huizinga had seen the macabre as symptomatic of a crisis ending the Middle Ages (the Black Death, the Hundred Years' War), Tenenti interprets it as the inverse expression of a vigorous love of life.

12 '[People] increasingly attached their self-esteem to worldly possessions, wishing to hold onto them to the grave and beyond.' Samuel K. Cohn, Jr, *The Cult of Remembrance and the Black Death: Six Renaissance Cities in Central Italy* (Baltimore: Johns Hopkins Univ. Press, 1992), 91.

13 Ariès, *Hour of Our Death*, 403.

14 Loren Partridge, *Michelangelo: The Sistine Chapel Ceiling, Rome* (New York: George Braziller, 1996), 16.

15 Ariès, *Western Attitudes*, 56–8. Ariès's 'remote and imminent death' is among his more controversial hypotheses. Lawrence Stone objects that Ariès's reason for inserting this stage is to impugn 'the effects of the Enlightenment, rationalism and science in stripping away the ancient controls over sex and death' (*The Past and the Present*, 252–3). Stone collapses this stage into 'one's own death,' which covers the entire period from the early Renaissance to the eighteenth century (as Ariès had done in the earlier of his two books on the subject, *Western Attitudes*). Cf. Cynthia Richards, 'The Body of Her Work, the Work of Her Body: Accounting for the Life and Death of Mary Wollstonecraft,' *Eighteenth Century Fiction*, 21, no. 4 (2009): 576.

16 Cf. John W. Draper, *The Funeral Elegy and the Rise of Romanticism* (New York: New York Univ. Press, 1929), 312.

17 Giuseppe Sertoli, 'Edmund Burke,' *The Johns Hopkins Guide to Literary Theory & Criticism*, ed. Michael Groden and Martin Kreiswirth (Baltimore: Johns Hopkins Univ. Press, 1994), 124. Cf. Sertoli, Presentazione, Burke, *Inchiesta sul Bello e il Sublime*, ed. Sertoli and Goffredo Miglietta (Palermo: Aesthetica Edizioni, 1985), 9–40.

18 Frederick S. Paxton comments that the burial of the dead within the church in the fifth century and their expulsion to a cemetery outside the city centre in the second half of the eighteenth century constitute Ariès's most significant example of the 'historical unity' of tame death (*Christianizing Death: The Creation of a Ritual Process in Early Medieval Europe* [Ithaca: Cornell Univ. Press, 1990], 17–18).

19 Ariès, *Western Attitudes*, 72, 73.

20 Roland Mortier has examined the passion for ruins that swept across Europe in the eighteenth and nineteenth centuries, often centred on Italian or imitation Italian ruins. *La poétique des ruines en France: Ses origines, ses variations de la Renaissance à Victor Hugo* (Geneva: Droz, 1974), 170–92. Cf. Bruce

C. Swaffield, *Rising from the Ruins: Roman Antiquities in Neoclassic Literature* (London: Cambridge Scholars Publishing, 2009).

21 Vovelle, *Piété baroque et déchristianisation*, 18, 101, 600–1, 605, 608, 612, 614; *La mort et l'Occident*, 367, 470.

22 As a consequence of scientific rationalism and individualism, 'the probability of personal extinction became at the same time more logically compelling and more emotionally unacceptable.' Stone, *The Past and the Present*, 244. Radicati di Passerano presented the logical side; Robert Blair, William Cowper, Joseph Wright, and Henry Fuseli treated emotional unacceptability. Adalberto Radicati di Passerano, *A Philosophical Dissertation upon Death* [1732], in *Politici ed economisti del primo settecento, Dal Muratori al Cesarotti* , vol. 44, pt. 5, *La letteratura italiana; Storia e testi* (Milan: Riccardo Ricciardi, 1978), 95–145. 'Beginning in the eighteenth century, however, affectivity was, from childhood, entirely concentrated on a few individuals, who became ... irreplaceable.' Ariès, *Hour of Our Death*, 472.

23 McManners, 'Death and the French Historians,' *Mirrors of Mortality*, 123.

24 Ariès, *Hour of Our Death*, 473, 610

25 Michael Wheeler, *Death and the Future Life in Victorian Literature and Theology* (Cambridge: Cambridge Univ. Press, 1990), 225.

26 'In the nineteenth century everyone seems to believe in the continuation of the friendships of life after death.' Ariès, *Hour of Our Death*, 471. The neo-Hegelian J.M.E. McTaggart argued that selves, at death, do not lose themselves like drops in the ocean, but maintain separate identities, enlarged and enlightened by love. Love at first sight signifies a shared soul in a previous life, and friends and lovers meet again in future lives.

27 Ariès, *Western Attitudes*, 60, 67. In a review of Ariès's *Hour of Our Death*, George Steiner writes that such wildness is out of place in the present age of 'agnostic hygiene' and 'emotional blandness'; then adds mistakenly that 'it is Mafia burials that preserve the flamboyant desolation of the romantics' (*New Yorker* [22 June 1981] 57: 114). With its religious rites, public spectacle, and emphasis on the survival of the family and clan, the southern Italian treatment of death is, in Ariès's terms, 'tame' and diametrically opposite to the intense inwardness of the Romantic cult of the dead.

28 Terry Castle, 'The Spectralization of the Other in *The Mysteries of Udolpho*,' in Felicity Nussbaum and Laura Brown, eds., *The New Eighteenth Century: Theory, Politics, English Literature* (New York: Metheun, 1987), 244. 'The fear of death in the modern era prompts an obsessional return to the world of memory – where the dead continue to "live"' (244).

29 Ariès, *Western Attitudes*, 88. 'The medicalization of death has generated a view of death as disease that can be overcome. Technology, however, has failed to provide a cure.' Badone, *Appointed Hour*, 14.

30 *The Works of John Ruskin,* ed. E.T. Cook and A. Wedderburn (London: 1903–12), 1:19. All following references, in text and notes, are to this edition.

31 *Works of Ruskin,* 1:18–19. As Dickens wrote of Italy in 1844: 'Everything is in extremes.... It seemed as if one had reached the end of all things.' Cited by Jan H.A. Lokin, 'The Wheel of Time Is Rolling for an End,' in Zweder Von Martels, *Travel Fact and Travel Fiction: Studies on Fiction, Literary Tradition, Scholarly Discovery and Observation in Travel Writing* (Leiden: Brill, 1994), 221; *The Letters of Charles Dickens,* vol. 4: *1844–1846,* ed. Kathleen Tillotson (Oxford: Clarendon Press, 1977), 160, 169 (22 July, 7 Aug. 1844).

32 *The Letters and Journals of James Fenimore Cooper,* ed. James Franklin Beard (Cambridge: Harvard Univ. Press, 1960), 1:345; 2:371 ; 3:233, 330; 5:179. In 1838 he wrote Horatio Greenough: 'I prefer the *dolce far niente* to go-ahead-ism' (3:330).

33 James Fenimore Cooper, *Gleanings in Europe: Italy* (1838), ed. John Conron and Constance Ayers Denne (Albany: State Univ. of New York Press 1981), 297. The lower classes are 'more gracious than the English, and more sincere than the French, and infinitely more refined than the Germans' (296).

34 Cooper, *Gleanings in Europe,* 297. 'I like the people of Italy, too. They are full of feeling, and grace, and poetry, and a vast number are filled with a piety that their maligners would do well to imitate' (*Letters and Journals,* 5:179).

35 Cited by Nathalia Wright: 'in the eleven works Cooper wrote before he went to Italy, allusions to foreign countries are negligible. In the thirty-two he wrote afterward, this country figures far more than any other' (*American Novelists in Italy: The Discoverers: Allston to James* [Philadelphia: Univ. of Pennsylvania Press 1965], 117, 125). 'Of all the European countries he visited,' writes Gaetano Prampolini, 'Italy is not only the one that most fascinated and delighted him, the one through which he found a more bountiful change in his creative work, and the only one which he left reluctantly and with dreams of revisiting ever after; but, above all, it is the country where he recognizes most fully that image of culture which, even while seeing it as the fruit of a millennial historical process, he would like to see flower as soon as possible in the United States.' 'Il Sud di James Fenimore Cooper,' in Emanuele Kanceff and Roberta Rampone, eds., *'Viaggio nel Sud' III: Il profondo Sud: Calabria e dintorni* (Geneva: Slatkine, Centro Interuniversitario di Ricerche del Viaggio in Italia, 1995), 2:465.

36 Cooper, *Gleanings in Europe,* 295: 'I felt that reluctance to separate, that one is apt to experience on quitting his own house' (295).

37 *The Bravo,* Leatherstocking ed. (New York: Putnam's, 1893); hereafter page numbers are cited in text and notes.

38 Cooper explores his constitutional standard in *Notions of an American* (1828)

and *The American Democrat* (1838). Emilio Goggio defends Cooper against the Italian reaction to *The Bravo*: 'one needs but read his account of his journey through Italy to be convinced at once that perhaps there never was a fairer and a more impartial observer of things Italian, nor a saner, a more appreciative, and a more sympathetic judge of Italy and her people than Cooper'; 'whatever knowledge nineteenth-century Italians had of America was due in a very large measure, if not almost exclusively, to James Fenimore Cooper's works.' 'Cooper's *Bravo* in Italy,' *Romanic Review*, 20, no. 3 (1929): 227, 230.

39 James S. Grubb, 'When Myths Lose Power: Four Decades of Venetian Historiography,' *Journal of Modern History*, 58, pt. 1 (1986): 43. 'Most of the elements used in *The Bravo*,' comments Rosella Mamoli Zorzi, 'can be traced back to literature and painting' ('The Text is the City: The Representation of Venice in Two Tales by Irving and Poe and a Novel by Cooper,' in Angela Vistarchi, ed., *The City as Text, RSA* [*Rivista di Studi Anglo-Americani*], 6, no. 8 [1990]: 293).

40 William J. Bouwsma, *Venice and the Defense of Republican Liberty: Renaissance Values in the Age of the Counter Reformation* (Berkeley: Univ. of California Press 1968), 93.

41 Cooper gave clues to date the historical action from 1710 to the 1730s. In the 'period of our tale' Venice is 'no longer mistress of the Mediterranean, nor even of the Adriatic,' but is 'still rich and powerful' (2). The Calabrian mariner Stefano speaks of 'Napoli ... with her constant change of masters' (12). Under Spain, Naples had no change of master from 1503 to 1705, after which in the space of twenty-nine-years, it went from Spain, to Austria, to an independent kingdom under a cadet branch of the Spanish Bourbons. The 'Spanish king' who wants to 'extend his sway' (165) in Italy would seem to denote Philip V in his military actions against Sicily (1717) and Sardinia (1718). Stefano also refers to the decline of Italy: 'Thou forgettest that Venezia has been –' and he is interrupted by his fellow Calabrian, the gondolier Gino: 'Zitto, zitto! that *has* been, caro mio, is a great word with all Italy' (12). Further, Gradenigo's palace has works by Titian, Veronese, and Tintoretto, 'relics of an age more happy in this respect than that of which we write' (44). If they are already 'relics,' one cannot speak of the action taking place in the Renaissance or immediately after.

42 Robert S. Levine, *Conspiracy and Romance: Studies in Brockden Brown, Cooper, Hawthorne, and Melville* (Cambridge: Cambridge Univ. Press, 1989), 78.

43 They apparently shared the same wet-nurse and grew up as friends.

44 From 1177 the Marriage of the Sea was an annual event (15 August) in which the Doge on the state barge *Bucentaur* (barge of gold and fabled man-

ox) threw a ring into the sea symbolizing the city's union and domination. Here the ceremony can be taken ironically in light of Venice's blocking the marriage of Violetta and Monforte.

45 For George Dekker, Antonio is the 'real hero of the novel' (*James Fenimore Cooper: The American Scott* [New York: Barnes and Noble, 1967], 132). Though Antonio has grand speeches, he is dead before the halfway point; the real hero of *The Bravo* is the bravo.

46 A former midshipman, Cooper was equally skilful with his descriptions in land and sea novels – with canoes as well as gondolas – and his Venetian novel may be said to have reaped the benefits of both talents: Violetta's abduction rivals the capture of Cora and Alice in *The Last of the Mohicans*.

47 Alberta Fabris Grube, 'La trilogia europea di J.F. Cooper,' *Studi americani*, 15 (1969): 36–7.

48 In *Gleanings in Europe* Cooper compares the gondola to a hearse as it glides 'with the silence of the grave,' a silence intensified by the occasional plashing of oars and the sound of water lapping at the boat (285). The comparison is remarkable for its combination of a visual with an auditory image, but otherwise it was not uncommon – it is found in De Staël, Byron, Shelley, Ruskin, and Barrès. Liszt wrote two piano pieces entitled *La Gondola lugubre*. The finest of Mendelssohn's four Venetian barcarolles are in the minor key. Wagner's funeral boat (*barca funebre*) hearse in Venice figures at the end of D'Annunzio's *Il Fuoco*.

49 Dekker, *Cooper*, 133–4; John Pemble, *Venice Rediscovered* (New York: Oxford Univ. Press, 1995), 88.

50 Giorgio Bassani, *The Garden of the Finzi-Continis*, trans. Isabel Quigly (New York: Atheneum, 1965), 100. 'Prati starts his *Edmenegarda* right there, in the Jewish cemetery of the Lido' says Ermanno Finzi-Contini; 'mind you say the old cemetery, where no one's been buried since the eighteenth century, and not the other one, the modern one, which is beside it but separate.'

51 William Beckford, *Dreams, Waking Thoughts, and Incidents*, ed. Robert J. Gemmett (Rutherford, NJ: Fairleigh Dickinson Press 1971), 122.

52 'Une île attendait sa tombe; une île est la vôtre' (Chateaubriand, *Mémoires d'outre-tombe*, eds. Maurice Levaillant and Georges Moulinier, Bibliothèque de la Pléiade [Paris: Gallimard, 1951], 2:1033). The notebook entries including the *Rêverie au Lido* (1833) were originally destined for a separate *Livre sur Venise*, book 40 of the *Mémoires d'outre-tombe* (see Maurice Levaillant, *Deux Livres des* Mémoires d'outre-tombe [Paris: Librarie Delagrave, 1936], 1:107–16; and Y. Batard, 'Chateaubriand et Venise,' in Carlo Pellegrini, ed., *Venezia nelle letterature moderne*. Atti del primo congresso dell'Associazione Internazionale di Letteratura Comparata (Venezia, 25–30

September 1955) (Venice, Rome: Istituto per la Collaborazione Culturale, 1961], 72–82. *Rêverie au Lido* is 'a gem in Chateaubriand's *art descriptif'* and a 'microcosm of the *Mémoires d'outre-tombe* as a whole,' writes Tom Conner, '[an epitome of] his most recurrent technique (the blending and development of present and past memories into a collage or mosaic of experiences more or less real that take place over an extended period of time)' (*Chateaubriand's* Mémoires d'outre-tombe: *A Portrait of the Artist as Exile* [New York: Peter Lang, 1995], 145, 150). In *Leone Leoni* George Sand set a scene in the Jewish cemetery.

53 Levine, *Conspiracy and Romance*, 91.

54 Kay Seymour House cites Cooper on Gradenigo: 'born with all the sympathies and natural kindliness of other men, but accident, and an education which had received a strong bias from the institutions of the self-styled Republic, had made him the creature of a conventional policy' (81). *Cooper's Americans* (Athens: Ohio State Univ. Press, 1965), 157. Cf. Marius Bewley. *The Eccentric Design: Form in the Classic American Novel* (New York: Columbia Univ. Press, 1959), 58

55 'Personal morality and the principles of just government are, to Cooper, identical.' Robert E. Spiller, *Fenimore Cooper: Critic of His Times* (New York: Russell and Russell, 1963), 219.

56 Wright, *American Novelists in Italy*, 120.

57 S.M. Ellis, qtd in Ivan Melada, *Sheridan Le Fanu* (Boston: Twayne, 1987), 12.

58 Dorothy L. Sayers, ed., *The Omnibus of Crime* (Garden City: Garden City Publishing, Brace, 1929), 1:22.

59 Melada, *Sheridan Le Fanu*, 128.

60 J. Sheridan Le Fanu, *Wylder's Hand* (London: Gollancz, 1963); page references are cited in the text.

61 'History of that Renowned Arch-Sorcerer, Dr. J. Faust, etc.,' in *The German Novelists*, trans. James Roscoe (1826; London, 1880), 132–4; James Hain Friswell, *Varia: Readings from Various Books* (London: 1866), 94; Emanuel Swedenborg, *The Apocalypse Revealed*, trans. and rev. Alice Spiers Sechrist (New York: Swedenborg Foundation, 1981), 954–5.

62 In *The Scholemaster* (1570) Roger Ascham warned against travel in Italy: 'Some *Circes* shall make him, of a plaine English man, a right Italian. And at length to hell, or to some hellish place, is he likelie to go.' Charles, second Lord Stanhope, insulted Sir Walter Raleigh by writing in the margin of a book: 'The originall of ye rude rauly / it is too base to tell / From Italy it came to us / to Italy from Hell.' Ctd in J.R. Hale, *England and the Italian Renaissance: The Growth of Interest in its History and Art* (London: Faber and Faber, 1954), 8, 20.

63 Emanuel Swedenborg, *Heaven and Hell* (1758), trans. J.C. Ager (London: 1958), par. 421, qtd in W.J. McCormack, *Sheridan Le Fanu and Victorian Ireland* (Oxford: Clarendon, 1980), 178. '*Heaven and Hell* is pervaded by the word "society" in one form or another, and the doctrine of correspondence sets up innumerable equations between the social world and the spiritual. The notion of judgment [is] that of rendering public that which has previously been private, and of regarding this transformation as itself a matter of reward or punishment.' W.J. McCormack, *Dissolute Characters: Irish Literary History through Balzac, Sheridan Le Fanu, Yeats and Bowen* (Manchester: Manchester Univ. Press, 1993), 99.

64 McCormack, *Sheridan Le Fanu and Victorian Ireland*, 178. Swedenborgian eschatology informs Le Fanu's 'Borrhomeo the Astrologer,' a satanic tale set in Milan and bearing parallels to Alessandro Manzoni's *Storia della colonna infame* (cf. *Borrhomeo the Astrologer: A Monkish Tale*, ed. W.J. McCormack [Edinburgh: Tragara Press, 1985]).

65 McCormack, *Sheridan Le Fanu and Victorian Ireland*, 193–4.

66 Michael H. Begnal, *Joseph Sheridan LeFanu* (Lewisburg: Bucknell Univ. Press, 1971), 54.

67 Ruskin, *Fors Clavigera*, Letter 69 (28.694).

68 Melada, *Sheridan Le Fanu*, 65.

69 The adjective is Georg Simmel's, ctd in Sergio Bettini, *Venezia* (Milan: Touring Club Italiano, 1963), 19.

70 Glen Cavaliero compares the final sentences to Ruskin in *The Stones of Venice* (*The Supernatural and English Fiction* [New York: Oxford Univ. Press, 1995], 45).

71 Ariès, *Hour of Our Death*, 457, 471: 'the next world becomes the scene of the reunion of those whom death has separated but who have never accepted this separation: a re-creation of the affections of earth, purged of their dross, assured of eternity. It is the paradise of Christians or the astral world of spiritualists and psychics. But it is also the world of the memories of nonbelievers and freethinkers who deny the reality of a life after death' (611).

72 McCormack, *Dissolute Characters*, 65.

73 As in so many other instances in the novel, things happen twice, e.g., the designation *humano major*, applied to the demonic and to the angelic: 'We have been accustomed to see another girl – bright and fair-haired Rachel Lake ... somehow in this low-roofed room, so small and homely, she looks like a displaced divinity – an exile under Juno's jealousy from the cloudy splendours of Olympus – dazzlingly melancholy, and "humano major" among the meannesses and trumperies of earth' (chap. 24).

74 Bryson Burroughs, 'The Island of the Dead by Arnold Böcklin,' *Bulletin of the Metropolitan Museum of Art*, 26 (1926): 146.

75 Fritz von Ostini, *Böcklin* (Bielefeld: Von Velhagen and Klasing, 1904), 102; *Arnold Böcklin e la cultura artistica in Toscana*, exh. cat., Fiesole, Palazzina Mangani, 24 July–30 Sept. 1980 (Rome: De Luca, 1980), 103.

76 Florens Deuchler, Marcel Roethlisberger, and Hans Lüthy, *Swiss Painting* (New York: Skira, Rizzoli, 1976), 168.

77 Franz Zelger, 'Invenzione, realizzazione, degenerazione: Motivi böckliniani e loro trasformazione su cartoline,' *I 'Deutsch-Römer': Il mito dell'Italia negli artisti tedeschi: 1850–1900*, exh. cat. (Milan: Mondadori, 1988), 290.

78 Michelle Facos, *Nationalism and the Nordic Imagination: Swedish Art of the 1890s* (Berkeley: Univ. of California Press, 1998), 123; Georg Nordensvan called it 'a painted poem' (122). Böcklin appealed to National Romantics like Viktor Rydberg who saw the artist as 'one of the very few in whom the myth-building imagination of prehistoric peoples has arisen anew in our bustling, practical era: one of those who feel what the primitive German was feeling in the holy forests at twilight' (123).

79 Barrie Martyn, *Rachmaninoff: Composer, Pianist, Conductor* (Aldershot: Scolar, 1990), 202. The painting inspired a movement in Max Reger's *Böcklin Suite* (1913).

80 Maurizio Fagiolo dell'Arco, 'Böcklin e De Chirico: la pittura letteraria,' in *Arnold Böcklin e la cultura artistica in Toscana*, 179–89. '[Dali] was so moved by the Metropolitan Museum's Böcklin, *Isle of the Dead*, that he returned home to paint *Interior Court of the 'Isle of the Dead'* and *Fountain of Böcklin*'; he referred to Modesto Urgell, one of his favourite local artists, as the 'Catalan Böcklin' (James Thrall Soby, *Salvador Dali: Paintings, Drawings, Printing* [New York: Museum of Modern Art, ca. 1941], 9, 21).

81 Hitler, when he saw Florence, told Speer that 'he finally understood Böcklin.' Speer's private name for Hitler's Berlin bunker was *Die Toteninsel*. Speer, *Inside the Third Reich: A Memoir*, trans. R. and C. Winston (New York: Macmillan, 1970), 473; qtd in Robert Harbison, *Deliberate Regression* (London: André Deutsch, 1980), 247.

82 Burroughs, 'The Island of the Dead by Arnold Böcklin,' 146, 148.

83 Christoph Heilmann, 'Note introduttive all'arte dei "Tedeschi-Romani,"' *I 'Deutsch-Römer,'* 4.

84 Elizabeth Tumasonis, 'Böcklin and Wagner: The Dragon Slain,' *Pantheon*, 44 (1986): 88. Böcklin's *Dragon in a Rocky Gorge* (1870) portrays travellers in the Alps startled to panic by a dragon. Tumasonis compares it to Karl Blechen's *Bau der Teufelsbrücke* (*Construction of the Devil's Bridge*), ca. 1830, which shows the dangerous Devil's Bridge in the St Gotthard Pass, over which travel-

lers crossed into Italy. In local legend, the bridge is named after the Devil, whom one must pay – originally with the life of an animal – to cross safely; but also the Devil guarding Italy, i.e., hell. For Turner's watercolour of Devil's Bridge, see Andrew Wilton, *Turner and the Sublime* (London: British Museum, 1980), cat. no. 19.

85 Georg Simmel, 'Böcklins Landschaften,' *Zur Philosophie der Kunst* (Potsdam: Gustav Kiepenheuer, 1922), 8, 11.

86 Giorgio de Chirico, 'Arnoldo Boecklin,' *Il Convegno*, 4 (May 1920): 50.

87 Qtd. in Zelger, 'Invenzione, realizzazione, degenerazione,' *I 'Deutsch-Römer,'* 288.

88 Jacob Burckhardt, *The Civilization of the Renaissance in Italy*, trans. S.G.C. Middlemore (New York: Penguin 1990), 98.

89 Marisa Volpi, 'Immaginazioni e realtà nel paesaggio dei "Tedeschi-Romani,"' *I 'Deutsch-Römer,'* 13.

90 Robin Ironside, 'Arnold Böcklin,' *Apollo*, 101 (March 1975): 184, 188.

91 Heinrich Wölfflin, qtd in Cristina Nuzzi, 'Aspetti del mito e della natura nell'opera di Arnold Böcklin,' in *Arnold Böcklin e la cultura artistica in Toscana*, 29.

92 Rudolf Schick, qtd in cat. no. 17, *I 'Deutsch-Römer,'*; cf. Von Ostini, *Böcklin*, 54.

93 Natalia Costa-Zalessow, 'Italy as a Victim: A Historical Appraisal of a Literary Theme,' *Italica*, 45 (1968): 216–40; 'The Personification of Italy from Dante through the Trecento,' *Italica*, 68 (1991): 316–31.

94 W. Ranke, qtd in *I 'Deutsch-Römer,'* cat. no. 17.

95 'Contemplation and creation constitute the higher forces, the Apollonian side of the grotto. But in a world also connected with Pan, Dionysian agents may rule. Surely primal elements are present in the association of caves with preterhuman existence – with rites of birth and death, magic ceremonies, mantic powers, erotic bacchanalian orgies – and in the ubiquity of water' (Naomi Miller, *Heavenly Caves: Reflections on the Garden Grotto* [New York: George Braziller, 1982], 11).

96 Simmel, *Zur Philosophie der Kunst*, 8–9.

97 Georg Simmel, 'The Ruin,' in Kurt H. Wolff, ed., *Essays on Sociology, Philosophy, and Aesthetics* (New York: Harper and Row, 1965), 260–1, 263: 'Nature has transformed the work of art into material for her own expression, as she had previously served as material for art' (262).

98 Volpi, 'Immaginazioni e realtà,' *I 'Deutsch-Römer,'* 14; on Böcklin's contrast and antithesis, see Hans Holenweg, 'Temi e tecnica di Böcklin,' in *Arnold Böcklin e la cultura artistica in Toscana*, 35.

99 Heinrich Wölfflin, *The Sense of Form in Art: A Comparative Psychological Study*,

trans. Alice Muehsam and Norma A. Shatan (1931; New York: Chelsea, 1958), 56, 86, 109, 117.

100 Nuzzi, 'Aspetti,' in *Arnold Böcklin e la cultura artistica in Toscana*, 28, 103.

101 Deuchler, Roethlisberger, and Lüthy, *Swiss Painting*, 167.

102 Herbert M. Vaughan, *The Naples Riviera* (London: Methuen, 1907), 276.

103 Alberto Savinio, *Operatic Lives*, trans. John Shepley (Marlboro, VT: Marlboro, 1987), 22.

104 This analysis concentrates upon the third version (1883), remarking upon divergences from the other versions where necessary. All five versions are reproduced in Rolf Andree, *Arnold Böcklin: Die Gemälde* (Basel: Friedrich Reinhardt and Prestel, 1977), nos. 343–7.

105 Sharon Hirsh, 'Arnold Böcklin,' *International Dictionary of Art and Artists*, ed. James Vinson (Chicago: St. James Press, 1990), 769. The dark cave was similarly the central locus in *Villa by the Sea* II.

106 Robert L. Delevoy, *Symbolists and Symbolism* (New York: Skira, Rizzoli, 1978), 54.

107 The Symbolist trope of silence represents 'the means of shutting out appearances in order to concentrate upon essence'; isolation is the 'condition through which the artist could ignore the material and thus be able to penetrate the spiritual.' Robert Goldwater, *Symbolism* (New York: Harper and Row, 1979), 1, 29. Cf. Ihab Hassan on silence in *The Dismemberment of Orpheus: Towards a Postmodern Literature* (New York: Oxford Univ. Press, 1971), 13–14.

108 Vaughan, *Naples Riviera*, 199.

109 R. Drew Griffith, *Mummy Wheat: Egyptian Influence on the Homeric View of the Afterlife and the Eleusinian Mysteries* (Lanham, MD: University Press of America, 2008), 20–3; Radcliffe G. Edmonds III, *Myths of the Underworld Journey: Plato, Aristophanes, and the 'Orphic' Gold Tablets* (Cambridge: Cambridge Univ. Press, 2004), 127.

110 Zelger, 'Invenzione, realizzazione, degenerazione,' *I 'Deutsch-Römer,'* 290.

111 Gert Schiff, 'An Epoch of Longing: An Introduction to German Painting of the Nineteenth Century,' *German Masters of the Nineteenth Century: Paintings and Drawings from the Federal Republic of Germany*, exh. cat. (New York: Metropolitan Museum of Art, 1981), 29. Cf. Hesiod, *The Momeric Hymns and Homerica*, trans. Hugh G. Evelyn-White, Loeb Classical Library (Cambridge: Harvard Univ. Press, 1967), 134.

112 Burroughs, 'The Island of the Dead by Arnold Böcklin,' 148.

113 Letter of 29 April 29 1880, qtd in cat. no. 17, *Arnold Böcklin e la cultura artistica in Toscana*, 103; and in cat. no. 30, *I 'Deutsch-Römer.'*

114 Trained as a landscape painter, Böcklin was weaker in his figures, though

they assumed increasing importance in his art (he did eighty-six portraits). 'The tragedy of Böcklin lies in the fact that he did not master figure drawing to the extent that he mastered landscape painting.' Holenweg, 'Temi e tecnica,' in *Arnold Böcklin e la cultura artistica in Toscana*, 31.

115 The term is taken from Mircea Eliade, *Patterns in Comparative Religion*, trans. Rosemary Sheed (Cleveland: World Publishing, 1963), 419–20.

116 Christiane Sourvinou-Inwood comments apropos Ariès in 'To Die and Enter the House of Hades: Homer, Before and After,' in *Mirrors of Mortality*: 'death is accepted as an inescapable evil, part of the life-cycle of the world, and of the community, in which the generations succeed each other, and the continuity of the community is contrasted with the discontinuity of the individual' (17).

117 Ironside, 'Arnold Böcklin,' 189.

118 Savinio, *Operatic Lives*, 22–3.

119 Ruskin, *The Poetry of Architecture*, 1.19 ; cf. 1.542.

120 Erwin Rohde, *Psyche: The Cult of Souls and Belief in Immortality among the Greeks* (London: Routledge and Kegan Paul, 1950), 57. Cf. Gregory Nagy, *The Best of the Achaeans: Concepts of the Hero in Archaic Greek Poetry* (Baltimore: Johns Hopkins Univ. Press, 1979), 193–5.

121 For another interpretation: 'In the versions of 1884 and 1886 Böcklin depicts the figure in white praying over the coffin. The silent conversation suggests that death is not the end of existence' (*Isle of the Dead* entry, *German Masters of the Nineteenth Century*). Actually, in the 1884 version the celebrant is holding out her hands; only in the last version is the celebrant bowing in prayer.

122 Rohde, *Psyche*, 55.

123 Sourvinou-Inwood writes: 'In Homer there is one dominant model of attitudes towards death, firmly rooted in the epic, and then signs of a tentative beginning of a partial movement away from it. The dominant model is the "familiar" or "traditional" type of attitude towards death, a version of the "Tamed Death" attitude analyzed by Ariès ... The new stirrings by contrast ... are the first beginnings of a series of developments which will gain momentum in the succeeding, archaic period (c. 700–c. 480) during which we can detect a (partial) shift away from familiar acceptance, towards a more individual, and anxious approach towards one's own death – broadly comparable to the change which occurred in the late Middle Ages in Europe.' The prophecy of Proteus and a passage on the immortality of the Dioscuri (*Od.* 11.300–304) represent 'the first signs of a challenge to the inescapable fate of death which in the following (archaic) period will grow and develop into an important new eschatological strand that will provide the

common man with a model of hope for a better life after death' ('To Die and Enter the House of Hades,' *Mirrors of Mortality*, 16–17, 20).

124 Rohde, *Psyche*, 66. This idea is suggested by Norbert Schneider, 'Böcklin's "Toteninsel,"' in *A. Böcklin, 1827–1901*, exh. cat. (Darmstadt, 1977), 120.

125 Nagy, *Best of the Achaeans*, 165; but later Achilles 'is regularly featured as having won immortality after death' (167).

126 Cedric H. Whitman, *Euripides and the Full Circle of Myth* (Cambridge: Harvard Univ. Press, 1974), 58.

127 Sourvinou-Inwood, 'To Die and Enter the House of Hades,' *Mirrors of Mortality*, 37.

128 Sourvinou-Inwood, 'To Die and Enter the House of Hades,' *Mirrors of Mortality*, 37–8.

129 Erwin Panofsky, *Tomb Sculpture: Four Lectures on Its Changing Aspects from Ancient Egypt to Bernini*, ed. H.W. Janson (New York: Abrams, 1963), 17.

130 Nagy, *Best of the Achaeans*, 208: 'Rohde, for one, thought that the concept of heroes being transported into a remote state of immortality is purely poetic and thus alien to the religious concept of heroes being venerated in cult. From the actual evidence of cult, however, we see that the two concepts are not at all treated as if they were at odds with each other' (189–90).

131 Pindar, *The Odes*, trans. Sir John Sandys, Loeb Classical Library (Cambridge: Harvard Univ. Press, 1930).

132 Panofsky, *Tomb Sculpture*, 22.

133 Nagy, *Best of the Achaeans*, 179. Cf. Timothy Gantz, *Early Greek Myth: A Guide to Literary and Artistic Sources* (Baltimore: Johns Hopkns Univ. Press, 1993), 132–3.

134 Delevoy, *Symbolists and Symbolism*, 54.

135 Adam Breysig, qtd. in Zelger, 'Invenzione, realizzazione, degenerazione,' *I 'Deutsch-Römer,'* 290.

136 Simmel, *Zur Philosophie der Kunst*, 11–12.

137 Charles Segal, 'Euripides' *Alcestis*: How to Die a Normal Death in Greek Tragedy,' in Sarah Webster Goodwin and Elisabeth Bronfen, eds., *Death and Representation* (Baltimore: Johns Hopkins Univ. Press, 1993), 227; 'it was the common claim of ancient poetry, especially of epic, that great deeds, if unsung, perished from the mind' (Cedric H. Whitman, *Homer and the Heroic Tradition* [Cambridge: Harvard Univ. Press, 1958], 17).

138 Tumasonis, 'Böcklin and Wagner,' 87; Ulrich Finke, *German Painting from Romanticism to Expressionism* (Boulder, CO: Westview, 1976), 139.

139 Schneider, *Arnold Böcklin*, 120; Zelger, 'Invenzione, realizzazione, degener-

azione,' *I 'Deutsch-Römer,'* 290; 'the focus of consolation is not on the hero's afterlife, but rather, on the eternal survival of the epic that glorifies him' (Nagy, *Best of the Achaeans*, 175).

140 Savinio, *Operatic Lives*, 23.

141 Simmel, *Zur Philosophie der Kunst*, 7–8: 'the sense of loneliness is not arbitrary, as a reflection of a particular scene which would change with different changes of lonely scenes, but is part of the inner essential configuration' (15).

142 Donald S. Walker, *A Geography of Italy*, 2d ed. (London: Methuen, 1967), 76–7. Cf. Jacques Béthemont and Jean Pelletier, *Italy: A Geographical Introduction*, trans. Eleonore Kofman (London: Longman, 1983), 178.

143 Adrian Stokes, *Stones of Rimini* (New York: Schocken: 1969), 40.

144 Robert L. Bates and Julia A. Jackson, *Dictionary of Geological Terms* (Garden City: Doubleday, 1984), 311. Giorgio de Chirico writes of Böcklin: 'seppe creare tutto in mondo suo di sorprendenti lirismi, combinando le apparizioni del paesaggio italiano con elementi architettonici' ('Arnoldo Boecklin,'52).

145 Stokes, *Stones of Rimini*, 42, 43.

146 The authors of the Böcklin entry (*German Masters of the Nineteenth Century*) argue that 'the artist appears to encourage a view of death as an impersonal phenomenon no more threatening than an event observed upon a stage.'

147 Simmel, *Essays on Sociology, Philosophy, and Aesthetics*, 261.

148 Simmel, *Essays on Sociology, Philosophy, and Aesthetics*, 262, 265.

149 Qtd. in cat. no. 30, *I 'Deutsch-Römer.'*

150 In *Modern Painters* III (pt. 4, chap. 12 [5.213]) Ruskin cites this example showing the closeness of Homeric death to what is here called the natural-metamorphic attitude: 'No; though Castor and Pollux be dead, yet the earth is our mother still, fruitful, life-giving. There are the facts of the thing. I see nothing else than these. Make what you will of them' (cf. *Modern Painters* V, pt. iv, chap. 2 [7.274–7] for an account of Homeric death that is tame.)

151 Burroughs, 'The Island of the Dead by Arnold Böcklin,'148.

152 Max Beerbohm, *More* (London: John Lane, 1899), 115, 107; Chesterton and Bierce ctd in Carl Van Vechten, introduction to Ouida, *In a Winter City* (New York: Boni and Liveright, 1923), vi, xi; Street ctd in Pamela K. Gilbert, *Disease, Desire, and the Body in Victorian Women's Popular Novels* (Cambridge: Cambridge Univ. Press, 1997), 87; Stephen Crane, 'Ouida's Masterpiece' (1897), in *The Works*, ed. Fredson Bowers (Charlottesville: Univ. of Virginia Press, 1972), 8:678; Norman Douglas, *Alone*, (London: Chapman and Hall, 1921), 113–17 ('abhorrence of meanness was her dominant

trait,' he writes, singling out for special praise *The Massarenes* and *In Marem-ma* ['haunting charm']).

153 Vernon Lee, *For Maurice: Five Unlikely Stories* (London: John Lane, 1927), xxxvii; Lee wrote on Ouida's influence in the *Westminster Gazette* in 1907, qtd in Elizabeth Lee, *Ouida: A Memoir* (London: Unwin, 1914), 270–1. Barbara Arnett Melchiori praises Ouida's *Fortnightly Review* essay on D'Annunzio ('The Early D'Annunzio in England,' in Patrizia Nerozzi Bell-man, ed., *Gabriele D'Annunzio e la cultura inglese e americana* [Chieti: Marino Solfanelli, 1990], 20–2).

154 Elaine Showalter, *A Literature of Their Own: British Women Novelists from Brontë to Lessing* (Princeton: Princeton Univ. Press, 1977), 162.

155 Quoted in Monica Stirling, *The Fine and the Wicked: The Life and Times of Ouida* (London: Gollancz, 1957), 215.

156 Lee, *Ouida*, 15, 18; Eileen Bigland, *Ouida: The Passionate Victorian* (New York: Duell, Sloan and Pearce, 1951), 14–15.

157 Bigland, *Ouida*, 67.

158 Natalie Schroeder, 'Feminine Sensationalism, Eroticism, and Self-Asser-tion,' *Tulsa Studies in Women's Litearture*, 7, no. 1 (1988): 87.

159 Sir Francis Vane, *Walks and People in Tuscany* (London: John Lane, 1910), 268.

160 Talia Schaffer, *The Forgotten Female Aesthetes: Literary Culture in Late-Victorian England* (Charlottesville: Univ. of Virginia Press 2000), 262; Ruskin ctd in Bigland, *Ouida*, 110.

161 E.E. Whipple, *A Famous Corner of Tuscany* (London: Jarrolds, 1928), 34. As a proprietress told Whipple, 'la signora Inglese era sempre molto gentile verso di noi ed anche, era la mama dei cani.'

162 Douglas, *Alone*, 117.

163 Vane, *Walks and People in Tuscany*, 269. Thanks to these travel writers, novel-ists, memoirists, etc., one can still "travel" in these decades from the major Italian cities to the most remote countryside.

164 Massimo Pallottino, *The Etruscans* (Harmondsworth: Penguin, 1978), 107–8.

165 Kenneth Churchill, *Italy and English Literature, 1764–1930* (Totowa: Barnes and Noble, 1980), 12, 53.

166 Ouida, *In Maremma*, in *Works*, 9 vols. (New York: Collier, 1890), 9:806. Hereafter page references are cited in parentheses in text and notes.

167 George Dennis, *Cities and Cemeteries of Etruria* (London: Dent, n.d.), 2:187, 196, 197, 230: 'Look over these luxuriant, variegated woods, these smiling lakes at your feet; admire them, rejoice in them – think not, know not, that for half the year they "exhale earth's rottenest vapours," and curdle the air with pestilence' (205).

168 Vernon Lee, *The Tower of the Mirrors, and Other Essays on the Spirit of Places* (London: John Lane, 1914), 210.

169 Churchill, *Italy and English Literature,* 164.

170 Churchill, *Italy and English Literature,* 163.

171 "Etruscan art always seemed to aim more at the fulfillment of religious and funerary beliefs on a purely practical level than at extolling the glory of the gods and the cities they protected.' Marie-Françoise Briguet, 'Art,' in Larissa Bonfante, ed., *Etruscan Life and Afterlife: A Handbook of Etruscan Studies* (Detroit: Wayne State Univ. Press, 1986), 101.

172 Dennis, *Cities and Cemeteries,* 2:229, 230, 235. Though Dennis extols the Etruscan sea-kings, the more powerful Carthaginians kept them out of the western Mediterranean.

173 Montgomery Carmichael, *In Tuscany* (London: Burns and Oates, 1906), 297.

174 Even small details like the death of the parish priest signify within the overall design: the priest 'father' is a male representative of the uncaring institution, a far cry from the religion of nature and the Etruscan mythology. His quick death might indicate his unworthiness of the secret. Despite violations to novelistic realism, writes Pamela Gilbert, 'there is an enduring charm in Ouida for tastes conditioned to intricacies, like an Elizabethan garden carefully planned and then allowed to run riot' (*Death, Desire, and the Body,* 159).

175 Michael Grant, *The Etruscans* (New York: Scribner's, 1980), 161.

176 Vernon Lee tells of a stone mason ca. 1847 called upon to open a Roman sarcophagus: 'the immense horned lid having been rolled off, there was seen, lying in the sarcophagus, a man in complete armour, his sword by his side and vizor up, who, as they cried out in astonishment, instantly fell to dust.' *Limbo and Other Essays* (1897), in *Ariadne in Mantua [and] Limbo and Other Essays* (London: John Lane, 1930), 171. A similar phenomenon occurs in the construction of the train tunnel in Fellini's *Roma.*

177 Sibylle von Cles-Reden, *The Buried People: A Study of the Etruscan World,* trans. C.M. Woodhouse (London: Rupert Hart-Davis, 1955), 95. The tomb celebrates the 'Etruscan need for blood to honor the dead.' R. Ross Holloway, *The Archaeology of Early Rome and Latium* (London: Routledge, 1994), 6–7.

178 H.H. Scullard, *The Etruscan Cities and Rome* (Ithaca: Cornell Univ. Press, 1967), 257. Cf. Mario Torelli, 'History: Land and People,' in Larissa Bonfante, *Etruscan Life and Afterlife,* 54–55; and Massimo Pallottino, *A History of Earliest Italy* (Ann Arbor: Univ. of Michigan Press 1991), 80.

179 Ouida alludes to this episode when Musa tends to the sickly Este (655).

180 In *Folle-Farine* the heroine sees herself in a mirror and a 'vain passion' creeps 'with all its poison into her veins.' Ctd in Schroeder, 'Feminine Sensationalism, Eroticism, and Self-Assertion,' 93.

181 Ellen Handler Spitz, 'Mothers and Daughters: Ancient and Modern Myths,' *Journal of Aesthetics and Art Criticism*, 48 (1990): 414; Efthymios G. Lazongas, 'Side: the Personification of the Pomegranate,' in *Personification in the Greek World: From Antiquity to Byzantium*, ed. Emma Stafford and Judith Herrin (Aldershot: Ashgate, 2005), 100.

182 Schaffer, *Forgotten Female Aesthetes*, 124.

183 Schroeder, 'Feminine Sensationalism, Eroticism, and Self-Assertion,' 90, 92. Showalter would add that 'the sensationalists and their women readers were less preoccupied with sexuality than with self-assertion and independence from the tedium and injustice of the feminine role in marriage and the family' (*Literature of Their Own*, 161). As Schroeder writes of Ouida's Folle-Farine from the eponymous novel, 'submission and self-abasement make her stronger than the three males who exploit and profit from her strength, but her death at the end of the novel confirms her earlier realization of the futility of women's self-assertion in a male-dominated society' (98). *Folle-Farine*'s epigraph is from Francesca's code of love in Dante, and could apply equally to *In Maremma*: 'Love which pardons no one loved from loving' (*Inf.* 5.103).

184 'The fascination of beautiful women already dead, especially if they had been great courtesans, wanton queens, or famous sinners ... suggested to the Romantics, probably under the influence of the vampire legend, the figure of the Fatal Woman who was successively incarnate in all ages and all lands, an archetype which united in itself all forms of seduction, all vices, and all delights' (Mario Praz, *The Romantic Agony*, trans. Angus Davidson, 2d ed. [Cleveland: World, 1968], 209–10).

185 Gilbert, *Disease, Desire, and the Body*, 85, 141; 'Her radicalism was aesthetic; beauty, and the artist's capacity to create it, was the one characteristic that could transcend class and national boundaries, conferring natural aristocracy on anyone' (86).

186 As Gilbert comments on Ouida's 'good' female protagonists, 'only through self-sacrifice (usually in the service of helping the male protagonist enter that same realm [of capitalist exchange] without loss of subjectivity), can they paradoxically "save" themselves, destroying their bodies to cancel out their shameful openness' (*Disease, Desire, and the Body*, 141).

187 *L'Oeuvre de Maurice Barrès*, ed. Philippe Barrès, 20 vols. (Paris: Club de l'Honnête Homme, 1965–68), 7:53. Works are cited from this edition in text and notes, excepting *Notes sur Italie* (Paris: Éditions des Horizons de France, 1929) and *Scènes et doctrines du nationalisme*, in J.S. McClelland, ed., *The French Right (from de Maistre to Maurras)* (London: Jonathan Cape, 1970), 159–195. Translations unless otherwise indicated are mine.

188 Apropos this cultural mood informing Thomas Mann's *Death in Venice*, Bernard Dieterle in 1995 contended that, whereas Barrès succumbed to the romantic myth of the artist in Venice, Mann resisted and narrated its end (ctd in Ellis Shookman, *Thomas Mann's* Death in Venice: *A Novella and Its Critics* [Rochester: Camden House, 2003], 204). Yet Dieterle had taken Barrès's travel writing at face value and not in dialectical relation with other sides of his biography. Years earlier, Mann, who recognized the mutual indebtedness of Barrès and himself to the romantic myth, acknowledged that each attempted to 'overcome decadence' in his fashion, Barrès by being 'political,' he himself by being '*moral*' (and 'nonpolitical' and aesthetic – irony, scepticism, psychological analyses, etc.) (*Reflections of a Nonpolitical Man*, trans. Walter D. Morris [1918: New York: Ungar, 1983], 145).

189 'To doubt and pessimism,' comments Zeev Sternhell, 'are opposed the certainties of history; to artifice, the cult of energy and vitality; to an aged civilization, that of youth; to disintegration and individualism, the sense of discipline. To scientific rationalism are opposed the forces of instinct' (*Maurice Barrès et le nationalisme français* [Paris: Armand Colin, 1972], 43); Philip Ouston, *The Imagination of Maurice Barrès* (Toronto: Univ. of Toronto Press, 1974), 114.

190 Ouston, *Imagination of Maurice Barrès*, 218–19.

191 Georges Valois, ctd in Zeev Sternhell, *Neither Right nor Left: Fascist Ideology in France*, trans. David Maisal (Berkeley: Univ. of California Press 1986), 8.

192 Fritz Ringer, *Fields of Knowledge: French Academic Culture in Comparative Perspective, 1890–1920* (Cambridge: Cambridge Univ. Press, 1992), 130–1.

193 'Barrès is not convinced by argument,' writes McClelland; 'he has to be moved' (*French Right*, 26). Some even questioned his idea of Lorraine: 'as the critic Berl wrote: "Who would realize on reading this citizen of Lorraine that he is describing a metallurgical country? He has seen the *mirabelliers* and neglected the blast-furnaces"' (143–4).

194 Pierre Boisdeffre, one of Barrès's biographers, points out that Barrès himself had only gained his reputation by leaving Lorraine for Paris: 'Is it so clear that one's original environment is always the best? Without the university, Pasteur would have tended cows' (ctd in Robert Soucy, *Fascism in France: The Case of Maurice Barrès* [Berkeley: Univ. of California Press, 1972], 98).

195 Ctd in Marie-Agnès Kirscher, *Relire Barrès* (Paris: Presses Universitaires du Septentrion, 1998), 30.

196 An intellectual is 'an individual who convinces himself that society should be founded on a basis of logic, and who fails to see that it rests on past exigencies that are perhaps foreign to the individual reason' (*Scènes*, 175).

197 Ctd in Soucy, *Fascism in France*, 323, his italics.

198 Ctd in Anthony Greaves, *Maurice Barrès* (Boston: G.K. Hall, 1978), 156.

199 Sternhell, *Maurice Barrès et le nationalisme français*, 51; Soucy, *Fascism in France*, 44.

200 Greaves, *Maurice Barrès*, 34–5.

201 *Un homme libre*, pref. 1904: 'The free man discerns and accepts his determinism' (1:139). At the same time, reassertions of the self provoke further insight, regarding which Venice again plays the role of initiator: 'the fever that I get there is very precious, for it enlarges my power of seeing to the point that my unconscious and my intellectual life mingle to become an immense reservoir of pleasure' (1:40).

202 C.M. Bowra, *The Heritage of Symbolism* (1943; New York: Schocken, 1961), 227: 'only the essential points are given ... there are no prosaic joints or interstices'; metaphor supplants simile. Cf. Philip R. Wood on Verlaine's 'le paradis au bout' ('Beyond the Simulacrum of Religion Versus Secularism: Modernist Aesthetic "Mysticism"; or, Why We Will Not Stop Revering "Great Books,"' *Religion and Literature*, 37:1 [2005]: 106).

203 Arthur Symons, *The Symbolist Movement in France*, qtd in David Perkins, *A History of Modern Poetry* (Cambridge: Harvard Univ. Press, 1977), 1:91.

204 'I have redirected my poetry from the heavens to the earth, the earth that contains my dead,' *Scènes et doctrines du nationalisme*, in McClelland, *The French Right*, 159.

205 Sternhell, *Maurice Barrès et le nationalisme français*, 47.

206 A.H. Lehmann, *The Symbolist Aesthetic in France, 1885–1895* (Oxford: Blackwell, 1950), 159.

207 Enzo Caramaschi, 'Maurice Barrès et Venise,' in Jean Schneider, ed., *Maurice Barrès, Actes du colloque organisé par la Faculté des lettres et des sciences humaines de l'Université de Nancy* (Nancy: Université de Nancy, 1963), 283.

208 The meeting between Barrès and D'Annunzio in 1916 is examined by Pierre Jourda: Barrès may well have envied D'Annunzio, 'who had been able to add to the prestige of the word that of the deed, to wear a uniform and spill his blood' ('La Venise de Maurice Barrès,' in Pellegrini, *Venezia nelle letterature moderne*, 200). Cf. Guy Tosi, 'Maurice Barrès regard d'Annunzio,' in *Maurice Barrès, Actes du colloque organisé*, 207–31.

209 Soucy, *Fascism in France*, 87.

210 Jules Bertaut, *L'Italie vue par les français* (Paris: Librarie des Annales politiques et littéraires, 1913), 333. As Barrès writes of Venice, 'nothing has value unless it reaches deep into my soul, wakes my dead, lightens my future' (7:14).

211 Edmond Pilon, *Maurice Barrès: Souvenirs, notes, et fragments de lettres inédites*

(Paris: Au Pigeonnier, 1926), 11. Barrès's writings are obsessed with images of hunting, bullfighting, slaughter, torture, illness, physical decomposition, and graveyards (Albert Thibaudet, ctd in Michael Curtis, *Three Against the Third Republic: Sorel, Barrès, and Maurras* [Princeton: Princeton Univ. Press, 1959], 55).

212 Henry James, *Letters 1883–1895*, ed. Leon Edel (Cambridge: Harvard Univ. Press, 1980), 3:228.

213 Caramaschi does not take the references to Taine *au pied de la lettre*; Barrès's syntheses of Taine's 'powerful schematization' and 'imperious simplifications' have an element of caricature and irony ('Maurice Barrès et Venise,' in *Maurice Barrès, Actes du colloque organisé*, 273).

214 As in Montesquieu on Rome, the word *equivocal* 'plays on two registers of meaning, one moral, the other physical' (Peter V. Conroy, Jr, *Montesquieu Revisited* [New York: Twayne, 1992], 65). Greaves takes it as residual Romanticism, 'linked with the decadent representatives of a race which has lived too long'; 'the real danger of Venice is that it will encourage his latent Romanticism' (*Maurice Barrès*, 108).

215 Bernard Berenson, *The Passionate Sightseer* (New York: Simon and Schuster, 1962), 164. Cf. Vernon Lee: 'Other places become solemn, sad, or merely beautiful at sunset. But Ravenna, it seems to me, grows actually ghostly; the Past takes it back at that moment, and the ghosts return to the surface' (*Limbo and Other Essays*, 176).

216 'Cities that gleamed too brightly attracted looters, while Ravenna's bricks did not,' comments William M. Johnston; 'to compound the irony, mud flats that furnished the brick also bred malaria, thus improving the protection' (*In Search of Italy: Foreign Writers in Northern Italy since 1800* [University Park: Pennsylvania State Univ. Press, 1990], 137).

217 Bertaut, *L'Italie vue par les français*, 335.

218 Abbé Joseph Barbier, '*La Colline inspirée*, roman historique ou poème symphonique,' in *Maurice Barrès, Actes du colloque organisé*, 189.

219 Cf. D'Annunzio, who in *Il Fuoco* expresses a 'concept of art suspended between an aspiration to transcend the misery of common existence and to "die of a nobler death"' (Guido di Pino, 'Venezia nell'opera di Gabriele D'Annunzio,' in Pellegrini, ed., *Venezia nelle letterature moderne*, 295).

220 Trans. Raymond Furness in 'Wagner and Decadence,' in Joan Tasker Grimbert, ed., *Tristan and Isolde: A Casebook* (Routledge: London, 2002), 406. Furness mistakenly refers to *Amori et dolori sacrum* as a 'novel' (405). When Barrès writes 'the orchestra attacks the prelude' (7:55), one thinks of the orchestral attack at the outset of the Prelude to *Tristan and Isolde*.

221 On the origins of this phrase, see Wladyslaw Folkierski, 'La rencontre post-

hume de Barrès et de Mickiewicz à Venise,' in Pellegrini, ed., *Venezia nelle letterature moderne*, 187.

222 'The feasts of Rome, says René, have something of an ancient poetry which places death at the side of pleasure' (Barrès, ctd in Bertaut, *L'Italie vue par les français*, 206).

223 Praz, *Romantic Agony*, 407.

224 Caramaschi, 'Maurice Barrès et Venise,' in *Maurice Barrès, Actes du colloque organisé*, 269.

225 Giulio Lorenzetti, *Venice and Its Lagoons*, trans. John Guthrie (Trieste: Lint, 1994), 413–14.

226 Lorenzetti, *Venice and Its Lagoons*, 414.

227 On his visit to Burano, Torcello, and Mazzorbo, William Beckford brought along musicians for his amusement. When he dined at a convent, the nuns who appeared at the grate 'all seemed to catch a gleam of pleasure from the music; two or three of them, probably the last immured, let fall a tear, and suffered the recollection of the world and its profane joys to interrupt for a moment their sacred tranquillity' (*The Travel-Diaries of William Beckford of Fonthill*, ed. Guy Chapman [Cambridge: Constable and Houghton Mifflin, 1928], 1:107). Beckford anticipates Barrès in the evening gondola ride, though Beckford on return rushed to hear an oratorio, music being his passion – or was this too a premonition of the Decadence?

4 From Italophilia to Italophobia: Italian Americans in the Gilded Age

1 Not to mention Italian American literature. Cf. the earliest novel published by an Italian American, Joseph Rocchietti's *Lorenzo and Oonalaska* (1835), in Carol Bonomo Albright and Elvira G. Di Fabio, eds., *Republican Ideals in the Selected Literary Works of Italian-American Joseph Rocchietti: 1835–1845* (Lewiston, NY: Edward Mellen, 2003); and Francesco Durante, ed., *Italo-americana: Storia e letteratura degli italiani negli Stati Uniti: 1776–1980*, 3 vols. (Milan: Mondadori, 2001–2008). By the 1850 census 3,645 Italians were living in the United States; in 1910, 1,343,125 (Emiliana P. Noether, 'As Others Saw Us,' *Transactions of the Connecticut Academy of Arts and Sciences*, 50 [Sept. 1990]: 125).

2 Richard H. Brodhead, 'The Double Dream of Italy in the American Gilded Age,' paper presented at the conference America's Italy, Washington, DC, 17–19 Sept. 1992, 11, reprinted as 'Strangers on a Train: The Double Dream of Italy in the American Gilded Age,' *Modernism/Modernity*, 1, no. 2 (1994): 1–19.

3 Brodhead, 'Double Dream of Italy,' 9.

4 Andrew M. Canepa demonstrates how the image of the Italian changed in English culture in one decade alone, the 1780s, in 'From Degenerate Scoundrel to Noble Savage: The Italian Stereotype in 18th-Century British Travel Literature,' *English Miscellany*, 22 (1971): 107–46.

5 He had to turn down the consulship in Rome because it came without a salary; the Venice post provided fifteen hundred dollars a year.

6 Ctd in James L. Woodress, Jr, *Howells and Italy* (Durham: Duke Univ. Press, 1952), 40.

7 William L. Vance, 'Seeing Italy: The Realistic Rediscovery by Twain, Howells, and James,' in Theodore E. Stebbins, Jr, ed., *The Lure of Italy: American Artists and the Italian Experience, 1760–1914* (Boston and New York: Museum of Fine Arts and Harry N. Abrams, 1992), 99.

8 Qtd in Woodress, Jr, *Howells and Italy*, 199.

9 Published with additions in 1887.

10 *Suburban Sketches* (1871; Boston: Osgood, 1872), 45. Hereafter page numbers are cited in parentheses in the text and notes. The distinction between *mordere* and *morsicare* is less pronounced in contemporary Italian.

11 William Dean Howells, *My Literary Passions* (1895; New York: Greenwood, 1969), 209–11.

12 Woodress, Jr, *Howells and Italy*, 131–2.

13 Nathalia Wright, *American Novelists in Italy: The Discoverers: Allston to James* (Philadelphia: Univ. of Pennsylvania Press, 1965), 195–6. Accusing Howells of careerism, Brodhead remarks that he exhibited shrewd self-interest in his pursuing the Italian theme, given the fascination with Italy in Boston literary circles, then deeply immersed in Dante and Italian culture ('Double Dream of Italy,' 12). This is unfair to Howells, whose ambition does not preclude a genuine interest in Italy and Italians. Cf. Woodress, Jr, *Howells and Italy*, 102, 113, 186, 198, 200–201.

14 Kenneth S. Lynn, *William Dean Howells: An American Life* (New York: Harcourt Brace Jovanovich, 1970), 206. See also *Suburban Sketches* (21); and James Russell Lowell, 'Leaves from My Journal in Italy and Elsewhere: III. Italy,' in *Fireside Travels* (Boston: Houghton Mifflin, 1904), 149.

15 Lynn, *William Dean Howells*, 199; Woodress, *Howells and Italy*, 63.

16 *Letters of James Russell Lowell*, ed. Charles Eliot Norton, 2 vols. (New York: Harper, 1894), 2:32.

17 'Doorstep Acquaintance' had first appeared in the *Atlantic* in 1869.

18 Though records are far from perfect, one can say from what is available that Italians ranked first among ethnic groups in repatriation between 1908 and 1931. Betty Boyd Caroli, *Italian Repatriation from the United States, 1900–1914* (New York: Center for Migration Studies, 1973), 9; see tables on

11 and 38 and the discussion of statistical problems, chaps. 1–2 passim. Of the so-called birds of passage syndrome R.F. Foerster explained: 'Between 1860 and 1880, as the fresh arrivals increased, the immigration assumed a much more definite character. Where before there had been individuals there were now types and classes. From small beginnings the contingent from South Italy had swelled to substantial proportions. After 1870, for the first time, it became evident that, following a somewhat indeterminate state, many repacked their chattels and went home again. No previous immigrants into this land of promise had done that' (*The Italian Emigration of Our Times* [Cambridge: Harvard Univ. Press, 1919], 324). Pino Arlacchi, citing this passage, locates the reasons for return-migration in 'balanced reciprocity,' a social system in crisis after the Unification (*Mafia, Peasants and Great Estates: Society in Traditional Calabria* [Cambridge: Cambridge Univ. Press, 1983], chap. 1). For return-migration see also Thomas Kessner, *The Golden Door: Italian and Jewish Immigrant Mobility in New York City, 1880–1915* (New York: Oxford Univ. Press, 1977), 27–8.

19 Arthur Mann, *Yankee Reformers in the Urban Age* (Cambridge: Harvard Univ. Press, 1954), 4. For the ethnic composition of the North End, see Anna Maria Martellone, *Una little Italy, nell'Atene d'America: La communità italiana di Boston dal 1880 al 1920* (Naples: Guida, 1973), 235–6. By 1900 there were twenty-five nationalities domiciled in the North End.

20 In the seventeenth and eighteenth centuries the ferry took people to and from Charlestown (Walter M. Whitehill, *Boston: A Topographical History* [Cambridge: Harvard Univ. Press, 1959)], 28–9).

21 Lynn refers to 'picturesque vignettes of Italian characters' (*William Dean Howells*, 199).

22 James criticized Howells for not writing about Italians 'as from equal to equal' in *Italian Journeys* (qtd in Lynn, *William Dean Howells*, 198). Thirty-five years later James would have a similar problem with the immigrants in *The American Scene*.

23 John F. Stack, Jr, commenting on Frederick A. Bushee's 'The Invading Host' (1902), in *International Conflict in an American City: Boston's Irish, Italians, and Jews, 1935–1944* (Westport: Greenwood, 1979), 24.

24 William Dean Howells, *The Rise of Silas Lapham*, in *Novels 1875–1886*, The Library of America (New York: Viking, 1982), 993.

25 Harvard adopted Botta for its course on the Revolution in 1839 (Noether, 'As Others Saw Us,' 133).

26 Stack, Jr, *International Conflict in an American City*, 24. This was the heyday of the Teutonic myth in Anglo-Saxon culture. In *Mont Saint Michel and Chartres* (1904) Henry Adams goes so far as to transform St Thomas Aquinas into a

Swabian-Norman, uniting 'the two most energetic strains in Europe,' as if
Italy could not produce a philosopher of such standing (Boston: Houghton
Mifflin, 1933), 343. See Edward N. Saveth, *American Historians and European
Immigrants, 1875–1925* (New York: Columbia Univ. Press, 1948), chaps. 1, 2.

27 Robert Anthony Orsi, *The Madonna of 115th Street: Faith and Community in
Italian Harlem, 1880–1950* (New Haven: Yale Univ. Press, 1985), 75 ff.

28 Douglas, *Alone*, 200.

29 Brodhead, 'Double Dream of Italy,' 14.

30 There were 35,287 Irish-born residents in Boston in 1850 compared to 134
Italians; by 1880 the number of Irish stood at 64,793 (an additional 8,366
in Cambridge) and Italians at 1,277 (36 in Cambridge) (Oscar Handlin,
Boston's Immigrants: A Study in Acculturation, rev. ed. [Cambridge: Harvard
Univ. Press, 1959], 243, 261). These figures may be compared with the 1875
Massachusetts Census, which lists 2,389 Italian residents in Boston (Stack, Jr,
International Conflict in an American City, 23).

31 The norm was otherwise, the Italians usually being compared unfavourably. 'The lowest Irish,' said John Fiske, 'are far above the level of these
creatures' (John Higham, *Strangers in the Land: Patterns of American Nativism,
1860–1925* [New York: Atheneum, 1963], 65).

32 Elsa Nettels, *Language, Race, and Social Class in Howells's America* (Lexington:
Univ. of Kentucky Press, 1988), 92.

33 Stack, *International Conflict in an American City*, 21.

34 Handlin, *Boston's Immigrants*, 191.

35 See John E. Zucchi, *The Little Slaves of the Harp: Italian Child Street Musicians
in Nineteenth-Century Paris, London, and New York* (Montreal and Kingston:
McGill-Queen's Univ. Press, 1992).

36 Oddly, Richard Gambino does not see the Italian as particularly graceful.
Commenting on black and Italian stereotypes, he remarks that black body
language is 'fluid, agile, graceful, easy, and seemingly relaxed and uninhibited,' whereas the Italian American 'stands and moves in a controlled,
guarded way'; 'his shoulders and hips remain locked even during the fastest
dancing, in contrast to the focus on pelvic movement of black dance. It is
a code of a self-contained rock-like body punctuated by deliberate staccato
movements' (*Blood of My Blood: The Dilemma of the Italian-Americans* [New
York: Doubleday, 1974], 303). The words 'controlled' and 'guarded' do not
spring to mind when one thinks of the *passeggiata*. Italians are known to be
excellent dancers: the Italian dancing master is a common type from the
eighteenth century onward in British and American novels (see n. 45 for an
example). In early nineteenth-century Palermo George Russell noted that
'the deportment of these lovely women, their dancing, and their attitudes,

are attractively elegant' (*A Tour through Sicily in the Year 1815* [London: 1819], 48).

37 Martin Burgess Green, *The Problem of Boston: Some Readings in Cultural History* (New York: Norton, 1966), 103: 'John S. Dwight, Boston's Yankee music critic, left town for the occasion.'

38 Handlin, *Boston's Immigrants*, 212.

39 Gambino, *Blood of My Blood*, 302–3.

40 Lynn, *William Dean Howells*, 197.

41 '"You don't call ... an Italian a white man?" a West Coast construction boss was asked. "No, sir," he answered, "an Italian is a Dago."' Ralph Waldo Emerson was 'thankful that immigration brought "the light complexion, the blue eyes of Europe"'; 'the black eyes, the black drop, the Europe of Europe is left' (Higham, *Strangers in the Land*, 65, 66). As James Fenimore Cooper saw the *lazzaroni* in Naples: 'Naked men, resemble Indians with breech cloths. Colour not very different' (*Letters and Journals*, ed. James Franklin Beard [Cambridge: Harvard Univ. Press, 1960], 1:380).

42 Mario Praz, *The Romantic Agony*, trans. Angus Davidson, 2d ed. (Cleveland: World, 1968), 209–10.

43 Mann, *Yankee Reformers in the Urban Age*, 5.

44 Wright, *American Novelists in Italy*, 187.

45 'Lorenzo Papanti, an exiled Italian count, established the one "proper Boston" dancing school of the century' (1214, note by Edwin H. Cady). Lapham's daughters take lessons in the public classes; the Brahmins presumably send their daughters to the private ones.

46 Ctd in William Dean Howells, *The Rise of Silas Lapham*, ed. Walter J. Meserve (Bloomington: Indiana Univ. Press, 1971), 385–6. The entire scene is an expression of the turmoil in Howells: 'In the spring [of 1885, shortly before the novel was published] a sudden overwhelming sense of guilt – a Swedenborgian "vastation" – turns Howells to Tolstoy and deeper, more radical social inquiries' (1205, note by Edwin H. Cady, Library of America edition).

47 Giuseppe Gadda Conti, *William Dean Howells* (Rome: Edizioni di Storia e Letteratura, 1971), 182.

48 William Dean Howells, *The Vacation of the Kelwyns* (New York: Houghton Mifflin, 1920), 51.

49 Wright, *American Novelists in Italy*, 195. In her chapter on Howells and Italy, Wright devotes only one paragraph to the Italians in America, Woodress in his book-length study even less (*Howells and Italy*, 63–4, 153).

50 Cf. Camillo von Klenze, *The Interpretation of Italy during the Last Two Centuries: A Contribution to the Study of Goethe's 'Italienische Reise'* (Chicago: Univ. of Chicago Press, 1907); and Herbert Barrows, 'Convention and Novelty in the Romantic Generation's Experience of Italy,' in *Literature as a Mode of Travel*,

Introduction by Warner G. Rice (New York: New York Public Library, 1963), 69–84.

51 *Impressions and Experiences*, qtd in Wright, *American Novelists in Italy*, 196. The Italians were not particularly 'fierce'; it took longer for them to receive their share of the 'pottage.'

52 I limit myself to these novels, though Bates's *The Puritans* (1898) has some of the same characters.

53 Arlo Bates, *The Pagans* (New York: Henry Holt, 1884; fac. rpt. Upper Saddle River, NJ: Literature House, 1970), 56, 211, 234–5.

54 Green, *The Problem of Boston*, 136.

55 According to Van Wyck Brooks, Boston's general suspicion of the plastic arts excepted portrait painting on account of its association with 'family pride,' 'wealth,' and 'public spirit' (*The Flowering of New England* [New York: Dutton, 1936], 3).

56 Arlo Bates, *The Philistines* (Boston: Ticknor, 1889), 324.

57 Helen Greyson's Roman art teacher is 'Flammenti,' another image of the fiery, passionate Italian (*Philistines*, 107).

58 Higham, *Strangers in the Land*, 90.

59 Arlacchi, *Mafia, Peasants and Great Estates*, 28.

60 Ctd in Mann, *Yankee Reformers in the Urban Age*, 4.

61 'While Italian women will receive an American parish visitor with a sweet smile, the next day they will tell the Italian pastor that they thought her somewhat crazy or at least very peculiar. There is such a chasm between the mentality of simple Italian women and that of the American lady visitor and there is such a strong tendency in the Anglo-Saxon race to enforce its views without much consideration for the views and traditions of the other race, that the results are not lasting' (Enrico C. Sartorio, *Social and Religious Life of Italians in America* [Boston: Christopher, 1918], republished [Clifton, NJ: A.M. Kelley, 1974], 123).

62 'Among the educated bourgeoisie [at the turn of the century], this quest for "real life" was the characteristic psychic project of the age. It energized the settlement house movement.' 'From Salvation to Self-Realization: Advertising and the Therapeutic Roots of the Consumer Culture, 1880–1930,' in Richard Wightman Fox and T.J. Jackson Lears, eds., *The Culture of Consumption* (New York: Pantheon, 1983), 10.

63 Martellone, *Una little Italy*, 203n, 487–8. As Allen F. Davis notes, 40 per cent (thirty-three) of the total number of settlement houses in the United States in 1911 were in Boston (*Spearheads for Reform: The Social Settlements and the Progressive Movement, 1890–1914* [New Brunswick: Rutgers Univ. Press, 1984], 268).

64 Martellone, *Una little Italy,*, 237–8.

65 Much of the social work was organized by the Protestant churches of Boston. See Francis D. De Bilio, 'Protestant Mission Work among Italians in Boston,' doctoral diss., School of Theology, Boston University, 1949; Antonio Mangano, *Religious Work among Italians in America: A Survey for the Home Missions Council* (New York: Missionary Education Movement of the United States and Canada, 1917). De Bilio writes that 'Our view of the American Christian world outside our slum was an extension of our experience with the solicitous American women who made up the *Ladies Auxiliary*, who were in turn the vital connection between the mission and the denomination. Christmas parties were a week or more after Christmas, so that the left-over or discarded Christmas gifts of parties in American churches could be collected and brought to the "poor mission children"' (165) (ctd in Martellone, *Una little Italy*, 452). Not to be outdone, the Italians usually went along to get the presents for their children at Christmas and Easter, but did not change their religion. Since Italians traditionally gave out gifts at the Epiphany (Jan. 6), the fact that they had to wait a week or two after Christmas would have made little difference to them.

66 Martellone, *Una little Italy* , 443.

67 The population of the North End rose from 16,904 in 1880 (perhaps less than 1,000 of them Italians) to 18,447 in 1890 and 30,546 in 1900 (when 13,738 are Italian).

68 There is an example of this trope in De Sica's film *Indiscretion of an American Wife* (*Stazione Termini*) (1954), where a married women from Philadelphia (Jennifer Jones) is tempted into an affair with an Italian (Montgomery Clift). She asks him whether, if she becomes his wife, he would beat her, and it appears that at some level the idea arouses her.

69 Cf. Martino Marazzi, *Misteri di Little Italy: Storie e Testi della Letteraturea italo-americana* (Milan: FrancoAngeli, 2001) and *Voices of Italian America: A History of Early Italian American Literature with a Critical Anthology*, trans. Ann Goldstein (Madison: Fairleigh Dickinson Univ. Press, 2004); Durante, *Italoamericana*; and Joseph Cosco, *Imagining Italians: The Clash in American Perceptions, 1880–1910* (Albany: State Univ. of New York Press, 2003).

70 Yellin, *Chadwick: Yankee Composer* (Washington: Smithsonian Institution Press, 1990).

71 Yellin, *Chadwick*, 211.

72 Yellin, *Chadwick*, 73, 212.

73 Yellin, *Chadwick*, 213.

74 Yellin, *Chadwick*, 218: 'When the American style was demanded during the New Deal days, it had to be reinvented.'

75 *Times Literary Supplement*, 26 Oct.–1 Nov. 1990, 1154.

76 Robert Joseph Garafolo, 'The Life and Works of Frederick Shepherd Converse, 1871–1940,' doctoral diss., Catholic Univ. of America, Washington, DC, 1969, 66–8.
77 Fred Langone, *The North End: Where It All Began* (Boston: *Post-Gazette*, American Independence, 1994), 20. Langone rankles defensively: 'What his book did to the North End was to make it look like everybody was in some kind of racket' (20). Actually Whyte was treating only one segment of North End life and did not examine, at any rate extensively, the role of women, family, health, education, or religion. Besides, far from being wholly negative, Whyte recognized in his corner boys the virtues of friendship, solidarity, fair-mindedness, patriotism, and community. Still, Whyte inaccurately referred to the North End as a 'slum.' See also Whyte's memoir 'My Friend, Angelo Ralph Orlandella,' *Italian Americana*, 13, no. 2 (1995): 166–76, and Orlandella's contribution in the same issue.
78 Walter Muir Whitehill, *Boston: A Topographical History*, 195.
79 Whitehill, *Boston: A Topographical History*, 2d ed. (Cambridge: Harvard Univ. Press, 1968), 201–2. In *Boston after Bulfinch: An Account of its Architecture: 1800–1900* (Cambridge: Harvard Univ. Press, 1946), 38, Walter Harrington Kilham praised the 'impressiveness' of Alexander Parris's St Joseph's Church (1834), 'standing as it does in the curve of [Chambers Street].' As Whitehill notes, 'that was lost when, thanks to the first efforts of the Boston Redevelopment Authority, the curve, the street, and all the neighboring buildings disappeared, leaving poor St. Joseph's forlorn and isolated in a great dump, later to become a parking lot' (275).
80 Whitehill, *Boston: A Topographical History*, 274.
81 Langone, *The North End*, 101.

5 Puccini's American Theme

1 Anna Maria Martellone, 'Italian Mass Emigration to the United States, 1876–1976: A Historical Survey,' in *Perspectives in American History*, 1, n.s. (1984), 380. 'Italy witnessed, from the 1870s until 1924, one of the largest migrations in modern history, yet Italian historians largely ignored it' (382). Not only did Italian historians ignore it, but Italians ignored it, Americans ignored it, and Puccini ignored it, at least in his public statements.
2 Francis Marion Crawford, *Ave Roma Immortalis* (1898; New York: Macmillan, 1899), 1:230. In this as in so many ways, Crawford earns Van Wyck Brooks's encomium: 'no other American, certainly, had ever possessed [Crawford's] knowledge of Rome' (*The Dream of Arcadia: American Writers and Artists in Italy: 1760–1915* [New York: Dutton, 1958], 162).

3 Mosco Carner, *Puccini: A Critical Biography*, 2d ed. (New York: Holmes and Meier, 1974), 218–19. 'The affairs of political and public life left him quite unmoved,' writes Richard Specht: 'all he wanted was to discover good texts for his operas, and, in the tranquil seclusion of Torre del Lago, to live for the work that he loved so passionately' (*Giacomo Puccini: The Man, His Life, His Work* [New York: Knopf, 1933], 21). See Vincent Seligman, *Puccini among Friends* (London: Macmillan, 1938), 290–1.

4 Harvey Sachs, *Music in Fascist Italy* (New York: W.W. Norton, 1987), 102.

5 Quoted in Seligman, *Puccini among Friends*, 155 (22 June 1908).

6 Eugenio Gara, ed., *Carteggi Pucciniani* (Milan: Ricordi, 1958), 483 (26 Mar. 1919) (my trans.). In addition to this collection, which contains over 900 letters, there are Giuseppe Adami, ed., *Letters of Giacomo Puccini*, trans. Ena Makin (Philadelphia: Lippincott, 1931) (240 letters); Arnaldo Marchetti, ed., *Puccini com'era* (Milan: Curci, 1973) (500 letters); and Giuseppe Pintorno, ed., *Puccini: 276 lettere inedite* (Milan: Nuove edizioni, 1974). Seligman (see n. 5) published many letters or parts of letters by Puccini to his mother Sybil Seligman. For a discussion of other collections see Howard Greenfeld, *Puccini* (New York: G.P. Putnam's, 1980), 13–14.

7 Adami, *Letters*, 289.

8 Sachs, *Music in Fascist Italy*, 106.

9 Carner, *Puccini*, 55.

10 Gara, *Carteggi Pucciniani*, 37. In an earlier letter (5 Jan. 1890) Puccini informed Michele that he was working on *Manon Lescaut*.

11 Gara, *Carteggi Pucciniani*, 38, 40.

12 Quoted in Dante Del Fiorentino, *Immortal Bohemian: An Intimate Memoir of Giacomo Puccini* (New York: Prentice-Hall, 1952), 63. For Michele's journey, see his letter to Nicolao Cerù (20 May 1890), *Puccini com'era*, 147–53.

13 Edoardo Aromatari to Puccini (25 May 1891), *Puccini com'era*, 166.

14 Greenfeld, *Puccini*, 58.

15 *Puccini com'era*, 159.

16 The *Harvard Brief Dictionary of Music* defines 'theme' as 'a melody which, by virtue of its characteristic design, prominent position, or special treatment becomes a basic element in the structure of a composition.' I use 'theme' both in its musical and its broader literary senses.

17 Charles Osborne, *The Complete Operas of Puccini* (New York: Athenaeum, 1982), 77.

18 Giacomo Puccini, *Manon Lescaut*, 1st ed. (Milan: Ricordi, 1893), 105 (piano score). The pages on which the heroic theme occurs in the score are 86–8 (act 2); 109 (Intermezzo); 117, 129, 134–5 (act 3); 136 (act 4).

19 Wilfrid Mellers, *Beethoven and the Voice of God* (New York: Oxford Univ. Press, 1983), 79.

20 Prévost says only 'They were looking then for young men who were disposed to join the colony voluntarily' (Abbé Prévost, *Manon Lescaut*, trans. Donald M. Frame [New York: Signet, 1961], 174). The captain's words were evidently supplied by Giulio Ricordi, one of the many who had a hand in the libretto (so many that no librettist was named on the title page) (*Carteggi Pucciniani*, 45, 72).

21 Carner, *Puccini*, 325.

22 Osborne, *Complete Operas*, 77; Carner, *Puccini*, 325; Mellers, *Beethoven*, 30.

23 Carner, *Puccini*, 320.

24 Michele Girardi, *Puccini: His International Art*, trans. Laura Basini (Chicago: Univ. of Chicago Press, 2000), 75. The commonest English designation is the one given in *Manon Lescaut* (ii), *The New Grove Dictionary of Opera*, ed. Stanley Sadie (London: Macmillan, 1992), 193: 'A vast desert near the outskirts of New Orleans.' This description has always struck music lovers as supremely quaint. The 1893 original Ricordi piano-vocal score gives the locale for atto quarto as 'Una landa interminata sui confini della Nuova Orleans.' It then sets the stage scene as 'Terreno brullo ed ondulato – Orrizonte vastissimo – Cielo annuvolato – Cade la sera.'

25 Adami, *Letters*, 149 (16 Nov. 1902).

26 Ben Lawton, 'Giuseppe Giacosa (1847–1906) and Giacomo Puccini (1858–1924),' in Marc Pachter, ed., *Abroad in America: Visitors to the New Nation, 1776–1914* (Washington, DC: National Portrait Gallery, Smithsonian Institution, 1976), 249.

27 Qtd in Lawton, 'Giacosa and Puccini,' 251. But the New York chief of police told Giacosa that 'of all the immigrant groups the Italian is that which produces the least number of assassins, thieves and trouble-makers of all kinds' (Giuseppe Giacosa, *Impressioni d'America* [Milan, 1898], 170–71).

28 Quoted in Lawton, 'Giacosa and Puccini,' 251; Giacosa, *Impressioni*, 171–72, 196 (my trans.).

29 Carner, *Puccini*, 398.

30 Specht, *Giacomo Puccini*, 189; Seligman, *Puccini among Friends*, 55.

31 In *Impressioni d'America* Giacosa treats home life and observes the American separation of working from residential environments. As Lawton notes, 'Whereas in Italy the two are identical, in America one must travel some distance between them.' Giacosa speculates whether this does not 'exacerbate the formidable American individualism.' The absence of the 'mitigating influence of the home … accustoms the American to an almost complete doubling of his nature … to a separation of his emotions from his will and his intellect,' which causes him to 'leave his loving, helpful humanity at home and to arm himself for business with a harsh, thankless selfishness' ('Giacosa and Puccini,' 250).

32 Adami, *Letters*, 144 (23 April 1902).

33 John Luther Long, 'Madame Butterfly,' *Century Magazine* (Jan. 1898), 385.
It takes a skillful actress to make the point of insecurity with only two initials
'F.B.' The librettists should have let her err by saying the full 'Franklin Ben-
jamin Pinkerton,' which would be clearly perceived as a (meaningful) error.
Operatic lore insists this error was unintentional, that they never meant it to
be 'F.B.'; today many sopranos sing 'B.F.' instead of 'F.B.'

34 Of a Rome congress on women's issues in 1908 he reported caustically,
'When are those chattering women going to finish?' (Adami, *Letters*, 179
[29 April 1908]). Carner traces Puccini's compulsive victimization of
women to a traumatic childhood event, the death of his father. At five, Puccini was surrounded by 'a wholly feminine environment presided over by a
relatively young mother' and five older sisters, virtual mother images; 'such
an atmosphere was likely to establish a particularly strong fixation on the
mother and cause an intolerable pressure on the fatherless boy.' In Carner's
analysis, Puccini tended to elevate the mother figure and then, in response
to his guilty love, chose 'unworthy' women in his personal life and his operas, then to pity and punish them (*Puccini*, 273–4).

35 Adami, *Letters*, 174 (15 July 1907).

36 Maria F. Rich, 'Opera USA – Perspective: Puccini in America,' *Opera Quarterly*, 2, no. 3 (1984): 28.

37 Adami, *Letters*, 164 (28 Dec. 1906).

38 Adami, *Letters*, 111, to Giulio Ricordi (15 May 1898); Puccini complained
that Verdi had not had to endure the duties of public life. But Ricordi replied: 'I read your litanies about invitations, dinners, receptions, presenta-
tions, etc. You cite Verdi but your citation is not exact. From his youth Verdi
was assiduous in frequenting the high society of Milan, and when he went to
Paris, Petersburg, London, Madrid, and Vienna for his operas, he submitted
to the necessary consequences!' (quoted in Greenfeld, *Puccini*, 108: 'The
publisher concluded by adding that times had changed, too; that in light of
greater competition, public relations was playing an increasingly large part
in artistic success.')

39 Metropolitan Opera Archives, cited in Rich, 'Opera USA,' 32.

40 George R. Marek, *Puccini* (London: Cassell, 1952), 220. Mascagni's tour
showed to what extent Italian Americans lionized the Italian composers.
As Alan Malloch writes: 'For the immigrant Italian community, largely impoverished and downtrodden, however, the composer's presence alone was
triumph enough. To Mascagni's amazement – he wrote to his friend Hirsch
that "he had no idea that he was so extraordinarily popular" – the Italians of
nearly every city in the eastern United States had their Mascagni Society or

their Mascagni band. The composer's arrival in each city became a festival of Italian solidarity, an opportunity for immigrants to remind themselves of their connections with their homeland and its great artistic tradition. In Philadelphia after midnight over 5000 Italians waited for his arrival at the Broad Street Station' ('The Mascagni Tour of 1902,' *Opera Quarterly*, 7, no. 4 [1990–91]: 23).

41 Quoted in Seligman, *Puccini among Friends*, 118 (18 Feb. 1907).

42 Rich, 'Opera USA,' 31.

43 *Carteggi Pucciniani*, 340 (18 Feb. 1907).

44 Girardi, *Puccini*, 326: 'the idea that the opera influenced films should be rejected, given the clear chronology of film history.'

45 Ctd in David Belasco, *My Own Story* (New York: International Magazine, 1915): 'I want the play! I have already the minstrel song in my head'; William Winter, *The Life of David Belasco*, 2 vols. (New York: Moffat, Yard, 1918, 1925), 1:75.

46 Qtd in Edward N. Saveth, *American Historians and European Immigrants, 1875–1925* (New York: Columbia Univ. Press, 1948), 126. In 1901 Turner wrote that the contribution of southern Italians to 'American racial characteristics' was 'of doubtful value judged from the ethical point of view of the stocks that have heretofore made the nation.' For him, Jews were even less assimilable since they were 'a city people'; life in crowded quarters 'produced a race capable of living under conditions that would exterminate men whom centuries of national selection had not adapted to endure squalor and the unsanitary and indecent conditions of a dangerously crowded population' (ctd in Saveth, *American Historians and European Immigrants*, 129).

47 Lawton, 'Giacosa and Puccini,' 247.

48 Girardi, *Puccini*, 289.

49 Leslie Fiedler, *Love and Death in the American Novel*, 2d ed. (New York: Stein and Day, 1966), 263.

50 Too much detail was Giovanni Pozza's (to my mind, unjustified) critique of the first act of *Madama Butterfly* in his review for *Corriere della Sera* (quoted in Greenfeld, *Puccini*, 145).

51 Leslie Fiedler, *No! in Thunder: Essays on Myth and Literature* (Boston: Beacon Press, 1960), 262.

52 Letter to Ervino Endvai, 7 April 1907, in Pintorno, *Puccini: 276 lettere*, 146: 'Magnifico soggetto!' Girardi considers it a 'mediocre libretto' (*Puccini*, 327).

53 Bert Levy, 'Puccini on the High Seas,' *Opera News*, 37 (20 Jan. 1973), 14.

54 Girardi, *Puccini*, 283, 286: Girardi justifies the experiment because 'the way

to renewal was not principally through the subject, but through the development of musical language'; the opera declares its entré into twentieth-century music by showing 'a detachment between the work of art and real feeling'; and, with its many influences, it looks ahead to 'generic blendings' (284, 327).

55 Ctd in Greenfeld, *Puccini*, 206.

56 Ctd in Girardi, *Puccini*, 281.

57 Quoted in Marek, *Puccini*, 239.

58 Gara, *Carteggi Pucciniani*, 38 (24 April 1890).

59 'If I could get a good Western American libretto, I would undoubtedly write the music for it. The Indian does not appeal to me, however. Real Americans mean much more' (quoted in Greenfeld, *Puccini*, 177).

60 Paul Fees, 'In Defense of Buffalo Bill: A Look at Cody In and Of His Time,' in *Myth of the West* (Seattle: The Henry Art Gallery and Univ. of Washington Press, 1991), 145. Nellie Snyder Yost says that Puccini's inspiration for the American West was not Belasco, but his seeing Buffalo Bill's Wild West Show in 1890 (*Buffalo Bill* [Chicago: Swallow, 1979], 224).

61 For an excellent description, see Nick Rossi, 'At Home with Puccini,' *Opera Quarterly*, 2, no. 3 (1984): 73–88.

62 Adami, *Letters*, 109 (10 May 1898).

63 Adami, *Letters*, 123 (31 July 1898).

64 Adami, *Letters*, 270 (10 Nov. 1920). 'He loathes the sophistication, the refinement, the nervous excitement of urban civilization, it induces in him an intolerable feeling of malaise and even nausea; yet his whole art is unthinkable away from the "decadence" of modern life in the big cities, of which it is indeed a highly characteristic product' (Carner, *Puccini*, 98).

65 Adami, *Letters*, Introduction, 16.

66 Seligman, *Puccini among Friends*, 95 (8 Nov. 1906); Adami, *Letters*, 192 (4 Oct. 1914).

67 Adami, *Letters*, 183 (21 Sept. 1908).

68 Marek, *Puccini*, 26.

69 A portrait of these evenings is recorded by Puccini's granddaughter, Simonetta Puccini, in 'Puccini and the Painters,' *Opera Quarterly*, 2, no. 3 (1984): 5–26.

70 Levy, 'Puccini on the High Seas, 14.

71 Adami, *Letters*, 133 (Dec. 1899), 124 (18 Aug. 1898); quoted in Seligman, *Puccini among Friends*, 343 (6 Jan. 1923); John Louis DiGaetani, 'Puccini the Poet,' *Opera Quarterly* 2, no. 3 (1984): 56; Marek, *Puccini*, 270.

72 In 1922, on a motor tour in Bavaria, he swallowed a goose bone that stuck in his throat; a doctor was summoned to remove it. After his death it was

suggested that 'an injury caused to his throat, either by the bone or in the process of removing it, might have set off the cancer of which he was to die two years later' (Carner, *Puccini*, 232).

73 Seligman, *Puccini among Friends*, 29. The accident delayed the completion of *Madama Butterfly* for months. In 1923, he won a suit against a ragtime composer whom he accused of plagiarism; he bragged about his victory trophy: 'I got a marvellous new car, an eight-cylinder limousine Lancia – 90,000 lire!' (quoted in Seligman, *Puccini among Friends*, 344 [26 Jan. 1923]). 'Ten months later he wants to trade it in for an *Hispano Suiza* with French bodywork of the Cabriolet type' (*Carteggi Pucciniani*, 544 [22 Nov. 1923]). He also purchased a new motorboat that 'does over twenty-five miles an hour' (quoted in Carner, *Puccini*, 231).

74 Adami, *Letters*, 176 (n.d.).

75 Robert K. Wallace, *Jane Austen and Mozart: Classical Equilibrium in Fiction and Music* (Athens: Univ. of Georgia Press, 1983), 44.

76 Wallace, *Jane Austen and Mozart*, 45.

77 According to Specht, Puccini was responsible for adding the 'hideous manhunt and the threats of torture' in the last act of *La fanciulla del West* (*Giacomo Puccini*, 118). William Winter (*Life of David Belasco*, 2:214) claims that Belasco had the idea and discarded it. Specht also argues plausibly that the love of hunting functions as a release of some suppressed element, which if allowed to fester would have produced an 'unpleasing effect, not only on his art, but perhaps on his everyday life too.'

78 Allan W. Atlas, 'Belasco and Puccini: "Old Dog Tray" and the Zuni Indians,' *The Music Quarterly*, 75 (Fall 1991): 378, 382–3.

79 Girardi places it second, after love as a redemptive force (*Puccini*, 292). From the first episode in the opera onwards 'the exposition of material follows the formal logic that enjoys an obvious autonomy, so much so as to make one think that the connotative value of the themes came into being only in retrospect' (293–4). If this is the case, then it divorces the plot from the music even further.

80 John Louis DiGaetani, 'Comedy and Redemption in *La fanciulla del West*,' *Opera Quarterly*, 2, no. 2 (1984): 91, 94.

81 Carner, *Puccini*, 256.

82 Specht, *Giacomo Puccini*, 128; Adami, *Letters*, 88; see also Marek, *Puccini*, 134.

6 'To Die Is Not Enough!' Hemingway and D'Annunzio

1 Henry James, *Italian Hours* (Boston: Houghton Mifflin, 1901), 3.

2 Rosella Mamoli Zorzi, 'The Text Is the City: The Representation of Venice

in Two Tales by Irving and Poe and a Novel by Cooper,' in Angela Vistarchi,, ed., *The City as Text, RSA (Rivista di Studi Anglo-Americani)*, 6, no. 8 (1990): 286.

3 Mamoli Zorzi, 'The Text Is the City,' 298.

4 Leslie Fiedler, *An End to Innocence: Essays on Culture and Politics* (Boston: Beacon Press, 1955), 194; Alberto Moravia, *Man as an End: A Defense of Humanism*, trans. Bernard Wall (1961; Westport: Greenwood, 1976), 234; Stephen L. Tanner, 'Wrath and Agony in *Across the River and Into the Trees*,' in Rena Sanderson, ed., *Hemingway's Italy: New Perspectives* (Baton Rouge: Louisiana State Univ. Press, 2006), 220; Agostino Lombardo, 'Hemingway in Italy,' *Hemingway Review*, 11, Special European Issue (Summer 1992):15.

5 Gina Fasoli, 'Nascita di un mito,' in *Studi storici in onore di Gioacchino Volpe per il suo 80 compleanno*, 2 vols. (Florence: Sansoni, 1958), 1:449.

6 Ctd in J.R. Hale, *England and the Italian Renaissance: The Growth of Interest in Its History and Art* (London: Faber and Faber, 1954), 30; see also 40–2.

7 Edward Muir, *Civil Ritual in Renaissance Venice* (Princeton: Princeton Univ. Press, 1984), 24; see also Andrew J. Kappel, 'Ezra Pound and the Myth of Venice,' *Clio*, 13, no. 3 (1983): 207.

8 Jacob Burckhardt, *The Civilization of the Renaissance in Italy*, trans. S.G.C. Middlemore (New York: Phaidon, 1960), 42.

9 Georg Simmel, ctd in Sergio Bettini, *Venezia* (Milan: Touring Club Italiano, 1963), 19; *Letters of Thomas Mann*, trans. Richard and Clara Winston (New York: Knopf, 1971), 76, 187; Paul Coates, *The Gorgon's Gaze: German Cinema, Expressionism, and the Image of Horror* (Cambridge: Cambridge Univ. Press, 1991), 1.

10 Robert W. Lewis, Jr, *Hemingway in Love* (Austin: Univ. of Texas Press, 1965), 183.

11 W.H. Auden, *The Enchafed Flood, or, The Romantic Iconography of the Sea* (New York: Random House, 1950), 7–8.

12 Robert Casillo, 'The Desert and the Swamp: Enlightenment, Orientalism, and the Jews in Ezra Pound,' *Modern Language Quarterly*, 45 (1984): 281, 285.

13 Giuseppe Baretti described in detail the 'odd way of killing quantities of the palmipedous birds' that are 'in great plenty' on the Venetian lagoons: 'Several empty and uncovered tubs are sunk in shallows within two or three inches of the brim, and placed at proper distance from each other. Many sportsmen, well provided with hand-guns ready loaded, and cartridges to load again in case of necessity, go in boats to those tubs before break of day; get into them, and send the boats away. As soon as the day-light approaches, the birds fly all about in search of their food. The sportsmen who stand peeping at the brim of their tubs, shoot at all those that come within reach.

The sport lasts a good part of the morning; and when it is over, the boatmen come to fetch the sportsmen out of the tubs; row about collecting the dead floating birds; then all go merrily together to land, where the game is fairly divided.' *An Account of the Manners and Customs of Italy; with Observations on the Mistakes of Some Travellers, with Regard to That Country*, 2 vols. (London: 1768), 2:230–1.

14 Ernest Hemingway, *Across the River and Into the Trees* (New York: Scribner's, 1950), 5. Hereafter the novel will be cited within parentheses in text and notes.

15 According to Charles M. Oliver, chap. 1 takes place on Sunday morning; chaps. 39–45 take place on Sunday evening ('Hemingway's Study of Impending Death: *Across the River and Into the Trees*,' in Robert W. Lewis, ed., *Hemingway in Italy and Other Essays* [New York: Praeger, 1990], 143). However, chap. 40 picks up when chap. 1 leaves off – it is still Sunday morning. In treating Sunday as 'time-present,' Oliver argues that chaps. 2 through 38 – virtually the entire novel – is a reminiscence or flashback by the 'omniscient narrator of Cantwell's memory' (148); 'at the beginning of chapters II and III there are past-perfect verbs that shift the story into its flashback sequence: "he *had taken* enough mannitol hexanitrate ..." etc. Hemingway does not continue the past-perfect narrative because once he has established the idea that events are taking place only in Cantwell's memory, it isn't necessary to continue what would eventually become an obtrusive verb tense structure' (145). The problem with this theory is that by convention Hemingway sometimes uses the free-indirect style to enter into Cantwell's thoughts and 'speak' through them, and at other times returns to the 'omniscient narrator' (e.g. chap. 40), and at still other times slides into the free-indirect style to portray, for instance, the driver Jackson's thoughts. Oliver's theory would seem to have Cantwell 'reminiscing' even about the thoughts of all the other characters in the novel. And Cantwell does not describe his actual death. Cf. Peter Lisca, 'The Structure of Hemingway's *Across the River and Into the Trees*,' *Modern Fiction Studies*, 12 (1966): 232–50.

16 Wirt Williams, *The Tragic Art of Ernest Hemingway* (Baton Rouge: Louisiana State Univ. Press, 1981), 161.

17 Lombardo, 'Hemingway in Italy,' 11.

18 Jane Harrison, *Mythology* (New York: Harcourt Brace, 1963), 48–9.

19 Guy Davenport, 'Persephone's Ezra,' in Eva Hesse, *New Approaches to Ezra Pound* (Berkeley: Univ. of California Press, 1989), 162.

20 Cantwell suffers from high blood pressure and angina pectoris and he has sustained numerous concussions in battle. Before his medical check-up he takes an extra large dose of mannitol hexanitrate in order to 'pass' and

be able to go on the duck-shoot. A longer-acting member of the nitrite family (nitroglycerin is a related drug), mannitol hexanitrate would have forestalled symptoms or signs on his cardiogram. In general, nitrites act on blood vessels (mainly arterioles, capillaries, veins) by 'causing muscle fibers to relax'; 'the lumen of the vessel is increased, the blood pressure is reduced, and the capillary flow is increased' (Elsie E. Krug, *Pharmacology in Nursing*, 8th ed. [St Louis: C.V. Mosby, 1960], 432). 'The primary effect on the heart is acceleration' (Solomon Solis-Cohen and Githens Thomas Stotesbury, *Pharmacotherapeutics: Materia Media and Drug Action* [New York: D. Appleton, 1928], 1330). Dilation of the retinal vessels may increase intra-ocular tension, and dilation of the meningeal vessels may increase intracranial pressure, causing severe headaches. Cantwell's overdose backfires. Not fooled by it, the 'skeptical' surgeon notes, after taking two readings, that the excessive medication is 'definitely contra-indicated in increased intra-ocular and intra-cranial pressure' (8) (Hemingway's art is illustrated by technical accuracy, conciseness, rhythm, and sonic texture with alliteration of *d*'s, *l*'s, and *in*'s). Cantwell cannot wait for the examination to end because he is suffering from nausea, a typical side-effect of large doses. Mannitol hexanitrate lasts for six to seven hours, roughly the intervals between which Cantwell takes the drug. Hemingway may have chosen this nitrite because of one of its unusual characteristics: it is 'very explosive' (Solis-Cohen, *Pharmacotherapeutics*, 1328–9). The surgeon tells Cantwell not to 'let any sparks strike' him when he is 'souped up' on his pills (9), another play on the pills/ammunition analogy, a parody of a soldier's death.

21 In Fellini's *La Strada* (1954), set like Hemingway's novel in the early postwar period, ten thousand lire is the price paid by Zampanò to Gelsomina's mother for putting her to work in his itinerant street act.

22 Hemingway also wrote 'Torcello Piece,' part of which he incorporated into *Across the River and Into the Trees* (item nos. 772 and 773, Hemingway Collection, John F. Kennedy Library, Boston).

23 Giulio Lorenzetti, *Venice and Its Lagoon*, trans. John Guthrie (Trieste: Lint, 1975), 834.

24 These comparisons point up a rather adolescent attitude on Cantwell's part. The fact that Cantwell and the driver Jackson are from only *neighbouring* western states lends a common reference, but underlines their difference. Also, both men have lost brothers in the Pacific theatre (22, 34–5).

25 An instance of Hemingway's typical romanticizing of waiters and their special 'knowledge,' which at any rate remains superficial. He condescends to waiters even as he pretends to glorify them.

26 In this count, a double equals two drinks; three of Cantwell's nine orders

are doubles. But it should be noted that Italian hard drinks are rarely at the strength of British or American drinks, even at Harry's.

27 Gabriele D'Annunzio, *Il fuoco* (Milan: Mondadori, 1982), 46, 117; Nicholas J. Perella, *Midday in Italian Literature: Variations on an Archetypal Theme* (Princeton: Princeton Univ. Press, 1979), 119, 133.

28 'Between a solid beginning and a solid end,' writes E.M. Halliday, 'we meander through a spongy middle of prolonged conversation wherein the hero expresses to his dream-girl contessa numerous prejudices, often malicious and often irrelevant to what meaning the book could have' ('Hemingway's Narrative Perspective,' *Sewanee Review*, 60 [1952]: 202–18). 'Spongy'? Those marshlands contain the clue to the work.

29 Mario Praz, *The Romantic Agony*, trans. Angus Davidson, 2d ed. (Cleveland: World, 1968), 197, 209–10, 221.

30 According to Tommaso Antongini, D'Annunzio referred to his 'women friends' in France as '*brother*' and earlier mistresses as '*sister*,' 'probably to enhance, with a vague savour of incest, his own sensations' (*D'Annunzio* [Boston: Little, Brown, 1938], 68). Antongini's book is in the Key West inventory (Michael S. Reynolds, *Hemingway's Reading: 1910–1940: An Inventory* [Princeton: Princeton Univ. Press, 1981], item 1943). Praz includes incest in the character portfolio of the Fatal Woman (*Romantic Agony*, 226–7). Nicholas Gerogiannis argues that Hemingway's Renata is a fusion of the caring daughter of *Notturno* and La Foscarina in *Il fuoco*, who possess 'wisdom,' 'sacrificing spirit,' and an 'erotic personality' ('Hemingway's Poetry: Angry Notes of an Ambivalent Overman,' in Bernard Oldsey, ed., *Ernest Hemingway: The Papers of a Writer* [New York: Garland, 1981], 76). Yet Hemingway's Renata would seem to have little wisdom or sense of sacrifice.

31 Praz, *Romantic Agony*, 266.

32 Robert W. Lewis (*Hemingway in Love*, 183) suggests that Renata may whisper of being pregnant, but surely they would have discussed a pregnancy – and his fatherhood – further. She stops Cantwell from taking off his 'tunic' (211) in his hotel room, a clear sign of a refusal that he reluctantly must accept. 'I am now inclined to think that the "disappointment" may be her period,' Lewis said (private communication, 8 Jan. 1988).

33 Praz, *Romantic Agony*, 204.

34 D'Annunzio, *Il fuoco*, 62.

35 Robert W. Lewis, Jr, private communication, 8 Jan. 1988.

36 D'Annunzio, *Il fuoco*, 84, 87: 'the soul of Venice ... is autumnal.'

37 Marina Gradoli, 'Italy in E. Hemingway's Fiction,' in Alfredo Rizzardi, ed., *Italy and Italians in America, RSA (Rivista di Studi Anglo-Americani)*, 3, nos. 4–5 (1984–5): 148.

38 On Dante's *Inferno* XV, the homosexuals and the new moon, see Kathleen Verdun, 'Hemingway's Dante: A Note on *Across the River and Into the Trees*,' *American Literature*, 57, no. 4 (1985): 633–40.

39 Harrison, *Mythology*, 88.

40 Maureen O'Shaughnessey, 'Painters and Painting in *Across the River and Into the Trees*,' in Sanderson, ed., *Hemingway's Italy*, 207. In her interpretation, Renata possesses 'Madonna-like purity and innocence' (208).

41 Yeats placed the passage at the beginning of his *Oxford Book of Modern Verse* (1939). 'What has been less routinely noticed,' writes Hugh Kenner on Hemingway, 'is the wholly aesthetic basis of all his values: aesthetic, decadent, in the fin-de-siècle sense: the sense of the forlorn aesthetes, Dowson and Symons, Pater and Oscar Wilde' (*A Homemade World: the American Modernist Writer* [New York: Knopf, 1979], 141–2).

42 Walter Pater, *The Renaissance* (New York: Boni and Liveright, 1929), 103.

43 Williams, *Tragic Art*, 158.

44 On De Staël's *Corinne*, Kenneth Churchill comments: 'everything in Venice becomes a symbol of sadness, of dissatisfaction with life: the lack of vegetation which other travellers had grumbled about as making them dis-oriented here becomes elegiac' (*Italy and English Literature, 1764–1930* [Totowa, NJ: Barnes and Noble, 1980], 28).

45 O'Shaughnessey does not raise this possibility in 'Painters and Painting in *Across the River and Into the Trees*,' 201–11. Hemingway owned twenty books on Italian art, and corresponded with Bernard Berenson while he was writing the novel (202–3).

46 Michael S. Reynolds, *The Young Hemingway* (Oxford: Blackwell, 1896), 126. For D'Annunzio's reputation in America, see Alberta Fabris Grube, 'La fortuna americana di D'Annunzio,' in Patrizia Bellman Nerozzi, ed., *Gabriele D'Annunzio e la cultura inglese e americana* (Chieti: Marino Solfanelli, 1990), 35–44.

47 Kenneth S. Lynn, *Hemingway* (New York: Simon and Schuster, 1897), 134.

48 Anthony Rhodes, *D'Annunzio: The Poet as Superman* (New York: McDowell, Obolensky, 1959), 175.

49 Lynn, *Hemingway*, 415.

50 Michael Ledeen, *The First Duce: D'Annunzio at Fiume* (Baltimore: Johns Hopkins Univ. Press, 1977), 7–8. Ledeen rejects Philippe Julian's suggestion (in *D'Annunzio* [New York: Viking, 1973], 23, 70–1) that D'Annunzio's appeal to both men and women lies in his buried bisexuality. Lynn reports that Hemingway's mother thought of her baby son as the 'twin' of his older sister, dressing him as a girl till he was six; and that Hemingway was obsessed with homosexuality, lesbianism, impotence, incest, transvestitism, and transexuality (*Hemingway*, 38–45, 57–8, 76–7, 286, 311, 541–4).

51 Praz, *Romantic Agony*, 386.
52 Moravia, *Man as an End*, 232. Moravia denigrates the 'myth' both writers built up of themselves, comparing them unfavourably with Malraux, 'a terribly serious European intellectual' (like himself) (233–4).
53 Eugenio Montale, 'William Faulkner,' *Selected Essays*, trans. G. Singh (Manchester: Carcanet, 1978), 139; in the same essay Hemingway is described as 'extrovert, bizarre, apparently anti-literary but in reality very cultured and up-to-date' (139). Hemingway is 'the most naturally European – Stendhalian – of the American writers' (Eugenio Montale, 'Uncle Ez,' *The Second Life of Art: Selected Essays*, trans. Jonathan Galassi [New York: Ecco, 1982], 204).
54 Montale, 'Hemingway – *Across the River and Into the Trees*,' *Selected Essays*, 136: 'Hemingway himself came to realize the dangers of that identification.'.
55 Terry Mort, *The Hemingway Patrols: Ernest Hemingway and His Hunt for U-boats* (New York: Scribner, 2009), 226: the epilogue is entitled 'The Meaning of Nothing.' Gerogiannis perpetuates the myth: 'Hemingway's last true heroic gesture was the wartime adventure aboard the *Pilar*' ('Hemingway's Poetry,' in *Ernest Hemingway*, 85).
56 Lynn, *Hemingway*, 502–4: 'a charade.'
57 Osbert Sitwell, 'Fiume and D'Annunzio,' *Discursions on Travel, Art and Life* (1925; Westport: Greenwood, 1970), 237. Hemingway appears to have read this essay (Reynolds, *Hemingway's Reading*, item 1943).
58 Hemingway, *88 Poems,* ed. Nicholas Gerogiannis (New York: Harcourt Brace Jovanovich, 1979), 28.
59 Cf. 'He tried to spit out the truth' ('Ultimately' [1922] [*88 Poems*, 39]).
60 Peter Griffin, *Along with Youth: Hemingway, The Early Years* (New York: Oxford Univ. Press, 1985), 123–4. The unpublished story is in the Hemingway Collection, item nos. 843 and 844 (fragments), John F. Kennedy Library, Boston (Hemingway counted 5,157 words).
61 Giovanni Checchin, 'Hemingway, Fulco Ruffo di Calabria, Enrico Serena e Bianca Maria Bèllia,' in Sergio Perosa, ed., *Hemingway e Venezia* (Florence: Olschki, 1988), 59.
62 Both Hemingway and D'Annunzio were indebted to Huysman. John Gaggin, *Hemingway and Nineteenth-Century Aestheticism* (Ann Arbor: UMI Research, 1988), 77–8. Huysman's *Against the Grain* is in the Key West inventory (Reynolds, *Hemingway's Reading*, item 1158).
63 Item no. 843, Hemingway Collection, John F. Kennedy Library, Boston. The story 'went through several versions, only the last of which has survived. It was essentially finished by the spring of 1920' (Reynolds, *Young Hemingway*, 265).
64 Thus Gaggin on Wilde's Dorian Gray: 'a decadent of the stereotyped variety,

squeezing a few drops of sensation from a culture that he, in a superficial way, perceives as vulgar and sterile. [Gray and Lord Henry] convey a *fin-de-siècle* sense that their society is enervated, that whatever vitality is available to people can be attained only by a forcible wringing of nearly desiccated cultural fabric' (*Hemingway and Nineteenth-Century Aestheticism*, 77).

65 Gabriele D'Annunzio, *Forse che sì forse che no* (Milan: Mondadori, 1982), 163–4.

66 Ledeen examines the D'Annunzian practice of employing 'religious symbols in traditionally secular contexts' (9, 145, 202): 'Fiume was the beginning of a spiritual blaze that would consume all of the rotting and decrepit Western world and that would purify the West, eventually transforming it into something finer and holier' (72).

67 Rhodes, *D'Annunzio*, 187.

68 Renzo De Felice, *D'Annunzio politico: 1918–1938* (Bari: Laterza, 1978), 148. The Shelleyan analogy should be qualified; the influence of Nietzsche strengthened D'Annunzio's distaste for the masses, rejection of democracy, and affirmation of a "privileged caste" in command of the state. See Mario Pomilio, 'D'Annunzio e l'Abruzzo,' in *L'arte di Gabriele D'Annunzio* (Milan: Mondadori, 1968), 614–15, ctd in Paolo Alatri, ed., *Scritti politici di Gabriele D'Annunzio* (Milan: Feltrinelli, 1980), 25.

69 Thomas Nelson Page, the American ambassador to Italy (1913–19) who was well disposed to Italian irredentist claims, felt that D'Annunzio's was a 'harebrained enterprise' that 'destroyed all chance of settling the matter immediately and complicated the situation beyond the possibility of pacific diplomatic adjustment' (*Italy and the World War* [New York: Scribner's, 1920], 402).

70 Cf. Tommaso Antongini, *Gli allegri filibustieri di D'Annunzio* (Milan: A. Martello, 1951) on the exploits of the *Uscocchi*.

71 John Buchan, *A History of the Great War*, 3 vols. (Boston: Houghton Mifflin, 1922), 3:543.

72 Enrico Mercatali and Guido Vicenzoni, *La guerra italiana: cronistoria illustrata degli avvenimenti*, 8 vols. (Milan: Sonzogno, 1915–18), 7:7, 66, 203, 223.

73 'The Mercenaries,' at least twice rejected and then withdrawn by Hemingway, was published in 1985 (Griffin, *Along with Youth*, 104–12).

74 Reynolds, *Young Hemingway*, 126.

75 Checchin, 'Hemingway, Fulco Ruffo di Calabria,' in *Hemingway e Venezia*, 60–61. There is further evidence tying an aunt of Fulco Ruffo to Agnes von Kurowsky, the nurse who turned down Hemingway's marriage proposal. Hence, Hemingway's revenge on Ruffo through Il Lupo (63–4).

76 Vito Salierno, *D'Annunzio e Mussolini: Storia di una cordiale inimicizia* (Milan:

Mursia, 1988), 9: As D'Annunzio addressed the people of Rome, 4 May 1919, 'Lupi di Firenzi, Lupi di Giovanni Randaccio, a chi la vittoria? I Lupi: "A noi!"'

77 Rhodes, *D'Annunzio*, 69–70.

78 D'Annunzio's 'theory was that fear is natural to the body, and that courage to control it belongs to the mind' (Rhodes, *D'Annunzio*, 180). Hemingway explained the relation between courage and imagination to his son in terms similar to Ricaud's explanation to Rinaldi (Lynn, *Hemingway*, 501).

79 Reynolds, *Young Hemingway*, 126.

80 'Etna to Sweden in Big Match Merger – D'Annunzio Coup Planned' (24 Feb. 1921 Ernest Hemingway, *Dateline: Toronto: The Complete* Toronto Star *Dispatches, 1920–24* (New York: Scribner's, 1985), 69.

81 D'Annunzio may have derived this use of the image for aesthetic creativity from Shelley, whom he read closely. In *Prometheus Unbound* Shelley places Demogorgon's cave in a terrain resembling Mt. Vesuvius, which he had visited. For references to volcanoes in *Il fuoco*, see *The Flame of Life*, trans. Kassandra Vivaria (New York: Boni and Liveright, 1900), 90, 121, 196, 372. Cf. Earl R. Wasserman, *Shelley's* Prometheus Unbound: *A Critical Reading* (Baltimore: Johns Hopkins Univ. Press, 1965), 156.

82 De Felice, *D'Annunzio politico: 1918–1938*, 104, 108, 147ff. De Felice rejects the notion that D'Annunzio is the 'John the Baptist of Fascism,' a role he assigns to Giolitti (cf. Salierno, *D'Annunzio e Mussolini*, 51, 58–9, 69–70, 77, 81, 103–4).

83 Ernest Hemingway, *Selected Letters*, ed. Carlos Baker (New York: Scribner's, 1981), 114.

84 For the relation between Cantwell's Renata and D'Annunzio's daughter Renata, see Adeline R. Tintner, 'The Significance of D'Annunzio in *Across the River and Into the Trees*,' *Hemingway Review*, 5, no. 1 (1985): 11.

85 D'Annunzio, *Il fuoco*, 164.

86 This is the second, kindly 'boatman' (42–3) in the novel, not to be confused with the surly Charon-like boatman. Hemingway thus divides the death symbol into 'good' and 'bad' components, in keeping with his consistently contradictory attitude towards death. As mentioned previously, both Cantwell and his driver Jackson have lost brothers to war (both in the Pacific). The three men are united by death.

87 'Dix jours en Italie,' in Philippe Barrès, ed., *L'Oeuvre de Maurice Barrès*, 20 vols. (Paris: Club de l'Honnête Homme, 1965–68), 9:115. Tintner points out that this 'little villa' is not the one in which D'Annunzio lived with Duse in 1896, but the one in which, with Renata at his side, he recovered from his war wound and wrote *Notturno* in 1916. Hemingway thus strengthens his

association with Renata and his fondness for this particular work ('The Significance of D'Annunzio,' 11).

88 Lynn, *Hemingway*, 59, 64, 168, 468, 480, 515, 516. In a dispatch to the *Toronto Star* (24 Oct. 1922), Hemingway said, 'The Jews claim that Kemal is a Jew. His thin rigid face does look Jewish. But the Jews also claim Gabriele D'Annunzio and Christopher Columbus and a thousand years or so from now may even be claiming Henry Ford. At any rate that rumor about Kemal is doing him no harm' (235).

89 Such mimetic hostility informs the relations between Jake Barnes and the 'Jewish' Cohn in *The Sun Also Rises*, resulting in Jake's projection of self-loathing onto Cohn.

90 Hemingway's self-hatred over his inability to place himself fully at risk in war, first set forth in 'The Woppian Way,' is one of the vexing questions in his biography. He put himself at some risk as an ambulance driver and engaged in riskier pursuits (game hunting), but he knew the difference. In 'The Woppian Way' the journalist, recalling his war-time service, protests that 'we were protected by the "Nothing can hit an ambulance" myth that some cheerful propagandist started in 1914'; it would appear that he wants to earn our sympathy for bravery.

91 'Se quello fu amore, che è mai questo che ci strazia e ci moltiplica? Se quello fu sacrificio, quale prova ci sarà oggi dimandata? quale siamo noi per dare? Morire non basta. Se morire è cessare di combattere, non si può morire. Bisogna rialzarsi.' Gabriele D'Annunzio, 'A una radunata di ufficiali d'ogni arma,' in *La Riscossa* (Milan: Bestetti and Tumminelli, 1918), 23. Cf. 'Italia o Morte' (9 Sept. 1919), in Gabriele D'Annunzio, *La penultima ventura: Scritti e discorsi fiumani* , ed. Renzo De Felice (Milan: Mondadori, 1974), 111: 'Ma, come nei giorni di Caporetto, morire non basta.'

92 Hemingway, *Dateline*, 'He is a fighter Lloyd George. But he knows the truth of what Gabriele D'Annunzio says, *"Morire non basta."* "It is not enough to die." You must survive to win' (320).

93 Ernest Hemingway, *A Farewell to Arms* (New York: Scribner's, 1929), 196.

94 Hemingway, *A Farewell to Arms*, 193. Also, the day on which Henry has this interior monologue is one of storms and rain. In Hemingway, rain is a common image for oppression and grief.

95 Early in the twentieth century *Il fuoco* was translated at least three times into English, testifying to the strength of D'Annunzio's reputation. See Barbara Arnette Melchiori, 'The Early D'Annunzio in England,' Robert Gordon, 'D'Annunzio sulla scena inglese,' and Alberta Fabris Grube, 'La fortuna americana di D'Annunzio,' all in Bellman Nerozzi, ed., *Gabriele D'Annunzio*; and Gerogiannis, 'Hemingway's Poetry,' in *Ernest Hemingway*, 86–7, nn. 14, 18).

96 *Notturno* is not in the Key West inventory. Having spoken on 'translations,' Cantwell may not have had enough Italian to read the original. There was a French translation (1923).

97 Eugenio Montale, interview with Ernest Hemingway, *Corriere della sera*, 25 March 1954: 'Ha letto D'Annunzio? Fa un salto sul letto e cerca di imitarlo gridando: "Vivere non è basta!" Poi ricorda, mi pare con lode, il *Notturno*.'

98 Hemingway's interest in D'Annunzio remained to the end; he owned a copy of Frances Winwar's *Wingless Victory: A Biography of Gabriele D'Annunzio and Eleonora Duse*, published in 1956 (see *Hemingway's Library: A Composite Record*, ed. James D. Brasch and Joseph Sigman [New York: Garland, 1981]).

7 The Hidden Godfather: Plenitude and Absence in Coppola's Trilogy

1 Mario Puzo, *The Godfather Papers and Other Confessions* (New York: Putnam's, 1972), 33. 'Never sufficiently credited,' Puzo 'created the mythic characters and primal narrative conceits that made Francis Ford Coppola's incomparable *Godfather* films possible' (Thomas J. Ferraro, 'Catholic Ethnicity and Modern American Arts,' in Pellegrino D'Acierno, ed., *The Italian American Heritage: A Companion to Literature and Arts* [New York: Garland, 1999], 349).

2 Pauline Kael, review (1972) of *Godfather I*, in *For Keeps* (New York: Plume, 1996), 434.

3 Puzo, *Godfather Papers*, 41.

4 T.S. Eliot, 'Tradition and the Individual Talent,' in *Selected Essays, 1917–1932* (New York: Harcourt Brace, 1950), 5.Throughout this essay *The Godfather* (1972), *The Godfather Part II* (1974), and *The Godfather Part III* (1990) will be referred to as *Godfather I, II,* and *III* in the text and notes.

5 Robert B. Ray, *A Certain Tendency of the Hollywood Cinema, 1930–1980* (Princeton: Princeton Univ. Press, 1985), 253–6, 328, 331–5, 341.

6 Harlan Lebo, *The Godfather Legacy* (New York: Simon & Schuster, 1997), 40–4, 96–7.

7 James Monaco, *How to Read a Film* (1977; New York: Oxford Univ. Press, 2009), 382; John Hess, '*Godfather II:* A Deal Coppola Couldn't Refuse,' in Bill Nichols, ed., *Movies and Methods: An Anthology*, 2 vols. (Berkeley: Univ. of California Press, 1976), 1:82; Nick Browne, 'Fearful A-Symmetries: Violence as History in the *Godfather* Films,' in Browne, ed., *Francis Ford Coppola's* The Godfather *Trilogy* (Cambridge: Cambridge Univ. Press, 2000), 1.

8 William Malyszko, *The Godfather* (London: York, 2001), 7.

9 Fran Mason, *American Gangster Cinema: from* Little Caesar *to* Pulp Fiction (New York: Palgrave, 2002), 130; Thomas J. Ferraro, *Feeling Italian: The Art of Ethnicity in America* (New York: New York Univ. Press, 2005), 107. The enduring popular success of the films indicates that their mythic appeal went well

beyond a specific ethnicity and claimed the support of other ethnicities, and even the mainstream.

10 Werner Jaeger, *Paideia*, 3 vols. (Chicago: Univ. of Chicago Press, 1943), 1:59. The gangster *as myth* traces to such films as Wallace McCutchen Jr's *The Black Hand* (1906) and D.W. Griffith's *The Musketeers of Pig Alley* (1912). By 1960, it had established itself through such films as *Little Caesar*, *Public Enemy*, *Scarface*, and *White Heat*, as well as the FBI and congressional investigations.

11 Pellegrino D'Acierno, 'Cinema Paradiso: The Italian American Presence in American Cinema,' in *Italian American Heritage*, 568–69. Richard A. Blake, SJ writes that *Godfather I* and *II* are 'too far removed in theme and style from the classics to fit into the category of Gangster film' with their seedy characters and Depression atmosphere. Yet this is to define the genre too narrowly; his remarks on the *Godfather* soundtrack are also off the mark: 'The rich color and Nino Rota's bouncy [!] Italian music undercut the gritty atmosphere of the classics' (*Screening America: Reflections on Five Classic Films* [New York: Paulist, 1991], 142).

12 Chris Messenger, *The Godfather and American Culture* (Albany: State Univ. of New York Press, 2002), 230; Mason, *American Gangster Cinema*, 129.

13 Stephen Farber, 'Coppola and *The Godfather*,' *Sight and Sound*, 41 (Autumn 1972): 223. Certainly the popular response to the films by various ethnicities and mainstream culture would seem to indicate that he had made his point.

14 C.M. Bowra, *Heroic Poetry* (New York: St. Martin's, 1966), 4, 132.

15 Farber, 'Coppola and *The Godfather*,' 223. Just to mention the gangster genre, in Hollywood film history godfather roles had gone to non-Italians, most memorably to Edward G. Robinson, Paul Muni, Luther Adler, Kirk Douglas – and Brando in *The Godfather*, which goes to show how long the tradition persisted. Eduardo Ciannelli in *Winterset* (1936) is an important exception.

16 George De Stefano, *An Offer We Can't Refuse: The Mafia in the Mind of America* (New York: Faber and Faber, 2006), 98, 107.

17 Ctd in Robert B. Ray, *The ABCs of Classic Hollywood* (New York: Oxford Univ. Press, 2008), 56–7.

18 Ray connects this theme to the Horatio Alger myth (*Certain Tendency*, 334).

19 Stephen Louis Karpf, *The Gangster Film: Emergence, Variation, and Decay of a Genre: 1930–40* (New York: Arno, 1973), 60: 'He bettered himself in the only way he understood. There was never indication that the more socially acceptable characters and their way of life were preferable to Rico and the road he had chosen' (p. 60).

20 Edmund Burke, *Reflections on the Revolution in France* (London: Macmillan, 1906), 85.

21 Robert Warshow, *The Immediate Experience* (New York: Atheneum, 1971), 131: 'for the gangster there is only the city; he must inhabit it in order to personify it: not the real city, but that dangerous and sad city of the imagination ... which is the modern world' (131).

22 Bowra, *Heroic Poetry*, 4.

23 Edmund Burke, *A Philosophical Inquiry into ... the Sublime and the Beautiful*, ed. James T. Boulton (Notre Dame: Univ. of Notre Dame Press, 1968), 82, 84.

24 *Godfather I* and *II* were in their originally released formats and times, 176 minutes and 200 minutes respectively; and *Godfather III* was issued in a director's cut that added 9 minutes to the original's 140. On a separate disk were thirty-four scenes or parts of scenes shot for the three films but not included in their final versions: nine from 1901–1927; ten from 1945; seven from 1947–1955; and eight from 1978–1997.

25 Georg Lukács, *The Theory of the Novel*, trans. Anna Bostock (Cambridge: MIT Press, 1971), 29.

26 Coppola's Mafia is a myth to which many Americans and Italian Americans subscribe, thanks to its marketing in film, television, fiction, etc. However, as the FBI, the police, most scholars, and Coppola himself (in his better moments) know, the real Mafia is different, and the Sicilian Mafia differs markedly from the American one, in social mores, in organization, and in relations to the state. For the Sicilian Mafia, see Diego Gambetta, *The Sicilian Mafia: The Business of Private Protection* (Cambridge: Harvard Univ. Press, 1993); Salvatore Lupo, *Storia della Mafia dalle origini ai giorni nostri* (Rome: Donzelli, 1993); Peter Robb, *Midnight in Sicily* (London: Faber and Faber, 1996); James Fentress, *Rebels and Mafiosi: Death in a Sicilian Landscape* (Ithaca: Cornell Univ. Press, 2000); Filippo Sabetti, *Village Politics and the Mafia in Sicily* (Montreal: McGill-Queen's Univ. Press, 2002); and John Dickie, *Cosa Nostra: A History of the Sicilian Mafia* (New York: Palgrave, 2004). For the American Mafia, see Stephen R. Fox, *Blood and Power: Organized Crime in Twentieth-Century America* (New York: W. Morrow, 1989); Howard Abadinsky, *Organized Crime*, 7th ed. (Belmont, CA: Wadsworth/Thomson Learning, 2003); and Thomas Reppetto, *American Mafia: A History of Its Rise to Power* (New York: Henry Holt, 2004).

27 In this respect, to the extent Italian Americans retain their ethnicity, they maintain *Gemeinschaft* values. 'Ethnicity,' writes Andrew Greeley, 'is one of the forms of *Gemeinschaft* that has survived in a rationalized, bureaucratized society.' Ctd by Joseph Lopreato and Timothy Alan Crippen, *Crisis in Sociology: The Need for Darwin* (New Brunswick, NJ: Transaction, 1999), 257.

28 Elias Canetti, *Crowds and Power*, trans. Carol Stewart (New York: Continuum, 1978), 290. Cf. the cinematic mise-en-scène of Vittorio De Seta's *Banditi a Orgosolo* (1960).

29 Wayland Young, 'The Montesi Affair,' *Encounter*, Sept. 1957, 30.

30 Robert Phillip Kolker, *A Cinema of Loneliness: Penn, Kubrick, Coppola, Scorsese, Altman* (New York: Oxford Univ. Press, 1980), 161.

31 Kael, *For Keeps*, 435.

32 William Simon, 'An Analysis of the Structure of *The Godfather, Part One*,' *Studies in the Literary Imagination*, 16 (1983): 78.

33 Irvin L. Child, *Italian or American? The Second Generation in Conflict* (New Haven: Yale Univ. Press, 1943), 76ff.

34 'What appears initially as opposition,' notes Simon, 'is progressively understood as dialectical' ('An Analysis,' 79).

35 Peter Biskind, *The Godfather Companion* (New York: HarperPerennial, 1990), 56.

36 Eduardo De Filippo's *Fortunella* (1958), with a script by De Filippo and Federico Fellini. See Franco Sciannameo, *Nino Rota, Federico Fellini, and the Making of an Italian Cinematic Folk Opera: Amarcord* (Lewiston: Mellen, 2005), 12.

37 The First Communion party scene was shot outdoors in October when the weather had turned cold, hence the quality of the light, which was aesthetically appropriate.

38 Coppola, ctd in Lebo, *Godfather Legacy*, 216. 'A careful reading of Part One,' writes Simon, 'makes it clear that this critical image of Michael and the values by which he lives have already been fully achieved' ('An Analysis,' 88–9).

39 Ctd in Hess, '*Godfather II*,' 1:83; and Farber, 'Coppola and *The Godfather*,' 223. For Frederic Jameson, 'the Mafia is not a substitution for American business, but the very thing itself,' the polarities being the Mafia as wild capitalism and the family as utopian fantasy; the tension is presented in *Godfather I* and deconstructed in *Godfather II;* Mason argues that deconstruction begins not in *Godfather II* but at the outset of *I* (*American Gangster Cinema*, 130).

40 Biskind, *Godfather Companion*, 61. The relation of the film to the Mafia, from pre-production to reception and beyond, would make a book in itself.

41 Ctd in Biskind, *Godfather Companion*, 117.

42 Ctd in Robert K. Johnson, *Francis Ford Coppola* (Boston: Twayne, 1977), 148; and Lebo, *Godfather Legacy*, 215.

43 Biskind, citing Judith Vogelsang on orange symbolism, provides numerous examples in *Godfather I* and *II ;* Richard Bright, who plays Al Neri in all three films, said 'The symbol of evil was a fuckin' orange' (*Godfather Companion*, 46–7, 112). See also Malyszko, *Godfather*, 42.

44 Thomas Schatz, *Hollywood Genres: Formulas, Filmmaking, and the Studio System* (Philadelphia: Temple Univ. Press, 2001), 82–3.

45 Ray, *ABCs of Classic Hollywood*, 19–20: 'for me,' writes Andrew Sarris, '*mise-en-*

scène is not merely the gap between what we see and feel on the screen and what we can express in words, but it also the gap between the intention of the director and his effect upon the spectator' (20).

46 Ctd in Johnson, *Francis Ford Coppola*, 111. Hess writes quite mistakenly that *Godfather II*'s 'real strength ... is its demonstration that the benefits of the family structure and the hope for community have been destroyed by capitalism'; 'American gangsterdom, the perfect microcosm of American capitalism' ('*Godfather II*,' 1:82, 89). But with the exception of a few ideological holdouts and Coppola himself (in Havana Michael acknowledges the strength of the Cuban revolutionary over the gangsters), it is impossible to lay the sins of the godfathers at the door of capitalism.

47 E.g., the Mafioso Don Ciccio in Pietro Germi's satirical *Divorzio all'italiana* (1961).

48 H.J. Treston, *Poine: A Study in Ancient Greek Blood Vengeance*, ctd in William Chase Greene, *Moira: Fate, Good, and Evil in Greek Thought* (New York: Harper, 1944), 405. The killing of Don Ciccio 'emphasizes Vito's connection to Old-World notions of justice' (Fred L. Gardaphé, *From Wise Guys to Wise Men: The Gangster and Italian American Masculinities* [London: Routledge, 2006], 39).

49 'He did the unthinkable Italian crime, he walked out on his family. They don't even have a name for this.' It is the chief sacrilege in the religion of the family (Don DeLillo, *Underworld* [New York: Scribner, 1997], 204).

50 Luigi Barzini, *The Italians* (New York: Atheneum, 1964), 273.

51 Don Vito 'is not only Godfather ... He is also, at least in the eyes of his dependents, no less than God the Father.' Robert Viscusi, 'Professions and Faiths: Critical Choices in the Italian American Novel,' in Remigio U. Pane, ed., *Italian Americans in the Professions* (New York: American Italian Historical Association, 1983), 50.

52 Canetti, *Crowds and Power*, 389–90. The symbolism persists in sitting courts and country seats; the *cathedra* of bishops and professors, from the Greek *kata*, 'down,' and *hedra*, 'seat'; chairs of departments, the Chair of Saint Peter, the Judgment Seat; and president, from the Latin *prae-sidere*, to 'sit before,' 'protect,' 'command,' even 'unseat.'

53 Kolker, *A Cinema of Loneliness*, 173–4.

54 Canetti, *Crowds and Power*, 394: 'Kneeling is always in some sense a prelude to a last moment. It is a form of flattery, and extreme because it has to attract attention' (394).

55 Canetti, *Crowds and Power*, 390.

56 Cf. Giovanni Verga, 'L'Asino di S. Giuseppe,' *Vita dei Campi* (1880).

57 Ctd in Hess, '*Godfather II*,' 1:86; Ray, *Certain Tendency*, 341.

58 Cf. Francesco Mulas's chapter 'Prolepsis in Mario Puzo's *The Godfather*,' *Studies on Italian-American Literature* (New York: Center for Migration Studies, 1995), 49–50.

59 Biskind, *Godfather Companion*, 117.

60 Hess, '*Godfather II*,' 1:85.

61 Coppola, ctd in Johnson, *Francis Ford Coppola*, 148.

62 Michael Ventre on *The Sopranos*, MS.NBC, 6 June 2007.

63 Jon Lewis, 'If History Has Taught Us Anything ... Francis Coppola, Paramount Studios, and *The Godfather Parts I, II,* and *III*,' in *Francis Ford Coppola's* The Godfather *Trilogy*, 47. Mancuso wanted the film ready for the 1990 Christmas season.

64 Michael Schumacher, *Francis Ford Coppola: A Filmmaker's Life* (New York: Crown, 1999), 417.

65 Script problems were compounded by severe weather, cost overruns, and Martin Sheen's heart attack. Eleanor Coppola wrote a memoir, *Notes* (New York: Simon and Schuster, 1979) and directed a documentary, *Hearts of Darkness* (1991), on the filming of *Apocalypse Now*.

66 Ctd in Biskind, *Godfather Companion*, 156.

67 'The Coppola family was spiritual to an extreme, but not religious,' writes Peter Cowie, 'attending church was a means of finding girls.' If the spiritual is 'to an extreme,' it should be examined, but Cowie goes off on another tangent, writing that 'August proved the ideal elder brother in such circumstances' (finding girls), and the thread is lost (*Coppola* [New York: Scribner's, 1990], 17).

68 Also in the background are Propaganda Due (P2), the secret Masonic lodge of high-echelon, influence-peddling Italians of all political and institutional stripes, and Banco Ambrosiano chairman Roberto Calvi, 'God's Banker,' found hanged beneath a bridge in 1982 (historically, Blackfriars in London; in the film, Ponte S. Angelo, Rome). The Banco Ambrosiano was accused of laundering Mafia money while defrauding the mismanaged Vatican out of hundreds of millions. For the ties among the Vatican, Paramount Pictures, Immobiliare, and the financiers Michele Sindona and Roberto Calvi, see Gene D. Phillips, *Godfather: The Intimate Francis Ford Coppola* (Lexington: Univ. Press of Kentucky, 2004), 135–9.

69 Another example of this habit is the inclusion of an inside family joke: Johnny Fontane says he is going to sing the godfather's favourite song 'Salsicce His Own,' 'To Each His Own.'

70 Yet Biskind writes 'oranges are more or less absent' in *Godfather III* (*Godfather Companion*, 177).

71 Geoff Fordham, 'A Study in Ambiguity: *The Godfather* and the American

Gangster Movie Tradition,' in Alain Silver and James Ursini, eds., *The Gangster Film Reader* (Pompton Plains, NJ: Limelight, 2007), 177.

72 Michael includes the Church hierarchy in his condemnation: 'they're the same problem ... they're connected.' Such remarks seem less intelligent than Michael – the script's fault.

73 He cites *King Lear* on bastards as liars to insult Vincent; Coppola had been reading Shakespeare and Greek drama to prepare himself for *Godfather III.*

74 Hagen was to have figured importantly in *Godfather III,* but Coppola and Paramount supposedly could not pay Robert Duvall's asking fee. B.J. Harrison, Connie, and Altobello share the consigliere duties. Scheduling prevented Frank Sinatra from playing Altobello; it would have been a memorable addition to the tableau.

75 For this we have not so much Coppola as Pacino to thank, for while his performance is authoritative and spellbinding, his lines are pitiful, e.g., responding to Kay's backing of Anthony becoming an opera singer instead of a lawyer: 'Well, music is great. I love music. But he should finish what he started.'

76 Antonio Meucci invented the telephone but was denied the honour, until the U.S. Congress interceded with a declaration in 1974.

77 Gilday is an Irish bishop; it would be more likely for Michael to have found an Irish American prelate with whom to make his move to legitimacy.

78 In the 1970s and 1980s the big corporations took over Las Vegas from the Mafia, so it is possible that Michael was paid off handsomely and then distributed some of the money in turn. Only the corporations could finance the increasingly popular mega-hotel resort casinos, beginning with Caesars Palace (1966).

79 'As a landowner in association with northern [Italian] businessmen and the church, [Michael] becomes the symbolic exploiter of his own people. In a sense, he returns to the past ... but now he is on the wrong side.' Vera Dika, 'The Representation of Ethnicity in *The Godfather,'* in *Francis Ford Coppola's The Godfather Trilogy,* 100.

80 Paramount used this heavy-handed line for promotion. It is a gangster film trope, e.g., 'I tried to go clean and you dragged me down,' spoken by mob boss Al Mungar (Martin Gabel) talking to his son in *Lady in Cement* (1968), the second of Sinatra's Tony Rome films. Like Don Vito, Mungar wants his son to succeed in the mainstream ('You're gonna make up for every lousy thing I was ashamed of'); and like Don Vito, he fails.

81 The poster on the opera house reads 14 April in the season 1978–79; the script, 1979–80.

82 Jeffrey Chown, *Hollywood Auteur: Francis Coppola* (New York: Praeger, 1988), 73.

83 An anachronism; the theatre was closed for repairs from 1974 to 1997.

84 Marilyn Yaquinto, *Pump 'em Full of Lead* (New York: Twayne, 1998), 167; I fail to read 'heartbreaking anguish' (167) on Connie's part.

85 Alan Mallach, *Pietro Mascagni and His Operas* (Boston: Northeastern Univ. Press, 2002), 66: 'There is no local color in *Cavalleria* … it was part of his design to avoid anything that might be perceived as exotic or folkloric, that would put distance between the audience and the immediacy of the events taking place' on stage' (68). But what of the traditional outfits, a *bettola*, a donkey cart, the knife? The whole 'Siciliana' – the piece Turiddu sings behind the curtain at the beginning of the opera, in the middle of the prelude – is traditionally sung in dialect.

86 In the opera, the challenge scene occurs late; but it is after this scene that Coppola sets an 'intermission.' His second 'act' is comprised of the Easter procession (which is much earlier in the opera) and Turiddu's farewell. The opera, in one act, has no formal intermission, but the Intermezzo serves a similar purpose. An unintended consequence of Coppola's decision to end his 'act' with the challenge is that the actors are left on stage without any music to guide them off; nor does the curtain drop. So Turiddu and the other singers must walk off without an accompaniment, as if at a dress rehearsal. Coppola could have spared his singers this awkwardness by cutting to another plotline.

87 It is one of the film's best moments; Zeffirelli merely has the chorus end its procession on a crowded church staircase. The risen Christ in *Godfather III* is or resembles one of the dead bodyguards.

88 Ronald Bergan, *Francis Ford Coppola* (New York: Thunder's Mouth, 1998), 93.

89 Walter Murch, 'Foreword: Collaborating with Coppola,' in Phillips, *Godfather*, xiii. He is wrong to say that after the scream 'the film – and the trilogy – is over'; there is the final scene, Michael's death.

90 The eighteenth-century debate between J.J. Winckelmann and G.F. Lessing focused upon the distinction between works of art that exist in space (painting, sculpture) and those that move in time (music, poetry). Winckelmann preferred the statue *Laocoon* to Virgil's Laocoon (*Aeneid* II) because in the statue the mouth of screaming Laocoon is only partly open – he shows stoic restraint in enduring his pain; in Virgil, one imagines the screaming mouth is open wide, which Winckelmann found aesthetically displeasing. Lessing countered that Virgil's Laocoon can scream because, in poetry, one does not have to 'see' his wide-open mouth, one assumes that a mouth is open wide to scream; in the *Laocoon*, which aims at a beautiful moment, the

statue's mouth must only be partly open or it would be grotesque. Pacino's gaping scream works because of the sudden silence, which derealizes or aestheticizes it, making it 'louder' than any naturalistic scream.

91 Mason's comment that the film is 'an attempt to return to the mythic ideology of the family as a cultural rather than criminal entity, embedded in its Sicilian traditions where it simply has the function of a paternalistic agency of protection' (*American Gangster Cinema*, 135) is reductive; does the Sicilian 'mythic ideology' mean 'simply' that the family is a 'paternalistic agency'?

92 Ctd in Bergan, *Francis Ford Coppola*, 90.

93 Pacino carries this film. His performance, not only in *Godfather III* but in the two previous films as well, represents an achievement against which American film actors will be measured for years to come. It may perhaps be the final testimony to Puzo's and Coppola's impoverished script and shoddy direction that Pacino was not even nominated for an Academy Award for Best Actor.

94 Michael Goodwin and Naomi Wise, *On the Edge: The Life and Times of Francis Coppola* (New York: William Morrow, 1988), 462–3.

95 Cowie, *Coppola*, 8. At one bash Ballard evidently 'drank too much, called Francis an asshole, and threw up all over the living room' (8–9).

96 Ctd in Bergan, *Francis Ford Coppola*, 7. '[I] was never the perfect wife, because at no time could I get into this "Italian" mode,' comments Eleanor Coppola; 'Francis is very conservative. He is a family man with old-fashioned Italian values, such as maintaining your wife, your family, and your children.' Ctd in Cowie, *Coppola*, 224. Yet he had a very public affair with an assistant during the filming of *Apocalypse Now*.

97 Cowie, *Coppola*, 126. In 1979 he celebrated his birthday: '"an unbelievable spectacular party," recalls Francis, "that went on for days and days!" More than a thousand guests put in an appearance, and the birthday cake, borne in on a stretcher, measured six feet in length' (145–6) – a birthday cake unwittingly delivered as if it were a sick person.

98 Cowie, *Coppola*, 3, 238.

99 Ctd in Bergan, *Francis Ford Coppola*, 92: the technological as opposed to the human side.

100 Cowie, *Coppola*, 5, 119, 161.

101 Jon Lewis, *Whom God Wishes to Destroy ... : Francis Coppola and the New Hollywood* (Durham: Duke Univ. Press, 1995), 22, 145, 146, 149, 153. Genius is not a thing that comes and goes; the editors are really saying, he never was a genius.

102 Michael Schumacher, *Francis Ford Coppola: A Filmmaker's Life* (New York: Crown, 1999), 409.

103 Phillips, *Coppola*, 141–2, 312.
104 Ctd in Goodwin and Wise, *On the Edge*, 273.
105 Ctd in Yaquinto, *Pump 'em Full of Lead*, 168.
106 Cf. Paul Levitt, 'Lucy Mancini, The New Woman,' *Italian Americana*, 27, no. 1 (2009): 83–5.
107 Ctd in Michael Sragow, 'Godfatherhood' (1997 interview), in Gene D. Phillips and Rodney Hill, ed., *Francis Ford Coppola: Interviews* (Jackson: Univ. Press of Mississippi, 2004), 169.
108 Michael Sragow, 'Godfatherhood,' 169.

8 The Representation of Italian Americans in American Cinema: From the Silent Film to *The Godfather*

1 Robert Casillo, *The Empire of Stereotypes: Germaine de Staël and the Idea of Italy* (New York: Palgrave Macmillan, 2006); Casillo, *Gangster Priest: The Italian American Cinema of Martin Scorsese* (Toronto: Univ. of Toronto Press, 2006); Andrew M. Canepa, 'From Degenerate Scoundrel to Noble Savage: The Italian Stereotype in Eighteenth-Century Travel Literature,' *English Miscellany*, 22 (1971): 107–46; John P. Diggins, *Mussolini and Fascism: The View from America* (Princeton: Princeton Univ. Press, 1972), 5–21; Roger Daniels, *Coming to America: A History of Immigration and Ethnicity in American Life* (New York: HarperCollins, 1990), 195–201; see also 188–201; Edward N, Saveth, *American Historians and European Immigrants, 1875–1925* (New York: Columbia Univ. Press, 1948), 40, 128–130, 133–4, 142–3, 179, 180, 181, 190, 213; Alan M. Kraut, *Silent Travelers: Germs, Genes, and the 'Immigrant Menace'* (New York: Basic Books, 1994), 4, 69, 105–35; John Higham, *Strangers in the Land: Patterns of American Nativism, 1860–1925* (New York: Atheneum, 1963), 90–1, 103, 110, 160, 166–7, 184–5; Allen L. Woll and Randall M. Miller, 'Italians,' in Woll and Miller, eds., *Ethnic and Racial Images in American Film and Television* (New York: Garland, 1987), 275–9, 289; Giuliana Muscio, *Piccole Italie, grandi schermi: Scambi cinematografiche tra Italia e Stati Uniti, 1895–1945* (Rome: Bulzoni, 2004), 10–11, 16–17, 26–7, 31–2, 37, 41–3, 46, 50–6, 68–70, 74, 99–101, 104, 104n, 105, 105n, 106, 107n, 108–16, 119, 126–8, 132–41, 145, 150–1, 152n, 171, 205; James M. O'Kane, *The Crooked Ladder: Gangsters, Ethnicity, and the American Dream* (New Brunswick, NJ: Transaction, 1992), 16–17; Lee Grieveson, 'Gangsters and Governance in the Silent Era,' in Lee Grieveson, Esther Sonnet, and Peter Stanfield, eds., *Mob Culture: Hidden Histories of the American Gangster Film* (New Brunswick: Rutgers Univ. Press, 2005), 13–14, 16, 18–19, 21, 38n; in the same volume: Giorgio Bertellini, 'Black Hands and White

Hearts: Southern Italian Immigrants, Crime, Race in Early American Cinema,' 207–17, 232n, 233n, 235n; Giorgio Bertellini, 'Duce/Divo: Masculinity, Racial Identity, and Politics among Italian Americans in 1920s New York City,' *Journal of Urban History*, 31, no. 5 (July 2005): 689–90, 698, 702; Richard Gambino, *Blood of My Blood: The Dilemma of Italian Americans* (New York: Doubleday, 1975), 274–312 and passim; Joseph Papaleo, 'Ethnic Pictures and Ethnic Fate: The Media Image of Italian America,' in Randall M. Miller, ed., *Ethnic Images in American Film and Television* (Philadelphia: The Balch Institute, 1978), 93–7 and passim; Thomas Monroe Pitkin and Francesco Cordasco, *The Black Hand: A Chapter in Ethnic Crime* (Totowa, NJ: Littlefield, Adams, 1977), Preface (by Pitkin), 2, 15–47, 115–16, 124–5, 168–9, 216–17; Salvatore J. LaGumina, *Wop!: A Documentary History of Anti-Italian Discrimination* (Toronto: Guernica, 1999); Lydio F. Tomasi, ed., *The Italian in America: The Progressive View, 1891–1914* (Staten Island: Center for Migration Studies, 1972): in this volume, see the essays by Broughton Brandenberg, Lilian Brandt, Rocco Brindisi, Alexander S. Cance, Kate Halladay Claghorn, Robert C. De Ward, Mina C. Ginger, I.W. Howarth, John Watrous Knight, Antonio Mangano, and Gino Speranza (the essays originally appeared in *Charities Review, Charities, Charities and the Commons,* and *The Survey* between 1894 and 1911); Michael Woodiwiss, *Crime, Crusades, and Corruption: Prohibitions in the United States* (Totowa, NJ: Barnes and Noble, 1988), 4; David Roediger, *The Wages of Whiteness: Race and the Making of the American Working Class* (London: Verso, 2007); Matthew Frye Jacobson, *Whiteness of a Different Color: European Immigrants and the Alchemy of Race* (Cambridge: Harvard Univ. Press, 1998); David A. Richards, *Italian American: The Racializing of an Ethnic Identity* (New York: New York Univ. Press, 1999); Matthew Pratt Guterl, *The Color of Race in America, 1900–1940* (Cambridge: Harvard Univ. Press, 2001); Jennifer Guglielmo and Salvatore Salerno, eds., *Are Italians White?: How Race is Made in America* (London: Routledge, 2003), 2–3 and passim; Thomas A. Guglielmo, *White on Arrival: Italians, Race, Color, and Power in Chicago, 1890–1945* (New York: Oxford Univ. Press, 2003).

2 On the question of the truth of stereotypes, see Casillo, *Empire of Stereotypes,* chap. 1, n. 14.

3 On nineteenth- and twentieth-century Americans' ambivalence towards Italy, see Diggins, *Mussolini and Fascism,* 5–21; Jacob Riis, *How the Other Half Lives: Studies among the Tenements of New York* (1890; rpt. New York: Dover, 1971), 37, 40–1, 43; Muscio, *Piccole Italie, grandi schermi,* 28, 64, 80, 105–6, 122–3.

4 The following discussion of the silent film draws on Lee Lourdeaux. *Italian and Irish Filmmakers in America: Ford, Capra, Coppola, and Scorsese* (Philadel-

phia: Temple Univ. Press, 1990), 3, 4, 16, 17, 18, 19, 26, 31, 32, 38–9, 42, 65–81; Paola Casella, *Hollywood Italian: Gli Italiani nell'America di celluloide* (Milan: Baldini and Castoldi, 1998), 21–46; Kevin Brownlow, *Behind the Mask of Innocence* (New York: Knopf, 1990), 308, 309–20; Ilaria Serra, *Immagini di un'immaginario: L'emigrazione italiana negli Stati Uniti fra i due secoli (1890–1924)* (Verona: Cierre, 1997), 103–59; Peter Bondanella, *Hollywood Italians: Dagos, Palookas, Romeos, Wiseguys, and Sopranos* (New York: Continuum, 2004), 21–8; Muscio, *Piccole Italie, grandi schermi,* 41–2, 66–9, 103–51; William K. Everson, *American Silent Film* (New York: Oxford Univ. Press, 1978); Grieveson, 'Gangsters and Governance in the Silent Era,' 13–40; Bertellini, 'Black Hands and White Hearts,' 216–28; Woll and Miller, 'Italians,' 276–8; Carlos Cortés, 'The Immigrant on Film: Evolution of an Illuminating Icon,' in Paul Loukides and Linda K. Fuller, eds., *Beyond the Stars: Stock Characters in American Popular Film* (Bowling Green, OH: Bowling Green State Univ. Press, 1990), 24–5; Gian Piero Brunetta, 'Breve viaggio con l'emigrato cinematografico,' *Cinema & Cinema,* 11 (Jan.–March, 1984): 7–8.

5 Kraut, *Silent Travelers,* 2, 50–77.

6 However, Herbert J. Gans found surprisingly little interest in opera among the second- and third-generation lower-middle-class Italians he studied in Boston's West End. See Gans, *The Urban Villagers: Group and Class in the Life of Italian Americans* (Glencoe: Free Press, 1962), 83n.

7 For Catholic theology, see Richard P. McBrien, *Catholicism* (San Francisco: HarperSanFrancisco, 1994), 9–12, 13, 15, 78, 108–9, 1250; Peter Berger, *The Sacred Canopy: Elements of Sociological Theory of Religion* (Garden City: Doubleday, 1969), 111–12, 121. The relative popularity of films on Catholic subjects is partly attributable to a growing fascination with Catholic ritual, symbology, imagery, and doctrine among American Protestants in quest of a less abstract form of religion gratifying to the senses, feelings, and imagination. See Jenny Franchot, *Roads to Rome: The Antebellum Protestant Encounter with Catholicism* (Berkeley: Univ. of California Press, 1994), passim.

8 For the *cicisbeo,* see Casillo, *Empire of Stereotypes,* 57–8, 68–9, 108–24, 290–1n.

9 On Valentino, see Bertellini, 'Duce/Divo,' 702, 704, 706–7, 709, 711–18; Bertellini, 'Black Hands and White Hearts,' 228; Gaylyn Studlar, 'Discourses of Gender and Ethnicity: The Construction and De(con)struction of Rudolph Valentino,' *Film Studies,* 13, no. 2 (Winter 1989): 18–29, 31, 32n; Miriam Hansen, 'Pleasure, Ambivalence, Identification: Valentino and Female Spectatorship,' *Cinema Journal,* 25, no. 4 (1986): 19; Muscio, *Piccole Italie, schermi grandi,* 89, 99–101. Bondanella rightly assumes not only that film audiences took Valentino to be Italian but that his appeal lay in his Italianate eroticism, whatever characters he portrayed. See Bondanella, *Hollywood Italians,* 134–5.

10 On Griffith's portrayal of ethnic groups, including Italians, see John Temple Kirby, 'D.W. Griffith's Racial Portraiture,' *Phylon*, no. 2 (2d qtr. 1978): 119.

11 Martin Clark observes that the decline of banditry in southern Italy during the later nineteenth and early twentieth century correlates with the rise of immigration, which acted as a 'great safety valve' for social and economic tensions. Anthropologically, banditry and immigration share the same dramatic, liminal, and transgressive character, each being a 'literal "rite of passage."' See Martin Clark, *Modern Italy, 1871–1982* (London: Longman, 1978), 70. The immigrants included a small percentage of ex-convicts as well as criminals and bandits (mainly Sicilian, Calabrian, and Sardinian) in flight from Italian justice. See Pitkin and Cordasco, *Black Hand*, 32–3, 95; Bertellini, 'Black Hands and White Hearts,' 232n, 234n.

12 On the Black Hand, see Pitkin and Cordasco, *Black Hand*, passim; Thomas Reppetto, *American Mafia: A History of Its Rise to Power* (New York: H. Holt, 2004), 36–53; Francis A.J. Ianni, *A Family Business: Kinship and Social Control in Organized Crime* (New York: Russell Sage Foundation, 1972), 50–2; David Critchley, *The Origins of Organized Crime in America: The New York City Mafia, 1891–1931* (New York: Routledge, 2009), 26–32.

13 Alba, *Italian Americans: Into the Twilight of Ethnicity (Englewood Cliffs: Prentice-Hall, 1980)*, 38, 97; Joseph L. Albini, *The American Mafia: Genesis of a Legend* (New York: Irvington, 1979), 6–7, 191–6; Pitkin and Cordasco, *Black Hand*, 12 (Cordasco, Foreword), 86–7, 92–3, 100–1, 132–4, 152–3, 164, 224–5, 228. Diego Gambetta, as cited by Critchley, believes that the Black Hand never existed in Italy. Yet whereas many scholars stress the organizational independence of the American Mafia from its Sicilian counterpart, arguing instead for a commonality in attitudes and values regarding family and state, Critchley contends that the American Mafia, though never under centralized Sicilian control, organized itself along familial lines closely reminiscent of Sicilian examples. He further holds, as do Pitkin and Cordasco, that the ranks of early Italian American criminal groups were swelled considerably by an influx of criminals, including Mafiosi, from southern Italy to the United States. See Ianni, *Family Business*, 43; Critchley, *Origins of Organized Crime*, 36, 60–2. For Petrosino's mission and murder, which Critchley believes to have been the only instance of joint planning between American and Sicilian criminal groups, see Critchley, 71; Pitkin and Cordasco, 106–37.

14 Thomas Kessner, *The Golden Door: Italian and Jewish Immigrant Mobility in New York City, 1880–1915* (New York: Oxford Univ. Press, 1977), 47–59, 67, 78–86, 93, 107–9, 111–19, 169–70, 174, 176.

15 Serra, *Immagini di un immaginario*, 106–9, 119; Lourdeaux, *Italian and Irish Filmmakers*, 46.

16 Giorgio Bertellini, 'New York City and the Representation of Italian Americans in the Cinema,' in Philip Cannistraro, ed., *The Italians of New York: Five Centuries of Struggle and Achievement* (New York: New-York Historical Society, 1999), 115–28, esp. 116, 118.

17 Francesca Canadé Sautman, 'Grey Shades, Black Tones: Italian Americans, Race, and Racism in American Film,' in Anna Camaiti Hostert and Anthony Julian Tamburri, eds., *Screening Ethnicity: Cinematic Representations of Italian Americans in the United States* (Boca Raton: Bordighera, 2001), 1–8.

18 Kessner, *Golden Door*, passim; James A. Crispino, *The Assimilation of Ethnic Groups: The Italian Case* (Staten Island: Center for Migration Studies, 1980), v–vi (Herbert J. Gans's Preface), xxii–xxiii, 8–10, 30, 34–5, 47–94, 134, 145–6, 150–1; Alba, *Italian Americans*, 12–17, 89–92, 110–13, 129–30, 132–4, 138–55; Joseph Lopreato, *Italian Americans* (New York: Random House, 1970), 148. As an alternative to Alba's and Crispino's acceptance of Milton Gordon's theory of straight-line assimilation, for which they provide abundant statistical evidence, Herbert Gans proposes a 'bumpy line' alternative that avoids the determinism implicit in the former theory while allowing for the individual ethnic's negotiation of his or her ethnicity vis-à-vis the mainstream. However, Gans acknowledges that ethnicity among third- and fourth-generation ethnics exhibits a largely symbolic, that is, superficial character, and his modest revision of the straight-line theory hardly negates the evident weakening of ethnicity among Italian Americans through increasing assimilation. See Herbert J. Gans, 'Ethnic Invention and Acculturation: A Bumpy-Line Approach,' *Journal of American Ethnic History*, 12, no. 1 (Fall 1992): 42–3.

19 On recent research into stereotypes, see in this volume Casillo, 'Stendhal and Italy,' Part 1, section 3.

20 According to Herbert Gans, Mafia and other negative stereotypes of the Italian American persisted into the third generation perhaps because Italian Americans did not suffer intolerable anti-Italian discrimination and thus failed to protest *en masse*. See Gans, 'Ethnic Invention and Acculturation,' 45–8. The question arises why, amid increasing Italian American assimilation, many negative stereotypes of the group (including that of the Mafia) have remained in place throughout the twentieth century, especially in cinema. A possible reason is that, having originated, intensified, accumulated, and solidified during Italy's decline, such stereotypes have acquired a life or momentum of their own, as part of the normal expectations of Anglo-America, to the point where they cannot easily be negated either by the reality of modern Italy's post-war successes or by the no less evident assimilation of the Italian Americans, which implies their acceptance within the American

mainstream. For whereas many favourable representations of Italian Americans have emerged only recently, the negative ones crystallize the reiterated prejudices of centuries, and it will therefore take at least several more decades, and perhaps longer, for such stereotypes to die out. As for the attractiveness of some long-standing Italian and Italian American stereotypes, this is probably explained by the Italians' unequaled suitability whether in reality or by traditional reputation for representing certain traits and behaviours to which northern European cultures are attracted but towards which they continue to feel inhibition or incapacity. These include not just eroticism but familial affection (including the maternal), emotionality, the natural and physical (whether grace of movement or virtuoso private violence), expressive musicality, gastronomy, gusto, social drama, sartorial flair (the famed *bella figura*), and the appreciation of leisure (the no less famed *dolce far niente*) as against mere free time. In short, the Italians stand for just about everything that goes by the name of life. Until another ethnic group seems better suited by cultural and historical association to embody such qualities, which is not likely given their mainly classical and Mediterranean provenience, Italians and Italian Americans will probably remain identified with them. See Muscio, *Piccole Italie, grandi schermi*, 276, 366.

21 Carlos Cortés, 'The Hollywood Curriculum on Italian Americans: Evolution of an Icon of Ethnicity,' in Lydio F. Tomasi, Pietro Gastaldo, and Thomas Row, eds., *The Columbus People: Perspectives on Italian Immigration to the Americas and Australia* (Staten Island: Center for Migration Studies, 1994), 91–2, 94. As Thomas Guglielmo observes, Italian immigrants were regarded officially as white upon their arrival in the United States, a categorization that had already been, and continued to be, endorsed in word and deed by the American public. To be sure, there were instances in which olive-skinned Italians were regarded suspiciously as a so-called 'in-between people,' and sometimes even despised by locals as non-white, as happened most often in the South, where extreme sensitivity in matters of colour had for obvious reasons been longstanding. However, such instances were comparatively infrequent, even in the South, and decreased to the point of non-existence as assimilation proceeded. On this issue as in all others it is a basic requirement to observe the 'total evidence rule,' by which standard there can be no question of the 'whiteness' of the Italians. According to Muscio in a highly tendentious argument, Italian Americans continued generally to be grouped 'racially' with Mexicans, Indians, Africans, and other 'coloured' ethnicities in the Hollywood films of the 1930s, and to be seen as exemplifying '*sangue impuro*' or impure blood. The argument is undermined by Muscio's own extensive evidence, which shows that many films treated in-

termarriage between Italians Americans and members of other white ethnic groups, including WASPS, along with instances of the adoption of Italian American children by WASP families or those of a different ethnicity. See Muscio, *Piccole Italie, grandi schermi*, 280.

22 On the question of Italian American cinema, see Casillo, *Gangster Priest*, 62–8, 435–9n; Casillo, 'Moments in Italian American Cinema: From *Little Caesar* to Coppola and Scorsese,' in Anthony Julian Tamburri, Paolo Giordano, and Fred L. Gardaphe, eds., *From the Margins: Writings in Italian Americana* (West Lafayette, IN: Purdue Univ. Press, 1991), 374–5; Jerre Mangione, 'American Artists of Italian Origin,' in Humbert S. Nelli, ed., *The United States and Italy: The First Two Hundred Years* (Proceedings of the Ninth Annual Conference of the American Italian Historical Association) (Staten Island: American Italian Historical Association, 1977), 212–13; Pellegrino d'Acierno, 'Cinema Paradiso: The Italian American Presence in American Cinema,' in D'Acierno, ed., *The Italian American Heritage: A Companion to Literature and Arts* (New York: Garland, 1999), 607–11. On Capra, see Vittorio Zagarrio, 'F.C.-F.C. Ovvero: Italian American Dream dal Film Muto alle Television,' in *Cinema & Cinema*, 38 (Jan.–March 1984): 37–40; Muscio, *Piccole Italie, grandi schermi*, 147–8.

23 Eugene Rosow, *Born to Lose: The Gangster Film in America* (New York: Oxford Univ. Press, 1978), 43, 104; Herbert Asbury, *The Gangs of New York* (New York: A.A. Knopf, 1928), passim; John D. Landesco, *Organized Crime in Chicago* (Chicago: Univ. of Chicago Press, 1929); Richard Maltby, 'Why Boys Go Wrong: Gangsters, Hoodlums, and the Natural History of Delinquent Careers,' in Grieveson, Sonnet, and Stanfield, *Mob Culture*, 46–7; David E. Ruth, *Inventing the Public Enemy: The Gangster in American Culture, 1918–1934* (Chicago: Univ. of Chicago Press, 1996), 1, 2, 28, 29, 45; O'Kane, *The Crooked Ladder*, 54–60, 62–78; Woll and Miller, 'Italians,' 292 (citing Everson). According to Muscio, the Italian American gangster became the prototype of the gangster generally. See Muscio, *Piccole Italie, grandi schermi*, 17.

24 Casillo, *Gangster Priest*, 494–5n; O'Kane, *The Crooked Ladder*, 77; Pitkin and Cordasco, *Black Hand*, 212. Many scholars, including Cressey, Ianni, Bell, and Nelli, have argued that, following the internecine Castellamarese War of 1930–31, the younger Mafia generation rejected Old World traditionalism in favour of a major and lasting modernization program characterized by increasing business rationalization, consolidation, specialization, expansion, efficiency, and centralized control, especially of violence. David Critchley rejects this interpretation, as in his view the Mafia remained diffuse, decentralized, improvisatory, and kinship based for many decades following the alleged transformation. See Critchley, *Origins of Organized Crime*, 140–1, 142–3, 164, 165, 186–7, 196–7, 198–204, 206, 208, 232–3, 236.

25 Ruth, *Inventing the Public Enemy*, 2, 27–8, 37, 40–57, 61–2; Dwight Smith, cited in Critchley, *Origins of Organized Crime*, 199.

26 Rosow, *Born to Lose*, 122–4; Andrew Sarris, 'Big Funerals: The Hollywood Gangster,' in Alain Silver and James Ursini, eds., *The Gangster Film Reader* (Pompton Plains, NJ: Limelight, 2007), 85–8; Everson, *American Silent Film*, 229–30; Muscio, *Piccole Italie, grandi schermi*, 153–4.

27 Alba, *Italian Americans*, 56.

28 On *Star Witness*, see Thomas Patrick Doherty, *Pre-Code Hollywood: Sex, Immorality, and Insurrection in American Cinema, 1930–1934* (New York: Columbia Univ. Press, 1999), 152; Carlos Clarens, *Crime Movies: An Illustrated History of the Gangster Genre from D.W. Griffith to Pulp Fiction* (New York: Da Capo, 1997), 73, 78–80, 79.

29 Jonathan Munby, *Public Enemies, Public Heroes: Screening the Gangster from 'Little Caesar' to 'Touch of Evil'* (Chicago: Univ. of Chicago Press, 1999), 5; Rosow, *Born to Lose*, 215–6; Clarens, *Crime Movies*, 60–1, 71; Richard Maltby, '"Grief in the Limelight": Al Capone, Howard Hughes, The Hays Code and the Politics of the Unstable Text,' in James Combs, ed., *Movies and Politics: The Dynamic Relationship* (New York: Garland, 1993), 158, 161–2, 164–5, 167–70; Gregory D. Black, *Hollywood Censored: Morality Codes, Catholics, and the Movies* (New York: Columbia Univ. Press, 1994), 31–46; William Bruce Johnson, *Miracles and Sacrilege: Roberto Rossellini, 'The Miracle,' and Film Censorship in Hollywood* (Toronto: Univ. of Toronto Press, 2007), 7–102, 103–10; Matthew Bernstein, Introduction to Bernstein, ed., *Controlling Hollywood: Censorship and Regulation in the Studio Era* (New Brunswick, NJ: Rutgers Univ. Press, 1999), 4–5, 6–7; in the same volume: Richard Maltby, '*The King of Kings* and the Czar of all the Rushes: The Propriety of the Christ Story,' 74–7; Richard Maltby, 'The Spectacle of Criminality,' in J. David Slocum, ed., *Violence and American Cinema* (New York: Routledge, 2001), 120–6; Richard Maltby, '"To Prevent the Prevalent Type of Book": Censorship and Adaptation in Hollywood, 1924–1934,' in Francis G. Couvares, ed., *Movie Censorship and American Culture* (Washington: Smithsonian Institution, 1996), 100, 101–2, 104–6; in the same volume: Francis G. Couvares, 'Hollywood, Main Street, and the Church,' 132–52; Leonard L. Leff and Jerold L. Simmons, *The Dame in the Kimono: Hollywood, Censorship, and the Production Code from the 1920s to the 1960s* (New York: Grove Weidenfeld, 1990), 4–17; Doherty, *Pre-Code Hollywood*, passim, esp. 347–67; Garth S. Jowett, 'Moral Responsibility and Commercial Entertainment: Social Control in the United States Film Industry, 1907–1968,' *Historical Journal of Film, Radio, and Television*, 10, no. 1 (1990): 10–12, 14, 15; Garth Jowett, 'Bullets, Beer and the Hays Office: *Public Enemy*,' in John E. O'Connor and Michael A. Jackson, eds., *American History/American Film* (New York: Continuum, 1988), 70; Ruth Vasey, *The*

World According to Hollywood, 1918–1939 (Madison: Univ of Wisconsin Press, 1997), 20–3, 29–62; Frank Walsh, *Sin and Censorship: The Catholic Church and the Motion Picture Industry* (New Haven: Yale Univ. Press, 1996), 23–65; Ruth, *Inventing the Public Enemy*, 19, 20, 29–30.

30 Influenced by the essays of Robert Warshow, critics have long defined the 'classic' gangster film as depicting the gangster as an individualist who, having gunned his way to the top of the underworld in a parody of the Horatio Alger myth, suffers a precipitously climactic downfall into death and disgrace. The 'classic' examples of the genre are widely seen as having had a brief heyday of less than four years after emerging more or less from nowhere around 1930. More recent critics, however, reject the idea of the 'classic' gangster film as a special yet universal type. Not only is it rooted historically in Prohibition, the rise of Al Capone, and the Chicago model of organized crime, but it represents a variation on formulae originating in the silent era. Nor does the standard definition account for other types of gangster films, some of a hybrid character, which appear contemporaneously with the small number of 'classic' examples (totalling about eleven by one estimate). See Robert Warshow, 'The Gangster as Tragic Hero,' in Warshow, *The Immediate Experience: Movies, Comics, Theater and Other Aspects of Popular Culture* (New York: Atheneum, 1970), 132–3; Thomas Schatz, *Hollywood Genres: Formulas, Filmmaking, and the Studio System* (Philadelphia: Temple Univ. Press, 1981), 86–95; Silver, Introduction to Silver and Ursini, *The Gangster Film Reader*, 1; in the same volume: Stuart Kaminsky, '*Little Caesar* and its Role in the Gangster Film Genre,' 47; Fran Mason, *American Gangster Cinema: From 'Little Caesar' to 'Pulp Fiction'* (New York: Palgrave Macmillan, 2002), xiv, 1–8, 31, 39; Stephen Louis Karpf, *The Gangster Film: Emergence, Variation, and Decay of a Genre* (New York: Arno, 1973), 25–7; Clarens, *Crime Movies*, 13; Thomas Leitch, *Crime Films* (Cambridge: Cambridge Univ. Press, 2002), 1–2, 23–6; Introduction to Grieveson, Sonnet, and Stanfield, *Mob Culture*, 2, 3; in the same volume: Grieveson, 'Gangsters and Governance in the Silent Era,' 34–5n; Esther Sonnet, 'Ladies Love Brutes: Reclaiming Female Pleasures in the Lost History of Hollywood Gangster Cycles, 1929–1931,' 93–4, 97–101, 106. The film discussed by Sonnett, *Ladies Love Brutes* (1930), differs from the 'classic' pattern. Having grown rich in his construction business without yielding to an extortionist mob boss, the Capone-like Mike Mendina, played by Stanley Fields, the Italian American Joe Forziati (George Bancroft) attempts to enter WASP high society only to be rejected because of his immigrant background. After attracting the interest of the bored Mimi (Mary Astor), a rich WASP divorcée, Forziati attempts to marry her by staging the kidnapping and rescue of her son by a previous marriage.

However, he is anticipated in the kidnapping by the mob boss, whom he defeats in a climactic confrontation, the life of Forziati's own son being now at stake. Yet the doors to high society remain closed to Forziati, as he and Mimi recognize the temporary nature of their mutual attraction. On this film see also Muscio, *Piccole Italie, grandi schermi*, 159.

31 W.R. Burnett, *Little Caesar* (New York: The Literary Guild of America, 1929): 'The first law of every being, is to preserve itself and live. You sow hemlock, and expect to see the ears of corn ripen.'

32 Jack Warner intended Rico as a 'thinly disguised portrait of Al Capone.' See Les Keyser and Barbara Keyser, *Hollywood and the Catholic Church: The Image of Roman Catholicism in American Movies* (Chicago: Loyola Univ. Press, 1984), 44.

33 Muscio, *Piccole Italie, grandi schermi*, 10, 89, 132, 153–4.

34 On Rico, see Golden, 'The Fate of La Famiglia,' in Randall M. Miller, ed., *The Kaleidoscopic Lens: How Hollywood Views Ethnic Groups* (Englewood, NJ: James S. Ozer, 1980), 81–2.

35 Walsh, *Sin and Censorship*, 70; Leff and Simmons, *Dame in the Kimono*, 15–16. Like many scholars, Thomas Patrick Doherty regards the use of moralistic labels in the gangster films of this period as homiletic hypocrisy served up to middle-class censors with the cynical aim of concealing the glorification of gangster violence for the sake of box-office profits. Doherty also contends as do many other scholars that these gangster films aimed to subvert the status quo, calling into question the injustices of class and inter-ethnic relationships under capitalism. However, Richard Maltby argues persuasively that such claims are ahistorical and offer no reliable evidence of subversive intent. Although Maltby acknowledges that a disparity may seem to exist between the films' stated intentions and their effects on an audience, he finds it highly unlikely that Hollywood sought to fool the censors by producing subversive films. Instead, the studios wanted to counter the recurrent accusation that they glorified criminality. Maltby further notes that in the early 1930s an enormous public backlash arose against gangsters, who had been widely admired in the previous decade as the incarnation of anti-Prohibition sentiment, but who now symbolized the licence, immorality, and corruption of the Roaring Twenties. See Doherty, *Pre-Code Hollywood*, 155; Munby, *Public Enemies, Public Heroes*, 51; Maltby, 'Spectacle of Criminality,' 118, 119, 120, 128–9, 132, 133, 140; Maltby, '"Grief in the Limelight,"' 140–6, 148–9, 154–5; Maltby, 'Why Boys Go Wrong,' 42.

36 Kaminsky, '*Little Caesar* and Its Role,' 51.

37 Ianni, *Family Business*, 16. Daniel Sembroff Golden errs in identifying Rico with the acquisitive American desirous above all of material success rather

than with the Mediterranean *uomo di rispetto* who values status and power. See Golden, 'Fate of la Famiglia,' 81.

38 On Italian American frugality, see Thomas Sowell, *Ethnic America: A History* (New York: Basic Books, 1981), 127.

39 For the gangster in association with consumption and excess, see Ruth, *Inventing the Public Enemy*, 2–3, 62–71, 82–3, 90, 105.

40 Bondanella, *Hollywood Italian*, 185. See also Kaminsky, '*Little Caesar* and Its Role,' 53; Sonnet, 'A Gunsel Is Being Beaten: Gangster Masculinity and the Homoerotics of the Crime Film, 1941–1942,' in Grieveson, Sonnet, and Stanfield, *Mob Culture*, 144n; in the same volume: Esther Sonnett and Peter Stanfield, '"Good Evening, Gentlemen, Can I Check Your Hats Please?": Masculinity, Dress, and the Retro Gangster Cycles of the 1990s,' 182; Doherty, *Pre-Code Hollywood*, 146–7; Black, *Hollywood Censored*, 114; Mason, *American Gangster Cinema*, 10.

41 Colin McArthur, *Underworld U.S.A.* (New York: Viking, 1972), 26, 28.

42 Golden, 'Fate of La Famiglia,' 78; Lee Bernstein, *The Greatest Menace: Organized Crime in Cold War America* (Amherst: Univ. of Massachusetts Press, 2002), 18.

43 Keyser and Keyser, *Hollywood and the Catholic Church*, 54; Black, *Hollywood Censored*, 124–5.

44 Keyser and Keyser, *Hollywood and the Catholic Church*, 56.

45 Ruth notes a 1931 *Cosmopolitan* article in which O.O. McIntyre compares invidiously the gunmen of the Old West with the current crop of urban criminals, whom he dismisses as effeminate, dandified, neurasthenic, cowardly, and flashily hedonic (qualities soon to be embodied in Tony Camonte), and among whom McIntyre implicitly numbers ethnic types. Ruth also notes, however, the atypicality of such a characterization, as the urban criminal was commonly seen as a tough guy. See Ruth, *Inventing the Public Enemy*, 91.

46 Munby, *Public Enemies, Public Heroes*, 10, 58–6; Maltby, '"Grief in the Limelight,"' 150–5; John McCarty, *Bullets over Hollywood: The American Gangster Picture from the Silents to The Sopranos* (Cambridge: Da Capo, 2004), 122, 123; Marilyn Yaquinto, *Pump 'em Full of Lead: A Look at the Gangster Film* (New York: Twayne, 1998), 38–43; Rosow, *Born to Lose*, 221; Bondanella, *Hollywood Italians*, 196; Walsh, *Sin and Censorship*, 71; Mason, *American Gangster Cinema*, 29; Leitch, *Crime Films*, 24–6; Doherty, *Pre-Code Hollywood*, 150, 153–4; Black, *Hollywood Censored*, 124–6, 129–31; Maltby, 'Spectacle of Criminality,' 118, 134–41.

47 The association of Italian criminality and opera appears in the story reported by the early nineteenth-century writer Charles MacFarlane of an operatic troupe held up by Italian banditti. Instead of robbing the singers,

the bandits demanded only a succession of arias and duets, after which they sent the troupe on its way. In addition to targeting the Italian tenor Tito Schipa for blackmail, Black Hand extortionists planted a bomb at a Caruso recital at New York's Metropolitan Opera House. Gangster films in which opera figures prominently include *Al Capone, Some Like It Hot,* Brian de Palma's *The Untouchables* (1987), in which Al Capone (Robert De Niro) weeps at the conclusion of *I Pagliacci,* and Coppola's *Godfather III* (1990), which concludes with a performance of Mascagni's *Cavalleria Rusticana* filmed at the Royal Opera House in Palermo. In many instances the common denominator between Italian criminality and Italian art is virtuosity, this association having long been commonplace in Anglo-American culture, as in Browning's 'My Last Duchess.' Although the fifteenth-century Florentine painter Andrea del Castagno was unfairly accused of killing a rival artist, Benvenuto Cellini is known to have been a murderer and brawler, as was Caravaggio. It has been alleged that the painter Pordenone wore a sword so as to fend off a possible assault from his rival, Titian. According to an apocryphal story told by James Jackson Jarves, the seventeenth-century artist Guido Reni achieved verisimilitude in a painting of Christ crucified by stabbing his model and then rendering his death agony, after which Reni fled Rome, only to expiate his crime through years of exile. Writing of Caravaggio's heyday, when 'noble masters' were replaced by 'gloomy ruffians ... gangsters, by modern description.' William Gaunt observes that Caravaggio was 'courteously received' in Naples by the painter Belisario Corenzio, who, with Ribera, otherwise known as 'Il Spagnoletto,' typified the city's 'brave new world of artist-gangsters.' Thus Ribera intimidated his rival, the great Bolognese painter Domenichino, into leaving Naples. According to Gaunt, Spanish misrule and widespread poverty promoted brigandage in southern Italy as well as gangsterism among such Neapolitan artists as the painter Tassi, who belonged to a gang of artist criminals. Salvator Rosa, the Lord Byron of his age, ventured among Calabrian bandits and heroized them in his picturesque landscapes as enemies of tyranny. Regarding cinematic examples, Johnny Rocco, the Italian American gang boss in John Huston's *Key Largo* (1949), smuggles into the United States high-quality counterfeit bills that call to mind the masterfully deceptive manual and mimetic skills long associated with Italian virtuosos. Exemplifying that peculiar mixture of aesthetic delectation and sadistic cruelty typified by such Italian Renaissance despots as Browning's Duke, the gangster Martinelli (Morris Carnovsky) in John Cromwell's *Dead Reckoning* (1947) enjoys his private art collection while, in full view within the same room, his two henchmen give Captain 'Rip' Murdock (Humphrey Bogart) a brutal working over. In *Johnny Cool*

(1963) Marc Lawrence plays Johnny Collini, a Lucky Luciano figure who, having been deported to Italy, plots vengeance in a palazzo worthy of a Renaissance potentate. Roger Corman's *The St. Valentine's Day Massacre* (1969) portrays Al Capone's living quarters as reminiscent of a Roman imperial or Renaissance palace. In Quentin Tarantino's *Reservoir Dogs* (1992), the office of a small-time Italian American crime boss (Lawrence Tierney) is decorated with a Canaletto landscape and Mantegna's St Sebastian, the latter work suggesting a connection, no doubt appealing to the director, between art and violence. See Charles MacFarlane, *The Lives and Exploits of Banditti and Robbers in All Parts of the World*, 3d ed. (London: T. Tegg, 1839), 187–9; Clarens, *Crime Movies*, 271; Pitkin and Cordasco, *Black Hand*, 223; W. Gaunt, *Bandits in a Landscape: A Study of Romantic Painting from Caravaggio to Delacroix* (London: Studio, 1937), 17–18, 23, 27–8, 29–35, 45. For Pordenone, see Giuseppe Tassini, *Curiosità veneziane* (Venice: Scarbellini, 1933), 672–3; William Dean Howells, *Venetian Life*, 3d ed. (New York: Hurd and Houghton, 1867), 166.

48 Robin Wood, *Howard Hawks* (Garden City: Doubleday, 1968), 59, 60.

49 Wood, *Howard Hawks*, 68. Camonte's vaguely ape-like appearance calls to mind the theories of the Italian criminologist Cesare Lombroso, who regarded many criminal types as atavistic throwbacks on the evolutionary scale, and who also claimed to find such traits in high degree among southern Italians. Lombroso's ideas, which were well known to American criminologists as well as nativist opponents of immigration, may have influenced the making of *Scarface*, whether consciously or unconsciously. See Nicole Rafter, *Shots in the Mirror: Crime Films and Society* (London: Oxford, 2000), 50–1; Kerry Soper, 'Classical Bodies versus the Criminal Carnival: Eugenics Ideology in 1930s Popular Art,' in Susan Currell and Christina Cogdell, eds., *Popular Eugenics: National Efficiency and American Mass Culture in the 1930s* (Athens, OH: Ohio Univ. Press, 2006), 272–4, 289, 297–8, 304.

50 On the vicissitudes of the Italian American family during this period, see Casillo, *Gangster Priest*, 14–20.

51 Micaela di Leonardo, *The Varieties of Ethnic Experience: Kinship, Class, and Gender* (Ithaca: Cornell Univ. Press, 1984), 177; Giuseppe Prezzolini, *Come gli americani scoprirono l'Italia, 1750–1850* (Milan: Fratelli Treves, 1933), 189. This stereotype probably owes something to the eighteenth and early nineteenth centuries, when the practice of the *cicisbeo* or *cavaliere sirvente* led foreigners to view the Italian family as corrupt.

52 Mason, *American Gangster Cinema*, 7–8.

53 Keyser and Keyser, *Hollywood and the Catholic Church*, 44.

54 Paul Giles, *American Catholic Arts and Fictions: Culture, Ideology, Aesthetics* (Cambridge: Cambridge Univ. Press, 1992), 155.

55 Wood, *Howard Hawks*, 61–2.

56 Keyser and Keyser, *Hollywood and the Catholic Church*, 53–4, 56.

57 For the stereotype of Italian effeminacy, see Casillo, *Empire of Stereotypes*, 49, 58, 83–6, 138–41, 300n.

58 Gerald Mast, *Howard Hawks, Storyteller* (New York: Oxford Univ. Press, 1982), 74; Maltby, '"Grief in the Limelight,"' 150.

59 David Ehrenstein, *The Scorsese Picture: The Art and Life of Martin Scorsese* (New York: Basic Books, 1992), 41.

60 Woodiwiss, *Crime, Crusades, and Corruption*, 24. For a survey of Capone's career and public image, see Ruth, *Inventing the Public Enemy*, 116–40.

61 Ianni, *Family Business*, 22–3; Stephen Fox, *Blood and Power: Organized Crime in Twentieth-Century America* (New York: William Morrow, 1989), 44–5.

62 Joseph Bonanno, *A Man of Honor* (New York: Pocket Books, 1972), 70, 102.

63 Martin P. Gosch and Richard Hammer, *The Last Testament of Lucky Luciano* (Boston: Little, Brown, 1975), 70; Sid Feder and Joachim Joesten, *The Luciano Story* (New York: Da Capo, 1994), 136.

64 John Cummings and Ernest Volkman, *Goombata: The Improbable Rise and Fall of John Gotti and His Gang* (Boston: Little Brown, 1990), 54, 103, 210.

65 However, Muscio identifies the flamboyant gangster with *sicilianità* rather than with Neapolitan behaviour patterns. See Muscio, *Piccole Italie, grandi schermi*, 319, 360.

66 Casella, *Hollywood Italian*, 56, 58; Karpf, *Gangster Film*, 211. For the claim that crime is Rico's only opportunity for self-advancement, see Randall M. Miller, Introduction to Miller, *Kaleidoscopic Lens*, 6; Muscio, *Piccole Italie, grandi schermi*, 154, 159.

67 Sarris, 'Big Funerals: The Hollywood Gangster, 1927–1933,' 88–91. Ruth notes that in the 1920s and early 1930s environmentalist and deterministic interpretations of crime were largely out of favour, as both moralists and the public preferred to view the individual criminal as a free moral agent. See Ruth, *Inventing the Public Enemy*, 20–5, 29, 73.

68 Alain Silver, Introduction to Silver and Ursini, *Gangster Film Reader*; in the same volume, John Baxter, 'The Gangster Film,' 29; Kaminsky, '*Little Caesar* and Its Role,' 49; Geoff Fordham, 'A Study in Ambiguity: *The Godfather* and the American Gangster Movie Tradition,' 165; Lewis Jacobs, *The Rise of the American Film: A Critical History* (New York: Teachers College Press, 1968), 510; Leitch, *Crime Films*, 24, 110–11; Bernstein, *The Greatest Menace*, 157; Fred Gardaphe, *From Wiseguys to Wise Men: The Gangster and Italian American Masculinities* (New York: Routledge, 2006), 13; Everson, *American Silent Film*, 232–3; Golden, 'Fate of La Famiglia,' 79, 80; Jowett, 'Bullets, Beer and the Hays Office,' 58, 69; Black, *Hollywood Censored*, 114; Ruth, *Inventing the Pub-*

lic Enemy, 2, 3, 4, 8, 18, 20, 37–40, 42–3, 61, 71, 73, 74, 88, 127–9; Munby,
Public Enemies, Public Heroes, 3, 5, 16–17, 20, 26, 27, 30, 32–3, 37, 43–51, 47n,
56, 60–2, 100, 103–4, 105, 107. On *Scarface*, see also Jowett, 'Bullets, Beer
and the Hays Office,' 67–9; Fordham, 'Study in Ambiguity,' 166, 168, 169,
170–1. On the nativist Protestant Crusade against alcohol consumption
among urban Catholic ethnics, see Fox, *Blood and Power*, 12–14, 51, 130–73;
Keyser and Keyser, *Hollywood and the Catholic Church*, 42–3. For an argument similar to Munby's, but stressing the 'racialized' identity of the Italian
American gangster, see Bertellini, 'Black Hands and White Hearts,' 229.
Drawing upon Daniel Bell's concept of crime as an 'American way of life'
and 'crooked ladder' to social advancement, James O'Kane argues similarly
to Munby that, for some Italian Americans, organized crime was the only to
way to escape the working-class neighbourhood. However, O'Kane regards
such individuals as anomalous, noting that the vast majority of Italian Americans achieved occupational and social mobility by legal means. See O'Kane,
Crooked Ladder, 23–50, 51–2, 58–9, 62–9.

69 Not only did New York congressman Fiorello Laguardia regard *Little Caesar*
as a slur against Italian Americans, charging that Hollywood would never
have allowed similar treatment of Jews, but *Scarface*, in addition to protests
by the Italian ambassador to the United States, brought down the denuncia-
tory wrath of fifty Italian American organizations for its 'libel on the Italian
race.' Fred Gardaphe therefore errs in claiming that there was little organized outcry by Italian American organizations over portrayals of Italian
American gangster before Puzo's *The Godfather*. This is not to deny that, in
Italian American neighbourhoods of the first and second generations, the
local gangster attained heroic status among some members of the working
class community for having won success at the expense of a mainstream
society perceived with considerable justification as anti–Italian American.
To them, it did not matter that the gangster exploited neighbourhood
residents. There is no evidence, however, that such attitudes translated into
an approval of the gangster film as a vehicle for ethnic protest, and in any
case the local gangster became increasingly anathematized among Italian
Americans the more they acculturated and assimilated, leaving the urban
ethnic neighbourhood behind. See Mark Haller, 'Organized Crime in Urban Society: Chicago in the Twentieth Century,' *Journal of Social History*, 5
(1971): 210–34, esp. 227–9; Maltby, 'Spectacle of Criminality,' 132, 134,
140, 147n; Maltby, '"Grief in the Limelight,"' 141; Vasey, *World According to
Hollywood*, 120, 143–4; Gardaphe, *From Wiseguys to Wisemen*, xiii, 57; O'Kane,
Crooked Ladder, 1, 48–9, 63, 77–8, 83–6, 111–13, 118–19, 121–6; Robert Orsi,
The Madonna of 115th Street: Faith and Community in Italian Harlem, 1880–

1950 (New Haven: Yale Univ. Press, 1985), 31, 103–4, 127–8; Muscio, *Piccole Italie, grandi schermi,* 157.

70 Munby, *Public Enemies, Public Heroes,* 47. Burnett said: 'I treated 'em [gangsters] like human beings.' See also Black, *Hollywood Censored,* 111.

71 D'Acierno, 'Cinema Paradiso,' xlviii–xlix, 592, 631, 761n.

72 Alba, *Italian Americans,* 49–51, 84–6; Lopreato, *Italian Americans,* 106, 113; Gans, *Urban Villagers,* 104–11, 294–8.

73 Johnson, *Miracles and Sacrilege,* 108–36; Silver, Introduction to *Gangster Film Reader,* 2, 6n; Sonnet, 'A Gunsel Is Being Beaten,' 120; Walsh, *Sin and Censorship,* 66–117; Leff and Simmons, *Dame in the Kimono,* xiii, 16–17, 18–9, 34–56; Doherty, *Pre-Code Hollywood,* 1, 2, 8–11, 319–42; Jowett, 'Moral Responsibility and Commercial Entertainment,' 12–13, 16, 17, 18–19; Jowett, 'Bullets, Beer and the Hays Office,' 70–1; Black, *Hollywood Censored,* 1, 2, 5–6, 108, 110–11, 122–6, 129–32, 144–5; Vasey, *World According to Hollywood,* 5–6, 10–11, 120, 127–40; Bondanella, *Hollywood Italians,* 196, 197; Munby, *Public Enemies, Public Heroes,* 5, 19, 83–4; Yaquinto, *Pump 'em Full of Lead,* 48–50; Rosow, *Born to Lose,* 220–1; Clarens, *Crime Movies,* 71, 103, 115, 271; Karpf, *Gangster Film,* 200; Sonnet, 'Ladies Love Brutes,' 117n; Maltby, 'Spectacle of Criminality,' 118, 133–4, 141–3; Maltby, '"Grief in the Limelight,"' 136–7, 138, 147, 151, 152, 154, 156, 169, 170; Woll and Miller, 'Italians,' 280–1; Lea Jacobs, 'Industry Self-Regulation and the Problem of Textual Determination,' in Bernstein, *Controlling Hollywood,* 87–99; Francis G. Couvares, Introduction to Couvares, *Movie Censorship and American Culture,* 4; Raymond Lee and B.C. Van Hecke, *Gangsters and Hoodlums: The Underworld in the Cinema* (New York: Castle, 1971), 13–14. Maltby cautions against thinking that 1934 marks an absolute division between an earlier period of unbridled licence and disorder and a later one of intrusive regulation, enforcement, and conformism under the production code. The period from 1930 to 1934 witnessed considerable self-regulation as well as studio enforcement of the code in response to public protests against underworld, sexual, and other offensive subject matter, as witness Hughes's difficulties in distributing *Scarface.*

74 Silver, Introduction to Silver and Ursini, *Gangster Film Reader,* 3; in the same volume: Frank Manchel, 'Post-Code Gangster Movies,' 99, 101; Vasey, *World According to Hollywood,* 143; Woll and Miller, 'Italians,' 281, 294; Mason, *American Gangster Cinema,* 53, 54; Bondanella, *Hollywood Italian,* 196–8. On environment, see Grieveson, 'Gangsters and Governance,' 28–33; Maltby, 'Why Boys Go Wrong,' 41–5, 54, 57, 59; Landesco, *Organized Crime in Chicago;* Louis Wirth, *The Ghetto* (Chicago: Univ. of Chicago Press, 1966); H.W. Zorbaugh, *The Gold Coast and the Slum: A Sociological Analysis of Chicago's Near*

North Side (Chicago: Univ. of Chicago Press, 1929); Frederic Milton Thrasher, *The Gang* (Chicago: Univ. of Chicago Press, 1936).

75 Munby, 'Why Boys Go Wrong,' 55; Vasey, *World According to Hollywood*, 143.

76 Esther Sonnet regards Johnny Eager as a WASP. See Sonnet, 'A Gunsel Is Being Beaten,' 136–9.

77 D'Acierno, 'Cinema Paradiso,' 597.

78 In a memoir of early twentieth-century London, Adrian Stokes attributes to the intermittent presence of an Italian organ-grinder with his barrel organ the vivification of an otherwise drab middle-class neighbourhood, which thus acquired momentarily something of the visual and auditory coherence of Italian urban spaces: 'I found in sound a most effective qualification of the visual world. A street became *informed* for me by the sounds of a barrel-organ. Everything had a new angle of light upon it, a new arrangement like a center pulsating with a heart. Thus the street ... became an organism, it came alive.' See Adrian Stokes, *Inside Out*, in Stokes, *The Collected Writings of Adrian Stokes*, vol. 2 (London: Thames and Hudson, 1978), 154.

79 Sembroff, 'Fate of La Famiglia,' 82–3.

80 Curiously, Muscio contends that Vanning fails to connote an Italian. See Muscio, *Piccole Italie, grandi schermi*, 312. For Luciano, as well as a brief discussion of *Marked Woman*, see Woodiwiss, *Crime, Crusaders, and Corruption*, 48–52, 55–7, 60–2; Gosch and Hammer, *Last Testament of Lucky Luciano*, passim; Humbert S. Nelli, *The Business of Crime: Italians and Syndicate Crime in the United States* (New York: Oxford Univ. Press, 1976), xii, 100–6, 139–40, 180–3, 199–200, 201–8, 239–41, 256–8; Feder and Joesten, *Luciano Story*, 135–75.

81 Nearly half a million Italian Americans served in the United States Army in World War II, the highest proportion of any ethnic group. See Gardaphe, *From Wiseguys to Wise Men*, 18.

82 On the pro-capitalism typical of Mafiosi, see Casillo, *Gangster Priest*, 470n.

83 George Raft and Jack LaRue (born Gaspere Biondolillo in 1902) are the only Italian American actors in whose filmographies gangster portrayals are heavily represented. See Muscio, *Piccole Italie, grandi schermi*, 158, 309, 315–19.

84 Gambino, *Blood of My Blood*, 288.

85 On *Cry of the City*, see Mason, *American Gangster Cinema*, 86, 87.

86 Gans, *Urban Villagers*, 90–1, 94–5, 108–9, 164, 236; Edward C. Banfield, *The Moral Basis of a Backward Society* (Glencoe: Free Press, 1958), 18, 28–9, 85, 98.

87 Casella, *Hollywood Italian*, 106–8.

88 Nelli, *Business of Crime*, 101–253; Ianni, *Family Business*, 56–9; James J.

Inciardi, *Careers in Crime* (Chicago: Rand-McNally, 1975), 116–21; Ralph Salerno and John S. Tompkins, *The Crime Confederation: Cosa Nostra and Allied Operations in Organized Crime* (Garden City: Doubleday, 1969), 87–9. As discussed previously, Critchley denies that organized crime was radically reorganized in the 1930s. See note 24.

89 Munby, *Public Enemies, Public Heroes*, 130n, 131–3, 134, 141; Schatz, *Hollywood Genres*, 102–3; Rosow, *Born to Lose*, 235, 271–2.

90 Dwight C. Smith, *The Mafia Mystique* (New York: Basic Books, 1975), 62–117, 121; Ianni, *Family Business*, 2–4; Pitkin and Cordasco, *Black Hand*, 220–3.

91 Carl Sifakis, *The Mafia Encyclopedia* (New York: Facts on File, 1987), 36–8; Pitkin and Cordasco, *Black Hand*, 88, 92–3, 135–6, 151–2, 165, 167, 225, 228; Ianni, *Family Business*, 50–2; Critchley, *Origins of Organized Crime*, 23.

92 As Critchley notes, some scholars such as Pitkin and Cordasco and Humbert Nelli believe that the Black Handers gravitated naturally into bootlegging with the defeat of the Black Hand and the coming of Prohibition – a common speculation for which Critchley finds no basis. Nor does he regard the Black Hand as an initial stage or launching pad for the Mafia, despite the fact that some Mafiosi started out as Black Handers. In his view, the Black Hand specialized in protection, that is, extortion, whereas the early Mafia opposed such criminality as a threat to the ethnic community it sought to protect. See Critchley, *Origins of Organized Crime*, 26–7, 34, 35.

93 Defendants charged with Black Hand activity employed such intimidating practices during court trials. See Pitkin and Cordasco, *Black Hand*, 177.

94 Smith, *Mafia Mystique*, 121–88, 217–40; William Howard Moore, *The Kefauver Committee and the Politics of Crime, 1950–19952* (Columbia, MI: Univ. of Missouri Press, 1974), 114, 120–6, 130–4; Ronald W. Wilson, 'Gang Busters: The Kefauver Crime Committee and the Syndicate Films of the 1950s,' in Grieveson, Sonnet, and Stanfield, *Mob Culture*, 67–89; Estes Kefauver, *Crime in America* (London: Victor Gollancz, 1952), 23–39, 52–3, 77, 81–94, 136–7, 148–51, 161, 170, 218–35, 236–54; Michael Woodiwiss, *Crime, Crusades and Corruption*, 7, 106–37, 143–7, 150, 159, 161; Michael Woodiwiss, 'Capone to Kefauver: Organized Crime in America,' *History Today*, 37, no. 6 (June 1987): 11–15; Feder and Joesten, *Luciano Story*, 85; Bernstein, *Greatest Menace*, 1–13, 53–4, 56–7, 66–7, 69–73, 92–3, 105, 172–5, 179; Mason, *America Gangster Cinema*, xvii, 105–6. John Baxter errs not only in regarding organized crime in the United States as a foreign import, but in supposing that Kefauver had clinched his case against the Mafia. See Baxter, 'The Gangster Film,' 30, 34–5.

95 For the syndicate film, see Baxter, 'Gangster Film,' 34–5.

96 On *Hoodlum Empire*, see Wilson, 'Gang Busters,' 77–9.

97 Jean Harlow is alleged to have been romantically involved with New Jersey crime boss 'Longy' Zwillman. See Sifakis, *Mafia Encylopedia*, 299.

98 Smith, *Mafia Mystique*, 152–88, 189–252; Moore, *Kefauver Committee*, 239–40. Contrary to the views of skeptics such as Michael Woodiwiss, the Mafia has over the last two decades been proved to exist not as a rationalized business organization on the model of a centralized corporation, as many observers had assumed, but as a loose and flexible association of criminals joined by common interests, commitment to the same values, fictitious familial relationships, and varying degrees of cooperation and directive authority among the upper echelons of the crime 'families.' See Woodiwiss, *Crime, Crusades, and Corruption*, 146–7, 157, 159–62; Casillo, *Gangster Priest*, Appendix, 401–11.

99 Phil Hardy, ed., *The Overlook Film Encyclopedia: The Gangster Film* (Westport, NY: Overlook, 1998), 189–90; McCarty, *Bullets over Hollywood*, 126–7.

100 Gambino, *Blood of My Blood*, 274.

101 Muscio, *Piccole Italie, grandi schermi*, 310.

102 For Black Hand plots against opera stars Caruso and Tito Schipa, see Pitkin and Cordasco, *Black Hand*, 138, 223. The plot against Caruso was foiled by the Italian squad rather than by Petrosino, who had already been assassinated.

103 Sifakis, *Mafia Encyclopedia*, 4, 7–9, 17, 21, 59–60, 117, 194–5, 222–3, 249, 290, 328–9, 347; John Kobler, *Capone: The Life and Times of Al Capone* (New York: G.P. Putnam's, 1971), 33–4; Kenneth Allsop, *The Bootleggers: The Story of Chicago's Prohibition Era* (New York: Arlington House, 1968), 81, 92–3, 125–30, 131–9; Feder and Joesten, *Luciano Story*, 85–7; Albini, *American Mafia*, 206–8; Critchley, *Origins of Organized Crime*, 171–2, 208–10; Peter Maas, *The Valachi Papers* (New York: G.P. Putnam's, 1965), 89.

104 Allsop, *Bootleggers*, 86.

105 Ehrenstein, *Scorsese Picture*, 41.

106 With the exception of Frank Ginetta, Fred Gardaphe's description of mob boss portrayals prior to that of Don Vito Corleone is correct. Don Vito is 'the first fictional gangster who is not presented as a psychopath,' and who remains free of sexual perversity. See Gardaphe, *From Wiseguys to Wise Men*, 21.

107 Ianni, *Family Business*, 18, 155–6; Gans, *Urban Villagers*, 200–1, 210–11; Donna Gabaccia, *From Sicily to Ellizabeth Street: Housing and Social Change, 1880–1930* (Albany: State Univ. of New York Press, 1988), 59–60, 78–9; Charlotte Gower Chapman, *Milocca: A Sicilian Village* (Cambridge, MA: Schenckman, 1971), 68, 70; Jane Schneider and Peter Schneider, *Culture and Political Economy in Western Sicily* (New York: Academic Press, 1976), 60, 87.

108 Nelli, *Business of Crime*, 180–3; Woodiwiss, *Crime, Crusades and Corruption*, 158–9; Critchley, *Origins of Organized Crime*, 180, 196, 199, 202, 207–8, 210.

109 Smith, *Mafia Mystique*, 19, 265, 315–16, 319–20; Ianni, *Family Business*, passim.

110 Howard Abadinsky, *The Criminal Elite: Professional and Organized Crime* (Westport, CT: Greenwood, 1983), 30–1. Like Ianni, upon whom he relies, Critchley argues for the centrality of family ties and loyalities in the organization of Mafia groups, which, whether in the United States or Sicily, he sees as valuing actual blood relationships over fictitious family bonds as established by loyalty oaths and ritual initiations. He notes marital connections between and within Mafia families as a source of solidarity and trust, as witness the alliance between the Bonannos and Profacis, as well as the preference shown family members in the assignment of key positions. Yet while there is no denying the fact of biological kinship as an organizational feature of some Mafia families, it seems to have diminished in importance over recent decades. As Critchley himself notes, recruits have been drawn increasingly from outside family blood lines. So too, members of Mafia families (in the fictitious sense) have often shown resentment of nepotism and other forms of favouritism enacted by mob bosses on behalf of their own kindred, an anti-meritocratic bias Critchley himself mentions. The members of the Los Angeles mob threatened violence against Louis Dragna, the family *consigliere*, when he announced his plan to elevate his son Tom Louis to leadership of the organization – a proposal he later retracted. The revolt of the Gallo brothers against the Profaci family was provoked by resentment of its apparent nepotism. When Joe Bonanno revealed his intention to make his incompetent son Bill the dynastic head of his crime family, a major Mafia war ensued. The killing of Gambino family boss Paul Castellano resulted partly because of the resentful perception that he had acquired supreme power chiefly for being the cousin of the previous boss, Carlo Gambino. Both succession and the distribution of power in many of the most important Mafia families, such as the Chicago Outfit, the Lucchese family, the Gambino family, and the family created by Lucky Luciano, do not appear to have been dictated primarily by blood relationships or nepotism. See Critchley, *Origins of Organized Crime*, 61–2, 71, 91, 92–4, 104, 145, 211–16, 229–30.

111 For Armetta, see Muscio, *Piccole Italie, grandi schermi*, 53–5, 152, 155, 159, 165, 166, 278–82. Projecting the image of the amiable, corpulent Italian driven to emotional extremes, Armetta in Muscio's view had become the virtual Italian American cinematic stereotype by the 1930s.

112 Simone Cinotto, *La famiglia che mangia insieme: Cibo ed etnicità nella comunità italoamericana di New York, 1820–1940* (Turin: OTTO, 2001), 393–8, 407–8. Cinotto cites Caroline F. Ware on the superficiality of the relations between ethnics and clients. On the fortunes of Italian food in the United

States, including its loss of authenticity through industrialization, see Cinotto, 264–80, 282, 288–302, 352–3, 359–71; Harvey A. Levenstein, 'The American Response to Italian Food, 1830–1930,' *Food and Folkways*, 1, no. 1 (1985): 1–24, esp. 2–6; Levenstein, *Revolution of the Table: The Transformation of the American Diet* (New York: Oxford Univ. Press, 1988), 146, 190–1; Donna R. Gabaccia, *We Are What We Eat: Ethnic Food and the Making of Americans* (Cambridge, MA: Harvard Univ. Press, 1998), 7, 9, 12, 51–4, 62, 66–7, 72–3, 81, 98–103, 111, 119–20, 128, 137, 150–1, 169, 185–6, 215–16.

113 On Italian American generational struggles, see Irwin L. Child, *Italian or American?: The Second Generation in Conflict* (New Haven: Yale Univ. Press, 1943); Humbert S. Nelli, *From Immigrants to Ethnics: The Italian Americans* (New York: Oxford Univ. Press, 1983); Phyllis H. Williams, *South Italian Folkways in Europe and America* (New Haven: Yale Univ. Press, 1938); Lopreato, *Italian Americans*; Jerre Mangione and Ben Morreale, *La Storia: Five Centuries of Italian American Experience* (New York: HarperCollins, 1993); Leonard Covello, *The Social Background of the Italo-American Child: A Study of the Southern Italian Family Mores and Their Effect on the School Situation in Italy and America* (Totowa, NJ: Rowman and Littlefield, 1972).

114 Space will not permit discussion of Edward Dmytryk's *Christ in Concrete* (1949), a well-known film on Italian American working-class life. The film is imbued with a leftist ideology that, proposing worker solidarity over capitalist individualism, has come to seem increasingly wrongheaded in recent decades, but which in any case most Italian Americans wisely disregarded in their pursuit of occupational and social mobility. On *Christ in Concrete*, see Bondanella, *Hollywood Italians*, 29–35.

115 Robert Ottoson, *A Reference Guide to the American Film Noir* (Metutchen, NJ: Scarecrow Press, 1981), 84–5; Alan Gevinson, ed., *Within Our Gates: Ethnicity in American Feature Films* (Berkeley: Univ. of California Press, 1997), 467–8.

116 Gevinson, *Within Our Gates*, 468.

117 On Italian fascism in America and Italian America, see Gaetano Salvemini, *Italian Fascist Activities in the United States* (Staten Island: Center for Migration Studies, 1977), 4, 8–9, 11–15, 18–21, 23–38, 38n, 39, 43–45, 47, 48, 51–2, 64, 70–6, 78, 83, 85, 91–2, 97, 99, 102, 105, 107–18, 124–29, 135–64, 167–9, 171, 175–187, 193–7, 200, 202, 205, 207–8, 210–45; Diggins, *Mussolini and Fascism*, xix, 79–81, 84–110, and passim; Bertellini, 'Duce/Divo,' 693–4, 697–8, 699, 701; Philip Cannistraro, *Blackshirts in Little Italy* (West Lafayette, IN: Bordighera, 1999), passim; Cannistraro, 'Fascism and Italian Americans,' in S.M. Tomasi, ed., *Perspectives on Italian Immigration and Ethnicity: Proceedings of the Symposium held at Casa Italiana, Columbia Univer-*

sity, May 21–23, 1976 (Staten Island: Center for Migration Studies, 1977), 51–66; Golden, 'Fate of La Famiglia,' 86; Muscio, *Piccole Italie, grandi schermi*, 146–7, 277, 277n, 307; Stefano Luconi, 'The Voice of the Motherland: Pro-Fascist Broadcasts for the Italian-American Communities in the United States,' *Journal of Radio Studies*, 8, no. 1 (Summer 2001): 61–80.

118 Italian and other immigrants were 'ignorant' and 'distrustful' of banks and 'often had their prejudices confirmed by their experiences here,' notes Roger Daniels. Local bankers prospered because of congested neighbourhoods, which enabled them to keep track of their clientele and to exploit those who fell into financial trouble. The great exception was San Francisco banker A.P. Giannini, who had the trust of his patrons, and who did not want to be identified with the Monettis. See Daniels, *Coming to America*, 194; Tomasi, *Italian in America*, 111–12, 68–9, 174, 175 (articles by Mangano and Speranza).

119 Because of such stereotypes Italian Americans have suffered a disadvantage as compared to Jews in the Nevada gambling industry. See Ronald A. Farrell and Carole Case, *The Black Book and the Mob: The Untold Story of the Control of Nevada's Casinos* (Madison: Univ. of Wisconsin Press, 1995), 4, 12, 24, 27n, 32, 52, 167, 169, 173–5, 219, 222, 228–9.

120 Apples symbolize WASP society in Guido D'Agostino's *Olives on the Apple Tree* (1940; New York: Arno, 1975), set in a New England town where Italian Americans attempt to come to terms with a non-ethnic environment.

121 Richard F. Leavitt, *The World of Tennessee Williams* (New York: G.P. Putnam's, 1978), 62–3, 106.

122 Tennessee Williams, *Memoirs* (London: Howard and Wyndham, 1976), 141–3; Philip C. Kolin, 'Sentiment and Humor in Equal Measure: Comic Form in *The Rose Tattoo*,' in George W. Crandell, ed., *The Critical Response to Tennessee Williams* (Westport: Greenwood, 1996), 94; Gene Phillips, *The Films of Tennessee Williams* (Philadelphia: Art Alliance Press, 1980), 104, 105; Tennessee Williams, *The Rose Tattoo*, in Williams, *Eight Plays* (Garden City: Nelson Doubleday, 1979), 307.

123 Daniel Sembroff Golden reads Serafina as combining two contradictory stereotypes of Italian and Italian American womanhood, the insatiable sexpot and the housebound matron. Nonetheless, Williams's portrayal of Serafina is so subtle that it transcends stereotypes. See Golden, 'Fate of La Famiglia,' 83.

124 Kolin, 'Sentiment and Humor in Equal Measure,' 94, 98. Sicilian audiences have been speechless with admiration for *The Rose Tattoo*. See Phillips, *Films of Tennessee Williams*, 104.

125 A. Barton Palmer, 'Hollywood in Crisis: Tennessee Williams and the Evolu-

tion of the Adult Film,' in Matthew C. Roudané, ed., *The Cambridge Companion to Tennessee Williams* (Cambridge: Cambridge Univ. Press, 1997), 223–4.

126 Signi Lenea Falk stresses Serafina's anti-dualism, noting that for her as for her daughter, physical love is 'more spiritual than religion.' See Falk, *Tennessee Williams* (New York: Twayne, 1978), 77.

127 Stan Berkowitz, 'Martin Ritt: A Shaper of the Medium Is Now Its Critic,' *Emmy Magazine*, July/August, 1985; Ronald Davis, 'A Conversation with Martin Ritt': both interviews in Gabriel Miller, ed., *Martin Ritt: Interviews* (Jackson: Univ. Press of Mississippi, 2002), 99, 162; Gabriel Miller, *The Films of Martin Ritt: Fanfare for the Common Man* (Jackson: Univ. Press of Mississippi, 2000), 205–6.

128 Orsi, *Madonna of 115th Street*, 28; Kraut, *Silent Travelers*, 182–5. The making of artificial flowers as a form of employment favoured by Italian immigrant women had been treated as early as 1926 in the silent film *Rose of the Tenements*. See Muscio, *Piccole Italie, grandi schermi*, 147.

129 Carlton Jackson, *Picking Up the Tab: The Life and Movies of Martin Ritt* (Bowling Green: Bowling Green Univ. Press, 1994), 55.

130 Lopreato, *Italian Americans*, 36–8.

131 Gabaccia, *From Sicily to Elizabeth Street*, 46; Chapman, *Milocca*, 40; Schneider and Schneider, *Culture and Political Economy*, 89–90.

132 Casella, *Hollywood Italian*, 218.

133 For the emphasis on honour and shame in Mediterranean and more especially southern Italian culture, see J.M. Peristiany, Introduction to Peristiany, ed., *Honour and Shame: The Values of Mediterranean Society* (Chicago: Univ. of Chicago Press, 1974), 9–18 and passim.

134 Casella, *Hollywood Italian*, 218.

135 The silent film *Defying the Law* (1924) is set in a community of Sicilian fishermen near San Francisco; *Song of the City* (1937) was partly shot in that city and concerns a family of kindly Italian fishermen; and *Fisherman's Wharf* (1939) depicts a community of Sicilian fishermen in the same area. See Muscio, *Piccole Italie, grandi schermi*, 145, 160, 167.

136 Andrew F. Rolle, *The Immigrant Upraised: Italian Adventurers and Colonists in an Expanding America* (Norman: Univ. of Oklahoma, 1968), passim.

137 Gans, *Urban Villagers*, 40–1, 65, 70–1, 74–103, 221.

138 Ann Parsons, 'Specific Patterns of Italian-American Life,' in Parsons, *Belief, Magic, and Anomie: Essays in Psychosocial Anthropology* (Glencoe: Free Press, 1969), 135–6.

139 Gans, *Urban Villagers*, 38–9, 40, 47–9, 51–3; Lopreato, *Italian Americans*, 80–1.

140 Paddy Chayefsky, '*Marty*: Two Choices of Material,' in Chayefsky, *Television Plays* (New York: Simon and Schuster, 1955), 173–7.

141 On Italian American homophilism, see Gambino, *Blood of My Blood*, 147.

142 Stephen Cooper, *Full of Life: A Biography of John Fante* (New York: North Court, 2000), 233–7.

143 Muscio, *Piccole Italie, grandi schermi*, 342.

144 Adrian Stokes, *Stones of Rimini*, in Stokes, *Critical Writings of Adrian Stokes*, 1:228–9 and passim.

145 Edited by George Horace Lorimer, the *Saturday Evening Post* strongly advocated immigration restriction during the period after World War I up to the passage of the Johnson-Reed Act in 1924. Kenneth Roberts, Lorimer's star correspondent on immigration issues, not only argued vehemently for restriction but asserted the racial inferiority of southern as opposed to northern Italians. See Rita J. Simon, *Public Opinion and the Immigrant: Print Media Coverage, 1880–1980* (Lexington: D.C. Heath, 1985), 52–3, 82–4, 85, 86, 216; Rita J. Simon and Susan H. Alexander, *The Ambivalent Welcome: Print Media, Public Opinion, and Immigration* (Westport: Praeger, 1993), 66–82, 248.

146 Orsi, *Madonna of 115th Street*, 3, 4, 22–3, 55, 57, 65, 69, 75–105, 163–231; Covello, *Social Background of the Italo-American School Child*, 103–45; Rudoph J. Vecoli, 'Cult and Occult in Italian American Culture: The Persistence of a Religious Heritage,' in Randall M. Miller and Thomas D. Marzik, eds., *Immigrants and Religion in Urban America* (Philadelphia: Temple Univ. Press, 1977), 25–42; Rudolph J. Vecoli, 'Prelates and Peasants: Italian Immigrants and the Catholic Church,' *Journal of Social History*, 2, no. 1 (Spring 1969): 217–68; Williams, *South Italian Folkways*, 135–59; Alba, *Italian Americans*, 33–4, 90–1; Chapman, *Milocca*, 42–4, 145–7, 158, 163–209; Lopreato, *Italian Americans*, 87–93; Mary Elizabeth Brown, 'Religion,' in Salvatore L. La Gumina, Frank Cavaioli, Salvatore Primeggia, and Joseph A. Varacalli, eds., *The Italian American Experience* (New York: Garland, 2000), 538–42; Casillo, *Gangster Priest*, 82–93, 449–457n.

147 On World War II as a catalyst of Italian American assimilation, see Muscio, *Piccole Italie, grandi schermi*, 356–7, 358n, 361n.

148 Gans, *Urban Villagers*, 36–41, 38, 64–8; William Foote Whyte, *Street Corner Society: The Social Structure of an Italian Slum* (Chicago: Univ. of Chicago Press, 1981), passim; Gabaccia, *From Sicily to Elizabeth Street*, 102.

149 Bondanella, *Hollywood Italians*, 116–8.

150 Golden, 'Fate of La Famiglia,' 90.

151 For the 'orientalization' of Italy, see Casillo, *Empire of Stereotypes*, 150–1, 182.

152 Michael Harper, *The American Indian in Film* (Metutchen, NJ: Scarecrow Press, 1986) (see index); Muscio, *Piccole Italie, grandi schermi*, 142. For Iron Eyes Cody (1909–1999), see Nick J. Milati, *Closet Italians: A Dazzling Collec-*

tion of Illustrious Italians with non-Italian Names (Bloomington, IN: Xlibris, 2004), 146–7.

153 James Fenimore Cooper, *Gleanings in Europe: Italy* (Albany: State Univ. of New York Press, 1981), 115. For the identification of American Indians, Roman Catholic 'infidels,' and Italians by nineteenth-century historians, including George Bancroft and Francis Parkman, see Franchot, *Roads to Rome*, 385n.

154 David Glassberg, *American Historical Pageantry: The Uses of Tradition in the Early Twentieth Century* (Chapel Hill: Univ. of North Carolina Press, 1990), 114.

155 Time/CNN, Sunday, 24 June 2001. According to Gardaphe, the eclipse of native Americans as America's evil 'other' has led to the substitution of the Italian Americans as the nation's demonic alien. See Gardaphe, 'A Class Act,' in Hostert and Tamburri, *Screening Ethnicity*, 59. Yet if Hollywood has Italianized its Indians, it has also de-Italianized its Roman epics. To quote Michael Grant, the 'rock-faced' ancient Romans 'were wildly excitable – a disconcerting blend between highly efficient Prussians and the most volatile of southerners.' It is impossible to recognize in this description most cinematic portrayals of ancient Romans, including those of Henry Wilcoxon (*Cleopatra*, 1930), Robert Taylor (*Quo Vadis*, 1951), Richard Burton (*The Robe*, 1953; *Cleopatra*, 1963), Stewart Granger (*Salomé*, 1953), Sir Laurence Olivier (*Spartacus*, 1960), Jack Hawkins (*Ben-Hur*, 1959), Rex Harrison (*Cleopatra*, 1963), and Sir Alec Guiness (*The Fall of the Roman Empire*, 1964). This disparity between historical reality and modern representation reflects the fact that Anglophilic Hollywood, repelled by the notion of Caesar and Mark Antony as emotional and sweaty Mediterranean pagans, prefers to portray them after an Anglo-American wish-fulfilment fantasy, in the idealized image of the British aristocrat, grave, stolid, and imperturbable. Apart from their prominent noses, which Stephen Bann decodes as the chief signifier in nineteenth-century Britain for *Romanità*, Hollywood Romans have nothing identifiably Italian about them to detract from their nobility, whose hallmark is a high British accent. Hollywood's custom of representing ancient Italians as British probably develops from the tendency in nineteenth-century Britain and America to dissociate Italy's 'Roman' and imperial legacy of Italy from its recent decadence. See Michael Grant, Introduction to Cicero, *Selected Political Speeches*, trans. Michael Grant (Harmondsworth: Penguin, 1989), 21; Stephen Bann, *The Clothing of Clio: A Study of the Representation of History in Nineteenth-Century Britain and France* (Cambridge: Cambridge Univ. Press, 1984), 164.

156 Ronald Hayman, *Tennessee Williams: Everyone Else Is an Audience* (New Ha-

ven: Yale Univ. Press, 1993), 157–8; Leavitt, *World of Tennessee Williams*, 64; Kenneth Holditch and Richard Freeman Leavitt, *Tennessee Williams and the South* (Jackson: Univ. Press of Mississippi, 2002), 52; Gene Phillips, *Films of Tennessee Williams*, 87–103.

157 See the essays by Enrico del Lago, Rick Halpern, Peter Kolchin, Piero Bevilaqua, Richard Follett, Marta Petrusiewicz, and Bruce Levine in Enrico dal Lago and Rick Halpern, eds., *The American South and the Italian Mezzogiorno: Essays in Comparative History* (New York: Palgrave Macmillan, 2002).

158 Leavitt, *World of Tennessee Williams*, 13.

159 Further points of resemblance include a strong reliance on oral tradition, superstitions (the Sicilian belief in witches calls to mind Williams's story 'The Yellow Bird'), and the frequency of natural catastrophes (Sicilian earthquakes and volcanoes, Delta floods). See Holditch and Leavitt, *Tennessee Williams and the South*, 39, 41–2.

160 Robert A. Orsi, 'The Religious Background of an Inbetween People: Street *Feste* and the Problem of the Dark-Skinned Other in Italian Harlem, 1920–1990,' *American Quarterly*, 44 (1992): 313–47.

161 Tennessee Williams, *Baby Doll* (New York: New Directions, 1956), 56.

162 On the association of Italians with improvisation, chiefly in relation to theatrical performances, see Casillo, *Empire of Stereotypes*, 35–42; Muscio, *Piccole Italie, grandi schermi*, 39, 65–6.

163 Phillips, *Films of Tennessee Williams*, 109, 205.

164 Tennessee Williams, *Orpheus Descending*, in Williams, *Eight Plays*, 606, 627.

165 Michael Woodiwiss remarks that, 'in the South,' the 'case for the banning of all intoxicating substances' was not only driven by 'fear and hatred of black Americans' but formed 'part of a wider movement to keep blacks passive and subordinate.' Regarding the tendency of immigrants to consort with blacks, which was bitterly resented by native Southern whites, John Higham observes: 'In the little town of Tallulah, Louisiana ... the coming of five Sicilian storekeepers disturbed the native whites because the Italians dealt mainly with the Negroes and associated with them nearly on terms of equality ... In a few years a quarrel over a goat resulted in the lynching of all five.' See Woodiwiss, *Crime, Crusades and Corruption*, 3, 4; Higham, *Strangers in the Land*, 169. According to Higham, 'the prohibition movement ... came alive in the South only when whites became convinced that cheap whiskey was responsible for turning blacks into ravenous beasts.' See Higham, 'Integrating America: The Problem of Assimilation,' in Higham, *Send These to Me: Immigrants in Urban America*, rev. ed. (Baltimore: Johns Hopkins Univ. Press, 1984), 195. For racism and Italian Americans in Louisiana, see G.E. Cunningham, 'Italians: A Hindrance to White Solidar-

ity in Louisiana, 1890–1898,' *Journal of Negro History*, 50 (Jan. 1965): 23–8, 33–6; Vincenza Scarpaci, 'Walking the Color Line: Italian Immigrants in Rural Louisiana, 1880–1910,' in Guglielmo and Salerno, *Are Italians White?*, 60–76.

166 Williams, *Orpheus Descending*, 550.

167 Williams, *Orpheus Descending*, 603.

168 Williams, *Orpheus Descending*, 627–8.

169 In view of Lady's father's Palermitan origin as stated in the play, it is worth noting that the fig tree is often taken as a symbol of Sicily. See Frances M. Malpezzi and William M. Clements, *Italian American Folklore* (Little Rock, AR: August House, 1992), 241.

170 Marcus Lee Hansen, *The Problem of the Third Generation Immigrant* (Rock Island, IL: Augustana Historical Society, 1938), 6–12; Muscio, *Piccole Italie, grandi schermi*, 362. It is now widely acknowledged that Hansen's so-called law of third-generation return admits of many exceptions. See Thomas J. Archdeacon, 'Hansen's Hypothesis of a Model of Immigrant Assimilation,' in Peter Kivisto and Dag Blanck, eds., *American Immigrants and Their Generations* (Urbana: Univ. of Illinois Press, 1980), 42, 45, 46, 48–52, 54, 58–60; see also in the same volume Peter Kivisto, 'Ethnicity and the Problem of Generations in American History,' 3.

171 Ronald Bergan, *Francis Ford Coppola: The Making of His Movies* (New York: Thunder's Mouth Press, 1997), 36, 39; Peter Cowie, *The Godfather Book* (London: Faber and Faber, 1997), 39–41.

172 John Paul Russo, 'The Hidden Godfather: Plenitude and Absence in Francis Ford Coppola's *Godfather* I and II,' in Joseph L. Tropea, James E. Miller, and Cheryl Beattie-Repetti, eds., *Support and Struggle: Italian-Americans in a Comparative Perspective* (Staten Island: American Italian Historical Association, 1986), 263–4.

173 McArthur, *Underworld USA*, 30, 32.

174 Robert K. Johnson, *Francis Ford Coppola* (Boston: Twayne, 1977), 109. For similar complaints that Coppola implies a Sicilian origin for the American Mafia, see Mangione and Morreale, *La Storia*, 413.

175 Keyser and Keyser, *Hollywood and the Catholic Church*, 88.

176 For *Godfather III*, see Robert Casillo, 'Registi italoamericani nel "tramonto dell'etnicità": Coppola, De Palma, Ferrara e Scorsese,' in Giuliana Muscio and Giovanni Spagnoletti, eds., *Quei bravi ragazzi: il cinema italoamericano contemporaneo* (Venice: Marsilio, 2007), 99–104. According to Geoff Fordham, *The Godfather* series shows the Church to be thoroughly corrupt. See Fordham, 'Study in Ambiguity,' 176.

177 Keyser and Keyser, *Hollywood and the Catholic Church*, 89.

178 Casella, *Hollywood Italian*, 256.

179 Gambino, *Blood of My Blood*, 16.

180 On the Mafia's segregation of business from domesticity, see Frederic J. Sondern, Jr, *Brotherhood of Evil: The Mafia* (New York: Farrar, Straus, Giroux, 1959), 24; Ianni, *Family Business*, 84.

181 Stephen Farber, 'Coppola and "The Godfather,"' *Sight and Sound*, Autumn 1972, 218.

182 William Malysjko, *The Godfather* (London: York, 2001), 78; Michael Sragow, 'Godfatherhood,' *New Yorker*, 24 March 1997, reprinted in Gene D. Phillips and Rodney Hill, eds., *Francis Ford Coppola: Interviews* (Jackson: Univ. Press of Mississippi, 2004), 171; Bergan, *Francis Ford Coppola*, 38; Cowie, *Godfather Book*, 10–1.

183 Bergan, *Francis Ford Coppola*, 48; Malyszko, *The Godfather*, 66; William Murray, '*Playboy* Interview: Francis Ford Coppola,' *Playboy*, July 1975, reprinted in Phillips and Hill, *Francis Ford Coppola: Interviews*, 19–20; Jeffrey Chown, *Hollywood Auteur: Francis Coppola* (New York: Praeger, 1984), 63.

184 Sragow, 'Godfatherhood,' 177.

185 Cowie, *Godfather Book*, 19.

186 Casella, *Hollywood Italian*, 247. Casella notes the protests by Italian Americans that *The Godfather* portrays Italian American women as submissive and emarginated, when in reality they often wield considerable power within their families; see 252. Randall M. Miller complains that the insider knowledge and accuracy in ethnic details displayed in *The Godfather* preserves and legitimates the untruth that most Italian Americans belong to the Mafia. See Miller, Introduction to Miller, *Kaleidoscopic Lens*, 11.

187 Despite giving the impression of deep familiarity with the mob, Puzo acquired his knowledge of the underworld through research. See Woodiwiss, *Crime, Crusades and Corruption*, 157.

188 Vera Dika, 'The Representation of Ethnicity in *The Godfather*,' in Nick Browne, ed., *Francis Ford Coppola's Godfather Trilogy* (Cambridge: Cambridge Univ. Press, 2000), 77–80, 89, 92.

189 Ianni, *Family Business*, 73. See also Pino Arlacchi, *Mafia Business: The Mafia Ethic and the Spirit of Capitalism* (London: Verso, 1986), 117–19; Sondern, *Brotherhood of Evil*, 11.

190 Doherty, *Pre-Code Hollywood*, 151; Mason, *American Gangster Cinema*, 105, 107, 110, 123–5; Wilson, 'Gang Busters,' 73–6, 78, 80, 86; Ruth, *Inventing the Public Enemy*, 37–62; Maltby, 'Spectacle of Criminality,' 127.

191 Coppola, qtd in Clarens, *Crime Movies*, 270.

192 Murray, '*Playboy* Interview: Francis Ford Coppola,' 26–7, 29.

193 Gambino, *Blood of My Blood*, 304.

194 Murray, '*Playboy* Interview: Francis Ford Coppola,' 27–8; Phillips, 'Francis Ford Coppola Interviewed,' in Phillips and Hill, *Francis Ford Coppola: Interviews*, 150–1; Chown, *Hollywood Auteur*, 60–1, 103, 109; Gene D. Philips, *Godfather: The Intimate Francis Ford Coppola* (Lexington: Univ. Press of Kentucky, 2004), 113; Glenn Man, 'Ideology and Genre in *The Godfather* Films,' in Browne, *Francis Ford Coppola's Godfather Trilogy*, 109, 110, 113, 117.

195 Fred Pasley, *Al Capone: The Biography of a Self-Made Man* (Binghamton, NY: Ives, Washburn, 1930), 349–50; Kobler, *Al Capone*, 214–5; Rosow, *Born to Lose*, 85, 88.

196 Bonanno, *A Man of Honor*, 61–2.

197 Giles, *American Catholic Arts and Fictions*, 495; Farber, 'Coppola and "The Godfather,"' 218.

198 Rosow, *Born to Lose*, 10–21, 27–35, 138–9, 272, 314.

199 Dickos, qtd in Phillips, *Godfather*, 109.

200 Man, 'Ideology and Genre,' 109, 113.

201 John Hess, '*Godfather II*: A Deal Coppola Couldn't Refuse,' in Bill Nichols, ed., *Movies and Methods: An Anthology* (Berkeley: Univ. of California Press, 1976), 88–9; Chris Messenger, *The Godfather and American Culture: How the Corleones Became 'Our Gang'* (Albany: State Univ. of New York Press, 2002), 44. For similar views, see Leitch, *Crime Films*, 68, 103, 111; Bernstein, *The Greatest Menace*, 18, 22–3.

202 Chown, *Hollywood Auteur*, 59.

203 Nelli, *Business of Crime*, 139–40.

204 Donald Cressey, *Theft of the Nation* (New York: Harper and Row, 1969), 109–61 and passim.

205 Ianni, *Family Business*, 111, 151–3; Albini, *American Mafia*, 243; Vincenzo Ruggiero, *Crimes and Markets: Essays in Anti-Criminology* (Cambridge: Cambridge Univ. Press, 2000), 18; Annelise Graebner Anderson, *The Business of Organized Crime* (Stanford: Hoover Institution, 1979), 44–6, 47–8, 49; Anderson, 'Organized Crime, Mafia, and Governments,' in Gianluca Fiorentini and Sam Peltzman, eds., *The Economics of Organized Crime* (Cambridge: Cambridge Univ. Press, 1995), 39–40. Coppola's description of the Mafia as a 'form of government' qualifies his view of it as a corporate business. See Cowie, *Godfather Book*, 80–1.

206 Albini, *American Mafia*, 9–10, 55–7, 61–2, 305; Abadinsky, *Criminal Elite*, 136, 143–4; Abadinsky, *Organized Crime*, 7th ed. (Belmont, CA: Wadsworth/ Thomson Learning, 2003), 222–6.

207 Casella, *Hollywood Italian*, 251.

208 Nick Browne, 'Fearful A-Symmetries: Violence as History in *The Godfather* Films,' in Browne, *Francis Ford Coppola's Godfather Trilogy*, 14, 15, 21.

209 Cawelti, ctd in Phillips, *Godfather*, 110; Man, 'Ideology and Genre,' 119.
210 Alessandro Camon, 'The Godfather and the Mythology of Mafia,' in Browne, *Francis Ford Coppola's Godfather Trilogy*, 60–1.
211 Cowie, *Godfather Book*, 153, 155, 157.
212 Bergan, *Francis Ford Coppola*, 42.
213 Rosow, *Born to Lose*, 272, 282, 372.
214 Martin Scorsese, *A Personal Journey with Martin Scorsese through American Movies* (Santa Monica, CA: Buena Vista Home Entertainment, 2000).
215 Bondanella, *Hollywood Italians*, 243, 246–7, 262–3, 273. Edward C. Banfield applies the phrase 'amoral familism' to what he sees as the characteristic inability or unwillingness of southern Italians (the regional group from which most Italian Americans derive) to join together cooperatively except to satisfy the short-term interests of either themselves or their nuclear families, thus ignoring the public or communal interest. Although Banfield's claims are disputed, Bondanella errs in describing the Corleones as amoral familists, for not only do they constitute an extended family, but their participation in a crime syndicate as well as their long-standing links to the legitimate power structure ill consort with amoral familism. See Edward C. Banfield, *The Moral Basis of a Backward Society* (Glencoe: Free Press, 1958), passim.
216 E.J. Hobsbawm, 'Robin Hoodo: A Review of Mario Puzo's *The Sicilian*,' *The New York Review of Books*, 14 Feb. 1985, 12–17; Frederic Jameson, 'Reification and Utopia in Mass Culture,' *Social Text*, 1 (1979): 130–48. See also Hess, '*Godfather II*: A Deal Coppola Couldn't Refuse,' 82–90; Thomas J. Ferraro, 'Blood in the Marketplace: The Business of Family in the *Godfather* Narratives,' in Thomas J. Ferraro, *Ethnic Passages: Literary Immigrants in Twentieth-Century America* (Chicago: Univ. of Chicago Press, 1993), 20–1, 24–7, 30–2, 37, 43.
217 Ianni, *Family Business*, 104–15, 152–5. Although Ianni's study appears in their bibliography, Mangione and Morreale seem to claim that no Italian American criminal group is organized on a familial basis. See *La Storia*, 242n.
218 Ferraro, 'Blood in the Marketplace,' 28–30, 32–3.
219 Ferraro, 'Blood in the Marketplace,' 41–3. The 'regressive sociology' to which Ferraro refers is possibly that of Max Weber, who is well known for having argued that the extended and smaller or nuclear family must inevitably pose perhaps insuperable obstacles to the development of a rationalized capitalism owing to the impeding presence within them of non-bureaucratic, personalistic, nepotistic, and communal features as against individualistic values. Yet far from being regressive, Weber's ideas on the

subject retain some currency. There is, however, considerable support for
Ferraro's position in the writings of the British social anthropologist Jack
Goody, who denies the universality of Weber's argument while offering
numerous counterexamples of successful family-operated businesses in the
West and more especially India and Asia into the present time. Indeed,
Goody contends that family firms have long been at the core of commercial and even industrial capitalism. See Goody, *The East in the West* (Cambridge: Cambridge Univ., 1996), 138–61, esp. 138, 158, 192–3; *The Eurasian
Miracle* (Malden, MA: Polity, 2010), 16, 17, 20, 24, 40; *Capitalism and Modernity* (Malden, MA: Polity, 2004), 101–2, 110–11. A similar debate has been
joined in Italian Renaissance studies, with some scholars identifying industrialism and the loss of familial and corporate ties with the modernization
supposedly ushered in by the Renaissance, whereas others hold that such
ties persisted and even flourished in the midst of modernization, being
fully compatible with it. See Ronald Weissman, 'Taking Patronage Seriously: Mediterranean Values in Renaissance Italy,' in F.W. Kent and Patricia
Simons, eds., *Patronage, Art, and Society in Renaissance Italy* (London: Oxford
Univ. Press, 1987), 25–45; Alison Brown, Introduction to Brown, ed., *Language and Images of Renaissance Italy* (Oxford: Clarendon, 1995), 17.

220 Ianni, *Family Business*, 172, 173.

221 Sifakis, *Mafia Encyclopedia*, 326; William F. Roemer, Jr, *The Enforcer: Spi-
lotro – The Chicago Mob's Man over Las Vegas* (New York: Donald L. Fine,
1994), 206; Ianni, *Family Business*, 173; Fred J. Cook, 'A Family Business:
Hijacking, Bookmaking, Policy, Dice Games, Loan-Sharking and Special
Contracts,' in Nicholas Gage, ed., *Mafia, U.S.A.* (New York: Playboy Press,
1972), 345–61. For Sicily, see Arlacchi, *Mafia Business*, 132.

222 Phillips, 'Francis Ford Coppola Interviewed,' 150.

223 Ianni, *Family Business*, 108; see also 131, 159, 162, 166.

224 Alba, *Italian Americans*, 151–3. On the decline of the Mafia, which many
observers believe to be in progress, but which others hesitate to predict,
see Casillo, *Gangster Priest*, 522–8n.

225 On the theme of the dispersion of the family, and the failure of Michael
Corleone to reconcile familial and business interests, see Leitch, *Crime
Films*, 117–24; Golden, 'Fate of Famiglia,' 88–9; Woll and Miller, 'Italians,'
284, 285; Mason, *American Gangster Cinema*, 130–4.

226 Clarens, *Crime Movies*, 285, 287.

227 Chown, *Hollywood Auteur*, 70, 71.

228 Johnson, *Francis Ford Coppola*, 110–11; Murray, '*Playboy* Interview: Francis
Ford Coppola,' 28.

229 William Pechter, '*Godfather II*,' *Commentary*, 59 (March,1975): 80; Ferraro, 'Blood in the Marketplace,' 41, 42, 206n; Chown, *Hollywood Auteur*, 110–11.

230 Cowie, *Godfather Book*, 94, 96; Phillips, *Godfather*, 117.

231 Johnson, *Francis Ford Coppola*, 154, 163.

232 Robert Phillip Kolker, *A Cinema of Loneliness: Penn, Kubrick, Coppola, Scorsese, Altman* (New York: Oxford Univ. Press, 1980), 174, 188, 189, 189n.

233 Giles, *American Catholic Arts and Fictions*, 500.

234 Intended as a characterization of southern Italian society, the epigraph to Banfield's *The Moral Basis of a Backward Society* is Hobbes's description of life in a state of nature as 'solitary, poor, nasty, brutish, and short' – a far cry from *Gemeinschaft*. According to Hobbes, such atomizing, antisocial conflict could only be resolved through the authoritarian state, an artificial or mechanical fabrication that Tönnies came to define as the antithesis of *Gemeinschaft* in the sense of an organically developing community. See Tönnies, *Fundamental Concepts of Sociology (Gemeinschaft und Gesellschaft)*, trans. Charles P. Loomis (New York: American Book Co., 1940), 154; Arthur Mitzman, *Sociology and Estrangement: Three Sociologists of Imperial Germany* (New York: Knopf, 1973), 46, 52–3, 58–63, 65–82. Robert D. Putnam essentially accepts Banfield's characterization of southern Italian society in referring to the 'Hobbesian outcome' of the Mezzogiorno. See Putnam, *Making Democracy Work: Civic Tradition in Modern Italy* (Princeton: Princeton Univ. Press, 1993), 183. However, Pino Arlacchi warns against characterizing the whole of southern Italy as amoral familist, noting the *Gemeinschaft*-like character of certain regions of Calabria. See Arlacchi, *Mafia, Peasants, and Great Estates: Society in Traditional Calabria*, trans. Jonathan Steinberg (Cambridge: Cambridge Univ. Press, 1983), 1–2.

Index